CALIFORNIA INDIAN LANGUAGES

CALIFORNIA INDIAN LANGUAGES

VICTOR GOLLA

UNIVERSITY OF CALIFORNIA PRESS
Berkeley   Los Angeles   London

University of California Press, one of the most distinguished
university presses in the United States, enriches lives around the
world by advancing scholarship in the humanities, social sciences,
and natural sciences. Its activities are supported by the UC Press
Foundation and by philanthropic contributions from individuals
and institutions. For more information, visit www.ucpress.edu.

For an electronic version of this book, see the press website.

University of California Press
Berkeley and Los Angeles, California

University of California Press, Ltd.
London, England

© 2011 by the Regents of the University of California

Library of Congress Cataloging-in-Publication Data

Golla, Victor.
    California Indian languages / Victor Golla.
        p. cm.
    Includes bibliographical references and index.
    ISBN 978-0-520-26667-4 (cloth : alk. paper)
    1. Indians of North America—California—Languages.   I. Title.

PM501.C2G65 2011
497.09794—dc23
                            2011019927

19 18 17 16 15 14 13 12 11
10 9 8 7 6 5 4 3 2 1

The paper used in this publication meets the minimum
requirements of ANSI/NISO Z39.48-1992 (R 1997) (*Permanence
of Paper*).

Central cover image: Louis Choris, "Habitants de Californie"
(Indians at Mission Dolores, 1816). Lithograph with hand
coloring prepared for *Voyage Pittoresque autour du Monde* (Paris,
1822). Courtesy of The Bancroft Library, University of California,
Berkeley.

Background cover image: John P. Harrington, field notes on
Chocheño (East Bay Costanoan), 1921. Courtesy of the Survey of
California and Other Indian Languages, University of California,
Berkeley.

To my colleagues, past, present and future

Tillotson was trying, mostly in vain, to make me understand Yuki grammar. Teaching me the language was not to be thought of in the same sense as everyday ethnography—it was a special gift of a magical nature which he made to me as a token of friendship. Just as the ability existed for a famous singer to pass on his songs to a protégé at his death, so could a man pass on his knowledge of language to a student from another culture. For the present I would learn a little Yuki, but not very much. But in a few years he would die, and his knowledge of the language would pass on to me. Then I would think about it, have it on my mind constantly, and if I should be in company with other Yuki, could join right in "just natural like". . . . Though a man might instruct several people in the art of Yuki conversation, only the one to whom he passed on the power would ever really understand it.

GEORGE M. FOSTER, *A Summary of Yuki Culture*, 1944

CONTENTS

PART FOUR
Typological and Areal Features: California as a Linguistic Area

Phonology / 204

Grammar / 209

Linguistic Culture / 218

PART FIVE
Linguistic Prehistory

PREFACE

This book is intended to be the reference of first resort for linguists, archaeologists, cultural anthropologists, ethnohistorians, and others who in the course of their work find themselves in need of a guide to what is known to scholarship about the indigenous languages of California.

Part 1, a short introductory essay, proposes a definition of the California linguistic area primarily in geographical and sociopolitical terms—a region in which a mosaic of language differences and a multitude of tiny village-level polities have evolved together in tandem for millennia.

Part 2 is a narrative history of the documentation and study of California languages from the contact period to the present, emphasizing the social and institutional contexts in which the work was carried out.

Part 3 is a detailed survey of the language diversity of California in the framework of the twenty-eight basic classificatory units[1] into which the languages of the region fall (either uncontroversial language families or subfamilies, such as Miwok or Takic, of no more than two to three thousand years' time depth, or classificatory isolated languages, such as Karuk or Takelma, that do not belong to such a group). The characteristic phonological and grammatical structures of each family or isolate are outlined, and information is provided on the geography and dialectology of each language of a given group, with a thorough summary of its documentation. These sections are divided into six groups, five for the larger classificatory units to which most of the languages of California have been assigned with varying degrees of certainty (the Algic, Na-Dene, and Uto-Aztecan superfamilies, and the Penutian and Hokan phyla) and a sixth for the small residuum of languages whose deeper affiliations have not been determined (the Yukian and Chumashan families, and the languages of the southern tip of Baja California). A short introductory essay on the nature and implications of these deeper classifications accompanies each section.

Part 4 provides a nontechnical summary of the structural features that characterize the languages of the California region, from phonology through discourse-level syntax, along with some consideration of the sociolinguistic profile of precontact speech communities and of the patterns of linguistic borrowing within the region.

Part 5 summarizes what is known (or has been speculated) about the linguistic prehistory of the California region, following the general classificatory outline of Part 3.

One of the principal goals of this book is to direct researchers to the full range of published and archival materials on California languages. Citations of the published literature, if not exhaustive, are as thorough as the author can make them, and special effort has been put into identifying the nature and location of archival materials and into untangling the history of research. Separate appendixes are devoted to the voluminous collections of data amassed by John P. Harrington and C. Hart Merriam.

"California" is defined here in the most inclusive sense. All the aboriginal languages originally spoken inside the present political boundaries of the state of California are covered, however small their toehold. Takelma is included, for instance, since a tiny part of the territory claimed by one of the Takelma-speaking communities extended a few miles south of the California border. Furthermore, since the principal unit of discussion is the language family, all the languages in contiguous states (Oregon, Nevada, and Arizona, as well as Baja California del Norte in Mexico) that belong to any family (or family-level branch of a superfamily or phylum) that is represented in modern California are covered, at least cursorily, no matter how disproportionate the balance. Thus, since Chetco-Tolowa was spoken in Del Norte County, California, all the other Oregon Athabaskan languages are discussed with equal thoroughness in ¶3.6, as, by a similar logic, are all of the Numic languages as far afield as Comanche in ¶3.31. Application of the same classificatory principle at a somewhat greater geographic distance leads to the inclusion of a short section on Lower Columbia Athabaskan (¶3.5), since it is usually grouped with Oregon and California Athabaskan in the Pacific Coast subfamily of Athabaskan, and of Cochimí and Seri, Hokan-affiliated languages of Baja California and Sonora respectively (¶3.19–3.20), insofar as they have sometimes been treated as members of an expanded Yuman language family. However, the other languages of northern Mexico (and beyond) that have been classified as Hokan are not within the purview of this book, nor are the other languages of Oregon and the Northwest that have been classified as Penutian, since in both cases their historical connections to California languages exist only as unproven hypotheses at the phylum level. These criteria have been relaxed only for Waikuri and the otherwise minimally attested languages of southern Baja California, a short section on which (¶3.37) seems warranted by the light these isolates might shed on the deep prehistory of the region (see ¶5.1).

Whatever merit this work may have as a guidebook to California Indian linguistics, its ultimate value derives from the generations of amateur and professional observers whose documentation of the languages of the First Californians is described and utilized in these pages. Among these, four extraordinary men stand out: Alfred L. Kroeber, Edward Sapir, John P. Harrington, and C. Hart Merriam. Without the decades of focused work that all four men devoted to the task, each in his own way, what has been preserved for us of the variety and complexity of aboriginal California languages would be much diminished. Their names are everywhere in this book.

The published record is dominated by Kroeber and Sapir and their academic descendents. Quite literally, neither California ethnography nor California linguistics would exist in their modern forms without these paradigm-creating giants.[2] The massive collections of Merriam and Harrington, in contrast, made largely outside the academic research paradigm and deliberately kept private by their creators, had little impact on the field before the 1970s. Today, microfilm editions of these collections (Merriam 1898–1938; Harrington 1982–1990) provide wide access to data of previously unsuspected richness on languages long thought dead. Twenty-first-century students of Californian linguistics, especially those with ties to Native communities, are likely to know and care more about Harrington than about Kroeber, as the success of the University of California, Davis, Harrington project testifies (Macri, Golla, and Woodward 2004). Less attention has been paid to Merriam's work, but its value as a detailed and comprehensive survey of California dialectology—the only one ever carried out—is coming to be appreciated.

Beside this heroic quartet, it seems invidious to single out any others. But insofar as this book is also a contribution to the history of California ethnolinguistics, I cannot leave unmentioned the name of Robert F. Heizer (1915–1979). Bob Heizer understood, long before the rest of his twentieth-century colleagues, that the ethnography of the California Indians had become a historical discipline. While remaining an enormously productive archaeologist, he devoted a significant part of his intellectual energy to locating and publishing neglected gems of nineteenth- and early-twentieth-century documentation of California languages and cultures. It was Heizer who single-handedly rescued from obscurity Stephen Powers's vivid accounts of California Indian life in the 1870s. It was he who collated and published Pinart's and Henshaw's Mission vocabularies. And it was he who, for thirty years, served as the vigilant custodian of C. Hart Merriam's massive collection of linguistic and ethnographic materials.

·   ·   ·   ·   ·

This is a book that has been long in coming. That it has finally appeared, after decades of procrastination, is in no small part due to the encouragement of two good friends, Robert L. Bettinger of the University of California, Davis, and Andrew Garrett of the University of California, Berkeley, and to the enthusiasm of my editor at the University of California Press, Hannah Love. I also deeply appreciate the support of Lyle Campbell and Ives Goddard, coeditors of the University of Utah/Smithsonian Publications in American Indian Linguistics, the series for which an earlier version of this volume was drafted.

My sincere thanks go to all those Californianist colleagues who answered my queries, read drafts of chapters, patiently corrected my errors of fact and interpretation, referred me to publications and documents I had overlooked, or otherwise gave me much-needed help in this enterprise. These include, in alphabetical order, Richard Applegate, Juliette Blevins, Loren Bommelyn, Gary Breschini, the late William Bright, Catherine A. Callaghan, Lisa Conathan, Scott DeLancey, Catherine Fowler, Geoffrey Gamble, Jane Hill, Kenneth Hill, Leanne Hinton, Ira Jacknis, William H. Jacobsen, Jr., Carmen Jany, John Johnson, Terrence S. Kaufman, the late Daythal Kendall, Kathryn A. Klar, the late Sheldon Klein, Don Laylander, Charles Li, Christopher Loether, Steven Marlett, John E. McLaughlin, Sally McLendon, Amy Miller, Randall Milliken, Marianne Mithun, Mauricio Mixco, Pamela Munro, Bruce Nevin, Marc Okrand, the late Robert L. Oswalt, the late Harvey Pitkin, William Poser, William Seaburg, David L. Shaul, Alice Shepherd, the late William F. Shipley, Shirley K. Silver, Norval Smith, Sheri Tatsch, the late Karl V. Teeter, Sandra A. Thompson, Rudolph Troike, Katherine Turner, William Weigel, Kenneth Whistler, and Lisa Woodward. If I have omitted anyone's name, it is inadvertent.

Portions of the book have also benefited from the feedback I received from students at the University of California, Berkeley, who used a preliminary version as their textbook in a graduate course in California Indian languages, taught by Andrew Garrett in the spring semester of 2007.

I am also greatly indebted to the archivists and librarians who have guided me to the not always obvious documentary resources on California Indian languages, with particular thanks to Lauren Lassleben and Susan Snyder of the Bancroft Library; Joan Berman of the Humboldt State University Library; Robert Leopold, Director of the National Anthropological Archives; and Alicja Egbert of the Hearst Museum of Anthropology. I am, in addition, grateful to the three talented individuals—Nathaniel Haas, Burt Dyer, and especially Jackie Honig Bjorkman—who gave concrete form to my inchoate cartographic musings in the maps that illustrate the sections of Part 3.

Martha Macri, the founder and director of the Native American Language Center at the University of California, Davis, deserves special mention. Her firm belief that the documentation of the native languages of California should be made as accessible as possible is what first gave me the idea of writing this book.

But the most special mention of all goes to my wife, Ellen Golla, for her sustaining love and for her endless patience with the obsessions of scholarship.

Trinidad, California
May 2010

PHONETIC ORTHOGRAPHY USED IN THIS BOOK

Throughout this book, words and elements cited from Indian languages are written in italics in the normalized phonetic orthography that is detailed in Table 1 (for other phonetic orthographies that have been used in transcribing California languages, see Appendix C). When names and occasionally other words are cited in their traditional spelling, these forms are not italicized and are sometimes enclosed in double quotes.

Here are a few additional conventions:

¶   indicates a cross-reference to another section of this book

[ ]   (enclosing an Indian form) indicates a phonetic transcription

*   (preceding an Indian form) indicates that it is reconstructed or hypothetical

TABLE 1A
Consonants

	Bilabial	Inter-dental	Dental-Alveolar	Retro-flex	Lateral	Palatal	Velar	Labio-velar	Post-velar	Laryngeal
Stops										
Plain	p		t	ṭ			k	kʷ	q	ʔ
Aspirated	pʰ		tʰ	ṭʰ			kʰ	kʰʷ	qʰ	
Glottalized	p'		t'	ṭ'			k'	k'ʷ	q'	
Voiced	b		d	ḍ			g	gʷ	ġ	
Fricatives										
Plain	ɸ, f	θ	s	ṣ	ł	š	x	xʷ	x̣	h
Voiced	β, v	ð	z	ẓ		ž	γ	γʷ	γ̣	
Affricates										
Plain			c	ç	ƛ	č				
Aspirated			cʰ	çʰ	ƛʰ	čʰ				
Glottalized			c'	ç'	ƛ'	č'				
Voiced			ȝ			ǯ				
Nasals										
Voiced	m		n			nʸ	ŋ	ŋʷ		
Voiceless	M		N				ŋ̣			

(continued)

	Bilabial	Inter-dental	Dental-Alveolar	Retro-flex	Lateral	Palatal	Velar	Labio-velar	Post-velar	Laryngeal
Approximants										
Voiced	w			r	l	y				
Voiceless	W			R	L	Y				

Palatalization

  k^y or k̲ (velars), l^y (laterals), t^y n^y s^y (dental-alveolars).*

Trills and taps

  r̃ (trill), ɾ (tap or flap).

Prenasalized voiced stops

  ^{n}d, etc.

Glottalized nasals and approximants

  'm, etc. (glottal stop released as nasal or approximant segment), m' (nasal or approximant segment closed by glottal stop), ṁ (nasal or approximant segment with simultaneous glottal stricture). Where there is allophonic variation or the exact phonetic representation of the phoneme is not clear, ṁ, etc. is used as a cover symbol except for glottalized laterals, where for typographic reasons l' is used.

Gemination (contrastive consonant length)

  marked by doubling the letter (patta).

Rare consonants

  s^h (aspirated/fortis voiceless fricative, occurs in Central Chumash); ħ (voiceless pharyngeal fricative, occurs in Achumawi); kx (velar affricate, reconstituted Esselen phoneme).

*A y superscript is used systematically by linguists working with Yuman languages to mark the palatalized nasals (n^y), laterals (l^y), and velar stops (k^y) that are phonemically distinct in many of those languages. This usage is generalized in this book except in California Athabaskan, where an alternative symbol with a subscript semicircle (k̲) is employed for the palatalized velar stop in order to avoid awkward double superscripts where aspiration or glottalization must also be marked.

	Front		Nonfront/Back	
	Unrounded	Rounded	Unrounded	Rounded
High	i	ü	ï	u
Lower-high	ɪ			ʊ
Higher-mid	e	ö	ë	o
Lower-mid	ɛ	ö̈	ə	ɔ
Higher-low	æ		ʌ	
Low	a		ɑ	ɒ

Contrastive vowel length

  marked by a colon (a:, e:)

Nasalization

  marked by a superscript tilde; occurs in the California region only in Northern Yukian, where it is a secondary feature of the reduced central vowel (ə) [ə̃].

R-color

  marked by superscript r in Serrano-Vanyume (a^r, e^r); the r-colored central vowel [ə^r] that occurs in Yurok is written as r with an underdot (r̩).

PART 1

INTRODUCTION

Defining California as a Sociolinguistic Area

Anyone who has paid the slightest attention to the aboriginal languages of California knows that there were a lot of them. In the core region west of the Sierra Nevada and the Mohave Desert, a significantly larger number of mutually unintelligible linguistic systems were in use than could reasonably be predicted from differences in ecology, subsistence strategy, or social organization. Instead, the primary factor generating linguistic diversity seems to have been the evolution, over millennia, of a sociopolitical landscape that consisted of a mosaic of *tribelets*—tiny but independent societies, typically numbering no more than a few hundred individuals, that utilized the resources of a highly circumscribed territory. Too small to survive as primary ethnolinguistic units on their own, tribelets were linked symbolically, but not in any political sense, to the others that spoke varieties of the same language, promoting an ideology that defined language boundaries as unalterable natural features inherent in the land rather than as negotiable social facts reflecting (potential) tribal or national units. Ironically, then, it was the arbitrary, relatively functionless nature of language boundaries that tended to promote their survival and deepening over time. But if the abrupt discontinuities of language that were scattered almost randomly across California had only an abstract meaning to the people who experienced them in precontact times, we today can see them as fossilized traces of past migrations and expansions that provide a uniquely valuable window into the past.

1.1 Diversity

The precontact linguistic diversity of the New World was especially great along the Pacific coast of North America, reflecting both the complex ecology of the West Coast and its position as the gateway to the Americas. Nowhere was this hyperdiversity more extreme than in the fertile strip that lies between the coast and the interior deserts from approximately 31°30′ N in Baja California to 43° N in south-central Oregon, from Ensenada to Cape Blanco. Nearly a thousand miles long, and in places more than 200 miles wide, this bountiful region—the California of this book—was home to an extraordinary variety of village-dwelling but nonfarming peoples who spoke seventy-eight mutually unintelligible languages (Map 1), nearly a third of the indigenous languages known to have been spoken in North America north of Mesoamerica (Golla 2007a). More than a few of these languages are clearly related to languages spoken elsewhere on the continent, indicating that some proportion of the ethnic and linguistic diversity of aboriginal California is to be accounted for by population movements in recent millennia. The majority of California languages, however, have only the most tenuous of relationships to languages spoken anywhere else—mostly through hints of an attachment to the hypothetical Hokan and Penutian phyla, which, if historically valid classifications, probably ramify across the entire hemisphere. These distinctively Californian languages stand a good chance of being, like the lifeways of the people who created them, the products of unbroken sequences of local events that extend back to the initial human settlement of the Americas.

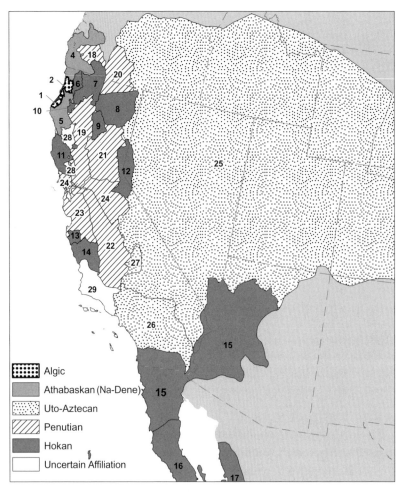

MAP 1. Language families and isolates of the California region.

Algic
1. Wiyot
2. Yurok

Athabaskan (Na-Dene)
3. Lower Columbia Athabaskan
4. Oregon Athabaskan (not shown)
5. California Athabaskan

Hokan
6. Karuk
7. Shastan
8. Palaihnihan
9. Yana
10. Chimariko
11. Pomo
12. Washo
13. Esselen
14. Salinan
15. Yuman
16. Cochimí
17. Seri

Penutian
18. Takelma
19. Wintuan
20. Klamath-Modoc
21. Maiduan
22. Yokuts
23. Costanoan
24. Miwok

Uto-Aztecan
25. Numic
26. Takic
27. Tubatulabal

Uncertain affiliation
28. Yukian
29. Chumash
30. Waikuri (and other languages of the
    southernmost part of Baja California)
    (not shown)

1.2 Tribelet and Language

While most Californian languages shared a number of structural traits (discussed in detail in Part 4), the most important of the defining features of the California language area was not linguistic but sociopolitical. More precisely, it was the absence of a congruence between the linguistic and the sociopolitical. In this region, uniquely in North America, the idea that a distinct common language is the social glue that holds together a tribe or nation played no significant role. In only one small part of aboriginal California did language boundaries and political boundaries normally coincide, and that was on the far southeastern periphery of the region, along the lower Colorado River. The varieties of Yuman spoken there—Mojave, Quechan, and Cocopa, as well as Halchidhoma before its speakers were forced to relocate among the Maricopa in the early nineteenth century—were distinct languages spoken by members of well-defined tribes (Kroeber 1925:727). When the Chemehuevi, who spoke a dialect of Southern Paiute, resettled along the Colorado near the Mojave in the early nineteenth century, their dialect also became a tribe-defining language of similar status.[1]

For all other California Indians in prewhite times, with the possible exception of the Diegueño or Kumeyaay (the only Yuman-speaking group on the California coast; see ¶3.18.3), the defining social unit was not a tribe but a small village community, or "tribelet" (Kroeber 1961). Comprising a few hundred individuals settled in a clearly demarcated territory that seldom encompassed more than 200 square miles—smaller than the present-day city and county of San Francisco—the tribelet was the economic and social building block of aboriginal California. Linked by close ties of kinship, the people of a tribelet were the direct owners of the land and its resources, most importantly the oak woodlands from which they gathered their staple food, the acorn (Basgall 1987). While there could be a half dozen or more permanent settlements within a tribelet's borders, there was usually only one of any significance. The headman or "captain" and his immediate family resided there, and the group was usually referred to by the name of that village.

A. L. Kroeber introduced the village community model of California political organization in the *Handbook of the Indians of California,* using the Yuki and the Pomo as his ethnographic examples (Kroeber 1925:160–163, 228–230, 234–235). He developed the idea more fully, and proposed the term "tribelet," in a monograph on the Patwin (Kroeber 1932:257–270). In his most extensive discussion of the model—the testimony he prepared for the Indian Claims Commission in 1954 (published as Kroeber 1961)—he estimated that most tribelets on average had about two hundred fifty members and that there were between five hundred and six hundred such miniature polities in aboriginal California. Over the last twenty years the tribelet concept has found a new popularity with ecologically oriented archaeologists who see in it the social expression of a distinctive Californian subsistence strategy that focused on the intensive exploitation of local resources (Basgall 1987; Raab and Jones 2004).

By contrast, the territory within which a given California language was spoken was almost always larger than a single tribelet, sometimes, as in the case of Yokuts or Northern Paiute, vastly larger. This language community, however, was largely an abstraction. It did not define a tribe or nation in any political sense, nor did it necessarily imply a common culture. At best, it fostered a sense of common destiny, often expressed in a strongly held belief that the relationship that existed between a particular region and a particular

language was spiritually ordained. At worst, it meant that some of your most dangerous enemies spoke the same language you did.

The disconnection between language and society in aboriginal California was brought home to me recently when, going through Pliny Earle Goddard's 1903–1908 ethnogeographical notes on the Sinkyone Athabaskans of the Eel River, I came across a brief statement in which an old man called "Little Charlie" described the social world he had grown up in before the whites came. Charlie was a survivor of the *tolankok* tribelet, whose territory lay along South Fork from Phillipsville to where it joins the main Eel at Dyerville. Their principal village, *tolanki,* was at the mouth of Bull Creek. Imagining himself a ten-year-old boy again at *tolanki,* Charlie told Goddard:

> If Mattole, [main] Eel River Indians, or Garberville Indians come they fight them. Long way off Indian never come this place. Garberville they talk like us. Wailaki talk pretty near us but too tight. Can't understand Mattole, "awful tight". Long time ago can't go to Mattole. Can go Bull Creek. Don't go Van Duzen. They kill me right there. Can't go Briceland nor Garberville. (Goddard 1902–1922a, Sinkyone notebook 1, p. 29)

With the exception of the Mattole on the coast, who had a distinct language, all the groups Charlie listed were speakers of mutually intelligible tribelet varieties of what can be called the Eel River Athabaskan language (¶3.7.3). On another page in the same notebook, Goddard recorded Charlie's precise identification of the upstream boundary of his tribelet:

> [At] Se-sûn-to, mile above Se-tcin-to-dûñ [between Miranda and Phillipsville], fishing there. People live there. Our kind of people. Can't go any further that way. Same kind of people. Same kind of talk. But can't go in early day. (Goddard 1902–1922a, Sinkyone notebook 1, p. 21)

There are reasons to believe that the relationships among the Eel River Athabaskan tribelets were more bellicose than among most California tribelets that shared a common language. Nevertheless, Charlie's fear that stepping outside his home territory in just about any direction would have had lethal consequences is entirely consistent with Kroeber's idea of the political self-sufficiency of the small tribelet unit.

The Kroeberian tribelet has not been without critics.[2] The most influential of these, Lowell John Bean, suggested that the model should be more flexible, pointing to evidence that the population of some tribelets could have been as high as one thousand, and arguing that the size of a tribelet's territory could have varied considerably according to the productivity of the area (Bean 1974). More importantly, Bean and others assembled persuasive evidence for the existence of political structures that went beyond the tribelet level to amalgamate several village communities into ad hoc chieftainships, especially in south-central California (Bean and Blackburn 1976). At the time of contact in the late 1760s, for example, a powerful leader (nicknamed "El Buchon" by the Spanish because of his prominent goiter) held sway over a substantial territory around San Luis Obispo (Jones et al. 2007:129).

Kroeber himself acknowledged that the single-tribelet society with little or no linguistic footprint was not universal in California, but rather the ideal toward which a variety of real-world situations gravitated. A particularly important set of exceptions were the Yokuts "dialect tribes" of the San Joaquin Valley, where a hereditary leader would often exercise authority over the headmen of two or more village communities (Kroeber 1925:474–475). These groups were referred to by special "tribal" names (like Yawdanchi, Chunut, or Chukchansi), not simply by the name of their central village (¶4.11.1), and each had a well-defined local dialect (Kroeber 1963). But despite having these tribe-like characteristics, Kroeber argued, Yokuts groups basically functioned like other California tribelets, as local residential units within a wider cultural matrix, rather than as independent, culturally self-contained social units like the "true" tribes of the Colorado. In particular, their dialectal idiosyncrasies were rudimentary, usually confined to vocabulary differences and a few slight divergences in phonology; they remained mere local varieties subsumed in a much wider—and unnamed—language.[3]

In general, where languages were spread over fairly wide territories, adjacent local varieties would often form a distinctive linguistic cluster, or regional dialect, with respect to other local varieties of the same language. Except in the Yokuts case, however, there is little if any evidence that these regional dialects reflected any formal sociopolitical unity above the village-community level.[4] Instead, regional dialect boundaries seem to have been correlated with networks of marriage and trade, and were thus ultimately determined by geography rather than political integration. A particularly complex development of this sort characterized Nisenan (Southern Maiduan) territory where the four well-defined regional dialects were correlated with riverine travel routes: Plains Nisenan, spoken in a dozen or more tribelet varieties along the Sacramento River, and three distinct Hill Nisenan dialects, Northern, Central, and Southern, each associated with the drainage of one of the streams flowing into the Sacramento from the Sierra foothills to the east.[5]

1.3 Symbolic Function of California Languages

Understanding the social function of a California language is primarily a matter of understanding the symbolic relationship between language and land. Attachment to the land was one of the fundamental characteristics of Native Californians, manifested most clearly in "their strong yearning to live, die, and be buried in the home of their fathers" (Powers 1877:249–250). In addition to fostering an almost obsessive internalization of the geography of one's native tribelet, this bond to the land was more abstractly symbolized by an extreme faithfulness to one's native language—or rather, to the language of the territory in which one was born. When a person had occasion to visit the territory in which another language was spoken—to trade, gamble, negotiate the purchase of a wife, attend a ceremony, or for some other compelling reason—the etiquette strictly required speaking the language of the hosts, since that was the language that "belonged" there. Although the individuals who typically went on these expeditions were either bi- or multilingual (see ¶1.5.1), or had to seek out someone with such skills to serve as an interpreter, facility with the languages of foreigners had only restricted social value in California Indian society. There were few occasions when any language other than the local one could appropriately be spoken in any given place. A foreign wife, in particular, was discouraged from continuing to speak her native language, however poorly she spoke her husband's, lest her children should acquire it.

The association of a particular language with a given tract of land was taken to be an immutable fact of nature. It is revealing that languages and the identities they symbolized were hardly ever lexicalized in California languages. This fact also was first noted by Powers:

> So contracted are their journeyings and their knowledge that they do not need a complicated system of names. If there are any people living twenty miles away they are not aware of their existence. In consequence of this it was almost impossible for me to learn any fixed names of tribes. (1877:315)

Even the Hupa, who traveled widely along the Trinity and Klamath Rivers, had no consistent names for the linguistic identities of the region. For their own Hupa-Chilula language, they made do with Dining'xine:wh ('those who speak like Dini people, i.e., Athabaskans'). One of the few apparent counterexamples, the term "Kashaya" that the speakers of Southwestern Pomo have long applied both to themseves and to their language, has recently been shown by Lightfoot (2005) to have its origin in the restructuring of this ethnic group—originally an uncoordinated group of at least two tribelets—as a work force for the Russian fur traders at Fort Ross during the early nineteenth century. Almost without exception, the names by which we now know the languages of the California region were created by whites, not infrequently by anthropologists and linguists.

The apparent arbitrariness of many language boundaries contributed to the aura of supernatural inevitability that attended them. While in some places they would run along mountain ridges or other natural dividing points, in others they would separate two adjacent village communities with long-standing ties of kinship and trade, as for example the northernmost Wiyot tribelet, Potawat, at the mouth of the Mad River, and the southernmost Yurok tribelet, Tsurai, ten miles to the north at Trinidad. That Wiyot and Yurok are the two branches of California Algic (¶3.1) imparts special historical interest to the location of this particular boundary, but it did little to explain it to Indians of the historic period.

Language boundaries were also remarkably impermeable. The normal processes of assimilation between adjacent languages were reduced to a minimum. Lexical borrowing was infrequent, at least in the form of overt loanwords, and confined to a few semantic domains (see ¶4.14), although covert metaphors and other styles of expression were probably to some extent shared.[6] Where phonological or grammatical borrowing can be suspected, it is more likely to be the result of language shift than of assimilation between adjacent languages. Even culturally shared subpatterns such as toponymy and counting systems tended to be sharply discontinuous at language boundaries; it was quite exceptional for a language not to have its own distinct place-names and numerals, even where the adjoining languages belonged to the same language family.[7]

It is a reasonable hypothesis that this close-fitting, symbolic Californian relationship between language and the land, operating over several millennia, was the primary cause of much of the structural diversity that is the primary subject matter of this book. Its effects are especially clear where the linguistic diversity in question is among languages belonging to a widespread North American family, such as Athabaskan, Uto-Aztecan, or Algic, which may be assumed to have intruded into the California linguistic matrix at a relatively late date.

Hill (2006), for example, has explored the possibility that the different patterns of internal diversity within the Takic and Numic branches of Uto-Aztecan might be in part explained because the former diversified in the California context while the latter did so mostly in the Great Basin. I have made similar observations about the surprisingly deep differences between the California and Oregon Athabaskan subfamilies, which can be the product of no more than fifteen hundred years of change (Golla 2000). One of the most interesting results of Hill's comparison of Numic and Takic is that a number of the "deep" discontinuities that a linguist tends to notice when comparing one Takic language to another appear much less important, or even to disappear, when they are coded according to the feature variants recognized by the *World Atlas of Linguistic Structures* (Haspelmath et al. 2005). While the WALS coding may be too blunt an instrument to capture the differences in structure that set the Takic languages apart in actual use, another possibility is that many of these differences are primarily sociolinguistic, not grammatical in the strict sense, and more to be attributed to the need for symbolic contrast between adjacent languages—the "California pattern" as it were—than to the accumulation of random changes in two speech communities that have lost contact with one another.

1.4 Languages and Migration

Ideology is not historic truth. Language boundaries were as much in flux in California as anywhere else in the world.

If the historical circumstances that established a linguistic boundary between Potawat and Tsurai are lost in the mists of time, the location of the eastern boundary of both tribelets is easily explainable as the actively contested frontier between the coastal peoples and the Athabaskans of the interior mountains. Early reports indicate that the Athabaskan Chilula were encroaching on Wiyot territory along the lower Mad River near Blue Lake, resulting in a steady shifting of the language boundary westward. While a nineteenth-century observer like Powers may have been too quick to extrapolate a long history of warfare throughout California from isolated incidents of raiding, in the areas where Athabaskans had settled there seems little doubt that a long-term process of expropriation and displacement was still at work at the time of contact.

Michael Moratto (1984) and others have made a persuasive case that the language geography of California may preserve the trace, at least in some part, of old frontiers of intergroup conflict. To a considerable extent I adopt this perspective in the conjectural outline of California linguistic prehistory that I present in Part 5. The Athabaskans almost certainly pushed into southern Oregon and northern California during the last fifteen hundred years, and we may suspect similar incursions and expansions over the past two or three millennia wherever we find single languages or shallowly differentiated language families occupying suspiciously large territories. This roster includes (but is not limited to) the Yokuts language in the San Joaquin Valley; the Wintuan languages in the Sacramento Valley; the string of Achumawi dialects along the Pit River; the Eastern Miwoks from Sacramento to Yosemite; the Shasta dialects, spread from Scott Valley to Shasta Valley and across the Siskiyous to Oregon; the Numic occupation of the Basin; and the Upland (Pai) dialects of Yuman.

By inverting the argument, where we find single languages or isolated families restricted to small territories, we may suspect them to be relics of much older movements of peoples. In this light, certain distributional regularities should be noted.

1. Although the region has an abundance of single-language families or "classificatory isolates"—for the most part orphaned branches of the ancient Hokan or Penutian phyla—none of these is confined to a single tribelet. Chimariko was spoken in at least three tribelet dialects, and the same minimal diversity can be observed in Takelma, Klamath-Modoc, Yana, Esselen, and Salinan. Washo, a Hokan isolate with no reported dialect diversity, is only an apparent exception, since its High Sierra environment led to the development of a seminomadic subsistence strategy more typical of the Basin or the subarctic than of resource-rich California.

2. The same absence of single-tribelet branches holds for the half-dozen moderately differentiated small language families that are so characteristic of the

region. Southeastern Pomo, spoken at the eastern end of Clear Lake in what was probably the smallest acreage associated with any California language, was split into three distinct tribelet speech communities, each on its own island (¶3.15.1). Cupeño within Takic, Hupa-Chilula within California Athabaskan, Chetco-Tolowa within Oregon Athabaskan, and Obispeño within Chumash are each composed of two or more tribelets.

3. Four California languages that apparently *were* confined to a single tribelet can be seen as the proverbial exceptions that prove the rule: Northeastern Pomo, spoken by the tribelet that controlled the salt deposits at Stonyford, northeast of Clear Lake; Kato, the distinctive variant of California Athabaskan spoken by the tribelet at Laytonville, at the center of a trade network connecting the coast with the interior and the Russian River with the Eel River; Karkin, the only Bay Area Costanoan language not to be a local dialect of San Francisco Bay Costanoan, spoken by the tribelet of "Carquines" (the word means 'traders' in some varieties of Costanoan) that controlled Carquinez Strait; and Konomihu, the distinctive Shastan language of the tribelet settled at Forks of Salmon, mediating the trade that flowed east and west between the Scott Valley Shasta and the peoples of the lower Klamath. Besides being the languages of important trading communities, at least two of four are known from ethnographic sources to have recently and fairly rapidly diverged from a much less distinctive local dialect (a variety of Northern Pomo in the case of the Stonyford tribelet and a variety of Eel River Athabaskan in the case of the Laytonville tribelet).

The following conclusions are suggested:

1. A minimum of several tribelets of speakers seems required if a relict language like Southeastern Pomo or Chimariko is to be maintained as the symbolic property of a district, and when the number falls to two or three, the language is unlikely to survive for more than a few generations. A combination of remoteness and rusticity seems to best account for the persistence of small enclaves of Hokan speech such as Chimariko, Yana, and Esselen. They can be interpreted historically as remnants of formerly more widespread language communities.

2. The identification of a single tribelet with a distinct language was the product of a very different phenomenon, rooted in the evolved ideology of the Late Period. These tribelets were typically trading centers, and their distinctive speech appears not to represent the survival of relict patterns but rapid innovation on the basis of an originally widely shared dialect or language, sometimes accompanied by social or geographical isolation.[8]

1.5 Multilingualism

An interesting—if poorly understood—corollary of the primarily symbolic nature of language boundaries in aboriginal California was the status of multilingualism. Two rather different situations can be distinguished: (1) *personal multilingualism*, the knowledge of the language of adjacent groups by a relatively small number of individuals who, as the result of intermarriage or trade, came into close contact with foreigners; and (2) *areal multilingualism*, the general use of two or more distinct languages in the same community or region.

1.5.1 Personal Multilingualism

At least a few individuals, both men and women, in most California groups were bi- or multilingual in nearby languages. Bilingual women were usually wives who had been raised in an adjacent foreign territory; in those areas where women were shamans, an accomplished doctor would not infrequently be hired to perform curing rituals outside her own territory and would be expected to have some acquaintance with foreign speech. Interpreters, however, appear to have usually been men, probably having learned one or more foreign languages in the course of trading. Since the social value of such multilingalism diminished quickly after Spanish and English became the lingua francas, ethnographic data are relatively sparse. However, Powers makes several interesting allusions to the social function of personal multilingualism in aboriginal times:

> The Kelta [the South Fork Hupa] are per force polyglots; and I saw a curious specimen of this class of inter-tribal interpreters so peculiar to California. . . . He had one eye and six languages in his head. (1877:89)
>
> The Wappo display great readiness in learning their neighbors' tongues. Old Colorado was said by the whites to have spoken in his prime fourteen languages and dialects. (1877:198)
>
> [The Yurok] have . . . much the same customs as their up-river neighbors [the Karuk], but a totally different language. They usually learn each other's language, and two of them will sit and patter gossip for hours, each speaking in his own tongue. (1877:44)

Alice Shepherd has reported a special type of personal multilingualism among Wintu shamans, who would sometimes shift to another language when channeling a spirit, particularly a malevolent one, during doctoring. In the example that she analyzed, the shaman apparently employed a variety of the neighboring Shasta language. Other shamans were said to use Achomawi, or even English. A translator would usually be at hand while the shaman was in a trance to interpret the foreign speech of evil spirits for the benefit of the monolinguals in the audience (Schlichter [Shepherd] 1981a:105–106).

1.5.2 Areal Multilingualism

Given the overriding principle that only the language that "belonged" to that place could ordinarily be spoken there, it is not surprising that certain areas along the border between two language territories should be considered neutral territory where the two languages could both legitimately be spoken. There is at least one report of such an overlap being restricted to a specific part of a single village.[9] More typically, the overlap included an area up to the size of an entire tribelet. While most seem to represent the long-term expansion of one language at the expense of another, these areas of overlap appear to have been perceived by the people of any given generation as natural and permanent features of the linguistic landscape, just like language territories themselves.

Several such dual-language areas are attested in southwestern Oregon and northwestern California, where Shasta, Wintu, and several Athabaskan languages appear to have been expanding their territories at the time of contact. These included the following:

1. The Illinois River Valley in the vicinity of Cave Junction, Oregon, where the original Takelma-speaking inhabitants seem to have been in transition to Rogue River Athabaskan (Gray 1987).

2. The Klamath River between Happy Camp and Hamburg, where both a "rustic" dialect of Karuk and a distinct dialect of Shasta were said to have been spoken. Whether this area was in transition from Karuk to Shasta or vice versa is not clear, although the former seems more likely given the general pattern of Shasta expansion. The Klamath River goes through a narrow canyon here; the widely scattered villages probably constituted two tribelets, known to the Shasta as Kammatwa and Watiru (¶3.11.1).

3. The valley of Bear Creek between Ashland and Medford, Oregon, which was being "fought over" by the Shasta and the Takelma, according to early historical reports. Takelma was undoubtedly the earlier language of this area, and its inhabitants were probably increasingly bilingual in Shasta.

4. The valley of New River, around present-day Denny, where speakers of the local variety of Chimariko were in transition to Hupa. Powers's highly colored description of the language shift occurring in this area has been quoted by several authors:

   > Although most of the petty tributaries [of the Hupa] had their own tongues originally, so vigorously were they put to school in the language of their masters that most of their vocabularies were sapped and reduced to bald categories of names. They had the dry bones of subsantives, but the flesh and blood of verbs were sucked out of them by the Hupâ. A . . . pioneer well acquainted with the Chi-mal´-a-kwe [New River Chimariko], who once had an entirely distinct tongue,

told me that before they became extinct they scarcely employed a verb which was not Hupâ. (1877:72)

The Chimarikos who lived along the Trinity River east of Burnt Ranch between Del Loma and Junction City were apparently undergoing a similar transition to Wintu (Chase-Dunn and Mann 1998), as were the South Fork Chimariko around Hyampom (Merriam and Talbot 1974:12; Bauman 1980a).

The resettlement of a number of Mono speakers across the Sierra crest in the century or two preceding contact (Kroeber 1959a:265–269) gave rise to a more balanced Yokuts-Mono bilingualism in the foothills between the Fresno and Kaweah Rivers. As described by Gayton (1948), the situation at the time of contact appears to have been fluid, with families speaking different languages living side by side in the same villages. In the majority of communities the immigrant Western Mono lineages were in the process of adopting a Yokuts identity; in a few, however, the process was going in the other direction, and the original Yokuts lineages were slowly switching to Western Mono. The most thoroughly bilingual community, the Entimbich, whose territory was along Mill Creek in Dunlap Valley, south of Kings River, appeared to Gayton to be midway in a transition from Yokuts to Mono (1948:254–255; see ¶3.31.1).

In at least four cases, a more or less stable multilingualism seems to have developed as the result of intensive trading and intervisitation:

SOUTH FORK OF THE EEL RIVER

The South Fork of the Eel River south of Garberville, and the adjacent coast, was the territory of the groups known ethnographically as the Southern (or Shelter Cove) Sinkyone and the Kato, but it was also an area in which Northern Pomo and one or more varieties of Northern Yukian were spoken. Powers referred to the Southern Sinkyone and the Kato as the "Kai Pomo" and the "Kato Pomo," respectively (1877:148–155), indicating that Pomo was their language of identification. Although Pliny Goddard (1903b) argued that Powers's nomenclature was incorrect, there is little doubt that Pomo was widely spoken by the Athabaskans of this region. As late as 1942, Harrington was able to collect a trilingual vocabulary (Kato, Northern Pomo, and Coast Yuki) during a brief visit to the Kato community in Laytonville (Mills 1985:9–15). Powers again provides a vivid description of the aboriginal multilingualism of the Kato:

> The Kato Pomo . . . do not speak Pomo entirely pure, but employ a mixture of that and Wailaki [i.e., Eel River Athabaskan]. . . . The men pay considerable attention to linguistic studies, and there is seldom one who cannot speak most of the Pomo dialects within a day's journey of his ancestral valley. The chiefs especially devote no little care to the training of their sons as polyglot diplomatists; and . . . they frequently send them to reside several months with the

chiefs of contiguous valleys to acquire the dialects there in vogue. . . . Like the Kai Pomo [Shelter Cove Sinkyone], their northern neighbors, they forbid their squaws from studying languages . . . principally, it is believed, in order to prevent them from gadding about and forming acquaintances in neighboring valleys. (1877:150)

EASTERN CLEAR LAKE

In the eastern end of the Clear Lake basin Patwin was widely used as a second language by the Southeastern (Sulphur Bank) Pomo and the Lake Miwok of upper Cache Creek, while the adjacent Cache Creek and Long Valley Patwin, cut off from the rest of the Patwin by a long canyon and a spur of the Coast Range, were fluent in both Pomo and Miwok. Intermarriage among the three linguistic communities was quite frequent, and they shared a distinctive version of the Kuksu religion (Loeb 1933:214–226). Observers as late as the beginning of the twentieth century found it difficult to distinguish them, often calling them all "Pomo."[10] Powers described the Southeastern Pomo under the Patwin name Makh´-el-chel, and the individuals he interviewed during his 1871 visit to Sulphur Bank apparently spoke Patwin in his presence. Curiously, however, he also noted that the Southeastern Pomo "heartily despised" their Patwin neighbors to the east (1877:214–216). The Lake Miwoks, whose language was permeated with Patwin borrowings (Callaghan 1964a), were usually considered Patwins before Barrett's work in the early twentieth century (1908a:363), while the southernmost Lake Miwoks, around Middletown, were also bilingual in Wappo (Merriam 1955:43–48).

NORTHEASTERN POMO

The Northeastern Pomo, at Stonyford, who were at the center of a salt trade that extended throughout the Sacramento Valley, had a high degree of bilingualism in the two adjacent Wintuan languages, Nomlaki and Patwin (Kroeber 1925:224; see ¶3.15.3).

CARQUINEZ STRAIT

Closely adjacent village communities on the north and south shores of Carquinez Strait spoke at least five distinct languages belonging to three different families: Suisun (Southern Patwin), Saclan (Bay Miwok), Alaguali (Coast Miwok), and Karkin and Huchiun (Costanoan) (Milliken 1995:24–26). Since these communities were either socially extinct or profoundly restructured before 1810 and little if any direct ethnographic information survives, the evidence for multilingualism in the area must be largely inferential.

1.6 Language Families and Phyla

Languages whose similar grammatical structures and patterned similarity in vocabulary provide definitive evidence of a historical origin in a single ancestral language are said to constitute a *language family*. A language that shows no such connection to another language is a classificatorily isolated language, or more succinctly a *language isolate*—that is, a language family in its own right. The majority of California Indian languages belong either to highly localized language families with two or three members (e.g., Yukian, Maiduan) or are language isolates (e.g., Karuk, Esselen). Of the remainder, most belong to the Uto-Aztecan family (¶3.30) or to the Athabaskan sub-family of the Na-Dene family (¶3.4), both widespread in western North America. Two others (Yurok and Wiyot) are outliers of the continent-wide Algic family (¶3.1). The California representatives of these "superfamilies" are further grouped into sub-units, or *branches*, although these are to some extent provisional classifications. Two Athabaskan branches are usually recognized (Oregon Athabaskan and California Athabaskan) and three Uto-Aztecan branches (Takic, Numic, and Tubatulabal). Yurok and Wiyot are treated by some scholars as independent branches of Algic, and by others as a single "Ritwan" branch. The ways in which the California branches of Athabaskan and Uto-Aztecan relate to more general subdivisions within these two families remains controversial and largely beyond the purview of this book. But whatever these relationships may be, they are distant. The Athabaskan, Algic, and Uto-Aztecan languages of the California region have adapted to the area in many details of phonology, grammar, lexicon, and sociolinguistic profile, and are unmistakably Californian.

Excluding the seven Californian branches of continental superfamilies, twenty-four linguistic units at the family or isolate level are attested in the California region as we maximally define it here. If we remove Waikuri and the two other barely-known languages of the southern tip of Baja California, we are still left with twenty-one, out of the fifty-eight roughly equivalent units attested for all of North America north of Mesoamerica (Golla 2007a). Languages confined to the California region thus accounted for approximately 36 percent of the family-level classificatory diversity in precontact North America.

With the exception of Yukian and Chumash, the localized language families and language isolates of California are usually assigned to one of two *phyla*, Hokan (¶3.8) or Penutian (¶3.21), on the basis of grammatical and lexical similarities that, while less than sufficient to establish a language family relationship, make the hypothesis of remote common origin not improbable. Although Hokan and Penutian were originally proposed by Dixon and Kroeber (1913, 1919) only to account for similarities among families and isolates in the California region, both phyla have subsequently been expanded to include languages as far afield as the Northwest Coast and Central America. Thus, at a deeper and much less certain historical level, the Hokan and Penutian relationships parallel the family-level connections between California and non-California languages represented by the Athabaskan, Uto-Aztecan, and

Algonquian relationships, and serve to link the linguistic diversity of the region to continent-wide (even hemisphere-wide) patterns of diversity that may date back to the earliest migrations into the hemisphere (see Part 5).

The Yukian and Chumash language families have resisted classification either as Hokan or as Penutian, although Chumash has sometimes been considered an outlier of Hokan. Nor do they constitute a third California phylum, although a few ancient loanwords seem to indicate a historical connection of some sort. While Yukian shows intriguing (if geographically puzzling) similarites to some of the languages of the Southeast, it is best considered, like Chumash, to be an isolate at the phylum level. What little is known of the languages (or language families) of the southernmost extremity of Baja California suggests that they, too, may have been deep classificatory isolates.

It should be emphasized that the significance of language family and phylum affiliation is almost entirely historical. Cultural and social correlations are virtually nonexistent. There was nothing to distinguish a "Hokan" from a "Penutian" lifestyle in aboriginal California, nor any significant cultural trait that united all "Uto-Aztecans" or "Athabaskans" other than that they spoke historically related languages. (The only exceptions are certain aspects of kinship terminology and fragments of mythic themes, which sometimes—and never exclusively—show some degree of correlation with language families; but kinship and myth, it could be argued, are themselves merely complex elements of a common linguistic heritage.)

The same is true of possible correlations between language classification and physical characteristics. What differences there were among California native populations in such morphological features as height, skin color, or head shape were seldom, if ever, coterminous with differences in language family or phylum. The often-noted "Yuki" physical type—short-statured and long-headed—was shared with the Eel River Athabaskans and the Yana, but was not at all characteristic of the Wappo, although they spoke a Yukian language. Similarly, the sharp discontinuity in the distribution of mtDNA haplogroups at the Chumash-Takic boundary (Eshleman and Smith 2007:296–298) is less likely to reflect an "intrusive wedge" of Uto-Aztecan languages expanding from the Great Basin to the Southern California coast than to mark a long-established cultural boundary between "upper" and "lower" California, the latter more deeply associated with Yuman-Cochimí than with Uto-Aztecan languages.

PART 2

HISTORY OF STUDY

Between Cabrillo's first exploration of the southern coast in 1542 and the raising of the Bear Flag at Sonoma three centuries later, little attempt was made to document the indigenous languages of the California region. It was only in the years following the Gold Rush that the nature and diversity of California languages came to be appreciated. But knowledge accumulated fast, and by the mid-1870s John Wesley Powell was able to compile an extensive comparative vocabulary and outline a family-level classification (see Box 4).

In 1901, the University of California launched a comprehensive program of California Indian ethnographic research and hired Alfred Kroeber as its first full-time anthropologist. Inspired by his mentor, Franz Boas, to place language at the center of culture, Kroeber devoted much of his long career at Berkeley to the documentation and analysis of California Indian languages. With the exception of two remarkable independent scholars, C. Hart Merriam and J. P. Harrington, who deserve their own chapters, the story of California Indian linguistics in the first half of the 20th century is largely Kroeber's.

Kroeber's own research was a mix of broad typological surveys and the intensive documentation of representative languages, such as Yurok and Mohave. Between 1912 and the early 1920s, he worked in close collaboration with Edward Sapir, primarily on historical and classificatory matters. This relationship endured into the next generation, as a significant number of Sapir's students took up work on California languages, culminating in the 1950s with the establishment at Berkeley of an autonomous Survey of California Indian Languages under the leadership of Mary Haas.

While recent decades have seen the study of American Indian languages firmly integrated into the research agenda of modern linguistics rather than anthropology, California Indian linguistics remains uniquely Kroeberian in spirit. This is especially true at Berkeley, where fresh work has been undertaken on such languages as Yurok and Hupa, and descendents of the "informants" of Kroeber's and Sapir's day are being trained as scholars of their own linguistic heritage.

Before Linguistics

2.1 Earliest Attestations

2.1.1 Juan Rodriguez Cabrillo, 1542–1543

Following the 1539 voyage of Francisco de Ulloa to the head of the Gulf of California, Juan Rodriguez Cabrillo was commissioned by Viceroy Mendoza to explore the Pacific coast farther north in the hope of finding a way to China. On June 27, 1542, a small fleet under Cabrillo's command set out from Navidad (now Acapulco) and reached the vicinity of San Diego on September 28. Progressing up the coast, Cabrillo sailed through the Santa Barbara Channel and around Point Conception, eventually reaching the mouth of the Russian River before storms forced him to turn back. The expedition returned in late November to "San Salvador" (one of the Channel Islands—Santa Catalina, San Miguel, and Santa Rosa have all been suggested) to make repairs, and there Cabrillo died on January 3, 1543, as the result of a fall. His second in command brought the remainder of the party back to Navidad, where they arrived April 14, 1543.

The expedition's report contains the earliest documentation of any California Indian language, primarily in the form of several dozen Chumash place-names from the Channel Islands and adjacent mainland.[1] Although the exact locations of the places named have been widely debated by scholars (see Kroeber 1925:552–556),[2] eight of them can be securely identified as Barbareño and Ventureño villages known in the twentieth century or attested in eighteenth- and nineteenth-century records: "Alloc" (*heliyïk*), Goleta; "Coloc" (*q'oloq'*), Carpenteria; "Mugu" (*muwu*), Point Mugu; "Siucut" (*syuxtun*), at the mouth of Mission Creek, Santa Barbara; "Susuquei" (*šišuč'i?*), between Refugio and Gaviota; "Xabagua" (*šalawa*), between Santa Barbara and Carpenteria; "Xexo" (*šišolop*), east of Point Conception; and "Xucu" (*šuku*), Rincon.

Three Chumash island names were recorded by the expedition: "Limu" (*limiw*), Santa Cruz Island; "Ciquimuymu," San Miguel Island; and "Nicalque," Santa Rosa Island. Only two of the eight village names attributed to Santa Cruz Island can be idenified with certainty, "Maxul" (*maščal*) on the north shore and "Xagua" (*šawa*) on the south shore.

It was reported that the Indians of the Gaviota area called maize "oep" and called a large animal, probably the elk, "cae," although neither word can be identified in later attestations of Chumash (Kelsey 1986:149). The expedition also noted that news of Coronado's depredations among the New Mexico pueblos in 1540–1541 had reached the California coast, and that terms for "Spaniard" were already in use in both Diegueño and Ventureño Chumash.[3]

2.1.2 Francis Drake, 1579

In the summer of 1579, the English explorer and privateer Francis Drake made landfall somewhere on the Northern California or Oregon coast, where he and his crew spent several weeks repairing a leak in his ship, *The Golden Hinde*. Most historians locate the landing site at or near Drake's Bay on Point Reyes, a few miles north of the Golden Gate, in territory that ethnographically belonged to the Marin Miwok. Two of the narratives of Drake's voyage—Francis Fletcher's *The World Encompassed* (1628) and a fragmentary account by Richard Maddox that was published in E. Taylor (1932)—contain transcriptions of a few Indian words or phrases. The relevant passages were published by Heizer (1947), who identified several of the Indian words as Marin Miwok (see also Heizer and Elmendorf 1942). The material has been reexamined in recent years by Callaghan and Bond (n.d.:11–13), who concur that the language is a dialect of Marin Miwok.

Fletcher records four words, "hioh" or "hyoh" 'king'; "tabah" or "tobah" 'an herb'; "petah" 'a roote whereof they make a kind of meale, and either bake it into bread, or eat it raw'; and "gnaah" 'an entreaty that we would sing'. He also notes that "oh" was uttered as 'a cry in unison during pauses in prayers'. Maddox provides another transcription of the word for king, "hioghe," and adds "cheepe" 'bread', "huchee kecharoh" 'sit downe', "nocharo mu" 'tuch me not', and "hodeli oh heigh oh heigh ho hodali oh" 'ther song when they worship god . . . one dauncing first wh his handes up, and al ye rest after lyke ye prest and people'.

Callaghan and Bond agree with Heizer that "hioh," "hyoh," and "hioghe" are variant transcriptions of Marin Miwok *hóypu* 'chief', and that "cheepe" is undoubtedly Marin Miwok *číppa* 'bread'. The other words and phrases are less certain. Heizer suggested that Maddox's "huchee kecharoh" 'sit downe' may actually have meant 'go into the house', Bodega Miwok *hóči kočcatto* (although Callaghan and Bond comment that this seems rather abrupt for an invitation). He also proposed that "nocharo mu" 'tuch me not' may actually have meant 'stay over there' (cf. Bodega Miwok *nótto* 'there' and *ṣuṭámmi* 'stay!') and speculated that Fletcher's "gnaah" could reflect Marin Miwok *koya* 'sing'.

2.2 Jesuit Missionaries in Baja California

The first Europeans to describe the aboriginal languages of California in any detail were missionaries of the Jesuit and Franciscan orders. Initially the focus was on Lower California, with an expansion into Upper California in 1769.

Although the Pacific coast as far north as Cape Mendocino was familiar from the mid-1560s to the pilots of the twice-yearly Manila-Acapulco galleons, no effort was made to incorporate any part of California into colonial Mexico until the end of the seventeenth century. After a preliminary expedition led by Isidro Atondo in 1683, permanent settlement of the southern gulf coast of Baja California

FIGURE 1. The Indians welcome Francis Drake to California in 1579. (From Theodore and John De Bry, *Collectiones Peregrationium . . .* Ser. I, *Historia Americae*, Pars VIII, 1599.) A composite rendering of events drawn by the artist from information recorded by Fletcher (Heizer 1974:49). The Hans P. Kraus Collection of Sir Francis Drake, Rare Book and Special Collections Division, Library of Congress.

began with Father Juan María Salvatierra's establishment of a mission at Loreto in 1697 (Map 2). This venture, along with Father Eusebio Kino's exploration of northern Sonora and the delta of the Colorado between 1698 and 1706, was financed by the Jesuits, who controlled most of the missionary activity in the region at the time. Four other missions were soon founded in the vicinity of Loreto, and by 1730 the system included a dozen establishments, extending from San José del Cabo at the southern cape to San Ignacio, deep in Cochimí territory. A northward expansion in the 1750s and 1760s took the mission frontier to Santa María, about eighty miles from the southern edge of Kiliwa (Yuman) territory.

The Jesuit missionaries who worked in Baja California during this period made serious efforts to learn and document the languages of their converts. It was a long-standing policy of the order, enunciated by Ignatius Loyola and incorporated into the constitution of the Society of Jesus, to use vernacular languages in communicating with the laity. (The Jesuits drew their members from an assortment of European nationalities, and many were multilingual.) All Jesuits assigned to New Spain were required to learn Nahuatl in preparation for tackling the local language of their parish. In Baja California, a missionary was expected to preach in the language of his mission and to pave the way for his successors by compiling a grammatical description along with translations of some of the basic prayers.[4]

Unfortunately, very little of what must have been a rich documentation survives. In the mid-eighteenth century the

Jesuit order, long suspected of having covert political and social agendas, came into open conflict with the Spanish authorities, and in 1767 King Carlos III ordered the Jesuits to cease all their activities in New Spain. Early the following year the Baja California missionaries were forcibly deported. It was apparently in the turmoil of this expulsion that the grammars, prayer books, dictionaries, and other linguistic manuscripts that had been compiled were lost. Some may have been carried away by the departing Jesuits, while those left at the missions were most likely neglected by the Dominicans who eventually took charge, whose interest in the local languages was minimal.[5] On their return to Europe, some of the former Jesuit missionaries wrote memoirs of their experiences, here and there including remarks about the indigenous languages they had learned. What is known about Baja California languages largely comes from these postexpulsion documents.

The most important of these accounts was written by **Jacob Baegert** (1717–1777), an Alsatian German who had been stationed at Mission San Luis Gonzaga, between Loreto and La Paz. In his *Nachrichten von der Amerikanischen Halbinsel Californien,* first published in Mannheim in 1771–1772 (Baegert 1952), Baegert included several pages of grammatical notes on the principal language of the mission, Waikuri, along with glossed texts of the Lord's Prayer and the Apostles' Creed (Zamponi 2004). This is the only surviving documentation of Waikuri, and it constitutes nearly all that is directly known of the languages of the southernmost part of the Baja California peninsula. At least two other distinct languages (or language families) are

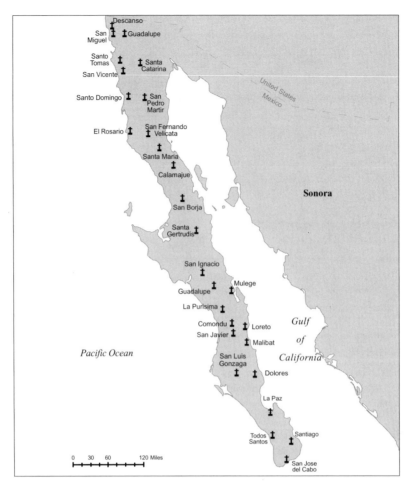

MAP 2. Missions of Baja California (after Laylander 1997).

known to have been spoken in this region, Pericú on the Southern Cape and Monqui on the east coast in the vicinity of Loreto, but except for some place-names and a few recordings of isolated words nothing of them survives (see ¶3.37).

In a short manuscript entitled *Specimina Linguae Californicae,* another exiled Jesuit, **Benno Ducrue,** who had been a missionary at La Purísima Cadegomó and Guadalupe, northwest of Loreto, provided the numerals from one to five together with twenty-six glossed phrases in a southern dialect of Cochimí (Burrus 1967:136–139; Mixco 1978:63–68). The most extensive Jesuit documentation of Cochimí, however, is found in the *Historia Natural y Crónica de la Antigua California,* written in Bologna in 1785 by **Miguel del Barco,** who had served at Mission San Javier Viggé for thirty years and spoke the Southern Cochimí dialect of that mission fluently (Barco 1973). In addition to translations of the basic prayers and a sermon composed in the language, Barco's manuscript includes a valuable outline of Cochimí grammar.[6]

The Franciscans who replaced the Jesuits in Baja California in 1768 were in turn replaced by Dominicans in 1773. From then onward, little attention was paid to the dwindling and increasingly Hispanicized mission communities in the southern and central areas, and emphasis was instead put on northward expansion. The Franciscans established San Fernando Velicatá, at the northern end of Cochimí territory, in 1768, and in the 1780s and 1790s the Dominicans founded a chain of eight missions in northwestern corner of the peninsula, for the most part in Kiliwa and southern Diegueño territory. The southernmost of these establishments were at El Rosario on the coast and San Pedro Mártir in the central highlands; the northernmost were at San Miguel and Descanso, near Ensenada. Little useful linguistic documentation is associated with any of these late northern Baja missions.

2.3 Franciscans in Alta California

2.3.1 Founding the Missions

Early in 1768 the Spanish government began formulating plans to secure Alta California, concerned that this remote territory might fall into the hands of the English or the

Russians. The Franciscans who had just been given charge of the former Jesuit missions in Baja California were asked to refocus their efforts on establishing new missions to the north, beginning with San Diego and Monterey, where good harbors had been noted by Sebastián Vizcaíno during his coastal reconnaisance in 1602. In May 1768, the Spanish Visitor General, José de Gálvez, issued orders for a full-scale expedition to be mounted the following year, with the newly appointed "Governor of the Californias," Don Gaspar de Portolá, in overall command.

Two ships and two overland parties were to meet at San Diego Bay. The first land party, led by Captain Fernando de Rivera, set out from the newly established Cochimí mission at San Fernando Velicatá on March 24, accompanied by Father Juan Crespí. A second, larger, party, led by Portolá himself, left Velicatá on May 15 and was accomanied by Father Junípero Serra, the president of the California missions, and three other Franciscans, together with a number of settlers and soldiers. Rivera's detachment reached San Diego in May, and Portolá's on June 29. Without delay, the combined expedition started north for Monterey on July 14, 1769. Led by Portolá, it included Captain Rivera and two other officers, Engineer Miguel Costansó and Lieutenant Pedro Fages, two of the Franciscans, Fathers Crespí and Gómez, and between fifty and sixty others—soldiers, mule drivers, and Christian Indians from Baja California.[7] Fathers Serra, Vizcaíno, and Parrón remained behind in San Diego to await a supply ship and to construct the first Alta California mission, San Diego Alcalá, which was formally established July 16 on Presidio Hill, overlooking Mission Valley (Map 3).

As the expedition moved north along the coastal plain, Crespí began noting linguistic variation. About twenty-five miles north of San Diego, the expedition crossed into Takic territory, where the usefulness of the expedition's Cochimí interpreters ceased.[8] Although the new idiom was "understood over a distance of some leagues," Crespí observed that "every day we can plainly recognize that there is a change in the language." On July 24, a few miles north of the site of Mission San Juan Capistrano, Crespí took down a list of thirty-one words, the first vocabulary ever recorded of an Alta California Indian language (Box 1).

By August 1 they were at the site of Los Angeles. Traveling northwest through the San Fernando and Santa Clara Valleys, they entered Chumash territory around Santa Susanna and reached the Santa Barbara area on August 19. The denser population and more complex material and social culture of the Chumash impressed them, as did the importance of the occangoing plank canoe, or *tomol*. At some point during the middle of August, as the expedition moved along the Santa Barbara Channel (or possibly during the expedition's return trip in January 1770), Miguel Costansó took down a short list of Barbareño words (Box 2). Included in his *Diario Histórico* (1770), the earliest published account of the expedition, this was the first vocabulary of a California language north of Baja California to reach print.[9]

BOX 1. CRESPÍ'S VOCABULARY OF JUANEÑO (1769)*

como se llama [what is it called?], *ybi*

agua [water], *pal*

osso [bear], *junut*

enzino [live oak], *uasal*

mano [hand], *ñima*

viene [come!], *ygage*

pescado [fish], *loquiuchi*

liebre [hare], *suichi*

venado [deer], *sucuat*

verrendo [antelope], *pat*

camino [trail], *petlou*

mar [sea], *momt*

ranchería [village], *esat*

sol [sun], *temete*

luna [moon], *muil*

chía [sage], *pasal*

cielo [sky], *tupachi*

canoa, o balza [canoe or "balsa"], *paut*

tierra [earth], *exel*

piedra [stone], *tot*

hombre [man], *potajo*

muger [woman], *sungal*

muchachito de pecho [small child in arms], *amaisicalla*

jícara, o batea [cup or bowl], *joil*

lumbre [fire], *cut*

tabaco [tobacco], *piut*

pipa [pipe], *cabalmel*

carriso [reed], *juiquichi*

pedernal [flint], *tacat*

flecha [arrow], *jul*

arco [bow], *cutapic*

*From A. Brown 2001:306–307.

Proceeding up the coast, the expedition reached the San Simeon area on September 13, then followed the Santa Lucia mountains through Salinan and Esselen territory, reaching the mouth of the Salinas River in Rumsen Costanoan territory on October 1. Although they had reached their goal, Monterey Bay, fog obscured the shoreline and they failed to recognize the landmarks described by Vizcaíno, and

Nucchù . . . . . . La Cabeza [head]

Kejuhé . . . . El Pecho [breast]

Huachajá . . . . . La Mano [hand]

Chipucú . . . . . . El Codo [elbow]

Tocholò . . . . . . El Sobaco [armpit]

Tononomò . . . . El Muslo [thigh]

Pistocù . . . . . . La Rodilla [knee]

Kippejuè . . . . . La Pierna [leg]

Acteme . . . . . . El Pie [foot]

Tomol . . . . Lancha, ò Canoa [boat or canoe]

Apa . . . . Rancheria [village]

Temí . . . . Capitan, ò Principal [chief or headman]

Amo . . . . No [no]

Pacà . . . . Uno [1]

Excò . . . . Dos [2]

Maseja . . . . Tres [3]

Scumu . . . . Quatro [4]

Itipaca . . . . Cinco [5]

Itixco . . . . Seis [6]

Itimasgo . . . . . Siete [7]

Malahua . . . . . Ocho [8]

Upax . . . . Nueve [9]

Kerxco . . . . Diez [10]

so continued north, discovering San Francisco Bay on October 31. After returning to San Diego to regroup early in 1770, a second expedition set out on April 17 to confirm the location of Monterey, found a mission there, and compile a list of potential sites for other missions. The party reached Monterey on May 18 and a mission, San Carlos Borromeo, was founded there on June 3, 1770.[10]

Another first attestation of a California language, a seventy-word vocabulary of Obispeño Chumash, was appended by Portolá's second in command, Pedro Fages, to the report he submitted to the Viceroy in 1775, summarizing what had been learned of the geography and aboriginal inhabitants of Alta California since the original 1769 expedition (Box 3).[11]

In the two years following the establishment of San Diego and Monterey, three other missions were established along the route followed by Portolá: San Antonio (July 14, 1771) on Salinan territory, San Gabriel (September 8, 1771) on Takic territory, and San Luis Obispo (September 1, 1772) on

Chumash territory. Another expansion occured four years later with the establishment of two missions on Costanoan territory, San Francisco de Asís (June 26, 1776) and Santa Clara (January 12, 1777), and a second Takic mission, San Juan Capistrano (November 1, 1776).

Six years later a second Chumash mission was built, San Buenaventura (March 31, 1782), soon followed by two others, Santa Barbara (December 4, 1786) and La Purisima (December 8, 1787). Then came four more missions on Costanoan territory, Santa Cruz (August 28, 1791), Soledad (October 9, 1791), San Jose (July 11, 1797), and San Juan Bautista (June 24, 1797), along with a second Salinan mission, San Miguel (July 25, 1797), and the third and fourth Takic missions, San Fernando Rey (September 8, 1797) and San Luis Rey (June 13, 1798).

The nineteenth century saw the founding of the fifth and last Chumash mission, Santa Ynez (September 17, 1840); a mission on Coast Miwok territory in Marin County, San Rafael (December 14, 1817); and finally a mission at Sonoma, San Francisco Solano (July 4, 1823), for the Western Miwok, Southern Pomo, Wappo, and Southern Patwin. The establishment of additional missions in the San Joaquin Valley and to the north of San Francisco Bay in Pomo and Patwin territory was envisaged, but these plans came to naught after Mexican independence brought the disestablishment and secularization of the mission system in the 1830s. Nevertheless, a substantial number of Yokuts and Miwoks from the Central Valley were recruited into some of the existing missions during their waning years.

2.3.2 Language Documentation at the Missions

The attitude of the Franciscan missionaries toward California languages was ambivalent. On the one hand, they had to carry out their work in the shadow of a 1795 Spanish royal decree that mandated the exclusive use of Spanish in missions and required the active supression of indigenous languages (Cook 1976:143, n. 10). Like the Jesuits, however, the Franciscans had a long tradition of teaching Christian doctrine in the native languages of their converts, and this continued to be done informally.[12] Spanish (and occasionally Latin) was the language of formal prayer, but the extent to which Indian languages might be used in less weighty contexts, especially to instruct new converts who knew little if any Spanish, was left up to the individual priests.

The results differed widely. In some cases, priests made no effort to communicate in anything other than Spanish. Visiting the church at Mission Dolores during the *Rurik*'s visit to San Francisco in 1816, Otto von Kotzebue found

several hundred half-naked Indians kneeling, who, though they understand neither Spanish nor Latin, are never permitted after their conversion to absent themselves from mass. As the missionaries do not trouble themselves to learn the language of the Indians, I cannot conceive in what

BOX 3. FAGES'S VOCABULARY OF OBISPEÑO CHUMASH*

Finally, I will put here in alphabetical order more than seventy Indian words, the meaning of which I understand very well; I learned them among the natives of the mission of San Luís and twenty leagues round about there. They are as follows:

Anejueso [Anajuesu]   A buckle, and anything made of iron.

Ascamaps [Ascamape]   Salt.

Asnudo [Asnunc]   Let us go for seeds.

Astu   Water.

Chaá   The teeth.

Chapé or Aspu   The earth.

Chele [Chete]   The tongue.

Chilipi   The skull.

China   The road.

Chilpiu   The clouds.

Chocono   The deer.

Cuscaxa [Cuxcaxa] or Ascamaps [Ciscamapi]   Noon.

Cusnatach   The sun has set.

Custoso or Luni   The daughter.

El Texo   Let us go to sleep.

Exetechs   All kinds of clothing.

Jamac or Ascuma   The sky.

Lapsú [omitted]   The hide (cotón) of a wolf.

Limi   Village.

Lucsi   It has dawned.

Lucsimu   The star.

Lune   A nursing child.

Masnax   The march.

Maxoch   To sleep.

Mil [omitted]   Shells.

Misleu   The arrow.

Misua [Misna]   Son.

Misuyo   Woman.

Miteme   The feet.

Mixacap [Mixacach]   The fingernails.

Moculten   To eat.

Nesmono   Boy.

Nipu   The fingers.

Nistapi   What is it called?

Paach or Maach   The weapon.

Peteche   The eyes.

Petit or Pitsmu   The head.

Pex or Meex   The mouth.

Pichiu or Miecau   The breast.

Piiassi [Pijawi] or Mixo   The hair (tresses).

Pismu   The tar (brea) chapopote.

Pocul   The nose.

Quexaquiex   The chin.

Sactasi   The handkerchief.

Sornilap   Large house.

Scsu   The moustache.

Suxuxu   Wooden tray.

Taa   The oak (Quercus rober).

Taach   The bow.

Tacua   The moon.

Taxamin [Tajamin]   The flint.

Tamacsuma   The tray with which women cover themselves.

Tames [Tame]   The shoes.

Tasquin   The reed tray.

Tassiqueu [Tavique, sister]   The sisters.

Tepú   The salt.

Texep   The stone.

Texssu [Texsu]   The alder tree.

Tiesnui [Ticsuni]   The hide (cotón) of the rabbit.

Timix   The branches.

Tissi [Tivi]   The brother.

Tixu   The large man.

Tlasicuyo [Tlavicuyo]   The tender (little) girl.

Tlaxpil   The cord.

Tarcom [Torcom]   The wildcat.

Tuxusqui   The bear.

Tupxononoque   Come here.

Tuquelequeytai [Tuquelequeytu]   Let us go to hunt.

Tussu [Tuvu] or Mogomel   The knee.

Tuxugo   The firewood

---

*From the translation in Priestley (1937:80–83), which is based on a transcript in the archives of the Museo Nacional in Mexico City. The original manuscript is in the Archivo General de Indias in Seville. The forms printed in brackets are the variants that appear in Ternaux-Compans's earlier publication of the Seville manuscript (1884:345–347).

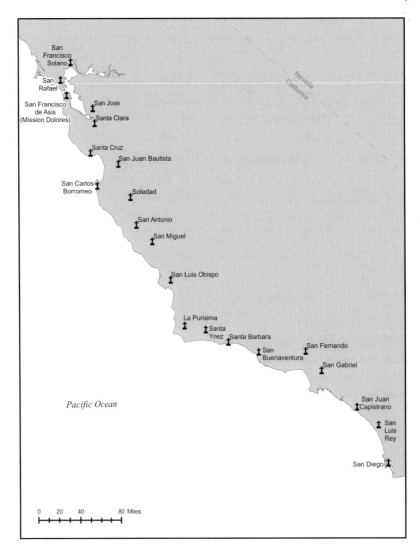

MAP 3. Missions of Alta California.

manner they have been instructed in the Christian religion; and there is probably but little light in the heads and hearts of these poor creatures, who can do nothing but imitate the external ceremonies which they observe by the eye. (1821.3:280)

But many priests appear to have followed the example of Father Lasuén, Junípero Serra's successor as president of the California missions, and acquired enough knowledge of the languages spoken by their converts to prepare translations of the basic catechism (*doctrina*) and of the most frequent prayers (the Pater Noster, Ave Maria, Apostles' Creed, and Salve Regina). A few also found it useful to compile a bilingual *confesionario,* a list of questions and responses that could be employed as a prompt during confession (Sandos 1985:115–119, 2004:96–98).

A number of translation manuscripts of this nature have survived. There are *doctrinas* in Rumsen and Esselen (Beeler 1978a:10–17; Shaul 1995a:192, 228–237), Barbareño

Chumash (Kelsey 1979), Soledad Costanoan (Sarría 1819), and a variety of San Francisco Bay Costanoan (Blevins and Golla 2005). *Confesionarios* have been preserved for Ventureño Chumash (Beeler 1967), Barbareño Chumash (Kelsey 1979), and Antoniano Salinan (Sitjar and Pieras 1771–1797b). Versions of the Pater Noster in several California languages survive in copies from now-lost mission manuscripts published by Duflot de Mofras (1844). Other mission translations still remain to be catalogued among Alexander S. Taylor's papers and in the large collection of mission documents copied by Pinart, and there are probably a number in archives in Mexico and Spain.

A handful of the California Franciscans, however, went beyond these ecclesiastical compositions to compile deliberate and systematic linguistic records of the languages they encountered. Among these was **Fermín de Lasuén,** the second president of the California missions, who in addition to writing a bilingual *doctrina* in Rumsen and Esselen that was used at Carmel, compiled a parallel vocabulary of

FIGURE 2. Father Gerónimo Boscana. From Alfred Robinson, *Life in California* (1849).

the two languages that survives among the records of the 1791–1792 Malaspina expedition (Cutter 1990:146–149). Especially notable was the documentation of Salinan compiled by a succession of priests at Mission San Antonio including **Buenaventura Sitjar** (1739–1808), **Miguel Pieras** (1741–1795), **Pedro Cabot** (1777–1836), and **Juan Bautista Sancho** (1772–1830). Their most impressive achievement was a dictionary of Antoniano (Sitjar and Pieras 1771–1797a), but a range of other materials in Antoniano Salinan have also been preserved.[13]

Gerónimo Boscana (1775–1831), who was stationed at Mission San Juan Capistrano from 1814 to 1826, was unique among the California Franciscans in taking a serious interest in the aboriginal customs and traditions of the Indians in his charge, and two versions of a lengthy scholarly treatise on Juaneño culture and pre-Christian religion were found among his papers. English translations of both versions have been published (Boscana 1846 and 1933, 1934). While the content of these manuscripts is primarily of ethnological interest, a significant amount of Juaneño vocabulary is included in the longer of the two versions.[14]

2.3.3 Felipe Arroyo de la Cuesta

By far the most enterprising of the Franciscan linguist-priests was Felipe Arroyo de la Cuesta (1780–1840). On his arrival in California in 1808 he was assigned to Mission San Juan Bautista, where he remained until 1833. Although by this time he was severely handicapped by what appears to have been rheumatoid arthritis, he chose to stay on in California, serving in an ancillary capacity at San Luis Obispo and San

Miguel (1833–1834), La Purisima (1834–1836), and finally Santa Ynez, where he died in September 1840.

Arroyo was a well-educated man by the standards of the California Franciscans, and had an inquiring and creative mind. His interest in the Costanoan and Yokuts languages spoken by the converts at San Juan Bautista was as much analytic and intellectual as it was practical. In 1817 the president of the missions, Vicente de Sarría, reported to his superiors:

> [Fray Arroyo de la Cuesta] has applied himself most assiduously to learning the respective languages [of his mission] with such success that I doubt whether there is another who has attained the same proficiency in understanding and describing its intricate syntax. He even reduced to some sort of rules the confusing formation of its verbs, adverbs and the rest of the parts of speech which I understand may serve likewise for the other missions. . . . I have animated him to compose a work on the subject. He has labored, as I understand, with good success. (Geiger 1969:19–20)

The lexicon and grammar of Mutsun Costanoan that Arroyo prepared with Sarría's encouragement constitute the best and most complete documentation of a California Indian language made in mission times.[15] The manuscript of the lexicon (Arroyo de la Cuesta 1815) contains 2,884 phrases and sentences in Mustun, translated into Spanish with Latin notes and explanations, along with a few sentences in the Wacharon variety of Rumsen and a number of prayers and other liturgical materials in Mutsun.[16] It was found at Santa Ynez in the 1850s by Alexander S. Taylor, who arranged for it to be published by the ecclesiastical historian John G. Shea in his "Library of American Linguistics." Shea's edition (Arroyo de la Cuesta 1862) included only the Mutsun phrases, omitting the religious texts and the Wacharon material.[17] The original manuscript was subsequently acquired by H. H. Bancroft and is now in the Bancroft Library at Berkeley (MS C-C 19). Mason published a grammatical sketch and vocabulary of Mutsun (1916a) based on an analysis and interpretation of the material in Shea's edition. Working both from the Shea edition and from the original manuscript, Harrington reelicited the entirety of Arroyo's Mutsun vocabulary from the last fluent speaker, Ascención Solórsano, in 1929 (Harrington 1982–1990, vol. 2, reels 41:150 to 57:188; see Appendix B). He also re-elicited the religious texts, both from her and from his Rumsen consultant, Isabelle Meadows (Harrington 1982–1990, vol. 2, reel 57:189–408).

The original manuscript of Arroyo's Mutsun grammar, apparently entitled *Gramatica Mutsun* or *Gramatica California*, has been lost. Taylor, however, found an extract of seventy-six pages that had been copied by another mission priest (identified on the manuscript only as a Catalan), and this was also published in Shea's series (Arroyo de la Cuesta 1861). The present location of this manuscript is

FIGURE 3. Mission of San Juan Bautista. Watercolor drawing made in 1862 by Edward Vischer, representing the mission as he remembered it from the 1840s, shortly after the departure of Father Arroyo de la Cuesta. Courtesy of the Bancroft Library UCB (039:29).

uncertain.[18] Harrington went over the published grammar with Ascención Solórsano and Isabel Meadows on two separate occasions (Harrington 1982–1990, vol. 2, reel 58:1–240 and reel 68:232–297). Besides showing considerable familiarity with the language, Arroyo's grammatical analysis of Mutsun is surprisingly sophisticated for its time and place, going beyond declensions and conjugations on the Latin model to discuss such matters as postpositions, metathesis, and sentence syntax.

Arroyo also kept a notebook for use in his priestly duties, titled *El Oro Molido* [Refined Gold] (1810–1819), containing a Mutsun *doctrina* and *confessionario* as well as various precepts, benedictions, and hymns. It also included extensive material on Nopṭinṭe Yokuts (see the next paragraph). Harrington "reheard" much of the Mutsun material with Ascención Solórsano in 1929, and a complete photostat copy of the original manuscript is interleaved with his notes (Harrington 1982–1990, vol. 2, reel 57:409–657). The prayers and hymns in Mutsun and Yokuts that Pinart (n.d.[a]) copied from unidentified mission documents were probably taken from *El Oro Molido*.

Arroyo's linguistic curiosity was not confined to Mutsun. He made a relatively thorough study of the varieties of Northern Valley Yokuts that were spoken by converts at his mission.[19] When the opportunity arose—unfortunately not often—he also collected samples of the languages spoken at other missions. Among his surviving manuscripts are the only attestations we shall ever have of Karkin Costanoan and the Saclan dialect of Bay Miwok, both collected on a rare trip to Mission Dolores in 1821 (Beeler 1955a, 1961b). During his semi-retirement after 1833 and reassignment to the Chumash missions, Arroyo was able to obtain a wider range of materials. In addition to several mission dialects of Chumash, these included vocabularies of Esselen, Luiseño, and of both Antoniano and Migueleño Salinan. Most of these miscellaneous

and comparative materials are preserved in a manuscript titled *Lecciones de Indios* [Indian Readings] (1837), a compilation that Arroyo made while he was at Mission Santa Ynez (Beeler 1971:14–15). It includes original data on Inezeño and Purisimeño Chumash, on which he was then still actively working, but otherwise consists of vocabularies that he had collected earlier from eleven other languages or dialects: Esselen; Antoniano and Migueleño Salinan; Obispeño Chumash; Nopṭinṭe Yokuts; Luiseño; and five languages from the San Francisco Bay area: Huimen (Marin Miwok), Juchiun (East Bay Costanoan), Saclan (Bay Miwok), Karkin (Costanoan), and Suisun (Southern Patwin).[20] Although the original manuscripts of these vocabularies have not survived, copies of three of the five Bay Area vocabularies (Huimen, Karkin, and Suisun) were independently made from Arroyo's originals in 1830 by a German visitor, Karl von Gerolt, and are preserved in the Humboldt Archives in Berlin (Gerolt 1830). Gerolt's copies differ in a number of details from Arroyo's own copies in *Lecciones de Indios*. The differences are especially noticeable in the Karkin vocabulary, Gerolt's copy of which includes three words not found in the *Lecciones* version (Golla 1996d).[21]

2.3.4 Pablo Tac and Giuseppe Cardinal Mezzofanti

Of particular interest is Pablo Tac (1822–1841), who bridged the divide between Indian convert and missionary priest. Tac, a native Luiseño, was born at Mission San Luis Rey to parents who were already Christians. He seems to have been a diligent student at the mission school, showing considerable promise for more advanced work. When Father Antonio Peyrí, the longtime priest at San Luis Rey, was forced to return to Mexico when his mission was secularized in 1832, he made secret arrangements for Tac and an older boy, Agapito Amamix, to travel with him. Peyrí enrolled the two

FIGURE 4. View of the mission of San Luis Rey. Drawing by Auguste Bernard Duhaut-Cilly, 1827, showing the Indian village in the foreground. From Duhaut-Cilly (1834–1835). Courtesy of the Bancroft Library UCB (039:34).

in the Franciscan mission college in Mexico City, but he grew dissatisfied with the education they were receiving and withdrew them after eighteen months. Despite his failing health and meager resources, Peyrí was able to escort the boys back to Spain, and from there send them on to Rome. In September 1834 they were admitted to the College for the Propagation of the Faith (*Propaganda Fide*), the training ground for the church's missionary elite. Unfortunately, the malaria-ridden Roman summers took their toll. Amamix died in 1837, at the age of seventeen, while Tac, who survived four more years and went on to complete courses in Latin grammar, rhetoric, humanities, and philosophy, died in December 1841 a few weeks short of his twentieth birthday.

Not long after their arrival in Rome the two young California Indians attracted the attention of Giuseppe Cardinal Mezzofanti (1774–1849), the head of the Vatican Library and an eminent linguist and polyglot. Mezzofanti, who had a passion for acquiring exotic languages, personally tutored Tac, helping him prepare a grammatical sketch and dictionary of Luiseño, while himself learning to speak the language with some fluency.[22] Tac's manuscripts—his grammar and dictionary (the latter only partially completed), and a short cultural and historical sketch of Indian life at San Luis Rey—were preserved by Mezzofanti, and at his death in 1849 they passed into the custody of the archdiocesan library of Bologna, where they remain. The manuscripts were published, in the original Spanish text with Italian notes, by Carlo Tagliavini (1926, 1930a, 1930b). An English version of the grammar, along with a sketch of Tac's life, was published by Kroeber as an appendix to Sparkman's grammar of Luiseño (Kroeber and Grace 1960:221–237), while an English translation of Tac's "Conversión de los San Luiseños de la Alta California" was published by Minna and Gordon Hewes in 1952. Although of only limited value as an attestation of mission-era Luiseño

(Chung 1994), Tac's fragmentary grammar and dictionary constitute the earliest substantial record of the language.

2.3.5 Responses to the Questionnaire of 1812

In 1812 Spain's Department of Overseas Colonies compiled a formal questionnaire (*preguntas*) designed to elicit a broad range of information about native peoples throughout the Spanish dominions in the Americas and elsewhere. The questionnaire reached the president of the California missions, Fray José Señán, late in 1813, and copies were forwarded to all eighteen missions then in operation. Responses (*respuestas*) were received over the ensuing two years, but were apparently never sent to Spain; the original manuscripts still reside in the Santa Barbara Mission Archives. The *respuestas* collectively constitute one of the most revealing documents of the mission period and have been widely consulted by historians and ethnographers. A complete English translation is available (Geiger and Meighan 1976), to which the following page citations refer.[23]

The *respuestas* are of interest to students of California languages primarily for the sociolinguistic information they contain, although transcriptions of a few dozen native words and place-names are scattered through the manuscripts (these have been collected by Geiger and Meighan on pp. 155–159).[24] The responses to the only direct question on language (question 3, "What languages do these people generally speak?") show the missionaries to have been aware of considerable tribelet-level diversity. The response from Santa Cruz, for example, reports that the Indians there

speak as many dialects as the number of villages of their origin. It is indeed a matter of surprise that although one village is only two leagues or less away from another, the Indians of the said villages not being allies, yet the dialects are so distinct that generally not a great deal can be understood of one by the other. (p. 21)

Arroyo de la Cuesta's response from San Juan Bautista is in a similar vein, but emphasizes the potential of interdialectal intelligibility across Costanoan:

> The Indians of this mission and of this region speak the language of the area where they were born. Though they appear to speak distinct languages this is only accidentally true; that is, some of the words are different only because of the manner of pronunciation. . . . Hence it is that the Indians living in a circumference of thirty or forty leagues understand one another. (pp. 20–21)

Question 11 asks if there are "catechisms of Christian doctrine . . . in the diverse and various languages." The responses indicate that an Indian language *doctrina* (and sometimes two or more) had been prepared at most of the missions, and they shed light on the context in which this work was done. Perhaps the most elucidating reply comes from Father President Señán himself, who writes for San Buenaventura:

> There are catechisms of Christian doctrine in the language of the neophytes and they are used alternately with the catechism in the Castilian language. They have not the approbation of any bishop for it would not only be difficult but next to impossible to review them in so many and in such strange, barbarous and unknown dialects as are to be found in this country and of which there is no grammar or dictionary to aid in the work. (These Indian catechisms contain only the most essential doctrines and practices. They are not printed and were intended only for private use.) It costs even the immediate superiors here indescribable labor and patience to understand them and then only with the help of the most experienced missionaries or by their assistance and knowledge with the aid of interpreters whom they have well trained. (p. 53)

Arroyo de la Cuesta, always the applied linguist, appended a comment to his response from San Juan Bautista suggesting the compilation of a standard catechism for all of Costanoan:

> It seems to me it would be easy with the aid of interpreters and some of the missionary fathers who know the language of the Indians to compose a catechism that could serve three or four missions, still another for as many more missions[,] for the languages are not so numerous as it appears[,] as was stated in [question 3]. In syntax and method they are the same with little or slight differences. (p. 54)

A scattering of ethnolinguistic observations are found in the *respuestas*. An aboriginal mnemonic system is said to have been used by the Salinans at Mission San Antonio (p. 36), and taboos on speaking the names of the dead are reported from San Luis Obispo (p. 94) and San Fernando (p. 97).

2.4 Visitors and Collectors, 1780–1880

2.4.1 Scientific Expeditions: Spanish, French, British, and Russian

During the mission period, California ports, especially Monterey, were frequently visited by naval expeditions sent out to explore the West Coast of North America and the islands of the Pacific. Although these voyages were usually under military command and sailed under national flags—British, French, and Russian, as well as Spanish (the American expedition under Charles Wilkes is discussed separately in the following section)—they were broadly scientific in purpose, and much of the distinctive flora and fauna of California was first described by the botanists and zoologists who accompanied them. In addition, limited, but nonetheless valuable, information was obtained on the native peoples of the California coast, and some of the expedition reports contain interesting vignettes of life at the missions. The California portion of the diary kept by the physician and botanist Archibald Menzies, who sailed with Captain George Vancouver (Menzies 1924), for instance, contains a vivid portrait of Fermin de Lasuén, and the account in *The Voyage of the "Blossom"* of an overland trip from San Francisco to Monterey and back (Beechey 1831) includes an unforgettable description of the party's overnight stay with Arroyo de la Cuesta at San Juan Bautista. Of particular interest to ethnographers are the paintings and sketches of Indian scenes made by expedition artists, most notably José Cardero, who accompanied Malaspina in 1791 (Cutter 1960:11–21), and Louis Choris, the artist on the voyage of the *Rurik,* a Russo-German expedition that visited San Francisco in 1816 (Choris 1822; Mahr 1932).

Linguistic data, however, are very sparse in these reports. Only four expeditions are known to have obtained vocabularies or other materials on California languages—La Pérouse in 1786, Malaspina in 1791–1792, Wrangell in 1833, and Voznesenskii in 1840–41—and the most extensive and accurate of these were not collected directly but were provided by the mission priests.

The earliest of the linguistic collections was made by **Robert de Lamanon,** a naturalist accompanying the ill-fated expedition led by the **Comte de la Pérouse,** during the party's short stay in Monterey in September 1786. La Pérouse and his companions perished in a shipwreck in the Solomon Islands in 1788, but fortunately a substantial number of the expedition's papers had already been sent back to Europe. La Pérouse's journal (1799), in addition to valuable information on the Indians at Monterey and Carmel, contains Lamanon's vocabularies of both Esselen and Rumsen ("Achastlien"). Both vocabularies are brief (fewer than two dozen words each), but they are the first attestations of these languages.

FIGURE 5. The reception of Jean-François de la Pérouse at Mission Carmel in 1786. Copied in 1791 or 1792 by José Cardero, artist of the Malaspina expedition, from a painting that La Pérouse had presented to the mission priests. The Indian converts stand in a formal line as La Pérouse and his officers are ushered across the plaza to the church. Courtesy of the Bancroft Library UCB (1963:002:1311).

A similarly ambitious Spanish expedition to the Pacific, under the overall command of **Alejandro Malaspina,** visited Monterey in 1791, and a special contingent, the schooners *Sutíl* and *Mexicana,* under the command of **Dionisio Alcalá Galiano** and **Cayetano Valdés,** made a second call at Monterey in the summer of 1792 on their return from a survey of Vancouver Island. On both occasions Father Lasuén, the president of the California missions, went to considerable lengths to provide his distinguished visitors with ethnographic data, sending out Indians to collect botanical specimens, making interpreters available, and even requesting that a collection of Chumash baskets and other artifacts be sent up from Santa Barbara (Cutter 1960; David et al. 2003). To document the two principal languages of Mission Carmel, Esselen and Rumsen, Lasuén compiled an extensive comparative word list and a bilingual catechism. These manuscripts were presented to Galiano and Valdés during the 1792 visit and were partially published in the account of their voyage (Anonymous 1802); full versions have only recently become available (Cutter 1990).[25]

In 1812, the Russian American Company established an outpost at Fort Ross, in Kashaya Pomo territory on the Sonoma County coast north of the Russian River. This stimulated a series of Russian explorations of the California coast, primarily to locate sources of sea otter and fur seals (Farris 1989). None of these, as far as is known, produced any information on the Indian languages of the area The first collection of linguistic data dates to 1833, when **Baron**

Ferdinand von Wrangell, chief manager of the company, made an inspection visit to Fort Ross. The information he obtained included a detailed report compiled by the local manager, **Peter S. Kostromitinov,** on the native people of the area, accompanied by vocabularies of Kashaya Pomo and the Bodega dialect of Coast Miwok. Kostromitinov's report and vocabularies were included in Wrangell's summary of statistical and ethnographic data on Russian America (Wrangell and Kostromitinov 1839).

Shortly before Fort Ross was closed down by the Russians in 1841, **I. G. Voznesenskii,** a young naturalist on an extended scientific tour of Russian America for the Imperial Academy of Sciences, visited northern California for 13 months (July 1840–August 1841) and collected a substantial amount of information on the Indians of the region (Liapunova 1967; Alekseev 1987:15–30). Voznesenskii traveled as far south as Santa Clara and as far north as Cape Mendocino and visited Sutter at New Helvetia. In addition to journals, correspondence, and sketches, Voznesenskii's California materials—housed in the Museum of Anthropology and Ethnography of the Russian Academy of Sciences in St. Petersburg—include more than 150 artifacts as well as a substantial number of natural history specimens (Bates 1983). Since he was under orders to collect a native name for each artifact or specimen that he obtained, some valuable vocabulary may be documented. To date, however, only a few samples of this material have been published.[26]

FIGURE 6. View of the Russian establishment of Bodega [Fort Ross] by Auguste Bernard Duhaut-Cilly, 1827. From Duhaut-Cilly (1834–1835). Courtesy of the Bancroft Library UCB (G440.B48 v.2).

2.4.2 William Fraser Tolmie, Thomas Coulter, and John Scouler

In 1841, John Scouler, a Scottish physician and natural historian, published a set of vocabularies from California and the Northwest Coast that had been collected during the previous decade by two fellow natural historians, William Fraser Tolmie and Thomas Coulter. Tolmie's vocabularies, primarily of languages spoken in British Columbia, included one of Upper Umpqua (Oregon Athabaskan). Six of Coulter's seven vocabularies (short samples, to be more accurate: the list has sixty-one entries) were of California languages, including Ipai Diegueño, Juaneño, Gabrielino, Barbareño and Obispeño Chumash, and Antoniano Salinan.

Tolmie, like Scouler a Scottish physician, worked as a fur trader with the Hudson's Bay Company for several decades, beginning in 1833. The vocabularies of his that Scouler published, although rough-and-ready in their phonetic accuracy, are in many cases the first attestation in print of a particular language. This description also applies to Tolmie's 111-word vocabulary of Upper Umpqua, which was collected a few years before Hale's and is thus the earliest recording of either Oregon or California Athabaskan.

Coulter, an Irish botanist and unsuccessful businessman, lived in California from late 1831 to 1835 (E. Nelson and Probert 1994). His word lists, although short, are well-organized (the numerals 1–16 and 20, some common nouns, mostly natural phenomena and kinship terms, and a few adjectives) and his orthography simple but unambiguous. His attestations of Gabrielino and Obispeño are especially valuable.[27]

2.4.3 Horatio Hale and the Wilkes Expedition, 1838–1842

Horatio Hale (1817–1896) was the first American linguist and ethnographer to visit California. Born into a well-known New England literary family, Hale had developed an interest in Indian languages at an early age, collecting and publishing an Algonquian vocabulary while still a student at Harvard.[28] Immediately after his graduation in 1837, at the age of twenty, he was invited to accompany the United States Exploring Expedition to the Pacific and the Oregon Territory, under the command of Lieutenant Charles Wilkes, probably the most ambitious American scientific enterprise of the first half of the nineteenth century (Stanton 1975). As "philologist" of the expedition, Hale was able to carry out groundbreaking linguistic work on Australian and Polynesian languages and on the Indian languages of the Northwest, as well as sample the linguistic diversity of California. After the publication of his Wilkes Expedition report in 1846, Hale all but disappeared from the scientific scene for several decades. After traveling extensively in Europe he took up the practice of law, first in Chicago and later in southern Ontario. However, late in life he returned to American Indian linguistics, publishing a series of monographs and papers on Iroquoian languages and a pioneering study of Chinook Jargon (1890). In his seventies he directed the young Franz Boas's research in Western Canada for the British Association for the Advancement of Science (Gruber 1967).

The Wilkes Expedition devoted its final eight months, April to November 1841, to making a survey of the Oregon and Washington coast—with a few forrays into the interior—from a base at Astoria at the mouth of the Columbia. During this time Hale was able to collect data on Chinookan, Coast Salish, Alsea ("Jakon"), and Lower Columbia Athabaskan, and learn Chinook Jargon. Feeling that he needed more information about the languages and peoples of the interior, Hale arranged to stay behind for several months after the others had sailed for home. As he described it to Boas, many years later, "I had but about three months for a large territory of whose ethnology hardly anything was known.

FIGURE 7. Horatio Hale. Courtesy of National Anthropological Archives, Smithsonian Institution (28-58600).

I had to travel hundreds of miles through a wild country, with no companions but Indians and half-breeds, and often very few interpreters. I gave my attention chiefly to languages" (quoted in Gruber 1967:26). Little is known of his itinerary,[29] but the vocabularies and accompanying ethnographic notes that he published in the Wilkes Expedition's report (1846) indicate that, in addition to traveling along the middle and upper Columbia documenting Sahaptian and Salishan languages, he must also have visited parts of central and southern Oregon, where he obtained vocabularies of Upper Umpqua Athabaskan, Northern Paiute ("Wihinasht"), Klamath-Modoc ("Lutuami") and Achumawi ("Palaihnih"). Hale ended his stay on the West Coast by accompanying Duflot de Mofras (see ¶2.4.4) to California, where he collected short vocabularies of Marin Miwok, Chalon Costanoan, Migueleño Salinan, Gabrielino ("Kij"), and Juaneño ("Netela"). In his published report, Hale added the vocabularies of Shasta, Wintu, Plains Miwok, and three varieties of Nisenan that were collected by another member of the expedition, the geologist James Dwight Dana, during the latter's overland journey along the Siskiyou Trail from Oregon to the Sacramento Valley in September and October 1841 (Hale 1846:218, 569–633; Stanton 1975:259–265).

Hale was a talented field linguist, and his data are considerably more accurate than those collected by most of his contemporaries, or by nearly any fieldworker before the establishment of the Bureau of American Ethnology in 1879. He constructed his own phonetic alphabet—using, for example, Greek chi (χ) to represent a velar fricative or French c-cedilla (ç) to represent a voiceless lateral fricative—and attempted to collect information on grammatical structure in addition to vocabulary lists.

2.4.4 Count Eugène Duflot de Mofras

Hale's companion during his brief visit to California at the end of 1841 was Count Eugène Duflot de Mofras. Born in 1810, Duflot de Mofras was a cultivated French diplomat who, while still a young man, had acquired a considerable reputation as an expert on Spain and its former colonial empire in the New World. In 1839 the French government sent him to Mexico to conduct investigations along the Pacific coast "for the purpose of procuring reliable information regarding political and commercial conditions in these lands" (Willys 1929). Although his instructions made it clear that his principal task was to scout out the prospects for a French toehold in California and Oregon, it was not until May 1841 that Duflot de Mofras finally reached the area. Once in California, however, his investigations were thorough. He spent the summer and fall traveling the length of El Camino Real, visiting nearly all the missions and pueblos between San Diego and Sonoma. In mid-October he sailed on to Oregon, where he encountered the Wilkes Expedition during the final weeks of their Northwest Coast work. He also met Sir George Simpson, governor of the Hudson's Bay Company, who was conducting his own inspection tour of the West Coast. After visiting outposts along the Columbia and the Willamette, he returned to San Francisco in late December, accompanied by Simpson and Hale. A few days later he and Hale sailed for Monterey, where they boarded a ship bound for Mexico, stopping along the way at Santa Barbara and San Diego.

Duflot de Mofras's interest in Indian languages was not great, but he was an astute observer of the social conditions in the postmission communities of the period. His published report also includes copies of a few mission documents, including versions of the Pater Noster in Ineseño Chumash, Mutsun and San Francisco Bay Costanoan, and two varieties of Marin Miwok (Duflot de Mofras 1844, vol. 2:392–393), along with sets of numerals in Esselen, Rumsen and Chalon Costanoan, Obispeño Chumash, Juaneño, and Gabrielino (1844, vol. 2:401). The Marin Miwok, Esselen, and San Francisco Costanoan data he obtained constitute significant attestations of these poorly documented languages.

2.4.5 Survey Expeditions of the 1850s and 1860s

During the 1850s and 1860s the United States government sent out a series of expeditions to survey the vast territory in the Southwest that had been acquired from Mexico as a result of the Mexican War. While these expeditions had a variety of purposes, most were encouraged to collect information on the Indian languages of the regions through which they passed. Some of the earliest records of the Yuman and Northern Uto-Aztecan languages come from the reports of these expeditions.

The earliest of the southwestern survey expeditions was that of the commission charged with establishing the new boundary with Mexico between Texas and the Pacific in

1850–1853. Commissioner *John Russell Bartlett* (1805–1886), a man with wide interests in language—remembered in particular for his *Dictionary of Americanisms* (1848)—collected a number of vocabularies in northwestern Mexico and in southern California, as well as in northern California (Bartlett 1854). These vocabularies (Bartlett n.d.) have never been published in full, although many of them were incorporated by Powell into the linguistic appendix to Powers's *Tribes of California* (1877); see Box 4.

One of the military officers accompanying Bartlett on the Boundary Commission survey was *Lieutenant Amiel W. Whipple* (1817–1863), who collected vocabularies of two Yuman languages in Southern California in 1850 (Whipple 1850). In 1853–1854, Whipple was placed in charge of an expedition to identify a possible transcontinental railroad route from Fort Smith, Arkansas, to Los Angeles, and to collect various scientific data along the way. Whipple himself took responsibility for information on Indian languages and collected vocabularies of Shoshone, Comanche, Chemehuevi, Cahuilla, Luiseño, Juaneño, Quechan, Mojave, Maricopa, and Diegueño. Published in the expedition's report together with a commentary by the expedition's natural historian, William W. Turner (Whipple 1855), Whipple's vocabularies provided the first detailed information on the extent and diversity of the "Shoshonean" (i.e., Northern Uto-Aztecan) languages.

During the winter of 1857–1858, *Lieutenant Joseph C. Ives* ascended the Colorado River to a point five hundred miles from its mouth in a small iron steamer in order to demonstrate the practicability of navigating the Colorado. The report of the Ives Expedition, the first extensive survey of Colorado River Yuman territory, contains some ethnographic and linguistic observations on the Cocopa, Quechan, and Mojave (Ives 1860).

The last and most extensive of the military surveys of the Southwest was carried out between 1871 and 1879 under the command of *Lieutenant George M. Wheeler*. Formally styled the "U.S. Geographical Survey West of the One Hundredth Meridian," the overall goal of the Wheeler Expedition was to make a detailed geographical survey—primarily in the form of topographic maps—of the region between the eastern boundary of Colorado and New Mexico and California, including mineral resources, economic potential, and information on Indians. In all, Wheeler made fourteen separate trips, including visits to northeastern California, western Nevada, and southern California. The task of collecting Indian vocabularies fell to the German chemist *Oscar Loew,* the botanist of the survey, who solicited the help of Albert Gatschet in preparing them for publication in the expedition's formal reports (Gatschet 1876a, 1879a). Loew's vocabularies from the California region include attestations of nine Uto-Aztecan languages (Shoshoni, Ute, Northern Paiute, Chemehuevi, Serrano, Cahuilla, Juaneño, Gabrielino, and Luiseño); five Yuman languages (Upland Yuman, Hualapai, Mojave, Diegueño, and Quechan); two Chumash languages (Barbareño and

Island); and Wintu (obtained from displaced "Digger" Indians whom Loew encountered in Huerfano, Colorado).

2.4.6 George Gibbs and the Treaty Party of 1851

George Gibbs (1815–1873) was the first ethnographer to make systematic collections of Indian language data in California. Born into a wealthy and prominent New York family, Gibbs, like Horatio Hale before him, studied at Harvard, although he left without a degree in 1834.[30] After practicing law in New York for a few years with little enthusiasm, he began to devote his energies to research and writing. An interest in ethnography and Indian languages was kindled by his friendship with the elderly Albert Gallatin, and a family connection to Richard Henry Dana, author of *Two Years Before the Mast*, stimulated his curiosity about the West Coast. Emigrating to Oregon in September 1849, he secured a patronage appointment as assistant collector of customs, in Astoria, and began taking notes on local Indians and Indian languages, in particular Chinook Jargon. In November 1850, Gibbs joined the commission that had been set up to make treaties with the tribes of the Willamette Valley, allowing him to expand his ethnographic and linguistic researches to the Kalapuya. When the commission's work ended, in June 1851, Gibbs traveled to California to visit his younger brother, a military officer stationed at Sonoma.

By chance, Gibbs reached California just as the three "commissioners" who had been appointed by the Interior Department to make conciliatory treaties with the California Indians were beginning their work. The three—Redick McKee, George W. Barbour, and Dr. Oliver M. Wozencraft—took up their uncertain assignment in March 1851, first working together as a team in the San Joaquin Valley, then dividing in the late summer into three exploratory parties. The North Coast party, under McKee, was being formed at Sonoma when Gibbs fortuitously arrived. McKee hired Gibbs on the spot, delighted to obtain the services of a man already experienced in treaty work and acquainted with Indian languages.

Between mid-August and early November 1851 the treaty party traveled north, via Clear Lake and the Eel River, to Humboldt Bay, then inland up the Klamath River to Shasta territory. Gibbs obtained vocabularies from fifteen of the languages they encountered along the route, including Coast Miwok, Hill Patwin, four Pomo languages, two dialects of Wiyot, Yurok, Hupa, Tolowa, Karuk, Scotts Valley Shasta, a variety of Rogue River Athabaskan ("Nabiltse"), and an additional Oregon language, "How-te-te-oh," that is probably either Oregon Shasta or Upper Takelma.[31] In many instances Gibbs's vocabulary was the first attestation of the language in question. Twelve of the vocabularies (Gibbs 1853b), together with Gibbs's journal of the expedition (1853a), were published in Schoolcraft (1851–1857, vol. 3:99–177, 428–445), and the same twelve vocabularies, edited somewhat by Powell, were reprinted in Powers

FIGURE 8. George Gibbs in the 1860s, at the time he was organizing the Smithsonian's linguistic materials. Courtesy of the Smithsonian Institution Archives.

(1877). The vocabularies of Shasta, Rogue River Athabaskan, and "How-te-te-oh" were inexplicably omitted.[32]

Gibbs spent the winter in San Francisco preparing his report of the expedition. In April 1852, when this had been submitted, he returned to northwestern California to try his hand at mining. He spent May and June on a claim at Orleans, and from July through October prospected along the Salmon River. During these months he collected further linguistic and ethnographic notes on the Karuk, Yurok, and Hupa, of which only a compact trilingual English-Yurok, Hupa dictionary survives (Gibbs 1852).

Gibbs returned to Astoria in December 1852, where he served again as collector of customs for a few months and resumed linguistic and ethnographic work in the Northwest. From 1853 to 1855, he held the position of geologist and ethnologist on the Pacific Railroad Survey of the 47th and 49th parallels under the command of Governor Isaac Stevens, and his published report on the Indians of Washington Territory (1854) established his reputation as the expert on this subject. In 1857 Gibbs joined the Northwest Boundary Survey as geologist and linguist, serving until 1861, by which time he had returned to the east and settled in Washington, DC.

After his connection with the Northwest Boundary Survey came to an end, Gibbs was invited by his friend Joseph Henry to organze the ethnographic and linguistic materials that had been accumulating in the Smithsonian Institution's archives. During the Civil War and the years immediately following, Gibbs functioned, on a voluntary basis, as the Smithsonian's linguistic curator. He compiled a circular for field researchers (Gibbs 1863a) that became the model for Powell's more comprehensive word list, invited William

Dwight Whitney to develop a standard orthography for American Indian languages, and collaborated with the historian John G. Shea in developing a publication series for Americanist linguistic work.[33] In declining health, Gibbs left Washington in 1868 to resettle in his native New York, where he died in April 1873.

2.4.7 Alexander S. Taylor

Alexander S. Taylor (1817–1876), the most prolific writer on California Indians during the Gold Rush period, was born and educated in Charleston, South Carolina, where his father was a naval officer of some distinction. In his early twenties he left home to take up a wandering life, according to his own account visiting "the West Indies, England, India, the Red Sea, China, Singapore, and Ceylon" and making and losing several fortunes (R. Cowan 1933:18). He arrived in California from Hong Kong in September 1848, but appears not to have spent any time in the goldfields. From 1849 to 1860 he lived in Monterey, where he made a modest living as clerk of the U.S. District Court. In 1860 he moved to Santa Barbara, where he married the daughter of Daniel Hill, an American settler who had married into a Californio family. Hill had received a large land grant near Santa Barbara, and Taylor and his wife took up residence on the portion of "Hill's Ranch" known as "La Patera." Taylor died there in 1876, in scholarly seclusion, having spent his later years on miscellaneous literary and historical projects and working on a general bibliography of California (R. Cowan 1933; Powell 1967:3–11).

In the early 1850s, when few others had any interest in the subject, Taylor became fascinated by the early history of California and began collecting materials relating to Spanish and Mexican settlement and to the Indians. He eventually amassed nearly six thousand documents, including numerous original letters and manuscripts from the Franciscan missions. Using these and other sources, he began writing articles on various historical topics, most of which after 1855 appeared in the *California Farmer*, a weekly newspaper owned and edited by his friend Colonel James L. Warren.

Between 1860 and 1863 the *California Farmer* published a long series of reports by Taylor on the history, languages, and customs of the native peoples of the state, under the general title of "Indianology of California."[34] A number of these reports contained vocabularies and other linguistic material. Most of these data were original, either collected by Taylor himself or copied from unpublished manuscripts that had come into his hands. Among the languages attested are Santa Cruz Costanoan (a vocabulary collected by Comellas); Antoniano Salinan (copied from Sitjar's manuscripts); Gabrielino; Diegueño; Santa Clara Costanoan (collected by Mengarini); Delta Yokuts; Ineseño Chumash; Santa Cruz Island Chumash (collected by Jimeno); San Francisco Costanoan (collected by Adam Johnston); Karuk (collected by G. W. Taggart); Marin Miwok; Sierra Miwok; and Nomlaki. Nearly all of Taylor's published vocabularies are marred by numerous typographical errors (his copy was apparently not proofread) and must be used with extreme caution. They were reprinted, with errors uncorrected, by Lucy-Fossarieu (1881); some were also reprinted in Heizer (1973). Fortunately, most of the manuscripts on which the "Indianology of California" was based are preserved in the Bancroft Library, as is Taylor's own bound copy of the printed articles and an 1864 map of California tribes (Heizer 1941a). More than seventy years ago, Robert Ernest Cowan lamented that "notwithstanding [the Indianology's] pretentious purpose and voluminous extent, it has seldom been cited by later ethnologists. It remains entombed in the forgotten files of the *Farmer*, from which it has never been reprinted" (1933:21). This assessment still holds in 2011.[35]

Around 1860, Taylor made contact with John Gilmary Shea (1824–1892), the leading historian of Catholic missionary work in North America, who—in collaboration with George Gibbs—was launching a publication series devoted to American Indian languages, the Library of American Linguistics. Taylor conveyed several mission documents on California languages to Shea, three of which were published in the series: the dictionary of Salinan compiled at Mission San Antonio (Sitjar 1861), and Arroyo de la Cuesta's grammar and vocabulary of Mutsun Costanoan (1861, 1862). Several shorter mission documents that were sent to Shea remain unpublished. These include a Salinan *confesionario* (Sitjar and Pieras 1771–1797b) and materials on Costanoan (Sarría 1819; Taylor 1860, 1862a) and Chumash (Cortés 1798–1805; Taylor 1862b). Most of these are now part of the Shea Collection in the Georgetown University Library.

2.4.8 Stephen Powers

A unique, substantial, and still not fully appreciated contribution to California Indian linguistic studies was made by the writer Stephen Powers (1840–1904) during his relatively brief sojourn in the state during the first half of the 1870s. Although a university graduate thoroughly at home in Latin and Greek, Powers could claim no scholarly or scientific expertise in either linguistics or ethnography; his primary skill was that of a sharp-eyed observer. In his early years he made a living as a journalist and popular writer, working for a while as European correspondent for the *New York Times*. An avid walker, Powers arrived in California by foot in October 1869 after a ten-month trek across the continent, recounted in *Afoot and Alone: A Walk from Sea to Sea* (1872), a bestseller in its day. He remained in California for five years, devoting himself largely to writing a series of essays for *The Overland Monthly* on the native people of the region, based on information that he gathered, in typical fashion, by walking the back-country trails of northern and central California. Most of Powers's material was collected in the summers of 1871 and 1872, with his essays appearing only a few months after his visits. Their accuracy and perceptiveness soon gained Powers a

FIGURE 9. Stephen Powers, 1881. Courtesy of the Bancroft Library, UCB.

reputation as an ethnographer, and in 1874 John Wesley Powell arranged for their republication in book form by the Smithsonian (Powers 1877), with a 170-page appendix on California languages edited by Powell (Park 1975).

Powers was a surprisingly astute collector of ethnolinguistic data, and unlike most later investigators he had the opportunity to hear California languages being used in a wide range of everyday communicative functions. Powers was also able to note and characterize broad areal differences in speech. To Powers, ethnographic "California" only began south of Mount Shasta. North of there, beginning with Shastan and Palaihnihan, the languages were "harsh and sesquipedelian," while in California proper they were "not only distinguished for that affluence of vowel sounds which is more or less characteristic of all tongues spoken in warm climates, but most of them are also remarkable for their special striving after harmony. . . . beautiful for their simplicity, the brevity of their words, their melody, and their harmonic sequences." Moreover, while "the Californians almost universally learn each other's languages or dialects, which is easy on account of their similarity of structure and their possession of words in common," between Shasta and Wintu "the separating chasm is so wide that both prefer to use English" (1877:15–16, 245).

The patient reader will find in Powers many such ethnolinguistic gems. He is especially insightful regarding multilingualism and the relative prestige of adjacent languages (see ¶1.5). He also collected a number of vocabularies, using the transcription system recommended by Gibbs (1863a; see Powers 1877:17). These are all included in the linguistic appendix to *Tribes of California* (Box 4), and a number of individual words and linguistic samples are scattered through the text.

Vocabularies reprinted from earlier publications are marked with an asterisk (*). Otherwise, citations are to the original manuscripts. The absence of a citation (as with all of Powers's vocabularies) indicates that the location of the original is unknown.

Ka´-rok family (447–459)

1. Ka´-rok. Stephen Powers. Scotts's Bar, 1872. ("From Pa-chi´-ta, a chief.")
2. Arra-arra. Lieutenant George Crook. (Crook 1852–1861)
3. Arra-arra. George Gibbs. 1852. (Gibbs 1852–1853)
4. Peh´-tsik. Lieutenant Edward Ross. Red Cap's Bar, Upper Klamath.
*5. Eh-nek. George Gibbs. (Gibbs 1853b)

Yu´-rok family (460–473)

1. Al-i-kwa. George Gibbs. Weitchpec, 1852. (Gibbs 1852)
*2. Al-i-kwa. George Gibbs. Weitchpec, 1851. (Gibbs 1853b)
3. Klamath, or Sa-ag-its. Thomas F. Azpell. Hoopa, 1870. (Azpell 1870)
4. Yu´rok. Stephen Powers. Hoopa, 1875. ("From a very intelligent Indian, who was, I believe, the only Yurok on the reservation.")
5. Al-i-kwa. George Crook. (Crook 1852–1861)
6. Yu´-rok. Stephen Powers. Weitchpec, 1872. ("From Salmon Billy.")

Chim-a-ri´-ko family (474–477)

1. Stephen Powers. December 1875. ("Collected at Martin's Ferry, Trinity River, from a person who was said to be one of the last three women of the tribe.")

Wish-osk family (478–482)

*1. Wish-osk. George Gibbs. 1851. (Gibbs 1853b)
*2. Wi-yot. George Gibbs. 1851. (Gibbs 1853b)
3. Ko-wilth. Ezra Williams. Near Humboldt Bay.

Yu´-ki (483–489)

1. Yu´-ki. Stephen Powers. Round Valley, November 1875. ("From two members of the tribe, with 'Tony' as interpreter.")
2. Huch´-nom. Stephen Powers. Round Valley, November 1875. ("From 'Tony,' the Indian judge of the reservation.")
3. Yuke. Lieutenant Edward Ross. Round Valley. ("With some words taken from the Historical Magazine of New York, April, 1863, which were not in the Smithsonian copy.") (Gibbs 1863b)
4. [Wappo.] John Russell Bartlett. 1850–1853. ("A tribe living near Knight's farm, at the head of the valley toward Clear Lake.") [Apparently a variety of Wappo.] (Bartlett n.d.)

Pomo (490–517)

1. Pomo. Stephen Powers. Round Valley, December 1875. ("From José, the 'marshal' of the reservation.")
2. Gal-li-no-me´-ro. Stephen Powers. Healdsburg, 1872 and December 1875. ("From Ventura, Andres, and Pinito, all of whom were well versed in Spanish, and the latter in English also.")
3. Yo-kai´-a. Ukiah, December 1875. ("From two Indians of the tribe.")
*4. Ba-tem-da-kaii. George Gibbs. 1851. (Gibbs 1853b)
*5. Chau-i-shek. George Gibbs. 1851. (Gibbs 1853b)
*6. Yu-kai. George Gibbs. 1851. (Gibbs 1853b)
*7. Ku-la-na-po. George Gibbs. 1851. (Gibbs 1853b)
8. H'hana. John Russell Bartlett. San Diego. ("From the servant of an officer. He said his people lived on the Sacramento River.") (Bartlett n.d.)
9. Venaamkakaiia. Governor J. Furu[h]jelm. ("From Indians who, twenty or thirty years ago, inhabited the country round about the Russian settlement, Ross.") [J. Hjalmar Furuhjelm, Governor of Russian America, was in correspondence with George Gibbs ca. 1860–1862.]
10. Ka´-bi-na-pek. Stephen Powers. Near Kelseyville, 1872. ("From two women of the tribe.")
*11. Chwachamaju. Kostromilov [Peter S. Kostromitinov]. (Transcribed from Wrangell and Kostromitinov 1839, with notes, by Professor F.L.O. Roehrig.)

Win-tūn´ family (518–534)

1. Win-tūn´. Stephen Powers. Tehema, 1872. ("From Shasta Frank, an educated and very intelligent member of the tribe.")
*2. Near to Mag. Reading's. . . . Adam Johnston. (Johnston 1854)
3. Trinity Indians. Dr. William A. Gabb. Upper Trinity River, 1866.
4. Noema, Wylacker. John Rusell Bartlett. Between the Sacramento River and Clear Lake. ("Obtained from H. B. Brown.") (Bartlett n.d.)
5. Colouse. John Russell Bartlett. Between the Sacramento River and Clear Lake. ("Obtained from H. B. Brown.") (Bartlett n.d.)
6. Tehema. John Russell Bartlett. ("Obtained from H. B. Brown.") (Bartlett n.d.)
7. Nome Lackee. ("Copied by Mr. Israel S. Diehl from Mrs. Van Tassel's scrap-book.")
*8. Ko-pé. George Gibbs. Putos [Putah] Creek, 1851. (Gibbs 1853b)
*9. Digger. Dr. Oscar Loew. ("From some Indians who came from California, and settled in Huerfano Park, Colorado.") (Gatschet 1876b)
10. Pat-wīn´. Stephen Powers. Long Valley, near Cedar Lake, 1872. ("From Antonio, chief of the Chenposel tribe, and one of his men.")
11. Num´-su. Stephen Powers. Mad River, 1871. ("From a woman of the tribe.")
*12. Win-tūn´. Livingston Stone. McCloud River, 1872. (Heizer 1973)

(continued)

BOX 4. (continued)

Mūt´-sūn family (535–559)

1. Miwok. Stephen Powers. Calaveras River. ("From an Indian of the tribe and his wife.")
*2. Tuolumne [Sierra Miwok]. Adam Johnston. (Johnston 1854)
*3. Costano. Adam Johnston. (Johnston 1852a)
*4. Tcho-ko-yem [Coast Miwok]. George Gibbs. 1851. (Gibbs 1853b)
5. Mūtsūn. Arroyo de la Cuesta. ("Copied by Mr. Buckingham Smith from the writing of Padre Aroyo [sic]. Mr. Smith says it is the dialect of San Jean [sic] Bautista. The spelling has not been changed.")
*6. Santa Clara [Costanoan]. Gregory Mengarini. (Mengarini 1860)
*7. Santa Cruz [Costanoan]. Juan Comelias. (Comelias 1860)
8. Chum-te´-ya [Sierra Miwok]. Albert S. Gatschet. New York, 1877. ("From Charles Manning, a Miwok [Chumteya band], who was stopping in New York, March, 1877. His tribe were in Mariposa Co.")
*9. Kawéya. ("Collected by 'T. H. R.' in the vicinity of Four Creeks, California, and published in the San Francisco *Wide West*, July, 1856, and reprinted in Taylor's *California Farmer*. It has been transliterated by Mr. Albert Gatschet into the Smithsonian alphabet.") (A. Taylor 1860–1863)
*10. San Raphael Mission [Coast Miwok]. Horatio Hale. 1842. (Hale 1846)
*11. Talatui [Plains Miwok]. James Dwight Dana. 1841. (Dana 1846)
*12. Olamentke [Bodega Miwok, from Peter S. Kostromitinov]. (Transcribed from Wrangell and Kostromitinov 1839, with notes, by Professor F.L.O. Roehrig.)

Santa Barbara [Chumash] (560–567)

*1. Kasuá. Dr. Oscar Loew. Santa Barbara. ("From an intelligent Indian named Vincente Garcia, 3 miles from the Santa Barbara Mission.") (Gatschet 1876a)
*2. Santa Inez. Alexander S. Taylor. 1856. ("From an Indian, 35 years of age, born near the Santa Inez Mission.") (A. Taylor 1860–1863)
*3. Island of Santa Cruz. Antonio Timmeno [error for Jimeno]. 1856. (Jimeno 1856)
*4. Santa Barbara. Portolá Expedition [Miguel Costansó]. Santa Barbara, 1769. (Costansó 1770)

San Antonio [Salinan] (568–569)

*1. [Vocabulary extracted from Sitjar 1861.]

Yo´-kuts family (570–585)

1. Yo´kuts. Stephen Powers. Tule River Reservation, November 1875. ("From Pedro, an Indian well versed in English and Spanish. Mr. Powers says they originally lived on the Kaweah River.")

2. Wi´chi-kik. Stephen Powers. Coarse Gold Gulch, 1872. ("From Tu´ -eh, an Indian of the tribe.")
3. Tin´linne. Stephen Powers. Tule River Reservation. ("From an Indian of the tribe, with Pedro as interpreter.")
*4. King's River. Adam Johnston. (Johnston 1854)
*5. Coconoons. Adam Johnston. (Johnston 1854)
*6. Calaveras [County]. Alexander S. Taylor. Rancheria Ta-kin near Dent's Ferry of the Stanislaus, 1856. (A. Taylor 1856)

Mai´du family (586–600)

1. Kon´kaw. Stephen Powers. Round Valley Reservation, November 1875. ("From Captain George and Charley Munson.")
2. Hol-o´-la-pai. Stephen Powers. Feather River, a little below Oroville, 1872.
3. Na´-kum. Stephen Powers. Susanville, October 1875.
4. Ni´-shi-nam. Stephen Powers. Bear River, above Sheridan, 1874. ("From Paung´ -lo and a Ni´ -shi-nam woman, Margaret.")
5. "Digger." H. B. Brown. (Bartlett n.d.)
*6. Cushna [N. Hill Nisenan]. Adam Johnston. South Yuba River, upper Sacramento Valley. (Johnston 1852b)
7. Nishinan. Israel S. Diehl. Placerville, 1854. ("From Mr. J. C. Johnson.") (Diehl 1854)
*8. Yuba or Nevada. Lieutenant Edward Ross. Yuba River. ("Published in the History Magazine of New York, 1863, p. 123.") (Gibbs 1863b)
*9. Punjuni [Valley Nisenan]. James Dwight Dana. 1841. (Dana 1846)
*10. Sekumné [Valley Nisenan]. James Dwight Dana. 1841. (Dana 1846)
*11. Tsamak [Valley Nisenan]. James Dwight Dana. 1841. (Dana 1846)

A-cho-mâ´-wi family (601–606)

1. Achomâ´wi. Stephen Powers. Round Valley, December, 1875. ("From two intelligent members of the tribe, who spoke good English.")
2. Lutuami [error for "Pitt River"]. George Gibbs. Washington, DC, 1861–1862. ("From Ie-op-to-mi, an Indian brought to Washington. from A-pui band. forks of Pitt and Fall Rivers.") (Gibbs 1861–1862)

Shas´ta family (607–613)

1. Shas-ti´-ka. Stephen Powers. Yreka, 1872. ("From a number of men and women of the tribe.")
2. Shas-te. Edward Ross. At the ferry on the Upper Klamath River.
3. Shasta. George Crook. Fort Lane, Oregon, May 7, 1856.
4. Shasta. William B. Hazen. Rogue River, Oregon, 1857. (Hazen 1857)
*5. Shastie. James Dwight Dana. 1841. (Dana 1846)

FIGURE 10. Alphonse Pinart. Courtesy of the Bancroft Library, UCB.

2.4.9 Alphonse Louis Pinart

During the late 1870s, California was visited by the French linguist and explorer Alphonse Louis Pinart (1852–1911). The only son of a wealthy factory owner, Pinart showed a stong interest in exotic languages and cultures from an early age. In his teens he met and became the disciple of the Abbé Brasseur de Bourbourg, one of the most influential Americanists of the nineteenth century. Brasseur encouraged the financially independent young man (Pinart's father had died in 1859, leaving him a substantial fortune) to carry out a comprehensive study of the languages of the Western Hemisphere in order to determine their origins. Under Brasseur's tutelage, Pinart equipped himself for this work by acquiring, among other special skills, a command of the phonetic transcription system that had been developed by the German Egyptologist Karl Richard Lepsius.[36]

In 1871 the young Pinart traveled to Alaska to begin work on the languages closest to Asia. Sailing on a salmon schooner, he first visited the Aleutians, then, after wintering on Kodiak Island, spent 1872 and part of 1873 along the southern coast of Alaska. He returned to France with a large collection of linguistic and ethnographic material, including an impressive array of Northwest Coast artifacts. Shortly afterward he set out for Russia, where he spent two years studying Tatar and other Central Asian languages to see what light they might throw on ancient connections with American languages. Back in France for a few months in

early 1875, he launched a publication series devoted to aboriginal American languages and cultures.[37]

Later that year, Pinart traveled across Canada from Nova Scotia to the Northwest Coast, then dipped south for a four-month sojourn in Arizona (Pinart and Wagner 1962). Although his stay on the West Coast was relatively brief, the linguistic diversity of the region left a strong impression, and on his return to France he made plans to mount an expedition to study the linguistics, ethnography, and archaeology of the region (Heizer 1951; Reichlen and Heizer 1963).

The preparations for this ambitious project, which had the formal sponsorship of the French government and included an ethnologist-archaeologist, Léon de Cessac, exhausted what remained of Pinart's personal fortune. When Pinart and Cessac finally rendezvoused in Santa Barbara in July 1878, the elaborate plans they had made for collaborative research had to be scrapped. Both men carried out a certain amount of independent work, however, and it was during this period that Pinart collected his most valuable documentation of California languages, a series of vocabularies collected at the former missions. The originals of these, together with Pinart's detailed diary, were obtained by H. H. Bancroft, possibly as collateral for a loan, and are now in the Bancroft Library (Pinart 1870–1885). Most of this collection was edited and published by Heizer (1952). Especially valuable are Pinart's vocabularies of Esselen (1878a) and Santa Cruz Island Chumash (1878l), each constituting the most extensive and phonetically accurate attestation of that language that has survived. Although omitted from Heizer's publication, Pinart's vocabularies of two long-extinct dialects of Yokuts are also of great value.[38]

Cessac, who had apparently collected some linguistic materials of his own, returned to France during the winter of 1878–1879, while Pinart retreated to northern Mexico. Pinart returned to San Francisco in 1879 to court the young heiress Zelia Nuttall, whom he married in May 1880. Financially reinvigorated by his wife's fortune, he resumed his collecting activities and obtained, among other materials, a vocabulary of the Yachikamne variety of Delta Yokuts. A version of this vocabulary appeared in print in 1894 (see also Merriam 1955:133–138), and a copy of the manuscript is preserved among his papers in the Beinecke Library at Yale, but otherwise none of the linguistic notes from his 1879–1880 California visit, and nothing of what Cessac is known to have collected, can now be located.[39]

Pinart subsequently traveled in the West Indies, the Southwest, and Panama. He returned to France in 1885, by this time separated from Nuttall (who divorced him in 1888) and again impoverished. He continued to write and publish, drawing on his extensive collections, but died in obscurity in 1911.[40]

Linguistic Scholarship

2.5 Early Research Linguistics, 1865–1900

2.5.1 Beginning of Research Linguistics in the United States

The years immediately after the Civil War were an important turning point in American Indian linguistics. Until this time, the documentation and comparison of the native languages of North America had been dominated by the practical goals of missionaries and military officers, and the little scientific attention that was paid to these languages came from scholars—or scholarly amateurs, such as Thomas Jefferson, Albert Gallatin, Stephen Duponceau, and John Pickering—who relied almost entirely on data collected by others. The only significant exception was Horatio Hale, whose detailed report on the languages of the Northwest (1846) was based on the materials he had collected at first hand during the Wilkes Expedition. But Hale's work had no imitators, and he himself largely abandoned linguistics for the practice of law until well into the 1870s. In a lecture delivered at the Smithsonan in 1862, William Dwight Whitney, at the time America's most eminent student of languages, could still say,

Europeans accuse us, with too much reason, of indifference and inefficiency with regard to preserving memorials of the races whom we have dispossessed and are dispossesing, and to promoting a thorough comprehension of their history. Indian scholars, and associations which devote themselves to gathering together and making public linguistic and other archaeological materials for construction of the proper ethnology of the continent, are far rarer than they should be among us. Not a literary institution in our country has among its teachers one whose business it is to investigate the languages of our aboriginal populations, and to acquire and diffuse true knowledge respecting them and their history. So much the more reason have we to be grateful to the few who are endeavouring to make up our deficiencies by self-prompted study, and especially to those self-denying men who, under circumstances of no small difficulty, are or have been devoting themselves to the work of collecting and giving to the world original materials. (Whitney 1867:362–363)

In the late 1860s, however, a new generation of scholar-explorers came on the scene, of whom John Wesley Powell was the most influential.

2.5.2 John Wesley Powell and the Bureau of American Ethnology

John Wesley Powell was born in 1834 in upstate New York, the son of a Methodist preacher with strong abolitionist

views, and grew up in Ohio, Wisconsin, and Illinois. Like most young men who came of age west of the Appalachians in the 1840s and 1850s, Powell had only limited opportunities for a formal education, but he read voraciously, particularly in the natural sciences, and by his early twenties was carrying out field research in biology and geology. He was well advanced in a career as a schoolteacher when the Civil War broke out. He joined the 20th Illinois Volunteer Infantry (commanded by Ulysses S. Grant), and fought in several campaigns, losing his right forearm at the battle of Shiloh.

After leaving the army in 1865 with the rank of major, Powell was appointed professor of geology at the newly established Illinois Wesleyan University, and he soon began laying plans for a scientific survey of the vast tract of territory between the High Plains and the Sierras. The time was ripe for such ventures, and Powell soon was one of the leading figures in the exploration of the American West. An expedition to the Dakota Badlands and the Rocky Mountains in the summer of 1867 was followed in 1868–1869 by a more ambitious exploration of the Colorado Plateau and, in the summer of 1869, by a boat trip down the Green and Colorado Rivers and through the Grand Canyon. This exploit

FIGURE 11. John Wesley Powell with a Southern Paiute man near the Kaibab Plateau. Photo by John K. Hillers, 1873. Courtesy of the National Anthropological Archives, Smithsonian Institution (16-03507).

received national publicity, and in 1870 Powell was awarded government funding for the establishment of the Geographical and Topographical Survey of the Rocky Mountains; further appropriations were forthcoming, and the survey continued until 1879, when its work was incorporated into that of the U.S. Geological Survey, for which Powell served as the first director.

The documentation of Indian languages made up an important part of the scientific survey work of Powell's expeditions. Influenced by the social evolutionary thinking of the period, especially the writings of Lewis Henry Morgan, Powell treated the cultures and languages of aboriginal peoples as an essential feature of the natural history of the regions he explored. An understanding of their prehistoric connections was a scientific activity akin to paleontology, and the collection of extensive and accurate data was imperative. Powell's own focus was on the Numic-speaking groups, and he carried out the pioneering documentation of several Numic languages, including Southern Paiute (1871–1872, 1873b), Chemehuevi (n.d.), and Northern Paiute (1873a, 1880c, 1880d, 1880e), and also collected substantial data on Shoshoni and Ute (D. Fowler and Fowler 1971). He also obtained a vocabulary of Mohave (1873c), made the first documentation of Yana (1880a), and collected a Wintu vocabulary and some mythological texts (1880b). In 1875, Powell joined forces with Stephen Powers to prepare the first overall classification of California languages, published as the "Linguistics" appendix to Powers's *Tribes of California* (Powell 1877a). In 1877, he hired the philologist Albert S. Gatschet to carry out full-time linguistic research for the survey, involving both extensive field collection and classificatory work.

In 1879, Powell was instrumental in setting up a federal agency, the Bureau of American Ethnology, to coordinate all government-funded research on Indian languages and cultures. Under Powell's direction, the BAE focused on a comprehensive survey of North American Indian languages, emphasizing the collection of new materials, particulary extensive vocabularies, with the aim of compiling a definitive continent-wide classification. To carry out this agenda, a staff of field researchers was assembled, starting with Gatschet.[41]

Researchers deployed by the BAE to the California area included Gatschet himself, Jeremiah Curtin, J. Owen Dorsey, and Henry W. Henshaw. Gatschet undertook several projects, most importantly the intensive documentation of Klamath-Modoc, but also survey work in the Sacramento Valley and on Yuman. Curtin was assigned the languages of northern California and Dorsey those of the Oregon Athabaskans, while Henshaw undertook a survey of the languages of the mission region on the central and southern coast, from Miwok to Diegueño. After 1880, Powell's own anthropological fieldwork was sporadic and usually incidental to his administrative duties. He spent several weeks on the Pacific Coast during the summer of 1893, but it is not clear which tribes he visited, and there are no manuscripts in the Smithsonian archives relating to this work.

2.5.3 Albert Samuel Gatschet

Born in Switzerland in 1832, Albert Samuel Gatschet (see Figure 58) attended the universities of Bern and Berlin, where he received a thorough training in philology. He emigrated to America in 1868, settling in New York, where he taught languages and contributed articles to scientific journals. In 1872, Oscar Loew, a German botanist and chemist, asked Gatschet to examine the vocabularies of the languages of California and the Southwest that he been collecting for the Wheeler Expedition (¶2.4.5). Gatschet's early reports on these materials (especially 1876a) attracted Powell's attention, and in March 1877 he offered Gatschet a position on his Rocky Mountain Survey. Gatschet's first assignment took him to the West Coast, where he collected data on Chico Maidu (1877d), Shasta (1877a), Achumawi (1877f), Molala (1877e), Kalapuya (1877g), and Upper Umpqua Athabaskan (1877b), and began the long-term study of Klamath (1878, 1890).

When the Bureau of American Ethnology was established in 1879, Powell assigned Gatschet the primary responsibility for classificatory work. He was able to return to the Klamath for an extended period in 1882–1884, providing the basis for a massive two-volume study of Klamath language and culture (1890). Otherwise, however, most of his BAE field research was devoted to a series of short but demanding projects scattered across the continent, many of them in the Southeast. He retired in 1905 and died not long afterward.

In addition to Klamath-Modoc and the field data on the languages mentioned, Gatschet's most important contribution to the study of California-area languages was his pioneering comparative work, first arising out of his analysis of Loew's vocabularies (1879a) and culminating in a detailed study of Yuman and Yuman-Cochimí relationships (1877c, 1883, 1886, 1892a, 1900). He also carried out some further field work on Achumawi (1892b) and made a brief study of Wintu (1889).[42]

2.5.4 Jeremiah Curtin

Jeremiah Curtin (1835–1906), a well-known literary figure, traveler, and polyglot, spent several years during the 1880s on the BAE staff. Although he devoted a considerable amount of time to work on the Iroquoian languages, the primary focus of his field research was on the languages of Northern California and Oregon. He made two visits to the region under BAE auspices, the first in 1884–1885, the second in 1888–1889. During these trips he collected extensive material, primarily vocabularies but also narrative texts (although many of these are in English), from more than a dozen languages. These included, in rough chronological order, Yana (Curtin 1884a, 1884–1889a, 1884–1889b), Wintu (1884b, 1884c, 1884–1889c,

FIGURE 12. Jeremiah Curtin. 1871. Courtesy of the Milwaukee County Historical Society.

1884–1889d, 1888–1889a, 1888–1889b), Atsugewi (1884d), Shasta (1885a, 1885b), Achumawi (1885c, 1889j), Hupa (1888–1889c, 1888–1889d, 1888–1889e), "Saia" [Nongatl] (1884e), Chimariko (1889a), Yurok (1889b), Karuk (1889c, 1889d, 1889e), Wiyot (1889f, 1889g), and Yuki (1889h, 1889i). In addition to the materials he obtained on Klamath-Modoc in Oregon during his 1884–1885 visit, he documented the Modoc dialect during an earlier visit to Oklahoma (1884–1885a, 1884–1885b, 1884–1885c). He also collected smaller amounts of data on a number of other California languages, including Wailaki, Plains Miwok, Coast Miwok, Suisun Patwin, Chocheño Costanoan, and the "Tamukan" and "Tawitci" dialects of Delta Yokuts (1884f, 1889k). In his posthumously published *Memoirs*, Curtin provides an entertaining, if not always fully accurate, record of his travel experiences during these field expeditions (Curtin 1940:324–380, 412–441).[43]

Curtin's documentation of many of these languages represents their first detailed attestation. This is especially true of Yana, which was all but unknown before Curtin's work. None of this material has ever been published, however, other than the English versions of a number of traditional narratives that Curtin incorporated into his study of *Creation Myths of Primitive America* (1898).[44]

Curtin was one of the rare polyglots to work as a field linguist, and his facility for acquiring languages easily and quickly served him well in his California work. When he was able to devote more than a few days to a language—as with Wintu, Yana, and Hupa—he apparently learned to speak it before filling out the "schedules" in Powell's questionnaire. Although he only sporadically transcribed glottalization and sometimes missed other phonemic contrasts to which his ear was not attuned, Curtin's field transcriptions are among the most reliable of the period. His documentation in general is remarkable for its depth of coverage, frequently including bilingual texts as well as lexical data.[45]

2.5.5 Henry Wetherbee Henshaw

Henry Wetherbee Henshaw (1850–1930) was trained as a biologist and in 1872 joined the Wheeler Expedition as a naturalist. It was under these auspices that he first visited California in the summer of 1875, as assistant to the archaeologist Paul Schumaker. Powell recruited him for the BAE in 1880 and sent him to California on multiple occasions over the following decade. In 1883 he collected vocabularies of Washo (1883a) and Panamint (1883b), and in an extended visit in 1884 he obtained substantial data on a number of languages in the former mission area (1884a–1884n, 1884–1888). During an 1888 visit to the San Francisco–Monterey area he collected especially valuable vocabularies of the Coast Miwok dialect of Tomales Bay (1888a), of the Costanoan and Delta Yokus dialects spoken at Mission Santa Cruz (1888b), of Esselen (1888c), and of Soledad Costanoan (1888d), and was the first to recognize the isolated classificatory status of Esselen (1890). He returned to California in 1892–1893, collecting materials on Northern Pomo (1892), Diegueño (1892–1893), and Cahuilla (1893). Henshaw's health failed in the mid-1890s, and he left the BAE to convalesce in Hawaii for several years. On his return to Washington in 1904, he became C. Hart Merriam's deputy in the Biological Survey, succeeding Merriam as chief in 1910.[46]

Although Henshaw regarded himself primarily as a field biologist—an ornithologist, more specifically—and made no pretensions to linguistic expertise, his influence on the work of the BAE in the 1880s and early 1890s was considerable. Kroeber has suggested that Powell relied more on Henshaw than on the more linguistically knowledgeable members of his staff in making the crucial decisions for the 1891 classification and map (Kroeber 1960b). Certainly there is little doubt that Henshaw's hand can be seen in Powell's decision to name North American linguistic stocks by the same rule of nomenclatural precedence that applied in biological taxonomy. Whatever his administrative and organization skills, however, Henshaw was no match for Gatschet, Dorsey, and Curtin as a field linguist. His transcriptions were amateurish, and on more than one occasion he mistook the identity of the language he was transcribing.[47] Nonetheless, his vocabularies of California languages often make up in their breadth of coverage and orderliness for what they lack in linguistic finesse, not unlike those collected by Merriam.

2.5.6 Rev. James Owen Dorsey

Rev. James Owen Dorsey (1848–1895), an Episcopal deacon who had been a missionary to the Poncas in the early 1870s, was invited by Powell in 1877 to join his Rocky Mountain Survey as an expert on Siouan languages (Hinsley 1981:172–177). After his position was transferred to the BAE, he was asked to take on other projects, and in 1884 he was sent to Oregon. During a four-month stay on the Siletz Reservation,

FIGURE 13. Henry Wetherbee Henshaw, Camp Bidwell, California, 1878. Ruthven Deane Collection, Library of Congress.

FIGURE 14. J. Owen Dorsey. Courtesy of the National Anthropological Archives, Smithsonian Institution (28-55500).

to where many of the Indians of western Oregon had been moved in the 1850s, Dorsey collected data on most of the languages of the region, including the Oregon Athabaskan languages (1884a–1884o), Takelma (1884p), and Shasta (1884q).

Dorsey was probably the best field linguist on the BAE staff—according to Kroeber he "virtually heard phonemically decades before the idea of phonemics was formulated" (1960b:1)—and his documentation of the languages of southwestern Oregon is masterly. In the case of Oregon Athabaskan, where Dorsey's meticulous record of dialect differences is remarkably complete, the material remains uniquely valuable, although (except for a few words quoted in Dorsey 1890) it remains entirely unpublished.

2.5.7 The Powell Classification

The classification of 1891—a collaborative effort by the BAE staff, with Henshaw taking a particularly important role (Kroeber 1960b; Sturtevant 1959; Hymes 1961a; D. Fowler and Fowler 1971:283, n. 8)—was by far the most important and influential work in American Indian linguistics to come out of the Powell era. More than a century after its publication, most of the classificatory scheme remains intact, although many of Powell's language family names (particularly those based on an application of the rule of precedence followed in biological taxonomy) have long been abandoned (Table 2).

2.6 The Kroeber Era, 1900 to World War II

2.6.1 Alfred L. Kroeber

No single individual has ever exerted a more powerful and enduring influence on the study—particularly the historical study—of California Indian languages than Alfred L. Kroeber

TABLE 2

Obsolete Names for California Language Families or
Isolates Used in the Powell Classification

Powell 1891	Present Work	Other Variants
Copehan	Wintuan	Wintun
Kulanapan	Pomo	Pomoan
Lutuamian	Klamath-Modoc	Klamath
Mariposan	Yokuts	Yokutsan
Moquelumnan	Miwok	Miwokan
Pujunan	Maiduan	Maidun
Quoratean	Karuk	Karok
Sastean	Shastan	
Shoshonean	Northern Uto-Aztecan	
Weitspekan	Yurok	
Wishoskan	Wiyot	

(1876–1960). A man of broad vision and immense capacity
for work, Kroeber had the good fortune to begin his
career during the decades when anthropology was being
transformed from an intellectual hobby into a research-
oriented academic discipline. He was the first professionally
trained anthropologist to establish himself in California, and
as such had the opportunity to create the institutional
structure within which anthropological research would be
carried out for decades to come.[48]

Kroeber received his anthropological training between
1897 and 1900 at Columbia University, where he was Franz
Boas's first (and in many ways most influential) student.
Boas, the founder of modern American anthropology, saw it
as a sociopsychological discipline within which the analysis
of language had a central role. He impressed on his students
the importance of detailed linguistic documentation that
went far beyond the collection of culturally important
vocabulary. His preferred method of work was to transcribe
long narrative texts—myths, legends, stories—in a close
phonetic transcription, and then work through these with a
bilingual interpreter, coming in this way to an understanding
both of the formal structure of the language and of the
modes of expression speakers of the language habitually
used. It was demanding work, but the majority of Boas's
students, regardless of their natural talents in language,
adopted the text-based approach to the documentation of
Indian languages and cultures.

Kroeber carried out his dissertation fieldwork in 1898–
1899 among the Arapaho of Wyoming, where he immersed
himself, following Boas's prescription, in a detailed study of
the Arapaho language as well as general Arapaho culture.
(His dissertation was a study of symbolic designs.) In the
spring of 1900, immediately after leaving Arapaho country,
Kroeber accepted an appointment as curator of anthropology at the California Academy of Sciences in San Francisco.
He carried out some preliminary fieldwork in the Klamath

River area of northern California, but after several months
the position unexpectedly terminated and he returned to
New York to finish his dissertation.

Early in 1901, Kroeber was invited to return to California
as a member of the University of California's newly
established Museum of Anthropology. Although Frederic
Ward Putnam, curator of the Peabody Museum at Harvard,
had been named the director of the museum and professor of
anthropology, his appointment was largely pro forma, and
he was expected to make only brief visits to California.
Kroeber was hired to be Putnam's resident assistant, in
charge of the practical administration of the museum and
the collection and study of California ethnological material.[49]

With the museum generously funded by Phoebe Apperson
Hearst during its first few years, Kroeber was able to embark
on a wide-ranging survey of California Indian cultures and
languages. Kroeber proved to be an astute adminsitrator as
well as a dedicated research scholar, and by 1915 the
University of California's anthropology department was one
of the most productive in North America. Besides Kroeber,
the staff included, at various times, P. E. Goddard, whose
focus was on the California Athabaskans; S. A. Barrett, who
studied the Pomo and Miwok; and T. T. Waterman, who
worked with groups as diverse as the Yurok, Yana, and

FIGURE 15. A. L. Kroeber, visiting Ishi's homeland
in the summer of 1914. Courtesy of the Hearst
Museum of Anthropology and the Regents of UC.

Unless otherwise specified, the original materials are archived in the A. L. Kroeber Papers (BANC MSS C-B 925), Bancroft Library, University of California, Berkeley, access to which is normally by microfilm (BANC FILM 2049; specific reel and frame numbers are given in square brackets). Publications of the linguistic data are noted in parentheses.

Atsugewi 1900 [98:147–309] (Kroeber 1958).

Cahuilla 1904–1907 [97:116–227; 119:34–137] (Kroeber 1907b:67–92, 151–152; 1908c; 1909a:236–246).

Chimariko 1901–1902 [96:323–580].

Chumash languages 1901–1912 [96:581–697; 97:2–68; 121:229–368] (Kroeber 1904:31–43; 1910:264–271).

Cocopa 1930 [125:723–762] (Kroeber 1943).

Costanoan languages 1901–1914 [96:670 ff.; 97:89–115; 119:138–256] (Kroeber 1904:69–80; 1910:239–263)

Diegueño 1904–1912 [97:116–291; 163:189–196] (Kroeber and Harrington 1914).

Esselen 1901–1902 [96:670 ff.] (Kroeber 1904:49–68).

Gabrielino 1904–1912 [97:35–68; 98:74–146] (Kroeber 1907b:67–92, 140–145; 1909a:251–253)

Hupa 1901–1924 [96:405–500; 98:310–330].

Karuk 1901–1951 [96:405–500; 98:331 ff.; 99; 100:2–572; 116:127–199; 120:2–87; 127:175–353] (Kroeber 1911a:427–435; 1936; Kroeber and Gifford 1980).

Kato n.d. [100:573–578]. See also Kroeber n.d.[a].

Kaxwan (Yuman) 1930 [102:132–171] (Kroeber 1943).

Luiseño 1902–1957 [97:116–227; 100:586 ff.; 101:2–674] (Kroeber 1907b:67–92, 145–149).

Maidu 1909–1923, n.d. [101:675 ff.; 102:2–101; 121:486–575]

Maricopa 1930 [102:132 ff.] (Kroeber 1943).

Miwok, Coast 1904–1914 [97:69–82; 119:138–256] (Kroeber 1911a:292–319).

Miwok, Sierra 1904–1923 [101:675 ff.; 116:200–208; 119:138–256; 121:369–485] (Kroeber 1906a; 1911a:278–291).

Mohave 1900–1960 [103–115; 116:2–115] (Kroeber 1911b; 1943; 1948).

Mono/Monache 1903–1904 [116:116–126] (Kroeber 1907b:67–92, 114–122).

Nisenan 1925. Kroeber's Nisenan notes are integrated into Kroeber, Gayton and Freeland (1925) and are not included in BANC MSS C-B 925 or BANC FILM 2049. (Some materials published in Kroeber 1929).

Numic languages (Kawaiisu, [Northern] Paiute) 1911–1916 [116:262–277]. See also Kroeber n.d.[b].

Patwin 1900–1924. Kroeber's Patwin notes are not in BANC MSS C-B 925 or BANC FILM 2049; see Kroeber 1900–1924, 1909b.

Pomo languages 1901–1910 [97:292–307; 116:209–262; 118:162–261] (Kroeber 1911a:320–347).

Quechan (Yuma) 1930 [125:687–762] (Kroeber 1943).

Salinan (Migueleño) 1901–1902. The location of these notes is unknown; see Kroeber 1904:43–47.

Serrano 1907 [119:34–82] (Kroeber 1909a:253–256).

Shasta 1902, n.d. [99:180–324; 119:18–33].

Shasta, New River 1901 [96:405–500; 116:127–199].

Takic, Numic and Tubatulabal ("Shoshonean") languages 1903–1912, n.d. [97:35–68, 228–269; 119:83–137; 121:229–575, 633–704] (Kroeber 1907b; 1909a).

Tolowa 1901, n.d. [119:257–265; 163:274–278].

Wappo 1908 [116:278–361].

Washo 1902–1903 [119:306–378] (Kroeber 1907c).

Wintu 1901, n.d. [96:405–500; 119:379–396].

Wiyot 1901–1923 [119:397 ff.; 120:2–140; 127:354–490, 602–710] (Kroeber 1911a:384–413).

Yokuts 1900–1960 [119:285–305; 120:482 ff.; 121–124; 125:2–660] (Kroeber 1906b; 1907a; 1963).

Yuki 1900–1912, n.d. [125:661–686; 163:351 ff.] (Kroeber 1906b; 1911a:348–83; 1959c). Most of Kroeber's Yuki linguistic materials are not included in BANC FILM 2049, although the original notes, which were separated from the Kroeber papers in the early 1960s, have now been reunited with BANC MSS C-B 925; see Kroeber 1900–1958. See also Uldall 1931–1932.

Yurok 1900–1940 [96:501–603; 125:763 ff.; 126–146; 147:2–271] (Kroeber 1911a:414–26; 1934; 1960a; 1976). See also Blevins and Garrett (n.d.), which contains a reel-by-reel synopsis of Kroeber's Yurok materials (Conathan and Wood n.d.)

Diegueño. In addition, Edward Sapir spent a year in California (1907–1908) as a research fellow, working on Yana (returning in the summer of 1915 to document Ishi's Yahi dialect). A significant proportion of the research carried out by Kroeber and his team was linguistic.

Kroeber himself collected basic data on more than two dozen California languages (Box 5). Much of this work was carried out very early. Kroeber devoted a substantial portion of his field time between 1901 and 1907 to conducting a broad survey of the diversity of California languages, with special attention to grammatical structure. He shared this work with the Harvard anthropologist R. B. Dixon (see ¶2.6.2), who had been carrying out linguistic and ethnological fieldwork in northern California since 1899. Dixon took responsibility for describing the Maiduan, Palaihnihan, and Shastan languages, as well as Wintu, Yana, and Chimariko. Kroeber dealt with the remainder of the state, including the coast both north and south of San Francisco Bay, the Central Valley south of the Wintu, the Sierras south of the Maiduans, and all of southern California. Kroeber reported on the languages of his area in short sketches grouped into volumes largely by region: Costanoan, Esselen, Salinan, and Chumash, that is, the coast south of San Francisco (1904); Yokuts and Yuki (1906b); Takic, Numic, and Tubatulabal, that is, the "Shoshonean" languages (1907b, 1909a); Washo (1907c); Chumash and Costanoan again (1910); and Miwok, Pomo, Yukian, Wiyot, Yurok, and Karuk, that is, the coast north of San Francisco (1911a). These short but insightful summaries of phonological, grammatical, and lexical structure—in many cases, the first grammatical description ever attempted for the language in question—with one significant exception constitute the major portion of Kroeber's published documentation of California Indian languages.

The exception is Kroeber's monograph on Yokuts (1907a), which contains a survey of the interrelation of the multitude of Yokuts dialects, a detailed grammatical analysis and lexicon of the Yawdanchi dialect with analyzed texts, and a somewhat less detailed parallel treatment of the Yawelmani dialect. Much of the data, particularly on Yawdanchi, was obtained in 1903 from a speaker who was brought to San Francisco for a month of intensive work. After the publication of this monograph Kroeber continued his investigation of Yokuts with an extensive field investigation of Yokuts dialect diversity, the results of which, however, were not finally readied for publication until the late 1950s (Kroeber 1963). Kroeber also collected more substantial data than appeared in his survey sketches for four other languages—Yurok, Yuki, Mojave, and Patwin—but hardly any of this was published during his lifetime.[50]

Dixon and Kroeber published a preliminary synopsis of their linguistic survey in 1903, sorting the languages of the region into groups defined largely in terms of a rudimentary morphological typology. This was followed in 1907 by a survey of the numeral systems of the region and, in 1913, by their groundbreaking classification of the large majority of the independent language families of California into the Hokan and Penutian phyla. The preliminary announcement of this classification was bolstered in 1919 by a monograph-length volume with substantial supporting data, largely lexical resemblances.

After the publication of this volume and the completion of his *Handbook of the Indians of California* (Kroeber 1925), which used the Hokan and Penutian classifications as its framework (most influentially in the accompanying map), Kroeber largely ceased to play an active part in California Indian linguistics. His interests were drawn to other topics,[51] and he also may have felt the work was best left to the professional linguists who were being trained by Sapir and others. During the 1930s and 1940s his own linguistic research was limited to collecting cultural vocabulary or dialectal data, as with Patwin (Kroeber 1932), or to investigating the internal classification of a language families, as with Yuman (Kroeber 1943). His enthusiasm for phylum-level classification was much diminished, and he found little value in expanding the Penutian and Hokan classifications beyond California (Kroeber 1940).

In the 1950s, with the establishment of an independent department of linguistics at Berkeley with a research focus on California Indian languages (see ¶2.9), Kroeber seems to have experienced a rekindling of his earlier enthusiasm for linguistic work. He returned to several language-based projects that he had allowed to languish for decades: editing Sparkman's Luiseño materials (Kroeber and Grace 1960); organizing the results of his 1906 Yokuts dialect survey for publication (Kroeber 1963); and preparing his massive collection of Yurok texts for publication (Kroeber 1976).[52]

In retrospect, Kroeber's contribution to the documentation of California Indian languages resides primarily in the typological and comparative schemata he constructed, rather than in the data he himself collected and processed. While the latter are not negligible, he wrote no comprehensive grammar and compiled no dictionary, and even the substantial collections of texts that he made for Yurok, Mohave, and Karuk were never readied for publication except in English translation.[53] But as director of the principal institution carrying out research on the languages of aboriginal California during the crucial decades when the fundamental data were being accumulated, Kroeber was able to structure the nature of this activity well beyond his own efforts. It was Kroeber who invented the concept of tribelet, who standardized the nomenclature of languages and dialects, and who invented Hokan and Penutian. For better or for worse, California Indian linguistics, together with the model of aboriginal California society it implies, has an indelible Kroeberian imprint.

2.6.2 Roland B. Dixon

Kroeber's closest professional colleague during his early years in California was Roland B. Dixon (1875–1934). After graduating from Harvard in 1897, Dixon took up archaeol-

FIGURE 16. Roland B. Dixon. © 2008 Harvard University, Peabody Museum (2004.24.32546).

ogy and ethnology, and in 1898 he began carrying out ethnographic and linguistic survey work for the American Museum of Natural History under the supervision of Franz Boas. After several months in British Columbia and Alaska, Boas assigned Dixon northeastern California as his primary field of operation. Over the next six years he worked with the Northeastern Maidu, the Northern and Central Yana, the Wintu, the Chimariko, and nearly all the Palaihnihan and Shastan groups, collecting both ethnographic and linguistic data. He received a doctorate from Harvard in 1900 with a dissertation on the Northeastern Maidu language that was largely directed by Boas.[54]

In addition to sharing an academic mentor in Boas, both Dixon and Kroeber had an institutional connection to Frederic Ward Putnam, who was simultaneously the director of the Peabody Museum at Harvard (where Dixon had an academic appointment from 1901) and professor of anthropology at the University of California. It was thus relatively easy for Dixon and Kroeber to coordinate their work. They made an explicit agreement not to duplicate one another's ethnographic activities—Dixon was to cover northeastern California and the northern Sierra Nevada, Kroeber the remainder of the state—and they pooled their data in a series of general linguistic surveys: linguistic typology (Dixon and Kroeber 1903), numeral systems (Dixon and Kroeber 1907), and language family relationships (Dixon and Kroeber 1913, 1919).

Although Dixon's primary interest was not language, and his skills as a field linguist were modest at best,[55] he strove to make as complete a record as he could of the languages he encountered. In addition to Maidu, he collected substantial material on Chimariko, Shastan, Palaihnihan, Wintu, and Yana, although much of it was never published.[56]

Dixon's interest in discovering historical connections among languages was greater than his concern with the details of the languages themselves. The 1905 paper in which Dixon proposed a genetic relationship between Shastan and Palaihnihan (his "Shasta-Achomawi" stock) inaugurated the "lumping" that led ultimately to the Hokan hypothesis (Dixon 1905b), and while the details of their collaboration have never been fully explored, it is possible that it was Dixon rather than Kroeber who first glimpsed the possibility of the two great phylum-level relationships to which their names have become attached.[57]

After 1906, Dixon's commitment to primary research in California tapered off. After World War I he was chiefly concerned with large-scale questions of geographic distribution and racial differences, and returned to California matters only in a brief exchange with Merriam about the identity of ethnolinguistic groups in the New River area (Dixon 1931).

2.6.3 Pliny Earle Goddard

Kroeber's first faculty colleague at Berkeley was Pliny Earle Goddard (1869–1928).[58] Born in Maine into a Quaker family, Goddard studied classical languages at Earlham College in Richmond, Indiana, graduating in 1892. During the next four years he taught in secondary schools in Indiana and Kansas, but in 1896, finding himself without employment during an economic downturn, he accepted an offer from the Indian Aid Society to serve as interdenominational missionary to the Hupas. Settling in Hoopa Valley with his family in 1897, he soon learned enough Hupa to preach in

FIGURE 17. Pliny Earle Goddard, during his New York years (1910–1928). Courtesy of the Division of Anthropology, American Museum of Natural History (PH 1/88).

and began the organized collection of information on Hupa grammar and traditional literature. Encouraged by the ethnographer Stewart Culin, who visited the area in 1899, Goddard approached Benjamin Ide Wheeler, a fellow classicist who had recently been named president of the University of California and, with Wheeler's encouragement and support, enrolled as a postgraduate student at Berkeley in 1900. The following year he was appointed an instructor and joined Kroeber on the faculty of the newly formed department of anthropology.

After completing his doctoral dissertation, a grammar of Hupa (Goddard 1905), he was promoted to assistant professor and by 1906 had responsibility for most of the undergraduate instruction offered by the department. Between 1900 and 1909, Goddard carried out extensive field research on Hupa and other Athabaskan languages of the California region, following Boas's technique of working from texts.[59] Two substantial works on Hupa language and culture (Goddard 1903a, 1904) made up the first volume of the *University of California Publications in American Archaeology and Ethnology* (UC-PAAE).

Kroeber and Goddard were only accidental colleagues, and their personal relationship was never a close one. Goddard had little interest in museum work or in ethnographic field studies beyond the California Athabaskan groups he was familiar with. Instead, he developed a strong interest in instrumental phonetics, and envisioned the growth of a program of teaching and research focused largely on linguistics. When Phoebe Apperson Hearst's private endowment of the Museum of Anthropology came to an end in 1908, Kroeber and Goddard openly feuded over the future direction of the department, with Kroeber ultimately triumphing.[60]

In 1909, Goddard left California for the American Museum of Natural History in New York, where he became curator of North American ethnology in 1914. As Franz Boas's close associate, he exerted wide influence as a writer on general ethnological topics and as the editor of the *American Anthropologist* (1915–1920). In 1917, Boas and Goddard cofounded the *International Journal of American Linguistics* as an outlet for American Indian linguistic scholarship, and Goddard served as the primary editor of the journal until his death in 1928.

From his new base in New York, Goddard continued his Athabaskan linguistic research with extended visits to the Southwest and Canada. In 1922 he accompanied Boas's student **Gladys A. Reichard** (1893–1955) on a field trip to northwestern California, where Reichard worked on Wiyot[61] and Goddard collected data on the Bear River dialect of the Mattole–Bear River language (Goddard 1929).

2.6.4 Thomas Talbot Waterman

Thomas Talbot Waterman (1885–1936) was Kroeber's student and, after 1910, junior colleague at Berkeley. A clergyman's son who took his BA in divinity, he switched to anthropology for graduate study. He worked as a museum

FIGURE 18. T. T. Waterman and Ishi, visiting Ishi's homeland in the summer of 1914. Courtesy of the Hearst Museum of Anthropology and the Regents of UC (15-5843).

assistant from 1907 to 1909 while carrying out extensive field research on Yurok ethnography and linguistics, then spent the academic year 1909–1910 in New York studying with Boas, taking his doctorate at Columbia in 1913 with a dissertation on comparative folklore.[62]

Waterman taught at Berkeley from 1910 to 1918, and again in 1920–1921. Between 1911 and 1915 his research focused on Ishi, the speaker of the Yahi dialect of Southern Yana who resided during those years at the Museum of Anthropology, and included the recording of many hours of wax cylinders of Ishi's speech. During the summer of 1915, Ishi lived in the Watermans' house in Berkeley while working intensively with Edward Sapir (Sapir 1915e; Golla 2003). He also worked on Northern Paiute (Waterman 1911).

Waterman was a talented ethnographer, and his monograph on Yurok geography (1920) is one of the classics of California anthropology. A later study of Oregon Athabaskan territory (1925) is also of considerable value. In his later years, however, his career splintered, and he held a series of teaching and research appointments of decreasing consequence, and at his death, at the early age of fifty-one, he was the territorial archivist of Hawaii.[63]

2.6.5 Paul Radin

Paul Radin (1883–1959),[64] a Boasian anthropologist with unusually strong literary and linguistic interests, left a rich legacy of California Indian research, although he only briefly held an academic appointment in California. After a precocious childhood and adolescence that included serious intellectual flirtations with zoology and history, Radin took up the study of anthropology in 1907, receiving his doctorate from Columbia in 1910 with a dissertation on the Winnebago medicine society. Although he remained a student of Winnebago culture and traditional literature for the rest of his life, Radin's interests were exceedingly broad and his career a series of sudden turns.

After a brief and unhappy association with the Smithsonian, Radin spent a year in Mexico studying the Zapotecs and then took a research position in Ottawa where he worked on Iroquoian ethnography and linguistics under the direction of Edward Sapir. A close friend of Kroeber and Lowie as well as Sapir, he was invited to California in 1917 on a visiting appointment that ultimately was extended for three years. During this time he carried out extensive linguistic and ethnographic work with the Achumawi (Radin 1919–1920) and the Wappo (Radin 1924, 1929), and—at the height of speculation about phylum-level connections such as Hokan, Penutian, and Na-Dene—published a brilliant but unpersuasive monograph that attempted to show the ultimate interrelationship of all North American linguistic families (Radin 1919).[65]

Radin spent the early 1920s in England, taught at Fisk University in Nashville for a few years, spent more time in Mexico, then returned to Europe. From 1930 to 1950 he maintained a residence in Berkeley, where his brother Max Radin was an influential member of the law faculty. Although without steady academic employment, he continued to write and to pursue research, including extensive

fieldwork on Patwin (Radin 1932–1949). During his last decade he returned once again to Europe, spending several years in Switzerland and Italy, but was back in the United States, teaching at Brandeis University, when he died in 1959. For a good biographical sketch see Du Bois (1960).

2.6.6 Other Colleagues and Students of Kroeber

Samuel A. Barrett (1879–1965) was Kroeber's first graduate student. After taking a BS at Berkeley in 1905, Barrett worked in the Museum of Anthropology for two years as a curatorial assistant and field collector, and wrote a doctoral dissertation on Pomo basketry. A methodical man, most at home in the classification of items of material culture, his linguistic work was largely confined to the collection of vocabularies and of detailed ethnogeographical data and is best represented in his survey of the territories of the Pomo and adjacent groups (1908a). Following a year's postdoctoral work in New York with Boas and a further year in South America on a research fellowship, Barrett accepted a curatorial appointment at the Milwaukee Public Museum, where he worked until his retirement. He returned to California in 1959, where he briefly resumed his ethnographic work, most notably a project to record various aspects of traditional California Indian culture on film.

Edward W. Gifford (1887–1959) joined the staff of the Museum of Anthropology in 1912 as a preparator. With only a high school degree, he seemed an unlikely candidate for academic research, but he soon proved to be a skilled ethnographer and synthesizer and soon developed a wide range of anthropological interests. He became a curator in

FIGURE 19. Participants at a meeting of the Anthropology Section of the AAAS, San Francisco, December 1916. *Left to right:* Leo J. Frachtenberg, J. P. Harrington, A. L. Kroeber, T. T. Waterman, and J. Alden Mason. Courtesy of the Hearst Museum of Anthropology and the Regents of UC.

1925, and he suceeded Kroeber as director after the latter's retirement in 1945. Gifford's contibutions to the study of California languages are for the most part embedded in his more general anthropological works. These include ethnographies of the Western Mono (1932b), of several Yuman groups (1932a, 1933, 1936), and of the Coast Yuki (1939); a groundbreaking study of Miwok social organization (1916); and a comprehensive survey of California kin-term systems (1922).

J. Alden Mason (1885–1967), a native of Philadelphia, received his BA from the University of Pennsylvania in 1907 and began graduate work there the same year. Although he had a strong interest in archaeology, he chose to work closely with Edward Sapir, who joined the Pennsylvania faculty in 1908, and traveled with Sapir to the Southwest in the summer of 1909 to carry out fieldwork on Southern Numic dialects in Colorado and Utah. After Sapir's departure for a position in Canada in 1910, Mason transferred to California, where he took his doctorate in 1911 with a dissertation on Salinan ethnography (Mason 1912). He returned to the Salinans in 1916 to do linguistic work, which resulted in a solid monograph on the language (Mason 1918). The remainder of his career was largely devoted to Latin American archaeology, in which he became a leading figure. In 1917 he was appointed to a curatorship at the Field Museum in Chicago, moving to the American Museum of Natural History in 1924, and finally to the University of Pennsylvania in 1926.

Robert H. Lowie (1883–1957), Kroeber's principal colleague at Berkeley during the second half of his career, was a fellow student of Franz Boas (receiving his doctorate at Columbia in 1908 with a dissertation on the Crow) and a highly regarded social theorist. Before moving to Berkeley permanently in 1921, he held a curatorial position at the American Museum of Natural History and was in frequent contact with Sapir and Radin, both of whom were close friends.[66] Lowie's interest in linguistics was limited, but focused, and he collected a significant amount of material in the Crow language during his dissertation field work. In California, his only important fieldwork was among the Washo, from whom he collected a set of texts that were published posthumously (1963).

Hans Jørgen Uldall (1907–1957), a Danish-British phonetician who had studied under Otto Jespersen and Daniel Jones, was invited in 1930 by the Committee on Native American Languages to carry out a field investigation of a California language. Working under Kroeber's direction, he spent several months during 1930–1932 working primarily on Nisenan, but also on Yuki and Achumawi, in the latter case in collaboration with Jaime de Angulo. He went to Columbia University in 1932 as a lecturer in phonetics, and then returned to Europe. Although he wrote only two short papers on the phonetics of Achumawi (1933) and Nisenan (1954), he left a large corpus of unpublished material on Nisenan from which a dictionary and a set of texts were edited for publication by Shipley (1966).

Dorothy Demetracopoulou, later *Dorothy D. Lee* (1905–1975), was, after Carl Voegelin (¶2.8.2), Kroeber's most talented linguistics student in the late 1920s and early 1930s. Born in Greece, Demetracopoulou began graduate work at Berkeley in 1927, contemporary with *Cora Du Bois* (1903–1991), with whom she conducted joint fieldwork on the Wintu in 1929–1930. Although her dissertation was on a folkloric topic ("The Loon Woman Myth: A Study in Synthesis," published in 1933), her collection of Wintu linguistic data was large and sophisticated. She drew on it over the next two decades for a series of papers on the relationship between Wintu linguistic categories and habitual thought (Lee 1938, 1940, 1942, 1943, 1944a, 1944b, 1946), several of which are reprinted in her influential book, *Freedom and Culture* (1959).

2.7 Independent Scholars, 1900–1940

2.7.1 Clinton Hart Merriam

Clinton Hart Merriam (1855–1942), one of America's great naturalists, devoted the later decades of his life to a massive, privately funded documentation of California Indian languages and traditional culture.[67]

FIGURE 20. C. Hart Merriam in his Washington residence at 1919 Sixteenthth Street Northwest, February 1930. Photograph by Vernon Bailey. Courtesy of the National Anthropological Archives, Smithsonian Institution (02862500).

An avid birdwatcher from childhood, Merriam was still in his teens when he accompanied the Hayden Survey of the Yellowstone region and published a fifty-page report on the birds and mammals that the expedition encountered. After graduating from Yale he studied medicine and was in practice for a few years, but he continued to devote considerable time to field biology. In 1882 he published the first volume of a monumental study of the mammals of the Adirondacs, and the following year he helped found the American Ornithologists' Union. In 1885 he gave up his medical career to join the Division of Entomology and Mammalogy in the Department of Agriculture, where he soon became chief of the U. S. Biological Survey. In this position he carried out pioneering research on the wildlife and ecology of the West and Southwest and formulated the concept of life zones.

In 1899, Merriam was invited by E. H. Harriman, president of the Union Pacific Railroad, to organize a summer expedition to Alaska. Under Merriam's direction the Harriman Alaska Expedition became one of the most productive scientific surveys of the period. Many prominent naturalists, scientists, and artists accompanied the expedition, among them John Burroughs, John Muir, and William H. Dall, and the twelve-volume report, which Merriam edited, portrayed the Alaskan environment in vivid detail. The success of the expedition led to a lasting friendship between Merriam and Harriman, and on the latter's death in 1909 his widow established a trust fund, administered by the Smithsonian Institution, that provided Merriam with a substantial independent income for the remainder of his life and the resources to pursue whatever scientific research he chose.

Retiring from the Biological Survey, Merriam used his financial freedom to begin an ambitious field study of the Indians of California. He had already worked extensively in California as a naturalist, and during that time he had met a number of Indians and made some miscellaneous ethnographic observations. Alongside his prodigious output as a biologist he had found time to publish several short papers on California Indian basketry, religion, and geography, as well as a book of traditional Miwok stories, *The Dawn of the World* (1910). He now set out to gather systematic data on the aboriginal "distribution" of the "varieties" or "types" of Indian society in California. This project entailed collecting precise data on tribal territories and subdivisions, including the names and locations of all known aboriginal villages, and—most importantly—establishing the basic classificatory units by means of differences in speech. His main tools in this work were extensive vocabulary lists.

Merriam continued this research well into the 1930s. He built a house at Lagunitas, in the redwoods of western Marin County, which he made his base of operations for five or six months each year as he roamed the state collecting data. His plan was to complete two vocabulary lists (in booklets he had printed for the purpose—one for general vocabulary

and ethnogeographical data, the other for animal and plant terms) for every identifiable tribe/dialect for which a reliable source of information could be found, and he left few gaps. He also kept a daily journal, and when the opportunity presented itself took detailed notes on various aspects of material and social culture.

Working on his own time and with self-defined goals, Merriam maintained an intellectual distance from others working with California Indians during this period, especially Kroeber and his students. The only anthropologist or linguist with whom he was on collegial terms was J. P. Harrington, who himself pursued an eccentrically independent course. Not surprisingly, Merriam published relatively few of the results of his ethnographic and linguistic work. His most substantial publication was a study of Achumawi ethnogeography and dialectology (Merriam 1926a), but he achieved his greatest noteriety among Californianists for his claim that he had identified an entirely new "stock" (i.e., language family) in the mountainous New River country of northwestern California, which he labeled Tlo-hom-tah-hoi (Merriam 1930a). The substantial objections to this identification that were raised by anthropologists familiar with the area (most notably Dixon 1931; see ¶3.11.4) served only to increase Merriam's estrangement from the academic anthropology of his time.

Given his concern with taxonomy and distribution, as well as his almost total lack of concern with linguistics and philology, it is not surprising that Merriam went to little trouble to acquaint himself with the phonological and morphological features of the languages he recorded. He deliberately (and to most linguists, infuriatingly) used a vastly oversimplified transcriptional system, derived from the pronouncing key of Webster's dictionary, in all his work. Arguing that the technical phonetic alphabets employed by linguists and anthropologists imposed "a formidable barrier between the professional ethnologist on the one hand and the average, educated American on the other" (1966: 24), Merriam consistently transcribed the words of all California languages, with their multitude of phonetic details, with the consonants and vowels of standard American English. The inevitable result is that Merriam's vast documentation is largely useless for precise phonological comparison. Nevertheless, his extraordinarily thorough lexical coverage and meticulous attention to dialectal differences provide many invaluable insights for the researcher who is willing to deal with the material on its own terms.

It is fair to say that the breadth and accuracy of Merriam's documentation of California Indian languages has, to date, been considerably underappreciated. Put off by his "aggravatingly unscientific spelling" (Dixon 1931), linguists have often been too quick to dismiss Merriam's work as hopelessly amateurish. However, even scholars who have approached the Merriam corpus with an open mind have, until recently, found it difficult to gain access to. The completion of a full microfilm edition of Merriam's ethnographic and linguistic papers in the Bancroft Library has now alleviated this problem (see Appendix A).

Merriam's own publication of his California ethnographic work was, as already noted, slim at best, especially when compared with his published work in biology. In addition to the previously mentioned study of Achumawi ethnogeography (1926a), papers of possible interest to readers of this book include "Distribution and Classification of the Mewan [Miwok] Stock" (1907), "Application of the Athapaskan Term Nung-kahhl" (1923), "Source of the Name Shasta" (1926b), "The Cop-éh of Gibbs" (1929), "The New River Indians Tló-hom-tah´-hoi" (1930a), "A Remarkable Case of Word Borrowing among California Indians" (1930b), and "The Em´-tim´-bitch, a Shoshonean Tribe" (1930c).

During his stewardship of the Merriam collection between 1950 and 1979, Robert Heizer published several books derived from Merriam's manuscripts. The earliest of these, *Studies of California Indians* (Merriam 1955), contains twenty-one papers on ethnology, material culture, and lexical topics that Merriam left in final or near-final draft form. Those of particular interest to students of California languages are "Tribes of Wintoon Stock" (3–25), "The Tuleyome" [Lake Miwok] (43–48), "The Beñemé of Garcés" [Chemehuevi] (93–95), "Pinart's Tcholovone Vocabulary" [Far Northern Yokuts] (133–138), "Words for Tobacco and Pipe" (139–148), "Shoshonean Tribal Names" (149–174), "Tribal Names of theTuleyome" [Lake Miwok] (175–187), and "California Mission Baptismal Records" (188–225). A decade later Heizer edited three further volumes of Merriam's writings, published as *Ethnographic Notes on California Indian Tribes*, Report 68 of the University of California Archaeological Survey, Parts 1, 2, and 3 (Merriam 1966, 1967a, 1967b). The first volume contains nineteen short papers, of which the most important to California ethnolinguistics is "Distribution and Classification of Wintoon Tribes" (1966:52–59, 76). The second and third volumes are devoted to ethnological notes extracted from Merriam's notes (northern and southern tribes in the second, central tribes in the third), some but not all of which incorporate linguistic and geographical observations. Of special interest are the notes on the Konomihu (1967a:230–243) and the New River tribe (1967a:244–249), the latter containing the correspondence between Merriam and Dixon on the possibility that Merriam's "Tló-hom-tah´-hoi" represented a separate linguistic family. The notes on Chimariko (1967a:226–229) are extracted from letters written to Merriam by J. P. Harrington.

Heizer also compiled a summary of Merriam's classification (Heizer 1966) and published a compendium of Merriam's vocabularies of plant and animal4 terms (Merriam 1979), lists of village names that Merriam extracted from mission records (Merriam 1968), and an ethnogeographical manuscript that Merriam had prepared in collaboration with his daughter (Merriam and Talbot 1974).

FIGURE 21. Jaime de Angulo as a medical student at Johns Hopkins, ca. 1912. Courtesy of UCLA Charles E. Young Research Library, Department of Special Collections. © Regents of UC, UCLA Library.

2.7.2 Jaime de Angulo and Lucy S. Freeland

Beyond any doubt the most colorful figure ever to do research on California Indian languages was Jaime de Angulo (1887–1950).[68] A bohemian French intellectual from a family with Spanish roots, de Angulo emigrated to America in 1905, where he worked as a ranch hand in Colorado and tried his hand at a variety of other jobs in California and Central America before finally deciding to study medicine. After taking his medical degree at Johns Hopkins in 1912, he returned to California where, after briefly working as a research scientist, he settled in the Monterey area, adopted the style of a Spanish California ranchero—shirts open to the waist, a red velvet cummerbund—and homesteaded in the rugged mountains near Big Sur. Developing an interest in American Indian cultures and languages, he struck up friendships with several Berkeley anthropologists, particularly Paul Radin, and read widely in cross-cultural psychiatry and ethnosemantics. In the early 1920s, with encouragement from Radin, and at least initially from Kroeber, de Angulo began undertaking linguistic studies of California Indian languages.

His first field trip, in the autumn of 1921, was to Modoc County to work on Achumawi. He found the work extraordinarily stimulating, and after two months he had collected enough data to draft a preliminary grammar of the language. Kroeber, and later Sapir and Boas, found this

FIGURE 22. Jaime de Angulo and his principal Achumawi consultant, Jack Folsom, in the yard of de Angulo and Lucy S. (Nancy) Freeland's house in the Berkeley Hills, ca. 1925. Courtesy of Gui Mayo.

manuscript quite impressive, leading the following summer to an invitation from the anthropologist Manuel Gamio to join him as a field assistant in Mexico. De Angulo spent the academic year 1922–1923 in Oaxaca, working intensively on Mixe, Chontal de Oaxaca (Tequistlatecan), and several Zapotecan languages, developing an expertise in these languages that was reflected in a number of publications in subsequent years. The rigors of fieldwork, however, precipitated an emotional crisis, and in the spring of 1923, de Angulo suddenly resigned his assistantship and returned to the United States, where with equal suddenness he married Lucy S. (Nancy) Freeland, a fellow linguist who was working on a grammar of Sierra Miwok for her doctoral dissertation at Berkeley.[69]

By breaking his contract with Gamio, de Angulo caused Kroeber deep professional embarrassment, and his marriage to one of Kroeber's most promising students only compounded the offense. From then on, according to Gui de Angulo, Kroeber "despised" her father "to an extraordinary degree" and took "a great deal of trouble to undermine his career" (1995:201).[70] Further academic support for de Angulo was out of the question, and even Freeland had to suspend her Miwok work, returning to it only in the 1930s in collaboration with Hans Jørgen Uldall (¶2.6.6).[71] The couple instead embarked on a series of independent collaborative studies of California languages. At the beginning this work was self-financed, but after 1927 de Angulo and Freeland received generous funding from the Rockefeller-funded Committee on Research in Native American Languages, whose most influential members were Boas and Sapir (Leeds-Hurwitz 2004). Boas in particular was strongly supportive of de Angulo and commissioned several major studies of California languages from him, including

grammars of Shasta, Achumawi, and Atsugewi, a comparative study of the Pomo languages, and a number of substantial collections of texts (Box 6).[72]

The accidental death of de Angulo's son in an automobile accident in 1933 dealt him an emotional blow from which he never recovered. He ceased fieldwork and withdrew to his mountaintop ranch at Big Sur, cultivating an eccentricity that Henry Miller vividly describes in *Big Sur and the Oranges of Hieronymous Bosch* (1957). In his last years, immediately after World War II, he wrote two books for a general audience, *Indians in Overalls* (1950), a irreverent portrayal of the Achumawi as he knew them in the 1920s, and *Indian Tales* (1953), a children's book woven out of episodes from various Northern California Indian stories. Recordings of de Angulo reading from *Indian Tales,* made for radio station KPFA in Berkeley in 1949, the year before he died, are still occasionally rebroadcast.

De Angulo and Freeland's scholarly work remains greatly underappreciated. Only a small amount of the linguistic material that they produced for Boas's committee was published, largely because of financial constraints. The much-delayed publication of Freeland's independently carried out Miwok work (1951) established her reputation as a linguist of considerable gifts, but it came too late in life to have an impact on her career.

De Angulo's descriptive studies of California languages are idiosyncratic but deeply engaged and occasionally illuminated by brilliant insights. He was particularly interested in the semantics of grammatical systems ("semasiology" in his terminology), but he was also a resourceful practical phonetician—one of the few in his generation to accurately describe tonal phenomena in American Indian languages—and a pioneer in the study of discourse. His "conversational" texts stand out in an era when otherwise nearly all texts were formally dictated narratives. The only linguist in recent decades to look closely at de Angulo's work has been Olmsted, who incorporated some of de Angulo's Achumawi material into his own Palaihnihan studies (Olmsted 1966:1–7).

2.7.3 John Peabody Harrington[73]

John Peabody Harrington (1884–1961) was one of those rare individuals seemingly predestined for his life's work. Raised in a well-educated Santa Barbara family of modest means, he developed at an early age a dual interest in languages and the local mission Indians. He attended Stanford on a scholarship, graduating in 1905 with a degree

in German and classics. In addition to his brilliance in the classroom, he showed himself to be a natural polyglot—besides the usual European languages he picked up Russian and Armenian in his spare time—and was fascinated by phonetics. On the recommendation of his Stanford mentor, the eminent classicist H. R. Fairclough, Harrington was offered a Rhodes Scholarship, but he turned it down in order to pursue graduate work in comparative philology and phonetics in Germany. Around this time he resolved to dedicate his career to the study of American Indian languages, and in particular to the collection of extensive and accurate data on the poorly documented and nearly extinct aboriginal languages of his native Southern California.

Returning to the United States in 1906, he launched into this work with the single-mindedness that was to become his dominant characteristic. To support himself he took a job as a high school language teacher in Santa Ana, California, but he devoted most of his spare time, and all of his summers, to the intensive documentation of such nearby languages as Mohave, Yuma, and Diegueño. Within a year or two, the high quality of his first publications, and his evident qualifications for the task, had caught the attention of other American Indian specialists. He soon acquired several influential supporters, including Matilda Coxe Stevenson of the Bureau of American Ethnology, C. F. Lummis of the Southwest Museum, and especially Edgar Lee Hewett of the Archaeological Institute of America in Santa Fe. By 1909, Harrington was employed by Hewett as a full-time research worker, assigned to document the languages of the Pueblo Indians of New Mexico and Arizona. In 1915, by now a well-established professional, Harrington was hired by the Bureau of American Ethnology as a research ethnologist, one of the most desirable positions in American linguistic anthropology at the time.

From then until his retirement, nearly forty years later, Harrington had—subject always to the vagaries of the Smithsonian's annual appropriation for field research—virtually unbounded freedom to wander the North American continent carrying out his mission of linguistic and cultural documentation (his assignment to "strategic" languages and cryptography during World War II being the only significant interruption). He took maximum advantage of this opportunity. Surely no linguistic field worker before or since clocked more months and years of field research. Harrington would move from language to language, informant to informant, without any intermission or vacation except for the necessary travel time. When it was bureaucratically unavoidable, he grudgingly put in a period of residence at the Smithsonian. But even then he would sometimes arrange to bring an informant with him to Washington so he could continue gathering data on evenings and weekends.

From 1916 to 1921 he was married to Carobeth Tucker (later Carobeth Laird), and they had a daughter, Awona. But these commitments made little difference to Harrington's research schedule or his dedication to his work. The wedding

FIGURE 23. John Peabody Harrington in the field, 1918. Courtesy of the National Anthropological Archives, Smithsonian Institution. (75-12221).

took place during a field trip to work on Obispeño Chumash, and the pair spent most of their brief marriage carrying out research together. Carobeth, late in her life, published a vivid portrait of the obsessed genius she knew during these years (Laird 1975); limited in scope though it is, this remains the best biographical treatment of Harrington.[74]

It is one of the ironies of Harrington's career that as he settled into the role of anthropological linguistic field collector par excellence, American anthropology and linguistics began moving away from the Boasian emphasis on amassing data and toward more interpretive modes of study. His devotion to field research began to look old-fashioned even as early as the 1920s, and it gained him little academic recognition during his lifetime (an honorary doctorate from the University of Southern California in 1934 was the only significant exception). As he grew older, he published less and less, and his scholarly visibility shrank to the vanishing point.[75]

Even before he retired in 1954, most anthropologists or linguists, if they had heard of him at all, considered Harrington little more than an obscure footnote in the history of American Indian studies. When he died in 1961, incapacitated by arthritis and Parkinson's disease, the one obituary that was published in an academic journal (Stirling and Glemser 1963) was more an anecdote-filled reminiscence than a serious assessment of his contributions to American linguistics and ethnology.

Harrington's eccentricities contributed more than a little to his obscurity. Always fanatically dedicated to his work

and intolerant of interruptions, by midcareer he had developed the traits of a secretive recluse. After his death, as Smithsonian curators began cataloguing his papers, it was revealed that the larger part of the documentation Harrington had been accumulating had been deliberately kept hidden from his colleagues. Suspicious to the point of paranoia that others would steal and publish them (see, for example, the anecdote related in Langdon 1997b), he had brought only a small part of his field notes and other collections to Washington. Most of them had been stored in warehouses, garages, and other caches up and down the West Coast. Harrington had even filed misleading or incomplete reports with his supervisors, so that they would not know the true extent of the work he had done.

By the late 1960s, with the bulk of Harrington's materials finally located and consolidated, it became clear that Harrington's extensive, accurate notes were a linguistic treasure of the highest order. The value of the documentation was especially great for languages like Chimariko, Costanoan, Salinan, and Chumash, written off as extinct by most scholars as early as the turn of the twentieth century, but for which the intrepid Harrington had discovered several aged speakers. His material—often the product of months of field work—was more than sufficient to allow a considerable amount of new analytic work to be undertaken on these languages.[76]

Harrington's documentation is by no means restricted to these languages; while focusing his energies on languages nearing extinction, he managed to collect at least some data on scores of languages in California and the Far West (see Appendix B), supplementing his written record with hundreds of sound recordings (wax cylinders in the early days, aluminum discs after about 1930; cf. Glenn 1991a). He also extended his work into traditional culture, particularly mythology and geography. He avidly collected place-names (often going on long auto or hiking trips with his informants to identify the sites named), and he took thousands of photographs.

An obscure and professionally marginal figure during his lifetime, since his death, as his unparalleled collection has become known and accessible, Harrington's reputation has risen enormously. He is now deservedly counted among the most significant figures of twentieth-century California Indian language studies.[77]

2.7.4 Edward S. Curtis and William E. Myers

The twenty volumes of Edward S. Curtis's *The North American Indian* (1907–1930), probably the most massive publication that American Indian studies has ever produced without government or institutional sponsorship, contain extensive original ethnographic and linguistic data. The bulk of these data were collected by William E. Myers, a talented field worker whose name has almost vanished from scholarly bibliographies.

Curtis himself was a society photographer from Seattle who had gained a reputation for Indian photography while

FIGURE 24. William E. Myers (*second from left*), ethnographer for the Curtis expedition, at the field camp in Sioux country, 1907. Seated in front is Chief Red Cloud. Photograph by Fred R. Meyer. Courtesy MSCUA, University of Washington Libraries. Edmond S. Meany Photograph Collection no. 132, negative UW17995.

accompanying the Harriman Expedition to Alaska in 1899. His original conception of *The North American Indian* was as a purely photographic documentation, but he was able to secure the financial backing of J. Pierpont Morgan and the support of such patrons as Theodore Roosevelt only by assuring them that the project would also include the collection of a substantial amount of new ethnographic material. To this end, Curtis recruited Frederick Webb Hodge, head of the BAE and editor of the *Handbook of American Indians*, to serve as general editor of the volumes, and assembled a small field team for an anthropological survey (Gidley 1998, 2003).

Myers was hired to supervise the latter project. Born in Springfield, Ohio, in 1877, Myers had graduated Phi Beta Kappa from Northwestern University, majoring in Greek. He began graduate work, but apparently was compelled by economic necessity to drop out before finishing a thesis. He was living in Seattle, working as a newspaper reporter, when he joined the *TNAI* project in 1906. He soon proved to be a good field ethnographer and a linguist of considerable skill.

The *TNAI* project worked with Indian groups in the California region during a series of field trips between 1906 and 1920. During these visits Myers collected extensive vocabularies and geographical nomenclature in more than thirty languages, including Lower Columbia Athabaskan, Hupa, Tolowa, Shasta, Achumawi, Karuk, Yurok, Wiyot, Klamath, Kato, Wailaki, Yuki, Wappo, Eastern, Northern, and Central Pomo, Wintu, Nomlaki, Patwin, Chico and Konkow Maidu,

Central and Southern Sierra Miwok, Chukchansi Yokuts, Mono, Northern Paiute ("Paviotso"), Washo, Cupeño, Luiseño, Cahuilla, Northern (Ipai) Diegueño, Mohave, and Quechan.[78]

The evidence is abundant that, the photographs aside, the enduring documentary value of all but the last two volumes of *TNAI* must largely be attributed to Myers. (He resigned from the project before the fieldwork in Oklahoma and Alaska was carried out.) Hodge, recalling his days as editorial overseer of the *TNAI* volumes, told an interviewer that although he "checked every word of it" before it went to the printer, "Mr. Myers . . . was the one who really wrote the text" (Gidley 1998:137). By the time the project shut down in 1930, Myers had published detailed ethnographic and ethnohistorical profiles of more than one hundred tribes, most of them accompanied by extensive original vocabularies and ethnogeographic data.

While the artistry of Curtis's photographs is widely recognized, the scholarly value of *TNAI* is far less recognized. Only a few hundred copies were printed, bound in tooled leather and sold to wealthy subscribers as a way of generating funds for the costly fieldwork. The work only became generally available after the original copyright expired in the late 1960s. But if the 1970 reprint of *TNAI* has made the publication more familiar to Americanists, the name of the man who actually carried out the scientific work is still rarely mentioned. While Myers was known to a few professional colleagues—A. L. Kroeber met Myers around 1914, and the two corresponded frequently for several years, particularly on comparative linguistics and kinship systems—he worked in isolation, as Curtis's employee, and received only the most minimal acknowledgement of his contributions. The ethnographic chapters and the linguistic appendices of *TNAI* are usually cited as if they were the work of Curtis, since he is the only author listed on the title page, with Hodge as editor. Myers is merely thanked for his "valuable assistance" in the preface to some of the volumes. Since Myers never published any report on his research elsewhere, even when encouraged to do so by admirers like Kroeber, his authorship has vanished almost without a trace.[79]

When Myers left the project in 1926, he severed all ties with American Indian ethnography and linguistics, living out his remaining years in the San Francisco area. He made a bad real estate investment in the late 1920s and survived the Depression by working for a soft-drinks company. In the 1940s he managed a series of small motels, the last near Petaluma. The short obituary that appeared in the Santa Rosa *Press Democrat* at his death in 1949 made no mention of his work with Curtis.

2.8 Structural Linguists

2.8.1 Edward Sapir as a Californianist

Twentieth-century American linguistics was largely the creation of two brilliant men, Edward Sapir (1884–1939) and Leonard Bloomfield (1887–1949), both of whom devoted the bulk of their own research to the descriptive and comparative study of American Indian languages. In Sapir's case, this research largely focused on the California region (Boxes 7 and 8). His documentation of Takelma, Yana, Hupa (California Athabaskan), and Ute and Southern Paiute (Numic) made these languages among the best known in North America. Much of what we know about the interrelationships of the Uto-Aztecan, Penutian, Hokan, Athabaskan, and Algic languages is the result of Sapir's foundational work on these families or phyla. It is hard to imagine how diminished our understanding of California Indian linguistics would be had Sapir not been a Californianist. And in addition to his own substantial work, we owe much of what has subsequently been accomplished in California Indian linguistics to Sapir's students and his students' students.

But if Sapir was the most productive and influential linguist ever to work on California Indian languages, he did so without an institutional base in the region. Employed by the University of Pennsylvania (1908–1910), the Geological Survey of Canada (1910–1925), the University of Chicago (1925–1931), and Yale (1931–1939), Sapir spent a total of less than eighteen months in California and Oregon, much of that time in the field.

Sapir's career as an Americanist began at the age of twenty, just as he was embarking on graduate work in comparative Germanic and Indo-European at Columbia University. Sometime during the academic year 1904–1905, Sapir had several (in retrospect, momentous) conversations with Franz Boas, who persuaded the young scholar to redirect his talents to the documentation and analysis of American Indian languages. Boas arranged for the Bureau of American Ethnology to send Sapir to northern Oregon during the summer of 1905 to collect data on Wishram Chinook at the Warm Springs Reservation (Sapir 1907b). Sapir's career as a Californianist began the following summer, when he returned to Oregon, again with BAE support, to document Takelma. While still working on his Wishram and Takelma materials (the latter forming the basis of his dissertation[80]), Sapir was invited by Kroeber to spend the academic year 1907–1908 as a research fellow at the University of California. This stay, his first and only extended visit to California, included three solid months of fieldwork on Northern and Central Yana (Sapir 1910a).[81]

Sapir returned to California only twice after that: in the summer of 1915 to document Ishi's Southern Yana (Sapir 1915e, 1923b) and in the summer of 1927, together with his student Li Fang-Kuei, to carry out a study of Hupa and other Northwest California languages (Golla and O'Neill 2001). His work on Southern Numic (Sapir 1930–1931) did not take him to California: after a visit to the Utes in Colorado in the summer of 1909, he spent the winter of 1909–1910 working with a young Southern Paiute speaker from the Carlisle Indian School in Pennsylvania.

Although Sapir's only face-to-face collaboration with Kroeber was during his 1907–1908 research fellowship, the two men—both students of Boas—developed a close intellectual relationship, reflected in an extensive lifelong

FIGURE 25. Edward Sapir at Hoopa, summer of 1927. Courtesy of the Sapir family.

BOX 7. SAPIR'S DOCUMENTATION OF
CALIFORNIA LANGUAGES

Athabaskan, Oregon (Chasta Costa variety of Lower Rogue River): Siletz Reservation, Oregon, Summer 1906 (Sapir 1914)

Athabaskan, California (Kato): Berkeley, Winter 1907–1908, with P.E. Goddard (Sapir 1907–1908)

Athabaskan, California (Hupa): Hoopa Valley Reservation, Summer 1927 (Sapir 1927b, 1928, 1936a; Sapir and Golla 2001)

Chimariko: Burnt Ranch and Hyampom, Trinity County, Summer 1927 (Berman 2001c)

Numic, Southern (Uintah and Ouray Ute): Colorado, Summer 1909 (Sapir 1930–1931)

Numic, Southern (Southern Paiute): Philadelphia and Carlisle, Pennsylvania, Winter 1909–1910 (Sapir 1930–1931)

Takelma: Siletz Reservation, Oregon, Summer 1906 (Sapir 1907a, 1909, 1910b, 1922a)

Yana, Northern and Central: Montgomery Creek, Summer and Fall 1907 (Sapir 1910a, 1917a, 1918, 1922b, 1923b, 1929a; Sapir and Spier 1943)

Yana, Southern (Yahi): Berkeley, Summer 1915 (Sapir 1923b; Golla 2003)

Yurok: Hoopa Valley Reservation, Summer 1927 (Berman 2001b)

BOX 8. SAPIR'S WORK ON THE
CLASSIFICATION OF CALIFORNIA LANGUAGES

Algic: The relationship of Yurok and Wiyot to Algonquian (Sapir 1913a, 1915b, 1915c; see also Golla 1986 and I. Goddard 1986)

Athabaskan: Hupa and Athabaskan (Sapir 1928); general classification of Athabaskan (Sapir 1931); Athabaskan migrations from the Canadian north (Sapir 1936b); affiliation of Athabaskan with other North American language families (Sapir 1915d); affiliation of Athabaskan with Sino-Tibetan (Golla 1984:374–384)

Hokan: Yana and Hokan (Sapir 1917a, 1918); Washo and Hokan (Sapir 1917b, 1921b); Chimariko and Hokan (Sapir 1920b); Salinan and Hokan (Sapir 1920c, 1921b); general classification of Hokan (Sapir 1920a, 1921c, 1925a, 1929b); collaboration with Kroeber (Golla 1984)

Penutian: General classification of Penutian (Sapir 1920a, 1921a, 1929b); the relationship of Oregon and California Penutian (Sapir and Swadesh 1953); collaboration with Kroeber (Golla 1984)

Uto-Aztecan: General classification of Uto-Aztecan (Sapir 1913b, 1915a)

Yukian: The relationship between Yukian and Hokan (Golla 1984:289–290, 421–422)

---

personal correspondence (Golla 1984). Sapir was an early and enthusiastic supporter of Dixon and Kroeber's proposals for phylum-level relationships among California linguistic families, which he bolstered with evidence that Yurok and Wiyot were distant offshoots of Algonquian (Sapir 1913a).[82] After 1915, Sapir took the lead in identifying further candidates for the Hokan and Penutian phyla, extending the scope of both far outside of California (see ¶3.8 and ¶3.21). After the mid-1920s, however, both Sapir and Kroeber grew more cautious about long-range comparative linguistics (see especially Kroeber 1940).

It is evident from the Sapir-Kroeber correspondence that Sapir had hopes of obtaining an appointment at Berkeley and joining with Kroeber to build a research program in which California Indian language studies would have a central role. As time went by, however, Kroeber's earlier interest in California linguistics waned, and in the Depression years of the 1930s, when programmatic contraction became necessary at Berkeley, support for Indian language research was drastically curtailed. Meanwhile, Sapir's academic success at Chicago and Yale made a position at Berkeley less attractive to him than it might have been earlier. It was not until a decade after Sapir's death in 1939 that Mary Haas

and other former students and associates of Sapir established at Berkeley something close to the research hub that Sapir had envisioned, the Survey of California Indian Languages (see ¶2.9).

2.8.2 Linguists of the 1930s

During the half century between the founding of the BAE in 1879 and the establishment of the Linguistic Society of America in 1924, institutionally sponsored research on American Indian languages was carried out almost exclusively by scholars who identified themselves as anthropologists. From the beginning, however, a handful of researchers who had been trained in phonetics and comparative philology were responsible for a disproportionately large share of the work accomplished. Thus in the California region, as we have seen, the contributions of five men—Albert Gatschet, J. P. Harrington, A. L. Kroeber, P. E. Goddard, and Edward Sapir—account for the vast majority of the linguistically sophisticated material collected before 1930. Although both through their own work and in their critique of the work of others the small band linguist-anthropologists gradually raised the standards of analytical rigor, it was abundantly clear as early as the beginning of the twentieth century that more focused training was needed.[83]

With the founding of the LSA, the way was paved for the establishment of university departments and research programs specifically focused on the scientific study of language and the training of a new generation of students in the methods and theories of structural linguistics. A major role in this institutional transition was played by Edward Sapir, who in 1925 left his long-term research position in Canada to join the department of anthropology at the University of Chicago (1925–1931), moving to Yale University in 1931, where he helped create the first academically independent department of linguistics in North America. At both Chicago and Yale, Sapir set up academic research programs for American Indian linguistics. Emphasizing descriptivist rigor, Sapir required his graduate students to master the formal tools of the emerging discipline of structural linguistics, including thorough training in phonetics and grammatical analysis, and to demonstrate these skills in extensive fieldwork on a specific language, almost always an American Indian language.[84]

Between 1925 and 1940 four linguists trained in this new academic paradigm—two directly by Sapir, two indirectly—carried out research on California languages: Li Fang-Kuei, Carl Voegelin, Stanley Newman, and A. M. Halpern. Strictly speaking, they were the first linguists (as opposed to anthropologists doing linguistic research) to work on California Indian languages.

FIGURE 26. Li Fang-Kuei, Seattle, 1960. Photograph by Melville Jacobs. Courtesy of William R. Seaburg.

who has become the literary executor of Li's California Athabaskan materials (cf. Seaburg 1977a).

LI FANG-KUEI

Li Fang-Kuei (1902–1987)[85] was Sapir's first graduate student at Chicago. Born in Canton, he prepared in Peking for study in the United States, graduating from the University of Michigan in 1926. He enrolled at the University of Chicago to do graduate work in comparative Indo-European under Carl Darling Buck, but Sapir quickly persuaded him to take up the study of American Indian languages. In the summer of 1927 he accompanied Sapir on a field trip to Northwest California to work on California Athabaskan languages. While Sapir worked on Hupa, Li carried out independent work on Mattole and Wailaki (Sapir 1927a). The Mattole material formed the basis of his dissertation (1930), the first structural linguistic study of a Pacific Coast Athabaskan language.

Li subsequently carried out pioneering field research on Athabaskan languages in Canada (Chipewyan in 1928 and Hare in 1929), and later worked on Eyak. On returning to China in 1929, he applied his training in both historical and field linguistics to Chinese dialectology and to the study of unwritten minority languages. Reestablishing himself in the United States in 1946, Li taught at Harvard and Yale, and in 1949 accepted a permanent position at the University of Washington. Following his retirement from Washington in 1969, he taught for several additional years at the University of Hawaii, where among his students was William Seaburg,

CHARLES F. (CARL) VOEGELIN

Charles F. (Carl) Voegelin (1906–1986) was Kroeber's last linguistics student. A New Yorker who had come west for his education, Voegelin graduated from Stanford with a degree in psychology in 1927. After a trip to the South Pacific kindled an interest in anthropology, he enrolled as a graduate student at Berkeley in 1928, at first planning to specialize in ethnomusicology. Kroeber, however, sensed his talent for linguistic work and urged him to specialize in language instead, sending him to the Tubatulabal to collect data. He remained in the field for a full year (1930–1931)—an unprecedented amount of time for doctoral fieldwork at the time—and submitted a sophisticated descriptive grammar as his dissertation in 1932 (published as Voegelin 1935a).[86] His wife, Erminie Wheeler Voegelin, a fellow student in Berkeley's anthropology department, accompanied Voegelin to the field and carried out a parallel study of Tubatulabal ethnography (E. Voegelin 1938). The two also worked together on Klamath-Modoc and Palaihnihan language and culture in 1936 (Voegelin 1946; E. Voegelin 1942).

After receiving his doctorate, Voegelin spent three years at Yale, supported by a series of postdoctoral fellowships, primarily in order to study under Sapir. He quickly became a member of the inner crcle of Sapir's theoretically sophisticated students, which at that time included Morris Swadesh, Mary Haas, Stanley Newman, and Benjamin L.

FIGURE 27. Carl Voegelin (*right*), Erminie Wheeler Voegelin (*center*), their daughter Gail (*seated with dog*), and an unidentified graduate student, Depauw University, ca. 1937. Photograph by Carleton T. Hodge. Courtesy of the Newberry Library.

B. Kendall, James Redden, and Akira Yamamoto. Voegelin continued to be strongly interested in Uto-Aztecan and devoted much of his research after 1950 to the languages of Arizona (see ¶2.9.4). Between 1944 and 1980 he wielded considerable influence as the second editor (after Franz Boas, who founded the journal in 1917) of the *International Journal of American Linguistics*.

STANLEY S. NEWMAN

Stanley S. Newman (1905–1984), an almost exact contemporary of Voegelin, was one of Sapir's graduate students in linguistics at the University of Chicago, beginning in 1929. A chance encounter with Kroeber's 1907 grammar of Yokuts during a seminar sparked his interest, and he decided to work on a Yokuts dialect for his dissertation. He began fieldwork in 1930. After trying unsuccessfully to find a fluent speaker of Palewyami (Poso Creek)—a divergent dialect that Kroeber had not been able to document extensively—he settled on Yawelmani, returning in 1931 to record material on six other dialects (Chawchila, Choynimni, Chukchansi, Gashowu, Dumna, and Wikchamni).

His dissertation was an intricate structural analysis of Yokuts grammar, with the particulars of dialectal variation intricately subordinated to a single overall scheme. In a letter to Sapir in 1935 he was modest, even self-deprecating, about this work:

> the machine design of Yokuts . . . is deceivingly simple; but when the machine is in operation, all the wheels seem to move at once, with confusing alternations in their relationship to each other. I must confess . . . to an uncomfortable suspicion that my treatment of Yokuts is due largely to my own disinclination for the neat logical order,

Whorf. Voegelin developed particularly close friendships with Whorf, with whom he shared a deep interest in Uto-Aztecan linguistics, and with Newman, who had carried out fieldwork on Yokuts at Tule River during the same years that the Voegelins had worked on adjacent Tubatulabal.[87]

In 1936, Voegelin joined the faculty of DePauw University in Indiana, where, with the support of the philanthropist and Indian enthusiast Eli Lilly, he carried out extensive field studies of Delaware, Shawnee, and other Algonquian languages of the region. Much of this research was done in Oklahoma, where Voegelin regularly spent half of each year.[88] In 1941, Voegelin moved to Indiana University, in Bloomington, where he established what was to become one of the most important research centers for American Indian linguistics in the postwar period. Among the students Voegelin trained at Indiana in the 1950s and 1960s were several who worked on languages of the California region, most notably David Olmsted, Kenneth Hale, Dell Hymes, Martha

FIGURE 28. Stanley S. Newman (*left*) with his University of New Mexico colleague Harry Basehart, ca. 1965. The two were the joint editors of the *Southwestern Journal of Anthropology* from 1962 to 1970. Courtesy of the Maxwell Museum of Anthropology, UNM.

to my kinesthetic pleasure in having things whirl about and intertwine in an intricate mess. (quoted in Gamble 1992:310–311)

Newman's grammar of Yokuts (1944, 1946) was widely considered to be the most structurally perceptive and analytically complete description of an American Indian language up to that time, and it has stimulated an extensive secondary literature (Harris 1944, 1947; Hockett 1973).

Newman followed Sapir to Yale in 1931 (taking his doctorate from there in 1932), and stayed on during the 1930s as a research fellow, working closely with Sapir on a structural analysis of Modern English. His later academic career was spent at the University of New Mexico, where his descriptive work focused on Zuni.

ABRAHAM M. HALPERN

In many ways the most productive of the California linguists of the 1930s was Abraham M. Halpern (1914-1985). Soon after graduating from Harvard at the precocious age of nineteen, Halpern began graduate work in anthropological linguistics at Berkeley. In 1935–1936—in the depths of the Depression—he worked steadily for nearly a year, primarily on Quechan, as part of a State Emergency Relief project designed to teach elders to write their language and record their traditional literature.[89] The following year he began an ambitious project to compile a thorough structural linguistic documentation of each the Pomo languages. By 1937, however, it became clear that he needed further support for his work than Berkeley was able to offer. He withdrew from the Berkeley program and enrolled as a graduate student at the University of Chicago, where he was able to study under Harry Hoijer, an early student of Sapir (see ¶2.9.3). With Chicago's support he returned to work further on Quechan in 1938 and on Pomo in 1939–1940 (Halpern 1964). His dissertation, a grammar of Quechan, completed in 1940 and published in 1946–1947, was the first detailed grammar of a Yuman language and set the paradigm for future research on the family (Langdon 1997a).

Halpern's American Indian work—like the work of nearly all of his contemporaries—was interrupted by World War II. He spent the war years devising and supervising a course on Japanese for army and navy officers, and during the immediate postwar years worked as an adviser to the U.S. occupation forces in Japan. During the decades that followed Halpern pursued a career as a research analyst on contemporary Asian affairs for several nongovernmental organizations, most notably the RAND Corporation. After his retirement in 1976, he reestablished his ties both with academic linguistics and with the Quechan tribe, and during his remaining years carried out further fieldwork both on Quechan (1978–1981) and Pomo (1982–1984).

FIGURE 29. Abraham M. Halpern. Photograph by Margaret Langdon, ca. 1980. Courtesy of Loni Langdon.

2.9 Survey of California (and Other) Indian Languages

It was not until well after World War II that Berkeley finally saw the establishment of a research program in California Indian linguistics. The Survey of California Indian Languages, housed in a newly created Department of Linguistics, was primarily the creation of two linguists from the Chicago-Yale school, Mary R. Haas (1910–1996), a student of Sapir who had worked primarily on the Indian languages of the Southeast, and **Murray B. Emeneau** (1904–2005), a Sanskritist who had carried out postdoctoral linguistic research among the Todas of India under Sapir's direction.

2.9.1 Mary R. Haas

Mary Haas, a native of Richmond, Indiana, and a graduate of the local college,[90] encountered Sapir during her first postgraduate year at the University of Chicago in 1930–1931. She soon became one of his small band of devoted graduate students and not long afterward married Sapir's brilliant protégé Morris Swadesh.[91] She and Swadesh, together with several other students, followed Sapir to Yale in the fall of 1931, and shortly afterward she began fieldwork on Tunica, an endangered language of Louisiana. After finishing her doctoral work in 1935, she received fellowship support for continued fieldwork on Natchez and several of the Muskogean languages, and by the end of the decade she had become the leading scholar on the languages of the Southeast.

It was Haas's wartime involvement with the study of Thai, however, rather than her achievements as an American Indianist, that led to an appointment at Berkeley. Recruited by the War Department in 1941 to prepare materials in Thai, she was invited to Berkeley in 1943 to join the Army Specialized Training Program, which had been set up, under

FIGURE 30. Mary R. Haas, ca. 1975. Courtesy of the Department of Linguistics, UC Berkeley.

the direction of A. L. Kroeber, to teach strategic languages to servicemen. After the war ended, she stayed on in the department of Oriental languages, and in the late 1940s she joined forces with her erstwhile Yale compatriot, Murray Emeneau, to develop a graduate program in linguistics. Supervised in its early years by an interdepartmental committee on linguistics that included, besides Haas and Emeneau, specialists such as Yakov Malkiel in Romance philology, Yuen-Ren Chao in Oriental languages, Madison Beeler in German, and Francis Whitfield in Slavic, the program was modeled on the Yale program of the 1930s. Grounding in historical and comparative linguistics— particularly in Indo-European—was balanced by training in the latest analytical tools of descriptive theory, and students were expected to make a commitment to the long-term study of a particular language. Although other possibilities existed, students were strongly encouraged to work on an American Indian language, more particularly a California language, and in 1953 the Survey of California Indian Languages was formally established, with Mary Haas as director, as the principal research arm of a newly created department of linguistics.[92]

2.9.2 Survey Research at the University of California, Berkeley

During its first half century of existence—and in particular during its first two decades—the Survey of California (and Other) Indian Languages supported field research on nearly all California languages for which fluent speakers survived (Box 9). Before 1975 most of this work was carried out by doctoral students in Berkeley's linguistics department, and

although the expectation was that survey researchers would complete a tripartite documentation—a full descriptive grammar, a collection of narrative texts, and a dictionary— the grammar alone was usually submitted as a dissertation. The monographs prepared under survey auspices usually appeared as numbers in the *University of California Publications in Linguistics*. The coverage and structure of the "Californian grammars" that came to typify published survey research have been commented on by Hamp (1966a) and Silverstein (1975).

2.9.3 California Language Research on Other UC Campuses

The creation of a graduate program in linguistics at Berkeley in the early 1950s was an important landmark in the establishment of linguistics as an independent academic discipline. During the next two decades formal programs in linguistics, at both the graduate and undergraduate levels, were set up at most of the research universities in North America. In California this trend coincided with the rapid expansion of the University of California into a multicampus institution, and by the end of the 1960s there were thriving linguistics programs on at least two UC campuses besides Berkeley—UCLA and UC San Diego—and dissertation-level research on California Indian languages was being sponsored at both. A third UC graduate program in linguistics, established at Santa Barbara in the 1980s, has also become an important center of California Indian language research.

UNIVERSITY OF CALIFORNIA, LOS ANGELES

As early as the 1940s the UCLA anthropology faculty included a prominent Americanist linguist, Harry Hoijer, one of Sapir's early students at the University of Chicago. A specialist in Athabaskan languages, Hoijer's research focused on Navajo and the Apache dialects, but in the 1950s, encouraged by his colleagues at Berkeley to turn his attention to languages of the California region, he carried out field research on Chetco-Tolowa and the Galice variety of Rogue River Athabaskan (Hoijer 1966, 1973) and encouraged a student (Mary Woodward) to begin work on Hupa.[93] In the 1960s, Hoijer was joined on the UCLA faculty by William Bright (see Figure 41), whose documentation of Karuk (Bright 1957) was the first fieldwork on a California language sponsored by the linguistics committee at Berkeley. Hoijer and Bright urged their graduate students to carry out documentary research on Southern California languages. Hoijer supervised a dissertation on the Yuman language Paipai (Joël 1966),[94] while Bright supervised the work of Kenneth and Jane H. Hill, who worked, respectively, on Serrano (K. Hill 1967) and Cupeño (J. Hill 1966, 2005); John Davis, who worked on Luiseño (Davis 1973); and Margaret Press, who worked on Chemehuevi (Press 1979). Bright also directed Alice Anderton's dissertation on extinct Kitanemuk, based on the materials collected by Harrington (Anderton

Algic

Berkeley Yurok Project—Yurok, 2001 and continuing
(Blevins 2003, 2004, 2005b; Garrett, Blevins,
and Conathan 2005. See also linguistics.berkeley.
edu/~yurok/)

Berman, Howard—Yurok (Berman 1982b)

Bright, William—Yurok, 1950

Fletcher, Stuart—Wiyot, 1954

Haas, Mary—Yurok, 1950–1960

Lamb, Sydney—Wiyot, 1955

Perry, Jean—Yurok, 1988

Proulx, Paul—Yurok, 1980 (Proulx 1985b)

Robins, Robert H.—Yurok, 1951 (Robins 1958)

Teeter, Karl V.—Wiyot, 1956–1959 (Teeter 1964;
Teeter and Nichols 1993)

Athabaskan

Berkeley Hupa Documentation Project (Amy Campbell,
Lindsey Newbold, Kayla Carpenter, Ramon
Escamilla, Justin Spence)—2008 and continuing

Golla, Victor—Hupa, 1962–1965; Tututni, 1962–1964
(Golla 1970, 1976, 1996a; Sapir and Golla 2001)

Haas, Mary R.—Hupa, 1950; Mattole, 1954

Hoijer, Harry—Galice, 1956 (Hoijer 1966, 1973)

Woodward, Mary—Hupa and Tolowa, 1953 (M.
Woodward 1964)

Chumash

Beeler, Madison—Barbareño, 1954–1963 (Beeler 1976)

Bright, William—Barbareño, 1950

Karuk

Bright, William—Karuk, 1949–1951, 1954 (Bright
1958)[†]

Klamath-Modoc

Barker, M.A.R. (Philip R.)—Klamath-Modoc,
1955–1957 (Barker 1963a, 1963b, 1964)

Maiduan

Shipley, William F.—Northeastern Maidu, 1954–1957
(Shipley 1963, 1964)

Smith, Richard A.—Nisenan, 1965–1966, 1971–1978
(Eatough 1999)[‡]

Ultan, Russell—Konkow, 1961–1964 (R. Ultan 1967)

Miwok

Broadbent, Sylvia M.—Sierra Miwok, 1955–1958, 1961
(Broadbent 1964)

Callaghan, Catherine A.—Lake, Bodega, Plains, and
Northern Sierra Miwok, 1956–1964 (Callaghan
1965, 1970, 1984, 1987)

Hoffman, Meredith—Central Sierra Miwok, 1978

Numic

Berkeley Northern Paiute Language Project (Molly
Babel, Andrew Garrett, Michael J. Houser, Maziar

Toosarvandani)—2006 and continuing (linguistics.
berkeley.edu/~paiute/project_publications.html)

Berkeley Kawaiisu Grammar Project (Jocelyn Ahlers,
Hannah Pritchett, Justin Spence)—2009 and
continuing

Dayley, Jon P.—Central Numic (Panamint, Shoshoni),
1971 (Dayley 1989, 1990)

Good, Dwight A.—Panamint, 1964

Klein, Sheldon—Kawaiisu, 1958

Lamb, Sydney M.—Mono, 1953–1955 (Lamb 1958b)

Nichols, Michael J. P.—Northern Paiute, 1968–1970

Rackley, W. Ray—Panamint, ca. 1966

Palaihnihan

McFarland, Teresa—Achumawi (Hewisi), 2002

Paster, Mary—Achumawi (Hewisi), 2002

Silver, Shirley—Achumawi, 1970–1976

Talmy, Leonard—Atsugewi, 1965–1966, 1970 (Talmy
1972)

Walters, Diane Guilfoy—Atsugewi, 1976 (Walters 1977)

Pomo

Grekoff, George—Southeastern Pomo, 1957

Halpern, A. M.—Southern, Central, and Southeastern
Pomo, 1982–1984[§]

McLendon, Sally—Eastern Pomo, 1958–1970
(McLendon 1975, 1996)

Mithun, Marianne—Central Pomo, 1984–1986 (Mithun
1988, 1990a, 1993, 1998b)

Moshinsky, Julius—Southeastern Pomo, 1965–1968
(Moshinsky 1974)

O'Connor, Mary Catherine—Northern Pomo,
1980–1990 (O'Connor 1992)

Oswalt, Robert L.—Kashaya Pomo, 1957–1964 (Oswalt
1961, 1964b)

Siniard, Roy—Southern Pomo, 1966–1968

Vihman, Eero—Northern Pomo, 1966–1967 (Vihman
1976)

Salinan

Jacobsen, William H., Jr.—Antoniano, 1954

Shastan

Bright, William—Shasta, 1950 (Bright and Olmsted
1959)

Silver, Shirley—Shasta, 1957–1961 (Silver 1966)

Takic

Miller, Wick R.—Serrano, 1959

Seiler, Hansjakob—Cahuilla, 1955 (Seiler 1970, 1977)

Tubatulabal

Lamb, Sydney, and Hansjakob Seiler—1954

Washo

Jacobsen, William H., Jr.—Washo, 1955–1968
(Jacobsen 1964, 1996a)

(*continued*)

BOX 9. (continued)

Wintuan

Bright, Elizabeth—Patwin, 1952

Pitkin, Harvey—Wintu, 1956–1959 (Pitkin 1984, 1985)

Schlichter [Shepherd], Alice—Wintu, 1975–1982 (Schlichter 1981b; Shepherd 1989)

Ultan, Donald—Patwin, 1961–1962

Whistler, Kenneth W.—Patwin, 1975–1979 (Whistler 1980a)

Yokuts

Broadbent, Sylvia—Chukchansi, 1955–1957

Collord, Thomas L.—Chukchansi, 1965 (Collord 1968)

Gamble, Geoffrey—Wikchamni, 1970–1973 (Gamble 1978)

Weigel, William F.—Yawelmani (Yowlumne), 2000–2005 (Weigel 2006)

Yukian

Lamb, Sydney M.—Yuki (Huchnom), 1955

Sawyer, Jesse O.—Wappo, 1959–1984; Yuki, 1967–1976 (Sawyer 1965, 1991; Sawyer and Schlichter 1984)

Silver, Shirley—Yuki, 1972–1976

Siniard, Roy—Yuki, 1966–1968

Yuman

Crawford, James M.—Cocopa, 1963–1965 (Crawford 1966, 1983, 1989)

Crawford, Judith Gray—various Yuman languages, 1967–1972

Hayes, Alfred—Diegueño, 1953

Hinton, Leanne—Havasupai, 1965–1985 (Hinton 1984)

Langdon, Margaret—Diegueño, 1963–1965 (Langdon 1970)

Mixco, Mauricio J. —Kiliwa, 1966–1969 (Mixco 1971, 1983, 1985, 2000)

Shaterian, Alan—Yavapai, Havasupai, 1965

---

*Citations are of the major publication(s), if any, of material collected during the field work: descriptive grammars, collections of texts, dictionaries, and similar documentary work. In most cases, copies of the fieldworker's original notes are on deposit in the survey archives (www.linguistics.berkeley.edu/Survey/archives.html). Sound recordings made during survey fieldwork are archived in the Berkeley Language Center (www.mip.berkeley.edu/blc/la/index.html). Recent survey-sponsored research on languages of the California region is described on the Projects page of the survey's Web site (linguistics.berkeley.edu/~survey/activities/projects.php).

---

†Bright's Karuk fieldwork was undertaken before the survey was formally established. It was considered a "pilot project" for the survey and funded directly by the university administration.
‡Smith began his Nisenan field research under survey auspices while still an undergraduate. Since Smith's death in 1987 his linguistic notes have been in the possession of William Shipley. Eatough's outline grammar of Nisenan is based on Smith's notes.
§Halpern's survey-sponsored work on Pomo in the 1980s followed on more extensive work that was carried out in the 1930s, before the establishment of the survey (see Halpern 1964).

FIGURE 31. Harry Hoijer, ca. 1970. Courtesy of the American Anthropological Association.

1988). In the 1970s, Pamela Munro, who had received her doctorate at UC San Diego with a dissertation on Mojave (see next section), joined the UCLA faculty and directed dissertation research on two other Yuman languages, Tolkapaya Yavapai (Heather Hardy 1979) and Maricopa (Lynn Gordon 1986).

UNIVERSITY OF CALIFORNIA, SAN DIEGO

A department of linguistics was included in the original design for the UCSD campus that opened in 1964, and Margaret Langdon (1926–2005), whose fieldwork on Ipai Diegueño had been sponsored by the survey (Langdon 1970), was a member of the UCSD founding faculty. Langdon established a program modeled on the Berkeley survey that supported dissertation research by half a dozen UCSD graduate students on languages and dialects of the Yuman family, including Leanne Hinton (1970, 1984), Pamela Munro (1976), Larry Gorbet (1976), Brigitte Bendixen (1980), Susan Norwood (1981), and Amy Miller (2001). Langdon

FIGURE 32. Margaret Langdon, ca. 1985. Courtesy of Loni Langdon.

also collaborated with her colleague Ronald W. Langacker in supporting research that resulted in three monographs on the Takic languages (Roderick Jacobs 1975; Susan Steele 1990; and Eric Elliott 1999) as well as Stephen Marlett's dissertation on Seri (1981). In 1970, UCSD hosted the first Conference on Hokan Languages (Langdon 1974:77; Langdon and Silver 1976), and during the next two decades the annual follow-up meetings of this group functioned as the primary venue for historical and comparative linguistics on California languages.

UNIVERSITY OF CALIFORNIA, SANTA BARBARA

A department of linguistics was established at UCSB in the mid-1980s, explicitly committed to "empirical research." Two members of the founding faculty had important ties to American Indian linguistics, Wallace Chafe and Marianne Mithun, the leading specialists in Iroquoian languages. Soon after joining the Santa Barbara faculty, Mithun began field research on a California language, Central Pomo. Two of the other founders of the department, Sandra Thompson and Charles Li, had long been working on a comprehensive descriptive grammar of Wappo (Thompson, Park, and Li 2006). In the ensuing years, UCSB has sponsored a major research project on Barbareño Chumash, resulting in a dissertation on Chumash syntax (Suzanne Wash 2001).

2.9.4 Research on California Indian Languages Outside California

Between 1928 and his death in 1971, Melville Jacobs, a student of Boas's, maintained a very active research program at the *University of Washington,* in Seattle, that focused on the languages and oral literature of the native people of Washington and Oregon (Seaburg and Amoss 2000). Jacobs's interest in Penutian and Athabaskan languages was especially strong and tied in well with research agendas of his contemporaries at Berkeley, particularly Mary Haas (Jacobs

1937, 1954). Other than his wife, Elizabeth, who carried out independent fieldwork on Oregon Athabaskan, Jacobs had no students or protegés who developed an interest in Oregon languages. He did have considerable indirect influence on Dell Hymes and on younger scholars such as Michael Silverstein; through them, a number of students, such as Daythal Kendall and Rob Moore, became active Oregonianists and students of comparative Penutian linguistics. In the early 1970s William Seaburg, a student of Fang Kuei Li's at the University of Hawaii—where Li had retired after a teaching career in Oriental Languages at Seattle—became interested in Li's earlier work in Athabaskan linguistics. With Li's encouragement, Seaburg transferred to the University of Washington. After taking a degree in Library Science, he became one of the custodians of Jacobs' papers and helped found the Jacobs Research Fund, which supports work on the indigenous languages and literatures of the Northwest. He later undertook his own work in both Oregon and California Athabaskan.

The *University of Oregon*, in Eugene, and the *University of Nevada at Reno* have been active sponsors of research on the languages of southern Oregon and western Nevada. At the University of Oregon, Scott DeLancey, a Tibeto-Burmanist with a strong secondary interest in American Indian languages, has been carrying out significant research on Klamath-Modoc and other Penutian languages. Students who have worked under him have completed dissertations on Klamath (Janne Underriner 2002) and Northern Paiute (Timothy Thornes 2003). His colleague Tom Givón has worked on Tolowa in collaboration with a student from the Tolowa community, culminating in an MA thesis (Loren Bommelyn 1997). At the University of Nevada at Reno, Catherine Fowler, an ethnobiologist and applied linguist, has worked closely with Numic-speaking communities and carried out considerable research on Northern Paiute. Her now-retired colleague, William Jacobsen, has continued through nearly five decades the research on Washo that he began as a graduate student at Berkeley in the 1950s and remains actively involved in Washo revitalization efforts.

From the 1950s through the 1970s, *Indiana University* maintained a summer research station at the Museum of Northern Arizona in Flagstaff, where Carl Voegelin (¶2.8.2) and his wife, Florence M. Voegelin, supervised the work of a number of students on languages of the Southwest. In addition to studies of Uto-Aztecan and Tanoan languages, this included several dissertation projects on Yuman languages: Martha B. Kendall on Yavapai (1976), James Redden on Hualapai (1966), and William Seiden (1963) and Edwin Kozlowski (1972) on Havasupai.

California Indian linguistics has also continued to attract the attention of scholars based in institutions outside the region. In some cases they have conducted research on California languages in collaboration with California institutions, as did the British linguist R. H. Robins (1922–2000), who carried out a field study of Yurok in 1951 under the auspices of the Survey of California and Other Indian

Languages at Berkeley. Subsequent work on Yurok by two independent scholars from outside California, Paul Proulx and Howard Berman, as well as earlier work by Berman on Sierra Miwok, was also sponsored by the Survey. Other notable visitors have included Hans Jakob Seiler, from the University of Cologne, who carried out extensive research on Cahuilla, and Werner Winter, from the University of Kiel, who has done important research on the Yuman languages.

2.10 The Contemporary Scene: Continuing Documentation and Research within and beyond the Academy

Many of the California languages that survived into the twentith century have become extinct in the last two generations, while most of those that remain are spoken fluently only by a few elderly people. Box 10 summarizes the situation as of 2010. The documentation activities that are currently being carried out are probably the last that will ever be undertaken.

Recognition of this fact has stimulated a gratifying burst of new descriptive activity in the last few years, accompanied by the rise of a fresh generation of Californianist linguists at UC Berkeley, UC Santa Barbara, and a few other institutions with a long historical commitment to Indian language research. Especially notable are the Yurok and Hupa documentation projects sponsored by the Survey of California and Other Indian Languages at Berkeley. To a considerable degree this work continues in the humanistic and anthropological tradition whose accomplishments are surveyed in this book, but informed by greater theoretical sophistication and with access to data-processing tools undreamt of in Kroeber's time, or even my own graduate student years in the 1960s. The speed with which the full extant documentation of a given California language can now be retrieved, searched, and factored into new research gives current work a scholarly breadth and historical context that were impossible in previous generations.

An equally important characteristic of the present era, however, is the enormous growth of serious interest in indigenous languages on the part of native people. Continuing

FIGURE 33. Violet Super teaching Luke Supahan, her great-grandnephew, to play cards in Karuk, 2003. Courtesy of Terry Supahan.

documentation of California languages is now usually conducted in close coordination with—or indeed as an integral part of—tribally sponsored cultural programs whose goal is the revitalization of the group's heritage language. Considerations of pedagogical usefulness often shape research priorities: dictionaries are favored over grammars, archiving (especially digital) is favored over analysis. With increasing frequency the researchers themselves are members of the tribe whose language is being documented (see, for example, the discussion of Havasupai and Yawelmani documentation in Hinton and Weigel 2002, and of Western Mono documentation in Kroskrity 2002). Details of specific tribal documentation and revitalization projects, to the extent I have information about them, are noted in Part 3.

BOX 10. SURVIVAL OF CALIFORNIA INDIAN LANGUAGES

Languages extinct before 1950

Athabaskan, California: all except Hupa and Kato

Athabaskan, Oregon: all except Tolowa, Tututni, and Galice

Chumash: all except Barbareño

Cochimí

Costanoan

Esselen

Maiduan: Chico Maidu

Miwok: Bay Miwok, Marin Miwok

Shastan: all except Shasta

Takelma

Takic: Gabrielino, Tataviam, Kitanemuk, Juaneño variety of Luiseño-Juaneño

Waikuri

Yana

Yokuts: Poso Creek and Buena Vista dialect groups

Languages that ceased to be spoken between 1950 and 2010*

Algic: Wiyot (1961)

Athabaskan, California: Mattole (1950s), Kato (1960s), Eel River (1970s)

Athabaskan, Oregon: Galice (1960s), Tututni (1980s), Tolowa (1990s)

Chimariko (1950s)

Chumash: Barbareño (1965)

Klamath-Modoc (2003)

_____

*Year or decade of death of last known fluent speaker in parentheses.

Maiduan: Nisenan (1980s)

Miwok: Coast Miwok (1970s), Plains Miwok (1990s)

Palaihnihan: Atsugewi (1988)

Pomo: Northeastern Pomo (1961), Southern Pomo (1990s), Southeastern Pomo (1990s), Northern Pomo (1990s)

Salinan (1950s or 1960s)

Shastan: Shasta (1970s or 1980s)

Takic: Cupeño (1987)

Wintuan: Nomlaki (1990s?)

Yukian: Yuki (1980s), Wappo (1990s)

Languages with at least one fluent speaker as of 2010

Algic: Yurok

Athabaskan, California: Hupa

Karuk

Maiduan: Konkow, Northeastern Maidu (?)

Miwok: Sierra Miwok, Lake Miwok (?)

Numic: Kuwaiisu, Chemehuevi, Panamint, Mono, Northern Paiute

Palaihnihan: Achumawi

Pomo: Kashaya, Eastern Pomo, Central Pomo (?)

Takic: Cahuilla, Luiseño, Serrano (?)

Tubatulabal

Washo

Wintuan: Wintu (?), Patwin (?)

Yokuts: Tule-Kaweah (Wikchamni), Kings River (Choynimni), Valley (Yawelmani, Tachi)

Yuman: Cocopa, Diegueño (Ipai, Tipai, and Kumeyaay), Kiliwa (?), Quechan, Maricopa, Mojave, Upland Yuman (Hualapai, Havasupai, Yavapai), Paipai

PART 3

LANGUAGES AND LANGUAGE FAMILIES

In Part 3 will be found the descriptive details of the approximately eighty languages of the California region, including their territories, subdivisions, and cultural associations; a summary of their linguistic documentation; and a short, semitechnical sketch of their principal phonological and grammatical characteristics. The presentation of this information is organized in twenty-three sections, each, in general, corresponding to one of the first-order ("inspectionally obvious") historical units, or families, into which John Wesley Powell and his coworkers grouped the languages of California in the first complete classification of North American Indian languages (Powell 1891; cf. ¶2.5.7).

While the internal history of a few of the more diversified of the Powell classification's California families (e.g., Pomo, Yuman) has attracted a certain amount of scholarly attention, much of the historical and comparative work on California languages has focused on exploring second-order phylogenetic connections among groups of Powell families. These deeper families or phyla, in alphabetical order, provide the overall framework of the presentation. Two of the Powell families, Yukian and Chumash, are treated as unaffiliated at this classificatory level, as are the poorly documented languages spoken at the southern tip of the Baja California peninsula.

Algic Languages

3.1 California Algic Languages (Ritwan)

Wiyot and Yurok were spoken in adjacent territories on the heavily forested northwest coast of California from a few miles north of the mouth of the Klamath River to a few miles south of the mouth of the Eel River. A family relationship between Wiyot and Yurok was recognized by R. B. Dixon and A. L. Kroeber (1913), who dubbed it "Ritwan," a coinage based on the cognate stems for 'two' in the two languages (Wiyot *rit-*, Yurok *neʔe-*; cf. Dixon and Kroeber 1919:54). Edward Sapir's claim (1913a, 1923a) that the two languages are also distantly related to the Algonquian family, although controversial at first (Michelson 1914, 1915), is now considered to be proven (Haas 1958; I. Goddard 1975, 1986). The relationship that includes Wiyot, Yurok, and

Algonquian has been referred to by several names, three of which are still in wide use: *Algic*, *Algonquian-Ritwan*, and *Wiyot-Yurok-Algonquian*. Sapir's original proposal that the family name Algonquian (or "Algonkin") be extended to the larger grouping did not meet with favor among Algonquianists, and the term is now seldom used in this sense by linguists. In this book the Wiyot-Yurok-Algonquian relationship will be called the *Algic* superfamily (Map 4).

Algic was assumed at first to be a binary relationship between Dixon and Kroeber's Ritwan on the one hand and Algonquian on the other, but the historical validity of Ritwan has become less certain as more accurate descriptive data have accumulated. While some continue to believe a Ritwan branch is justified (Berman 1982a, 1984, 1990), Proulx, who gave the question his sustained attention, found the evidence

MAP 4. Yurok and Wiyot within the Algic superfamily.

unconvincing and treated Wiyot, Yurok, and Algonquian as three equally old branches of Algic (Proulx 1984:166, 1994:152–153). Most specialists would probably follow Haas (1966:103) in leaving the question open. To that end, Wiyot and Yurok will be referred to as the "California Algic" languages in this book rather than the "Ritwan" languages.

That the position of Wiyot and Yurok within Algic should be so uncertain indicates how deep the differences are between the two California Algic languages. Although they share a compex system of verb-stem derivation, including many specific lexical and affixal elements, much of this structure is also shared with Proto-Algonquian (Teeter 1974; Proulx 1985a, 1985b; Garrett 2004). If lexical similarities likely to reflect recent borrowing are set aside, the percentage of cognate core vocabulary between Wiyot and Yurok is not significantly greater than that between either of these languages and Proto-Algonquian (Proulx 1994:152). Phonologically, the two languages show many differences, with Wiyot, on the one hand, lacking the glottalized consonants present in Yurok but, on the other hand, having an aspirated stop series that Yurok lacks.[1]

3.2 Wiyot

3.2.1 Geography

The Wiyot speech area was restricted to a narrow coastal strip around Humboldt Bay, extending from Little River, a few miles north of the mouth of the Mad River, to the Bear

River mountains south of the mouth of the Eel River. Wiyot territory reached inland only to the foot of the first major ridge in the Coast Range, nowhere more than fifteen miles from the coast (Loud 1918:249; see Map 5).

Despite the severe disruption of traditional life after 1850, the names and locations of about twenty Wiyot villages have been recorded (Loud 1918:259–275; Curtis 1907–1930, vol. 13:226–227; Nomland and Kroeber 1936). Although each village was largely independent, three geographical clusters or "districts" existed, each distinguished by a name and apparently by shallow dialect differences (Kroeber 1911a:384; Loud 1918:249, 300; Curtis 1907–1930, vol. 13:67; Reichard 1925:8). The northern district, **Patawat** (*patəwat*), was focused on the lower Mad River from the river mouth to Blue Lake, and south along Mad River Slough. Important villages included *hətwelakaw* on the south bank near the river mouth, *kʷəsakʷ* ('on the hill') on the north bank west of Mill Creek, and *tatikʷəɣək* ('trail descending') at Blue Lake. The central district, **Wiki,** included all the villages around the marshy shores of Humboldt Bay, the most important being *tuləwat* on Indian Island (known also as Gunther Island) opposite Eureka, *kucuwaɫik* at the site of Bucksport, and *pimir* on the South Spit. The southern district, **Wiyat,** included the villages along the lower Eel River from the coast to where the Van Duzen joins the Eel above Rohnerville. The principal village of this district, *təratpeɫik*, was located on the south side of the river near the old cannery site at Port Kenyon, about three miles northwest of Ferndale.

The Mad River Wiyots were in close contact with the Yuroks at Trinidad and other coastal Yuroks to the north. Intermarriage between the two groups was common and Yurok-Wiyot bilinguals must have been numerous. Nevertheless, the language boundary, which lay just south of Little River, appears to have been quite stable. Relations were apparently less friendly between the Wiyots and the Athabaskan-speaking groups to the east and south (Chilula, Whilkut, Nongatl, Sinkyone, and Mattole–Bear River). The Chilulas of Redwood Creek were especially hostile, and attacks by the Chilulas on Wiyot (and coastal Yurok) villages were not uncommon, accompanied by a gradual encroachment on Wiyot territory. Chilula pressure was especially strong around Blue Lake, and shortly before white settlement the Chilulas established their own village close to the Wiyot settlement to give themselves direct access to the resources of the lower Mad River (Loud 1918:251–252). The Nongatls on the Van Duzen River and the Sinkyones on the Eel River were somewhat less aggressive toward the Wiyots, perhaps because the dense redwood forest along Eel River between Scotia and the mouth of Larabee Creek created a buffer between the two groups (Nomland and Kroeber 1936:40).

3.2.2 Documentation and Survival

The first attestation of Wiyot was in two vocabularies ("Wee-yot" from the lower Eel River and "Wish-osk" from

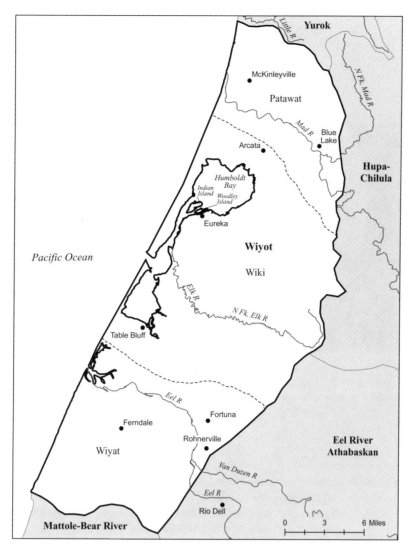

MAP 5. Wiyot territory and dialects.

Humboldt Bay) collected by George Gibbs during the McKee Expedition in 1851, published by Schoolcraft (Gibbs 1853b, 1853c) and reprinted in Powers (1877:478–482). The earliest substantial documentation is a pair of Bureau of American Ethnology survey lists collected by Jeremiah Curtin, one obtained from an Eel River speaker (1889f) and the other the only direct attestation of the Patawat variety spoken along Mad River (1889g). Merriam collected a general Wiyot vocabulary and a natural history wordlist between 1910 and 1923 (¶Appendix A: C-3a-c), explicitly including data from more than one dialect. The most extensive documentation was made by Gladys Reichard in 1922–1923. She collected texts, vocabulary, and a considerable amount of grammatical information from speakers of both the Humboldt Bay and Eel River dialects, nearly all of which she published in a comprehensive volume (Reichard 1925). In 1956–1959 the UC Berkeley linguist Karl Teeter worked with Della Prince, an Eel River Wiyot and the last fluent speaker of the language, who died in

1962. He published a grammatical sketch with a set of texts (1964), and a glossary/concordance (Teeter and Nichols 1993). Although Teeter's documentation is more linguistically sophisticated than Reichard's, it is derived from a single elderly speaker and lacks the cultural richness of the earlier collection (see also I. Goddard 1966).

Other published sources of Wiyot data include the vocabulary and grammatical notes in Kroeber's preliminary sketch of the language (1911a:384–413); extensive but poorly transcribed geographical and general vocabulary in Loud (1918); and a long vocabulary of the Humboldt Bay dialect in Curtis (1907–1930, vol. 13:263-272), obtained by Myers from Reichard's principal source, Jerry James. In addition to the Curtin and Merriam vocabularies, the most significant unpublished attestation of the language is in the miscellaneous materials, including ethnogeographical data "reheard" from Loud (1918), that were collected by Harrington during two short visits in 1926 and 1942 (Mills 1985:3–9).

FIGURE 34. Jerry James and his wife Birdie, Humboldt Bay, 1910. Wiyot consultants for Gladys Reichard in 1922–1923. C. Hart Merriam collection of Native American photographs (C/3c/P1 no.4). Courtesy of Bancroft Library UCB.

Wiyot is the heritage language of the Wiyot tribe, whose principal modern community is at Table Bluff Rancheria near Loleta, where a modest language-revival program is under way.

3.2.3 Linguistic Structure

The standard descriptive grammar of Wiyot is Teeter (1964), but it is not well organized and is overly brief in places. Ives Goddard's extended review (1966) should be consulted. Reichard's prestructural treatment (1925), with its abundance of data, sheds light on various aspects of the language not fully covered by Teeter.

Wiyot has six series of stops and affricates (*p, t, c* [ts], *č, k, kʷ*), each occurring plain and aspirated (Table 3). There are five fricatives, three voiceless (*s, š, ł*) and two voiced (*β, γ*); two nasals (*m, n*); four approximants (*l, r* [ɹ], *w, y*); and two laryngeals (*ʔ, h*). There is also an alveolar tap or flap *ɾ* (written *d* by Teeter). In the speech of the last native speakers (ca. 1920–1960) the two voiced bilabial obstruents (*β* and *m*) freely varied in initial position and may not have been in phonemic contrast in any position; the data indicate that a sound change *m > β* was in progress (Conathan 2004:120–125). There are four full vowels (*i, e, a, u*), with allophonic differences in length, and a reduced vowel (*ə*) that is always short. Wiyot has a pitch accent system, but the existing descriptions do not make its operation clear.[2]

Wiyot has a system of consonant alternations involving the *t, c,* and *č* series of stops and affricates, the fricatives *s* and *š*, and the approximants *l* and *r* (Teeter 1964: 21–22). These alternations are used lexically to symbolize diminutive—and possibly augmentative—semantic contrasts, sometimes (but not always) reinforced by a suffix *-ac* or *-ač*. For example, *ritətk* 'two round objects', *ricəck* 'two small round objects (such as peas)', and *ričəčk* 'two large round objects (such as watermelons)'; *lalisw-* 'sing', *rarišw-ac-* 'hum'; or *tʰuʔl* 'pestle', *čʰaʔr-ač* 'bottle' (see ¶4.12.1 and Haas 1970).

Wiyot morphology is complex and strongly reminiscent of both Yurok and Algonquian. Nouns can have simple stems, but most are made up of two or more elements and are derived either from other nouns ("subordinative themes") or from verbs and verb phrases. Nouns are inflected for first and second person possessor with pronominal prefixes. Alienable nouns take *ru(ʔ)-* first person, *kʰu(ʔ)-* second person. Inalienable nouns take *r-* first person, *kʰ-* second person if the stem begins in a vowel, but if the stem begins in a consonant these are left unmarked for first person and marked for second person by aspiration of the initial consonant. To mark a third person possessor, alienable nouns take the prefix *hu(ʔ)-*, inalienable nouns the prefix *w-* if vowel-initial but no prefix if consonant-initial. Nouns with a third person possessor are treated as subordinative themes and inflected with agentive verbal suffixes (*-aʔl* definite, *-ik* indefinite). Vowel-initial inalienable nouns can also mark the absence of specific possession with the prefix *β-*. Examples: *pas* 'basket plate', *rupas* 'my basket plate', *kʰupas* 'your basket plate', *hupasaʔl* 'his basket plate', *hupasik* 'one's basket plate'; *rit* 'my tongue', *kʰit* 'your tongue', *witəʔl* 'his tongue', *witik* 'one's tongue', *βit* 'a (detached, unpossessed) tongue'; *čul* 'my (maternal) aunt', *čʰul* 'your aunt', *čuləʔl* 'his aunt', *čulik* 'one's aunt'.[3]

Verb stems are often analyzable into three derivational elements, as in the Algonquian languages: an initial element indicating a general action or direction (e.g., *tʰiγ-* 'out', *takʷ-* 'strike'), a medial element that is often classificatory in meaning, including a set of body-part elements (e.g., *-ətal-* 'one person goes, walks', *-eʔsan-* 'hand'), and a final element that marks thematic class (e.g., *-aʔw*, transitive). Subject

TABLE 3
Wiyot Phonemes (Teeter 1964)

Consonants									Vowels	
p	t	c			č	k	kʷ	ʔ	i	u
pʰ	tʰ	cʰ			čʰ	kʰ	kʰʷ			ə
		s		ł	š			h	e	a
β						γ				
m	n									
w			r, ɾ	l	y					

and object inflection is marked by suffixes, with considerable allomorphy. Preverbal particles express negative, prohibitive, and various aspectual, modal, and adverbial meanings. Verb themes are divided into active and stative classes, with the latter having passive, impersonal, or adjectival meanings. An important subclass of statives, called "descriptive compounds" by Teeter, have adjectival initials and classificatory medials (e.g., *rat-βəl-* 'to be a large building', *rat-ak^h-* 'to be a large long object'). The numerals 1 to 4 always occur in classificatory themes of this type, such as *kuc-βəl-* '(to be) one building' or *rit-ak^h-* '(to be) two long objects'.

3.2.4 Nomenclature

Wiyot speakers called themselves *sulatelak*. "Wiyot" is derived from the Wiyot name for the Eel River, and was first recorded by George Gibbs in September 1851 during the McKee treaty expedition (Gibbs 1853b). Gibbs collected two vocabularies, one of which he labelled "Wee-yot" (*wiyat*), noting that this was "the name given to Eel river, by the Indians at its mouth, and here applied to their dialect of [the otherwise unnamed language] common to the river, and to Humboldt bay." Gibbs labeled the second vocabulary ("the dialect of the upper part of the bay") "Wish-osk," which he identified as "the name given to the Bay and Mad river Indians by those of Eel river" (1853b:422)—a misunderstanding, since *wišask* is actually the Wiyot term for 'Athabaskan woman'. In cataloging the Smithsonian's manuscripts in the 1860s, Gibbs, unaware of this error, designated both vocabularies as attestations of "Wishosk." The misnomer was made official when Powell (1891), following his usual rule of precedence, adopted "Wishoskan" as the formal designation of the language family. The mistake was finally discovered by Kroeber, who quickly substituted "Wiyot" for "Wishosk," justifying the extension of the name of a single district to the entire linguistic group by noting that the Yurok and Karuk appeared to do the same (Kroeber 1911a:384). Yurok *weyet* and Karuk *váyat*, however, may originally have designated only the Eel River tribelet and dialect; it is noteworthy that as late as the 1870s Powers considered the "Patawāt" of the lower Mad River and Arcata and the "Viard" of lower Humboldt Bay and Eel River to be different "tribes" and treated them in separate chapters (1877:96–106).

3.3 Yurok

3.3.1 Geography

Yurok was spoken aboriginally in a chain of villages along the Klamath River, extending from the mouth of the river at Requa (*rek^woy* 'river mouth') to a few miles above Weitchpec (*wečpus* 'confluence'), about forty miles upstream; north along the coast a few miles to the village of Omen (*ʔomen*); and south along the coast to Little River, a few miles south of Trinidad (Map 6). The Yuroks along the Klamath River and north to Omen spoke minimally differentiated local varieties of a single dialect, which may be called **River Yurok** (Quinby 2003). The Yuroks along the coast south of Requa, who were collectively referred to as Coast Yurok or Nererner (*nrʔrnrh*), spoke at least two distinct dialects. **Lagoon Yurok** was spoken at Orick (*ʔoʔrek^w*), near the mouth of Redwood Creek, and at the villages around Freshwater and Stone Lagoons, and **Trinidad Yurok** was spoken at Tsurai (*čurey*), the village at Trinidad Head. It is not clear from the surviving documentation whether the speech of the villages on Big Lagoon was closer to the Trinidad or the Lagoon dialect. Similarly uncertain is the dialectal affiliation of the village of Espau, between Orick and Requa. These somewhat blurred local differences were overshadowed in social importance by a distinction between "ordinary" Yurok speech and a specialized style ("high language") that was employed on formal occasions by socially prominent individuals (see ¶4.13.1).

The Yurok were the prestige group at the center of a small and tightly integrated culture along the lower Klamath River and adjacent area. They shared this small territory with speakers of four other languages, Tolowa, Wiyot, Karuk, and Hupa-Chilula, visiting one another frequently, participating in one another's ceremonies, trading, and intermarrying. Many Yuroks, especially members of wealthy families, were bilingual or multilingual, while Yurok was known by many wealthy Hupas and Karuks, as well as by at least some Tolowas, Chilulas, and Wiyots. However, despite this extensive areal multilingualism, which was perhaps unique in the linguistic geography of aboriginal California, there is very little evidence of lexical borrowing between Yurok and adjacent languages, or of phonological and morphological influence. Nevertheless, some degree of semantic convergence in grammatical categories and general lexical structure has been noted among all northwestern California languages (Haas 1967; O'Neill 2001; Conathan 2004:32–93), and a system of diminutive consonant symbolism was partially shared (Haas 1970).

3.3.2 Documentation and Survival

Although Yurok traditional culture has been the focus of considerable ethnographic investigation for more than a century, the published documentation of the Yurok language has been rather modest until recently. The ongoing work of UC Berkeley's Yurok Language Project (see ¶3.3.3) is remedying this deficiency. The first attestations of the language were made in 1851 and include word lists collected at Trinidad by J. Goldsborough Bruff and Carl Meyer (Heizer and Mills 1952:113–117) and a vocabulary collected at Weitchpec by George Gibbs during the McKee expedition's visit (Gibbs 1853b). Gibbs also collected a more substantial vocabulary the following year, and both this and his 1851 vocabulary were published in Powers (1877: 460–473) together with vocabularies obtained by Crook

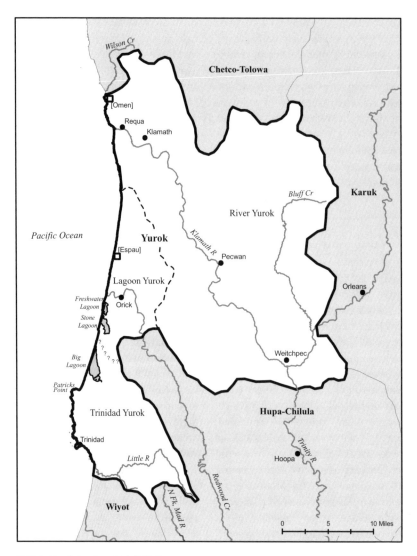

MAP 6. Yurok territory and dialects.

(1852–1861), Azpell (1870), and by Powers himself. Jeremiah Curtin's BAE survey list (1889b), collected during a three-month stay at Hoopa, was the most substantial documentation of Yurok made during the nineteenth century.

Research on Yurok during the twentith century was dominated by A. L. Kroeber, who made the Yurok the focus of his most intensive ethnographic and linguistic work. During the course of at least six field visits between 1900 and 1908 (cf. Thoresen 1976), Kroeber collected a large corpus of traditional narrative texts (many of them on wax cylinder recordings), as well as many lexical and grammatical data. Of this material, however, Kroeber published only a short sketch of the grammar (Kroeber 1911a:414–426), and a volume of texts (in English translation) reached print only after his death (Kroeber 1976).[4] T. T. Waterman, who worked under Kroeber's direction beginning in 1907, collected further materials and began drafting a full grammar of the language. In the end, however, he published only a

list of affixes (1923), although his justly celebrated monograph on Yurok geography (1920) contains a considerable amount of linguistic information. Between 1910 and 1922, Merriam collected vocabularies and natural history word lists from both a Coast and a River variety (¶Appendix A: B-2a, B-2b). Sapir worked briefly with a Yurok speaker during his Hupa fieldwork in the summer of 1927, and the three short texts he collected were edited and published by Howard Berman (2001b).

The British linguist R. H. Robins studied Yurok in the field during the spring of 1951 and published a moderately comprehensive description (1958), followed by a series of short papers elaborating on various aspects of the grammar (1962, 1966, 1980, 1985a, 1985b, 1985c). In the early 1970s Berman collected additional lexical material (Berman 1982b), and in 1980 Paul Proulx collected extensive new data on derivational morphology (Proulx 1985b).

Since 2001, linguists from the University of California, Berkeley, have been working in collaboration with the Yurok

FIGURE 35. A. L. Kroeber, his Yurok colleague Robert Spott, and the psychologist Erik H. Erikson, visiting Requa in the early 1940s. Courtesy of the Bancroft Library, UCB.

Tribe on a long-term documentation and revitalization project. An important component of this work is archival, focusing on the retranscription and analysis of the unpublished materials collected by Kroeber and Waterman (Kroeber 1900–1940; Kroeber and Waterman 1917–1918). A preliminary dictionary has been compiled from all available sources (Garrett, Blevins, and Conathan 2005). Several papers have appeared (Garrett 2001, 2004; Blevins 2002, 2003, 2004, 2005b), and other materials are posted on the project's website (linguistics.berkeley.edu/~yurok/).

Yurok is the heritage language of the Yurok Tribe of northwestern California and of three nearby independent rancherias, Reseghini, Big Lagoon, and Trinidad (Cher-Ae). Only a dozen or fewer elderly people have full first-language fluency in a combined tribal enrollment of nearly five thousand, although there are perhaps three times as many semispeakers and passive speakers, all middle-aged or older. In addition, several individuals, not all of them Indians, have acquired second-language fluency, and many younger Yuroks have an acquaintance with the language through local school programs that have been in place since the 1970s at both the primary and secondary levels. A distinctive writing system based on English phonetics ("Unifon") was employed in classroom teaching between 1970 and 2000, but this has been superseded by a tribally sponsored orthography based on the Roman alphabet.

3.3.3 Linguistic Structure

Robins (1958) remains the only comprehensive structural description of Yurok, but it should be used in combination with the dictionary compiled by the UC Berkeley Yurok Language Project (Garrett, Blevins, and Conathan 2005).

Yurok has five series of stops and affricates (*p, t, č, k, kʷ*), each occurring both plain and glottalized, although the

glottalized member of each series is relatively rare in the lexicon (Table 4). The articulation of the affricate series (*č, č'*) is now almost exclusively palatal [tʃ], but transcriptions made in the early twentith century indicate that some speakers favored a palatal and dental/alveolar [ts] articulation in at least some environments. There are four fricatives (*s, ł, š, γ*), two nasals (*m, n*), four approximants (*l, r, w, y*), and two laryngeals (*ʔ, h*). A voiceless velar fricative (*x*) occurs rarely and may be a sound-symbolic variant of *h* (Robins 1958:5, fn. 3). Fricatives and sonorants coarticulated with a glottal stop or constriction are treated as single phonemes (*s', ł', š', 'γ, 'm, 'n, 'w, 'l, 'r, 'y*).[5]

Six vowel qualities are distinguished (*i, e, ɹ, a, o, u*), all of which except *e* occur long as well as short. The phonetic realization of *e* varies between [e] and [ɛ], sometimes approaching [æ], and English speakers can easily mistake a low allophone of *e* for a fronted variety of *a*. Syllables closed by *r, w,* and *y* are frequent. The rhotic vowel (*ɹ*) is a rhotacized schwa [ɚ], similar to the vowel of Midwestern American English *bird*. The prevalence of *ɹ* and of syllables closed by consonantal *r* gives Yurok speech an unusually rhotic character (e.g., *wɹ'yɹs* 'girl', *čirʔɹ'y* 'bear', *ʔe'γu'r* 'basket used in the Jump Dance', *kɹmɹtɹw* 'little finger', *pr'ypr'w* 'be sour'). In a small number of lexemes, *ɹ* can be substituted for a nonhigh vowel (*e, a, o*) to convey a diminutive meaning, sometimes in combination with consonant substitutions that have the same semantic force, e.g., *pontet* 'ashes' > *pɹnčɹč* 'dust' (Haas 1970; Berman 1986b; see also ¶4.12.1).

Although many Yurok noun stems resist analysis, including most body-part and kin terms, a good number are derived from morphologically complex verb stems, while others show an iterative infix; reduplication is also found, albeit infrequently. Nouns are inflected for pronominal possessor by a set of prefixes marking first, second, and third

TABLE 4
Yurok Phonemes (Robins 1958; Garrett, Blevins, and Conathan 2005)

Consonants							Vowels		
p	t		č	k	kʷ	ʔ	i / i:		u / u:
p'	t'		č'	k'	k'ʷ		e	ṛ / ṛ:	o / o:
	s	ł	š	(x)		h	a / a:		
	s'	ł'	š'						
				γ					
				'γ					
m	n								
'm	'n								
w	r	l	y						
'w	'r	'l	'y						

persons and—for inalienable body-part terms and a few others—an indefinite or unknown possessor (e.g., *'netepo:* 'my, our tree', *k'etepo:* 'your tree', *'wetepo:* 'his, her, their tree'; *'nelin* 'my, our eyes', *k'elin* 'your eyes', *'welin* 'his, her, their eyes', *melin* 'somebody's eyes'). Locative case is marked by a suffix, basically *-oł* (e.g., *lo:ɣin* 'fish-dam, weir', *lo:ɣinoł* 'at the fish-dam'). Nominal phrases are formed with two articles (*k'i* 'this', *ku* 'that'). In addition to noun stems, verbs conjugated in the attributive paradigm can be the heads of nominal phrases and can be inflected for possessor.

Verbs are inflected for subject, object, and voice in three modal paradigms (imperative, indicative, and subjunctive) by complex sets of suffixes whose morphological components are difficult to analyze (Robins 1958:30–80). A separate attributive paradigm produces forms that function syntactically as relative clauses or nouns. Tense and aspect categories are marked by independent preverbal particles. An iterative form of the verb stem, marking plurality, iteration or intensification of the basic lexical meaning, is derived by infixation or vowel lengthening (e.g., *kemol-* 'to steal' > *keɣemol-* 'to be a thief'; *čwin-* 'say, speak' > *čweɣin-* 'talk a lot, negotiate'; *hes-* 'think, intend' > *hi:s-* 'always think, be intending'). A repetitive form with similar meaning is derived from a number of verb stems by reduplication of the initial syllable (e.g., *tekʷs-* 'to cut' > *tekʷtekʷs-* 'to cut up into pieces') (Garrett 2001).

Although the morphological components are often fused and difficult to identify, Yurok verb stems appear to have a tripartite structure. An initial lexical element is followed by an optional "medial" element, generally classificatory nature, and a "final" element that is grammatical in function (e.g., *loʔoɣ-e'n-on-* 'be charred' < *loʔoɣ-* 'black' + *-e'n-* 'having to do with trees, sticks' + *-on*, stative; *tk-ohp-et* 'thicken (something liquid)' < *tk-* 'thick, sticky' + *-ohp-* 'having to do with water, liquid' + *-et*, transitive). All Yurok verb stems can occur in a "noninflected" form, without inflection or a final stem element. Noninflected verbs are used as the syntactic equivalents of inflected verbs under conditions that are not completely understood but that are probably defined by discourse structure and pragmatics (Garrett 2004).

3.3.4 Nomenclature

The Yurok for 'speak Yurok' is *sa:ʔaɣoč*, but this has rarely been used in an ethnographic context to designate either the language or its speakers (although note "Sa-ag-its" in the title of Azpell's 1870 vocabulary). The earliest formal documentation of the Yurok language, collected by George Gibbs in September 1851 during the McKee treaty expedition (Gibbs 1853b), was labeled simply "Weits-pek" after the village in which it was obtained. In subsequent decades the Yuroks were variously referred to as "Aliquah" or other versions of Yurok *ʔo:lekʷoh(ł)* 'people, human beings' (Crook 1852–1861); "Klamath (River) Indians" (Azpell 1870); or versions of *pulik-la:* 'downriver people', the term used by the Yuroks to distinguish themselves from the Karuk or *pečik-la:* 'upriver people' (Gibbs 1852, 1852–1853, and Curtin 1889b). By the 1870s the Karuk equivalents of *pulik* and *pečik, yuruk* and *karuk,* were in general use by local whites and were adopted by Powers (spelled "Euroc" and "Cahroc" in his early reporting, and "Yu´-rok" and "Ka´-rok" in 1877). Although Powell, following his rule of precedence, designated the language family "Weitspekan" in his 1891 classification, by the beginning of the twentieth century Powers's "Yurok" had gained wide acceptance, and it was adopted by Kroeber as the standard ethnographic and linguistic name.

Athabaskan (Na-Dene) Languages

3.4 The Pacific Coast Athabaskan Languages

The approximately forty languages of the Athabaskan family, although spread across western North America from Alaska to Mexico, are all closely related, reflecting a series of migrations out of a homeland in northwestern Canada within the last 1,000 to 1,500 years (Krauss and Golla 1981). The Athabaskan language family as a whole is more remotely related to two classificatory isolates along the southern Alaska coast, Eyak (now extinct) and Tlingit, the three

MAP 7. Pacific Coast Athabaskan within the Na-Dene phylum.

constituting the **Na-Dene** superfamily (Map 7), a loose relationship of uncertain time depth which a few scholars further extend to include Haida, the language of the Queen Charlotte Islands.[6] Na-Dene, in turn, has recently been demonstrated to have a historical connection to the Yeniseian languages of south-central Siberia (Vajda 2009), giving substance to at least one of the long-suspected links between Na-Dene and certain Eurasian languages. Besides Yeniseian these have included three other small groups of problematic affiliation, Burashaski, Caucasian, and Basque (Starostin 1989), as well as the vast Sino-Tibetan phylum (Sapir 1925b). With the exception of Haida, however, no relationship has been seriously proposed between the Na-Dene languages and any other American Indian language family or isolate. The evidence thus suggests that Athabaskan and the other Na-Dene languages are relatively recent additions to the linguistic diversity of the Western Hemisphere.

The eight Athabaskan languages that form the Pacific Coast subgroup were spoken in three noncontiguous enclaves along the Coast Range from southern Washington to northern California (Hoijer 1960). In geographical order these were **Lower Columbia Athabaskan,** a single language spoken, with little dialectal variation, by the Kwalhioqua of southwestern Washington and the Tlatskanai of northwestern Oregon; **Oregon Athabaskan,** a cluster of three shallowly diversified languages in southwestern Oregon and far northwestern California, including Upper Umpqua, Rogue River, and Chetco-Tolowa; and **California Athabaskan,** a slightly more diversified cluster of four languages in

Humboldt and Mendocino Counties, California, including Hupa-Chilula, Mattole–Bear River, Eel River, and Kato. While internally showing only modest differentiation, these three enclaves of Athabaskan speech are sharply distinguished from one another by extensive phonological, grammatical, and lexical differences and share few common innovations beyond a general tendency to simplify and restructure inherited features. Rather than being treated as a classificatory node, the Pacific Coast Athabaskan languages are probably best viewed as a geographically defined group of isolated and divergent forms of Athabaskan that, at most, partially share a common history of southward migration from Canada.[7] Some early episodes of this common history may also be shared with two other divergent classificatory nodes on the southern periphery of Canadian Athabaskan, the Ts'utina (Sarsi) language of southern Alberta and the Apachean subfamily of the Southwest.[8]

3.5 Lower Columbia Athabaskan (Kwalhioqua-Tlatskanai)

The Lower Columbia language, the only branch of Pacific Coast Athabaskan that was not in the California region as defined in this book, was formerly spoken near the mouth of the Columbia River by two small groups, one on the north side of the river and the other on the south side, in an area primarily dominated by speakers of Lower Chinook (Krauss 1990), and secondarily by the Coast Salish. Horatio Hale, who in 1841 was the first ethnographer to take note of these isolated Athabaskans, wrote that neither of the groups "comprise more than a hundred individuals. . . . They build no permanent habitations, but wander in the woods, subsisting on game, berries, and roots. As might be expected, they are somewhat more bold and hardy than the tribes on the river and coast, and, at the same time, more wild and savage" (Hale 1846:204). The group on the northern side of the Columbia, the **Kwalhioqua** (kʷəlxióḱʷa [?]), was further subdivided into an upland band on the prairies at the headwaters of the Chehalis and Willopah Rivers (called *šuwal* by their Salishan neighbors) and a band lower down the Willopah. The group on the south side of the Columbia, the **Tlatskanai** (ɫáts'kənəy [?]), lived in the mountains northwest of Portland (present-day Clatskanie County). There were some minor dialectal differences between Kwalhioqua and Tlatskanai, and between the speech of the upstream and downstream subgroups of the Kwalhioqua, but there is little doubt that all these were shallowly differentiated varieties of the same language. This similarity probably indicates that the intrusion of Athabaskans into this area had occurred only a few generations earlier. Hale (1846:204) notes that the groups kept in touch with one another across the Columbia, and that "a connexion of some kind" apparently also existed between the Tlatskanai and the Upper Umpqua, 150 miles to the south.

The history of the documentation of Lower Columbia Athabaskan is surprisingly complex, although much of it consists of short word lists of less-than-adequate phonetic accuracy. The earliest, and in some ways the best, attestation is by Horatio Hale, who collected a vocabulary of 276 words from both Kwalhioqua and Tlatskanai speakers in 1841 (Hale 1846:569–629). Other early or amateur vocabularies were collected by Gibbs (1856), Anderson (1857), and Wickersham (1888). Later, more professional, collections were made by Boas (1895:588–592), Teit (1910), Frachtenberg (1910), and Myers (in Curtis 1907–1930, vol. 9:199–200). The last native speakers died not long after 1910, but Melville Jacobs and J. P. Harrington were able to find nonnative speakers who knew a few words as late as the 1940s (Mills 1981:47–54).

An extensive compilation of the data on Lower Columbia was published by Boas and Goddard in 1924, but it was marred by unreliable editing. Krauss (1976) made a thorough study of all of the surviving documentation and systematically reconstituted the phonology and (so far as it is attested) the nominal and verbal morphology. Although this study remains unpublished, it is available in the Alaska Native Language Center Archives.

3.6 Oregon Athabaskan Languages

The Oregon Athabaskan languages were spoken in five contiguous but geographically distinct areas: (1) the upper valley of the Umpqua River in the vicinity of modern Roseburg; (2) the upper valley of the Coquille River; (3) parts of the Rogue River valley west and south of Grants Pass, along Applegate River and Galice Creek, and probably also along the Illinois River; (4) the lower Rogue River from the Illinois River to the ocean, together with the coast between Cape Blanco on the north and Cape Ferrelo on the south; and (5) the coastal area south of Cape Ferrelo, from Brookings, Oregon, to Crescent City, California (Map 8). Different varieties of Oregon Athabaskan were spoken in each of these areas, but only at the geographical extremes— *Upper Umpqua* in the north and *Chetco-Tolowa* in the south—were they distinct enough from adjacent Athabaskan varieties to be considered separate languages (Table 5). Between these the Upper Coquille, Galice-Applegate, and Lower Rogue River dialects (the latter two with several local varieties) formed a dialect network, *Rogue River Athabaskan,* whose diversity may be compared to the traditional rural dialects of England. The time depth of the Rogue River dialects is a few hundred years; the separation between them and Upper Umpqua or Chetco-Tolowa cannot be older than nine hundred or a thousand years.

The events of the Rogue River War of 1855–1856 led to the forced removal of the entire Indian population of southwestern Oregon—primarily the Oregon Athabaskans, but also the Takelma—to two reservations in northwestern Oregon, at Siletz and Grand Ronde (Beckham 1971; Douthit 2002). This resettlement of a large and diverse population had social and linguistic consequences that, while perhaps milder, were not dissimilar to those that followed on the

TABLE 5
Oregon Athabaskan Languages, Dialects,
and Attested Local Varieties

Upper Umpqua language

Rogue River dialect network

    Upper Coquille dialect

    Lower Rogue River dialect

        Tututni (Joshua)

        Mikwanutni

        Chasta Costa

        Euchre Creek

        Sixes

        Pistol River

    Upper Rogue River (Galice-Applegate) dialect

        Applegate River (Dakobe)

        Galice Creek (Taldash)

        Nabiltse (?)

Chetco-Tolowa language

missionization of Indian groups in California. Certainly it needs to be borne in mind that, except for Upper Umpqua and the Tolowa variety of Chetco-Tolowa, nearly all the information that is preserved on Oregon Athabaskan languages comes from individuals who spent much, if not all, of their lives on government land far from their ancestral territory. Upper Umpqua is an exception only because the documentation of this long-extinct language commenced in the early 1840s, more than a decade before the Rogue River War, after which they too were resettled on the Grand Ronde Reservation northeast of Siletz. Of the speakers of Oregon Athabaskan in the 1850s, only the Tolowa, who had the (qualified) good fortune to live south of the California border, were able to preserve something of their original speech community.

3.6.1 Upper Umpqua

Almost nothing is known about the aboriginal culture of the Athabaskans of the Umpqua River drainage. With the exception of the Cow Creek area in the south, which belonged to the Takelma, their original territory apparently included the entire Umpqua River valley above the head of tidewater in the vicinity of Scottsburg, about fifteen miles from the coast. The lower course of the river belonged to a Siuslaw-speaking group, usually known as the Lower Umpqua, with whom the Athabaskans (the "Upper Umpqua") traded and occasionally intermarried. They were also in sporadic contact with the Kalapuya to the north,

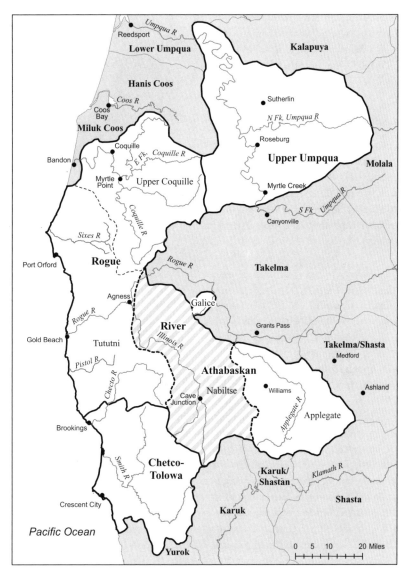

MAP 8. Oregon Athabaskan languages and dialects.

the Hanis Coos and Upper Coquille Athabaskans to the southwest, and the Takelma to the south. Their principal settlements were along the south fork of the Umpqua in the Roseburg area.

The surviving documentation of the Upper Umpqua language indicates that it possessed a number of distinctive lexical and phonological features that set it apart from all other varieties of Oregon Athabaskan. Even speakers of Upper Coquille, living only a few dozen miles closer to the coast, could understand Upper Umpqua only with difficulty (Seaburg 1994:232). In many of these points of difference, especially in vocabulary, Upper Umpqua tends to preserve older forms and thus tends to bear a superficially closer resemblance to the California Athabaskan languages than do the Rogue River dialects or Chetco-Tolowa.

Although the documentation of Upper Umpqua began only a few years after the establishment of a fur-trading post

on the Umpqua River in 1832, the corpus is scanty and largely confined to nineteenth-century vocabulary lists, of which the two earliest are the most substantial. The first was collected, probably in 1840, by Dr. William F. Tolmie, a Hudson's Bay Company employee (Scouler 1841:215–251; A. Grant 1993). The second was one of the survey vocabularies that Horatio Hale, "ethnologist and philologist" of the Wilkes Expedition (¶2.4.3), collected in the Oregon Country in 1841–1842 (Hale 1846:570 629). Both vocabularies were published not long after they were obtained, and until the first appearance of material on Navajo around 1850 they provided the only widely available data on the Athabaskan languages south of Canada. Important later collections (all of which remain unpublished) were made by Milhau (1856), Barnhardt (1859), Gatschet (1877b), and E. Jacobs and Jacobs (ca. 1935). The last known speaker of the language, John Warren, was interviewed by J. P. Harrington in 1940.

Although Harrington's transcriptions are undoubtedly the most accurate we shall ever possess for Upper Umpqua, he spent most of his time with Warren futilely attempting to retrieve information on Lower Columbia Athabaskan (Mills 1981:49).

3.6.2 Rogue River Athabaskan

Nine varieties of Rogue River Athabaskan are documented. These can be grouped into three regional dialects, Upper Coquille, Lower Rogue, and Galice-Applegate. The differences among these dialects are mainly lexical, although the attested varieties of the Galice-Applegate dialect show minor phonological differences both from the other Rogue River dialects and from each other.

UPPER COQUILLE

The northern dialect, **Upper Coquille** (*miši-kʷʰət-meʔ-tən̩e* 'Mishi creek people'), was spoken in a tribelet or cluster of tribelets on the Coquille River and its tributaries in the densely forested and swampy area around Myrtle Point (Youst and Seaburg 2002: Appendix 2). Athabaskan speech prevailed downstream to the junction of Beaver Slough, about four miles beyond the present town of Coquille City. The lowermost few miles of the Coquille River, as well as the coast north of the Coos-Curry county line, was in Miluk Coos territory, although the ethnic and linguistic status of this area may have been in flux; the people of *xʷeštən*, about six miles upriver from the coast at Bandon, were said to speak a variety of Lower Rogue River Athabaskan (R. Hall 1992; Youst and Seaburg 2002:268–270). To the east, the Upper Coquille were in contact with the Upper Umpqua, but as already noted the speech of the two groups differed to such a degree that mutual intelligibility was difficult.[9] By contrast, Upper Coquille seems to have been very similar to the Lower Rogue River varieties that were spoken to the south, although some uncertainty surrounds this issue. Upper Coquille is mainly attested in materials from a single individual, Coquelle Thompson (ca.1848–1946), who worked with several linguists and anthropologists, beginning with J. Owen Dorsey in 1884 (Youst and Seaburg 2002). Thompson was a lifelong resident of Siletz, and Dorsey thought it possible that his speech had been influenced by the Lower Rogue River dialect that served as the lingua franca in the reservation community. However, "the pure Coquelle" that he subsequently collected from an older speaker did not appreciably differ from what he obtained from Thompson (Dorsey 1884e; Seaburg 1994:67).

GALICE-APPLEGATE

The eastern dialect of Rogue River Athabaskan, Galice-Applegate, was spoken in at least two distinct varieties in the lower part of the inland valley of the Rogue, near Grants Pass. Although lexically very similar to the Lower Rogue

FIGURE 36. Hoxie Simmons, last speaker of the Galice Creek dialect of Rogue River Athabaskan. Photograph by Victor Golla, 1962.

River dialect, it is characterized by several phonological innovations, the most distinctive of which is the denasalization of *m* and *n* to the voiced stops *b* and *d*, respectively. Our knowledge of the variety spoken by the Applegate River tribelet, **Dakobe** (*daʔkʰoh-beʔ),* comes to us almost entirely through the vocabularies collected by Hazen (1857) and Dorsey (1884b), although Harrington recorded a few words remembered by a Galice speaker (Mills 1981:76–80). The Galice Creek tribelet variety, **Taldash** (*tʰaːldaš*), by contrast, is quite well documented, thanks to the work of Melville Jacobs in 1935–1939 and Harry Hoijer in 1956 with the last surviving speaker, Hoxie Simmons (Hoijer 1966, 1973; M. Jacobs 1968). An especially valuable part of this attestation is Jacobs's large collection of narrative texts (Seaburg 1982:16). J. P. Harrington also worked briefly with Simmons in 1940 (Mills 1981:76–77). There is also an earlier vocabulary from Dorsey (1884c), as well as mixed ethnographic and linguistic materials collected by Goddard around 1903–1904 (Seaburg 1982:16).

It was George Gibbs's belief that the short vocabulary of a language called **Nabiltse** that he collected "from a young Indian at the upper ferry on the Klamath" during the McKee Expedition (Gibbs 1851–1852, 1853c) was an attestation of the Applegate variety (see his letter in Hazen 1857). J. Owen Dorsey's judgment, however, was that the Nabiltse vocabulary represented a separate unidentified Athabaskan language (Dorsey 1886). A close inspection of the data in the context of what is now known of Oregon Athabaskan variation shows Gibbs to have been more nearly correct. Nabiltse appears to be a conservative variety of the inland dialect of Rogue River Athabaskan, closer to Applegate than to Galice but with sufficient differences from both to indicate that it was spoken by a separate group. Where this group was located can only be guessed; the name "Nabiltse" is not otherwise attested. My own speculation is that they lived in the Illinois River valley to the southwest of the Applegate River. Although Dorsey identified this as Takelma territory, his evidence is equivocal. It is equally likely to have been occupied by Athabaskan speakers linked to the Galice and Applegate tribelets (Gray 1987:20–24).[10]

LOWER ROGUE RIVER

All of the other known varieties of Rogue River Athabaskan belong to the **Lower Rogue River** dialect cluster, sometimes referred to collectively as "Tututni" (see Miller and Seaburg 1990:580), although that term is used here in a more restricted sense (see the next paragraph). Varieties belonging to the Lower Rogue River dialect were spoken in the numerous village communities or tribelets that occupied the last twenty miles of the Rogue River—the famous "Mail Boat" route—between Agness and Gold Beach, as well as a short stretch of the coast both north and south of the river mouth. Six distinct varieties are attested:

Joshua (from *yəšuči* 'river-mouth') or **Tututni** (in the narrow sense), the speech of the lowermost tribelet on the Rogue River, centering on the village of Dututun (*tutʰu-tən* 'freshwater lagoon-place') located on the north bank a short distance upstream from Wedderburn. Joshua-Tututni territory included the present site of Gold Beach and extended south along the coast to Cape Sebastian.

Mikwanutni, the variety spoken in and around the major village of Mikwanudun (*mikʷʼənu-tən* 'white clover-place'), about twelve miles upstream on the Rogue from Dutudun.

Chasta Costa (*šista kʷʼəsta*, etymology unclear; Sapir 1914:274), the variety associated with tribelet located at the confluence of Illinois River and Rogue River about twenty miles upstream from Dutudun, near the present-day town of Agness. Dorsey (1890:228) locates the principal Chasta Costa village on the Rogue well above the Illinois River, but according to Sapir (1907a:253, n. 2) they occupied the river no farther east than Leaf Creek. Upstream from here the Rogue flows through a narrow canyon renowned for its dangerous rapids, a barrier to communication that marked the boundary between the Lower Rogue River varieties and the Galice-Applegate varieties of the interior.

Euchre Creek (from *yuki* or *yukʷʼi* 'mouth of the stream'), the speech of the tribelet at the mouth of Euchre Creek, on the coast about nine miles north of the Rogue River.

Sixes (from the name of the Sixes River, *səkʷe* 'wide open'), the variety spoken on the coast from Port Orford to Sixes River, twenty-five miles north of the Rogue River. Their territory extended north a few miles past Cape Blanco, where it adjoined Miluk Coos territory.

Pistol River (*naltʰəne-təne*, etymology uncertain), the variety of a tribelet on the coast south of Cape Sebastian. Spoken in an isolated coastal river valley midway between the Lower Rogue River and Chetco-Tolowa dialect areas, the Pistol River variety might be expected to be transitional between the two, but the data, although sparse, show it to have been very similar to the Joshua-Tututni variety of Lower Rogue River, and quite distinct from Chetco-Tolowa.

Much of our knowledge of the internal diversity of Lower Rogue River Athabaskan is derived from a linguistic survey that J. Owen Dorsey, working for the Bureau of American Ethnology, carried out on the Siletz Reservation in 1884 (see Dorsey 1890). Although nearly thirty years had passed since the resettlement of the Lower Rogue River Indians at Siletz, Dorsey found many of the old intervillage linguistic distinctions still maintained and was able to collect extensive parallel vocabularies (in the "Powell schedules" format[11]) of Joshua-Tututni (1884h–1884k), Mikwanutni (1884g), Chasta Costa (1884d), Euchre Creek (1884l), Sixes (1884m), and Pistol River (1884n). A slightly earlier vocabulary by Everett (1882) of "Tu-u-tene," also in the Powell schedules, apparently documents the Joshua-Tututni variety. The twentieth century saw an important attestation of the Chasta Costa variety by Sapir (1914) and significant collections of data by Harrington from speakers of Chasta Costa and Joshua-Tututni (Mills 1981:69–77), and by Elizabeth Jacobs and myself (on separate occasions, about thirty years apart) from Ida Bensell, a speaker of the Euchre Creek variety and the last fluent speaker of any Oregon Athabaskan dialect other than Tolowa (Seaburg 1982:17; Golla 1976). A Lower Rogue River dictionary that I compiled from the data collected by Jacobs and myself from Mrs. Bensell (Golla n.d.) is being used in revitalization efforts, and an expanded version is being readied for publication in 2012. Extensive tape recordings were made of the then-surviving speakers of Rogue River Athabaskan by Joe E. Pierce in the early 1960s (Pierce 196263; Pierce and Ryherd 1964). These are now in the archives of Oregon State University in Corvallis.

FIGURE 37. Elizabeth (Bess) Jacobs and Melville Jacobs. Courtesy of William Seaburg.

3.6.3 Chetco-Tolowa

Chetco-Tolowa was spoken in two shallowly differentiated local varieties. **Chetco** was associated with a small area around the mouth of the Chetco River at Brookings, Oregon, from Cape Ferrelo on the north to the Winchuck River at the California-Oregon state line on the south. **Tolowa** was spoken in the far northwestern corner of California, principally along the lower Smith River and the shores of Lake Earl (a large ocean lagoon south of Smith River), as well as along the coast in the Point St. George and Crescent City areas. The differences between the two dialects as attested in the nineteenth and twentieth centuries may to some extent reflect the social disruption caused by the removal of most of the Chetco population to northwestern Oregon following the Rogue River War of 1855–1856.

A few miles southeast of Crescent City the Tolowa adjoined the Yurok, with whom they traded and intermarried, although the coastline here is rocky and densely forested and most travel had to be in oceangoing canoes. The Tolowa also had close ties to the Karuk, whose Klamath River territory they reached using trails across the Siskiyou Mountains (Waterman 1925:528). They appear as well to have been in fairly close contact with the Takelma and the Galice-Applegate Athabaskans in the interior valleys to the northeast.

Along the coast to the north, the linguistic boundary between Chetco-Tolowa and the Rogue River dialect complex lay between Cape Ferrelo and Pistol River, and was surprisingly abrupt, indicating that contacts across this boundary were limited. (That the Chetco River marks the northern boundary of the thick forests of coast redwood, *Sequoia sempervirens*, may not be accidental.) Chetco-Tolowa has undergone a number of unique phonological and morphological restructurings (e.g., Collins 1989; Givón and Bommelyn 2000), which, while relatively superficial and apparently recent, are significant enough to impede communication with speakers of any of the adjoining Rogue River dialects.[12] Phonological innovations include the secondary lengthening of schwa in open syllables, a complex pitch accent system, and the strong palatalization and rhoticism of what elsewere in Oregon Athabaskan is a set of slightly retroflexed apicals. Chetco-Tolowa also has a number of apparent loanwords from non-Athabaskan languages (Conathan 2004). Influence from a substratal language, most likely Yurok or a closely related extinct Algic language, may account for some of these distinctive traits, while others may be the result of rapid linguistic evolution in relative isolation from the other Oregon Athabaskans.

Chetco-Tolowa is the best-documented variety of Oregon Athabaskan, although what purports to be the earliest attestation—the vocabulary of "Tah-le-wah" collected by Gibbs in 1851 from a Sregon Yurok (Gibbs 1853b, 1853c:422)—is in fact almost entirely a documentation of Yurok. Much of the earlier material on Chetco-Tolowa reflects the Chetco variety and was obtained in the displaced reservation communities at Siletz and Grand Ronde by J. Owen Dorsey (1884f, 1884o), J. P. Harrington (Mills 1981:69–76), and Elizabeth Jacobs (1968, 1977; cf. Seaburg 1982:15). The Tolowa speech community that remained in situ at Smith River in northwest California was extensively documented by P. E. Goddard (1902–1903, 1902–1922b no. 7), Merriam (Appendix A: A-1a), and Jane Bright (1964), and the survival of a few speakers and semispeakers allowed at least limited documentary work to continue there as late as 1990 (cf. Seaburg 1976–1982; Collins 1985, 1989). Especially notable is the work of Loren Bommelyn, himself a Smith River Tolowa, who acquired second-language fluency through apprenticeship to the last first-language speakers and compiled a learner's dictionary and other pedagogical materials (Bommelyn 1989, 1997). Much of Bommelyn's more recent work draws on his own acquired competence and thus reflects what may more accurately be called "New Tolowa." Some of this work has been carried out in collaboration with Tom Givón, with whom he studied at the University of Oregon (Bommelyn and Givón 1998; Givón and Bommelyn 2000).

3.6.4 Survival

With the exception of two or three elderly rememberers of Tolowa at Smith River or of Lower Rogue River at Siletz, no native speaker of any Oregon Athabaskan variety survives in 2010. The last fully fluent first-language speakers of Chetco-Tolowa and Rogue River died before 1990; the last person to have even partial fluency in Upper Umpqua died around 1945. Since 1980 a number of learners have acquired some degree of second-language fluency in Tolowa, and to a lesser extent in Lower Rogue River, through language classes and other educational initiatives. Much of the success of the Tolowa language revival is due to Loren Bommelyn, and the revitalization effort he spearheads has a broad cultural and religious base (Bommelyn 1995; Collins 1998). For Lower Rogue River, in addition to tribally sponsored initiatives at Siletz, a number of Rogue River Athabaskan descendants living in southern Oregon have held summer immersion camps in recent years, and classes have been held at Lane Community College in Eugene.

3.6.5 Linguistic Structure

Proto–Oregon Athabaskan can be reconstructed with five series of stops and affricates (*t, c, ç, č, k*), each possessing a plain and a glottalized member (*c* is a dental-alveolar affricate [ts]~[tθ]; *ç* is a retroflex affricate [tṣ]; and *č* is a palatal affricate [tʃ]). The dental-alevolar stop series and the palatal affricate series further distinguished an aspirated member (*tʰ, čʰ*). The *c, ç, č,* and *k* series were paired with fricatives that occurred both voiceless (*s, ṣ, š, x*) and voiced (*z, ẓ, ž, γ*). There was also a lateral fricative (*ł*) which was paired with a glottalized lateral affricate (*ƛ'*), but no corresponding plain or aspirated lateral affricate existed.

There were two nasals (*m, n*), three approximants (*l, w, y*), and two laryngeals (*h, ʔ*).

This system was modified and simplified in various ways during the diversification of the Oregon subfamily (Table 6). The plain members of both the *c* and *ç* series merged with the corresponding fricatives (*s, ṣ*) in Chetco-Tolowa and in all Rogue River varieties except Applegate and Nabiltse. In Applegate and Nabiltse, and also in Upper Umpqua, this merger appears to have been under way but was not complete at the time these varieties became moribund in the late nineteenth century. Phonetically, *s* and *c'* have a tendency to be fronted to interdental position ([θ] and [tθ']) in some varieties of the Lower Rogue River dialect (most notably Chasta Costa), while in Chetco-Tolowa *ṣ* and *ç'*, which elsewhere have an apical retroflex articulation, are palatalized and strongly r-colored ([ʃʳ] and [tʃʳ']). The full set of voiceless and voiced fricatives was preserved only in Upper Umpqua; in the other languages the contrasts between *s* and *z*, between *ṣ* and *ẓ*, and between *š* and *ž* were lost. In Chetco-Tolowa *ƛ'* merges with *t'*. In the eastern dialect of Rogue River (Galice, Applegate, and Nabiltse) the nasals are denasalized in many phonetic environments to voiced stops [b, d], or sometimes to prenasalized stops [ᵐb, ⁿd]. In addition, all the languages have a plain bilabial stop (*p*) in a few marginal words, most of them probably borrowed from adjacent non-Athabaskan languages. A secondary labiovelar series (*kʷ*) has developed as the result of several phonological processes., as well as a labialized glottal stop [ʔʷ] (or glottalized labial approximant [w']).

Four full vowels can be reconstructed (*i, e, a, u*), occurring both short and long, and one reduced vowel (*ə*) that is always short. Length contrasts in full vowels are predictable from syllable structure in most if not all dialects. A velar stop or fricative that opens or closes a closed syllable with *u* is replaced in all languages by the corresponding labiovelar, and the *u* is reduced to *ə* (e.g., *xus > xʷəs, tuk > təkʷ*). In Chetco-Tolowa, when *ə* occurs in an open syllable, it becomes a (phonetically long) full vowel, either *e* or *a* (the choice determined by the phonetic environment): for example, *mən? 'house', ši-šme(:)ne? 'my house'*. In Chetco-Tolowa and Rogue River, a full vowel in a syllable closed with a nasal is nasalized and the nasal lost; in the Lower Rogue and Upper Coquille dialects of Rogue River the resulting vowel also loses its distinctive nasalization. In many Rogue River varieties a full vowel in a syllable closed by a laryngeal (either *h* or *ʔ*) is marked by a falling pitch. A pitch accent has also developed in Chetco-Tolowa in similar if not identical circumstances.

Oregon Athabaskan morphology deviates in several minor but distinctive ways from the general Pacific Coast Athabaskan pattern shared with the California group. In nouns, the possessive prefixes tend to be phonologically reduced. The first and second person singular possessors are nonsyllabic *š-* and *n-*, respectively, resulting in word-initial consonant clusters that are morphologically resyllabified by attaching a proclitic independent pronoun (e.g., Lower

Rogue River *ši-škaneʔ* 'my arm', *ši-šʔat* 'his wife', *ni-ntaʔ* 'your mouth'). In the third person, the original phonetic form of the possessor, nonsyllabic *w-*, is preserved only in Upper Umpqua and in Galice, and only before certain stem-initial consonants. Otherwise, it is realized as *m-* before a stem-initial vowel (Lower Rogue River *mineʔ* 'his, her back, spine') and as the labialization of a stem-initial velar or laryngeal (*kʷaneʔ* 'his, her arm', *ʔʷat* 'his wife'), but is entirely lost before other stem-initial consonants (*laʔ* 'his, her hand', *taʔ* 'his, her mouth'). The indefinite possessor is marked by syllabic *xo-* before a consonant (*xotaʔ* 'someone's mouth'), *xʷ-* before a vowel (*xʷineʔ* 'someone's back'). A thematic (specific, understood) possessor is marked by syllabic *č'ə-*. The same prefix set is used to mark verbal objects, except for the third person (which, as elsewhere in Athabaskan, is unmarked, or marked by *y-* when the subject is also third person). The thematic object is reduced to a phonemic glottal stop (represented phonetically by falling pitch and glottal constriction) when following a prefix ending in a full vowel (e.g., **tʰa-č'ə-ɣi-š-ʔa* 'I set a net', lit. 'I put a specific object into the water' > *tʰaʔyišʔa*).

In verbs, the phonological leveling that has simplified stem alternation patterns generally in Pacific Coast Athabaskan has made further inroads in Oregon, with the alternation of reduced and full stem vowels automatically conditioned by phonological rules. However, the glottalization of stems is fully preserved in Ida Bensell's Lower Rogue River (and probably in all other Oregon varieties if we had sufficiently precise transcriptions) as subtle glottal constriction and falling pitch, and alternations between voiceless and voiced fricative finals are preserved to an extent in Upper Umpqua. Many tense-aspect categories that are marked in California Athabaskan and elsewhere by combinations of a mode-aspect prefix and a distinctive stem shape are marked in Oregon Athabaskan by enclitics. Dual number in both subject and object is regularly marked (by the prefix *xə-*), and several intransitive verbs of motion have a distinct suppletive stem for the dual category as well as for the plural (*-t'uh* 'one person swims', *-l-ʔ eɬ* 'two people swim', *-l-xat* 'three or more people swim').

TABLE 6

Lower Rogue River Athabaskan Phonemes (Golla 1976)

Consonants											Vowels	
p	t				č	k	(kʷ)	ʔ	(ʔʷ)		i	u
	tʰ				čʰ							ə
	t'	ƛ'	c'	ç'	č'	k'	(k'ʷ)				e	a
	ɬ	s	ṣ	š	x	(xʷ)	h					
						γ	(γʷ)					
m	n											
w	l			y								

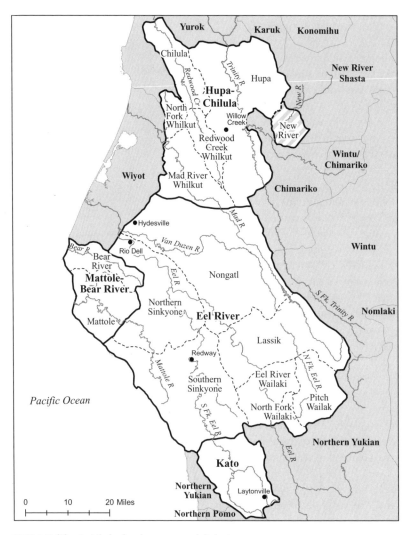

MAP 9. California Athabaskan languages and dialects.

3.7 California Athabaskan Languages

The California Athabaskan languages were spoken in northwestern California between Yuki territory in Round Valley and Yurok and Wiyot territory along the Klamath River and Humboldt Bay, including all or most of the drainage of the Mattole River, the Eel River, the Van Duzen River, the upper Mad River, and Redwood Creek, as well as the lowermost twenty miles of the Trinity River (Map 9). *Hupa-Chilula* in the north, *Kato* in the south, and *Mattole–Bear River* on the coast near Cape Mendocino are well demarcated languages with little internal diversity. The *Eel River* dialects constituted a network that can be considered a fourth language (Table 7).

The most divergent language of the group is Hupa-Chilula, which could not be understood by any other California Athabaskans. Kato, although spoken at the headwaters of the South Fork of the Eel, has a number of specialized lexical and grammatical features that made intercommunication with other Eel River speakers difficult. Mattole–Bear River speakers and Eel River speakers could make themselves understood to

one another, but the differences were substantial. In general, California Athabaskan differentiation can be compared to the continuum of Dutch and German local dialects along the Rhine from Holland to Switzerland, with Hupa-Chilula analogous to Amsterdam Dutch and Kato to the Swiss German of Zürich. A time depth of nine hundred to a thousand years seems likely.

The ethnogeography of the California Athabaskan area was surveyed by Baumhoff (1958), who utilized the detailed toponymic data collected for most of the groups by Merriam, supplementing this with data from Pliny Goddard's publications and field notes.

3.7.1 Hupa-Chilula

The Hupa-Chilula language had two shallowly differentiated local dialects: Hupa (including New River Hupa) and Chilula-Whilkut.

Hupa (from Yurok *hup'o* 'Hoopa Valley') was spoken in about a dozen villages along the lower Trinity River, from the lower South Fork, near Salyer, to the canyon at the north end of Hoopa Valley (P. Goddard 1903a). The largest and

TABLE 7
California Athabaskan Languages and Attested Dialects or Local Varieties

Hupa-Chilula language
  Hupa
  Chilula-Whilkut
Mattole–Bear River language
  Mattole
  Bear River
Eel River dialect network
  Sinkyone (South Fork)
  Nongatl (Van Duzen)
  Lassik (Lower Main Eel)
  Wailaki (Upper Main Eel)
Kato language

most important of these were Ɫe:lding or "Hleldin" (ɫe:ltiŋ 'confluence place') at the mouth of South Fork, Ta'k'miɫding or "Hostler Ranch" (tʰaʔḳ'imiɫtiŋ 'acorn cooking place') in the northern half of Hoopa Valley, and Me'dilding or "Matilton" (meʔtiltiŋ 'canoe place') in the southern half of the valley. These were the central villages of three tribelet-like groups, the ɫe:lxʷe: 'confluence people', tʰaʔḳ'imiɫxʷe: 'acorn cooking people', and meʔtilxʷe: 'canoe people', respectively (Baumhoff 1958:209–215). These regional divisions had mainly ceremonial functions, however, and no territorial rights or subdialect distinctions existed.[13]

Both on the main Trinity and on South Fork, the upstream boundary of Hupa territory abutted on Chimariko territory. On the main Trinity the boundary was about four miles above Ɫe:lding, while on South Fork it lay about ten miles upstream, at the upper end of an uninhabited canyon. Hupa was widely spoken as a second language in the Chimariko villages along the Trinity River. It was also spoken along New River, a small stream that joins the Trinity from the north opposite Burnt Ranch, about fifteen miles upstream from Ɫe:lding. At the time of contact in 1850 the upland valley of New River, around Denny—the territory of the northernmost of the Chimariko subgroups, the Chimalakwe or New River Chimariko (¶3.10.1)—was evidently being incorporated into Hupa territory. The population of this area was almost completely bilingual, with Hupa the dominant language (a "conquest" vividly described by Powers 1877:72, 92). Documentation of New River Hupa speech is scant, but there is no indication it was significantly distinct from the remainder of Hupa.

Non-Hupa varieties of Hupa-Chilula were spoken by several tribelets between Hoopa Valley and the Wiyot and Yurok settlements on the coast. Of these only the Chilula dialect (from Yurok č'ilu-la 'Bald Hills people') is adequately described (Goddard 1914b). The villages of the Chilula lay along lower Redwood Creek, on the grassy slopes of the "Bald Hills" to the east of the heavily forested stream. As their ethnographic designation implies, they seem to have been in closer contact with the Yurok along the Klamath than with the Hupa, who considered them hillbillies. The Hupa-Chilula speakers who lived along Redwood Creek upstream from the Chilula are somewhat inaccurately referred to in the ethnographic literature as the "Whilkut." The term is taken from xʷiyɫq'it, which is the Hupa name for the whole of Redwood Creek canyon, including Chilula territory (the usual Hupa name for the Chilula was xʷiyɫq'it-xʷe: 'Redwood Creek people'). Merriam calls the Whilkut living on upper Redwood Creek the "Kloki Whilkut" (presumably ƛ'o:q'i-xiyɫq'it 'prairie Whilkut'). Goddard notes that same dialect was also spoken further west, along the middle course of the Mad River and its tributaries, Maple Creek and Boulder Creek (Goddard 1914a). Merriam recorded the name of the Mad River "Whilkut" tribelet as "Ma-we-nok" (probably me:w-yinaq 'underneath it (i.e., under a large rock or cliff) upstream'; Baumhoff 1958:201–209). Although poorly attested, some small degree of varietal differentiation seems to have characterized the speech of these local groups (Goddard 1914b:291).

To the north, Hupa and Chilula territory adjoined Yurok territory, and to the northeast the Hupa were in frequent contact with the Karuk. The Hupa, and to a lesser extent the Chilula, were core participants in a close-knit intertribal culture that centered on the Yurok and Karuk and peripherally included the Tolowa and Wiyot (Kroeber 1925:5–8, 910–912; Kroeber and Gifford 1949). These close social and ceremonial ties, reinforced by frequent intergroup marriage, produced a sharp awareness of language differences and a moderate degree of multilingualism. In these circumstances it is surprising how few of the distinctive phonological, lexical, or grammatical features of Hupa-Chilula can be attributed to direct Yurok or Karuk influence (O'Neill 2001, 2008; Conathan 2004). Lexical borrowings are almost nonexistent, and the grammatical convergences that can be identified (for example, in directional systems) are all relatively superficial. In phonology, the most that can be said is that a language with some of the phonological properties of Karuk or Wiyot—but not of Yurok—seems to have played a role in a few distinctive Hupa-Chilula sound shifts, most notably the labialization seen in *γ > w and *š > W (Bauman and Silver 1975). This influence was probably early and substratal, however, and not due to contact in recent generations. There also appears to be a small amount of Chimariko substratal influence, including a handful of Hupa-Chilula place-names that are calques on their Chimariko counterparts.[14]

Hupa-Chilula has been extensively documented, beginning with the vocabulary collected by George Gibbs in 1851, during the McKee Expedition, and first published in Schoolcraft (Gibbs 1853b). A second, longer, vocabulary was obtained by Gibbs when he returned to the region the

FIGURE 38. Sam Brown (*left*), Edward Sapir's principal Hupa consultant in 1927, photographed in 1907 with his brother Oscar Brown, the source of several of Pliny Earle Goddard's *Hupa Texts* (1904). Courtesy of the Hearst Museum of Anthropology and the Regents of UC (15-3751).

following year (Gibbs 1852). Jeremiah Curtin collected a full BAE survey list and a text (1888–1889c to 1888–1889e) during an extended stay in Hoopa Valley in the winter of 1888–1889, when he apparently learned to speak the language. The most valuable materials collected during the nineteenth and early twentith centuries come from the anthropologist Pliny Earle Goddard, who lived in Hoopa Valley as an interdenominational missionary from 1897 to 1900. Goddard published two grammars (1905, 1911) and a large collection of traditional narrative texts (1904).[15]

In the summer of 1927, Edward Sapir carried out a field study of Hupa, the full results of which were published only in the last decade, edited and annotated by myself (Sapir and Golla 2001). I studied Hupa in the field in 1962–1965 and made it the focus of my dissertation (1970); I have also published a grammatical sketch (1996a) and a pedagogical dictionary (1996b). My student Sean O'Neill worked with some of the last fluent speakers in 1997–2001 and incorporated extensive Hupa data into his dissertation, which is a comparative semantic study of Hupa, Karuk, and Yurok (O'Neill 2001; see also O'Neill 2006, 2008). More narrowly focused investigations have been carried out by Jocelyn Ahlers on Hupa metaphorical speech (1999) and Matthew Gordon on Hupa phonetics (Gordon 1996, 2001; Gordon and Luna 2004).

In 2005 the Survey of California and Other Indian Languages, University of California, Berkeley, initiated a collaborative project to extend and organize the documentation of Hupa, involving extensive new fieldwork (made feasible by the reappearance of a fluent speaker who had been living in Oregon for several decades) and the digitization of the extant corpus. An on-line dictionary is in preparation.

There is some documentation of the dialect variation within Hupa-Chilula in Goddard (1901–1908, 1902–1907,

1914b) and in vocabularies collected by Merriam (Appendix A: A-1b, A-1d). New River Hupa is sporadically attested by Harrington in his transcription of the speech of Saxy Kidd, a multilingual native of the New River area (Mills 1985:49–55, 63–80).

Hupa is the heritage language both of the Hoopa Valley Tribe and of the Chimariko descendants who have organized as the (not yet federally acknowledged) Tsnungwe Tribe. In 2010, in addition to the fluent native speaker mentioned previously, in her mid-seventies, Hupa-Chilula had a rapidly dwindling number of less fluent native speakers (none younger than seventy). There were also about a dozen second-language speakers with conversational competence and a larger number with lesser degrees of fluency. The Hoopa Valley Tribe has maintained an active language education program since the 1970s, and has published a dictionary (Golla 1996b) and various pedagogical materials, including a phrase book with an accompanying cassette recording. Beginning and intermediate classes in Hupa are regularly offered at Hoopa High School. The Tsnungwe Tribe maintains a website with information on the Hupa language (www.dcn.davis.ca.us/~ammon/danny/Hupa/HupaLanguage.html).

3.7.2 Mattole–Bear River

The Mattole–Bear River language was spoken in two dialects, a southern one in the Mattole River valley and along the adjacent coast, and a northern one along Bear River, near Cape Mendocino. The Mattole dialect was spoken in two tribelets, the larger and more important of which centered on the northern part of Mattole River valley around modern Petrolia, the smaller one located to the south along Cooskie Creek and in parts of the upper Matttole River and its tributaries (Baumhoff 1958:195–200). Subdialect differences between thse two Mattole groups, if any existed, are unattested. There appears to have been a single Bear River tribelet, whose dialect was clearly marked off from Mattole (Nomland 1938).

With their coastal orientation and isolated location, the speakers of Mattole–Bear River were somewhat cut off from other California Athabaskans. The Bear River people had some contact with the people living along the lower Eel River—both Nongatl and Wiyot—and a village at the mouth of the Van Duzen River, near Carlotta, was said to be allied to the Bear River tribelet and to have a bilingual population (Goddard 1929:291). Extensive intermarriage between Bear River and Wiyot families has been common in recent generations, but it is not clear if this practice reflects the aboriginal pattern. The external contacts of the Mattole tribelets were primarily with the Shelter Cove Sinkyone to the south and the Briceland Sinkyone to the east, but these relationships were not close, and the Mattole–Bear River and Eel River languages were barely, if at all, mutually intelligible (Merriam, in Baumhoff 1958:196). There was an important trade route, primarily for abalone shells, from the

FIGURE 39. Ike Duncan, Li Fang-Kuei's Mattole consultant in 1927. Petrolia, 1923. C. Hart Merriam collection of Native American photographs (A/1f/P2 no.1). Courtesy of Bancroft Library UCB.

Mattole area northeastward to the Hupa and other groups in the Klamath-Trinity drainage, but the contact was probably not direct (Nomland 1938:105).

Merriam collected vocabularies and natural history word lists from both the Mattole and Bear River dialects (Appendix A: A-1f, A-1n). The Mattole dialect was documented by Sapir's student Li Fang-Kuei in 1927; the resulting publication, Li's doctoral dissertation (1930), is a comprehensive phonological and grammatical sketch and includes nearly all the data he collected. P. E. Goddard collected material from a speaker of the Bear River dialect in 1907 and, working with Reichard, from two other Bear River speakers in 1923 (Goddard 1907, 1929). J. P. Harrington collected a small amount of material from speakers of both the Mattole and the Bear River dialects in 1942 (Mills 1985:3–9).

Mattole–Bear River has no surviving native speakers. Some descendants of the Mattole and Bear River communities are members of the Bear River Band of the Rohnerville Rancheria, near Loleta, where there is interest in initiating language classes for both children and adults.

3.7.3 Eel River Dialects

Most of the drainage of the Eel River and its tributary the Van Duzen River, as well as the upper portions of the Mad River, was occupied by speakers of a network of closely related local dialects of California Athabaskan. Although there may have been as many as thirty-four separate tribelets in this area (Elsasser 1978:191–192), the ethnographic and linguistic literature usually assigns them to four major dialect divisions: Sinkyone, Nongatl, Lassik, and Wailaki, with the eighteen Wailaki tribelets separated into three regional groups, the Eel River Wailaki, the North Fork Wailaki, and the Pitch Wailaki.[16]

SINKYONE

The Sinkyone dialect was spoken along the South Fork of the Eel River and adjacent areas by two well-defined groups of tribelets, although the difference in speech between these groups appears to have been minimal. The Northern Sinkyone ("Lo-lahn´-kok" in Merriam's nomenclature, taken from the name of the tribelet whose principal village was at the mouth of Bull Creek) lived in the heavily forested territory along South Fork from above Miranda to its confluence with the main Eel at Dyerville. They also had settlements on Salmon Creek, a western tributary of South Fork, and for some distance along the main Eel both above and below Dyerville. The Southern or Shelter Cove Sinkyone (Merriam's "To-cho´-be") lived along South Fork in the less heavily forested region between Phillipsville and Garberville, with another tribelet to the west around Briceland. A third tribelet occupied the rocky and thinly populated coast from north of Shelter Cove to Usal Creek, where Coast Yuki territory began, and there was apparently a fourth tribelet along the upper reaches of South Fork between Garberville and Leggett, the border of Kato territory.

There is disagreement regarding the Northern Sinkyone occupation of the main Eel River between South Fork and Scotia. Goddard and Merriam placed the northern boundary of Sinkyone territory near Scotia, but Nomland (1935:150), following Powers (1877:107), assigned the Eel River downstream from Dyerville to speakers of Mattole–Bear River. Since this was an area of dense redwood forest, with few permanent settlements, it is quite possible that it was one of the neutral areas between adjoining groups that were frequently found in the California region (¶1.5.2).

Wherever the boundary between them lay, the Northern Sinkyone were in fairly close contact with the Wiyot, and there was some intermarriage and individual bilingualism between the two groups. The Southern Sinkyone, however, were the trading partners and allies of the Coast Yuki. As for other Athabaskans, mutual hostility seems to have been the rule. Each of the Sinkyone groups disliked the other, and both were supicious of the Mattole and Bear River groups across the steep mountains to the west, who spoke a different language and whom they encountered only rarely. And both had a strong antipathy to the Lassik and Wailaki on the main Eel, who were apparently encroaching on their territory from the east.

NONGATL

The Nongatl dialect (Merriam's "Kit-tel") was spoken along the Van Duzen River from near its confluence with the Eel below Scotia to its headwaters above Dinsmore—the route of State Highway 36—as well as in a few small villages on Larabee Creek north of Blocksburg. It was also spoken on Yager Creek, and as far north as the Iaqua Buttes. The ethnogeography of Nongatl territory is more poorly documented than that of the other Eel River dialect divisions. There was apparently a distinct subgroup around Blocksburg and another around Bridgeville. The latter, referred to as the Nai'ai-chi ('the ones who fly around') by other Eel River people, had the reputation of being roving marauders (Essene 1942:91–92; Baumhoff 1958:181). Many speakers of Nongatl were brought to the Hoopa Reservation in the 1860s, where they were called "Saia" (Powers 1877:122–124; P. Goddard 1910).

LASSIK

The Lassik dialect (Merriam's "Set-ten-bi´-den") was spoken along the main Eel River in the area to the east of the redwood forest, from Dobbyn Creek south to the border of Wailaki territory at Kekawaka Creek. The major village was at Alderpoint. There were smaller Lassik villages along Dobbyn Creek and in the area around Zenia and Kettenpom. During the summer the Lassik hunted and foraged in the rugged country to the east, in the Soldier Basin area and as far as the upper Mad River around Ruth, where they sometimes encountered the Hayfork Wintu (Essene 1942:84). Some of the place-names in Lassik territory (as well as the name "Lassik" itself) are of Wintu or Nomlaki origin, and it is possible that Powers was correct in reporting that the Athabaskans had only recently taken control of the region (Powers 1877:114).

WAILAKI

The people known as the Wailaki differed from other Eel River Athabaskan speakers insofar as their tribelets were loosely grouped into named regional "divisions" or small-scale tribes (P. Goddard 1923a; Baumhoff 1958:169–170). Three such divisions are distinguished in the ethnographic literature, but whether these were correlated with subdialects is not known. The **Eel River Wailaki** (Merriam's "Tsen-nah´-ken-nes") lived in nine communities along a short stretch of the main Eel River above Lassik territory, between Kekawaka Creek and Bell Springs Creek, with summer camps on the grassy ridges to the west. The **North Fork Wailaki** (Merriam's "Bah´-ne-kut") had six villages along the lower four or five miles of the North Fork of the Eel. The **Pitch Wailaki** (Merriam's "Che-teg-ge-kah") occupied the wilder country upstream on North Fork, and along Hull and Casoose Creeks (P. Goddard 1924). All three Wailaki divisions lived to the east of the redwood forest and

FIGURE 40. Lucy Young, the best-documented speaker of the Lassik dialect of Eel River Athabaskan, with Yellowjacket (Jack French), a Pitch Wailaki. Zenia, July 1922. In the foreground is Young's great-granddaughter, Marie (Clark). C. Hart Merriam collection of Native American photographs (A/1j/P1 no.4). Courtesy of the Bancroft Library UCB.

had a close relationship with the Yukis of Round Valley, a dozen or so miles to the south. It is likely that the Wailaki had earlier spoken Yuki and had shifted to Athabaskan in recent centuries. They shared many of the features of Yuki ceremonial and social culture and had the distinctive Yuki body type, very short of stature with narrow heads (Gifford 1926).

DOCUMENTATION AND SURVIVAL

The Eel River Athabaskan dialects are not well documented. Only Wailaki has been adequately recorded (F. Li 1927), and only a small portion of this material has been published (Seaburg 1977a, 1977b). Other published data include P. E. Goddard's collection of Wailaki texts (1923b); an extensive vocabulary of Wailaki in Curtis (1907–1930, vol. 14:201–207), collected by Myers; and Essene's vocabulary of Lassik (from Lucy Young), which is integrated with a vocabulary of Kato in his *Culture Element Distributions* monograph on Round Valley (Essene 1942:85–89). The major unpublished documentation is Goddard's substantial collection of raw lexical and textual data on Sinkyone (1903–1908), Nongatl (1907–1908), Lassik (Seaburg 1982:17), and Wailaki (1906).[17] Also of importance are the vocabularies and natural history word lists that Merriam obtained from speakers of both subdialects of Sinkyone (Appendix A: A-1g, A-1h), Nongatl (A-1i), Lassik (A-1j), and two varieties of Wailaki (A-1k). The earliest attestation of Eel River Athabaskan is Jeremiah Curtin's substantial BAE survey vocabulary of "Saia" (Curtin 1884e), but which Eel River dialect it documents cannot be determined without a closer inspection of the manuscript.

The only modern tribe that explicity indentifies some of its members as descendants of the Eel River Athabaskan communities is the Round Valley Tribe at Covelo, where they are known as "Wailakis" whatever their origin. There is also a group of unenrolled "Wailakis" in the Garberville area, and the Bear River Band of the Rohnerville Rancheria, north of Fortuna, claims the entire Eel and Van Duzen drainage as part of its heritage area. While no native speakers of any variety of Eel River Athabaskan could be identified in 2010, all the groups listed here have an interest in revitalizing the language, and there are several serious learners.

3.7.4 Kato

Kato was spoken along the upper reaches of the South Fork of the Eel and its tributary, Tenmile Creek, mainly in Cahto Valley and Long Valley between Branscomb and Laytonville. There were also some Kato speakers living about fifteen to twenty miles downstream along South Fork in the vicinity of Leggett. Powers treated the latter as a separate tribe, the "Kai Pomo" as distinguished from the "Kato Pomo," but there was apparently no difference in speech between the two groups (Powers 1877:148–155; P. Goddard 1909:67). Kato territory was bordered by Yuki and Huchnom territory on the east and Coast Yuki territory on the west, but contacts between the Kato and their Yukian neighbors were more a matter of necessity than of choice. Instead, the most important cultural and social relationships of the Kato were with the Northern Pomo immediately to the south. There was extensive Kato–Northern Pomo bilingualism, leading Powers and other early observers to mistake the Kato for a Pomo group, as indicated in the terminology cited earlier (see P. Goddard 1903b). By contrast, the relationship between the Kato and the Sinkyone and Wailaki, their Athabaskan kinsmen to the north, was often hostile, and linguistic differences impeded communication (P. Goddard 1909:67–68).

Kato was moderately well documented in 1906–1908 by P. E. Goddard (1902–1906, 1902-1922a, 1902-1922b), who published a grammar (1912) and a set of texts (1909). Although this work does not come up to the standard that Goddard set in his documentation of Hupa, it identifies most of the lexical and grammatical features that distinguish Kato from other varieties of California Athabaskan. Also of use are the ethnographic vocabularies of Kato that were

collected by Myers (published in Curtis 1907–1930, vol. 14:201–207) and by Essene (1942:85–89), and the general and natural history word lists collected by Merriam in 1920–1922 (Appendix A: A-1o). Harrington collected a small amount of miscellaneous data in 1942, largely ethnogeographical in nature, valuable principally for the accuracy of the phonetic transcription (Mills 1985:9–15). Some important phonological insights are also provided in the detailed transcriptions of several dozen words that Sapir made while assisting Goddard in collecting instrumental phonetic data from a Kato speaker at Berkeley in 1908 (Sapir 1907–1908; see P. Goddard 1909:68, 1912:86–176).

No fluent native speakers of Kato remain, although members of the Cahto Tribe (Laytonville Rancheria) preserve some knowledge of the language. An independent consultant, Sally Anderson, has worked with the tribe to make data on Kato accessible online (www.billabbie.com/calath/caindex.html).

3.7.5 Linguistic Structure

Proto–California Athabaskan can be reconstructed with five stops and affricates (t, c [ts], $\check{c}$, k^y, k), each occurring plain, aspirated, and glottalized, except for the k series, which lacked an aspirated member. There were two voiceless fricatives (s, $\check{s}$), paired with c and $\check{c}$, respectively, and a voiced velar fricative (γ). In addition there was a lateral fricative (t) paired with a glottalized lateral affricate (λ'), but no corresponding plain or aspirated lateral affricate. There was one bilabial obstruent ($p \sim m$); one nasal (n, but phonetically [ŋ] when word-final or before a velar); two laryngeals (h, $ʔ$); and three approximants (l, w, y).

The fricative and affricates of the $\check{c}$ series ($\check{c}$, $\check{c}^h$, $\check{c}$', and $\check{s}$) develop a distinct phonetic realization in each of the four languages. In the Eel River dialects both the fricative and the affricates have palatal articulation [ʃ] ~ [tʃ], and phonemically merge in some dialects with the palatals that develop from the front velar ($\underline{k}$) series. In Kato both fricative and affricates have apical retroflex articulation [ṣ] ~ [tṣ]. In Mattole–Bear River the affricates remain palatal, but the fricative is articulated as a voiceless front-velar fricative [x̲], which apparently acquires a labial feature [x̲ʷ] in the Bear River dialect (P. Goddard 1929:293). In Hupa-Chilula both the fricative and the aspiration of the affricate $\check{c}^h$ are articulated as labialized breath ("voiceless w"), nearly identical to English wh; they are transcribed here as W and $\check{c}^w$, respectively (Table 8).

Other language- or dialect-defining consonantal developments include the following: In Hupa-Chilula the voiced velar fricative (γ) merges with w; in the other languages it merges with the plain velar stop (k). In all languages except Hupa-Chilula the voiceless velar fricative (x) is usually realized as an aspirated velar stop [kʰ]. The stops of the front velar $\underline{k}$ series are retained as such in Hupa-Chilula and in some Eel River dialects [$\underline{k}$, $\underline{k}^h$, $\underline{k}$']; in Mattole–Bear River they are realized as palatalized dental-alveolar affricates

TABLE 8

Hupa Phonemes (Sapir and Golla 2001)

Consonants								Vowels	
(p)	t	c	č	ḵ	(k)*	q	ʔ	i / e:	o / o:
	tʰ	cʰ	čʷ	ḵʰ	(kʰ)			a / a:	
	t'	ƛ' c'	č'	ḵ'	(k')	q'			
	ł	s				x	h		
						xʷ			
m	n					ŋ			
w	l	y							
W									

*Midvelar stops—phonemically distinct from both front and back velars—replace the corresponding front velars in Hupa words affected by diminutive consonant symbolism (e.g., Wiḵʰaːy 'my daughter's child [woman speaking]', but ʔiskʰaːy 'darling grandchild!'). See ¶4.12.1.

[tṣ]; while in Kato and in some Eel River dialects they are realized as palatal affricates [tʃ], merging with the affricates of the palatal č series in Eel River but kept distinct in Kato, where the č series developed retroflex articulation. The glottalized lateral affricate (ƛ') merges with t' in all Eel River dialects except Nongatl; the same merger occurs sporadically in Kato. The bilabial obstruent is articulated as a plain stop (p) in most of the languages, but as a nasal (m) in Hupa-Chilula except in a few marginal words (e.g., ʔičipeh! 'I'm scared!').

Four full vowels can be reconstructed (i, e, a, u), which occur both short and long, and an intrinsically short reduced vowel (ə). In Hupa-Chilula, the high vowels are phonetically lowered, the phonemic contrast between i and e is lost, and ə merges with the short variant of the merged front vowel. These changes result in a system of three long vowels (e:, a:, o:) and three short vowels (i, a, o), with considerable allophonic variation in the short front vowel. Hupa-Chilula and Mattole–Bear River are also characterized by a phonological contrast between "light" and "heavy" syllables (historically closed versus open syllables, but obscured synchronically by a phonological rule that elides final short vowels), and light syllables with basically long vowels develop a postvocalic laryngeal increment (h or ʔ).

Some California Athabaskan languages have innovated distinctive morphological features within the basic Athabaskan framework. A customary or habitual aspect (marked by ʔi-, or "breaking" the prestem syllable) has been innovated in Hupa-Chilula. In Hupa-Chilula and Mattole–Bear River, the distinction between "light" and "heavy" stem syllables has been recruited to mark modal or aspectual distinctions in verb stem alternations. The Athabaskan indefinite pronoun set, represented in California Athabaskan as č'ə- subject, xo- object/possessor, is reinterpreted in Hupa-Chilula and Kato (but not in Mattole–Bear River or the Eel River dialects) as an animate or proximate third person, contrasting with a less-animate or obviative third person marked for subject by the inherited third person subject-object prefix (yə-), for direct object by zero, and for postpositional object or possessor by pə- (Hupa-Chilula mi-).[18]

Hokan Languages

3.8 The Hokan Phylum

The name "Hokan" was coined in 1913 by R. B. Dixon and A. L. Kroeber to label a phylum-level relationship they believed to exist among six California language families or isolates: Karuk, Shastan, Chimariko, Palaihnihan, Yana, and Pomo (Map 10).[19] With the exception of Shastan and Palaihnihan, whose relationship to one another Dixon had proposed a few years earlier (1905b, 1906), all had previously been treated as independent classificatory units. Over the next decade, a number of other families and isolates in North and Central America were added to the Hokan roster, including Yuman, Chumash, Washo, and Salinan in California; Seri, Tequistlatecan (Oaxaca Chontal), and Tlapanec in Mexico; and Subtiaba in Nicaragua (Kroeber 1915b; Sapir 1917b, 1920b, 1920c, 1921b, 1925a; Dixon and Kroeber 1919).[20]

The first detailed exploration of the Hokan relationship was carried out by Edward Sapir, who collected several hundred potential cognate sets and proposed the outlines of a common Hokan grammatical structure (most fully in Sapir 1917a, 1925a). According to Sapir, a fundamental—and diagnostic—feature of Hokan morphosyntax was the tendency (admittedly obscured by later developments in some languages) to have nominal and verbal stems with initial vowels preceded by single-consonant prefixes with grammatical or derivational functions (nominal, adjectival, intransitive, transitive). He identified what appeared to be cognate structures of this type in languages as diverse as Subtiaba, Salinan, and Washo (1925a).

Sapir also presented evidence that suggested the long-extinct "Coahuiltecan" languages of southern Texas and northeastern Mexico were distantly related to Hokan, the two groups perhaps forming coordinate branches of a broader "Hokan-Coahuiltecan" phylum (Sapir 1920a).[21] In 1920, Sapir further proposed that the Hokan-Coahuiltecan languages were part of an even more ancient and widespread relationship to which he gave the name "Hokan-Siouan" (1920d, 1921c, 1929b). In addition to the Hokan and Coahuiltecan branches, he saw Hokan-Siouan comprising (1) the Yukian family of California; (2) the Keresan family of the Pueblo Southwest; (3) the isolate languages Atakapa, Tunica, and Chitimacha along the lower Mississippi River and Gulf Coast; (4) the Caddoan and Iroquois families of the Plains and eastern woodlands; and (5) the Muskogean-Natchez, Siouan, and Yuchi languages of the Southeast and the Mississippi Valley. This bold proposal was part of a general classificatory scheme in which Sapir assigned all attested North American Indian languages to one of six "superstocks" (Golla 1986), and it was controversial from the start. Although it remained under discussion as late as the 1970s (Swadesh 1954a; Haas 1969), it never enjoyed wide acceptance.[22]

Sapir's classificatory proposals for the core Hokan relationship, however, continue to exert influence. He initially proposed (1921c) a tripartite subgrouping of the phylum: (1) Northern Hokan, with three geographical subdivisions; (2) Esselen, Yuman, and Cochimí; and (3) Salinan and Seri. As further data accumulated, he added Washo, Chumash, Tequistlatecan, and Subtiaba to the third of these subgroups (1925a:504).[23] His final classificatory scheme is shown in Table 9.[24]

The only major subsequent addition to the roster of Hokan languages was Jicaque (Tol) of Honduras, proposed by Greenberg and Swadesh (1953). Beginning in the late 1960s, Margaret Langdon, a student of Yuman languages, together

TABLE 9
Sapir's Classification of Hokan (1925a)

Northern Hokan

    Karuk, Chimariko, Shastan, and Palaihnihan

    Yana

    Pomo

Esselen-Yuman

    Esselen

    Yuman-Cochimí

Southern Hokan

    Washo

    Salinan-Seri

    Chumash

    Tequistlatecan (Chontal of Oaxaca)

    Subtiaba-Tlapanec (Nicaragua)

with colleagues working on other Hokan languages in California and Mexico, resumed active exploration of the Hokan (or Hokan-Coahuiltecan) classifications in a series of meetings and collaborative projects collectively known as the "Hokan Conference."[25] An early fruit of this second wave of interest in the relationship was Langdon's *Comparative Hokan-Coahuiltecan Studies* (1974), which provided a critical survey of work to that date. While not formally proposing a revision to the scope and internal structure of Sapir's Hokan-Coahuiltecan phylum, Langdon summed up the consensus of her colleagues that Sapir's hypothesis had "withstood the test of time fairly well." The only subtraction clearly required was that of Tonkawa and Karankawa from the Coahuiltecan branch. The addition of Jicaque, on the other hand, seemed clearly warranted, and new evidence seemed to bolster Sapir's "Southern Hokan" subgrouping (1974:86).[26]

In recent decades, although further doubt has been cast on the Hokan status of any of the Coahuiltecan languages (I. Goddard 1979), the essence of Sapir's Hokan hypothesis continues to be used as a framework for historical and typological investigation (Jacobsen 1979a; Mithun 1999; Poser 1995; Mixco 1997b; Campbell 1997). Important phylum-wide syntheses have been undertaken by the German comparativist Karl-Heinz Gursky and the Mesoamericanist Terrence Kaufman.

Gursky's goal has been to demonstrate the validity of the phylum by assembling a comprehensive database of several hundred potential cognate sets, both from his own comparative work and from previous scholarship (Gursky 1974, 1988). Gursky, however, sees the Hokan phylum as part of a wider relationship among North American languages on the scale of (but different from) Sapir's "Hokan-Siouan" hypothesis (Gursky 1965, 1966b, 1968), and his

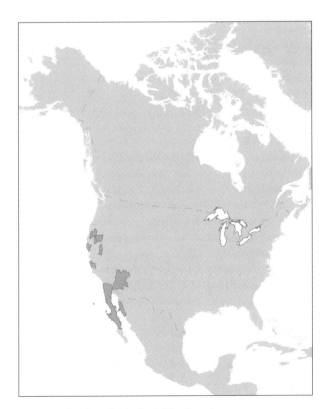

MAP 10. Hokan branches in the California region.

criteria for Hokan affiliation in the narrow sense are somewhat vague.

Kaufman (1988) has proposed a much tighter model of Hokan. Working from Gursky's materials and from his own comparative data, he has assembled a substantial number of potential cognates. Unlike any of his predecesors, however, he has abstracted a comprehensive scheme of phonemic correspondences from these cognates, on the basis of which he reconstructs a proto-Hokan lexicon of approximately one thousand items. Kaufman admits into Hokan only those languages that are linked to the others by a substantial number of core etymologies exhibiting regular phonemic correspondences. The absence of such evidence leads him to exclude Chumash from the relationship, as well as all the subbranches of Coahuiltecan except two—the Coahuilteco (Pajalate) isolate and Comecrudoan family (Comecrudo, Garza, and Mamulique). He also finds the evidence for the inclusion of Subtiaba and Tlapanec far too slim, and follows Rensch (1977) and Suárez (1983) in assigning these languages to Otomanguean (although leaving open the possibility of an ancient relationship between Otomanguean and Hokan). Nevertheless, Kaufman sees plentiful evidence for retaining Tequistlatecan within the Hokan grouping, together with Jicaque, whose relationship to Tequistlatecan has been independently demonstrated in recent years (Campbell and Oltrogge 1980:221–223). But if Kaufman's comparative method allows him to draw a clear line around the languages that constitute the phylum, it provides little support for classificatory subgrouping. He sees no good evidence for anything more than a flat classification into sixteen independent nodes, only two of which (Shastan-Palaihnihan and Yuman-Cochimí) represent more than a single language or a shallowly differentiated family. He sorts these into eight clusters on purely geographical grounds (Table 10).

3.9 Karuk

The Karuk language is a classificatory isolate within the Hokan phylum. It was spoken in a territory that extended about sixty miles along the Klamath River in western Siskiyou County and northeastern Humboldt County, adjoining Yurok territory downstream and Shasta territory upstream. To the east, a short distance up the Salmon River, the Karuk bordered on the Shastan-speaking Konomihu of the Forks of Salmon area. To the west and northwest, over the high mountains of the Coast Range, they were in frequent contact with the Oregon Athabaskans. To the south, in addition to adjoining the Yuroks on the Klamath River, they often intervisited with the Hupa in Hoopa Valley, usually traveling there over a trail up Redcap Creek.

3.9.1 Geography

Karuk territory along the Klamath can be divided into four districts, or village clusters (Kroeber 1936; Map 11). The district farthest downstream centered on the area between

TABLE 10

Kaufman's Sixteen Hokan Classificatory Units in Their Geographical Clusters (1988)

Northern Coast Range

1. Pomo

Northern California

2. Chimariko

3. Yana

4. Karuk

5–6. Shastan-Palaihnihan

Great Basin

7. Washo

Central California Coast

8. Esselen

9. Salinan

Southwest

10–11. Yuman-Cochimí

12. Seri

Northeast Mexico

13. Coahuilteco

14. Comecrudan

Oaxaca

15. Tequistlatecan (Chontal)

Honduras

16. Jicaque (Tol)

the mouth of Camp Creek and the modern town of Orleans. The principal village in this cluster was Panamnik (panámni:k, 'the flat place' [?]), at the site of modern Orleans. The next cluster upstream, four or five miles to the north, centered on the villages of Katimin (ka?ti:m?i:n 'upriver edge falls') and Amekyaram (ame:kyá:ra:m 'salmon making place'), near the mouth of the Salmon River. Although villages were few and relatively small along the next twenty miles of the Klamath, they appear to have constituted a separate geographical and social unit. Beyond this lay an upstream cluster of villages centering on Inam (ina:m 'world-renewal celebrating place'), at the mouth of Clear Creek, about five miles south of Happy Camp. While there were no dialect differences acknowledged by speakers to be correlated with these four districts, Harrington made note of a Clear Creek variety that was distinct in certain details from "Lower River" speech (Mills 1985:30, fn.2).

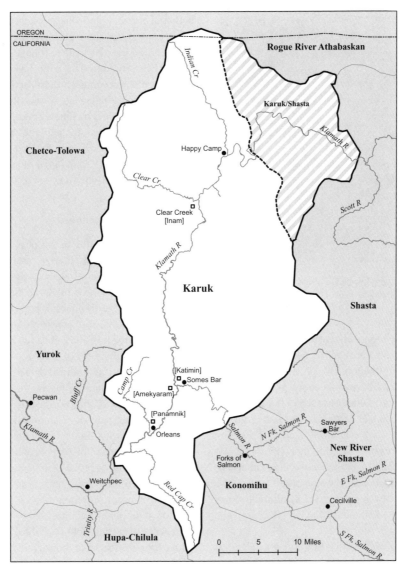

OREGON
CALIFORNIA

Rogue River Athabaskan

Indian Cr

Karuk/Shasta

Chetco-Tolowa

Happy Camp ●

Klamath R

Clear Cr

Scott R

Clear Creek
[Inam] □

Klamath R

Karuk

Shasta

Yurok

□ [Katimin]
□ Somes Bar

□ [Amekyaram]

Camp Cr

Bluff Cr

Pecwan ●

□ [Panamnik]
● Orleans

Klamath R

Sawyers
Bar ●

N Fk, Salmon R

**New River
Shasta**

Salmon R

E Fk, Salmon R

Weitchpec ●

Red Cap Cr

Konomihu

Forks of
Salmon ●

Cecilville ●

Trinity R

Hupa-Chilula

0   5   10 Miles

S Fk, Salmon R

MAP 11. Karuk territory.

Indian Creek (*aθiθúf* 'cedar creek'), at Happy Camp, traditionally marked the upper boundary of Karuk territory. The people of the thinly populated area between Happy Camp and Hamburg (*ka:kamî:č va?ára:r* 'people a little upriver'), including Seiad Valley (*sâ:may*), spoke a distinct upriver variety of Karuk, but apparently were also bilingual in Shasta (Kroeber 1936:35–37). Merriam collected a vocabulary of this upriver variety (Appendix A: I-8b, "Kah-rah´-ko-hah"); it may also be the "Happy Camp" dialect referred to in various places in Harrington's notes (Mills 1985:30). By contrast, the border between Karuk and Yurok territory was sharply demarcated—it lay a few hundred yards to the south of Bluff Creek—and there was no intermediate area of bilingualism.

3.9.2 Documentation and Survival

Karuk is extensively documented and well represented in the published scholarly literature. The first attestation was made

by George Gibbs in 1851 during the McKee Expedition and published by Schoolcraft (Gibbs 1863b, "Eh-nek"). Gibbs collected a more substantial vocabulary when he returned to northwestern California as a gold miner in 1852 (Gibbs 1852–1853), and both this and the 1851 vocabulary were published in Powers (1877:447–459), together with vocabularies collected later in the 1850s by Crook and Ross and a vocabulary collected by Powers himself in 1872. Jeremiah Curtin collected two substantial BAE survey lists (1889d, 1889e) and fifteen narrative texts (1889c). A. L. Kroeber carried out an ethnographic and linguistic survey of the area in 1902–1903 and collected a number of Karuk narrative texts in addition to other materials. He published a brief grammatical sketch (1911a:427–435) and later prepared an English-only edition of the texts (published posthumously in Kroeber and Gifford 1980:1–103). Between 1910 and 1921, Merriam collected vocabularies and natural history word lists from two dialects (Appendix A: I-8a-b). J. P. Harrington collected extensive materials, including

FIGURE 41. William Bright with Elizabeth Case, Karuk medicine woman and language consultant, ca. 1989. Courtesy of Lise Menn.

numerous texts, during repeated visits between 1925 and 1929; he also worked with a speaker, Phoebe Maddux, who accompanied him to Washington, DC, in 1928–1929 (Mills 1985: 29–49). He published two collections of texts (1930, 1932b) and a bilingual Karuk-English study of the traditional use of tobbaco (1932a). Jaime de Angulo and L. S. Freeland collected materials on Karuk in 1929 and published a collection of texts with notes on grammar (1931). E. W. Gifford collected incidental but valuable linguistic materials during ethnographic fieldwork between 1939 and 1942. These included numerous narrative texts, although they were for the most part dictated in English (Kroeber and Gifford 1980:105–329).

The most thorough documentation of Karuk was made by William Bright, who began fieldwork in 1949 and continued working with the community in a language revitalization program until his death in 2006. Early along he published a structural grammar, accompanied by a selection of texts and a full lexicon (1957). His later work focused on literary and ethnopoetic analysis of Karuk discourse (1977, 1979a, 1980a, 1980b, 1984), and on the preparation of reference materials in collaboration with the Karuk Tribe (Bright and Gehr 2004). Beginning in the 1980s, Monica Macaulay, combining new fieldwork with a close examination of the text corpus,[27] has furthered the analysis of various phonological and grammatical features (1989, 1992, 1993, 2000, 2004; see also Brugman and Macaulay 2009).

Karuk is the heritage language of the Karuk Tribe of the Klamath River in northwestern California. There are fewer than a dozen fluent first-language speakers, along with a larger number of semispeakers and passive speakers. Up to thirty people have some degree of second-language fluency, including a near-traditional command of the language on the part of a small group of tribal scholars and cultural revival activists. In addition, many children have acquired a degree of familiarity with Karuk in school-based programs at both the primary and the secondary level, and through a tribally sponsored summer immersion camp. Several pairs of speakers and learners have participated in the AICLS Master-Apprentice program. The tribe has a language committee that coordinates some of these activities, and a standard alphabet was adopted in 1988 (Richardson and Burcell 1993). Recent efforts include a grant from the Administration for Native Americans to help the tribe republish, update, and distribute the lexicon in Bright (1957) and to compile a full dictionary of the language; a preliminary version has been circulated (Bright and Gehr 2004).

3.9.3 Linguistic Structure

Bright (1957) provides a thorough structural analysis of Karuk phonology, morphology, and phrasal syntax (Table 11). Macaulay, whose work represents the only major addition to the analysis of Karuk since Bright, accepts the latter's descriptive framework but views the linguistic system from the vantage of contemporary linguistic theory.

The phonemic inventory of Karuk is quite small. There are four stops and affricates (p, t, č, k), with no distinction either in aspiration or in glottalization. There are five fricatives (f, θ, s, š, x), with f varying between bilabial and labiodental, and with š in most (but not all) of its occurrences being a predictable alternate of s. There are two laryngeals (h, ʔ), two nasals (m, n), a flapped r [ɾ], and two approximants (v, y), with v phonetically varying between a voiced bilabial fricative [β] and a labial semivowel [w]. There are three vowels (i, a, u) that occur both short and long, and two mid vowels that occur only long (e:, o:). Long vowels may carry one of two pitch accents—acute (v́:), characterized by high pitch in nonfinal syllables or by falling pitch with glottalization in monosyllables or final syllables (púk 'fog', pú:fič 'deer', ipšé:k 'be heavy'), or circumflex (v̂:), characterized by falling pitch without glottalization (pû:č

TABLE 11
Karuk Phonemes (Bright 1957)

Consonants					Vowels		
p	t	č	k	ʔ	i / i:		u / u:
f	θ	š	x	h	e:		o:
v						a / a:	
m	n						
	r	y					

	Long	Short
Pitch Accents		
Unaccented	v:	v
Acute (high)	v́:	v́
Circumflex (high falling)	v̂:	

'boot', *pûːviš* 'sack, bag', *pihnîːč* 'old man')—or can occur unaccented (*puːn* 'cherry', *puːhara* 'no', *pahaːv* 'green manzanita'). Short vowels may have an acute accent with high pitch (*púrip* 'cherry tree') or can occur unaccented (*puxič* 'very much').[28]

Compared to this uncomplicated phonology, the morphology of Karuk nouns and verbs is relatively complex. Some nouns are simple roots (*áːh* 'fire', *θaːm* 'meadow', *íːš* 'meat, flesh', *yúːp* 'eye'), but the number of these is small. The majority of nominal forms are either compounds or are derived from verbs (*ávʔiːš* 'cheek', lit. 'face-flesh'; *θantápar* 'sifting basket', lit. 'sifting-instrument'). Many of these are made opaque by a variety of phonological processes (cf. *púrip* 'cherry tree' < *puːn* 'cherry' + *iːp* 'tree, bush'; *xunyêːp* 'tan oak', lit. 'acorn soup-good-tree' < *xuːn* 'acorn soup' + *yav* 'be good' + *iːp* 'tree, bush'). Possession is marked by a nonobligatory set of pronominal prefixes: *nani-/nini-* 'my', *mi-* 'your (sg.)', *mu-* 'his. her', *nanu-* ~ *nunu-* 'our', *mikun-* 'your (pl.)', *mukun-* 'their', and *va-* or *kuma-* ~ *ku-* 'its'.

Verbs stems are frequently compounded. A number of synchronically monomorphemic stems are historically analyzable as "bipartite" compounds involving instrumental and classificatory elements (Bright 1957:86–87; Haas 1980; see ¶4.8.2), and Macaulay (1993) has argued that this historical analysis continues to have synchronic relevance, manifested in patterns of reduplication. Locational-directional stem complements are found with most verbs of motion, situating the action of the verb in a spatial frame that is in many cases intimately linked to the riverine topography of Karuk territory (e.g., *ikpúːh-varak* 'to swim hither from upriver', *ikpúːh-roːvu* 'to swim upriverward', *ikpúːh-kara* 'to swim across the river'; see Macaulay 2004). Verbal inflection and derivation, both prefixal and suffixal, are rich and complex, with pronominal subject and object categories marked by complicated sets of only partially analyzable prefixes. In a recent series of papers Macaulay has shown how many of the apparently arbitrary features of the pronominal system can be explained by an animacy hierarchy that favors the marking of the more animate entity in transitive verbs, a pattern that can be "inverted" by adding the suffix element *-ap* and that interacts with the enclitic *ʔîin* to mark ergativity and a type of obviation (Macaulay 1992, 2000).

3.9.4 Nomenclature

Gibbs, who published the first vocabulary of Karuk (Schoolcraft 1851–1857.3:422), called it "Ehnek" (from *ʔenek*, the Yurok name of the village of Amekyaram), noting that while this was "the name of a band at the mouth of the Salmon, or Quoratem river, [the] latter name may perhaps be considered as proper to be given to the family." "Quoratem," which is actually the Yurok name for the Jumping Dance site on the south side of the mouth of the Salmon River (Karuk *asápiːpmaːm* 'behind the black cottonwood'; Kroeber 1925:100), was consequently

given priority by Powell (1891:100–101), who proposed "Quoratean" as the classificatory name. As with many of Powell's coinages, this term has rarely been used. Curtin (1889a) used "Ehnikan," from the same source as Gibbs's Ehnek. Merriam called the principal dialect (as opposed to the Happy Camp dialect) "Arʹrah-ahʹrah" (Appendix A: I-8a-b) from Karuk *áraːr* 'person'. Powers (1877:19) called the tribe and language "Karok," derived from a Karuk directional term (*káruk* 'upstream'), which along with "Yurok" (from *yúruk* 'downstream') had come into general use in the local white community. Kroeber adopted Powers's name and spelling, and these became standard in California anthropology for much of the twentieth century. The Karuk Tribe of California prefers the spelling with "u" (which was also used by Harrington), and this preference is now widely followed.

3.10 Chimariko

3.10.1 Geography

The Chimariko language, a classificatory isolate within the Hokan phylum, was spoken in a small territory in the mountainous region of northwestern Trinity County (Bauman 1980a). At the beginning of the historical period, Chimariko cultural independence was under considerable pressure from the neighboring Hupa and Wintu, and many, perhaps most, Chimariko speakers were bilingual in one of those languages. The Chimariko nation in 1850 was actually three distinct regional entities, lying roughly in a north-to-south chain, each of which was experiencing a different pattern of linguistic and cultural assimilation (Map 12).

NEW RIVER HUPA/CHIMARIKO

The northern group, the New River Chimariko (Power's "Chimalakwe"), occupied the upland valley of New River around Denny as far north as the New River forks. At the beginning of the historic period a shift to Hupa was apparently well under way in this area, reflecting a cultural dominance to which Powers alludes when he calls the Hupas "the Romans of California" (1877:92; see ¶1.5.2). The New River Shasta (called by the Hupa *ƛ'oh mitʰahxʷe:* 'people [living] in the grass'), who hunted and foraged in the mountain meadows near the headwaters of New River and Salmon River, may also have spoken both Hupa and Chimariko, but were ethnically distinct from the New River Chimariko (see ¶3.11.4).

TRINITY RIVER CHIMARIKO

In the center were the Trinity River Chimariko, or Chimariko proper, who lived along the deep canyon of the main Trinity River east of Salyer. Their territory began about four miles upstream from the large and important Hupa village of Hleldin (*ƚeːltiŋ* 'confluence place') at the mouth of South

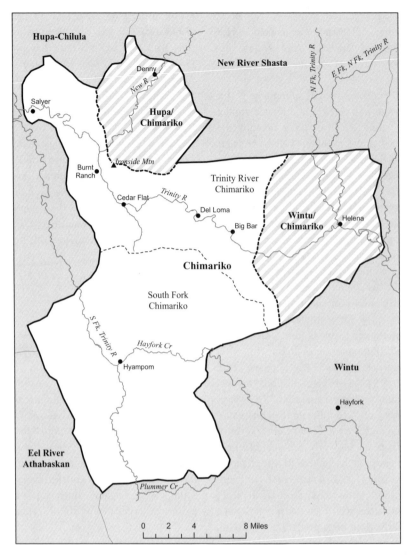

MAP 12. Chimariko territory, showing bilingual areas.

Fork, and Hupa influence was strong. The principal Trinity River Chimariko village was at Burnt Ranch, on the south(west) bank of the Trinity opposite Ironside Mountain, about ten miles above Hleldin. The eastern extent of their territory is not precisely known. Dixon (1910:295–296) stated that the last Chimariko village upstream on the Trinity was at Taylor's Flat, near modern Del Loma. Bauman (1980a), relying on Harrington's data, places it fifteen miles to the east, in the vicinity of North Fork at Helena, while Merriam (1967b:257–281) locates it still further upstream, at Canyon Creek near Junction City. This uncertainty is probably a consequence of the depopulation that followed the heavy mining activity of the 1850s.

SOUTH FORK CHIMARIKO

The southern group, the South Fork Chimariko, had several villages around Hyampom, at the confluence of Hayfork Creek and South Fork. Their northern boundary was at

Cedar Flat, about ten miles north of Hyampom, and their southern boundary was at Plummer Creek. The location of their eastern boundary, where they adjoined the Hayfork Wintu, is less certain, but was probably closer to Hayfork than to Hyampom. The South Fork Chimariko kept in close contact with the Trinity River Chimariko of the Burnt Ranch area by an overland trail, but while the latter were under heavy linguistic and cultural influence from the Hupa, the South Fork people oriented themselves toward the Hayfork Wintu. It is noteworthy that several of the American-era place-names in South Fork Chimariko territory, including Hyampom itself (*xayi:n-p^hom* 'slippery place'), are of Wintu origin. Kroeber (1925:352) assigned nearly the entire South Fork to the Wintu, but Merriam's and Harrington's substantial ethnogeographic data make clear that the Hyampom area was basically Chimariko, although it was probably undergoing an ethnic and linguistic shift to Wintu (Merriam and Talbot 1974:12; Bauman 1980a).

These three Chimariko groups were probably separate tribelets with distinct dialects, but the attestations of the language, coming as they do from a few survivors of the upheavals of the Gold Rush period, are insufficient—or have not yet been evaluated closely enough—to make a determination.[29]

3.10.2 Documentation and Survival

Although the Chimariko language has been extinct since about 1950, something approaching an adequate linguistic record exists, although the most important materials are unpublished. The earliest word list was collected by Stephen Powers in 1875 (published in Powers 1877:474–477). The first substantial documentation was made by Jeremiah Curtin (1889a), followed in 1906 by R. B. Dixon, whose short sketch of the language (Dixon 1910:307–380), inadequate in many ways, remained the only published general description for more than a century.[30] Edward Sapir commented insightfully on Dixon's analysis (Sapir 1911, 1920a) and collected some incidental Chimariko data during work on Hupa in 1927 (published in Berman 2001c). Merriam collected a vocabulary (Appendix A: K-10a).

By far the most valuable and extensive documentation of Chimariko is J. P. Harrington's. He devoted several months between 1921 and 1928 to fieldwork with six Chimariko speakers, one of whom, Sally Noble, was quite fluent (Mills 1985:49–56, 63–81). Except for some place-names (Bauman 1980a) and citations in recent analytic work (Jany 2007), none of Harringon's material has been published. George Grekoff collated Dixon's, Sapir's, and at least some of Harrington's data, with the intention of writing a full grammatical description (cf. Grekoff 1997), but the study was unfinished at the time of his death.[31] Building on Grekoff's work and a further examination of Harrington's notes, Lisa Conathan (2002) and Carmen Jany (2007, 2009) have recently made considerable progress in analyzing Chimariko grammar.

The last speaker of Chimariko, Martha Ziegler, died in the early 1950s. Modern Chimariko descendants, organized as the Tsnungwe Tribe (from Hupa *cʰe:niŋxʷe:* 'Ironside Mountain people') and seeking federal acknowledgement,[32] consider both Hupa and Chimariko to be their heritage languages, but emphasize Hupa for purposes of cultural revitalization. No efforts are known to be under way to learn or teach Chimariko.

3.10.3 Linguistic Structure

As analyzed by Grekoff and summarized in Jany (2009), Chimariko has five series of stops (*p, t, ṭ, k, q*) and two series of affricates (*c* [ts], *č*), all of which occur aspirated and glottalized as well as plain (Table 12).[33] There are three fricatives (*s, š, x*), two nasals (*m, n*), two laryngeals (*h, ʔ*), a flap (*r*), and three approximants (*l, w, y*). The flapped *r* may

FIGURE 42. Sally Noble, the last fluent speaker of Chimariko. Photograph by Mrs. J. J. Dailey, 1921. C. Hart Merriam collection of Native American photographs (K/10a/P2 no.1). Courtesy of the Bancroft Library, UCB.

be an allophone of *l*. The vowels include only the basic five (*i, e, a, o, u*), and length appears not to be distinctive.

Chimariko nouns are inflected for pronominal possessor by either a set of prefixes (if alienable) or a set of suffixes (if inalienable)—for example, *čʰu-sam* 'my ear', *mi-sam* 'your (sg) ear', *hi-sam* 'his ear', *čʰa-sam* 'our ears', *qʰa-sam* 'your (pl) ears'; but *ʔawa-ʔi* 'my house', *ʔawa-mi* 'your (sg) house', *ʔawa-yta* 'his, their house', *ʔawa-ʔčʰi* 'our house', and *ʔawa-mqʰi* 'your (pl) house'.

Pronominal categories are marked in verbs by a single affix which is either prefixed or suffixed depending on the verb stem, stems requiring prefixation being by far the more numerous. When prefixed, the affix is either (1) a single consonant, followed by the initial vowel of the stem if the stem is vowel-initial (e.g., *čʰ-akʰo-xana-n* 'he is going to kill me', *m-exači-t* 'you stole it') or by an epenthetic *i* or *u* if the stem is consonant-initial (e.g., *čʰ-u-k'o'-nan* 'he talks to me', *m-i-k'o'-nan* 'he/they talk to you'); or (2) a consonant-vowel (CV) syllable whose vowel replaces the initial vowel of a

TABLE 12
Chimariko Phonemes (Grekoff 1997; Jany 2009)

Consonants								Vowels	
p	t	ṭ	c	č	k	q	ʔ	i	u
pʰ	tʰ	ṭʰ	cʰ	čʰ	kʰ	qʰ		e	o
p'	t'	ṭ'	c'	č'	k'	q'			a
			s	š	x		h		
m	n								
		(r)							
w	l		y						

TABLE 13
Chimariko Pronominal Affixes (Jany 2009)

	Singular		Plural	
	Prefix	Suffix	Prefix	Suffix
1 intransitive ("voluntary") 1 transitive, acting on 2 or 3	y-, ʔi-	-ʔ(i)	ya-	?
1 intransitive ("involuntary") 3 transitive, acting on 1	čʰ(u)-	-čʰ(u)	čʰa-	-čʰa
2 transitive, acting on 1	me-	-m(V)	qʰo-	-qʰV
2 intransitive 2 transitive, acting on 2/3	m(i)-	-m(V)	qʰ(u)-	-qʰV
3 intransitive 3 transitive, acting on 2/3	h(i)-	-h/zero	h(i)-	-h/zero

vowel-initial stem (e.g., *ya-k'oʔ-nan* 'we talk to him', *ya-xači-t* 'we stole it' < *ya-exači-t*). This affix expresses either the subject in intransitives or a specific combination of agent and patient categories in transitives. The greatest number of distinctions are made in verbs inflected for first person categories, where three sets of pronouns are used. One set marks the first person subject of "voluntary" intransitives (e.g., *ʔi-sekmu-t* 'I swallow') or, in transitives, the combination of a first person agent with a second or third person patient (*ʔi-k'oʔ-nan* 'I talk to him, you', *ya-k'oʔ-nan* 'we talk to him, you'). A second set is used either to express the first person subject of intransitive verbs denoting involuntary states or actions (*čʰ-u-saxni-t* 'I cough', *čʰa-kučʰen* 'we don't want to'), or with transitive verbs to express the combination of a third person agent and a first person patient (*čʰ-u-hatni* 'he pokes me', *čʰa-hatni* 'he pokes us').[34] A third set is used only with transitive verbs to express the combination of a second person agent and a first person patient (*me-k'oʔ-nan* 'you talk to me, us', *qʰo-k'oʔ-nan* 'you pl talk to me, us'). By contrast, in verbs that are not inflected for a first person category the only distinctions marked are person and plurality (see Table 13).

Verbs stems display the polysynthetic tendency typical of the northern Hokan languages (¶4.8.2), often compounding two or more instrumental, classificatory, and locational-directional elements. For example, *-tʰu-kʰ-* 'roll with the hand', *-miči-kʰ-* 'roll with the foot', *-tʰu-kluš-* 'knock over with the hand', *-miči-kluš-* 'knock over with the foot, kick over', *-tʰu-kʰ-tam-* 'roll down with the hand'. Verbs are inflected for tense, mode, and aspect by a system of suffixes of moderate complexity.

3.10.4 Nomenclature

Powers (1877:91–95) briefly described the "Chimalakwe" (New River) and "Chimariko" (Trinity River) tribelets and provided a vocabulary from the latter (1877:474). Powell (1891:63) adopted "Chimarikan" as the family name. From Kroeber onward only "Chimariko" has been used. Both Chimalakwe and Chimariko are native formations derived from the verb base *č'imar* 'be an Indian'.

3.11 Shastan Languages

The Shastan language family includes the **Shasta** and **Konomihu** languages, and probably a third language, **New River Shasta**, all spoken in the central and western parts of Siskiyou County (Map 13). A group known as the "Okwanuchu," living at the head of the Sacramento River immediately south of Mount Shasta, may have spoken a fourth Shastan language, but it is more likely that this was a speech community in which a variety of Shasta was spoken together (and perhaps mixed) with some non-Shastan language. The details of the Shastan relationship are not well understood, in large part because the languages other than Shasta are not well documented—in the case of New River Shasta and Okwanuchu, only in short word lists. The situation is further complicated by the fact that Shasta was the dominant language throughout the region, and loans from Shasta into other languages are difficult to distinguish from cognates.

The Shastan family has been grouped with Chimariko, Karuk, Yana, and Palaihnihan as Northern Hokan (Bright 1954; Haas 1976; Silver 1976). The close relationship between Shastan and Palaihnihan that was once widely accepted (Dixon 1905b; Haas 1963) is now rejected by most specialists (Olmsted 1956, 1957, 1959), along with the use of "Shastan" to label a Shastan-Palaihnihan subgroup within Hokan.

3.11.1 Geography

The Shasta language was spoken in a relatively large territory that stretched from the junction of Bear Creek and the Rogue River, near Jacksonville, Oregon, across the Siskiyou Mountains to the upper Klamath River canyon in

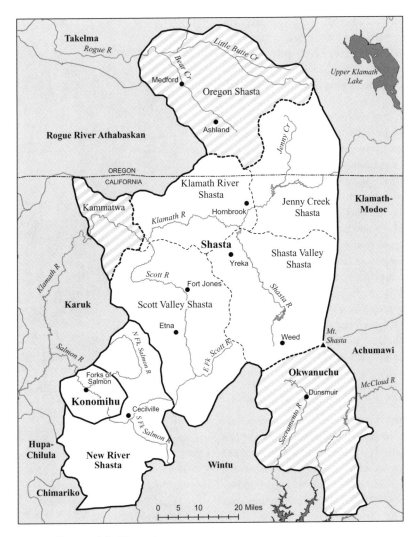

MAP 13. Shasta and the Shastan languages.

California, and southward up the Shasta and Scott Rivers to their headwaters. Shasta territory was bounded on the east by the crest of the Cascades from Mount McLoughlin to Mount Shasta, while easy communication with groups to the west was cut off by the rugged Salmon and Marble Mountains. Along the Klamath River, the canyon between Hamburg and Happy Camp served as a buffer between the Shasta and the Karuk downstream. Only in the north, where the ethnohistorical record indicates that there was considerable hostility between the Shasta and the Takelma, were the Shasta in close and sustained contact with other groups (Heizer and Hester 1970:141–144).

The Shasta were loosely organized into four divisions, apparently correlated with shallowly differentiated regional dialects. These included (1) the **Oregon Shasta** (*ikirakáccu* 'people from back behind'), along Bear Creek from its headwaters south of Ashland to its confluence with the Rogue River north of Medford; (2) the **Klamath River Shasta** (*iruhikwá:cu* 'people from along the river upstream'), along the Klamath between Hornbrook on the east and the mouth of Scott River on the west; (3) the **Scott Valley Shasta**

(*uwá:tuhúccu* 'people from the other side'), occupying the large valley on the upper Scott River between Fort Jones and Callaghan, as well as a portion of the upper Salmon River around Cecilville; and (4) the **Shasta Valley Shasta** (*ahútireʔe:cu* 'people from the open place'), from north of Yreka to the headwaters of Shasta River near Weed (Holt 1946:301; Silver 1978:223).

The names and locations of 156 villages are known, largely owing to Merriam's investigations (collated in Heizer and Hester 1970:119–131), but information on tribelet groupings and boundaries has not been preserved. Merriam noted that several villages were "large" or "important," and these probably represent divisional or regional centers. Among these are Kowachaha, at the mouth of Scott River ("home of a chief and a great place for fishing"); Hasnit, on the Klamath River above the mouth of Shasta River; Kwapesasera, in Scott Valley at the present site of Fort Jones; Ukyukwyaka, in Scott Valley four miles south of Etna; and Apone, on Shasta River northwest of Montague. Although villages had considerable autonomy, each of the four divisions recognized the loose authority of a headman or chief, whose position was hereditary in at least the Oregon division. At the beginning of the historical period the chief of the Oregon division exercised a limited authority over all four divisions, and was turned to as a mediator when there were serious disputes between divisions (Silver 1978:211–213).

At both the upstream and downstream ends of Klamath River Shasta territory there were Shasta-speaking villages whose speech apparently differed from any of the four dialectal divisions noted previously. At the upstream end, the **Jenny Creek Shastas,** who had villages along the Klamath between Hornbrook and Beswick as well as along Jenny Creek, were said to speak a divergent variety of Klamath River Shasta. At the downstream end, the people of the villages between Hamburg and Seiad Valley, referred to as the **Kammatwa** (*K'amat'wa*), are reported to have been bilingual in Shasta and an unattested second language (Curtis 1907–1930, vol. 13:232) and were scorned for their inability to speak Shasta properly. A similar group, the **Watiru**, living in the canyon from Seiad Valley west to Happy Camp, were said to speak the same unknown language as the Kammatwa but were bilingual in Karuk (Silver 1978:211).[35]

3.11.2 Documentation and Survival

Shasta is moderately well documented, although relatively little material has been published. The first attestation is a vocabulary collected in 1841 by James Dwight Dana, the geologist of the Wilkes Expedition, while exploring the Siskiyou Trail (Hale 1846:218, 569). This was reprinted by Stephen Powers (1877:607–613) along with vocabularies obtained in the 1850s by Crook, Hazen, and Ross, and a vocabulary collected by Powers himself in 1872. Survey lists were collected for the BAE by A. S. Gatschet (1877a), J. Owen Dorsey (1884q), and Jeremiah Curtin (1885a, 1885b). Extensive texts and other materials were obtained by R. B. Dixon (1908–1910; see also Dixon and Freeland 1928–1930) and by Jaime de Angulo and L. S. Freeland (1928–1930). Merriam collected two sets of vocabularies and natural history word lists, one from speakers of the Shasta Valley dialect (Appendix A: G-6c) and another from a speaker of the Scott Valley Shasta spoken in the Cecilville region on the upper Salmon River (Appendix A: G-6e). Shirley Silver worked extensively with the last speakers in 1957–1960, and has written a grammar (Silver 1966) and published an analyzed text (Silver and Wicks 1977). A short dictionary was published by William Bright and David Olmsted (1959), incorporating material from most of the older sources as well as from their own fieldwork in the 1950s.

Although Shasta survived into the mid-twentieth century, the last fluent speaker, Clara Wicks, died in 1978. In the absence of a federally recognized Shasta Tribe, many Shasta descendants have merged their political and cultural identity with the Karuk Tribe and now often consider Karuk their heritage language.

FIGURE 43. Sargent Sambo, Klamath River Shasta, principal source of ethnographic and linguistic data for Roland B. Dixon (1907, 1908–1910) and later investigators. Photograph by Cecile Jacobs, Hornbrook, ca. 1958. Courtesy of Shirley Silver.

FIGURE 44. Clara Wicks, the last fluent speaker of Shasta and Shirley Silver's principal consultant. Courtesy Shirley Silver.

3.11.3 Konomihu

The Konomihu were a small group on the lower Salmon River whose territory centered on the area around Forks of Salmon. The names and locations of twenty-one Konomihu villages have been preserved (Merriam 1967a:239–240), nearly all of them located along the Salmon River within ten miles of Forks of Salmon. The westernmost village was at Butler Flat, the easternmost at the mouth of Plummer Creek. In precontact times the Konomihu were culturally dominated by the Karuk on the Klamath River, only a few miles west of their territory. The Salmon River region was heavily impacted by mining activity in the 1850s, however, and in subsequent decades the Konomihu were culturally absorbed by Scott Valley Shastas who resettled in the area. By the 1860s the language of the "Etna people" had become the lingua franca of the area (Larsson 1987:235). Thus the extensive vocabularies and ethnogeographical data that Merriam collected from the Konomihu in 1919 and 1921 documented a Shasta-speaking community (Appendix A: G-6a; cf. Merriam 1967a:230–249).

Nevertheless, sufficient material has been recovered to allow the general nature of the language earlier spoken in Konomihu territory to be outlined. In 1903, Dixon was able to gather about seventy-five words and phrases of "the old people's talk" from two Konomihu women, Susan Brazille and her sister Ellen (Mrs. Hugh Grant) (Dixon 1905b:213–214, 1907:497–498).[36] Although both "were emphatic in declaring that they knew of no one then living [in 1903] who could speak the language" (Dixon 1931:266), they remembered fragments of the older Konomihu they had learned as children from their maternal grandfather (Larsson 1987; Silver 1980).

The Brazille sisters, who lived into the early 1940s, were subsequently visited by two other researchers. Jaime de Angulo obtained a short word list from Susan Brazille in 1928, but it was almost identical to the one that Dixon had collected. J. P. Harrington, however, working with characteristic perseverance during extended field visits in 1928 and 1933, obtained a considerable amount of new material from both sisters (Mills 1985:29–48; Larsson 1987:234–235).

Although the language remembered by Susan and Ellen Brazille appears to have been a divergent member of the Shastan family (Silver 1980), its structural differences from Shasta are considerable (see ¶3.11.6). This fact led Olmsted to suggest that it might be better to consider it a separate Hokan branch (1959:638).

3.11.4 New River Shasta

At the time of white contact in the 1850s, a distinct ethnographic and linguistic group appears to have been thinly dispersed across the rugged Salmon Mountains east and south of the Konomihu, including the North Fork of the Salmon above Sawyers Bar, the South Fork of the Salmon in the vicinity of Cecilville, and the upper drainage of New River as far south as Denny (P. Goddard 1903a:8; Dixon 1907; Kroeber 1925:282–283). This group—somewhat inexactly referred to as the "New River Shasta"—has been

FIGURE 45. Mrs. Hugh Grant (née Ellen Brazille or Bussel), one of two sisters from whom Roland B. Dixon, Jaime de Angulo, and J. P. Harrington were able to recover fragments of Konomihu. Butler Flat on the Salmon River, September 1921. C. Hart Merriam collection of Native American photographs (G/6a/P2 no.1). Courtesy of the Bancroft Library UCB.

FIGURE 46. Saxy Kidd, Hupa-Chimariko bilingual and the son of Malinda Kidd, the last documented speaker of New River Shasta. 1926. C. Hart Merriam collection of Native American photographs (G/6f/P1 no.6). Courtesy of the Bancroft Library UCB.

FIGURE 47. C. Hart Merriam collecting an Okwanuchu vocabulary from Lottie O'Neal. Squaw Creek, Shasta County, 1925. C. Hart Merriam collection of Native American photographs (G/6d/P1 no.7). Courtesy of the Bancroft Library UCB.

culturally extinct for nearly 150 years, and the documentation of their language is, not surprisingly, scanty and open to interpretation. Merriam further muddied the situation by claiming that this mountainous backcountry harbored not one but two distinctive languages, one spoken on the New River above the Chimariko, which he called "Tlo-hom-tah-hoi," and the other spoken on the Salmon River above the Konomihu, which he called "Hah-to-ke-he-wuk" or "Kah-hoo-tin-e-rook" (Merriam 1930a, 1967a:241–243; Dixon 1931).

A good part of the confusion can be attributed to the fact that the already weak sociolinguistic cohesion of the thin "New River Shasta" population seems to have been totally destroyed by the disruptive events of the Gold Rush period. By the late nineteenth century, (Scott Valley) Shasta and Hupa had become the dominant Indian languages of the Salmon Mountain region, and the few New River Shastas who remained when data began to be collected around 1900 were primarily speakers of these intrusive languages. Thus the vocabulary of "Hah-to-ke-he-wuk" that Merriam obtained from a speaker from Cecilville (Appendix A: G-6e) merely attests a Shasta dialect, as does most of the vocabulary collected in the same area by P. E. Goddard (1902b).[37] Of the twenty-seven items in Dixon's 1903 New River Shasta vocabulary, thirteen resemble Shasta closely enough to be loanwords (Dixon 1931). The "Tlo-hom-tah-hoi" vocabulary collected by Merriam (Appendix A: J-9a) consists largely of Chimariko and Konomihu forms.

Only one individual with any degree of fluency in the distinctive New River Shasta language, Malinda Kidd, survived into the twentieth century. Three short attestations of her speech were made between 1901 and 1903. The most extensive and phonetically reliable of these is an unpublished

vocabulary of approximately sixty-five words and phrases collected by Kroeber (1901). A few supplementary items were added by Goddard in a brief visit the following summer (1902a). A vocabulary of twenty-seven items was collected by Dixon in 1903, fifteen of which he published (Dixon 1909, 1931; Merriam 1967a:245); the remainder have been lost with the original manuscript.[38]

3.11.5 Okwanuchu

The language of the Okwanuchu, who lived at the head of the Sacramento River, around Mount Shasta City and Dunsmuir, and to the east on the upper McCloud River, is known only through a list of about seventy-five words collected by Merriam in 1925 (Appendix A: G-6d; cf. 1979:62-3) and seven words published by R. B. Dixon (1905b) that he excerpted from a longer list that is now lost. In both Merriam's and Dixon's attestations, Okwanuchu vocabulary is sharply divided into words that are almost identical to Shasta and other words that show no resemblance to Shasta or to any other language in the region. Unlike Konomihu and New River Shasta, moreover, "the general phonetic character" of Okwanuchu differed "quite a little in some points from the Shasta, particularly in its fondness for nasals" (Dixon 1905b:215).[39]

The most likely explanation for the mixed nature of the Okwanuchu linguistic corpus is that it documents a community undergoing language shift. A hint of what the sociolinguistic circumstances might have been in this area are given by Du Bois, who in her ethnographic survey of the Wintu area in the early 1930s discovered an elderly woman from a group that the Wintu called the *Waymaq* ('northern people'), who had been all but exterminated by the Modoc

TABLE 14
Shasta Phonemes (Silver 1966)
All consonants other than the approximants (*w, r, y*) can occur geminated between vowels.

Consonants						Vowels	
p	t	c	č	k	?	i / i:	u / u:
p'	t'	c'	č'	k'		e / e:	a / a:
		s		x	h		
m	n						
w	r		y				

Pitch Accents
v́ high
v (unmarked) low

in a retaliatory raid during the Modoc War. These people, who had lived on the McCloud River above Nosoni Creek (near the head of the McCloud River Arm of the present Shasta Lake), were "supposed to have spoken two languages, their own (or Shastan) and Wintu." The woman recalled a few words and phrases of her traditional language, at least three of which (*atsa* 'water', *au-u* 'wood', and *katisuk* 'bring') are clearly Shasta. Du Bois suggested that the Waymaq of the upper McCloud and the Okwanuchu of the upper Sacramento were essentially the same people, a "transitional" group "among whom one tribal unit gradually faded into another" (Du Bois 1935:8). But since the non-Shasta words in Dixon's attestation of Okwanuchu are not of Wintu origin, but come from some unidentified source, this explanation is probably oversimplified.

3.11.6 Linguistic Structure

Of the Shastan languages, only Shasta is well enough documented to allow a structural summary, although Silver (1980) has made a tentative analysis of Konomihu phonology.

Shasta has five stops and affricates (*p, t, c* [ts], *č, k*), which occur both plain and glottalized (Table 14). There are two fricatives (*s, x*), two nasals (*m, n*), three approximants (*r, w, y*), and two laryngeals (*h, ?*). There are four vowels (*i, e, a, u*). All vowels, and all medial consonants other than approximants, can be either short or long, and all syllables are either high (v́) or low (unmarked) in pitch.

In Konomihu, aspirated stops and affricates occur in addition to the plain and glottalized sets, but these may be secondary, resulting from vowel deletion conditioned by the placement of the pitch accent. The distinction between *c* and *č* is not certain, and there may only be a single affricate series. Konomihu also appears to lack *r*, and to have *v* (or a bilabial fricative [β], as in Karuk) in place of *w*.

Shasta noun morphology is simple, largely restricted to suffixes or enclitics marking possessive, locative, and other

oblique case relationships, and collective plurality. Konomihu has two frequently occurring noun prefixes, apparently of demonstrative force (and possibly proclitics).

Shasta verbs are quite complex. An obligatory set of unanalyzable prefixes marks various combinations of tense, mode, person, and number (e.g., *t-* 'let me . . .', *s-* 'I might . . .', *sw-* 'I am . . .', *kw-* 'I have . . .', *p'-* 'I used to . . .'). Third person prefixes in addition mark evidentiality (e.g., *k'wáhussi:k* 'he talked [so I have perceived]', *táhussi:k* 'he talked [so it is said]'). Stems, which are usually vowel-initial, consist of a root of general verbal meaning that is often followed by an attributive suffix that marks salient properties of the verbal action, as for example in *-ehé-čukku-* 'jump from one place to another', *-ehé-ka:ru-* 'bob up and down', or *-ehé-:nu-* 'shoot up into the air' (based on the root *-ehé-* 'jump, move suddenly'); and in *-a:?a:-kaká-* 'drag something' or *-a:?a:-kwitti-* 'break a rigid, long object' (based on *-a:?a:-* 'handle something with force'). Stems may also be extended by a suffix that marks the location or direction of the action (e.g., *-učč'i-wa:k-* 'fall into the water', *-učč'i-čw-* 'fall off of something', *-ehe-:nu-čw-* 'shoot up into the air off of something', *-a:?a:-kaká-wa:k-* 'drag something into the water'). Several further classes of suffixes mark various derivational categories, with aspect obligatorily marked by a final suffix.

3.11.7 Nomenclature

The Wilkes Expedition geologist James Dwight Dana, who was the first to collect a vocabulary from a Shastan language (apparently the Oregon dialect of Shasta), called it "Saste," from Klamath *seste* 'Shasta Indians', although he (or Hale) called the people "Shasty" or "Shasties" (Hale 1846:218, 569). Stephen Powers (1877:243) claimed "Shastika" to be the original term, but acknowledged "Shasta" to be the name by which the tribe and its language had generally come to be known by the 1870s. Since Dana's name had priority, Powell (1891:105–106) called the family "Sastean." R. B. Dixon, however, preferred "Shasta" (1907), and his usage prevailed. He and A. L. Kroeber later used "Shastan" to label a larger family that included the four "Shasta" or "Sastean" languages and the two Palaihnihan languages (Kroeber 1925:279). Since this grouping is no longer widely accepted, "Shastan" is now usually restricted to Dixon's Shasta group.

3.12 Palaihnihan Languages

The Palaihnihan language family consists of two distinct languages spoken along the Pit River and its tributaries in the plateau region of northeastern California. *Achumawi*, a cluster of nine local dialects, was spoken along Pit River from Big Bend in Shasta County to Goose Lake and the Warner Mountains near the Nevada border. *Atsugewi* was spoken to the south of Pit River in two dialect areas, along Hat Creek to the west and in Dixie Valley to the east.

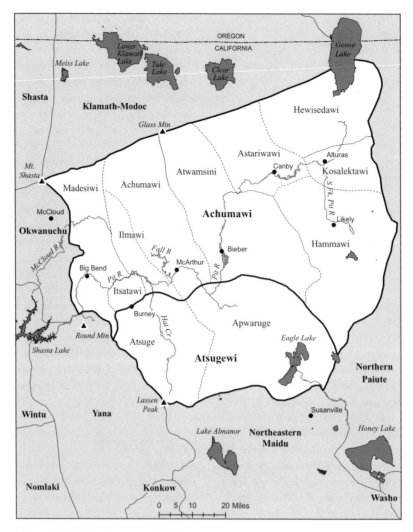

MAP 14. Palaihnihan languages and dialects.

The split between Achumawi and Atsugewi is surprisingly deep. While the 1100–1500 BC date of separation that Baumhoff and Olmsted calculated (1963, 1964) is almost certainly too early, de Angulo and Freeland, who knew the languages well, estimated them to be as deeply differentiated as French and Spanish, "perhaps even more" (1930:78). The two linguistic communities were nevertheless in close contact—Cayton Valley Achumawi and Hat Creek Atsugewi villages were separated by only a few miles—and inter-marriage was frequent. Many Atsugewi speakers were bilingual in Achumawi, although not vice versa (Voegelin 1946; Olmsted 1954), and Atsugewi has a number of obvious Achumawi loanwords, particularly for items of material culture (Merriam 1926a:5–11).[40]

The linguistic details of the Palaihnihan relationship were explored by Olmsted, who worked out the phonemic correspondences beween the two languages and reconstructed 205 Proto-Palaihnihan forms (1964:36–48). Good, McFarland, and Paster (2003) have revisited and refined some of Olmsted's correspondences on the basis of more recent and accurate data. The proposal that Palaihnihan

and Shastan form a subgroup within Hokan (Dixon 1905b; Bright 1954) is no longer widely accepted, although Kaufman (1988) still finds some merit in the hypothesis.

3.12.1 Achumawi

GEOGRAPHY

The nine Achumawi groups were located along the mountainous course of Pit River, extending more than 150 miles from the densely forested margins of the northern Sacramento Valley to the river's headwaters in the high, arid grassland around Alturas (Map 14). Settlements were concentrated in valleys, often separated from one another by rocky canyons. The river was not easily navigable by canoe for long distances, and communication between groups was restricted. Each group had its own local dialect, although these were very shallowly differentiated.[41]

An important cultural distinction can be drawn between the downriver (western) and upriver (eastern) Achumawi-speaking groups. The four western groups, along with the

Hat Creek Atsugewi, were divided into autonomous tribelets, focused their subsistence activities on acorns, and in many other respects formed part of the Central California culture area (Kniffen 1928:319). By contrast, the Achumawi groups to the east of Fall River, along with the Dixie Valley Atsugewi, had hereditary band chiefs, focused their gathering activities on camass and other tubers, and generally participated in the culture of the Plateau and Basin. The Achumawi local dialects fall into two clusters—upiver and downriver—that more or less conform to this cultural and ecological division, the boundary falling between the Achumawi (proper) and Atwamsini dialects (Nevin 1998:2–3).

Downriver Dialect Groups

The **Madesiwi** (*madé:siwí*), or Big Bend Achumawi, were the westernmost Achumawi group. Their main settlement, Mades (*madé:si*), was located just east of the mouth of Kosk Creek on the north side of Pit River at Big Bend. The area had abundant resources and was the most densely populated part of Achumawi territory. The Madesiwi were on friendly terms with the Wintu to the west (Chase-Dunn and Mann 1998), much of whose culture they shared, and also with the Northern Yana at Montgomery Creek, but they were wary of the Yana who lived in the rough country to the south, who were said to have sometimes raided Madesiwi villages.

The **Itsatawi** (*ʔič'á:tay̓éwawí* 'Goose Valley people'), or Goose Valley Achumawi, were a small group whose territory centered on the Goose Valley and lower Burney Creek area. They were closely connected to the Madesiwi.

The **Ilmawi** (*ilmé:wí* 'people of the village of Ilma'), or Cayton Valley Achumawi, occupied Pit River from the mouth of Burney Creek to a few miles below Fall River Mills. This was an especially well-endowed area, with important salmon fishing sites and abundant acorns, and it contained several large villages. The Hat Creek Atsugewi were directly to the south of Ilmawi territory, and the two groups were in close contact, although not always on friendly terms.

The **Achumawi** proper (*ačúmmá:wí* 'river people'), or Fall River Achumawi, lived in the Fall River Valley, which marked the upstream limit of acorn oaks and salmon fishing sites. Settlements were scattered along Fall River and Pit River in the vicinity of Glenburn, McArthur, and Pittville. The territory of the Fall River Achumawi also extended north into the lava beds. They sometimes visited Glass Mountain, the principal source of obsidian in this area, where they occasionally fought with the Modoc. Their more frequent encounters with the Modoc were in the Fall River area, however, which the Modoc raided constantly to capture slaves (Kniffen 1928:312).

Upriver Dialect Groups

The **Atwamwi** (*atw̓amwí* 'valley people') or **Atwamsini** (*atw̓amsini* 'valley dwellers'), the Big Valley Achumawi, occupied the high valley to the east of the Big Valley Mountains around Bieber and Nubieber, and also the Ash Creek area to the north, around Lookout. Tule and seed-bearing grasses were abundant, and edible roots plentiful, and people from adjacent groups often visited to utilize these resources. About twenty small settlements were spread across the area.

The **Astariwawi** (*ʔasda:qíʔwí* 'hot [springs] people'), or Hot Springs Achumawi, lived along Pit River upstream from Big Valley to about eight miles west of Alturas. They had four major sites, somewhat separated from one another. The most important of these was at the hot springs east of Canby, where the band chief lived. Fishing was important in this region. Like the Fall River Achumawi, the Astariwawi were subjected to frequent slave raids by the Modoc.

The **Kosalektawi** (*q'óssiʔálléq'taʔwí* 'juniper-liking people'), or Alturas Achumawi, occupied a relatively small area where the north and south forks of Pit River join. Their principal settlement was near the site of present-day Alturas, and the headman of the band lived there. Hunting and fishing were the principal subsistence activities. As with the Likely Achumawi to the south of them, the territory of the Alturas Achumawi extended up to the crest of the Warner Mountains, the eastern side of which was in Northern Paiute territory. Their relations with the Paiutes were hostile, and they were sometimes attacked by them.

The **Hammawi** (*ħammá:wí* 'south fork of Pit River people'), or Likely Achumawi, lived along the south fork of Pit River in the semiarid region to the south of Alturas. Their principal settlement was in the vicinity of the present town of Likely, near the Modoc-Butte county line. Their life style was seminomadic, and their basic social unit was essentially a foraging band.

The **Hewisedawi** (*hé:wíssídé:wí* 'the ones who live high up'), or Goose Lake Achumawi, lived in scattered locations in the high, mostly arid territory along the north fork of Pit River, north of Alturas. They also utilized the shallow waters of Goose Lake during the periods when it was not dry. Little is known about the Goose Lake group other than that their principal settlement was on a mesa about ten miles north of Alturas.

DOCUMENTATION AND SURVIVAL

Achumawi has a substantial history of study, although much of the collected material remains unpublished. The first attestation was a vocabulary collected by Horatio Hale in 1841 and labeled by him "Palaihnih" (Hale 1846; see ¶3.12.4). A vocabulary was collected by George Gibbs in the early 1860s from a member of the "A-pui band at the forks of Pitt and Fall Rivers" who had been brought to Washington, DC (Gibbs 1861–1862); it was published by Powers (1877:601–606), together with an Achumawi vocabulary obtained by Powers himself in 1875. Jeremiah Curtin completed a BAE survey list for the Ilmawi variety (1889j) and obtained a small collection of myth texts (1885c).

FIGURE 48. Ruby Miles, a speaker of the Hammawi variety of upriver Achumawi, working with Shirley Silver. Photograph by Scott Patterson, 1982. Courtesy of Shirley Silver and Victoria K. Patterson.

The substantial twentieth-century documentation includes materials collected by Paul Radin from a speaker of a downriver variety in 1919–1920; Jaime de Angulo's extensive documentation of the Hammawi and Atwamsini varieties, made between 1921 and 1931; H. J. Uldall's precise observations of Achumawi phonetics during joint fieldwork with de Angulo in 1931; Abe Halpern's State Emergency Relief Project collection of texts and anecdotes in Hammawi and other varieties (Halpern 1936b); David Olmsted's fieldwork in the 1950s on six varieties, in particular Fall River; work by James Bauman and Shirley Silver in 1970 with speakers of several downriver varieties and in 1976–1979 and 1982 by Silver alone with speakers of Kosalektawi and Hammawi; and an extensive field investigation of Madesi and Itsatawi carried out by Bruce Nevin in 1970–1974 for his doctoral dissertation (Nevin 1998). The only major publications arising from this work include an idiosyncratic but insightful grammatical sketch by de Angulo and Freeland (1930) and a dictionary partially based on de Angulo's data (Olmsted 1966).[42]

A nontechnical introductory survey and a learner's dictionary have also been published (Bauman 1980b; Bauman, Miles, and Leaf 1979). Important unpublished manuscripts include notes for a grammatical sketch (Radin 1919–1920), a comparative grammar of Achumawi and Pomo (de Angulo ca. 1931), a collection of texts (de Angulo and Freeland ca. 1931), a phonetic sketch (Uldall 1933), and a comprehensive study of Achumawi phonology and phonetics (Nevin 1998). Merriam also collected extensive comparative vocabularies of at least five dialects (partially published in Merriam 1979:64–74 and in Olmsted 1966:143–158).

Achumawi is spoken by fewer than ten elderly people, most of them semispeakers or passive speakers. There are noticeable differences among local varieties. Instructional materials were prepared for a language program in the 1980s, but this program is apparently no longer in operation.

3.12.2 Atsugewi

GEOGRAPHY

The territory belonging to the speakers of Atsugewi lay to the south of Pit River, and was divided, like Achumawi territory, into a western area in which acorn processing and salmon fishing were the dominant subsistence activities, and an eastern area where the inhabitants were largely dependent on hunting and the collection of roots and tubers (Map 14).

The **Atsuge** (*aču-keyi* 'pine tree people'), or Hat Creek Atsugewi, were the western group. Their territory included the Hat Creek Valley south of Cassel and the upper Burney Valley, and extended south to Lassen Peak. The four settlement sites were in the lower Hat Creek Valley and at Burney, the upper valleys and mountains being visited only in the summer. Each settlement had its own hereditary chief. They had little involvement with the Yana and Maidu. They had friendly trade relationships with the Dixie Valley Atsugewi and the Goose Creek Achumawi, but were frequently at odds with their closest neighbors, the Ilmawi, or Cayton Valley Achumawi, who occupied Pit River around the mouth of Hat Creek.

The **Apwaruge** (*apwaru-keyi* 'Dixie Valley people'), or Dixie Valley Atsugewi, lived in several isolated locations in the high, barren plain that stretched from Pit River near Big Valley southeast toward Susanville. The most important winter village sites were situated along Horse Creek, in or near Dixie Valley (*apwaru*). In the summer the they hunted and foraged as far south as Eagle Lake and Willow Creek. They were friendly with the Hat Creek Atsugewi, from whom they got acorns, and with the downriver Achumawi, from whom they got salmon. They were also on good terms with the Northern Paiute, but hostile to the upriver Achumawi groups who frequently fought the Paiute.

DOCUMENTATION AND SURVIVAL

Atsugewi has been moderately well documented, but only a small portion of the material that has been collected is published or easily accessible. The first important attestation of Atsugewi as a language distinct from Achumawi was a BAE survey list collected by Jeremiah Curtin (1884d). Jaime de Angulo collected data on Atsugewi in the late 1920s to parallel his work on Achumawi, and he and L. S. Freeland completed a grammatical sketch (1929). David Olmsted collected material on Atsugewi as part of his Pit River fieldwork in 1953–1959 and published two papers (1958, 1961) and a lexicon (1984). Diane Walters worked with the last speaker of the Dixie Valley dialect in the 1970s (Walters 1977). The most detailed and accurate data come from Leonard Talmy, who carried out extensive fieldwork in the

FIGURE 49. Selena LaMarr, Leonard Talmy's primary Atsugewi consultant, describing her culture to visitors at Lassen Volcanic National Park. Photograph by John Robinson, 1953. Courtesy of the National Park Service.

1960s with Selena LaMarr, the last fluent speaker of the Hat Creek dialect, as part of his dissertation research on comparative semantic structures (Talmy 1972, 1985).

According to Talmy, at the time of his fieldwork Atsugewi was "spoken impeccably by perhaps only one person and well by no more than five—none of them young" (1972:6). The last of these individuals passed away in 1988, and no revitalization effort is known to be under way at the present time.

3.12.3 Linguistic Structure

Nevin (1998) provides a detailed description of Achumawi phonology, with remarks on Atsugewi. The small amount of published information on Palaihnihan morphosyntax that is available focuses on Atsugewi (Olmsted 1961; Talmy 1972; Walters 1977).

The phonemic inventories of Achumawi and Atsugewi are very similar, although not identical (Table 15). Both languages have five series of oral stops and affricates (*p, t, č, k, q*), each with a plain, aspirated, and glottalized member, except for the back velar series which lacks an aspirated member; the affricate *č* varies in articulation from dental-alveolar [ts] to palatal [tʃ].[43] There are two fricatives (*s, x̣*); two nasals (*m, n*); three approximants (*l, w, y*); two laryngeals (*h, ʔ*); and a pharyngeal or epiglottal fricative (*ħ*).[44] All nasals and approximants occur both plain and glottalized (*ṁ, ṅ, l', ẇ, ẏ*). There are five full vowels (*i, e, a, o, u*) that occur both short and long, and a short epenthetic central vowel (*ə*). Atsugewi differs from Achumawi in having an aspirated back velar stop in place of a back velar fricative,

and in lacking the pharyngeal/epiglottal fricative (*ħ*); cognate forms have *h* with a lowered vowel in place of *ħ* (Good, McFarland, and Paster 2003). It also apparently has a rhotic liquid (*r*) that contrasts with *l*. In Achumawi, all syllables have either high pitch (*v́*) or low pitch (unmarked); a pitch contrast is not noted in Atsugewi.

Palaihnihan verb structure is classically polysynthetic. Verbs are inflected for subject, mode, tense, and such derivational categories as causative by sets of prefixes and suffixes that are remarkable for their irregularity and phonological complexity, often fusing with stem elements. Although some verb stems are unanalyzable (Atsugewi *-ičm-* 'sleep', *-ye:č-* 'sing'), they are often morphemically complex, particularly when expressing motions or physical actions. In Talmy's analysis (1972), Atsugewi verb stems can include as many as three morphological components: (1) a "figure-specifying" prefix that defines the instrumental or physical profile of the action (e.g., *ma-* 'with the feet'); (2) a root that specifies the class of entity in motion (e.g., *-swal-* 'limp material'); and (3) one or more suffixes marking the direction or location of the action (e.g., *-ič't* 'into liquid') (see ¶4.8.2).

Nominalized verbs frequently function as nouns (e.g., *ye:č-i* 'song' < *ye:č* 'sing'), but there are many root nouns, typically di- or trisyllabic (*ehew* 'mountain', *ači* 'water', *aẇteh* 'person', *yehči* 'land', *ismiči* 'girl', *minuri* 'woman'). Atsugewi noun phrases are normally marked by a proclitic article *č(ə)* (e.g., *č-ači* 'the water', *č-itki ači* 'the big water, ocean', *čə-č'nehẇa* 'the moon').

3.12.4 Nomenclature

The name "Palaihnihan" was bestowed on the family by Powell (1891), basing it on "Palaihnih," the name Hale gave to his vocabulary of Achumawi (1846), apparently Klamath-Modoc *playkʰni:* 'people from above'. Although *playkʰni:* is recorded ethnographically as the name of a

TABLE 15
Achumawi Phonemes (Nevin 1998)
Most consonants can be geminated in medial position.

Consonants							Vowels			
p	t	č	k	q		(ʔ)	i / i:			i / u:
pʰ	tʰ	čʰ	kʰ				e /e:		(ə)	o / o:
p'	t'	č'	k'	q'					a / a:	
	s	š		x̣	ħ	h				
m	n									
ṁ	ṅ									
w	l	y								
ẇ	l'	ẏ								

Pitch Accents
v́ high pitch
v low pitch

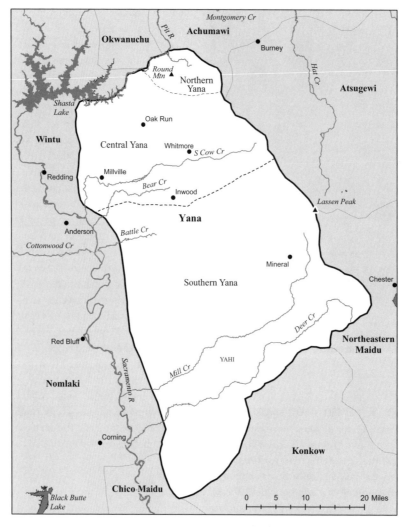

MAP 15. Yana territory and dialects.

Klamath-speaking group on the upper Sprague River in Oregon, near the modern town of Bly (¶3.23.1), Hale probably obtained his vocabulary in Modoc territory, in northeastern California, where Achumawi was indeed the language spoken at higher elevations to the southeast.

The language names "Achumawi" and "Atsugewi" are generalized from the names of two local dialect groups: Achumawi from the name of the Fall River group, Atsugewi from the name of the Hat Creek group. This usage, while confusing, is entrenched in the literature. In a creative attempt to overcome the ambiguity, Olmsted, in most of his published work, consistently distinguished between the "Achumawi" language and the "Ajumawi" dialect, although these are merely two spellings of the same word.

3.13 Yana

Yana is a classificatory isolate within the Hokan phylum (Sapir 1917a). A single language with three moderately differentiated dialects, it was spoken in the hills and canyons that border the northeastern corner of the Sacramento

Valley, between Pit River on the north and roughly the Tehama-Butte county line on the south. The northernmost Yanas, around Montgomery Creek, lived closely adjacent to the territory of the Madesi Achomawi; the Yahi subgroup at the opposite end of Yana territory bordered on the Maiduan-speaking Hill Konkows. To the east, the crest of the Cascades, dominated by the active volcano Lassen Peak, separated the Yana from the Atsugewi and the Northeastern Maidu, while on the west, Yana territory extended to within a few miles of the Sacramento River, although the river itself belonged to the Wintu and the Nomlaki. With the partial exception of the Achumawi, the Yanas had a generally hostile relationship with all neighboring groups, from whom they were physically as well as linguistically distinct, and were on particularly bad terms with the Wintu.[45]

3.13.1 Geography

Three dialects of Yana are usually distinguished (Map 15). **Northern Yana** was spoken in a relatively small territory along Montgomery Creek and Cedar Creek, tributaries of the

FIGURE 50. Ishi with (*left to right*) T. T. Waterman, Paul Radin, Robert Lowie, and Edward Sapir. On the UC campus, Berkeley, August 1915. Courtesy of the Hearst Museum of Anthropology and the Regents of UC (15-16977).

Pit River, reaching south to Bullskin Ridge and including Round Mountain. *Central Yana* was spoken along the branches of Cow Creek and Bear Creek, tributaries of the Sacramento, in the vicinity of the modern communities of Millville, Oak Run, Whitmore, and Inwood. The speakers of these two dialects were culturally similar to the Madesi and other western Achumawi groups. A third dialect, *Southern Yana*, was spoken in a number of subdialects, each associated with a small nomadic band, in the dry, lava-strewn country that extends from Battle Creek to the southern end of Yana territory. Only one of the Southern Yana subdialects, *Yahi*, the variety spoken by Ishi, is more than minimally documented.

This tripartite nomenclature obscures the deep split between Northern and Central Yana on the one hand and Southern Yana on the other. Northern and Central Yana, while clearly distinct from one another, differed mainly in vocabulary and were easily mutually intelligible. Southern Yana, as attested in Yahi, differed from both Northern and Central Yana in many lexical, grammatical, and phonological particulars and was understood by Northern and Central Yana speakers only with difficulty.[46]

3.13.2 Documentation and Survival

Yana is remarkably well documented, although the language seems to have escaped the notice of linguists before John Wesley Powell collected a vocabulary in 1880 (Powell 1880a, 1891:135). In the course of the next decade, Jeremiah Curtin, working at Powell's direction under BAE auspices, collected a large amount of data on Yana during

his survey of northern California languages (Curtin 1884a, 1884–1889a, 1884–1889b). He also transcribed a number of mythological narratives, largely in English (published in Curtin 1898:281–484). In 1900, R. B. Dixon obtained a small amount of linguistic material and further mythological narratives (published in Sapir 1910a:209–235). Merriam collected a general and a natural history word list from Northern Yana speakers in visits to Round Mountain between 1907 and 1926 (Appendix A: L-11a), while Harrington collected a considerable amount of data, principally Northern Yana vocabulary and place-names, during several months of fieldwork in the same area in 1922 and 1931 (Mills 1985:56–81).

By far the most important documentation of Yana was made by Edward Sapir, who studied Northern and Central Yana in the field during the summer and fall of 1907 and worked with Ishi in Berkeley during the summer of 1915. Sapir published a volume of Central and Northern Yana texts (1910a), a study of Yana kinship terminology (1918), an outline of Northern Yana grammar (1922b), an exposition of the major points of difference among the three dialects in the form of comparative text analyses (1923b), and a description of gender-based speech styles (1929a). A dictionary, primarily of the Northern and Central dialects, was assembled from Sapir's notes after his death (Sapir and Swadesh 1960). Sapir's materials on Ishi's Yahi subdialect of Southern Yana are being readied for publication.[47]

The last known speakers of Yana died before 1940. Although there is wide interest in the story of Ishi (T. Kroeber 1961), no modern tribal group claims to be

TABLE 16
Yana Phonemes (Sapir 1922b)

Consonants					Vowels		
p	t	c	k	ʔ	i / iː		u / uː
pʰ	tʰ	cʰ	kʰ		e / eː		o / oː
p'	t'	c'	k'			a / aː	
		s	x	h			
m	n						
ṁ	ṅ						
w	r	l	y				
ẇ		l'	ẏ				

primarily of Yana descent and no attempts are currently being made to revive the language.[48]

3.13.3 Linguistic Structure

Although a comprehensive linguistic description of Yana does not exist, Sapir's sketch of Northern Yana morphology (1922b) can serve as a basic analytic framework, and his detailed annotation of three short text samples, one from each dialect (1923b), provides a wealth of information about both phonology and grammar. Leanne Hinton (1988) has also published a useful synopsis of Sapir's morphosyntactic scheme. Herbert Luthin has made a thorough study of Yana discourse structure as it is represented in Sapir's texts (Luthin 1988, 1991).

Yana has three series of stops (*p, t, k*) and a postalevolar affricate series (*c* [ṭṣ]), each with a plain, aspirated, and glottalized member (Table 16). There are two fricatives (*s, x*), with *s* usually postalveolar [ṣ]. There is a voiced trill (*r*), two nasals (*m, n*), three approximants (*l, w, y*), and two laryngeals (*ʔ, h*). Nasals and approximants occur both plain and glottalized. There are five vowels (*i, e, a, o, u*), all of which occur both short and long. All three dialects have basically the same phonology, but in Northern Yana the nasals are denasalized to plain *p* and *t* when syllable-final, *ṁ* and *ṅ* becoming *p + ʔ* and *t + ʔ*.

Noun phrases are made up of an inflected pronoun or article and an uninflected, although sometimes derivationally complex, noun. Typical pronoun/articles are *ay* 'the, it', *aykʰ* 'his, her, its'(possesive), *ayki* 'to it, on it' (oblique), *aye* 'that yonder' (distal), *ayekʰ* 'of that yonder' (distal possessive). Typical noun phrases are *ay ʔiːkunna* 'the sweathouse', *ayki ʔiːkunna* 'at, in, by the sweathouse', *ayeki ʔiːkunna* 'at, in, by that sweathouse yonder', *aykʰ ʔiːkunna* 'his sweathouse'.

Verb stems are usually complex, exhibiting a variety of the "bipartite" stem structure that is widespread in this region (¶4.8.2). The root, which is initial, is often instrumental or classificatory in meaning (e.g., *lay-* 'hard round object lies', *me-* 'handle wood', *ho-* 'do with a long object') and is often followed by a secondary root of more

concrete semantics (e.g., *-k'aw-* 'cut, break', *-t'aṅ-* 'crack, mash'). Derivational stem suffixes mark locational and directional categories (e.g., *-tu* 'back', *-wil* 'across', *-ri* 'down'), more than one of which may occur in a given stem. An important subset of these suffixes specifies movement to or from one of the four cardinal directions (e.g., *-kapʰ-* 'to the north', *-tkʰi-* 'from the east', *-haw-* 'to the east'). The stem and its derivational suffixes are followed by one or more inflectional elements, marking aspect, evidentiality, causativity, mode, and tense, with pronominal subject and object marked by a complex set of word-final suffixes.

Formally marked gender-linked registers are attested in Yana (Sapir 1929a). The male register ("men's speech") is used only by men when speaking to other men, the female register ("women's speech") by women in nearly all contexts except when quoting men, and by men when speaking to women. The male register is characterized by full and deliberate forms, the female register by abbreviated forms. In monosyllabic nouns or any noun ending in a long vowel, diphthong, or consonant, the male register adds an enclitic (*-na*, sometimes assimilated to *-la*, in Northern and Central Yana, and either *-na* (*-la*) or *-hi* in Ishi's Southern Yana). Typical male/female register pairs are *imampa/imampʰ(a)* 'deer liver', *ayeʔe/aye* 'that one yonder', *ʔiːsi/ʔiːs(i)* 'man', *yucʰay-na/yuːcʰayh* 'acorn', *yaː-na/yah* 'person' (*yaː-hi/yah* in Southern Yana).

3.13.4 Nomenclature

The Northern and Central Yana were first known as the "Nozi" or "Noje," from Northeastern Maidu *nusí* or *nisí* 'the short (ones)', and were so designated in Powers (1877) and by Powell, who obtained the first full vocabulary (1880a). Powers distinguished the Southern Yana as the "Kombo," from Maidu *k'ómbo*, of obscure etymology. "Yana" is from Yana *yaː* 'person, people' with the male-register absolutive enclitic *-na*, and was first applied to the people and language by Curtin (1884a). Powell adopted "Yana(n)" as the family name in his classification (1891:135), and this usage has been universally followed since. Kroeber used "Yahi" (from *yaː* 'person, people' with *-hi*, the variant of the male-register absolutive enclitic used with this noun in Southern Yana) for the far-southern band from which Ishi came and for Ishi's local variety of the Southern Yana dialect. Since Southern Yana is not otherwise attested except for a few fragments of dubious status, the distinction between it and "Yahi" is academic, and the two terms are often used interchangeably.

3.14 Washo

3.14.1 Geography

Washo is a single language constituting a classificatory isolate in the Hokan phylum and was the only language spoken by a Great Basin group that did not belong to the

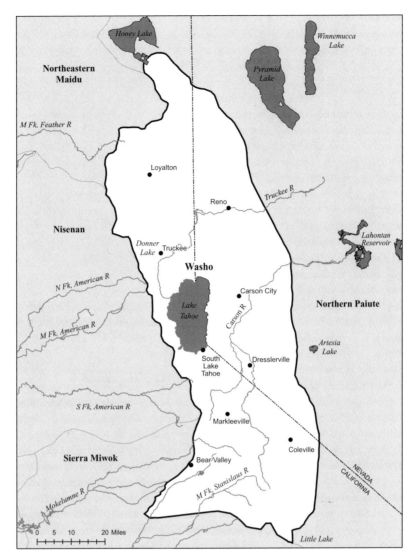

MAP 16. Washo territory.

Numic branch of Uto-Aztecan. Washo territory lay along the eastern slope of the Sierra Nevada between Honey Lake on the north and Antelope Valley on the south (Map 16). Permanent settlements were located along fishing streams in a series of valleys: Long Valley, south of Honey Lake; Sierra Valley at the head of the Feather River; the valley of the Truckee River from Donner Lake to Reno; Washoe and Carson Valleys, around Carson City; the valley of the upper Carson River, around Woolfords and Markleeville; and Antelope Valley, around Coleville. At various times during the year small groups from these settlements ranged over a much wider territory that extended east to Pyamid and Walker Lakes, and west into the Lake Tahoe basin and down the Feather, American, Mokelumne, and Stanislaus Rivers, deep into Konkaw, Nisenan, and Miwok territory. The Washo frequently traded and intermarried with the Northern Paiute and the Sierra Miwok; their relations with Maiduan peoples were less close (D'Azevedo 1986).

Washo has very little internal diversity. The small amount of dialectal variation that exists indicates a shallow differentation between a northern and a southern dialect, but this was not correlated with any sociopolitical boundary; in general, a relatively high level of social integration and intercommunication was maintained throughout Washo territory. A number of borrowings reflect long-standing intergroup contacts, in particular with speakers of Numic and Miwok languages (Jacobsen 1978, 1986a:108–110, 1986b).

Interaction with neighboring languages is also indicated by a number of phonological and grammatical parallels. The majority of these similarities, however, link Washo to the Penutian and Hokan languages rather than to Numic, apparently reflecting a long-term residence in northern California rather than in the Great Basin (¶5.2.9). Of particular interest is the occurrence in Washo of a fully voiced set of stops (b, d, g), a trait shared with Maiduan, Wintuan, and Pomo, as well as with Tubatulabal, and of complex verb stems with analyzable elements of instrumental and classificatory force. These "bipartite" stems resemble in general structure the polysynthetic stems characteristic of other northern California Hokan languages, as well as of certain Penutian languages such as Maiduan and Klamath-Modoc (Jacobsen 1980; DeLancey 1996; see ¶4.8.2).

3.14.2 Documentation and Survival

The first data on Washo appear to have been collected by Stephen Powers (1876), although too late to be published in the linguistic appendix to his *Tribes of California* (1877). Classified by Powell (1891:131) as a distinct "Washoan" stock, Washo was first linked to the Hokan phylum (through a connection to Chumash) by Harrington (1917), who was joined shortly afterward by Sapir (1917b). Confirming data were published by Dixon and Kroeber (1919:104–108) and Sapir (Dixon and Kroeber 1919:108–112; Sapir 1921b:72).

Washo is relatively well documented, but no comprehensive grammar is easily available. William H. Jacobsen, Jr., whose extensive work on Washo—begun in 1955—is still continuing, completed a grammar as his dissertation (1964), but it has not been published. His work is otherwise represented in a short pedagogical grammar (1996a) and in a series of technical articles (1977, 1979b, 1979c, 1980, 1996b, 1998). Since 2004, the Washo Documentation and Revitalization Project at the University of Chicago, directed by Alan C. L. Yu, has been developing an online resource for Washo, including an analytic and cultural dictionary with sound files (washo.uchicago.edu). Yu and his students have also been carrying out technical studies of Washo phonetics (Midtlyng 2005; Midtlyng and Yu 2005; Murphy and Yu 2007; Yu 2005).

The most comprehensive earlier documentation is by Grace Dangberg, who published two volumes of texts (1927, 1968) and a short grammatical sketch (1922), and completed the manuscript of a longer grammar (1925). A. L. Kroeber collected some grammatical, lexical, and textual material on Washo during a brief visit to Reno in 1905, which he published in full, with an extensive discussion (1907c). Robert Lowie obtained miscellaneous linguistic data during ethnographic fieldwork (1939), and subsequently collected a series of texts (1963). The most significant archival documents are two BAE vocabularies collected by H. W. Henshaw (1883a, 1883b) and the general and natural history word lists collected by Merriam between 1903 and 1936 (¶Appendix A: P-15a).

As of 2008 there were about twenty fluent first-language speakers of Washo, all middle-aged or elderly, out of a total population of more than fifteen hundred that is divided among four small reservations (or "colonies") in Nevada and California. The Washoe Tribe sponsors a language-retention project that emphasizes master-apprentice learning and (since 1994) a small but successful immersion school in the Dresslerville Colony (Washiw Wagayaya Mangal), where students use Washo as the medium of instruction from kindergarten through eighth grade. A number of children and young adults have acquired moderate second-language fluency through these initiatives. Curricular materials have

TABLE 17
Washo Phonemes (Jacobsen 1996a)

Consonants						Vowels		
p	t			k	ʔ	i / i:	ï / ï:	u / u:
p'	t'	c'		k'		e / e:		o / o:
b	d	ʒ		g			a / a:	
		s	š		h			
m	n			ŋ				
M				ŋ̊				
w	l		y					
W	L		Y					

Stress Accent
ˊv

also been prepared for use in community classes and for a course that is given from time to time at at the University of Nevada in Reno.

3.14.3 Linguistic Structure

Washo has a somewhat unusual phonemic inventory (Table 17). There are three series of stops (*p, t, k*), each with a plain, glottalized, and fully voiced member; a single apical affricate (*c* [ts]) that occurs glottalized and voiced, but not plain; two fricatives (*s, š*); two laryngeals (*ʔ, h*); and six resonants—three nasals (*m, n, ŋ*) and three approximants (*l, w, y*)—all of which except *n* occur both voiced and voiceless (the latter written by Jacobsen with the corresponding capital letters—M, L, etc.). There are six vowels (*i, e, a, o, u, i*), both short and long. The high back unrounded vowel (*i*) is relatively rare.

Vowel-initial noun and verb stems are common. When unpossessed, a vowel-initial noun has the prefix *d-* (*d-aŋal* 'a house'); otherwise, the pronominal possessor is marked by the prefixes for first, second and third person categories (*l-aŋal* 'my house, our house', *m-aŋal* 'your house', *t'-aŋal* 'his, her, its, their house'). Consonant-initial stems have no prefix when unpossessed and are marked for possessor by a different set of prefixes (*k'omol* 'a ball', *di-k'omol* 'my, our ball', *ʔum-k'omol* 'your ball', *da-k'omol* 'his, her, its, their ball'). The same prefixes mark first and second person subjects in both intransitive and transitive verbs (e.g., *l-ešm-i* 'I am singing', *ʔum-da:mal-i* 'you hear it'). A third person intransitive subject is unmarked in consonant-initial stems, and marked by *ʔ-* in vowel-initial stems (e.g., *t'a:Yaŋ-i* 'he is hunting', *ʔ-a:saw-i* 'he is laughing'). A third person transitive subject is marked in the same way when an object is overtly expressed (*l-a:du ʔ-alŋ-i* 'it's licking my hand', *memde:wi bali?-i* 'he shot the deer'), but when no object is expressed vowel-initial stems take *k'-* and consonant-initial stems take *ga-* or *ge-* (*k'-alŋ-i* 'it's licking something', *ga-bali?-i* 'he shot him').

MAP 17. Pomo languages and their major dialects.

Tense, causality, negation, and several other categories are marked by suffixes (e.g., *l-emlu-yi* 'I'm eating', *m-emlu-he:š-i* 'are you eating?', *l-emlu-ye:s-i* 'I am not eating', *l-emlu-še* 'let's (both) eat!', *l-emlu-yaša?-i* 'I'm going to eat'). Many verb stems have a "bipartite" structure (Jacobsen 1980) and most consonant-initial verb stems can be analyzed into a lexical prefix (C- or CVC-) and a dependent verb stem (see ¶4.8.2).

3.14.4 Nomenclature

The Washos' self-designation, *wá:šiw,* was anglicized as "Washoe" by early settlers and was used in the spelling "Washo" by Powers (1876) for both the people and the language. Powell followed this precedent and adopted "Washo(an)" in his 1891 classification. The spelling "Washo" has remained the standard usage among linguists and anthropologists, usually pronounced with the second

syllable rhyming with "show." In part to avoid this mispronunciation, the spellings "Washiw" and "Washoe" are preferred by the native community.

3.15 Pomo Languages

The Pomo family constitutes an independent branch of the Hokan phylum, although a number of lexical and grammatical similarities suggest that it has a relatively close connection to Chimariko and Yana. Pomo, however, is not part of the Northern Hokan lexical diffusion area that includes Karuk, Chimariko, Shastan, Palaihnihan, and Yana (¶5.2.1).

Pomo includes seven distinct and sharply bounded languages (Map 17). Samuel A. Barrett, in his pioneering geographical survey and classification (1908a), referred to them as "dialects," but there was no mutual intelligibility among them, except to a limited extent between the languages of the Southern Group of Western Pomo, and

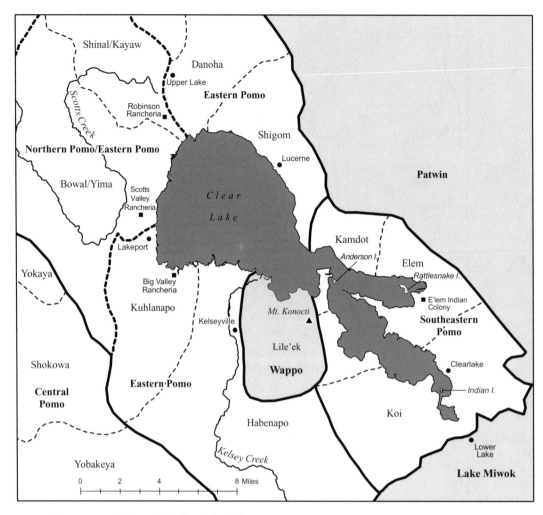

MAP 18. Languages and dialects of the Clear Lake Basin.

TABLE 18
Classification of the Pomo Languages (Oswalt 1964a)

Southeastern Pomo

Eastern Pomo

Northeastern Pomo

Western Pomo

   Northern Pomo

   Southern Group

      Central Pomo

      Southern Pomo

      Kashaya (Southwestern Pomo)

lexicostatistical analysis, is the one most widely accepted (Table 18).

Oswalt distinguishes four branches: one for each of the two languages spoken around Clear Lake (Southeastern and Eastern Pomo; see Map 18); a third for Northeastern Pomo, spoken in an isolated location on the west side of the Sacramento Valley; and a Western Pomo branch that includes the four languages spoken along the Russian River. He subdivides Western Pomo into Northern Pomo and a Southern Group that includes Central Pomo, Southern Pomo, and Kashaya (or Southwestern Pomo). Oswalt estimates the time depth of the Southern Group to be similar to that of the Western Romance languages (less than 1,250 years), and the division between Northern Pomo and the Southern Group to be about as old as the split between Western Romance and Romanian (somewhat over 1,500 years). The divisions among the four branches appear to be little more than 750 to 1,000 years older.

Halpern's classification, based on phonological and morphological shifts, is essentially in agreement with Oswalt's, differing mainly in the placement of Northeastern Pomo. Instead of considering it an independent branch of

perhaps also between Northern and Northeastern Pomo. In addition to Barrett's, classifications of Pomo have been put forward by A. L. Kroeber (1925:227), A. M. Halpern (1964), Robert Oswalt (1964a), Nancy Webb (1971), and Julius Moshinsky (1976). Oswalt's classification, based on a

FIGURE 51. Abraham Halpern and Clifford Salvador, Southeastern Pomo, 1936. Courtesy of Sally McLendon.

the family, Halpern groups it with the four Western languages but leaves open the question of whether it forms its own branch of that group or is to be subgrouped with Northern Pomo: "Certain elusive similarities between Northern and Northeastern Pomo . . . may be interpreted either as genetic similarities or as products of diffusion" (Halpern 1964:91). A linkage between Northeastern and Northern Pomo accords with Kroeber's and Barrett's ethnographic observation that speakers of the two languages shared some degree of mutual intelligibility (Barrett 1908a:100; Kroeber 1932:364).

3.15.1 Southeastern Pomo

Southeastern Pomo was spoken in a tiny territory at the eastern end of Clear Lake by three distinct tribelets. These are usually refered to by the names of their principal villages, each of which was located on a small island: *Kamdot* (*qámdot*), on Anderson Island, off Buckingham Point; *Elem* (*ʔalém*), on Rattlesnake (or Sulphur Bank) Island in East Lake; and *Koi* (*xaqóyi*), on Indian Island in Lower Lake. Slight dialect differences seem to have existed among the tribelets but were not considered significant by the speakers (Halpern 1988:1). Although the Southeastern Pomo shared the lake with the Eastern Pomo and intermarried with them, their languages were deeply divergent with no possibility of mutual intelligibllity. The two groups also differed considerably in many aspects of culture (McLendon and Lowy 1978:306). Patwin influence was quite strong in the Southeastern Pomo area, with Patwin-Pomo bilingualism common. Until the twentieth century nearly all observers considered the Southeastern Pomo to be a Patwin group, and Powers (1877:214) referred to them as the "Makh´-el-chel," a name of Patwin derivation.

Southeastern Pomo was extensively documented by A. M. Halpern (1936–1937, 1939–1984), although little of his material has so far been published (Halpern 1964, 1982, 1988). Julius Moshinsky restudied the language in 1965–1968 and published a comprehensive grammar (1974). The language has at least one elderly speaker, and work has recently been carried out with her by Jocelyn Ahlers (2006, 2007) and by students working under Leanne Hinton at Berkeley. The most important earlier materials are the lexical and ethnogeographical data collected by S. A. Barrett (1908a), and the vocabulary and natural history word list collected by Merriam from speakers of the Koi dialect between 1904 and 1927 (Appendix A: M-12cc).

3.15.2 Eastern Pomo

There were five Eastern Pomo tribelets in the western portion of the Clear Lake basin, with their principal settlements located along streams well back from the shoreline. These included *Kuhlanapo* (*qu:xána:pʰò*) in Big Valley, south of Lakeport; *Habenapo* (*xa:béna:pʰò*) on the south shore of the lake along Kelsey Creek; *Danoha* (*da:nóxà*) in Clover Valley northeast of Upper Lake; *Howalek* (*xówalekʰ*) along Middle Creek in Upper Lake Valley; and *Shigom* (*ší:kom*) on the north shore of the lake near Lucerne. In addition, the *Shinal* (N Pomo *šinál* 'at the head') or *Kayaw* (E Pomo *kʰa:yáw*, same meaning) tribelet west of Upper Lake and the *Bowal* (N Pomo *bówal* 'west side') or *Yima* (E Pomo *yi:má:* 'gristle, sinew') tribelet along Scotts Creek northwest of Lakeport represented recent amalgamations of Northern and Eastern Pomo populations and were bilingual in the historic period. There was a noticeable dialect difference between the two south shore districts (Kuhlanapo and Habenapo) and those on the upper lake.

Eastern Pomo is one of the best documented of the Pomo languages. The first attestation of any Pomo language was George Gibbs's vocabulary of the Kuhlanapo variety of Eastern Pomo, collected in 1851 during the McKee Expedition and first published by Schoolcraft (Gibbs 1853b). In 1875, Stephen Powers collected a vocabulary of the Habenapo variety (1877:490–517). Between 1906 and 1924, Merriam collected Eastern Pomo vocabularies and natural history word lists from both south shore and upper lake ("Han-nah-bah-ch") varieties (Appendix A: M-12w-y and M-12z-aa). There were two important collections made during the 1920s and 1930s, both almost entirely unpublished. One is from Jaime de Angulo and L. S. Freeland, who worked with the Habenapo tribal scholar William Ralganal Benson between 1920 and 1935 (de Angulo and Freeland 1920–1935; de Angulo ca. 1935b); the other is from survey work carried out by A. M. Halpern in 1939–1940 (Halpern 1964). Sally McLendon began work on Eastern Pomo in 1959 and continues to collect data. She has published a grammar (1975), a grammatical sketch (1996), and a discussion of the case system (1978a), as well as two analyzed texts (1977, 1978b) and two papers on discourse structure (1979, 1982).

FIGURE 52. Sally McLendon and Ralph Holder, Eastern Pomo. Photo by Julia Tucker, 1973. Courtesy of Sally McLendon.

As of 2008, Eastern Pomo had a handful of semifluent speakers at the Robinson and Big Valley Rancherias at the west end of Clear Lake. None of these speakers was younger than sixty.

3.15.3 Northeastern Pomo

The Northeastern Pomo (or "Salt Pomo") lived in a compact area along Stony Creek in Colusa County, on the western edge of the Sacramento Valley. They appear to have constituted a single tribelet, with a principal settlement near Stonyford (čʰeʔe:tiʔdo: 'salt-field', Patwin *bakamtati*). The Northeastern Pomo were separated from the Northern Pomo by the uninhabited hinterland along the Rice Fork of the Eel River, an area claimed by the Yuki, and from the Pomo at Clear Lake by the rugged territory along Bartlett Creek, which was sparsely settled by speakers of Patwin. Despite their geographical separation from other Pomos, they were not entirely out of contact with them, since they controlled the largest salt deposit in the area and were frequently visited by trading parties from the Russian River. Their most intensive contacts, however, were with the Nomlaki to the north and the Hill Patwin to the south, and most Northeastern Pomo speakers were probably bilingual in Nomlaki or Patwin (Kroeber 1925:224). According to Kroeber, speakers of Northeastern Pomo could "partly understand Northern Pomo, but not the Eastern and Southeastern languages," an observation which led him to surmise that they "separated from their kinsmen in upper Russian river drainage, not on nearer Clear Lake" (1932:364).

Northeastern Pomo is the least well documented of the Pomo languages, and unfortunately it must remain so; the last fluent speaker died in 1961. The first certain attestation appears to be the lexical and ethnogeographical data that

S. A. Barrett collected in 1903–1906 for his comparative study of the family (1908a). Merriam collected a vocabulary and natural history word list in the course of several visits between 1903 and 1928 (Appendix A: M-12bb). In 1923–1924, A. L. Kroeber collected a small amount of cultural vocabulary, published in his ethnographic report on the group (1932:364–366). The most extensive documentation was made by A. M. Halpern during a short field trip in 1940 (Halpern 1964; Bean and Theodoratus 1978:304–305).

3.15.4 Western Pomo

The Western Pomo languages were the languages of the Russian River, from Northern Pomo at its headwaters above Redwood and Potter Valleys to Kashaya at its mouth at Jenner. The adjacent coastline of Mendocino and Sonoma counties was also part of Western Pomo territory, but, except for the Kashaya, coastal communities were small and spoke the same language as the Russian River tribelets to the east of them. Arranged in a north-to-south chain, the Western Pomo languages adjoined one another at seemingly arbitrary boundaries with no intermediate dialectal gradations. Northern Pomo was especially sharply marked off from Central, Southern, and Kashaya Pomo, which can be said to form a Southern Group. There was no mutual intelligibility between Northern Pomo and the languages of the Southern Group, while a small degree of intercommunication was sometimes possible among speakers of the latter.

NORTHERN POMO

Northern Pomo was spoken over the largest territory of any Pomo language and had the greatest internal diversity. Several Northern Pomo tribelets can be distinguished, each of which spoke a distinct variety. In the far northwest, adjoining Kato Athabaskan territory, was **Mato** (*ma:ṭʰóʔ*), centered on Sherwood Valley. A few miles to the southeast was **Mitom** (*miṭʰóm*), on Outlet Creek (a tributary of the Eel) in the Willits and Little Lake area; their northern neighbors were the Huchnom Yuki. The **Kacha** (*kʰacʰa:*) occupied Redwood Valley. To their south, near Calpella, were the **Masut** (*masút'*). **Balokay** (*baló?kʰáy*) was the district in and around Potter Valley, containing the large and important villages of Shanel, Sedam, and Pomo. **Shodakay** (*šo:dakʰáy*) was the tribelet of Coyote Valley, now submerged by Lake Mendocino. Much of the territory of the southernmost Northern Pomo tribelet, **Komli** (*k'ómli*), just north of Ukiah, appears to have been in dispute with the Yokaya tribelet of Central Pomo.

Northern Pomo territory also extended into the Clear Lake Basin, where there were two areas of Eastern Pomo/ Northern Pomo bilingualism, the tribelet of **Shinal** (N. Pomo *šinál* 'at the head') in Bachelor Valley and on Tule Lake, to the west of Upper Lake, and the tribelet of **Bowal** (N Pomo *bówal* 'west side') in Scotts Valley, which had a small frontage on the western shore of the lake to the north of Lakeport. These linguistically mixed groups had apparently resulted from postcontact nineteenth century relocations. Many of the Northern Pomos at Bowal were originally from the Komli tribelet near Ukiah.

The coastline in Northern Pomo territory—from the Navarro River to the Noyo River—was not occupied on a permanent basis, but was regularly visited, particularly in the summer, by people from the Mato and Mitom tribelets. These areas were also used by the Coast Yuki and the Boya Central Pomo.

Northern Pomo is well documented, although relatively little material is published. The first attestation of the language was made in 1851 by George Gibbs, who collected vocabularies of two varieties spoken "on heads of Eel River" in villages whose names he recorded as "Chow-e-shak" and "Batem-da-kai-ee" (Gibbs 1853b, 1853c). The vocabulary that Stephen Powers collected from a Pomo speaker in Round Valley in 1875 is also apparently Northern Pomo (1877:490–517). In the early twentieth century, Merriam collected vocabularies and natural history word lists from four dialects: Sherwood Valley (Appendix A: M-12a), Little Lake (M-12b), Potter Valley (M-12d), and Upper Lake (M-12g). Since the 1930s, three linguists have made extensive collections of Northern Pomo data: A. M. Halpern in 1939–1940 (Halpern 1964), Eero Vihman in 1966–1967 (Buzzard-Welcher and Hinton 2002), and M. Catherine O'Connor, beginning in the early 1980s. O'Connor's published dissertation (1992) is a grammar of the language, and she has also written separately on various special topics, including case (1981), tense-aspect (1990b), and switch reference and discourse structure (1982, 1986, 1990a). A digital database is being prepared from O'Connor's texts and lexical materials (O'Connor and Deal 2005).

As of 2001, Northern Pomo had a single elderly speaker, living at Sherwood Rancheria, near Willits. Since 1993, O'Connor has been engaged in preparing language learning materials (written and video) for the Coyote Valley and Pinoleville Tribes.

CENTRAL POMO

Central Pomo territory, like that of Northern Pomo, centered on the Russian River, but since the terrain here is somewhat less rugged and less heavily forested than to the north, permanent settlements were also located along the coast and in the valleys between the coast and the Russian River. Along the river were three well-defined tribelets or districts, each with a distinct dialect. The northernmost was **Yokaya** (*yóqʰa:ya* 'south valley [people]'), in the southern part of Ukiah Valley; **Shokowa** (*šóqowa* 'east valley [people]') was in Hopland Valley, where the principal village was Shanel (*šanél* 'at the ceremonial house'); and farthest south was **Yobakeya** (*yowba:kʰeya* 'people from Yowba'), close to the Sonoma County line. Between the Russian River and the coast was a large and not well-defined district whose inhabitants were known as **Bokeya** (*bo?kʰeya* 'western people'), with villages around Yorkville and in Anderson Valley. **Boya** (*bó:ya*), the coastal district, had villages at Manchester, Point Arena, and at the mouth of the Gualala River.

Central Pomo has been well documented. Early vocabularies of the Yokaya dialect were collected by George Gibbs in 1851 (Gibbs 1853b) and by Stephen Powers in 1875 (1877:490–517). Merriam collected vocabularies and natural history word lists from four dialects: Boya (Appendix A: M-12h), Anderson Valley (M-12i), Yokaya (M-12l), and Hopland (M-12n). Jaime de Angulo collected the autobiography of the multilingual Eastern Pomo chief, William Benson, in the Yokaya dialect of Central Pomo (de Angulo ca.1935a). Major linguistic studies since the 1930s include A. M. Halpern in 1939–1940 (Halpern 1964); Robert Oswalt in 1958–1968, on the Boya and Yokaya dialects; and Marianne Mithun from 1985 onward, primarily on the Hopland dialect. Mithun has published several papers on various grammatical topics (1988, 1990a, 1990b, 1993, 1998b) and is preparing a full grammar.

Central Pomo still has several speakers in the Hopland area and at Manchester and Point Arena on the coast.

SOUTHERN POMO

The aboriginal linguistic geography of the Southern Pomo is known in less detail than that of the other Pomo-speaking groups, because of the disruptive effects of the missions and of early Mexican and American settlement. The language (also referred to in earlier sources as "Gallinomero") was apparently spoken only in the interior, along the lower Russian River from Cloverdale to Guerneville and in the

FIGURE 53. Robert Oswalt and Essie Parrish, Kashaya Pomo, 1960. Courtesy of the Oswalt family.

adjoining Dry Creek Valley and Santa Rosa plain. The thick redwood forest that lay between this area and the coast, as well as the coast itself as far north as Central Pomo territory, belonged to the Kashaya.

A dialect district known as **Makahmo** (*ma:kʰahmo* 'salmon hole') was centered in the Cloverdale area, with a large village where Big Sulphur Creek joins the Russian River. The district in Dry Creek Valley (west of, and parallel to, the stretch of the Russian River in the Geyserville area that belonged to the Wappo) was called **Mahilkaune** (*mihhilaʔkʰawna* 'west creek'). Further downstream no district names or boundaries are certain, but a distinctive dialect was spoken around Healdsburg, **Kale** (*kʰalle* 'in the midst of the water'), and there were dialect differences associated with groups of villages near Santa Rosa and Sebastopol. The Southern Pomo speakers who lived in the upper Gualala River drainage, between the Russian River Valley and the coast, were known as the **Wishachamay** (*wiššahčamay* 'ridge people').

Southern Pomo was first attested by Stephen Powers, who collected a vocabulary of "Gallinomero" at Healdsburg in 1872 (Powers 1877:490–517). Merriam collected four sets of vocabularies and natural history word lists: Cloverdale (Appendix A: M-12r), Wishachamay (M-12t), and two varieties of the Healdsburg–Santa Rosa dialect (M-12r). The language was extensively documented by A. M. Halpern in 1939–1940 (cf. Halpern 1964) and again in the early 1980s,[49] and by Robert Oswalt in 1963–1968. None of Halpern's material has been published; Oswalt published an analyzed text (1977) and prepared a partial lexicon.

As of the early 2000s, Southern Pomo was reported to have two or three semispeakers living in the Cloverdale and Geyserville area, but Elsie Allen, who was generally considered to be the last fluent speaker of the language, died in 1990.

KASHAYA

Kashaya (or Southwestern Pomo) was the language of the Sonoma County coast, from a few miles north of Bodega Bay to the area around Stewart's Point and Annapolis. The name Kashaya (*k'ahšá:ya*) is a native word, referring both to the language and to the people who speak it—unusual for a California language (see ¶1.3). Aboriginal linguistic geography is not well known, but most of the settlements whose names are preserved were on the coast north of Fort Ross or along the South Fork of the Gualala River, which parallels the coast. During the first half of the nineteenth century the Kashaya had extensive contact with the Russian, Aleut, and Alaskan Indian employees of the Russian American Company at Fort Ross (Oswalt 1958, 1988b; Lightfoot 2005).

Kashaya is one of the best documented of the Pomo languages, primarily owing to the work of Robert Oswalt, which he began in 1957 and continued for the remainder of his long research career. Oswalt wrote a full grammar (1961), published a collection of texts (1964b), and published papers on Kashaya lexical semantics (1981), switch reference (1983), evidentials (1986), pitch accent (1988a), aspect (1990), and syllable structure (1998). Building on Oswalt's work, a 1989–1990 UC Berkeley seminar carried out further documentation and analysis of Kashaya, resulting in papers on switch reference (Gamon 1991), animacy (K. Hall 1991), and phonology (E. Buckley 1991, 1994).

Important early docmentation dates to the Fort Ross period (1811 to 1842), including a vocabulary collected by Peter Kostromitinov, the local manager of the Russian American Company (Wrangell and Kostromitinov 1839), and an anonymous vocabulary that was transmitted to George Gibbs by the governor of Russian America in the early 1860s (Powers 1877:490–517). Other materials include substantial lexical and ethnogeographical data collected by Barrett for a comparative study (1908a), material collected by Halpern in 1939–1940 (see Halpern 1964), and a Kashaya vocabulary and natural history word list collected by Merriam (Appendix A: M-12q).

Kashaya, the the most vigorously surviving of the Pomo languages, is spoken in varying degrees of fluency by several dozen people in 2010. A small-scale language education program is under way, and a practical orthography has been devised.

3.15.5 Linguistic Structure

There are noticeable differences in both phonological and grammatical structure among the major branches of Pomo, although they all share the same basic patterns. There is an outline of comparative Pomo phonology in McLendon (1973) and of comparative verb morphology in Oswalt (1976a). Full analyses of Pomo morphology and syntax are most easily accessible in the published grammars of Northern Pomo (O'Connor 1992), Eastern Pomo (McLendon 1975, 1996), and Southeastern Pomo (Moshinsky 1974). No comprehensive dictionary of any Pomo language exists. Barrett's *Ethno-Geography of the Pomo* (1908a) includes a comparative lexicon of 282 items in all seven languages (pp. 56–68), but the transcriptions are poor; an extensive glossary also accompanies Barrett's collection of Pomo myths (1933:494–538).

The consonantal inventory is quite large (Table 19). The basic system of stops and affricates makes six distinctions (*p, t, ṭ, č, k, q*), all of which occur plain, aspirated, and glottalized; voiced stops occur as well in the labial and dental positions (*b, d*). Northern, Southern, and Northeastern Pomo lack the postvelar stop series (*q, qʰ, q'*). Otherwise, all series are found, with full sets of plain, aspirated, and glottalized contrasts in all languages except Southeastern Pomo (which has no aspirated stops or affricates), Northern Pomo (which lacks *čʰ*), Northeastern Pomo (which lacks *pʰ* and *p'*), and Eastern Pomo (which lacks *qʰ*). The phonetic nature of the basic affricate series varies between apical [ts] and palatal [tʃ], and in Southern, Northern, and Northeastern Pomo there is a phonemic distinction between the two series. There are two basic fricatives (*s, š*). Southeastern Pomo also has *f, x,* and *x̣* (corresponding to aspirated *pʰ, kʰ,* and *qʰ* in other Pomo languages), and Eastern Pomo has *x* (corresponding to *qʰ* in other Pomo languages). All languages have two laryngeals (*h, ʔ*), and at least two nasals (*m, n*) and three approximants (*l, w, y*). Northeastern Pomo also has *r*, and Eastern Pomo has a full set of voiceless nasals and approximants (written *M, N, L, W, Y* by McLendon).

The vowel system is the same throughout Pomo: five vowels (*i, e, a, o, u*) both short and long. Stress patterns vary from language to language, and pitch accent has developed (apparently separately) in Northern Pomo and Kashaya (Vihman 1976; Oswalt 1988a).

TABLE 19
Eastern Pomo Phonemes (McLendon 1996)

Consonants							Vowels	
p	t	ṭ	č	k	q	ʔ	i / i:	u / u:
pʰ	tʰ	ṭʰ	čʰ	kʰ			e / e:	o / o:
p'	t'	ṭ'	č'	k'	q'		a / a:	
b	d							
		s	š	x		h		
m	n							
M	N							
w	l	y						
W	L	Y						

Pomo has a somewhat less synthetic morphology than many other Hokan languages. Pronouns are independent words, and together with nouns are inflected for case (Table 20). Verbs can take locational-directional proclitics, and verb stems often incorporate instrumental prefixes (¶4.8.2). Derivational suffixes mark various modal and adverbial categories, and a word-final set of suffixes marks aspectual differences (basically imperfective versus perfective, but further elaborated in some languages). There is also a well-developed system of evidential enclitics. Marking of "switch reference" (¶4.9) is found in all Pomo languages and is reconstructible to Proto Pomo (Oswalt 1976a).

3.15.6 Nomenclature

The word "Pomo" has two plausible native sources, both in Northern Pomo. One is the place-name *pʰo:mo* 'at the hole (where) ochre (is found)', a village in the Potter Valley district. The other is *pʰoʔmaʔ* 'people of (a certain place)', a common formant of Northern Pomo ethnonyms (e.g, *miṭʰo:m-pʰoʔmaʔ* 'the people of Little Lake', the tribelet at Willits). It is likely that the adoption in the 1850s of "Pomo" or "Poma" as the general designation of the Northern Pomos owes someting to both sources. Powers (1877:146–195) broadened the term to include all Western Pomo groups, but excluded the Clear Lake groups, whose connection to the others he considered "slight" (1877:204). Powell (1891), who was the first to recognize the unity of the entire language family, proposed that it should be named "Kulanapuan" (from *qu:Lá-na:pʰò*, the name of the Eastern Pomo tribelet from which Gibbs collected the first Pomo vocabulary in 1851). Kroeber and other anthropologists working in California, favoring local usage in this case as elsewhere, rejected Powell's coinage in favor of a further extension of Powers's term (e.g., Dixon and Kroeber 1903). Except for Kashaya (Southwestern Pomo), none of the Pomo languages has a traditional native name, and the directional nomenclature that is now generally used was instituted by Barrett (1908a).

TABLE 20
Eastern Pomo Case Marking (McLendon 1996)

Pronouns

	Agent	Patient	Possessive (Alienable)	Possessive (Inalienable)*
1 sg	ha:	wí	wáx	wíma:-
2 sg	má	mí	mí:bax ~ míx	mi:-
1 pl	wá:	wá:l	wáybax ~ wáyx	wáyma:-
2 pl	má:	má:l	máybax ~ máyx	máymi:-
3 sg masculine	mí:p'	mí:pal	mí:pibax ~ mí:pix	há:mi:-
3 sg feminine	mí:t'	mí:ral	mí:ribax ~ mí:rix	há:mi:-
3 pl	bé:kʰ	bé:kal	bé:kibax ~ bé:kix	há:mi:-
3 sg anaphoric	hí:	hí:	hí:bax ~ híx	ma:-
3 pl anaphoric	k'e:héy	hé:kal	hé:kibax ~ hé:kix	ma:-

Nouns†

	Agent	Patient	Possessive
'mother'	-tʰé	-tʰel	-tʰélbax
'bear'	bu:ráqalla:	bu:raqal	bu:raqalbax
'snake'	xá:su:la:	xa:s	xa:sbax

*The inalienable possessive pronouns are used only with kinship terms, to which they are prefixed.
†Kinship terms, like pronouns, must be explicitly marked when they refer to the patient but are usually unmarked when they refer to the agent. Conversely, most other nouns are explicitly marked as agents but unmarked as patients.

3.16 Esselen

3.16.1 Geography

Esselen is a long-extinct classificatory isolate belonging to the Hokan phylum, spoken at the time of European contact by several tribelets in the northern Santa Lucia Range in Monterey County (Map 19). The best known of these, the **Excelen**, occupied the upper portion of the Carmel River Valley, southeast of Monterey. Several other tribelets adjoined the Excelen on the east and south. These included the **Eslenahan** and **Aspasniahan**, who occupied the Salinas Valley and the lower Arroyo Seco around the site of Mission Soledad and the modern town of Greenfield; the **Imunahan** on the upper Arroyo Seco, in the mountains to the west and south of Soledad; and the **Ekheahan,** who lived along the mountainous coast south of Big Sur, in the vicinity of Julia Pfeiffer Burns State Park (Milliken 1990).[50] Richard Levy (cited in Hester 1978) would also assign the **Sarhentaruc** tribelet on the lower Big Sur River and Point Sur to the Esselen, but this is more likely to have been a Rumsen Costanoan–speaking group (Milliken 1990:27–33) or possibly an area of Rumsen-Esselen bilingualism (Breschini and Haversat 1994). There is little attestation of intertribelet dialect differences, although the vocabulary collected by Arroyo de la Cuesta at Mission Soledad deviates from the other recordings in a few particulars (Beeler 1977:41; Shaul 1995a:192).

The Esselens who belonged to the Excelen tribelet were in close contact with the Rumsen Costanoans at Monterey, and similarly the Arroyo Seco–Salinas River Esselens with the Chalon and Ensen Costanoans in the northern Salinas Valley. While this contact was often hostile—the mutual antipathy between the Rumsens and Esselens in the Indian community at Carmel is a recurring theme in mission-era documents (cf. Cutter 1990:149)—Esselen-Costanoan bilingualism appears to have been common. Some of the historically attested bilingualism, however, may reflect the postcontact absorption of much of the aboriginal Esselen population into the missions at Carmel and Soledad, where Costanoan speakers were in the majority. The Ekheahan tribelet was also in contact with the Salinans to the south, and there were a number of converts from this group at Mission San Antonio (Cook 1974; Beeler 1978a:36; Milliken 1990:51–58).

3.16.2 Documentation and Survival

Although some memory of the language survived until the 1930s (Shaul 1995b), Esselen ceased to be spoken in the mid-nineteenth century and is very poorly documented.

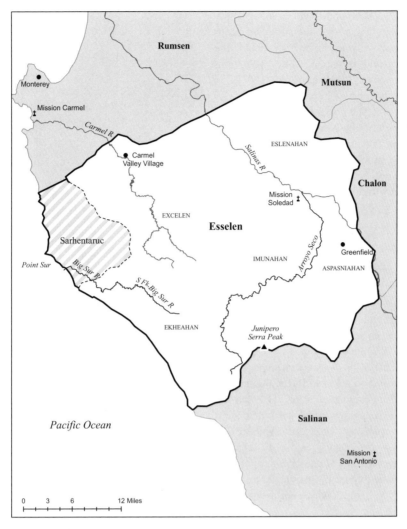

MAP 19. Esselen territory.

Preserved from the mission period are a trilingual (Spanish-Esselen-Rumsen) catechism and associated vocabulary (Cutter 1990:151–155; Shaul 1995a); a few lines from another catechism (Shaul 1995a); a sentence quoted in the Carmel mission's *respuesta* to the questionnaire of 1812 (Geiger and Meighan 1976:20; see ¶2.3.5); a vocabulary taken down by Arroyo de la Cuesta at Soledad during a visit in 1833; and two short word lists collected by early visitors to Monterey (published, together with the Arroyo vocabulary, in Kroeber 1904:49–57).[51] The most valuable of these early materials is the trilingual catechism/vocabulary, which was compiled by Father Lasuén at the request of the Malaspina Expedition and collected by Alcalá Galiano and Valdés during their visit to Monterey in 1792 (see ¶2.4.1).[52]

The best attestations of Esselen are the post-mission-period vocabularies collected from the last semispeakers by Alphonse Pinart (1878a) and H. W. Henshaw (1888c). Pinart's vocabulary (published in Heizer 1952:73–82) was obtained from an elderly Rumsen woman named Omesia, whose husband was from the rancheria of "Ex´sien or 'the rock'," which can be identified as the Excelen tribelet (Levy,

cited in Hester 1978). The principal source of Henshaw's data (published in Kroeber 1904:49–57) was Eulalia, a Rumsen Costanoan woman whose mother had been Esselen. He subsequently found "an aged and blind Indian" living near Soledad, Pacifico Belisano, who recalled a few more Esselen words and verified many of those given by Eulalia (Henshaw 1888d, 1890).

By the beginning of the twentieth century Esselen was extinct, the first native California language family to suffer this fate. A. L. Kroeber in 1902 (1904:50, 52) and Merriam in 1906 (Appendix A: Q-16a) were able to recover only a few words and phrases, dimly remembered by elderly people who had never spoken the language fluently. In the 1920s and 1930s, J. P. Harrington made repeated attempts to find a speaker or rememberer of Esselen, but his only success was to discover that his principal Rumsen consultant, Isabel Meadows, had heard the language when she was a child. Although Meadows had no actual command of Esselen, Harrington dictated the extant corpus to her and transcribed her repronunciations and comments (Shaul 1995b).

Madison Beeler (1977, 1978a) and David L. Shaul (1982, 1983, 1995a) independently surveyed the surviving documentation and summarized what is known about the language. An earlier synthesis compiled by Harrington (1916) is also of some interest (Turner and Shaul 1981).

With no known speakers in over a hundred years and with such scanty documentation, the prospect for the revival of Esselen would appear to be dim. Nevertheless, a group of individuals of Esselen descent, the Ohlone/Costanoan Esselen Nation of the Monterey-Carmel area (www.ohlone-costanoanesselennation.org) is making efforts to regain what can be salvaged of their traditional language and culture (Leventhal et al. 1994).[53]

3.16.3 Linguistic Structure

The consonant inventory of Esselen includes at least three stops (*p, t, k*); three affricates (*c* [ts], *č, kx*); four fricatives (*f, s, š, x*); two nasals (*m* and *n*); three approximants (*l, w, y*); and two laryngeals (*h* and *ʔ*) (Table 21). It is also likely that a postalveolar/retroflex stop (*ṭ*) contrasts with dental *t*, and that a flapped or tapped *r* [ɾ] contrasts with *l*. Beeler (1978a:20) argued that *f*, which appears to alternate with *p*, is in fact an affricate [pf], quite unusual for a California Indian language; Shaul (1995a:196–197), however, argues from the same data that it is phonetic [f], but an allophone of *p*. There is no evidence that Esselen has glottalized consonants or a distinctively aspirated series of stops. Geminated consonants appear to occur frequently and to be important in syllable structure. There are five vowels (*i, e, a, o, u*), which occur both short and long.

Esselen morphology, insofar as it can be reconstituted from the fragmentary data, is relatively uncomplex. Noun suffixes mark instrumental, comitative, and locative concepts. In verbs, suffixes mark various derivational and tense-aspect categories. Pronominal subjects (and probably objects, although examples are few and confusing) are marked by a set of independent pronouns: *enni ~ ni* 'I', *nemi* 'you (sg)', *lex* 'we', *lax* 'they'. The possessor of a noun is marked by a proclitic pronoun followed by an element *-š-* or *-s-* (*ni-š-exe* 'my man, husband', *nemi-š-iya* 'your bone', *lex-s-kacia Santa Yglesia* 'our mother the Holy Church').

3.16.4 Nomenclature

Father Lasuén reported in 1792 that the Indians of Mission San Carlos belonged to two nations, one speaking "Eslen" and the other "Runsien" (Cutter 1990:149). In their response to the questionnaire of 1812 the mission priests identified seven nations, two of which, the "Excelen" and the "Egeac," were said to be "from inland" and to "have one and the same language or speech . . . called Excelen" (Kroeber 1908b:20–21). "Excelen," which Pinart (1878a) transcribed "Ex´xeien" and "Ex´seien" and called a dialect of the "Esselen" language ("dialecto del idioma Esselen"), was apparently the name of

TABLE 21
Esselen Phonemes (Shaul 1995a)

Consonants								Vowels		
p	t	(ṭ)	c	č	k	kx	ʔ	i / i:		u / u:
(f)			s	š	x		h	e / e:		o / o:
m	n								a / a:	
w	l	(r)	y							

the village or tribelet in the upper Carmel Valley from which many of the Esselen speakers at Carmel had come (Milliken 1990). "Eslen" is possibly the Rumsen version of the same name, adopted by the missionaries as a general term for the language. However, there is evidence in the records at both Carmel and Soledad that the Esselen-speaking tribelet on Arroyo Seco, near Soledad, was called "Eslenagan" or "Eslenajan," which is presumably "Eslen" with the suffix *-xan* that is seen in several other Esselen tribelet or village names. Whatever its aboriginal etymology, the mission term "Esselen" was still in use in the Indian community at Monterey at the time of Pinart's and Henshaw's visits in the 1870s and 1880s and was subsequently adopted by anthropologists as the standard ethnonym and language name. Shaul (1995a) cites evidence that "Huelel" was the term used by Esselen speakers to refer to their own language, but this may simply be the general noun meaning 'tongue' or 'speech' that is transcribed "villel" in the Lasuén vocabulary.

3.17 Salinan

Salinan is a single language, forming a classificatory isolate in the Hokan phylum. It was formerly spoken in the southern part of the Salinas River Valley and adjacent mountain ranges in Monterey and San Luis Obispo counties. Two shallowly differentiated dialects are attested, **Antoniano** (or Antoniaño) to the north and west, associated with Mission San Antonio (founded in 1771), and **Migueleño** (or Miguelino) to the south and east, associated with Mission San Miguel (founded in 1797). These probably represent mission-era standardizations of a more complex picture of local variation that originally encompassed numerous distinct village or tribelet dialects (Mason 1912:105–106).

3.17.1 Geography

Working from mission records, the ethnohistorians Randall Milliken and John Johnson (2003) have identified more than a dozen tribelets or "districts" in Salinan territory (Map 20). The boundaries of these districts are best documented in the upper valley of San Antonio River (now mostly inside the Hunter Liggett Military Reservation), which formed the western portion of the territory in which the Antoniano dialect was spoken. There were at least four districts in this

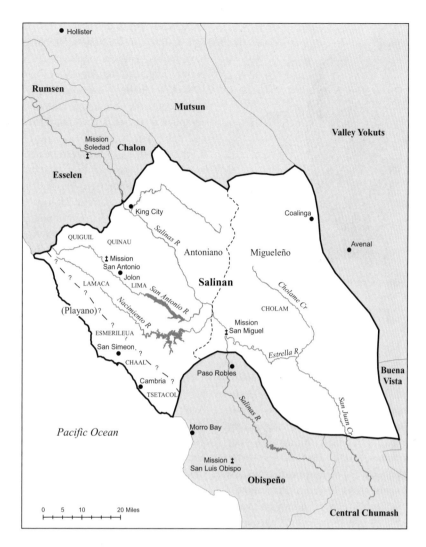

MAP 20. Salinan territory and dialects.

area. **Lima** was in the immediate vicinity of San Antonio mission and the modern town of Jolon; **Quiguil** (or **Kigil**) was in the mountains to the northwest of the mission; **Lamaca** lay to the southwest, on the upper reaches of the Nacimiento River; and **Quinau** (**Kinaw**) lay to the northeast, between the mission and the Salinas River (Rivers and Jones 1993).[54]

The northernmost area of Salinan speech was in the vicinity of King City and bordered on Esselen-speaking tribelets in the Greenfield and Soledad areas (Milliken 1990:66–69). On the south, Milliken and Johnson (2003:134–136) agree with Robert Gibson (1983) in placing the precontact border between Salinan and Obispeño Chumash territory only a few miles south of Mission San Miguel, arguing that the information that led Mason (1912), Kroeber (1925), and other earlier authorities to assign the entire upper Salinas River to the Salinans reflected resettlement during mission times. On the east, Salinans occupied the Coast Range mountains of eastern San Luis Obispo County to the edge of the San Joaquin Valley and

Yokuts territory. The most important Salinan district in this eastern area was **Cholam,** on Cholame Creek and in the northern portion of the drainage of the Estrella River.

The linguistic geography of Salinan territory is complicated by references in mission documents at both San Antonio and San Miguel—in particular the responses to the questionnaire of 1812—to a distinct language spoken by **los playanos** 'the beach people' who lived to the west (Kroeber 1908b:13; Geiger and Meighan 1976:20). Mason (1912:105) believed that this referred either to a divergent dialect of Salinan or to a second Salinan language, an interpretation that seems to be corroborated by statements in Harrington's notes that a distinct variety of Salinan was spoken in the coastal mountains from Point Lopez to Cambria (summarized in Milliken and Johnson 2003:130–132). It is also possible that the language referred to was Esselen, since converts from the coastal Esselen tribelet of Ekheahan on the coast south of Big Sur are known to have formed part of the mission population at San Antonio (Milliken 1990:51–58). However, speakers of the "Playano" language were also

FIGURE 54. Pedro Encinales, one of
J. Alden Mason's Salinan consultants in
1910. Courtesy of the Hearst Museum
of Anthropology and the Regents of UC
(15-5285).

reported to be at Mission San Miguel, where there were no
coastal Esselen converts (Milliken and Johnson 2003:19).
Gibson (1983) has proposed that "Playano" was used to
designate a Northern Chumash subgroup that occupied the
coast as far north as Ragged Point, near the Monterey County
line. Milliken and Johnson (2003:128–130, 134) find
Gibson's arguments for such a dramatic northward extension
of Chumash weak and suggest that a better interpretation of
the evidence is that "Playano" referred narrowly to the
people of the **Tsetacol** district or tribelet, which appears to
have been located along the coast from Estero Point to
Cambria, and possibly to the people of the **Chaal** and
Esmerileua regions immediately to the north. Tsetacol
speech could have been Salinan, Chumash, or a relict
language completely different from either. Milliken and
Johnson suggest that analysis of personal names in the
mission records is the only avenue open for determining
"Playano" linguistic affiliation.

The Salinans seem to have been on relatively friendly terms
with the Esselens, with whom they shared the northern Santa
Lucia Range and the Salinas Valley, but like the Esselens they
had a hostile relationship with the Costanoan-speaking groups
farther north. Their relationship with the Obispeño Chumash
to the south was also marked by hostility and frequent
intergroup raiding. By contrast, the Salinans were close
trading partners with the Valley Yokuts to the east. Some
degree of Yokuts-Salinan bilingualism seems to have existed
in the Cholam area, although this could also have been the
product of language mixture in the mission period.

3.17.2 Documentation and Survival

Salinan is one of the few California languages to have
been documented in more than a perfunctory way by

Franciscan priests during the mission period. Both Mission
San Antonio and Mission San Miguel were fortunate to
have had several able missionaries who served for lengthy
periods and acquired fluency in the native language (Geiger
1969:224). Fathers Buenaventura Sitjar and Miguel Pieras,
who were the founding missionaries at San Antonio,
compiled a well-organized bilingual dictionary (later edited
and published by Shea [Sitjar 1861]). They also composed
a long *confesionario,* a question and response dialogue for
use in the confessional (see I. Goddard 1996a:41, fig. 15).
Two later missionaries, Fathers Pedro Cabot and Juan
Sancho (who served from 1804 to 1834 and from 1804 to
1830, respectively), continued Sitjar and Pieras's
lexicographic work on Antoniano and also translated a
number of religious texts into that dialect.[55] Comparable
documents may have been produced at San Miguel by Father
Juan Martín, who is known to have acquired a good
knowledge of the language of the mission he administered
for twenty years, but if so they have been lost (Geiger
1969:149–150). Most of the known manuscript sources for
Salinan have been described and assessed by Katherine
Turner (1988a).[56]

Other early attestations include a vocabulary of Antoniano
by Thomas Coulter (1841) and vocabularies of both
Antoniano and Migueleño by Horatio Hale (1846). The first
trained investigators to document Salinan were Alphonse
Pinart, who collected a vocabulary of Antoniano (1878d),
and H. W. Henshaw, who collected vocabularies of both
dialects (Henshaw 1884f). Shortly after the turn of the twentieth century, A. L. Kroeber gathered and published a small
amount of lexical and grammatical material on Migueleño
(Kroeber 1904:43–49). J. Alden Mason, working under
Kroeber, collected extensive data on both Antoniano and
Migueleño during field trips in 1910 and 1916 and published
a grammatical study and a number of texts (Mason 1918; see
also Sapir 1920b). During visits in 1902 and 1933–1934,
Merriam collected vocabularies from speakers of both
dialects (Appendix A: R-17a-b). Harrington carried out field
investigations on both dialects during several extended visits
between 1922 and 1933, collecting lexical and grammatical
data and recording a number of narrative texts on long-
playing aluminum discs (Mills 1985:130–139; Glenn 1991a).
He also collected a substantial amount of ethnogeographical
information, some of which has been analyzed and published
(Rivers and Jones 1993; Jones et al. 2000). Working with
the last speakers in the 1950s, William H. Jacobsen, Jr.,
obtained a small but valuable collection of data, including
tape recordings, that is now in the archives of the Survey of
California and Other Indian Languages at the University of
California, Berkeley.

The last native speakers of both Salinan dialects died in
the late 1950s or early 1960s. Although Salinan descendants
have no federally acknowledged tribe, they maintain a
continuing identity, particularly in the area around Jolon.
During the past decade the group has made efforts to revive
traditional culture and language.

TABLE 22
Salinan Phonemes (K. Turner 1980)

Consonants							Vowels		
p	t	ṭ	c	č	k	ʔ	i / iː		u / uː
p'	t'	ṭ'	c'	č'	k'		(e / eː)		(o / oː)
			s	š	x	h		a / aː	
		r							
m	n								
ṁ	ṅ								
w	l			y					
ẇ	l'			ẏ					

TABLE 23
Salinan Pronouns (Mason 1918)

	1 sg	2 sg	3 sg	1 pl	2 pl	3 pl
Subject (independent or enclitic)						
	heʔk	moʔ	heyoʔ	haʔk	moːm	heyoʔt
Object (suffixed)						
	-(h)ak	-ka	-(k)o	-t'ak	-t'kam	-(k)ot ~ -tko
Possessive (infixed after ṭ- or suffixed)						
	(unmarked)	-m-	-o	-a-	-k(o)-	-ot

3.17.3 Linguistic Structure

Katherine Turner (1987) provides a summary of the phonology and morphology of Antoniano as it was attested by Mason (1918) and in the data collected by Harrington and Jacobsen. There is also a useful discussion of some aspects of Salinan structure in Poser (1992).

The phonology of Salinan is moderately complex (Table 22). There are four positions of stops, *p, t, ṭ* (post-alveolar or "retroflex"), and *k*, and two affricates (*c* [ts] and *č*). There are two nasals (*m* and *n*); and three approximants (*l, w, y*). All of these occur in both plain and glottalized form. (A plain versus glottalized contrast in nasals and approximants is an areal feature shared with both Yokuts and Chumash.) In addition there are three fricatives (*s, š, x*), a flap (*r*), and two laryngeals (*h, ʔ*). In Turner's analysis, there are three phonemic vowels (*i, a,* and *u*), which occur both long and short. Mid vowels (*e, o*) are analyzed as allophones of the high vowels (Turner 1980).

Salinan morphology is fusional, using both prefixes and suffixes, and clitics abound (Table 23). It shares with a number of other Hokan languages a tendency to have vowel-initial stems, both nominal and verbal, although consonant-initial stems are also abundant. Stems are usually preceded by one of a small number of stem-deriving prefixes, most of them consisting of a single consonant. Nominalized verbs are marked by the prefix *ṭ-* (e.g., *-axay* 'to fear', *ṭ-axaẏ* 'bear';

-kaw 'to sleep', *ṭ-kawi* 'sleep'). Possessed nouns are marked by the same nominalizing prefix (e.g., *ṭ-aːk* '[my] head', *ṭ-saːnat'* '[my] skin, hide'), following which the 2 sg and 1 and 2 pl possessive pronouns are infixed (*ṭ-m-saːnat'* 'your [sg] hide', *ṭ-a-saːnat'* 'our hide', *ṭ-k-saːnat'* 'your [pl] hide'); in 3 sg/pl forms the pronominal possessor is marked by a suffix (*ṭ-saːnat'-o* 'his, her hide', *ṭ-saːnat'-ot* 'their hide'), while in 1 sg forms it is marked only by the presence of the nominalizing prefix (*ṭ-saːnat'* 'my hide').

In verbs, active or transitive forms are marked by a prefix *p-* (e.g., *p-šik'ay-ka=heyoʔ* 'he kicked you', *p-awiːlo-ko=heyoʔ* 'she heated it'), while stative or intransitive verbs are marked by a prefix *k-* (e.g., *k-ekoł=heʔk* 'I am hungry', *k-aːmpło* 'it came out'). Pronominal objects are marked by suffixes, as are such categories as passive, reflexive, and causative. The subject is expressed by an independent pronoun that usually follows the verb and is often enclitic on it, particularly in transitive forms (*p-aleːl-hak=moʔ* 'you asked me', *p-šik'ay-ak=moʔ* 'you kicked me').

Probably the most complicated area of Salinan morphology is the formation of noun plurals and of pluractional forms of verbs (see ¶4.7.2). Plural variants are lexically specified and employ a variety of different processes, including ablaut, infixation, and reduplication in addition to suffixation. For example, *ṭ-aːm* 'house', *ṭ-emhal* 'houses'; *išxeːw* 'foot', *išxepaːl* 'feet'; *xuč* 'dog', *xosten* 'dogs'; *kaxota* 'hunt (a single animal)', *kaxoten* 'hunt (several animals)', *kaxonilet* 'several hunt (several animals)'.

3.17.4 Nomenclature

Antoniano and Migueleño were placed by the English comparativist R. G. Latham (1856:85) in a "Salinas" family (named after the river) to which he also assigned Esselen, Rumsen and Chalon Costanoan, and "Guiloco" (an attestation of Wappo; see ¶3.35.2). Powell (1891:101–102) moved the other members of this heterogeneous group to more appropriate families and left Antoniano and Migueleño with the name "Salinan."

3.18 Yuman Languages

Yuman is a family of eight closely related languages, spoken along the lower Colorado River from the Grand Canyon to the Gulf of California, as well as on the plateau of northwestern Arizona and westward to the Pacific coast of San Diego County and adjacent Baja California (M. Kendall 1983; see Table 24 and Map 21). **Kiliwa,** in Baja California, is the most divergent language in the family and constitutes an independent subgroup. The other seven languages are usually divided into four subgroups: **Paipai,** in northeastern Baja California; **Delta-California** (Cocopa in the delta of the Colorado, and Diegueño in northwestern Baja California and San Diego County, California); **River** (Quechan, Maricopa, and Mojave, on the lower Colorado River north of the Cocopa, and on the lower Gila River); and **Upland Yuman** or

TABLE 24
Classification of the Yuman Languages

Kiliwa

General Yuman

  Paipai

  Delta-California group

    Cocopa

    Diegueño (Kumeyaay)

      Ipai ('Iipay)

      Tipai (Tiipay)

  River group

    Quechan (Yuma)

    Maricopa

    Mojave

  Upland Yuman (Pai)

    Hualapai (Walapai)

    Havasupai

    Yavapai

Pai (a cluster of dialects on the plateau of northwestern Arizona, usually referred to individually as **Havasupai, Hualapai,** and **Yavapai**). Paipai is sometimes classified as a member of the Pai subgroup, but since it is spoken at a considerable distance from the Northern Pai dialect cluster, this grouping is problematic (see ¶3.18.2). The time depth of Yuman diversification is shallow, probably no greater than 1,500–2,000 years (K. Hale and Harris 1979:172). The Yuman family as a whole has a distant but well-established relationship to the Cochimí family of the Baja California peninsula, and Yuman-Cochimí in turn constitutes a branch of the Hokan phylum (see ¶3.19).

3.18.1 Kiliwa

Aboriginal **Kiliwa** territory centered on the Sierra San Pedro Martir, the high, forested mountain range in the middle of the Baja California peninsula approximately 75 to 100 miles south of the U.S.-Mexico border. The Kiliwa were hunter-gatherers who migrated seasonally from the mountains to the desert beaches of the Gulf of California or to the Pacific coast (Meigs 1939). Although the descendants of the Dominican mission community of San Pedro Mártir now account for what remains of Kiliwa ethnic and linguistic identity, ethnohistorical data suggest that in the eighteenth century dialects of Kiliwa or Kiliwa-like languages were more widely spoken, in particular to the south and west of San Pedro Mártir (Joël 1964:102). J. P. Harrington, in the 1920s, was able to collect a vocabulary of about a hundred

words in "Domingueño," or **Ñakipa,** the speech of Mission Santo Domingo, north of Rosario. It is virtually identical to Kiliwa (Mixco 1977c).

On the north the Kiliwa bordered the Paipai, whom they regarded as friends and with whom they intermarried (Gifford and Lowie 1928:351). The precontact border between the two groups appears to have been in the vicinity of Arroyo San Rafael, but in mission times a number of Kiliwa were among the converts at the principal Paipai mission, Santa Catarina, about fifty miles farther north. Despite the close contacts between the Kiliwa and the Paipai in the historic period, however, the similarities between the two languages are no greater than those between Kiliwa and the Delta-California group, indicating a long period of independent development.

In both phonology and grammar, Kiliwa is quite distinct from all other Yuman languages, and only a small number of Kiliwa stems have clear Yuman cognates. Cultural connections with Cochimí speakers to the south seem to have been of considerable long-term importance, although the nature and degree of Cochimí influence on Kiliwa, or even where the boundary between the two languages in fact lay, is difficult to determine from the scanty attestation of Northern Cochimí that survives (Joël 1964:103; Mixco 1979).

Kiliwa has been documented by Mauricio Mixco in extensive fieldwork that began in 1966. His dissertation (1971) was a grammar of the language, and he has published two grammatical sketches (1996, 2000), a dictionary (1985), and a collection of texts (1983).

The fewer than ten speakers of Kiliwa that survive now share the Santa Catarina community with speakers of Paipai. No language retention efforts are reported.

3.18.2 Paipai (Akwa'ala)

The territory of the **Paipai** (referred in earlier literature by their Mojave name, **Akwa'ala**) lies in the Baja California mountains to the north of Kiliwa territory. Most of the remaining Paipai—many of whom are fluent speakers of their traditional language (Joël 1976:84)—live in the vicinity of the former Dominican mission at Santa Catarina, founded in 1797. Gifford and Lowie (1928:340) elicited a list of seventeen named Paipai lineages, at least some of which may originally have been local groups speaking distinct varieties. One of these lineages, the **Yakakwal,** was apparently the group living on the Pacific Coast near the former mission at San Vicente, southwest of Santa Catarina, between Santo Domingo and Santo Tomás. Two fragmentary attestations of the speech of this area were collected by J. P. Harrington around 1925. A vocabulary of about one hundred words in "Jaka?akwal" is nearly identical to Paipai; a second vocabulary, consisting of only the numerals 1–10 and labeled "San Vicente Paipai," is more divergent, showing Diegueño or Cocopa influence (Mixco 1977c).

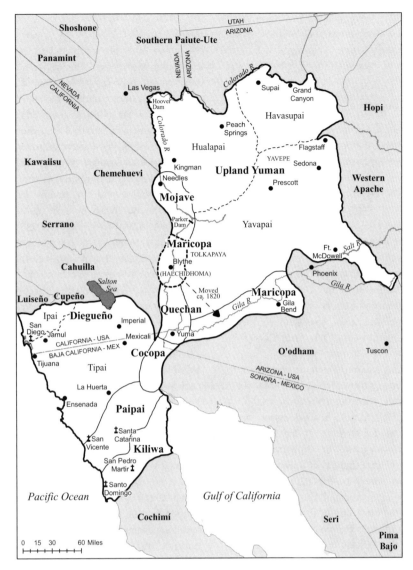

MAP 21. Yuman languages.

Paipai was well documented in the late 1950s by Judith Joël, who prepared a study of Paipai phonology and morphology for her dissertation (1966). Of earlier materials, the most important are a vocabulary of Henshaw's (1884l) and the notes collected by Harrington around 1925 (Mills and Brickfield 1986:116–137).

The classification of Paipai has been a subject of considerable debate among Yuman specialists. Although the Paipai were on friendly terms with the Kiliwa to the south of them, the two languages, as noted earlier, differ sharply. The lexical and grammatical similarities to Diegueño or Cocopa are somewhat greater, but Paipai cannot be considered part of the Delta-California subgroup. The closest connection appears to be with Upland Yuman in northwestern Arizona, in particular Yavapai, with which Paipai shares several phonological isoglosses and some distinctive vocabulary (Kroeber 1943:24–25). This linguistic resemblance lends credence to intertribal traditions of

a relationship between the Upland Yuman and Paipai peoples, and Werner Winter (1967) proposed that a relatively recent tribal fission in the Yavapai community led to the migration of the Paipai into their historic territory. The hypothesis was taken up by Alan Shaterian (1983:8–16), who found that modern Yavapai speakers could understand Paipai with no difficulty (but see M. Kendall 1983:8). Joël (1964), however, following Kroeber (1943), thought it more likely that the Upland Yuman–Paipai similarity was attributable to the relative conservatism of two geographically peripheral languages whose "generalized Yuman" speech had not been affected by the innovations characteristic of the Colorado River languages. The lack of shared borrowings from Spanish, indicating that the languages have not been in contact during historical times (Joël 1998), lends significant support to Kroeber's and Joël's interpretation, but the question still remains open.

Paipai is still spoken in several small communities in northern Baja California, near San Miguel, Santa Catarina, and San Isodoro. There are possibly as many as a hundred speakers, although most of them are in their fifties or older.

3.18.3 Delta-California Subgroup

The languages of the Delta-California subgroup, Cocopa and Diegueño, were spoken from the delta of the Colorado River west to the Pacific coast, on both sides of the U.S.-Mexico border.

COCOPA

Cocopa was restricted to a small but resource-rich territory that lay along the lowermost fifty miles of the Colorado River and its delta branches, from near the modern city of Yuma, Arizona, to the head of the Gulf of California. Although dialect variation had largely disappeared before serious documentation began in the twentieth century, it was reported that the speech of the "Mountain Cocopa" of the western delta, near the Cocopah Mountains, used to differ from that of the Cocopa along the main channel of the river, and that the Hwanyak group of the lower delta region had a distinctive dialect (Gifford 1933:260–261; J. M. Crawford 1966:3). The Colorado River immediately to the north of the Cocopa was the territory of the **Kahwan** or "Cajuenches" and the **Halyikwamai** or "Jalliquamai," who were said to have spoken either dialects of Cocopa or closely related languages (Kroeber 1943:21–22). The only attestations of Kahwan—two vocabularies obtained from speakers living among the Maricopa in the Phoenix area—are not significantly different from Cocopa, and James Crawford believed that the Kahwan were "a clan or a group of clans who spoke the same language as the Cocopa, but who lived separately from the main tribe" (1966:4). No record survives of the language of the Halyikwamai, but the Kahwan speaker whom Kroeber interviewed claimed that it was identical to her language (1943:21–22).

While there are only scattered earlier attestations, Cocopa was abundantly documented in the 1960s by James Crawford, who carried out extensive fieldwork. He wrote a full grammar as his dissertation (1966) and subsequently published a collection of texts (1983) and a dictionary (1989). There is also a phonological study by Brigitte Bendixen (1980).

The language is spoken today by between 150 and three hundred of the approximately seven hundred members of the Cocopah Tribe, who have a reservation near Yuma, Arizona, and by an equal or greater number of Mexican *Cucapás* in communities in Baja California and Sonora. In Arizona, most Cocopas over fifty are fluent, and a number of younger people are semispeakers, including at least some children. There is a summer program with some language retention activities, and a course in Cocopa is offered at Yuma Community College.

DIEGUEÑO (KUMEYAAY)

Diegueño (now often referred to as "Kumeyaay," although this term is also used for a specific Diegueño dialect, see next paragraph) was spoken in the southern two-thirds of San Diego County and in the northwestern part of Baja California as far south as Ensenada. The eastern extent of Diegueño territory in aboriginal times is uncertain. Despite the close linguistic connection between Diegueño and Cocopa, the two groups seem not to have directly adjoined. A group known historically as the "Kamia" occupied the Imperial Valley and the region around Mexicali in Baja California, and were in close contact with the Quechan (Gifford 1931). While Kroeber (1925) and others treated the Kamia as a Diegueño subgroup, there is no firm evidence in support of this approach, although the name they are known by appears to be a variant of "Kumeyaay" (Langdon 1975a).[57] With this possible exception, all of the groups definitely known to have spoken varieties of Diegueño were located west of the present San Diego–Imperial County line or in Baja California west of the Sierra de Juarez.

Diegueño is currently spoken in at least sixteen communities in San Diego County and in Baja California, each using a distinct local variety. At least two dialects or dialect clusters have long been recognized, referred to in the earlier literature as Northern and Southern Diegueño (Kroeber 1943) but since the 1970s usually designated *Ipai* (or 'Iipay) and *Tipai* (or Tiipay) after the words for 'person' in the two groups. Although Ipai and Tipai are to some extent mutually intelligible, they show numerous differences in vocabulary and structure (for a comparison of Mesa Grande Ipai and Jamul Tipai see A. Miller 2001:359–363) and have sometimes been treated as separate languages. Winter (1957), who called Tipai "Campo," judged it to be no closer to (Northern) Diegueño than to Cocopa. The most recent classification (Langdon 1991; A. Miller 2001:1–4) distinguishes the Ipai and Tipai band dialects ("languages") from wider Ipai and Tipai dialect clusters ("language clusters"), and adds a third dialect cluster intermediate between the other two, somewhat confusingly named **Kumeyaay**.[58] In this scheme, Ipai proper is spoken in northern San Diego County in the communities at Mesa Grande, Santa Ysabel, and Barona, while the Ipai dialect cluster also includes the varieties of Iñaja and San Pasqual. Tipai proper is spoken at Jamul in southern San Diego County and in the communities of Tecate, San José, and La Huerta in Baja California, while other varieties of the Tipai cluster are spoken in three other Baja California Diegueño communities—Naji, Ha'a, and San José de la Zorra. The Kumayaay dialect is spoken at Campo, Manzanita, and Cuyapaipe in southeastern San Diego County. The variety spoken in the central San Diego County community of Baron Long is classified as intermediate between the Ipai dialect cluster and the Kumeyaay dialect.

The best documented variety of Diegueño is Mesa Grande Ipai, which was the focus of Margaret Langdon's extensive

FIGURE 55. Ted Couro, one of the last speakers of Ipay (Northern Diegueño) and coauthor, with Christina Hutcheson, of the *Dictionary of Mesa Grande Diegueño* (1973). Courtesy of Loni Langdon.

fieldwork in the 1960s. Langdon published a Mesa Grande grammar (1970) and helped to prepare a teaching grammar (Couro and Langdon 1975) and a dictionary (Couro and Hutcheson 1973). Langdon and Hymes (1998) also collaborated on a study of Mesa Grande oratory and narrative. Jamul Tipai is well documented in Amy Miller's work (Miller 1990, 2001). Baja California Tipai is best represented in the notes on the La Huerta variety collected by Leanne Hinton (1970, 1976; Hinton and Langdon 1976).

Earlier documentation includes a vocabulary collected by Alexander Taylor at San Luis Rey (Taylor 1860–1863; Langdon 1993); three long vocabularies collected in Powell schedules by H. W. Henshaw (1884j, 1884k, 1892–1893); general and natural history vocabularies collected by Merriam between 1903 and 1933 (Appendix A: O-14b); an Ipai vocabulary collected by A. L. Kroeber from a Mesa Grande speaker in 1912 (1943:26–30); and a range of materials collected by J. P. Harrington, much of it in Baja California, between 1913 and 1933 (Mills and Brickfield 1986:129–135). Kroeber and Harrington collaborated on an early study of Diegueño (specifically Ipai) phonetics (1914; see Langdon 1994).

Ipai is still spoken by a small number of elderly people. Kumeyaay has between forty and fifty fluent speakers. Tipai is spoken by approximately one hundred people, who live in several locations in northern Baja California and at Jamul near San Diego.

3.18.4 River Subgroup

The River subgroup includes the Yuman languages spoken in the Colorado River valley, from the vicinity of Yuma, Arizona, to southern Nevada, and on the Gila River from its confluence with the Colorado upstream to the Phoenix area. While three languages are usually distinguished in the River subgroup, Quechan (Yuma), Maricopa, and Mojave, they are all mutually intelligible to some extent (Biggs 1957:61–62), and the relationship between Quechan and Maricopa is especially close. Externally, the languages of the River group most closely resemble the Delta-California languages, in particular Cocopa, but this similarity may be more the result of the extensive contacts among the tribes settled along the Colorado than an indication of a common origin of the two subgroups within the Yuman family.

QUECHAN (YUMA)

The Quechan, or "Kwtsaan" (k^wca:n),[59] earlier known as the **Yuma,** occupied the strategically important stretch of the Colorado at the mouth of the Gila, where a major trade route from the Southwest to California crossed the Colorado. Although scattered in a number of settlements north and south of the Gila, the Quechan had a strong tribal identity and frequently joined in alliances to fight with or against neighboring tribes. Their main allies were the Mojave to the north and the Kamia to the west, while their enemies were usually the Cocopa on the lower Colorado to the south and, most frequently, the Maricopa on the Gila to the east (Bee 1983:93). Despite the historic enmity of the two tribes, however, the Quechan and Maricopa languages are very close, perhaps better classified as dialects of a single language (Harwell and Kelly 1983:71; M. Kendall 1983:9).

Quechan is one of the best documented Yuman languages, owing to the efforts of A. M. Halpern, who carried out fieldwork on Quechan in the 1930s (Halpern 1935) and again in 1978–1985. He published a grammatical sketch (1946a) and a fuller study (1946b, 1947), both based on his earlier work. A posthumous collection of ethnographic texts with a short grammatical sketch (1997) is based on his later work. Other attestations of Quechan include vocabularies collected by Whipple (1850, 1855) and Loew (Gatschet 1876a), and survey materials collected by Kroeber in 1930 (Kroeber 1943). Merriam collected general and natural history vocabularies in 1933 (Appendix A: O-14d), and J. P. Harrington collected incidental material on Quechan while working on Mojave (Mills and Brickfield 1986:116–129).

Quechan is currently spoken by 150 to two hundred of the three thousand members of the Quechan Indian Nation of southeastern California, whose reservation is adjacent to Yuma, Arizona. Most fluent speakers are middle-aged or elderly, but fluency in the language retains considerable social prestige, particularly in ceremonial contexts, and there are a number of younger semispeakers. Language retention is largely a traditional concern, and there is no systematic attempt to teach Quechan in the schools, although there is a Quechan culture course at the high school where some vocabulary is taught.

Maricopa is primarily the language of the tribe of the same name, whose present homeland is on the Gila River just east of its confluence with the Salt River, southwest of Phoenix, Arizona. The Maricopa earlier lived along the lower Colorado River, where several distinct Maricopa-speaking groups occupied the territory between the Quechan and the Mojave in the eighteenth century and before. The last to leave the Colorado and resettle on the Gila were the *Halchidhoma,* who were forced to abandon the area around Blythe in the 1820s, owing to constant attacks from the Quechan and Mojave (K. Stewart 1983:55). Although in the twentieth century the Halchidhoma continued to be distinguished from the Maricopa proper, and both were distinguished from the *Kaveltcadom* who had settled downstream from the main body of Maricopas around Gila Bend, they spoke only "barely separable" dialects (L. Spier 1933:ix). In addition to the Maricopa-speaking Halchidhoma and Kaveltcadom, the Gila River Maricopa also absorbed two groups of Cocopa refugees, the Kahwan and the Halyikwamai, some of whom appear to have continued to speak Cocopa for several generations (see ¶3.18.3).

The earliest attestation of Maricopa is a vocabulary collected by Whipple (1855). Kroeber collected a survey vocabulary in 1930 (Kroeber 1943:26–30). Maricopa was moderately well documented by Leslie Spier, who published vocabularies and texts collected incidentally to his ethnographic work (1946), and it was restudied a generation later by Lynn Gordon, who published a descriptive grammar (1986).

Maricopa is currently spoken by perhaps as few as one hundred of the approximately eight hundred members of the Maricopa (or Pee-Posh) tribe of Arizona, most of whom live either in the Maricopa Colony at Laveen, on the Gila River Reservation south of Phoenix, or in the community of Lehi on the Salt River Reservation northeast of Phoenix. There is a language program at Lehi, where the language is referred to as "Piipaash."

MOJAVE (MOHAVE)

Mojave (or Mohave) is the language of the Mojave (or Mohave) Tribe,[60] whose territory extended in the mid-nineteenth century along the Colorado River from north of Davis Dam in Nevada to the vicinity of Blythe, California, and Ehrenberg, Arizona, where they adjoined the Quechan. Prior to that time, Mojave territory was centered on the Mohave Valley around present-day Needles, extending south into the Chemehuevi Valley only as far as Parker. The river below Parker was occupied by the Maricopa-speaking Halchidhoma, whom the Mojave and the Quechan, after protracted warfare, forced out sometime before 1830 (K. Stewart 1983:55). Following the exodus of the Halchidhoma, their former territory was partly settled by the Numic-speaking Chemehuevi.

Although structurally and lexically very similar to Maricopa and Quechan, Mojave is distinct enough not to be easily intelligible to speakers of either (L. Spier 1933:ix; Biggs 1957). Long-standing connections with speakers of the Upland Yuman (Pai) languages to the northeast have had some influence on Mojave, most strikingly in a sound shift—the fronting of alveolar [s] to [θ]—that probably dates to the nineteenth century (Hinton 1979).

The documentation of Mojave is rich and varied and extends over a century and a half. Early vocabularies were collected by Lieutenant A. W. Whipple (1855), Oscar Loew (1874–1875; see Gatschet 1876a), and William Corbusier (1885). A. L. Kroeber spent a large amount of time with the Mojaves between 1900 and 1911, but with the exception of a technical study of Mojave phonetics (1911b) and the vocabulary incorporated into his comparative study of Yuman languages (1943:26–30), his linguistic data seem largely to have been collected incidentally to his ethnographic work. The long mythic narratives he published (1948) were dictated in English.

The first substantial documentation of the language was made by J. P. Harrington, who worked on Mojave intermittently for more than fifty years, from 1906 to 1957, most intensively in 1910–1911 (Mills and Brickfield 1986:116–129). None of his materials, however, have been published.[61] Merriam collected general and natural history vocabularies (Appendix A: O-14a) during visits between 1905 and 1919. In the late 1940s the psychiatrist and anthropologist George Devereux carried out research in the Mojave community, some of it ethnolinguistic in focus (1949, 1951). Pamela Munro has worked extensively on the language since the early 1970s, and has published a study of Mojave syntax (1976), supervised the preparation of a Mojave dictionary (Munro, Brown, and Crawford 1989), and written numerous technical papers.

Mojave is the heritage language of both the Fort Mojave Tribe, near Needles, California, and of the Mojave members of the Colorado River Indian Tribes, near Parker, Arizona. In the two communities combined there are fewer than a hundred fluent first-language speakers, nearly all of them elderly, in a total Mojave population of more than two thousand. A practical orthography has been developed, and language classes are offered in both communities. At Fort Mojave the language program is sponsored by the AhaMakav Cultural Society.

3.18.5 Upland Yuman (Pai)

The Upland Yuman (or Pai) subgroup consists of a single language with three dialects, *Hualapai* (or *Walapai*), *Havasupai,* and *Yavapai,* spoken in the high desert and plateau area of northwestern Arizona between the Grand Canyon and the Gila River valley. Hualapai territory lies to the north of Bill Williams River, Yavapai territory to the south of it. Havasupai territory is restricted to a single village community situated below the south rim of the Grand

TABLE 25
Yuman Phonemic Systems

Consonants											Vowels		

Quechan (Halpern 1946b, 1997)

p	t	ṭ	(tʸ)	c	kʸ	k	kʷ	q	qʷ	ʔ	i / i:		u / u:
β	s	ṣ				x	xʷ				e / e:	(ə)	o / o:
m	n		nʸ								a / a:		
w		r	y										
		l	lʸ										

Jamul Tipai (Miller 2001)

p	t	ṭ	č	k	kʷ	ʔ					i / i:		u / u:
	s		š	x	xʷ							ə	
m	n		nʸ								a / a:		
w		r	y										
		l	lʸ										
		ł	łʸ										

Canyon. Hualapai and Havasupai (sometmes referred to as **Northern Pai**) are especially close, and their separation can only be two or three centuries deep. Yavapai has several well-differentiated subdialects: **Yavepe** (Central Yavapai) in the area around present-day Prescott and Jerome; **Wipukpaya** (Northeastern Yavapai) in the middle Verde Valley and the Sedona area; **Tolkapaya** (Western Yavapai) from the western slopes of the Bradshaw Mountains to the Colorado River; and **Keweevkapaya** (Southeastern Yavapai) in the lower Verde Valley around the Fort McDowell Reservation (Gifford 1932a, 1936; M. Kendall 1983:5–7).

Upland Yuman is extensively documented. Survey vocabularies and other materials were collected by Loew (Gatschet 1876a, 1876b), Corbusier (1873–75, 1923–24), and Kroeber (1943:26–30). More recent materials include a full reference grammar of Hualapai (Watahomigie et al. 2001); structural summaries of Havasupai phonology and morphology (Seiden 1963) and basic syntax (Kozlowski 1972); discussions of various points of Hualapai grammar (Redden 1966, 1976, 1981, 1982, 1983, 1986a, 1986b; 1986c, 1990); a sketch of Tolkapaya Yavapai morphology (Munro 1996); syntactic studies of Western Yavapai (Hardy 1979) and Northeastern Yavapai (M. Kendall 1976); and a phonology and dictionary of Southeastern Yavapai (Shaterian 1983). There is also an ethnomusicological study of Havasupai songs (Hinton 1984) and an older but useful comparative vocabulary of Havasupai and Yavapai (L. Spier 1946).

The Upland Yuman languages, particularly Hualapai and Havasupai, all retain substantial numbers of speakers. Hualapai is spoken at the Hualapai Indian Reservation in Peach Springs by approximately one thousand people, slightly more than half the total population. Speakers are of all ages, and at least some children continue to acquire Hualapai as their first language. There has been an active bilingual education program in the Peach Springs schools for more than twenty-five years, and extensive teaching materials have been prepared. Havasupai is spoken by more than five hundred people of all ages, nearly the entire population of the village of Supai in Havasu Canyon, at the western end of the Grand Canyon. The tribally controlled school offers bilingual education courses, and there is extensive literacy in the dialect. Yavapai is spoken in four small reservation communities, Prescott, Fort McDowell, Camp Verde, and Clarkdale. Local varieties, however, reflect the pre-reservation subtribes (Yavepe, Tolkapaya, Keweevkapaya, and Wipukpaya), and speakers of all of these are found in each of the four communities. None of the Yavapai varieties is thriving as well as Hualapai or Havasupai, and most of the estimated one hundred to 150 speakers (out of a total population of about a thousand) are middle-aged or older. Yavapai is taught in the reservation school in Prescott.

3.18.6 Linguistic Structure

The Yuman consonant system is characterized by a lack of laryngeal feature contrasts in voicing, aspiration, or glottalization (Table 25), although in some languages the phonemic sequence of a stop and *h* produces a phonetic aspirated stop. The single set of stops and affricates has basically six articulatory contrasts, as in Kiliwa: *p, t, č, k, kʷ, q*. A distinction between dental or interdental [t̪] and alveolar or postalveolar [t] stops is allophonic in the majority of the languages, but the contrast is phonemic (with low functional load) in Diegueño, Cocopa, Quechan, and Maricopa. A palatalized velar (*kʸ*) and a labialized uvular (q^w) are also phonemically distinct in most languages of the River subgroup. Four basic fricatives are distinguished: two sibilants—one dental or interdental ([s̪]~[θ]), the other alveolar, postalveolar, or palatal ([s]~[ṣ]~[š]), the pattern of articulations varying considerably from language to language (cf. Hinton 1979, 1981)—and two velar fricatives, plain and labialized (x, x^w). In the River and Upland Yuman subgroups a voiced bilabial fricative (v [β]) is added, and in the River subgroup a voiced interdental fricative (ð) as well.[62] Most languages have three nasals (m, n, $ñ$)—Ipai Diegueño adds a distinction between a dental n and a (rare) alveolar $ṇ$—and at least four liquids (l, r, w, y). Languages of the Delta-California and River groups also have a contrast between plain and palatalized laterals (l, l^y), and the Delta-California languages further distinguish a series of voiceless laterals, both plain and palatalized ($ł$, $ł^y$). To its basic r (written $ṛ$), described as a "voiced apico-postdental trill," Ipai Diegueño contrasts a second r (written r), "similar to English 'r' but more tense and occasionally spirantal" (Langdon 1970:25, 32). Although all Yuman languages have a phonemic laryngeal stop (ʔ), in many languages the phonemic status of the laryngeal fricative h is marginal, with most occurrences of [h] representing either an epenthetic onset in vowel-initial words or the primary allophone of the velar fricative x. In Kiliwa, however, there is a basic phonemic contrast between velar and laryngeal fricatives, including labialized versions of both (x, x^w and h, h^w) (Mixco 1977b).

Kiliwa and the Delta-California languages have three primary vowel contrasts (i, a, u), each with a phonemic contrast in length. A phonologically secondary schwa is often inserted to break up consonant clusters; the phonemic status of this "inorganic" vowel differs from language to language (Langdon 1970:37–40; A. Miller 2001:20–21). To this system the River and Upland Yuman languages add two mid vowels (e, o), which occur both short and long.

Verb and noun stems are based on a monosyllabic root, (C)V(C). A few verb stems in every Yuman language consist of unmodified roots (e.g., Tipay Diegueño *pap* 'to bake', *kuł* 'to climb'), but most incorporate an element termed a "lexical prefix" by Yuman specialists. Although some of these prefixes seem to have instrumental meanings (e.g., Tipay Diegueño *š-* 'with the hand or a handheld instrument', *k-* 'on or by the feet'), many are semantically vague or opaque, and none are synchronically productive (see ¶4.8.2). Lexical suffixes are occasionally used to mark direction (e.g., Tipay Diegueño *čša:-k* 'bring', *čša:-m* 'take away'). There are a few root nouns (e.g., Tipay Diegueño *ma:t* 'body', *wa* 'house'), but many noun stems are compounds or can be analyzed as having a prefixed formative (e.g., Tipay Diegueño *xaṭ-pa* 'coyote' < *xaṭ* 'dog' + *ʔi:-pa* 'man'; *ł^y-tut* 'spider', *ł^y-tiš* 'bug sp.' < *ł^y-* 'insect'). The semantic transparency of many of these compounds is minimal, however, and the recognition of a dissyllabic noun root may be preferable in some cases (Winter 1998). In addition, a number of noun stems are nominalized verbs (e.g., Tipay Diegueño *k^wə-č-čəya:w* 'singer' < *čəyaw* 'sing').

Verb stems are marked for various derivative categories by a multiplicity of irregular or semiregular morphological processes. In Tipay Diegueño, a causative stem is formed in about 90 percent of stems by the prefixation of *a:-* to the root or the infixation of *-a:-* after the initial consonant of the lexical prefix nearest the root, in many (but not all) cases accompanied by the further prefixation of *t-, č-,* or *š-*, and the suffixation of *-i* or *-a* (*yiw* 'come' > *a:yiw* 'bring', *xəmi:* 'grow, be born' > *txa:mi:a* 'make grow', *pʔaw* 'step, stand' > *špa[:]ʔawa* 'stand [it] up'). Plural and pluractional stems are similarly derived by several different and unpredictable processes (*sʔaw* 'give birth' > *suʔa:w* 'several give birth', *stəʔa:w* 'give birth on several occasions'; *i:ma* 'dance' > *i:mač* 'several dance', *ičma:č* 'dance repeatedly, be a dancer'; see ¶4.7.2).

In contrast to the complexity and irregularity of derivation, inflectional categories are few and regular. Most verbs are inflected for subject and, when transitive, for object. The basic subject prefixes in Tipay Diegueño are *ʔ-* first person, *m-* second person (declarative), *k-* second person (imperative), *w- ~ -u:-* third person. First person is unmarked before any consonant-initial stem, third person umarked before a lexical prefix. In transitive verbs, single prefixes mark specific combinations of subject person and object person (*ñ-* 'I . . . you', *ñəm-* 'you . . . me', etc.). First and second person subject and object categories, differentiated for number, are also marked by independent pronouns (*ña:č* 'I', *ña:p* 'me', *ñaʔwač* 'we', etc.). Case is otherwise indicated by clitics which follow the last element of the noun phrase, with the object (or absolute) case left unmarked (*-č* subject, *-i* locative, *-m* instrumental/comitative, *-k* ablative/locative, *-ł^y* inessive). Inalienable nouns are usually inflected for first and second person pronominal possessor with the intransitive verb subject prefixes (e.g., Maricopa *ʔ-i:ša:l^y* 'my hand', *m-i:ša:l^y* 'your hand'); a third person possessor is either left unmarked or marked with a proclitic demonstrative or indefinite. Possessed alienable nouns are additionally marked as such by a distinct prefix (Maricopa *βa* 'house', *ʔ-ñ-βa* 'my house', *m-ñ-βa* 'your house', *ñ-βa* 'his/her house'). These forms are possibly verbal in origin (Langdon 1978b). In some languages a number of nouns can indicate a possessor only through a periphrastic syntactic construction with an auxiliary verb meaning 'have' or 'possess'.

Yuman syntax is characterized by the occurrence of a variety of biclausal constructions that are usually described as Main Clause + Auxiliary Clause constructions (Langdon 1978a; Langacker 1998). The verb of the auxiliary clause is often grammaticized in its function, is typically restricted in its inflectional and derivational properties, and is sometimes phonologically dependent on the main clause. For example, Diegueño *-a:*, which means 'go' when used in a main clause, has an inchoative function in an auxiliary clause (*ña:č aʔ-šay ʔ-a:* 'I am getting fat'); the auxiliary verb *-a:r* in similar fashion serves as an intensifier (*mi: ləʔuñ w-a:r* 'his legs are very short').

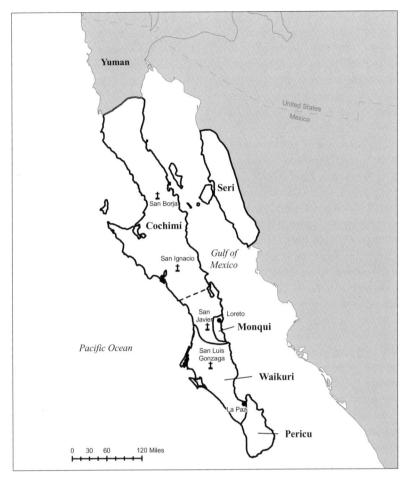

MAP 22. Seri, Cochimí, and languages of southern Baja California (after Laylander 1997).

3.18.7 Nomenclature

"Yuma" was the name by which the Spanish knew the Quechan, from Kino's visit in 1699 onward. It appears to have been borrowed from O'odham *yu:mi* 'Quechan' (Goddard in Bee 1983:97). "Yuma" was first employed in a broader sense by William W. Turner (in Whipple 1855:55) to designate the relationship between Quechan, Maricopa, Mojave, and Diegueño that he saw reflected in the vocabularies collected by Lieutenant Whipple.[63] Gatschet (1877c etc.) extended the relationhip, as well as the term "Yuma," to all the languages now recognized as Yuman, as well as to Cochimí and Seri, and in his 1891 classification Powell formally adopted "Yuman" as the name of this larger grouping. Kroeber (1925, 1943) was the first to use "Yuman" consistently and systematically as the name of the family in the current sense, including Kiliwa but excluding Cochimí and Seri.

3.19 Cochimí and the Cochimí-Yuman Relationship

Cochimí is the name given to the dialects spoken by the small nomadic groups who lived in the four hundred miles

of arid desert that stretch across central Baja California between Rosario (about two hundred miles south of San Diego) and Loreto (Map 22). Extinct as a spoken language since the nineteenth century, Cochimí appears to have been a dialect complex with moderate internal variation; the Jesuit missionary Miguel del Barco compared its diversity to that of the Iberian languages (Mixco 1979:39). The northern half of Cochimí territory was occupied by speakers of a single dialect, usually referred to as **Borjeño** or **Borjino** after the principal mission in the area, San Francisco Borja Adac, and extending down the peninsula to the territory of Mission San Ignacio. In the southern half, the dialect diversity seems to have been somewhat greater, and distinctions are usually drawn between **Cadegomeño** (at La Purísima Cadegomó), **Laymón** or **Javicroño** (around San Javier Viggé and San José Comondú, in the interior of the peninsula west of Loreto), and sometimes **Didiu** (on the east coast of the peninsula between Loreto and Mulegé). The last mentioned, however, is not directly attested, and may represent a confusion with Monqui, the non-Cochimí language of the Loreto-Malibat area (¶3.37).

Most of the data on Cochimí come from the Jesuit missionaries who worked in Baja California between 1697 and 1768 (see Clavigero 1789; the manuscripts are collated and discussed in Mixco 1978). To this can be added a 176-item vocabulary of Borjeño that was collected by the naturalist William Gabb in 1867 (Gatschet 1886, 1892a). The last attempt to document the language was made in the mid-1920s by J. P. Harrington, who was able to collect only a few dimly remembered words from the Borjeño area (Mixco 1977a).

Although sparse, the surviving lexical and grammatical data are sufficient to show that Cochimí has a distant but secure connection to the Yuman family (Troike 1976). Mauricio Mixco, the scholar most familiar with Cochimí and Baja California Yuman, sees the relationship as a straightforward family tree, with the two language groups representing collateral branches of a Yuman-Cochimí stock (Mixco 1978, 1979, 2006). Clouding this picture, however, is the uncertain status of Kiliwa, the southernmost Yuman language. After the establishment of the missions in northern Baja California in the late eighteenth century, Kiliwa was primarily associated with a small area in the Sierra San Pedro Mártir. There is reason to believe, however, that before this time other Kiliwa dialects or Kiliwa-like languages were spoken further to the south and that these may have shaded into the northernmost Cochimí varieties (Joël 1964:102; Mixco 1977c).[64] Furthermore, although attested Kiliwa is phonologically and grammatically Yuman, a substantial percentage of its vocabulary is not cognate with other Yuman languages. This observation raises the possibility of substantial borrowing from Cochimí, although the meager documentation of northern Cochimí does not permit this to be demonstrated.

Mixco (1978:13–19) attributes to the Cochimí reflected in mission-era records five stops and affricates (*p, t, č, k, kʷ*), four fricatives (*s, š, x, xʷ*), four nasals (*m, n, ñ, ŋ*, the last occurring only word-finally), four approximants (*l, r, w, y*), and one laryngeal (*ʔ*). Lenited or voiced variants of the labial, dental, and velar stops (*b, d, g*) may also have had phonemic status, although the evidence is equivocal. There were at least three phonemic vowels (*i, a, u*), and possibly also *e* and *o*.

3.20 Seri

The Seri were the inhabitants of the arid coastal region of the Mexican state of Sonora from Puerto Lobos to Guaymas, including the islands of Tiburón and San Esteban in the Gulf of California (Bowen 1983:230). In both language and culture they were sharply differentiated from all adjoining groups and were the only aboriginal people of Sonora not to cultivate maize.

The Seri language can be fairly securely assigned to Hokan (Kroeber 1915b; Kaufman 1988:58)—Marlett (2001) demurring—but its exact position within the phylum is unclear. A close connection to Yuman-Cochimí is suggested by geography, and the inclusion of Seri in an expanded

"Yuman" family was in fact proposed by Brinton (1891:111) and accepted by Powell in his general classification (1891). But the lack of solid lexical evidence for this hypothesis soon became apparent, and both Hewitt (in McGee 1898:300) and Gatschet (1900:558) separated Seri from Yuman-Cochimí. Kroeber, however, continued to explore a Yuman-Seri relationship, both in the context of a larger group of Hokan-affiliated languages that also included Tequistlatecan (Kroeber 1915b) and as a bilateral relationship (1931). The accumulation in recent decades of extensive and accurate data both on Seri and on the Yuman languages has made it clear that the split between them is ancient (J. G. Crawford 1976; K. Hale and Harris 1979:173). Sapir, in his general comparative work on Hokan, saw evidence for grouping Yuman with Esselen, while he felt that Seri belonged with Salinan and Chumash (Sapir 1925a:525). Although this classification has received some substantiation from lexicostatistics (Bright 1956), it has not been widely accepted and has been undermined by recent studies that have excluded Chumash (although not Salinan) from the Hokan relationship.[65] Meanwhile, Kroeber's proposal that Seri might belong to the same Hokan subgroup as Tequistlatecan remains under discussion—sympathetically explored by one specialist (Waterhouse 1976:339–340) but rejected by another (P. Turner 1967, 1976). The fact that Chontal, Seri, Salinan, and, to some extent, Yuman share an elaborate system of marking plurality and pluractionality (see ¶4.7.2) may have relevance for subgrouping. Pending further studies, however, Seri is best considered a classificatory isolate within Hokan.

3.20.1 Geography

Seri tradition recognizes six regional bands who spoke three mutually intelligible dialects. Two of these dialects (the one spoken by the band living in the mangrove swamps near Punta Sargento and the one spoken by the inhabitants of the extremely hot and arid areas on the west side of Tiburón Island and San Esteban Island) are said to have become extinct in the nineteenth century. Whatever the earlier diversity, attested Seri only reflects the speech of eastern Tiburón Island and the adjacent mainland (Moser 1963; Felger and Moser 1985:8, 96–99). On the mainland the immediate neighbors of the Seri were speakers of Southern Uto-Aztecan languages—Upper Piman (Pima-Papago, O'odham) and Lower Piman (Pima Bajo) to the north and east, Yaqui to the south—but relations between these groups and the Seri were infrequent and inconsequential, except in the north around Puerto Libertad and Puerto Lobos. There the Seri and the O'odham often mixed, sometimes camping together as far north as the mouth of the Colorado. The Seri were also in contact with the Cochimí across the Gulf of California and closely resembled these and other Baja Californians in their simple material culture and nomadic foraging lifestyle.

FIGURE 56. Edward Moser transcribing Seri from his consultant Pancho Contreras, as a Seri boy looks on. Photograph by Mary B. Moser, 1952. Courtesy of Mary B. Moser and Cathy Marlett.

3.20.2 Documentation and Survival

Despite their remote and inhospitable location, the Seri were the object of ethnographic and linguistic study as early as the 1870s, when the language was first documented by Pinart (n.d.[b], Box 2, Folder 11). W. J. McGee led an anthropological expedition to Seri counry in the 1890s, and his report (McGee 1898) contains miscellaneous linguistic material. Seri continues to be spoken by most of the few hundred surviving Seris. It has been well documented by Edward and Mary Beck Moser and their son-in-law Stephen Marlett, linguists associated with the Summer Institute of Linguistics who have worked in the Seri community since the 1950s. Publications are numerous and include a preliminary dictionary (Moser and Moser 1961), a technical grammar (Marlett 1981), a grammatical sketch (Moser and Marlett 1996), a dictionary in semantic format (Marlett and Moser 1996), a full Seri-Spanish-English dictionary (Moser and Marlett 2005), and two typological sketches (Marlett 2000, 2005).

The descendants of the aboriginal Seri live in two villages, El Desemboque del Río San Ignacio and Punta Chueca, on the Gulf coast of Sonora. Most of the seven hundred Seris still regularly speak the language, including most children, making it one of the more vigorously surviving languages of the region. A writing system devised by the Mosers is in general use.

3.20.3 Linguistic Structure

Seri consonantal phonology resembles Yuman in its lack of laryngeal feature contrasts in voicing, aspiration, or glottalization (Table 26). Other than a glottal stop, only four stop phonemes are distinguished (*p, t, k, kʷ*). There are no affricates, but there is a rich set of voiceless fricatives, including a labial (*f*, usually bilabial [ɸ]), an alveolar (*s*), a palatal (*š*), a lateral (*ł*), and a velar and a postvelar, both plain and labialized (*x, xʷ, x̣, x̣ʷ*). There are two nasals (*m, n*); only one approximant (*y*); and only one laryngeal, the glottal stop (*ʔ*). Two marginal phonemes occur, a very rare lateral approximant (*l*) and a tapped *r* [ɾ] that is found only in loanwords. There are four vowels, two front (*i, e*) and two back (*o, a*), all of which occur both short and long. Stress is phonemic.[66]

Except for the marking of plurality in stem alternates (see ¶4.7.2), Seri noun morphology is relatively uncomplex. Inalienable nouns (body-part terms, kinship terms, and relational nouns) are marked for possessor by a set of prefixes: *ʔi-* first person, *mi-/ma-* second person, *i-/a-* third person, *k-i-* unspecified or indefinite possessor ("someone's"), and *ʔa-/ʔap-* absolutive or unpossessed. Verbs, by contrast, are highly inflected, marked for subject and object by pronominal prefixes (the object prefix preceding the subject), and for certain tense/mood categories by prefixes that follow the subject. Finite verbs (used in main clauses) are morphologically distinct from nominalized verbs (used in relative and complement clauses), and there are distinct imperative and infinitive forms.

3.20.4 Nomenclature

The indigenous ethnonym is Cmiique (*kmíke*) '(Seri) person', plural Comcáac (*komká:k*) '(Seri) people'; the language is called Cmiique Iitom (*kmíke i:tom*). "Seri," of uncertain but possibly Opata origin, is the name by which the group has long been known to adjacent Uto-Aztecan speakers. It was adopted by the Spanish as early as the seventeenth century.

TABLE 26
Seri Phonemes (Marlett 2005)

Consonants									Vowels	
p	t			k	kʷ			ʔ	i / i:	o / o:
ɸ	s	ł	š	x	xʷ	x̣	x̣ʷ		e /e:	a / a:
m	n									
	(r)	(l)	y							

Stress Accent
v́

Penutian Languages

3.21 The Penutian Phylum[67]

The name "Penutian" was created by Dixon and Kroeber (1913) to label the phylum-level relationship that they believed to exist among the Costanoan, Miwok, Maiduan, Yokuts, and Wintuan language families (Golla 2002). In the full presentation of their comparative evidence (1919:55–69) they cited 171 "cognate stems" and some other lexical resemblances, from which they derived a small set of sound correspondences. Sapir (1920d, 1921c) extended the Penutian relationship (and the name) to include a number of small language families in the Northwest, from Takelma and Klamath-Modoc in southern Oregon to Tsimshianic on the northern coast of British Columbia. He later (1929b) added two groups in southern Mexico, the Mixe-Zoque family and the isolate Huave. Since the 1930s several scholars have attached "Penutian" or "Macro-Penutian" to even broader phylum-level proposals, such as the one put forward by Greenberg (1987), whose "Penutian" includes Mayan, Yukian, and the Gulf languages in addition to Sapir's core group or Swadesh's lexicostatistical exploration of a chain of "long-range" relationships among "Penutioid stocks" from Tsimshianic to Quechua (1956).

For most North American linguists in recent decades, however, the Penutian hypothesis has usually been understood to be the relationship that was proposed by Sapir in 1920–1921. Specifically, it includes *Tsimshianic* in British Columbia, *Chinookan* on the lower Columbia River, and three geographic clusters in the California-Oregon area that may or may not be classificatorily significant units: *California Penutian*, consisting of Utian (Miwok-Costanoan), Yokuts, Maiduan, and Wintuan; *Oregon Penutian,* consisting of Takelma, Coastal Oregon Penutian (Coosan, Siuslawan, Alsea), and Kalapuyan; and *Plateau Penutian*, consisting of Sahaptian, Molala (and Cayuse), and Klamath-Modoc.[68]

Although Sapir published only one short paper specifically on comparative Penutian (1921a), he believed there was solid grammatical and lexical support for his hypothesis and, most importantly, a uniting typological pattern. According to Sapir, the Penutian languages

> are far less cumbersome in structure than [Eskimo-Aleut, Algonkin-Wakashan, and Na-Dene] but are more tightly knit, presenting many analogies to the Indo-European languages; make use of suffixes of formal, rather than concrete, significance; show many types of inner stem change; and possess true nominal cases, for the most part. Chinook seems to have developed a secondary "polysynthetic" form on the basis of a broken down form of Penutian; while Tsimshian and Maidu have probably been considerably influenced by contact with Mosan and with Shoshonean and Hokan respectively. (Sapir 1929b:140)

Since Sapir's day the potential relationships among the Penutian languages have received a considerable amount of attention from linguists (for a synopsis of comparative Penutian research see DeLancey and Golla 1997). Since much of this scholarship has focused on specific pairs or groups of languages rather than on a comprehensive synthesis, scholarly opinion remains divided as to whether a Penutian phylum in Sapir's sense has been proven (Shipley 1980b; Campbell 1997:309–322). It seems fair to say, however, that the Penutian hypothesis, in its broad outlines, is much more likely to be true than the contrary hypothesis: that no historical relationships exist among the languages concerned. Penutian, like Hokan, is a historical construct that should be treated with caution, but it has elucidated much more than it has obscured.

3.21.1 Subgrouping

Of particular interest in comparative Penutian research is the question of the historical unity of the California Penutian languages. While a fair amount of comparative lexical and grammatical data supports the view that these languages are related as members of the Penutian phylum, the more specific claim that they represent a classificatory subunit within Penutian has rarely been directly tested. Since Dixon and Kroeber's original classificatory work (1913, 1919) was arbitrarily restricted in scope to language families indigenous to California, "Penutian" was by default a grouping of the five California families (see also Berman 1983, 1989). As soon as languages of Penutian affiliation outside California were taken into consideration, there was no compelling reason to treat "California Penutian" as a node in the classification of the phylum. The current understanding of Penutian subgroups, particularly those involving the languages of the California region (Map 23), is outlined in Table 27.

PLATEAU PENUTIAN AND MAIDUAN

Sapir's proposed "Plateau Penutian" has fared well in the face of later research. While the place of Cayuse, because of limitations of data, may never be conclusively established, the relatively close relationship of Klamath-Modoc and Sahaptian, first explored by Melville Jacobs (1931), is now well supported (Aoki 1963; Rude 1987; DeLancey 1988b; DeLancey et al. 1988), and Molala has been firmly attached to this grouping by Berman's recent studies (1996). Geographical and archaeological considerations make this the most likely place to look for the deeper affiliation of Maiduan, and there is indeed some suggestive lexical and structural evidence for this grouping (DeLancey 1996).[69]

Shipley and Smith (1979a) have provided evidence for the Basin or Plateau origin of Maiduan, which, as Whistler does Wintuan (later), they see as relatively recent in California.

MAP 23. Penutian branches.

Lexical evidence has long been noted indicating a relatively close relationship between Takelma and Kalapuyan (Frachtenberg 1918; Swadesh 1965; Shipley 1969). Investigation of this relationship has been resumed in recent years by Daythal Kendall (1997) and Marie-Louise Tarpent (1997), who have found evidence that Tsimshianic is a third member of this group (see also Tarpent and Kendall 1998).

WINTUAN AND OREGON

One of the more important developments in Penutian studies in recent decades is Kenneth Whistler's (1977a) convincing demonstration that the ethnographic locations of the Wintuan languages represent relatively recent migration from Oregon. In an exemplary exercise in linguistic paleontology, Whistler identified sets of plant and animal species names in the Wintuan languages that are, on the

TABLE 27
Provisional Subgroups of the Penutian Phylum

Tsimshianic

Chinookan

Coastal Oregon Penutian

  Alsea

  Siuslaw-Lower Umpqua

  Coosan

    Hanis

    Miluk

Kalapuya-Takelman

  Kalapuya

  Takelma

Plateau Penutian

  Sahaptian

    Sahaptin

    Nez Perce

  Molala

  Klamath-Modoc

Maiduan

Wintuan

Yok-Utian

  Utian

    Miwok

    Costanoan

  Yokuts

They show that the three Maiduan languages have a significantly lower rate of cognacy for plant and animal names than for body-part terms and other basic vocabulary, suggesting that many plant and animal names are recent innovations in the three languages and implying that the family originated in an ecological setting different from the one that Maiduan speakers now inhabit in the Sierra Nevada.

TAKELMA AND THE WESTERN OREGON LANGUAGES

In Sapir's original formulation, "Oregon Penutian" included as distinct subbranches Takelma, Kalapuyan, and the Coastal Oregon group, Coosan, Siuslawan, and Alsea (Yakonan). All these languages have been extinct for many years, and the philological research necessary for a more comprehensive understanding of their structures and interelations has progressed more slowly than with other Penutian languages. Our present understanding of their position within Penutian is consequently more preliminary and speculative. The Coastal Oregon languages certainly show more lexical and structural connections with one another than have been adduced between any of them and anything else (the connection of Alsea with Wintuan notwithstanding; many of the close resemblances may be due to borrowing), and Sapir's grouping them together as a unit may be considered the default hypothesis, although far from being established.

one hand, reconstructible for Proto-Wintuan and, on the other, borrowed from neighboring California languages. He showed that terms for various prominent species characteristic of the Central Valley are borrowed, whereas the Proto-Wintuan nomenclature is more consistent with an environment to the north: "I reach the probable conclusion that the Proto-Wintuan language was spoken by a people living in interior Northwest California or Southwest Oregon. The drainage of the upper Rogue River seems the most likely candidate, with the middle Klamath or the South Umpqua drainages also possible" (Whistler 1977a:166). Whistler also infers, on the basis of the extensive borrowing of species names into Patwin from Miwok, that the diversification of Wintuan took place prior to the Wintuan entry into the Central Valley, and that the ancestral Patwin and Northern Wintuan communities probably entered California separately (1977a:170–171). (For further details see ¶5.3.4.)

Support for Whistler's hypothesis of a recent Wintuan connection to western Oregon has been provided by two subsequent studies. DeLancey (1987, 1988a) has pointed out striking morphological congruences between the Wintu and Klamath personal pronouns that appear to be the result of recent borrowing, and I, myself, (Golla 1997) have presented and commented on a significant body of close lexical resemblances between Northern Wintuan and Alsea, again likely borrowings.

"Yok-Utian" is the designation proposed by Geoffrey Gamble (1991b) for a branch of Penutian that would include the Utian languages and Yokuts. Catherine Callaghan has published substantial, if not entirely conclusive, evidence for this classification in two articles (1997a, 2001), in which she also argues that very little evidence supports linking either Maiduan or Wintuan to the Yok-Utian group.

It is Callaghan's view that, while the accumulating evidence is highly suggestive of a close relationship, it is still too early to assert that a Yok-Utian grouping has been substantiated. The resemblant words show many unresolved phonological irregularities, and extensive borrowing cannot be ruled out. A full demonstration of the relationship will need to explain the considerable differences in both phonology and morphosyntax between the two language families. The Utian languages are unique within Penutian in basically lacking laryngeal feature contrasts in stops and affricates. In Yokuts, however, all stops and affricates show a three-way contrast between plain, aspirated, and glottalized articulations, with the plain versus glottalized contrast also extended to resonants.

An intriguing aspect of the Yok-Utian relationship is the role played by contact with Numic. Of the thirteen Yokuts-Utian resemblant sets for plant and animal terms that have so far been identified by Callaghan, all but two (the words for 'bat' and 'turtle') closely resemble the corresponding word in Mono or Northern Paiute. Further research is needed

to determine if these words are more likely to have been borrowed from Numic into Yokuts and Utian or vice versa, but whatever the direction of the borrowing it is difficult to construct a scenario in which it could have occurred in California. Instead, a Yok-Utian "homeland" in western Nevada is suggested. This would be consistent with similarities that archaeologists have long noted between Yokuts and Utian cultural patterns and those seen in the pre-Numic Lovelock culture of northwestern Nevada, as well as with recently noted similarities in mitochondrial DNA haplogroup frequencies among the same modern and ancient populations (Kaestle and Smith 2001; Eshleman et al. 2004). Also supportive of an extra-California location for the early Yok-Utian community is the fact that there are no resemblant sets of Yokuts and Utian words for plants and animals found widely in central California but almost totally absent in adjacent regions such as Nevada.[70] Although an abundance of such terms can be reconstructed to Proto-Utian (strongly indicating that Proto-Utian was spoken in the California environment), not a single one matches the corresponding term in Yokuts.

3.22 Takelma

Takelma, an isolated Penutian language with some shallow dialectal diversity, was spoken in the central and eastern parts of the Rogue River Valley of southern Oregon. It has been grouped with the Kalapuyan family of the Willamette Valley in the "Takelman" (or "Takelma-Kalapuyan") subphylum (Swadesh 1965; Shipley 1969; Kendall 1997). Although this classification has been challenged by Tarpent and Kendall (1998), it is clear that the substantial similarities between the two language groups at the very least reflect a period of close contact.

3.22.1 Geography

The speakers of Takelma proper, or **Lowland Takelma,** occupied the north bank of Rogue River from Table Rock and the mouth of Bear Creek downstream as far as Grave Creek (Map 24). To the west and south they bordered on the Athabaskans who lived along Galice Creek and Applegate River. Although the Takelmas were said by earlier authorities to have occupied the area south of the Rogue between Galice Creek and Applegate River, including most of the valley of the Illinois River, more recent studies favor assigning this area to Athabaskans (Gray 1987:20–24). On the north, where the Takelmas bordered on another Athabaskan group, the Upper Umpquas, their territory extended beyond the drainage of Rogue River to include at least the upper portion of Cow Creek, and perhaps the entire Cow Creek drainage to its confluence with the Umpqua River near Riddle. The uncertainty of these boundaries in part reflects the disruption of traditional life that followed the Rogue River War of 1855–1856 and the removal of the Indians of southwestern Oregon to the Siletz and Grand Ronde Reservations several

MAP 24. Takelma territory and dialects.

hundred miles to the north, but it also may indicate that the inhabitants of these areas had dual linguistic and ethnic identities (see ¶1.5.2). Athabaskan territory throughout southern Oregon and northern California was characterized by such transitional zones along its borders.[71]

The mountainous area east of Table Rock along Little Butte Creek belonged to the **Upland Takelmas** (or **Latgawas**), a separate group who spoke a distinct dialect (Sapir 1910b; Drucker 1937:294–296, n.d.). Gray (1987:24–25) further distinguishes a **Northern Takelma** (or **Hanesakh**) dialect area along the upper Rogue River and in the Trail and Elk Creek region. Daythal Kendall (1990:589) also sees evidence for dialectal complexity in the easternmost part of Takelma territory. Upland Takelma territory may also at one time have extended south along Bear Creek into the Ashland area, but at the time of contact the Shastas occupied most of Bear Creek Valley and were fighting the Takelmas for control of territory as far north as Little Butte Creek (Kroeber 1925:285–286; Heizer and Hester 1970:138–144).

3.22.2 Documentation

The first attestation of Takelma was a short vocabulary collected by William Hazen in 1857. The first significant documentation was made by J. Owen Dorsey, who collected a BAE survey vocabulary at Siletz in 1884 (Dorsey 1884p). The language was thoroughly documented by Edward Sapir in 1906, working with Frances Johnson, the most fluent of the remaining handful of speakers of Lowland Takelma, and he published a full grammar (1922a) and a collection of narrative texts with an accompanying lexicon (1909). Sapir also collected a few forms in the Upland Takelma dialect from Mrs. Johnson (Sapir 1907a:252–253). In 1933, working with Sapir's consultant and with a woman who recalled some Upland Takelma, J. P. Harrington collected additional material from both dialects, primarily place-names and other ethnogeographical information (Mills 1981:78–80). With the death of Frances Johnson in the late 1930s, Takelma ceased to be spoken. Using Sapir's materials,

FIGURE 57. Frances Johnson, Takelma. Photograph by Edward Sapir, Siletz, Oregon 1906. Courtesy of the Sapir family.

Daythal Kendall (1977) and Borim Lee (1991) have carried out modern theory-based studies of Takelma syntax and morphophonology, respectively.

3.22.3 Linguistic Structure

The phonology and grammar of Takelma are known primarily through the published work of Sapir (1909, 1922a), which is remarkably thorough and accurate (D. Kendall 1982). The transcription used here follows a phonemicization proposed by Sapir in a seminar at Yale in 1936 (Shipley 1969:227; Hymes 1990:596; see Table 28).[72]

Takelma has three series of stops (*p, t, k*), each with plain, aspirated, and glottalized members. Sequences of velar stop + *w* are treated by Sapir as a fourth stop series (*kʷ, kʰʷ, k'ʷ*). An affricate, varying in articulation between alveolar [ts] and front-palatal [tʃʸ], occurs only glottalized (*c'*). There are two fricatives (*s*, which like the corresponding affricate varies between [s] and [ʃʸ], and *x*). There are two nasals (*m, n*), three approximants (*l, w, y*), and two laryngeals (*ʔ, h*). A voiceless lateral fricative (*ł*) is used only in the recitation of myths, where it is prefixed to words spoken by Bear (Sapir 1922a:8; Hymes 1979).

The vowel system of Takelma is somewhat more elaborate than that of most nearby languages. There are five vowel qualities (*i, e, a, o, u*), which occur both short and long, the latter with a distinct rearticulation (e.g., *a:* is [aᵃ]). Bimoraic and trimoraic syllables are formed with vowels (short or long) + *w, y, l, m, n*. There is an accentual contrast in stressed syllables between a high or rising pitch (*v́*) and a falling pitch (*v̀*). For example *xí* 'water', *tán* 'rock', *tíːpʰ* 'camass', *tʰká:* 'earth, land', and *kʷáːy* 'grass', but *skìsi* 'coyote', *pàkʰpa:* 'woodpecker', *kamkàm* 'four', *tìːs* 'gopher', *tʰkʷalàː* 'hoot owl'.[73]

Takelma noun morphology is relatively complex. Many nouns have special stem variants for locative and possessive constructions, formed with both affixation and ablaut. For example, *tʰká:* 'earth', *ha-tʰká:w* 'in the earth'; *kʷáːn* 'trail', *ha-kʷaːlám* 'in the trail', *kʷaːlám-tʰkʰ* 'my trail'; *puːpán* 'arm', *puːpinítʰkʰ* 'my arm', *puːpinìx-takʷa* 'his own arm'. Possession is marked by a set of affixes, for the most part suffixes, that fall into four declensional sets (Table 29).

Takelma verbs—or more accurately, verbal phrases—typically consist of one or more proclitic elements that mark various locative and instrumental categories, including loosely incorporated nominal objects, preceding a tightly constructed verbal word that marks tense, mode, various adverbial categories, and pronominal subject and object. Among the proclitics perhaps the most distinctive is a set of body-part locatives that have both a literal and a formal (locative) value and function somewhat like verbal classifiers (e.g., *takʰ=* 'head, above, on top of' in *takʰ=c'ayá:pʰteʔ* 'I washed my head', *takʰ=waːkàʔn* 'I finish it', lit. 'I bring it on top'; *kʷel=* 'leg, under, away from view' in *kʷel=c'ayá:pʰ* 'he washed his legs', *kʷel=mac'ákʰ* 'they put it away'). Body-part proclitics also occur with their locative meaning in nominal phrases (*takʰ=wilí:* 'over the house', *kʷel=xiyá* 'under water') but cannot be used as noun stems without the suffixation of a stem formant and sometimes other phonological alteration (*tàk-ax-* 'head', *kʷéːl-x-* 'leg'). The stem of the verbal word has two ablaut variants—a special stem that occurs with the "aorist" inflectional paradigm (basically expressing the narrative past tense) and a general stem that occurs with all other tenses and modes. The patterns of vowel and consonant alternation between these variants are irregular and must be specified for each stem—for example, *t'omon-* (aorist), *to:m-* (general) 'to kill'; *yowo-* (aorist), *yu-* (general) 'to run'. Secondary repetitive and frequentative stems are formed from these by full or partial reduplication (e.g., *lepe-* 'pick up and eat seeds' > *lèːpʰlapʰ-* 'pick up and eat many seeds'; *he:l-* 'sing' > *helèhelʔ-* 'used to sing'). Complex verb-final suffixes mark pronominal subject (and object in transitives) in six tense-mode paradigms (aorist, future, potential, inferential, present imperative, and future imperative). Subjects and objects can in addition be marked by a

TABLE 28
Takelma Phonemes (Sapir 1922a; Shipley 1969)

Consonants						Vowels		
p	t		k	kʷ	ʔ	i / i:		u / u:
pʰ	tʰ		kʰ	kʰʷ		e / e:		o / o:
p'	t'	c'	k'	k'ʷ			a / a:	
	(ł)	s	x		h			
m	n							
w	l	y						

Pitch Accents
Rising or high v́
Falling v̀

TABLE 29
Takelma Possessive Affixes (Sapir 1922a)

	1 sg	*2 sg*	*3 sg/pl*	*1 pl*	*2 pl* reflexive	*3 sg* reflexive	*3 pl*
I*	*wi-*	*`-ʔtʰ*	*-(x)a*	*-tàm*	*-ʔtʰpan*	*-(x)akʷa*	*-(x)akʷan*
II†	*-t/tʰekʰ*	*-t/tʰeʔ*	*-t/tʰa*	*-tàm*	*-t/tʰapaʔn*	*-t/tʰakʷa*	*-t/tʰakʷan*
III‡	*´-tʰkʰ*	*`-ʔtʰ*	*`-(tʰ)*	*-tàm*	*`-ʔtʰpan*	*`-tʰkʷa*	*`-tʰkʷan*
IV§	*-téː*	*-taʔ*	*`-ta*	*-tàm*	*-tapaʔn*	*`-takʷa*	*`-takʷan*
					`-ʔtʰpan	*`-tʰkʷa*	*`-tʰkʷan*

*Set I is used only with kinship terms: *wi-wá:* 'my younger brother', *wà:-ʔtʰ* 'your younger brother', *wá:-xa* 'his younger brother'.

†Set II is used with bare stems or stems having the formant *-x*: *hèːl* 'song', *hèːl-tʰekʰ* 'my song', *hèːl-tʰa* 'his song'; *tàkax-tekʰ* 'my head', *tàkax-ta* 'his head'. (The alternation between *-t* and *-tʰ* in set II and IV suffixes is regular and predictable.)

‡Set III is used with stems having other formants: *xáːn* 'urine', *xa:lám-tʰkʰ* 'my urine', *xa:làm* 'his urine'; *tán* 'rock', *taná-tʰkʰ* 'my rock', *tanà:* 'his rock'; *p'áː-n* 'liver', *p'áːn-tʰkʰ* 'my liver', *p'àːn-tʰ* 'his liver'.

§Set IV is used in locative constructions: *ha=wili-téː* 'in my house' (compare *wilí-tʰkʰ* 'my house'), *xa:=kʷel-téː* 'between my legs' (compare *kʷéːlx-tekʰ* 'my legs'), *wa-téː* 'to me'.

set of independent pronouns: 1 sg *kíː*, 2 sg *má ~ maː*, 3 sg *áːkʰ*, 1 pl *kóːm*, 2 pl *máːpʰ*, 3 pl *aːy ~ xilamaná*.

3.22.4 Nomenclature

Takelma is an Anglicization of the self-designation of the Lower Takelma, *ta:kelmàʔn* 'those living along the (Rogue) river' (< *ta:=kelám* 'along the river' + *-àʔn* 'person coming from'). It was first recorded by Hazen in 1857 as "Ta-kil-ma," and this spelling was adopted by Gatschet (1882) in his survey of the languages of the region. Dorsey, who collected the first full vocabulary of the language (1884p), recorded the name as "Takelma" but continued to use Gatschet's spelling for the "Takilman" language family, as did Powell (1891). Since Sapir, both the language and the isolate-family have been referred to simply as Takelma. "Takelman" was reintroduced by Shipley (1969) as the name for the Takelma-Kalapuya relationship, but this usage has not been widely adopted.

3.23 Klamath-Modoc

3.23.1 Geography

Klamath-Modoc is the only language of the Plateau Penutian subphylum whose territory extends into the California region as here defined (the others are Molala, Sahaptin, and Nez Perce; see ¶3.21.1). It was spoken in two closely related dialects, Klamath and Modoc, immediately to the east of the Cascades between Crater Lake and Mount Shasta (Map 25). This region is geographically dominated by the freshwater lakes at the headwaters of the Klamath River, and permanent settlements clustered around these lake and along the streams that fed them. The **Klamath** dialect was spoken to the north of present-day Klamath Falls on Upper Klamath

Lake and Agency Lake, in the Klamath Marsh, and on the Williamson and Sprague Rivers. The **Modoc** dialect (from *mo:wat'a:k* 'south') was spoken south and east of Klamath Falls at Lower Klamath and Tule Lakes and along the Lost River. Although the two dialects were quite similar, speakers were conscious of their distinguishing features (the Klamath verb *koýa* means 'to speak Klamath with a Modoc accent'). As of 2006 there were no fluent native speakers of either dialect.

Both dialectal groups were divided into named, autonomous subgroups occupying well-defined territories and possibly showing small subdialectal differences. The thirty-four villages of the Klamath Marsh people (*ʔewksi-kʰniː*) constituted the largest and most important of the Klamath subgroups. The fourteen villages of the Klamath Falls people (*ʔiWLaLLo:n-kʰniː*), who occupied the southern half of Upper Klamath Lake, were next in importance. Between these were three much smaller subgroups, the Agency Lake people (*qoWasti-kʰniː*), the Lower Williamson River people (*tokʰwa-kʰniː*), and the Pelican Bay people (*kompat-kʰniː*), while the Upland Klamath (*play-kʰniː* 'people from above') lived to the east on the upper Sprague and Sycan rivers.[74] The three Modoc subgroups were located in the Lower Klamath Lake and Tule Lake area (*kompatʰ-waːs*), along the lower Lost River (*pʰaskan-waːs*), and along the upper Lost River as far east as Goose Lake (*qoqe-waːs* 'river place') (Spier 1930; Ray 1963; Stern 1998).

3.23.2 Documentation

Klamath-Modoc, particularly the Klamath dialect, is well documented. The standard description is by Philip R. Barker, based on fieldwork he conducted in the 1950s, and includes a full grammar (1964), a dictionary (1963b), and a volume of narrative texts (1963a).[75] The most important earlier

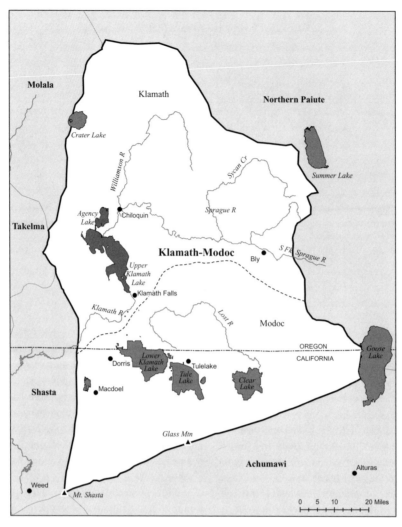

MAP 25. Klamath-Modoc territory.

documentation—and in some respects the richest source of data on Klamath-Modoc from any period—are the materials collected by the BAE linguist Albert S. Gatschet between 1877 and 1892, both in Oregon and in Oklahoma, where many of the survivors of the Modoc War of 1872–1873 had been relocated. He published several papers, culminating in a massive two-volume study incorporating a dictionary, grammatical sketch, and texts (Gatschet 1890).

The earliest attestation of Klamath-Modoc is a vocabulary of Modoc ("Lutuami") collected by Horatio Hale in 1841 during the Wilkes Expedition (1846:569–629). Jeremiah Curtin collected BAE survey vocabularies from both dialects (1884–1885b), as well as numerous myth texts (1884–1885a, 1884–1885c). Jaime de Angulo collected data on Klamath-Modoc in 1926 and published a grammatical sketch and some short texts (de Angulo and Freeland 1931b; see also Leeds-Hurwitz 2004:218–219). Substantial vocabularies were also collected by Merriam (Appendix A: F-5a) and by Myers (in Curtis 1907–1930, vol. 13:272–276). Swadesh and Melton (1953) made tape recordings of Klamath for the Penutian Vocabulary Survey (Swadesh 1954b).[76]

After the Modoc War of 1872–1873, about 150 Modocs were relocated in Oklahoma, the remainder merging into the Klamath community. The Modoc dialect is extinct in Oklahoma. The Klamath dialect continued to be spoken in and around the principal tribal community at Chiloquin, Oregon, until the death of the last fluent speaker in September 2003. Revitalization efforts have been made at Chiloquin, in informal liaison with anthropologists and linguists from the University of Oregon who have drawn on the extensive documentation of the language by Gatschet in the late nineteenth century and Barker in the 1950s. These efforts have included language lessons in the tribal Head Start program, weekly classes in the local primary school and after-school program, and weekly community meetings. About half a dozen adult second-language speakers have been produced, two of whom are moderately fluent.

3.23.3 Linguistic Structure

Barker's grammar (1964) is the standard description, although it is obscured by a complex and often redundant structural

FIGURE 58. Albert Samuel Gatschet, field linguist for the Bureau of American Ethnology, whose two-volume study of Klamath (1890) is especially notable for its attention to sociolinguistic detail. Courtesy of the National Anthropological Archives, Smithsonian Institution.

formalism. Gatschet's older and less theory-dominated study (1890) can sometimes be more elucidating. DeLancey (1991, 1999) has attempted to bring some order to the complexity of verb suffix and stem morphology as described by Gatschet and Barker. He maintains the useful Klamath-Modoc Linguistics Page (www.uoregon.edu/~delancey/klamath.html), where copies of his papers and other materials are available, although it has not been updated in recent years. Underriner (2002) has explored the relationship between prosody, syntax, and pragmatics by doing a pitch-tracking analysis of seven texts recorded by Barker. There is also a large secondary literature concerned with the formal restatement of Klamath phonology as represented by Barker (see, for example, Darden 1985; Blevins 1993; and White 1973).

Klamath-Modoc has a complex phonology (Table 30). Segmental phonemes include five series of stops or affricates (*p, t, č, k, q*), each with a plain, aspirated, and glottalized member.[77] There are two series of nasals (*m, n*) and three series of approximants (*l, w, y*), each with a plain, voiceless, and glottalized member. There is one nonlaryngeal fricative (*s*) and two laryngeal consonants (*ʔ, h*). (The voiceless lateral approximant, L, may alternatively be considered a lateral fricative, *ł*.) Consonant clusters of two and three members are numerous. Of particular note are word-initial clusters of plain stops or approximants (*p, k, q, l*) + glottal stop, which are phonemically distinct from the corresponding glottalized stops or approximants (*p', k', q', l'*)—for example, *pʔomčʰip* 'cousin', *p'o:sis* 'cat'; *lʔeka* 'get drunk', *l'o:ks* 'lizard'. There are four vowels (*i, e, a, o*), short and long. In addition, plain nasals and approximants are syllabic when they occur between consonants or initially before a consonant (e.g., *l* [ḷ] or [lə] in *lṁač* 'metate' or *w* [wᵘ] in *wso* 'chest').

As in most Penutian languages, nouns and pronouns in Klamath are inflected for case—subject (unmarked in nouns), object and possessive (Table 31)—and for instrumental and locative relations. Approximately half of the attested noun stems are formed with a nominalizing suffix -(V)*s* (e.g., *ẇa-s* 'coyote', *ʔew-s* 'lake', *lo:k-s* 'slave', *yamn-as* 'bead'; compare *som* 'mouth', *tʰoqi* 'horn', *maksa* 'basket'), but nouns otherwise show little derivational complexity except for secondary reduplication to mark certain modes. Verb stems, by contrast, are nearly always morphologically complex, the majority having a "bipartite" pattern of stem compounding (DeLancey 1999; see ¶4.8.2). Various suffixes mark aspectual and modal categories. Pronominal arguments are marked (when marked at all) by case-inflected nouns and free pronouns; unemphatic third person singular arguments can be left unmarked.

3.23.4 Nomenclature

Hale (1846:218) mistook the Achumawi name for the Tule Lake Modoc (*lut'wa:mi* 'lake people') for "the proper designation of the people in their own language" and published his Klamath-Modoc vocabulary—the first attestation of the language—as "Lutuami." Following the rule of nomenclatural precedence, Powell (1891) adopted "Lutuamian" as the family name. "Klamath," a rendition of *łamat* 'they of the river', the Upper Chinook (Wasco-Wishram) name for the Klamaths, was used by local whites in the nineteenth and early twentieth centuries to designate some or all of the Indians of the Klamath River Basin, including the Klamaths, the Shastas, the Karuks, and the Yuroks. Gatschet used "Klamath" as the specific ethnographic name for the Indians of the reservation on Upper Klamath Lake and for their dialect of Klamath-Modoc, and this usage soon became standard among anthropologists. There was reluctance, however, to extend the term to the Modocs, who had been treated as a separate tribe since the Modoc War of 1872–1873 and their subsequent removal to Oklahoma. ("Modoc" is an Anglicization of the initial syllables of Klamath-Modoc *mo:wat'a:k-kʰni:* 'southern people'.) As a

TABLE 30
Klamath Phonemes (Barker 1964)

Consonants						Vowels	
p	t	č	k	q	ʔ	i / i:	o / o:
pʰ	tʰ	čʰ	kʰ	qʰ		e / e:	a / a:
p'	t'	č'	k'	q'			
	s				h		
m	n						
M	N						
ṁ	ṅ						
w	l	y					
W	L	Y					
ẇ	l'	ẏ					

TABLE 31
Klamath Case Inflection (Barker 1964)

Nouns

	Subject	Object	Possessive
	(unmarked)	-s, -(?)as	-m, -(?)am, -lm
'coyote'	ẇas	ẇasas	ẇasam ~ ẇas?am
'slave'	lo:ks	lo:ksas	lo:ksam
'chief'	laqi	laqẏas	laqẏam
'housefly'	manq	manqas	manq?am
'basket cap'	qʰma	qʰma?as	qʰmalm

Pronouns

	Subject	Object	Possessive
1 sg			
(emphatic)	no:	no:s	kew
(unemphatic)	ni	nis	kew
2 sg	?i	mis	mi
3 sg			
(emphatic)	pi	po:s	mna
1 pl	na:t	na:l's ~ na:ts	na:l'am
2 pl	?a:t	ma:ts	ma:l'am
3 pl			
(emphatic)	pa:t	mna:l's	mna:l'am
(unemphatic)	sa	sas	sam

result, Powell's "Lutuamian" continued in use as the anthropological designation of the overall Klamath-Modoc ethnic group and their language as late as the 1930s (see, for example, de Angulo and Freeland 1931b). In recent decades linguists have called the language either "Klamath" or "Klamath-Modoc." Given the ambiguity of the former in older sources, the latter has been adopted here.

3.24 Maiduan Languages

Maiduan (or Maidun) is a family of four closely related Penutian languages that were spoken in a territory that extended from the Sacramento River between Sacramento and Chico eastward to the crest of the Sierra Nevada (Map 26). They included **Konkow, Chico Maidu, Northeastern** or **"Mountain" Maidu** (often referred to simply as "Maidu"), and **Nisenan.** Their relationship is a historically shallow one, comparable perhaps to West Germanic (R. Ultan 1964), and some degree of mutual intelligibility probably existed among all Maiduan speakers. In terms of lexical similarity, Northeastern Maidu and Chico Maidu are closest, with Nisenan the most divergent from them. Nevertheless,

Northeastern Maidu stands apart from the other three languages in a number of grammatical features (Shipley 1961:46). In general, the grammatical differences among the Maiduan languages are more significant than either the phonological or the lexical differences and appear to reflect different external (and probably substratal) influences: Washo and Palaihnihan in the case of Northeastern Maidu, Northern Wintuan in the case of Konkow and Chico Maidu, and Eastern Miwok in the case of Nisenan (Dixon 1911:683; Shipley and Smith 1979a).

3.24.1 Konkow

Konkow was spoken along the Feather River and adjacent areas in Butte County, from about twenty miles south of Oroville to near the Plumas County line, including the lower part of the Feather River Canyon. Meyer (in Curtis 1907–1930, vol. 14:194–195) identified the names and locations of twelve Konkow tribelets, from Yupa at Yuba City (which may have been in Nisenan territory) to Hakama, north of Feather Falls on the Middle Fork of the Feather. There was a cultural boundary, probably marked by a dialect boundary,

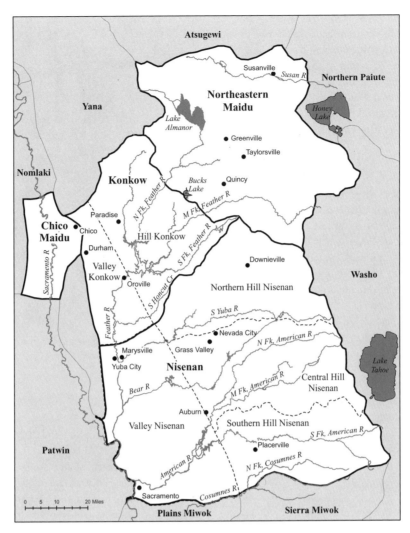

MAP 26. Maiduan languages and major dialects.

between the **Hill Konkows** above Oroville (called "Hill Maidu" by Kroeber 1932) and the **Valley Konkows** north and south of Oroville on the flat plain of the Sacramento Valley. The latter had close social and ceremonial ties to the Valley Nisenan and the Valley Patwin, as well as to the Chico Maidu. According to Merriam (1967b:314), the boundary between the Chico Maidu and the Valley Konkow (whom he called the "Ti-mah") lay only a few miles east of Chico. Kroeber identified four Valley Konkow tribelets: O'da-wi, between Chico and the foothills to the northeast; Esken, between Durham and the foothills; Shiudi, southwest of Oroville; and Kulu, south of Oroville. The villages in the Honcut Creek area, between the Feather and Yuba Rivers, may have constituted a fifth Valley Konkow tribelet, although Kroeber thought it possible that the variety spoken in this region was a transitional dialect between Konkow and Nisenan (1925:393, 1932:266–267).

The modern Konkows, who are mostly of Hill Konkow origin, recognize six subdivisions. These include the Na Tok Ya or "North People" from Bucks Lake; the Eskimonica, from the area between the Middle Fork of the Feather River and

the town of Challenge, now associated with Enterprise Rancheria; the Taime, who lived in the area ranging from Stringtown Mountain to Walker's Plain, now associated with Berry Creek Rancheria; the Tanka of the Feather Falls area, now associated with Mooretown Rancheria; the Toku or "Valley People," who lived in the area ranging from Stringtown Mountain to Chico; and the Pulga, from the area around Pulga and Paradise, also known as the Nimshew (Forbes n.d.: 4–5).

The earliest attestation of Konkow is a vocabulary collected by Stephen Powers in 1875 from speakers who had been resettled on the Round Valley Reservation (1877:586–600). Early in the twentieth century vocabularies of Hill Konkow were collected by Merriam (Appendix A: U-20i), Myers (Curtis 1907–1930, vol. 14:229–237), and Halpern (1936c), and a vocabulary of the variety of Valley Konkow (or possibly Nisenan) spoken in the Brownsville area on South Honcut Creek was collected by Merriam (Appendix A: U-20g). Swadesh and Melton (1953) made a tape recording of Konkaw for the Penutian Vocabulary Survey (Swadesh 1954b). The most substantial documentation (focusing on the Hill Konkow dialect) was made by Russell Ultan in 1961–1963, and his dissertation is a grammar of the language (Ultan 1967). His only publication on the language, however, is a short paper on sound symbolism (1973).

The principal modern Konkow community is at the Mooretown Rancheria, near Feather Falls east of Oroville. There are a few elderly speakers, who participate in the Konkow Language Preservation Group.

3.24.2 Chico Maidu

Chico Maidu was spoken in several tribelets along the Sacramento River in Butte and Glenn Counties, from south of Vina to Butte City, and east as far as Chico. The area was evidently heavily populated. Meyer (in Curtis 1907–1930, vol. 14:194–195) lists nineteen Chico Maidu villages. Kroeber (1932:266–267) identifies six tribelets along the river and a seventh tribelet (Michópdo) at Chico.

The language is attested in a substantial vocabulary collected by A. S. Gatschet (1877d, 1879b) at Michúpda (or Michópdo) on Bidwell's Ranch, a few miles south of Chico, and in vocabularies collected by Merriam (Appendix A: U-20a) and Myers (in Curtis 1907–1930, vol. 14:229–237) from descendants of the same community. There is some doubt whether Chico Maidu is a separate language or a divergent dialect of Konkow. On cultural rather than linguistic grounds, Kroeber (1932) grouped the Valley Konkow and the Chico Maidu together as "Valley Maidu."

3.24.3 Northeastern Maidu

Northeastern Maidu (also known as Mountain Maidu, or simply Maidu) was spoken in several high mountain valleys between Lassen Peak and Sierra Valley in Plumas County, and on the high plateau to the northeast around Susanville and Honey Lake in Lassen County. The principal areas of permanent settlement were Big Meadows (the site of Lake Almanor), Mountain Meadows, Butt Valley (*k'áwbatim koyó* 'flat ground valley'), Indian Valley (*tasím koyó*, between Greenville and Taylorsville), Genesee Valley, American Valley (*silóm koyó*, around Quincy), and along the Susan River from Susanville to Honey Lake. Mohawk Valley and Sierra Valley on the upper Middle Fork of the Feather River were visited seasonally. No significant dialect differences are reported, although each area was considered a separate social entity (Riddell 1978:371–372).

Northeastern Maidu is the best documented of the Maiduan languages, and one of the better known languages in California as a whole, thanks to extensive fieldwork carried out by R. B. Dixon between 1899 and 1903 and by William Shipley beginning in 1955. This work has resulted in three grammars (Dixon 1900, 1911; Shipley 1964), a dictionary (Shipley 1963), and two major collections of narrative texts (Dixon 1912; Shipley 1963). The earliest published attestation of Northeastern Maidu is a vocabulary of the Susanville variety ("Na-kum") collected in 1875 by

FIGURE 59. William Shipley and his principal Northeastern Maidu consultant, Maym Gallagher. Paynes Creek, California, Summer 1955. Courtesy of William Shipley.

Stephen Powers (1877:586–600). Merriam also collected vocabularies between 1903 and 1926 from a speaker at Big Meadows (Appendix A: U-20b).

Some Northeastern Maidu descendants are members of the small Susanville and Greenville Rancherias, but most live away from tribal land in scattered locations in Plumas and Lassen Counties. Only a few semispeakers of Maidu remain, but there is considerable interest in revitalization. William Shipley, who acquired second-language fluency during his documentation of Maidu in the 1950s, was one of the best remaining speakers at the time of his death in 2011, and he mentored several community members in the language (Holbrook 2001).

3.24.4 Nisenan

Nisenan was spoken to the south of the three other Maiduan languages, in a large territory that included the drainages of the American, Bear, and Yuba Rivers from their confluence with the Sacramento east to their headwaters. There were four major dialects, with quite sharp boundaries (Beals 1933:338–339); the differences were grammatical as well as lexical (R. Smith 1977:132).

Valley Nisenan was spoken in several village tribelets that clustered along the Sacramento and Feather Rivers, and on the lowermost twenty miles of the American River. Among the most important villages (and presumably tribelet centers) were Pusune, on the Sacramento River within the boundaries of modern Sacramento; Yuba, near Marysville; and Hok, on the lower Feather River south of Marysville.

The Hill dialects were distributed along the major streams, with territories roughly approximating the modern counties of the area. **Northern Hill Nisenan** was spoken in Nevada County on the middle and upper Yuba River, with a southern boundary somewhere in the neighborhood of Bear River. **Central Hill Nisenan** was spoken in Placer County in the area around Auburn, on the North and Middle Forks of the American River. **Southern Hill Nisenan** was spoken in El Dorado County from the South Fork of the American River to the North and Middle Forks of the Cosumnes River, including the area around Placerville.

All four dialects are attested, although the coverage is uneven. Valley Nisenan was documented earliest, but not extensively. The first materials published on any Maiduan language are three short vocabularies that the Wilkes Expedition geologist James Dwight Dana collected at John A. Sutter's New Helvetia colony in 1841, documenting the Valley Nisenan subdialects of the villages or tribelets of "Pujūni" (Pusune), "Sekumné" (Sek), and "Tsamak" (Sama), all located close to Sacramento (Dana 1846). Stephen Powers—who owned a ranch nearby—collected a vocabulary of the "Hololapai" variety on the Feather River below Oroville in 1872 (1877:586–600). A. L. Kroeber's monograph on the Valley Nisenan (1929) contains a substantial vocabulary of the lower American River variety arranged topically (most of the data extracted from Kroeber, Gayton, and Freeland 1925). Merriam also collected a Valley Nisenan vocabulary (Appendix A: U-20l).

Of the three Hill dialects, Southern Hill was extensively documented by Uldall in the 1930s (Uldall and Shipley 1966) and Central Hill by Richard Smith in the 1960s (R. Smith 1977; Eatough 1999). Northern Hill Nisenan appears to be directly documented only in two vocabularies, one collected at Cushna on the upper Yuba River shortly after the Gold Rush (Johnston 1852b), the other by Merriam (Appendix A: U-20h). There is some further documentation of Nisenan dialectology in several early vocabularies printed in Powers (1877:586–600); in materials that Kroeber's student, Hugh Littlejohn, collected for his unfinished ethnogeographical study (1928a, 1928b, 1928c); in notes collected by A. M. Halpern (1936c) during a linguistic survey; and in Merriam's vocabularies of the southernmost varieties of Nisenan (Appendix A: U-20m–U-20o).[78]

Nisenan descendants live at Auburn Rancheria in Placer County, Shingle Springs Rancheria in El Dorado County, and in various other locations in the area. There are no fluent speakers, but a language program is under way at Shingle Springs, with classroom instruction.

3.24.5 Linguistic Structure

Maiduan structure is known primarily through Shipley's grammar of Northeastern Maidu (Shipley 1964), supplemented by three comparative papers (Shipley 1961; Shipley and Smith 1979b, 1982).

TABLE 32
Northeastern Maidu Phonemes (Shipley 1964)

Consonants					Vowels		
p	t	c	k	?	i	ï	u
p'	t'	c'	k'		e	a	o
b	d						
	s			h			
m	n						
w	l	y					

Stress Accent
 v́

All Maiduan languages have basically the same uncomplicated phonology (Table 32). In all four languages there are two full sets of oral stops, plain (*p, t, c, k*) and glottalized (*p', t', c' k'*), with the alveo-palatal series (*c* and *c'*) varying between stop and affricate articulation. In addition there are two fully voiced stops (*b, d*), which are often pronounced with a slight implosion. There is only one fricative (*s*), which is apical and usually slightly retroflexed [ṣ]. There are two laryngeals (*h, ?*), two nasals (*m, n*), and three approximants (*l, w, y*). There are six vowels—two front unrounded (*i, e*), two back unrounded (*ï, a*), and two back rounded (*u, o*). Nisenan and Konkow distinguish three rather than two back unrounded vowels (*ï, ə, a*) and contrast short and long vowels. Nisenan consistently places stress on initial syllables; in the other Maiduan languages the placement of stress is unpredictable.

Nouns and independent pronouns must always be inflected for case. The subject, object, possessive, and locative forms of nouns and the independent pronouns are illustrated in Table 33.[79] Other case suffixes or case-like postpositions include -*k'an*, comitative (*wépak'an* 'along with the coyote'); -*ni*, instrumental (*wépani* 'by means of the coyote'); -*na*, allative (*wépana* 'toward the coyote'); and -*nan*, ablative (*wépanan* 'from the coyote').

Some verb stems consist of a single morpheme (*sol*- 'sing', *c'ukút*- 'wash', -*?idí* 'do along with, eat with'), but compounding is frequent (*sól-?idi*- 'sing along with', *sól-wek'oy*- 'seem to be singing'). An important set of complex stems are "bipartite" verbs of motion or direction (DeLancey 1999; see ¶4.8.2).

3.24.6 Nomenclature

Although Powers (1877) used "Maidu" (in some earlier publications spelled "Meidoo"), from Northeastern Maidu *maydï* 'man, person', as the ethnonym for speakers of the northern Maiduan language cluster, distinguishing the speakers of the southern Maiduan language as "Nishenam." Powell, in the linguistic appendix to the same volume, treated both languages as part of the "Maidu family"

TABLE 33
Northeastern Maidu Case Inflection (Shipley 1964)

Nouns

	Subject	Object	Possessive	Locative
	-(i)m	-(i)	-(i)k'i	-di
'song'	sólim	sóli	sólik'i	sóldi
'mountain'	yamánim	yamáni	yamánik'i	yamándi
'coyote'	wépam	wépa	wépak'i	wépadi
'light'	banák'am	banák'a	banák'ak'i	banák'adi

Independent Pronouns

	Subject	Object	Possessive	Locative
1 sg	ni 'I'	nik 'me'	nik'í 'my'	nikdí 'at me'
2 sg	mi 'you (sg)'	min	mínk'i	míndi
3 sg	mïm 'that one'	mï	mïk'í	mïdí
1 du	nisám 'we two'	nisá	nisák'i	nisádi
2 du	mínc'em 'you two'	mínc'e	mínc'ek'i	mínc'edi
3 du	máyc'om 'they two'	máyc'o	máyc'ok'i	máyc'odi
	mïsám 'those two'	mïsá	mïsák'í	mïsádi
1 pl	nisém 'we all'	nisé	nisék'i	nisédi
2 pl	míncïm 'you all'	míncï	míncik'i	míncïdi
3 pl	máysem 'they all'	máyse	máysek'i	máysedi
	mïsém 'those all'	mïsé	mïsék'í	mïsédi

(1877:586). In his 1891 classification, Powell substituted "Pujunan" for the family name, from *Pujūni*, the first-listed of Dana's 1841 Valley Nisenan vocabularies as published in Hale (1846:631); Latham had earlier used the same term for Valley Nisenan (1860:346). This application of the rule of taxonomic precedence, however, found little favor among Californianists. Dixon rejected Pujunan ("derived from the name of an insignificant village") in favor of Powell's earlier and "more rational" use of Maidu, proposing that the constituent language or dialect groups be labeled geographically ("Northwestern Maidu" for Konkow and Chico, "Northeastern Maidu" for Maidu proper, and "Southern Maidu" for Nisenan) (Dixon 1905a:123–125). Kroeber adopted Dixon's nomenclature, and it remained in general use among California anthropologists into the 1950s. "Konkow," "Maidu," and "Nisenan," however, also gained acceptance as names of the language-defined "tribes." In the late 1950s, Shipley, influenced by the latter usage, published his work on Northeastern Maiduan as a description of the "Maidu" language, and to disambiguate the term he proposed that "Maidun" be employed for the language family. This practice is now generally followed, although while Shipley has consistently spelled the term "Maidun," others, including the editors of the *Handbook of North American Indians*, have preferred the more analytic "Maiduan," which is the spelling adopted here.

3.25 Wintuan Languages

Wintuan is a moderately diversified Penutian language family with two quite distinct branches, **Northern Wintuan** (or **Wintu-Nomlaki**) and **Southern Wintuan** (or **Patwin**). Northern Wintuan is further divided into two dialect complexes, **Wintu,** a relatively homogeneous cluster of varieties spoken in the far northern Sacramento Valley and the mountains to the north and west, and **Nomlaki** (also called "Wintun"), spoken in Tehama and Glenn Counties in the north-central Sacramento Valley. Southern Wintuan is basically one language, **Patwin,** spoken in two distinct dialects—**River Patwin** and **Hill Patwin**—in Colusa and northern Yolo Counties. A poorly attested third dialect, **Southern Patwin,** that was spoken in southern Yolo County, in Solano County, and in the vicinity of Napa, may be divergent enough to be considered an emergent language.

The degree of difference between the two branches of Wintuan is similar to that separating Romanian from a Western Romance language such as Spanish, suggesting a time depth of approximately 1,500 to 2,000 years (Whistler 1980a:17).[80] The differences are phonological and grammatical as well as lexical and reflect an extended period of separate development. The presence of an important cultural boundary halfway down the Sacramento Valley

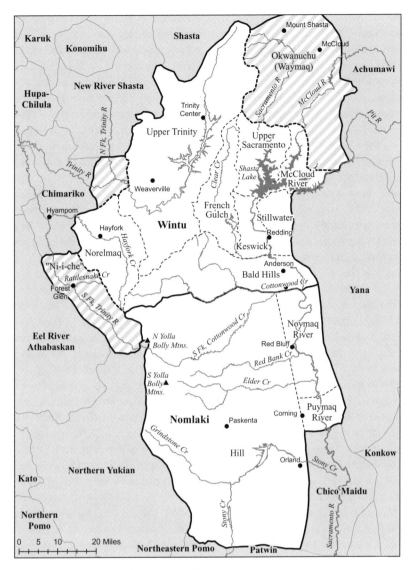

MAP 27. Northern Wintuan languages and dialects.

seems to be indicated, with different substratal influences north and south of this line. It is also possible that some of the differentiation between Northern and Southern Wintuan may have occurred outside California. There is good evidence that the Wintuan languages entered California from southwestern Oregon around 500 AD and that the family has a closer relationship to some Oregon Penutian languages than to its Penutian neighbors in California (see ¶5.3.4).

3.25.1 Northern Wintuan (Wintu-Nomlaki)

WINTU

Wintu, the more northerly of the two Northern Wintuan dialect groups, was spoken in a number of village communities in the upper end of the Sacramento Valley north of Cottonwood Creek, in the mountainous region to the north

on the upper Sacramento River and its tributaries, and to the west in the upper drainage of the Trinity River (Map 27).

The exact number and locations of the Wintu subgroups at the time of contact is uncertain. The most detailed information was gathered by Cora Du Bois in the early 1930s. She identified eight Wintu "subareas" (1935:6–8), which seem for the most part to correspond to tribelets: (1) ***Upper Sacramento River*** (*nomtipom* 'on the other side of the hill west'), including the Sacramento River canyon from roughly the present Shasta Lake to between Le Moine and Dunsmuir; (2) ***McCloud River*** (*wenem-mem* 'middle river'), the resource-rich area where the lower McCloud River joins the Pit River, now largely submerged by Shasta Lake; (3) ***Stillwater Valley*** (*dawpom* 'flat place'), the plateau north of Redding; (4) ***Keswick*** (*ʔelpom* 'inside place'), the area along the Sacramento River west of Redding; (5) ***French Gulch*** (*ƛ'aba:lpom* [meaning uncertain]), the valley at the upper end of Clear Creek, north of Whiskeytown; (6) ***Upper Trinity***

River (*nomsuːs* 'those who live in the west'), the valley of the upper Trinity River from Trinity Center to Lewiston, much of it now submerged by Trinity Lake; (7) **Bald Hills** (*dawnom* 'flat to the west'), the flat valley area south of Redding, around Anderson and Cottonwood and west to Ono; and (8) the **Hayfork Wintu** (*norelmaq* 'south uphill people'), centered on Hayfork Valley, about fifteen miles southwest of Weaverville.

Dialect variation among these subgroups appears to have been minimal, and boundaries are hard to draw. Du Bois, relying mainly on the statements of speakers about the difficulty they experienced in understanding people from other subareas, proposed no dialect lines and saw differences accumulating with distance, particularly in the Sacramento Valley (see her statement about the Bald Hills dialect under the heading "Nomlaki"). Merriam, who collected vocabularies from many of the Wintu areas, grouped subareas 1–5 together as the "Wintoon proper" and treated the speech of each of the three other areas as independent dialects (Heizer 1966:42). The linguist Alice Shepherd, however, believes that Wintu internal variation was almost entirely social and individual, not dialectal; according to her data, even Hayfork Wintu, which Du Bois reported to be "incomprehensible" to the McCloud River Wintu, diverged only slightly from other attested Wintu speech (Schlichter [Shepherd] 1979; Shepherd 2005:2).

The ethnogeographic situation seems to have been in flux at the time of contact. There is evidence of the existence of bilingual tribelets and of shifting language boundaries on both the northern and western margins of Wintu territory. In the north, Du Bois noted a group that formerly lived in the vicinity of present-day McCloud, whom the McCloud River Wintu considered Wintu and called **Waymaq** ('north people'). Du Bois believed the Waymaq were closely related to, if not identical with, the Shastan Okwanuchu; the survivor of the group whom she interviewed gave her a short vocabulary that included words of Shasta origin (Du Bois 1935:8).[81]

In the west, Merriam located a Wintu tribelet that he called the "Ni-i-che" on the South Fork of the Trinity between Plummer Creek and Post Creek, near Forest Glen (Heizer 1966:42; Merriam and Talbot 1974:28). This is usually claimed to be Athabaskan territory, but Merriam apparently had evidence that Wintu was spoken there as well. The occurrence of Wintu place-names and personal names in historic Athabaskan territory even further south and west (Kettenpom, Yolla Bolly, Lassik) suggests that the boundary between the two language families was not stable in this area, and that Powers's report (1877:114) that the Athabaskan Wailaki had recently captured this region from the Wintu might well have a basis in fact. Only on the east, where relations between the Wintu and the Yana were generally hostile, was the Wintu language boundary sharply defined and relatively stable.

Wintu received considerable attention from linguists in the twentieth century. Kroeber's student Dorothy Demetracopoulou (later Dorothy Lee) collected linguistic material during the fieldwork that she carried out in collaboration with Cora Du Bois in 1929–1930, most importantly a substantial corpus of traditional narrative texts. Her original interest was comparative mythology, and the early publications derived from her Wintu work reflect this (Du Bois and Demetracopoulou 1931; Demetracopoulou and Du Bois 1932; Demetracopoulou 1933). Demetracopoulou (as Dorothy Lee) later reported on Wintu linguistics in a series of papers that focused on semantics and worldview (Lee 1938, 1940, 1942, 1943, 1944a, 1944b, 1946). Most of her data remain unpublished, including the Wintu-language versions of the texts. Work on Wintu was resumed in the 1950s by Harvey Pitkin, who carried out fieldwork with several speakers in the Redding area between 1956 and 1959. Pitkin incorporated much of Lee's data into his published grammar (1984) and dictionary (1985). Alice Schlichter (later Shepherd) worked with a speaker of the Hayfork variety between 1975 and 1982 and published a dictionary (1981b) and an extensive collection of texts (1989). Schlichter also published and commented on a text of Lee's that documents the shamanistic jargon used in Wintu traditional curing (1981a).

Other documentation includes a word list obtained in 1841 by James Dwight Dana during the Wilkes Expedition (Hale 1846); a McCloud River vocabulary collected by Livingston Stone in 1872 (Heizer 1973); vocabularies and myth texts collected by J. W. Powell (1880b); substantial materials, including texts, collected by Jeremiah Curtin during two extended BAE survey visits (1884b, 1884c, 1884–1889c, 1884–1889d, 1888–1889a, 1888–1889b); and a short grammatical sketch by R. B. Dixon (1909). Other early vocabularies are printed in Powers (1877:518–534). Merriam collected vocabularies from two varieties of the dialect he called "Numʹ-te-pomʹ or Wintoon proper" (Appendix A: T-19b). He also collected vocabularies of two varieties of the Upper Trinity River dialect (Num'-soos, T-19a) and a vocabulary from Hay Fork (Nor'-rel-muk, T-19c). A Trinity River variety ("Numsu") is also attested in a vocabulary collected by Powers in 1871 (1877:518–34). Swadesh and Melton (1953) made sound recordings of Wintu for their Penutian Vocabulary Survey (Swadesh 1954b).

There is a substantial community of Wintu descendants in Shasta and Trinity Counties. Some are enrolled at Redding Rancheria, the only federally recognized entity which is currently associated with the Wintu, but which also includes members of Pit River and Yana descent. The majority of the present-day Wintu are affiliated with one of seven unrecognized groups (stopwintufraud.blogspot.com). The two most active of these are the Wintu Tribe of Northern California (organized as the Toyon-Wintu Center) and the Winnemem, or McCloud River Wintu (organized as the Winnemem Wintu Organization). The latter is a culturally conservative group active in the preservation of Wintu cultural and religious sites, language, and ceremonies. There is also a Wintu organization in Hayfork, Trinity County, seeking federal

FIGURE 60. Carrie B. Dixon, Harvey Pitkin's principal source of Wintu data in 1956–1959 and later one of the consultants for Alice Schlichter's dictionary (1981b). Photograph ca. 1958 courtesy of the estate of Harvey Pitkin.

acknowledgement as the Nor Rel Muk Nation. Although the last fluent speaker of Wintu, the Winnemem shaman Flora Jones, passed away in 2003, there remain several less-fluent speakers as well as a number of learners. Several master-apprentice pairs have been sponsored and a learner-oriented dictionary is in preparation (Liedtke 2004).

NOMLAKI

Nomlaki, or "Wintun," is a distinct dialect area—or emergent language—within Northern Wintuan, adjoining Wintu territory to the south in the Sacramento Valley. Wintu and Nomlaki may have graded into one another in the southernmost Wintu dialect (Bald Hills). Du Bois reports that Bald Hills speakers had no difficulty in understanding Nomlaki, whereas speakers of the more northerly McCloud River dialect considered Nomlaki incomprehensible. Bald Hills speakers had "a slight shift in vocabulary" and had a general term (*waybos* 'northerners') for all other Wintu (1935:5–8). Kroeber reports that Wintu was intelligible to Nomlaki speakers "including all those of Trinity County and as far as Mt. Shasta" (1932:355). Nevertheless, according to Shepherd, there were distinct isoglosses separating Wintu from Nomlaki (2005:3). To the south, however, the linguistic boundary was much sharper and "the speech . . . of the Patwin was unintelligible" (Kroeber 1932:355).

Nomlaki territory extended from the Shasta-Tehama county line at Cottonwood Creek to south of Grindstone Creek in Glenn County. There were two Nomlaki divisions. The **River Nomlaki** lived along the Sacramento River as far as Vina, in the vicinity of Corning, below which point the river was in Chico Maidu territory. The **Hill Nomlaki** occupied the dry valley floor and foothills to the west. There

were two River Nomlaki divisions, each apparently with a separate dialect: Noymaq in the north, near Red Bluff, and Puymaq in the south (the latter including the village or tribelet from which the name Tehama is derived). The Hill Nomlaki, who spoke a single dialect, were divided into four tribelets or subdialect groups by creek drainage: Red Bank Creek, west of Red Bluff; Elder Creek, west of Gerber; Thomes Creek, near Paskenta; and Grindstone Creek, west of Orland (Kroeber 1932:264–266; Goldschmidt 1978:341).

The documentation of Nomlaki is fragmentary. The first attestation is a short list of words in "the language spoken by the Indians of that [Sacramento] river, at about two hunded and fifty miles above its mouth" obtained by James Dwight Dana in 1841 during the Wilkes Expedition (Hale 1846:630). Three vocabularies were collected in the early 1850s, one by the Indian agent Adam Johnston (Johnston 1854) and the others ("Noema" and "Tehama") by H. B. Brown, transmitted by J. R. Bartlett (Bartlett n.d.). All three were printed in Powers (1877:518–534), together with a vocabulary collected at Tehama by Powers himself in 1872. S. A. Barrett, as part of his survey of Pomo and surrounding languages, collected a vocabulary of Nomlaki in 1903–1906 (1908a:81–87, "Northerly dialect"). In 1919, Merriam collected a vocabulary from speakers of the Thomes Creek (Paskenta) and Grindstone Creek varieties of Hill Nomlaki (Appendix A: T-19f). Between 1915 and 1924, Myers, working for Curtis, obtained a good sample of Nomlaki ("Central Wintun") at Paskenta (Curtis 1907–1930, vol. 14:220–229). In 1923–1924, A. L. Kroeber collected a substantial amount of Nomlaki ("Wintun") cultural vocabulary, which he incorporated into his published ethnographic report (1932:355–364). Swadesh and Melton (1953) made a sound recording of Nomlaki for their Penutian Vocabulary Survey (Swadesh 1954b). Jesse Sawyer (1975) and Kenneth Whistler (1976) carried out some limited fieldwork with the last speakers.

Most Nomlaki descendants are associated with the Grindstone Rancheria and the Paskenta Band, in Tehama County, although there is also a Nomlaki community on the Round Valley Reservation. At least one partial speaker of Nomlaki is said to remain, but no details are known.

3.25.2 Southern Wintuan (Patwin)

RIVER AND HILL PATWIN

The only well-attested Southern Wintuan language, Patwin, is divided into two distinct dialect complexes, each with further subdialectal variation (Map 28). **River Patwin** was spoken is a string of tribelets located along the banks of the Sacramento River in Colusa County. Their names and boundaries are known with some precision through Kroeber's work (1932:259–261). The River Patwin tribelets fell into two divisions, each associated with a subdialect. The northern or Colusa (Koru) division included six tribelets, the most important of which included the site of

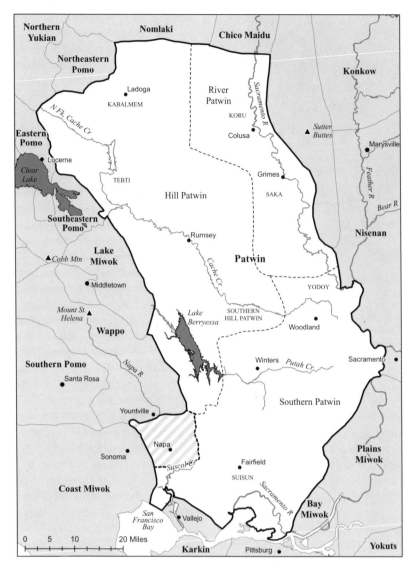

MAP 28. Patwin (Southern Wintuan) territory and dialects.

the present-day city of Colusa, where a salmon-fishing weir was built. Somewhere around Sycamore and Meridian one entered the territory of the southern or Grimes (Saka) division. The most important tribelet of the southern division centered on the village of Saka, about a mile south of Grimes, where another salmon-fishing weir was built. River Patwin territory ended at approximately the Yolo County line, where Southern Patwin territory began. **Hill Patwin** was spoken in the grassy plains and foothills to the west of the River Patwin area, in three distinct subdialects. Kabalmem, the northernmost subdialect, was spoken in the Ladoga area of northwestern Colusa County, bordering on the territory of the Northeastern Pomo. The Tebti subdialect was spoken along upper Cache Creek and Long Valley in eastern Lake County. The Southern Hill Patwin subdialect was spoken across the remainder of Hill Patwin territory, which included the Cortina Creek area in southwestern Colusa County, lower Cache Creek and the Capay Valley in northwestern

Yolo County (in the vicinity of Rumsey), and the Berryessa Valley on upper Putah Creek (now submerged by Lake Berryessa).

There is also some evidence that a Hill Patwin group held a small part of the Napa Valley. Their principal village appears to have been Tulocay, close to Napa, and their speech was said to be distinct both from the Wappo spoken further up Napa Valley and from the language spoken at Suscol, a few miles to the south of Napa, which may have been Southern Patwin (Merriam 1967b:270–272).

The first attestation of Patwin was a vocabulary of a variety ("Kopeh") of Southern Hill Patwin, obtained by George Gibbs at Clear Lake in 1851 during the McKee Expedition (Gibbs 1853b, 1853c). It was reprinted by Stephen Powers (1877:518–534), along with Powers's own vocabulary of the Long Valley variety of Hill Patwin, collected in 1872. In the early twentieth century survey vocabularies were collected by S. A. Barrett from an unspecified variety (1908a:81–87,

FIGURE 61. C. Hart Merriam and Bill Wiley at Cachil Dehe rancheria, on the Sacramento River north of Colusa (Korusi, River Patwin), 1931–1935. C. Hart Merriam collection of Native American photographs (T/19r/P6 no.32). Courtesy of the Bancroft Library UCB.

Patwin descendants live on small rancherias at Cortina and Colusa, and on the Rumsey (Cache Creek) Rancheria west of Woodland. In 2003 at least one speaker of the Hill dialect remained.

SOUTHERN PATWIN

Southern Patwin (called "Poo-e-win" [puywin], according to Merriam 1967b:270–272) is poorly attested, and its status is not clear. It is probably best classified as a third dialect of Patwin, although it may be sufficiently divergent from the Hill and River dialects to be considered a separate Southern Wintuan language. It was spoken from central Yolo County to Suisun Bay and west at least as far as the lower Napa River. The best attested subdialect is *Suisun* (or Suyisun), spoken by a tribelet whose territory lay along the marshy edges of Suisun Bay, southwest of Fairfield. Although it is not directly attested, a distinct Knights Landing (or Yodoy) subdialect is known to have been spoken on a short stretch of the Sacramento River south of River Patwin territory, as well as west of the river toward Woodland. Older sources mention several other tribelet groups who apparently spoke the same dialect, including Liwaito (a name, interestingly enough, of Lake Miwok origin), on lower Putah Creek near Winters; Ululato, in the vicinity of Vacaville and on the plains to the east; Malaca, on the Suisun plains east of Fairfield; Tolena, in Gordon Valley, northeast of Fairfield; and probably the Napa, or Suscol, tribelet on the Napa River south of the present city of Napa (Powers 1877:218–219, Milliken 1995:228–261, Merriam 1967b:270–272).

There is conflicting evidence regarding the language affiliation of the Sonoma region. On the one hand, Merriam (1967b:270–272) collected a Southern Patwin vocabulary near Sonoma, as well as other information indicating that Southern Patwin territory extended west to that town, whose name, derived from the nickname of an early nineteenth-century headman of the nearby Chocuyen or Chocoime tribelet, could well be based on Southern Patwin *sono* 'nose' (Kroeber 1932:354; Beeler 1954:268–272). On the other hand, Gibbs's vocabulary of the Chocuyen dialect (Schoolcraft 1851–1857, vol. 3:428) is clearly Coast Miwok, as is the "Napa" vocabulary that Curtin collected from a descendant of the "Alamitca" tribelet (1884f), possibly to be identified with the Alaguali who lived at the mouth of Sonoma Creek (Milliken 1995:234). A possible explanation for this confusion is that the Sonoma Creek area may have originally belonged to the Coast Miwok, but when Southern Patwin speakers were brought in by the Spanish after the establishment of the mission at Sonoma in 1823, their language became dominant in what remained of the local Indian community (Kroeber 1957:215–216).

The very sparse documentation of Southern Patwin includes a vocabulary of about fifty words in the Suisun subdialect collected on an 1821 visit to Mission Dolores by Padre Arroyo de la Cuesta (Arroyo 1837); a one-hundred-word vocabulary of Suisun collected by Jeremiah Curtin

"Southerly dialect"), and by Myers from the Cortina variety of Hill Patwin and the Colusa variety of "Valley Patwin" (Curtis 1907–1930, vol. 14:220–229). From the late 1920s to the early 1960s, Patwin was extensively documented by several linguists, including Jaime de Angulo (1929), Paul Radin (1932–1949), A. M. Halpern (1936a), Elizabeth Bright (1952), and Donald Ultan (1961–1962, n.d.). Nearly all of this documentation remains unpublished. The last linguist to work with Patwin, Kenneth Whistler, carried out extensive fieldwork in 1975–1979 with the few remaining speakers (all of them Hill Patwins) and reported on the language in his dissertation (1980a), in some short papers (1981a, 1986), and in two analyzed texts (1977b, 1978).

Vocabularies and natural history word lists collected by Merriam in the early twentieth century are especially valuable for the light they shed on Patwin internal diversity. Merriam's attestations of Hill Patwin include the varieties spoken at Ladoga (Appendix A: T-19l), Long Valley (T-19m), Cortina (T-19o), and Rumsey (T-19p). His attestations of River Patwin are of both the Koru and Saka ("Patwin") varieties (Appendix A: T-19r-s). Comparative word lists and other data on the Colusa, Rumsey, and Stonyford varieties were also collected by Halpern (1936a), and Swadesh and Melton (1953) made sound recordings of Patwin for their Penutian Vocabulary Survey (Swadesh 1954b).

(1884f); a vocabulary and natural history word list collected by Merriam in 1906 from a speaker living near Sonoma and supplemented in 1917 with items from two other speakers (Appendix A: T-19t); miscellaneous notes on Suisun in a manuscript written in the 1890s by Platon Vallejo, the son of General M. G. Vallejo (Pitkin 1962:48, item 54); and a short vocabulary elicited from Platon Vallejo by J. Alden Mason in 1916 (Mason 1916b; Kroeber 1932:354–355).

3.25.3 Linguistic Structure

The phonologies of Northern and Southern Wintuan differ significantly (Table 34). Northern Wintuan (for which Wintu is cited here) has the larger phonemic inventory, which includes four basic stops (*p, t, k, q*) and a palatal affricate *č* (written *c* by Pitkin), all occurring both plain and glottalized. The labial and alveolar stops also occur aspirated (*p^h, t^h*) and voiced (*b, d*). There are four fricatives (*ł, s, x, x̣*), with the lateral fricative *ł* (sometimes affricated, hence written λ by Pitkin) paired with a glottalized lateral affricate (*λ'*). There are also two nasals (*m* and *n*), four approximants (*l, r, w, y*), and two laryngeals (*h* and *ʔ*). The *r* is a voiced trill [r̄], usually reduced to a flap [ɾ] when between vowels. The five vowels (*i, e, a, o, u*) occur both short and long. In Patwin, there are only three basic stops (*p, t, k*) and a palatal affricate *č*, occurring both plain and glottalized. As in Wintu, the labial and apical stops also occur aspirated and voiced. In addition, Patwin has an aspirated velar stop (*k^h*). Patwin has only two fricatives (*s, ł*), again with the lateral fricative paired with a glottalized lateral affricate (*λ'*). The Patwin nasals, approximants, and laryngeals are as in Wintu, as are the five vowels, short and long.

Shepherd (2005), following Whistler (1980a), reconstructs a Proto-Wintuan consonant system with the points of articulation as in Wintu, but with a complete series of aspirated stops. The points of articulation of the Patwin system are the result of fronting of the velars (PWin *q, *q' > Win *q, q'*, Pat *k, k'* and PWin *k, *k' > Win *k, k'*, Pat *č, č'*), while the aspirated velar stops have been fricativized in Wintu (PWin *q^h > Win *x̣*, Pat *k^h* and PWin *k^h > Win *x*, Pat *č*).

Northern and Southern Wintuan also show differences in morphology, although the basic patterns are similar. In both languages nouns and pronouns are inflected for four cases—subject, object, possessive, and locative—as illustrated in Table 35. In Wintu, all nouns and pronouns can be either particular or generic in aspect, with the particular form usually marked by suffixed *-h* or the devoicing of the stem-final consonant. The semantic contrast is often one of animacy or specificity—for example, *nurh* 'a live salmon' (particular) versus *nur* 'salmon meat to eat' (generic)'; *č'epkax̣* 'a bad person' (particular) versus *č'epkal* 'a bad thing, wrongness' (generic); *seh* 'one hand, finger' (particular) versus *sem* 'hands' (generic). This is an unusual distinction in California languages and one with interesting implications for discourse (D. Lee 1944a; Wash 1991). Contrasts in

TABLE 34
Wintuan Phonemic Systems

Consonants						Vowels		

Wintu (Pitkin 1984)

p	t		č	k	q	ʔ	i / i:		u / u:
p^h	t^h						e / e:		o / o:
p'	t'	λ'	č'	k'	q'			a / a:	
b	d								
	s	ł		x	x̣	h			
m	n								
w	r	l	y						

Hill Patwin (Whistler 1977b)

p	t		č	k	ʔ	i / i:		u / u:
p^h	t^h		č^h	k^h		e / e:		o / o:
p'	t'	λ'	č'	k'			a / a:	
b	d							
	s	ł			h			
m	n							
w	r	l	y					

nominal aspect are lacking in Patwin, although remnants of a formerly productive system can be identified (e.g., Whistler 1977b:176, n. 22).

In both branches of Wintuan, pronouns are numerous and morphologically complex (Table 36). A Proto-Wintuan personal pronominal system can be reconstructed with distinct forms for first person (*ni-*), second person (*mi-*), third person proximal (*ʔe-w-*), third person distal (*ʔu-*), and third person neutral (*pi- ~ *pu-*). In each of these categories there are sets of pronouns contrasting in number (singular, dual, plural) and in case (subject, object, genitive, possessive). A special set of pronominal possessive noun prefixes makes no distinction in number but does distinguish between those prefixed to (inalienable) kinship terms and those prefixed to all other (alienable) nouns (Schlichter [Shepherd] 1981c; Shepherd 2005). Both in specific forms and as a system the Wintuan personal pronouns closely resemble those of Klamath-Modoc (DeLancey 1987; see ¶5.3.5).

In both languages, verb roots are often augmented with a prefixed element indicating location or direction (e.g., Wintu *nom-wana:* 'be in, move west', *nor-wana:* 'be in, move south', *puy-wana:* 'be in, move east', *pat-k'uda* 'go outside', *x̣an-k'uda* 'go away, step off'). In Wintu, roots, both simple and augmented, are further marked for one of three classes (indicative, imperative, nominal) by a stem-forming suffix. Distinctive sets of inflectional suffixes occur with each of these stem classes, marking pronominal categories, certain modes, and several evidential categories. Similar sets of verbal inflectional suffixes occur in Patwin, but not all are

TABLE 35
Case and Aspect Marking in Wintu Nouns (Pitkin 1984; Shepherd 2005)

Common Nouns

		Subject	Object	Possessive	Locative
		(unmarked)	-(u)m	-(u)n	-in
'stone'	(generic)	son	sonum	sonun	sonin
	(particular)	soh	sohum	sohun	sohin
'acorn'	(generic)	ʔi:w	ʔi:wum	ʔi:wun	ʔi:win
	(particular)	ʔi:h	ʔi:hum	ʔi:wun	ʔi:hin
'fingernail'	(generic)	k'ahay	k'ahayum	k'ahayun	k'ahayin
	(particular)	k'ahah	k'ahahum	k'ahahun	k'ahahin
'hat'	(generic)	tʰaki	tʰakitum	tʰakitun	tʰakitin
	(particular)	tʰakit	tʰakim	tʰakin	tʰaki:n
'coyote'	(generic)	sedet	sedetum	sedetun	sedetin
	(particular)	sedet	sedem	seden	sede:n

Kinship Nouns

		Subject	Object	Possessive	Locative
		(unmarked)	-t	-r	-in
'older sister'	(generic)	lay	layat	layar	layin
	(particular)	lah	lahat	lahar	lahin

cognate with their Wintu counterparts, and the patterns of formation are different.

3.25.4 Nomenclature

"Wintun" (often spelled Wintoon), was in use as the general term for the Northern Wintuan people and language as early as the mid-1850s, and it was employed by Powers in this sense (1877:229). It is probably a direct borrowing into English of Wintu *wintʰu:h* 'person' (particular aspect) in its locative case form, *wintʰu:n,* although it is also possible that it was borrowed indirectly through Maidu *wint'um maydï* 'Wintu people'. Powers introduced the parallel term "Patwin" for the Southern Wintuans, explicitly modeling it on their word for 'person' (1877:218). Following the rule of taxonomic precedence, Powell (1891:145–146) proposed "Copehan" as the name for the overall language family, which had been first identified by Latham (1856:79) and named by him "Copeh" after the title of Gibbs's vocabulary of the Cache Creek subdialect of Southern Hill Patwin (Schoolcraft 1851–1857, vol. 3:421). To avoid this cumbersome term, Kroeber extended the name "Wintun" to the entire language family, distinguishing among "Northern Wintun," "Central Wintun," and "Southern Wintun" dialects (1925:353–355). In the 1930s, as the distinctiveness of the languages became clearer, Kroeber and his students began to use "Wintu" for the northern language, "Nomlaki" for the central language, and Powell's "Patwin" for the southern language. This nomenclature has now become standard among anthropologists and linguists, but the continuing nonacademic use of "Wintun" in its older sense, or as a synonym for "Nomlaki," frequently leads to confusion. As a consequence, many scholars prefer to follow the *Handbook of North American Indians* and employ the unambiguous "Wintuan" in place of "Wintun" as the language family name, as is done in this book, and to avoid "Wintun" altogether.

3.26 Yokuts

Yokuts is a single Penutian language with an extraordinarily large number of local dialects and subdialectal varieties (Map 29). Yokuts-speaking peoples occupied the entire southern half of the Central Valley, from the Delta to Tejon Pass, including both the valley floor and the lower elevations of the southern Sierra foothills. There were nearly forty tribe-like social units in the Yokuts area (for the distinction between these microtribes and "tribelets" see ¶1.2), which, although mostly restricted to very small territories, had distinct national identities and characteristic dialects. Contact among speakers from different dialect-tribes was frequent, and there was extensive ceremonial reciprocity, intermarriage, and long-distance trade. The salient linguistic

TABLE 36
Wintu Pronouns (Pitkin 1984; Shepherd 2005)

Independent Pronouns

	Subject	Object	Possessive
1 sg	ni, niyo	nis	ner
2 sg	mi, miyo	mis	mar
3 sg proximate			
(generic)	ʔew	ʔewet	ʔewer
(particular)	ʔeh		
3 sg nonproximate	pi, piyo	put	pir
1 dual			
(generic)	neːlel	neːlem	neːlen
(particular)	neːlet	neːlet	
2 dual			
(generic)	maːlel	maːlem	
(particular)	maːlet	maːletum	
3 dual	ʔewelel	ʔeweletam	
1 pl			
(generic)	niteːrum	neleːt-p'urum	
(particular)	neleːt		
2 pl			
(generic)	miteːrum	maːlet-p'urum	
(particular)	maleːt		
3 pl	ʔebas-p'urum	ʔebaːn-p'urum	

Possessive Prefixes

	With Kinship Terms	With Other Nouns
1 sg/pl	net-nen 'my mother'	neto-baːs 'my food'
2 sg/pl	mat-tan 'your father'	mato-sono 'your nose'
3 sg/pl proximate	ʔewer-somoːn 'his brother-in-law'	ʔewetun-suku 'his dog'
3 sg/pl nonproximate	pur-soh 'his younger sister'	putun-k'elek'ele 'his knife'

differences were primarily lexical rather than phonological or grammatical (Kroeber 1963). In addition to this internal diversity, Yokuts speakers living in the Sierra foothills were in close contact with the Western Mono groups who lived at higher elevations in the mountains.

Kroeber (1907a, 1963) sorted the Yokuts dialects into six subgroups: (1) Poso Creek, attested only in the Palewyami tribelet dialect in the southernmost foothill region. (2) The Buena Vista and Kern Lake tribelet dialects, Tulamni and Hometwoli. (3) The dialects of the foothill tribelets on the Tule and Kaweah Rivers, principally Yawdanchi and Wikchamni. (4) The dialects of the foothill tribelets on Kings River, the best known of which is Choynimni. (5) The Gashowu tribelet dialect, in the foothills to the north of the Kings River subgroup. (6) All remaining dialects, including Chukchansi and two or three others in the foothills to the north of Gashowu, and all the tribelet dialects of the valley floor (excepting those in subgroup 2).

More generally, Kroeber saw the dialects divided into two branches, a Foothill branch that included subgroups 1–5 and a Valley branch containing only the languages of subgroup 6. Kenneth Whistler and I (Whistler and Golla 1986), while accepting the validity of Kroeber's subgroups, rearranged them in a taxonomic hierarchy (Table 37). We saw the deepest split between **Poso Creek** (Kroeber's subgroup 1) and the rest, which we labeled General Yokuts. This group is in turn divided into **Buena Vista** (Kroeber's subgroup 2) and the rest, which we called Nim-Yokuts.[82] Nim-Yokuts is

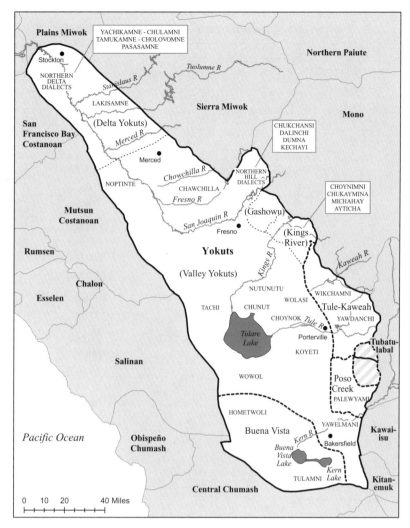

MAP 29. Yokuts territory and dialect groups.

divided into **Tule-Kaweah** (Kroeber's subgroup 3) and Northern Yokuts (his subgroups 4–6), whose three branches, **King's River, Gashowu,** and **Valley,** are coordinate. The Valley branch of Northern Yokuts has two divisions, **Northern Valley** and **Southern Valley.** The poorly attested **Delta** dialects can be treated either as a third division of Valley Yokuts (as in Whistler and Golla 1986) or as a fourth branch of Northern Yokuts (as in the present study).

3.26.1 Poso Creek

Palewyami, the only attested dialect of the Poso Creek subgroup, was spoken by a tribe whose principal village was at Altaw ('salt grass place'), on lower Poso Creek, a short distance above the valley floor to the northeast of Bakersfield. Tribal lands extended up Poso Creek to Poso Flat and possibly as far as Linns Valley. The drainage of Poso Creek above Cedar Creek, including Linns Valley, seems however to have belonged to another Yokuts tribe, the **Kumachisi,** who are usually assumed to have spoken a second Poso Creek dialect, although there is no attestation of it. Since it is known that

the Kumachisi intermarried with the Tubatulabal-speaking Bankalachi who lived at the head of Deer Creek, a few miles to the north, they were probably bilingual. The Kumachisi have occasionally been identified as the "Giamina," a small group in this area who appear to have spoken a distinct Uto-Aztecan language intermediate between Tubatulabal and Takic (¶3.34).

Palewyami is documented only in word lists, none of them extensive. The best materials were collected by Kroeber (1963) and Harrington (Gamble 1991a) during the first two decades of the twentieth century. These are supplemented by the general and natural history vocabularies obtained by Merriam in 1932 from the same speaker that Harrington had interviewed (Appendix A: W-22aa; see Berman 2002).

3.26.2 Buena Vista

Two named tribes are known to have spoken dialects of the Buena Vista subgroup. The **Tulamni** (plural, **Tulalmina**) lived in the area around Buena Vista Lake (now dry), about fifteen miles southwest of Bakersfield. Their principal

TABLE 37
Classification of Yokuts Dialects (Whistler and Golla 1986)

Primary Branches	Intermediate Subgroups	Attested Dialects
A. Poso Creek		Palewyami
B. General Yokuts	1. Buena Vista	Tulamni
		Hometwoli
	2. Nim-Yokuts	
	a. Tule-Kaweah	Yawdanchi
		Wikchamni
	b. Northern Yokuts	
	(1) Kings River	Choynimni
		Chukaimina
		Michahay
		Ayticha
	(2) Gashowu	Gashowu
	(3) Valley Yokuts	
	(a) Southern Valley	Tachi
		Chunut
		Wowol
		Yawelmani
		Nutunutu
		Wolasi
		Choynok
		Koyeti
	(b) Northern Hill/Valley	
	Northern Hill	Dumna
		Kechayi
		Chukchansi
	NorthernValley	Chawchila
		Noptịnṭe
	(4) Delta Yokuts	
	(a) Northwestern Delta	Yachikamne
		Cholovome-Tamcan
	(b) Southeastern Delta	Lakisamne
		Santa Cruz Mission

village, Tulamniw, was at the western end of the lake. The tribe known ethnographically as the **Hometwoli** (*xometwoli* 'southerners')—probably not their own name—lived around Kern Lake (also now dry), a few miles east of the Tulamni. A third tribe, the Tuholi, probably spoke a dialect belonging to this group, but there is no direct documentation of it. Their territory was immediately to the north of the Tulamni, along Kern River in the vicinity of Buttonwillow.

Documentation of the Buena Vista dialects is sparse. The earliest known attestation is a vocabulary, apparently of Hometwoli, obtained by Pinart in 1878 from a "Tejon" Indian said to be from the "rancheria of Tanesac" (1878n). Word lists

from both Tulamni and Hometwoli were collected by Kroeber in 1906 in the course of his dialect survey (1963), and Harrington obtained some miscellaneous data on both dialects in 1916–1917 (Mills 1985:141–160). Merriam's general and natural history vocabularies of Tulamni (Appendix A: W-22ee), obtained in 1905, are the most extensive attestation.

3.26.3 Tule-Kaweah

There are two attested dialects belonging to the Tule-Kaweah subgroup. **Yawdanchi** was spoken by a tribe that lived along Tule River from just east of Porterville to the headwaters of the North Fork. The South Fork of Tule River—the territory that became the Tule River Indian Reservation—belonged to another tribe, the Bokninwad, whose unattested dialect is said to have been close to Yawdanchi. **Wikchamni** was the dialect of a tribe on the Kaweah River, east of Visalia, one of a tight cluster of named groups in this resource-rich area. The principal Wikchamni village was in the vicinity of Lemoncove. The two groups immediately to the west of the Wikchamni, the Yokod and the Kawia (or Gawia), probably spoke other dialects of the Tule-Kaweah group. A few miles upstream on the Kaweah River were two Western Mono–speaking groups, the Patwisha on the Middle Fork and the Waksachi on the North Fork, with both of whom the Wikchamni were on good terms (see ¶3.31.1).

Yawdanchi was moderately well documented by Kroeber, who published a grammatical sketch of the dialect accompanied by a substantial vocabulary and eight texts (1907a:173–278). Wikchamni is one of the best documented of the Yokuts dialects, having been the focus of Gamble's research since 1970. He has published a grammar (1978) and several narrative texts (1980, 1994:46–61), and is preparing a dictionary. The earliest attestation of a Tule-Kaweah dialect is a vocabulary (dialect uncertain) collected in 1875 by Powers (1877:570–585, no. 1). There are also vocabularies from Merriam for both Yawdanchi (Appendix A: W-22x) and Wikchamni (W-22r).

3.26.4 Kings River

The best known dialect of the Kings River subgroup is **Choynimni,** spoken in a territory situated along a ten-mile stretch of Kings River between Mill Creek and Sanger. The principal Choynimni village was Tishechu, at the mouth of Mill Creek. Upstream on Mill Creek were the **Chukaymina,** centering on Squaw Valley, and to their south the **Michahay,** in the Drumm Valley area. Further up Mill Creek, in the vicinity of Dunlap, were the Entimbich, whose dialect has been reported to be either Western Mono or Kings River Yokuts. Both the Entimbich and Michahay are likely to have been bilingual, and their underlying ethnic affiliation remains unclear (R. Spier 1978b:426; see ¶1.5.2). Adjoining the Choynimni upstream on Kings River, above the present Pine Flat Reservoir, were the Western Mono Wobonuch. One further dialect of the Kings River group is attested, **Aiticha,** spoken south of Kings River downstream from the Choynimni, a few miles east of Sanger. On the north side of Kings River in the same area were the Toyhicha, whose undocumented dialect almost certainly belonged to the Kings River group as well.

The documentation of the Kings River dialects is relatively scanty. It consists largely of the comparative vocabularies that Kroeber collected during his 1906 dialect survey (Kroeber 1963) and the general and natural history vocabularies that Merriam collected for Choynimni and Chukaymina (Appendix A: W-22m, W-22o, and W-22m-o). Stanley Newman also collected a small amount of data on Choynimni, which he incorporated into his Yokuts grammar (1944).

FIGURE 62. Steve Soto, source of Palewyami data for C. Hart Merriam and J. P. Harrington. Tule River, June 1932. C. Hart Merriam collection of Native American photographs (W/22aa/P1 no.3). Courtesy of the Bancroft Library UCB.

FIGURE 63. Cecile Silva, Geoffrey Gamble's primary source of Wikchamni data. Courtesy of Geoffrey Gamble.

3.26.5 Gashowu

The Gashowu subgroup is attested only in the dialect of a single tribe, the **Gashowu.** Their small territory was located in the foothills southeast of the site of Friant Dam, a few miles east of Fresno on the upper reaches of Dry Creek and Little Dry Creek. The Gashowu dialect was documented by Kroeber in his 1906 dialect survey (1963) and by Merriam in a vocabulary from 1903 (Appendix A: W-22j). Newman also collected a scattering of data, most of it incorporated into his Yokuts grammar (1944).

3.26.6 Valley Yokuts

At least twenty attested tribal dialects are classified as Valley Yokuts, divided into two regional dialect networks, **Southern Valley** and **Northern Valley.** The **Delta** (or **Far Northern Valley**) dialect network is here treated separately (¶3.26.7). Since many of these groups were located on land that was occupied by Mexican and American settlers at an early date, boundaries are much less certain than in the foothills.

SOUTHERN VALLEY

Three of the Southern Valley dialect-tribes were clustered around Tulare Lake, whose abundance of fish and birds supported a large population. These included the **Tachi** to the north and west of the lake, the **Chunut** to the northeast, and the **Wowol** to the southeast.

The only Southern Valley dialect spoken to the south of these was **Yawelmani** (singular **Yawlamne**), which belonged to a—for the Yokuts—unusually large, mobile group that occupied an extensive territory at the far southern end of the San Joaquin Valley between Bakersfield and Rancho Tejon (they were often called the Tejoneños). Kroeber speculated (1959a:275) that the historic location of the Yawelmani, separating the Buena Vista and Poso Creek dialect groups, indicated their recent southward displacement from the Tulare Lake area.

To the north and east of Tulare Lake several tribes speaking Southern Valley dialects occupied land along the streams flowing out of the foothills into the sloughs and marshes of the valley floor. Five of these dialects are attested: **Nutunutu** along the south side of Kings River in the vicinity of Hanford, **Telamni** between Visalia and Goshen, **Wolasi** along Cameron Creek south of Visalia, **Choynok** along Inside and Bayou Creeks southeast of Tulare, and **Koyeti** along the Tule River west of Porterville.

The Southern Valley dialects are the best known varieties of Yokuts. The documentation of Yawelmani is especially extensive, beginning with a vocabulary ("Tinlinne") collected by Powers (1877:570–585). Kroeber collected enough data on Yawelmani to allow him to compose a short grammatical sketch of the language (1907a:279–307), and Newman made it the focus of his extensive fieldwork in

FIGURE 64. Ross Ellis, Stanley Newman's principal Yawelmani consultant, with his son. Tule River, June 1932. C. Hart Merriam collection of Native American photographs (W/22cc/P1 no.4). Courtesy of the Bancroft Library UCB.

1930–1931 (Newman 1932, 1944, 1946). Weigel worked with the last fluent speakers of Yawelmani, focusing on aspects of grammar, particularly syntax, not covered by previous investigators (Weigel 2006). Other dialects are also represented. In his 1906 survey, Kroeber collected vocabularies of Wechihit, Nutunutu, Tachi, Chunut, Wolasi, and Choynok (1963). Harrington, in addition to abundant data on "Tejoneño" (i.e., Yawelmani), collected material on Tachi, Chunut, Wowol, Nutunutu, Choynok, and Koyeti (Mills 1985:141–160). Merriam obtained general and natural history vocabularies of Nutunutu (Appendix A: W-22p), Tachi (W-22q), Chunut (W-22u), Koyeti (W-22z), and two varieties of Telamni (W-22s, W-22t), as well as of Yawelmani (W-22cc, W-22dd). The earliest attestation of Southern Valley Yokuts is a vocabulary collected near Tulare Lake by Adam Johnston around 1850 (Johnston 1854).

NORTHERN VALLEY AND NORTHERN HILL

The Northern Valley dialects were spoken along the San Joaquin River and its tributaries, from about fifteen miles above Friant Dam to the vicinity of Merced. Exclusive of the Northern Hill cluster (see next paragraph) only three dialects are clearly known: **Chawchila,** spoken along the Chowchilla River by a tribelet renowned for its fierceness in warfare (Kroeber 1925:485); the **"Ta-kin"** dialect attested in a vocabulary collected by Taylor (1856) at Knight's Ferry (then known as Dent's Ferry) on the Stanislaus, but evidently spoken originally somewhat further south;[83] and **Noptinte** (or **Nopthrinthre**), spoken at Mission San Juan Bautista by converts who came from a tribelet located on the west bank of the San Joaquin in the vicinity of Los Banos (Beeler 1971). Arroyo de la Cuesta (1837) listed several tribelets to the east and south of the Noptinte who also spoke what he called "Lathruunun" (apparently his term for Northern Valley Yokuts). Besides "Chausila" (clearly Chawchila) the list includes only one other name that can be identified from later sources, "Geuche," Kroeber's Heuchi, a tribelet he locates on the Fresno River near Madera (1925:484). Kroeber also included the Hoyima, Pitkachi, and Wakichi on the upper San Joaquin among the tribelets speaking Northern Valley dialects, but the only documentation of any of these is a few phrases in Hoyima (1907a:359).

The Northern Hill cluster, as its name implies, is a subgroup of Northern Valley tribelet dialects that were spoken in the Sierra foothills rather than on the valley floor. The areas along the upper San Joaquin and Fresno Rivers occupied by the Northern Hill tribelets lay only a few miles north of Gashowu territory, but the social connections of these communities were primarily with the valley tribelets downstream, and the linguistic discontinuity with Gashowu was abrupt. Kroeber reports that Northern Hill speakers could understand Gashowu only with difficulty (1925:481). The attested Northern Hill dialects are **Dumna** and **Kechayi**, spoken by two tribelets on the San Joaquin River above the present site of Millerton Lake; **Dalinchi**, spoken by the tribelet on Fine Gold Creek to the north of the Dumna and Kechayi; and **Chukchansi**, spoken by the tribelet on Coarsegold Creek, a tributary of the Fresno River, about fifteen miles to the north. The Chukchansi were in close contact with the Southern Sierra Miwok, and the dialect has many Miwok loanwords.

Another dialect belonging to the Northern Hill cluster is reported to have been spoken upstream from the rest on the San Joaquin. The only documentation of this dialect, known as **Toltichi**, is a short vocabulary that Kroeber obtained in 1906 from the old woman who was his source for Dumna (1907a:354–357, 1963:180–181). She did not, in fact, know Toltichi, but remembered some of the words used by the last speaker, a relative of hers who had died thirty years earlier. Although most of the vocabulary closely resembles Dumna and other Northern Hill dialects, the forms are obscured by radical phonetic shifts more characteristic of a speech impediment or of conscious word play than of normal sound change. A handful of the words, however, are completely different from their Northern Hill equivalents, and two of these—the numerals for 'one' and 'two', *nas* and *bis*—are identical to the same numerals in the special "old time" count collected by Harrington from a speaker of Chunut, a Southern Valley dialect near Tulare Lake (Gamble 1980:51–55; ¶4.10.4). In light of this discovery, and in the absence of any corroborating data, it seems unlikely that the "Toltichi"

vocabulary actually represents the normal speech of that local group. More likely it attests, at least in part, elements of a mission-era trading jargon (see ¶4.15.1).

Chawchila is documented by a vocabulary from Kroeber's dialect survey (1963) and by data collected by Newman and incorporated into his Yokuts grammar (1944). Noptinte is known from materials collected at Mission San Juan Bautista by Father Arroyo de la Cuesta (1810–1819, 1837; Beeler 1971). The dialects of the Northern Hill cluster are documented largely by materials on Chukchansi, the most extensive of which were obtained by Kroeber (1963), Newman (1944), and Collord (1968). One of the earliest attestations of Yokuts was a vocabulary of Chuckchansi ("Wichikik") collected in 1872 by Powers (1877:570–585), and Myers, working for Curtis, also collected a substantial Chukchansi vocabulary between 1915 and 1924 (Curtis 1907–1930, vol. 14:244–247). Dumna and Kechayi are attested in the comparative vocabularies in Kroeber's dialect survey (1963). In addition to general and natural history vocabularies of Chukchansi (Appendix A: W-22c), Merriam collected vocabularies of Dalinchi (W-22e) and Kechayi (W-22h).

3.26.7 Delta Yokuts

The Delta (or Far Northern Valley) dialects were spoken along the lower course of the San Joaquin River from its confluence with the Merced River east of Newman to the delta sloughs north of Stockton. Only fragmentary information exists on the tribelets and dialects of this area, because of early missionary activity and Euro-American settlement, and all the linguistic documentation comes from nineteenth- and early twentieth-century word lists (Kroeber 1959a:269–270, 1959b). There are nine Delta Yokuts tribelets whose local dialects are attested, and several others are known by name.[84] Farthest north were the **Yachikamne**, whose principal village (Yachik) was at Stockton. (Kroeber's informant called them "Chulamni," implying a connection to the Plains Miwok–speaking Chilamne on the Calaveras River some twenty miles to the east of Stockton.) A closely related group, the **Pasasamne**, was located near Lathrop, ten miles south of Stockton. About fifteen miles to the west, on the opposite side of the slough, were the **Tamukamne** (also known by their Costanoan name, **Tamcan**), and a few miles south of them, at Banta, east of Tracy, the **Cholovomne**. Upstream from the sloughs, on the lower Stanislaus River, lay the territory of the **Lakisamne**. Further south, in the vicinity of Turlock and Atwater, lay the territory of the **Atsnil**. Along the Merced River where it emerged from the foothills was a group whose name is variously rendered **Coconoon, Cucunun,** and **Huocon**. Along both banks of the San Joaquin between the mouth of the Stanislaus and the mouth of the Merced were two or three tribelets who probably also spoke varieties of Delta Yokuts. Members of these groups were brought to Mission Santa Cruz, along with some speakers of Atsnil and Coconoon, and it was from elderly survivors of the Indian community at Santa Cruz that Pinart and Henshaw collected the most important documentation of Delta Yokuts (Pinart 1878e; Henshaw 1888b).[85]

Although the scanty material that survives indicates that the Delta dialects can be classified as Valley Yokuts on phonological and morphological grounds, a small but significant portion of their lexicon is not cognate with that of other Yokuts languages. Some of these words are borrowings from adjacent Miwok and Costanoan languages, but most are unique to Delta Yokuts.

The attested Delta Yokuts dialects fall into two subgroups: (1) a smaller northwestern group along the edges of the Delta marshes, comprising Yachikamne, Tamukamne, and probably Cholovomne, and (2) a larger southeastern group upstream from the marshes, both along the San Joaquin and along the major rivers flowing west from the foothills, including Pasasamne, Lakisamne, and the southern dialects represented at Santa Cruz. The defining feature of the southeastern group is the regular replacement of the nasals (*m, n*) by the corresponding plain stops, usually but not always with prenasalization (ᵐp, ⁿt). For example Yachikamne *ponoy* '2', *šo:pʰin* '3', but Pasasamne *poⁿtoy* '2', *šo:pʰiⁿt* '3'. There are also some differences in vocabulary between the two groups.[86]

Yachikamne is documented in vocabularies collected by Pinart in 1880 (Pinart 1894; Merriam 1955:133–138) and by Kroeber in 1909 (Kroeber 1959b) from descendants of Yokuts converts at Mission San Jose. The only attestation of Tamukamne is about twenty words collected by Curtin (1884f; N. Smith 2007). A brief vocabulary of Pasasamne ("Lathrop"), collected by Barrett in 1906, was published by Kroeber (1908a:372). Lakisamne appears to be attested in a second vocabulary of Barrett's (Kroeber 1908a:373–374) and in a longer vocabulary of Gifford's (Kroeber 1959b, vocab. D), both collected at Knight's Ferry on the Stanislaus. Atsnil and other varieties from both sides of the San Joaquin near the mouth of the Merced are documented in a vocabulary collected by Pinart (1878e) and two vocabularies collected by Henshaw (1888b) at the Indian settlement near the former mission at Santa Cruz. A variety of Delta Yokuts is also attested in a vocabulary of the "Coconoons . . . a remnant of three bands under their chief, Nuella, on the Merced River" that was recorded by the Indian agent Adam Johnston around 1850 and printed in Schoolcraft (Johnston 1854).

Kroeber (1959b) collated and assessed the records of Delta Yokuts that were known to him in the 1950s, which included most of the preceding except for Henshaw's Santa Cruz vocabularies (1888b). The most recent addition to this small corpus consists of some words and phrases in Delta Yokuts and Spanish that were identified in 2002 on the endpapers of a San Francisco Bay Costanoan catechism from Mission Santa Clara. The dialect belongs to the northwestern (Yachikamne-Tamukamne) subgroup (Blevins and Golla 2005:57–61).

3.26.8 Survival

The Poso Creek, Buena Vista, and Gashowu subgroups have been extinct since the 1930s. Fewer than ten speakers of the Wikchamni (locally referred to as "Wukchumne") dialect of the Tule-Kaweah subgroup remain, most of them living on the Tule River Reservation near Porterville. A Wukchumne preschool has been started, weekly adult classes are given by elders, and several speakers and learners have participated in master-apprentice teaching. Half a dozen elderly speakers or partial speakers of the Choynimni ("Choinumne") dialect of the Kings River subgroup live in scattered locations in and around their traditional homeland. There are speakers of at least three Valley Yokuts dialects, including up to twenty-five fluent and semifluent speakers of Yawelmani ("Yowlumne") on the Tule River Reservation, a few speakers of Chukchansi at the Picayune and Table Mountain Rancherias in the foothills northeast of Fresno, and a few speakers of Tachi at the Santa Rosa Rancheria near Lemoore. Some language revival activity has occurred in the Chukchansi and Tachi communities, and several Yawelmani speakers and learners have formed master-apprentice partnerships.

3.26.9 Linguistic Structure

The best guide to Yokuts structure is Newman's grammar (1944). Although based primarily on Yawelmani, a Southern Valley dialect, it incorporates data from five other dialects and covers four of the six major classificatory subgroups; only Poso Creek and Buena Vista are lacking. Gamble's study of Wikchamni (1978) is written in a more accessible style but follows Newman's analysis closely. Weigel (2006)

TABLE 38
Yokuts Phonemes (Newman 1944)

Consonants							Vowels			
p	t	ṭ	c	č	k	ʔ	i / i:	(ï / ï:)*	u / u:
pʰ	tʰ	ṭʰ	cʰ	čʰ	kʰ		e / e:	(ə / ə:)	o / o:
p'	t'	ṭ'	c'	č'	k'			a / a:	
	s	ṣ			x	h			
m	n				(ŋ)†				
ṁ	ṅ				(ṅ)				
w	l		y						
ẇ	l'		ẏ						

*Unrounded high and mid central vowels are phonemically distinct only in the dialects of the Tule-Kaweah subgroup and in Hometwoli in the Buena Vista subgroup. Cognate forms in other dialects have front vowels.

†Velar nasals are phonemically distinct only in the Poso Creek, Buena Vista, and Tule-Kaweah subgroups. Cognate forms in the other subgroups have dental nasals.

provides an analysis of Yawelmani grammatical relations and reference tracking. There is a significant secondary literature on Yokuts devoted to theory-based reinterpretations of Newman's description of Yawelmani (e.g., Harris 1944, 1947; Kuroda 1967; Hockett 1967; see Pullum 1973 for a complete list to that date), but the narrow range of data on which some of this work focuses leaves it open to criticism (Blevins 2004; Hockett 1973).

Yokuts phonology is complex (Table 38). The basic phonemic inventory distinguishes four stops, *p, t, ṭ* (postalveolar or "retroflex"), and *k*, and two affricates, *c* [ts] and *č*, each series including a plain, aspirated, and glottalized member. The affricate contrasts have a low functional load and are unstable. They are best preserved in the Tule-Kaweah dialects (such as Wikchamni).[87] In many Southern Valley Yokuts dialects (such as Yawelmani) the palatal affricate has apical postalveolar (retroflex) articulation, *ç* [ṭṣ]. In many other dialects the two affricate series have merged, usually as a palatal series. Two nasals (*m* and *n*) occur both plain and glottalized, as do the approximants (*l, w, y*). There are three fricatives (*s, ṣ, x*). The two laryngeals (*h* and *ʔ*) are found in most positions, but *h* does not occur finally. In the Poso Creek, Buena Vista, and Tule-Kaweah subgroups there is also a velar nasal (*ŋ*), both plain and glottalized. In some Delta dialects the nasals are denasalized to plain stops, and in the Tule-Kaweah group *l* merges with

plain *t*. There are also a few mergers and shifts among the dialects involving the fricatives and affricates.

Most dialects have five vowels (*i, e, a, o, u*), both short and long. In all dialects of the Tule-Kaweah subgroup, and in the Hometwoli dialect of the Buena Vista branch, slightly rounded high and mid central vowels also occur ([ï] and [ə], written *ï* and *ë* in Gamble's Wikchamni orthography), possibly reflecting Numic influence (Kroeber 1907a:173–174; Gamble 1978:22–23; Whistler and Golla 1986:335–341). There is extensive vowel ablaut, involving harmony in height and frontness/backness between stem vowels and suffix vowels, as well as relationships involving length and laryngeal insertion. These ablaut patterns, described by Newman (1944), have been much discussed in the theoretical literature (cf. Kuroda 1967; Hockett 1973).

Yokuts noun and verb morphology is entirely suffixing, and there is considerable fusion between suffixes and stems owing to ablaut processes. Nouns, pronouns, and demonstratives are inflected for six cases (Table 39). Verbs consist of a stem, an optional thematizing suffix (marking such categories as passive, comitative, benefactive, and reflexive, as well as mode and aspect), and an obligatory final suffix marking mode, tense, or subordination. Subject and object are marked only by independent pronouns.

The complexity of the fusional morphology of the Yokuts verb is legendary among linguists (Hockett 1967). Nearly all

TABLE 39
Wikchamni Case Marking (Gamble 1978)

	Subject	Object	Possessive	Dative	Ablative	Locative
	(unmarked)	-V	-in	-ŋi	-nitʰ	-Vw
Nouns						
'bone'	č'iy	č'iya	č'iyin	č'iya: ŋi	č'iya:nitʰ	č'iyaw
'house'	ṭʰiʔ	ṭʰe:ʔi	ṭʰe:ʔin	ṭʰe:ŋi	ṭʰe:nitʰ	ṭʰew
'mouse'	p'ič'tu	p'ič'tuʔ	p'ič'tuʔun	p'ič'tuŋ	p'ič'tunutʰ	p'ič'tuw
'fire'	ʔusitʰ	ʔostʰo	ʔostʰin	ʔostʰoŋ	ʔostʰonitʰ	ʔostʰow
'hand'	pʰuṭʰoŋ	pʰuṭʰo:ŋa	pʰuṭʰo:ŋin	pʰuṭʰo:ŋaŋ	pʰuṭʰo:ŋanitʰ	pʰuṭʰo:ŋaw
'root'	ho:pʰut	ho:pʰut	ho:pʰutun	ho:pʰutŋu	ho:pʰutnitʰ	ho:pʰutaw
'dancer'	kʰaṁa:ʔač'	kʰaṁaʔč'i	kʰaṁaʔč'in	kʰaṁaʔč'iŋ	kʰaṁaʔč'initʰ	kʰaṁaʔč'iw
Pronouns						
1 sg	naʔ	nan	nim	na:naŋ	na:nanitʰ	na:naw
2 sg	maʔ	mam	min	ma:maŋ	ma:manitʰ	ma:maw
1 du inc	mak'	makʰwa	ma:kʰin	makʰwaŋ	makʰwanitʰ	makʰwaw
1 du exc	naʔak'	na:nak'	nimkʰin	na:nakʰŋi	na:nakʰnitʰ	na:nakiw
2 du	maʔak'	ma:mak'	minkʰin	ma:makʰŋi	ma:makʰnitʰ	ma:makiw
1 pl inc	maẏ	maẏwa	ma:ẏin	maẏwaŋ	maẏwanitʰ	maẏaw
1 pl exc	naʔan	na:nunwa	nimik'	na:nunwaŋ	na:nunwanitʰ	na:nunwaw
2 pl	maʔan	ma:munwa	minik'	ma:munwaŋ	ma:munwanitʰ	ma:munwaw

verb stems are basically disyllabic, and may be either open (CVCV) or closed (CVCVC). Six stem types are distinguished according to the length of the basic vowels (two long-vowel syllables are not permitted), illustrated by Wikchamni *tuyu-* 'to eat' (CVCV), *ʔi:pʰi-* 'to swim'(CV:CV), *hoyo:-* 'to name' (CVCV:), *pʰïwïs-* 'to pound' (CVCVC), *pi:win-* 'to sew" (CV:CVC), and *hiwi:tʰ-* 'to walk' (CVCVC:). Suffixes fall into different phonological classes according to the ablaut grade that they require the basic vowels of the stem to assume (lengthened, shortened, a-colored, zeroed, etc.). The interaction of the basic shape of a given stem with the ablaut-class requirements of a given suffix—sometimes further modified by rules of vowel harmony—typically results in an occurring form that, while theoretically predictable, is for all practical purposes idiomatic to that combination of stem and suffix. For example, in Wikchamni the suffixes *-iš* 'aorist tense', *-itʰ* 'passive aorist', and *-ʔič'* 'agentive' combine with the stem *pʰičʰiw-* 'to grab' to produce *pʰičʰiwiš* 'grabbed', *pʰičʰwitʰ* 'was grabbed', and *pʰičʰe:wič'* 'policeman' (< 'one who grabs'). The same suffixes combine with the stem *ʔu:šu-* 'to steal' to produce *ʔoššu* 'stole', *ʔusa:ʔitʰ* 'stolen', and *ʔuso:ʔuč'* 'thief', and with *t'oyox-* 'to doctor' to produce *t'uyixši* 'doctored', *t'uyxitʰ* 'was doctored', and *t'oyo:xač'* 'one who doctors'.

3.26.10 Nomenclature

"Yokuts" [yókəts] is from Southern Valley Yokuts *yokʰoc'* 'person', and has been in wide use as the name of the people and language since at least the time of Powers (1877:369). During the mission period the Yokuts were usually referred to as *los Tulareños* 'those of the tules'. Powell's proposal (1891:90–91) that "Mariposan" be adopted as the name of the stock was not widely accepted, nor has the technical coinage "Yokutsan" (e.g., Shipley 1978:93) found favor. The back-formation "Yokut" (taking Yokuts as an English collective plural) is heard with increasing frequency, but is etymologically incorrect.

3.27 Miwok Languages

Miwok is a family of five moderately diverse languages, two of which (Coast Miwok and Sierra Miwok) have significant regional dialects (Table 40). The languages fall into two distinct branches, **Western Miwok,** in Marin, Sonoma, and Lake Counties, and **Eastern Miwok,** from Contra Costa County east into the Sierra Nevada. The Miwok languages have been extensively studied, and the family is one of the best understood in California (see Broadbent and Callaghan 1960; Callaghan 1972). Catherine Callaghan, the modern scholar most familiar with the family, estimates that it has a time depth of 2,500 to 3,000 years (1997a:18), which accords with the lexicostatistical calculations cited by Levy (1978a) that indicate Western and Eastern Miwok began to diverge about 500 BC.

TABLE 40
Classification of the Miwok Languages

Western Miwok
    Coast Miwok
        Bodega Miwok
        Marin Miwok (Nicasio, Tomales)
    Lake Miwok
Eastern Miwok
    Bay Miwok (only Saclan attested)
    Plains Miwok
    Sierra Miwok
        Northern Sierra Miwok
        Central Sierra Miwok
        Southern Sierra Miwok

3.27.1 Western Miwok

COAST MIWOK

Coast Miwok was spoken in a number of local dialects from Bodega Bay across the Petaluma Plain to Sonoma Valley and the lower Napa River (Kroeber 1957:215–216; see Map 30). According to Gibbs, who provides the earliest ethnogeographic account of Coast Miwok territory, the southernmost part of the Marin peninsula belonged to another people ("called by the Spanish Tulares"), presumably a tribelet of San Francisco Bay Costanoans (Gibbs 1853c:421).[88] The principal division seems to have been between the interior and the coast; the people from Tomales Bay to Bodega Bay were collectively called *tamal-ko* 'coast people' (cf. *tamal-payiṣ* 'coast mountain', Mount Tamalpais).

Coast Miwok was one of the first California Indian languages to be encountered by Europeans—at Drake's Bay in 1579 (Heizer 1947).[89] With the exception of the Bodega Bay dialect, however, the language is attested only in short word lists and a few scraps of text. Callaghan and Bond (n.d.) have brought together many of the extant data. Their sources include Arroyo de la Cuesta (1837), Barrett (1908a:68–80, "Southern Moquelumnan"), Callaghan (1964b), Duflot de Mofras (1844), Hale (1846), Henshaw (1888a), Kelly (1931–1932), Kroeber (1911a:315–318), and Sawyer (1960), as well as the words and phrases reported in accounts of Drake's voyage (collated in Heizer 1947). Not included in this compilation is the Sonoma Valley ("Tchoko-yem") vocabulary collected by Gibbs in 1851 (1853b), a vocabulary of the Napa dialect collected by Curtin (1884f; see also numerals in 1889k), and the vocabularies that Merriam collected from speakers of the Tomales Bay dialect (Appendix A: V-21r). During her ethnographic survey of the area in 1931–1932, Isabel Kelly was able to find two

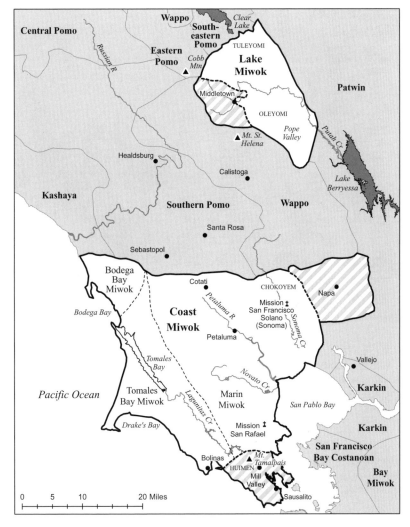

MAP 30. Western Miwok languages and dialects.

relatively fluent speakers, María Copa Freas (Nicasio) and Tom Smith (Bodega Bay), but collected only terms of ethnographic relevance; Kelly's notes have been published by Collier and Thalman (1996).

The only linguistically accurate attestations of Coast Miwok are a short Nicasio vocabulary collected from María Copa Freas's daughter, Julia Elgin, by Jesse Sawyer (1960), and much more extensive lexical data from the Bodega Bay dialect collected from Tom Smith's daughter, Sarah Ballard, by Callaghan (published in dictionary format as Callaghan 1970) and later by Richard Applegate (available online in Applegate n.d.).[90] Earlier documentation of the Bodega Bay dialect includes a vocabulary ("Olamentke") collected in the 1830s by Peter Kostromitinov, manager of the Russian American Company's outpost at Fort Ross (Wrangell and Kostromitinov 1839:233–254); a survey vocabulary collected by S. A. Barrett between 1903 and 1906 (1908a:68–80, "Western Moquelumnan"); and a vocabulary collected by Merriam (Appendix A: V-21s).

LAKE MIWOK

Lake Miwok was spoken in a small area southeast of Clear Lake, separated from Coast Miwok territory by the Yukian-speaking Wappos of Napa Valley. There were two Lake Miwok tribelets, *Tuleyomi,* with a major village on Cache Creek about four miles south of Lower Lake, and *Oleyomi,* in Coyote Valley on upper Putah Creek and in Pope Valley, with a major village near Middletown (Merriam 1907; Barrett 1908a:314–318; Callaghan 1978a:264). The Oleyomi had close connections to the Wappo, and the area around Middletown was apparently bilingual. It was included in Wappo territory by Barrett (1908a) and Kroeber (1925), but Merriam persuasively argued that the dominant language of the tribelet was Lake Miwok (1955:43–48).

Despite their geographical separation, the Coast and Lake Miwoks appear to have maintained regular trading contact, and even intermarried. Nevertheless, the two languages, while closely related, are quite distinct both phonologically

FIGURE 65. María Copa Freas, Isabel Kelly's main consultant for Marin Miwok (1931–1932), with her daughter Julia (Elgin). Lytton, Sonoma County, September 1927. C. Hart Merriam collection of Native American photographs (V/21r/P1 no.2). Courtesy of the Bancroft Library UCB.

FIGURE 66. Henry Knight and his sons at Oleyome, near Middletown, August 1927. Henry Knight was an important source of Lake Miwok data for C. Hart Merriam and L. S. Freeland, and his sons John and James Knight were Catherine Callaghan's primary consultants in the 1950s and 1960s. C. Hart Merriam collection of Native American photographs (V/21q/P3 no.5). Courtesy of the Bancroft Library UCB.

and lexically, comparable in this regard to Spanish and Italian. Many of the differences can be attributed to a strong influence on Lake Miwok from adjoining non-Miwok languages, in particular from Hill Patwin. In addition to having a substantial number of loanwords from Patwin, Lake Miwok has a very un-Miwok-like phonemic inventory that closely resembles Patwin (and to a lesser extent Pomo) in including aspirated and glottalized stops and affricates, a lateral fricative and affricate, and voiced *b* and *d* (Callaghan 1964a).[91]

The Patwin influence on Lake Miwok reflects a more general cultural penetration of the Clear Lake basin from the Sacramento Valley in the late prehistoric period, typified by the spread of elaborate Kuksu ceremonialism from Southern Patwin and Valley Nisenan territory. A language shift from Miwok to Patwin seems to have occurred relatively recently in the western portions of the Hill Patwin area, where several Patwin place-names, including the name of a village on Putah Creek near Winters (Liwai-to), have plausible Western Miwok etymologies (Callaghan n.d.[a]). Whistler (1977a) has pointed to evidence of an older Miwok substratum throughout Patwin territory, particularly in terms for local flora (¶5.3.4).

Lake Miwok has been extensively documented by Catherine Callaghan, whose unpublished dissertation (1963) is a grammar of the language. She has published a dictionary (1965) and three analyzed texts (1977, 1978b, 1980a). L. S. Freeland published several texts and a brief grammatical

sketch, based on fieldwork carried out in the 1920s and 1930s (Freeland 1947). There is earlier documentation by S. A. Barrett (1908a:68–80, "Northern Moquelumnan") and Merriam (Appendix A: V-21q).

3.27.2 Eastern Miwok

Western and Eastern Miwok, although similar phonologically, are quite distinct in vocabulary and grammar. While the Western Miwok languages, like Costanoan, have a relatively simple verbal morphology, the Eastern (particularly the Sierra) Miwok languages have quite complex verbal paradigms. Callaghan likens the differences to those distinguishing English from German (1980b), and a long period of communicative separation is indicated. According to Freeland, "the Miwok of the Sierras . . . had no contact with the groups to the west, and apparently did not know of their existence" (1951:iii). Despite the depth of the split, however, the westernmost Eastern Miwok language, Bay Miwok, was spoken in villages in western Contra Costa County that lay only a few miles from Coast Miwok villages on the north shore of San Pablo Bay (Map 31).

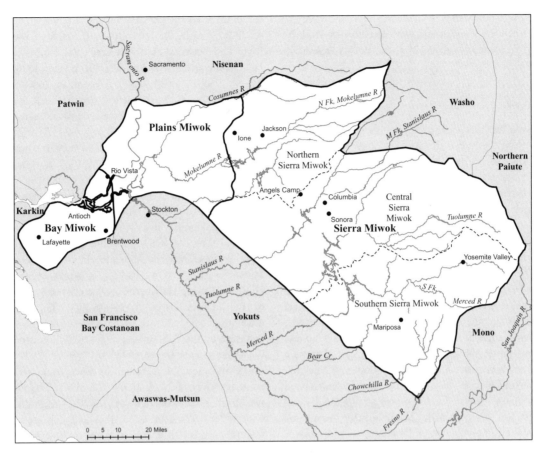

MAP 31. Eastern Miwok languages and dialects.

BAY MIWOK

Very little is known about Bay Miwok, which is recorded only in a short vocabulary collected by Arroyo de la Cuesta in 1821 (Arroyo 1837; see also Beeler 1955a, 1959; Callaghan 1971). Arroyo's vocabulary reflects the speech of the *Saclan* tribelet, whose territory was located in the vicinity of Lafayette and Walnut Creek.[92] Personal names and other information in the mission records indicate that other varieties of the same language were spoken across Contra Costa County from the East Bay hills to Antioch and Brentwood (Milliken 1995:228–261; Callaghan 1997b). The Saclan vocabulary documents a language that is clearly Eastern Miwok in phonology and lexicon, as well as in morphology to the extent it is attested, but which is also clearly distinct from either Sierra or Plains Miwok, although slightly closer to the latter (Callaghan 1971). Seven of the sixty-three attested words are unique to Bay Miwok, including the numerals 'five' and 'ten' (Beeler 1955a).

PLAINS MIWOK

Plains Miwok is a distinct language, quite different from adjoining Sierra Miwok in vocabulary, although very similar in phonology and grammar (Berman 1986a:305–306). The differences between Plains and Bay Miwok are harder to judge, owing to the paucity of data on the latter. The territory of the Plains Miwok in the nineteenth century was on the east bank of the Sacramento River, from the city of Sacramento on the north to Rio Vista on the south, and reached eastward to the first line of hills, where Sierra Miwok territory began. Following Merriam's (1968) analysis of mission records, Levy (1978a:399) locates twenty-eight Plains Miwok tribelets, eleven on the Sacramento, nine on the lower Mokelumne, and eight on the lower Cosumnes. Although the details of precontact ethnogeography in the Delta area are speculative, there is good evidence that Plains Miwok speakers (rather than Southern Patwin) formerly occupied areas on both the east and west banks of the Sacramento south of Rio Vista and thus directly bordered on Bay Miwok territory in the vicinity of Antioch (Bennyhoff 1977; Kroeber 1957:217).[93]

Plains Miwok has been extensively documented by Callaghan, and she has published a full dictionary (1984). The speakers with whom she worked spoke the dialects of Jackson Valley (west of Ione) and of Lockeford (between Ione and Stockton). Earlier documentation is sparse, the most important publications being a vocabulary by Barrett (1908b) and comparative notes by Kroeber (1911a:292–319). Merriam collected vocabularies from the Lockeford dialect (Appendix A: V-21l), the Mokosumni dialect (V-21g), and the Sherman Island dialect ("Wi-pa" or Guaypem,

V-21i). The first attestation of Plains Miwok is a vocabulary ("Talatui") collected at Sutter's New Helvetia in 1841 by James Dwight Dana, the geologist of the Wilkes Expedition (Dana 1846).

SIERRA MIWOK

Sierra Miwok territory extended from the Cosumnes River on the north to the Fresno River on the south and included both the foothills and the higher elevations of the Sierra Nevada. The adjacent valley floor was occupied by Yokuts speakers. This appears to have been a single language area within which three well-differentiated dialects, or emergent languages, were spoken—Northern, Central, and Southern Sierra Miwok.[94]

Although distinct on linguistic grounds, it is not clear to what extent the three major Sierra Miwok dialects represented significant social facts in precontact times. They were not named, and they had no apparent sociopolitical correlates. Callaghan compares the differentiation of the Sierra Miwok dialects to that of Swedish, Danish, and Norwegian, noting that there was at least partial mutual intelligibility throughout the dialect continuum (Callaghan 1987:5).[95] Subdialectal varieties also existed, correlated with individual tribelets. The differences among the dialects and subdialects are primarily phonetic and lexical; all varieties of Sierra Miwok are similar enough in morphosyntactic structure to be easily describable in a single grammatical model (Freeland 1951).

Northern Sierra Miwok was spoken over much of Amador County and northern Calaveras County, along the upper Mokelumne and Calaveras rivers and along the south fork of the Cosumnes. The middle and north forks of the Cosumnes were in Nisenan territory. On the west, Northern Sierra Miwok territory adjoined Plains Miwok territory at the first line of foothills. On the east it reached high into the Sierra Nevada, although not to the headwaters of the Mokelumne River, which was in Washo territory. Levy (1978a:400) identifies twenty-three lineage settlements, probably representing eight tribelets: Omo Ranch and Plymouth-Fiddletown on the south fork of the Cosumnes; Ione–Sutter Creek; Buena Vista; Jackson Creek; West Point on the Mokelumne; and Rail Road Flat and San Andreas on the Calaveras.

Central Sierra Miwok was spoken in the southern part of Calaveras County and in most of Tuolumne County, along the Stanislaus and Tuolomne Rivers. Levy (1978a:400) identifies fifty-seven lineage settlements. One significant cluster, possibly representing a single tribelet, was in the lower foothills near Knight's Ferry on the Stanislaus River. Most of the other settlements were located at higher elevations on the Stanislaus in the vicinity of Angels Camp and Columbia or on the north fork of the Tuolumne.

Southern Sierra Miwok was spoken over much of Mariposa County, between the Merced and Chowchilla Rivers. Levy (1978a:400) identifies thirty-nine lineage settlements, which appear to represent seven tribelets. Three of these were in the lower foothills, on the lower Merced River and between Mariposa Creek and Chowchilla River. Each of these tribelets had numerous lineage settlements, as did the tribelet on the upper Merced, in Yosemite Valley. The remaining three tribelets (on Bull Creek, Bear Creek, and the south fork of the Merced) consisted of only one or two settlements.

Sierra Miwok is relatively well documented. Barrett published comparative vocabularies of the three Sierra dialects that he collected in 1906 (1908b:362–368), and Kroeber published a sketch of the West Point variety of Northern Sierra Miwok, with comparative notes on Central Sierra and Plains Miwok, based on materials collected in 1908 (1911a:278–319). Merriam collected vocabularies from Northern Miwok (Appendix A: V-21a), Central Sierra Miwok (V-21c), and two varieties of Southern Sierra Miwok (V-21d, V-21e). Harrington collected some materials on Northern Sierra Miwok in 1939 (Mills 1985:21–24). Earlier attestations include a vocabulary collected by Adam Johnston on the Tuolumne around 1850 (Johnston 1854), a Calaveras vocabuary collected by Powers (1877:535–559, no.1), and materials obtained by Gatschet in 1877 from a Southern Sierra Miwok of the "Chumteya" band while he was visiting New York (Powers 1877:535–559, no.8).

Between 1921 and 1932, Freeland collected extensive materials on all three dialects. She published a grammar (Freeland 1951) based primarily on the Knights Ferry variety of the Central Sierra dialect, but also including information from one of the eastern varieties of the same dialect (apparently the upper Stanislaus River), the West Point variety of Northern Sierra dialect, and the Yosemite variety of the Southern Sierra dialect. Later, both a Central Sierra dictionary with texts (Freeland and Broadbent 1960) and a second set of Central Sierra and Southern Sierra texts (Berman 1982a) were published from Freeland's materials.

In visits beginning in 1956 and extending over three decades, Callaghan extensively documented the three surviving varieties of Northern Sierra Miwok—Camanche (Lower Mokelumne), Fiddletown, and Ione—and published a full dictionary based on her materials (1987). Sylvia Broadbent documented the Southern Sierra dialect during fieldwork between 1955 and 1961 and published a grammar with texts and a dictionary (1964). Her primary consultant spoke the Yosemite variety, but she also worked with speakers of the Mariposa and Bootjack varieties (Mariposa Creek and Chowchilla River).

3.27.3 Survival

Coast Miwok is now extinct. As of 2008, two or three partial speakers of Lake Miwok were living at the Middletown Rancheria southeast of Clear Lake, but none of them actively used the language.

Two of the Eastern Miwok languages, Bay Miwok and Plains Miwok, have no surviving native speakers. A number

FIGURE 67. Sylvia Broadbent being honored in 2003 for her work on Southern Sierra Miwok. Tribal member Sandra Chapman in foreground. Photo by James Lin, University of California, Riverside.

of descendants of the Sierra Miwoks (many of whom prefer the name "Miwuk") live in a scattering of small communities in and around their historic territory in Amador, Calaveras, Tuolumne, and Mariposa Counties. The most thriving of the dialects is Northern Sierra Miwok, spoken at the Jackson Rancheria, near West Point in Calaveras County. It is estimated that there are between six and twelve speakers, only one of whom has active conversational fluency. There is a sustained community interest in language revival, and several of the speakers meet regularly as an informal language forum. In the 1980s a practical orthography was established, and elementary curricular materials were prepared for a (now-terminated) bilingual program in the San Juan Unified School District in Carmichael, near Sacramento, where a number of Sierra Miwok families have relocated. Suzanne Wash, a linguist working closely with the Northern Sierra Miwok community, has extensively documented the language in recent years and has collected numerous audiotapes and videotapes of speakers. Central Sierra Miwok and Southern Sierra Miwok have a few semispeakers or passive speakers, but no overt community activity appears to be focused on their survival or revitalization.

3.27.4 Linguistic Structure

Although the Miwok lexicon is quite well documented and accessible in several published dictionaries, the only general presentations of Miwok grammar are Freeland's older but still useful study of Sierra Miwok (1951), Broadbent's sketch of Southern Sierra Miwok (1964:11–139; see also Hamp 1966b), and Callaghan's unpublished dissertation on Lake Miwok (1963). There is also a short synopsis of Northern Sierra Miwok phonology and morphology in Callaghan's dictionary of that dialect (1987:16–31). Callaghan has published a series of comparative papers on Miwok phonology

(1972), numerals (1979, 1994), nominal cases (1980b), ablaut (1986a), and cardinal directions (1986b).

Except for Lake Miwok, the phonology of the Miwok languages is characterized by a very small phonemic inventory (Table 41). The four stops, *p, t* (dental or alveolar), *ṭ* (postalveolar or "retroflex"), and *k,* have no laryngeal feature contrasts. There is one affricate, varying from dialect to dialect between dental *c* [ts], postalveolar *c̣* [ṭṣ], and palatal *č*; two fricatives (*s* and either *ṣ* or *š*), merging into a single phoneme in some dialects; two basic nasals (*m, n*), with a velar nasal (*ŋ*) also phonemically distinct in Sierra Miwok; three approximants (*l, w, y*); and two laryngeals (*h, ?*). Lake Miwok sharply deviates from this pattern by distinguishing aspirated and glottalized members for all four stop series, as well as voiced members for the labial and dental series (*b, d*). It also has a lateral fricative (*ł*) and a glottalized lateral affricate (*ƛ'*). All these phonemic contrasts have entered the language through numerous lexical borrowings from neighboring Hill Patwin or Southeastern Pomo, primarily the former (Callaghan 1964a). All Miwok languages have *i, e, a, o,* and *u,* with an additional high central vowel *ï* (written *y* by Callaghan and Broadbent) in Sierra Miwok, and both a high and a mid central vowel (*ï, ə*) in Plains Miwok. All vowels have phonemic contrasts for length. All consonants can be geminated in medial position.

The Miwok languages have a suffixing morphology, characterized by a system of stem ablaut in which the consonants and vowels of stems vary in length according to the suffixes that follow (Callaghan 1986a). Nouns are inflected for case, with as many as nine cases distinguished (Table 42). Possessed nouns are marked for person and number of possessor by a set of suffixes that usually follow case markers (Northern Sierra: *koca-ṭ* 'my house', *koca?-nï* 'your sg. house', *koca?-sï* 'his/her house', *koca?-mas* 'our house', *koca?-mok* 'your pl. house', *koca?-ko* 'their house'). Verbs are marked for a variety of derivational categories by thematic suffixes. Pronominal arguments are marked by a set of independent pronouns, inflected for case. In Eastern Miwok, verbs are also inflected for subject and object by final suffixes, with separate sets of pronominal suffixes used in declarative, possessive, volitional, and nominal verbs. The fusion of categories in Eastern Miwok verb suffixes is reminiscent of the complex verb endings found in many Indo-European languages (Callaghan 1980b).

TABLE 41

Sierra Miwok Phonemes (Freeland 1951; Broadbent 1964)

All consonants can be geminated in medial position

Consonants						Vowels		
p	t	ṭ	č	k	?	i / i:	ï / ï:	u / u:
		s		š	h	e / e:		o / o:
m	n			ŋ			a / a:	
w	l		y					

TABLE 42
Northern Sierra Miwok Case Inflection (Callaghan 1987b)

Nouns

		naŋŋa- 'man'	waka:l-ï- 'creek'
Subject	-ʔ	naŋŋaʔ	waka:liʔ
Object	-y	naŋŋay	waka:liy
Possessive	-ŋ	naŋŋaŋ	waka:liŋ
Allative	-(t)t(o) ("toward . . .")	naŋŋato	waka:lït
Locative	-m/-mï-ʔ ("at, on, in . . .")	naŋŋam	waka:lïm, wakalmïʔ
Ablative	-mmï-ʔ ("from, out of . . .")	naŋŋammïʔ	waka:lïmmïʔ
Instrumental	-ssï ("by means of . . .")	naŋŋassï	waka:lïssï

Independent Pronouns

	1 sg	2 sg	3 sg	1 pl	2 pl	3 pl
Subject	kanniʔ	miʔ	ʔissakiʔ	massiʔ	mikoʔ	ʔissakkoʔ
Object	kanniy	mi:niy	ʔissakïy	massiy	mikoy	ʔissakkoy
Possessive	kanïŋ	mi:nïŋ	ʔissakïŋ	masiŋ	mikoŋ	ʔissakkoŋ

As with Yokuts (¶3.26.9), there is an extensive secondary literature on (Sierra) Miwok morphophonology, based mainly on forms cited in Freeland (1951) and Broadbent (1964) (e.g., N. Smith 1985; Sloan 1991; J. Brown 2003).

3.27.5 Nomenclature

The name "Miwok" [míwɔk] or "Miwuk" [míwək], from Sierra Miwok miwwïk 'people, Indians', was applied by Powers only to the Plains and Sierra Miwok people and language (1877:346–347). Powell, in the linguistic classification he appended to Powers (see Box 4), grouped Sierra, Plains, and Coast Miwok together with Costanoan in the "Mutsun" family—essentially Utian. In his general classification, however, Powell separated Miwok and Costanoan, calling the former "Moquelumnan" (1891:92–93), the term earlier proposed by the English comparativist Latham (1856:81). Unlike the majority of Powell's coinages, this name gained some acceptance among Californianists and was employed by Kroeber and others as late as 1907. Barrett (1908b), however, returned to Powers's extended use of "Miwok," and he was soon followed by most specialists. The only dissenter was Merriam, who instead fashioned a terminology to reflect native nomenclature: "Miwuk" for Sierra Miwok, "Mewko" for Plains and Bay Miwok (from Plains Miwok miwkoʔ 'people'), "Inneko" for Western Miwok, and "Mewan" for the family as a whole (Merriam 1907).

3.28 Costanoan (Ohlone) Languages

Costanoan is a family of six not very deeply differentiated languages or dialect clusters (Table 43). All of these are now extinct, and only three varieties (Mutsun, Rumsen, and Chocheño) survived long enough to be accurately documented by a twentieth-century linguist. The subdivisions of the family constitute a rough north-south chain (Map 32), within which three languages stand out with some degree of clarity: *San Francisco Bay Costanoan* (the San Francisco Bay varieties exclusive of Karkin); *Mutsun,* the language of the Pajaro River valley from the ocean near Castroville to east of Hollister; and the *Rumsen* dialect cluster of the Monterey and Carmel area. Mutsun and Rumsen, although quite distinct, appear to share a common core of innovations and are often grouped as "Southern Costanoan."[96] The classification of the remaining varieties is

TABLE 43
Classification of the Costanoan Languages

Karkin

San Francisco Bay Costanoan

    Ramaytush (San Francisco Costanoan)

    Chocheño (East Bay Costanoan)

    Tamyen (Santa Clara Costanoan)

Mutsun-Awaswas

    Awaswas (Santa Cruz Costanoan)

    Mutsun (San Juan Bautista Costanoan)

Rumsen (Monterey-Carmel Costanoan)

Chalon (Soledad Costanoan)

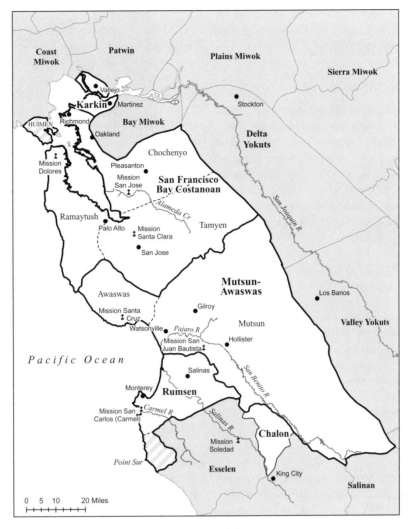

MAP 32. Costanoan languages and major attested dialects.

less certain. The northernmost dialect, **Karkin,** which was spoken along Carquinez Strait, is very poorly attested but appears to be distinct enough from the other varieties spoken around San Francisco Bay to warrant classification as a separate language. The **Awaswas** varieties attested from Mission Santa Cruz show features characteristic both of Mutsun and of San Francisco Bay Costanoan and could be grouped with either, or could be treated as an intermediate language. The **Chalon** dialect, spoken in the remote southeastern corner of Costanoan territory, is lexically similar to Mutsun and Rumsen but has phonological and grammatical features that align it with the more northerly Costanoan languages; thus, like Karkin, it is usually classified as a separate unit.

All these divisions are shallow. Lexicostatistical estimates indicate that the attested diversity is the product of no more than 1,500 to 2,000 years (Levy 1978b:486; Callaghan 1992b), and although not all varieties were mutually intelligibile on first hearing, the degree of similarity among them seems to have allowed at least restricted communication. The postcontact consolidation of Costanoan dialectal variation into a small number of mission-based lingua francas, as well as the loss of intermediate dialect varieties, may have artificially sharpened dialect differences, as suggested by Milliken (1995:24–26).

3.28.1 Karkin

The northernmost variety of Costanoan, Karkin, was spoken in a single tribelet ("los Carquines" is the only name that has survived) whose territory included villages on both the northern and southern shores of Carquinez Strait in the vicinity of modern Crockett, Martinez, and Vallejo (Kroeber 1957.217; Milliken 1995:238). The sole attestation of Karkin is a short vocabulary that was obtained by Arroyo de la Cuesta during a visit to San Francisco in 1821 (Beeler 1961b; Callaghan 1988a).[97] The distinctive lexical and grammatical features that Arroyo's word list exhibits indicate that Karkin was quite distinct from the other Costanoan varieties spoken around San Francisco Bay, and most specialists follow Beeler (1961b) in considering it a separate language. Among the unique features of Karkin are the words for 'man' and 'woman', which differ from those found elsewhere in Costanoan and are said by Beeler to resemble the Esselen forms (Beeler 1977:44; see ¶5.2.11).

3.28.2 San Francisco Bay Costanoan

With the exception of Karkin, all the varieties of Costanoan attested from the San Francisco Bay area represent mildly divergent (and undoubtedly mutually intelligible) local varieties of a single type of Costanoan speech (Kroeber 1910:241). Variation within San Francisco Bay Costanoan is usually treated in terms of the dialects, or more accurately the clusters of local varieties, that were associated with the three missions of the area: *Chocheño* or *Chochenyo* (Mission San Jose),[98] *Tamyen* (Mission Santa Clara), and *Ramaytush* (Mission Dolores).

CHOCHEÑO

The Chocheño varieties were spoken along the eastern shore of San Francisco Bay from the Richmond–San Pablo area (where the *Huchiun* or *Juchiun* variety is attested)[99] to Hayward (the Irgin or Yrgin tribelet along San Lorenzo Creek)[100] and Fremont (the Tuibun and Alson tribelets along lower Alameda Creek and to the south). Closely related local varieties were spoken in the interior of Alameda County in tribelets in the San Ramon and Dublin area, and in the Livermore Valley (for names and probable locations see Milliken 1995; 2008).

There is some uncertainty in the mission records about the linguistic affiliation and exact location of the Jalquin tribelet (Milliken 1995:244–246; 2008:32–41). The Jalquins lived in the hills east of Oakland, where they were apparently affiliated with the Saclans, who are definitely known to have been speakers of Bay Miwok (¶3.27.2). But there is also reason to believe that the Jalquins shared territory with the Irgins, or that the two names were synonyms for the same people. In either case, some degree of Miwok-Costanoan bilingualism is indicated in the Hayward–San Lorenzo area, which tallies with references in Font's diary of the 1776 Anza expedition to a sharp language boundary between Fremont and Hayward (Cook 1957:132–133; Beeler 1961b:195, fn.16). The two Chocheño speakers that Harrington worked with in the 1920s (discussed later in this section), who ordinarily made a distinction only between Chocheño and other mission dialects ("Clareño" for the speech of the Indians at Mission Santa Clara, "Doloreño" for the Indians at Mission Dolores in San Francisco), consistently distinguished an "Estereño" dialect that was apparently spoken in the estuaries along the East Bay shoreline north of Hayward. The significance of this remains to be assessed, but one likely explanation is that the Jalquins are meant, most of whom joined Mission Dolores (Milliken 2008:35).

Mission San Jose was not established until 1797. Prior to then, many East Bay Costanoans were recruited into the San Francisco and Santa Clara missions. The earliest known

FIGURE 68. María de los Angeles Colós, J. P. Harrington's principal source of data on Chocheño (San Francisco Bay Costanoan). Courtesy of the National Anthropological Archives, Smithsonian Institution (91-30287).

attestation of the Chocheño dialect is a copy of a short vocabulary of the Juchiun variety (mislabeled "Juichun") that was obtained by Arroyo de la Cuesta in 1821 from an Indian at Mission Dolores (Arroyo 1837; Beeler 1961b:192–193). After 1797, however, Mission San Jose (on former Tuibun territory in present-day Fremont) was the principal mission at which Chocheño was spoken (Milliken 2002). Short vocabularies of Chocheño were collected from former members of the Mission San Jose community in the late nineteenth century by Curtin (1884f, "Niles"; see also Beeler 1961b:192; Milliken 2008:91–92) and in the early twentieth century by Kroeber (1910:242–249), Merriam (¶Appendix A: S-18a), and Mason (1916a:470–472).

These fragmentary attestations are overshadowed by the extensive and accurate data amassed by Harrington in 1921 and 1929 from Angela (María de los Angeles) Colós and José Guzman. The last speakers of Chocheño (or of any variety of San Francisco Bay Costanoan), they lived in the postmission community of Alisal near Pleasanton (Mills 1985:81–82, 87–89; Ortiz 1994:100–104). (Kroeber's and Merriam's vocabularies were also obtained from Colós and Guzman.) A preliminary dictionary of Chocheño based on the Harrington materials was compiled by Levy (1978c); a much more extensive dictionary, together with a grammatical sketch, is in preparation (A. Miller and Callaghan n.d.; A. Miller n.d.).

TAMYEN

San Francisco Bay Costanoan varieties belonging to the Tamyen group were spoken by the Tamyen tribelet in the immediate vicinity of Mission Santa Clara and by as many as half a dozen other tribelets in the South Bay area. It is unambiguously attested only in a vocabulary of about 180 items that was collected in 1856 by Gregory Mengarini, a former Jesuit missionary to the Flathead of Montana who was teaching at the College of Santa Clara (Mengarini 1860). Mengarini's source was "an old Chief born at the Mission, named Marcellino," and the careful transcription reflects his prior experience with Indian languages. An extensive vocabulary collected by Henshaw (1884d) and identified as the dialect of Mission Santa Clara is of dubious authenticity.[101] One of the two Costanoan translations of the Lord's Prayer transcribed from Santa Clara mission documents by Duflot de Mofras in 1841 may reflect Tamyen (Kroeber 1910: 253–256), as may also a mission-era catechism recently discovered in Zacatecas (Blevins and Golla 2005).[102] It is quite possible, however, that one or both of these is an attestation of Chocheño.

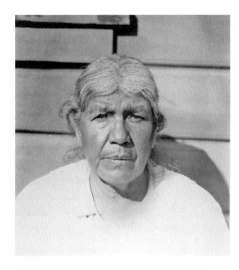

FIGURE 69. Ascención Solórsano de Cervantes, the last fluent speaker of Mutsun Costanoan. Courtesy of the National Anthropological Archives, Smithsonian Institution (91-30315).

RAMAYTUSH

Ramaytush (*rammay-tuš* 'people from the west') is the term that the Chocheños applied to the people who lived on the opposite shore of San Francisco Bay. It was adopted by Levy (1976) as the common label for the San Francisco Bay Costanoan varieties that were spoken by the tribelets of the San Francisco peninsula as far south as Palo Alto and Pescadero. (One of the tribelets in the latter area, on San Gregorio Creek north of Pescadero Point, was known as *Oljon*, apparently the source of "Ohlone"; see ¶3.28.8.) A variety of Ramaytush may also have been spoken by the Huimen tribelet in Marin County immediately to the north of the Golden Gate (Beeler 1972a; A. Brown 1973), but the one vocabulary that is clearly attributed to that tribelet (Arroyo 1837) attests a variety of Coast Miwok (¶3.27.1). The documention of Ramaytush is very scant. It consists of twenty-six words recorded by Father Vicente Santa María, chaplain of a Spanish naval vessel anchored at San Francisco in 1775 (Beeler 1972a); a vocabulary collected by the Indian agent Adam Johnston from Pedro Alcantara at Mission Dolores in 1850 (Johnston 1852a); and a list of twenty words and two phrases in "Doloreño" obtained by Harrington in 1912 from an elderly man in San Luis Obispo, Ysidro Solis, who also recalled words in Marin Miwok (Okrand 1991).[103] In addition a few Ramaytush words are scattered through Harrington's Chocheño notes, but these have not yet been collated.

3.28.3 Mutsun and Awaswas

Varieties of **Mutsun** were spoken by the tribelet at Mission San Juan Bautista (Motsun) and by the other tribelets in the drainage of the Pajaro River—west to Monterey Bay (Calendaruc), north to Gilroy (Unijaima), east to Hollister (Ausaima), and southeast toward Indian Canyon and the Pinnacles (Pagcin).[104]

Felipe Arroyo de la Cuesta, the mission priest at San Juan Bautista from 1808 to 1833, compiled a phrase book and short grammar of Mutsun—the latter remarkably thorough and analytical for its time—both of which have been published (Arroyo 1861, 1862; see also Mason 1916a).[105] The only other nineteenth-century documentation of the language, a vocabulary collected by Henshaw (1884e), is much less substantial. Between 1902 and 1904, Merriam collected a vocabulary and a natural history word list from a speaker of the "Hoo-mon-twash" variety (¶Appendix A: S-18b-c).[106] Between 1922 and 1930, Harrington collected a substantial amount of data from the last speaker of Mutsun, Ascención Solórsano de Cervantes, although much of it consisted of reelicitations of Arroyo's transcriptions (Mills 1985:82–83). Okrand has written a comprehensive grammar of Mutsun based largely on Harrington's materials (Okrand 1977). The combination of Arroyo's and Harrington's documentation makes Mutsun the most extensively and accurately recorded Costanoan language.

Mutsun speakers referred to Costanoans who lived on the north shore of Monterey Bay and in the mountains to the northwest as **Awaswas,** from *ʔawas-was* 'north-people from there' and this term is applied to the varieties of Mission Santa Cruz Costanoan documented in postmission times (Shipley 2002). However, no standard variety seems to have emerged during the two decades that Costanoan speakers were in the majority at this notoriously troubled mission, which in any event after 1810 was dominated by substantial numbers of Yokuts speakers brought in from the San Joaquin Valley. Although the tribelets most frequently referred to in the Santa Cruz mission records are the nearby Cotoni, Uypi, and Aptos (Milliken 1995), converts from more distant Costanoan-speaking areas, including parts of the San Francisco Peninsula, seem to have made up a portion of the mission community from the beginning. Whatever the reason, the "Awaswas" word lists collected in the second half of the nineteenth century by Comelias (1860), Pinart (1878f), and Henshaw (1888b), appear to attest more than one dialect.[107]

While Awaswas shares with the San Francisco Bay dialects the merger of medial *č and *kʷ with *y* and *w* (e.g., *payan* 'blood' and *ruwa* 'house') it also shares a significant number of lexical innovations with Mutsun (Levy 1976, tables 12 and 13). Since the lenition of medial *č and *kʷ is the default case for Costanoan, with only Mutsun and Rumsen preserving the original obstruents, I must agree with Levy (1976) that the documentation of Awaswas, sparse and confusing as it is, points to a dialect cluster that from a cladistic perspective is closer to Mutsun than to the San Francisco Bay dialects.[108]

3.28.4 Rumsen

Varieties of **Rumsen** (also known as **Rumsien**) appear to have been spoken in four tribelets, whose names and locations Milliken identifies as Achasta or Rumsen, on the Monterey Peninsula and along the lower Carmel River; Ensen, in the Salinas–Fort Ord area; Wacharon, in the vicinity of Castroville; and Sarhentaruc, from the Carmel Valley to the coast near Point Sur (Milliken 1987, 1990, 2002).[109] The upper part of Carmel Valley belonged to the Esselen, with whom the Rumsen were in close (and usually hostile) contact. There apparently was widespread Rumsen-Esselen bilingualism in the Sarhentaruc region near Point Sur, and perhaps elsewhere, although the occurrence of Esselen loanwords in attested Rumsen more likely reflects the ethnic mixture at Carmel mission (Levy 1976; Breschini and Haversat 1997b; Callaghan 2006).

Earlier substratal influences from Esselen, however, may in part be responsible for the considerable lexical distinctiveness shown by Rumsen vis-à-vis the other Costanoan languages (Levy 1976:38; Shaul 1988; Callaghan 2006). The language is also phonologically innovating, with the loss of vowels in word-final syllables resulting in distinctive final consonant clusters (Callaghan 1992a). Pre-Rumsen—the starting point for these innovations—shares a number of distinctive features with Mutsun, and the two languages are sometimes grouped together as "Southern Costanoan."

Rumsen was documented by several investigators from the late eighteenth century through the early twentieth century. The earliest attestation is a mission-era vocabulary and short catechism (with parallel Esselen translations) that was prepared for the Malaspina expedtion in 1791–1792 by Fermin de Lasuén, Serra's sucessor as president of the California missions (Cutter 1990). In the late nineteenth and early twentieth centuries, vocabularies were collected by Pinart (1878b), Henshaw (1884g), and Kroeber (1910:242–249), and in 1906, Merriam collected a vocabulary and natural history word list that attested the southern or "Kahˊ-koon" variety from Point Sur (Appendix A: S-18e). Using these materials, Broadbent (1957) reconstituted a combined

FIGURE 70. Isabelle Meadows, J. P. Harrington's primary Rumsen consultant. Courtesy of the National Anthropological Archives, Smithsonian Institution (91-30298).

vocabulary of about 390 items (for an assessment see Okrand 1980).

Only after Broadbent had completed her study did the extensive notes obtained by Harrington in the 1920s and 1930s become available. Although Harrington worked with the last, elderly speakers of the language, his materials far outweigh in importance any earlier attestation (Mills 1985:85–87, 100–112). Particularly valuable are the extensive notes he collected from Isabelle Meadows (1846–1939), whose mother was a Rumsen from Carmel mission and whose father was an English seaman. Studies of Rumsen that incorporate Harrington's data include Callaghan (1992a) and Shipley (1980a). Amy Miller has completed a full dictionary of Rumsen based primarily on Harrington's material (A. Miller n.d.).

3.28.5 Chalon

Chalon was the dialect of Costanoan spoken by the Chalon and Noptac tribelets along Chalone Creek in the Gabilan Range east of the Salinas River near Mission Soledad. It is possible that related varieties were spoken by tribelets to the northeast of these, along the upper San Benito River. It was formerly thought (e.g., Kroeber 1925:548) that Chalon was the language of the tribelet in the immediate vicinity of Mission Soledad and that it was spoken along the Salinas River as far south as King City, but Milliken has shown from mission records that all the villages in this area were Esselen-speaking (1990:66–69).

Chalon is documented only by a fragment of a mission-era catechism (Sarría 1819) and by nineteenth-century vocabularies collected by Hale (1846:633–634), Pinart (1878c), and Henshaw (1888d).

The classificatory status of the geographically isolated Chalon dialect is problematic. Kroeber (1910) grouped it with Mutsun and Rumsen as a "Southern Costanoan" language on the basis of shared lexical items. Richard Levy, who prefers to see Costanoan relationships in terms of a dialect network rather than as branching subgroups, finds Chalon to be close both to Rumsen (1976:38–39) and to Awaswas (1978b:468). Catherine Callaghan, citing unpublished work by her student Catherine Schambach, is inclined to believe that Chalon "may be a Northern Costanoan language with a heavy overlay of Southern Costanoan loanwords." Not only does the development of medial -y- and -w- from Proto Costanoan *č and *kʷ link Chalon to Northern Costanoan (which in Callaghan's classification includes Awaswas), but the Chalon "pronominal particles are also strikingly Northern" (Callaghan 1988a:436–437). Marc Okrand, finally, has suggested that the features that Callaghan and Schambach see Chalon sharing with Northern Costanoan may be better interpreted as retentions or independent developments from Proto Costanoan (Okrand 1989).

3.28.6 Survival and Revitalization

Although no Costanoan tribe has so far gained federal acknowledgement, Costanoan descendants have not been reluctant to assert their ethnic identity, and many are interested in reviving their traditional languages. A group of Mutsun descendants has established the Mutsun Language Foundation (www.mutsunlanguage.com), a nonprofit organization that works collaboratively with linguists at the University of Arizona and elsewhere to develop pedagogical materials (Warner, Luna, and Butler 2007). The Muwekma Ohlone Tribe, which includes descendants of the Indian communities at Mission San Jose and Mission Santa Clara, sponsors a class in Chocheño in which several students have acquired conversational abilities; work on a dictionary is being planned. Linda Yamane, a poet and artist of Rumsen descent, has acquired considerable familiarity with her ancestral language through working with Harrington's data and has published a small book of traditional stories in English translation (Yamane 1995).

3.28.7 Linguistic Structure

Only Mutsun, Rumsen, and Chocheño are sufficiently well documented to permit a definitive linguistic analysis. The standard description is Okrand's Mutsun grammar (1977; see also Adams 1985), derived primarily from Harrington's data. Some aspects of Rumsen structure are covered by Callaghan (1992a) and Shipley (1980a). Amy Miller (n.d.) and Miller and Callaghan (n.d.) provide an analysis of Chocheño.

Costanoan phonology is characterized by an unusually high number of phonemic contrasts between apical and palatal consonants (Table 44). In Mutsun, the most conservative

TABLE 44

Mutsun Phonemes (Okrand 1977)

All consonants except *c*, *nʸ*, *lʸ*, *r*, *w*, and *ʔ* can be geminated in medial position

Consonants								Vowels		
p	t	tʸ	c	ṭ	č	k	ʔ	i / i:		u / u:
	s	ṣʸ					h	e / e:		o / o:
m	n	nʸ							a / a:	
w	l	lʸ		r	y					

of the adequately documented languages, the stop and affricate articulations, in addition to *p* and *k*, are *t* (dental), *ṭ* (postalveolar or "retroflex"), *tʸ* (palatalized apical or alveolar), *c* (dental affricate [ts]), and *č* (palatal affricate [tʃ]). There are, however, no phonemic laryngeal feature contrasts (aspiration, glottalization, or voicing). There are two fricatives (*s*, *ṣʸ*); three nasals (*m*, *n*, *nʸ* [ñ]); four approximants (*l*, *lʸ*, *w*, *y*); a flapped *r* [ɾ]; and two laryngeals (*h*, *ʔ*). All consonants can occur geminated in medial position except *c*, *nʸ*, *lʸ*, *r*, *w*, and *ʔ*. There are five vowels (*i*, *e*, *a*, *o*, *u*), which occur both long and short. Morphological alternations between geminated consonants and long vowels are found in all three languages, but are particularly common in Rumsen (Shipley 1980a; Callaghan 1992a:41–48). Rumsen and Chocheño (and probably most other Costanoan languages) lack palatalized apical consonants (*tʸ*, *ṣʸ*, *nʸ*, *lʸ*) and have a palatal fricative (*š*). In Rumsen, a velar fricative (*x*) developed from *h* in most positions.

Costanoan languages have an agglutinative, largely suffixing morphology, with only minimal fusion. Nouns are inflected for case: subject, direct object, instrumental, and locative are distinguished everywhere, and a few additional categories are marked sporadically in specific languages (Table 45).[110] Pronouns marking subject and object can occur either as independent words or as enclitics following the first word of a sentence, whatever this word may be (e.g., Mutsun *huske-k* 'he is playing the flute' < *huske* 'play the flute', *yete-ka tursin* 'I will get cold later' < *yete* 'later'). An object pronoun is not infrequently enclitic on an independent subject pronoun (e.g., Mutsun *ka:n-mes muyṣʸin* 'I like you'). Constructions with enclitic pronouns are syntactically equivalent to constructions with free pronouns; the difference appears to be in topicality or focus (Okrand 1977:173–174). Possessive pronouns are prefixed to nouns (e.g., Mutsun *kan-to:ṭe* 'my meat', *me-tokko* 'your mat', *wak-mo:hel* 'his head', *mak-ʔama* 'our bodies').

Verbs are inflected for aspect, voice, and mode, and often for tense. In addition, derivational suffixes mark such categories as causation, benefaction, reflexivity, reciprocity, and directionality. Verb stems sometimes occur with the final VC metathesized to CV, depending on the suffix that follows (Okrand 1979).

TABLE 45
Mutsun Case Inflection (Okrand 1977)

Nouns

		ʔissu 'hand'	*sottow 'bow'*
Subject	(unmarked)	*ʔissu*	*sottow*
Object	*-(s)e*	*ʔissuse*	*sottowe*
Instrumental	*-(s)um* ("by means of . . .")	*ʔissusum*	*sottowum*
Locative	*-tka ~ -tak* ("at, on . . .")	*ʔissutka*	*sottowtak*

Independent Pronouns

	1 sg	*2 sg*	*3 sg*	*1 pl incl*	*1 pl excl*	*2 pl*	*3 pl*
Subject	*ka:n*	*me:n*	*wa:k*	*makke*	*makse*	*makam*	*haysa*
Object	*kannis*	*me:se*	*wa:kse*	*makkes*	*maksen*	*makamse*	*haysan*

Enclitic Pronouns

	1 sg/pl	*2 sg/pl*	*3 sg/pl*
Subject	*-ka*	*-m(e)*	*-(a)k*
Object	*-kas* (rare)	*-mes*	*-was*

3.28.8 Nomenclature

The published version of Adam Johnston's 1850 vocabulary of a variety of Ramaytush is titled, without further explanation, "Olhones or Costanos" (Schoolcraft 1851–1857, vol. 2:494-506). Apparently *costanos*, a colonial California variant of standard Spanish *costeños* 'inhabitants of the coast', was used at Mission Dolores to refer to the *Oljones*, the converts from the tribelet of *Oljon* [olxon], located on the coastal side of the San Francisco peninsula (Milliken 1995). Latham (1856:52), perhaps believing it to be a more general ethnonym, adopted "Costano" as the overall designation of the language or languages that he saw represented in five early vocabularies from the San Francisco Bay area. Gatschet (1877h) subsequently joined Mutsun, Rumsen, and the Miwok languages to Latham's Costano to form the "Mutsun" family, equivalent to modern Utian. In his definitive classification, however, Powell (1891:70–71) removed Miwok (his "Moquelumnan" family) from this grouping and designated the remainder—Mutsun, Rumsen, and Costano—the "Costanoan" family. Although Kroeber rejected many of Powell's cumbersome family names, he accepted "Costanoan" (cf. Dixon and Kroeber 1903), and as a consequence it became standard anthropological usage. Only Merriam, who preferred to use native designations for tribes and languages wherever possible, idiosyncratically employed "Olhonean" (modeled on Johnston's "Olhones")

in place of "Costanoan."[111] Modern Costanoan descendants call themselves "Ohlone" [olóni], a neologism probably based on a misreading of "Olhones," although other etymologies have been offered. Whatever its origin, "Ohlone" has gained wide currency, and it or "Ohlonean" is used with increasing frequency by many anthropologists and linguists in place of "Costanoan."[112]

3.29 Utian

Utian is the term coined by Catherine Callaghan, and adopted by most other researchers, to label a classificatory unit within Penutian consisting of the Miwok and Costanoan families. The validity of this classification is supported by numerous cognates showing regular sound correspondences. The first compilation of these was published by Kroeber (1910:260–262), and although this evidence was more suggestive than compelling, Dixon and Kroeber (1913) took as given the existence of a "Uti" (or Miwok-Costanoan) subdivision of their proposed Penutian phylum, as did Sapir in his own later discussions of Penutian (1921a:60). Callaghan (1962, 1967, 1982, 1983, 1986c, 1986d, 1988b, 1992b) has conclusively demonstrated the validity of a Utian grouping through a meticulous comparative analysis of the lexical and morphosyntacic evidence. A comprehensive study is in an advanced stage of preparation (Callaghan n.d.[b]).

Uto-Aztecan Languages

3.30 Uto-Aztecan and Northern Uto-Aztecan

Uto-Aztecan is one of the largest and most diversified of proven American language families, extending well beyond Southern California and the Great Basin to include languages from the Great Plains to Central America (Map 33). It is, in fact, a superfamily, with several subgroups that are families in their own right. Despite the great diversity of Uto-Aztecan, however, the underlying similarities uniting it were recognized by Buschmann as early as 1859 and discussed by Latham (1860), Bancroft (1874–1876), and others. Daniel G. Brinton (1891:118–119) coined the name "Uto-Aztecan" and grouped the languages into three broad divisions— "Shoshonean" in California and the Great Basin, "Sonoran" in southern Arizona and northern Mexico, and Nahuatl. Powell, taking a typically conservative stance, judged that the evidence for a historical relationship among Brinton's divisions was insufficient and included separate "Shoshonean" and "Piman" families in his general classification of North American languages (1891:98–99, 108–110). (Barrows 1900 has a useful summary of this earlier work, with special attention to the California languages.) Kroeber (1907b:154–163) reasserted the validity of Uto-Aztecan, and Sapir (1913b, 1915a) closed the debate with a masterful series of papers on comparative Uto-Aztecan phonology and grammar, citing a substantial number of Uto-Aztecan cognates supported by regular sound correspondences.

There is a rich scholarly literature on comparative Uto-Aztecan linguistics, surveyed in Lamb (1964) and Steele (1979). While there has long been a general agreement on what languages and small families are included in the Uto-Aztecan superfamily, a firm higher-order classification has been elusive. Brinton's "Shoshonean" group—Hopi, Numic, Takic, and Tubatulabal—has been one of the more enduring subgroups. The classification that is currently in widest use (Campbell 1997:134) divides Uto-Aztecan into a Northern (i.e., Shoshonean) and a Southern subfamily (Table 46). Alternative classifications that treat each of the four Northern branches as an independent classificatory unit within Uto-Aztecan were proposed by Whorf (1935), Lamb (1964), and Wick Miller (1984), and these continue to have adherents. Kenneth Hale and David Harris (1979) staked out a middle ground, accepting the classificatory validity of Northern Uto-Aztecan but arguing that there were deep structural differences between an Eastern subgroup (Hopi, Numic) and a Western subgroup (Takic, Tubatulabal) that reflected an early split between languages associated with the farming societies of the southern Great Basin and Pueblo Southwest, and those associated with the sedentary foraging societies of the California region.

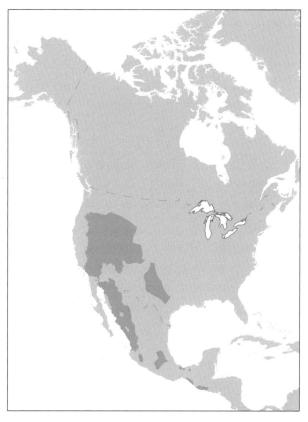

MAP 33. Uto-Aztecan branches of Northern Mexico and the Southwest United States.

Manaster Ramer (1992a), however, has greatly strengthened the case for a unified Northern branch by identifying a phonological innovation that appears to be shared by all and only the Northern languages, the lenition of intervocalic *-c- (i.e., the affricate *-ts-) to -y-. Joining Manaster Ramer in this view has been Jane Hill, who for over a decade has been mustering both linguistic and nonlinguistic evidence to support the hypothesis that a migration of Uto-Aztecan speakers from Mesoamerica bought maize horticulture to the Southwest (Hill 2001; see ¶5.4.1). In a recent paper (Hill 2009) she has experimentally reclassified the Uto-Aztecan languages using only "the most conservative possible criterion" of the comparative method, shared innovation in phonology. Her results strongly reaffirm the Northern Uto-Aztecan classificatory node, which she finds supported by three phonological innovations in addition to the one already proposed by Manaster Ramer. They also reaffirm Hale and Harris's identification of an East-West division in Northern Uto-Aztecan that separates Numic and Hopi from Takic and Tubatulabal, and further suggest that the latter, rather than being independent branches of Northern Uto-Aztecan,

TABLE 46
General Classification of the Uto-Aztecan Languages
(Campbell 1997:134)*

Northern Uto-Aztecan

    Hopi

    Numic (see Table 47)

    Takic (see Table 49)

    Tubatulabal

Southern Uto-Aztecan

    Tepiman

        O'odham (Pima-Papago)

        Pima Bajo

        Tepehuan (Northern Tepehuan, Southern Tepehuan)

        Tepecano

    Taracahitic

        Tarahumaran (Tarahumara, Guarijio)

        Cahitan (Yaqui, Mayo, Cahita)

        Opata-Eudeve

    Corachol-Aztecan

        Cora-Huichol

        Nahuatl

*Similar classifications have been proposed by Heath (1977) and Kaufman (1974).

constitute a single intertwined classificatory unit, which Hill calls "Californian."

3.31 Numic Languages

The territory in which the Numic languages were spoken (and to some extent continue to be) includes most of the Great Basin and the Colorado Plateau, as well as portions of the High Plains (Table 47). However, all but one (Comanche) of the Numic languages were spoken in or closely adjacent to the California culture area, and three of them (Mono, Panamint, and Kawaiisu) were spoken almost entirely within the present-day borders of the state of California (Map 34).

The internal diversity of Numic is relatively shallow, with a maximum time depth of between 1,500 and 2,000 years (W. Miller 1986:100). There are three branches—Western, Central, and Southern Numic[113]each consisting of a dialect chain along which two or three dialect clusters or emergent languages can be identified. These clusters are most distinct along the eastern slope of the Sierra Nevada between Mono Lake and Tehachapi Pass, where all three Numic chains converge. In the **Western Numic** chain, which extends north from Owens Valley through western Nevada to eastern Oregon and southern Idaho, the Mono dialects of the Owens Valley area form a compact localized group vis-à-vis the widespread and shallowly differentiated Northern Paiute dialect area. In the **Central Numic** chain, which extends east from Owens Lake through central Nevada to Utah, Idaho, and Wyoming, the well-defined Panamint dialects immediately to the east of Owens Lake and north of Death Valley can be distinguished from the vast Shoshoni dialect area. (At the eastern end of the chain, Comanche, which has been spoken on the High Plains since the eighteenth century, is also sharply distinct.) In the **Southern Numic** chain, which extends from the southern end of the Sierras across the Mojave Desert to southern Nevada and Utah and into western Colorado, a clear boundary separates the language of the Kawaiisu, spoken in the vicinity of Tehachapi Pass,

TABLE 47
Numic Languages and Dialects

Western Numic ("Mono-Paviotso") dialect chain

    Mono (Owens Valley Paiute and Western Mono/"Monache") cluster

        Northeastern Mono (Upper Owens Valley) dialect

        Northwestern Mono (San Joaquin and Kings River) dialect

        Southeastern Mono (Lower Owens Valley; Kaweah?) dialect

    Northern Paiute dialect area

        Nevada Northern Paiute ("Paviotso") dialect subarea

        Oregon Northern Paiute (including Bannock) dialect subarea

Central Numic ("Shoshoni-Comanche") dialect chain

    Panamint cluster

    Shoshoni dialect area

        Western Shoshoni dialect subarea

        Gosiute dialect subarea

        Northern (Fort Hall) Shoshoni dialect subarea

        Eastern (Wind River) Shoshoni dialect subarea

    Comanche language

Southern Numic ("Ute-Chemehuevi") dialect chain

    Kawaiisu language

    Southern Paiute-Ute dialect area ("Colorado River Numic")

        Chemehuevi dialect

        Southern Paiute dialect subarea

        Southern Ute dialect subarea

        Uintah-Ouray Ute dialect subarea

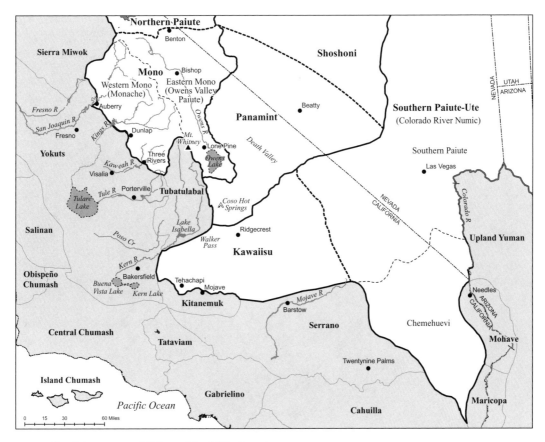

MAP 34. Numic languages and dialects of the California region.

from the dialect continuum that stretches from Chemehuevi to Northern Ute.

For general surveys of Numic diversity see Kroeber (1907b, 1925:574–580); Steward (1937); W. Miller (1964); Freeze and Iannucci (1979); and Campbell (1997: 133–138).

3.31.1 Western Numic

MONO

Mono is the term used in the linguistic literature for the cluster of dialects spoken at the southern end of the Western Numic dialect chain, on both the eastern and western side of the Sierra Nevada (Map 35). An environment more favorable than the rest of the Great Basin to permanent settlements gave rise in the Mono area to several distinct local varieties (Liljeblad and Fowler 1986:412). Three major precontact dialect groups can be distinguished.[114]

Varieties of **Western Mono,** or "Monache," were spoken west of the Sierra crest in at least two tribelets. One was on the upper San Joaquin River, with villages near Auberry and North Fork, adjacent to the Chukchansi Yokuts. The other was on or near Kings River, with villages at Sycamore Valley (Wobonuch) and Dunlap (Entimbich). On the east side of the Sierra Nevada two distinct varieties of **Eastern Mono,** or

"Owens Valley Paiute," were spoken. **Northeastern Mono** was spoken in communities along the upper Owens River and around Benton, along the middle Owens River near Bishop, and east of the White Mountains in Deep Springs and Fish Lake Valleys. **Southeastern Mono** was spoken along the lower Owens River at Big Pine, Independence, and Lone Pine, where its speakers were in contact with the Panamint. Lamb (as reported by Kroeber 1959a:266) claims that this dialect, which he prefers to call "Southern Mono," was also spoken along the Kaweah River on the west side of the Sierra by the Waksachi in Eshom Valley and the Patwisha at Three Rivers. However, the available data on the Waksachi and Patwisha varieties (Merriam, in Appendix A: X-23n; Gayton 1948:213–290) have not been fully studied, and the dialectological status of these communities remains undetermined (R. Spier 1978b:426).

Complicating this picture is the fact that all the Mono groups west of the Sierra Nevada lived in close proximity to one or more Yokuts groups and were thoroughly bilingual (see Map 35). This linguistic overlap may not have been due in all instances to acculturation on the part of immigrating Monos but may have proceeded in both directions. The ethnographer Anna Gayton suggested that the Entimbich were quite possibly a Yokuts group that had been "overwhelmed" by the Mono.[115] The Michahay, a Yokuts tribe of the Kings River subgroup who had begun to intermarry with the

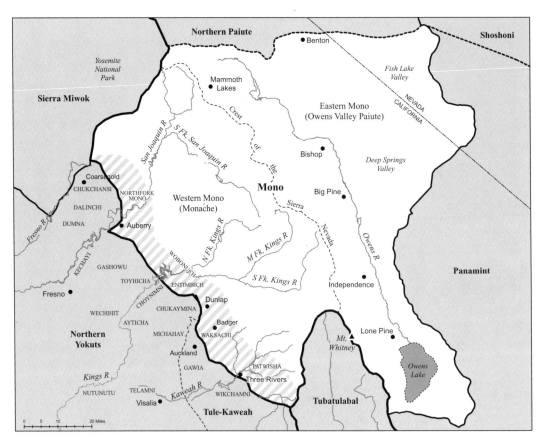

MAP 35. Mono territory, showing Western Mono communities.

FIGURE 71. C. Hart Merriam taking a vocabulary of the Waksachi variety of Monache (Western Mono) from Blind Sam Osborn. Eshom Valley, Kaweah River, October 1935. C. Hart Merriam collection of Native American photographs (X/23n/P1 no.2). Courtesy of Bancroft Library UCB.

Waksachi, may have been in an earlier stage of the same process (Gayton 1948:213–253; see ¶1.5.2).

Contact between the Western and Eastern Mono was frequent, following established trails across the Sierra crest. The primary motivation for this contact was economic, with acorns, clamshell beads, and other central California items being traded for obsidian from several major sources east of the mountains (Moratto 1984:288).[116]

Mono is well documented, although relatively little of the material is easily accessible. Lamb carried out extensive fieldwork in the mid-1950s, focusing on Western Mono. He compiled a grammar (1958b) and a dictionary (1957), neither of which has been published. Liljeblad collected extensive linguistic and ethnographic materials between 1960 and 1980, now in the archives of the University of Nevada, Reno. In the 1970s, Norris carried out a field study of Eastern Mono, preparing a syntactic sketch as his MA thesis (1976) and a full grammar as his dissertation (1986), and published a paper on instrumental prefixes (1980). The Mono Language Program, a collaboration between the Northfork (Western) Mono community and UCLA, has produced a dictionary (Bethel et al. 1993) and a CD-ROM (Kroskrity, Bethel, and Reynolds 2002; see also Kroskrity 2002). Loether has written on Western Mono verbal art (1991); he has also carried out extensive fieldwork on

Owens Valley Paiute and written a pedagogically oriented descriptive grammar (Loether 2003). Of earlier work, perhaps the most valuable is the dialect survey implicit in Merriam's collection of vocabularies from six Western Mono communities (Appendix A: X-23d-n) and three Owens Valley communities (X-23r-t).

Western Mono continues to be spoken at North Fork and Auberry (Big Sandy Rancheria), each of which had in the early twenty-first century at least ten fully fluent speakers, the youngest in his fifties. There are also a few speakers at Tollhouse (Cold Springs Rancheria) and Dunlap. In addition, one hundred or more people have some passive or second-language knowledge of the language. Local language retention efforts are coordinated by the Sierra Mono Museum in North Fork and are integrated with other cultural revitalization activities. Eastern Mono (or Owens Valley Paiute) is still spoken in the Indian communities at Bishop, Big Pine, Lone Pine, and Fort Independence. All Eastern Mono speakers are elderly and number not more than thirty in a total population of about a thousand. Language revival programs in the Owens Valley area are being coordinated by the Nüümü Yadoha Program at Bishop.[117]

NORTHERN PAIUTE

The Western Numic dialects other than Mono are referred to collectively as Northern Paiute. Although there are some differences in grammatical structure between Northern Paiute and Mono, the phonology and vocabulary are quite similar, and the boundary is not sharply defined sociolinguistically (Liljeblad and Fowler 1986:412). The degree of intelligibility across the boundary seems largely to be a function of distance. Julian Steward reported in the 1930s that the Mono Lake variety of Northern Paiute that was spoken at Bridgeport was easily understood by speakers of the Benton variety of Northeastern Mono as well as by Western Monos from Northfork. Speakers of Southeastern Mono from the lower Owens Valley, however, found Bridgeport speech more difficult to follow, and the Northern Paiute spoken at Walker Lake, fifty miles north of Mono Lake, was barely intelligible to them (Steward 1933:236). The UC Berkeley Northern Paiute Language Project (discussed later) considers the varieties spoken in the four southernmost communities (Mono Lake, Bridgeport, Coleville, and Sweetwater) to constitute a distinct dialect of the language.

Varieties of Northern Paiute were spoken across a wide territory that extended from the vicinity of Mammoth, south of Mono Lake, to the John Day River in Oregon, including most of the western third of Nevada and parts of northeastern California. At least twenty-two Northern Paiute subgroups are known to have existed (O. Stewart 1939), each with a distinctive speech variety. These are often divided into two dialect areas, **Oregon Northern Paiute** and **Nevada Northern Paiute,** with the dividing line lying in the vicinity of Pyramid Lake (Nichols 1974:4–5; C. Fowler and Liljeblad 1986:435).

Speakers of Shoshoni and Mono sometimes refer to the Nevada Northern Paiute varieties as **Paviotso,** a term that Lamb (1958a) unsuccessfully tried to extend to all of Northern Paiute in order to avoid confusion with Southern Paiute. The **Bannock** of the Fort Hall Reservation in Idaho represent an eastward expansion during historic times of some groups of Oregon Northern Paiute speakers into Shoshoni territory on the Snake River Plain. All varieties of Northern Paiute are mutually intelligible, and none of the differences are as deep-rooted as those that distinguish the three major Mono dialects.

On the east, from southern Nevada to Idaho, the Northern Paiute adjoined the Shoshoni. The relationship was generally friendly, with occasional intermarriage, and individual bilingualism was common along the boundary (C. Fowler and Liljeblad 1986:435). To the west, the Northern Paiute bordered on several California and Oregon groups. The Walker Lake, Pyramid Lake, and Honey Lake Paiute had the Washo as neighbors, with whom they were on moderately good terms. The Honey Lake Paiute fought with the Northeastern Maidu for control of the area around the lake. The Surprise Valley Paiute, east of the Warner Mountains, were in contact with the Atsugewi, the Achumawi, the Modoc, and the Klamath, with one or more of whom they were frequently on a hostile footing, particularly after the acquisition of the horse in the early historical period. The Harney Valley Paiute in the Burns area of north-central Oregon were in contact with the Umatilla Sahaptin.

Northern Paiute is moderately well documented. The earliest attestation is a vocabulary that Hale collected in eastern Oregon during the Wilkes Expedition, titled "Wihinasht" (Hale 1846; Gallatin 1848). The foundational work on the language was done by Powell, who collected several Nevada "Paviotso" vocabularies (1873a, 1880c, 1880d, 1880e; see D. Fowler and Fowler 1971:30–31, 210–249). Waterman worked with a speaker from Pyramid Lake at Berkeley in 1910, primarily studying phonetics and making wax cylinder recordings (Waterman 1911), and he subsequently collaborated with W. C. Marsden, a physician from Burns, Oregon who had accumulated a large amount of data on Oregon Northern Paiute. A publication resulted (Mardsen 1923), but much unpublished material remains in the Bancroft Library. Gilbert Natches, a Northern Paiute speaker from Pyramid Lake, was brought to Berkeley to aid in this work, and later wrote a short paper on Northern Paiute verbs (1923). Merriam collected vocabularies at Pyramid and Walker Lakes (Appendix A: X-23a), and from the southernmost Northern Paiute community at Mono Lake and Bridgeport (X-23b) at various times between 1900 and 1938. De Angulo and Freeland made brief observations on the Surprise Valley dialect during their work on neighboring Achomawi (de Angulo and Freeland 1929a).

In recent decades the pace of research on Northern Paiute, one of the few Indian languages in the California region that still remain widely spoken, has accelerated. Between 1940 and 1980 the leading researcher was the Swedish expatriate

Sven Liljeblad, who carried out extensive fieldwork across the Northern Paiute area (W. Davis 1970); his voluminous notes and several unpublished manuscripts are housed in the Special Collections Department, Getchell Library, University of Nevada, Reno. Michael Nichols worked on the Bannock, Harney Valley, and Honey Lake dialects in 1968–1970; his doctoral dissertation (1974), although primarily a historical and comparative study, has a considerable amount of Northern Paiute data. Poldervaart, a linguist associated with the Summer Institute of Linguistics, has worked with the Yerington dialect and published a grammatical sketch (Dick, Williams, and Poldervaart 1987) and a dictionary (Poldervaart 2004). The most recent major work is by Thornes, whose dissertation (2003) is a full grammar of Burns Paiute (Harney Valley) in eastern Oregon. During the academic year 2005–2006, a University of California, Berkeley, field class under the direction of Andrew Garrett worked with speakers of the Bridgeport variety, near Mono Lake. Continuing research by members of that group has been organized as the Northern Paiute Language Project of the Survey of Calfornia and Other Indian Languages (linguistics.berkeley.edu/~paiute/index.html).

Northern Paiute is the most vigorously surviving indigenous language in the California region. Speakers of Northern Paiute are found in a number of reservation communities in Oregon, Nevada, California, and Idaho, as well as in urban locations in these states. The principal communities in Oregon are at Warm Springs and Burns; in Nevada at Fort McDermitt, Owyhee, Winnemucca, Pyramid Lake, Reno-Sparks, Lovelock, Fallon, Yerington, and Walker River; and in California at Bridgeport, Lee Vining, and Fort Bidwell. The Bannock variety continues to be spoken by a few elderly people at Fort Hall, Idaho, where Shoshoni is otherwise the heritage language. Fluency in all communities except Fort McDermitt is confined to speakers sixty years of age and older, with a total of about three hundred speakers. At Fort McDermitt, however, at least four hundred individuals are fluent in Northern Paiute, roughly half the community, and from 20 to 30 percent of children acquire it as their first language. Semispeakers from all areas add another four hundred to these figures.

During the past twenty-five years nearly all Northern Paiute communities have initiated teaching programs, but only a few of these have flourished. The most sustained efforts have been undertaken by the communities at Warm Springs, Reno-Sparks, and Pyramid Lake. They have produced phrase books, some audio and video tapes, dictionaries, and a series of lessons, all designed to be used in classroom settings. These materials use a standard orthography, with some variations due to local dialect differences and other idiosyncracies. A few communities have also used the master-apprentice approach and other activities, but none has an immersion school. All these efforts have increased language awareness and resulted in some language activity, but no new fluent speakers. The State of Nevada approved awarding of high school credit in Great Basin languages in

1998, but thus far only the tribal high school at Pyramid Lake and the state high school at McDermitt have regularly scheduled classes.[118]

The UC Berkeley Northern Paiute Language Project, which focuses on the varieties spoken in the Mono Lake area, has the goal of developing an online dictionary and an interconnected text corpus (linguistics.berkeley.edu/~survey/activities/projects.php).

3.31.2 Central Numic

PANAMINT

Panamint is the usual ethnographic term—although Kroeber preferred "Koso"[119]—for the groups speaking the westernmost Central Numic dialects. Panamint territory adjoined Mono territory on the southeast. It included the southern end of Owens Valley around Owens Lake; the Coso Range and Indian Wells Valley as far south as Little Lake; the Inyo Mountains and Saline Valley to the east; northern Panamint Valley and the Panamint Mountains; the Last Chance Range; Death Valley as far south as Furnace Creek; the Grapevine Mountains and Funeral Range; and the Amargosa Valley east to Beatty, Nevada. Most of this area is arid desert, in summer typically recording the highest teperatures in North America, and during much of the year individual Panamint families wandered independently, foraging for food. Several families congregated in the fall for communal hunting and pine nut gathering, and wintered together. The Koso Panamint controlled the most important obsidian resource in south central California, at Coso Hot Springs, and were in frequent contact with the Tubatulabal to the west and shared the Owens Lake area with the Mono. The Panamint band in Saline Valley likewise controlled the local supply of salt and often visited the lower Owens Valley Mono.

There were noticeable differences in speech from valley to valley, and further variation among winter village groups (Dayley 1989:3–6). Panamint has two main dialects, although intervening varieties show a gradation between them. **Eastern Panamint** includes the community around Beatty, Nevada. **Western Panamint** includes the communities permanently living in Lone Pine and Darwin, California. The **Tümpisa** (or **Timbisha**) community in Death Valley and Lone Pine is transitional between Eastern and Western Panamint. The Beatty variety, which shares many features with Shoshoni dialects further east, was the most distinct (McLaughlin 1987). Although no variety of Panamint is mutually intelligible with the Shoshoni spoken in northern Nevada and southern Idaho, there is a transitional zone in southwestern Nevada in which both languages are understood. It is not clear, however, whether this reflects a dialect continuum or an area in which most people were bilingual (Dayley 1990:xvi).

McLaughlin carried out fieldwork on the Beatty dialect, and his dissertation is a phonological and morphological analysis (1987). Dayley studied the Death Valley dialect and has published a full grammar (1989), as well as a dictionary (1990) that incorporates most of the other extant lexical data on Panamint. Earlier documentation is sparse, but includes vocabularies collected by Merriam from speakers of two varieties between 1902 and 1932 (Appendix A: X-23u-v).

No monolingual speakers of Panamint remain, and no speakers who did not also learn English as small children. The "pure" Eastern and Western dialects from Lone Pine and Beatty are almost extinct. The majority of no more than twenty speakers speak the Death Valley variety, and all are elderly. There are very few, if any, passive speakers, since there is a strong tendency to marry outside the tribe. There is interest in revitalizing the language, but funding is scarce and will require distance education techniques because of the widely scattered nature of the tribe. Literacy in the language is very rare.[120]

SHOSHONI AND COMANCHE

With the exception of Comanche, the Central Numic dialects to the east of Panamint form a continuum that reaches from southern Nevada to western Wyoming with no significant break. All these dialects are mutually intelligible and constitute a single language, **Shoshoni**.[121] Several dialect clusters are often referred to by separate names, most frequently *Gosiute* for the northern Utah dialects, but also *Western Shoshoni* (Nevada, or sometimes Nevada and Utah), *Northern Shoshoni* (Idaho), and *Eastern Shoshoni* or *Wind River Shoshoni* (Wyoming). The boundaries separating these clusters are to some extent arbitrary. Shoshoni groups were (and continue to be) characterized by considerable mobility, and their dialects interlock and overlap (W. Miller 1970, 1986:99–100; McLaughlin 2000). However, the dialect spoken by the **Comanche,** who adopted a High Plains lifestyle in the late eighteenth century and moved south into New Mexico and Texas, has become quite distinct and is usually treated as a separate language. Further consideration of Comanche lies beyond the scope of this book.[122]

Shoshoni has been extensively documented. Although Powell's early surveys established the principal language and dialect boundaries (D. Fowler and Fowler 1971), the most significant and comprehensive documentation was provided by the extensive work of Wick Miller, beginning in the 1960s (Shipley 1995). He published a grammatical sketch (1996), but most of his materials, including numerous texts, are in the University of Utah archives. Much of the recent documentation of Shoshoni is pedagogical in focus and owes much to the initiative of tribal scholars, particularly Beverly Crum for Western Shoshoni (Crum and Dayley 1993) and Drusilla Gould for Northern Shoshoni (Gould and Loether 2002). Comanche has a separate history of documentation (cf. Charney 1993).

Currently, there are around a thousand actively fluent speakers of Shoshoni, and perhaps another thousand with more restricted competence. The largest surviving Shoshoni speech community is at Fort Hall, Idaho. While a few children still learn Shoshoni as a first language in the Duck Valley and Gosiute communities, most speakers are in their fifties or older. There are about the same number of passive speakers. There is a strong interest in maintaining or revitalizing the language in most communities, but the efforts are scattered, and there has been little intercommunity coordination. Idaho State University in Pocatello offers a two-year Shoshoni language program that satisfies university second-language requirements, and publishes a Shoshoni language newsletter. About one-third of the students are passive speakers who want to achieve a speaking fluency and literacy; another one-third are Shoshonis who have no knowledge of the language; and a final one-third are non-Shoshonis. Shoshoni-language literacy is increasing, with two major orthographies in use—one used in the Western Shoshoni and Gosiute areas, another used in Northern Shoshoni areas.[123]

3.31.3 Southern Numic

KAWAIISU

The Kawaiisu spoke the westernmost dialect of Southern Numic. They occupied the southern end of the Sierra Nevada between the Tehachapi and Piute Mountains, primarily the area around Tehachapi Pass, and also foraged in a large tract of desert to the east of the Sierra crest. The eastern boundary of this foraging territory lay between the southern end of Death Valley and the Mojave River, where in theory they adjoined the Chemehuevi, but there is no evidence that the two groups were in contact in the historical period. To the south of Tehachapi Pass and in the western Mojave Desert the Kawaiisu adjoined the Takic-speaking Kitanemuk and Vanyume Serrano. To the north, they adjoined the Tubatulabal in the mountains and the Panamint in the desert. On the western side of Tehachapi Pass they were in contact with the Yokuts.

Their closest cultural ties were with the Tubatulabal, and the Kawaiisu were as much semisedentary participants in central California culture as they were Great Basin nomadic foragers (Kroeber 1925:601; Zigmond 1986). As a result of this cultural orientation, as well as geographical separation, the speakers of Kawaiisu formed a sharply demarcated unit vis-à-vis the continuum of Southern Numic subdialectal varieties that extends from Chemehuevi to Ute, and Kawaiisu is usually treated as a separate language.

The most important collection of data on Kawaiisu was made by Maurice Zigmond during two periods of fieldwork, 1936–1940 and 1970–1974. A grammar and dictionary have been published based on these materials (Zigmond, Booth, and Munro 1990), as well as an ethnobotanical study (Zigmond 1981). Sheldon Klein collected extensive data on Kawaiisu in 1958 and again in 1981–1984, but only a small amount has so far been published (Klein 1959, 1988). Although Klein died in 2005, files with some of Klein's sound recordings and notes, and a description of Kawaiisu morphosyntax formulated in Zellig Harris's categorial grammar notation remained available in 2011 for downloading at his website (www.cs.wisc.edu/~sklein, see Klein 2002). Earlier documentation includes general and natural history vocabularies collected by Merriam (Appendix A: X-23w) at various times between 1902 and 1935.

Kawaiisu is the heritage language of a small unrecognized tribe located in the Tehachapi-Tejon region. In 2009 the Kawaiisu Language and Cultural Committee was awarded a grant to develop a practical grammar of Kawaiisu. A team of linguists from UC Berkeley is providing technical assistance (linguistics.berkeley.edu/~survey/activities/projects. php).

OTHER SOUTHERN NUMIC

Exclusive of Kawaiisu, Southern Numic consists of a chain of mildly diversified dialects or subdialectal varieties extending from the eastern Mojave Desert to western Colorado. Several regional dialect clusters are usually distinguished in this continuum: **Southern Paiute,** the dialects from southeastern California to the high plateau northeast of the Grand Canyon, including southwestern Utah; **Southern Ute,** the dialects of southern Utah and southwestern Colorado; and **Northern Ute** (or **Uintah-Ouray Ute**), the dialects of north-central Utah and northwestern Colorado. The westernmost Southern Paiute groups, the Las Vegas Paiute and the Chemehuevi, traveled widely and maintained friendly contacts with groups as far west as the Serrano, Cahuilla, and Diegueño. In the nineteenth century the **Chemehuevi** established an especially close relationship with the Mojave and other Colorado River Yumans, and their speech, which has a number of Mojave loanwords, is often treated separately from the other varieties of Southern Paiute. This distinction is social and cultural, however, not primarily linguistic. All varieties spoken in the dialect chain from Chemehuevi to Northern Ute remain mutually intelligible and constitute a single language. No name for this dialect chain is in general use, although "Colorado River Numic" has been proposed.[124]

Southern Numic is exceptionally well documented. The most comprehensive study is Sapir's, who worked with both Northern Ute and Southern Paiute in 1909–1910 and published a full grammar, dictionary, and collection of narrative texts (Sapir 1930–1931). Published grammars and dictionaries are also available for Chemehuevi (Press 1979) and Southern Ute (Givón 1979, 1980). James Goss prepared a grammatical study of Ute as his dissertation (1972). Pamela Bunte has carried out exensive fieldwork on the San Juan variety of Southern Paiute since the mid-1970s and prepared a study of syntax and semantics as her dissertation (1979). An online Chemehuevi dictionary is being prepared by Dirk Elzinga (n.d.; see also H. Nelson, Manookin, and Elzinga 2004). Margaret Press's notebooks and audio tapes from her 1973–1974 fieldwork on Chemehuevi, as well as her 1974 dissertation, are available online at www.cheme-

FIGURE 72. George Laird, Chemehuevi consultant for J. P. Harrington and his wife, Carobeth, who later divorced Harrington and married Laird. Courtesy National Anthropological Archives, Smithsonian Institution (81-14104).

huevilanguage.org/. Further documentation of Chemehuevi is ongoing (Major 2005).

The principal earlier documentation is by John Wesley Powell, who collected data on the Kaibab (1871–1872), Las Vegas (1873b), and Chemehuevi (n.d.) varieties of Southern Paiute during his exploration of the Grand Canyon. Merriam collected vocabularies of Southern Paiute (Appendix A: X-23y) and Chemehuevi (X-23z) at various times between 1906 and 1933. J. P. Harrington worked briefly on Ute in 1909 and on Chemehuevi in 1910–1911; his wife, Carobeth Tucker Harrington, carried out more extensive research on Chemehuevi in 1918–1920 under Harrington's direction (Mills and Brickfield 1986:105–116), continuing independently after divorcing Harrington and marrying her Chemehuevi informant, George Laird (Laird 1975). Late in life she published several books and articles on the Chemehuevi that incorporate some of her linguistic data (Laird 1976, 1984).

Southern Ute is spoken in the reservation community at Ignacio, Colorado, where there about a hundred first-language speakers, the youngest about fifty-five, out of a total population of thirteen hundred. Ute Mountain Ute is spoken at Towaoc, Colorado, where there are about five hundred first-language speakers, the youngest about twenty-five, out of a total population of fifteen hundred. Uintah and Ouray (Northern) Ute is spoken on the Fort Duchesne Reservation, Utah, where there are about three hundred first-language speakers, the youngest about forty-five, out of a total population of two thousand. There are tribally sponsored language programs at all three reservations, and substantial reference materials have been produced for Southern Ute, but efforts to date have resulted in few if any second-language speakers or literate first-language speakers.

Southern Paiute dialects (other than Chemehuevi) are currently spoken in ten widely separated communities in Utah, Arizona, and Nevada. The five Utah communities constitute the Paiute Tribe of Utah and have a total population of about six hundred. The San Juan Paiute Tribe is settled on the Navajo Reservation in Utah and Arizona and has a population of 220. The Kaibab Paiute Tribe, with a reservation north of the Grand Canyon, has a population of 212. The three southern Nevada tribes (Moapa, Las Vegas, and Pahrump) have a combined population of more than four hundred. The language is spoken to a varying extent in all communities, but only in the San Juan tribe are children still acquiring it as their first language. There are no active language education programs, although there is considerable interest in recording and videotaping traditional storytellers.

The Chemehuevi dialect is spoken on the Colorado River Indian Reservation at Parker, Arizona (which the Chemehuevis share with Mohaves, Navajos, and Hopis), and on the neighboring Chemehuevi Reservation in California. There are fewer than twenty first-language speakers, with the youngest nearly forty. The Arizona Chemehuevis have started a language-revitalization program, but there are few materials and no agreement on orthography. One woman is learning Chemehuevi as a second language from her mother in a master-apprentice program.[125]

3.31.4 Linguistic Structure

A relatively large number of descriptively adequate studies of Numic phonology and grammar are available. The primary resource for Southern Numic (and for Numic generally) is Sapir's classic grammar of Southern Paiute (1930–1931); good grammars of Chemehuevi (Press 1979), Kawaiisu (Zigmond, Booth, and Munro 1990), and Ute (Givón 1980) can also be consulted. For Central Numic, there are McLaughlin's (1987) and Dayley's (1989) independent studies of Panamint, and Wick Miller's (1996) compact sketch and Crum and Daley's (1993) reference grammar of Western Shoshoni. Western Numic structure is treated in two unpublished dissertations, Lamb's study of Western Mono (1958b, written, regrettably, in a theoretical metalanguage that is almost impenetrable to modern readers) and Thornes's comprehensive description of Harney Valley Northern Paiute (2003). There is also a grammatical sketch of Northern Paiute by Snapp, Anderson, and Anderson (1982).

The phonemic inventories of the Numic languages are quite small, although the devoicing of short vowels, particularly in final position, the fricativization and voicing of stop and affricate consonants in intervocalic position, and other subtle allophonic variation renders Numic speech much more complex at the phonetic level (Table 48). There are few phonemic differences, all of them dialectal within the branches rather than distinguishing the branches from one another.

TABLE 48
Western Mono Phonemes (Loether 2003)

Consonants							Vowels		
p	t	c	k	kʷ		ʔ	i / iː	ï / ïː	u / uː
(β)	(ð)	(ʒ)	(ɣ)	(ɣʷ)			e / eː	a / aː	o / oː
		s	x			h			
m	n		ŋ	(ŋʷ)					
w		y							

The basic phonemic inventory can be seen in Western Shoshoni, which has four plain oral stops (*p, t, k, kʷ*), an affricate (*c*) and a sibilant fricative (*s*) that vary in articulation between dental and palatal, two nasals (*m, n,*), two approximants (*w, y*), and two laryngeals (*ʔ, h*). The stops, affricate, and nasals may be geminated in word-medial position. There are six vowels (*i, e, a, o, u, ï*), which may be short and long. To these contrasts, many dialects add a velar nasal (*ŋ*) and a velar fricative (*x*). A labialized velar nasal (*ŋʷ*) is phonemic in Panamint and in Owens Valley Paiute. The phonemic status of *e* is uncertain in some dialects.

The weakening of nongeminated stops and the affricate *c* between vowels results in a set of lenis voiced consonants (Western Shoshoni [β], [ð], [ʒ], [ɣ], [ɣʷ] for *p, t, c, k, kʷ*, respectively), which in some analyses—and in many of the practical writing systems that have been created for Numic languages—are treated as separate phonemes. Sapir called attention to the theoretical implications of this phonological process in his classic paper on the psychological reality of phonemes (1933).

In Southern and Western Numic, nouns mark possessors with a set of pronominal prefixes—for example, Western Mono *ʔi-* 'my', *ʔih-* 'your (sg.)', *ʔah-* 'his, her, its', *tïh-* 'his, her, its own', *ta-* ~ *tanih-* 'our (inclusive)', *niːh-* 'our (exclusive)', *ʔïhnih-* 'your (pl.)', *ʔanih-* 'their', *tïhih-* 'their own'. In Central Numic, pronominal possession is always marked by the possessive case of the independent personal pronouns—for example, Western Shoshoni *niam* 'my', *ïn* ~ *ïmmïn* 'your (sg.)', *man* ~ *un* 'his, her, its', *pïn* 'his, her, its own', *tammïn* 'our (inclusive)', *nïmmïn* 'our (exclusive)', *mïmmïn* 'your (pl.)', *pïmmïn* 'their own'. When nouns are not possessed or compounded they are marked with an absolutive suffix, basically *-pi* in all Numic languages but with many secondary forms. Compound noun stems are common. Typical formations include noun + noun, adjective + noun, and verb + noun—for example, Shoshoni *punku-kahni* 'barn' (< 'horse, pet' + 'house'), *ontïm-pa:* 'whiskey' (< 'brown' + 'water'), *tïmï:h-kahni* 'store' (< 'buy' + 'house').

Numic verb stems are sometimes compounded with nominal elements (see ¶4.8.2). About twenty stem prefixes with instrumental reference are used in every Numic language—for example, Western Shoshoni *kï-* 'with the mouth or teeth'

MAP 36. Takic languages and dialects.

(*kï-kkopah* 'bite [rigid object] in two, break with teeth'), *ma-* 'with the open hand' (*ma-sunka:h* 'feel with the hand'), *ta-* 'with the feet' (*ta-kkopah* 'break with the feet', *ta-sunka:h* 'feel with the feet'). A number of verb stems incorporate a nominal object—for example, Shoshoni *tutua-pa?i* 'children-have', *tïpam-mahai* 'pine nut–gather'. Conjoined verb stems are also common—for example, Western Shoshoni *taikwa-wïnnï* 'stand talking' (< 'talk-stand'), *tïkka-suan* 'want to eat' (< 'eat-want'). Subject and object pronouns are expressed by independent pronouns marked for subjective and objective case. Verb suffixes mark tense and aspect.

3.31.5 Nomenclature

Gallatin (1848), seeing close similarities between the Northern Paiute vocabulary obtained by Hale during the Wilkes Expedition (Hale 1846) and earlier vocabularies of Bannock and Northern Shoshoni, grouped these together as "Shoshonee," noting further resemblances to the Juaneño and Gabrielino vocabularies that Hale had collected during his brief visit to California. As the documentation of Southwestern ethnolinguistic diversity accumulated over the following decades, a number of other languages were placed under this rubric, including all of those now known as Numic, most of the Takic languages, and Hopi. In presenting his own field research on Numic and Hopi, Powell (D. Fowler and Fowler 1971) substituted "Numa" (based on the general

Numic word for 'person', *nïmï*) for Gallatin's classificatory "Shoshonee," and Gatschet (1879a) adopted the same usage. In his 1891 classification, strictly following the rule of nomenclatural precedence, Powell reverted to "Shoshone(an)" to designate the Northern division of Uto-Aztecan, which he treated as an independent family; the term still remains in occasional use in this meaning. Kroeber (1907b) proposed that Powell's Shoshonean should be divided into four branches, one of which, "Plateau Shoshonean," is modern Numic. Kroeber's nomenclature remained in general use until the early 1960s, when Lamb's proposal (1958a, 1964) to replace "Plateau Shoshonean" with Powell's "Numa" in the adjectival form "Numic" gained quick acceptance among both linguists and anthropologists.

3.32 Takic Languages

The Takic languages were spoken along the Southern California coast from Malibu to Carlsbad, and in the mountains and valleys of the interior from northern Los Angeles County to northern San Diego County, including the semiarid Coachella Valley as far south as the Salton Sea (Map 36). The southwestern part of the Mojave Desert, and the Tehachapi Mountains to the north, were also in Takic territory, as were Santa Catalina and San Clemente Islands, and probably also San Nicolas Island. Takic speakers were in contact with the Ventureño Chumash along the coast to the

TABLE 49
Takic Languages and Dialects

Serrano-Kitanemuk group

    Serrano-Vanyume language

        Serrano dialect

        Vanyume (Desert Serrano) dialect

    Kitanemuk language

Tataviam language (?)

Gabrielino-Fernandeño (Tongva) language

    Gabrielino dialect cluster

    Fernandeño dialect

Cupan group

    Luiseño-Juaneño language

        Luiseño dialect cluster

        Juaneño (Ajachemem) dialect

    Cahuilla language

        Mountain Cahuilla dialect

        Pass Cahuilla dialect

        Desert Chuilla dialect

    Cupeño language

---

northwest; with the Yokuts to the north of the Tehachapi Mountains; with the Chemehuevi (Southern Numic), Mojave, and other River Yumans across the Mojave Desert to the east; and with the Diegueño in the mountains of San Diego County to the south.

Takic is a subfamily of Uto-Aztecan and is grouped with Numic, Tubatulabal, and Hopi in the Northern Uto-Aztecan branch of the family (¶3.30). Three Takic subgroups are usually distinguished (Table 49): Serrano-Kitanemuk; Gabrielino (including the Fernandeño dialect); and Cupan (including Luiseño-Juaneño, Cupeño, and Cahuilla). Tataviam, the poorly documented Takic language of the upper Santa Clara River valley around Newhall, may constitute a fourth subgroup, but the data can also be interpreted to support the view that it belongs to the Serrano-Kitanemuk subgroup (Munro and Johnson 2001). Gabrielino appears to be transitional between Serrano-Kitanemuk and Cupan. Wick Miller (1984), on strictly lexical evidence, grouped Gabrielino with Serrano-Kitanemuk in a "Serrano-Gabrielino" branch, a classification that is in accord with statements by older speakers of Serrano that Gabrielino was partially intelligible to them. More recently, however, Munro (1990:218, fn.2), following Bright (1974), has proposed grouping Gabrielino with Cupan. Giamina, a very poorly documented language that was spoken in the San Joaquin Valley near the Poso Creek Yokuts, may possibly represent another Takic subgroup, but the data are too sparse to confirm this (see ¶3.34).[126]

Takic has a moderately deep internal diversity. Wick Miller, evaluating only lexical resemblances, estimated that the split between Serrano-Kitanemuk and the other Takic languages could be as old as 3,750 years (1983:119). Linguists more familiar with the details of Takic consider its time depth to be roughly comparable to that of the Romance languages, or approximately two thousand years. The diversity of the Cupan branch resembles that of Spanish, Portuguese, and Italian, with Luiseño corresponding to Italian and Cahuilla-Cupeño to Spanish and Portuguese (R. Jacobs 1975:5).

3.32.1 Gabrielino-Fernandeño (Tongva)

Gabrielino takes its name from Mission San Gabriel, near Los Angeles, where it was the dominant language of the Indian converts. Many Gabrielino descendants now prefer to be called **Tongva,** and the language is now often referred to by that name.[127] It was spoken throughout the Los Angeles basin and in northern Orange County as far south as Irvine. On the north, Gabrielino territory extended to the San Gabriel Mountains. How far east Gabrielino was spoken is unclear, but it appears to have been the language of at least the western portion of the San Bernardino Valley, from Ontario to Corona. The Serrano appear to have moved into the north and east of the valley in the nineteenth century, after the establishment of a mission station between San Bernardino and Redlands.

A dialect of Gabrielino, spoken in the San Fernando Valley, was the dominant language of the converts at Mission San Fernando and is usually referred to as **Fernandeño.** William McCawley (1996:90) also notes the possibility of a dialectal distinction between the interior areas around San Gabriel and Whittier, possibly dominated by the major village of Shevanga, and the coastal area around San Pedro and Long Beach. The variety spoken in the San Pedro–Long Beach area may have been close to the Gabrielino that was said to have been spoken on Santa Catalina and the other southern Channel Islands (Harrington 1962).

The names and locations of about fifty precontact Gabrielino-Fernandeño settlements are known (Kroeber 1925, plate 57; B. Johnston 1962; W. McCawley 1996:35–87). Although the aboriginal sociopolitical divisions can only be guessed at, there are hints that some Gabrielino village communities were organized into districts that recognized the authority of the hereditary chief of a central village. One such district seems to have been located north of the Puente Hills, centered on the village of Ahwinga (*ʔahwi:-ŋa* 'burned brush place'?). Other villages that may have been district centers include Shevanga (*šiva:-ŋa* 'stone, flint place'?), near San Gabriel Mission; Pasheknga (*paše:k-ŋa*), near San Fernando Mission; and Povunga (*povu:ʔ-ŋa*), at Rancho Los Alamitos near the mouth of the San Gabriel River, in Long Beach. Povunga was also an

FIGURE 73. Mrs. James V. Rosemeyre. Bakersfield, July 1905. One of the last speakers of Gabrielino and the source of C. Hart Merriam's extensive vocabulary. C. Hart Merriam collection of Native American photographs (Y/24a/P2 no.1). Courtesy of Bancroft Library UCB.

important ceremonial site, the traditional birthplace of the god Chinigchinich (Boscana 1933:32–33; W. McCawley 1996:69–71).

Gabrielino-Fernandeño is not well documented. No mission-era manuscript is known. There are early word lists by Horatio Hale (1846:566–567, "Kij"), Alexander Taylor (1860–1863), Oscar Loew (1875), and (a very short one) by H. W. Henshaw (1884m), all of them collected at or near the former mission at San Gabriel. The most valuable attestation is by Merriam, who found a speaker living near Bakersfield in 1903 and collected vocabularies of general and natural history terms totaling about fifteen hundred words (Appendix A: Y-24a). William McCawley (1996) has published complete transcripts of the Merriam vocabularies and of the four earlier wordlists. In 1903–1904, Kroeber collected a brief vocabulary of Gabrielino at Highland, near Riverside, and a vocabulary of Fernandeño at Tejon ranch (1907b:70–89). Between 1914 and 1933, Harrington collected additional material from several elderly Gabrielino speakers, as well as from one semispeaker of Fernandeño (Mills and Brickfield 1986: 67–76). Working primarily with Harrington's data, Munro has made a preliminary morphological analysis (see Munro 2000) and is at work on a full lexical compendium (n.d.).

Gabrielino has been extinct since at least the late 1930s. There are three modern Gabrielino-Fernandeño descendant communities, the Gabrielino-Tongva Tribe (www.tongvatribe.org), the Gabrieleno/Tongva Tribal Council of San Gabriel (www.tongva.com), and the Fernandeño-Tataviam Band of Mission Indians (www.tataviam.org). None of these has federal acknowledgement. Language revival efforts are intermittent.

3.32.2 Luiseño and Juaneño

Raymond White (1963:110) estimates that there were approximately fifty autonomous village communities (i.e., tribelets) in precontact Luiseño-Juaneño territory. Knowledge of the names and locations of a number of these communities has survived into recent generations, despite the repeated uprootings and resettlements of the eighteenth and nineteenth centuries. Although independent and fiercely defensive of their territories, the villages appear to have clustered in at least three groups.

The most important villages were located on the San Luis Rey River, from the coast to its headwaters above present-day Lake Henshaw, and to the south of the river in the Valley Center region. Among these were Keishla (Quechla, Quechinga) near Mission San Luis Rey; Wiasamai (Ojauminga), about five miles to the east; Pumusi, further upstream; Pala, at the *misión asistencia* of the same name; Pauma (Paumega), in Pauma Valley; Pakwi, near Lilac; Souma and Kaulawut, near Valley Center; Kuka (Cuqui) and Huyulkum, on the present-day La Jolla Indian Reservation; and Ngorivo (Curila, Guariba), east of Lake Henshaw, northwest of Cupeño territory. South along the coast, at the mouth of San Marcos Creek, was Bataquitos. In present Camp Pendleton to the north, Topome was on the Santa Margarita River, and Uchme on the coast at Las Flores (J. R. Johnson and Crawford 1999).

There was a second cluster of villages on the upper Santa Margarita River and in the Lake Elsinore–Temecula area, including Pechanga, Temecula, and Paxavxa. According to Kroeber (1907b:146) the dry upland to the east, on upper Temecula Creek around Aguanga and on the San Jacinto River as far as Soboba, also belonged to the Luiseño. The information that White collected in the 1960s, however, indicated that this sparsely inhabited area was more likely to have belomged to the Cahuilla or Serrano in precontact times, although some Luiseño people took refuge there in the nineteenth century after being forced off of their original lands by Mexican and American settlement (R. C. White 1963:105).

San Juan Creek and its tributaries in southern Orange County were the focus of a third cluster of villages. These people are usually referred to as the Juaneño, after Mission San Juan Capistrano, which was established on their territory in 1776, adjacent to the villages of Putuidem and Ahachmai. In the 1820s, Gerónimo Boscana, the mission priest at San Juan Capistrano, compiled a list of fourteen Juaneño villages (1934:60).

There were distinctions among local varieties in each cluster, but whether the village clusters were associated with distinct regional dialects is uncertain. The amalgamation at the missions of people from different villages and regions leveled most of the original linguistic variation before any record was made. The principal documented variation reflects the different standardizations that arose in the two mission communities: *Luiseño,* based on the Keishla variety at San Luis Rey, and *Juaneño,* based on the Ahachmai variety at San Juan Capistrano. During the postmission era, secondary local varieties of Mission Luiseño developed in the reservation communities of Rincón, Pauma, La Jolla, Pechanga, and Soboba, but it is unlikely that these have any significant connection with the pre-mission-era varieties distinctive of these areas.

Luiseño-Juaneño is one of the best documented Indian languages in California. The Rincón variety has been especially well attested in recent years by Eric Elliott in a massive dictionary (1999) and a fourteen-hundred-page series of texts in Luiseño and English (Hyde and Elliott 1994), and further work is in progress (Elliott n.d.). The older documentation of the language is also rich and varied.

The earliest surviving attestation is the vocabulary collected by Crespí near the site of Mission San Juan Capistrano on July 24, 1769 (see Box 1), the first formal documentation of an Alta California language. Another early vocabulary was collected by Father Arroyo de la Cuesta in the late 1830s from two Luiseño visitors at Mission Santa Ynez (Arroyo 1837). A short grammar and dictionary were compiled around 1840 by Pablo Tac, one of two young Luiseño men who had been taken to Rome to prepare for the priesthood (Tagliavini 1926, 1930b; Kroeber and Grace 1960:221–237; see ¶2.3.4). Horatio Hale collected a short vocabulary at Mission San Juan Capistrano in 1841 (Hale 1846:566–567, "Netela"). H. W. Henshaw collected a sizable vocabulary (1884l) during his BAE survey in the 1880s.

Beginning in 1898, Philip Stedman Sparkman, a storekeeper at Rincón and a self-taught linguist of considerable talent, devoted much of his spare time to compiling a detailed grammar and dictionary of Luiseño. He was in contact with A. L. Kroeber, who encouraged his efforts, and with Kroeber's sponsorship he published a short grammatical sketch (Sparkman 1905). When Sparkman was murdered near his store by an unknown assailant in May 1907, Kroeber took Sparkman's manuscripts into his care with the intention of seeing them into print. A nearly finished paper on Luiseño culture was published in 1908, but Sparkman's grammar, edited by Kroeber and his student George Grace, appeared only in 1960. The manuscript of Sparkman's dictionary, which had been augmented by Kroeber and Grace with their own materials, was published after Kroeber's death by William Bright (1968) in an edition that incorporated further data collected by Harrington, Malécot, and himself.[128]

Merriam documented the dialect diversity of the 1910 1930 period in sets of vocabularies collected at La Jolla, Pechanga, and Soboba (Appendix A: X-23nn-pp). In 1932–1934, Harrington devoted a considerable amount of time to field research on Luiseño and Juaneño (Mills and Brickfield 1986:85–103; Bright 1994). He also edited, and wrote a long and detailed introduction to, Boscana's mission-era description of traditional Juaneño religious beliefs and

practices (Boscana 1933), and shortly afterward discovered and published a different version of the manuscript (Boscana 1934).[129] In 1958–1960, André Malécot conducted fieldwork with a speaker from Pauma and published a structural analysis in a series of articles (1963–1964); Bright worked briefly with the same speaker and obtained somewhat different results (1965c). In the late 1960s a research team at UC San Diego worked in collaboration with a Luiseño speaker to prepare a teaching grammar for Tribal purposes (Hyde 1971). Roderick Jacobs's study of comparative Cupan (1975) and Susan Steele's research on Luiseño syntax (1990) have their origin in this project. John Davis carried out fieldwork in the early 1970s, resulting in his UCLA dissertation on Luiseño syntax (1973) and a paper on Luiseño phonology (1976).

Approximately 2,500 Luiseño and Juaneño descendants live on or around the La Jolla, Rincon, Pauma, Pechanga, and Pala Reservations, and in the town of San Juan Capistrano. Elliott (n.d.) reports that there are no longer any speakers whose primary vehicle of expression is Luiseño, although there are partial and passive speakers of the Rincón, La Jolla, and Pauma dialects. The Takic Language Program, a joint venture of UC Riverside and the Pechanga Band at Temecula, sponsors the teaching of Luiseño to adults, the teaching of Luiseño in preschool and after-school immersion programs, and the translation and transcription of older Luiseño and other Takic language data. Classes in Luiseño are a regular part of Palomar College's Program in American Indian Studies. The Acjachemen Nation at San Juan Capistrano has a small language preservation program focused on the Juaneño dialect; an extensive Juaneño vocabulary, prepared by William Bright on the basis of Harrington's notes, is posted at the tribal Web site (Bright 1994).

3.32.3 Cupeño

Cupeño is a distinct language originally spoken in a small area near the headwaters of San Luis Rey River, at the foot of Hot Springs Mountain. There were only three Cupeño villages, the largest of which was Kupa, near Warner Springs. Two smaller settlements, Wilaqalpa and Paloqla, were on San Ysidro Creek a few miles to the southeast. Despite the small scale of Cupeño territory, there were clear dialectal differences between Kupa and the other two villages (Jacobs 1975:7).

The Cupeño were in close contact with the Cahuilla to the north and east, and the conservative Mountain dialect of Cahuilla was almost—but not quite—mutually intelligible with Cupeño. The Cupeño and Mountain Cahuilla both have an oral tradition that the Cupeño were originally a Cahuilla group. The Cupeño were on less close terms with the Luiseño to the west, and the languages were significantly different (Bright and Hill 1967; R. Jacobs 1975:5). Their closest contacts were with the Ipai Diegueño to the south, and many Cupeño speakers, especially in Wilaqalpa, were bilingual in

Ipai. These relationships were disrupted in 1903 when the Cupeño community was expelled from the Warner Springs area and resettled among the Luiseño on the Pala Reservation.

Cupeño is well documented. Jane Hill made a thorough study of the Kupa dialect in the early 1960s, and her doctoral dissertation (1966) is a formal grammar and a lexicon. She has recently published a fully revised and much expanded version of this technical study (J. Hill 2005), and there is a more pedagogical presentation in Hill and Nolasquez (1973). The major archival documentation is the collection made by Paul Louis Faye between 1919 and 1927, working under Kroeber's supervision (Faye 1919–1920, 1919–1927). It contains a number of narrative texts as well as extensive grammatical and ethnographic notes. Other documentation includes general and natural history vocabularies collected by Merriam (¶Appendix A: X-23mm) and various material collected by Harrington (Mills and Brickfield 1986:103–105). The only significant documentation of the Wilaqalpa dialect was made by Roderick Jacobs (1975:7).

The last fluent speaker of Cupeño died in 1987 at the age of ninety-four, although several people still remember a few words and phrases, and there was one elderly semispeaker as of 2001. A collection of texts and a dictionary have been prepared for community use, and classes in Cupeño are a regular part of Palomar College's Program in American Indian Studies.

3.32.4 Cahuilla

Cahuilla is the easternmost of the Takic languages. Cahuilla traditional territory extended east from Riverside and Banning through San Gorgonio Pass and south through the Coachella Valley to the vicinity of the Salton Sea. It was also spoken in the Soboba area west of the San Jacinto Mountains and along Temecula and Cahuilla Creeks between the Palomar and Santa Rosa Mountains.

In this arid territory, village communities centered on springs and other scarce water resources and were largely self-sufficient, although linked to one another by a social and ceremonial system that emphasized reciprocity between the Wildcat and Coyote moieties. Cahuilla communities fell into three geographical divisions, correlated with clear dialect differences (Seiler 1977:6–7).

The *Pass* (or *Wanikik*) *Cahuilla* occupied San Gorgonio Pass, around Banning and the present-day Morongo Reservation. The Pass Cahuilla were in close contact with the Serrano in the San Bernardino Mountains to the north, and in the postcontact period the linguistic and ethnic identity of the Indian communities in this region has become mixed. The lower part of the Morongo Reservation, called Malki in Cahuilla, is predominantly Cahuilla, while the Mission Creek and Morongo Valley areas to the northeast identify themselves as Serrano (Kroeber 1908c:35–36; 1925:693–694). The same dialect of Cahuilla is also spoken in the Palm Springs area, a few miles to the east of San Gorgonio Pass at the foot of Mount San Jacinto.

The *Desert Cahuilla* occupied the low Colorado Desert (now the heavily irrigated Coachella Valley) southeast of Palm Springs, centering on the area around Indio. Although the Colorado Desert is fiercely hot in the summer, water could easily be obtained in springs and shallow wells, mesquite trees were abundant, and the aboriginal Desert Cahuilla were relatively numerous. Modern descendant communities include the Cabazon Reservation in Indio and the Torres-Martinez Reservation in Thermal.

The *Mountain Cahuilla* lived on the less arid western slopes of the San Jacinto and Santa Rosa Mountains from Soboba to the Cahuilla Valley, and along Temecula Creek around Aguanga, east of Mount Palomar. Modern descendant communities include the Cahuilla and Santa Rosa Reservations in Riverside County, and the Los Coyotes Reservation in San Diego County.

The differences among the dialects sometimes hinder but do not prevent mutual intelligibility (R. Jacobs 1975:6). Of the three, Mountain Cahuilla is the most conservative and Pass Cahuilla the most innovative in both grammar and vocabulary. Desert Cahuilla more closely resembles Mountain Cahuilla than Pass Cahuilla.

Cahuilla has been well documented, most extensively by the German linguist Hans-Jakob Seiler, who conducted fieldwork between 1955 and 1974 and published a grammar (1977), a dictionary (Seiler and Hioki 1979), and a collection of narrative texts (1970). His materials principally represent the Desert dialect (for a Cahuilla assessment of his work see Saubel and Munro 1980). A 1977 UCLA project, directed by Pamela Munro and Katherine Siva Saubel, collected a considerable amount of data on the Mountain dialect and compiled a pedagogical grammar (Saubel and Munro 1981). Since 1990, Saubel has been working in collaboration with Eric Elliott, resulting in a two-volume collection of bilingual texts (Saubel and Elliott 2004) and a dictionary of Mountain Cahuilla in manuscript (see Elliott n.d.).

The most significant earlier work is an ethnobotanical study by Barrows (1900), one of the most thorough for any California linguistic group. Between the mid-1920s and the early 1950s, Harrington collected a large amount of Cahuilla data from Adan Castillo, a prominent Mission Indian spokesman who worked with Harrington during frequent visits to Washington, DC; it is not clear which dialect he spoke (Mills and Brickfield 1986:76–85). Merriam collected general and natural history vocabularies from all three dialects (Appendix A: X-23ff-kk).

While there are no longer any speakers of Pass Cahuilla, five native speakers of Mountain Cahuilla survived as of 2004, as did one fully fluent and perhaps a dozen or so nearly fluent speakers of Desert Cahuilla. A practical orthography was introduced in 1980, and extensive teaching materials were prepared, including a full introductory textbook (Saubel and Munro 1981). The Malki Museum, on the Morongo Reservation in Banning, has played an important role in Cahuilla language preservation.

3.32.5 Serrano and Vanyume

The Serrano occupied the San Bernardino Mountains and parts of the Mojave Desert immediately to the north of the mountains. Their territory extended from Cajon Pass on the west, where they adjoined the Gabrielino, to Twentynine Palms, deep in the Mojave Desert, on the east. The loosely articulated nature of Serrano society makes it difficult to assign definitive boundaries to their territory, and in the historical period they seem to have moved into Cahuilla territory in San Gorgonio Pass, and into either Gabrielino and Cahuilla territory in the San Bernardino Valley south of Cajon Pass (Kroeber 1907b:132–133, 1908c:32–34).

Serrano is moderately well documented. Kenneth Hill carried out fieldwork on the language in the early 1960s; his dissertation (1967) is a full descriptive grammar (see also K. Hill 1978). More recently Serrano has been studied by Eric Elliott, who has published a nine-hundred-page collection of narrative texts with a grammatical sketch, in collaboration with the last fluent speaker (Ramón and Elliott 2000). Elliott also has in preparation a bilingual (Serrano/English, English/Serrano) dictionary and a textbook of Basic Serrano that is approximately four hundred pages in length (see Elliott n.d.). Earlier documentation includes some material collected by Harrington in 1918 (Mills and Brickfield 1986:64–67) and vocabularies of at least two varieties of Serrano collected by Merriam at several locations between 1907 and 1933 (Appendix A: X-23cc-dd).

Serrano settlements in the Mojave Desert were primarily located along the Mojave River, at least to Victorville and possibly as far as Barstow and Daggett. Further north, with very uncertain boundaries, lay the territory of a group known to the Mojaves as the **Vanyume,** who considered themselves a separate but related tribe (Kroeber 1925: 614–615, 1959:299–305). The Vanyume were all but exterminated sometime before 1840, and very few data on their speech have been preserved (see Kroeber 1907b:70–89, 139–140, under "Möhineyam"). The existing evidence suggests that the Vanyume dialect was very close to Serrano, although it also seems to have shared some features with Kitanemuk.[130]

3.32.6 Kitanemuk

The Kitanemuk occupied the Tehachapi Pass area and the western end of the Mojave Desert as far east as present-day Edwards Air Force Base. Hardly anything is known about Kitanemuk settlements. To the southwest were the inland outposts of the Central Chumash, and to the north the Kawaiisu and the Tubatulabal. According to Harrington's data, the Kitanemuk were linked to all these mountain neighbors in a complex ritual and trading alliance (Blackburn and Bean 1978:564). They had a more distant, often hostile, relationship with the Yokuts in the San Joaquin Valley, and with the Serrano, Vanyume, and Tataviam in the desert and mountains to the south. They were friendly with the Mojave, however, who often made the long trip across the desert to visit and trade with them (Kroeber 1907b:135–136).

Although usually treated as a separate language, Kitanemuk was easily understood by a speaker of Serrano (Kroeber 1907b:140) and may be considered a third dialect of Serrano-Vanyume. The earliest attestations of Kitanemuk come from the early twentieth century. Merriam collected general and natural history vocabularies in 1903–1905 (Appendix A: X-23aa) and Kroeber collected a vocabulary in 1906 (1907b:69, 71–89). Most of the information on Kitanemuk society, culture, and language comes from data collected by Harrington in 1916–1917 (Mills and Brickfield 1986:60–64), with additional documentation of the language by Zigmond in 1937. Although the language has been extinct for several decades, Anderton (1988, 1991) was able to compile a grammar and dictionary on the basis of Harrington's and Zigmond's data.

3.32.7 Tataviam

The Tataviam lived on the Santa Clara River above Sespe and Piru, and along Piru and Castaic Creeks into the Sawmill and Tehachapi Mountains (J. R. Johnson and Earle 1990). They were in close contact with the Fernandeño to the south, and like them were recruited into Mission San Fernando. On the northeast their territory adjoined that of the Kitanemuk. On the west they bordered on the Ventureño Chumash, and to the north they were in contact with Interior Chumash and Southern Valley Yokuts around Castac Lake and Fort Tejon.

The language of the Tataviam was first attested by a single phrase ('where are you going?') and a place-name (the Tataviam equivalent of "Piru"), both collected by Kroeber in 1912 from a Kitanemuk speaker who remembered only these scraps of a language spoken by his grandparents (Kroeber 1915a). Harrington reelicited these forms from the same individual the following year, and in 1916–1917 collected a few more words or phrases said to be Tataviam from speakers of other languages in the area (Bright 1975; Mills and Brickfield 1986:60–64). Kroeber thought Tataviam would most likely turn out to be a variety of Serrano. Bright (1975), however, believed Harrington's data either attested a Takic language that was distinct from all others, or was the remnant, influenced by Takic, of an otherwise unknown language family. Munro and Johnson (2001), reexamining the data available to Bright, a small amount of additional material culled from Harrington's notes, and some place-names from the San Fernando mission records, have returned to Kroeber's view that the language probably belongs to the Serrano-Vanyume-Kitanemuk subgroup of Takic, and most closely resembles Kitanemuk.

The situation is complicated by a vocabulary collected by Merriam of a language he identified as "Alliklik Chumash." Beeler and Klar (1977) have shown this vocabulary to represent a variety of Chumash very close to Ventureño but with many borrowings from Kitanemuk. Taking this evidence into account, Bright (1975:236) tentatively concluded that there were two types of speech in the upper Santa Clara Valley, a Chumash dialect (which could be called "Alliklik") and a language with Takic affinities (which could be called "Tataviam"). But as Hudson (1982) cautioned, the surviving attestations of their speech are probably too small and too problematic ever to allow a definitive understanding of the linguistic profile of the Tataviam.

3.32.8 Island Takic

The three inhibited Southern Channel Islands—Santa Catalina, San Clemente, and San Nicolas—were occupied at the time of contact by speakers of one or more Takic languages. A variety of Gabrielino was apparently spoken on Santa Catalina (Gabrielino Pimu, Luiseño Pipimar) and possibly also on San Clemente (Gabrielino Kinki or Kinkipar, Luiseño Khesh). According to Kroeber, however, the Luiseño claimed that San Clemente had been "inhabited by people speaking their own language, who, after having been brought to the mainland by the Franciscans, were settled at a place three miles below San Luis Rey Mission, to which they gave the same name, Khesh" (1907b:153).[131] San Nicolas, the most remote of the islands, may have been occupied by speakers of a distinct Takic language, but it is attested only in four poorly transcribed words and two songs that were obtained in 1853 from a woman who had been abandoned on the island for eeighteen years (Heizer and Elsasser 1961). Analysis of the data confirms that the language is Takic, but it appears to be more similar to the languages of the Cupan subgroup than to Gabrielino (Munro 2002).

3.32.9 Linguistic Structure

Modern grammatical descriptions are available for most of the Takic languages: Cahuilla (Seiler 1977), Cupeño (J. Hill 1966, 2005), Kitanemuk (Anderton 1988), Luiseño (Elliott 1999; Steele 1990), and Serrano (K. Hill 1967; Ramón and Elliott 2000). Munro provides an outline of Gabrielino structure in a paper focusing on the pronominal enclitics (Munro 2000). Bright (1965a) provides a nontechnical survey of the sound systems of Cahuilla, Cupeño, and Luiseño.

In phonology, the Takic languages all share a basic pattern, but with some significant differences. The simplest phonemic system is found in Cahuilla (Table 50), which has five plain oral stops (*p, t, k, q, qʷ*), a palatal affricate (*č*), four plain fricatives (*s, š, x, xʷ*) and a voiced labial fricative (*β*), four nasals (*m, n, nʸ, ŋ*), four approximants (*l, lʸ, w, y*), and two laryngeals (*h, ʔ*). A flap (*ɾ*), mostly restricted to loanwords from Spanish, occurs in a few non-Spanish words. There are four vowels (*i, e, a, u*), which occur both short and long, and stress is phonemic. To this phonemic inventory Luiseño adds a fifth vowel (*o*) and a front-velar labiovelar

TABLE 50

Cahuilla Phonemes (Bright 1965b)

Consonants							Vowels		
p	t	č	k	q	qʷ	ʔ	i / i:		u / u:
(f)	s	š	x		xʷ	h	e / e:		(o:)
β								a / a:	
	(ɾ)								
m	n	nʸ	ŋ						
	l	lʸ							
w		y							

(*kʷ*), but lacks the palatal nasal (*nʸ*) and palatal lateral (*lʸ*); Gabrielino apparently had the same system. A phonemic contrast exists in Luiseño and Cupeño between a postalveolar and a palatal fricative (*ṣ, š*), but it has a low functional load (Bright 1965c). Cupeño further adds a high central unrounded vowel (*i*). Serrano has the phonemic inventory of Gabrielino and Luiseño, plus a retroflex stop (*ṭ*) and three r-colored vowels (*iʳ, aʳ, oʳ*).

Takic nouns are marked for possessor by a set of pronominal prefixes—for example, Cahuilla *ne-* 'my', *ʔe-* 'your (sg.)', *he-* 'his, her, its', *čeme-* 'our', *ʔeme-* 'your (pl.)', *hem-* 'their'. They are also inflected for plurality (Cahuilla *-m ~ -em*) and objective case (Cahuilla *-i ~ -y*), while various locative, directional, and instrumental relationships are marked by suffixes that fuse with the stem somewhat more loosely (Cahuilla *-ŋa* 'at', *-ika* 'toward', *-ax* 'from'). When not possessed or in compounds—and thus with contextually isolated and sometimes specialized meanings—nouns are usually marked with a lexically specified absolutive suffix (in Cahuilla basically *-it, -iš, -il, -ilʸ*; cognate forms are found in all Takic languages, cf. Luiseño *-t ~ -ta, -š ~ -ča, -l ~ -la*) (see Seiler 1985). For example, Cahuilla *né-wiw* 'my acorn mush' versus *wíw-iš* 'acorn mush', *ne-húya* 'my arrow' versus *húya-l* 'arrows, anybody's arrow', *hé-puš* 'his eye' versus *púč-il* 'the eye; a seed'; Luiseño *no-ku:tapi* 'my bow' versus *ku:tapi-š* 'bow', *no-paw* 'my water' versus *pa:-la* 'water'.

Verb morphology differs considerably among the Takic languages. In Luiseño and Cupeño, verbs lack prefixes but have a relatively complex suffixal morphology marking various derivational categories and aspect. Subject and object pronouns are expressed in independent words that are marked for case. In Cahuilla, however, verbs are inflected for subject and object by sets of prefixes similar to those used to mark possessor in nouns, and a small number of aspectual and subordinating suffixes follow the stem. Most temporal, aspectual, and other modifying concepts are expressed in adverbs that often are enclitic to the inflected verb. In both Gabrielino-Fernandeño and Serrano-Kitanemuk, pronominal subject and object categories are marked by a complex set of phrasal enclitics (not cognate between the two groups) that also mark the indicative, subjunctive, and interrogative moods (Munro 2000).

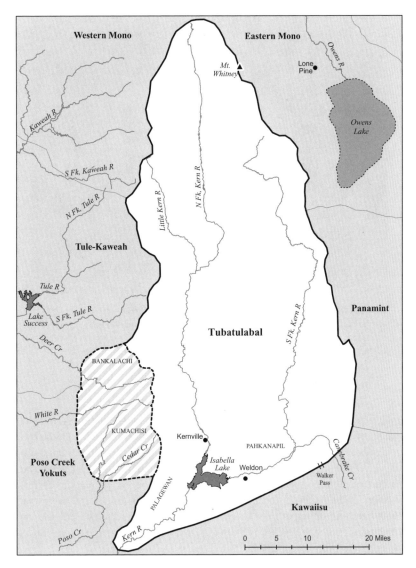

MAP 37. Tubatulabal territory

3.32.10 Nomenclature

"Takic," a term based on the word for 'person' in all Takic languages (and borne by the indigenous Luiseño linguist Pablo Tac; see ¶2.3.4), was introduced as the family name by Wick Miller (1961), replacing Kroeber's "Southern California Shoshonean" and paralleling the replacement of "Plateau Shoshonean" by "Numic" (Lamb 1958a).

3.33 Tubatulabal

Tubatulabal is a language[132] of the Uto-Aztecan family, usually classified, like Hopi, as an independent branch of the Northern Uto-Aztecan subfamily, and thus coordinate with, rather than a member of, Numic or Takic. Manaster Ramer (1992b) and Jane Hill (2009), however, arguing strictly from phonological evidence, believe Tubatulabal to belong to a subgroup with Gabrielino and Cupan that split away from

Serrano-Kitanemuk at the earliest stage in the differentiation of a "Californian" branch of Northern Uto-Aztecan.

3.33.1 Geography

Tubatulabal was spoken along the upper Kern River northeast of Bakersfield, both along the main Kern (or "North Fork") and along its principal tributary, South Fork (Map 37). There were two principal tribelets or districts, correlated with "a slight dialectic difference" (Voegelin 1935a:v). The **Palagewan** (*pa:lage:wan*), or North Fork Tubatulabal, claimed the main Kern River from Kern Canyon, a few miles northeast of Bakersfield, to the headwaters near Mount Whitney. Their permanent villages, however, were concentrated in Kern Valley, a fourteen-mile stretch of the river around the mouth of South Fork. The **Pahkanapil** (*pahkanapï:l*), or Tubatulabal proper, lived along the South Fork as far east as Canebrake Creek, with the majority of their villages located in South

FIGURE 74. Pahkanapil Tubatulabal chief Steban Miranda (*left*), with his son Mike and family. Weldon, Kern Valley, 1932. Mike Miranda was Carl Voegelin's primary consultant for Tubatulabal; Steban Miranda was the source of Harringon's Giamina (Omomil) data. C. Hart Merriam collection of Native American photographs (Z/25b/P1 no.2). Courtesy of the Bancroft Library UCB.

Fork Valley, on the lowermost few miles of the stream (E. Voegelin 1938:41–43). Many Palagewan and Pahkanapil village sites have been flooded by the reservoir behind Isabella Dam (completed in 1953). A third Tubatulabal-speaking group, the **Toloim** or **Toloip** (more commonly known by their Yokuts name, ***Bankalachi***),[133] occupied a small territory around the hot springs on upper Deer Creek, west of the Greenhorn Mountains, only a few miles north of the headwaters of Poso Creek. According to Kroeber, "the majority of the little tribe are likely to have been bilingual; at any rate they were extensively intermarried with the Yokuts" (1925:610). The Kumachisi on upper Poso Creek (¶3.26.1) were probably also Tubatulabal-Yokuts bilinguals, a fact which would help explain the confusion between the two tribelets in the ethnographic record (cf. Kroeber 1907b:126). Probably located somewhere in this area as well (if they were not the Kumachisi by another name) were the Giamina, or Omomil, who appear to have spoken an otherwise unattested Uto-Aztecan language, related to but quite distinct from Tubatulabal (see ¶3.34).

The Tubatulabal often traveled outside their territory to trade and gather food, and interaction with speakers of other languages, particularly Uto-Aztecan languages, was frequent (E. Voegelin 1938:51–52). The most important external contacts were to the northeast, with the Western Numic–speaking Owens Valley Paiute and the Central Numic–speaking Koso Panamint. The latter, whom the Tubatulabal reached across Walker Pass, controlled an important obsidian resource at Coso Hot Springs. To the south the Tubatulabal were in contact with the Southern Numic–speaking Kawaiisu and, more distantly, with the Takic-speaking Kitanemuk and Serrano-Vanyume, and even with the Mojave (Kroeber 1925:607). There are reports of Tubatulabals journeying as far south as Ventureño Chumash territory to obtain olivella shells and steatite, with Chumash traders occasionally making reciprocal visits (E. Voegelin 1938:52). Relations were less friendly with the Poso Creek and Southern Valley Yokuts, who sometimes raided Tubatulabal territory (E. Voegelin 1938:49).

3.33.2 Documentation and Survival

Ignored by nineteenth-century investigators (except for a listing of the numerals 1–10 in Powers 1877:399), Tubatulabal was first documented by Merriam, who began collecting a vocabulary of Pahkanapil in 1902 (Appendix A: Z-25b), continuing work intermittently through 1935 and adding a vocabulary of Bankalachi in 1932 (Z-25a). Kroeber collected vocabularies of both Pahkanapil and Bankalachi in 1906 and was the first to describe the language in print (1907b:69, 71–89). T. T. Waterman carried out a field reconnaisance around 1910–1912, collecting texts, vocabulary, and ethnographic data, including some material on Bankalachi (Waterman n.d.[a]). Harrington obtained a Tubatulabal vocabulary in 1916 while working on Kitanemuk, and gathered further data in 1933–1934, much of it ethnogeographical in nature (Mills and Brickfield 1986:56–59). The language is best known from the work of C. F. Voegelin, who made an extensive field study of the Pahkanapil dialect in 1931–1933 and published a grammar (1935a), a short dictionary (1958), and a collection of texts (1935b).

There is no formally organized Tubatulabal tribe, but many descendants belong to the Kern Valley Indian Council, in Lake Isabella (www.navatech.org/KVIC.htm), which is petitioning for federal acknowledgement. In October 2004 a group of Tubatulabal descendants from the White Blanket Allotment on the South Fork established the Pakanapul Language Program (Mount Mesa, California) with private grant funding. As of 2005, Betsy Johnson, the project coordinator, and four others were studying the language with Jim Andreas, 74, the only remaining speaker of the South Fork dialect (his mother was raised in the Bull Run area near Kernville). A media technician videotaped all teaching sessions. One of the principal goals of the Pakanapul project is to develop teaching materials for the local school curriculum.

3.33.3 Linguistic Structure

The only linguistically adequate general description of Tubatulabal is Voegelin's (1935a). There is a significant secondary literature on the phonological analysis of the language, based on data derived entirely from Voegelin (Swadesh and Voegelin 1939; J. McCawley 1969; Lightner 1971; Jensen 1973; Heath 1981). Manaster Ramer (1984, 1993) has analyzed Tubatulabal phonology from a comparative Uto-Aztecan perspective.

The phonemes of Tubatulabal (Table 51) include three oral stops (*p, t, k*) and two affricates (*c* [ts], *č*), which are uniformly voiceless in initial and final position but show a voiced:voiceless contrast between vowels (historically the product of allophonic lenition; see Manaster Ramer 1984); a plain palatal fricative (*š*); three nasals (*m, n, ŋ*); three approximants (*l, w, y*); and two laryngeals (*ʔ, h*). There are six vowels (*i, e, a, o, u, ï*), which can be phonemically short or long. Stress is not distinctive.

Nouns are marked for possessor by a set of pronominal suffixes: *-niʔïŋ* 'my', *-ïŋ* 'your (sg.)', *-n* 'his, her, its', *-č* 'our (two)', *-c* 'our (pl.)', *-ulu* 'your (pl.)', *-p* 'their'. When unpossessed, nouns are marked by one of two absolute suffixes (*-l* or *-t*) or are unmarked, the choice being lexically determined (e.g., *hani:-niʔïŋ* 'my house' versus *hani:-l* 'the house', *mu:š-niʔïŋ* 'my fish spear' versus *mu:š-t* 'the fish spear', *co:h-niʔïŋ* 'my fish' versus *co:h* 'the fish'). Three syntactic cases are distinguished: subject (unmarked), object (*-a ~ -i*), and genitive (*-ïŋ ~ -aʔaŋ*), which combine in sometimes complex ways with the possessive and absolute suffixes. Secondary cases are formed by suffixing postpositions to nouns in the objective case—for example, *hani:-l-a-p* 'to, in the house', *hani:-l-a-bacu* 'from the house', *hani:-bacu:-niʔïŋ* 'from my house'.

Tubatulabal verb stems have two forms, called by Voegelin (1935a:94) "telic" and "atelic," which are essentially aspectual variants (momentaneous versus durative). The atelic variant usually has the phonologically basic form, the telic variant being derived from it by initial reduplication: *ʔela-* 'jump, be jumping' versus *ʔeʔela-* 'jump (once)'; *tik-*

TABLE 51

Consonants						Vowels		
p	t	c	č	k	ʔ	i / i:	ï / ï:	u / u:
-b-	-d-	-ʒ-	-ǰ-	-g-		e / e:	a / a:	o / o:
			š		h			
m	n			ŋ				
w	l		y					

'eat, be eating' versus *ʔitik-* 'eat (once)'. The atelic stem must always be accompanied by inflectional and derivational suffixes marking tense, voice, and such categories as causative and benefactive; the telic stem, while it may have suffixes, often stands alone. Subject and object are marked by sets of pronouns that can be enclitic to the verb, be enclitic to a word that precedes the verb, or take the form of an independent pronominal word. For example, the subject pronoun *nik ~ -gi ~ -ki* 'I' is enclitic to the verb in *tika-ki tapiši:la* 'I am eating the bread', but it could also be enclitic to the nominal object (*tapiši:la-gi tïkat*), or it could be expressed as an independent pronoun (*nik tïkat tapiši:la*).

3.33.4 Nomenclature

"Tübatulabal" was said by Kroeber (1907b:124) to be the Tubatulabal self-designation and to be derived from the Numic term for pine nut (cf. Mono *tïpah* 'piñon pine nut'). E. Voegelin's consultants told her it was not a Tubatulabal word, but had been "applied like a nickname by other tribes such as the Chumash, Kawaiisu, and some Yokuts groups" to the Pahkanapil tribelet (1938:8). It first appeared in print in Powers (1877:393) in the form "Ti-pa-to-la´-pa." The spelling with "ü" (representing the high central vowel *ï*) was introduced by Kroeber and followed by Voegelin, but "Tubatulabal" is now common among anthropologists and linguists. The academic tradition is to stress the word on the final syllable; as Powers's transcription suggests, in a more authentic pronunciation the stress would fall on the penult.

3.34 Giamina (Omomil)

Giamina, or Omomil, was the Uto-Aztecan language of a small group living somewhere adjacent to, and probably to the west of, Tubatulabal territory. The language is very poorly attested. In 1905, Kroeber (1907b:126–128) collected twenty words from an elderly speaker of Yokuts on the Tule River Reservation but was unable to elicit much further information about the language or the group. Referring to them as the *Giamina* (probably their Yokuts name), the old man located their territory a few miles northeast of Bakersfield, between Poso Creek and the Kern River, downstream from Kern Falls (see Map 37). In this area they would have been surrounded by Yokuts-speaking groups, including the Poso Creek tribelets on the east and north, and the Yawelmani on the west and south. Later, however, the same informant said they were the same group as the Kumachisi tribelet of Poso Creek Yokuts, on the upper White River. Here they would have been close neighbors to the Bankalachi Tubatulabal on Deer Creek.

A number of resemblances to Takic suggested to Kroeber that the "Giamina" vocabulary might represent nothing more than "miscellaneous Yokuts corruptions, either individual or tribal, [of] one or more Shoshonean dialects" (1909a:263–265). However, he left open the possibility that it was "the vanishing trace of a distinctive Shoshonean language and group" (1925:610). The case for this was strengthened when, in 1933–1934, Harrington was able to collect a number of additional words in what was clearly the same language (Mills and Brickfield 1986:56). The source of his information, Steban Miranda (see Figure 74), was apparently the grandson of the man from whom Kroeber obtained his 1905 Giamina word list. Miranda referred to the language by a Tubatulabal name, *Omomil,* and said that it was formerly spoken in the territory that lay between the

"rio grande" (the Kern River) and the "rio chiquito," by which he could have meant either the South Fork of the Kern on the east or Poso Creek on the west. If the latter, which seems to be the more likely possibility, this generally agrees with the location indicated by his grandfather.

Alexis Manaster Ramer, who has examined the Giamina/Omomil corpus in detail (Manaster Ramer n.d.), believes that it represents an independent Northern Uto-Aztecan language that could be a historic link between Tubatulabal and Takic. The data, however, remain too meager for a definitive assessment. Whatever the classificatory status of Giamina/Omomil, the possible existence of so distinct a Uto-Aztecan language in the southern San Joaquin Valley indicates that this area may well have displayed more ethnolinguistic diversity in late precontact times than Kroeber recognized when he assigned nearly all of it to the Yokuts. He may have been too quick to dismiss Powers's report that in relatively recent times "the Paiuti tribes, swarming through [the Sierra Nevada] passes, seized and occupied Kern River, White River, Posa Creek and Kern Lake, thus completely severing the Yokuts nation" (Powers 1877:369; Kroeber 1907b:124).

Languages of Uncertain Affiliation

3.35 Yukian Languages

The Yukian family consists of two quite divergent, geographically separated languages, **Northern Yukian** and **Wappo,** with Northern Yukian divided into three distinct dialects or emergent languages, Yuki, Huchnom, and Coast Yuki (Map 38). Despite the many differences between Northern Yukian and Wappo, the unity of Yukian was recognized as early as the 1870s (Powers 1877:197). Although the validity of this grouping was challenged by Sawyer (see ¶3.35.4), the Yukian family can be considered securely demonstrated. A substantial comparative vocabulary of Northern Yukian (all three dialects) and Wappo can be found in Elmendorf (1968:22–35).

The Yukian family is not a member of either the Penutian or the Hokan phylum. Except for recent borrowings from Pomo and a number of widely distributed loanwords, lexical resemblances between Yukian and other California languages are minimal (Shipley 1957; Oswalt 1979). Yukian does, however, show numerous lexical similarities to Siouan and Yuchi (Elmendorf 1963, 1964), as well as to the Gulf languages of the Southeast, particularly Atakapa, Tunica, and Chitimacha (Munro 1994; Golla 1996c). Data published by Radin on Yukian-Siouan resemblances (1919) led Sapir to classify Yukian as an independent branch of the Hokan-Siouan stock in his proposed general classification of North American languages (1921c). The Gulf resemblances, which appear to have been

first noticed by Swadesh (1954a), similarly led Greenberg (1987) to assign Yukian to the (Macro-)Penutian branch of his proposed Amerind macrostock. Although neither Sapir's nor Greenberg's classification has enjoyed wide acceptance, it is not unlikely that future comparative work will eventually confirm some ancient connection between Yukian, Siouan-Yuchi, and the Gulf languages.[134]

Kroeber (1959c) noted several structural similarities (but no specific lexical resemblances) between Yukian—especially Northern Yukian—and Athabaskan, including tonal phenomena, monosyllabic stems, and classificatory verbs, and suggested that these features may have diffused into Northern Yukian from adjacent Athabaskan languages such as Wailaki. However, the California Athabaskan languages are one of several subgroups of Athabaskan that have never developed tone, and the other features Kroeber cites are unlikely to have been borrowed during the few centuries that Yuki and Wailaki were in contact. However, tonal contrasts and some of the other "Athabaskan" traits characteristic of Yukian are also found in Siouan and many Southeastern languages, as is Yuki's distinctly un-Californian nasalized central vowel.

3.35.1 Northern Yukian

Northern Yukian was spoken in the mountanous area of northern Mendocino County, from the high ridges of the Coast

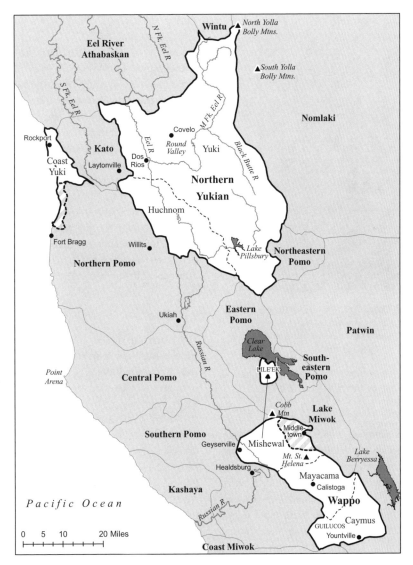

MAP 38. Yukian languages and dialects.

Range bordering the Sacramento Valley to the rocky coast north of Fort Bragg. Its three dialects were well marked off from one another by lexical and phonological differences, although they were nearly identical in grammar. Elmendorf has characterized them as "language-like dialects" that formed a chain of relationship from east to west (1968 [1993]:178). The comparative phonology of Northern Yukian was worked out in detail by Schlichter [Shepherd] (1985), who reconstructed a substantial Proto (Northern) Yukian lexicon.

YUKI

The principal dialect of Northern Yukian was Yuki, most of whose speakers lived in and around Round Valley in the upper drainage of the Middle Fork of the Eel River. There were six tribelets in Yuki territory, each associated with a shallowly differentiated subdialect. The most populous and

important of these was ***Ukom-no'm*** (*u:k'om-nom* 'valley people'), centered on Round Valley. According to Foster (1994:159–161) the others were ***Ta'-no'm*** ('slope people'), downstream from Dos Rios on the Middle Fork; ***Witukom-no'm*** ('Eden Valley people'), in and around Eden Valley; ***Huitit-no'm*** ('middle ridge people'), on Black Butte Creek; ***Sukshaltatam-no'm*** ('nicely shaped pine tree people'), at the headwaters of the Middle Fork; and ***Onkolukom-no'm*** ('ground in another valley people'), at the headwaters of the South Eel River near modern Lake Pillsbury. Subdialectal differences between tribelets were associated (as elsewhere in California) with a certain degree of social rivalry:

The word hálsi (to put more with) was used with reference to the language of subgroups other than that of the speaker. Strange dialects sounded complicated, and their speakers were thought to make them so simply for the sake of effect. Tillotson [Foster's principal informant] thought the

FIGURE 75. Ralph Moore, A. L. Kroeber's primary source of Yuki data. Photographed by Philip M. Jones, ca. 1900. Courtesy of the Hearst Museum of Anthropology and the Regents of UC.

Huititno'm were especially guilty of this: conversely, they considered their dialect to be the most pure of all Yuki speech. (Foster 1944:161)

While Yuki speakers were on relatively friendly terms with the Athabaskan-speaking Wailaki to the north, with whom they traded and intermarried, they had notoriously hostile relationships with most other surrounding peoples, including their Yukian kinsmen, the Huchnom (Kroeber 1925: 167–168). Besides the Huchnom, wars were fought with the Kato, the Pomo, and in particular the Wintuan Nomlaki of the Sacramento Valley. (The name "Yuki" is from Nomlaki *yuki* 'enemy'.) Powers, with his characteristic mix of insight and hyperbole, described the Yuki as "a pure democracy, fierce and truculent . . . and indisputably the worst tribe among the California Indians" (1877:125).

The first attestation of Yuki is a short vocabulary collected by Lieutenant Edward Ross in the 1850s, published by Gibbs (1863b), and reprinted by Powers (1877:483–489) along with a vocabulary collected by Powers himself in 1875. The first scientific observer to record Yuki was Jeremiah Curtin, who collected a BAE survey vocabulary (1889h, 1889i). The language was extensively documented by A. L. Kroeber between 1900 and 1917, and by Kroeber in collaboration with the Danish phonetician H. J. Uldall in 1931–1932 (Kroeber 1900–1958; Uldall 1931–1932, 1932); only a small portion of this material, most of which was obtained from a single speaker, Ralph Moore, has been published (Kroeber 1906b, 1911a, 1959c).[135] Harrington compiled an English-Yuki vocabulary (Harrington n.d.), and Merriam collected a vocabulary and a natural history word list from speakers of both the Round Valley ("Oo-kom-nom") and Eden Valley ("We-too-kom-nom") subdialects (Appendix A: D-4b-c). W. E. Myers, working for Curtis, obtained a good lexical sample

during ethnographic survey work in 1915–1924 (Curtis 1907–1930, vol. 14:207–214), and there is a considerable amount of cultural vocabulary scattered through Foster's ethnographic monograph (1944). Sydney Lamb collected some Yuki data during a linguistic survey of the area (1955), and extensive tape-recorded interviews were conducted by Jesse Sawyer, Roy Siniard, and Shirley Silver between 1966 and 1976 with the last two speakers, Minnie Fulweider and Arthur Anderson (see Schlichter 1985:8). All the lexical data gathered by Lamb and by Sawyer, Siniard, and Silver, together with much of the earlier material (except for Kroeber's), can be found in the cumulative lexicon compiled by Sawyer and Schlichter (1984).[136]

Arthur Anderson, the last known speaker, died around 1990. Yuki descendants share the Round Valley Reservation with several other tribes, and no language revitalization effort specifically focused on Yuki is known to be under way.

HUCHNOM

The Huchnom dialect was spoken by the people of a single tribelet (*huč-nom̓* 'outside people'), sometimes referred to as the "Redwood Indians" (Foster 1944:225–237). They lived in the heavily forested area along the lower part of South Eel River, northeast of Willits, separated from Yuki territory by the steep Sanhedrin Range. There was also one Huchnom village at the far northern end of Potter Valley, which was otherwise in Northern Pomo territory. According to Barrett (1908a:258), Huchnom cultural affinities were with the Pomo, while those of the Yuki were more with the Athabaskans to the north, although Foster (1944:225) notes that the similarities among all the Northern Yukian groups far exceeded their differences.

Sources of data on the Huchnom dialect include a vocabulary collected by Powers in 1875 (1877:483–489), a survey vocabulary collected by Barrett in 1903–1906 (1908a:68–80; see also 93, fn. 67), some data in Kroeber's collection (1900–1958), and the material collected from the last speaker, Lulu Johnson, by Lamb (in Lamb 1955). Lamb's notes are described by Schlichter (1985:13) as "the largest and most reliable body of data" on the dialect.

COAST YUKI

The Coast Yuki dialect was spoken in eleven village communities or small tribelets scattered along a forty-mile stretch of rocky coastline between Fort Bragg and Usal Creek. Although their foraging territory extended inland to Outlet Creek, close to Huchnom territory, the Coast Yuki were only sporadically in contact with other Northern Yukian speakers or with the Northern Pomo. By contrast, their interaction with adjacent Athabaskans—the Kato in the Branscomb and Laytonville area, and the Shelter Cove Sinkyone to the north of Usal Creek—were friendly and frequent, and most Coast Yukis understood or spoke Sinkyone and Kato (Gifford 1939 [1965]:14).

The most extensive and reliable attestation of Coast Yuki is Kroeber's (in Kroeber 1900–1958); the Coast Yuki survey vocabulary in Barrett (1908a:68–80) was almost entirely supplied by Kroeber (see Barrett's footnote 67 on p. 93). The only other sources are the general and natural history word lists collected by Merriam (Appendix A: D-4a), the cultural vocabulary included in E. W. Gifford's ethnographic sketch (1939) (but note the caution in Schlichter 1985:13), and some miscellaneous words and place-names that Harrington collected incidentally during a very brief visit to Laytonville in 1942 (Mills 1985:18–21).

3.35.2 Wappo

Wappo, the only Southern Yukian language, was spoken in a territory separated from Northern Yukian by the Pomo groups of Clear Lake and the upper Russian River. The Wappo occupied Alexander Valley, most of Napa Valley, and the northern portion of Sonoma Valley. There were several regional subgroups, each with a distinct but not deeply differentiated dialect. The **Mishewal** (*míše:wal*) were the people of Alexander Valley and Knights Valley (*mútis-t'ul* 'berry sp.–valley'). Their territory also included a stretch of the Russian River between Asti and Healdsburg, the southern part of which they took from the Southern Pomo in a series of conflicts around 1830 (Barrett 1908a:265–266; Kroeber 1925:219–220). The **Mayacama** held the upper Napa Valley, with their major village (*maya?kma*) located near Calistoga. The **Caymus** were centered on a village at Yountville (*kaymus*). Over the mountains to the west, at the head of Sonoma Creek, there was a Wappo-speaking group referred to in the Spanish-Mexican records as the **Guilicos** or **Guilucos,** after *wí:lok* 'dusty', the Miwok name of their principal village (Barrett 1908a:263–274; Merriam 1955:43). There was another Wappo enclave, or more accurately a colony, on the south shore of Clear Lake around Mount Konocti, where a group speaking the Alexander Valley dialect settled about 1800 (Barrett 1908a:274–278). This group was called the **Lile'ek** by the Clear Lake Pomo, a name which may have been derived from their self-designation (cf. Wappo *lel* 'rock'). Barrett (1908a:273) and Kroeber (1925:219) also assigned the area around Middletown, north of Mount St. Helena, to a Wappo subgroup variously called "Guenoc" or "Loknoma." Merriam (1955:43–48) argued that these were merely Wappo names for the southern, or Oleyomi, subgroup of Lake Miwoks. The area was probably bilingual.

Reliable ethnographic and linguistic data exist only for the Mishewal and Mayacama subgroups. The first attestation of the language was a vocabulary of the Knight's Valley variety of Mishewal that was collected in the early 1850s by John Russell Bartlett, published in Powers (1877:483–489). During visits between 1905 and 1929, Merriam collected a vocabulary and a natural history word list from speakers of both Mishewal and Mayacama (Appendix A: E-4h-j), and at some date between 1915 and 1924, W. E. Myers collected a similar general vocabulary (Curtis 1907–1930, vol. 14:207–

FIGURE 76. Laura Fish Somersal, last fluent speaker of Wappo and consultant for Jesse Sawyer, and later Charles Li and Sandra Thompson. Courtesy of Ralph Shanks.

214). The first extensive data on Wappo were collected by Paul Radin in 1917, resulting in the publication of a volume of traditional narrative texts (1924) and a grammar (1929). Radin's sources, Jim Tripo and Joe McCloud, were from Alexander Valley, and Tripo, who was also fluent in Eastern Pomo and Spanish, was the last speaker to have extensive knowledge of Wappo traditional myths and the "high language" in which they were couched (Radin 1929:7–8). Radin's documentation was refined and expanded between 1960 and 1985 by Jesse Sawyer, and between 1975 and 1985 by Charles Li and Sandra Thompson, working (independently) with Laura Fish Somersal, the last fluent speaker of the language. Sawyer published a short lexicon (1965) and prepared two analytical papers that were edited and published posthumously (1991). Li and Thompson published a series of technical papers on Wappo syntax (1977, 1978; Li, Thompson, and Sawyer 1977), culminating in a reference grammar (Thompson, Park, and Li 2006).

Although a few elderly individuals retain some knowledge of the language, none has a speaking knowledge, and Wappo is near extinction. Since there is no modern group for which Wappo is the heritage language, no retention effort is under way.

3.35.3 Linguistic Structure

Schlichter (1985:21–65) provides a grammatical summary of Proto-[Northern] Yukian, covering phonology and verbal and nominal morphology, but Kroeber's sketch (1911a) remains useful. Sawyer's short, informal sketch of Wappo

TABLE 52

Yukian Phonemic Systems

Consonants	Vowels

Yuki (Schlichter 1985)

p	t	ṭ	č	k	ʔ		i		u
p'	t'	ṭ'	č'	k'				ə	
		s	š		h		a		o
		-s'							
m	n								
-ṁ	-ṅ								
w	l		y						
-ẇ	-l'		-ẏ						

Wappo (Sawyer 1965; S. Thompson, Park, and Lee 2006)

p	t	ṭ	c	č	k	ʔ		i / i:		u / u:
pʰ	tʰ	ṭʰ	cʰ	čʰ	kʰ			e / e:		o / o:
p'	t'	ṭ'	c'	č'	k'				a / a:	
			s	š		h				
m	n									
ṁ	ṅ									
w	l		y							
ẇ	l'		ẏ							

phonemics and grammar (1991:11–84) is informative but idiosyncratic and leaves many topics untouched. The Wappo reference grammar by S. Thompson, Park, and Li (2006) focuses on syntax.

Northern Yukian languages have five basic stops and affricates (p, t, ṭ, č, k), all of which occur both plain and glottalized. There are two fricatives (s, š), two laryngeals (h, ʔ), two nasals (m, n), and three approximants (l, w, y). The fricative s, the nasals, and the approximants have glottalized equivalents that occur only in morpheme-final position. In addition to four basic vowels, two high (i, u) and two low (a, o), Northern Yukian languages also have a phonemically distinct central vowel (ə), which in Yuki is nasalized ([ə̃] or [ã]). A midfront vowel (e) is frequently written in transcriptions of Yuki, but its phonemic status is doubtful. Length was probably not phonemic in the protolanguage but may be in Yuki. Pitch differences are clearly present at the phonetic level, but their contrastive function is uncertain. Uldall and Kroeber (Uldall 1932; Kroeber 1959c) made a case for Yuki being a tone language, while Sawyer and Schlichter (1984:11) believed pitch differences were a secondary effect of stress.

The Wappo consonant system can be seen as an elaboration of the Northern Yukian system in the direction of Pomo (Table 52). To the preceding inventory of consonants it adds a contrast between two series of affricates (c [ts] and č), and distinguishes an aspirated set of stops and affricates in addition to the plain and glottalized sets. In addition, the glottalized nasals and approximants occur medially as well as finally. The Wappo five-vowel system (i, e, a, o, u) is identical to the vowel system found throughout Pomo but differs from Northern Yukian in lacking a central (nasalized) vowel, in having a distinction between i and e, and in making phonemic distinctions in length.[137] The pitch differences noted in Northern Yukian are absent in Wappo.

Morphologically, both Yuki and Wappo lie at the analytic end of the typological spectrum of California languages (¶4.5.2). In Yuki, all roots can occur as independent words, and compounding is frequent. Nouns are inflected for case, although some case endings may be better analyzed as postpositions or clitics (¶4.6.2). Pronouns are independent words and distinguish case in an subject/object paradigm (Table 53). As in the Pomo languages, agents are marked as "objects" rather than "subjects" when their relationship to the action or state described by the verb is involuntary (¶4.6.3). Verb roots are often derived with a suffix marking various voice and transitivity relationships, and are inflected for aspect and mode. Affixation is agglutinative rather than synthetic, and enclitics rather than suffixes may be involved in many morphological constructions.

Wappo roots, like Yuki roots, are often used as independent words, particularly as nouns, and are frequently compounded. Pronominal possession of nouns is marked by a set of prefixes not found in Northern Yukian; case relationships are marked by loosely bound suffixes or enclitics (see ¶4.6.2). Pronouns other than possessives are free words, and distinguish number and case. A class of adjectives is distinguished. Wappo verbs are morphologically complex, with more similarities to Pomo than to Northern Yukian. Well-developed sets of prefixes that are entirely lacking in Yuki mark direct object, direction, and instrument; suffixes mark tense and aspect.

3.35.4 The Yukian Relationship

Wappo differs markedly from Northern Yukian, not only in phonology and grammar, but also in lexicon—less than 20 percent of basic vocabulary is shared. Elmendorf characterized the "separate character" of the two languages as

> comparable to that of Italian to German, or of German to Russian. That is to say, Wappo constitutes a distinct "branch" (in Indo-European terms) of the Yukian family. (Elmendorf 1968 [1993]:177)

Elmendorf also noted that the percentage of likely cognates between Northern Yukian and Wappo varies considerably among the major semantic areas. Shared vocabulary is highest for plants (42 percent) and natural phenomena (30 percent), lowest for animals (9 percent) and items of technology (17 percent). He suggested that these differences in rate of retention might be explained by migration and differential culture change (1968 [1993]:186). Since the

TABLE 53
Yuki and Wappo Pronouns (Elmendorf 1981a)

	Subject	Object	Possessive (alienable)	Possessive (inalienable)
Yuki				
1 sg	ʔəp	ʔi	ʔitin	ʔi(t) ~ ʔin
2 sg	miʔ	mis	mit	mit
3 sg near	ka	kaʔa	kaʔat	kaʔat
3 sg distant	ki	kiʔa	kiʔat	kiʔat
1 pl inclusive	mi	miya	miyat	miyat
1 pl exclusive	ʔus	ʔusa	ʔusat	ʔusat
2 pl	moʔos	moʔosiya	moʔosiyat	moʔosiyat
3 pl near	kamasi	kamasa	kamasat	kamasat
3 pl distant	kimasi	kimasa	kimasat	kimasat
Wappo				
1 sg	ʔáh	ʔí-	ʔímeʔ	ʔi:-
2 sg	míʔ	mí-	mímeʔ	mi:-
3 sg near	hépʰi	té- ~ mé-	témeʔ ~ mémeʔ	te- ~ me-
3 sg distant	cépʰi	té- ~ mé-	témeʔ ~ mémeʔ	te- ~ me-
1 pl	ʔísi	ʔísa	ʔísa:meʔ	ʔi:sa-
2 pl	mísi	mísa	mísa:meʔ	mi:sa-
3 pl near	héko:ti	héko:to	héko:tomeʔ	héko:to
3 pl distant	céko:ti	céko:to	céko:tomeʔ	céko:t

highest retention rates are in domains connected with women's activities, and the lowest in those connected with men's activities, Elmendorf thought it possible, for example, that there was a period during the evolution of Wappo when Wappo-speaking women regularly married non-Wappo-speaking men.

Sawyer (1980), considering the same range of data, argued that borrowing could have operated in the reverse direction, and proposed that Wappo should be considered a non-Yukian language that has heavily borrowed from Northern Yukian:

> Yuki and Wappo . . . are not descended from any common or proto-language. . . . [T]heir putative relationship has been based on areal features and borrowings that reflect an intimate, extensive, and possibly unfriendly coexistence that predates European contact but may have slightly overlapped the earliest European contacts. (Sawyer 1980:210)

The evidence that Sawyer assembled to support his hypothesis of "non-genetic relationship" was addressed by Elmendorf and Shepherd (1999), who pointed out that the Wappo words that Sawyer claimed to be borrowings represented at most 6.9 percent of the full corpus of resemblant lexical sets. In another paper, Elmendorf (1997)

showed that the regularity of sound correspondences, whose lack Sawyer used as part of his argument for borrowing, can be masked by morphological processes that go back to Proto-Yukian.

3.35.5 Nomenclature

The Wintu and Nomlaki used the term *yukeh* 'enemy, hostile people' to designate any adjacent group with whom they were on a hostile footing, applying it indiscriminately to the Modoc, Shasta, Achumawi, and Yana, as well as to the group now called Yuki. Early white settlers in the Sacramento Valley borrowed the word in the same loose sense. It was Powers who made it the ethnic label for the previously undesignated Yuki because "this tribe alone acknowledge the title and use it" (1877:126). In Powers's usage, the term applied only to the Round Valley Yuki, but he recognized their linguistic affinity to the Huchnom ("Tatu") and the Wappo ("Ashochimi"), a relationship that he labeled the "Yuki-Wappo" family (1877:197). Powell simplified "Yuki-Wappo" to "Yukian" (1891:135), and this remains in general use.

"Wappo" is apparently borrowed from Spanish *guapo* 'handsome, gutsy, cocky'. According to Powers (1877:196), the epithet was bestowed on the Wappo by General Vallejo's troops after they had been repulsed by the Indians in a skirmish near Healdsburg in the 1840s.

3.36 Chumash Languages

The Chumash (or Chumashan) languages form a close-knit independent family, formerly believed to be of Hokan affiliation but now generally considered to be a classificatory isolate. Three branches of the family are usually recognized (Table 54): (1) **Obispeño,** or Northern Chumash, is a single language spoken by the village communities around Mission San Luis Obispo; (2) **Central Chumash** is a group of at least four distinct dialect clusters or emergent languages that are each associated with a mission: Purisimeño (Mission La Purisima, near Lompoc); Inezeño (Mission Santa Ynez); Barbareño (Mission Santa Barbara); and Ventureño (Mission San Buenaventura); (3) **Island Chumash** is the language spoken on the three inhabited islands in the Santa Barbara Channel—Santa Cruz, Santa Rosa, and San Miguel. These branches roughly correspond to the three broad ecological zones of Chumash territory (Map 39): (1) the relatively unproductive area north of Point Conception; (2) the resource-rich coast between Point Conception and Malibu; and (3) the unique ecology of the northern Channel Islands (Arnold 2001:12).

TABLE 54

Chumash Languages and Central Chumash Mission Dialects

Obispeño

Central Chumash

    Purisimeño

    Inezeño (Samala)

    Barbareño

    Ventureño

    Interior Chumash (?)

Island Chumash

    Cruzeño

The difference between Obispeño and the other Chumash languages is considerable, and there was little possibility of intelligibility between speakers of Obispeño and Purisimeño, the adjacent variety of Central Chumash. The paucity of data makes it difficult to assess the degree of difference between Island Chumash and the Barbareño and Ventureño varieties of Central Chumash spoken on the mainland opposite, but intercommunication was apparently difficult.

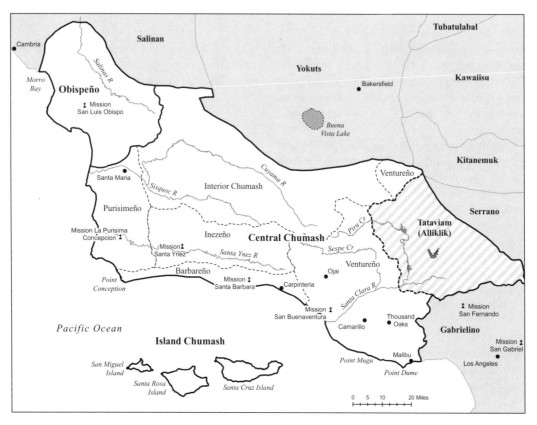

MAP 39. Chumash languages and mission dialects.

3.36.1 Obispeño

Obispeño differs markedly from the other attested Chumash languages in both phonology and grammar. Although much of its vocabulary is cognate with Central Chumash, the relationship is obscured by a number of sound changes, leading the earliest scientific observer, H. W. Henshaw, to initially assume that the language was not Chumash (Klar, Whistler, and McLendon 1999:24). The phonological divergence between Obispeño and Central Chumash, which is comparable to that between the modern standard varieties of French and Spanish, is underscored by a number of morphological differences in which Obispeño generally shows a greater similarity to Island Chumash than to adjacent Central Chumash.

The available data do not permit determination of the exact boundaries and internal diversity of Obispeño territory, but it seems clear that there was some degree of dialect diversity (Kroeber 1908:16, fn. 39; Klar 1971:20–22) as well as bilingualism with Salinan to the north.[138] Several of the phonological and morphological specializations of Obispeño within Chumash seem best explained by assuming a Salinan substratum to have existed throughout Obispeño territory (Kroeber 1910:268; Klar 1971:36–40).[139] Klar has also pointed out a number of possible borrowings into Obispeño from Uto-Aztecan, including the numeral 'one', which closely resembles the Numic form (Klar 1980:115). If these resemblances are more than accidental, they may testify to a Uto-Aztecan and/or Chumash presence in the southern San Joaquin Valley before the spread of Valley Yokuts (see M. Nichols 1981 for further exploration of this possibility).

The documentation of Obispeño extends over three centuries, but is relatively thin. A vocabulary of about seventy words and phrases was collected by Pedro Fages sometime before 1775 (Priestley 1937:80–83; see ¶2.3). Three mission-era word lists exist, two from travelers (Coulter 1841; Duflot de Mofras 1844) and one from the indefatigable linguist-priest Arroyo de la Cuesta (1837). Henshaw (1884–1888) collected an extensive postmission vocabulary from a speaker living near San Luis Obispo.[140] Although the language was nearly extinct by the end of the nineteenth century, Harrington fortunately discovered one surviving speaker, Rosario Cooper, living near Arroyo Grande in 1913. He worked with her intermittently until shortly before her death in 1917 (Mills and Brickfield 1986:4–6, 8–12; Klar 1991). Harrington's Obispeño materials have not been published as such, but Kathryn Klar incorporated many of Harrington's data into her comparative work on the language (Klar 1971, 1977).

3.36.2 Central Chumash

The varieties usually known as *Purisimeño, Inezeño, Barbareño,* and *Ventureño* represent mission-era restructuring of a dialect continuum that extended from

FIGURE 77. J. P. Harrington with Rosario Cooper, the last speaker of Obispeño Chumash, ca. 1915. Courtesy of National Anthropological Archives, Smithsonian Institution (91-31418).

Santa Maria to Malibu. Although the original internal boundaries within this continuum must remain conjectural, it is clear that the eastern region was considerably more diversified than the western, and that there was at least one inland dialect, Cuyama, that was not directly represented in the mission varieties. All attested varieties of Central Chumash share a common phonological and grammatical system and a considerable amount of vocabulary. All were probably mutually intelligible, although communication between speakers at the geographical extremes—Purisimeño and inland varieties of Ventureño—could well have been difficult.

PURISIMEÑO

The varieties of Central Chumash spoken around Mission La Purisima, near modern Lompoc, are the most northerly in the dialect continuum and the least well attested. No sharp boundary existed between Inezeño and Purisimeño territory, and the Purisimeño varieties along the lower Santa Ynez River seem merely to have been the western extension of the Inezeño dialect network. Beyond this area most of the territory usually ascribed to the Purisimeño—the windswept coast north of Point Conception and the interior plain as far as Santa Maria—was resource-poor and relatively thinly populated in comparison to the rest of Central Chumash territory (Greenwood 1978:521). The groups of this marginal region appear to been transitional between the cultural complex that developed on the Santa Barbara Channel after 700 AD and the simpler material and social culture of the Obispeños and Salinans.

The only significant linguistic records of Purisimeño are the early vocabularies collected by Arroyo de la Cuesta (1837), Alphonse Pinart (1878m), and H. W. Henshaw (1884c). There is also some miscellaneous material collected by Harrington in 1914 and 1916, primarily on place-names (Mills and Brickfield 1986:5, 12–14).

INEZEÑO (SAMALA)

Inezeño, or Samala (s^hamala), the ancestral name now pre-ferred by members of the Santa Ynez Band, was the Central Chumash variety spoken in the mission community at Santa Ynez, reflecting the speech of the middle portion of the Santa Ynez River. On the west, these varieties shaded into Purisimeño, while to the east and across the Santa Ynez mountains to the south they shaded into Barbareño (Applegate 1972a:1–2, 1974). Most Inezeño communities were in close contact with the Barbareño groups on the coast, with whom they had extensive trading and marriage relationships (J. R. Johnson 1988). This connection was further emphasized in mission times by the transfer of a number of converts from Mission Santa Barbara to Mission Santa Ynez (C. Grant 1978b:518). Perhaps as a result of these ties, the attestations of Inezeño more closely resemble those of Barbareño than of Purisimeño, at least in vocabulary.

The earliest known linguistic records of Inezeño are a short vocabulary collected by Arroyo de la Cuesta (1837) and a text of the Lord's Prayer copied from a mission manuscript in 1841 by Duflot de Mofras (1844, vol. 2:393; reprinted in Kroeber 1910:269–270). Alexander Taylor collected a vocabulary at Santa Ynez in 1856 that is reprinted in Powers (1877:560–567). Pinart (1878h) and Henshaw (1884b) both obtained extensive vocabularies. Kroeber's two brief overviews of Chumash (1904:31–43, 1910:264–271) heavily rely on material he collected at Santa Ynez in 1901–1902. Merriam also collected an Inezeño vocabulary and natural history word list (Appendix A: N-13c). By far, however, the most important documentation is Harrington's, who obtained extensive materials from the last speakers between 1914 and 1919 (Mills and Brickfield 1986:5–6, 14–20). Working primarily with Harrington's materials, Richard Applegate compiled a full grammar and dictionary (1972a, 1972b), the most complete description to date of any Chumash language.[141]

BARBAREÑO

The varieties of Central Chumash that are represented in the Barbareño dialect were spoken along the Santa Barbara Channel from Point Conception to Rincon Point, east of Carpenteria. The **Santa Barbara Mission** variety, reflected in most attestations, was based on the speech of the heavily populated area around Santa Barbara (Burton Mound) and Goleta Slough. There are a few atteststions of at least one different variety, centering on the important villages at **Dos Pueblos,** to the west of Santa Barbara (Klar, Whistler, and McLendon 1999:24). As noted later, the **Emigdiano** variety of "Interior Chumash" that was spoken by a nineteenth-century Chumash community in the San Joaquin Valley

FIGURE 78. Mrs. Mary Yee, the last speaker of Barbareño Chumash. Photographed by Madison Beeler, ca. 1958. Courtesy of National Anthropological Archives, Smithsonian Institution (91-31333).

was a mixture of Barbareño and Yokuts, but this almost certainly reflects mission-era trading connections and postsecularization resettlement, not an inland extension of the Barbareño dialect in precontact times.

More than a dozen Barbareño place-names and a few other words and phrases are noted in the report of Cabrillo's 1542–1543 voyage along the California coast, one of the earliest records of any California Indian language (¶2.1). Costansó's short list of Barbareño words, collected in 1769–1770 during the Portolá expedition, was the first vocabulary of an Alta California language to be published (Costansó 1770; see ¶2.3). A catechism and confessional aid, composed by Father Juan Cortés between 1798 and 1805, survive from the mission period (Kelsey 1979). A survey vocabulary was collected by Oscar Loew for the Wheeler Expedition, published in Gatschet (1876a) and in Powers (1877:560–567). More substantial vocabularies were collected by Pinart (1878j) and Henshaw (1884c, 1884h).

All other documentation of Barbareño is put in the shade, however, by the voluminous notes and sound recordings collected by J. P. Harrington during the course of nearly half a century of investigation (Mills and Brickfield 1986:2–8, 20–33). Harrington worked intensively with several speakers, the most important of whom was Juan de Jesús Justo, beginning in 1913. His consultants also included three generations of women from the same family—Luisa Ignacio, a contemporary of Juan Justo's; her daughter Lucrecia García; and her granddaughter Mary Yee, with whom Harrington continued working until his final illness in 1961. Mrs. Yee, who was the last fluent speaker of any variety of Chumash, developed her own orthography and kept extensive notebooks based on her work with Harrington. Between 1954 and 1961, she also served as a consultant for Madison Beeler, whose notes and tape recordings, now in the Archives of the Survey of California and Other Indian Languages at Berkeley, provide an important supplement to Harrington's documentation. Beeler published a short grammatical sketch (1976) and an annotated text with some lexical data (1979). Harrington's rich materials, however, will remain the primary source of information on the dialect. To facilitate access, a digital database of Harrington's Barbareño has been created at UC Santa Barbara. Two major studies of Barbareño grammar have been prepared using it (Wash 1995, 2001), and Mithun has drawn on it for phonological data (1998a).

FIGURE 79. Fernando Librado, Ventureño Chumash. Courtesy of National Anthropological Archives, Smithsonian Institution (91-31301).

VENTUREÑO

The term "Ventureño" is a geographical cover term for the varieties of Chumash spoken in the eastern third of Central Chumash territory (Whistler 1981b; Klar, Whistler, and McLendon 1999:24–25). Along the coast from Carpenteria to Malibu three dialect areas can be distinguished. Historically the most important was the northern or **Ventura** variety, which became the lingua franca of the Chumash speakers at Mission San Buenaventura.[142] Farther south, noticeably different varieties were associated with the **Mugu** (*muwu*) and **Malibu** (*humaliwo*) areas. In the mountains to the north, well-differentiated dialects were spoken in the **Ojai** (*ʔawhaẏ*) and **Matilija** (*mat'ilha*) areas. In the far northeast of Ventureño territory, a quite distinct **Castac** dialect was spoken at Cashtéc (*kaštiq*), on Castac Lake at the head of Grapevine Canyon (J. R. Johnson 1978). In the central and eastern parts of Ventureño territory, a number of local varieties of **Interior Ventureño** were spoken. These appear to have fallen into two dialect clusters: **Cayetano,** including the varieties spoken around Saticoy (*satik'oy*), Santa Paula (*mupu*), Sizar Creek (*sis'a*), Piru (*kaštu*), and Camulos (*kamulus*); and **El Conejo,** including the varieties spoken around Thousand Oaks (*s'apwi*) and Camarillo (*kayïwïš*), and in Simi Valley (*šimiyi*).[143]

Another Ventureño dialect may have been spoken along the upper Santa Clara River, documented by Merriam in a vocabulary of what he called "Alliklik Chumash." The language attested appears to be Ventureño with many borrowings from Kitanemuk (Beeler and Klar 1977).[144] However, other evidence indicates that the inhabitants of this area were primarily speakers of Tataviam, another Takic language (Hudson 1982; J. R. Johnson and Earle 1990; see ¶3.32.7).

The documentation of Ventureño began early. Ventureño as well as Barbareño place-names are recorded in the report of Cabrillo's voyage, along with a Ventureño word for 'Spaniard' (see ¶2.1). From the mission period there survives a *confesionario* in Spanish and Ventureño compiled around 1812–1815 by Father José Señán at San Buenaventura (Beeler 1963:16–18, 1964). During the postmission period, Alphonse Pinart collected two vocabularies, one documenting the dialect of the mission at Ventura (1878g), the other the dialect of the Santa Paula area (1878i). H. W. Henshaw collected a long vocabulary (1884i) from Juan Estevan Pico, an educated native speaker of Ventureño who was literate in Spanish. With Henshaw's encouragement, Pico himself transcribed further vocabularies and texts, using a phonemically accurate orthography of his own devising (Heizer 1955:187–193).[145] Merriam collected a vocabulary and natural history word list (Appendix A: N-13e) during a series of brief visits to Ventura beginning in 1905, and Kroeber collected a brief vocabulary at about the same time (1910:265–268).

Between 1912 and 1919, Harrington worked intensively with the few surviving Ventureño speakers, most notably Fernando Librado, who had been born during the mission period and also spoke Island Chumash (Appendix B; Mills and Brickfield 1986:2–4, 35–44). On the basis of these materials Harrington prepared a manuscript dictionary and the outline of a grammar.[146] Harrington also collected numerous ethnographic texts from Librado, many of which have been edited and published in translation (Blackburn 1975; Hudson 1979; Hudson et al. 1977). In the early 1980s, Kenneth Whistler began a long-term project to collate and analyze Harrington's documentation of Ventureño with the ultimate goal of preparing a full dictionary of the language (Whistler 1981b).

Varieties of Chumash are known to have been spoken to the north and west of Central Chumash territory, along the Sisquoc and Cuyama Rivers, and as far north as the San Joaquin Valley. The "Interior Chumash" of this region is attested only in a few place-names, and its relationship to the rest of the Chumash family cannot be determined, with the exception of a dialect spoken at San Emigdio, near Buena Vista Lake southwest of Bakersfield. This **Emigdiano** dialect, attested in short word lists collected from a single speaker by Merriam in 1905 (Appendix A: N-13f) and Kroeber in 1906, has been shown to be a variety of Barbareño, strongly influenced by Buena Vista Yokuts (Beeler and Klar 1977). While this finding could be taken to indicate a long-standing connection between the coast and the interior, the Emigdianos were probably nineteenth-century refugees from Mission Santa Barbara (C. Grant 1978a:507).

3.36.3 Island Chumash

A distinct language, Island Chumash (or Isleño), was spoken on Santa Cruz, Santa Rosa, and San Miguel Islands, apparently with some island-by-island variation (**Cruzeño, Roseño,** and **Migueleño**).[147] In those aspects of its inflectional morphology that are attested, Island Chumash appears more closely to resemble Obispeño than Central Chumash. Its phonology, however, is basically that of a Central Chumash language, and much of its vocabulary is nearly identical to Ventureño. However, a significant residue of the attested Island Chumash vocabulary is completely different from mainland Chumash, and ethnohistorical testimony is unequivocal that the speech of the islanders was difficult if not impossible for other Chumash speakers to understand (Klar 2002). The complex network of trade and exchange relationships that existed between the northern Channel Islands and the Central Chumash–speaking mainland must therefore have required extensive bilingualism (Arnold 2001:18).

Four vocabularies of Island Chumash were collected in the second half of the nineteenth century from elderly speakers living on the mainland. Two of these were attestations of Cruzeño: a short vocabulary obtained by Father Antonio Jimeno at Mission Santa Barbara (Jimeno 1856) and a much more extensive vocabulary collected by Alphonse Pinart (1878l). The other two were attestations of Roseño: a second long vocabulary by Pinart (1878k) and a vocabulary collected by a Santa Barbara businessman, George H. Gould (in Roberts 1888).[148] The most extensive and accurate documentation of the language was made by Harrington between 1912 and 1915, working with his Ventureño consultant, Fernando Librado. Librado had grown up at Mission San Buenaventura speaking Ventureño and Spanish, but he remembered a good deal of the Island Chumash spoken by his parents, who had been born on Santa Cruz Island (Mills and Brickfield 1986:2–4, 33–35). Although this

was primarily a documentation of Cruzeño, Harrington was able to obtain at least some information on Roseño and Migueleño. In addition, Librado noted differences between two village or tribelet varieties of Cruzeño, Swaxil, at the eastern tip of the island, and Kaxas (or Xaxas), on the north shore. A full study of the documentation of Island Chumash is in preparation by Kathryn Klar (Beeler and Klar n.d.).

3.36.4 Survival and Revitalization

Since the death in 1965 of Mary Yee, the last speaker of Barbareño, Chumash has been without native speakers. There is, however, considerable interest among Chumash descendants in restoring their traditional culture and language. Since 2002 the Santa Ynez Band has used some of its gaming income to support a tribal language program, the centerpiece of which has been a weekly class taught by Richard Applegate. As part of this effort Applegate has prepared extensive pedagogical materials on Inezeño, most of which are accessible at a website maintained by the Santa Ynez Band (www.chumashlanguage.com).

3.36.5 Linguistic Structure

Applegate's grammar and dictionary of Inezeño (1972a, 1972b) provide a comprehensive overview of Central Chumash phonology, grammatical structure, and lexicon, which can be supplemented with the sketches of Barbareño grammar by Beeler (1976) and by Wash (2001:30–114). Analyses of Obispeño and Island Chumash linguistic structure are not available, although Klar's comparative studies (1971, 1977, 1981) yield a fair amount of descriptive data on Obispeño.

The Central Chumash languages have nearly identical phonologies (Table 55). The consonant inventory includes four stops (p, t, k, q), two affricates (c [ts] and č), and three fricatives (s, š, x), all of which occur plain, glottalized, and

TABLE 55
Ventureño Phonemes (Whistler 1981b)

Consonants								Vowels		
p	t	c	č	k		q	ʔ	i	ï	u
pʰ	tʰ	(cʰ)	(čʰ)	kʰ		qʰ		e		o
p'	t'	c'	č'	k'		q'			a	
		s	š		x		h			
		(sʰ)	(šʰ)							
		(s')	(š')		x'					
m	n									
ṁ	ṅ									
w	l		y							
ẇ	(l')		ẏ							

TABLE 56
Barbareño Pronouns (Beeler 1976; Wash 2001)

| | Singular | Nonsingular | |
		Dual	Plural
Independent			
1st person	*no?*	*kiškï ~ kiški*	*kiykï*
2nd person	*pi?*	*piškï ~ piški*	*piykï*
Subject Prefixes			
1st person	*k-*	*kiš-*	*kiy-*
2nd person	*p-*	*piš-*	*piy-*
3rd person	*s-*	*siš-*	*siy-*
3rd person indef	*(s)am-*	*(s)am-*	*(s)am-*
Object Suffixes			
1st person	*-it*		*-iyuw*
2nd person	*-in*		*-iyuw*
3rd person	(unmarked)		*-wun*
	-us		*-uswun*

(except for *x*) aspirated; two nasals (*m* and *n*) and three approximants (*l, w, y*), all of which occur both plain and glottalized; and two laryngeals (*h* and *?*). The glottalization of fricatives is unusual in California languages, and the aspiration of fricatives (*sʰ, šʰ*) is unparalleled. These consonants are secondary, however; aspirated sibilants fricatives and affricates (*sʰ, šʰ, cʰ, čʰ*) and glottalized sibilant fricatives (*s', š'*) occur only as the result of the operation of phonological rules at morpheme boundaries. A pervasive and characteristic Central Chumash feature is a rule of sibilant harmony, which requires that all sibilants within a word be either apical (*s, c, cʰ, c'*) or palatal (*š, č, čʰ, č'*) (Beeler 1970; Harrington 1974). There are six vowels (*i, ï, u, e, a, o*), with no contrasts in length. Several vowel harmony processes are active, typified by the Inezeño assimilation of a low vowel (*e, a, o*) in a prefix to a low vowel in the initial syllable of the stem (e.g., *s-aqta=p'ow* > *soqtop'ow* '[a projectile] veers off').

In addition to the consonants found in Central Chumash, Obispeño has a set of retroflex stops (*ṭ, ṭʰ, ṭ'*), which Klar thinks may reflect a palatalized velar (*kʸ) set in Proto-Chumash (1971:14–16, 1993). Obispeño also differs from Central Chumash in lacking a productive sibilant harmony rule.

Central Chumash noun morphology is limited to marking the possessor with a set of pronominal prefixes in which singular, dual, and plural numbers are fully distinguished; an indefinite third person is also marked. In Obispeño, unpossessed nouns

can also take a prefix or proclitic (usually *ṭ-*) that apparently marks them as absolutive (Kroeber 1910:268).

Central Chumash verbs are inflected for intransitive subject or transitive agent with the same prefixes that mark possession in nouns, and transitive verbs are inflected for object with a separate set of suffixes marking only singular and nonsingular (Table 56). Subject prefixes can be preceded by a few "outer" prefixes that mark tense (e.g., *sa?-* 'future') or that serve to nominalize or relativize the verb. In Inezeño the basic nominalizing or relativizing prefix (*ma-*) also functions as the general marker of a nominal phrase (e.g., *ma-qaq'* 'the raven', *ma-k-popoč'* 'my paternal grandfather', *ma-l-am-ašïn* 'food' < 'what one eats'). One or more "inner" prefixes can occur after the subject prefixes and before the verbal root. Some of these have straightforward grammatical functions (e.g., *?al-* 'agentive'; *su-* 'causative'), but many mark instrumental, classificatory, locative-directional, and other largely lexical categories and are best treated as stem formatives (e.g., Inezeño *aq-/ax-* 'with the mouth', *pal-* 'with a pliable object', *akti-* 'motion toward the speaker-hearer', *wašti-* 'of a flow, of liquid in motion', *qili-/qulu-* 'of seeing, vision'). Suffixes mark various tense and aspect categories (e.g., *-waš* 'past', *-š* 'imperfective').

Reduplication is widespread in nouns and verbs alike, both as a lexical feature (e.g., Barbareño *kopkop* 'toad', *xïxï?* 'cactus') and as a grammatical process (e.g., *tentent'ey* 'keep pressing' < *tent'ey* 'press').

3.36.6 Nomenclature

"Chumash" (usually pronounced [čúmæš]) is from Central Chumash čʰumaš 'islander', specifically an inhabitant of the Channel Islands (called mi-čʰumaš 'islander place'). The name first given to the language family was "Santa Barbara" (Latham 1856:85), which Powell adopted in the linguistic appendix to Powers (1877). For the purposes of his general North American classification, however, Powell felt compelled to reject this label on the grounds that it was a "compound name," prohibited by the nomenclatural rules he was following. For "a suitable substitute" he turned to "Chumash . . . the name of the Santa Rosa Islanders [and] a term widely known among the Indians of this family" (Powell 1891:67). Powell's adjectival form "Chumashan" is now rarely used, since "Chumash" has fallen out of use as a designation for Island Chumash and no ambiguity arises when it is used as the family name.

3.37 Southern Baja California Languages: Monqui, Waikuri, and Pericú

Speakers of Cochimí occupied the arid central portion of the Baja California peninsula as far south as the mission of San Javier, west of Loreto and Malibat (see ¶3.19 and Map 22). Between there and Cabo San Lucas, however, at least three other quite different languages are known to have been spoken, **Monqui, Waikuri** (or **Guaycura**[149]), and **Pericú** (Laylander 1997). Monqui was spoken in a relatively small area on the east coast of the peninsula around the missions at Loreto and Malibat. Waikuri was spoken in the territory served by Mission San Luis Gonzaga, in the interior between Malibat and La Paz, and south across the Magdalena Plain to the Pacific coast in the vicinity of Todos Santos. Pericú was spoken in the mountainous region at the southern tip of the peninsula around the mission at San José del Cabo, on the southeastern coast from Santiago to La Paz, and on the islands along the east coast of the peninsula as far north as Isla San José. Of these languages, Waikuri is attested by a short vocabulary, fragmentary text, and paradigm that Jacob Baegert, the Jesuit priest at Mission San Luis Gonzaga between 1750 and 1767, incorporated into his memoirs (Baegert 1952[1771]:94–104).[150] Of the other two languages even less remains: four words and ten place-names in Pericú, fourteen place-names in Monqui (Laylander 1997:79–80).

Given the lack of data, any statement regarding the possible relationship of Monqui, Waikuri, and Pericú to one another or to other language families can only be speculative. The first thorough examination of the evidence was made by Massey (1949), who proposed that Waikuri and Pericú, together with "Uchití"—a group of dialects that he believed constituted a language intermediate between Waikuri and Pericú—be considered the "Guaycuran" language family.[151] Reassessing the same material in the light of subsequent scholarship (León-Portilla 1976; Ibarra Rivera 1991),

TABLE 57
Waikuri Phonemes (Zamponi 2004)

Consonants					Vowels	
p	t	č	k	(ʔ)	i	u
b	d				e	a
m	n	nʸ				
	ſ					
w	řˇ	y				

Laylander (1997:14–29, 68) has concluded that Massey's Uchití dialects were merely varieties of either Pericú or Waikuri, and that the two languages were unrelated.[152] Raoul Zamponi (2004:157–158) reaches much the same conclusion, although he prefers to treat the Waikuri varieties of Uchití as a separate language within the same family. As for Monqui, the almost total absence of direct data makes any determination speculative. The ethnohistorical evidence led Massey to conclude that it was a dialect of the "Didiu" language spoken around San Bruno, to the north of Loreto, which in turn was said to be close to Cochimí, if not merely a dialect of that language (¶3.19). Laylander, however, believes it more likely that Monqui was quite distinct from Didiu and possibly related to Waikuri (Laylander 1997:33–40, 68).

There have been several attempts to establish a relationship between Waikuri and Cochimí-Yuman, Seri, or the Hokan phylum more broadly (for a survey of this work see Gursky 1966a:41–42). Although some points of resemblance have been noted, a definite connection to Cochimí-Yuman or Seri cannot be demonstrated with the data available. A remote affiliation to Hokan remains a possibility (Gursky 1966a; Kaufman 1988:56).

3.37.1 Waikuri Linguistic Structure

The outlines of Waikuri phonology and morphology can be derived from Baegert's data (Zamponi 2004; see Tables 57 and 58). The language had four basic stop and affricate contrasts (p, t, č, k), with a distinction in the labial and dental stops between variants that Baegert writes p versus b and t versus d. While this may have been, as the orthography suggests, a distinction between voiceless and voiced stops, it is also possible, since Baegert does not otherwise write any fricatives, that it was between a plain stop and a lenis voiced fricative ([β] and [ð]), as in the Numic languages (¶3.31). In addition to the stops and affricates, there were three nasals (m, n, nʸ), two approximants (w, y), and two distinct rhotic consonants, probably a tap (ſ) and a trill (řˇ). The presence of an intervocalic glottal stop may be inferred from such transcriptions as aëna 'above'. There were apparently four

TABLE 58
Waikuri Pronouns (Zamponi 2004)

	Subject	Object	Possessive (alienable)	Possessive (inalienable)
1 sg	*be*	?	*bekún*	*be- ~ m-*
2 sg	*eʔi*	*eʔi* (?)	*ekún*	*e-*
3 sg	?	?	?	*ti- ~ t-*
1 pl	*katé*	*kepe*	*kepekún*	*kepe-*
2 pl	*peté*	?	?	?
3 pl	?	?	*kikún*	?

vowels (*i, e, a, u*), but whether there were contrasts in length cannot be recovered from Baegert's orthography.

Independent pronouns were inflected for subject, object, and possessive relationships; inalienable pronominal possessors were marked by a related set of noun prefixes. Complex verb suffixes, difficult to analyze from the surviving data, marked various categories of tense, aspect, and negation. The plurality of verbal subjects was regularly marked by a prefixed *ku- ~ k-*. The same prefix appears to have been employed to form plural or collective nouns (*anaʔi* 'woman', *kanaʔi* 'women').

PART 4

TYPOLOGICAL AND AREAL FEATURES
California as a Linguistic Area

Varied though their histories may be, the languages of the California region share a number of characteristics that may be called "Californian." Some of these features are localized enough to define a California linguistic area or a significant subgroup of languages within such an area. Others are more widespread, but they are given special emphasis in the region, or they form patterns with other features in a distinctively Californian way. Certain features, particularly some of those associated with the Athabaskan languages, tend in their very deviation from the California norm to serve as negative definers of it.

These characteristics, both linguistic and sociolinguistic, are discussed in detail in the sections that follow, but a brief preliminary outline may be useful.

Phonology In consonantal phonology (¶4.1) the theme is one of elaboration: many California languages have three or even four modes of articulation (plain, voiced, aspirated, and glottalized), and most distinguish multiple points of dental-alveolar and palatal articulation, often involving retroflection. Vowel systems (¶4.2), in contrast, are simple, rarely involving oral/nasal contrasts, and while pitch accent is present (especially in the northern tier of languages), it is not a defining trait (¶4.3).

Grammar Morphologically (¶4.4), suffixation, sometimes fused with stem ablaut, is the dominant pattern; prefixation is a defining characteristic only of the intrusive Athabaskan languages. Reduplication is not uncommon but is only marginally grammaticized, while suppletive pluralization is a historically significant trait of a subset of Hokan languages: Salinan, Yuman, and Seri (¶4.7).

In basic structural pattern (¶4.5), California languages fall into two distinct structural types: dependent-marking languages that employ elaborate systems of syntactic (although never ergative-absolutive) case marking (¶4.6); and head-marking languages that are characterized by morphologically complex verb stems, often involving the compounding of classificatory-instrumental and locational-directional elements (¶4.8). The California Penutian group is defined by dependent-marking syntax, but the pattern is shared more widely, most notably with the Pomo languages. While an extreme development of morphologically complex verbs and other features linked with head-marking syntax is characteristic of a subset of Hokan languages at the northern end of the region, other undoubted members of the Hokan phylum, such as Karuk and Washo, show these traits in a much milder form, and it is totally absent in the subgroup of Hokan languages that, as noted previously, mark the plurality of nouns by suppletion.

The most typically Californian syntactic feature is the "switch reference" marking of continuity or discontinuity of the subject between clauses (¶4.9). Notably absent in California is the ergative-absolutive coding of case relationships, common elsewhere in the Americas. However, something similar to the foregrounding of passive voice that is typical of ergative-absolutive grammars is found in the Pomo languages, and probably also in Yukian and Chimariko, where a fundamental distinction is made between verbs predicating actions that can be initiated or controlled by an agent and verbs predicating actions or states that lie outside of deliberate agentive control (¶4.6.3). Although semantically similar to the active-passive distinction made in languages throughout the world, the control/noncontrol contrast found in these Californian languages is primarily encoded lexically—certain verbal ideas being treated as open to control by a conscious human actor while others are treated as essentially uncontrollable.

Linguistic Culture Some of the lexical subsystems found in California languages have distinctive areal characteristics. Numeral systems (¶4.10) are especially diverse, with decimal, quinary, and vigesimal counts all widely found, and a quaternary or octonary count attested in a few languages—a diversity that may reflect a late-developing cultural need (primarily in monetary transactions) for a systematic mode of counting beyond the digits of one hand. Toponyms (¶4.11.1) are overwhelmingly focused on village names, with other geographic features (mountains, rivers, lakes) usually named in reference to settlements, if named at all. Abstract topographical terms are rare, and the primary directions are often riverine (upstream/downstream). Personal names (¶4.11.2), surrounded as they are by notions of privacy and secrecy, tend to be phonologically and morphologically aberrant. They often form part of the "diminutive" (or more accurately "affective") register, char-

acteristic of many California languages, that is used in conversation with relatives or close friends and marked by "sound-symbolic" shifts in the articulation of the phonemes of certain salient words (¶4.12).

The sociolinguistic profile that might have characterized California speech communities prior to their destruction in the eighteenth and nineteenth centuries is poorly known. Only the employment of prestige dialects, such as "High Yurok" or "Court Gabrielino," is widely enough attested to be noted as characteristic of the region (¶4.13). In both pre- and postcontact periods, lexical borrowing appears not to have played an important role in defining a California speech area (¶4.14–4.15). With the exception of the poorly attested spread of a Spanish-based jargon in mission times, no trade language or intertribal language seems to have been in regular use, although the archaeological evidence of wide-reaching intergroup contacts in the Late Period is substantial. This would seem to indicate that bi- or multilingualism was common, but if this was the case the evidence for it is patchy and largely anecdotal.

Phonology

4.1 Consonants

4.1.1 Laryngeal Feature Contrasts: Aspiration, Glottalization, and Voicing

Languages of the California area show considerable variation in the employment of phonemic contrasts in the laryngeal articulation of stops and affricates (i.e., distinctive aspiration, glottalization, or voicing). A substantial number of languages do without any laryngeal feature contrasts, having only a single "plain" type of stop or affricate. Four of the Hokan branches—Karuk, Esselen, Seri, and Cochimí—belong to this group, as probably did Proto Yuman, although Upland Yuman and Kiliwa have independently innovated a plain versus aspirated contrast. While most Penutian branches have a rich array of laryngeal feature contrasts, both Utian sub-branches have only plain stops and affricates, with the exception of Lake Miwok, which has developed a four-way contrast through the influence of neighboring Patwin and Pomo (Callaghan 1964a).

The three Uto-Aztecan branches represented in the California area—Numic, Takic, and Tubatulabal—are often described as lacking any phonemic contrast in laryngeal features, although they all have phonetically distinct voiced stops, affricates, and fricatives in intervocalic position. These distinctions are usually treated phonemically as contrasts in consonantal length (the voiced segments simplex, the voiceless segments geminate) or between plain versus lenited or weakened segments, although some

specialists—particularly in Numic—prefer to describe these as limited phonemic contrasts between plain and voiced obstruents. A similar phonetic and structural situation may also be present in Cochimí.

Only one California language, Wiyot, has a basic two-way contrast between plain and aspirated stops and affricates, although as noted earlier, Upland Yuman and Kiliwa appear to have developed such a contrast.

A basic two-way contrast between plain and glottalized (ejective) stops and affricates is found in Yurok and Salinan. It is also found in Shasta within Shastan and in Northern Yukian (Yuki and Coast Yuki) within Yukian, but in both these cases another member of the family (Konomihu within Shastan and Wappo within Yukian) has a three-way contrast in laryngeal articulation—plain versus glottalized versus aspirated—and it is not clear which is the older pattern within the family.

A basic three-way contrast between plain, glottalized, and aspirated stops and affricates is the most widespread pattern in California languages. Families or isolates for which this is the case include Athabaskan (both the California and Oregon branches), Chimariko, Chumash, Klamath-Modoc, Palaihnihan, Takelma, Yana, and Yokuts. As noted previously, Wappo within Yukian and Konomihu within Shastan also follow this pattern. With the exception of the Athabaskan languages, which are undoubtedly intrusive at a late date, languages with this three-way laryngeal feature contrast fall into two areal clusters in California: (1) a northern cluster that includes languages belonging to four Hokan branches—Chimariko, Palaihnihan, Yana, and Konomihu Shastan—and two Penutian branches—Klamath-Modoc and Takelma; and (2) a south-central cluster that includes Wappo, Yokuts, and Chumash. Outside California, in addition to being an ancient feature of the Athabaskan-Eyak and Tlingit languages in the Northwest, this three-way contrast is also found in Molala, a Penutian language of Oregon, in the Keresan languages of the Pueblo Southwest, and in Siouan.

Voicing, as noted earlier, can be seen as marginally contrastive in a two-way pattern (plain versus voiced) in the Uto-Aztecan branches, and possibly also in Cochimí, but this pattern does not occur otherwise in the California region. Voicing is a fully contrastive laryngeal feature only in three- and four-way patterns. A basic three-way contrast between plain, glottalized, and voiced stops and affricates is shared by Maiduan and Washo. A basic four-way contrast (plain versus glottalized versus aspirated versus voiced) is found in Wintuan and is the underlying pattern in Pomo, although in Southeastern Pomo the aspirated stops and affricates have secondarily developed into the corresponding fricatives. Lake Miwok, as noted before, has the same basic four-way contrast, clearly borrowed from adjacent Wintuan or Pomo languages. All the languages in which voicing is a fully contrastive feature are contiguous and form a well-defined cluster in north-central California. It is likely that the trait was borrowed into intrusive Penutian languages (Wintuan and Maiduan) from a Hokan substratum.

4.1.2 Stop and Affricate Positions

BASIC CONTRASTS

All California languages distinguish phonemic stops in bilabial, apical, and velar positions, and at least one affricate that is either apical (c) or palatal (č) in position:

$$p \quad t \quad c \sim č \quad k$$

Languages possessing *only* these four stop and affricate distinctions include Karuk, Yana, Washo, Maiduan, and Patwin.

There are (partial) exceptions to the universality of these contrasts in marginal Seri and in the intrusive Athabaskan languages. In Seri no apical or palatal affricate is phonemically distinguished. In both California and Oregon Athabaskan the bilabial stop is structurally distinct from other stops. In California Athabaskan, each language has either *m* or *p*, but never both, while in Oregon Athabaskan, although *p* is phonemically distinct from *m* (and *w*), it is of relatively rare occurrence and is most frequent in borrowed words. In both Oregon and California Athabaskan, furthermore, the bilabial stop is never distinctively aspirated or glottalized, whereas a three-way contrast (plain versus aspirated versus glottalized) is found in all other stop positions.

APICAL VERSUS PALATAL AFFRICATES

A number of languages phonemically distinguish apical from palatal affricates:

$$c \quad č$$

Languages or language families that make this distinction include California and Oregon Athabaskan, Shastan, Esselen, Salinan, Chumash, and most but not all varieties of Yokuts.

BACKED APICALS

A number of languages make a phonemic distinction between a fronted (dental or interdental) apical stop and a backed (alveolar, postalveolar, or retroflex) apical stop, which is sometimes allophonically affricated (Langdon and Silver 1984):

$$t \quad ṭ \sim [ṭ\underline{s}]$$

Languages or language families having this distinction include Yukian (both Yuki and Wappo), Chimariko, Pomo, Yokuts, Miwok, Costanoan, Salinan, and probably Esselen. In addition, Serrano and possibly Kitanemuk within Takic, Diegueño, Cocopa, Quechan, and Maricopa within Yuman, and Obispeño within Chumash have this contrast. Except for Chimariko and the Yuman languages, these languages form a contiguous cluster in the Coast Range and Central Valley.

In addition, a backed apical affricate occurs as a phoneme in its own right in many varieties of Southern Valley Yokuts, in phonemic contrast both with a backed apical stop and with a fronted apical affricate:

$$t \quad ṭ \quad c \quad c̣ \, [ṭ\underline{s}]$$

In most varieties of Oregon Athabaskan, a glottalized backed apical affricate is in phonemic contrast with a glottalized fronted apical affricate; neither affricate occurs plain or aspirated:

$$c' \quad c̣'$$

BACKED VELARS

A number of languages have a phonemic distinction between a fronted (velar or front velar) dorsal stop and a backed (postvelar or uvular) dorsal stop:

$$k \quad q$$

Languages or language families with this distinction include Klamath-Modoc, Palaihnihan, Chimariko, Pomo, Chumash, Takic (except Kitanemuk), Yuman, and Seri, along with

Northern Wintuan (Wintu and Nomlaki) within Wintuan, Lake Miwok within Miwok, and Hupa-Chilula and some Eel River dialects within California Athabaskan. These languages form three clusters: (1) a northwestern cluster including California Athabaskan, Chimariko, Northern Wintuan, Pomo, and Lake Miwok; (2) a northeastern cluster including Klamath-Modoc and Palaihnihan; and (3) a southwestern cluster including Chumash, Takic, and Yuman. Clusters 1 and 2 adjoin along the Wintu-Achumawi boundary and are probably historically linked.

LABIOVELARS

A few languages distinguish labiovelars from plain velars:

$$k \quad k^w \quad (q \quad q^w)$$

Languages or language families with a plain velar versus labiovelar distinction include: both branches of California Algic (Yurok and Wiyot), Oregon Athabaskan, Takelma, Numic, Takic, Yuman, Cochimí, and Seri. These fall into two obvious clusters: (1) a northern cluster including California Algic, Oregon Athabaskan, and Takelma, all of which have relatively recent historical connections with languages to the north, where this contrast is much more common; and (2) a southern cluster including Numic, Takic, Yuman, Cochimí, and Seri.

LATERAL AFFRICATE

A glottalized lateral affricate (λ') is distinguished in Oregon and California Athabaskan and in Wintuan, but in neither language group is it paired with a plain affricate.

4.1.3 Fricatives

All California languages have at least one sibilant fricative. Where only one sibilant is distinguished, it is voiceless and typically varies in articulation between apical and palatal positions, often including an apico-postvelar variant (Bright 1978b):

$$s \sim \underset{.}{s} \sim \check{s}$$

Languages or language families having a sibilant only of this type include Takelma, Klamath-Modoc, Yurok, Karuk, Shastan, Yana, Wintuan, most Miwok languages, Numic, and Tubatulabal. Of these, Klamath-Modoc, Maiduan, and Tubatulabal possess only this one fricative.

A large number of California languages distinguish two phonemic voiceless sibilants, one with a fronted articulation (varying between apico-dental and interdental) and one with a backed articulation (varying between apico-postalveolar and palatal):

$$s \sim \theta \quad \underset{.}{s} \sim \check{s}$$

Languages or language families with this contrast include Wiyot, Karuk, Oregon Athabaskan, California Athabaskan, Chimariko, Palaihnihan, Pomo, Yukian, Washo, Yokuts, Miwok, Costanoan, Esselen, Salinan, Chumash, Takic, Yuman, and Seri.

The great majority of California languages also have a voiceless *velar* fricative (x). The only languages or language families that lack this phoneme are Wiyot, Washo, Yukian, most Pomo languages, Klamath-Modoc, Maiduan, Miwok, Costanoan, and Tubatulabal. Esselen is sometimes described as having a voiceless velar affricate [kx] rather than a voiceless velar fricative. In Yuman, the voiceless velar fricative phoneme is often pronounced as a laryngeal [h], with which it does not phonemcally contrast in most Yuman languages.

Languages or language families that possess only two fricatives, a voiceless sibilant and a voiceless velar fricative, are Takelma, Shastan, and Yana. Languages or language families that possess only three fricatives—a fronted and a backed sibilant and a voiceless velar fricative—are Chimariko, Salinan, Yokuts, and Chumash. Other fricatives that occur in California languages include the following:

A voiceless lateral fricative ($\textstyle\unicode{0x142}$) is found in Wiyot, Yurok, Oregon Athabaskan, California Athabaskan, Wintuan, and Seri. The voiceless lateral approximant (L) in Klamath-Modoc and Washo is sometimes fricative in pronunciation.

A postvelar (or uvular) fricative that is phonemically distinct from the velar fricative (x versus $\underset{.}{x}$) is found in Wintuan and Seri. It also occurs in Southeastern Pomo, where it has developed from an earlier aspirated postvelar stop (q^h).

A labiovelar fricative (x^w) contrasts with a plain velar fricative (x) in Oregon Athabaskan, Takic, Yuman, and Seri. In Seri, where both velar and uvular fricatives are phonemically distinguished, both have labialized equivalants.

A pharyngeal fricative ($\hbar$) is attested in the California region only in Achumawi.

A voiceless bilabial or labiodental fricative (ϕ or f) occurs in Karuk, Esselen, and Seri. It is also found in Southeastern Pomo, where it has developed from an earlier aspirated bilabial stop (p^h).

Voiced fricatives are rare in California. A voiced bilabial or labiodental fricative (β or v) occurs in Wiyot (where it is a dialectal variant of m), Karuk (where it is a dialectal variant of w), Takic, and the River and Upland branches of Yuman. A voiced velar (and where the distinction is made, labiovelar) fricative (γ, γ^w) is found in Wiyot, Yurok, Oregon Athabaskan, and in some California Athabaskan. Voiced bilabial, velar, and labiovelar fricatives also occur intervocalically in Numic, where they are usually phonemically analyzed as allophones of nongeminate bilabial and velar stops.

4.1.4 Nasals

Nearly all California languages have a class of nasal phonemes and distinguish a bilabial nasal from an apico-dental or apico-alveolar nasal (*m* versus *n*). The exceptions are California Athabaskan where, except in Hupa-Chilula, *m* can be analyzed as an allophone of the bilabial stop (*p*), and some of the Delta varieties of Yokuts in which all nasals have either been denasalized to the equivalent plain stops (*p* and *t*) or are pronounced as prenasalized voiced stops (*ᵐb* and *ⁿd*).

Several languages or language families distinguish a palatal nasal (*ñ*). These include Yuman and Cochimí, as well as Cahuilla, Cupeño, and Serrano in Takic, and Mutsun in Costanoan.

Some languages or language families also distinguish a velar nasal (*ŋ*). These include Washo, Sierra Miwok, Tubatulabal, Numic, Takic, and Cochimí.

Contrasts in laryngeal articulation are found among nasals in a few languages. Voiceless nasals (*M, N*) are phonemically distinct from plain (voiced) nasals in Klamath-Modoc, Washo, and Eastern Pomo. Glottalized nasals, either preglottalized (*'m, 'n*) or postglottalized (*m', n'*), are phonemically distinct in Yurok, Klamath-Modoc, California Athabaskan, Yukian, Chumash, Salinan and Yokuts.

4.1.5 Approximants and Flaps

All California languages have at least three approximants: two semivowels (*w, y*) and either a lateral (*l*) or a rhotic approximant (*r*), the lateral being far more common than the rhotic. Only Karuk and Shasta are described as having *w, y*, and *r* but not *l*. Languages with both *l* and *r* are more plentiful, and these include Wiyot, Yurok, Chimariko, Wintuan, Yana, Esselen, Salinan, Costanoan, Yuman, and Cochimí, as well as Serrano, Luiseño, and Cupeño in Takic, and Northeastern Pomo.

A few California languages make a phonemic distinction between a plain *l* and a palatalized *lʸ*, including Mutsun in Costanoan, all Takic languages except Luiseño, and the Delta-California and River branches of Yuman.

The rhotic approximant varies in articulation from language to language, sometimes being a rhotic semivowel [ɚ], sometimes a postalveolar trill [ř], and sometimes a *flap* [ɾ]. In Wiyot, a rhotic flap (written *d*) phonemically contrasts with a rhotic semivowel (written *r*).

Contrasts in laryngeal articulation are found among approximants in a few languages. A set of voiceless approximants (*W, Y, L*) is phonemically distinct from the plain (voiced) set in Klamath-Modoc, Washo, and Eastern Pomo. The voiceless semivowel *W* is phonemically distinct from voiced *w* in Hupa-Chilula within California Athabaskan. A set of glottalized approximants is phonemically distinct from the plain approximants in Yurok, California Athabaskan, Yukian, Salinan, Chumash, and Yokuts, and from both the plain and the voiceless approximants in Klamath-Modoc. These can be (depending on the language) preglottalized (*'w, 'y, 'l*), postglottalized (*w', y', l'*), or with glottal constriction during the vocalic segment (*ẇ* or *ẏ*)

4.1.6 Laryngeals

In medial and final position in words, the glottal stop (*ʔ*) functions as a distinct consonantal phoneme in all attested California languages. In phrase-initial position before a vowel, however, the situation is more varied. While in nearly all California languages no phonemic distinction is made between an initial vowel and an initial glottal stop + vowel, in some languages an underlying initial glottal stop manifests itself when a vowel-final prefix is added, and in other languages it does not. In Karuk, both possibilities exist (Bright 1957:32–33).

The glottal fricative or voiceless vowel (*h*) functons as a distinct consonantal phoneme in most California languages. In the Yuman languages, however, the phonemic status of *h* is marginal. Its presence is usually predictable in initial position, and in other positions it is the structural equivalent of a voiceless velar fricative (*x*).

The relationship between postvocalic laryngeals, vowel length, and syllable weight is a complex phonological issue in a number of California languages in the northern Coast Range, including Pomo, Northern Yukian, California Athabaskan, Wiyot, Yurok, and perhaps others. In discussions of Pomo phonology, the term "laryngeal increment" is often used to describe postvocalic *h* or *ʔ* (Oswalt 1976a:20, 1998).

4.1.7 Contrasts in Length (Gemination)

A few California languages or language families regularly distinguish between plain and long (geminate) consonants in intervocalic position. These include Shastan, Miwok, Costanoan, and probably Esselen. In Miwok and Costanoan, alternations between plain and geminate consonants are governed by complex relationships between stems and affixes or between ablaut grades of the stem, and are usually correlated with complementary alternations in vowel length. In the Numic languages, phonetic alternations between intervocalic plain and voiced stops or between stops and fricatives are often analyzed as the expression of an underlying contrast between geminate and nongeminate (or plain and lenited) consonants.

4.2 Vowels

4.2.1 Basic Contrasts

FIVE-VOWEL SYSTEMS

The majority of California languages distinguish five vowel qualities, two high vowels (*i, u*), two mid vowels (*e, o*), and a low vowel (*a*):

```
        i    u

      e      o

          a
```

Languages or language families with this vowel pattern are found throughout the region and include Takelma, Wiyot, Karuk, Chimariko, Yana, Wintuan, Pomo, Wappo within Yukian, Western Miwok, Costanoan, Esselen, most varieties of Yokuts, River and Upland Yuman, and Luiseño and Gabrielino within Takic. The Palaihnihan languages follow this pattern as well, but also have an epenthetic schwa.

SIX-VOWEL SYSTEMS

The second most common pattern of vowel contrasts in California distinguishes the same five vowels but adds a sixth, a high central unrounded (or slightly rounded) vowel (ï). In these languages the fundamental opposition is between high and low vowels, each set distinguishing vowels in front, central, and back positions:

```
      i    ï    u

        e    a    o
```

Most of the languages or language families with this pattern are found in the Sierra Nevada and adjacent Great Basin, and include Washo, Northeastern Maidu within Maiduan, Sierra Miwok, Tubatulabal, Numic, Cupeño within Takic, and Chumash.

SEVEN-VOWEL SYSTEMS

A few languages have a more elaborate version of this pattern in which a low central vowel (a) is distinguished from both a high and a mid central vowel (ï, ə):

```
      i    ï    u

        e    ə    o

            a
```

This pattern is found in Nisenan and Konkow within Maiduan, Plains Miwok, and the Tule-Kaweah and Homotwoli varieties of Yokuts.

FOUR-VOWEL SYSTEMS

A small group of languages and language families have vowel systems that distinguish four qualities, two front vowels (i, e) and two nonfront vowels (u, a) or (o, a):

```
      i    u (or o)

        e    a
```

Most of the languages with this vowel pattern are in the northernmost part of the California region and include Klamath-Modoc, Shastan, Oregon Athabaskan, and California Athabaskan (with the exception of Hupa-Chilula). Otherwise it is found only in Cahuilla within Takic. In Klamath-Modoc, epenthetic schwa or syllabified resonants are phonetically present in addition to the four full vowel qualities. Oregon Athabaskan (except for Chetco-Tolowa) and California Athabaskan also have a reduced vowel (usually phonetic schwa) that does not automatically lengthen in open syllables.

THREE-VOWEL SYSTEMS

Three Hokan branches in the California region appear to have a basic three-vowel system, distinguishing a front and a back high vowel (i, u) from a low vowel:

```
        i    u

          a
```

This system is found in Salinan, Yuman (except for the River and Upland languages), and Cochimí. In all three cases, however, a restructuring of this pattern into a five-vowel system seems to have been under way, probably under the influence of Spanish.

An unusual three-vowel system occurs in the Hupa-Chilula varieties of California Athabaskan as the result of the merger of *i and *e in a basic four-vowel system of the type described in the preceding subsection:

```
        e    o

          a
```

In addition to three full vowels, which vary in length with position, Hupa-Chilula also has three reduced vowels that never lengthen, with phonetic qualities matching the full vowels:

```
      [ɪ] ~ [ɛ]    [ʊ]

            [ʌ]
```

SYSTEMS WITH RHOTIC VOWELS

Two languages have vowel systems with one or more rhotic vowels. In Yurok a five-vowel pattern is supplemented by a sixth vowel, a rhotacized schwa ([ɚ] written ɹ), resulting in a pattern structurally identical to the six-vowel system described earlier:

```
      i    ɹ    u

        e    a    o
```

In Serrano within Takic, the five-vowel system found in Gabrielino and Luiseño has three additional rhotic low vowels:

$$
\begin{array}{ccc}
i & & u \\
e & a & o \\
e^r & a^r & o^r \\
\end{array}
$$

THE NORTHERN YUKIAN SYSTEM

Northern Yukian has a unique pattern in which a central unrounded vowel (nasalized in some varieties) is distinguished from both back rounded vowels and nonback unrounded vowels (Schlichter 1985:30–31):

$$
\begin{array}{ccc}
i & & u \\
& ə & \\
a & & o \\
\end{array}
$$

4.2.2 Length

A phonemic contrast between short and long vowels is made in most California languages. The only languages that definitely lack length contrasts in vowels are Oregon Athabaskan, Wiyot, Chimariko, Chumash, Northern Maiduan, and Yukian.

4.2.3 Reduced and Epenthetic Vowels

A reduced vowel, usually phonetic schwa (ə), occurs in Oregon Athabaskan (except for Chetco-Tolowa) and in California Athabaskan, contrasting with full vowels by not automatically lengthening in open syllables. In the Hupa-Chilula varieties of California Athabaskan, there are three reduced vowels: a widely occurring front vowel of highly variable quality (i), and relatively rare low and back vowels (a and o). An epenthetic short schwa—not basically present but phonetically predictable in specific phonological environments, typically in clusters of consonants—is recognized in the phonologies of Palaihnihan, most Yuman languages, and Southeastern Pomo. In Klamath-Modoc, as analyzed by Barker, the set of full vowel contrasts is supplemented by epenthetic schwa or the syllabification of resonants.

4.2.4 Nasalized Vowels

Phonemically distinct nasalized vowels are very rare in California. Only some varieties of Oregon Athabaskan, most notably Chetco-Tolowa, have a set of nasalized full vowels (ĩ, ẽ, ã, ũ) that phonemically contrast with the set of oral full vowels. The schwa in the Yuki dialects of Northern Yukian is consistently nasalized, but this is a secondary feature.

4.2.5 Rhotic Vowels

Vowels with strong r-coloring are phonemically distinct in two California languages, Yurok and Serrano (Takic). In both cases a rhotic vowel (in Serrano, three contrasting rhotic vowels, e^r, a^r, o^r) is most likely to have developed from an earlier schwa or unrounded central vowel.

4.3 Pitch Accent and Tone

Accentual uses of pitch and tonal phenomena occur widely in the languages of the northern part of the California region, but in most instances the documentation is poor. The following languages or language families have been noted to have pitch accent or tone: Wiyot, Oregon Athabaskan, Karuk, Palaihnihan, Pomo, Shastan, Takelma, and Northern Yukian.

Grammar

4.4 Morphological Processes

Most morphologically complex words in California Indian languages are formed by prefixing or suffixing dependent elements to a stem. Suffixation is the preferred technique in the majority of them, including all the Penutian and Uto-Aztecan languages, the California Algic languages, and two Hokan languages, Pomo and Yana. The other Hokan languages and Chumash use both prefixes and suffixes in rough balance, with Seri and the Yuman languages generally favoring the former over the latter. In the California region only the Athabaskan languages rely almost entirely on prefixes for marking inflectional and derivational categories.[1]

In addition to affixation, three other morphological processes are used to varying degrees: reduplication (the full or partial repetition of part of the stem), ablaut (a systematic change in the vowels or consonants of the stem), and suppletion (replacing the stem with a totally unpredictable alternate form).

4.4.1 Reduplication

Reduplication (most frequently the partial reduplication either of the initial or final phonemes of the stem) is unevenly represented in the California region. On one hand, it is an important component of the inflectional and derivational morphology of Chumash, Tubatulabal, most Takic languages, the California Algic languages, and many of the Penutian and Hokan languages. On the other hand, it is totally absent as a productive morphological process in the Athabaskan and Yukian languages, and is either absent or represented only in nonproductive lexical forms in a substantial minority of Hokan languages.[2]

As a productive grammatical process, reduplication is most frequently employed in marking habitual, repetitive, and distributive categories, in both nouns and verbs. For example, Barbareño Chumash *tent'ey* 'to press' > *tentent'ey* 'to keep pressing'; Yurok *tekʷs-* 'to cut' > *tekʷtekʷs-* 'to cut up into pieces'; Takelma *lepe-* 'pick up and eat seeds' > *lè:pʰlapʰ-* 'pick up and eat many seeds'; or Karuk *ikmař* 'hit with one's fist' > *ikmánmař* 'beat up'. Reduplication is especially widespread in Klamath, where in addition to deriving verbal and nominal stems marked for categories such as distributive or habitual (e.g., *ka:ma* 'grind [with mortar and pestle]' > *kaka:ma* 'several grind, grind on several occasions', *hiswaqs* 'man' > *hihaswaqs* 'several men'), it is used to mark intensity or to derive a set of "affectionate" kinship terms used in direct address (e.g., *loks* 'grandfather' > *lol'aks* 'granddad!').

Reduplicated forms do not always have such iconic or symbolic meanings, however. In Tubatulabal, initial reduplication of the verb stem is used to derive a secondary stem with momentaneous force ("telic" in Voegelin's terminology; cf. ¶3.33.3) from a basically durative verb, as in *ʔela-* 'jump, be jumping' > *ʔeʔela-* 'jump (once)', or *tik-* 'eat, be eating' > *ʔitïk-* 'eat (once)'.

4.4.2 Ablaut

Changing the vowels or consonants of a stem to mark a change in meaning or function is relatively common in California languages. Changes in vowel quality and vowel or consonant length are part of the derivational and inflectional morphology of nearly all the Penutian languages of the region, and are especially elaborate in the languages of the Yok-Utian subgroup. In Wikchamni Yokuts, for example, the stem of the verb 'to steal' can be *ʔu:šu-*, *ʔoš-*, *ʔuša:-*, or *ʔušo-* and the stem of 'to doctor' *t'oyox-*, *t'uyix-*, *t'uyx-*, or *t'oyo:x-*, while in Costanoan the metathesis of the stem vowel sometimes derives a deverbal noun (e.g., Chocheño Costanoan *ʔirko* 'to defecate', *ʔirok* 'feces'). In Takelma, all verb stems have two ablaut variants, a special stem that occurs with the past tense (the "aorist" stem, in Sapir's terminology) inflectional paradigm and a general stem that occurs elsewhere, as in *t'omon-* (aorist), *to:m-* (general) 'to kill' or *yowo-* (aorist), *yu-* (general) 'to run'. The Penutian languages also tend to have families of semantically similar words differing only in vocalic or consonantal ablaut, such as Klamath *q'al'-* 'bend, fold', *čq'a:l'-* 'coil up (like a snake)', and *q'oliʔ* 'to bend (intr.)' or Wintu *daq-al* 'to be burned', *daq-ča* 'scorch, heat', *duč-a:* 'make fire' and *doči-* 'coals' (DeLancey 2006). Compare also Lake Miwok *ʔúṣṣu* 'to drink' and *ʔú:ṣu* 'to drink to excess', or *múla* 'to hit once' and *múlla*

'to spank, whip' (Callaghan 1987, personal communication). Similar ablaut processes are also found sporadically in some Hokan languages, particularly in plural formations, as for example in Salinan *ṭ-a:m* 'house', *ṭ-em-hal* 'houses'.

4.4.3 Suppletion

Completely irregular changes in the form of a stem, as in the past tense forms *went* and *did* in English, are rare in languages nearly everywhere. In California, suppletive changes are for the most part confined to the Hokan languages, particularly Salinan, Yuman, and Seri, where they play an important role in the formation of plurals, both in nouns and verbs. Typical are such formations as Salinan *xuč* 'dog' > *xosten* 'dogs' or Seri *-koi* 'bring' > *-koa:tim* 'bring (repeatedly)'.

4.5 Structural Patterns

4.5.1 Morphological Marking of Subject and Object

The locus of the morphological marking of syntactic relationships, in particular the marking of the subject and object of the main verb of the clause, generally follows one of four patterns. In **head-marking** languages, the predominant type in North America, the verb includes affixes agreeing with the subject and object, while the nouns representing these entities are left unmarked. In **dependent-marking** languages, which are well represented in the California region but infrequently found elsewhere on the continent, the verb has no agreement markers, but the subject and object nouns are marked as such by case affixes. The **double-marking** pattern, in which both verbal agreement affixes and nominal case markers are used, is widespread in the world but relatively uncommon in California languages. A fourth pattern, **zero marking**, in which no morphological marking is used either in the verb or on the nouns (word order usually being relied on to distinguish subject from object) is not found in California and is rare elsewhere in the Americas.[3]

Head marking is typical of the Hokan languages, with the sole exception of Pomo. Also following the head-marking pattern are the Athabaskan languages, the California Algic languages, and Chumash. Only one Penutian language in the California region, Takelma, is head marking. Otherwise the Penutian languages are dependent marking, with the exception of the Eastern branch of Miwok, which is double marking. Also dependent marking are the Yukian languages, the Pomo languages, and all of the Uto-Aztecan languages of the region except Cahuilla and Tubatulabal, which are double marking.

The three double-marking languages—Tubatulabal, Cahuilla, and Eastern Miwok—were all apparently in transition from dependent marking to head marking. In Tubatulabal, while subject and object can be marked by independent pronominal words or by nouns inflected for case, they can also be marked by pronominal particles that can be enclitic either to the verb or to a word of any category preceding the verb. The loosely bound pronominal prefixes of Cahuilla probably represent a somewhat more advanced stage of a similar development, while the complex systems of verbal pronominal suffixes of Takelma and the Eastern Miwok languages can be seen as the end products of a parallel restructuring process in Penutian, accompanied in Takelma by the loss of case markers on nouns, completing the shift to full head marking.

If the head-marking pattern found universally elsewhere in Hokan was once typical of Pomo, it represents a language that has completed a full transition in the opposite direction from Takelma, adding case markers to nouns and completely losing pronominal agreement affixes in verbs.

4.5.2 Morphological Complexity

The degree of morphological complexity within words varies considerably among California languages. Following Bickel and Nichols (2005a, 2005b, 2005c), we may distinguish three typological variables in morphological complexity: phonological *fusion*, the *exponence* of grammatical markers, and the degree of *synthesis* within words.

Languages differ in the degree to which markers of the basic grammatical categories (case, plurality, tense, aspect, mood) phonologically merge with the word or stem they are syntactically dependent on. An *isolating* marker is a well-demarcated phonological word; a *concatenative* marker is phonologically dependent on the stem to which it is attached (i.e., affixation); and a *nonlinear* marker cannot be segmented from the stem, and involves either a systematic alternation of one or more of the consonants or vowels of the stem (i.e., ablaut) or the addition or change of a tonal feature. With the exception of Yukian, in all the indigenous languages of California basic grammatical categories are expressed either exclusively by concatenation (in Athabaskan, Algic, Uto-Aztecan, Chumash, and Hokan) or by a combination of concatenation and ablaut (in Penutian).

In both Northern Yukian and in Wappo, unmodified roots are often used as independent words, particularly as nouns, and the compounding of roots is the most frequently used morphological process. Otherwise, there are a few case markers in nouns and an uncomplicated system of voice, transitivity, aspect, and mode marking in verbs. But these markers show little if any phonological fusion with the stems to which they are attached and may better be described as syntactic constructions.

EXPONENCE

Exponence refers to the number of categories that are expressed by a single marker. While in most languages most grammatical markers express only one category (*monoexponential*), in some languages *polyexponential* or *cumulative* markers occur that simultaneously code more than one category (such as the case-number-gender affixes of many Indo-European languages). In the California region, polyexponential grammatical markers appear to be characteristic of languages belonging to the Hokan phylum. An especially complex example is the simultaneous expression of tense, mode, person, and number in a paradigm of stem-initial prefixes in Shasta (e.g., *t-* 'let me . . .', *s-* 'I might . . .', *sw-* 'I am . . .', *kw-* 'I have . . .', *p'-* 'I used to . . .').

SYNTHESIS

The measure of synthesis in a morphological construction is the number of grammatical categories it expresses, regardless of the degree of fusion or exponence. The *degree of synthesis* characteristic of a language can be represented by the maximal number of categories per word (the "cpw value") of a diagnostic complex word, typically the verb. In the worldwide survey of synthesis carried out by Bickel and Nichols (2005c), the cpw values of the five California languages in their sample varied between a low of 4–5 (Sierra Miwok, Kashaya Pomo) and a high of 8–9 (Karuk, Maricopa), with Yurok in the middle with 6–7 cpw. These values place California languages in the midrange of synthesis among the world's languages. Other North American languages have much higher cpw values (Wishram Chinook 10–11, Wichita 12–13), while many Indo-European languages, including English, have cpw values of 2–3, and "isolating" languages like Mandarin or Vietnamese have 0 (i.e., no morphological constructions).

4.6 Case Marking

Languages with a basic dependent-marking or double-marking typological pattern (¶4.5.1) distinguish subjects, objects, and other syntactic relationships through the morphological modification of the noun (or independent pronoun), usually by affixation or cliticization. In California, this is universally suffixation or enclisis. The relationships marked differ somewhat from language to language.

4.6.1 Penutian Case Marking

The basic case marking systems found in the Penutian languages of the California region bear enough similarity to one another to support the reconstruction of case marking in Proto Penutian. Table 59 shows the cases found in the dependent-marking Penutian languages of the California area and the basic shapes of the suffixes used to mark them in nouns. All are nominative-accusative in pattern, with the nominative normally being unmarked. The exceptional Maiduan system, where the accusative is unmarked and the nominative is marked by an *-m* that would be more expected as the marker of possessive case, is perhaps the vestige of an

TABLE 59

Penutian Case Marking: Nouns

	Klamath	Maiduan	Wintuan	Miwok	Costanoan	Yokuts
	(Klamath)	(Northeastern Maidu)	(Wintu)	(Northern Sierra)	(Mutsun)	(Wikchamni)
Subject	(unmarked)	-m	(unmarked)	-ʔ	(unmarked)	(unmarked)
Object	-s	-(i)	-m	-y	-(s)e	-V
Possessive	-m	-ki	-n	-ŋ	—	-in
Locative	—	-di	-in	-m	-tak	-Vw
Dative	—	—	—	-t(o)	—	-ŋi
Ablative	—	—	—	-miʔ	—	-nitʰ
Instrumental	—	—	—	-sï	-(s)um	—

older ergative-absolute system of case marking of the type found in Oregon Penutian languages to the north of Klamath-Modoc and Takelma (DeLancey and Golla 1997).

The same categories are marked in pronouns, although with a considerable amount of phonetic fusion and irregularity. The singular forms for subject, object, and possessive case are shown in Table 60.

4.6.2 Yukian Case Marking

The case-marking system in both Wappo and Northern Yukian is nominative-accusative, with accusative unmarked. The basic Wappo markers are shown in Table 61. There are, in addition, more than a dozen locative enclitics that combine with nouns and noun phrases to form locative phrases (e.g., *mot'a-pi* 'from the mountain', *hol-ompi* 'under the tree', *kʰeye-newe:la* 'inside the boat'). All the Wappo case markers should perhaps be treated as enclitic particles. Note, for example, the position of the subject marker -*i* in such complex noun phrases as *ečču mey-i* 'river water' (< *ečču* 'river' + *mey* 'water' + *-i*) and *ce k'ew hučewiš-i* 'that happy guy' (< *ce* 'that' + *k'ew* 'man' + *hučewiš* 'happy' + *-i*). Nevertheless, the lexically specified fusion of vowel-final stems with the subject case marker in such forms as *k'eši* 'deer' (<*k'ešu* + *i*) and *met'a:yi* 'woman' (< *met'e* + *i*) can be taken as evidence for the morphological status of this construction (S. Thompson, Park, and Li 2006:10–18). Kroeber's comment on the structurally parallel (but for the most part noncognate) markers of case in Yuki holds for all of Yukian (1911a:356–357):

> These suffixes show a complete transition from purely formal or grammatical case-endings, such as the objective, through locative suffixes such as -op or -ki, to whole stems used as suffixes with prepositional meaning. The employment of all is however exactly alike; so that if the designation of 'case' is denied to -mik'al, around, and

-op, on, it must also be denied to objective -a and possessive -at.

Yukian independent pronouns are for the most part unanalyzable, but distinguish subject, object, and possessive forms (see Table 53).

4.6.3 Pomo Case Marking and the Marking of Agent "Control"

The Pomo languages stand apart from all other Hokan languages in their development of dependent marking (¶4.5.1). Three basic cases—agent, patient, and possessor—are distinguished in the independent pronouns (see Table 20) and are also marked on nouns, although the system is weakly developed and intertwined with the marking of a contrast in the degree of "control" an agent exerts on an action (Mithun 1991:518–523). Nouns or pronouns marked as objects are used instead of subject-marked forms with verbs denoting mental, emotional, or bodily states, or with active verbs where the agent is not in control of the situation. Thus in Eastern Pomo, *wi* 'me', the first person singular object case pronoun, is used in place of *ha:* 'I', the first person singular subject case pronoun, in *wi ʔečkiya* 'I sneezed', *wi da:šula* 'I lost something', and *wi ba:tsc'ki* 'I got bumped (accidentally)' (McLendon 1996:534).

The same type of marking of the degree of agent control has been noted in Yuki (Kroeber 1911a:371–372). As in Pomo, object forms are used as subjects with verbs expressing mental, emotional, or bodily states, or with active verbs if the subject is not in control of the situation (e.g., *ʔi ʔohtik* 'I vomit', but *ʔap ʔohtlik* 'I spit it out'). When such "noncontrol" constructions are transitive, the grammatical object is expressed by a possessive form (*ʔi mit nanak'u* 'I knew you'). Chimariko may mark a similar distinction with contrasting sets of pronominal prefixes in verbs (¶3.10.3).

TABLE 60
Penutian Case Marking: Pronouns

	Klamath	Maiduan	Wintuan	Miwok	Costanoan	Yokuts
	(Klamath)	(Northeastern Maidu)	(Wintu)	(Northern Sierra)	(Mutsun)	(Wikchamni)
Subject						
1	no: ~ ni	ni	ni ~ niyo	kanni?	ka:n ~ -ka	na?
2	?i	mi	mi ~ miyo	mi?	me:n ~ -m(e)	ma?
3	pi	mïm	pi ~ piyo	?issaki?	wa:k ~ -(a)k	xi
Object						
1	nos ~ nis	nik	nis	kanniy	kannis ~ -kas	nan
2	mis	min	mis	mi:niy	me:se ~ -mes	mam
3	po:s	mï	put	?issakkoy	wa:kse ~ -was	xiŋ
Possessive						
1	kew	nikí	ner	kanïŋ	—	nim
2	mi	mínki	mar	mi:nïŋ	—	min
3	mna	mïkí	pir	?issakkoŋ	—	xi?an

TABLE 61
Wappo Case Marking (S. Thompson, Park, and Li 2006)

		pol'e? 'boy'	k'ešu 'deer'	met'e 'woman'
Subject	-i	pol'e?i	k'eši	met'a:yi
Object	(unmarked)	pol'e?	k'ešu	met'e
Possessive	-me?	pol'e?me?	k'ešume?	met'eme?
Dative	-tʰu	pol'e?tʰu	k'ešutʰu	met'etʰu
Benefactive	-ma	pol'e?ma	k'ešuma	met'ema
Instrumental	-tʰi	pol'e?tʰi	k'ešutʰi	met'etʰi
Comitative	-k'a	pol'e?k'a	k'ešuk'a	met'ek'a

4.7 Marking of Plurality

4.7.1. Collective Plurals

In all languages of the California region except some of those belonging to the Hokan phylum, whose plural formations are described in the following section, plurality of subject and object is an optionally marked grammatical category of relatively infrequent occurrence in normal discourse. When it is marked on the noun, the reference typically is to a group of people (most frequently kinsmen) who are the collective subject or object of an action. In Sierra Miwok, for example, the pluralizing suffix -yya- is attested only in personal nouns, such as ?ésleyya? 'children', míw?ïyya? 'people', náŋ?ayya?

'men', ?óš?ayya? 'women', and támlïyya? 'northerners' (Freeland 1951:57–58). Similarly in Ineseño Chumash, both nominal pluralizers—the suffix -wuṅ and initial stem reduplication—are restricted to collective terms such as makičtïṅïwuṅ 'my children', ?alapšawawuṅ 'people from šawa (village)', and mak'ank'aniš 'my paternal uncles' (Applegate 1972a:230–235). Formations of this type frequently serve as tribal and ethnic designations, as in Hupa, where -ni (usually reduced to -n), which marks a collective plural in cʰamehsƛ'on '(a group of) women' (<cʰamehsƛ'o:n-ni), also occurs in a number of ethnonyms such as ḳ'inasn 'Karuk people' and yita:č'in (<yita:č'in-ni 'hither from downstream–pl.') 'Yurok people' (Sapir and Golla 2001:860).

In some languages a related verb marker can indicate the plurality of the subject or object, although in most cases it shades into a more general marker of "pluractionality" by means of such concepts as repetition and distribution. Thus in Karuk, the verbal suffix -va, in addition to pluralizing subjects or objects—*ivrú·htih* '(one object) to be floating', *ivruhti·h-va* '(several objects) to be floating'; *pasnápisrih* 'to glue down', *pasnapisri·h-va* 'to glue down (plural objects)'— can also mark the repetition of the action: *ikre·myáhis(rih)* 'to start to blow', *ikre·myahisrih-va* 'to blow off and on'; *taknah* 'to hop', *takná·h-va* 'to play hopscotch' (Bright 1957:92–93; Conathan and Wood 2003). In Inezeño Chumash, the pluralizing noun suffix *-wuṅ* is paralleled by a verbal suffix *-wun* that marks plurality of object (e.g., *skutiwun* 'he sees them'), and the same initial reduplication that marks collective plurality in nouns can be used in verbs with "repetitive, distributive, intensive, or continuative force" (e.g., *štelmemen* 'he touches it', *šteltelmemen* 'he is groping around'). Both pluralizers occur in *šteltelmemenuwun* 'he is touching them (one after another)' (Applegate 1972a:284– 286, 383–384). Wood (2007) has recently surveyed the typology of pluractionality, with a case study of the marking of the category in Yurok.

4.7.2. Plural Stems in Hokan Languages

The plurality of the subject or object, and sometimes also verbal pluractionality, are marked in many Hokan languages by irregular and often phonetically complex stem derivation (including infixation and ablaut). Highly lexicalized marking of plurality, together with its extension to verbal pluractionality, appears to be an ancient trait of the Hokan languages, and its occurrence in Tequistlatecan (P. Turner 1967) and Coahuiltecan (Troike 1996:654–655) languages is one of the most persuasive arguments for the inclusion of these groups in the Hokan phylum. Among the California Hokan languages the development (or retention) of a system of plural stem formation is most prominent in Yuman, Salinan, and Seri.

YUMAN

Yuman plural marking may be illustrated by Jamul Diegueño (A. Miller 2001:100–116). Here the marking occurs primarily on verb stems, with two types of plural verbs distinguished. "Plural-subject plurals" indicate action taken by a plural subject either collectively on a single object or independently on many objects, or intransitive action by a plural subject. "Distributive action plurals" indicate the distribution of an action across a number of objects, locations, or times. Plural-subject verb stems are derived from their singular counterparts by a variety of processes of prefixation, suffixation, and ablaut, in various combinations—for example, *axkay* 'to go across' > *naxkay*; *xap* 'to enter' > *nəkxap*; *a:lʸap* 'to hit' > *ačuːlʸap*; *xtup* 'to jump' > *xuːtuːp*; *xənu* 'to be sick' > *xiːnuːč*. Although some

of these formations follow similar patterns, in general they are unpredictable and lexically specified, and a few can only be described as suppletive—for example, *wa* 'to be located' > *nyəway*; *yaw* 'to pick up' > *suːtuːč*. Distributive action plural stems are formed by similar but differently specified processes. For example, compare *a:tuk* 'to pour, spill' > *čuːtuːk* (plural-subject), *ačtuːk* (distributive action); *šəma* 'to sleep' > *šuːmaːp* (plural-subject), *stəmač* (distributive action). A few noun stems referring to people and kin are also marked for plurality—for example, *kur'ak* 'old man' > *kʷəčər'ak*; *xuːmaːy* '(man's) son' > *čəxmáya*.

SALINAN

In Salinan, plurality and distributive action are marked in both nouns and verbs, and the "great irregularity and complexity" of this marking is noted by Mason as "one of the most striking peculiarities" of the language (1918:22–28). Mason's further remark that "the details are very variant and almost inexplicable" is justified by the data that he presents, where some verbs are observed to occur with three distinct plural stems and at least one noun (*ṭaːm* 'house') in as many as seven plural variants.

The most common plural formatives in nouns are the suffixes *-ten*, *-lax*, and *-neł* (e.g., *wakiṭ* 'frog' > *wakiṭen*; *keṭpoy* 'cedar' > *keṭpoylax*; *at* 'acorn' > *atneł*) and the infixes *-il-*, *-t(e)-*, and *-he-* (e.g., *kpat'ak* 'dancer' > *kpat'ilax*; *kaxap* 'corpse' > *kaxatep*; *let* 'tooth' > *lehet*). Suppletion is common (e.g., *stexa* 'boy' > *sentam*), but a number of forms that appear to be irregular, such as *taken* 'shaman' > *tanta*, may in fact be the product of complex rules that cannot be recovered from the extant data (compare the treatment of the Spanish borrowing *kuwayo* 'horse' > *kuyata*).

In verbs, plurality of both subject and object are marked by distinct stem variants that are partially analyzable at best. Mason cites the following examples from Sitjar's dictionary:

> *kaxota* 'a man hunts an animal'
>
> *kaxoten* 'a man hunts many animals'
>
> *kaxotota* 'many men hunt an animal'
>
> *kaxonilet* 'many men hunt many animals'

Frequentative and distributive meanings are apparently also marked:

> *amalek* 'give alms'
>
> *amolek* 'give alms frequently'

Mason also notes an infix *-t(e)-* with iterative force in the following:

> *kmaltox* 'jump again' < *kmalox* 'jump'
>
> *pale'ltko* 'inquire again' < *pale'lko* 'inquire'

As with nouns, however, many verbs have plural formations that defy a ready analysis:

liyax 'shoot', *litax* (pl.)

komiyota 'lie down', *ko'kiyutne* (pl.)

SERI

The marking of singular versus plural number in both noun and verb stems plays an unusually large role in Seri grammar (Moser and Moser 1976; Marlett 1990). Nearly all noun stems have plural alternates, for the most part formed by irregular suffixation (e.g., *nop, nópxam* 'wildcat, wildcats'; *ná:pxa, ná:pxaxk* 'buzzard, buzzards', *ši:k, ší:kaxka* 'coyote, coyotes'). With possessed nouns, the basic plural alternate of the noun stem marks plurality of the possessor: *ʔikakám* 'my son in law', *ʔikakámtoxka* 'our son-in law' (*ʔi-* first person possessor); *itakx* 'its surface, above it', *itakax* 'their surface, above them' (*i-* third person possessor). Kinship nouns and some body-part terms have a second plural stem indicating plurality of the possessed object (e.g., *ʔitoa:* 'my leg', *ʔitoit* 'my legs', *ʔitoa:tx* 'our legs').

In the Seri verb, the plurality of the subject and the pluractionality of the action or event are both marked. Most verb stems have four alternates: singular subject semelfactive, singular subject repetitive, plural subject semelfactive, and plural subject repetitive. For example, *ʔayokapx* 'I chewed it (once)!', *ʔayokapapxax* 'we chewed it (once)!', *ʔayokapapxim* 'I chewed it (repeatedly)!', *ʔayokapapxoxka* 'we chewed it (repeatedly)!' (*ʔa-* first person subject, *-yo-* distal realis). The forms are complex and unpredictable. Although most stem alternates are formed by suffixation, this is often accompanied by other phonological processes, such as ablaut and infixation: *-koi* 'bring', *-koa:tim* 'bring (repeatedly)', *-koit* '(several) bring', *-koa:tam* '(several) bring (repeatedly); *-i:p* 'carry on the head', *-i:ptim* 'carry on the head (repeatedly), *-i:tópax^w* '(several) carry on the head'. *-i:tópaxka* '(several) carry on the head (repeatedly)'.

4.8 Stem Derivation

Complex verb stems are common in the languages of the California region. Only the Yukian languages, two Hokan isolates (Esselen and Salinan), and two Penutian families (Costanoan—but not Miwok—and Yokuts), appear to wholly lack productive processes of verb stem composition. In all of the rest, at least some polymorphemic stems occur, although the range of variation in productivity and complexity is considerable. A distinction needs to be drawn between languages in which complex stems are derived from simplex stems only by markers of formal and adverbial categories, and those in which stems can also incorporate nominal (usually instrumental or classificatory) elements.

4.8.1 Formal and Adverbial Derivation

Sierra Miwok provides a good example of a California language with relatively complex verb stem morphology, but in which that complexity nowhere involves compounding (Freeland 1951:105–146). Although a variety of morphological processes are employed, all are derivational in function. Some of the derived stems are formed by consonantal and vocalic ablaut:

sakkawï:- 'tear up several, repeatedly' (< *sakwa-* 'tear up [one]')

maʔʔatï:- 'kill several' (< *maʔta-* 'kill')

In a few instances part of the stem is reduplicated:

šilettetti 'fly about' (< *šile:t-* 'fly')

The great majority of derived verb stems, however, are formed by suffixation. A few of these create verb stems from nouns:

-ŋki- denominative: *haya:po-ŋki-* 'be a chief'

-pušnu- inchoative: *šawa:-pušnu-* 'become a rock'

Most mark adverbial and formal categories:

-puttu- continuative: *milliʔ-puttu-* 'keep on singing'

-iči:- continuative, stative: *hiŋŋ-iči:-* 'be sitting'

-ta:nï- conative: *ʔuppi:-ta:nï-* 'try to dive'

-mešnï- 'on the way': *sunu:-mešnï-* 'get wood on the way'

-nnukku- causative: *ʔupi-nnukku-* 'make dive'

-na- causative: *čamiš-na-* 'cause to die'

-ynï- inceptive: *šïlte-ynï-* 'take flight, fly off'

-teynï- 'here and there': *mï:liʔ-teynï-* 'sing here and there'

-ka- benefactive: *wel-ka-* 'get for someone'

-tukku- malefactive: *ʔïwï:-tukku-* 'eat at someone else's expense'

-ene:- directive: *well-ene:-* 'tell someone to get'

-kkï- desiderative: *ʔiwʔi-kkï-* 'wish to eat'

-pokšu- reflexive: *wï:ku-pokšu-* 'burn oneself'

-mši- reciprocal: *yilli-mši-* 'bite each other'

-ŋŋe- passive: *yïnna-ŋŋe-* 'get killed'

A less elaborate pattern of stem derivation is seen in the Takic languages. In Cupeño (J. Hill 2005:260–293), a small number of suffixes—most if not all of them grammaticalized verb stems in origin—derive secondary verb forms from primary stems. Two of these change the valence of the verb

(-*nin* causative, and -*max* benefactive). The remainder subordinate the stem-defined action to a verb of motion or intention:

-*lu* 'go in order to do': *aṣ-lu* 'go to take a bath' (*aṣ* 'take a bath')

-*ŋiy* 'go off doing, go around doing': *ʔamu-ŋiy* 'go off hunting' (*ʔamu* 'hunt')

-*nəq* 'come [verb]-ing': *yaw-nəq* 'bring' (lit. 'come carrying'; *yaw* 'carry')

-*βənəq* 'come along [verb]-ing': *čaṣwin-βənəq* 'come crawling' (*čaṣwin* 'crawl')

-*miʔaw* 'arrive doing': *yaw-miʔaw* 'bring' (lit. 'arrive carrying'; *yaw* 'carry')

-*βiču* 'want to [verb]': *ŋiy-βiču* 'want to go' (*ŋiy* 'go')

In addition, three suffixes derive verb stems from nouns (-*či* unaccusative and causative, -*čo* inchoative, and -*lu* ~ -*tu* denominal).

4.8.2 Stem Compounding

In a large number of California languages, complex verb stems are not only the product of formal and adverbial derivation but also show a type of "polysynthetic" stem compounding in which elements of largely nominal force are incorporated into the verbal base. The languages showing this feature are more common in the northern part of the region. In central and southern California, stem compounding is relatively rare, and in its most elaborate form is restricted to Chumash. Among the Hokan subgroups, Karuk, Shastan, Chimariko, Palaihnihan, Yana, Washo, and Pomo all show complex stem compounding, whereas in the central and southern areas only Yuman has compound verb stems (at least historically; their synchronic analyzability is often doubtful), while Esselen, Salinan, and Seri appear to lack the feature entirely. Among Penutian families, Takelman, Klamath-Modoc, Wintuan, and Maiduan have compound stems similar in their polysynthetic complexity to those of adjacent Hokan languages. In Yokuts and Utian, by contrast, stem compounding of any sort is completely absent. Of the Uto-Aztecan families of the California region, only Numic has any form of stem compounding (¶3.31.4).

INSTRUMENTAL AFFIXES

Stem compounding is not uncommon among North American languages in the form of "instrumental" affixation—the incorporation into the stem of an element that "indexes the shape or other semantic features of an absolutive or instrumental argument of the verb" (Delancey 1999:56). Instrumental affixation is found in languages as far from California as Siouan and Haida, and has a long history of discussion in American Indian linguistics (cf. Sapir 1916a).

Of the languages of the California region, the Numic family most clearly exemplifies the generic pattern of incorporating instrumental elements into the verb stem. In Shoshoni (W. Miller 1996:702–703), for example, a fairly well-defined class of verbs of hitting, breaking, cutting, and surface contact occur only with a prefixed element specifying the instrument of the action:

ta-nnua-hkʷa (with foot–move–Momentaneous) '(he) pushed (it) with his foot'

ci-kkaʔa-hkʷa (with sharp point–cut–Momentaneous) '(he) cut (it) with a knife'

ku-kkipa-hkʷa (by heat–break–Momentaneous) '(it) broke by burning'

BIPARTITE STEMS

More characteristic of the California region is the "bipartite" stem (Jacobsen 1980; DeLancey 1996, 1999), in which two interdependent elements of roughly equal lexical status fuse in a polysynthetic unit. The first element in such a stem—the "lexical prefix" in DeLancey's terminology (1999:57)—usually identifies the class of entity (often a body part) involved in the verbal action or state, while the second element refers to a type of motion or position or is descriptive of some attribute. Although the first element in a bipartite stem is often difficult to distinguish semantically from an instrumental prefix of the type found in Numic, its morphological relationship to the second element is usually more complex and the semantic relationship more abstract.[4]

Bipartite stem fusion is well illustrated in McLendon's grammatical sketch of Eastern Pomo (1996). In her analysis, the typical Eastern Pomo verb stem contains one of eighteen instrumental prefixes (e.g., *du:-* 'with or affecting the fingertips', *mu:-* 'from inside out')[5] and a monosyllabic "root" that refers to abstract types of motion, action, process, or state (e.g., -*di-* 'place or maintain in a specific appropriate position', -*da-* 'force open, expose', -*qʼa-* 'applying pressure'):

du:-di- 'push with the hands'

du:-da- 'split open with the fingers'

mu:-da- 'split open (like a ripe melon)'

du:-qʼa- 'tighten, close off (faucet)'

mu:-qʼa- 'be knocked unconscious or dead'

These prefix-root combinations are then further modified by one of twenty-one "manner" suffixes of modal or aspectual meaning (e.g., -*kʰ-* 'punctual', -*l-* 'durative', -*tʰ-* 'intermittently', -*s-* 'sharply, with intensity'). The interaction of any given combination of instrumental prefix, root, and manner suffix is only partly definable as a morphological process. The resulting forms are highly lexicalized:

ma:-di-ll- (with the foot–place in position–Continuative) 'step on something (such as a car's accelerator)'

kʰi:-di-ll- (with a rope or strap–place in position–Continuative) 'carry in a basket held in place (on one's back) with a strap'

Not infrequently the same complex stem can be applied to different situations that, from the point of view of an English speaker, seem only arbitrarily associated:

si:-qa-l- (in liquid medium–transform–Durative) 'be pure, cleaned off, all of one kind, homogeneous' *or* 'to lick (ice cream) off (fingers)'

pʰa:-q'a-ṭ'- (with kinetic energy–apply pressure–Intensive) 'to pry (abalones) loose (from rocks with crowbar)' *or* 'high water to wash (house) away'.

Conversely, a single act or event can often be described by more than one stem, according to which aspects of the event are focused on. Thus the act of poking a snake with a stick could equally grammatically be described as *ša:-nu-l-kʰ* with the prefix *ša:-* 'with a long pointed object' or as *pʰa:-nu-l-kʰ* with the prefix *pʰa:-* 'with kinetic energy' (McLendon 1996:515–522).

In Washo, the morphological fusion of a similar set of bipartite stem elements is far advanced.[6] Most consonant-initial verb stems can be analyzed into what Jacobsen (1980) calls a "lexical prefix" (C- or CVC-) and a "dependent verb stem." These fall into two types:

1. The stem specifies a type of motion or position, and the prefix identifies the class of entity involved (e.g., *tuʔm-áŋaʔ* 'to have one's foot on something' < *tuʔm-* 'with the foot' + *-aŋaʔ* 'be on something'; *wed-ípïs* 'for a long object to stand up from a surface' < *wed-* 'long object standing' + *-ips* 'be up from a surface').

2. The stem is descriptive of some physical attribute or change of state, and the prefix expresses the entity (often a body part) that possesses the attribute or that causes the change of state—for example, *k'-ípeš* 'to have a black face' < *k'-* 'face' + *-ipš* 'be black'; *d-á:baš* 'to kill (pl.) by shooting' < *d-* '(with) arrow, bullet' + *-a:baš* 'kill (pl.)'.

In Yuman languages, many consonant-initial dissyllabic verb stems appear to be open to a similar analysis. In Tipay Diegueño, for example, *š-* 'with the hand or a handheld instrument' seems analyzable in such stems as *ša:win* 'hold onto', *šemalʸ* 'touch', *šemkʷin* 'pinch (someone)', and *šu:kʷïl* 'sew'; similarly *k-* 'by speaking' in such stems as *ka:na:p* 'tell', *kena:p* 'ask about' and *ki:nap* 'gossip' (A. Miller 2001:52–69). However, these and most other similar analyses are not productive in any modern Yuman language,

and if a bipartite stem construction was originally involved, it has long been fossilized.

Although in Bright's analysis of Karuk a class of bipartite verb stems is not recognized synchronically, he suggested (1957:86–87) the "sub-morphemic" analyzability of elements such as **im* 'involving fire or heat' or **ʔak* 'with the hand' that closely resemble the lexical prefixes of Washo. Haas (1980) argued that the methods of internal reconstruction allowed a bipartite stem-compounding system to be recovered from such elements, which Macaulay (1993) supported by demonstrating that certain patterns of stem reduplication can most easily be explained by assuming the synchronic reality of a bipartite analysis.

Bipartite stems are especially characteristic of the languages of the southern Cascades and northern Sierra Nevada, from Klamath-Modoc to Maiduan and Washo, an area DeLancey (1996) has called the "Bipartite Stem Belt." Klamath verb stems are frequently bipartite in structure, with a classificatory or instrumental element preposed to an element with locative-directive meaning: *l-apa:tʰa* 'put a round object up on shore', *l-oli:na* 'put a round object off the edge'; *tʰ-q'eẇa* 'break with a blow, kick', *n-q'eẇa* 'break with a round instrument'; *l'očʰ-wa* 'put/have knee in water', *č'oqʰ-wa* 'put/have buttocks in water' (DeLancey 1999). In Maiduan, a widely used subset of verbs of motion are bipartite, the second element indicating direction. For example, Northeastern Maidu *c'ídoy* 'grab up something in the hand' (< *c'ï-* 'action with the hand' + *-doy* 'upward'), *yodá* 'make a hit, hit the mark, split sticks in preparation for basketweaving' (< *yo-* '[hit] with the hand' + *-da* 'down, off'), and *tïppin* 'jump in this direction' (< *tïp-* 'jump' + *-pin* 'hither') (Shipley 1963, 1964).

These Penutian languages have probably borrowed their bipartite stem formations from adjacent or substratal Hokan languages. The pattern has its most exuberant expression in Palaihnihan and Yana. In Talmy's analysis (1972), most Atsugewi verb stems are in fact tripartite, with (1) a "figure-specifying" prefix that defines the instrumental or physical profile of the action (e.g, *ma-* 'with the feet'), (2) a root that specifies the class of entity in motion (e.g., *-swal-* 'limp material'), and (3) one or more slightly less tightly integrated suffixes that mark the direction or location of the action (e.g., *-ičʰt* 'into liquid'). Typical formations of this type are *sẁa:póqʰ* 'I kicked up the dirt' (< *s-'-w-*, 1 sg subject, factual mode + *ma-puq* 'with the feet–dust moves'), *sẁoscʹákʹčʰu* 'I swung the axe down onto (the stump) by the handle' (< *s-'-w-*, 1 sg subject, factual mode + *uh-sčʹakʹ-čïsu-im* 'by swinging–sharp linear object moves–down against a solid object–thither'), and *čʹwaswálmičʹ* 'the (clothes) blew down from (the clothesline)' (< *'-w-* 3 sg subject, factual mode + *ča-swal-mičʹ* 'by wind blowing–limp material moves–down to the ground').

ALGIC STEM COMPOUNDING

Although the morphological components are often fused and difficult to identify, Wiyot and Yurok verb stems appear to reflect the same tripartite structure that is found in Algonquian verb stems (I. Goddard 1975; Proulx 1985a). An initial lexical element (e.g., Wiyot *tʰɨɣ-* 'out', *takʷ-* 'strike'; Yurok *loʔoɣ-* 'black', *tk-* 'thick, sticky') is followed by an optional "medial" element, generally classificatory in nature and including a set of body-part elements (e.g., Wiyot *-ətal-* 'one person goes, walks', *-eʔsan-* 'hand'; Yurok *-eʔn-* 'trees, sticks', *-ohp-* 'water, liquid'), and a "final" element that is grammatical in function (e.g., Wiyot *-aʔw*, transitive; Yurok *-on*, stative, *-et*, transitive). Although this system has the same general polysynthetic nature as the bipartite, classificatory compound stem of the California region, it clearly has a very different origin.

4.9 Switch Reference

A set of "switch reference" enclitic markers, which indicate whether the subject of a subordinated verb is the same or different from that of the main verb (as well as some other interclausal relationships), is found in all Pomo languages. In Eastern Pomo (McLendon 1996:539), for example, the main clause has the Coreference marker *-y* when the subect of the dependent clause remains the same, but has the Switch Reference marker *-qan* when the subject of the dependent clause is different:

> *há: káluhu-y, mérqaki:hi* 'I went home, and (I) went to bed'
>
> *há: káluhu-qan, mí:p' mérqaki:hi* 'I went home, and he went to bed'

This syntactic device, as well as its specific markers, can be reconstructed in Proto-Pomo (Oswalt 1976a). Similar systems of interclausal subject marking are found in some other California Hokan languages, most notably Washo (Jacobsen 1967) and Yuman (Langdon and Munro 1979), as well as in a few non-Hokan languages such as Maiduan (Oswalt 1976b) and Yuki (Kroeber 1911a:378–380). In most of these cases the (dis)continuity of the subject between adjoining clauses is marked by a difference either in the conjunction that links the two clauses or (as in Eastern Pomo) in a particle enclitic to the first clause. Differences in this particle are sometimes used to distinguish other categories as well. In Jamul Diegueño (A. Miller 2001: 228–232), there are two sets of switch reference markers, differing according to the mood of

the first clause. When it is realis, an unchanged subject in the following clause is marked by *-č*, a switched subject by *-čm* (phonetically [čəm]):

> *wesi-č wa:m* 'He drank it and went off'
>
> *wesaw-čm uwi:w tu:yaw* 'They ate while he stood and watched them'

When the clause is in the irrealis mood, however, the markers are *-k* and *-km* [kəm]:

> *may tekewan-k uwi:w xema:w* 'He didn't turn around and look'
>
> *nʸačaw-km sawma* 'When I finish, we can eat'

In Yuki, switch reference is marked in the "dubitative" particle, a conjunction that is used in myths to indicate that the narrative does not rest on the personal experience of the narrator. This particle takes the form *səʔi* when the subject of the verb is the same as that of the finite verb in the preceding sentence, but *siʔi* when the subject of the verb is different from the subject of the preceding verb (Kroeber 1911a:378).

Switch reference constructions often occur in long chains, particularly in stories and anecdotes, where they are an important mechanism for expressing the coherence of the narrated events. In Jamul Diegueño, sequences such as the following are frequently encountered in narrative discourse:

> *nʸasʔa:y-čm, kʷakpu čamɬʸ stu:-č, nʸa:čan-č, a:a:-č, sa:kɬʸ šu:wi:-č, nʸaučaw-č, a:a:-č, šuʔak.* '. . . when it was dry, when she had gathered all the meat, and taken it down, she took it, and put it in a sack, and then took (the sack), and hung it up'. (A. Miller 2001:235)

Related syntactic phenomena have been identified in several other American Indian languages, for the most part in languages for which a Hokan or Hokan-Siouan affiliation has been hypothesized (Jacobsen 1983; Mixco 1997a; Mithun 1999:269–271). While the marking of subject continuity between clauses is attested elsewhere in the world (see Haiman and Munro 1983), the distinctiveness in form and function that it assumes in the Hokan languages seems to reflect a long history in that phylum.[7]

Linguistic Culture

4.10 Numerals

4.10.1 Decimal and Quinary Systems

All attested California languages possess systems of enumeration fully adequate for counting into the hundreds

and beyond. The great majority of these systems are ***decimal*** in their overall plan—that is, the basic set of numerals is 1–10, with higher numbers expressed as multiples of ten. The lexical structure of the basic decimal numerals differs from language to language, however. In a few languages all ten are etymologically distinct, as they are in European languages. These include the California Algic languages, the California and Oregon subfamilies of Athabaskan, and two Penutian language families, Yokuts and Miwok (but not Costanoan). Although these are, in the main, languages that we know (or suspect) were spoken by groups who entered the California region in relatively recent times, it can be stated with assurance only of the Athabaskans that they brought a full-fledged decimal count with them. The basic ten numerals are cognate among all Pacific Coast Athabaskan subfamilies, from California to the Columbia River.[8] By contrast, no numerals over five can be reconstructed for Proto-Algic, or even Proto–California Algic, and hardly any numeral at all can be attributed to a hypothetical "Yok-Utian." There is thus no linguistic reason to suppose that the decimal systems used by the speakers of Yurok, Wiyot, Yokuts, or Miwok in historical times were part of the cultural traditions of these peoples before their arrival in California.

It seems unlikely, in fact, that routine counting beyond the digits of one hand played a significant role in traditional California society before the beginning of the Late Period, circa 800–1000 AD in most areas. Higher numerals may well have been constructed for special occasions (the pattern preserved in Cupeño indicates one form such impromptu counting could have taken; see Box 11), but there could have been few occasions where numbers like "forty" or "one hundred"—or even "eleven"—would have been indispensable. The regular use of lexified higher numbers almost certainly had to await the development of an intergroup trading economy in which values were set in a standard, countable medium of exchange—strings of dentalia, clamshell disk beads, or olivella shell necklaces.[9]

When that trading economy got under way, speakers of most California languages seem to have rapidly innovated systematic patterns of counting to higher numbers. Only the first few numbers of the typical California numeral system consist of basic roots: in most cases these can be taken to be the remnants of an earlier one-hand count.[10] Numerals above five variously define a number as the product of an arithmetic operation (e.g., "two threes" for six); describe the gestures used in counting it (e.g., "two fingers held in the opposite hand" for seven); or refer to it as a stage in a metaphorical process (e.g., "almost there" for nine). Ten is often expressed as "two hands" or "two fives."

Dixon and Kroeber (1907) called such numeral systems *quinary*. For most California languages with "quinary" numerals, however, the label must be taken in the etymological sense, not as a characterization of the actual counting scheme. Only in some of the Takic languages of Southern California, exemplified by Cupeño in Box 11, did counting literally proceed by fives. In these languages the basic set of numerals names the five digits of a single hand, and all higher numerals are constructed by adding limbs and digits with extreme literalness.[11] Besides Cupeño, Gabrielino-Fernandeño, Juaneño, and Luiseño all followed this scheme.

BOX 11. CUPEÑO QUINARY COUNTING
(J. HILL 2005:210–214)

1 *sulit, suplewet*
2 *wih*
3 *pah*
4 *wičiw*
5 *nema kʷanaŋax* ('my handsworth [of fingers], a hand's supply of my [fingers]')
6 *nema kʷanaŋax paʔax supluwet* ('one on top of my handsworth')
7 *nema kʷanaŋax paʔax wih* ('two on top of my handsworth')
8 *nema kʷanaŋax paʔax pah* ('three on top of my handsworth')
9 *nema kʷanaŋax paʔax wičiw* ('four on top of my handsworth')
10 *nema tulwenet* ('my hand[s] finished')
11 *nema tulwenet supluwet namyaxwen* ('my hand[s] finished [with] one crossing')
12 *nema tulwenet wih . . .* (etc.)
15 *nema tulwenet nema kʷanaŋax namyaxwen* ('my hand[s] finished [with] my handsworth crossing')
16 *nema tulwenet nema kʷanaŋax pa'ax supluwet namyaxwen* ('my hand[s] finished [with] one on top of my handsworth crossing')
17 *nema tulwenet nema kʷanaŋax pa'ax wih . . .* (etc.)
20 *wis nema tulwenet* ('two times my hand[s] finished')

That these were the groups involved in the Chinigchinich religion has often been noted, but it is probably coincidental.[12]

4.10.2 Vigesimal Systems

Across most of the remainder of the California region, the higher count is either decimal or proceeds by twenties or "scores"—40 is "two twenties," 60 "three twenties," and so on. The languages in which such **vigesimal** counting prevails are found only in the northern third of California, centering on the Sacramento Valley. Kroeber thought it was significant that the southern portion of this area, stretching from Nisenan and Sierra Miwok to Pomo, was the region within which the Kuksu religion was dominant at the time of contact (1925:878). But the occurrence of vigesimal systems of counting as far afield as Wintu, Shasta, Achumawi, and Yana makes it more likely that the determining factor was the use of clamshell disk beads as the medium of exchange (Farris 1990:179). From a core area in Coast Miwok and Pomo country, clamshell beads were traded up the

Sacramento Valley and are attested ethnographically both along the Pit River and in the Rogue Valley of southern Oregon (J. T. Davis 1961). They were also traded as far up the coast as the Tolowa (Driver 1939:336).[13] Throughout this area, wherever they were used as money, twenty beads and four hundred beads (20 × 20) were the basic pricing units.

Many of the vigesimal systems of this region (Wintu, Shasta, Takelma, etc.) lexify 20 as 'person', that is, the digits of both hands and both feet. However, in Eastern Pomo, 20 is *xay* 'stick': *xáy-di:lè:ma* 'twenty' (='a full stick'), *xóča-xày* 'forty' (='two sticks'), *xó:mk'a-xày* 'sixty' (= 'three sticks'), and so on. The lexification of 20 as 'stick' (and 400 as 'big stick') reflects the use of stick counters in reckoning monetary sums.[14] The same lexification is attested for Mattole (V. Hymes 1955:43), an Athabaskan language where the count is unambiguously decimal but clamshell disk necklaces were also used.[15] In Oregon Athabaskan, as well as in the California Athabaskan languages north and east of Mattole, 'stick' is used only for 100, not 20 (V. Hymes 1955:41–45).[16] In this area the basic unit of money was a single string of ten dentalia shells, and apparently the larger 'stick' sum was ten of these.

4.10.3 Quaternary and Octonary Systems

A small residue of counting schemes that cannot be classed as quinary, decimal, or vigesimal are found in Northern Yukian, Salinan, and Chumash (Appendix D: 3.9, 6, and 7). In all three language groups the count is by fours, either straightforwardly *quaternary* (based on four, in Salinan and Chumash) or *octonary* (based on eight, in Northern Yukian). Counting by fours apparently had its origin in an old practice, attested ethnographically among the Yuki (Kroeber 1925:878–879), of counting sticks held between the fingers rather than counting the fingers themselves. The first four numerals of a quaternary/octonary count thus add up to a hand in the same way as the first five numerals of a quinary/decimal count.[17] It was immaterial, however, whether sticks continued to be used in this way in the actual practice of counting (the Salinans and the Chumash denied any knowledge of it), since the toting up of large sums characteristic of Late Period trading and other complex activities went far beyond simply counting a few fingers. Numbers into the hundreds often required, and the logic of a quaternary/octonary system could be just as efficient as a quinary/decimal one in generating these sums. The only difference lay in the lexical form of the count and the numerical base on which large numbers were constructed. Some people counted by tens and hundreds, others by eights and sixty-fours.[18]

4.10.4 Traces of Senary Counting

Beeler (1961a) argued that the widespread borrowing of numerals for 7–9 in the Bay and Delta region (see ¶4.14.5) indicated that a *senary* system, in which the basic set of

numerals stopped at six, had earlier been used in this area, by both Miwok and Costanoan speakers, and perhaps by others. Callaghan's reconstruction of *šakken* 'six' as the highest numeral in Proto-Costanoan appears to fit this pattern (Callaghan 1990). Blevins (2005a), revisiting this question, believes the evidence for Proto-Costanoan *šakken* 'six' is weak, and that the occurring forms in Costanoan are better explained as the borrowing of a form *ṣakken that can quite plausibly be reconstructed with the same meaning in Proto–Eastern Miwok.[19] Thus, if she is correct, only the numerals for 1–3 can be reconstructed in Proto-Costanoan, and only Eastern Miwok shows traces of senary counting.

In laying out his case for senary counting in the Delta region, Beeler pointed out that the decimal system of at least one of the Yokuts dialects spoken in this area (Tamukamne, as recorded by Jeremiah Curtin) lacked the usual Yokuts cognates for numerals beyond 1–3, replacing 4–6 with borrowings from Costanoan and 7–10 with borrowings from Plains Miwok (Appendix D: 4.6 to 4.9). Although this could be seen as little more than a late borrowing, the possibility that senary counting was more generally practiced in earlier Yokuts was greatly bolstered by Gamble (1980), who convincingly showed that the "old time" count that was remembered by Harrington's Chunut (Southern Valley Yokuts) informant was undoubtedly senary in structure. Interestingly, at least two of the numerals associated with this alternative counting system are attested in the highly aberrant short vocabulary that Kroeber collected in 1906 from a woman who "remembered" it as Toltichi, an otherwise unattested Northern Hill dialect (see ¶3.26.6). As a count, however, the sequence of "Toltichi" numerals, at least as it is represented in its one dubious attestation, cannot be analyzed as having a senary basis.[20]

4.11 Names[21]

4.11.1 Toponyms and Ethnonyms

Throughout California, village names were the primary toponyms. This was especially the case with the riverine societies of the northwestern part of the state, where the Hupa, Karuk, and Yurok often named mountains, lakes, and other features of the backcountry after the creeks that flow from them, with a creek in turn being named after the village closest to its mouth (Waterman 1920). Village names sometimes refer to mythical incidents supposed to have taken place there, but more typically are derived from some natural or man-made feature that characterized the site. Sawyer (1978:257) lists among the most common morphemes in Wappo village names: *nóma* 'camp, place'; *nuy'* 'sand'; *lel* 'stone'; *ʔéyču* 'creek'; *méy* 'water'; *meynán* 'spring'; *hóc'a* 'sweathouse, dancehouse'; *t'ul* 'field, valley'; *mót'a* 'mountain'; *hól* 'tree, stick, wood'; *hólma* 'woods'; and *péti* 'barbecue pit'. Village names, like place-names generally, usually take the form of locative phrases. Thus Kashaya Pomo villages bear names like *muča:-wi* 'grain place', súlkʰeya:-wi 'at the condor's nest', and k'olómmal-li 'hollowed out place' (McLendon and Oswalt 1978:279). Similarly, a substantial proportion of the attested village names in Gabrielino territory are formed with the locative enclitic -ŋa, as in kawéʔ-ŋa 'rock place', ʔahwi:-ŋa 'burned brush place' (?), šiva:-ŋa 'flint place' (?), or the Gabrielino originals of Cucamonga and Topanga.

Even where settlements appear to be long established, a very large proportion of California village names are analyzable. The principal villages of Hoopa Valley are probably typical: yehwilin-tiŋ 'where (the river) flows into (the canyon)'; xonsah-tiŋ 'where (the river) is deep'; cʰe:-na:lʔa:-tiŋ 'where the rocks hang down'; k̓inčʷiW-q'it 'on (high ground that resembles) a nose'; mis-q'it 'on the bluff'; tʰaʔk̓'imił-tiŋ 'where they stir acorn mush (in cooking)'; cʰe:wina:l-tiŋ, not fully analyzable but apparently containing cʰe: 'rocks' and referring to them being turned over; tʰołc'aʔc'-tiŋ, not fully analyzable but apparently referring to the seepage of water; meʔtil-tiŋ 'where there are canoes'; xowaŋ-q'it 'on (what resembles) her vulva'; and tiš-tʰa:ŋʔa:-tiŋ 'where tiš extends out into (the river)'. The only element in any of these names that is not fully meaningful or whose original meaning cannot at least be guessed at is tiš in the last village name listed. Not only is this syllable not a Hupa morpheme, but it also contains the marginal phoneme š, which otherwise is found only in a few exclamations (e.g., ša:n!, said at the end of a story) or when imitating the blubber-lipped speech of mythical Frog (see ¶4.12.3). But even this mysterious form ultimately yields to philological investigation. Like ša:n, which is evidently an archaic variant of modern Hupa Wa:n(e:) 'only, just (so)' (Hupa-Chilula underwent a sound shift a few hundred years ago in which the palatal fricative š became a voiceless w), tiš can be explained as a fossilized form of the California Athabaskan word for 'quail', represented in modern Hupa by tiW- in tiW-k̓ʰoh 'grouse', originally 'big quail'. In short, tiš-tʰa:ŋʔa:-tiŋ is 'Quail Point'.

Although in many areas tribelets are known simply by the name of their central village, a number of California languages have developed distinctive forms for tribelet names. In Hill Patwin, most tribelet names are formed with -sel 'people', frequently—but not always—suffixed to the name of the principal village of the group. Thus the Tebti-sel ('Tebti people') tribelet of Long Valley Creek was centered on the village of Tebti at the mouth of Bartlett Creek; the adjoining tribelet on Long Valley Creek was Lol-sel ('tobacco people') (Kroeber 1932:262–263). Yuki -no'm and Plains Miwok -amne have basically the same function. The Pomo languages distinguish tribelet names less overtly, although Northern Pomo -pʰóʔmaʔ 'people of . . .' and Southeastern Pomo -mfo appear to have been taking on that role.[22]

Among the Yokuts and Western Mono, whose sociopolitical organization is more "tribal" than that of most adjoining groups (see ¶1.2), names for "dialect-tribes" are usually sui generis, unconnected to the name of the principal village. Many of these are formed with a suffix -amni, plural -ma:ni

(e.g., Yawlamni, Yawelmani) that is clearly connected historically to the Plains Miwok tribelet-name formant, -amne (e.g., Tuolumne), most likely borrowed by the Plains Miwok from the Delta Yokuts. Another common Yokuts tribal-name formant is -či (e.g., Tachi, Yawdanchi).

Good ethnogeographic studies exist for the Yurok (Waterman 1920), the Achomawi (Kniffen 1928), and several Pomo groups (Kniffen 1939; O. Stewart 1943). Of these, Waterman's Yurok Geography (1920) stands out for its thoroughness and ethnographic contextualization, although the linguistic transcriptions are sometimes inaccurate, and it is best used in conjunction with Garrett, Blevins, and Conathan (2005). In addition, extensive lists of place-names have been published for a number of northern and central California groups. These include Tolowa and Tututni (Waterman 1925); California Athabaskan in general (Baumhoff 1958); Hupa (Sapir and Golla 2001:1002–1011); Karuk (Bright 1957, 1958; Kroeber 1936); Shasta (Heizer and Hester 1970); Wiyot (Loud 1918; Nomland and Kroeber 1936); Wintu (Du Bois 1935); Palaihnihan (Merriam 1926a); Pomo (Barrett 1908a); Wappo (Driver 1936); Nisenan (Kroeber 1929); Patwin (Kroeber 1932); and Chumash (Heizer 1975a). Barrett's Pomo compilation (1908a) also includes Wappo and Western Miwok place-names, and Kroeber's notes on Patwin geography (1932) extend to cover the Southeastern and Northeastern Pomo, the Nomlaki, and the Chico and Konkow Maidu. Numic, Takic, and Yuman groups are less well represented in the ethnogeographic literature, although Steward (1933) has data on Owens Valley Paiute (Mono) names, Couro and Hutcheson's Ipai Diegueño dictionary (1973) includes extensive information on place-names, and there is some documentation of Cocopa place-names in Gifford (1933).

Merriam was fascinated by place-names, as was Harrington, and both researchers collected them extensively throughout their California work. Merriam published some of his Miwok and Palaihnihan place-name data (1907, 1926a), and more has appeared posthumously (inter alia in Merriam 1966, 1967a, 1967b; Merriam and Talbot 1974; Heizer 1975a; Baumhoff 1958). Harrington's place-name data were almost entirely unpublished at the time of his death in 1961. Since then, Applegate (1974, 1975) and Hudson (1977) have compiled and published his Chumash data, Gibson (1985) and Rivers and Jones (1993) his Salinan, and Bauman (1980a) his Chimariko.

A considerable amount of information on the precontact ethnogeography of the missionized groups of central and southern California has been recovered from ethnohistorical documents. Close study of the mission registers of baptisms and marriages has enabled Milliken to recover tribelet, village, and personal names—and infer patterns of trade and intermarriage—for much of the area in which Costanoan, Northern Valley and Delta Yokuts, Bay Miwok, Esselen, and Salinan were spoken (Milliken 1987, 1990, 1994, 1995, 2002, 2008; Milliken and Johnson 2003). John Johnson has recovered similar data from Southern California mission records for the Chumash, Southern Valley Yokuts, and Takic area (Johnson 1978; Johnson and Crawford 1999; Johnson and Earle 1990). Bennyhoff, using a wide range of historical sources, was able to reconstruct a detailed picture of the aboriginal geography of the Plains Miwok and Delta Yokuts area (Bennyhoff 1977).

4.11.2 Personal Names

Personal naming practices differed considerably across the California region. The only universal feature was an avoidance of speaking the name of a recently deceased individual, although in many groups the name could be formally reassigned to a child and the taboo lifted.[23]

In the northern half of California, personal names were considered private attributes, and their use was circumscribed. The etiquette followed by the Achumawi was typical:

> Achumawi personal names, while not secret or sacred in any respect, were not ordinarily terms of address. Rather they were used for reference when not in the presence of the person named. Terms of address were kin terms like aunt or brother for the appropriate relatives and nicknames for covillagers not nameable by kin terms; strangers were addressed by the names of their tribelets or villages. Calling a man by his personal name was . . . considered rude, insolent and provocative.[24] (Olmsted and Stewart 1978:231)

In northwestern California, a personal name was often treated as an item of property that could be inherited, donated, or sold. It was normal for a child to go without a name—to be referred to as "baby" or "child"—for months, sometimes years, until an appropriate name was negotiated. A Hupa family would sometimes delay the conferral of a personal name for up to five years (Wallace 1978:172), and among the Tolowa it was expected that the naming ritual for the child of an upper-class man would be performed in public and accompanied by a potlatch-style feast (R. Gould 1978:133–134).

Hupa names may be taken as typical of this region.[25] Nearly all are structurally unusual, many being marked as "diminutive" by symbolic consonant shifts (¶4.12.1). Some have an enclitic -(i)ŋ which occurs only in personal names and in a few archaic terms referring to people, and some women's names have an enclitic -č'eʔ. Probably the largest set are descriptive phrases of obscure metaphorical reference: misče:-nint'ik' 'fog extends in a string (dim.)'; tʰo:-me:we:-c 'under the water (dim.)'; yehna:tyo:s-iŋ 'it pulls back inside-person'; ʔa:ta:ne:sił 'it hides itself'; me:wi-č'eʔna:W 'he comes out from underneath it'; yehna:xine:W-iŋ 'into the house it talks–person'. Others refer to personal attributes or habits (although not necessarily that of the current bearer): kʰile:xič-ne:s 'boy (dim.)-tall', i.e., "Tall Boy"; k'itaʔ-łiq'eʔ 'lips-doughlike', i.e., "Flabby Mouth"; kʰan-se:l 'belly (dim.)–

warm'. In a few cases, wealthy men were referred to by the name of their house, as with tʰo:-xote:l-tiŋ 'water–flows close to him–place', or "Captain John" of Matilton. Some names show the characteristic signs of antiquity in their aberrant phonetics and morphological obscurity: ʔayheʔ (unanalyzable, and with an infrequently occurring medial -h-); xoʔtekeʔ (unanalyzable); tʰah-se:n-č'eʔ 'into the water–?–woman'. It is probably no accident that this last set of names belonged to a family of considerable prestige that included a ceremonial dance leader and a prominent doctor. Of particular interest is kʰö:peh, the name of a very traditional old man, nearly every segment of which is phonetically atypical.[26]

Among the Patwin and adjacent groups in the Sacramento Valley, the name a person bore was linked to his or her stage of life, and it was normal to be called by several names during one's lifetime. The naming patterns of the Konkow Maidu were probably typical of the area. Children went without distinctive names—being called simply "boy," "girl," or "baby"—until they were about one or two years old, at which time their parents or relatives gave them descriptive names like "snoring bird" or "running girl" that reflected some personal characteristic or habit. A boy continued all his life to be addressed this way by his parents, but in adolescence, on being initiated into the Kuksu religion, he would receive a more formal name. These names were passed down through families and were bestowed by his initiated older kinsmen (Kroeber 1932:376). Examples are "Vomiting Basket," "Wing Tied Up," "Licking Deer," "Pinenut Eater," and "Licking Head." In the case of a girl, the family term changed as she grew older, a new name being given her at puberty, then at childbirth, and again in old age (Dixon 1905a:230–231).[27]

In the Pomo and Yuki area, children were given a permanent name very early in life, usually the name of a deceased kinsman, with the hope that the child would become like the person whose name was taken. The name of a grandparent who had lived to an advanced age was especially favored.[28] In some cases a living person would give his or her name to the child and cease to use that name (Loeb 1926:259–261; Foster 1944:250).[29]

The Eastern Miwoks (and probably also the Western Miwoks, Costanoans, and Yokuts) had a moiety organization, with each lineage belonging either to the "land side" or to the "water side." The moieties were associated with certain animals, and one's personal name always contained an implied reference to an animal or object appropriate to one's moiety. Personal names of people in the water moiety frequently referred to deer, salmon, and valley quail, while people in the land moiety had names referring to bear and chicken hawk (Levy 1978a:411). Although the Miwoks did not participate in the Kuksu religion, each group did have complex initiation rituals, particularly for young men, and apparently moiety-identifying names (the Coast Miwoks called them yali 'real') were acquired in early adulthood (Kelly 1978:419).

Among the Takic- and Chumash-speaking groups of Southern California, personal names were similarly associated with lineages and were bestowed in public ceremonies within a year of birth. Among the Gabrielino, patrilineal names were formally bestowed during the annual mourning ceremony on all the children born during the previous year (Bean and Smith 1978:546). Among the Chumash, an astrologer-like official named newborn children at a ceremony conducted under the auspices of the ʔantap secret society (Blackburn 1974:100).

Throughout the California region, nicknames were very frequently employed between nonrelatives in place of personal names. Among the Yuki, who were probably typical in this respect, nicknames were given informally, but once accepted they were rarely changed. Although many of the nicknames were humorously obscene, they "were used by both sexes without any feeling of indecency" (Foster 1944:182). Examples of Yuki male nicknames are šunósomi 'wrinkled skin' (referring to genitalia); pilwási 'standing in the snow'; tátkoy 'that's good!' (applied because the expression was constantly used by the namee); šampalhólsi 'wags his ears'; mipan-wilak 'toes together' (referring to webbed toes); sišúhi 'sitting on his buttocks'; malwósak 'penis bent over'; k'ask'ənsi 'buttocks chafing'; minsilkaówak 'big liar'; malhot 'big penis'; həčtántstil 'shakes his forehead'; and ʔust'ót 'low pressure urine'. Some female nicknames are silpitnaóhil 'looks at genitalia'; sitinlíli 'quivering buttocks'; šiltašómi 'crackling vagina'; čílak 'legs spread out'; hatámi 'small vagina'; and həwolp'ú 'wringing deer snare net' (Foster 1944:182; transcriptions and translations are his). There is a similar collection of Klamath nicknames in Gatschet (1890, Part 1:xxxviii), who comments that "these sketch the Indian in a striking and often an unenviable light, because they generally depict the extremes observed on certain individuals."

4.12 Diminutive and Other Expressive Symbolism

4.12.1 Diminutives

Marking utterances to symbolize their use in special expressive functions is a characteristic feature of North American languages. It is particularly common to mark *diminutive* affect—that is, the speaker's perception of the smallness (and consequent need for protection and nurturing) of children, small animals, or, by extension, any small object. In the languages of the California region, words and phrases are typically marked as diminutive by a combination of affixal morphology and regular patterns of alternation in phonetic shape, primarily shifts in consonant articulation.

Diminutive affixes in California languages often have an undoubtedly sound-symbolic palatal or apical consonant (e.g., Hupa -č, Karuk -ič and -iš, Sierra Miwok -kči, -tti). In some languages the representation is more arbitrary (e.g., Shasta -xí:yáx). Sometimes more than one diminutive-like

category is symbolized. In Takelma, the prefixes s- and ł-, which Sapir had described as being used in stories to mark the speech of Coyote and Bear, respectively (1922a:8, n. 2), are probably more accurately analyzed as expressions of two distinct varieties of the diminutive attitude, the s- prefix marking the sympathy and affection that Coyote often shows, the ł- prefix marking Grizzly Bear's characteristic "disdain for coarseness and stupidity" (Hymes 1979). Reichard describes a complex interplay of diminutive processes in Wiyot that affect both nominal and verbal forms, and that "as a literary device, give delicacy and variety to the language" (1925:29–35).

Closely linked to the diminutive, in many California languages, are two semantically distinct categories, ***pitifulness,*** encompassing such ideas as weakness, impoverishment, and the feebleness of age, and ***cessation,*** referring to the termination brought about by the death of an individual, the rupture of a social bond, or the destruction or loss of an artifact or tool. In Sierra Miwok both these categories are marked morphologically by a single affix -šší- 'past' that resembles the diminutive in shape and function and that occurs productively in such words as čukú-ššu:-t 'my former dog, the dog I used to have' and ʔamáčči-šší 'our poor old grandmother' (Freeland 1951:161–162). The Shasta suffix -əpsi 'pitiful' also appears to mark both categories in such forms as súk'k'axapsi 'a pitiful boy, a bachelor' and yappúk'upsi 'a bucket belonging to someone who is dead' (Silver 1966:192–193). In Karuk, in at least a few lexicalized forms, the same semantic conflation is directly marked by a diminutive affix, for example, kê:mačko (or ko:hímačko) 'poor, pitiable; deceased father', derived from the adjective stem kê:m 'bad, homely' by the widely occurring diminutive suffix -(a)č, and kê:miša 'something supernaturally dangerous; a deceased person', derived from the same stem by a second diminutive suffix -iš (Bright 1957).[30] In several languages only the cessation category (but not pitifulness) is overtly marked, as in Wikchamni Yokuts by -mam 'decedent', in nipač'mam 'deceased older brother' and ʔaŋaťʰmam 'deceased doctor' (Gamble 1978:96). In Hupa, the past tense verbal enclitic -neʔin has this function in such nominal phrases as Witʰaʔ-neʔin 'my late father', Waʔat-neʔin 'my ex-wife', hay ḵʰiŋʔa:ḵa:n-neʔin 'her pipe (that she had lost)' (Sapir and Golla 2001:858).

A few California languages also mark the category of ***augmentative,*** which in addition to sheer size often implies power, particularly supernatural power. Thus Northern Sierra Miwok -ṭṭi- (often reduplicated) functions as an augmentative marker in such formations as ʔóssaṭṭiṭṭiʔ 'a great big woman' (from ʔóssaʔ 'woman', cf. ʔóssaṭṭiʔ 'girl', diminutive) and tínniṭṭiʔ 'a monster or supernatural being' (literally 'a great something, a great unknown' from tínniʔ, indefinite pronoun, 'something') (Freeland 1951: 160–161). Wiyot has been described by one investigator as having an augmentative affix (Teeter 1964:21–22), but its existence is explicitly denied by another (Reichard 1925:29).

BOX 12. DIMINUTIVE PHONETIC SHIFTS IN CALIFORNIA LANGUAGES

1. Algic Languages

Yurok (Robins 1958:14, 189): Shift of *t* to *č*, and *l* to *r*, with no diminutive affix but in a few cases accompanied by a shift of vowel to *ṛ*: For example, *pontet* 'ashes' *>pṛnčṛč* 'dust'; *-'lep* 'hair' *>-'rep* 'eyebrows'.

Wiyot (Teeter 1959:41–42): Shift of *t, tʰ* to diminutive *c, cʰ* and augmentative (?) *č, čʰ*; *s* to diminutive (or augmentative) *š; l* to diminutive (or augmentative) *r*. Sometimes with diminutive suffixes *-ic, -oc, -oč* or augmentative suffix *-ačk*. (For examples, see ¶3.2.3.)*

2. Athabaskan Languages

Hupa (Sapir and Golla 2001:869–870): Shift of *č, čʷ, č'* to *c, cʰ, c'*; *W* to *s; k̲, k̲ʰ, k̲'* to *k, kʰ, k*. For example, *čime:l* 'lizard' *>cime:l* '(cute) little lizard'; *Wičʷo:* 'my maternal grandmother' *>ʔiscʰo:* 'grandma!' (in address); *Wik̲ʰa:y* 'my (woman's) daughter's child' *>ʔiskʰa:y* 'darling grandchild!' (in address).

3. Hokan Languages

Karuk (Bright 1957:76–79): Shift of *θ* to *č*, *r* to *n*, and, very rarely, *v* to *m*; usually with suffixes *-ič, -ač, -iš*. For example, *iθari:p* 'fir tree' *>ičani:pič* 'small fir'.

---

*Reichard, unlike Teeter, did not ascribe an augmentative function to Wiyot sound symbolic consonant shifts and affixation. She found the shift to *č* to signal "diminutive in the sense of 'young'" whereas the shift to *c* "has the idea of 'small, tiny'" (Reichard 1925:30).

Yana (Sapir and Swadesh 1960:8): Shift of *l* to *n*, with diminutive suffixes *-p'a*, singular, and *-c'e:ki ~ -c'ki*, plural. For example, *lal-* 'foot' *>nanp'a* 'little foot'.

Ipay Diegueño (Langdon 1971): Shift of *ɬ, ɬʸ* to *l, lʸ; r̥* (voiceless trill) to *r* (rhotic apico-postdental fricative). For example, *cəkuɬk* 'hole through something' *>cəkulk* 'small hole through something'; *ʔəsaɬʸ* 'my hand, arm' *>ʔəsalʸ* 'my little hand, arm'; *yar̥əyar̥* 'to be circular' *>yarəyar* 'to be small and circular'.

Cocopa (Crawford 1966:114, 135): Shift of *č* to *t* in roots taking the diminutive verbal prefix *n, nʸ-*. For example, *ɬʸčaš* 'be small' *>ɬʸnʸtuš ~ ɬʸnʸtaš ~ ɬʸnʸtiš* 'be very little'.

4. Penutian Languages

Konkow (R. Ultan 1973): Shift of *a, o* to *i, c*, with *ə* sometimes representing a middle term. For example, *law* 'lift a large object' *>lew* 'lift a small object'; *c'á:ʔat'in* 'creak' (low pitch) *>c'ə:ʔat'in* 'creak' (mid pitch), *c'í:ʔit'in* 'squeak'; *wótc'ot'in* 'chop a notch with, e.g., an axe' *>wetc'et'in* 'crack open a small object'; *hódo* 'there, later' *>hćde* 'here, now'.

5. Uto-Aztecan Languages

Luiseño (Kroeber and Grace 1960:23–25): Shift of *ṣ* to *s*, sometimes also *r* to *ð*, in nouns taking the diminutive suffix *-mal*. For example, *maṣla* '(large) brake fern' *>masmal* 'small fern'; *ŋaruŋruš* 'pot with medium-sized mouth' *>ŋaðuŋðumal ~ ŋaruŋrumal* 'pot with small mouth'.

In addition to affixal morphology, many California languages symbolize diminutive and related meanings with distinctive, regular phonetic shifts. Although they often co-occur with a diminutive affix, such phonetic shifts not infrequently suffice to convey diminutive meaning by themselves. California languages for which diminutive phonetic shifts have been described are listed in Box 12. Most of these utilize shifts in consonant articulation, as is also generally the case in the Northwest.[31] The use of vowel ablaut to mark diminutive or other expressive features is relatively infrequent throughout western North America, and it may not be accidental that the one case that has been described at any length (Konkow Maiduan) is a Penutian language.

4.12.2 Baby Talk

Diminutive forms are used in a variety of situations, basically wherever the speaker wishes to signal an emotional closeness with the person addressed or the object named. In some groups, the derivational morphology and phonetic modifications used to form diminutive variants are generalized to mark a style of speaking used by adults in talking or referring to small children. The best described "baby talk" register of this nature in the California region is that used by speakers of Cocopa (J. M. Crawford 1970, 1978). To transform normal Cocopa adult speech to baby talk, several phonological rules are systematically applied (Silver and Miller 1997:159–164). Most importantly, the nonlaryngeal-stop contrasts are reduced from eight (*p, t, ṭ, c, k, kʷ, q, qʷ*) to three (*p, t, k*); the fricative contrasts are reduced from seven (*s, ṣ, š, x, xʷ, ɬ, ɬʸ*) to three (*s, x, ɬ*); the nasals are reduced from three (*m, n, nʸ*) to two (*m, n*); and the approximants are reduced from five (*l, lʸ, r, w, y*) to three (*l, w, y*). In addition, the initial consonant of the stressed syllable in a polysyllabic word is replaced by a voiced bilabial fricative (*β*), and an *-n-* is infixed. Optionally, the initial consonant of a prefix—or the entire prefix—is elided. Typical Cocopa baby talk formations are the following:

Adult Speech	Baby Talk	
aṣú: ikm	anβú: ikm	'later'
umic wa:yá:c	unβít anyá:t	'she goes around crying'
kʷanʸuk	kanβúk	'baby'
xasánʸ	βán	'little girl'
nʸi:šá:łʸ	ninβá:ł	'her hand'

4.12.3 The Speech of Mythical Animals and "Animal Talk"

In at least a few California languages, certain mythical animals are represented in stories as speaking in a characteristically distorted fashion, usually taking the form of stereotyped phonetic shifts and interpolations. Thus in Hupa, mythic Frog is personified by a "mushy" way of enunciating words that is represented by shifting *s* to *š*, as for example in *tiwitwa:s ʔo:k̲'iłn* (normal) ~ *tiwitwa:š ʔo:k̲'iłn* (spoken by Frog) 'Watch out! The abalone shells might break!' (Golla 1977:24, n. 59). Coyote is the character that most frequently is made to "speak in a funny voice" (Hinton 1994:45). For example, in Ishi's tellings of Southern Yana stories Coyote not only substitutes shibilant *š* for sibilant *s*, like Frog in Hupa, but replaces both *l* and *r* with *n*, as in *yap'lasa:sitʰi* (normal) ~ *yap'naša:šitʰi* (spoken by Coyote) 'It is well done.' In Takelma narratives, Coyote and Bear are characterized by prefixation of *s-* and *ł-*, respectively, to their reported utterances (Sapir 1922a:8, n. 2, and Hymes 1979; but see also ¶4.12.1).

This pattern of stereotyping of the speech of mythical animals is most prevalent in the northernmost tier of California languages, linking them to an ethnolinguistic area in the Northwest in which phonetic play of this nature was a salient feature of the oral tradition, classically described by Sapir for Nootka (1915f).[32] For most languages of central and southern California, the feature was either absent or not well developed.[33] At the southern end of the area, however, it reappears in relatively well-developed form in the Yuman languages.

In Hualapai, Hinton reports, Coyote's leitmotif is the voiceless interdental fricative (*θ*), which he uses in place of *s* and suffixes to words in which no *s* occurs. In addition, his words "have an extra long *iiiii* sound, said in a high falling voice that sounds like the howl of a coyote," as for example in

miβiyama (normal) ~ *miβiyamiiiiiθ* (spoken by Coyote) 'Run!' (Hinton 1994:45 46).

In Quechan it is the palatal lateral (*lʸ*) that characteristically marks Coyote's speech:

maʔancí:na (normal) ~ *ma:lʸʔancí:na* (spoken by Coyote) 'You, my older brothers' (Halpern 1976:24).

In adjacent Cocopa, *lʸ* is similarly "introduced in every word of the discourse in [Coyote's] style either in replacement of one of the normal consonants or in addition to the normal segments":

xumá:ka, xumá:ka (normal) ~ *xulʸmá:ka, xulʸmá:ka* (spoken by Coyote) 'My son, my son!' (Langdon 1978c:11).

Although the usages are now archaic, older speakers of Cocopa recall that Mountain Lion's "favorite sound" was *r* and that Rabbit's speech was marked by the segment *f* (otherwise not a phoneme in Cocopa).

Interestingly, in modern Cocopa, as described by James Crawford (1966), alongside Coyote's distinctive *lʸ* a distorted version of phonemically contrasting voiceless *ł̓ʸ* (typically spoken out of the side of the mouth) is used in an identical manner to mark what might be called an "animal talk" register—a type of speech that is attributed to animals in ordinary day-to-day affairs, including horses, chickens, and domestic cats, and in turn is used by humans to address them:

makáy mwayá:c myu (normal) ~ *makáłʸ mł̓ʸá:c mł̓ʸu:* (spoken to or by an animal) 'Where have you been?'

ksánʸkic (normal) ~ *kł̓ʸánʸkic* (spoken to or by an animal) 'Get down!'

4.12.4 Song Texts

Throughout the world, song texts are usually characterized by phonetic distortions and grammatical and lexical substitutions that clearly distinguish the language of song from everyday speech. The cumulative effect of these distortions is an increase in "resonance" (Shaul 1989), a process which, when carried to its logical conclusion, results in the complete replacement of the segmental phonological structure of song words by clusters of highly resonant vowels and nasals—"vocables" in ethnomusicological parlance—that no longer have any linguistic function. The ethnographic literature on California Indian song texts in suggests that the complete replacement of song words by vocables is perhaps more frequent here than in other parts of the continent (Hinton 1994:145–151). This characteristic is probably correlated, as Hinton has proposed, with the frequent exchange of songs across tribal and linguistic boundaries (1994:43).

There are indications, however, that linguistically analyzible song texts were a more important part of the precontact linguistic repertoire than more recent documentation would suggest. Gatschet, working in the 1870s and 1880s, collected the texts of nearly two hundred Klamath and Modoc songs, most of them at least partially analyzible (Gatschet 1890, Part I:153–197). However, many of these songs were connected to the shamanistic tradition (see ¶4.13.2), and their texts interlarded with obscure and archaic words known only to initiated Indian doctors.[34]

In the Northwest California "medicine formula" tradition analyzed by Keeling (1992), nonshamanistic cures

were effected by the use of herbal or other curative substances during the recitation of a short verbal narrative
invoking the spirit who originated the cure. These verbal
formulas were usually accompanied by "medicine songs,"
which were

> mimetic and imitated the utterance of the spirit-person
> who originally sung them. Songs of this type were often
> delivered in a form of heightened speech rather than
> employing clearly focused tones as in other types of singing.
> Others seem to re-create the crying of spirit-persons as they
> hoped for things. (Keeling 1992:132)

Ethnographic observations and sound recordings dating to
the early twentieth century appear to indicate that both
"heightened speech" and melodic (often plaintive) songs
with vocables rather than words had a place in the recitation
of medicine formulas. Clearly something more subtle than a
single opposition in genre (song versus ordinary speech) was
involved, with linguistic ramifications that are probably not
fully recoverable.

In the Yuman and Southern Numic tribes along the
Colorado River, and to an extent in the Takic-speaking area,
a strong tradition of song texts with recognizable linguistic
structure has persisted into recent generations. But even
here, the tendency to increase "resonance" by phonetic substitutions is strong. In her study of Havasupai songs, Hinton
(1984) describes the many phonological shifts that
characterize song words: high vowels are lowered, vowels
are inserted, vowels normally deleted in surface phonology
are retained, and stops frequently shift to fricatives. Purely
vocable syllables are also interpolated to fill out the rhythmic
line. For example,

nʸač eβah (normal) ~ βe nʸač o eβah a (sung) 'I will feel it'

kiyu ʔim (normal) ~ keyo ye ʔim e wa (sung) 'That is what
I desire' (Hinton 1994:149)

Since here as elsewhere songs are frequently exchanged
across linguistic boundaries, singers not infrequently sing
words and phrases in languages they do not understand.

4.13 Social and Situational Varieties

4.13.1 "High" Languages

In communities throughout the California region, special
styles or registers are reported to have been employed by
prestigious individuals on certain formal occasions. These
ranged in complexity from a few distinctive words or turns
of phrase that might be employed by a polished storyteller
to elaborate semisecret jargons used by religious initiates.
Although detailed attestations of these usages are relatively
rare, it seems likely that the basic phenomenon was
widespread, if not universal. Examples can be cited from one
end of the region to the other.[35]

Wealthy Yuroks, both men and women, used an oratorical
"high language" in moralistic speeches delivered at World
Renewal dances, in the recitation of medicine formulas, and
in legal and philosphical discussions. It was derived from
ordinary speech by metaphorical lexical substitutions,
descriptive circumlocutions, and semantic shifts (Kroeber
1960a; T. Buckley 1984). Most of the Yurok speakers who
provided data to linguists and anthropologists in the mid to
late twentieth century retained little or no command of this
register, but it is extensively documented in many of the
unpublished texts collected by Kroeber in 1906 and 1907 (T.
Buckley 1984:485, fn. 3).

A very similar tradition is reported from the Takic area.
Boscana wrote of the Juaneño at Mission San Juan
Capistrano that

> all their knowledge is from tradition, which they preserve in
> songs for their dances, and these are introduced by a chief at
> their festivities in a language distinct from that in common
> use. Others unite with them but without understanding the
> meaning of what they do or articulate; perhaps the songs
> thus introduced are in the primitive language. (Boscana
> 1933:17; see also Harrington 1933:107, n. 11)

Regarding the adjacent Gabrielino, Hugo Reid wrote in
1852 that "there is now at San Gabriel an old woman named
Bona, who takes pride in speaking sometimes the 'court
language' to the young ones, to stultify their intelligence"
(1852 [1968]:14). Since it is otherwise known that members
of the Gabrielino elite participated in secret religious
ceremonies not open to commoners (Bean 1974:29), it seems
likely that this was the context in which this "court language"
was learned.

An important component of the ceremonial language of
the Luiseño and Juaneño was the use of "semantic couplets,"
the stylized juxtaposition of two words or phrases of nearly
identical meaning, for example yú:vayniti tó:wayniti 'dark-
ness-dusk' or nó:t sówkišla 'chief–principal chief'. Gods were
often known by "double names" of this type, as for example
Kyuvish Atavish (kíwviš ʔatáxviš 'unoccupied-empty'), the
Luiseño creator, or Whaiahat Piwahat (xʷáykit píwkit 'white–
whitish gray'), another primal divinity (DuBois 1908:129).
This stylistic device bears a remarkable similarity in form
and function to the difrasismo of Classical Nahuatl and
Mayan literary texts (Garibay 1970; Bright 1990b).[36]

The Yuki had a name, k'oni hót ('talk high'), for a way of
speaking that was, according to the ethnographer George
Foster,

> a refined speech, spoken by the well-educated—those who
> had gone to the Taikomol-woknam [training for ceremonial
> initiates]. It was not a secret language, since some of both
> sexes knew it thoroughly, and those of lower class were
> acquainted with some of the expressions. The distinction
> is similar to that in our own society between a college
> graduate and one whose schooling has ended at the fifth
> grade. (Foster 1944:161)

Callaghan identifies a very similar "high narrative style" in Lake Miwok, used by skilled storytellers in the recitation of sacred or mythic narratives (2004:226–230). It was marked by a rhythmic, declamatory style, a "high" vocabulary, and the use of distinctive sentential particles and adverbs. Jane Hill also reports that a "chiefly" style was formerly used by Cupeño ceremonial leaders, primarily characterized by the extensive use of complex sentences and especially of relative clauses (2005:416).

4.13.2 Shamanistic Jargon

A closely connected, if not identical, "high" register is reported to have been used by shamans in several northern California groups. The most detailed account is given in a Wintu text on shamanism collected by Dorothy Demetracopoulou Lee, analyzed by Schlichter [Shepherd] (1981a) and Hinton and Shepherd (1998). According to Schlichter, the register employed by shamans during doctoring differed from the speech used in everyday conversation not only in increased formality—special idioms and metaphors, more "polite" words for concepts considered taboo, understatement, archaisms, repetition, and longer sentences with more syntactic subordination—but also in phonological features reminiscent of glossolalia, including the favoring of words with lower vowels (*e* and *o* rather than *i* and *u*) and voiced high-frequency consonants. Alliteration and assonance were also employed.

Powers was probably alluding to the same kind of register among Shasta shamans when he wrote that "there is a class of priests or rain-makers, who have an occult language not understood by the common Indians" (1877:249).

4.13.3 Men's and Women's Speech

There are fewer reports of clear differences in speech patterns related to gender. The patterned differences between men's and women's speech that Sapir noted among the Yana (1929a) possibly had their equivalents elsewhere in California, but if so they were almost entirely overlooked by anthropologists and linguists. The difference was not dialectal but stylistic. Yana men were expected to speak to other men in more formally complete words than they used when speaking to women or than woman used when speaking among themselves. In particular, "men's language" employed the full form of the definite article, which in Yana is an enclitic (-*na:* in the Northern and Central dialects), while women used an abbreviated form (*h*).

4.14 Precontact Lexical Borrowing

Lexical borrowing was relatively rare in the California region during precontact times, even in areas where encounters between speakers of different languages were frequent and multilingualism common. In Lake Miwok, a language that came under especially heavy influence from neighboring Patwin, Pomo, and Wappo, fewer than a hundred probable loanwords can be identified (Callaghan and Gamble 1996:115). Although in the Lake Miwok case, a few terms for body parts and some verbs of operation such as 'split', 'peel', and 'knock on' were borrowed, here as elsewhere in California lexical exchange was largely confined to a few semantic domains directly relating to trade, bartering, or gambling. These included numerals and other terms of valuation; names of birds, particularly those whose feathers were prized for decoration or whose cry was very distinctive; words for certain frequently traded items, such as baskets, bows and arrows, and salt; and some of the terminology associated with shamanism and the Kuksu and Toloache ceremonial religions.

Precontact lexical borrowing has not been widely studied. The following sets of examples are intended only to illustrate the potential for future investigation.

4.14.1 'Dog' Terms

The dog was the only mammal for which a term was widely borrowed in the California region in precontact times. Six basic forms (three of them forming a subset with a likely common origin) account for the majority of the 'dog' terms that are attested between the Southern California coast and Oregon:

1. <č'iši>: Takelma *c'îxi* (from earlier *c'ìši), Karuk *čiši:h*, Yurok *č'iš*, Yokuts (non-Valley dialects) *č'e:šaš*. Chimariko *sič'ella* may belong here as well.

2a. <čučo> Plains Miwok *čú:ču?*, San Francisco Bay Costanoan *čuču~ čučo*, Esselen *šo:šo*.[37]

2b. <suku> ~ <čuku> ~ <čuču>: Wintu *suku-h*, Patwin *suku-t*, Washo *súku?*, Sierra Miwok *čuku*, San Francisco Bay Costanoan *čuku*.[38]

2c. <su>: Maidu *sï* (from earlier *su), Yana *su:su*. (?) Shasta *?á:psu*.[39]

3. <hayu>: Pomo (all languages) *hayu ~ hayyu*, Wappo *háyyu*, Lake Miwok *háyu*, Marin Miwok *hayusa*.

4. <xuč> ~ <wuč>: Mutsun and Soledad Costanoan *xučeknis̟*, Esselen *huč(u)mas*, Salinan *xuč*, Ineseño and Purisimeño Chumash *hučru*, Island Chumash *(k)wočo*, Gabrielino *woši?*, Serrano *kuči*, Kitanemuk *kuci*.

Except for Gabrielino, Serrano, and Kitanemuk, the California Uto-Aztecan languages are outside this diffusion area, using for 'dog' either an inherited term that is cognate with Hopi *puhku* (e.g., Western Mono *puhku*, Northern Paiute *pukku*, Kawaiisu *pukuc*, Tubatulabal *puŋgu-l*), or an innovation (Luiseño *?awá:-l*).[40] So too are the Yuman languages, all of which use a form reflecting Proto-Yuman *əxat. At the northern edge of the area, the Athabaskan languages, the Palaihnihan languages, and Klamath-Modoc follow the Plateau pattern of lexicalizing 'dog' with a more inclusive term for 'pet', later extended to the horse.[41]

4.14.2 Other Animal (Bird) Names

The names of game animals were rarely if ever borrowed in precontact California. The names of animals important in myth, such as the coyote, bear, and eagle, were sometimes borrowed, but primarily in the context of the intergroup ceremonial religions of the late precontact period—the Kuksu religion or "Bighead Dance" that united the groups north and east of San Francisco Bay and the Chinigchinich religion of the Southern California coast. In both cases, however, it was primarily esoteric ceremonial names that were borrowed, not words in common use.[42] Except for terms used interchangeably by bilingual speakers in communities such as the Western Mono villages in the Sierra Nevada foothills, where social and linguistic fusion was well under way, there were few instances of the diffusion across language boundaries of ordinary animal terms. One salient exception is the name of the lynx or wildcat (*Lynx rufus*):

> <tolomə>: Esselen *toloma* 'wildcat'; Chocheño *to:romi* 'wildcat'; Plains Miwok *tollomma* 'bobcat'; Southern Pomo *do:lon* 'wildcat'; Western Mono *tono:wi* 'wildcat'.

This term appears to have spread across a relatively compact area in north-central California independently of the Kuksu religion. It is possible but unlikely that it is historically connected to Proto-Yuman *n^{y}əmi 'wildcat, bobcat'.

Bird names, by contrast, were relatively widely diffused in precontact California. Some of these were the names of birds of economic or religious significance, but the key factor in diffusion seems to have been the practice of naming birds with an onomatopoeic interpretation of their cry. The following are the most common of these "natural" names. The extremely wide distribution of several of them indicates a considerable time depth.

1. <č'ay-ʔ-s> 'California bluejay' (*Aphelocoma* sp.): Takelma *c'àyʔs* 'bluejay'; Wintu *č'ayk, č'ayi:(k)* 'scrub jay'; Yuki *č'ə̀ʔəy* 'jay'; Southern Pomo *s'a:yi* 'scrub jay'; Plains Miwok *saysi* 'bluejay'; Chocheño *saysi* 'jay, sp.'; Salinan *ṭ'ay* 'bluejay'; Yawelmani Yokuts *ṭ'ayṭ'ay*, Wikchamni Yokuts *č'ayis-ṅa* 'bluejay'; Chumash *č'ay̓* 'jay'.

2. <səwal> 'crested jay' (*Cyanocitta* sp.): Southern Pomo *sa:wa:la* 'crested jay'; Yana *c'iwal-la* 'bluejay'.

3. <tə-kakə> ~ <sə-kakə> ~ <kə-kakə> 'valley quail' (*Lophortyx* sp.): Klamath *tika:kaʔ* '(mountain[?]) quail'; Takelma *t^{h}kohóx* 'quail'; Karuk *takâ:ka:* '(valley) quail'; Shasta *t'aka:ka:* '(valley) quail'; Yurok *trkrkuʔ* 'quail'; Wiyot *təko:k^h* 'quail'; Yana *sika:ka* 'quail'; Southern Pomo *šakka:ka*

'(California, valley) quail'; Plains Miwok *takka:ta* 'quail'; Southern Valley Yokuts *sak^{h}a:k^{h}a* ~ *tahak^{h}a* '(valley) quail'; Wikchamni Yokuts *t^{h}ak^{h}ak-ṅa* 'California quail'; Inezeño and Barbareño Chumash *takak* 'quail'; Island (Cruzeño) Chumash *tkaka* 'quail'; Southern Paiute *kahkata* 'quail'; Cocopa *kuká:k* 'Gambel quail'.

4. <xumul> 'mountain quail': Esselen *kumul* 'quail'; Antoniano Salinan *xomlik* 'quail'; Yawelmani Yokuts *humnul* 'quail'; Diegueño *xamamuɬ* '(mountain) quail'.

5. <kərat> ~ <kərak> 'woodpecker': Karuk *kúrat* 'California woodpecker'; Shasta *kure:tat* 'woodpecker' (*Melanerpes* sp.); Yana *c'ara:tu* '(red-headed) woodpecker'; Southern Pomo *k'aṭṭak'* 'woodpecker'.

6. <pəlatat> ~ <pəlakak> 'woodpecker': Plains Miwok *palattata* 'yellowhammer'; Chocheño *para:tat* 'woodpecker sp.'; Western Mono *pahna:htataʔ* 'California woodpecker'; General Yokuts *pala:t'at'* 'woodpecker'; Yawelmani Yokuts *pala:k'ak'* 'woodpecker'; Salinan *pelá:kaʔ* ~ *palá:kak'* 'woodpecker'; Inezeño Chumash *pulak'ak'* 'woodpecker (spp.)'.

4.14.3 Bow and Arrow Terms

There is abundant archaeological evidence to support the hypothesis that knowledge of the bow and arrow diffused into California from the north and east at the beginning of the Late Period, about 1500 BP (Jones and Klar 2007:306). It is not surprising that the terminology associated with this culturally important tool appears to have been widely borrowed across language boundaries that were well established by the time the bow and arrow appeared. At least four sets of borrowed lexemes can be identified. It is perhaps worthy of note that most of the languages involved in these sets are Penutian.[43]

1. <nok'V>: Northeastern Maidu *nok'ó* 'arrow'; Patwin *nok'o* 'arrow(head)'; Wappo *lúk'a* 'bow'; Plains Miwok *tanukka* ~ *tonukka* 'bow, bow and arrow'; San Francisco Bay Costanoan *tanúkam, pa nu ka* 'bow'; Valley Yokuts *nuk'on* 'bow', *ne:k'i-* 'draw a bow'. Possibly also connected are Yurok *nrẃk^{w}rč* 'arrow', Northern Wintuan *no:-* 'arrow' (Wintu *no:t*, Nomlaki *nawt'*), and Patwin *nu(:)n* 'bow, gun'.

2. <kVl>: Takelma *kalʔ* 'bow'; Wintu *k'ulul* 'bow'; Poso Creek (Palewyami) Yokuts *k'elk'el* 'arrow'. Possibly also connected is Patwin *k'áli* 'string, twine" (cf. *nuɬabe k'ali* 'bowstring').

3. <kič>: Plains Miwok, Northern Sierra Miwok *kicca* 'bow'; Central, Southern Sierra Miwok *kiče* 'arrowhead'; Valley Yokuts *k'ac'* 'arrowhead'; Poso Creek (Palewyami) Yokuts *keṭ(i)ŋal* 'bow', Buena Vista Yokuts *kaciŋil* 'bow' (for -ŋal and -ŋil compare

Southern Sierra Miwok *ʔuŋli* 'bow'). Possibly also connected are Lake Miwok *cícca* 'arrowhead' and Alsea *mu:kuc'u* 'bow'.

4. <wasV> ~ <posV>: Klamath *mposaks* 'obsidian'; Northeastern Maidu *bosó* 'arrowhead'; Nisenan *wa:se* 'arrowhead'.[44]

4.14.4 Borrowed Numerals: Finger Counting

The most widely diffused numeral in the California region probably dates back to quite early times and seems to be connected with finger counting by fours. It has the shape <pVk(V)> and is used primarily as the numeral for 'one' and as an adverb meaning 'once', 'only', or 'alone'. In some languages it functions as the numeral for 'four' (i.e., one hand, in stick counting) or 'nine' (i.e., the first number of the second octonary count). It is found in these various usages both in Northern Yukian and in most of the Chumash languages, as well as in Yana, Esselen, Mutsun and Rumsen Costanoan, and Gabrielino. The instances of its occurrence are these:

Yuki	*pək* '(person) by himself, alone'
Yana	*-pʰku-* 'each one'
Mutsun Costanoan	*pakki* 'nine'
Rumsen Costanoan	*pak* 'nine'
Esselen	*pek* 'one'
Obispeño Chumash	*paksi* 'four'
Central Chumash	*pak'a(s)* 'one'
Gabrielino	*pukú* 'one'

Related forms in *-w* or *-y* occur in Yukian and Yana:

Yuki	*powi ~ pəwi* 'one' (in counting)
Wappo	*páwi ~ pay ~ pa-* 'one'
Yana	*pay-* 'one'

It is worthy of note that Obispeño Chumash *paksi*, the cognate of Central Chumash *pak'a(s)* 'one', has the meaning 'four', while 'one' is *sumo*, apparently a borrowing from Numic (compare Panamint *sïmï* 'one', *sï:mo:* 'ten'). Obispeño has several other words likely to be of Numic origin (Klar 1980).

The numerals above 'five' were particularly susceptible to borrowing when decimal or octonary systems were being restructured out of earlier one-hand counts (see ¶4.10). The Chumash languages, in creating numeral systems based on an original 1–4 count, appear to have borrowed at least two terms for higher numbers from neighboring Yokuts (see Appendix D: 4.7 and 7):

Central Chumash *yiti-*, Island Chumash *(na)s-yet'-* in 5–7 < Yokuts *yet'* 1

Obispeño *tiyeni* 5 (?), Central Chumash *č'iya(w)* 10 < Yokuts *ṭ'iyew* 10

4.14.5 Borrowed Numerals: The Bay and Delta Region

The languages spoken around San Francisco Bay and in the Sacramento–San Joaquin Delta, one of the most active trading corridors in California, show several instances of the borrowing of numerals (see Appendix D: 4.6 to 4.9).

1. The numerals 7–9 in the Costanoan languages of the Bay Area (e.g., Chocheño *kene:tiš* 7, *ʔoša:tiš* 8, *tellektiš* 9) originated in the Western Miwok hand-count numerals 1, 2, and 3, respectively (e.g., Bodega Miwok *kénne* 1, *ʔóṣṣa* 2, *telé:ka* 3), while 7–9 in the northwestern dialect of Delta Yokuts (*kine ~ kiⁿde* 7, *kawinta* 8, *woʔe* 9) were borrowed from their Plains or Sierra Miwok equivalents (e.g., Plains Miwok *kenekkak* 7 'one again', *kawwinta* 8 'in the middle', *woʔe* 9).

2. In Saclan (the only attested variety of Bay Miwok) the numerals 7–9 (*keneʔke* 7, *ʔosokasi* 8, *telekaki* 9), like the equivalent numerals in adjacent San Francisco Bay Costanoan (e.g., Chocheño *kene:tiš* 7, *ʔoša:tiš* 8, *tellektiš* 9), as already noted, are derived from the hand-count numerals 1–3 in Western Miwok, not the hand-count numerals in Saclan itself (*luṭi* 1, *ʔowoṭo* 2, *tolokoṭo* 3). Thus Bay Miwok 7–9, although ultimately originating in Miwok, seem to have been proximately borrowed from Costanoan (Beeler 1961a:4; Callaghan 1994:169).

3. Blevins (2005a) has proposed that San Francisco Bay Costanoan *šakken* 6 and Northern Delta Yokuts *šaken* 6 are both borrowings of the unattested reflex of Proto-Eastern Miwok **ṣa:ken* 'six, all (of the count)', which can be reconstructed on the basis of Sierra Miwok words for 'twelve' and 'eighteen' (see ¶4.10.4).

4. All attested varieties of Western Miwok have an unanalyzable numeral 7 (e.g., Bodega Miwok *se:lówih*, Lake Miwok *ṣemlá:wi*) that closely resembles the analyzable numeral 8 in geographically distant Northern Wintuan (e.g., Wintu *se-ƛ'awi-t* 'double four') but has no resemblance to 7, 8, or any other numeral in adjacent Southern Wintuan (Patwin and Southern Patwin; see Appendix D: 4.4 and 4.5).[45] At least two explanations seem plausible. One is that in earlier times Western Miwok speakers and Northern Wintuan speakers were in more frequent contact, perhaps around the salt deposits in the foothills to the northeast of Clear Lake. The other is that the numeral 7 was borrowed into Western Miwok from an extinct variety of Patwin that preserved an older form of the numeral 8 that has been replaced in all attested forms of Patwin by an innovated form.

4.15 Postcontact Lexical Borrowing

4.15.1 Borrowing from Spanish

All the languages of the California region as far north as Yuki, Nomlaki, and Maidu and as far east as Numic absorbed some loanwords from Spanish during the mission period. The number of borrowed words varied with the distance from the primary area of missionization along the south and central coast, but the semantic areas affected were generally the same for each language: the domestic animals and crops brought in by the Spanish, European tools and clothing, quantitative concepts (sometimes the numerals themselves) having to do with counting time and money, and general categories of ethnic identity such as "white" and "Indian." Surprisingly few terms directly associated with religious belief and practice were borrowed from Spanish, and no terms for firearms. The bulk of the borrowed vocabulary reflects the social status of nearly all Indians in central and southern California during the Spanish-Mexican period: a ready source of unskilled labor for an agrarian economy based on vast ranchos. The Spanish loanwords reported for Patwin by William and Elizabeth Bright (Table 62) can be taken as representative.[46]

During the Spanish-Mexican period the majority of Indians who lived as converts in the missions or as field laborers on the ranchos appear to have communicated with their Spanish-speaking masters in semipidginized varieties of Spanish (see ¶2.3.2). While no direct attestation of this practice survives, traces of it can be seen in J. P. Harrington's transcriptions of the Californio Spanish spoken by such informants as Ascención Solórsano de Cervantes and Fernando Librado, who had either lived in the missions or been raised by parents who had (Hinkson 1980).

It is probable that elements of this or a similar pidgin were used as a contact and trade jargon in the regions beyond direct mission control. It was certainly the case that knowledge of a few words of Spanish derivation extended deep into the interior of California. Among the most widespread of these were *mahel* or *mahela* 'Indian woman, squaw' and *hindil* 'Indian man, person', ultimately from *mujer* and *gentil* (the term used in the missions for a non-Christian Indian).[47] The terms for 'dog' belonging to the <suku> set (2b), found throughout the Sacramento Valley and adjacent Sierra Nevada, may have a similar history (see ¶4.14.1), as may also some of the "alternative" numerals (*nas* 'one', *bis* 'two') attested in Chunut Yokuts (Gamble 1980:51–55), Toltichi Yokuts (see ¶3.26.6), and possibly also in Klamath *Nas* 'one'.[48]

Documentation of this jargon, given the circumstances of its use and spread, is understandably all but nonexistent. One of the few glimpses we catch of it is in the speech of Ishi, who was otherwise apparently a monolingual speaker of Southern Yana. During the years he lived at the Museum of Anthropology in San Francisco he preferred to speak his own language to the uncomprehending anthropologists, making no attempt to acquire any fluency in English. Only when absolutely necessary did he resort to an ad hoc pidgin that consisted of a few dozen English nouns, verbs, and phrases, liberally garnished with the Yana quotative enclitic (e.g., *candy-tee* 'what-you-call "candy"').[49] In the list of these fragments that was compiled by Saxton Pope (1920: 188–189), four words of Spanish origin stand out: *camisa* (shirt), *paka* (cow), *papello* (paper), and *mahale* (woman), the last presumably being Pope's transcription of Ishi's [məhe:l]. According to Kroeber these (and possibly other) Spanish words were acquired by Ishi "from his own people and considered by him part of his native tongue" (1925:343).[50]

4.15.2 Borrowing from English

Lexical borrowing from English is far less significant in the California region than borrowing from Spanish, and in general it affected only the languages of southern Oregon and California north of Yuki, Nomlaki, and Valley Maidu. The terms borrowed reflect the rapid incorporation of Indians only one or two generations after contact, and still speaking their aboriginal languages, into the agrarian economy of late-nineteenth-century California. The range of this borrowing is illustrated in Box 13 by the Karuk words of English origin in the lexicon of William Bright's *The Karok Language* (1957).

4.15.3 Borrowing from Russian and Alaskan Languages

During the three decades (1812–1841) that the Russian American Company maintained a fur-trading outpost at Fort Ross in Sonoma County, the nearby Kashaya Pomo had extensive interactions with the Russian merchants and the native employees they brought with them from Alaska (Lightfoot 2005). A number of Russian words were borrowed into Kashaya, as well as a few from Alutiiq Eskimo or other Alaskan languages (Oswalt 1958, 1988b). The Kashaya words in Box 14 have been identified as having a Russian or Alaskan origin.

4.15.4 Borrowing from California Indian Languages

Except as place-names, very few words of California Indian origin have been borrowed into Euro-American languages. Two Southern Costanoan (Rumsen or Mutsun) terms were borrowed into California Spanish during the mission period and later made their way into English: Costanoan *ʔawlun* 'Haliotis' into Spanish as *aulón* (English *abalone* is apparently based on the Spanish plural *aulones*); and Costanoan *točon* 'California holly bush, Christmas berry' into Spanish (and English) as *toyon* (Harrington 1944:37). Similarly, Salinan

TABLE 62
Spanish Loanwords in Patwin (Bright and Bright 1959)

	Patwin	Spanish Source
Domestic animals	*čuču* 'dog'	*chucho* 'dog '(dial.)
	ka:tu 'cat'	*gato*
	kawayo 'horse'	*caballo*
	kaye:na 'chicken'	*gallina* 'hen'
	mansu 'tame (animal)'	*manso*
	wore:ka 'lamb'	*borrega*
	wuholo:te 'turkey'	*guajolote*
	ye:wa 'mare'	*yegua*
Foods and crops	*aro:s* 'rice'	*arroz*
	le:čo '(cow's) milk'	*leche*
	nara:ho 'orange'	*naranjo*
	owas 'grapes'	*uvas*
	pa:pa 'potato'	*papa*
	sa:r 'salt'	*sal*
	sepira-man 'onion'	*cebolla*
Tools and clothing	*awha ~ awho* 'needle'	*aguja*
	čiko:te 'rope'	*chicote*
	ha:če 'axe'	*jacha* 'axe, hatchet' (dial.)
	kalaw 'nail'	*clavo*
	kalera 'ladder'	*escalera*
	kanowa 'boat'	*canoa* 'canoe'
	kostal 'sack'	*costal*
	la:ča 'axe'	*el hache*
	lame:sa 'table'	*la mesa*
	lema:te 'oar'	*remo* (?)
	lewi:ta 'blouse'	*levita* 'frock coat'
	pa:ha 'belt'	*faja* 'waistband'
	pila:te 'dish'	*plato*
	sapa:te 'shoe'	*zapato*
	tara:po 'cloth'	*trapo* 'rag'
	ti:nta 'paint'	*tinta* 'ink'
	winta:no 'window'	*ventana*
	wo:te 'boat'	*bote*
	wute:ya 'bottle'	*botella*
Money and counting	*ayno* 'year'	*año*
	dewer 'to owe'	*deber*
	monču ~ monča 'many'	*muncho* 'many' (dial.)
	serial 'ten cents'	*se* 'one' + *real*
	watorel 'fifty cents'	*cuatro reales*
People	*meka:nu* 'white man'	*americano*
	payno:l 'Mexican'	*español*
	sorto 'deaf'	*sordo*
Religion	*saltu* 'spirit'	*santo* (may not be a loanword)
	yawlo 'devil'	*diablo*

BOX 13. ENGLISH LOANWORDS IN KARUK
(BRIGHT 1957)

ʔápus 'apple(s)'

čániman 'Chinese' ("Chinaman")

čî:š 'cheese'

ʔé:kɔ:ns 'acorns' (borrowed to fill the lack of a generic term in Karuk)

fîš 'fish' (used as a generic term)

fúpič 'fifty cents' ("four bits")

háma 'hammer'

káfih 'coffee'

kâ:h 'car'

kê:ks 'cake(s)'

kî:h 'key'

kô:n 'corn'

mákay 'white man' (from Alexander McKay, an early explorer; Bright 1967)

murá:sis 'molasses'

níka 'Negro'

pâ:y 'pie'

píčas 'peach(es)'

pí:n 'pin'

pí:nšura 'bean(s)' (-*ura* is not identifiable; see *vírusura*)

prâms 'plum(s)'

pû:č 'boot(s)'

púsih 'cat' ("pussy")

putíruh 'potato'

sárarih 'Saturday'

síkspič 'seventy-five cents' ("six bits")

sirik- (in compounds) 'silk'

tákta 'doctor, shaman'

tíripu:s 'cat' ("kitty-puss")

tô:nak 'town' (-*ak*, locative)

tumé:tus 'tomato(es)'

túpič 'twenty-five cents' ("two bits")

vánpit 'penny' ("one penny," or perhaps "one bit")

vantára 'dollar' ("one dollar")

vínika 'vinegar'

vírusura 'pear(s)' (-*ura* is not identifiable; see *pí:nšura*)

BOX 14. RUSSIAN AND ALASKAN LOANWORDS IN KASHAYA POMO (OSWALT 1958, 1988B)

Eskimo (several languages) *agyu-*	*ʔayayo* '(Christian) cross'
Central Yupik *čama-i*	*čamay* 'hello'
Russian чашка 'cup'	*čaška* 'dishes'
Alutiiq *čawik*	*čawik* 'iron, metal, nail'
Russian чайник	*čaynik* 'teakettle'
Russian чай, чаю 'some tea'	*čayu* 'tea'
Dena'ina *iqšak* or Alutiiq *iqsak*	*ʔeqše* 'fishook'
Alutiiq or Aleut *kalikaq*	*kalikak* 'paper, book, letter'
Russian каша	*kaša* 'gruel'
Alutiiq *kičak*	*kičak* 'anchor'
Russian корова 'cow', via Alutiiq *kuluwat* 'cows'	*kuluwet* 'cattle'
Russian кошка	*kuška* 'cat'
Russian мешук	*mišuk* 'bag'
Alutiiq *heqkaq* 'prepared food'	*nukkuk* 'jerky'
Russian парус 'sail'	*parus* 'canvas'
Russian печка 'oven'	*pečka* 'brick'
Russian бутылка 'bottle'	*putilka* 'broken glass'
Eastern Aleut *šakitar* 'murre'	*šakitaq* 'ocean bird (sp.)'
Russian тали	*tali* 'pulley'
Alutiiq *taqmak* or Dena'ina *tahmak*	*taqma* 'woman's dress'
Russian топор, via Alutiiq *tupulu-q*	*tupulu* 'axe'
Russian огородь, via Alutiiq *ukuluta-q*	*ʔukuluta* 'fence, garden'

sluẏ 'hollyleaf cherry' was borrowed into California Spanish as *islay*, and thence into English (Harrington 1944:38). A rare borrowing directly into English is found in the local speech of Humboldt and Siskiyou Counties, where the World Renewal ceremonies of the Karuks and adjoining tribes are called *pikiawish*, based on the Karuk phrase *ʔiθívθaːneːn*

ʔupikyâːviš 'he (the priest) is going to fix the world' (Bright 1957:374).

By contrast, California Indian languages have left a considerable mark on the toponymy of the region. The list of approximately 150 place-names of native origin in Box 15 is far from being exhaustive.

Acalanes. Bay Miwok *saklan*, 'Saclan', tribal name. The original Spanish version of the name, *los Sacalanes*, was reinterpreted as *los Acalanes* in the Acalanes land grant of 1834 (Beeler 1955a, 1959).

Ahwahnee. Sierra Miwok *awo:ni* or *owo:ni* 'Yosemite Valley', from *awwo* or *owwo* 'mouth'.

Anacapa. Chumash *anyapax* 'mirage, illusion' (Applegate 1975, 27).

Aptos. Santa Cruz Costanoan *apṭos* 'meeting of two streams' (?), village name.

Arcata. Yurok *oket'oh* 'where there is a lagoon, smooth water'. Originally the name of the village at Big Lagoon.

Azusa. Gabrielino *ašúkša-ŋa* '(?)-place', village name.

Bally (also **Bolly**, **Bully**). Wintu *buli* 'mountain'. In several mountain names, principally in Trinity County; see **Yolla Bolly**.

Bly. Klamath *play* 'above, up high' (see ¶3.23.1).

Bolinas. Older Spanish spelling, *(los) Baulenes*, apparently reflecting a tribal name *pawlen*. Of uncertain origin but probably Coast Miwok.

Cahto. Northern Pomo *kʰaṭo* 'lake'.

Cahuenga. Gabrielino *kawéʔ-ŋa* 'rock-place', village name.

Calpella. Northern Pomo *kʰál pʰíːla* 'carrying mussels down'.

Camulos. Ventureño Chumash *kamulus* 'the juniper' (Applegate 1975, 31).

Capay. Hill Patwin *kapáy* 'creek'.

Capell. Yurok *kep'el*, village name.

Carquinez. From the Spanish version *(los Carquines)* of the Costanoan ethnonym *karkin*, said to mean 'trade, barter' (Beeler 1954).

Castac, Castaic. Ventureño Chumash *kaštïq* 'the eye, the face' (Applegate 1975, 32).

Chalone. Costanoan *čalon*, meaning unknown.

Cher Ae. Yurok *č'urey* 'mountain', village name.

Chetco. Chetco-Tolowa *čʰetxu* 'at the mouth of the river'.

Chiloquin. Klamath *či:loqin*, a man's name.

Cholame. Salinan *c'olám* 'evil people' (?), village name.

Chowchilla. Northern Valley Yokuts *čawsila* or *čawšila*, tribal name.

Colma. San Francisco Bay Costanoan *kolma* 'moon' (Beeler 1954).

Coloma. From a Nisenan village name.

Colusa. Patwin *koru*, village name.

Cortina. Nomlaki *kotina*, personal name of the headman of a nearby village.

Coso. Panamint *koso:wa* 'steamy', referring to hot springs in the area.

Cosumnes. Plains or Sierra Miwok *ko:so-mne*, 'toyon berry–people', tribal name.

Cotati. Coast Miwok *kotati*, village name.

Cottaneva. Kato *kʰa:-tʰəne:-piʔ* 'where the trail goes over the hill' (?), from *tʰəne:* 'trail'.

Cucamonga. Gabrielino *kúkamo-ŋa* '(?)-place', village name.

Cuyama. Chumash *kuyam* 'clam' (Applegate 1975, 34).

Cuyamaca. Diegueño *ʔekwi:yemak* 'behind the clouds'.

Cuyapipe, Cuyapaipa. Diegueño *ʔewi:ya:pa:yp* 'leaning rock'.

Gualala. Kashaya Pomo *wala:li* or *qʰawala:li*, village name, from *ahqʰa wala:li* 'water go-down-place' (Oswalt 1960).

Guenoc. Lake Miwok *wénok*, name of a lake, possibly from *wéne* 'medicine'.

Guilicos. Originally spelled *Guilucos*, based on a tribal or village name apparently derived from Lake Miwok *wí:lok* 'dusty'.

Havasu. Mohave *havasú:* 'blue'.

Hetch Hetchy. Southern Sierra Miwok *aččačča* 'magpie' (?).

Hoopa, Hupa. Yurok *hup'o:* 'Hoopa Valley'.

Horse Linto. Hupa *xahslin-tiŋ*, 'place where there is a riffle', village name. Possibly also *xahslin-tʰaw* 'heron', lit. 'the one (who stays) around a riffle'.

Hueneme. Ventureño Chumash *weneʔmu* 'sleeping place' (Applegate 1975:45; Beeler 1967).

Hyampom. Wintu *xayi:n-pʰom* 'slippery place'.

Iaqua. Yurok *oyekʷi*, Karuk *ayuki:* '(greetings) friend!'

Inam. Karuk *ina:m*, village name, site of a World Renewal ceremony.

Inyo. Probably from Panamint *ïnï-yun* 'it's dangerous' (Bright and McLaughlin 2000) although Beeler (1972b, 1978b) argued for a derivation from Spanish *indio* 'Indian'.

Ishi Pishi. Karuk *išipiš* '(trail) extending down', village name.

Jacumba. Diegueño village name.

Jalama. Purisimeño Chumash *xalam*, 'bundle', village name.

BOX 15. (continued)

Jamacha. Diegueño *həməča:* 'a type of gourd used for soap', village name.

Jamul. Diegueño *həmuł* 'foam, lather', village name.

Jolon. Salinan *xolon* '(water) leaks through'.

Jonata. Barbareño Chumash *xonxoñata* 'tall oak', village name.

Jurupa. Gabrielino *horúv-pa* 'sagebrush place'.

Kanick, Kenick. Yurok *kenek*, village name.

Katimin. Karuk *ka?tim?í:n* 'upper edge falls', village name, site of a World Renewal ceremony.

Kettenpom. Wintu *xetʰin-pʰom* 'camas place'.

Klamath. Upper Chinook *łamał* 'Indians of the Klamath River Basin', lit. 'those of the river'. Columbia River tribes were in frequent contact with the Klamath and groups to the south after the acquisition of the horse in the early nineteenth century.

Konocti. Southeastern Pomo *kno-qțay* 'mountain (of) old women' (Barrett 1908a:183).

Loleta. Wiyot *hóš wiwítak* 'let's have sexual intercourse!' "In 1893 a resident, Mrs. Rufus F. Herrick, chose the present name, supposed to be from the local Wiyot Indian language. The Indian name was in fact *katawóło?t*, but an elderly Indian played a joke on Mrs. Herrick by telling her that the name was [as above]—the latter part of which she interpreted in baby-talk fashion as *Loleta*" (Bright 2004:254; Teeter 1958).

Lompoc. Purisimeño Chumash *(o)lompo?* 'stagnant water' (?) (Applegate 1975:34).

Malibu. Ventureño Chumash *(u)maliwu* 'it makes a loud noise all the time over there' (referring to the surf), village name (Beeler 1957).

Matilton. Hupa *me?til-tiŋ* 'canoe place', village name.

Mayacamas. Wappo *maya?kma*, village name.

Mettah. Yurok *meta:*, village name.

Modoc. Klamath-Modoc *mo:wat'a:k* 'south' (see ¶3.23.4).

Mojave. Mojave *hamakha:v* 'Mojave Indians'.

Mokelumne. Plains Miwok *mokel-umne* '(?)-people', name of a village near Lockeford, possibly from *moke* 'fish net'.

Monache. Yokuts *monačʰi* 'Mono-speaking Indian'. See **Mono**.

Mono. A term of self-idenitification that is used by some speakers of the Western Numic language spoken from Mono Lake southward, primarily those living west of the Sierra crest in close proximity to the Yokuts. Those living east of the Sierra crest usually prefer to call themselves Paiute ("Owens Valley Paiute," "Mono Lake Paiute," etc.). The Yokuts call all Mono speakers *monačʰi*, which they folk-etymologize as *mo:ñay* 'fly' + *-čʰi* 'people (of that tribe)', alluding to the fly larvae they were said to eat.

Morongo. Serrano *ma:riŋa?*, the name of a Serrano lineage or clan.

Mugu. Ventureño Chumash *muwu* 'beach', village name.

Napa. Possibly from a Southern Patwin village or tribal name. In Hill Patwin, *nápa* is the term for 'bear doctor', that is, a shaman believed to have the ability to shape-shift into a bear.

Negit Island (Mono Lake). Mono *nikïtta* 'goose'.

Niguel. Juaneño *nawil* 'young girl' (Boscana 1933:83, 215–216).

Nipomo. Obispeño Chumash *nipumu?* 'house-place, village', from *(q)nipu* 'house' (Klar 1975).

Nopah. Said to be a hybrid of English *no* and Southern Paiute *pa:* 'water', that is, 'waterless, arid'.

Novato. Probably from *Novatus*, the baptismal name of a Coast Miwok chief (Merriam 1907:355).

Noyo. Northern Pomo *nó-yow* 'dust, ashes–under, in', village name.

Ojai. Ventureño Chumash *?awáy* 'moon'.

Olema. From a Coast Miwok village name, probably based on *óle* 'coyote'.

Olompali. Coast Miwok *ó:lum pálli*, village name, apparently containing *ólom* 'south'.

Orick. Yurok *?o:-'rekʷ* 'at the river mouth', village name. See also **Requa**.

Otay. Diegueño *?eta:y* 'big'.

Pacoima. Perhaps from a Gabrielino word meaning 'running water'.

Pahrump. Southern Paiute *pa-tïmpï* [parímpⁱ] 'water-rock'.

Paicines. Perhaps from Mutsun *paysen* 'get pregnant'.

Pala. Luiseño *pá:-la* 'water'.

Pamo. Diegueño *pá:mu:*, a place-name of unknown etymology.

Panamint. Southern Paiute *panïmïnt* 'Kawaiisu Indians', probably from *pa-nïwinci* 'water-people'; later applied to the Shoshoni speakers of the same area, also called *tïmpisa*.

Paoha Island (Mono Lake). Mono *pa-oha:* 'water baby', referring to a dangerous supernatural creature said to live in bodies of water.

Paskenta. Nomlaki *pʰas-kenti* 'under the cliff'.

Pauma. Probably from Luiseño *pá:-may* 'water-little'.

(continued)

BOX 15. (continued)

Pecwan. Yurok *pekʷan*, village name.

Petaluma. Coast Miwok *péta-lúːma* 'hillside-back(bone), ridge'.

Piru. Tataviam *piʔidhuku*, the name of a plant (Bright 1975).

Pismo. Obispeño Chumash *pismuʔ* 'tar, asphalt', from *pisoʔ* 'black, dark' (Klar 1975).

Potawot. From the name of the Wiyot group whose territory lay at the mouth of the Mad River.

Potwisha. From the name of the Western Mono group whose territory lay near the junction of the Marble and Middle Forks of Kaweah River.

Poway. Diegueño *pawiːy*. This is also the Diegueño word for 'arrowhead', but the resemblance may be accidental (Couro and Hutcheson 1973).

Putah. Lake Miwok *puṭa wuwwe* 'grassy creek' (Beeler 1974:141). The similarity to Spanish *puta* 'whore' is purely accidental.

Requa. Yurok *rekʷʷoy* 'river mouth', village name. See also **Orick**.

Saticoy. Ventureño Chumash *satik'oy*, village name.

Seiad. Earlier written *Sciad*. Of unidentified origin, but possibly from Shasta.

Sespe. Ventureño Chumash *seqpe*, village name.

Shasta. From "Sasty" or "Shasty," a name possibly of Klamath origin by which the Shasta tribe was known to explorers in the early nineteenth century (see ¶3.11.7).

Simi. Ventureño Chumash *šimiyi*, village name.

Siskiyou. A Chinook Jargon term for 'bob-tailed horse', apparently originating in Cree, and according to Gibbs (1863d) "ludicrously bestowed" on the Siskiyou Mountains by Alexander McLeod's party in 1828.

Sisquoc. Probably from a Barbareño Chumash term for 'quail'.

Sixes. Lower Rogue River Athabaskan *səkʷečʰeʔ* 'wide-open river mouth'.

Sonoma. From "Sonomas" or "Sonomi", the name of a group whose territory lay in or around the Valley of the Moon. Possibly from Patwin *sono* 'nose', via the name or nickname of a village headman (Kroeber 1932:354) or the name of a nose-shaped topographic feature (Beeler 1954:268–272).

Soquel. Probably from Santa Cruz Costanoan *sokkoč* 'laurel'.

Sotoyome. From Coast Miwok *yomi* 'village'. The first element is obscure, possibly the name of a chief. The earliest recorded spelling is "Satiyome."

Soulajulle. Coast Miwok *sówlas-húyye* 'laurel promintory'.

Suisun. From the name of the Southern Patwin group whose territory lay to the north of Suisun Bay.

Surgone. Yurok *sregon*, village name.

Suscol. From the name of a Southern Patwin village.

Sycan. Klamath *saːyk'a(n)* 'plain, clearing'.

Sycuan. Diegueño *sekwan*, the name of a kind of bush.

Taboose. Mono or Northern Paiute *tïpattsi*, diminutive of *tïpa* 'pine nut'.

Tahoe. Washo *daʔaw* 'lake'.

Tahquitz. Luiseño *táːkʷiš*, the name of a supernatural being said to manifest itself as a fireball in the mountains.

Talawa. Yurok *toloweł* 'Tolowa tribe'.

Tamalpais. Coast Miwok *tamal-payis* 'west, coast mountain'.

Tecate. Probably from Diegueño *tuːkatt* 'cut with an axe'.

Tectah. Yurok *tektoh* 'log', village name.

Tecuya. Possibly from Yokuts *tʰokya* 'Chumash, westerners', based on *tʰoxil* 'west'.

Tehachapi. Kawaiisu *tïhačïpía* 'difficult climbing'.

Tehama. From the name of a Nomlaki village on the Sacramento River.

Temecula. Luiseño *temeku*, village name.

Tenaya. Southern Sierra Miwok *tïyenna* 'sleeping place'.

Tijuana. From the name of a Diegueño village. The etymology *Tia Juana* 'Aunt Jane' is not historically correct.

Tish Tang a Tang. Hupa *tiš-tʰaːŋʔaːtiŋ* 'tiš promontory'. The unanalyzable element *tiš* is an archaic form of *tiW-* 'quail' or 'pheasant'.

Toiyabe. Shoshoni *toyapi* 'mountain'.

Tomales. From the name of a Coast Miwok group, based on *tamal* 'west, coast'.

Topanga. Gabrielino *topa-ŋa* '(?)-place', village name.

Topock. Mojave *tuːpák*, from *tapák* 'drive piles'.

Tujunga. Gabrielino *tuhu-ŋa* '(?)-place', village name.

Tuolumne. Central Sierra Miwok *ṭaːwalïmni* 'squirrel place'.

Ukiah. Central Pomo *yóqʰaːya* 'south valley' (Oswalt 1980).

Ukonom. Karuk *yuhnaːm* 'downriver flat', village name.

BOX 15. (continued)

Ulatis. A shortened form of Ululatos, the name given by the Spanish to a Southern Patwin group.

Umunhum. Probably from the Southern Costanoan word for 'hummingbird', cf. Mutsun *humu:nya*, Rumsen *ummun* (Beeler 1954).

Usal. Northern Pomo *yo:sal*, perhaps containing *yo:-* 'south'.

Wahtoke. Yokuts *watʰak'* 'pine nut'.

Waucoba. Mono *wokóbï* 'bull pine'.

Wawona. Southern Sierra Miwok *wohwohna* 'redwood tree'.

Weitchpec. Yurok *wečpek* 'confluence'.

Weott. Wiyot *wiyat* 'Eel River'.

Winema. Modoc woman's name.

Winnemucca. From Northern Paiute, perhaps containing *moko* 'shoe'.

Yolla Bolly. Wintu *yo:la buli* 'snow mountain'.

Yolo. Patwin *yoloy* or *yodoy*, the name of a village on the Sacramento River at Knight's Landing.

Yonna. Klamath *yana:* 'below'.

Yontockett. Tolowa *yanʔtakət* 'southward uphill', village name.

Yosemite. Southern Sierra Miwok *yoṣṣeʔmeti* 'the killers', a name given to the people of Yosemite Valley.

Yreka. Shasta *wáik'a* 'Mount Shasta'.

Yuba. Konkow *yupu*, name of the village at the mouth of Feather River.

Yucaipa. Supposedly from a Serrano word meaning 'wet or marshy land'.

Yuma. O'odham *yu:mi* 'Quechan' (see ¶3.18.7).

PART 5

LINGUISTIC PREHISTORY

Part 5 summarizes the work of linguists and archaeologists who have attempted to infer certain prehistoric connections and movements in California and adjacent areas from the patterns of diversity within languages, language families, and phyla, and from the distribution of loanwords and other shared linguistic features. Possible correlations are noted with the models of California prehistory that have been constructed by archaeologists, and more recently by geneticists, but no attempt is made to bring the diversity of facts and interpretations together in a single integrated scheme. Apart from an abbreviated version of this survey that was published as Golla (2007b), the only previous overall evaluation of the linguistic evidence for California prehistory was the chapter on linguistic prehistory in Michael J. Moratto's *California Archaeology* (1984:529–574). My debt to Moratto, as well as to the work of Kenneth Whistler on which Moratto draws, will be apparent to anyone familiar with the field. Less apparent, perhaps, is my debt to Richard E. Hughes, whose critique of the facile migrationism that pervades so much linguistic prehistory (Hughes 1992) is never far from my mind.

A word should be said here regarding the evidentiary value of the two phylum-level classifications of California languages, Hokan (¶3.8) and Penutian (¶3.21). My position on the historical validity of these hypothetical relationships is somewhat more positive than that of such methodological conservatives as Lyle Campbell (1997), although considerably more cautious than that of such enthusiasts as Paul Radin (1919), Morris Swadesh (1959), and Joseph Greenberg (1987), or even Edward Sapir in his less restrained moments (as, for example, in Sapir 1921c). While the categories "Hokan" and "Penutian" are undoubtedly meaningful—no one would ever classify Shastan as Penutian or Klamath-Modoc as Hokan, and the consensus is now clear that Chumash and Yukian belong to neither (nor to a phylum of their own)—we continue to debate the nature of the historical relationships these categories imply. Readers of this section must take into account that I am more adventuresome than some of my colleagues in entertaining what seem to me plausible speculations about Hokan and Penutian subgrouping (more particularly the latter), and about the overall expansion and interinfluence of the phylum-level groupings in the deep prehistory of the region. I hope, however, that I make clear the highly speculative nature of such hypotheses, and I try to indulge my predilection for them only when, in my view, they appear to cast some useful light on the past.

5.1 The Oldest Stratum? Waikuri, Chumash, Yukian

Most of the indigenous languages of the California region belong to one of five widespread North American language groups—the Hokan and Penutian phyla, and the Uto-Aztecan, Algic, and Athabaskan language families. The distribution and internal diversity of four of these groups suggest that their original centers of dispersal were outside, or peripheral to, the core territory of California—that is, the Central Valley, the Sierra Nevada, the Coast Range from Cape Mendocino to Point Conception, and the Southern California coast and islands. Only languages of the Hokan phylum can plausibly be traced back to populations inhabiting parts of this core region during the Archaic, and there are hints of connections between certain branches of Hokan, such as that between Salinan and Seri, that suggest that at least some Hokan languages could have been brought into California by later immigrants, primarily from the Southwest and northwestern Mexico.

Three widely separated clusters of California languages, however, resist inclusion in any of these five groups. These are, from south to north, the pocket of languages at the southern tip of the Baja California peninsula, of which *Waikuri* is the only attested representative; the languages of the *Chumash* family of the Santa Barbara Channel; and the *Yukian* languages, Northern Yukian and Wappo, in the Coast Range north of San Francisco Bay. It is intriguing that all three of these groups of languages were spoken in areas where there is evidence of long-established populations of a distinctive physical type—small-bodied people with dolichocephalic crania.[1]

5.1.1 Unclassified Languages of Southern Baja California

Although the southern tip of the Baja California peninsula is far removed from what has been characterized here as the "core territory" of California, it is a geographical cul-de-sac where direct descendents of very early populations, and possibly their languages, could well have survived. Massey (1966) described the Baja California peninsula precisely in these terms, arguing that it had been entered by a succession of major population movements from the north. In his view, the oldest stratum was represented by the speakers of the languages of the southern cape region (Waikuri, Uchití, and Pericú). North of Loreto this stratum—or at least Waikuri—was overlaid by the southward expansion of speakers of Cochimí, which was in turn overlaid in the far north by a Yuman expansion into the San Pedro Mártir highlands. Laylander (1997), however, in reviewing the scanty evidence, found little linguistic support for Massey's stratification hypothesis. He sees no reason to believe that linguistic movement within the peninsula has been consistently unidirectional from north to south. There are significant east-west linguistic and cultural divisions along the length of the peninsula, and communication with the mainland of Mexico via the islands of the middle Gulf was feasible in precontact times.

This debate must remain largely hypothetical, since of the languages spoken in the southern tip of Baja California only Waikuri is documented, and not very extensively (¶3.37).

5.1.2 Chumash

The artifactual and skeletal evidence that has been analyzed to date indicates an extraordinary demographic and cultural stability in the northern Channel Islands and adjacent mainland from the early Holocene (10,000 to 12,500 years ago) to the historic period (Arnold 2001:13–14; Jones et al.

2002). The absence of a demonstrable relationship between Chumash and any other language or language family in North America similarly suggests that it has deep roots in its present territory.

Since, however, the internal diversity of the Chumash family is no greater than that of Germanic or Romance, it appears to represent the expansion during the last two millennia of a language originally confined to only one part of that territory, replacing an earlier, much more complex diversity. The pattern of Chumash internal differentiation, moreover, suggests that this expansion occurred in two waves. A first expansion, early in the first millennium AD, if not before, appears to have brought the language into much of its historic territory, the northwestern part of which seems to have been previously occupied by speakers of a Hokan language related to Salinan; Obispeño shows both lexical and structural evidence of having replaced such a language in much of its territory. This first expansion probably did not have any major impact on the Channel Islands, which would have remained linguistically quite distinct from the mainland.

A second expansion, probably from coastal Ventureño territory, appears to have introduced a single relatively undifferentiated Central Chumash language as far north as the historic Purisimeño-Obispeño boundary, overlaying whatever diversity had accumulated in this area after the earlier Chumash expansion. This expansion reached the Channel Islands, resulting in a mixed language (or possibly a bilingual speech community) based on both Central Chumash and the preexisting language. The diversity within Central Chumash is consistent with a time depth of between 1,000 and 1,200 years, making it a reasonable supposition that the rapid expansion of the language—and in particular its extension to the Channel Islands—was in part facilitated by the medium-distance trading networks that developed in this area after 700 AD (J. R. Johnson 1988, 2000; Arnold 2001). These networks were dependent on oceangoing sewn-plank canoes, which appear about this time, and Klar and Jones (2005) have recently revived the hypothesis, first seriously entertained by Heizer (1941b, 1941c), that the Chumash-Gabrielino plank canoe was introduced by direct contact with seafarers from Eastern Polynesia. The linguistic data in particular are intriguing, including a possible Tahitian origin for Central Chumash *tomol* 'plank canoe', but specialists in Polynesian navigation remain unconvinced (Anderson 2006).

The mixed nature of Island Chumash possibly sheds light on the more remote linguistic prehistory of the Chumash area (Klar 2002:657). While much of the attested Island Chumash vocabulary closely resembles that of the Ventureño or Barbareño dialects of Central Chumash, a significant number of the words are unique to island speech. This local vocabulary is noticeably non-Chumash in phonology, includes many words with basic meanings such as 'water' and 'house', and accounts for a higher proportion of the attested Island Chumash lexicon than does the unique vocabulary of otherwise quite divergent Obispeño.[2] The linguistically most probable explanation for this lexical discontinuity is that what we know as Island Chumash was a variety of Central Chumash that borrowed heavily from an otherwise unknown Channel Island language that was quite distinct from Chumash.[3] The presence of such a language on the Channel Islands would hardly be surprising. Although the northern Channel Islands have been inhabited continuously for at least ten millennia, the archaeological evidence does not indicate a close relationship with the mainland until late in the first millennium AD (Arnold 2001:14–15). Like the southernmost part of the Baja California peninsula, the Channel Islands are the kind of geographical cul-de-sac in which one might well expect to find evidence of direct linguistic continuity from some of the earliest human settlements in the Western Hemisphere.

5.1.3 Yukian

The early history of the Yukian-speaking peoples is shrouded in mystery. The physical characteristics of the (Northern) Yukians and their immediate Athabaskan neighbors—most notably longheadedness and short stature—suggest an isolated gene pool that could well be, as Kroeber proposed (1925:159), a relict population from the earliest human settlement of California. The widely attested hostile relationships between Yukians and neighboring groups could be seen a social adaptation that promoted long-term ethnic survival.

There is some evidence that languages related to Yukian might have formed the basal linguistic stratum in a significant part of California, particularly along the coast to the south. In an unpublished paper, Elmendorf (1984) compiled a list of Yukian words that closely resemble words of similar meaning in other California languages and that seem likely to be borrowings in one direction or the other. He found thirty or more words shared with adjacent Wintuan, Pomo (many with Proto Pomo), and Miwok (many with Proto Miwok). Among nonadjacent languages, the largest number of sharings was with Wiyot (23), Yokuts ("a fair number"), Chumashan (25–30), and Uto-Aztecan (35 or more). Smaller numbers were shared with Chimariko (14) and Maiduan (12). Few or none were shared with Karuk, Shasta, and Palaihnihan. Nor were there many pairs of resemblant words between Yukian and Salinan or Esselen, with the interesting exception of the numeral 'one', which is nearly identical in Yuki and Esselen and has resemblant forms in Yana, Southern Costanoan, Chumash, and Gabrielino (¶4.14.4).

A radically different explanation of Yukian uniqueness has been put forward by Swadesh (1954a:324) and more recently by Munro (1994). They propose that Yukian speech entered California with a relatively recent immigrant population, basing this hypothesis on the striking lexical resemblances that have been noted by several scholars, beginning with Radin, between Yukian and the Siouan, Yuchi, and Gulf languages (¶3.35). These resemblances

cannot easily be dismissed, and it is not unlikely that they in part reflect ancient historical connections. But the residue of a phylum-level relationship that might reach back to the Archaic must be distinguished from evidence of a direct historical link to specific languages spoken far outside of California. It is difficult to construct a realistic prehistoric scenario that could have brought a group from the Mississippi Valley or the Gulf Coast to the North Coast Range, and unless substantial new evidence—genetic, archaeological, linguistic, or ethnographic—comes to light, a Yukian entry into California within the last one or two millennia must be considered much less likely than very ancient residence.

The internal diversity of Yukian is also open to different interpretations. Early observations on the Yuki-Wappo relationship suggested a rather shallow time depth, perhaps only a few hundred years (Kroeber 1925:218). Elmendorf's glottochronological calculations, however, indicated that the separation of Northern Yukian and Wappo took place between 1950 and 1100 BC (1968 [1993]:178; 1981a:13, fn.7). Although this interpretation gives the split a much greater antiquity than earlier estimates, it fits well with recent syntheses of North Coast Range archaeology. Thus Fredrickson (1984:510), on the basis of archaeological correlations, dates the expansion of Pomo groups into the Russian River valley to the Middle Archaic period, between 3000 BC and 1000 BC. If the pre-Pomo language of this area was Yukian, this expansion could have been the catalyst that separated early Wappo from the rest of Yukian around the date that Elmendorf's calculations suggest. A 3,000-to-5,000-year time depth for Western Pomo expansion, however, flies in the face of most linguistic estimates of the age of the entire Pomo family, which are on the order of 2,000 to 2,500 years (see ¶5.2.10). More work on the historical linguistics of both Yukian and Pomo remains to be done before correlations such as these can be given much weight.

Whenever and wherever Wappo diverged from Northern Yukian, it seems to have involved substantial influence from Pomo, since a number of the phonological and grammatical differences between Northern Yukian and Wappo are best explained as a "Pomoization" of the latter.[4] Miwok influence on Wappo, by contrast, is largely confined to superficial lexical borrowing. This finding is consistent with a late date for the Wappo occupation of the Napa Valley, where an older Miwok population appears to have been absorbed. A correlation of a Wappo intrusion with the beginning of the Saint Helena Aspect of the Augustine Pattern, around 500 AD, is generally accepted (Fredrickson 1984:511). The dialectal divisions within Wappo, so far as they are attested, seem to be consistent with this date, or even a later one. As for the Northern Yukian languages, the chain relationship of Yuki, Huchnom, and Coast Yuki dialects suggests that they differentiated in much the same locations as their historical ones (Elmendorf 1968 [1993]:176). The divisions do not appear to be older than a thousand years.

5.2 Hokan

The time depth of the "core" Hokan relationship among California and Mesoamerican language as defined by Kaufman (see ¶3.8) must be at least equal to that of the Indo-European family, which is usually estimated to be around six thousand years.[5] Kaufman himself considers eight thousand years to be "a fairly good guess" (1988:59), and even earlier dates have been suggested. Given this time depth, and an overall distribution of the surviving Hokan branches that suggests a long-standing connection with the intermontane West, Moratto's correlation of ancient Hokan with the Western Pluvial Lakes Tradition of eight thousand to eleven thousand years ago, and more generally with the big-game-hunting Folsom-Clovis culture out of which it grew, remains a plausible speculation (1984:90–103, 544). The Post Pattern assemblage from the Borax Lake site at Clear Lake—reflecting a fluted-point-manufacturing, big-game-hunting society that was beginning to adapt to lakeside gathering and hunting—can similarly be associated with an early Hokan occupation of the Central Valley and adjacent areas ultimately ancestral to Pomo, Chimariko, Yana, and Washo. By contrast, the apparently earlier (ca. 10,250 BP) coastal adaptation revealed at the Cross Creek site in San Luis Obispo County, with its milling equipment and shell middens (Jones et al. 2002), is less likely to be connected with early Hokan-speaking groups than with early speakers of the coastal or near-coastal isolates, Chumash and Yukian (see ¶5.1).

Of the sixteen Hokan branches that Kaufman recognizes, ten are single languages with few if any dialects (Karuk, Chimariko, Yana, Washo, Esselen, Salinan, Seri, Coahuilteco, Chontal, and Jicaque), and three others are language families whose shallow internal diversity reflects time depths of 1,500 years or less (Shastan, Palaihnihan, and Comecrudan). Only two (Pomo and Yuman-Cochimí) show deeper internal divisions, and neither is apparently the product of more than 2,500 years of differentiation.

Subgrouping the Hokan languages, along with reconstructing the outlines of a general Hokan linguistic prehistory, has proved very difficult. At the beginning of the historic period the Hokan branches, especially those with little or no internal diversity, were largely relegated to what Johanna Nichols has called "residual zones"—culturally and geographically peripheral areas, often mountainous, where the observable linguistic diversity reflects the slow aggregation of the remnants of formerly more widespread language communities rather than in situ diversification from a single ancestral language (J. Nichols 1992:13–16, 2004).

5.2.1 The Northern California Diffusion Area

The most complex of these mountain refuges includes the territories of Karuk, Chimariko, Shastan, Palaihnihan, and Yana, which lie in a contiguous arc across far northern California from the lower Klamath River to the upper Pit River. While Shastan and Palaihnihan show resemblances that have led some to suggest that they form a subgroup descended from Proto-Shastan-Palaihnihan (Campbell 1997:123), the phonologies and grammars of the languages in this Northern California (or "Northern Hokan") cluster are almost as diverse as those of a random selection of any five Hokan languages. Although all five of the Northern California branches have similarly structured "bipartite" polysynthetic verb stems (¶4.8.2), they share this feature with both Pomo and Washo as well as several adjacent Penutian languages. If Chimariko is to be grouped with another Hokan branch on phonological, morphosyntactic, and lexical criteria, Pomo is the most likely candidate (Berman 2001c:1052–1053), not neighboring Shastan; Karuk is deeply different from both Chimariko and Shastan, and in some ways more closely resembles Yuman and Cochimí; Yana's connections seem to be to Washo (Jacobsen 1976).

Despite these structural (and presumably historical) differences, the Northern California branches share a small but significant portion of their vocabularies. Kaufman (1988) identifies several dozen sets of closely resemblant words shared between two or more languages of the cluster. Most of these words lack direct cognates elsewhere in Hokan, and it can be presumed that they were borrowed across an area of similar Hokan culture subsequent to the coalescence of the Northern California refuge area. They include words for local fauna and flora (such as Yana *wixlay*, Chimariko *wisila* 'chipmunk'; Yana *cawʔi*, Shasta *ʔaccáwʔwi:huʔ* 'sugar pine'; Yana *cʼimcʼimʔi*, Achumawi *čʼimčʼimalo:* 'spruce'; see Silver 1974) and for a number of items of material culture (such as Yana *lumi* 'spear shaft', Achumawi *lo:mi* 'fish spear'). The borrowed cultural terms reflect a relatively recent period: shared terms for 'upstream' and 'downstream' and for various nets and tools indicate a riverine fishing orientation; the bow and arrow was known; clamshell disc beads and dentalium were used in exchange.[6] It seems fair to conclude that, whatever their previous histories, the Hokan-speaking groups of far-northern California came into much closer contact with one another during the Late Period. It could also be speculated that this coming together may in part have been the result of the intrusion of Algic, Wintuan, and Athabaskan speakers, who surrounded and isolated formerly more widespread Hokan groups.[7]

5.2.2 The Central California Coast Diffusion Area

Another refuge cluster is on the Central California Coast, where speakers of Esselen and Salinan shared a common boundary in the rugged Santa Lucia mountains. Few unique lexical sharings have been identified between this pair of languages, partly because of the scanty attestation of the Esselen lexicon. Kaufman (1988) identifies only two uniquely Central Coast lexical sets, one for 'pestle and mortar' and the other for 'bow', both terms for relatively recent cultural traits, particularly the latter.[8] As with the

Northern California refuge cluster, however, whatever the extent of recent shared vocabulary, the phonological and morphological evidence strongly suggests that the deeper connections of Esselen and Salinan were with languages outside the area rather than with each other: Esselen with Yuman, Cochimí, and Pomo; Salinan with Seri (but see Marlett 2008b), and possibly Washo.

5.2.3 More Ancient Diffusion

A few elements of a more ancient stratum of California Hokan culture can be reconstructed from sets of cognate (or possibly borrowed) words that are shared among two or more languages from two or more of the four geographical refuges in northern and central California—the Northern California group as defined previously, the Esselen-Salinan cluster, Pomo, and Washo—but otherwise not found in Hokan. These words can be assumed to reflect the culture of all or part of the Hokan-speaking region in northern and central California before the influx of Penutian speakers and the retreat of Hokan-speaking communities to their present-day locations. The sets of such shared words that Kaufman (1988) identifies indicate a cultural environment in which acorns of several varieties of oaks, along with buckeye, were being gathered and processed; beliefs about shamans, poisoning, dreams, and ghosts were being elaborated; and beads were being exchanged.[9]

Finally, cognate words shared between any language from the four California Hokan refuge areas and any language in any of the four other geographically separated clusters of Hokan languages—the Southwest (Yuman-Cochimí and Seri), Northeast Mexico ("Coahuiltecan"), Chontal, and Jicaque—can reasonably be supposed to have evolved from a common original term that existed either in Proto-Hokan or in some early branch of the stock. The vocabulary thus inferred can be assumed to reflect the culture of the Hokan speech community in its earliest stage. From the lexical sets that Kaufman (1988) has assembled, it appears that this community must have been located in an environment in which the cottonwood, yellow pine, tule, manzanita, and at least one variety of oak were present, and bears, coyotes, jackrabbits, gophers, mountain lions, and foxes were abundant. Members of this community gathered pine nuts and dug for soaproot and Indian potatoes. They twined baskets, ground seeds and nuts in bedrock mortars, and had trading relations with other groups.[10]

This comparative linguistic evidence, while admittedly thin, seems to support a Proto-Hokan homeland in the interior of the continent with old connections to Mexico and Central America. The more northerly and westerly parts of the California region are less likely to have been part of this homeland than to have been occupied at a later date by successive waves of Hokan speakers from the south and east. These immigrants would have intermingled and redistributed themselves in secondary clusters, most of which are now

separated from one another by large tracts of territory in which languages of non-Hokan origin are spoken. This reconstruction (which follows in general outline the one proposed by Moratto 1984) is bolstered by Richard Keeling's research on music and culture history in northwestern California (Keeling 1992, 1993). Keeling finds a surprising discontinuity in musical style between the otherwise culturally homogeneous Yuroks and the Karuks. An important genre of Yurok songs shows stylistic traits that link it to what Keeling calls the "Arctic-Asian" substratum, while the parallel—but very differently profiled—Karuk genre can be linked to a South American substratum. He speculates that this profound structural distinction in musical tradition, like the distinction between Hokan and non-Hokan language, may be the buried trace of an ancient fault line that "divided northern hunting cultures from more southerly seed-gathering ones in Paleo-Indian times" (1993:231).

5.2.4 Karuk

There are few clues to Karuk linguistic prehistory, other than its ultimate Hokan derivation. Lexical sharings with Shastan, Chimariko, Palaihnihan, and Yana indeed indicate extensive contact between speakers of Karuk and other Northern California Hokan languages, but this seems to have been confined to the late prehistoric period (see ¶5.2.1). Attempts to demonstrate an old "Northern Hokan" subgroup of which Karuk is a part have largely been fruitless (Bright 1954; Haas 1964; Silver 1976). The handful of terms (mainly for plants and animals) that are shared between Karuk and Yurok seem all to have originated in Karuk, and this finding could be taken as evidence for a Karuk substratum in Yurok territory. More interesting are the resemblances in phonology between Wiyot and Karuk, including the absence of glottalized consonants, the presence of a voiced bilabial fricative, and a pitch accent system (Bauman and Silver 1975). These resemblances indicate a longer history of interaction between these two languages than between Yurok and Karuk, probably because speakers of Karuk formerly occupied some of the territory historically occupied by the California Athabaskans.

In lacking either glottalized or aspirated consonants but possessing bilabial (f, v) and interdental (θ) fricatives, the phonology of Karuk more closely resembles that of Esselen, Yuman-Cochimí, and Seri than that of most other Hokan languages, including contiguous languages in the Northern California cluster. This resemblance might possibly indicate an old affinity among these languages within Hokan, but an equally plausible explanation would be that all these languages, being on the western fringe of Hokan territory, were separately influenced by now extinct languages of a different phonological type from Proto-Hokan, spoken by the descendents of coastal settlers who had established themselves in these areas before Hokan intrusion from the interior.[11]

5.2.5 Chimariko

Although undoubtedly a Hokan language, Chimariko does not strongly resemble either of its immediate Hokan neighbors, the Shastan languages and Karuk. As noted earlier (¶5.2.1), the geographical cluster of five Northern California Hokan branches to which Chimariko belongs appears not to represent a classificatory subgroup, although significant lexical borrowings have spread across it in recent centuries. For Chimariko, structural resemblances suggest a different grouping. Both phonologically, with its full array of plain, aspirated, and glottalized stops and affricates, and morphologically in the overall pattern of its polysynthetic verb stem, Chimariko most closely resembles the languages of the Pomo branch, and less closely Yana. In addition, there are some striking lexical similarities to Pomo, and more distantly Yuman (Langdon 1979; Berman 2001c:1052–1053).[12] While these resemblances may be no more than an accident of shared conservatism, when taken together with the fact that much of the intervening territory was occupied in historic times by intrusive Athabaskans and Wintuans, the possibility suggests itself that Chimariko, Pomo, and Yana may once have formed a geographically contiguous "North Central Hokan" subgroup separate from Karuk and the Shastan languages. This would be a fruitful hypothesis for someone to explore now that fuller materials on Chimariko lexicon and grammar are available (Jany 2009).

The very restricted area in which Chimariko was spoken at the time of contact suggests recent language shifts in adjacent territory. Neither the California Athabaskans nor the Wintu are likely to have entered the Trinity River drainage much before 800–1000 AD, in the case of the Wintu perhaps as late as 1300 AD if their incursion is to be linked to the spread of the Augustine Pattern (or Shasta Complex). Their predecessors were very likely to have been speakers of Chimariko. Chase-Dunn and Mann (1998:125–127) argue that the numerous Wintu place-names along the upper Trinity that are direct translations of the Chimariko names for the same places constitue evidence for a slow, peaceful supplanting of Chimariko by Wintu. Several places in Hupa territory also have names that are translations of their Chimariko equivalents, including the principal village in Hoopa Valley, whose Hupa name, Ta'k'imiłding (*tʰaʔķ'imiłtiŋ* 'acorn soup cooking place'), is modeled on Chimariko *hopetači* 'acorn soup place', from *hopew* 'acorn soup'. It is not unlikely that this is the ultimate source of *hup'o*, the Yurok name for Hoopa Valley (and the source of the modern place-name), suggesting that the Yuroks first knew it as a place where the Chimariko language prevailed.

5.2.6 Shastan

The prehistory of the Shastan family is unclear except that it must ultimately figure in the prehistory of the Hokan languages. Dixon was convinced that the Shastan and

Palaihnihan languages were closely related (1905b), even going so far as to extend the name "Shastan" to the relationship. This grouping was challenged by Bright (1954), and Olmsted took the view that Shastan and Palaihnihan were independent branches of Hokan (1959:643–644). Many of the lexical resemblances on which Dixon relied are now seen as relatively recent borrowings among adjacent Northern California Hokan languages (see ¶5.2.1). However, a significant residuum of lexical resemblances that are difficult to dismiss as borrowings, together with a number of grammatical resemblances, points to a unique historical connection of some nature between the two families (Kaufman 1988).

Within Shastan, the deepest division is between the Shasta dialect chain and Konomihu. Shasta-Konomihu cognates show the effects of a number of sound changes involving ablaut, contraction, and other systematic phonological processes, as well as a significant amount of morphological restructuring (Silver 1980). The relationship thus appears to be old, possibly two thousand years or more. However, Shasta dialect differences are very shallow, suggesting a recent spread of that language over much of its historic territory. The fact that Konomihu (and New River Shasta) was spoken to the south and west of the Shastas suggests that the southwestern portion of Shasta territory—Scott Valley and the immediately adjacent parts of the Klamath River—may have been its historic core, and that Shasta Valley, the upper Klamath River, and the Bear Creek–Upper Rogue Valley region of southern Oregon were areas of more recent expansion. If some of this territory, particularly in the Mount Shasta area, was earlier occupied by Palaihnihan speakers, a Shasta expansion may have been the vector that brought northwestern cultural influences to the Pit River area after 500 AD (Baumhoff and Olmsted 1964:10).[13] The hypothesis of a Shasta expansion to the north and east is also consistent with the relative stability of the relationship between the Shasta and the Karuk along the Klamath River, which sharply contrasts with the raiding and small-scale warfare that the Shasta engaged in with the Takelma, Modoc, and Achumawi (Heizer and Hester 1970:133–148).

5.2.7 Palaihnihan

Baumhoff and Olmsted (1964) constructed a detailed account of Palaihnihan prehistory on the basis of both linguistic and archaeological evidence. In their scenario, a pre-Palaihnihan Hokan population in north-central California was displaced or marginalized to the lower Pit River area by Penutian immigrants around 2000 BC. Subsequently, dialect diversification led to a north-south split between Achumawi and Atsugewi, and at some relatively recent date speakers of both languages moved further upriver onto the arid Modoc Plateau, displacing the Northern Paiute. An essential element of their scheme is the archaeological discontinuity between central California and northeastern California. Whereas after 2000 BC most of central California entered the Middle Horizon, characterized by much greater use of river and wetland resources, the evidence (at least as of 1964) from sites along Pit River indicated that the Palaihnihan area remained associated with the Early Horizon, and that later developments aligned its culture more with those of Eastern Oregon and Idaho than with the rest of California.

During the first half of the first millennium AD, northeastern California was affected by the widespread technological and demographic changes associated with the introduction of the bow and arrow (marked by the appearance of Gunther points). These influences appear to have entered the area from the northwest, through historic Shasta territory, and were accompanied by a number of specific cultural traits that ethnographically link northeastern California with the Oregon and California coast (Baumhoff and Olmsted 1964:10). This may have been correlated with an expansion of Shasta territory from a base in Scott Valley eastward along the Klamath River, into Shasta Valley, and south and east of Mount Shasta (assuming that poorly documented Okwanuchu is a dialect of Shasta, or a mixed language, not a separate Shastan language; see ¶3.11.5). It is plausible that much of this territory was earlier occupied by Palaihnihan speakers; some of it remained contested into historical times.

The widespread warfare and slave raiding that characterized northeastern California in the early historical period—involving long-distance attacks by the Klamath and Modoc on various Pit River communities and frequent bloody skirmishes between the Northern Paiute and the upriver Achumawi—was due in large part to the introduction of the horse. However, it could only have represented a magnification of older patterns of intergroup hostility, and it seems likely that the Modoc Plateau and the northwestern Great Basin had been in contention for many centuries between speakers of Palaihnihan, Klamath-Modoc, and Western Numic. On the west, by contrast, there seems to have been little outright hostility between the Achumawi and the Wintu, and the same spirit of neutrality seems to have characterized Atsugewi–Northeastern Maidu relations. Although the Yana, particularly the Southern Yana, were hated and feared by their Maiduan and Wintuan neighbors, they seem to have had a stable relationship with the Achumawi, at least around Montgomery Creek. Only in the northwest, with the Shasta, did the Achumawi show the same aggressiveness toward a neighboring group as they did toward the Klamath-Modoc.

5.2.8 Yana

The relationship of Yana to other Hokan languages in Northern California, while firmly established by Sapir (1917a), is nevertheless a distant one. There is no clear evidence that Yana belongs in any proposed Hokan subgroup, although, as noted above, it shares some features with Chimariko and Pomo. The ethnographic territory of the Yana partially adjoined a block of Hokan speech in far

northern California, including Palaihnihan, Shastan, Chimariko, and Karuk, and as noted in ¶5.2.1, the languages in this cluster share a number of evidently borrowed terms for local flora and fauna and for some relatively recent cultural features. Neither Pomo nor Washo is part of this diffusion area, indicating that it dates back no farther than the time when incoming Wintuan, Maiduan, and Athabaskan-speaking groups occupied the intervening territory, probably little more than a millennium ago (discussed later in this section).

A somewhat deeper connection with northeastern California is suggested by morphological structure. Yana is part of a chain of language families that extends along the Cascades from the southern Columbia Plateau to the northern Sierra Nevada that have developed a typologically distinctive "bipartite" pattern of verb stem formation (Jacobsen 1980; DeLancey 1996; see ¶4.8.2). In this type of polysynthesis, the verb stem is often made up of two semantically interpenetrating elements—a lexical first element (typically with instrumental and classificatory meaning) and a locative-directional second element that specifies vectors of motion. In Yana this structure is manifested in the relationship between the stem (which itself can be complex) and the locational-directional stem suffixes. Bipartite stem morphology links Yana with some nearby Hokan branches—Shastan, Washo, Palaihnihan, and Chimariko[14]—but also with several Penutian branches, most notably Maiduan and the Plateau Penutian languages.

This firm typological association with the languages of the southern Cascades, along with the absence of close ties to other Hokan branches, suggests that the ancestral Yana were long resident in northeastern California. They can plausibly be identified with (part of) the population that occupied the northern Sacramento Valley and surrounding mountains before intensive riverine fishing and associated elements of the Augustine Pattern (locally called the Shasta Complex) were introduced circa 600–800 AD, most likely by immigrating Wintuan and Maiduan speakers (Clewett and Sundahl 1990:41–44). The distinctive short stature of the Yana, which set them off sharply from surrounding peoples in the historic period, suggests a connection with the short-statured and long-headed Yukis of the northern Coast Range.[15] The fierce hostility that persisted into the nineteenth century between the Wintu and Nomlaki on the valley floor and the Yana and Yuki in the mountains, on both the east and west sides of the valley, can be seen as the final stage in a long struggle between incoming Penutians and the long-resident Hokan and Yukian peoples whom they displaced and marginalized.

5.2.9 Washo

On one hand, Washo, although clearly Hokan in affiliation, is not closely connected to any other Hokan language, including those found in the same general area of central California—Yana, Pomo, Esselen, and Salinan. On the other hand, the Washo lexicon contains numerous loanwords from adjacent Numic and Miwok languages, and Washo grammar shows significant convergences in phonological and grammatical structure with Maiduan, Wintuan, and Pomo. Jacobsen's conclusion that Washo "has long been in approximately the same area in which it is now found" (1986a:107) seems well justified. The precursors of the ethnographic Washo could plausibly be associated with Archaic adaptations in the northern portion of the east slope of the Sierra Nevada as far back as the beginning of the Spooner Phase, around 5000 BC (Elston 1986:141). They were almost certainly participants in the Middle Archaic Martis Complex, which developed in this area after 2000 BC (Elston 1986:143).

Walter W. Taylor (1961), elaborating on a suggestion of Sapir's (1920a:290, 1921b:72), argued that the historical Washo speech community was the only surviving remnant of a widespread Hokan subgroup that occupied much of the Great Basin during the Archaic. Subsequent archaeological and linguistic work has not lent support to this hypothesis. From the beginning of the Martis Complex, if not earlier, the characteristic cultural developments in historic Washo territory have been quite distinct even from an area as close as the Lahontan Basin, the sink into which the Truckee and Humboldt Rivers drain. Instead, the Lovelock Culture of the Middle Archaic Lahontan Basin shows many similarities to the early stages of the Utian-associated Windmiller Pattern of the Sacramento–San Joaquin Delta, suggesting that substantial portions of the Great Basin were Penutian rather than Hokan in speech (Moratto 1984:552). Rather than coming from the Basin, the Middle and Late Archaic culture of the Washo area appears to have its roots in the Sierras, where a Martis or Martis-affiliated tradition dominated in historical Maidu and Nisenan territory as far west as the Sacramento Valley (Moratto 1984:302–303). It seems a likely scenario that bearers of the early Martis tradition spoke Hokan languages that included the precursor to Washo, and possibly also to Yana. Subsequently, however, much of the Martis region came to be occupied by speakers of Penutian languages. Perhaps as early as 1000 BC, Miwok speakers began infiltrating the Sierras from the southwest; and after 500 AD, Maiduans appear to have moved into the northern Sierra from the Basin, at first displacing Washo on the upper Feather River and then overlaying an earlier Miwok occupation in what became Nisenan territory.

The relationship of Washo to Uto-Aztecan is interesting. The Northern Paiutes who lived immediately to the east of the Washo in historical times were relatively new in that area, and their dialects had only a small impact on Washo. However, in the Sierras south of Lake Tahoe and around Walker and Mono Lakes, the ancestral Washo community appears to have had sustained contact with Uto-Aztecans. Lexical borrowings into Washo from Numic include several words no longer found in recent Western Numic dialects, indicating that they entered Washo at a period when Numic was less differentiated than it is now, or when Washo

speakers were in direct contact with speakers of Central and Southern Numic, and possibly even Tubatulabal. For example, Washo *mu:c'uk* 'medicine' (no resemblant form in Northern Paiute, but cf. Southern Paiute *mucuttukkʷi*); Washo *-aŋal* 'house', *kaŋa* 'cave' (no resemblant forms in Northern Paiute, but cf. Southern Paiute *kani* 'house', Tubatulabal *hani:-l* 'the house') (Jacobsen 1986a:109–110).

5.2.10 Pomo

As noted in ¶3.15, Robert Oswalt, whose views on Pomo differentiation and classification are the most widely accepted by linguists, estimated the time depth of Western Pomo to be comparable to that of the Romance languages including Romanian (somewhat over 1,500 years), while the division between Eastern and Southeastern Pomo, or between either of these and Western Pomo, appeared to him to date back between 2,250 and 2,500 years (Oswalt 1964a). The relative antiquity of the Eastern Pomo–Southeastern Pomo split has led most researchers (except for Webb) to assume that the Pomo occupation of the Clear Lake Basin is older than that of the Russian River. Oswalt himself unequivocally saw Clear Lake as the Proto-Pomo homeland, with subsequent dispersals of Pomo speakers to the northeast (Northeastern Pomo) and to the west, and with the Russian River valley first occupied by Pomo-speaking people around 500 AD.

A. M. Halpern's classification (1964) implies a different scenario, particularly if his grouping of Northern and Northeastern Pomo is accepted. If the Western Pomo languages represent a migration westward from a Clear Lake homeland, then the Northeastern Pomos would have had to reach their historical location in the Sacramento Valley by a back-migration from the Russian River valley. Possibly corroborating this interpretation are the Pomo words for 'arrow' (a weapon that was introduced into Central California not much earlier than 500 AD): one form is shared by the Western Pomo languages and Northeastern Pomo, but a quite different form (probably borrowed between them) is shared by Eastern and Southeastern Pomo.

Nancy Webb's classification (1971) is based in part on a glottochronological study that shows the deepest divergence (between 1,600 and 1,900 years) to be between Northeastern Pomo and the others. She locates the Pomo homeland along the Russian River, with the Northeastern Pomo cleaving off first, followed by a Lake group that split into the Eastern and Southeastern Pomo only after settling around Clear Lake. Webb's classification, and the scenario it implies, is not widely accepted.

Kenneth Whistler (1988) sees further evidence for a Clear Lake homeland in McLendon's (1973) reconstructed Proto-Pomo terms for plants, animals, and especially fish. However, noting the unbroken continuity of the Late Borax Lake Pattern in the Clear Lake Basin, he further proposes that Proto-Pomo was spoken there as early as 3000 BC, and that "Pre-Proto-Pomo" may go back as far as the beginning of the (Early) Borax Lake Pattern at Clear Lake around 5000 BC. Whistler also correlates the first movement of the Pomo into the Russian River drainage with the expansion of the Borax Lake Pattern into that area, around 2000 BC. Fredrickson (1984:510), making the same correlation, more cautiously dates it only to the Middle Archaic Period, between 3000 BC and 1000 BC. Although Whistler's and Fredrickson's scenario makes an interesting fit with the archaeological record, the dates they assign to it are difficult to reconcile with observed Pomo linguistic diversity, which suggests that Proto-Pomo was spoken not much earlier than 250 to 500 BC.[16]

The Pomo languages have been in contact with Yukian, Miwok, and Wintuan languages for a long period, and borrowing has taken place in both directions.

There are numerous Yukian loanwords in Pomo, some apparently borrowed by Proto-Pomo at an early date, others borrowed more recently by individual Pomo languages (Elmendorf 1984). The earlier borrowings are consistent with the view held by many archaeologists that a Yukian occupation preceded all others in the North Coast Ranges (Fredrickson 1984:509). However, substratal Pomo influence on a southward-migrating group of Yukian speakers may have been an important factor in the development of Wappo (see ¶5.1.3).

Miwok influence on Pomo, by contrast, is not extensive. Lake Miwok has had some influence on Southeastern Pomo, although borrowings from Pomo into Lake Miwok are probably more consequential. Coast Miwok has had some influence on Southern Pomo, which probably replaced it in some parts of Sonoma County.

Pomo and Wintuan share several phonological and grammatical features implying an old and important relationship that is not well understood. Pomo and Wintuan, for instance, are the only language families in California to have a four-way contrast in laryngeal features: plain, aspirated, glottalized, and voiced (¶4.1.1).[17] Since other evidence strongly suggests that the speakers of the Wintuan languages first entered California from southwestern Oregon around 500 AD, the borrowing—if there was any—must have taken place after that date, and since Pomo differention seems to have begun no later than 2,000 to 2,500 years ago, it could only have been from Pomo into Wintuan. One possible scenario is that all or part of the territory in the Sacramento Valley that became the homeland of the early Wintuans was previously occupied by speakers of Pomo, of which Northeastern Pomo may be the surviving (Patwinized) remnant. It should be noted, however, that there is little evidence in Wintuan of early lexical borrowing from Pomo, whereas there has been substantial recent borrowing into Northeastern and Southeastern Pomo from Patwin.

5.2.11 Esselen and Salinan

Although both Esselen and Salinan are included in the Hokan phylum by most specialists (Kaufman 1988), the two languages differ significantly in phonology and grammar, and no cognates other than those that indicate a general Hokan affiliation have been identified. Sapir (1925a:525) suggested that Salinan (and possibly Chumash) belonged to the same Hokan subgroup as Seri of northwestern Mexico, while Esselen was to be grouped with Yuman. While Sapir himself cited no evidence for this classification, it has received some substantiation from lexicostatistics (Bright 1956); it is not, however, considered definitive.[18]

Salinan and Esselen, whatever their ultimate connections within the phylum, are clearly the product of millennia of local specialization following an early Hokan occupation of central California. This occupation probably involved several waves of immigration, all generally representing the northwestward movement of desert hunters and foragers during the early Archaic (Moratto 1984:544–547). By 2000 BC, much of the historic territory of the Utian, Yokuts, and Chumash languages was probably occupied by speakers of Hokan languages related to Esselen and Salinan.

There is a some evidence that Esselen—or an extinct language closely connected to Esselen—was the linguistic substrate in most or all of Costanoan territory. Although some resemblances between Costanoan and Esselen can be attributed to recent borrowing by Esselen from Rumsen and other adjacent Costanoan languages,[19] Beeler (1961b, 1978a:35–36), Shaul (1984, 1988), and Callaghan (2006) have noted similarities in the vocabularies of nonadjacent Costanoan languages that are more likely to be borrowings from Esselen. Among these is a resemblance between the terms for 'man' and 'woman' in Esselen and Karkin, the northernmost Costanoan language: Esselen *(e)xe-noče* or *xe-noṭe* 'man', *ta-noč(e)* or *ta-noṭe* 'woman' = Karkin "junathramuhue" (? *xu-naṭa-muwe*) 'man', "runathramuwe" (? *ru-naṭa-muwe*) 'woman' (Beeler 1961b:197).[20] Callaghan (2006) also compares Esselen *imila* 'sea' to Chocheño *ʔommu* and Karkin "umunuth" (? *ʔumunu-ṭ*) 'sea'; Esselen *walkošex* 'canoe' to Awaswas *wali*, Tamyen *walin* 'canoe', and Ramaytush "wah lee" 'tule boat'; and Esselen *cila* 'watertight basket' to Mutsun *tilai* 'basket with a good base'. Given the shallow diversity of Costanoan—a time depth of fifteen hundred years would be a maximal estimate—Levy's correlation of the Costanoan displacement of Esselen in the San Francisco and Monterey Bay areas with the beginning of the Late Horizon thus seems quite plausible. The linguistic evidence is less supportive of the models proposed by Moratto (1984:246–247, 553–557) and Breschini and Haversat (1997b), who correlate the shift from Esselen to Costanoan with the transition between the Early and Middle Horizon, around 500 BC.

In addition to its lexical connections to Costanoan, Esselen shares a number of typological features with the Utian languages in general, Miwok as well as Costanoan. These include the absence of a glottalized series of stops, the structural importance of geminate consonants, and (late developments in the Eastern Miwok languages aside) a relatively analytic morphosyntax. The general similarity of this typological profile to that of the Uto-Aztecan languages is probably not accidental and suggests the existence of an ancient linguistic area stretching from the central Sierra Nevada through the Sacramento–San Joaquin Delta to San Francisco Bay.

Salinan territory, like Esselen territory, was almost certainly larger in the past. The location of the Salinan-Costanoan boundary southeast of Soledad in the Salinas Valley appears to reflect the southward expansion of Chalon Costanoans in the mountains to the east of Salinas Valley at a relatively recent date, at the expense both of Salinans and Esselens. A similar erosion of the Salinan speech area seems to have been in progress in the south, where Obispeño Chumash speakers were slowly absorbing Salinan communities between La Cuesta Summit and Paso Robles (Milliken and Johnson 2003). Some of the phonological specialization of Obispeño within Chumash may be accounted for by assuming a Salinan substratum as far south as the Santa Maria River.

5.2.12 Yuman

The time depth of the Yuman family is at most two thousand years, the earliest estimate of the date of the split between Kiliwa and the remainder of the family. The other three divisions—Delta-California, River, and Upland Yuman—appear not to have become distinct from one another before about 700 AD. Although the River and Delta-California branches share some phonological and grammatical innovations that might point to an earlier River-Delta versus "Pai" split, these are more likely correlated with the rapid cultural changes that followed the adoption of agriculture by the Colorado River tribes, which could have occurred as late as 800–1000 AD (Joël 1964:103–105).

Joël (1978) has called attention to the fact that, while most of the Yuman farming vocabulary is of native origin, with semantic shifts from older nonagricultural references, the word for 'bean' (maɾík or closely resemblant forms) is likely to have been borrowed from Hopi móri. Found throughout Yuman (except for Kiliwa), but too similar from language to language to be reconstructible to Proto-Yuman, the word must have spread southward along the Colorado River after the acquisition of farming. If the Hopi provenance is correct (and Joël's evidence is persuasive), it would appear to indicate that farming reached the Yumans not down the Gila but by way of the Western Anasazi farmers who as late as 1000 AD occupied most of the territory where Southern Paiute was spoken historically. Conversely, it lends independent support to the hypothesis that the language of these western Puebloans was a variety of Hopi, which has been suspected on other grounds (see ¶5.4.2).

The pattern of Yuman differentiation, together with the ancient connection between the Yuman family as a whole and Cochimí, points to a late prehistoric expansion of Yuman-speaking peoples north and east from a homeland in the mountains of northern Baja California. This expansion may have been stimulated by a growth of population around prehistoric Lake Cahuilla, which covered most of what is now the Imperial Valley between 1100 and 1550 AD (Joël 1964:103–105, 1998:34–35). Whatever its impetus, the northward expansion of Yuman was apparently not confined to the Colorado River Valley, but carried the language family deep into historic Takic territory. The Coachella Valley and the adjacent Santa Rosa Mountains are likely to have been occupied by Yuman speakers before the Cahuilla and Cupeño entered this area from the north and west (Hinton 1991), and River Yuman influences on Serrano and Kitanemuk testify to the presence of early Mojave or Maricopa speakers in the Mojave Desert as far west as Antelope Valley and the Tehachapi Mountains.

The last stages of Yuman expansion were in the northeast. Archaeological data indicate that the ancestors of the Hualapai and Havasupai began moving into their modern locations west and south of the Grand Canyon around 1150 AD (Euler 1975), possibly displacing a Hopi-speaking population in this area. This displacement may have been contemporary with the Southern Numic expansion into Virgin Anasazi territory north of the Grand Canyon (Voegelin, Voegelin, and Schutz 1967:421). The Yavapai reached the central and eastern parts of their historic territory, including the Verde Valley, no earlier than 1400 AD (Joël 1998:34).

5.2.13 Seri

Historic Seri territory represents an isolated Hokan enclave in a region that is otherwise largely occupied by speakers of Southern Uto-Aztecan languages of the Piman branch. Kroeber (1931) speculated that the Seri originally came from Baja California, but if so the migration must have been an early one, given the lack of linguistic evidence for a close connection between Seri and Yuman-Cochimí. A distinctive Seri pottery style, Tiburón Plain, has been characteristic of the Seri area since the beginning of ceramic times, about two thousand years ago, indicating a long in situ development of Seri culture and language (Bowen and Moser 1968; Bowen 1976). The most likely—although quite speculative—prehistoric scenario for Seri is that it is the remnant of a formerly widespread branch of Hokan in northwestern Mexico, replaced in most areas by southward-migrating Uto-Aztecans before 1000 BC.[21] Sapir's suggestion (1925a:525) that Seri and Salinan belong to a separate Hokan subgroup from Yuman-Cochimí, raises the possibility that at a very early period languages of the "Salinan-Seri" type were spoken in a continuous band from south-central California to Sonora and that the Yuman-Cochimí homeland lay to the southwest of this region, in the mountains of San Diego County and in the Sierra de San Pedro Mártir of northern Baja California.

5.3 Penutian

5.3.1 Penutian Origins

Attempts to identify deeper relationships between the Penutian phylum and other American Indian language groups have largely focused on Mesoamerica. Penutian connections have been proposed for Huave, Mixe-Zoquean, Totonacan, and the Mayan family (for a roster see Campbell 1997:320, 323–324), with possible deeper connections either to Uto-Aztecan (Whorf 1935:608) or to Yukian and Gulf (Greenberg 1987:143–144). Few of these proposals have been taken seriously, and hardly any are supported by any substantial data.[22]

Equally plausible (or implausible) relationships have been suggested across the Bering Strait, where the typological similarities between many Penutian languages and the languages of the Uralic family in Siberia and northeastern Europe have long attracted the attention of both professional and amateur linguists. In a series of papers and books that appeared beginning in the 1970s, the Indo-Europeanist Otto Sadovsky attempted to demonstrate a specific historical relationship between the Ob-Ugric branch of Uralic (ancestral to Hungarian as well as to Vogul and Ostyak on the Ob River in western Siberia) and the Penutian languages of Californa, in particular Miwok and Wintuan (Sadovsky 1976, 1996). The numerous lexical similarities and grammatical parallels adduced by Sadovsky are impressive (see Siegl 1994), but his historical explanation—a coastal voyage three thousand years ago from the Arctic coast of Siberia to San Francisco Bay—is highly improbable. If there is a "Cal-Ugrian" connection, it is much more likely to reflect a common historical source for the Penutian Phylum as a whole (including possible remoter affiliations, as with Mayan) and for the Uralic family as a whole, perhaps also involving Mongolian, Korean, and Japanese (Fortescue 1999). The time depth for such a connection would have to be at least ten thousand years. Two other interhemispheric connections for specific Penutian languages that have been proposed in recent years should be evaluated in the same light: N. Davis's hypothesis (2000) that Zuni is related to Japanese and Yu's proposal (2004) of a historical connection between Sahaptian and Mongolian.

5.3.2 Penutian Subgroups

Moratto (1984:545) equates the Western Pluvial Lakes Tradition in the Great Basin with early Hokan and places the ancestral Penutians relatively far north on the Columbia Plateau. The linguistic evidence is more equivocal. Klamath-Modoc (and the Plateau Penutian languages), Maiduan, and Yok-Utian appear either to have had a common origin as a distinct subgroup of Penutian or to have been in sustained contact with each other for a considerable period of time. Either case is compatible with long residence east of the Cascades in southern Oregon and northwestern Nevada. But

if so, what is the older connection between this *transmontane* cluster of Penutian branches and Chinookan, the Coastal Oregon languages, Wintuan, Takelma, and Kalapuya, which might be called the *cismontane* cluster? Or the connection between either or both of these clusters and Tsimshianic? Are the branches west of the Cascades offshoots from an original Plateau stock? Or was the ancestor of the transmontane languages a secondary inland specialization of an older coastal prototype? Our current understanding of the Penutian relationship—including the possibility of connections to Eurasiatic or Mesoamerican languages—is far too incomplete to allow these questions to be addressed in a meaningful way. Confining ourselves to the Penutian branches found in the California region, the best that can be said at present is that they sort themselves into two distinct groups: Takelma and Wintuan on the one hand, Klamath-Modoc, Maiduan, and Yok-Utian on the other. The latter show signs of a common history—most likely in the northern Great Basin—that Takelma and Wintuan do not share.

5.3.3 Takelma

Numerous lexical resemblances to Kalapuya—either loanwords or cognates deriving from Proto-Takelma-Kalapuyan—provide abundant evidence that at some point in the past Takelma and the Kalapuyan languages were in close contact. This suggests that Takelma represents a southward intrusion of Penutian speech into a formerly Hokan-speaking region. If so, the language replaced was probably related to Karuk. A tonal accent (a distinct falling pitch on certain phonologically prominent syllables) is a regional characteristic that links Takelma, Karuk, Rogue River Athabaskan, and Chetco-Tolowa Athabaskan, and seems best explained by assuming a Karuk-like language to have been substratal throughout the Rogue River valley and adjacent coast.

The sudden replacement of the Old Cordilleran Glade Tradition by the Siskiyou Pattern in this area around 300 AD possibly marks the arrival of the Penutian Takelmas. The subsequent intrusion of Athabaskans into western Oregon around 800–900 AD, as well as their settlement in the Umpqua River valley, would have isolated the Takelmas from the Kalapuyas. The Takelmas of Cow Creek are probably the remnant of an earlier Takelma occupation of much of the upper valley of the Umpqua.

It is also possible, however, that the sharp cultural transition to the Siskiyou Pattern in the Rogue Valley was associated with the immigration not of the Takelmas but of either Wintuan or early Algic-speaking groups. Both could have entered the area from the east, and several of the diagnostic traits of the Siskiyou Pattern—nucleated pit-house villages, predominant use of metates and hopper mortars, small side-notched and basally notched projectile points, and a flourishing of long-distance trade in olivella shells and obsidian—point more to the Great Basin and

Plateau than to the Willamette valley. A Wintuan occupation of the Rogue River valley from circa 300 to 800 AD, followed by a chain of southward displacements stimulated by the Athabaskans—Takelma speakers from the Umpqua valley into the Rogue valley, Wintuan speakers from the Rogue valley into the Sacramento valley—is a plausible scenario.

5.3.4 Wintuan

The most probable homeland of the Wintuan family before 500 AD is the interior of southwestern Oregon, somewhere between the Rogue and Umpqua Rivers. The best evidence for this hypothesis was put forward by Whistler (1977a), who noted that most of the plant and animal terms that are cognate between Wintu-Nomlaki and Patwin, and can thus be reconstructed in Proto-Wintuan, are for species that are found both in California and western Oregon (e.g., Wintu *qalaw*, Patwin *kalaw* 'alder'; Wintu *sumu*, Patwin *sumu-tʰoːk* 'sugar pine'; Wintu *patet*, Patwin *pate* 'mountain lion'). By contrast, plants and animals that are found in the Sacramento Valley but not in western Oregon, are usually named quite differently in the two Wintuan branches, with the Patwin form often being a borrowing from Miwok. For example, Wintu *čati*, Patwin *čusak* 'digger pine' (cf. Proto–Eastern Miwok *sakkɨ); Wintu *pʰaqa*, Patwin *ʔeːye* 'manzanita' (cf. Proto-Miwok *ʔeyye); Wintu *wuːqwuq*, Patwin *moːlok* 'condor' (cf. Sierra Miwok *mollok*). Such a pattern of retention and innovation in plant and animal vocabulary strongly suggests that the speakers of Proto-Wintuan lived in an environment that more closely resembled western Oregon than the Central Valley of California.

Significant borrowings from two Oregon Penutian languages also serve to locate Proto-Wintuan to the north and west of the Central Valley of California. On the one hand, certain features of Wintuan morphology, most notably the complex system of pronouns, are closely paralleled in Klamath-Modoc (DeLancey 1987, 1988a) and seem to be best explained by assuming that they were borrowed into Proto-Wintuan. The most likely circumstance under which such structural borrowing might have taken place is the absorption by the southward-migrating Wintuans of a Klamath-Modoc speech community in Shasta Valley and along the upper Klamath River (for further discussion of this topic, see ¶5.3.5).

A quite different episode of linguistic borrowing from an Oregon language is attested in a substantial number of Wintuan words and lexical elements that closely resemble equivalent forms in Alsea, a language spoken in the historic period in a small enclave on the north-central Oregon coast (Golla 1997). Like Klamath-Modoc, Alsea is a Penutian language, but the resemblant words are phonetically too close and culturally too specific to represent shared retentions from Proto-Penutian. (For example, Alsea *tsuːlqw* 'blanket', Wintu *suloq* 'blanket, bedding', Patwin *suːx* 'blanket, mat'; Alsea *tluːqw* 'stagger, walk with a cane', Wintu *toloq* 'staff, cane'; Alsea *tqiːsa* 'acorn flour', Wintu *teqes* 'sifting basket'.) Unlike the structural borrowing of the Klamath-Modoc pronoun system, which probably resulted from the amalgamation of two speech communities, the shared Alsea-Wintuan vocabulary appears to represent a long-term trading relationship between adjacent groups.[23]

A final piece of linguistic evidence that locates the homeland of the Wintuan languages well outside of north-central California is negative—the absence in Wintuan of the polysynthethic "bipartite" verb stems that otherwise characterize all the languages of this region, both Hokan and Penutian (¶4.8.2). The most obvious explanation is that at the time the features of bipartite stem structure were diffusing through the California-Oregon area, the Wintuan speech community was beyond the range of these influences, probably somewhere to the north of the Takelma (DeLancey 1996). Interestingly, Wintuan does have a set of verb affixes that have locational-directional meaning, semantically equivalent to the final elements of typical bipartite verb stems, but these are prefixes or proclitics in Wintuan and clearly different in origin.

An estimated time depth of fifteen hundred years for the split between Northern and Southern Wintuan correlates well with the inception of the Augustine Pattern in the southern Sacramento Valley around 500–600 AD (Moratto 1984: 211–212). Among the distinctive features of the culture represented by the Augustine Pattern were intensive riverine fishing and the use of the bow and arrow, and it is widely interpreted to reflect the incursion of a new population into the area. In the northern part of the Sacramento Valley the archaeological record indicates a later development of the full Augustine Pattern (or Shasta Complex), around 800 AD, but the bow and arrow arrived independently a few centuries earlier, with the Tehama Pattern, which otherwise is a continuation of much older archaeological traditions usually associated with Hokan-speaking peoples (Clewett and Sundahl 1990:41–44).

The most likely scenario is that Wintuan-speaking invaders, armed with the bow and arrow, began entering parts of the Sacramento Valley from southern Oregon sometime before 500 AD. The area they first occupied— probably north of Colusa County—was probably Hokan territory, most likely Pomo, accounting for certain resemblances between Wintuan and Pomo phonology. They subsequently expanded into historic Patwin territory in the southwestern portion of the valley, encountering Miwok speakers from whom they borrowed many terms for the distinctive flora and fauna of the region (Whistler 1977a). The Patwin were still encroaching on Miwok and Pomo territory at the beginning of the historic period, most notably in the lower Napa Valley and along the north shore of San Pablo Bay as far west as Sonoma. In the Clear Lake region there is place-name evidence for a relatively recent expansion of Hill Patwin into formerly Miwok territory along Cache Creek, and the historic Lake Miwok speech community was under heavy influence from Patwin. This was in part associated with the diffusion of the Kuksu Cult, an elaborate intertribal ceremonial system that centered on

River Patwin territory in the southern Sacramento Valley (Kroeber 1932:391–420).

In the Wintu area, the absence of significant dialect boundaries in the mountainous areas to the north and west, contrasting with a clear dialectal layering in the upper Sacramento Valley, suggests the relatively recent expansion of Wintu out of a core territory south and east of Redding. This can be correlated with the spread of the Augustine Pattern north from Tehama county after 800 AD, almost certainly into a region previously occupied by Yana speakers (Clewett and Sundahl 1990:41–44). The movement was slow, possibly because of resistance from the Yana, who seem to have been displaced to the east rather than assimilated. It seems unlikely that Wintu speech was fully established in the more northerly and westerly parts of its historic territory any earlier than a few hundred years ago. The displacement or assimilation of Shastan speakers on the upper McCloud River and of the Chimariko in the Trinity drainage was still under way at the time of contact (Chase-Dunn and Mann 1998:119–123).

5.3.5 Klamath-Modoc

The Klamath Basin has been an area of extraordinary cultural stability since the beginning of the Archaic (Cressman 1956, 1977). The lakeside and marshland adaptations characteristic of the region developed early and were evidently shared with much of the Great Basin until the pluvial lakes began to contract during the dry conditions of the Altithermal. After 2500 BC, only in the Klamath Basin—in the shadow of the Cascades and with the external drainage of the Klamath River—was the lacustrine culture of the preceding millennia able to continue without significant alteration. Given this cultural and environmental continuity, it is likely that language has been equally stable, and that Klamath-Modoc, and more broadly the Plateau Penutian branch of the Penutian Phylum, has been associated with the Klamath Basin since at least 5000 BC.

Much of the eastern Oregon region occupied by the Northern Paiute in historic times was probably Plateau Penutian in linguistic affiliation until after 1000 AD, and perhaps as late as 1500 AD. There seems little doubt that Klamath-Modoc territory extended much farther to the east until comparatively recent times. According to an oral tradition reported by Isabel Kelly (1932:72, 186), the entire territory of the Groundhog-Eaters band of Northern Paiutes, including Surprise and Warner Valleys, belonged to the Klamath until the Northern Paiutes moved west of Steens Mountain and drove them out. Further south, the origin of the Maiduan family—which appears to be either part of, or closely connected to, the Plateau Penutian group—is probably to be sought in northeastern Nevada, east of Honey Lake, from where expanding Numic peoples are likely to have pushed them westward into the northern Sierra Nevada (Moratto 1984:562).

Speakers of other Penutian languages may well have occupied regions even further south and east in the Great Basin, including languages historically connected to Utian and Yokuts (Hattori 1982:208; Moratto 1984:552). It is entirely plausible, although far from demonstrable, that much of the territory into which the Western and Central Numic languages expanded was previously occupied by Penutians, and that Western Numic (Northern Paiute) mostly displaced languages closely related to Klamath-Modoc.

The presence of a few striking morphological borrowings from Klamath-Modoc into Wintuan, most notably the near-identity of a significant number of personal pronouns (DeLancey 1987, 1988a), is difficult to explain given the lack of any other evidence of sustained contact between speakers of the two languages.[24] The most likely explanation for the borrowing of a pronominal system in the absence of other lexical borrowing is that for a relatively short period in the past the speech community ancestral to modern Wintuan included substantial numbers of Klamath-Wintuan bilinguals.[25] The only region in which such an event could plausibly be imagined is Shasta Valley and the adjacent area along the upper Klamath River. This is historically the eastern part of Shasta territory, but the modern Shasta presence quite likely represents the recent repopulation of an area frequently affected by volcanic activity (the last major eruption of Mount Shasta occurred in 1786). At an earlier date Shasta Valley could well have been the homeland of a group of Klamath-Modoc speakers, overwhelmed and absorbed by southward-migrating Wintuans from western Oregon around 500 AD.

5.3.6 Maiduan

The likelihood that Maiduan either belongs to or is closely associated with the Plateau Penutian branch suggests that, before the speakers of proto-Maiduan moved into the Sierra Nevada, they were located somewhere in the northern Great Basin adjacent to speakers of Klamath-Modoc and/or Sahaptian. Since the diversification of Maiduan probably began around 800 AD, there is a possibility that the westward displacement of the Maiduan speech community was stimulated by the expansion of the Numic languages (Moratto 1984:562).

That three of the four historic Maiduan languages were located in the northern third of Maiduan territory indicates a southward spread, probably from a Proto-Maiduan homeland in the Feather River drainage. Given the quite shallow differences among the languages, this spread could not have begun before 800–1000 AD. It is significant that the ethnographically salient boundary between foothill and valley cultures (cf. Kroeber 1929) cuts across both the Konkow and Nisenan languages and is reflected only by low-order dialectal differences. This situation interestingly contrasts with the presence of a sharp language (or even language family) discontinuity elsewhere along the eastern edge of the Central Valley—that is, the boundary that separates the Wintu from the Yana, the Plains Miwok from the Sierra Miwok, the Northern Valley and Delta Yokuts from the Sierra Miwok, and the Southern Valley Yokuts from the Foothill Yokuts. All these linguistic boundaries were well established before the beginning of the cultural elaborations of the Late Period circa 1400 AD. Nisenan and Konkow, however, seem to have spread westward only in the last few centuries, long after the large villages along the Sacramento and lower Feather Rivers had developed a society quite distinct from that of the foothills.

The presence in Nisenan, but not in the three other Maiduan languages, of a significant number of widespread Central California loanwords, argues for a recent non-Maiduan, probably Miwok, substratum in the Nisenan area. At a historically deeper level, all Maiduan languages have a set of fully voiced stops, an unusual phonological feature among the languages of the Far West that is otherwise found only in Washo, Wintuan, Pomo, and Tubatulabal. Of these, only Washo is like Maiduan in contrasting the voiced stops with plain and glottalized stops, while lacking aspirated stops. The probability is high that this phonological profile diffused from Washo into Maiduan, most likely through Washo being substratal in all or part of Proto-Maiduan territory.

5.3.7 Yok-Utian

There is increasing evidence that Yokuts and Utian constitute a distinct "Yok-Utian" branch of Penutian (Callaghan 1997a, 2001). If so, two lines of evidence suggest that the homeland of the group lay in the Great Basin, not in California. On the one hand, archaeological connections between the Windmiller Pattern and northern Great Basin and Plateau traditions, most notably the Lovelock Culture of northwestern Nevada, suggest a migration into California from the east and northeast around 2500 BC (Moratto 1984:552), which is approximately the estimated time depth of Proto-Yok-Utian. On the other hand, Callaghan (personal communication) has noted that, while a considerable range of semantic areas is represented in the apparently cognate Yok-Utian vocabulary, terms for the distinctive flora and fauna of Central California are noticeably lacking; by contrast, a number of reconstructed Proto-Utian words refer to characteristic features of the California ecosystem. The most likely scenario, therefore, is that the split between Proto-Utian and Proto-Yokuts occurred when the people who gave rise to the Utians moved into California, around 2500 BC. The ancestors of the Yokuts would have remained in the Great Basin and entered California later, probably by a separate and more southerly route.

5.3.8 Yokuts

The fact that few significant phonological and grammatical differences separate the Yokuts dialect subgroups, along with the likelihood that most if not all of the scores of

dialects were mutually intelligible, indicates a relatively recent date for Proto-Yokuts, conceivably as late as 600 to 700 AD (Kroeber 1963). If the linguistic ancestors of the Yokuts were those Yok-Utians who remained in the western Great Basin after the migration of the Utians into California at the beginning of the Windmiller period, Yokuts can represent only a small fraction of the linguistic diversity that must have accumulated in this speech community over the millennia after the Yokuts-Utian split. Proto-Yokuts probably was but one of a multitude of Great Basin Yok-Utian languages—the dialect of a few hundred people who resettled across the crest of the southern Sierra Nevada, possibly around Tehachapi Pass. However, none of the other languages survive: all eradicated, one can hypothesize, by the Numic expansion.[26]

Kroeber (1959a:269–275) believed that the ethnographic locations of the major dialect subgroups were best explained by assuming that the original diversification of the language took place in the southern half of the valley. In his reconstruction, dialects ancestral to the Poso Creek, Tule-Kaweah, Kings River, and Valley subgroups were spoken in a south-to-north chain in the Sierra foothills. Another chain of dialects, of which only the Buena Vista subgroup survived into the historic period, was spoken around Tulare, Buena Vista, and Kern Lakes on the valley floor. About five hundred years ago, speakers of Western Mono moving across across the Sierra Nevada from Owens Valley pushed the northernmost Foothill group downstream into the valley. Some moved south, displacing speakers of Buena Vista dialects around Tulare Lake and eventually (as the ethnographic Koyeti and Yawelmani) reaching the bottom of the valley. Others moved north, down the San Joaquin River, where they probably replaced Miwoks and Wintuans in the Delta region north of the Merced.

Whether or not Kroeber's scenario is accurate in all its details, some such rearrangement in relatively recent times of an original north-to-south chain of Yokuts dialects seems likely. Further, the fact that the most specialized of the dialect subgroups (Poso Creek and Buena Vista) were spoken at the southern end of Yokuts territory suggests that the Proto-Yokuts homeland was located in the vicinity of the lower Kern River and Tehachapi Pass.

The friendly relationships in the historic period among the Valley Yokuts, the Salinans, and the Chumash, including some degree of Yokuts-Salinan bilingualism in Migueleño Salinan territory, appears to have been of long standing. This fact, and a degree of phonological convergence among the three languages, supports the hypothesis that Salinan-like and Chumash-like languages formed the substratum for Proto-Yokuts in the southern San Joaquin Valley.

5.3.9 Utian

The time depth of the Miwok-Costanoan split appears to be on the order of 3,000 to 3,500 years. The reconstructed plant and animal lexicon of Proto-Utian suggests that the homeland of the family was located somewhere in the interior of central California, most likely in the Sacramento–San Joaquin Delta. The linguistic evidence thus indicates a correlation between the Proto-Utian community and the cultural features of the Windmiller Pattern, which developed in the Delta area after 2500 BC. The expansion of the Windmiller Pattern into the Coast Range and the San Francisco Bay area after 2000 BC can be taken as tracking the westward expansion of Utian speech at this period. Moratto suggests that the emergence of the Berkeley Pattern "represents a fusion of older Hokan (mostly Esselen?) and intrusive Utian cultural elements in the Bay Area" (1984:553).

5.3.10 Miwok

In the most likely scenario, Proto-Miwok became a distinct dialect of Utian, separate from the precursor of Costanoan, sometime between 1000 and 500 BC and probably in the mountains north of San Francisco Bay between Napa County and the Sacramento Valley. Reconstructible plant terms indicate a noncoastal environment with access to high mountains, foothills, woodlands, wet slopes, and probably valley grasslands (Callaghan 1997a:18–19). A subsequent spread into Marin and southern Sonoma Counties seems to have been accompanied by the borrowing or innovation of terms for the distinctive plants and animals of the coastal ecosystem; there is some indication that Yukian (early Wappo) may have been the precursor language in part of this area. Miwok speakers also spread eastward into the Central Valley, which Moratto (1984:555–557) correlates with the spread of the Berkeley Pattern into the Central Valley, displacing the Windmiller Pattern, after 500 BC. The linguistic data indicate that the split between the Eastern and Western branches of Miwok began about this time, initially representing dialectal divisions correlated with the diverse environments in which the language had come to be spoken.

Whistler (1977a) has identified a number of words for plants and animals in Patwin that have no cognates in Wintu but that resemble forms with similar meanings in Miwok, many of them reconstructible to Proto-Miwok. Although the Patwin were in contact in the historical period with both Lake (Western) and Plains (Eastern) Miwok, Whistler believes these borrowings are from an early Miwok language that occupied the southern Sacramento Valley before the Patwin. Several of the words refer to the distinctive environment of Central California (including terms for digger pine, live oak, manzanita, buckeye, and redwood), and he sees them as evidence that the Wintuan languages were originally spoken in an area with a distinctly different ecology, most likely southwestern Oregon (see ¶5.3.4).

If Whistler is correct, it seems likely that many of the distinctive differences between Western and Eastern Miwok are attributable to the geographical separation of the two groups by the Patwin intrusion, which appears to have begun shortly after 500 AD (Moratto 1984:211–214). This is also roughly the time depth of the Sierra Miwok split from Plains Miwok. The speakers of Sierra Miwok apparently remained in a small, linguistically undifferentiated area for several centuries before spreading southward and developing the modern dialect boundaries, none of which appear to be more than five hundred to seven hundred years old.

The linguistic differences between Coast Miwok and Lake Miwok can be accounted for by assuming that the initial expansion of the early Western Miwoks reached as far north as Lake County, including both historic Lake Miwok territory and much or all of Wappo territory. After the Yukian Wappos occupied the Alexander and Napa Valleys around 500 AD, the now-isolated Lake Miwok community came under heavy Patwin cultural influence, resulting in extensive borrowing of vocabulary and rapid phonological change.

5.3.11 Costanoan

If Proto-Miwok became a distinct Utian language not long after 1000 BC in the area to the north of San Francisco Bay, the shallow time depth of Costanoan diversification suggests that it may be the sole survivor of a more deeply differentiated group of non-Miwok Utian languages that developed elsewhere in Utian territory. Levy (1978b:486) locates the Proto-Costanoan homeland in in the Sacramento–San Joaquin Delta and proposes that an expansion west and south from there was correlated with the cultural changes of the Late Horizon. The likely presence of borrowings from Esselen in Karkin and other San Francisco Bay Costanoan languages (see ¶5.2.11) may indicate that some of this expansion was into territory not previously occupied by Utians.

In an alternative speculation, Moratto (1984:553–557) sees an early movement of (Proto) Utian speakers into the San Francisco Bay area around 2000 BC, where they were responsible for the distinctive archaeological innovations of the Berkeley Pattern after 1500 BC. The Costanoan-Miwok split would have occurred in the Bay Area not long after this time, but the diversity within the historic Costanoan family would not have begun to accumulate until after 500 BC, when Costanoan speakers began moving south into the Monterey Bay area. This date, however, is too early to be easily correlated with the attested diversity of Costanoan, which cannot be more than two thousand years old, and is probably closer to fifteen hundred. Levy's correlation of Costanoan expansion with the beginning of the Late Horizon seems more plausible.

Whatever the earlier scenario, nearly all archaeological speculation envisages a late expansion of Costanoan south into the Monterey Bay area at the expense of one or more Hokan languages, the most likely candidate being Esselen. Substratal influences from Esselen are especially visible in Rumsen (see ¶3.28.4).

5.4 Uto-Aztecan

5.4.1 The Uto-Aztecan Homeland and Early Migrations

The time depth of the Uto-Aztecan family is generally estimated to be in excess of five thousand years, and it is often compared to that of Indo-European. In a series of studies, Fowler (1972a, 1972b, 1983) argued that the plant and animal terms that can be attributed to the Proto-Uto-Aztecan vocabulary strongly suggest that the center of Uto-Aztecan dispersal was located somewhere between the eastern Mojave Desert and northern Sonora and Chihuahua, identifying the Proto-Uto-Aztecans with the Desert Archaic Culture of the Southwest about 3000 BC. Over the ensuing two millennia these foragers slowly spread southward, establishing communities ancestral to Tepiman and Taracahitic across much of northwestern Mexico and bringing the ancestral Aztecans, Cora, and Huichol to the border of Mesoamerica. By 500 BC, speakers of Aztecan dialects had begun to infiltrate Mesoamerica itself, eventually establishing the Toltec and Aztec empires of the Classic and Post-Classic period.

In this view, which is widely held by both linguists and archaeologists and is reflected also in the work of Goss (1968) and Kenneth Hale (1958–1959), the division between the Northern and Southern branches of Uto-Aztecan is the result of the gradual separation from the Proto-Uto-Aztecan speech community of the migrants into western and central Mexico. Meanwhile, Northern Uto-Aztecan (which, rather than being a separate geolinguistic entity, may never have been more than the northern dialects in a contiguous Proto-Uto-Aztecan chain) began to diversify into a western subgroup associated with the sedentary seed-processing societies of central and southern California and an eastern subgroup associated with the development and diffusion of Hohokam and Anasazi irrigation horticulture. The northward expansion of Yuman languages along the Colorado and into northern Arizona may also have played a role in this division, but whether as a cause or as a consequence is uncertain.

Several alternative to this scenario have been proposed, two of which—Michael J. P. Nichols's Northern Basin hypothesis and Jane Hill's Mesoamerican hypothesis—warrant our attention here.

Nichols (1981), arguing that numerous lexical similarities between California languages and Uto-Aztecan indicate an ancient period of borrowing between Uto-Aztecan and "Old California" languages, proposed that the Proto-Uto-Aztecan homeland did not lie in Arizona or Sonora, as Fowler's studies have suggested, but in the northwestern Great Basin in historic Northern Paiute territory. In Nichols's scenario, early Uto-Aztecan speakers moved westward as the Basin grew increasingly desiccated and eventually came to occupy much of central California, including the entire Central Valley. These "Old California Uto-Aztecans," as Nichols styles them, were followed by a second wave of immigrants from the Basin, mainly Penutian speakers, who displaced the Uto-Aztecans from nearly all of the Central Valley, except on the upper Kern River, where the ancestors of the Tubatulabal held out.

Although supported by little systematic evidence (Nichols 1981 was followed up only by one slim paper in 1998), the Old California hypothesis has attracted support from some archaeologists, most notably Sutton, whose recent model of the Takic expansion (Sutton 2009) has Uto-Aztecan speakers entering Southern California about 1500 BC from the north, pushed out of the Central Valley by Penutians.

Jane Hill, by contrast, locates the Uto-Aztecan homeland as far to the south of Arizona and Sonora as Nichols located it to the north, in early maize-farming communities on the northern periphery of Mesoamerica. She has laid out this scenario in a series of papers (most importantly, Hill 2001, but see also 2002a, 2003, 2008), all rich in linguistic data. Her strongest evidence is a set of Hopi terms relating to maize farming that are cognate with Southern Uto-Aztecan terms with the same or closely related meanings. This shared agricultural vocabulary, she argues, must either be attributed to Proto-Uto-Aztecan or represent the early intrusion of Uto-Aztecan farmers into the Southwest.[27] She prefers the former hypothesis and argues that the ancestors of the four Northern Uto-Aztecan groups and the Tepiman group of Southern Uto-Aztecans introduced maize cultivation into the Southwest when they entered the Southwest from Mexico between 1500 and 1000 BC. Loanwords indicate that they passed along maize cultivation to the ancestral Kiowa Tanoan at an early date,[28] but apparently not to other groups, since the maize vocabularies of the Yuman languages, Zuni, and Keresan seem all to be quite independent both of one another and of Uto-Aztecan. However, there is evidence of Uto-Aztecan (primarily Tepiman) involvement in the development of an area-wide religious and ritual system culture during the Hohokam period (after 200 AD) in the form of numerous loanwords shared among Yuman, Tepiman, Keresan, and Zuni that appear to date to this time (Shaul and Hill 1998).[29]

5.4.2 Northern Uto-Aztecan and the Sierra Nevada

In the historic period, languages belonging to three of the four generally recognized branches of Northern Uto-Aztecan—Numic, Takic, Tubatulabal—adjoined one another in the southern Sierra Nevada between Kern River and Tejon Pass. Only Hopi was absent. Also spoken in this area was the very poorly attested Giamina/Omomil language, which possibly represents a fifth Northern Uto-Aztecan branch. Such a concentration of diversity in itself suggests that the homeland of Proto–Northern Uto-Aztecan, which Wick Miller (1983) estimated to have existed around 3500 BP, at least included—if it was not entirely restricted to—the southern Sierra Nevada. This is the position taken by Sutton (2009), and it appears to be corroborated by internal diversity in both Numic and Takic that can be interpreted as reflecting relatively recent expansion northeastward (in the case of Numic) and southwestward (in the case of Takic) from a southern Sierra Nevada base. From the same perspective, Tubatulabal (possibly together with Giamina/Omomil) can be seen as the product of in situ development near the center of dispersal of the Numic and Takic branches.

Any such scenario, however, must also explain the location of Hopi, the remaining Northern Uto-Aztecan branch. In the historic period Hopi was spoken only in the Pueblo villages on the Hopi mesas east of the Grand Canyon, nearly five hundred miles from the southern Sierra Nevada. The linking territory—the high plateau north and west of the modern Hopi, from the Four Corners to the Mojave Desert—was occupied in historic times by speakers of Southern Paiute, hunters and gatherers who reached the area as part of the Numic expansion around 1200 AD (Lyneis 1995). Their predecessors were Western Anasazi village farmers, who had developed and maintained small-scale agriculture in the area northwest of the Colorado River for at least two millennia. If the Northern Uto-Aztecan homeland lay in California, then the ancestors of the Hopis could have followed a route similar to the one followed by the ancestors of the Southern Paiutes centuries later, adopting a farming culture as they entered the Western Anasazi area and merging with the bearers of that tradition.

The more likely possibility is that the ancestral Hopi *were* the originators of the Western Anasazi tradition and that at one point—perhaps before the northward migration of the Yumans had brought them into the Colorado River Valley—there existed "an east-west continuum of [Northern] Uto-Aztecans extending from the Hopi in Arizona (probably in the area of the later Western or Kayenta Anasazi development) to Takic in California" (K. Hale and Harris 1979:175). A similar position has been espoused by Jane Hill, who goes further to argue that the Western Anasazi region was the homeland of *all* Northern Uto-Aztecan linguistic groups. In her scenario, speakers of the early Northern Uto-Aztecan dialects ancestral to Takic, Numic, and Tubatulabal migrated westward, gradually abandoning farming as they moved into regions where it was difficult to sustain.[30] Hill identifies her Proto-Northern Uto-Aztecan community archaeologically with the early maize farmers of Western Basketmaker II, which would date them to around 1500 BC (J. Hill 2002a, 2006). While this estimate is consistent with linguistic estimates of the time depth of Northern Uto-Aztecan (K. Hale 1958–1959:101–107), it does not correlate well with the archaeological evidence for a substantial population displacement that took place in southern California at about the same time, unless the intrusive population spoke a relatively undifferentiated Northern Uto-Aztecan. If, however, Tubatulabal, Takic, and Numic became established in California later than 1500 BC, the apparently deep linguistic differences among them require explanation. One possibility is that these differences could reflect diversity that had evolved before the migration. Another, somewhat more controversial, possbility is that the diversity could be attributed to rapid linguistic change stimulated by communicative isolation and by the special sociolinguistic conditions in the California culture area (Golla 2000; J. Hill 2006).

5.4.3 Takic and Tubatulabal

The deepest split in the Takic branch is between Serrano-Kitanemuk and the rest. The split is so deep that Jane Hill (2009), following a proposal made earlier by Manaster Ramer (1992b), suggests abandoning "Takic" entirely for a model that would identify a "Californian" branch whose first subbranching would be between Serrano-Kitanemuk on the one hand and Tubatulabal-Gabrielino-Cupan on the other. In contrast to this great diversity in the northern half of Takic territory, the Cupan languages (Luiseño-Juaneño, Cupeño, and Cahuilla) are quite close to one another, at least in phonology and lexicon, and seem to represent a relatively recent southward spread of Takic speech. It is likely that the Cupan expansion began on the southern and eastern borders of Gabrielino territory with the precursors of the Juaneño and Luiseño moving south along the coast, and the precursors of the Cahuilla and Cupeño moving through the interior. The presence of Yuman-like features in Cupan phonology and grammar suggests that at least part of Cupan territory was previously occupied by speakers of Diegueño or other Yuman languages (Sproat 1981; Hinton 1991; Elliott 1994), although lexical evidence for a Yuman substratum is sparse (W. Bright and M. Bright 1969).[31]

A period of (renewed) contact between Hopi and the Takic languages seems to have begun around 500 AD. At this time the archaeology of the eastern Mojave Desert shows a major discontinuity that appears to be linked to the expansion of the Western Anasazi from the Virgin River area of southern Nevada as far west as Halloran Spring and Soda Lake (Warren and Crabtree 1986:189–191). Since the Western Anasazi were closely connected to the ancestral Hopi, some of the distinctly "Puebloid" features of Takic religion and ceremony, possibly including complex ritual speech patterns (see ¶4.13.1), might have found their way into California around this time.

5.4.4 Numic

It was Kroeber's belief, at least in his early work, that varieties of the "Plateau branch of Shoshonean" (i.e., the Numic branch of Northern Uto-Aztecan) had been spoken in the Great Basin "from time immemorial" (1925:580) and that the shallow diversification of the modern Numic languages represented a situation of linguistic stasıs, a "steady state" of dialect diversity that was correlated with the nomadic band societies of the region and, like them, had persisted over millennia. The growth of linguistic and archaeological data, as well as more recent views of the linguistic dynamics of thinly populated regions, have made Kroeber's scenario increasingly unlikely. By far the most plausible explanation for the relative lack of linguistic diversity in the Great Basin is that speakers of Numic dialects have only recently occupied the region.

The currently favored model of Numic expansion locates the center of dispersal in the southwestern Basin. The fact that the three Numic dialect chains radiate out from a small area along the east side of the Sierra Nevada, and that the dialects are most differentiated at the southwestern end of each chain, can be taken as evidence for an expansion of Numic north and east from the area between Mono Lake and Owens Lake that was historically occupied by speakers of Mono, Panamint, and Kawaiisu (Lamb 1958a). The estimate of a thousand years for the time depth of the split between the Numic dialect chains correlates well with archaeological indications of a change of subsistence strategies and social structures in the Great Basin beginning about 1200 AD (Bettinger and Baumhoff 1982). The three subbranches, in addition to being correlated with three different population movements, may also reflect different substratal languages. Western and Central Numic probably replaced either Penutian languages (Maiduan, Klamath-Modoc, Molala, and Sahaptian) or Hokan languages (Washo and Palaihnihan). Southern Numic, however, expanded into territory in which Anasazi Pueblo influence had been strong, and possibly replaced either a Kiowa-Tanoan language or another Northern Uto-Aztecan language, most likely connected to Hopi.

Several lines of linguistic and cultural evidence support this model. That the Numic homeland was located near the Sierra Nevada is supported by reconstructed terms for plants and animals, which suggest an environment with oaks and piñons and well supplied with water (Fowler 1972b). An earlier Numic occupation of the western and southern Basin and a later occupation of the north and east is indicated by an increase in the analyzability of place-names as one moves eastward (Goss 1968). Oral tradition—particularly origin myths and tales of population movements—yields evidence that the Numic peoples moved north and east into the Great Basin from its southwest corner (Sutton 1993). Of particular interest is the claim made by the Northern Paiute of the Humboldt Sink that they encountered a foreign tribe called the Saidukah or Sairuqa when they first entered the area from the south. The two groups fought, and the Saidukah were eventually expelled after a final battle at Lovelock Cave (Heizer 1970:241–242).[32]

An ancient relationship between the Great Basin and the southern Sierra Nevada is also indicated by a close resemblance between the otherwise unique twined basketry of all Numic-speaking groups and that of the Tubatulabal and Yokuts (Fowler and Dawson 1986:728–729).

An alternative hypothesis, locating the Numic homeland in and around the territory of the Virgin River Anasazi in southern Nevada and southwestern Utah, has had its adherents (Gunnerson 1962). A variant of this proposal has recently been put forward by Jane Hill (2003), as a component of her more general hypothesis that the Uto-Aztecan family originated in Mesoamerica (see ¶5.4.1). In her reconstruction, Proto-Numic arose out of the dialects that were spoken on the northern edge of the territory in the Southwest that had been occupied since 1000 BC by Uto-Aztecan-speaking cultivators moving north from Mexico. The reconstructibility in Proto-Numic of a number of words that point to a former acquaintance with horticulture seems to support her argument. Like Gunnerson earlier, she sees a "devolution" from farming to foraging in this area, followed by the expansion northward of groups who would become the Shoshoni, northwestward by groups who would become the Mono and Northern Paiute, and southwestward by groups that would become the western Southern Paiute, the Chemehuevi, and the Kawaiisu. She explains the dialectal complexity of the Mono-Panamint-Kawaiisu area as the result of rapid innovation as Numic dialects were incorporated into the communicational matrix of the California area.[33]

5.5 Algic

Specialists in Algonquian linguistics generally estimate the time depth of that family to be about three thousand years (Proulx 1981:14; M. Foster 1996:98–100). Algic as a whole is perhaps a millennium older. If Algonquian, Wiyot, and Yurok are coordinate branches of Algic, the differentiation of Yurok and Wiyot could have been under way as early as 2000 BC. If Ritwan is a valid subgroup, the split between the two languages would have begun more recently, possibly as late as the 300 BC date calculated by Swadesh (1959) on the basis of resemblances in vocabulary.

That the divergence between Yurok and Wiyot may date back four millennia, and that the lowest estimate is around 2,300 years, presents a considerable problem for prehistoric reconstruction. The most straightforward interpretation of the linguistic evidence would locate the Proto-Algic homeland in or near northern California, but this is a considerable distance from the westernmost of the proposed Proto-Algonquian homelands, on the northern Plains.[34] However, it is equally difficult to imagine circumstances under which Pre-Yurok and Pre-Wiyot speakers would have migrated separately to the same remote part of the northern California coast from a distant starting point. The hypothetical Proto-Algic homeland that would best fit the geographical facts would be on the Columbia Plateau, somewhere in the region historically occupied by the Sahaptians and the Interior Salish.[35] From here, people ancestral to the speakers of Proto-Algonquians could have expanded east to the Plains and beyond, while the ancestors of the Yuroks and Wiyots could have followed several plausible routes to the Oregon and northern California coast (Denny 1991; M. Foster 1996:97).

Archaeologists have frequently speculated that the appearance of the sophisticated fishing technology of the Gunther Complex in northwestern California between 500 and 900 AD might somehow be correlated with the arrival in the area of Yurok-, Wiyot- and Athabaskan-speaking groups from the north. One possible scenario would locate a "Ritwan" speech community ancestral to Yurok and Wiyot in north-central Oregon, roughly in the area occupied in the historic period by the Upper Chinook and Molala. In this location they would have been on the southern periphery of Northwest Coast cultural developments, thus explaining fundamental structural similarities in kin term systems that the Yurok and Wiyot share with the Coast Salish-, Chimakuan-, and Wakashan-speaking peoples of Puget Sound and Vancouver Island (Kroeber 1934). A "Ritwan" homeland in Oregon is also consistent with Moratto's observation of the "remarkable likeness of [late prehistoric northwest California] assemblages to those of the mid–Columbia River country" (1984:564–565, Table 11.3). This early Yurok-Wiyot community in northern Oregon would have been displaced to the south by intrusive Athabaskan raiders and other population movements around 500–700 AD.

For this scenario to be correct, given the deep differences between the two languages, the ancestors of the Wiyots and Yuroks would have had to enter northwestern California as two linguistically well-differentiated groups which, purely by chance, settled in small territories immediately adjacent to one another. The only other possibility is that the structural differences between the two languages are not, as they would seem, the product of several millennia of accumulated change, but result from special local processes of linguistic change and differentiation that operated with unprecedented speed. Neither alternative is clearly indicated by the data.[36]

A more plausible reconstruction would separate the recent prehistory of the Wiyots and the Yuroks, and would have speakers of early Wiyot establishing themselves in the Humboldt Bay area considerably earlier than ancestral Yurok speakers did in the Klamath River area. If we imagine an early "Ritwan" speech community occupying in pre-Gunther Complex times not just north-central Oregon but a territory that extended (not necessarily continuously) south along the Coast Range to Cape Mendocino, historic Wiyot might represent the survival of a southerly segment of this chain more or less in situ. Historic Yurok, however, could represent the speech of a group originally located much further north that was displaced to the Klamath River several centuries later as a consequence of the Athabaskan invasion. The appearance of the Gunther Complex in northwestern California would thus be linked to the arrival of Yurok speakers in particular, not of the "Ritwan" languages in general.[37]

Further support for the hypothesis that Wiyot has a longer history in northwestern California than Yurok comes from the structural resemblances that exist between Wiyot and Karuk—a language likely to have been established in the area for several millennia—and that are not shared with Yurok, although the Wiyots in the historic period were separated from the Karuks by Yurok territory. These resemblances are especially striking in phonology: Wiyot and Karuk are the only languages of the area to lack glottalized consonants; they both have a voiced bilabial fricative; they both have a flap r [ɾ]; and they both have a pitch-accent system involving a contrast between a stressed high-pitch syllable and a stressed falling-pitch syllable (cf. also Bauman and Silver 1975).

5.6 Athabaskan

The Athabaskan language family is second only to Uto-Aztecan in the extent of its dispersal in aboriginal North America. In addition to the branches in northwestern California and southwestern Oregon, Athabaskan languages were (and largely continue to be) spoken from the Yukon River to western Texas, and from the Pacific Coast to Hudson Bay. Unlike Uto-Aztecan, however, Athabaskan is not deeply diversified. Estimates of its time depth range between 1,500 and 2,200 years (Hoijer 1956; Hymes 1957; Kroeber 1959a:241–258; Krauss and Golla 1981:68). This shallow diversity reflects the rapid spread of Athabaskan-speaking foraging bands from a prehistoric homeland in the subarctic forests of northwestern Canada.

5.6.1 Pacific Coast Athabaskans

All three of the Pacific Coast branches probably had their origin in central British Columbia. The southward movement of ancestral Pacific Coast Athabaskan speakers probably began early in the Athabaskan diaspora and seems to have been complete by 1200 AD. Moving in small raiding parties, their general route must have followed the Columbia River across the Plateau and through the Cascades to the Pacific.[38] After reaching the lower Columbia River, some of these early Athabaskan migrants apparently struck south along either the Cascades or the Coast Range, and possibly both, encountering and displacing Penutian, Hokan, and Algic speakers in various parts of western Oregon and northwestern California.

There is no linguistic evidence (such as shared lexical innovations for the distinctive flora, fauna, and cultural features of the region) to suggest that the ancestors of the California, Oregon, and Lower Columbia Athabaskans had a common homeland along the Pacific Coast. It is thus a plausible assumption that the Pacific Coast Athabaskan migration occurred in two or more stages or pulses. The different degrees of internal diversity within the branches indicate that California Athabaskans may have been settled in their historic area by 700 AD, while the Oregon Athabaskans may not have arrived until around 1000 AD. The homogeneity of Lower Columbia River Athabaskan suggests an even later arrival. That there was some connection between the Athabaskan invasions and other ethnic movements in southern Oregon and northern California at roughly the same date seems highly likely (see in particular the discussion of Wintuan prehistory in ¶5.3.4).

5.6.2 Later Developments in Southwest Oregon and Northwest California

Southward-migrating Athabaskans rapidly infiltrated the eastern side of the coast range from the Umpqua Valley south to the Illinois Valley, displacing earlier Kalapuyan, Takelma, and possibly Wintuan and Algic inhabitants. A largely in situ differentiation into a dialect chain then followed, with Upper Umpqua, Upper Coquille, and Galice-Applegate representing the continuation of this core area into the historical period. Occupation of the Curry and Del Norte County coastline resulted from a slow, secondary expansion downstream along the Coquille, Rogue, and Smith Rivers, which probably absorbed Coosan-speaking populations in the north and Ritwan speakers further south. Chetco-Tolowa, with its numerous distinctive traits, probably represents the rapid transformation of a Rogue River dialect in a multilingual setting where the majority of speakers were non-Athabaskans.

Since California Athabaskan languages share their terms for "bow" and "arrow" (as well as words for specific details of bow-and-arrow technology) with Athabaskan languages in Canada and Alaska, there can be little doubt that the first Athabaskans to settle in northwestern California arrived no earlier than 500–600 AD, the estimated date of the first appearance in the region of projectile points associated with the bow and arrow (Blitz 1988). Since the internal differentiation in California Athabaskan reflects a time depth of about a thousand years, the most likely date of Athabaskan entry thus lies between 700 and 900 AD. The pattern of diversification suggests an early split between Hupa-Chilula and the rest, but since at least one important grammatical innovation (the reinterpretation of the indefinite subject and areal object/possessor prefixes as animate third person prefixes) links Hupa-Chilula to Kato, the dialectal groups may possibly have had a different geographical relationship during early stages of differentiation. (An equally likely explanation of the Hupa-Kato innovation, however, is that it was separately stimulated by a period of bilingualism with an adjacent Hokan language: Chimariko in the case of Hupa-Chilula, Northern Pomo in the case of Kato. See Golla 2011.)

The pre-Athabaskan distribution of languages in northwestern Californa may be partially inferred from patterns of differentiation among the Athabaskan dialects. As noted earlier, some of the distinctive phonological traits of Hupa-Chilula may be due to substratal Karuk or Wiyot influence (Bauman and Silver 1975). The merger of the lateral affricate ƛ' with t' in most of the Eel River dialects, together with the identical merger in Chetco-Tolowa, is possibly to be explained by a Ritwan substratum in both areas (both Yurok and Wiyot have a lateral fricative [ɬ] but lack the corresponding affricate). A Yukian substratum beneath Wailaki and Kato is likely on cultural and geographical grounds, but specific linguistic influences from Yukian are not easy to identify in either language, other than a few Yuki loanwords in Kato such as ʔal 'firewood' (Golla 2000).

C. Hart Merriam's Vocabularies and Natural History
Word Lists for California Indian Languages

A.1 The Merriam Papers

Most of C. Hart Merriam's data on California Indian languages (see ¶2.7.1) are contained in standardized vocabularies of two types, general word lists and natural history word lists, both of which he collected in printed booklets devised for the purpose. His methods and goals were essentially the same ones that guided his field collection of animal and plant specimens, that is, to document the variation in a species (in this case a language "stock") by collecting a standard sample of each of its identifiable variants or types (its "dialects"). His usual working procedure was to visit speakers of a given dialect on repeated occasions, often years apart, adding words to the vocabulary lists until they were filled out as completely as possible.

The dialect that each vocabulary represented was coded and filed according to Merriam's own classificatory scheme, which evolved as his data accumulated. The classification that he was using in the 1930s, near the end of his work, is shown in Table A.1.

Merriam made duplicate copies of all of his vocabulary booklets and kept these at his Washington, DC, residence. The originals remained in California at the house in Lagunitas, Marin County, which served as his base for California fieldwork. After his death in 1942, the duplicate vocabularies, together with all his other papers in Washington, were donated by Merriam's heirs to the Library of Congress. The originals in Lagunitas, however, were turned over to Robert Heizer, whom the Smithsonian Institution—the trustee of the fund that had been set up by E. H. Harriman to subsidize Merriam's research—appointed the custodian and editor of the material. Over the course of the next twnety-five years Heizer supervised the publication of substantial portions of the vocabularies and associated manuscripts (see ¶2.7.1), but access to the original materials was limited (Table A.1).[1] Following Heizer's death in 1979, the Merriam manuscripts that had been in his charge were transferred to the Bancroft Library, where they are now accessible in a microfilm edition (Merriam 1898–1938). The Washington materials (which include Merriam's field journals as well as the copies he made of his vocabularies) are available for study in the Manuscripts Division of the Library of Congress (http://lccn.loc.gov/mm 82032698). A complete photocopy of Merriam's field journals is on file in the Anthropology Collections, Department of Anthropology, UC Davis.

A.2 List of Vocabularies

All the vocabularies listed here, whether they are archived in the Bancroft Libary or in the Library of Congress, bear a catalog number in the following format:

Stock/dialect/manuscript type and number

The stock and dialect are identified by an initial capital letter, followed after a slash by a number and lowercase letter that locates the dialect in the classification outlined in Table A.1. Following a second slash, the type of manuscript is identified—V (vocabulary), NH (natural history word list), or in a few instances BL (brief linguistic recordings, i.e., short files of miscellaneous data)—and is assigned a manuscript number. Manuscripts of a given type are numbered sequentially (V1, V2, etc).

Vocabularies in the Bancroft Library at the University of California, Berkeley (UCB) are further identified by a reel number in square brackets, referring to the location of the manuscript in the microfilm of the collection. Vocabularies in the Manuscripts Division of the Library of Congress (LC) are further identifed by their storage carton number.

Although the arrangement of the vocabularies follows Merriam's classification, the names of language families and languages are the ones used elsewhere in this book. If it differs, Merriam's "stock" name is given in quotation marks. Merriam's version of the language or dialect name, as it appears on the manuscript, is given in italics.

A. Athapascan Stock

  1a. Tolowa or Huss

  Hoopa Group

  1b. Hoopa or Tin'-nung-hen-na'-o

  1c. Ma'-we-nok

  1d. 'Hwil'-kut

  1e. Tsa'-nung-wha

  Wilakke Group or Nung'-hahl

  1f. Mat-tol'

  1g. Lo-lahn'-kok

  1h. To-cho'-be

  1i. Lassick or Ket-tel'

  1j. Set-ten-bi'-den

  1k. Tsen-nah'-ken-nes

  1l. Che-teg'-ge-kah

  1m. Bah-ne-ko ke'-ah

  1n. Nek'-kan-ni

  1o. Kahto or To-chil-pe-ke'ah-hahng

B. Polikla Stock [Yurok]

  2a. Ner'-er-ner'

  2b. Polikla

C. Soolahteluk Stock [Wiyot]

  3a. Pah'-te-wat

  3b. We'-ke

  3c. We'-yot

D. Yukean Stock [Northern Yukian]

  Northwestern or Coast Division [Coast Yuki]

  4a. Oo'-ko-ton-til'-kah

  Round Valley Division [Yuki]

  4b. Oo'-ko-ton-til'-kah

  4c. Kah'-shut-sit'-nu

  Upper South Eel Division [Hutchnom]

  4d. Hootch'-nom

  4e. Wet-oo'-kum-nom

  4f. Tah'-too or Nar'-ko-po-mah

  4g. On-kal-oo'-kum-nom

E. Mi-yahk'-mah [Wappo]

  4h. Mish'-a-wel band

4i. Moo'-tis'-tool band

4j. Mi-yahk-mah band

4k. Lil'-lak [Clear Lake]

F. Lutuamean Stock [Klamath-Modoc]

  5a. Mo'-dok

G. Shastan Stock

  6a. Ko'-no-me'-ho

  6b. Wah-te'-roo

  6c. Ke'-kahts

  6d. O-kwahn'-noo-choo

  6e. Hah-to-ke'-he-wuk

  6f. Tlo'-hom-tah'-hoi [Also classed separately as J]

H. Achomawan Stock [Palaihnihan]

  7a. A-choo'-mah'-we

  7b. As-tah-ke-wi'-che

  7c. At-wum'-we

  7d. Ham-mah'-we

  7e. Ha'-we-si'-doo

  7f. Il-mah'-we

  7g. Ko-se-al-lek'-te

  7h. Mo-des'-se

  7i. To-mal-lin'-che-moi'

  7j. At-soo-ka-e [Atsugewi]

  7k. Ap-woo'-ro-ka'-e

  7l. A-me'-che

  7m. E-poo'-de

I. Karok Stock

  8a. Ar'-rahr

  8b. Kah-rah'-ko-hah

J. Tlohomtahhoi Stock [New River Shasta; also classed as part of G]

  9a. Tlo'-hom-tah'-hoi

K. Chemareko Stock

  10a. Chemareko

L. Yahnah Stock

  11a. Yah'-nah

M. Pomo Stock

   Northern Division or Family [Northern Pomo]

      12a. Mah'-to-po'-mah

      12b. Me-tum'-mah

      12c. Kah'-be-tsim'-me-po'-mah

      12d. Po-mo'-ke-chah'

      12e. Mah-soo'-tah-ke'-ah

      12f. Mah-too'-go

      12g. Ki-yow'-bahch

   Yokiah-Boyah Division [Central Pomo]

      12h. Boyah

      12i. Tah'-bah-ta'

      12j. Lah'-ta

      12k. Kan-no'-ah

      12l. Yo-ki'-ah

      12m. She-a'-ko

      12n. Sho-ko'-ah or Sha-nel

      12o. Den-nol'-yo-keah

      12p. Yo-buk'-ka'-ah

   Kah-chi'-ah Division [Kashaya]

      12q. Kah-chi-ah

   Mah'-kah-mo-chum'-mi or We-shum'-tat-tah Division
[Southern Pomo]

      12r. Mah-kah-mo-chum'-mi

      12s. Shah-kow'-we-chum'-mi

      12t. We'-shah'-chum-mi

      12u. Me-hin-kow'-nah

      12v. We-shum'-tat-tah

   Han-nah-bah-ch or Clear Lake Division [E Pomo]

      12w. Dan-no'-kah

      12x. She'-kum

      12y. Bo-al-ke'-ah

      12z. Ku'-lan-na'-po

      12aa. Ha'-be-nap'-po

   Sho-te'-ah or Stony Creek Division [Northeastern Pomo]

      12bb. Sho-te'-ah

   Ham-fo or Lower Lake Division [Southeastern Pomo]

      12cc. Ham'-fo

N. Chumash Stock

      13a. Ah'-moo

      13b. Kah'-she-nahs-moo

      13c. Kah'-sah-kom-pe'-ah

      13d. Kas'-swah

      13e. Chu-mahs

      13f. Hool'-koo-koo

      13g. Tso-yin'-ne ah-koo

O. Yuman Stock

      14a. Mohave

      14b. Kam'-me-i

      14c. Tis-se'-pah

      14d. Diegueño

      14f. Es-kah'-ti

P. Washoo Stock [Washo]

      15a. Washoo

Q. Esselen Stock

      16a. Esselen

R. Ennesen Stock [Salinan]

      17a. Antoniano or Kah-tri-tam

      17b. Migueleno or Te-po-trahl

      17c. Lahm-kah-trahm

S. Olhonean Stock [Costanoan]

      18a. Hor-de-on

      18b. Hoo'-mon-twash

      18c. Moot-soon'

      18d. Achestah

      18e. Kah'-koon or Room-se-en

      18f. Yak-shoon

T. Wintoon Stock [Wintuan]

   Northern Wintoon [Wintu]

      19a. Wintu or Num'soos Wintoo

      19b. Num'-te-pom' or Wintoon proper

      19c. Nor' rel-muk

      19d. Ni-i'-che

      19e. Daw'-pum

   Nom-lak-ke or Central Division

      19f. Nom'-lak-ke

      19g. Wi-e'-ker'-ril band

      19h. Dah'-chin-chin'-ne

19i. Te-ha'-mah

19j. No-e-muk

19k. No-mel'-te-ke'-we

Southern Division [Patwin]

19l. Choo-hel'-mem-shel

19m. Chen'-po-sel

19n. Lol'-sel band

19o. Klet'-win

19p. Ko-pa or Win

19q. Nan'-noo-ta'-we or Nap'-pa

19r. Ko'-roo

19s. Pat'-win

19t. Poo'-e-win

U. Midoo Stock [Maiduan]

Northern Division [Chico Maidu and Northeastern Maidu]

20a. Mitchopdo

20b. No'-to-koi-yu

20c. Sa-ap-kahn-ko band

20e. Oso'-ko band

Central Division [Konkow]

20f. Kon'-kow or Ti'-mah

20g. Tahn'-kum

20h. Kow'-wahk

20i. Kum-mo'-win

Southern Division or Nissenan [Nisenan]

20j. To-sim'-me-nan

20k. Ho'-mah band

20l. Nis'-sim Pa'-we-nan

20m. Nis'-se-nan

20n. No-to'-mus'-se band

20o. Es'-to Nis' e-nan band

V. Mewan Stock [Miwok]

Me-wuk or Sierra Tribes [Sierra Miwok]

21a. Northern Me'-wuk

21b. Hoo-ka-go band

21c. Middle Me'-wuk

21d. Southern Me'-wuk

21e. Po-ho'-ne-che band

Mew-ko or Plains Tribes [Plains and Bay Miwok]

21f. Hul-pom'-ne

21g. Mo-koz'-um-ne

21h. O'-che-hak

21i. Wi'-pa

21j. Han-ne'-suk

21k.Yatch-a-chum'-ne

21l. Mo-kal'-um-ne

21m. Chil-um'-ne

21n. Si'-a-kum'-ne

21o. Tu-ol'-um-ne

21p. Saclan

In-ne-ko or Coast Tribes [Lake and Coast Miwok]

21q. Tu-le-yo'-me

21r. Hoo-koo c'-ko

21s. Olamentko

21t. Le-kah'-te-wuk

W. Yokut Stock

22a. Heu'-che

22b. Chow-chil'-lah

22c. Chuck-chan'-sy

22d. To-ko'-lo band

22e. Tal-lin'-che

22f. Pit-kah'-che

22g. Toom'-nah band

22h. Ketch-a'-ye

22i. Kum'-nah

22j. Kosh-sho'-o or Ko-shon

22k. Ho-ye'-mah

22l. Chu-ki'-ah

22m. Cho-e-nim'-ne

22n. Wa'-cha-kut

22o. Cho-ki'-min-nah

22p. No-to'-no-to

22q. Tah'-che

22r. Wik-chum'-ne

22s. Ka-we'-ahs

22t. Ta-dum'-ne

22u. Choo'-nut

22v. Choi'-nook or Cho'-nook or Choo'-enu or Wa-da'-she

22w. Yo'-kol or Yo-o'-kul or Yo'-a-kud'-dy

22x. Yow-lan'-che

22y. No-chan'-itch band

22z. Ko-yet'-te

22aa Pal-low'-yam'-me

22bb. Wo'-wul

22cc. Yow'-el-man'-ne

22dd. Tin'-lin-ne

22ee. Too-lol'-min

22ff. Ye-wum'-ne or Pah-ah'-se

22gg. Ham-met-wel'-le

22hh. Tu-lum'-ne

X. Shoshone Stock [Numic and Takic]

23a. Northern Piute

23b. Koo-tsab'-be dik'-ka

23c. Pahng'-we-hoo'-tse

Monache Piute/Western Monache [Western Mono]

23d. Nim or Monache

23e. Posh-ge'-sha

23f. Kwe'-tah

23g. Too-hook'-mutch

23h. Ko-ko-he'-ba band

23i. Toi-ne'-che band

23j. Hol'-ko-mah band

23k. To-win-che'-ba band

23l. Wo'-pon-nutch

23m. En'-tim-bitch

23n. Wuksa-che'

23o. Pot-wish'-ah

Owens Lake Monache Piute [Eastern Mono]

23p. Kwe'-nah-pat'-se band

23q. Ut'-te-ur-re-we'-te

23r. To'-bo-ah-hax-ze

23s. Chuk'-ke-sher-ra'-ka

23t. No'-no-pi-ah

Panamints

23u. Pak'-wa-sitch

23v. Moo-et'-tah

Southern Piute

23w. New-oo'-ah [Kawaiisu]

23x. Tol-chin'-ne

23y. Nu-vah'-an-dits

23z. Chem-e-we'-ve'

Ke-tahn-na-mwits or Serrano

23aa. Ke-tah'-na'-mwits

23bb. Pur'-ve'-tum or Pur-vit-tem

23cc. Yo-hah'-ve-tum

23dd. Mah'-re-ah-ne-um or Mah'-ring-i-um or Mo'-he-ah'-ne-um

Kah-we-sik-tem or Cahuilla

23ee. Koos'-tam

23ff. Wah'-ne-ke'-tam or Mahl'-ke

23gg. Kah-we-sik'-tem

23hh. Pan'-yik-tem

23ii Wah-ko-chim'-kut-tem

23jj. Sow'-wis-pah-kik'-tem

23kk. Pow'-we-yam

23ll. We-is'-tem

Koo'-pah [Cupeño]

23mm. Koo'-pah

A-katch'-mah or Luiseño

23nn. A-katch'-mah

23oo. Pi-yum'-ko

23pp. So-bo'-ba

Y. Tongva Stock [Gabrielino]

24a. Tongva

Z. Tubotelobela Stock [Tubatulabal]

25a. Pahn'-ka-la'-che

25b. Tu'-bot-e-lob'-e-la

A. Athabaskan ("Athapascan")

[OREGON ATHABASKAN]

A-1a **Tolowa** (*Hah´-wung-kwut*, Huss or Tolowa. Crescent City. Sam Lopez, 1910–1938.)
  * UCB: A/1a/V1 [reel 30] and A/1a/NH1 [reel 52]
  * LC: carton 26–27

[CALIFORNIA ATHABASKAN]

A-1b **Hupa** (*Tin´-nung-hen-na´-o*, Hoopa. Burnt Ranch, Hoopa Valley. James Chesbro, Mrs. Abraham Jack and Mrs. Freda Norton, 1921–1934.)
  * UCB: A/1b/V2 [reel 30] and A/1b/NH2 [reel 52]
  * LC: carton 25–26

A-1d **Whilkut** (*Hwil´-kut* or *Hoil´-kut*. Redwood Creek. John Stevens, Laura Stevens, Ohaniel Bailey, etc., 1910–1920.)
  * UCB: A/1d/V3 [reel 30] and A/1d/NH3 [reel 52]
  * LC: carton 25–26

A-1f **Mattole** (*Bet-tol´*, commonly called *Mat-tol´*. Mattole River region. Joe Duncan and son Ike, 1923.)
  * UCB: A/1f/V4 [reel 30] and A/1f/NH4 [reel 52]
  * LC: carton 26–27

A-1g **Northern Sinkyone** (*Lo-lahn´-kok*. Bull Creek and South Fork Eel River. George Burt, 1921–1923.)
  * UCB: A/1g/V5 [reel 30] and A/1g/NH5 [reel 52]
  * LC: carton 25–26

A-1h **Southern Sinkyone** (*To-cho´-be ke´-ah*. Garberville to Shelter Cove, Briceland and region. Sally Bell, 1923.)
  * UCB: A/1h/V6 [reel 30] and A/1h/NH6 [reel 52]
  * LC: carton 26–27

A-1i **Nongatl** (*Kit-tel*. Iaqua to Dobbin Creek and Bridgeville, lower Van Duzen. Mrs. George Burt, 1921–1923.)
  * UCB: A/1i/V7 [reel 30] and A/1i/NH7 [reel 52]
  * LC: carton 25–26

A-1j **Lassik** (*Set-ten-bi´-den*. Zenia. Lucy Young, 1922.)
  * UCB: A/1j/V8 [reel 31] and A/1j/NH10 [reel 52]
  * LC: carton 26–27
  Lassik (*To-kub´-be ke´-ah*, closely related to *Set´-ten-bi´-den ke´-ah*. East branch South Fork Eel River. Albert Smith, 1921–1922.)
  * UCB: A/1j/V9 [reel 31] and A/1j/NH9 [reel 52]
  * LC: carton 26–27

A-1k **Wailaki** (*Tsen-nah´-ken-nes*. Blue and Bell Springs region. Wylakke Tip, Fred Major and Nancy Doty, 1922–1924.)
  * UCB: A/1k/V10 [reel 31] and A/1k/NH11 [reel 52]

Wailaki (*Ken´-nes-te´ wi´-lak-ke´*. Garberville, South Fork Eel River. Sarah Carl, 1920.)
  * UCB: A/1k/BL2 [reel 51] and A/1j/NH8 [reel 52]
  * LC: carton 25–26

A-1n **Bear River** (*Nek´-kan-ni*. Bear River region, Cape Mendocino. Mrs. Prince, etc., 1920–23.)
  * UCB: A/1n/V11 [reel 31], A/1m/BL3 [reel 51], and A/1n/NH12 [reel 52]
  * LC: carton 26–27

A-1o **Kato** (*To-chil´-pe ke´-ah-hahng*, Kahto. Kahto and Long Valleys. Mrs. Martinez Bell and others, 1920–1922.)
  * UCB: A/1o/V12 [reel 31] and A/1o/NH13 [reel 52]
  * LC: carton 25–26

B. Yurok ("Polikla")

B-2a **Coast Yurok** (*Ner´-er-ner´*. Trinidad Bay. Liza Warren Lindgren and Maggie Skirk, 1920–1921.)
  * UCB: B/2a/V13 [reel 31], B/2a/BL4 [reel 51], and B/2a/NH14 [reel 52]
  * LC: carton 32

B-2b **River Yurok** (*Helth-kik-lah, Po-lik´-lah*, Lower Klamath River. 1910–1922.)
  * UCB: B/2a-b/V14 [reel 31] and B/2b/NH15 [reel 52]

C. Wiyot ("Soolahteluk")

C-3a-c **Wiyot** (*Soo-lah´-te-luk*, including *We´-yot*, Humboldt Bay and Lower Eel River)
  * UCB: C/3a-c/V15 [reel 32] and C/3a-c/NH16 [reel 52]
  * LC: carton 41

D-E. Yukian ("Yukean")

D-4a **Coast Yuki** (*Oo´-ko-ton-til´-kah* or *Oo´-ko-ton-til´-lik-kah*)
  * UCB: D/4a/V16 [reel 32] and D/4a/NH17 [reel 52]
  * LC: carton 46

D-4b-c **Yuki** (Oo-kom-nom, Round Valley dialect, We-too-kom-nom, Eden Valley dialect)
  * UCB: D/4b-c/V17 [reel 32] and D/4b-c/NH18 [reel 52]
  * LC: carton 46

E-4h-j **Wappo** (*Mish´-a-wel* and mi-yahk-mah [Mayacama] dialects)
  * UCB: E/4h-j/V18 [reel 32] and D/4h-k/NH19 [reel 52]
  * LC: carton 46 ("Mi-yah-kah-mah")

F. Klamath-Modoc ("Lutuamian")

F-5a   **Klamath** (*Yah-nah´k-ne*. Klamath. 1912. Collected in Riverside, CA, from Luella George.)
* UCB: F/5a/V19 [reel 32] and F/5a/NH20 [reel 53]
* LC: carton 27–28

         Modoc (*Mo´-dok.*)
* LC: carton 27–28 [missing]

G. Shastan

G-6a   **Konomihu** (*Ko´-no-me´-ho*. Salmon River, Siskiyou County. 1919–1921. From Fred Kearney and Mrs. Hugh Grant.)
* UCB: G/6a/V20 [reel 32], G/6a/BL5 [reel 51], and G/6a/NH21 [reel 53]
* LC: carton 35

G-6c   **Shasta** (*Shas´-te, Ke´-kahts*. Yreka and Shasta Valleys, Klamath Canyon, Siskiyou County. 1907–1919. From Bogus Tom and wife, Shasta Jake, and Mrs. Cynthia Mike.)
* UCB: G/6c/V21 [reel 33] and G/6c/NH22 [reel 53]
* LC: carton 35

G-6d   **Okwanuchu** (*O-kwahn´-noo-choo, wi-muk* or *A-te*. Squaw Creek and Upper McCloud River. 1925. From Lottie O'Neal and Rosa Ryan.)
* UCB: G/6d/V22 [reel 33] and G/6d/NH23 [reel 53]
* LC: carton 35

G-6e   **Salmon River Shasta** (*Hah-to-ke´-he-wuk*. Cecilville region, South Fork Salmon River, Siskiyou County. 1929. From Mrs. George.)
* UCB: G/6e/V23 [reel 33] and G/6e/NH24 [reel 53]
* LC: carton 35

H. Palaihnihan ("Achomawan")

H-7a-m   Palaihnihan in general (Achomawan stock.)
* UCB: H/7a-m/BL6 [reel 51]

[ACHUMAWI]

H-7a   —————— (*Ah-choo-mah´-we*. Fall River, Lassen County. 1903–1928. From Charles Green, Davis Mike and wife.)
* UCB: H/7a/V24 [reel 33] and H/7a/NH25 [reel 53]
* LC: cartons 24–35

H-7b   —————— (*As-tah-ke-wi´-che* or *As´-tah-ke-wi´-se*. Warm Springs Valley [Canby Valley], Modoc County. 1925–1926. From Sam Spring and Robin Spring.)
* UCB: H/7b/V25 [reel 33] and H/7b/NH26 [reel 53]
* LC: cartons 24–25

H-7c   —————— (*At-wum´-we*. Big Valley, Lassen and Modoc counties. 1924–1926. From Billy Quinn and wife, Harry George, etc.)
* UCB: H/7c/V26 [reel 33] and H/7c/NH27 [reel 53]
* LC: carton 25

H-7d   —————— (*Ham-mah´-we*. Likely Valley and Madeline Plains, South Fork Pit River, Modoc County. 1924–1928. From Susie Evans, Cha-cha-ha [Old Pete], Jack Williams, chief, etc.)
* UCB: H/7d/V27 [reel 34] and H/7d/NH28 [reel 53]

H-7h   (*Mo-des´-se*. Big Bend, Pit River, Shasta County. 1907–1924.)
* UCB: H/7h/V28 [reel 34] and H/7h/NH29 [reel 53]
* LC: carton 25

[ATSUGEWI]

H-7j   —————— (*Ah´-tsoo-ka´-e*. Hat Creek, Shasta County. 1907. From several members of tribe.)
* UCB: H/7j/V29 [reel 34] and H/7j/NH30 [reel 53]
* LC: carton 24–25

H-7k   —————— (*Ap-woo´-ro-ka´-e*. Dixie Valley, Lassen County. 1924–1926. From Robert Rivis and Harry Wilson.)
* UCB: H/7k/V30 [reel 34] and H/7k/NH31 [reel 53]
* LC: carton 24–25

I. Karuk ("Karok")

I-8a-b   **Karuk** (*Ar´-rahr* and *Kah-rah´-ko-hah*. Klamath River, Happy Camp to Bluff Creek, Siskiyou County. 1910–1922.)
* UCB: I/8a-b/V31 [reel 34], I/8a-b/BL7 [reel 51], and I/8a/NH32 [reel 53]
* LC: carton 27–28

I-8b   **Karuk** (*Kah-rah´-ko-hah*. Happy Camp on Klamath River, Siskiyou County. 1910–1918.)
* UCB: I/8b/V32 [reel 34] and I/8b/NH33 [reel 53]
* LC: carton 27–28

J. New River Shasta ("Tlohomtahoi")

J-9a   **New River Shasta** (*Tlo´-hom-tah´-hoi*, New River Shasta. New River. 1926–1929. From Saxy Kid.)
* UCB: J/9a/V33 [reel 34] and J/9a/NH34 [reel 53]
* LC: carton 41

K. Chimariko ("Chemareko")

K-10a   **Chimariko** (*Che-mar´-re-ko*. Trinity River, Burnt Ranch and lower New River; Trinity River from Big Bar to 7–8 miles of South Fork. 1920-21. From Sally Noble.)
* UCB: K/10a/V34 [reel 35], K/10a/BL8 [reel 51], and K/10a/NH35 [reel 53]
* LC: carton 27

L. Yana ("Yahnah")

L-11a **(Northern) Yana** (*Yah´-nah* or *Nos´-se.* Round Mountain, Shasta County. 1907–1926.)
    * UCB: L/11a/V35 [reel 35], L/11a/BL9 [reel 51], and L/11a/NH36 [reel 53]

M. Pomo

M-12a-cc Pomo in general (Pomo stock.)
    * UCB: M/12a-cc/BL10 [reel 51]

M-12a **Northern Pomo** (*Mah´-to po´-mah.* Sherwood Valley, Mendocino County. 1925.)
    * UCB: M/12a/V36 [reel 35] and M/12a/NH37 [reel 54]
    * LC: carton 33–34

M-12b **Northern Pomo** (*Me-tum´-ki* or *Me-tum´-mah.* Little Lake Valley. 1921–1922.)
    * UCB: M/12b/V37 [reel 35] and M/12b/NH38 [reel 54]

M-12d **Northern Pomo** (*Po-mo´-ke-chah´.* Potter Valley, Mendocino County. 1916–1921.)
    * UCB: M/12d/V38 [reel 35] and M/12d/NH39 ("Bal´-lo-ki subtribe") [reel 54]
    * LC: carton 34

M-12g **Northern Pomo** (*Ki-yow´-bahch.* Tule Lake, Blue Lakes, and Batchelor Valley, Lake County; Upper Lake Rancheria, Clear Lake. 1924.)
    * UCB: M/12g/V39 [reel 35] and M/12g/NH40 [reel 54]
    * LC: carton 33–34

M-12h **Central Pomo** (*Boyah.* Coast from Navarro Ridge to Gualala River. 1922.)
    * UCB: M/12h/V40 [reel 35]
    * LC: carton 32–33

M-12i **Central Pomo** (*Tah´-bah-ta´.* Anderson Valley; Boonville-Philo region, Mendocino County. 1924.)
    * UCB: M/12i/V41 [reel 35] and M/12i/NH41 [reel 54]
    * LC: carton 34

M-12l **Central Pomo** (*Yo-ki´-ah* and Hopland. Upper Russian River Valley near Ukiah, Mendocino County. 1918–1925. From Jim Calico and Stephen Knight.)
    * UCB: M/12l/V42 [reel 36] and M/12l/NH42 (2 copies) [reel 54]
    * LC: carton 34

M-12n **Central Pomo** (*Sho-ko´-ah* or *Sha-nel.* Hopland Valley, Mendocino County.)
    * UCB: M/12n/V43 [reel 36] and M/12n/NH43 [reel 54]
    * LC: carton 34

M-12q **Kashaya** (*Kah-chi´-ah.* Stewarts Point south to Lower Russian River and adjacent coast. 1905–1925.)
    * UCB: M/12q/V44 (2 copies) [reel 36] and M/12q/NH44 [reel 54]
    * LC: carton 32–33

M-12r **Southern Pomo** (*Mah´-kah-mo chum´-mi.* Cloverdale Valley, Russian River, Sonoma County. From John Thompson. 1922–1925.)
    * UCB: M/12r/V45 (2 copies) [reel 36] and M/12r/NH45 [reel 54]
    * LC: carton 33–34

M-12t **Southern Pomo** (*We´-shah´-chum´-mi.* Rockpile to Annapolis and coast. From Dan Scott. 1925.)
    * UCB: M/12t/V46 [reel 36]
    * LC: carton 34

M-12v **Southern Pomo** (*Me´-dah-kah´-tum´-mi* band of *We-shum´-tat-tah.* Santa Rosa Plain. 1925. From Tom Boots.)
    * UCB: M/12r/V47 [reel 37] and M/12v/NH46 [reel 54]
    * LC: carton 34 ("Mé-dah-kah tum-ki")

    Southern Pomo (*Kah´-tah-we chum-mi.* Healdsburg region, Russian River. 1905–1925.)
    * UCB: M/12r/V48 [reel 37] and M/12v/NH47 [reel 54]
    * LC: carton 32–33

M-12w-y **Eastern Pomo** (*Han-nah -bah-ch* or Upper Lake Pomo: *Dan-no´-kah, She´-kum, Bo-al-ke´-ah.* Upper Lake, Lake County. 1916–1923.)
    * UCB: M/12w-y/V49 [reel 37] and M/12w-12aa/NH48 [reel 54]
    * LC: carton 32–33 ("Hah-nah-bahch")

M-12z-aa **Eastern Pomo** (*Hah-be´-nap´-po* and *Ko-lan´ nap´-po.* Big Valley near Kelseyville, Lake County. 1906–1924.)
    * UCB: M/12z-aa/V50 [reel 37] and M/12aa/NH49 [reel 54]
    * LC: carton 33–34 ("Kulanapo")

M-12bb **Northeastern Pomo** (*Sho-te´-ah* or Stony Creek Division: *Sha´-men.* Stony Ford, northwest Colusa County. 1903–1928. From Chief "San Diego.")
    * UCB: M/12bb/V51 [reel 37] and M/12bb/NH50 [reel 54]
    * LC: carton 34

M-12cc **Southeastern Pomo** (*Hram-fo* or Lower Lake Division: *Koi-im-fo* subtribe or band. *Koi-e* or Indian Island, Lower Lake, Lake County. 1904–1927.)
    * UCB: M/12cc/V52 [reel 37] and M/12cc/NH51 [reel 54]
    * LC: carton 32–33

N. Chumash

N-13a-g Chumash stock (general)
    * UCB: N/13a-g/BL11 [reel 51]

N-13c **Inezeño** (*Kah´-sah-kom-pe´-ah.* Santa Ynez Valley, Santa Barbara County. 1911–1934.)
    * UCB: N/13c/V53 [reel 37] and N/13c/NH52 [reel 55]
    * LC: carton 27

N-13e   Ventureño (*Chu-mahs*. Ventura.
        1905–1932.)
        * UCB: N/13e/V54 [reel 38] and N/13e/NH53
          [reel 55]
        * LC: carton 27

N-13f   Emigdiano (*Hool´-koo-koo*. San Emigdio. 1905.
        From Maria Ignacio.)
        * UCB: N/13f/V55 [reel 38] and N/13f/NH54
          [reel 55]
        * LC: carton 27

O. Yuman

O-14a-f   Yuman Stock (brief notes)
        * UCB: O/14a-f/BL12 [reel 51]

O-14a   Mojave (Needles and Mohave City.
        1905–1919.)
        * UCB: O/14a/V56 [reel 38] and O/14a/NH55
          [reel 55]
        * LC: carton 46–47

O-14b   Eastern Diegueño (*Kam´-me-i*. Colorado Desert,
        U.S.-Mexico border on Colorado River near
        Yuma. 1933. From "Indian Frank.")
        * UCB: O/14b/V57 [reel 38] and O/14b/NH56
          (vocabulary 1) [reel 55]
        * LC: carton 46-47

[″]   Tipai and Ipai Diegueño [and Paipai?]
        (*Kam´-me-i* and *A-whah´-kwahk*. Southern
        San Diego County and Lower California near
        Campo; Manzanita Mission Reservation; Mesa
        Grande and El Cajon. 1903–1933.)
        * UCB: O/14b/V58 [reel 38] and O/14b/NH56
          (vocabularies 2 and 3) [reel 55]
        * LC: carton 46–47

O-14d   Quechan (*Kwe-tsahn´*. Lower Colorado River.
        1933.)
        * UCB: Misc/Ariz/V135 [reel 49] and Misc/Ariz/
          NH143 [reel 61]
        * LC: carton 46–47

P. Washo ("Washoo")

P-15a   Washo (*Wah-shoo*. Sierra Valley to Antelope
        Valley; Lake Tahoe, Carson Valley, Sierra
        Valley, and Reno. 1903–1935.)
        * UCB: P/15a/V59 [reel 38] and P/15a/NH57
          [reel 55]
        * LC: carton 42

Q. Esselen

Q-16a   Esselen (brief notes)
        * UCB: Q/16a/BL14 [reel 51]

R. Salinan ("Ennesen")

R-17a-b   Antoniano and Migueleño (Milpitas Valley,
        Santa Lucia Mountains 20 miles northwest of
        Jolon, south to San Antonio Creek and Mission;
        San Miguel Mission, south to Toro Creek.
        1902–1934.)
        * UCB: R/17a/V60 [reel 38] (Antoniano)
        * UCB: R/17a&b/V61 [reel 38] and R/17a&b/
          NH58 [reel 55] (Antoniano and Migueleño
          mixed)
        * LC: carton 27–28 ("Ennesen" unidentified as to
          dialect)

S. Costanoan ("Olhonean")

S-18a-f   Costanoan (general)
        * UCB: S/18a-f/BL15 [reel 51]

S-18a   Chocheño (*Hor-de-on*. Pleasanton, Alameda
        County. 1904–1905. From Anhelo Colos.)
        * UCB: S/18a/V62 [reel 39]

S-18b-c   Mutsun (*Hoo´-mon-twash* and *Moot-soon´*. San
        Juan Valley, San Benito County. 1902–1904.)
        * UCB: S/18b&c/V63 [reel 39] and S/18b/NH59
          [reel 55]
        * LC: carton 32

S-18e   Rumsen (*Room´-se-en* or *Kah´-koon*. Monterey
        and Carmel. 1906–1933.)
        * UCB: S/18e/V64 [reel 39] and S/18e/NH60
          [reel 55]
        * LC: carton 32

T. Wintuan ("Wintoon")

T-19a-t   Wintuan (general)
        * UCB: T/19a-t/BL16 [reel 51]

T-19a   Trinity Wintu (*Num´-soos*. Salt Flat Rancheria,
        Trinity River near Lewiston; Trinity Center,
        Trinity County. 1918–1932. From "Jim Tye";
        Jim Fader.)
        * UCB: T/19a/V65 [reel 39] and T/19b/NH62
          [reel 56] ("Lewiston")
        * UCB: T/19a/NH61 [reel 56] (Kah-bal´-pum,
          Trinity Center)
        * LC: carton 43–44 ("Wintu [northwest]
          Num-soos")

T-19b   McCloud Wintu (*Num´-te-pom*, or Wintoon
        proper. Ono, Shasta County; McCloud and
        Upper Sacramento Rivers. 1903–1931. From
        Mrs. Roll Range and Mrs. Wash Fann, and
        others.)
        * UCB: T/19b/V66 [reel 39] and T/19b/NH63
          [reel 56] ("Ono")
        * UCB: T/19b/V67 [reel 39] and T/19b/NH64
          [reel 56] ("McCloud and Upper Sacramento")
        * LC: carton 43–44 ("Ono Wintun" and "Northern
          Wintun [McCloud River]")

T-19c   Hayfork Wintu (*Nor´-el-muk*. Hay Fork, Trinity
         County. 1921–1922. From Kate Luckie, etc.)
         * UCB: T/19c/V68 [reel 40] and T/19c/NH65
           [reel 56]
         * LC: carton 43

T-19f   Nomlaki (*Nom´-lik-kah* or *Nom´-lak-ke*. Upper
         Thomas Creek (near Paskenta), Tehama County;
         Grindstone Creek. 1919.)
         * UCB: T/19f/V69 [reel 40] and T/19f/NH66
           [reel 56]
         * LC: carton 43

T-19l   Hill Patwin (*Choo-hel´-mem-shel*. Ladoga, Indian
         Valley and Sites, Colusa County. 1923–1928.)
         * UCB: T/19l/V70 [reel 40] and T/19l/NH67
           [reel 56]
         * LC: carton 42–43

T-19m   Hill Patwin (*Chen´-po-sel*. Long Valley, Lake
         County. 1906–1907. From Anton Taylor
         [Hool´-pi].)
         * UCB: T/19m/V71 [reel 40] and T/19m/NH68
           [reel 56]
         * LC: carton 42–43

T-19o   Hill Patwin (*Klet´-win* or *´Klet-sel*. Cortina Valley
         region, Colusa County. 1903–1927.)
         * UCB: T/19o/V72 [reel 40; 2 copies] and T19o/
           NH69 [reel 56]
         * UCB: T/19r&o/V74 [reel 40] ("*Ko´-roo* [River
           Patwin] and *Klet´-win*")
         * LC: carton 42–43

T-19p   Hill Patwin (*Ko-peh´*. Rumsey, Capay Valley,
         Yolo County. 1904.)
         * UCB: T/19p/V73 [reel 40] and T/19p/NH70
           [reel 56]
         * LC: carton 43–44

T-19r-s River Patwin (*Ko´-roo* and *Pat´win*. West side
         Sacramento River, Colusa County; Colusa.
         1903–1936.)
         * UCB: T/19r&s/NH72 [reel 56] ("*Ko´-roo* or
           Pah´-tin, and *Pat´win*")
         * UCB: T/19r/V75 [reel 41] ("*Ko´-roo*")
         * UCB: T/19r & o/V74 [reel 40] ("*Ko´-roo* and
           Klet´-win [Hill Patwin]")
         * LC: carton 42–43 ("Ko-too")
         * LC: carton 43 ("Pat´-win")

T-19t   Southern Patwin (*Poo´-e-win*. Sonoma Valley.
         1906–1917.)
         * UCB: T/19t/V76 [reel 41] and T/19t/NH73
           [reel 56]
         * LC: carton 43

U. Maiduan ("Midoo")

U-20a   Chico Maidu (Mitchopdo. Chico region, Butte
         County. 1903–1923.)
         * UCB: U/20a/V77 [reel 41] and U/20a/NH74
           [reel 56]
         * LC: carton 30

U-20b   Mountain Maidu (*No´-to-koi´-yu*. American
         Valley, Big Meadows, Plumas County, now
         Lake Almanor. 1903–1926. From Mrs. Polly
         Jackson.)
         * UCB: U/20b/V78, U/20b/V79 [reel 41], and
           U/20b/NH75 [reel 56]
         * LC: carton 30–31

U-20g   Valley Konkow (*Tahn´-kum* [Oleepa]. South
         Honcut Creek and Stanfield Hill, Brownsville
         area, Yuba County [east of Oroville]. 1928.
         From Mrs. William Hughes and Henry
         Thompson.)
         * UCB: U/20g/V80 [reel 41] and U/20g/NH76
           [reel 56]
         * LC: carton 30–31

U-20h   Northern Hill Nisenan (*Ne´-sem kow´-wahk*:
         Sierra Nevada between American and Yuba
         Rivers, French Corral, and Nevada City
         (between Downieville on the east and Sheridan
         on the west). 1928. From Mrs. Anna Barron,
         Richard [Blind Dick] and Nellie Yamie.)
         * UCB: U/20h/V81 [reel 41] and U/20h/NH77
           [reel 56]
         * LC: carton 30

U-20i   Hill Konkow (*Kum-mo´-win*. Enterprise and Bald
         Rock, Mooretown, Middle and South Forks
         Feather River. 1924–1930. From Mim ["Billy
         Logan"], George Martin, and Sam Elbert and
         wives.)
         * UCB: U/20i/V82 [reel 42] and U/20i/NH78
           [reel 56]
         * LC: carton 30

U-20l   Valley Nisenan (*Nis´-sim Pa´-we-nan*.)
         * LC: carton 30–31

U-20m   Southern Hill Nisenan (*Ne´-se-non* or *Nis´-se-nan*.
         North Fork American River; between North and
         Middle Forks of Cosumnes River, El Dorado
         County, with supplementary names from Gold
         Hill. 1902–1904. From Chief Hunchup and
         wife.)
         * UCB: U/20m/V83, U/20m/V84 [reel 42], and
           U/20m/NH79 [reel 56]
         * LC: carton 30–31

U-20n   (Southern?) Hill Nisenan (*No-to´-mus-se* [around
         Folsom]. Lower American River, north side, 9
         [?] miles above its mouth. 1905.)
         * UCB: U/20n&o/V85 [reel 42] and U/20n/
           NH80 [reel 56]
         * LC: carton 30–31

U-20o   Southern Hill Nisenan (*Es´-tom nis´-se-non*.
         Middle Cosumnes–Deer Creek region. 1936.
         From Mrs. Ida Starkey.)
         * UCB: U/20n&o/V85 [reel 42] and U/20o/
           NH81 [reel 56]
         * LC: carton 30–31

V. Miwok ("Mewan")

V-21a-t Miwok (general)
         * UCB: V/21a-t/BL18 [reel 51]

V-21a   **Northern Sierra Miwok** (Northern *Me´-wuk*.
         Mokelumne River south to San Andreas; West
         Point, Calaveras County; Pleasant Valley, El
         Dorado County. 1905–1919. From Captain Eph;
         Johnson Hunter.)
         * UCB: V/21a/V86 and V/21a/V87 [reel 42] and
         V/21a/NH82 [reel 57]
         * LC: carton 29

V-21c   **Central Sierra Miwok** (Middle or *Po´-tah mew´-
         wah*. Murphy's and Angels; south to south side
         of Tuolumne River. 1902 and later dates.)
         * UCB: V/21c/V88 [reel 42] and V/21c/NH83
         [reel 57]
         * LC: carton 28

V-21d   **Southern Sierra Miwok** (variety)
         * LC: carton 29 ("Southern Mu´wah")

V-21e   **Southern Sierra Miwok** (variety)
         * LC: carton 28 ("Chow-chil-lah Mew-wuh")

V-21g   **Plains Miwok** (*Mo-koz-um-ne*, Mokosumni.)
         * LC: carton 29–30

V-21i   **Plains Miwok** (*Wi´-pa*, Guaypem. Sherman
         Island.)
         * LC: carton 29–30

V-21l   **Plains Miwok** (*Mo-kal´-um-ne*. Mokelumne River,
         1¼ miles west of Lockeford. 1903. From Lan´-
         nah-wis´-tah [Casus Oliver].)
         * UCB: V/21l/V89 [reel 43] and V/21l/NH84
         [reel 57]
         * LC: carton 29-30

V-21q   **Lake Miwok** (*O-la´-yo´-me* or *Tu´-le-yo´-me*. Putah
         Creek, Lake County. 1905–1927. From Hoo´-
         yum-ha´-yum, Salvado Cha-po, John Sebastian.)
         * UCB: V/21q/V90 [reel 43] and V/21q/NH85
         [reel 57]
         * LC: carton 29–30

V-21r   **Marin Miwok** (*Hoo´-koo-e´ko*. Tomales Bay.
         1905–1927.)
         * UCB: V21r/NH86 [reel 57]
         * LC: carton 28

V-21s   **Bodega Miwok** (*O-la ment´ ke*)
         * LC: carton 29–30

V-21   **Miwok** (variety uncertain)
         * LC: carton 29 ("Oleta")

W. Yokuts ("Yokut")

W-22c   **Chukchansi** [Northern Valley, Northern Hill
         cluster] (*Chuk-chan´-sy*. Picayune and Fresno
         Flats, south side of Fresno River; Coarse Gold.
         1902–1930. From Old Matilda Neal and Mrs.
         Sophie Jones.)
         * UCB: W/22c/V91 [reel 43] and W/22c/NH87
         [reel 58]
         * LC: carton 44–45

W-22e   **Dalinchi** [Northern Valley, Northern Hill cluster]
         (*Tal-lin´-che*. Coarse Gold, Fresno County. 1930.
         From Bill See.)
         * UCB: W/22e/NH88 [reel 58]
         * LC: carton 45

W-22h   **Kechayi** [Northern Valley, Northern Hill cluster]
         (*Ketch´-a´-ye*. San Joaquin, at Falls, Table
         Mountain, 9 miles above Sulphur Springs.
         1930.)
         * UCB: W/22h/NH89 [reel 58]
         * LC: carton 44–45

W-22j   **Gashowu** (*Kosh-sho´-o*. Table Mountain above
         Pollasky, south side San Joaquin River. 1903.
         From Mrs. Matthews.)
         * UCB: W/22j/V92 [reel 43] and W/22j/NH90
         [reel 58]
         * LC: carton 44–45

W-22m   **Choynimni** [Kings River] (*Cho-e-nim´-ne*. Mill
         Creek Valley near Kings River, Fresno.
         1930.)
         * UCB: W/22m/NH91 [reel 58]
         * LC: carton 44–45

W-22m-o **Choynimni and Chukaymina** [Kings River]
         (*Cho-e-nim´-ne* and *Cho-ki´-min-nah*. Squaw
         Valley, south of Kings River and Kings River
         at mouth of Mill Creek, Fresno County.
         1903–1930.)
         * UCB: W/22m and o/V93 [reel 43] and W/22m
         and 22o/NH92 [reel 58]
         * LC: carton 44–45

W-22o   **Chukaymina** [Kings River] (*Cho-ki´-min-nah*.
         Squaw Valley, Fresno County. 1930.)
         * UCB: W/22o/NH93 [reel 58]
         * LC: carton 44–45

W-22p   **Nutunutu** [Southern Valley] (*No-tu´-no-to*. Laton,
         lower Kings River, Fresno County. 1932. From
         Mary and Annie Tip.)
         * UCB: W/22p/V94 [reel 43] and W/22p/NH94
         [reel 58]
         * LC: carton 45

W-22q   **Tachi** [Southern Valley] (*Tah´-che*. Northeast side
         Tache or Tulare Lake. 1903–1932.)
         * UCB: W/22q/V95 [reel 44] and W/22q/NH95
         [reel 58]
         * LC: carton 45

W-22r   **Wikchamni** [Tule-Kaweah] (*Wik-tchum´-ne*.
         Kaweah River at Limekill, Lemon Cove.
         1902–1930. From Jim Harrison and family
         and Jim Breeches and family; Mrs. Eda
         I´-chow.)
         * UCB: W/22r/V96 [reel 44] and W/22r/NH96
         [reel 58]
         * LC: carton 45–46

W-22s   **Telamni or Tedamni** [Southern Valley]
         (*T'-dum-ne*. Near Tulare Lake. 1903–1931.)
         * UCB: W/22s/NH97 [reel 58]
         * LC: carton 45 ("Pa-dum-ne")

W-22t   **Telamni or Tedamni** [Southern Valley]
         (*Ta-dum´-ne*. Visalia, Tulare County.
         1902–1903.)
         * UCB: W/22t/V97 [reel 44]

W-22u   **Chunut** [Southern Valley] (*Choo´-nut*. Hanford
         and island in Tulare Lake. 1935. From Mrs. Jose
         Alonza [Yoi´-mut].)
         * UCB: W/22u/V98 [reel 44], W/22u/BL19 [reel
         51], and W/22u/NH98 [reel 58]

W-22x   **Yawdanchi or Yawlanchi** [Tule-Kaweah] (*Yow-lan´-che, Yow´-lan-che.* Tule River. 1932. From Philip Hunter, Mrs. Joe Vera.)
* UCB: W/22x/V99 [reel 44] and W/22x/NH99 [reel 58]
* LC: carton 45–46

W-22z   **Koyeti** [Southern Valley] (*Ko-yet´-te.* Tule River near and at Porterville. 1935. From Jose Vera.)
* UCB: W/22z/V100 [reel 44]
* LC: carton 45

W-22aa   **Palewyami** [Poso Creek] (*Pal-low´-yam´-me.* Poso Flat and northern part of Bakersfield Plain. 1932. From Steve Soto.)
* UCB: W/22aa/V101 [reel 44] and W/22aa/NH100 [reel 58]
* LC: carton 45

W-22cc   **Yawelmani** [Southern Valley] (*Yow´-el-man´-ne.* Bakersfield Plain, Kern County. 1903–1932. From Juan Immetrio.)
* UCB: W/22cc/V102 (2 copies) [reel 44] and W/22cc/NH101 [reel 58]
* LC: carton 45–46

W-22dd   **Yawelmani** [Southern Valley] (*Tin´-lin-ne.* Old Tejon (Tejon Viejo) on Tejon Ranch Creek. 1905. From Maria.)
* UCB: W/22dd/V103 [reel 45] and W/22dd/NH102 [reel 58]
* LC: carton 45–46

W-22ee   **Tulamni or Tulalmina** [Buena Vista] (*Too-lol´-min.* Buena Vista Lake and Kern Lake. 1905.)
* UCB: W/22ee/V104 [reel 45] and W/22ee/NH103 [reel 58]
* LC: carton 45–46

X. Numic and Takic (except Gabrielino) ("Shoshone")

[NUMIC]

X-23a   **Northern Paiute** (Northern Piute: Pyramid Lake, Walker Lake.)
* LC: carton 38

X-23b   **Northern Paiute** (Mono Lake Piute. *Koo-tsab´-be-dik´-ka.* Mono Lake, Mono County. 1903–1938.)
* UCB: X/23b/V105 (2 copies) [reel 45] and X/23b/NH104 [reel 59]
* LC: carton 37–38

   Northern Paiute (Bridgeport Piute. *Koo-tsab´-be-dik´-ka* or *Po-rah* and *Ye-pug´-gi.* Bridgeport Valley, Mono County. 1900–1938.)
* UCB: X/23b/V106 [reel 45] and X/23b/NH104 [reel 59]
* LC: carton 37–38

X-23d   **Western Mono** (Nim or Monache. North Fork San Joaquin River, Madera County. 1902–1937. From Chief Cheko and Mrs. Mary Teaford.)
* UCB: X/23d/V107 [reel 45] and X/23d/NH105 [reel 59]
* LC: carton 37

X-23h   **Western Mono** (*Ko´-ko-he´-bah.* Burr Valley and western side of Pine Ridge, west of Sycamore Creek, Fresno County. 1903–1931.)
* UCB: X/23h/V108 [reel 45] and X/23h/NH106 [reel 59]
* LC: carton 36–37

X-23j-k   **Western Mono** (*To-win-che´-bah* and *Hol-lo-kom-mah* or *Hoo´-doo-ge´-dah.* Pine Ridge and east of Sycamore Creek, Fresno County. 1903–1937.)
* UCB: X/23j and k/V109 [reel 46] and X/23k/NH107 [reel 59]
* LC: carton 36–37

X-23l   **Western Mono** (*Wo´-pon-nutch.* Mill Flat Valley, Ko-ho´-neje, Fresno County. 1930. From Joe Whaley and family.)
* UCB: X/23l/V110 [reel 46] and X/23l/NH108 [reel 59]
* LC: carton 37

X-23m   **Western Mono** (*En´-tim-bitch.* Mill Valley, Fresno County. 1903–1937. From "Tanner Dick" and Samson Dick.)
* UCB: X/23m/V111 [reel 46] and X23m/NH109 [reel 59]
* LC: carton 36–37

X-23n   **Western Mono** (*Wuksa-che´.* Eshom Valley, Tulare County. 1903–1935. From "Eshom Bob" Osborn.)
* UCB: X/23n/V112 [reel 46] and X/23n/NH110 [reel 59]
* LC: carton 37

X-23r   **Owens Valley Paiute** (*To´-bo-ah-hax-ze,* Bishop Piute, or *Pe-ton´-a-guat.* Bishop, Owens Valley. 1902–1937.)
* UCB: X/23r/V113 [reel 46; 2 copies] and X/23r/NH111 [missing]
* LC: carton 37–38

X-23r-t   **Owens Valley Paiute** (*To´-bo-ah-hax-ze* and *No´-no-pi-ah.* Lone Pine and Big Pine, Owens Valley, Inyo County. 1909–1935.)
* UCB: X/23r and t/V114 [reel 46] and X/23t/NH113 [missing]
* LC: carton 37–38

X-23s   **Owens Valley Paiute** (*Chuk´-ke-sher-ra´-ka,* Independence Piute. Independence, Owens Valley, Inyo County. 1938. From Mrs. Daisy Kruz and Hazel Richards.)
* UCB: X/23s/V115 [reel 47; 3 copies] and X/23s/NH112 [reel 59]
* LC: carton 37–38

X-23u-v   **Panamint** (*Pak´-wa-sitch* and *Moo-et´-tah,* Panamint Shoshone. Death and Panamint Valleys, Olancha, and east side of Owens Lake, Inyo County. 1902–1932.)
* UCB: X/23u/V116 and X/23u and v/V117 [reel 47]; X/23u/NH114 [reel 59]
* LC: carton 37

X-23w   **Kawaiisu** (*New-oo´-ah* and *Ow´-wah-tum new-oo´-ah.* Piute Mountain and Kelso Creek; Tehachapi Basin; Mohave River. 1902–1935. From Andrew and Rosalia Mace and Joanne Mike; "John.")

* UCB: X/23w/V118, X/23w/V119, and X/23w/
V120 [reel 47]; X/23w/NH115 and X/23w/
NH116 [reel 59]
* LC: carton 39

X-23y   **Southern Paiute** (*Nu-vah´-ahn-dits, Pi-yu´-che,*
and *Pa-nar-a-nap.* Ash Meadows, Amargosa
Desert, and Las Vegas. 1906–1931.)
* UCB: X/23y/NH117 [reel 59], Misc/Nev/V138
[reel 50]
* LC: carton 39–40

X-23z   **Chemehuevi** (*Chem-e-we´-ve, Na´-o.* Mara (29
Palms); Colorado River. 1912–1933. From
Mary Mack, Dorothy Ruiz, Mrs. Tom Morongo;
Charley Johnson and Lucy Smith.)
* UCB: X23z/V121 and X/23z/V122 [reel 47];
X/23z/NH118 [reel 59; 2 copies]
* LC: carton 39

[TAKIC]

X-23aa   **Kitanemuk** (*Ke-tan-a-mu-kum* or *Ke-tah´-na´-
mwits.* San Bernardino Mountains and Tejon
Canyon. 1903–1905. From Alto Mirando Vadio
and Mrs. J. V. Rosemyer.)
* UCB: X/23aa/V123 and X/23aa/V124 [reel 48];
X/23aa/NH119 [reel 60]
* LC: carton 36

X-23cc-dd   **Serrano-Vanyume** (*Mo-he-ah´-ne-um* and
Yo-hah´-ve-tum. San Bernardino and San Manuel
Reservation at Patton. 1907–1933.)
* UCB: X/23cc and dd/NH120 [reel 60]

X-23dd   **Serrano-Vanyume** (*Ma´-ring-am* and *Mo-he-ah´-
ne-yum.* San Bernardino Mountains, Morongo
Reservation. 1907–1933. From Joaquina
Moronga, Ida Miguel, Isaac Morongo, Valentine
Santiago, and Macario Marcos.)
* UCB: X/23dd/V125 [reel 48] and X/23dd/
NH121 [reel 60]
* LC: carton 36

X-23ff   **Pass Cahuilla** (*Wah´-ne-kik´-tem* or *Mahl´-ke.*
Northeast of Banning. 1910–1932. From
William Pablo and Juana Antonio.)
* UCB: X/23ff/V126 [reel 48] and X/23ff/
NH122 [reel 60]
* LC: carton 35–36

X-23gg   **Desert Cahuilla** (*Kah-we-sik´-tem.* Palm Springs.
1907–1932. From Francesco Patencio.)
* UCB: X/23gg/V127 [reel 48] and X/23gg/
NH123 [reel 60]
* LC: carton 35–36

X-23jj-kk   **Mountain Cahuilla** (*Pow´-we-yam* and *Sow´-
wis-pah-kik´-tem.* Cahuilla Valley and Santa
Rosa Mountain region. 1910–1934. From
Chief Leonicia Lugo, Lupy Lugo, Frank Albers,
Calistro Tortes and wife.)

* UCB: X/23jj and kk/V128 [reel 48] and
X/23kk/NH124 [reel 60]
* LC: carton 35–36

X-23mm   **Cupeño** (*Koo´-pah.* Agua Caliente, Warner Valley.
1909–1934. From Angelita Chaves, Rosinda
Nolasques, Francis Bosley, and Simma R.
Chavis.)
* UCB: X/23mm/V129 [reel 48] and X/23mm/
NH125 [reel 60]
* LC: carton 36

X-23nn-pp   **Luiseño** (*A-katch´-mah, Pi-yum´-ko,* and *So-bo´-ba.*
San Diego County. 1918–1936. From J. R.
Amago, Francisco Cuevas, and Antonio La
Chuza.)
* UCB: X/23nn-pp/V130 [reel 49]
* LC: carton 35–36

X-23nn   **Pechanga Luiseño** (*Chum-p´-wum.* Pechanga.
1919.)
* UCB: X/23nn/NH126 [reel 60]

X-23oo   **La Jolla and Soboba Luiseño** (*Pi-yum´-ko* and
So-bo´-ba. La Jolla Reservation and Soboba.
1907–1936.)
* UCB: X/23oo/NH127 [reel 60]

X-23pp   **Soboba Luiseño** (*So-bo´-ba.* San Jacinto River,
northeast of Hemet. 1933. From Isabel Erietta
and old Jesus Howro.)
* UCB: X/23pp/NH128 [reel 60]

Y. Gabrielino ("Tongva")

Y-24a   **Gabrielino** (*Tong-va.* San Gabriel [collected in
Bakersfield]. 1903. From Mrs. J. V. Rosemyer.)
* UCB: Y/24a/V130a [reel 49], Y/24a/BL21 [reel
51], and
Y/24a/NH129 [reel 60]
* LC: carton 41

Z. Tubatulabal ("Tubotelobela")

Z-25a   **Bankalachi-Toloim** (*Pahn´-ka-la´-che.* Upper Deer
Creek and Poso Flat. 1932–1935. From Mrs.
Louisa Francesco and Dan Williams.)
* UCB: Z/25a/V131 [reel 49] and Z/25a/NH130
[reel 60]
* LC: carton 42

Z-25b   **Pahkanapil-Tubatulabal** (*Tu-bot´-e-lob´-e-la.*
Kern Valley. 1902–1935.)
* UCB: Z/25b/V132 [reel 49] and Z/25b/NH131
[reel 60]
* LC: carton 42

Materials on California Indian Languages in
the Papers of John Peabody Harrington

B.1 The Harrington Papers

No single collection of archival material on California Indian languages rivals the Papers of John Peabody Harrington (1884–1961).[2] Largely consisting of the unprocessed notes that Harrington transcribed from speakers of more than a hundred languages during half a century of almost continual fieldwork, the Harrington Papers include the most thorough and accurate documentation we will ever have of several now-extinct California languages, including Chimariko, Chocheño and Rumsen Costanoan, Salinan, and several varieties of Chumash, as well as extremely valuable supplementary documentation for scores of others.

Since he was an employee of the Bureau of American Ethnography for most of his career, the bulk of Harrington's papers are federal documents and are archived in the National Anthropological Archives in Suitland, Maryland. During the 1980s most of the NAA's Harrington collection was cataloged and microfilmed under the supervision of Elaine Mills (Harrington 1982–1990; see Box B.1). At least a portion of the five-hundred-reel microfilm edition of the Harrington Papers is now available at many research libraries, particularly in California (see ¶B.6).

A small but significant portion of Harrington's manuscript notes, including a considerable part of his personal and academic correspondence, came to light too late for inclusion in the NAA microfilm. Some of these materials are in the NAA, separately cataloged, but the most important supplementary papers are archived in the Santa Barbara Museum of Natural History (see ¶B.4).

B.2 Work on the Materials

Users of the Harrington materials need to understand that many of the details of Harrington's fieldwork, including dates, locations, and even the names of the people from whom he obtained his material, often have to be inferred from the records themselves and from surviving correspondence. Harrington published little of the material he collected, and he was closemouthed about where, when, and on what languages he spent his research time. The official reports he submitted to the BAE were cursory and at times deliberately misleading. His supervisors in Washington were aware of only a small part of what he had obtained, primarily the materials that he kept in his Smithsonian office. The bulk of his collection, including many of the most valuable notes, was hidden away in a variety of locations: a small house he maintained in Santa Ana, a shed he owned in Santa Barbara, and storage units he rented in various warehouses, as well as in the care of various individuals, including in a few cases relatives of the people from whom he had obtained the data. Although most of the material has come to light, there is reason to believe that the location of some of it still remains unidentified.

In the fall of 1961, while still a graduate student at Berkeley, Catherine Callaghan was invited to spend several months in Washington helping the BAE archivist, Margaret Blaker, organize the notes that Harrington had left with the bureau. By the time of her arrival in Washington in January 1962, however, the BAE had begun to receive the tons of notes that Harrington had been storing in other locations, and the scope of Callaghan's cataloging work expanded to encompass a preliminary identification of all the languages represented in the material, packet by packet (Callaghan 1991). Working with Callaghan's inventory, Blaker and others compiled an index of the Harrington papers and related material in the BAE archives, and after the transfer of the BAE archives to the National Anthropological Archives in 1972, an archival assistant, Jane Walsh, prepared a detailed catalog focusing on the California materials (1976). By the 1970s the Harrington papers at the Smithsonian were accessible enough to attract the serious attention of anthropologists, and several manuscripts with data of ethnographic interest on the Chumash were edited for publication (Blackburn 1975; Hudson 1979; Hudson et al. 1977).[3]

executor. These included a considerable part of Harrington's field notes on Luiseño, Cahuilla, Serrano, Chumash, Kitanemuk, Tubatulabal, Salinan, Yokuts, Costanoan, and Chimariko. During the following decade these notes, whose primary value was linguistic rather than ethnographic, were the focus of considerable study, primarily by faculty and students at Berkeley. Several graduate students based their dissertations on portions of this material, including Richard Applegate 1972a, 1972b (Ineseño Chumash); Kenneth Hill 1967 (Serrano); Kathryn Klar 1971, 1977 (Obispeño and comparative Chumash); and Marc Okrand 1977 (Mutsun Costanoan). In addition, Geoffery Gamble worked through Harrington's Yokuts materials (Gamble 1991a); George Grekoff the Chimariko materials (Grekoff n.d.); William Bright the Luiseño materials (1965c, 1968); and Kenneth Whistler the Barbareño and Venureño Chumash materials (Whistler 1980b; Beeler and Whistler 1980). Several scholars worked extensively with Harrington's Chocheño and Rumsen Costanoan materials (see Callaghan 1992a; A. Miller n.d.; A. Miller and Callaghan n.d.; and Shipley 1980a). Also rooted in the Berkeley collection were the later dissertations of Alice Anderton 1988 (Kitanemuk) and Katherine Turner 1987 (Salinan).

B.3 The Microfilm Project

Beginning in the mid-1970s, the materials that had been housed in Berkeley were transferred to the Smithsonian to be consolidated with the materials there. In 1975, Geoffrey Gamble received a Smithsonian fellowship to work on the integration of the Washington and Berkeley materials, and the following year the National Anthropological Archives received a grant from the National Historical Publications and Records Commission for a five-year project to systematically catalog and microfilm the entire Harrington collection. Elaine Mills was appointed editor of this project, and between 1976 and 1981 several other Berkeley linguists followed Gamble as Smithsonian fellows to collaborate in the organizational work, including Kathryn Klar, Marc Okrand, and Kenneth Whistler; I also joined in this effort from my university position in Washington.

The first part of the *Papers of John Peabody Harrington in the Smithsonian Institution, 1907-1957* (Harrington 1982–1990), thirty microfilm reels of notes on the languages of Alaska and the Northwest Coast as far south as Oregon Athabaskan and Takelma, was released in 1981 (Mills 1981). It was followed by Part 2, 101 reels, covering the languages of Northern and Central California (Mills 1985), and Part 3, 182 reels, covering the languages of Southern California and the Basin (Mills and Brickfield 1986). Each part was accompanied by a *Guide to the Field Notes* prepared by Mills and her assistants. Four further parts, released between 1986 and 1988, covered Harrington's notes on the languages of the Southwest, the Plains, the Northeast and Southeast, and Mexico and Central and South America. Part

Around 1964–1965, some of the materials retrieved from Harrington's Santa Ana house and from other storage sites in California were entrusted to the linguistics department at UC Berkeley by Awona Harrington, his daughter and

8, including notes and writings on special linguistic studies, was released in 1989, and the series concluded in 1991 with Part 9, Harrington's correspondence and financial records. Overall, the collection includes 494 microfilm reels, with more than 750,000 frames, nearly 60 percent of which are devoted to Harrington's notes on languages of the California region. The microfilm and Mills's *Guides* are now available in many research libraries, especially in California, and are widely consulted by linguists, anthropologists, historians, and (increasingly) by Native Californians researching their tribal heritage.[4] The contents of the microfilm that are relevant to California languages are summarized in Box 16 and outlined in detail in ¶B.5.

In the 1990s, following completion of the microfilm project, a series of conferences were held at which scholars who were working with Harrington's materials shared information and discussed common problems. Five conferences were held: Santa Barbara, 1992; Washington, DC, 1993; San Juan Capistrano, 1994; Albuquerque, 1995; and Berkeley, 1996. Ten issues of a *Newsletter of the J. P. Harrington Conference* were circulated between 1991 and 1996, copies of which are still accessible online (www.rock-art.com/jph). A special issue of the journal *Anthropological Linguistics* was devoted to papers arising from the 1992 Santa Barbara meeting (Golla 1991b); other papers from this meeting were published in Redden 1993. Some of the papers from the 1996 Berkeley meeting were published in Hinton 1997.

In 2002, the *J. P. Harrington Database Project* was established in the Native American Language Center, department of Native American studies, UC Davis (http://nas.ucdavis.edu/NALC/JPH.html). The goal of the project (which has been funded by a series of National Science Foundation grants) is to increase access to the microfilm edition of Harrington's linguistic and ethnographic notes by transferring their contents to a searchable database. As the database is compiled, guides to the materials on each language are being prepared that will include dates and location of the fieldwork, with a list of all place-names mentioned; a full explanation of the orthography and symbols used for each language; biographical information on consultants and field assistants; cross-references to associated sound recordings, photographs, notes, and correspondence; and references to relevant linguistic and ethnographic publications.

B.4 Materials Not Included in the Microfilm Project

Harrington was a prolific collector of sound recordings. In his earlier work, between 1912 and 1930, the only practical recording device available to him was a wax cylinder phonograph, and the recordings he made are short and of relatively low fidelity. The subject matter is primarily songs. Much more important for the student of language are the approximately one thousand long-playing aluminum disks that Harrington (and field assistants working under his supervision) made on a custom-made machine between the mid-1930s and 1941 (Glenn 1991a). These recordings, which can be up to thirty minutes in length, are primarily of narrative texts or word lists. As the only extensive audio recordings of California languages before the advent of the tape recorder in the early 1950s, they have considerable potential value as linguistic documents, although to date relatively little use has been made of them. They are preserved in the National Anthropological Archives, but not indexed in the *Papers of John Peabody Harrington* microfilm or accompanying *Guides*. Their contents have all been transferred to reel-to-reel audio tapes, from which duplicate cassettes can be produced for researchers on demand. These recordings are catalogued in SIRIS (the Smithsonian Institution Research Information System, accessible online at www.siris.si.edu), and ordering information is posted at the NAA website (www.nmnh.si.edu/naa). Languages of the California region for which aluminum disc recordings exist include Cahuilla (32), Chimariko (1), Chumash languages (269), Costanoan languages (6), Oregon Athabaskan languages (34), Juaneño (145), Luiseño (118), Miwok languages (28), Salinan (55), Tubatulabal (19), other unidentified languages (101) (identifications as of 1992 as noted in Glenn 1991a).[5]

In the early 1980s, the Santa Barbara Museum of Natural History acquired several caches of papers from the estate of Harrington's daughter Awona. The collection includes approximately 1,000 pages (six boxes) of ethnographic and linguistic field notes, 4,500 letters, 1,185 photographs, 896 negatives, and numerous sound recordings, as well as a number of miscellaneous items (Johnson, Miller, and Agren 1991). Most of this material came to the Museum too late to be included in the Smithsonian's microfilming project. A detailed catalog of the ethnographic and linguistic notes has been compiled. In terms of volume and research importance, the Chumash materials may be the most significant. They include Harrington's original notes from the Ventureño speaker, Fernando Librado, recorded in 1912–1913, and a fair amount of Barbareño material from his work with Mary Yee in the 1950s.

B.5 Language Index to the California Materials on the Microfilm

References are to volume, reel, and frame of the microfilm as detailed in Mills (1981, 1985) and Mills and Brickfield (1986).

ALGIC (MILLS 1985, 3-9)
Wiyot (Amos Riley and Birdie James, 1926, 1942)

Vocabulary	2:1:317–323
Comparative vocabulary	2:1:324–717
Place-names	2:2:407–565

Yurok (Charlie Williams and Orick Bob, 1942)

Place-names   2:2:1–406

ATHABASKAN: OREGON ATHABASKAN
(MILLS 1981:47–54, 69–77)
Upper Umpqua (John Warren, 1940)

Rehearings of Kwalhioqua-Tlatskanai1:   19:2–287

Upper Coquille (Coquille Thompson, 1942); Lower Rogue River (Wolverton Orton and Lucy Smith, 1942); Chetco-Tolowa (several speakers, 1942)

Comparative vocabulary	1:25:2–1146
Tribe names and place-names	1:26:3–1268
Grammatical notes	1:27:2–209
Texts	1:27:210–487
Ethnographic notes	1:27:488–512
Historical notes	1:27:513–541
Miscellaneous	1:27:542–646

Galice-Applegate (Hoxie Simmons, 1940–1942)

Miscellaneous   1:28:2–120

ATHABASKAN: CALIFORNIA ATHABASKAN
(MILLS 1985:3–15, 49–56)
Hupa: New River variety (Saxy Kidd, 1928)

Interview   2:24:141–156

Mattole (Ike Duncan and Johnny Jackson, 1942)

Placenames   2:2:566–710

Bear River (Theodore Prince, 1942)

Comparative vocabulary   2:1:324–717

Kato (Gil Ray and Martina Bell, 1942)

Place-names	2:3:398–867; 2:4:1–163, 286–338
Rehearing of Esselen	2:4:339–485
Biographical and miscellaneous	2:4:495–559

CHIMARIKO (MILLS 1985:49–56)
Trinity River (Sally Noble and Martha Ziegler, 1921–1922)

Linguistic notes	2:20:1–1093
Grammar	2:20:1093–1168
Texts	2:21:1–539

Trinity River (Lucy Montgomery, 1926–1928)

Vocabulary	2:22:1–333
Rehearing of Sally Noble notes	2:23:1–1175
Ethnographic notes˙	2:24:1–141

New River (Saxy Kidd, 1928)

Interview   2:24:141-156

Hayfork (Billy George and Abe Bush, 1928, 1931–1932)

Wintu-Chimariko vocabulary	2:30:1–782; 2:31:1–178
Rehearing of Dixon (1910)	2:31:179–263
Place-names	2: 35:1–249

CHUMASH (MILLS AND BRICKFIELD 1986:1–55)
Obispeño (Juan Solano, 1912; Rosario Cooper, 1913-17)

Field notes	3:1:1-837
Secondary sources	3:1:838–921
Semantic slip file	3:2:1–761
Grammatical slip file	3:3:1–958; 3:4:1–818
Grammatical sketch	3:4:819–889
Copies of field notes	3:5:1–861
Miscellaneous notes	3:5:862–883

Barbareño (Juan de Jesús Justo, 1914–1915, 1919, 1923; Luisa and Juliana Ignacio, 1914–1915, 1923; Lucrecia García, 1929–1931; Mary Yee, 1952–1960)

Field notes	3:19:1–1006
Slip file	3:20:1–1147; 3:21:1–501
Linguistic notes	3:22:1–973
Rehearing of Ineseño notes	3:23:1:659 to 3:33:1–179
Grammatical notes	3:33:180–1188 to 3:49:1–787
Ethnobotany	3:50:1–277
Place-name trips	3:50:278–469
Rehearings of earlier vocabularies:	
Henshaw	3:50:470–847 to 3:52:1–499
Merriam	3:52:500–671
Pinart	3:52:672–1070 to 3:53:1–984
Portolá	3:53:985–1077
Taylor	3:54:1–172
(Unidentified)	3:54:173-223
Texts:	
Luisa Ignacio	3:54:224–345
Juan de Jesús Justo	3:54:346–816
Lucrecia García	3:55:1–559 to 3:58:1–746
Mary Yee	3:59:1–708 to 3:66:1–242
Ethnographic and historical notes	3:66:243–769
Secondary sources	3:67:1–466

Inezeño (María Solares, 1914–1916, 1919)

Field notes	3:7:1–1011 to 3:8:1–900
Texts	3:9:1–1154
Semantic slip file	3:10:1–0596 to 3:13:1–506
Miscellaneous slip file	3:13:507–775
Grammatical slip file	3:14:1–731 to 3:15:1–492
Dictionary	3:16:1–586 to 3:18:1–564
Miscellaneous notes and secondary sources	3:18:565–811

Purisimeño (María Solares, 1914–1916)

Field notes	3:6:1–212
Slip files	3:6:213–613
Notes for grammatical sketch	3:6:614–628
Secondary sources	3:6:629–860

Ventureño (Fernando Librado, 1912–1914; Simplicio Pico, José Juan Olivas, 1915–1933)

Field notes [1912–1913]	3:69:1–1107
Semantically arranged vocabulary	3:70:1–721 to 3:75:1–639
Semantic slip file	3:76:1–871 to 3:78:1–596
Encyclopedia	3:79:1–744; 3:80:1–737
Linguistic notes [1915–1918]	3:81:1–651 to 3:88:1–577
Dictionary [BAE MS 3039]	3:89:1–741 to 3:93:1–460
Grammar [BAE MS 2966, 3045, 3057]	3:94:1–923
Texts	3:95:1–85
Place-name trips	3:95:86–289
Secondary sources	3:95:290–434
Miscellaneous notes	3:95:435–610

Island Chumash (Fernando Librado, 1912–1913)

Rehearing of early vocabularies	3:68:1–454
Cruzeño linguistic notes	3:68:455–536
Cruzeño semantic slip file	3:68:537–712
Miscellaneous Chumash records, writings	3:95:611–807 to 3:96:1–672

Compilations of other sources; rehearings with Isabelle Meadows

Drafts of papers on Esselen	2:81:1–441
Primary and secondary sources	2:81:441–663
Slip file of vocabulary, cognates	2:81:664–982; 2:82:1–478
Rehearing of Esselen vocabulary	2:82:479–640; 2:83:1–425
Comparison of Esselen and Southern Pomo	2:83:426–450

Katimin (Fritz Hanson, Sylvester Donahue, and Phoebe Maddux, 1925–1929)

Vocabulary	2:6:1–915; 2:7:1–591
Ethnographic notes and place-names	2:8:1–767; 2:9:1–958
Grammar	2:10:1–1013; 2:11:1–658
Miscellaneous	2:11:658–835
Texts	2:13:1–885; 2:14:1–222
Songs	2:14:223–1024; 2:15:1–195

Klamath (Mr. and Mrs. Jesse Kirk, before 1946)

Rehearing of Gatschet	2:1:1–313

Nisenan (Lizzie Enos and others, 1939)

Vocabularies	2:5:353–477
Miscellaneous	2:5:478–569

Achumawi (James Hawkins, 1922)

Vocabulary	2:25:1–123
Texts	2:26.1–289
Ethnographic and biographical notes	2:26:392–431

Achumawi (Rosa Charles, Clara Grant, and Billy Wright, 1931)

Yana-Achumawi-Wintu vocabulary	2:27:1–928; 2:28:1–291
Place-names	2:32:1–343
Ethnographic and biographical notes	2:35:329–398

Atsugewi (Clara Grant, 1922)

Vocabulary and grammatical notes	2:25:124–451
Myths	2:26:289–340
Ethnographic and biographical notes	2:26:392–431

Northern Pomo: Sherwood (several speakers, 1942–1943)

Vocabulary and ethnographic notes	2:3:1–397
Place-names	2:3:398–867; 2:4:1–163, 286–338
Biographical and miscellaneous	2:4:495–559

Central Pomo: Point Arena (Harvey James, 1942–1943)

Place-names	2:4:163–285

Southern Pomo (Manuel Córdova, 1947)

Coast Miwok place-names	2:5:573–618

Southeastern Pomo/Kashaya (Henry Knight and Jake Knight, 1942)

Comparative vocabulary	2:5:162–349

Antoniano and Migueleño (Juan Solano and Pacífico Archuleta, 1912–1913; David and María Mora, 1922; María de los Angeles Ocarpia and Tito Encinales, 1930–1932)

Early Migueleño field notes	2:84:1–113
Migueleño slip file	2:84:114–257
Antoniano and Migueleño field notes	2:84:258–437
Antoniano and Migueleño vocabulary	2:85:1–1204; 2:86:1–380
Rehearing of Mason, "Ethnology"	2:86:381–489
Rehearing of Mason, "Language"	2:86:490–644
Rehearing of vocabulary	2:86:645–1190; 2:87:1–1001
Rehearing of Sitjar's vocabulary	2:88:1–413
Place-names	2:88:414–655
Miscellaneous notes	2:88:655–820

SHASTAN (MILLS 1985:29–49)

Konomihu (Mrs. Grant and Susan Brizelle, 1926–1928, 1933)

Word list	2:12:161–362
Place-names	2:12:363–703
Miscellaneous	2:12:704–815

Shasta: Scott Valley, Shasta Valley (Mrs. Grant and Susan Brizelle, 1928, 1933)

Vocabulary	2:12:1–161
Miscellaneous	2:12:704–815

TAKELMA (MILLS 1981:78–80)

Lowland Takelma, Upland Takelma (Frances Johnson, Molly Orcutt, 1933)

Linguistic and ethnographic notes	1:28:123–398
Place-name trips	1:28:399–887

UTIAN: COSTANOAN (MILLS 1985:81–120)

San Francisco Bay: Chocheño (Angela Colos, José Guzman, 1921, 1929–1930)

Chocheño and Mutsun song texts	2:36:1–111
Linguistic and ethnographic notes	2:36:112–711; 2:37:1–812
Notes from José Guzman	2:37:813–825

Mutsun (Tomás Torres, 1922; Ascención Solórsano, 1922, 1929–1930)

Dictionary	2:38:1–625 to 2:41:1–47
Rehearing of Merriam's vocabularies	2:41:47–91
Rehearing of Henshaw's vocabulary	2:41:92–110
Rehearing of mission records	2:41:110–150
Rehearing of Arroyo de la Cuesta's "Vocabulario" [BAE MS 4557]	2:41:150–792 to 2:57:1–188
Rehearing of religious texts in Arroyo's "Vocabulario"	2:57:189–408
Rehearing of Arroyo's "Oro Molido"	2:57:409–657
Rehearing of Arroyo's "Gramática"	2:58:1–240
Harrington's "San Juan Report" MS	2:58:240–996; 2:59:1–1126
Harrington's "Medicine Practices" MS	2:60:1–774; 2:61:1–525

Rumsen (Laura Ramírez, 1929–1930; Isabelle Meadows, 1932–1939)

Rehearing of early vocabularies	2:61:525–1116
Linguistic notes	2:62:1–392
Rehearing of Kroeber's notes	2:62:393–777; 2:63:1–352
Rehearing of Henshaw's vocabulary	2:63:353–602
Rehearing of Taylor's vocabulary	2:63:602–718
Rehearing of Pinart's vocabulary	2:64:1–1028 to 2:66:1–913
Rehearing of Pinart's Esselen-Rumsen vocabulary	2:66:914–1054; 2:67:1–126

Rehearing of Latham's article	2:67:127–131
Rehearing of Kroeber's articles	2:67:131–203
Tribe names and place-names	2:67:203–235
Rehearing of mission records	2:67:235–320
Rehearing of Bancroft documents	2:67:321–332
Dictionary	2:67:332–773
Place-names	2:68:1–232
Grammatical questionnaire	2:70:287–369
Texts	2:71:1–420
Miscellaneous notes	2:72:1–884 to 2:80:1–523

Other languages reheard with Mutsun and Rumsen speakers (1929–1939)

Arroyo's Mutsun grammar (with Isabelle Meadows)	2:68:232–297
Arroyo's San Francisco vocabularies	2:68:298–448
Johnston's San Francisco vocabulary	2:68:448–627
Henshaw's Santa Clara vocabulary	2:68:628–733
Mengarini's Santa Clara vocabulary	2:68:733–809
Duflot de Mofras's copy of the "Santa Clara" Lord's Prayer	2:68:810–903
Comelias's Santa Cruz vocabulary	2:69:1–116
Pinart's Santa Cruz vocabulary	2:69:117–338
Henshaw's Yokuts vocabularies from Santa Cruz	2:69:338–584
Hale's Soledad vocabulary	2:69:585–599
Henshaw's Soledad vocabulary	2:69:600–648; 2:70:1–144
Pinart's Soledad vocabulary	2:70:145–270
Pinart's Delta Yokuts vocabulary	2:70:270–284
Duflot de Mofras's copy of the "Tulareño" Lord's Prayer	2:70:284–286

UTIAN: MIWOK (MILLS 1985:16–18, 21–29)

Coast Miwok: Bodega and Nicasio (Mariano Miranda, 1939); Tomales (Julia Elgin, 1939)

Place-names	2:5:1–97
Historical and ethnographic notes	2:5:98–154
Miscellaneous	2:5:155–158

Coast Miwok: Bodega and Tomales (Henry Knight, Maggie Smith Johnson, 1942)

Comparative vocabulary	2:5:162–349
Materials on Drake's landfall	2:5:573–978

Lake Miwok (Henry Knight, 1942)

Comparative vocabulary	2:5:162–349

Northern Sierra Miwok (Mike Murray, 1939)

Vocabularies	2:5:353–477
Miscellaneous notes	2:5:478–569

UTO-AZTECAN: NUMIC (MILLS AND BRICKFIELD 1986:105–116, 137–141)

Chemehuevi (Jack Jones, George Johnson, and Ohue, 1910–1911)

Vocabulary	3:131:1–649

Chemehuevi (George Laird, Annie Laide, and Ben Paddock, 1919–1920)

Field notes of Carobeth T. Harrington	3:132:1–1006
Slip file	3:133:1–959 to 3:135:1–571
Grammar	3:136:1–798 to 3:145:1–516
Semantic vocabulary	3:146:1–116
Texts	3:146:117–1006; 3:147:1–378
Miscellaneous notes	3:147:379–518

Chemehuevi (Lucy Mike and Luisa, 1946)

Field notes	3:147:519–963

UTO-AZTECAN: TAKIC (MILLS AND BRICKFIELD 1986:60–104)
Kitanemuk (Eugenia Mendez, José Juan Olivas, and Magdalena Olivas, 1916–1917)

Linguistic and ethnographic notes	3:98:1–707
Semantic slip file	3:99:1–680 to 3:100:1–320
Dictionary	3:100:321–713
Grammar	3:100:714–914

Serrano (Manuel Santos and Tomás Manuel, 1918)

Linguistic and ethnographic notes	3:101:1–301
Semantic slip file	3:101:302–862

Gabrielino (José María Zalvidea, José de los Santos Juncos, and Felicita Serrano Montaño, 1914–1922; Jesús Jauro, 1932–1933)

Slip file	3:102:1–877
Linguistic and ethnographic notes	3:103:1–765 to 3:105:1–476
Song texts	3:105:477–555
Miscellaneous notes	3:105:556–715

Fernandeño (Setimo López, 1916)

Field notes	3:106:1–251

Luiseño-Juaneño (José Olivas Albañez, 1919, 1932–1934; Anastacia de Majel, 1933–1936)

Luiseño linguistic, ethnographic notes	3:115:1–322
Luiseño vocabulary	3:116:1–529 to 3:118:1–358
Luiseño place-name trips, interviews	3:119:1–435
Luiseño texts	3:120:1–671 to 3:121:1–336
Luiseño miscellaneous notes	3:121:337–451
Juaneño vocabulary	3:121:452–496
Juaneño linguistic, ethnographic notes	3:121:497–792 to 3:123:1–235
Rehearings of Sparkman	3:123:236–647; 3:124:1–754
Drafts and notes for *Chinigchinich*	3:125:1–950 to 3:127:1–304

Rehearings of notes for *Chinigchinich*	3:127:305–607; 3:128:1–293
Notes and drafts for a new version of Boscana's account	3:128:294–704; 3:129:1–824

Cupeño (Martin Blacktooth, 1915; Francisco Laws, Manuel Chuparosa, and Marcelino Cahuish, 1925)

Vocabulary, grammar [BAE MS 6062]	3:130:1–710
Text	3:130:711–712

Cahuilla (Adan Castillo, 1922, 1930–1952)

Comparative vocabulary	3:107:1–825
Grammar [BAE MS 6040, 6051–6052, 6061, 6064]	3:108:1–914 to 3:111:1–864
Texts [BAE MS 6050–6051]	3:112:1–528
Writings [BAE MS 6052, 6065]	3:113:1–760; 3:114:1–226
Miscellaneous linguistic notes	3:114:227–420

UTO-AZTECAN: TUBATULABAL (MILLS AND BRICKFIELD 1986:56–59)
Pahkanapil ["Rio Chiquito"] (Angela Lozada, 1916); Estévan Miranda, 1933–1934)

Vocabulary	3:97:1–118
Grammar	3:97:119–267
Linguistic and ethnographic notes	3:97:268–307
Place-name trips	3:97:308–352
Interviews	3:97:353–376

WINTUAN (MILLS 1985:63–81)
Wintu: Hayfork (Billy George and Abe Bush, 1928, 1931–1932)

Wintu-Chimariko vocabulary	2:30:1–782; 2:31:1–178
Rehearing of Dixon (1910)	2:31:179–263
Place-names: Hayfork, Hyampom	2:34:198–631

Wintu: Upper Sacramento and Upper Trinity (Charlie Daniels, Jim Feder, Fred and Tildy Griffin, and Martha Sperry, 1931)

Place-names: Upper Trinity region	2:32:343–805
Place-names: Upper Sacramento region	2:33:1–157

Wintu: McCloud River (Mary Nichols, 1931)

Yana Achumawi-Wintu vocabulary	2:27:1–928; 2:28:1–291
Place-names: McCloud River	2:33:157–487
Place-names: Lower Pit and Redding	2:34:1–197
Ethnographic and biographical notes	2:35:329–398

Wintu: Unidentified dialect [and Shasta?] (Sarah Kloochoo, 1931–1932)

Miscellaneous notes	2:35:399–465

YANA (MILLS 1985:56–81)

Montgomery Creek, Cassel (Kate Snooks, Albert Thomas, Walter Moody, and Mrs. Hank Haley, 1922)

Vocabulary	2:25:452–571
Myths	2:26:340–391

Montgomery Creek, Round Mountain (Grapevine Tom, 1931)

Yana-Achumawi-Wintu vocabulary	2:27:1–928; 2:28:1–291
Rehearing of Sapir, "Yana Texts"	2:28:292–612; 2:29:1–501
Rehearing of Sapir, "The Position of Yana in the Hokan Stock"	2:29:502–555
Rehearing of Sapir, "Yana Terms of Relationship"	2:29:555–613
Rehearing of Sapir, "Text Analyses of Three Yana Dialects"	2:29:613–627
Rehearing of Waterman, "The Yana Indians"	2:29:627–645
Rehearing of Esselen	2:29:645–685
Place-names	2:31:263–719
Ethnographic and biographical notes	2:35:329–398

YOKUTS (MILLS 1985:141–160)

Poso Creek: Palewyami (Estevan Soto, 1916–1917)

Linguistic and other notes	2:89:154–1504
Slip file	2:95:110–169

Buena Vista: Hometwoli (Maria Wheaton, 1916–1917)

Linguistic and other notes	2:89:154–1504

Yawdanchi, Wikchamni (Juana Dionisio and Francisca Lola, 1916–1917)

Linguistic and other notes	2:89:154–1504
Yawelmani-Koyeti-Yawdanchi-Wikchamni slip file	2:92:1–691 to 2:95:1–89
Miscellaneous slip files	2:95:170–356

Valley dialects (Bob Bautista, Joseph Brunell, Josefa Cordero, Josefa Damián, Rosendo Ellis, Francisca Lola, and others, 1914, 1916–1917)

Early field notes	2:89:1–153
Linguistic and other notes	2:89:154–1504
Chunut-Tachi slip file	2:90:1–833; 2:91:1–893
Yawelmani-Koyeti-Yawdanchi-Wikchamni slip file	2:92:1–691 to 2:95:1–89
Choynok slip file	2:95:89–109
Copies of Chunut and Tachi notes	2:96:1–799
Copies of Koyeti and Yawelmani notes	2:96:800–975
Yawelmani grammatical slip files	2:97:1–539 to 2:99:1–568
Yawelmani grammar	2:100:1–954
Tejon Ranch Case notes	2:100:954–1190; 2:101:1–145
Notes on recordings of songs (1916–1917)	2:101:146–437
Miscellaneous notes	2:101:438–706

YUKIAN (MILLS 1985:9–15, 18–21)

Yuki [Not on microfilm; see Harrington n.d.]

   Coast Yuki (Lucy Perez, 1942–1943)

Place-names	2:3:398–867; 2:4:1–163, 286–338
Rehearing of Esselen	2:4:339–485
Notes on myths	2:4:486–494
Biographical and miscellaneous	2:4:495–559

Wappo (Henry Knight and Jake Knight, 1942)

Comparative vocabulary	2:5:162–349

YUMAN-COCHIMÍ (MILLS AND BRICKFIELD 1986:116–137)

Cochimí: Borjeño, Rosareño, "Judillo" (Carmen Melendrez, Manuel Manriquez, and others, 1925[?]; see Mixco 1977a)

Linguistic and ethnographic notes	3:171:1–99

Diegueño: U.S. groups (Isidro Nejo, 1913; Angel Quilpe and others, 1925–1927)

Semantic slip file	3:169:1–064
Linguistic and ethnographic notes	3:169:65–568

Diegueño: Baja California (Feliciano Manteca, Bartelo Prieto, and others, 1925–1926, 1932)

Linguistic and ethnographic notes	3:170:1–340

Diegueño: U.S. and Baja California mixed

Notebooks	3:170:341–777

Kiliwa: San Pedro Mártir, Domingueño, Jaka?akwal (Manuel Manriquez and others, 1925[?]; see Mixco 1977a)

Linguistic and ethnographic notes	3:171:1–99

Mojave (Ferd Wagner, Lee Irving, and others, 1907–1914)

Linguistic and ethnographic notes	3:148:1–1077 to 3:156:1–571
Semantic slip file	3:157:1–717 to 3:158:1–808
Linguistic and ethnographic notebooks	3:159:1–386
Grammatical notes and slip file	3:159:387–540 to 3:160:1–519

Mojave (Hal Davidson, Mr. and Mrs. Harry Lewis, 1946)

Linguistic and ethnographic notes	3:162:1–807 to 3:164:1–852
Notes on material culture	3:165:1–604; 3:166:1–882
Notes on tribe names	3:167:1–383
Semantically arranged notes	3:167:384–812
Grammatical notes	3:168:1–244
Miscellaneous notes	3:168:245–423

Paipai (Various informants, 1925[?])

Linguistic and ethnographic notes	3:171:1–99

Various Yuman languages

Miscellaneous notes	3:161:1–354

B.6 Availability of the Harrington Microfilm in North American Research Libraries (Information as of 2007)

I. LIBRARIES HOLDING COMPLETE OR NEARLY COMPLETE SETS OF THE ENTIRE MICROFILM (PARTS 1–9)

Stanford University (Green Library, Humanities, Social Sciences)

University of California, Riverside

University of Arizona (Part 9, *Correspondence*, lacking)

University of Colorado, Boulder

Boston Public Library

University of Pittsburgh

McMaster University (Hamilton, Ontario)

Mashantucket Pequot Museum and Research Center

II. LIBRARIES HOLDING A PORTION OF THE CALIFORNIA REELS (PARTS 1–3)

Part 1 only:

University of California, Davis

University of Oregon

Lewis and Clark College

University of Hawaii, Manoa

Parts 1 and 2:

CSU East Bay (Hayward)

San Diego State University

Arizona State University (also has Part 9, *Correspondence*)

Central Washington University

Part 2 only:

CSU Chico

CSU Sacramento

San Jose State University

Parts 2 and 3:

CSU Northridge

Part 3 only:

Florida State University (also Part 4, *Southwest*, and Part 6, *Northeast/Southeast*)

Smaller holdings:

University of Nevada, Reno: Part 3, reels 131–147 and 171
Humboldt State University: Part 2, reels 1–24

Phonetic Transcription Systems Widely Used in California Indian Language Materials

C.1 Scientific and Nonscientific Transcription

Before 1880 nearly everyone who transcribed the speech of California Indians used a phonetic system of his own devising. Sometimes this was little more than an attempt to employ the Latin alphabet in a regular manner. A handful of experienced observers—Arroyo de la Cuesta, Horatio Hale, Alphonse Pinart—went beyond this to construct idiosyncratic but consistent representations for such non-European sounds as retroflex stops and fricatives, voiceless laterals, and on occasion glottalized stops and affricates. Philologists working with the manuscripts of this period must become familiar with the individual habits of each transcriber.

Pinart, working in the late 1870s, was the first to employ a more general phonetic alphabet, that of the influential German orientalist Richard Lepsius (1863). By the last decade of the nineteenth century, most transcribers of California Indian languages had received some amount of phonetic training and attempted to adhere to one or another standard phonetic orthography in their recordings. During the twentieth century, as linguistics advanced, orthographies became more precise and systematic, but also more diverse. During the ninety-year span between 1880 and 1970, when the bulk of our present documentation of California Indian languages was obtained, at least five distinct scientific systems were in common use at different times in various institutional traditions. The principal features of these systems are outlined in Table C.1 as a guide to researchers. The symbols in the rightmost column, the American Phonemic tradition, are those generally used in this book.

Two important collectors of data on California languages during the first half of the twentieth century, C. Hart Merriam and William Myers, carried out their work—to some extent deliberately—on the periphery of the anthropological-linguistic establishment. Despite their avowed scientific goals, both men continued to amass data in idiosyncratic

prescientific orthographies derived from the conventions of the English alphabet. As with material from the earlier period, those making use of these transcriptions, especially Merriam's, must take the time to familiarize themselves with the transcriber's usages. While these are usually internally consistent, they do not (especially in Merriam's case) map neatly onto scientific phonetic or phonemic transcriptions. Both men were self-taught linguists, and Merriam was particularly hostile to structuralist interpretations of speech.[6]

C.2 The Five Major Transcriptional Systems

IPA

Although the International Phonetic Alphabet was available to researchers as early as the 1880s, the IPA was rarely used for the transcription of California Indian languages until recent decades, and its use is still largely confined to technical discussions of phonetics.

BAE

The revised and expanded phonetic alphabet recommended by the Bureau of American Ethnology in the second edition of Powell's *Introduction to the Study of Indian Languages* (1880f), was used by Dorsey, Gatschet, Powell himself, and a few others for the transcription of California Indian languages between 1880 and 1900.

KROEBER

A revised version of the BAE orthography, used by anthropologists trained under Franz Boas, was widely employed in California by A. L. Kroeber and his students and colleagues between 1900 and 1935. For descriptions see Boas (1911) and Boas and colleagues (1916). The version of this orthography employed by Sapir is described in each volume of his *Collected Works*.

The orthography used by J. P. Harrington throughout his field career (1906–1960) was an eclectic mix of BAE and IPA practices. No full published description exists. Harrington described his phonetic practice as of 1912 in correspondence with Sapir and Kroeber that has been published in Golla (1984, 444–448).

AMERICAN PHONEMIC

This orthography, favored by American linguists and anthropologists beginning about 1935, is characterized by unit symbols for affricates and associated with phonemic structuralism. It continues to be used in most technical publications on California Indian languages, including volumes in the *University of California Publications in Linguistics* and *Reports of the Survey of California and Other Indian Languages*, and is the basis for the orthography used in this book. For a description see Herzog and colleagues (1934). It should be noted that a special version of the American Phonemic orthography has been used by Callaghan, Broadbent, and others in publications on Miwok and Costanoan, and by Shipley and his students in publications on Maiduan. In this version, the approximant [y] is written *j* (as in IPA) and the nonfront high unrounded vowel [ɨ] or [ï] is written *y*.

TABLE C.1

Principal Transcription Systems Used for California Indian Languages

	IPA	BAE	Kroeber	JPH	Phonemic
Stops					
Bilabial					
Plain	p	p	p	p	p
Voiced	b	b	b	b	b
Aspirated	pʰ	p‘	p‘	p‘	pʰ
Glottalized	p’	p’	p!	p’	p’
Dental-alveolar					
Plain	t	t	t	t	t
Voiced	d	d	d	d	d
Aspirated	tʰ	t‘	t‘	t‘	tʰ
Glottalized	t’	t’	t! / t’	t’	t’
Retroflex					
Plain	ṭ	(t)	t·	ṭ / tʳ	ṭ
Voiced	ḍ	(d)	d·	ḍ / dʳ	ḍ
Aspirated	ṭʰ	(t‘)	t·‘	ṭ‘	ṭʰ
Glottalized	ṭ’	(t’)	t·! / t·’	ṭ’	ṭ’
Velar					
Plain	k	k	k	k	k
Voiced	g	g	g	g	g
Aspirated	kʰ	k‘	k‘	k‘	kʰ
Glottalized	k’	k’	k! / k’	k’	k’
Postvelar-uvular					
Plain	q	(k)	q	ĸ	q
Voiced	ɢ	(g)	g̣	ɢ	ġ
Aspirated	qʰ	(k‘)	q‘	ĸ‘	qʰ
Glottalized	q’	(k’)	q! / q’	ĸ’	q’
Nasals					
Bilabial	m	m	m	m	m
Dental-alveolar	n	n	n	n	n
Postalveolar-palatal	ɲ	ny	ny	ñ	ñ / nʸ
Velar	ŋ	ñ	ñ	ŋ / ṇ	ŋ

TABLE C.1
(continued)

	IPA	BAE	Kroeber	JPH	Phonemic
Fricatives					
Bilabial					
Plain/voiceless	ɸ	f	f	ɸ	ɸ
Voiced	β	v	v	β	β
Interdental					
Plain/voiceless	θ	ç	ç	θ	θ
Voiced	ð	¢	¢	δ	ð
Dental-alveolar					
Plain/voiceless	s	s	s	s	s
Voiced	z	z	z	z	z
Retroflex					
Plain/voiceless	ṣ	(s)	s·	ʃʳ / ṣ	ṣ
Voiced	ẓ	(z)	z·	ʒʳ / ẓ	ẓ
Lateral (voiceless)	ɬ	hl	ɬ	ɬ	ɬ
Palato-alveolar					
Plain/voiceless	ʃ	c	c	ʃ	š
Voiced	ʒ	j	j	ʒ	ž
Velar					
Plain/voiceless	x	q	x	q	x
Voiced	ɣ	ɣ	ɣ	ɣ	ɣ
Postvelar-uvular					
Plain/voiceless	χ	(q)	x̣	χ	x̣
Voiced	ʁ	(ɣ)	ɣ̣	ɣ̣	ɣ̣
Affricates					
Dental-alveolar					
Plain	ts	ts	ts	ts	c
Voiced	dz	dz	dz	dz	ʒ
Retroflex	tṣ	(ts)	ts·	tṣ / tʃʳ	c̣
Lateral	tɬ	(tl)	ʟ	tɬ	ƛ
Postalveolar-palatal					
Plain	tʃ	tc	tc	tʃ	č
Voiced	ʤ	dj	dj	ʤ	ǯ
Approximants					
Labiovelar	w	w	w	w	w
Retroflex	r	r	r	r	r
Palatal	j	y	y	j	y / j
Lateral	l	l	l	l	l
Laryngeals					
Glottal stop	ʔ	—	ᴱ / '	'	ʔ
Voiceless vowel	h	h	'	h / '	h

TABLE C.1
(continued)

	IPA	BAE	Kroeber	JPH	Phonemic
Vowels					
Front unrounded					
High	i	i	i	i	i
Lower-high	ɩ	ĭ	ɪ	ɩ / ɪ	ɪ
Higher-mid	e	e	e	e	e
Lower-mid	ɛ	ĕ	ê	ɛ	ɛ
Higher-low	æ	ä	ä	æ	æ
Low	a	a	a	a	a
Nonfront unrounded					
High	ɨ / ɯ	—	ï	ɨ / ɯ	ï / y
Higher-mid	ɤ	—	ë	ɤ	ë
Mid	ə	û	ᴇ	ə	ə
Lower-mid	ʌ	û	α / ʌ	ʌ	ʌ
Low	ɑ	(a)	(â)	ɑ	ɑ
Front rounded					
High	y	ü	ü	y	ü
Higher-mid	ø	û	ö	ø	ö
Lower-mid	œ	—	ӧ	œ	ӧ
Back rounded					
High	u	u	u / ū	u	u
Lower-high	ɷ	ŭ	ʊ / ᴜ	ɷ / ᴜ	ᴜ
Higher-mid	o	o	o / ō	o	o
Lower-mid	ɔ	ŏ	o / ɔ	ɔ	ɔ
Low	ɒ	â	â	ɒ	ɒ

APPENDIX D

Basic Numerals in Selected California Languages

1
ALGIC

	1.1 Wiyot[7]	1.2 Yurok[8]
1	kúcər ('it is one thing')[9]	ko:raʔ ('it is one thing')[10]
2	rítər	naʔa'n
3	ríkʰər	nahkse'n
4	riyáʔwər	čo:ne'n
5	weʔsaɣ hələr ('there are five things')[11]	meruh čo:'m ('there are five things')[12]
6	təkɬəɬúk hələr	kohčew čo:'m
7	háʔləw hələr	čr̩wr̩sik' čo:'m
8	híwitəw hələr	knewetik' čo:'m
9	βəšərúk hələr	kr̩:mik' čo:'m
10	rəlúk hələr	weɬowa: čo:'m
11	βeʔ-kucər	
12	βeʔ-rítər	
20	retaβáʔ hələr	

2
ATHABASKAN[13]

	2.1 Oregon Athabaskan[14]	2.2 California Athabaskan[15]	
	Lower Rogue River	Hupa-Chilula	
1	ɬaʔ	ɬaʔ	ɬiwaŋ 'one person'
2	naxi	nahx	nahnin 'two people'
3	tʰak'i	t'ʰa:q'	tʰaq'in 'three people'
4	tənč'i	tiŋk̲'	tiŋk̲'in 'four people'
5	sxʷəla	čʷolaʔ	čʷolaʔn 'five people'
6	kʷəstʰane	xostʰa:n	xostʰan 'six people'
7	sč'ite	xohk̲'it	xohk̲'itin 'seven people'
8	naxə-nto ('lacking two')	k̲ʰe:nim	k̲ʰe:nimin 'eight people'
9	ɬaʔ-nto ('lacking one')		miq'ost'aw ('at its neck')
10	xʷese		minɬaŋ ('filled up')
100	ɬaʔ-čʰən ('one stick')[16]		tik̲ʰin (cf. k̲ʰiŋ 'stick, tree')[17]

3
HOKAN

	3.1 Karuk[18]	*3.2 Chimariko*[19]
1	yiθ	p'un
2	ʔáxak	xokʰu ~ xoqʰu ~ qoqʰu
3	kuyra:k	xutay ~ xut'ay
4	pi:θ	qʰuyku ~ kʰulku
5	itrô:p	ṭanehe ~ čanehe
6	ikrívkih	p'unčipom ~ p'unsipʰom
7	(ʔa)xakinívkih	xokʰišpom ~ xokʰuspʰom
8	kuyrakinívkih	xutayčipom ~ xut'ayčʰipʰom
9	itro:patíša:mnih	p'unčiku ~ p'unp'em
10	itráhyar	šanpun ~ saʔan-p'un ('one arrow')
12	ʔaxak-í:č-karu ('two only additional')	xokʰusut
20	ʔaxak-itráhyar ('two tens')	šanpunasut ~ xokʰumtun šanpun ('twice ten')
100	iθa-páčiš ('one throwing down')	

3.3 Shastan

3.4 Palaihnihan

	Shasta (Scott Valley)[20]	Achumawi	Atsugewi
1	c'á:ʔam(u)	ham'is	ciw
2	xúkkʷaʔ	hak'	hokʰi:
3	xácki	c'ásti	q'i:cqʰí:
4	ʔíraha:ya	hattá:má	hak'á:w
5	ʔe:cáʔ	láttíw	həra:pʰakína
6	c'u-wate:haʔ	láttíwate ham'is	cira-púcakʰi
7	xúkkʷa-wate:ha	láttíwate hak' a:yéq'ti	ho:kʰi-púcakʰi
8	xácki-wate:haʔ	láttíwate c'ásti a:yéq'ti	q'icqʰi-púcakʰi
9	ʔíraha:ya-wate:haʔ	láttíwate hattá:má a:yéq'ti	hak'á:w-wi
10	ʔeccahé:wiʔ	malússi	cuk'si:
20	c'é-hi:s ('one person')		
100	ʔe:cá-hi:s ('five people')		

3.5 Yana

3.6 Washo

	Central Yana		
1	*pay-* (~ *-pʰku-* 'each one')	*lák'aʔ*	*lék'iliŋ* ('one person')
2	*ux-*	*hésgeʔ*	*hésgilši* ('two people')
3	*pul-*	*hélmeʔ*	*hélmiw* 'three people'
4	*tawmi-*	*háʔwaʔ*	*háʔwaw* 'four people'
5	*ciman-*	*dubáldiʔ*	*dubáldiw* 'five people'
6	*pay-mami-*		*dubáldiʔ lak'* ('five-one')
7	*ux-mami-*		*dubáldiʔ hesgeʔ* ('five-two')
8	*pul-mami-*		*haʔwaʔ haʔwaʔ* ('four-four')
9	*tawmi-ma-*		*dubáldiʔidaʔ haʔwaʔ* ('five plus four')
10	*xa:can-*		*lák'aʔ muc'umi*

3.7 Pomo[21]

	Eastern Pomo	3.8 Esselen
1	k'áli	pek
2	xočʰ	xulax
3	xó:mk'a	xulep
4	dó:l	xamaxus
5	lé:ma ('full')	pemaxala
6	c'á:di	pek-walanai
7	kʰúlaxòčʰ	xulax-walanai
8	xókadò:l	xulep-walanai
9	hádaqal-šòm ('ten lacking [one]')	xamax-walanai
10	ṭék' ~ hádaqal	tomoila
20	xáy-di:lè:ma ('full stick')[22]	?

3.9 Salinan[23]

	Antoniano		3.10 Seri
1	t'ol	tášo	~ tó:xom[24]
2	kákiše	kó:kx	~ káxkom
3	lápay	kápχa	~ pxá:ʔom
4	kíša?	kšó:xʷk	~ šóxkom
5	ʔólṭaw	kóitom	~ xʷáitom
6	payá:nel ('three-plural')	isná:p kášox	~ nápšox
7	te?	tomkoi kʷkí:?	~ káxkʷi
8	šaʔá:nel ('four-plural')	kšóxolkam ('four-plural')	~ pxáxkʷi
9	teteṭóʔe (? 'one less than ten')	ksoi kʔánl	~ ksó:xʔanl
10	ṭóʔe (? 'five-plural')	kʔánl	~ xóhnal
11	ṭóʔetaxt'ol ('ten and one')		
12	lapaykša ('three fours')		
16	kpeš		

3.11 Yuman

	Cocopa	Mojave	Hualapai
1	ʔašiṭ	ʔaséntik	síta
2	xwak	haβík	hwákʰa
3	xmuk	hamók	hmúkʰa
4	spap	cimpáp	hupá
5	ṣrap	θaráp	θarápʰa
6	xmxu:k	sí:nta	tispʰéʔ
7	pxka:	βí:ka	hwakʰspʰéʔ
8	spxu:k	mú:ka	hmukʰspʰéʔ
9	xmxmuk	pá:ye	halθúy
10	ṣɑ:xú:k	arrapa	βwaβ

	4.1 Takelma[25]	4.2 Klamath-Modoc[26]
1	mì:ʔskaʔ	Na:s
2	kà:ʔm ~ kà:p'iní	la:p
3	xìpiní	ntan
4	kamkàm	woni:p
5	té:hal	tʰon'ip
6	haʔi:-mì:ʔs ('one in the hand')[27]	Nač-ksept ('one + five')
7	haʔi:-kà:ʔm ('two in the hand')	lap-ksept ('two + five')
8	haʔi:-xín ('three in the hand')	ntan-ksept ('three + five')
9	haʔi:-kó ('four [?] in the hand')[28]	Nač-q'e:k-s ('lacking one')
10	ixti:l ('two hands')[29]	tʰewn'ip
20	yap'a-mìʔs ('one person')	lap-n'i tʰewn'ip ('twice ten')
100	t'eimìʔs ('one male person' ?)[30]	tʰewn'ip-n'i tʰewn'ip ('ten times ten')

4.3 Maiduan[31]

	Northeastern Maidu	Konkow (Mooretown)	Nisenan
1	sítti (~ wɨk')	wikte	witte: (< *wik-te:)
2	péne	pene	pe:n
3	sáp'ɨ (~ say)	sap'i	sap'iy
4	c'ɨyɨ	c'iyi	c'i:y
5	má-wik'ɨ ('one hand')	ma-wik'ɨ	ma:-wik ('one hand')
6	sáy-c'ok'o ('three both sides')	say-c'ok'o	timbo:
7	top'ɨ[32]	top'i	top'iy
8	pén-c'ɨyɨ ('two fours')	pen-c'iy	pe:n-c'i:y
9	péliʔom	peliʔom	pe:n-liʔo
10	más-c'ok'o ('hands both sides')	ma-c'ok'o	ma:cam
12	wik'im-nok'ó ('one arrow')	wik'im-nok'o	pe:noto
20	penem-masc'ok'o ('two tens')	penem-nok'o ('two arrows')[33]	huye: ('string of beads')[34]

4.4 Northern Wintuan[35]

	Wintu	Nomlaki
1	k'ete:-t ~ k'ete:-m	k'ete:m
2	pa:lel	pale
3	panu(:)ł	pano(:)ł
4	ƛ'awi-t	ƛ'awit
5	č'an-sem ('one-side hand')	č'an-sem
6	se-panuł ('double three')	se-panoł
7	lolo:qi-t ('pointer')[36]	čumeł
8	se-ƛ'awi-t ('double four')	se-ƛ'awit
9	k'ete-t-ʔel ('one inside') ~ k'ete-m-ʔeles ('one less')	č'an-ƛ'awit ('one side + four')
10	tiqeles	sema ('hand')
20	k'ete-wintʰuh ('one person')	?

	Patwin	Southern Patwin (Suisun)
1	ʔete:-ta	eta
2	pampa-ta	papa-ta
3	pono:ɬ-ta	punol-ta
4	ʔemu:h-ta	emul-ta
5	ʔete-sem-ta ('one hand')	et-sem
6	ser-po:ɬ-ta	k'ače-ta
7	ser-pote:-ta ('six + one')[38]	kenetela
8	pan-ʔemu:h-ta ('twice four')	panomuya
9	pan-ʔemuhte:-ta ('twice four + one')[39]	kalapa-ta
10	pampa-sem-ta ('two hands')	papa-sem
20	ʔete-k'ayi ('one walk')	emu-sem ('four hands')

4.6 Costanoan[40]

	Karkin	Chocheño	Chalon (Soledad)	Mutsun	Rumsen
1	niṭhan	himhen	himič?a	hemeč?a	ʔimxala
2	ʔoṭhin	ʔuṭhin	ʔuṭi	ʔuṭhin	ʔuṭṭis
3	kaphan	kaphan	kapxa	kaphan	kappes
4	kaṭwaš	katwaš	ʔu:ṭit	ʔu:ṭit	ʔu:ṭitim
5	mišur(u)	miššur	parwiš	parwes	hale?is
6	tanipos	šakken	hemen-oksi	nakči	hali-šakken
7	kenetis	kene:tiš	ʔuṭh-oksi	ṭakči	ʔuṭu-mai-šakken
8	oṭonakantumus	ʔoša:tiš	tayitmin	tayitmin	kapxa-mai-šakken
9	talan (? talaw)	tellektiš	wa:cu	pakki ~ wacu	pak ~ pakke
10	tahṭeiṭis	ʔiwweš	ma:tusu	tansahte	tancaxt

4.7 Yokuts[41]

	Delta Yokuts[42]		Other Dialects
	NORTHWESTERN	SOUTHEASTERN	
1	yet'	yet'	yet'
2	ponoy	poⁿdoy	ponoy ~ poŋoy[43]
3	šo:pʰin ~ pelek	ṣo:pʰiⁿd	ṣo:pʰin
4	c'owoṭʰ	c'owo?aṭʰ	hot-ponoy ~ hot-poŋoy ~ tapaŋiy[44]
5	ṭʰanaṣwil	ṭʰaⁿdaṣwil ~ ṭʰaⁿdṣiway	yic'inil ~ yic'iŋil ~ yec'elay[45]
6	šaken	hat-ᵐbalsat	č'olipʰiy
7	kine ~ kiⁿde	ṭʰulukʰay	nomc'in ~ nomc'il [46]
8	kawinta	ⁿdo:ṣ	mun'os [47]
9	wo?e	kʰatʰil	ṣo:pʰin-hot ~ no:nipʰ ~ wuṭʰat' ~ likiyi? [48]
10	ʔekuke	ṭ'iyew	ṭ'iyew
11	?	?	yeč'am[49] ~ tiwa:p[50]
12	?	?	pučum ṣulokʰay ~ suyukʰay[51]
13	?	?	ṣopʰyom
14	?	?	hačpam
15	?	?	yit'ṣam
16	?	?	č'olpʰom
17	?	?	nomč'om
18	?	?	mun'čam
19	?	?	nonpʰom ~ ṣo:pʰinhot-min
20	?	?	ponoy-ṭ'iyew ('two tens')
100	?	?	pʰič'(a)[52]

4.8 Western Miwok[53]

	Coast Miwok (Bodega)	Lake Miwok
1	*kénne*	*kénne*
2	*ʔóṣṣa*	*ʔótṭa*
3	*telé:ka*	*telé:ka*
4	*húya*	*ʔoṭóṭṭa*
5	*kenékkuh* ('one hand')	*kedékku*
6	*pácciṭak*	*páccadak*
7	*ṣe:ló:wih*	*ṣemlá:wi*
8	*ʔóṣṣuwah* ('two fours')	*ʔótṭʰaya*
9	*kénnekotoh* ('one inside')	*kénnenhelak* ('one lacking')
10	*kíccih*	*ʔukú:koci* ('hand-dual')
12	*ʔóṣṣa-wállik* ('two increased')	*ʔótṭa-wállik*
20	*ʔóṣṣa-kíccih* ('two tens')	*ʔótṭa-tumay* ('two sticks')

4.9 Eastern Miwok[54]

	Bay Miwok (Saclan)	Plains Miwok	Sierra Miwok
1	*luṭi*	*kennati*	*kéŋŋe ~ lu:ṭi*
2	*ʔowoṭo*	*ʔo:yokko*	*ʔoṭi:ko*
3	*tolokoṭo*	*tellokko*	*tolo:koṭ*
4	*ʔoyisa*	*ʔoysekko*	*ʔoyyissa*
5	*(ʔu)supa*	*kassokko*	*maṣṣokka*
6	*hesmuʔi*	*teme:pu* ('big')[55]	*temmokka* ('across')
7	*keneʔke*	*kenekkak* ('one again')	*kenekkaki*
8	*ʔosokaṡi*	*kawwinta* ('in the middle')	*kawwinṭa*
9	*telekakɨ*	*woʔe*	*woʔe*
10	*ʔuṣ-ʔuṣuṣ* ('hand + hand')	*ʔekku-ke* ('hand')	*naʔa:ca*
12	?	*ʔoykoppa-*	*ʔoṭik-ṣake:n-i* ('two sixes'?)
20	?	*naʔʔa* ('enough')	*naʔʔa*

5
UTO-AZTECAN

5.1 Numic

	Northern Paiute	Tümpisa Panamint	Chemehuevi
1	*sɨmɨ*	*sɨmɨ*	*su:*
2	*waha*	*waha*	*waha*
3	*pahi*	*pahi*	*pahi*
4	*wacɨ*	*waccɨwi*	*wacɨw*
5	*manigɨ*	*maniki*	*manɨg*
6	*na:pahi*	*na:pai*	*nava*
7	*natakʷasɨ*	*ta:cciwi*	*mukʷɨs*
8	*namiwacɨ*	*wo:sɨwi*	*na:nci*
9	*sɨmɨ kadupɨ*	*wanikki*	*ʒuwip*
10	*sɨmɨ manoi*	*si:mo:*	*masɨw*

	5.2 Takic[56]	5.3 Tubatulabal
	Gabrielino	Cahuilla	
1	*puku*	*súplʸe*	*čiːč*
2	*wehe*	*wíh*	*woː*
3	*pahi*	*páh*	*paːy*
4	*wača*	*wíčiw*	*naːnaːw*
5	*mahar*	*namakʷánaŋ*	*maːhažiŋa*
6	*pabahi*	*kʷan-súplʸe*	*napaːy*
7	*puku-baivi*	*kʷan-wíh*	*nomnžin*
8	*wehe-baiva*	*kʷan-páh*	*naːbunžiŋa*
9	*baiš*	*kʷan-wíčiw*	*laːgiːh*
10	*weheš-mahar*	*namečúmi*	*amhayžiŋa*

6
YUKIAN

	6.1 Yuki	6.2 Wappo
1	*powi ~ pək'*[57]	*páw ~ pay ~ pa-*
2	*ʔopi*	*hópi*
3	*mólmi*	*hopóka*
4	*ʔopi mihəṭ* ('two forks')	*ʔóla*
5	*huy k'oʔ* ('middle inside')	*káta*
6	*mik'as č'ilkiʔ* ('even sprouting')	*pa-ténaʔukʰ* ('one added')
7	*mik'as koʔ* ('even go')	*hopi-ténaʔukʰ* ('two added')
8	*pow mipat'* ('one hand')	*hopi-hán* ('two less')
9	*hučam powi pan* ('beyond one hanging')	*pa-walákʰ* ('one lacking')
10	*hučam ʔopi šul* ('beyond two body')	*maʔháys*
11	*mólmi šul* ('three body')	
12	*ʔo(pi)mihəṭ šul* ('four body')	
13	*huyk'o šul* ('five body')	
14	*mik'as č'ilkiʔ šul* ('six body')	
15	*mik'as koʔ šul* ('seven body')	
16	*huy kot* ('middle none')	

	7.1 Obispeño[58]	*7.2 Central Chumash*	*7.3 Island Chumash*
		(Inezeño)	(Cruzeño)
1	*sumo*	*pak'aʔs*	*ʔismala*
2	*ʔestʸuʔ*	*ʔiškóm'*	*ʔiščom*
3	*misiʔ*	*masix*	*masix*
4	*paksi*	*skumu*	*skumu*
5	*tiyeni*	*yiti-pak'as*	*(na)syet'-isma*
6	*ksuw'astʸu*	*yiti-škóm'*	*(na)syet-iščom*
7	*ksuwasmisi*	*yiti-masix*	*(na)syet-masix*
8	*skom'o*	*malawa*	*malawa*
9	?	*spa*	*spaʔa*
10	*tutʸimli*	*č'iya(w)*	*kaškom*
11	*tiwapa*	*til'uʔ*	*telu*
12	*takotia*	*xayi-skumu*	*masix-pa-škumu*
13	*wak-sumo*	*ʔic'iyul*	?
14	*wak'-estʸuʔ*	?	?
15	*wak-misiʔ*	?	?
16	*peusi, pasi*	*p'et'aʔ*	?

NOTES

Frontmatter Notes

1. The number twenty-eight does not include Lower Columbia Athabaskan (¶3.5), the possible Giamina branch of Uto-Aztecan (¶3.34), or the languages of the southernmost part of Baja California (¶3.37). For the levels of linguistic classification used in this book, see ¶1.6.

2. For more than thirty years Sapir and Kroeber worked in tandem to create the intellectual framework—historical, typological, and structural—within which Californian languages and cultures came to be studied. The texture of this interdisciplinary collaboration is best seen in their voluminous correspondence, part of which I have published (Golla 1984).

Part 1 Notes

1. During the two centuries that Chemehuevi and Southern Paiute have been separated, "a considerable amount of vocabulary has diverged, as have portions of the tense-aspect system," and they "differ with respect to several phonological rules." Nevertheless they are "certainly mutually intelligible" (Press 1979:2; see also W. Miller, Elzinga, and McLaughlin 2005:414, fn.1). The tribe-defining function of Chemehuevi was recently underscored by a grant the tribe received from National Science Foundation's Documentation of Endangered Languages (DEL) program to collect a wide range of new data specifically on the Chemehuevi variety of what is one of the best-described languages in North America (Major 2005; see Sapir 1930–1931).

2. In recent years, it has become fashionable among Native Californian political activists to decry the isolated, self-sufficient tribelet as the linchpin of a willfully distorted construction of traditional California Indian society that has subverted the development of effective modern tribes. While not adopting the same conspiratorial tone, at least one anthropologist has criticized Kroeber's tribelet model (and the "memory culture ethnography" on which it was based) on sociopolitical grounds (Lightfoot 2005:42–48).

3. A case can be made that all attested "tribal dialects" of Yokuts fall into, at most, four language-level groups signifi-

cant enough to require an interpreter (Poso Creek, Buena Vista, Tule-Kaweah, and what Whistler and I call "Northern Yokuts"; see ¶3.26). Certainly Newman (1944) had little difficulty in accounting for the differences among six quite distinct "tribal" varieties in a single descriptive grammar (¶3.26.9). There are hints in the ethnographic record that the mobile Yokuts, who frequently encountered speakers of other dialects, used vocabulary differences as badges of local identity and (like modern Americans) would sometimes mock one another's local speech patterns.

4. The lingua francas that developed in the Mission communities, particularly in the Chumash area, are not to be mistaken for precontact regional dialects.

5. What Powers wrote of Nisenan regional diversity must have applied widely in California languages with distinct geographic dialects: "The Nishinam language varies greatly within itself. . . . Let an Indian go [from one village community to another] and, with the exception of the numerals, he may not at first understand one word in four or five or six. But with this small stock in common [and] a great many others nearly the same and recognizable after being spoken a few times, and the same laws of grammar to guide them, they pick up each others' dialects with amazing rapidity" (1877:314).

6. Sean O'Neill (2008) has explored the evidence for semantic convergence in certain aspects of Yurok, Hupa, and Karuk language use.

7. The Hupa, Yurok, and Karuk, for instance, maintained nearly complete sets of place-names for each other's territory (Sapir and Golla 2001:873–1011).

8. The linguistic distinctiveness of Northeastern Pomo, Kato, and Konomihu is well documented. Karkin is attested in a single vocabulary (Arroyo 1837), but this is sufficient to show how different it was from other varieties of Costanoan spoken around San Francisco Bay (¶3.28.1). The history of the Northeastern Pomos is the best understood. Their language, while not fully intelligible to speakers of any of the other six Pomo languages, shares many features with Northern Pomo, and Kroeber (1932:364) noted instances of partial intelligibility between speakers of the two languages. It is likely that Northeastern Pomo was originally the local variety of a group of Northern

Pomos who moved east to Stonyford to control the salt trade (see ¶3.15.3). A much-used trail north of Clear Lake connected the two areas.

9. My Hupa friend Gordon Bussell tells me that it was the practice in Northwest California to provide foreign wives an opportunity to learn something of the language of their new community at a "mixed village" that did not belong exclusively to either language. For the Hupa and the Yurok, this liminal space was the southern "suburb" of Weitchpec—near Pearson's Store on the right bank of the Trinity just above its confluence with the Klamath. An arrangement would have been made for a Yurok woman marrying into a Hupa family, or a Hupa woman marrying into a Yurok family, to live there for a month or two in a house where both languages could legitimately be spoken.

10. Mabel McKay, who was born in this area, identified herself as a "Cache Creek Pomo" (Sarris 1994).

Part 2 Notes

1. The official report of Cabrillo's expedition, prepared by the viceroy's secretary, Juan León, on the basis of eyewitness accounts, has been lost. What survives is a summary made by Andrés de Urdaneta in 1543 and now in the Archivo General de Indias in Seville, filed as *Patronato* 20, no. 5, ramo 13 (Kelsey 1986:168–170). A facsimile copy and translation can be found in Wagner (1929:72–93, 450–463). The León Urdaneta report condensed information from perhaps as many as five sources, including an account by Cabrillo himself, and is often confusing and repetitious.

2. Kelsey (1986:145–157) summarizes current views on the identification of the mainland names:

On Tuesday, October 10, 1542, the expedition anchored near the large village at **Mugu.** On Friday [13 October 1543] the ships . . . pass[ed] **Quelqueme** (Hueneme), **Misinagua** (Ventura), and **Xuco** (Rincón). . . . [This was] a province that the Indians called **Xucu. Xuco** was the . . . chief town in that group. Sunday, 15 October, the armada continued its slow voyage up the heavily populated coast, passing **Coloc** (or **Alloc**, as it was also called in the text), in the Carpinteria estuary, **Xabagua** (or **Xagua**) near present Montecito and *Cicacut* (also called **Ciucut, Xocotoc,** and **Yutum**) near present Santa Barbara. . . . This was a different province . . . **Xexu**, and **Cicacut** was the chief village. On 16 October the fleet sailed further westward, passing **Potoltuc** (also called **Partocac, Paltatre,** and **Paltocac**), **Anacbuc** (also called **Nacbuc**), and **Gwa**, the latter two of which were located on small islets adjoining the mainland. They stopped for the night at two villages, now called Dos Pueblos, but then named **Quanmu** or **Quiman.** On the evening of [26 October], with a fresh breeze from the south, the fleet was able to round [Point Conception] and explore the coast for a few leagues north of Point Arguello. But . . . they were unable to land at the village they called **Nocos** (near present Jalama). . . . After several days of fighting the elements, the ships turned back toward the channel villages, finally coming to rest . . . at a village below [Point Conception] . . . called **Xexo.** On Monday 6 November, sailing [toward Point Conception] . . . the Indians came out in their canoes greeting the Spaniards, and calling off the

names of their villages. These included **Aguin** (El Capitan Beach), **Casalic** (Cañada del Refugio), **Susuquei** (Quemada Canyon), and **Tucumu** (Arroyo Hondo). The armada anchored again at **Xexo.**

3. The Indians who came on board Cabrillo's ships at San Diego related (in sign language) that bearded men dressed just like those on the ships, armed with crossbows and swords, had killed many natives further inland. The Indians called these intruders by a term the Spanish thought sounded like "Guacamal" (Kelsey 1986:144), which can probably be identified with the stem seen in Mesa Grande Iipay *kwalkwaal* 'light in color' (Couro and Hutcheson 1973). The same story of bearded Christians marching through the interior was heard further up the coast at Mugu, where the local name for Christians sounded to Spanish ears like "Taquimine" (Kelsey 1986:146). No dictionary of Ventureño Chumash is available, but Applegate (1972b) records *takïmïn* 'hard, caked, covered with a shell' for Inezeño, making it likely that the Mugu term referred to Spanish armor.

4. For details of Jesuit linguistic practice in New Spain see Mixco (1978:9–10), who derives much of his information from the work of the Jesuit historian Ernest Burrus (see Burrus 1956; Burrus and Zubillaga 1982).

5. With the exception of the Franciscans, the non-Jesuit missionary orders followed the lead of the Crown and the ecclesiastical hierarchy in favoring the rapid Hispanicization of indigenous communities. Piccolo (1962:102–103, quoted in Mixco 1978:9) reports that the archbishop of Mexico was most distressed to learn that some Cochimí children knew their Christian doctrine only in Cochimí.

6. Mixco (1978) transcribes and analyzes Barco's texts, gives an English translation of Barco's grammatical notes, and provides photographic reproductions of the linguistic portions of Barco's original manuscript.

7. There are several eyewitness accounts of this famous *primera expedición* into Upper California. The most comprehensive is the official log compiled by Father Juan Crespí, a full version of which has only recently been published by Alan Brown (2001). Of interest for their linguistic content are the accounts of Fages (Priestley 1937) and Costansó (1770), both of which include Chumash vocabularies.

8. On the afternoon of July 18, near the future site of Mission San Luis Rey, "forty heathens all painted in all colors, naked, came up close to the camp, with, as they reached us, a long speech which we were unable to understand, since none of the Christian Indians that we have with us can understand a thing." Converts from the northern Cochimí missions accompanied Serra's party (A. Brown 2001:50, 275–277).

9. Costansó prefaces this wordlist with the observation that the Chumash language "is sonorous and of easy presentation" and that "some believe they find in it a certain connection with the Mexican in that the L and T are frequently sounded" ["Su Lengua es sonora, y de facil pronunciacion: creyeron algunos hallarle cierta conexion con la Mexicana en la que, la L, y T, suenan frequentemente . . ."] (1770:39). His recordings appear to be fairly accurate, considering the circumstances. The form given for 'hand' in fact means 'upper arm' (cf. Inezeño *wač'ax*), and the forms for 'chest', 'knee', 'leg', and 'foot' include the possessive prefixes *k-* 'my' or *p-* 'your'. Costansó's word for 'chief' is not attested in later sources, where the term is everywhere

wot', but it appears to be confirmed by *pirotomi,* the word for 'chief' given by Crespí (Brown 2001:406–407). The initial *u-* for the expected *s-* in the numeral '9' is presumably a printing error.

10. After a year at the site of the present Presido in Monterey, Mission San Carlos was moved to Carmel in 1771.

11. It is uncertain exactly when this vocabulary was collected. Fages, who succeeded Portolá as the military governor of California in 1770, was in Obispeño territory on several occasions between 1769 and 1775. He spent part of the summer of 1772 hunting bears on Los Osos Plain to provision the settlement at Monterey, and returned there with Father Serra at the beginning of September 1772 to formally establish Mission San Luis Obispo de Tolosa.

12. See, for example, the responses of the missionaries when asked about translations of the catechism in the Questionnaire of 1812 (¶2.3.5).

13. See the documents listed in K. Turner (1988a). Father Sancho, in addition to being a diligent linguist, was an accomplished musician, and he occasionally worked Salinan words and phrases into the masses and other works he composed for the mission choir (C. H. Russell 2004).

14. One of the two original manuscripts was discovered by Duflot de Mofras in 1841 and taken by him to France; it is now in the Bibliothèque National in Paris (Kessler 1979). The other came into the possession of Don José de la Guerra, and Alfred Robinson, de la Guerra's son-in-law, published a translation of this version as an appendix to his 1846 memoir, *Life in California,* under the title "Chinigchinich" (Boscana 1846); the present location of this manuscript is unknown. The Paris manuscript, published in translation by J. P. Harrington (Boscana 1934), is apparently the first draft of the de la Guerra manuscript. Harrington's edition of the Robinson translation of the latter (Boscana 1933) has extensive linguistic and ethnographic notes incorporating data from Harrington's own field research on Juaneño and Luiseño. Kroeber's discussion of the value of Boscana's treatise and of the differences between the two manuscripts is very useful (1959a:282–293). New light has recently been thrown on Boscana's work by the discovery in the Bancroft Library of a four-page outline in his handwriting (J. R. Johnson 2006).

15. See the assessments by Kroeber (1910:237), Mason (1916a:400–401), and Okrand (1977:3–4).

16. Andrew Garrett, who has inspected Arroyo's manuscript more closely than I have, reports:

The Mutsun-Spanish phrase book has Mutsun written on the left, in alphabetical order (by first word of the Mutsun), with Spanish translation immediately following on the same line. On the first page only of the ms, Arroyo or whoever actually wrote it down has also written a third version of each sentence, in "Guachirron"—the beginning of the third column of a trilingual phrase book. Those are then crossed out, and they do not continue after page 1. That first page is rather crowded, and one wonders if the reason why the Rumsen was not continued is simply because he decided it wouldn't fit, which would be tragic if true. At any rate, the alphabetical order says to me that it is all copied from some other source (file slips, as it were, then alphabetized), and thus that Arroyo possessed or had some access to a big ms. phrase book of Rumsen that has not survived. (personal communication 2007)

17. The Shea edition contains numerous typographical errors and should not be relied on for details (Andrew Garrett, personal communication 2007).

18. There is a manuscript Mutsun grammar in the Santa Barbara Mission Archives (Geiger and Meighan 1976:165, n. 32), which I regret I have not had the opportunity to see. It could be Arroyo's full original, but it is more likely to be the otherwise unlocated manuscript of the extract published by Shea. As for the authorship of the latter, Shea, in his introduction to the publication, refers to the manuscript as "Extracto de la gramatica Mutsun, ó de la lengua de los naturales de la mision de San Juan Bautista, compuesta por el Rev. Padre Fray Felipe Arroyo de la Cuesta . . . 1816." He tells us that the cover bore the following note in another hand: "Copia de la lengua Mutsun en estilo Catalan á causa la escribió un Catalan. La Castellana usa de la fuerza de la pronunciacion de letras de otro modo en sa alfabeto. Ve el original intitulado Gramatica California." [Copy of the Mutsun language in the Catalan style because it was written by a Catalan. Castillian empasizes the pronunciation of letters in a different way in its alphabet. See the original, titled Gramatica California.] Shea (or Taylor) mistakenly believed that the manuscript was in Arroyo's hand and that the cover note indicated that Arroyo was a native speaker of Catalan, as so many California Franciscans were. Arroyo was in fact a Castillian. The Catalan priest most likely to have made a copy of Arroyo's grammar was Estevan Tapis (1756–1825), who served with Arroyo at San Juan Bautista from 1815 to 1825.

19. By the 1820s most of the neophytes at San Juan Bautista were Yokuts speakers. Arroyo applied himself to analyzing Yokuts with the same industriousness that he had earlier applied to Mutsun, focusing on the Northern Valley dialect he called "Nopthrinthre" (*nopṭinṭe*). Beeler (1971) extracted and published most of the Nopṭinṭe material in Arroyo's manuscripts (1810–1819, 1837), although he omitted the discussion of the verb and some general observations on Northern Valley Yokuts dialectology that are found at the end of *Lecciones de Indios* (Arroyo 1837; pp. 132 ff. in the copy by Murray [Bancroft MS C-C 63b]).

20. For a discussion of the five Bay Area vocabularies, which Arroyo collected during a visit to Mission Dolores in 1821, see Beeler (1961b). Harrington reviewed these vocabularies with his Rumsen informant, Isabel Meadows, in 1934–1936 (Harrington 1982–1990, vol. 2, reel 68:298–448).

21. Little is known for certain about Karl von Gerolt or of his stay in California, other than that he was the older brother of Baron Friedrich von Gerolt, secretary to the Prussian consul-general in Mexico City and from 1846 to 1870 Prussian minister to the United States. Karl von Gerolt is mentioned in connection with the Dutch-German merchant Henry Virmond and seems to have resided at Santa Clara for a year or more around 1830, possibly as a commercial agent for Virmond. Since Friedrich von Gerolt was a close friend of Alexander von Humboldt, it seems likely that Karl sought out data on California languages at his brother's request. In the letter of transmittal that accompanied his copies of Arroyo's vocabularies, dated Santa Clara, December 1830, he states that they were "Mittheilungen von einem Padre, der diese Gegend seit 24 Jahren bewohnt und viele Notizen gesammelt hat" [communications from a padre who has lived in this vicinity for twenty-four years and collected many notes]. It continues, "Mit der Zeit kann ich Ew. mehr liefern und aus eigener Erfahrung mittheilen, was ich jetzt nur mit grosser Mühe

habe erhalten können" [In time I can supply something more and communicate on the basis of my own observations what I have been able to obtain so far only with great difficulty]. Since mission records indicate that "Carlos Gerolt" died in Santa Clara in 1831, it is unlikely that he carried this work any further.

22. Judging from its style and sophistication, it is likely that the grammatical sketch is largely Mezzofanti's work; his biographer includes "Californian" among the thirty-eight languages that the cardinal claimed to speak "perfectly" (C. W. Russell 1858). Chung (1994) assesses the coverage of the grammar in the light of what we now know of Luiseño. For a recent discussion of the Tac-Mezzofanti relationship see Kottman (2005).

23. Edited selections from the *respuestas* to the 1812 questionnaire were earlier translated and published by Kroeber (1908b). Meighan's "Anthropological Introduction" to the 1976 volume (pp. 3–9) is quite useful.

24. The most valuable linguistic data in the *respuestas* are the two sentences that Fray Juan Amorós included in his response to question 3 from Mission San Carlos (Carmel), one in Rumsen, the other in Esselen, both said to translate "Men who are good bowmen are esteemed and well-liked." The Esselen ("Excelen") sentence is one of the few recorded for that language (see ¶3.16.2).

25. On his return to Spain in 1794, Malaspina became embroiled in political intrigue, and in 1795 he was arrested and imprisoned. As a result, a full report of his expedition was never published, and the voluminous records of the voyage in the Museo Naval in Madrid are still yielding discoveries. The manuscripts of Lasuén's word list and part of his catechism came to light in the early 1970s (Beeler 1977:41), and the complete catechism only in the 1980s (Cutter 1990:147–155; Shaul 1995a). The importance of the Malaspina expedition in general has largely been overlooked, both in Spain and elsewhere, and a fully edited and annotated edition of Malaspina's journal is only now being published (David et al. 2003). Needless to say, many of the artifacts collected by the expedition have been irrecoverably lost, although some of the baskets and other objects collected in Monterey are in the Museo de America in Madrid, where they are frequently on display.

26. For Voznesenskii's instructions see Alekseev (1987: 6–7). A few words from California languages are quoted by Liapunova, e.g., from Voznesenskii's letter to E. I. Schrader, the vice president of the Imperial Academy of Sciences, dated February 16, 1841: "I have now the honor of reporting to Your Excellency the dispatch of a box, numbered 21, in which are found the following items pertaining to the Suizun Indian tribe [*k suizunskomu indejskomy plemeni*]: 1) a belt or sash, used at the time of celebratory games, *kala*; 2) a hair-pin, *sipek*; 3) ear-pendants, *alok*; 4) a headband, *uagl'ku*" (1967:16). Although these artifacts were presumably collected from the Suisun (Southern Patwin), the names given by Voznesenskii seem to be Coast Miwok: *kala* 'feather belt', *sapa* (?) 'hair', *ʔalok* 'ear', *tawaka* (?) 'headdress of flicker feathers' (Callaghan and Bond, n.d.).

27. For an assessment of Coulter's and Tolmie's vocabularies see A. Grant (1993). Grant also provides complete transcriptions, with suggested modern phonetic equivalents, for all of Coulter's vocabularies.

28. Hale has had no biographer, but his career as a linguist and ethnographer has been described and its significance assessed by Gruber (1967). Pilling, in his *Bibliography of the Algonquian Languages* (1891:219), gives the bibliographical details of Hale's undergraduate effort on Penobscot (1834), adding this note from Hale: "You may be amused to learn that this youthful production of mine was not only written at the age of seventeen, during my second year at Harvard, but was printed by myself. Some Indians from Maine came—I do not remember how or why—and encamped on the college grounds. I took down a vocabulary from them, and, having a knowledge of typesetting, I took it to a printing office, and there put it into type and printed off fifty copies, which I sent to persons whom I thought likely to be interested in it."

29. The location of Hale's Wilkes Expedition notebooks and papers is unknown, although Fenton and Gruber are apparently mistaken about their having been destroyed in a fire (Fenton 1963:xi; Gruber 1967:11). They were sold at auction in 1911 to a buyer whose name is recorded only as "Jones" (Henkels 1911, item 593). Some manuscripts of Hale's relating to his work in the Northwest have recently (summer 2006) been located in the archives of the California Historical Society in San Francisco, but they appear to be early drafts of his published report, not original field notes.

30. For a biography of Gibbs see Beckham (1969).

31. Gibbs describes the provenance of his vocabularies in a set of "Observations on Some of the Indian Dialects of Northern California" that Schoolcraft published separately (1853c). The Coast Miwok vocabulary is attributed to the "Tcho-ko-yem band of Sonoma valley," and the Hill Patwin vocabulary ("Co-peh") is of the dialect spoken "in the mountains at the head of Putos [i.e., Putah] creek." Both were apparently obtained at Sonoma before the expedition set out. Of the Pomo vocabularies, one ("Kula-napo," the Big Valley variety of Eastern Pomo) was collected at Clear Lake, a second ("Yu-kai," presumably the Yokaya dialect of Central Pomo) on Russian River, and the other two ("Chow-e-shak" and "Batem-da-kai-ee") in the vicinity of modern Willits, in Northern Pomo territory. The two Wiyot vocabularies are of "Wee-yot" at the mouth of Eel River and of "Wish-osk . . . the dialect of the upper part of the bay." The Shasta vocabulary is attributed to the "Watsa-he-wa" band (probably the village community at the mouth of Scott River whose name is reported in more modern sources as Kowachaha). The Oregon Athabaskan vocabulary, labeled "Nabil-tse," was obtained on the Klamath River in Shasta territory. The "How-te-te-oh" vocabulary was collected in Scott Valley "from some Indians who came over from the Rogue river ferry, where they lived" (1853c:423). It presumably represented the speech of the mixed Shasta-Takelma group living in the vicinity of Medford; "How-te-te-oh" seems to be a rendering of Shasta *ʔahut'iré:ʔi-cuʔ* 'valley-people'. The "Tah-le-wah" vocabulary is misleadingly labeled; it appears to be largely Yurok, not Athabaskan.

32. All three are enumerated by Gibbs in his "Observations" on the vocabularies (1853c:422–423), and their omission was presumably an editorial error on Schoolcraft's part. A copy of the Nabiltse vocabulary is in the Smithsonan archives (Gibbs 1851–1852), but the Shasta and "How-te-te-oh" vocabularies are lost. There may be copies among Schoolcraft's papers in the Manuscript Division of the Library of Congress; so far as I know, no one has searched for them there. There may also be copies among the documents relating to the 1851–1852 California Indian treaty expeditions in the National Archives. Gibbs's map

is there (Gibbs 1851). Gibbs's original field journals apparently have not survived, unless they too are in the National Archives. The treaties negotiated by McKee and his two colleagues were never ratified by the U.S. Senate. As Heizer observed, "Taken all together, one cannot imagine a more poorly conceived, more inaccurate, less informed, and less democratic process than the making of the 18 treaties in 1851–52 with the California Indians. It was a farce from beginning to end" (1972a:5). The story of the McKee expedition has been retold by Raphael (1993); he includes a copy of Gibbs's map, which shows the route in considerable detail.

33. Gibbs contributed two volumes to Shea's "Library of American Linguistics"—a dictionary of Chinook Jargon (Gibbs 1863c), also issued by the Smithsonian, and a lexicon of Clallam and Lummi (Gibbs 1863d)—and collaborated with Shea in editing Pandosy's Yakima grammar (Pandosy 1862). For a discussion of Gibbs's relationship to Shea see Beckham (1969:233–237).

34. About 140 separate articles appeared under this title in the *California Farmer*, the first on February 22, 1860, the last on October 30, 1863.

35. Cowan, who had possession of Taylor's "Indianology" manuscripts for five years before passing them on to the University of California in 1897, wrote that they "awaken curiosity and compel feelings akin to awe. Approximately they are 1100 pages written on paper of many sizes, shapes and hues. Scraps, backs of discarded envelopes, newspaper clippings, excerpts from magazines, with countless annotations and original MSS, they were arranged and classified under a system devised and known only by Taylor himself." As for the printing errors that disfigure the work, "The printers of that day command respect and invite admiration. . . . How they ever made use of that unique copy is beyond our powers of divination" (1933:21–22).

36. Lepsius's "Standard Alphabet," originally designed for African languages but soon expanded to cover most of the languages known to mid-nineteenth-century scholars (Lepsius 1863), was the first general phonetic orthography to achieve wide acceptance. Pinart's use of Lepsius's alphabet—with unit symbols such as *š* and *č* for sounds that could only be written in standard European orthographies with a confusing array of di- and trigraphic combinations such as *sh*, *ch*, *sch*, and *tsch*—put him at the forefront of descriptive linguists of his period. The International Phonetic Alphabet was not in wide use before the end of the nineteenth century.

37. Entitled *Bibliothèque de Linguistique et d'Ethnographie Américaines*, the series was projected to be an outlet both for original documentation and for old manuscripts. (Pinart had acquired Brasseur de Bourbourg's massive library and manuscript archive after the latter's death in 1874.) In the event, the only volumes published were an edition of two colonial manuscripts on Chapanec and Émile Petitot's *Dictionnaire de la Langue Dènè-Dindjié*.

38. These are the vocabulary of the "Chalostaca" variety of Delta Yokuts, collected at Santa Cruz (Pinart 1878e), and one of the two vocabularies ("Tanesac") collected from "Tejon" Indians, attesting the Hometwoli variety of Buena Vista Yokuts (1878n). (The second "Tejon" vocabulary ["Iauxlemne"] attests the well-known Yawelmani variety of Southern Valley Yokuts.) Heizer does not explain his decision to exclude Pinart's Yokuts vocabularies from the published edition.

39. The full contents of the Pinart papers in the Beinecke Library (Pinart n.d.[b]) have not been catalogued, but what I have seen of them (in a microfilm in the Anthropology Library at UC Berkeley) suggests that the California materials consist of copies that Pinart made of vocabularies collected by others, together with his copies of a few mission documents. This collection awaits the attention of a dedicated scholar. The disappearance of Léon de Cessac and his papers is described in Reichlen and Heizer (1963).

40. Most of Pinart's publications appeared in long forgotten French journals that are not easily found today even in France. Parmenter's bibliography (1966) is probably as complete as could be made, and is interwoven with a sketch of Pinart's life. There is also a short biography in Pinart and Wagner (1962). Zelia Nuttall, after divorcing Pinart, went on to have her own long and successful career as an Americanist (Tozzer 1933).

41. For the details of the formation of the BAE and the hiring of its staff see Hinsley (1981:145–189). The collection of data was standardized by a guide, *Introduction to the Study of Indian Languages* (Powell 1877b; 2nd ed., 1880f), which included dozens of vocabulary lists (or "schedules") to be collected, arranged by semantic category. The second edition also provided a phonetic orthography specially designed for Americanist work. The collection of primary data in "Powell schedules" was required of the researchers employed by the BAE, and independent collectors were also encouraged to use them.

42. The scant information that exists on Gatschet's reclusive life has been gathered by Landar (1974) and Hinsley (1976).

43. The manuscript edited by Joseph Schafer that was published as *The Memoirs of Jeremiah Curtin* by the State Historical Society of Wisconsin (Curtin 1940), was actually written by Curtin's widow, Alma, who seems to have supplied many of the details from her own diaries and recollections (she accompanied her husband on all his travels). The narrative has numerous gaps and chronological inconsistencies. Despite its lack of authenticity as a first-person account, the book contains much useful information on the circumstances of Curtin's field work and should be consulted by anyone using his data.

44. For a discussion of Curtin's use of his American Indian data in his work on comparative mythology see Karl Kroeber's introduction to the 2002 edition of *Creation Myths*.

45. For a further assessment of Curtin's California work and his contributions to American Indian linguistics see Olmsted (1975).

46. Henshaw's Costanoan and Chumash vocabularies were published by Heizer (1955). His Esselen vocabulary was published by Kroeber (1904). His Coast Miwok vocabulary has been integrated into Callaghan and Bond (n.d.).

47. What he recorded as Santa Rosa Island Chumash was actually Barbareño, although the speaker apparently also knew Roseño (see ¶3.36.3, note 148). Similarly, the "Santa Clara Costanoan" that Henshaw obtained from a man at Mission San Antonio is a largely useless hodgepodge. Both these vocabularies, unfortunately, are published in Heizer's edition of Henshaw's mission vocabularies (1955) without any indication of their incorrect attribution.

48. For a thorough and well-informed assesment of Kroeber's career from a linguistic perspective see Hymes (1961b).

49. The politics and personalities involved in the establishment of the University of California's anthropology

program and Kroeber's hiring have been described in detail by Thoresen (1975, 1976) and are also sketched, from Kroeber's point of view, in Theodora Kroeber's memoir of her husband (1970).

50. Kroeber's collection of Yurok narratives (cf. Kroeber 1900–1940) was published in English translation in 1976; the Yurok language texts are only analyzed as part of the Berkeley Yurok Project (Blevins and Garrett n.d.). The Yuki, Mojave, and Patwin materials (Kroeber 1900–1958, 1900–1910, and 1900–1924, respectively) still languish in the archives. Kroeber also took over responsibility for Sparkman's extensive unpublished materials on Luiseño after Sparkman's murder in 1907. An edited version of Sparkman's grammar was published the year of Kroeber's death (Kroeber and Grace 1960).

51. The manuscripts both of Dixon and Kroeber (1919) and of the *Handbook* were actually completed in 1917. By 1920, Kroeber had become deeply involved in Freudian psychology and took part-time leave from the university to open a psychoanalytic practice in San Francisco, which he maintained until 1922 (T. Kroeber 1970:105–107).

52. Even here, however, his focus was not on language per se, but on folk literary motifs and the personalities of the narrators. For a thorough evaluation of Kroeber's career as a linguist, see Hymes (1961b).

53. When asked by Boas to contribute a grammatical sketch to the first volume of the *Handbook of American Indian Languages* (Boas 1911), Kroeber at first demurred, then reluctantly submitted an outline of Yuki structure which Boas found inadequate for the purpose.

54. This grammatical study was subsequently published in Boas's *Handbook of American Indian Languages* (1911:679–734).

55. See for example Sapir's scathing assessment of Dixon's transcription and analysis of Chimariko in a letter to Kroeber (in Golla 1984:89–90).

56. Dixon published a sketch of Chimariko (1910) and a shorter outline of Wintu (1909), and Sapir incorporated Dixon's Yana texts into his own collection (Sapir 1910a), but a substantial collection of Shasta narratives (1908–1910), edited by Freeland, remains in manuscript. Many of Dixon's original field notes and other manuscripts have been lost; he is said to have destroyed them himself shortly before his death.

57. See also the discussion in Langdon (1974:22–36). The correspondence between Kroeber and Dixon that is preserved in the A. L. Kroeber Papers, Bancroft Library (now easily accessible by microfilm) needs the attention of a historian.

58. According to David Peri, Samuel Barrett's field assistant in the early 1960s, Barrett said that Goddard pronounced his first name /plátniy/, rhyming with *tiny*, the traditional schoolroom anglicization of Latin *plīnius*, with /ay/ for long *i*. However, David Goddard, P. E. Goddard's son, told me that his father had always pronounced his name /plíniy/, rhyming with *tinny*. Barrett also said that Berkeley students nicknamed him "Pliny, Earl of Goddam" after his fondness for expletives (unexpected in a former missionary).

59. The only significant published results of this work are collections of Chilula, Kato, and Wailaki texts (Goddard 1909, 1914b, 1923b) and a Kato grammar (Goddard 1912). Substantial unpublished data exist on these languages as well as Tolowa (1902–1903), Sinkyone (1903–1908), Mattole (1907), and Nongatl (1907–1908). See Kroeber (1967) for a somewhat unsympathetic account of Goddard's field methods and an assessment of the resulting materials.

60. Goddard proposed to President Benjamin Ide Wheeler that the department of anthropology be reorganized as a department of linguistics, with Goddard as the head. Kroeber fought this plan bitterly and effectively (see Kroeber's letter to F. W. Putnam dated 2/19/08 and his letters to Wheeler dated 2/24/09 and 3/2/09, A. L. Kroeber Papers, Bancroft Library). When, early in 1909, Goddard received Boas's invitation to join the American Museum of Natural History, he attempted to use this as a bargaining tool, but Kroeber called Goddard's bluff, and the latter resigned in April 1909.

61. Reichard made several trips to the Wiyot between the summer of 1922 and the spring of 1923. Goddard accompanied her only on the first visit. Reichard's collection of Wiyot data, particularly texts, was quite extensive for the time (see ¶3.2.2), but as a linguistic analyst she belonged to the prestructuralist school of the Boasian era.

62. The original plan was for Waterman to work with Boas on the grammatical analysis of Yurok, based on the materials collected by Kroeber between 1900 and 1907 as well as supplementary data Waterman himself had collected, and to submit a Yurok grammar as his dissertation. This proved impractical. The only published product of Waterman's work on Yurok grammar is an uninspiring study of Yurok affixes (1923).

63. Kroeber, in his obituary of Waterman, describes him as "simple, sincere, direct, always vigorous, often drastic" and noted that "some were offended by his brusqueness" (1937:528). Sapir was one of the latter, calling Waterman an "ass" in a letter to Kroeber (see Golla 1984:219–220).

64. Pronounced /reydn/, rhyming with *maiden*.

65. Among the more substantial pieces of evidence that Radin adduced in this fascinating work—which predated Joseph Greenberg's similar (and no better supported) claims for "Amerind" by nearly seventy years—are a number of striking parallels between Wappo and Yuki on the one hand and Siouan on the other. Radin knew Wappo from his California fieldwork and had become acquainted with Siouan linguistics through his dissertation research on the Winnebago, and was thus in a better position than any of his contemporaries to see structural resemblances between the two stocks. Sapir was sufficiently impressed by Radin's comparisons to include Yukian in his Hokan-Siouan phylum, but did not pursue the relationship further. (See Langdon 1986 and Munro 1994.)

66. Lowie's correspondence with Sapir, privately published by Lowie's widow (L. Lowie 1965), provides a fascinating glimpse into the social and intellectual networks of American anthropology at that period.

67. The best biography of Merriam is by Sterling (1974). See also Phillips, House, and Phillips (1988). An influential member of the scientific establishment in turn-of-the-century Washington, Merriam was close to Theodore Roosevelt—it was Merriam who named the Roosevelt elk in his honor—and advised Roosevelt on the reform of Indian policy (see Hagan 1997). For assessments of Merriam's California Indian work see Kroeber (1955) and Heizer (1966).

68. There is a good biography by de Angulo and Freeland's daughter, Gui de Angulo (1995). See also Olmsted (1966:1–7) and Leeds-Hurwitz (2004).

69. For biographical details see Leeds-Hurwitz (1982).

70. Rumor has it that Kroeber, a widower then in his mid-40s, was also romantically entangled with Freeland (Brightman 2004:178–179). De Angulo appears to confirm this in a 1950 letter to Ezra Pound quoted in Gui de Angulo's biography: "That bastard he couldn't make up his mind between Nancy and another girl (a pretty fast one). . . . i was still married then—& i fucked both N. and the other girl—and that awful gossip of Paul Radin—with his long nose—of cors he found it out and gave it a trolley-ride around Carmel and Berkeley—you bet K. loved me less than ever—The day I got my divorce i married N. . . . In those days i was still trying to get into academic circles—whenever i was on the point of landing a good job Kroeber wud spoil it for me—he wud go out of his way to blacken my character—i did fuck around a good deal—but what has that got to do with anthropology? . . . What a goddam son-of-a-bitch—But he was a good anthropologist" (G. de Angulo 1995:429–430).

71. The completed work, *Language of the Sierra Miwok,* was submitted to Kroeber in 1936, but Freeland was not awarded a doctorate, and the manuscript was not published in the UC-PAAE series; it appeared in 1951—the year after de Angulo's death—as an IJAL Memoir (Leeds-Hurwitz 1982; see also Brightman's discussion of the "strange tale of Freeland's dissertation" [2004:176–177]).

72. According to Leeds-Hurwitz (2004:52) "between 1927 and 1937 de Angulo was given more money and worked on more languages than any other researcher for the committee." Boas's annual reports list payments to de Angulo totaling $4,400, the equivalent of at least $75,000 in 2010 dollars. De Angulo described his relationship to Boas in a letter to Ezra Pound (July 20, 1950):

Boas didnt give a damn about my private morals as long as my phonetics were right So he took me up It was a joy to work for the Old Man . . . He had a golden heart but he was brusque One day I get a telegram "I need the Kalapooya language of the lower Columbia to settle a question of comparative linguistics. According to information there is only one man left who speaks that language. Lives somewhere on the Yakima Reservation and is drinking himself to death. Will you undertake it? I can get only $500 from Committee. When can you go?" I answered from Portland "I am on the way" I thot it rather amusing to send one drunkard looking for another drunkard "somewhere on the Yakima Reservation" But I was used to Indian ways and it took me only a week to locate him and I drove him back to Berkeley We arrived in the middle of the afternoon nobody at home When the gang returned they found a drunken anthropologist and a drunken Indian (last of his race) snoring in each other's arms. (quoted in G. de Angulo 1995:424–425)

Although this apparently was one of Jaime's favorite anecdotes, Gui de Angulo has told me (personal communication 2008) that it could not have occurred as Jaime describes it. While her father was a drinker, he was seldom drunk, and the Kalapuya speaker he brought to Berkeley, Konoi, was in fact a teetotaler.

73. This section is an abbreviated version of Golla (1991c).

74. The obituary by Mathew Stirling (Stirling and Glemser 1963), who headed the BAE during the latter part of Harrington's career there, also provides some firsthand information about Harrington's personality and working habits. Jane Walsh published a useful sketch of Harrington's life and work as part of a preliminary catalog of his linguistic notes (Walsh 1976). See also the assessments by Callaghan (1975), Heizer (1975, with replies from Callaghan 1976 and Klar 1976 , followed by a riposte from Heizer 1976), and Glenn (1991b). Detailed information about Harrington's research activities in California can be found in Elaine Mills's guides to the microfilm (Mills 1981, 1985; Mills and Brickfield 1986). Kathryn Klar has been working for several years on a full intellectual biography of Harrington.

75. Harrington's only significant publication of his California work, other than a report on the excavation of an archaeological site near Santa Barbara (1928), consists of three collections of Karuk narratives (1930, 1932a, 1932b); two editions of an important mission-era manuscript (Boscana 1933, 1934), only the first with annotations; and a checklist of Salinan and Chumash "cultural elements" for Kroeber's survey of western American Indian cultures (1942). He published next to nothing of his extensive and valuable data on Chimariko, Chumash, Costanoan, Salinan, Takic, Yokuts, and Yuman.

76. It is fair to say that nearly all we know of these languages beyond superficial details is due to Harrington's notes. The grammars that have been written in recent decades of Mutsun Costanoan (Okrand 1977), Salinan (Turner 1987), and Inezeño Chumash (Applegate 1972a) are largely derived from Harrington's data, as are Wash's studies of Barbareño Chumash (1995, 2001) and the grammar of Chimariko begun by Grekoff (n.d.) and recently completed by Jany (2009). Grammars and dictionaries of other varieties of Chumash and Costanoan can be expected in future years.

77. Harrington's modern reputation is probably higher among nonlinguists than linguists. Outside of the technicalities of phonetics, his linguistic acumen was at best modest, and he made no significant contribution to the systematic analysis of California Indian languages. His posthumous fame arises from the sheer magnitude of his compulsively obtained, furtively hoarded notes. For a negative assessment of Harrington's notes as scientific documentation see the exchange between Heizer (1975, 1976), Callaghan (1976), and Klar (1976). Moore (2006), while also skeptical of Harrington's science, explores reasons why both Harrington's *Nachlass* and the man himself have had strong appeal for Indian descendants concerned with personal and historical identity.

78. Vocabularies were published in appendixes to the ethnographic text, which also included numerous words and place-names. Mojave and Quechan vocabularies are in volume 2 (123–128). Volume 9 has a vocabulary of Lower Columbia Athabaskan (199–200). Volume 13 has vocabularies of Hupa and Tolowa (243–253); Shasta, Achumawi, and Karuk (253–262); Yurok and Wiyot (263–272); and Klamath (272–276). Volume 14 has vocabularies of Kato and Wailaki (201–207); Yuki and Wappo (207–214); Eastern, Northern and Central Pomo (214–220); Wintu, Nomlaki, and Patwin (220–229); Chico and Konkow Maidu (229–237); Central and Southern Sierra Miwok (237–243); and Chukchansi Yokuts (244–247). Volume 15 has vocabularies of Cupeño, Luiseño, and Cahuilla (173–179); Northern Diegueño (179–182); Mono and Northern Paiute (182–188); and Washo (188–192).

79. Myers's name does not appear in the index either to the *Languages* volume of the *Handbook of North American Indians* (I. Goddard 1996b) or to Marianne Mithun's comprehensive survey

of North American Indian linguistics (1999). In a rare exception to this silence, Dale Kinkade acknowledges Myers's contribution to the linguistics of the Northwest Coast (Kinkade 1990:101), comparing it to that of P. E. Goddard and J. P. Harrington. Myers's central role in *TNAI* has finally been clarified by Mick Gidley in his detailed study *Edward S. Curtis and the North American Indian, Incorporated* (1998) in which he reconstructs the chronology of the *TNAI* project, the negotiations to finance it and direct its course, and the intertwined lives of the principals. Among the still-unanswered questions, however, is the location of Myers's original field notebooks. Some papers may have been preserved by his family, but in 1978, when Gidley attempted to contact Myers's niece (his closest surviving relative at that time), she refused to meet with him.

80. Sapir's grammar of Takelma was submitted to Columbia University in 1908 as his doctoral dissertation, although not formally published for nearly fifteen years (Sapir 1922a). The Takelma texts he collected were published in 1909.

81. For the circumstances and some of the details of Sapir's fellowship year at Berkeley in 1907–1908 see Golla (1984:2–31). In addition to conducting his Yana research under Kroeber, Sapir also briefly worked with P. E. Goddard on Kato during this time (Sapir 1907–1908).

82. The intensity of the intellectual collaboration between Sapir and Kroeber was especially high during the weeks leading up to Sapir's discovery of the Yurok-Wiyot-Algonquian relationship. See Golla (1986) and Golla (1984:105–126).

83. After 1897, most American anthropologists who collected data on American Indian languages were students of Franz Boas, at Columbia University. Although Boas had a deep interest in linguistic analysis and published widely in the field, he did not see the necessity for general anthropologists to have formal training in linguistic analysis and grammatical description. All that was required, in his view, was sufficient skill in phonetic transcription to take rapid dictation of Indian language texts, and even that skill he felt was better acquired through apprenticeship than through the study of general phonetics. Before 1925, the only serious attempt to provide more technically grounded linguistic training for work with Indian languages was at the University of California, where P. E. Goddard and the president of the university, Benjamin Ide Wheeler, set up a short-lived department of linguistics in 1902. But since Kroeber, taking Boas's position, opposed the idea, it came to naught, and its failure was one of the factors in Goddard's leaving Berkeley for New York in 1909—ironically, to work with Boas (A. L. Kroeber to F. W. Putnam, February 19, 1908, A. L. Kroeber Papers, Bancroft Library).

84. In an article published in *The University of Chicago Magazine*, describing his and Li's work in Northwest California, Sapir (1927a) explained the nature and goals of academic linguistic research on American Indian languages as he envisaged it. In an article written for a Gallup, New Mexico, newspaper, Sapir (1929c) similarly described the Navajo research project that the University of Chicago had embarked on that year.

85. Li usually styled himself Fang-Kuei Li in his English-language publications.

86. Although not yet in personal contact with Sapir, Voegelin was deeply influenced by Sapir's grammar of Southern Paiute, which had just appeared (Sapir 1930–1931). At least in its published form, Voegelin's Tubatulabal grammar is far more Sapirian than Kroeberian.

87. For the influence of Voegelin's Tubatulabal analysis on Yale linguists of the 1930s see Whorf (1935), Swadesh and Voegelin (1939), and Lightner (1971).

88. Extensive fieldwork was included in the terms of Voegelin's appointment at DePauw, enabling him to acquire expertise in a wide range of American Indian languages. Kinkade (1989:728) lists more than a dozen Indian languages on which Voegelin worked "at some depth." For the relationship with Eli Lilly, see Tanner (1991).

89. Halpern's colleagues on this State Emergency Relief Administration project were two fellow Berkeley anthropology students, Frank Essene and Frederick Hulse. No published description of the project exists, but its voluminous results, both original manuscripts and typescripts, can be accessed in the microfilm edition of the Ethnological Documents of the Department and Museum of Anthropology, University of California, Berkeley, 1875–1958 (Bancroft Library, BANC FILM 2216). For Halpern's materials see Bancroft Library 2007:174–175.

90. Haas attended Earlham College in Richmond, graduating in 1930. In a curious coincidence, this small but academically distinguished Quaker school had also been Pliny Earle Goddard's alma mater (¶2.6.3).

91. The marriage was short-lived and they were divorced in 1937. While it lasted, they were apparently an impressive team. Sapir encouraged Kroeber to consider a joint appointment for the couple at Berkeley (cf. Sapir to Kroeber, June 17, 1935 and July 24, 1935, A. L. Kroeber Papers, Bancroft Library, UC Berkeley), and one can only imagine what the trajectory of California Indian linguistics would have been had both Haas and Swadesh been on the Berkeley faculty. In the event, Swadesh had few opportunities to work in California. World War II intervened, and in the early 1950s his academic and research career in the United States was brought to a halt by political difficulties (A. Grant 2009). He was, however, able to do some secondary work with the languages of the California region through editing Sapir's linguistic notes after the latter's death in 1939. He prepared a Yana dictionary from Sapir's files (edited by Haas and published as Sapir and Swadesh 1960), and began work on a detailed analysis of Sapir's Chimariko notes (Swadesh n.d., incorporated in part into Berman 2001b). In the mid-1950s, in an attempt to procure new data in support of Sapir's Penutian hypothesis, he carried out a privately supported field survey of the surviving California and Oregon Penutian languages (Swadesh 1954b).

92. The Survey was renamed the Survey of California and Other Indian Languages in the 1960s, as its scope expanded to cover research on North American Indian languages as far afield as Nez Perce, Blackfoot, and Wichita. For further details of Mary Haas's role in the establishment of the department and the survey see Shipley (1988) and Golla, Munro, and Matisoff (1997).

93. After a successful field season in the summer of 1954, personal difficulties compelled Woodward to discontinue her work on Hupa; her only publication on the language was a phonemic study (1964). My own name probably should be added here next to hers as a student of Harry Hoijer. When I decided in 1962 to make Hupa the focus of my doctoral research at Berkeley, Mary Haas suggested that I ask Hoijer to serve as an external member of my thesis committee and as the informal codirector of my work. He graciously consented, and I met with him frequently during my fieldwork in 1962–1965 as well as on a number of later occasions.

94. This was not the first dissertation Hoijer had directed on a Yuman language. In 1937–1940, while teaching at the University of Chicago, he had supervised A. M. Halpern's work on Quechan (Yuma). As noted earlier (¶2.8.2), Halpern transferred to Chicago from Berkeley midway in his graduate studies.

Part 3 Notes

1. A few shared phonological irregularities can nevertheless be identified, such as the unusual sandhi pattern whereby initial *h* in both languages surfaces as *l* after certain preverbs, reflecting an *l* in these preverbs in Proto-Algic (Blevins and Garrett 2007).

2. Teeter's phonemic orthography is somewhat idiosyncratic. In addition to writing the alveolar flap *r* as *d*, he writes the voiced fricatives *β* and *γ* as *b* and *g*, respectively. He writes the reduced vowel (*ə*) as *a* and the low back full vowel (*a*) as *o*. Arguing that they are in complementary distribution, he writes the two laryngeals (*ʔ* and *h*) with the same symbol, *h*. Thus what would be written here as *βaʔyəγəniɬ* 'he vomits' Teeter writes *bohyaganiɬ*.

3. In a handful of inalienable nouns with initial *k*, the third person stem has a labiovelar (< *w-k-), e.g., *kəɬ* 'my grandson (son's son)', *kʰəɬ* 'your grandson', *kʷəɬəʔl* 'his grandson' (Reichard 1925, 92; I. Goddard 1966, 401). Both in its overall pattern and in its distinctive irregularities, Wiyot possessive marking has a clear parallel in Algonquian. Discovery of this parallel is what convinced Sapir that Wiyot, Yurok, and Algonquian were genetically related (see Sapir 1913a, 633–637; Kroeber's letter to Sapir in Golla 1984, 112–113; and the discussion in I. Goddard 1986).

4. Kroeber's field notebooks are in the Bancroft Library (Kroeber 1900–1940, notebooks 9–10 [1901], 39–42 [1902], 66–67 [1906], and 70–84 [1907]). The wax cylinder recordings are in the Hearst Museum (Keeling 1991). The Berkeley Yurok Project has been retranscribing and analyzing these texts and other Yurok materials archived at UC Berkeley; a catalog is available online on the project's Web pages (www.linguistics. berkeley.edu/~yurok).

5. Glottalized sonorants are single preglottalized segments with the same phonological status as glottalized stops and affricates (Blevins 2003:10–11), although Robins (1958) writes them as glottal stop + sonorant. The same analysis can be extended to glottalized fricatives. When initial in a phonological word, a basic glottalized sonorant or fricative is often (but not always) pronounced as its plain equivalent; when a vowel-final prefix or particle is added, the preglottalization reappears (e.g., *'lumon* 'eel basket' [lumon] ~ [ʔlumon], *k'e-'lumon* 'your eel basket' [k'ɛʔlumon]).

6. Sapir's (1915d) original proposal that the Na-Dene relationship encompassed Haida was accepted uncritically for many decades. As more accurate data on Haida became available after new research in the 1970s and 1980s, it became apparent that many of Sapir's comparisons were based on incorrect analyses, leading the majority of scholars to view the resemblances between Haida and Athabaskan-Eyak-Tlingit as either accidental or the result of contact. However, John Enrico, the contemporary linguist with the deepest knowledge of Haida, continues to believe that a real, if distant, genetic relationship connects Haida to Na-Dene (Enrico 2004).

7. The Lower Columbia language (Kwalhioqua-Tlatskanai) may, indeed, have a largely separate history. According to Krauss, the scholar most familiar with the documentation of Lower Columbia, while the language "may share a few peculiarities" with the Oregon and California languages, it has "striking affinities" to Babine-Hagwilgate in north-central British Columbia, including a shared irregular marking of first person singular subjects in certain classes of verbs (Krauss 1979:870).

8. Among the historically intriguing lexemes uniquely shared between the California and Oregon groups and Apachean is a synchronically unanalyzable theme (both verbal and nominal) associated with the female puberty ceremony (Navajo kinaaldá [kʰina:ltá], Hupa kʰinahɬta). Another, with implications for migration routes, is the term for the yellow or ponderosa pine, *Pinus ponderosa* (Navajo dilchíí' [tilčʰíːʔ], Hupa tilčʷʰeːkʸ).

9. When the first party of white settlers entered Upper Coquille territory in May 1853, they hired an Upper Umpqua Indian to show them the way. When they reached the Upper Coquille villages near Myrtle Point, the guide found it so difficult to communicate to the residents that he had to ask an Upper Umpqua woman who was married into the Upper Coquilles to serve as his translator (Youst and Seaburg 2002:28–29).

10. As Dorsey recognized, it is likely that the Takelma were once the occupants of most of the interior of southwestern Oregon, but that "later on there was an invasion by the Athapascans, who established villages on all sides of them" (1890:235). See also Jacobs (1937).

11. Vocabulary collection for the BAE was standardized by J. W. Powell's *Introduction to the Study of Indian Languages* (Powell 1877b; 2nd ed., 1880), which included long lists (or "schedules") of words to be collected, arranged by semantic category. See ¶2.5.2.

12. My Lower Rogue River informant, Ida Bensell, who had often visited the Indian Shaker church at Smith River, claimed to be able to understand Chetco-Tolowa ("the way they talk down in California") but made clear that this ability was due to her long familiarity with it.

13. The *tʰaʔkʸimiɬxʷeː* ("Hostler Ranch") and *meʔtilxʷeː* ("Matilton") divisions in Hoopa Valley had—and continue to have—reciprocal social and ceremonial functions, exhibited most clearly in the World Renewal dances (Goldschmidt and Driver 1940; Kroeber and Gifford 1949). Merriam's identification of these divisions (summarized in Baumhoff 1958:211–213) is accurate in geographical terms, but the names he ascribes to them, "Natinuwhe" and "Tinuheneu," are incorrect. The former is *naːtʰinixʷeː* ('the people of Hoopa Valley'), while the latter is apparently *tiniŋʔxineːW* ('those who speak *tini* [i.e, "Dine" or Athabaskan]'). See Sapir and Golla 2001, esp. pp. 35–98.

14. Among these is Ta'k'imiɬding ('acorn cooking place'), the name of the principal village of the lower half of Hoopa Valley. It was the ceremonial center of Hupa culture, and its name alludes to the Acorn Feast that was held there, where the "first acorns" of the season were ritually cooked. The Chimariko name for Ta'k'imiɬding was *hoːpu-tače* 'acorn soup place', and if, as seems likely, this is the source of Yurok *hup'o* 'Hoopa Valley' there is little doubt that when the Yuroks first had contact with the people of Ta'k'imiɬding they spoke Chimariko.

15. See also Goddard 1903–1906.

16. The supgroups of the Eel River Athabaskans are largely of Goddard's and Kroeber's making. Kroeber speaks of them as "bodies of people into whom [they] appear naturally to divide"

(1925:143), and while he alludes to members of a particular subgroup having "perhaps some consciousness of their own separation," the classification is based on external linguistic observation, not internal social attitudes. The names are arbitrary, and varying usages can lead to confusion (see the synonymy in Elsasser 1978:203). "Nongatl" is especially problematic: Merriam observed that the term was used by the Eel River Athabaskans themselves as "a general or blanket name for all the . . . tribes from Iaqua and Yeager Creek on the north to the northern border of Round Valley on the south" (1923:276). "Lassik," the Wintu name of a Nongatl war leader in the early historic period, has been varously applied to the Nongatl, the Wailaki, and (in Goddard's usage, which has become standard) to a group located between the Nongatl and the Wailaki and distinct from both. Merriam's nomenclature, although cumbersome, is more precise, and I provide it as an alternative.

17. See also various materials in P. Goddard (1902–1922a, 1902–1922b), including the typescript of a substantial collection of Nongatl texts with interlinear translations (EDDMA CU-23.1, no. 12.3). Sally Anderson has extracted lexical information and texts from Goddard's notes on the Eel River dialects, which she has electronically published at her Web site "California Athabaskan Languages" (www.billabbie.com/calath). Anderson uses "Kuneste" (from *kʰonəst'eʔ* or *kʰonest'eʔ* 'person') in place of my "Eel River Athabaskan" to designate the Eel River dialect network. For general comments on Goddard's California Athabaskan fieldwork see Kroeber 1967.

18. The development in Hupa-Chilula and Kato of an animacy or obviation contrast in third person pronouns, with the erstwhile indefinite pronouns dramatically shifting their semantics to serve as the animate/proximate member of the pair, is a major restructuring that is unique to California Athabaskan. The closest parallel is the use of the indefinite (or "fourth person") in Navajo to refer to the main character in narratives (Willie 1991). But while reminiscent of the functional shift in the California languages, the topic-tracking function of the Navajo fourth person seems more to underscore the semantic and functional flexibility of the typical Athabaskan indefinite pronoun. While this occasionally allows its deployment as a marker of topical saliency (in addition to Navajo, see the examples in C. Thompson 1990 and Saxon 1993), it more frequently results in the extension of the "indefinite" category to include first person plural (Story 1989). What has happened to the indefinite in California is more akin to a semantic inversion than an incremental expansion of its core meaning. It must be admitted, however, that the origin of the Hupa-Chilula and Kato systems of third person pronominal marking is not fully understood and remains open to differing historical interpretations. Balodis (2009), relying mainly on general structural principles, argues that the animacy/obviation contrast seen in Kato and Hupa-Chilula must have been inherited from Proto-Athabaskan and that its absence in the other two California languages is to be attributed to a simplifying innovation. In a recent paper (Golla 2011) I argued that the comparative data suggest the opposite sequence of events. This leaves me to explain, however, how Hupa-Chilula and Kato, separated by approximately one hundred miles of Eel River and Mattole territory, could have independently developed almost identical animacy/obviation contrasts out of the inherited third person and indefinite pronouns. I hypothesize that this development reflects the influence of one or more long-established Hokan languages on the speech of Athabaskan newcomers in two well-populated and resource-rich areas, Hoopa Valley and Cahto Valley. In these situations of language shift and cultural assimilation, an old Hokan pattern of marking topical saliency, particularly in narrative (Mithun 1990a, in press; O'Connor 1990a), was carried over into the new Athabaskan idiom by redeploying the semantically labile indefinite pronoun.

19. "Hok-" was abstracted from the apparently cognate forms of the numeral 'two' found in all these languages (cf. Karok *ʔáxak*, Shasta *xúkkwaʔ*, Chimariko *xoku*, Atsugewi *hoʔki*, Yana *ux-*, and Eastern Pomo *xoč̓ʰ*).

20. For an overview of the construction of the Hokan hypothesis by Kroeber, Sapir, and others between 1900 and 1930, see Langdon 1974:22–47.

21. It was Swanton who first brought the Coahuiltecan group (Coahuilteco, Comecrudo, and Cotoname) to the attention of Americanist linguists (Swanton 1915). In his view, the more likely connections of the Coahuiltecan languages lay to the east, in Karankawa, Tonkawa, and Atakapa, and possibly Natchez and Muskogean. Sapir included data from some of these wider possibilities in his initial Hokan-Coahuiltecan comparisons (1920a), and in his later classification (1921c, 1929b) he proposed three branches for "Coahuiltecan"—Tonkawa, Coahuilteco-Cotoname-Comecrudo, and Karankawa. Atakapa and Natchez-Muskogean, however, were relegated to separate subgroups of "Hokan-Siouan."

22. For a somewhat more upbeat appraisal see Langdon (1986).

23. Sapir believed that the strongest evidence for a "Southern Hokan" grouping was a system of nominal and verbal prefixes shared by Salinan, Washo, Tequistlatecan, and Subtiaba, but "wanting or nearly so in the north": *t- nominal or absolute, *m- adjectival, *k- intransitive, and *p- transitive (1925a:504). Campbell, however, aptly remarks that "the fact that Subtiaba-Tlapanec clearly has been demonstrated to belong to the Otomanguean family, not to Hokan, shows just how speculative Sapir's Hokan morphology was" (Campbell 1997:292). It remains possible that the prefixes (and the categories they mark) were borrowed into Subtiaba-Tlapanec from some now-extinct central Mexican Hokan language, but this is a far less elegant scenario than the one Sapir originally proposed, which he bolstered with dozens of now-suspect lexical comparisons purporting to demonstrate the Hokan bona fides of Subtiaba.

24. The publication history of Sapir's work on comparative Hokan obscures the evolution of his thinking about the relationship. His initial paper on Hokan and Hokan-Coahuiltecan (Sapir 1920a) was actually written early in 1915 (Golla 1984:175–182). The classification that appeared in the 1929 edition of the *Encyclopedia Britannica* (Sapir 1929b) represents a minimally revised version of a paper he delivered in December 1920 (Sapir 1920d) and that was published in outline two months later (Sapir 1921c). Sapir's most evolved views on Hokan are to be found in his paper "The Hokan Affinity of Subtiaba in Nicaragua" (1925a).

25. The first "Conference on Hokan Languages" was held at UC San Diego in April 1970, supported by funds from the National Science Foundation (Langdon 1974:77; Langdon and Silver 1976). During the following two decades less formal meetings of the Hokan Conference (or Workshop) were held annually, combined after the early 1980s with a parallel gathering of Penutian specialists. After 1977 the proceedings of these meetings were published, until 1992 usually under the

editorship of James E. Redden. In the early 1990s enthusiasm for this project began to wane, and no "Hokan-Penutian Conference" has been held since 2000 (Buszard-Welcher 2002).

26. Langdon cites evidence to support a connection between Tequistlatecan and Seri, and between both of these and Chumash. In light of Kaufman's conclusion (discussed in this section) that the paucity of cognates supported by regular phonemic correspondences makes Chumash a doubtful member of the Hokan phylum, future scholars might want to explore the possibility that the connections (e.g., in plural formation) that Langdon sees between Chumash and Southern Hokan might be due to morphological borrowing from Salinan or a related language that was spoken across much of historic Northern and Central Chumash territory before the spread of an originally island-based Chumash.

27. The 132 texts that she examined included "Bright's (1957) grammar and its 92 texts, the 5 texts contained in Lang (1994), the 14 in Harrington (1930), the 12 in Harrington (1932b), the 8 in De Angulo and Freeland (1931a), and one unpublished text which was collected by William Bright in 1989." In addition, "the 284-page Harrington monograph (Harrington 1932a [*Tobacco among the Karuk*]) consists of discussions of tobacco usage among the Karuk, of which approximately half are given in Karuk" (Macaulay 2000:467, n. 7).

28. For more on Karuk pitch accent see Macaulay (1988).

29. For a recent assessment of the evidence for Chimariko dialects see Conathan 2006.

30. Carmen Jany's grammar (her dissertation) was published in 2009.

31. Grekoff's notes and manuscripts have been deposited in the Archives of the Survey of California and Other Indian Languages, University of California, Berkeley (cf. Wood and Hinton 2002).

32. The Tsnungwe Council maintains a website (as of 2011) at www.dcn.davis.ca.us/~ammon/tsnungwe/council.html.

33. Although precontact Chimariko probably had a phonemic contrast between the midvelar stop series (k) and the back-velar or uvular series (q), it was only marginally functional in the remnant speech community that survived into the early twentieth century. At least one of the semifluent speakers Sapir interviewed in 1927, Martha Ziegler, made no distinction whatsoever between the two velar stop positions, and the two who did—Abe Bush and Saxy Kidd—primarily spoke Wintu and Hupa, respectively, languages with a fully phonemic k : q contrast (Berman 2001c:1043–1044). Harrington regularly distinguished k from q in the materials he obtained in 1921 from Sally Noble, his oldest and best source (and Martha Ziegler's mother), but even in her speech the difference often seems to have been allophonic. Her pronunciation of the numeral 'two', for example, is closely transcribed as kok^hu in one place but as $q(^h)oq^hu$ in another (Harrington 1982–1990, vol. 2, reels 20:0005 and 21:0007).

34. The analysis is incomplete, but it seems likely that the verbs of "involuntary" actions and states in Chimariko function in much the same way as the "noncontrol" verbs of Pomo and Yuki (¶4.6.3).

35. "According to Sargent Sambo, a Klamath River Shasta, 'the Watiru talked to the Karok and the Kammatwa, the Kammatwa talked to the Watiru and the Shasta, but the Watiru and the Shasta could not talk to each other'" (Silver 1978:211–212). Except for general sociolinguistic observations of this kind,

absolutely nothing is known about the "Kammatwa-Watiru" language. One can speculate that it was what remained of a formerly more widespread language spoken on the Klamath River between the Karuk and the Shasta, at a somewhat more advanced stage of being absorbed by them as Chimariko was being absorbed by Hupa and Wintu. If so, the geography suggests that it was a Hokan language related to New River Shasta or Konomihu.

36. Brazille is also spelled "Brizell" and "Bussal," among other variants (my Humboldt colleague Suzanne Burcell is a member of the same extended family). Susan and Ellen's father, Francis (Frank) Brazille, was a French-Canadian (probably an employee of the Hudson's Bay Company) who settled in the area in the 1840s, where he married "Queen," who spoke her mother's Shasta. Queen's father, however, known as "Mowíma" (i.e., *mauweema*, the local English term for "chief" or "headman"), spoke the old Konomihu language, and the sisters—particularly Susan, the elder of the two, who was eleven years old when he died in 1858—learned words from him and listened to him tell stories (Larsson 1987, summarizing information in Harrington's notes).

37. Goddard's vocabulary was collected in July 1902 from Mrs. Mary Jordan, a self-described New River Shasta who lived near the head of the South Fork of the Salmon. Of its approximately 120 items, nearly 100 are almost entirely identical with the Scott Valley Shasta documented by Bright and Olmsted (1959); most of the fifteen to twenty non-Shasta items are Chimariko, and one word ('sucker') appears to be Konomihu. Merriam's Hah-to-ke´-he-wuk vocabularies, collected in 1929–1930 from "Mrs. George," near Cecilville, are almost entirely an attestation of Scott Valley Shasta.

38. Although Malinda Kidd was the mother of Saxy Kidd, the source of Merriam's "Tlo-hom-tah-hoi," her son's speech apparently preserved none of her distinctive vocabulary. The "one old woman" that Goddard counted as the last cultural survivor of the New River people (1903a:8) was undoubtedly Malinda Kidd.

39. Okwanuchu speech may also be attested in a scattering of words identified as "Wailaki on McCloud" (cf. Wintu *waylaki* 'north people') that Jeremiah Curtin recorded in the margins of a manuscript otherwise devoted to material from San Francisco Bay area languages (Curtin 1884f). A total of eighteen "McCloud" words are noted: *gü´ru* 'man', *ki´rikega* 'woman', *hänumaqa* 'old man', [*ki´rikega*] + *apci* 'old woman', *ä´toqe´äqa* 'young man', *kewatcaq* 'young woman' (p.77); *tse´gwa* 'one', *hoka* 'two', *qätski´* 'four', *tseapka* 'five' = 'one hand', *huk^{a}apka* 'six' (p.97); *tsuwara* 'sun', *kapqu´[r]wara* 'moon', *kau* 'snow', *atsa´* 'water', *gri´tuma* 'thunder', *itsa* 'rock', *tarak* [*terak*?] 'earth' (p.132). (Note that Curtin employed the BAE transcription system, in which q represents a velar fricative, not a velar stop.) Of these forms, five (man, old man, old, four, thunder) are not attested in any other variety of Shasta.

40. "The majority of Atsugewi (or at least a goodly number of them) speak Achumawi as well, while very few Achumawi speak Atsugewi. At all common meetings the speeches are always in Achumawi, and not translated" (de Angulo and Freeland 1930:78). See also Voegelin's comments on the "subtle negativism of Achumawi indivduals to the Atsugewi language" (1946:101).

41. De Angulo and Freeland remark on the exceptional—for California—uniformity of Achumawi (and Atsugewi): "the differences between the two extremes of the territory are

minimal: not more than the differences between the French of Paris and that of Tours" (1930:78; see also Voegelin 1946, Olmsted 1964:5).

42. For cautions on the accuracy of both de Angulo's and Olmsted's work see Nevin (1998). Gursky (1987) has also pointed out that Olmsted accidentally incorporated some of de Angulo's Eastern Pomo files into his 1966 Achumawi dictionary.

43. In Atsugewi, and probably also in Achumawi, surface phonemic aspirated consonants are the product of morphological rules, as are the mid vowels (*e, o*) and all long vowels (Walters 1977:155).

44. See Nevin 1998, Appendix A. The phonetic description of the pharyngeal/epiglottal fricative and the barred ħ symbol are from Uldall (1933). Voegelin (1946:99) called it a "voiceless fricative with laryngeal contraction" and wrote it with small cap н.

45. The Yanas were notable for their short stature and were called *nosi* 'the short ones' by their Maidu neighbors. Powers, with his typical mixture of hyperbole and fact, portrays the "Nozi" as a "constant terror" to the Wintu and Nomlaki. "With this fierce and restless tribe forever on their flank, always ready to pounce upon them, it is singular that the Wintun maintained such a long and narrow ribbon of villages on the east bank [of the Sacramento]. . . . The tormenting Nozi . . . though coming for fish . . . never neglected an opportunity to carry away women and children into the foothills for slaves" (Powers 1877:275).

46. Nevertheless, the differences between Northern/Central and Southern Yana seem not to have amounted to a language boundary. During Ishi's first few weeks in San Francisco, Sam Batwi, a speaker of Central Yana, served as Ishi's interpreter, and the two apparently conversed easily (Golla 2003). Sapir and Spier comment that "it is doubtful if a Northern or Central speaker could understand Yahi perfectly, but it is certain that he could make out practically all of it after a brief contact" (1943:244). This statement is partially based on Sapir's personal experience; he relied on Northern/Central Yana as a medium of communication during his work with Ishi in 1915 (Sapir 1923b:264).

47. See Golla (1988, 2003) for a description of these materials, which are housed in the Bancroft Library (Sapir 1915e). Work has been under way for a number of years to produce a publishable edition of the extended narrative texts they contain (Perry 2003; Luthin and Hinton 2003a, 2003b). Although Sapir's was the principal documentation of Ishi's Yahi made during his years at the University of California's Museum of Anthropology (1911–1916), Kroeber and Waterman also collected some materials, including extensive wax cylinder recordings (Jacknis 2003).

48. Although there is no federally acknowledged Yana tribe, a number of individuals who consider themselves to be of Yana descent are scattered across northern California, many of them enrolled in other tribes. For the tangled nature of modern Yana ethnic identity see Starn (2004).

49. Halpern described his later work on Southern Pomo in a letter to me, dated March 24, 1982, which I published in *COLN* (*California-Oregon Linguistics Newsletter*), vol. 5, no. 3, 1982, a mimeographed bulletin that circulated among a hundred or so Californianists for a few years. Since it is unlikely that many readers of this book will have access to *COLN*, I take the opportunity of reprinting Halpern's report here:

My period in the field was Feb. 1–March 4 [1982], financed by a Smithsonian Urgent Anthropology grant. . . . My So. Pomo work was successful beyond expectations. I collected a significant amount of new lexical and paradigmatic material, illuminating and at times complicating problems I had not previously worked out. In addition I now have on tape the content of nine texts, mostly brief, originally recorded in 1940 from Annie Burke. These were obtained by my reading my transcript of 1940 and having Elsie Allen repeat what I was reading. Further, Elsie contributed several new items in text, original material of her own, largely ethnographic and oral-historical in nature. The total is 6 one-hour tapes, though the amount of Pomo language material is of course less than 6 hours.

The success of this endeavor is due entirely to Elsie. Elsie is best known as one of the last competent basket makers and is literally besieged by phone calls from people eager to obtain instruction. She is also, it now seems to be confirmed, just about the last So. Pomo speaker with real facility in the language. Not only was Elsie willing to work long hours, putting aside other demands on her time, she also quickly perceived the nature of the problems I was working on, so that besides giving directly relevant answers to my questions she also volunteered data of great value beyond what it occurred to me to ask.

I look back on this period of field work, unfortunately limited in duration by schedule problems of my own, as a fine example of cooperative endeavor by investigator and informant. We inevitably left some loose ends. I hope for another opportunity to tie some of these up, though with some reluctance because of the interruption it entails in my work on Quechan. Quechan remains the center of the work I feel committed both personally and professionally to complete.

Incidentally in your report on the Sonoma State workshop of last summer [*COLN* 4, no. 5/6, November 1981] you quote me as agreeing with Oswalt that So-SW-CP [Southern Pomo–Kashaya–Central Pomo] constitute a sub-group within the family, distinct from the others. I'm not sure how you got that impression, but I certainly have reservations about it. I still don't feel I can improve on my conclusions, which are not final, as published in Bright [1964, 88–93].

50. The tribelet names and locations are from Milliken (1990) and reflect his detailed analysis of mission records. Milliken's identification of the two tribelets in the immediate neighborhood of Mission Soledad, the Eslenahan and Aspasniahan, as Esselen rather than Costanoan in speech is contestable, but his case is well argued.

51. These include a list of twenty-two words collected by Lamanon during la Pérouse's visit in 1786 and the numerals 1 to 10 collected—or, more likely, copied from a mission manuscript—by the French traveler Duflot de Mofras in 1841.

52. The richness of the data in Lasuén's manuscript only gradually came to light. Kroeber (1904) printed the vocabulary in the truncated form in which it appeared in the published report of Alcalá Galiano and Valdés's visit (Anonymous 1802), which included only 31 of the original 108 Esselen words. Beeler (1978a:10–15) and, with less accuracy, Cutter (1990:147–149) published the complete vocabulary as it appears in the original

manuscript in the Museo Naval in Madrid. The catechism was entirely omitted from the 1802 publication and was first noted by Beeler (1978a:41), who however had access only to an incomplete copy of the manuscript. The full text has been published by Shaul (1995a) and Cutter (1990:147–155).

53. The Esselen Tribe of Monterey County, apparently a separate group from the Esselen Nation, maintains an informative Web site (www.esselen.com) with support from Coyote Press (see Breschini and Haversat 2004). A comprehensive Esselen lexicon, compiled by David Shaul, is available at this site.

54. Turner (personal communication) points out that two of these dialect names are merely directional terms: *lima* is glossed by both Harrington and Kroeber as 'over there' or 'above', and *lamaka* is 'west' or 'toward the coast'.

55. Some of these were set to music by Father Sancho, who was a composer of considerable talent (C. H. Russell 2004).

56. Alexander S. Taylor came into possession of most of the surviving missionary manuscripts of Antoniano during the mid-1850s. This collection is now divided among three repositories. The original manuscript of Sitjar and Pieras's dictionary is in the Bancroft Library (Sitjar and Pieras 1771–1797a). The confessional is in the Special Collections Division of the Georgetown University Library in Washington, DC (Sitjar and Pieras 1771–1797b). The manuscript of another dictionary is in the Boston Athenaeum (Sitjar, Cabot, and Dumetz 1770–1835). In addition to these manuscripts, a prayer and song board, with texts in Salinan and Spanish, is preserved at the Smithsonian (NAA MS 1082). It was prepared by Cabot in 1817 for instructional purposes and as a prompting aid during choral singing (Ahlborn 1992; Cook and Marino 1988:477, fig.4).

57. Imperial Valley "Kamia" is primarily known through the miscellaneous terms that Gifford cites in his ethnographic sketch (1931). While concurring with Gifford that the variety was "only subdialectally distinguished from Diegueño," specifically Tipai, Langdon notes significant phonological and lexical influences from Quechan (Langdon 1975a:64). Merriam collected general and natural history vocabularies of "Eastern Diegueño" or "Kam´-me-i" from a speaker living in Yuma in 1933 (Appendix A: O-14b). These materials possibly represent an independent attestation of the language spoken by Gifford's "Kamia," but to my knowledge they have not been examined with this question in mind.

58. Spoken by groups in the mountains of eastern San Diego County, and not to be confused with the Kamia of Imperial Valley. Winter (1957) called this dialect cluster "Campo" and judged it to be no closer to other varieties of Diegueño than to Cocopa. According to the ethnohistorian Florence Shipek, "Kumeyaay"—which Langdon etymologizes as 'people of the cliffs' or 'highland people' (1975a)—was the name of the precontact tribe, the "Kumeyaay Nation," that incorporated all Diegueño speakers. They recognized the authority of a "national" leader or "general," *kuuchult kwataay*, whose duties resembled those of the "big leader" of a Colorado River tribe, including the maintenence of a system of relay runners that kept the coastal Diegueño in contact with the the interior. This integration was destroyed by missionization, but the term Kumeyaay—and perhaps some lingering sense of tribal identity—persisted among the remote interior bands (Shipek 1982, 1986). If Shipek's analysis is correct, the aboriginal Diegueño more closely resembled the Mojave, Quechan, and Cocopa in tribal cohesion, as well as

in identification of language with nation, than the more typically Californian Luiseño and Cahuilla to their north.

59. Phonetically [kʷətsá:n]; the cluster-breaking schwa is not considered phonemic in Halpern's analysis. Other spellings of the name are "Cuchan" and "Kwitsan."

60. There are two modern Mojave groups: the Fort Mojave Tribe, near Needles, California, and the Mohave members of the Colorado River Indian Tribes, near Parker, Arizona. The former prefer the spelling "Mojave" while the latter prefer "Mohave." For purposes of general reference, the Fort Mojave spelling is used in this book.

61. Harrington began collecting data on Mojave during summer vacations while teaching school in Santa Ana in 1906–1908. It was his first work on an American Indian language (Miles and Brickfield 1986:116–117).

62. Voiced stops and fricatives occur throughout Yuman as lenited variants of plain stops in certain morphophonologically "weak" positions (Langdon 1975b). In some Yuman languages this variation is subphonemic (as [p] ~ [b] in Tipay Diegueño, cf. A. Miller 2001:45–48), while in others it produces marginal phonemic contrasts (as p ~ β in Ipay Diegueño, restricted to a few enclitics). In the River and Upland Yuman languages some lenited variants have gained full phonemic status.

63. Latham recognized the relationship independently, as pointed out by Powell (1891:137), but he did not propose a family name.

64. Mixco notes, however, that when the Jesuit missionary and explorer Wenceslaus Linck reached the vicinity of Rosario during his expedition of 1766, he wrote in his diary that "it seems that this place marks the outermost limits of the Cochimí language. We heard these natives utter with exceptional speed a language which resembles in no way that used up to this point. . . . Our interpreters despite all their efforts could not understand a single word" (Burrus 1966, quoted in Mixco 1977a:42, 1977c:189).

65. Marlett (2008b), after examining Bright's data in the light of what is now known about Seri, concludes that a number of Seri-Salinan resemblant sets must be eliminated as spurious. The remaining "correlates," he argues, are too few to demonstrate a deep historical relationship.

66. In their published materials on Seri, Marlett and the Mosers write /k/ as c or qu and /x/ as j, following Spanish spelling conventions; /χ/ is written as x; and /kʷ/, /xʷ/, and /χʷ/ are written as cö, jö, and xö, respectively. The glottal stop is written as h, the palatal fricative /š/ is written as z, and long vowels are written doubled. Thus what they write *ziix icácötim* 'blanket' is to be interpreted as phonemic /ši:χ ikákʷtim/, *hasatoj* 'stones' as /ʔasatoh/, and *czóoxöc* 'four' as /kšó:χʷk/.

67. This section is derived in part from DeLancey and Golla 1997. For another survey see Silverstein 1979a.

68. Zuni should possibly be added to this list. Sapir left it unclassified in 1921, and later tentatively placed it in Hokan-Siouan, but Newman, who had worked extensively with both Zuni and Yokuts, assembled an interesting body of lexical and grammatical comparisons suggesting a distant relationship between Zuni and some of the California Penutian languages, primarily Yokuts and Miwok (Newman 1964). Except for Hamp (1975), who found the hypothesis quite promising, most linguistic historians appear to agree with Campbell (1997:321) that it "fails to be convincing." The story that has circulated since Newman's death, that the paper was a spoof intended to

satirize the futility of long-range comparative work, is probably a canard.

69. As early as the 1880s, Gatschet had noted the existence of "an uncommon number of affinities . . . between Klamath and the Maídu dialects" (1890, Part 1:li). Although he dismissed the prospect of establishing a genetic relatonship between Klamath-Modoc and any nearby language or family, Gatschet found the evidence for what we now know as Plateau Penutian (Klamath-Modoc plus Sahaptin, Cayuse, and Molala) to be "real and not fanciful." Before coming to his negative conclusion, he devoted several pages of the introduction to his *Klamath Language* to "radicals which Klamath holds in common with other families" (1890, Part 1:xlvii–l). These sets include some of the most frequently cited Penutian etymologies, including 'mouth', in which Gatschet identified forms "parallel" to Klamath *som* in Plateau Penutian, Maiduan, and Yokuts, and noted resemblant words in Wintuan and Costanoan (as well as Yuki, Chumash, and Quechua). But rather than see this as evidence for a Penutian phylum, Gatschet chose to interpret these resemblances as widespread borrowings "disseminated through many of the Pacific coast languages" (1890, Part 1:xlix).

70. For example, such plants as the gray pine, the valley oak, and poison oak, which are virtually diagnostic of California west of the Sierras.

71. See R. Hall (1992) for the Athabaskan-Coos border on the lower Coquille River. For further discussion of the Takelma-Athabaskan border, see ¶3.6.2.

72. Sapir writes the Takelma plain stops as *b, d,* and *g,* and the aspirated stops as *p, t,* and *k.* For the sake of consistency within this volume these have been rewritten as *p, t, k* and *pʰ, tʰ, kʰ,* respectively.

73. Sapir writes high pitch, which occurs only on short vowels, as v̀ (e.g., *xì* 'water'); rising pitch, which occurs only on long vowels, as ṽ (e.g., *dīp'* 'camass', *k!wāi* 'grass'); and falling pitch on both short and long vowels as v́ (e.g., *sgísi* 'coyote', *t'ī'ʼs* 'gopher').

74. This is apparently the source of "Palaihnih,", the name Horatio Hale gave to his Achumawi vocabulary (1846) and on which Powell based "Palaihnihan" (¶3.12.4). The town of Bly, Oregon, also takes its name from Klamath *play* 'upland'.

75. Although Barker, a convert to Islam, published these under the name Muhammad Abd-al-Rahman (or M. A. R.) Barker, he is still known to his friends and colleagues as "Phil." Now in his eighties and retired from an academic career in South Asian linguistics at McGill and Minnesota, Barker has achieved a degree of fame as the inventor of the fantasy world Tékumel (www.tekumel.com).

76. For a comprehensive bibliography and other resources on Klamath-Modoc linguistics, see the Klamath/Modoc Linguistics Page maintained by Scott Delancey at the University of Oregon (www.uoregon.edu/~delancey/klamath.html).

77. Barker writes the plain stop/affricates—which are voiced when occurring between voiced segments—as *b, d, j, g, ġ,* and writes the aspirated stop/affricates as *p, t, č, k, q.* Since plain and aspirated stops and affricates are in phonemic contrast only before vowels and voiced resonants, their phonemic assignment in other environments is arbitrary. Barker chooses to treat these noncontrasting stop/affricates as aspirated; here they are treated as plain.

78. Tatsch (2006) has recently collated all of the extant data on Nisenan dialectology and ethnogeography. She sees evidence for nine political "districts," which were probably also dialectally distinct to one degree or another:

1. Notomusse, along the American River from Sacramento to Auburn.
2. Nisem Pawenan, along the Sacrameno River from a few miles south of the American River to Verona at the mouth of the Feather River.
3. Eskanamusse, between the South Fork of the American River and the Cosumnes River, from Coloma on the northeast to Latrobe on the southwest.
4. Southern Nishenan, in the mountainous area east of Placerville.
5. Nisem K'auwak', in the Nevada City and Grass Valley area.
6. Tahnkum, from Brown's Valley north to Honcut Creek and Lake Oroville.
7. Northern Nishenan, a large division that included four subdivisions—Auburn, Colfax, Sugar Pine Hill, and Clipper Gap—all under the political influence of the Auburn group.
8. Estom Nisenan, a small group near Sloughhouse, southeast of Sacramento.
9. Yupumusse, along the Feather River in the vicinity of Marysville and Yuba City.

Tatsch's divisions 1, 2, and 9 are included in my Valley Nisenan, while her divisions 5, 7, and 4 correspond to my Northern, Central, and Southern Hill Nisenan, respectively. Her Eskanamusse (3) and Estom Nisenan (8), the most southwesterly dialect districts in Nisenan territory, attested only in Merriam's vocabularies, appear to be transitional between Southern Hill and Valley Nisenan, while Tahnkum (6) was a Nisenan area heavily influenced by Konkow and probably transitional between the two languages. Tatsch thus largely agrees with the standard tripartite scheme of the "Hill Nisenan" dialects, as outlined here, but finds reasons (particularly in the ethnogeographic data collected by Merriam and Littlejohn) to split "Valley Nisenan" into several distinct politico-linguistic subgroups.

79. Maiduan is the only branch of Penutian in which the subject case is marked by an overt suffix, while the object is left unmarked. In form, the Maiduan subject marker *-(i)m* appears to correspond to Plateau Penutian *-Vm*, the marker of the possessive case (see the Klamath forms in Table 31). In the Sahaptian languages the same suffix is also used to mark the ergative case, that is, the agent of a transitive verb as distinct from the subject of a transitive verb. (For the details of Sahaptin and Nez Perce ergatives see Rude 1987. Rude is ambivalent about the historical identity of the ergative and possessive case markers.) It is possible that Pre-Maiduan had an ergative-absolute system of case marking similar to that of Sahaptian, and that this was restructured into the typically Californian nominative-accusative case system of historic Maiduan. More likely, however, the Maiduan *-(i)m* subject marker represents the generalization of a passive or passive-like construction, widespread in Penutian, in which the agent is marked by the possessive case (DeLancey and Golla 1997:189–191).

80. Shepherd estimates a time depth of "perhaps 2000–2500 years," but still compares the divergence to that of the Romance languages (2005:1).

81. For further discussion of the Okwanuchu-Waymaq question see ¶3.11.5.

82. The name Nim-Yokuts is taken from *nim*, the form of the 1 sg possessive pronoun ("my") in the dialects of subgroups 3 through 6. In the dialects of the Buena Vista subgroup the form is *ken*; in Poso Creek it is *mik*.

83. Norval Smith and Randall Milliken (p.c.) have identified "José Patricio," the source of Taylor's vocabulary, as Juan José Patricio, a man born at Mission Santa Clara in 1835. The mission records indicate that his father, Narciso/Pililis, belonged to the rancheria of Mayemas, which seems to have been located on the west bank of the San Joaquin near Vernalis, opposite the mouth of the Stanislaus River. If this information is correct, and the vocabulary that Taylor collected accurately represents the speech of that village, then Northern Valley Yokuts was spoken much further north than has previously been thought. Since there seems little doubt that Delta Yokuts dialects were spoken as far south as the mouth of the Merced, the San Joaquin River may have been the boundary between Northern Valley Yokuts (on the west bank) and Delta Yokuts (on the east bank) in nearly all of Stanislaus County.

84. The most useful information about the linguistic geography of the Delta Yokuts area comes from Pinart, who attached the following note to his Yachikamne vocabulary (Pinart 1894; Merriam 1955:134): "Jačikamne [was] beside the town of Stockton. . . . [O]ther rancherias . . . speaking the same dialect were: Pašašamne, Nututamne, Tammukamne, Helutamne, Taniamne, Sanaiamne, Xosmitame. All these rancherias were within the limits of San Joaquin county. A little farther up the San Joaquin river and on its branches were the Lakkisamnes, the Notunamnes, [and] the Tuolumnes, who all spoke dialects very close to that of the Jačikamne." In locating some of these village-tribelets more precisely, I have followed the reconstruction, based on mission records, in Milliken 2008 (especially the map in figure 2). For the suffix *-(a)mne* see Kroeber (1908a).

85. Both Pinart and Henshaw found Delta Yokuts speakers among the survivors of the former Mission Santa Cruz community. Pinart attributed the extensive vocabulary he collected (1878e) to the "rancheria de Chalostaca" or "Cholastaca," but this appears to refer to the Costanoan tribelet in the vicinity of the Mission: "Chaloctac" (Costanoan *-tak*, locative) was the name of a village on Loma Prieta Creek in the Santa Cruz Mountains (Milliken 1995:238). As for the original Yokuts dialect groups, Pinart noted only that "il est probable que la tribu parlant cette langue habitait vers le Sn. Joaquin sur la rive gauche dans les contés de Stanislaus ou Merced" [it is probable that the tribe speaking this language lived toward the San Joaquin on the left bank in the counties of Stanislaus or Merced]. A search of the Mission baptismal records reveals that Eulogia, the old woman who was the source of Pinart's data, was from the Atsnil tribelet near Turlock (SCr-Bapt 1680; Milliken personal communication 2009). Henshaw's even more extensive parallel vocabularies from two individuals (1888b) attest the same general type of Delta Yokuts, presumably also from tribelets along the lower Merced River or on the adjacent west bank of the San Joaquin in the vicinity of Newman and Gustine.

86. These intergroup vocabulary differences appear, at least in part, to reflect stronger non-Yokuts influences on the northwestern subgroup. Compare, for example, the two counts 1–10 attested in Delta Yokuts: 1–5 are the same in both subgroups, with 1–3 the general Yokuts cognates and 4–5 unique to the Delta dialects. In 6–9, however, while the southeastern forms appear to be Delta innovations, the northwestern forms are borrowed from Costanoan or Plains Miwok. For 10, the southeastern subgroup retains the general Yokuts form, but the northwestern subgroup again has a Miwok borrowing.

87. At least according to Newman (1944:13–15). Gamble, however, describes Wikchamni as having only a palatal affricate series (1978:21–22, n. 4). The functional load of this contrast is low, and there seems to be considerable interdialectal variation.

88. For what little is known about the Huimen tribelet of southern Marin see Beeler (1972a), A. Brown (1973), and Milliken (1995:244). Confusing the issue, the vocabulary that Arroyo de la Cuesta collected from a Huimen speaker while he was in San Francisco in 1821 is in fact an attestation of Coast Miwok (Arroyo 1837). The Huimen may well have been bilingual. Gibbs also notes a postcontact population replacement in the North Bay area: "In Petaloma valley, the original inhabitants are reduced to almost nothing, and they have been replaced by the Indians of Suisun, from the bay of that name, above Benicia" (1853c:421). See the discussion of the southwestern boundary of Southern Patwin territory in ¶3.25.2.

89. About a dozen Indian words and phrases are quoted in the accounts of Drake's landing on the California coast (see ¶2.1.2).

90. Sarah Ballard was at first reluctant to collaborate. She finally agreed to provide linguistic data to Callaghan only on the condition that her name would not appear in any resulting publication; the source of Callaghan's Bodega Bay dictionary (1970) is anonymous. After Mrs. Ballard's death, Applegate combined his data (obtained separately in 1974) with Callaghan's for presentation in an online Coast Miwok tutorial (www.jamatra.com/cm/), where the source is fully acknowledged. Julia Elgin, who was probably more fluent in Nicasio than Mrs. Ballard was in Bodega Bay, similarly refused to let her language be documented extensively, and unlike Mrs. Ballard could not be budged. Neither woman wanted her Indian background to become known to her white middle-class friends and neighbors.

91. So heavy is the Patwin influence on Lake Miwok that it was considered a Wintuan language before Barrett's work (Barrett 1908a:363, n. 379). It is interesting to note, however, that the historic Lake Miwok and Hill Patwin were only in sporadic contact and appear to have known very little about one another (Barrett 1908a:115, n. 99). Furthermore, in Kroeber's assessment, "the general culture of the Lake Miwok was of Pomo rather than of Patwin cast" (1932:369). The multilayered history of cultural and linguistic contact in the eastern Clear Lake Basin deserves further investigation.

92. A truncated version of "Saclan" is preserved in the name adopted by the Acalanes Union High School District in 1940. The spelling was taken from *Rancho Acalanes*, the Mexican land grant in the area, whose name apparently was derived from a misunderstanding of "Los Sacalanes" as "Los Aclanes."

93. In interviews with elderly members of the ex–Mission San Jose community at Pleasanton between 1905 and 1910, Merriam was able to determine that mutually intelligible varieties of Eastern Miwok were spoken by a cluster of tribelets along the lower Sacramento River that included "O-che-hak" (apparently Ochejamne, on Grand Island, upriver from Rio Vista), "Wi-pa" (Guaypem, which Merriam locates on Sherman Island, near Antioch), "Han-ne-suk" (Anizumne), and "Hool-poom-man-ne" (Julpun). The latter two were said to be located to the south of the Wi-pa/Guaypem, probably in the Antioch-Pittsburg and Brentwood areas, respectively, and could have been

eastern tribelets of the Bay Miwok group (Merriam 1967b:367–368).

94. These were first identified by Barrett (1908b), who called them the Amador, Tuolomne, and Mariposa dialects, respectively.

95. While acknowledging their partial mutual intelligibility, Callaghan prefers to refer to the Sierra Miwok dialects as "languages," as did also Broadbent (1964:vi), "since the term 'dialect' is so misused" (personal communication). Powers, on the other hand, is quite explicit about the interintelligibility of the Sierra Miwok dialects "from the Cosumnes to the Fresno" and comments that "to one who has been traveling months in regions where a new language has to be looked to every ten miles sometimes, this state of affairs is a great relief" (1877:346–347).

96. Southern Costanoan is phonologically defined by the preservation of the obstruent quality of Proto Costanoan medial *č as *tʸ (in Mutsun) or as *č (in Rumsen) and of medial *kʷ as *k (in both languages). Elsewhere in Costanoan *-č- merges with *-y- and *-kʷ- merges with *-w-.

97. The original manuscript of this vocabulary has not survived. Arroyo copied (most of) it into a compendium, *Lecciones de Indios*, that he prepared late in his life (Arroyo 1837). The German traveler Karl von Gerolt, who visited Arroyo in 1830, made his own copy of the original, respelling many of the words according to German conventions and including three words that Arroyo seems accidentally to have left out of the copy he made for *Lecciones de Indios* (Golla 1996d; see also ¶2.3.3). The etymology of *karkin* is interesting. In a note accompanying the vocabulary in *Lecciones de Indios*, Arroyo states that the term is derived from the verb 'to trade, barter' (Spanish *trocar*), presumably referring to the Costanoan stem *karkʷe. The San Francisco Bay Costanoan reflex of this stem, with the expected lenited *kʷ, is seen in Chocheño *karwe* 'to lend, borrow'. Since Karkin also shows lenition of *kʷ in *muwe* 'man, person' (< *mukʷe) the Karkin reflex of *karkʷe must have been similar if not identical to that of Chocheño. The evident source of Arroyo's *karkin* is Mutsun, where the unlenited (but delabialized) reflex of *karkʷe is *karki* 'bargain, trade, barter' (Mason 1916a:459), with final -n deriving a mediopassive stem. (There is no attested cognate in Rumsen, the only other Costanoan language in which medial *kʷ did not merge with *w.) It is hardly a surprise that Arroyo would cite the ethnonym (or nickname) in the Costanoan dialect he was most familiar with. What is surprising is that the Karkins were known by this epithet as far south as San Juan Bautista.

98. *Chocheño* (not the expected *Joseño) was the California Spanish term for 'Indian of Mission San José'. Compare *Clareño* 'Indian of Mission Santa Clara' and *Doloreño* 'Indian of Mission Dolores'.

99. Milliken (1995:243–244) identifies two distinct Costanoan-speaking tribelets in this area, the Huchiun (Juchiun) to the south and the Huchiun-Aguasto to the north. In his most recent work (2008), Milliken locates the Huchiun-Aguasto both on the southeast shore of San Pablo Bay and across Carquinez Strait on Mare Island, similar to the straits-straddling Karkin a few miles to the east.

100. Levy (1978b:485) calls this tribelet, and by extension all speakers of East Bay Costanoan, "Lisyan." This is an error, and can be traced to an ambiguity in Harrington's Chocheño notes, where *lisyan* is glossed as 'Chocheño; Indian of Mission San José.' This term is from (Northern) Sierra Miwok *lisyaniḱ*

'Pleasanton Indians; speakers of the Pleasanton dialect of Plains Miwok' (Callaghan 1987:132) and refers to the Plains Miwok–speaking converts from the Sacramento area who accounted for as much as 60 percent of the Indian community at Mission San Jose in its final years (Milliken 1995:247; 2008:71).

101. Henshaw's source, Félix Buelna, a Californio of mixed blood and uncertain background, was the caretaker of the former Mission San Antonio, in Salinan territory, when Henshaw interviewed him there in 1884. Although Buelna claimed to be a fluent speaker of San Francisco Bay Costanoan, records show that he was unable to identify the locative suffix *-tak(a)* in a Santa Clara place name when he was called as a witness in a land case in the late 1860s (A. Brown 1994:38).

102. One of Duflot de Mofras's Santa Clara Paternosters is labeled "Vallée de los Tulares" (Tulare Valley, i.e., Yokuts) and the other "Mission Santa Clara" (Kroeber 1910:253–256). The latter is actually written in a variety of Mutsun-Awaswas, while the former is in a variety of San Francisco Bay Costanoan. The Zacatecas catechism is undoubtedly in some form of San Francisco Bay Costanoan. The endpapers of the eight-page, bound manuscript contain some words and phrases in Yokuts written in a hand that Randall Milliken, the leading expert on California mission records, believes to be that of Padre José Viader, who served at Mission Santa Clara for thirty-seven years. The catechism itself, however, is carefully written in a less easily identified hand.

103. The notes Harrington collected from Solis are interfiled with his rehearings of Arroyo de la Cuesta's five short vocabularies of San Francisco Bay languages (Harrington 1982–1990 [reel 2:68:298–448]; see Mills 1985:107–108).

104. Tribelet territories and designations are from Milliken (2002).

105. For further discussion of Arroyo's linguistic work on Mutsun and other California languages see ¶2.3.3.

106. According to Harrington, this is *hu:mon-ta(k)-was* 'west-at-people from there', that is, 'Westerners', a term used at San Juan Bautista to designate the Mutsun speakers who lived along the lower Pajaro River (Merriam 1967b:384–386).

107. Shipley (2002) has collated the Pinart and Henshaw materials into a vocabulary of approximately seven hundred items. He also includes the "Niles" vocabulary collected by Curtin (1884f), which is an attestation of Chocheño.

108. It is theoretically possible that the development of medial consonants moved historically in the opposite direction, with Proto Costanoan medial *y and *w innovating an obstruent component ("hardening" to č and k) in Mutsun and Rumsen. In this case, it would be better to consider Awaswas a separate language, sharing lexical innovations with Mutsun but not sharing the distinctive Mutsun-Rumsen phonological innovation.

109. Merriam was told by two women from the southern tribelet whom he interviewed in 1906 that "Sargent-a-ruk" (*sarhen-ta-ruk*) was the name of a village on the Carmel River (called Sargent's Ranch in local English; -ta-ruk is a sequence of locative suffixes perhaps best translated as "rancheria"). This village was also called "Tap-per." The village community near Point Sur was called "Kah-koon-ti-rook" (*kaku:n-ta-ruk* 'south rancheria') (Merriam 1967b:372).

110. In addition to those shown in Table 45, other cases or case-like constructions attested in Mutsun include the attributive (*-was* "having the attributes of...": *čisnan-was lullup* 'elderwood flute', cf. *čisnan* 'elder tree'); the ablative (*-tum*

"away from . . .": *ʔirek-tak-tum* 'away from (at) the rock'); and the comitative (-*ṭuk* "along with . . .": *me:s-ṭuk* 'along with you'). For further examples see Okrand 1977.

111. This was a principled decision on Merriam's part. "In choosing tribal names, my aim has always been to adopt, whenever feasible, that name applied by the tribe to itself. . . . Many anthropologists have adopted Spanish names, not only for tribes but also for stocks. My system revolts so strongly against this practice that I have not been able to acquire a frame of mind sufficiently cosmopolitan to permit the use of such terms as Costanoan, Serrano, Cupeño, Luiseño, Diegueño, and so on" (Merriam 1966:23).

112. Alan Brown (1973:188–189, 1994:29–38) reconstructs a plausible chain of misunderstandings and reinterpretations leading from Johnston's tribelet name "Olhones" to the modern ethnonym "Ohlone." The -lh- spelling appears in Bancroft's *Native Races of the Pacific States* (1874–1876, vol. 1:453), possibly influenced by the same typographical error in an 1861 article by Alexander Taylor in *The California Farmer* (A. Brown 1994:38, fn. 90). Bancroft's misspelling was given wide dissemination and authority when it was used on a commemorative plaque installed at Mission San Jose in the 1930s.

113. Kroeber (1907b), who was the first to define these branches, labeled them "Mono-Paviotso," "Shoshoni-Comanche," and "Ute-Chemehuevi," respectively. The Numic subfamily he called "Plateau Shoshonean," one of the four divisions of "Shoshonean," that is, Northern Uto-Aztecan. The present nomenclature for the Numic branches was first proposed by Wick Miller (1966:78), and "Numic" itself, in place of "Shoshonean," by Lamb (1958a, 1964).

114. Lamb carried out a dialectological survey of Mono territory between 1953 and 1955, the results of which are summarized by Kroeber (1959a:265–266). The full notes are apparently still in Lamb's possession, although there are ten hours of tape recordings in the Berkeley Language Center archives (Lamb 1953–1955).

115. Gayton's perceptive comments on Entimbich bilingualism are worth quoting at length.

The Entimbich have been classed both as Yokuts and as Western Mono, but I think that the wording may be revised to state that they are both Yokuts and Western Mono. . . . My Entimbich informant D.S. used a Shoshonean dialect continuously until I asked for kinship terms, which she suddenly and spontaneously gave in Penutian. The obvious answer, though not necessarily the correct one, is that the Entimbich, like the Waksachi and Patwisha, are a tribe with lineages of both Yokuts and Mono descent. Which was the basic group and which the interloper is difficult to tell. There seems no doubt that the Waksachi and Patwisha were originally Shoshonean-speakers; of the Entimbich I feel some doubt, since it is the Wobunuch neighbors to the east who have moved in and married into the Entimbich area whereas Yokuts neighbors to the west have not (according to my genealogies). How, then, do the Entimbich come to speak Yokuts so often, if they were not originally Yokuts who have recently been overwhelmed by Mono neighbors? (Gayton 1948:254–255).

116. See Gifford (1932b:19) and Gayton (1948:160) for the trail connecting the Northfork Mono with the Mammoth area south of Mono Lake. Parties of Northfork Mono frequently made the nine-day trip in order to gather pine nuts, while Eastern Mono would come down to Auberry to trade. Gayton (1948:214–215, 258–259) describes the route followed by the Eastern Mono to reach the Wobonuch and Waksachi, crossing the Sierra at Piute Pass near the headwaters of the Middle Fork of Kings River. The Eastern Mono visited the Waksachi only to trade, not for social functions, "the Ghost Dance of 1870 being the first contact of a social order." These visits were not usually reciprocated, although "on rare occasions two or three young men might go over to visit as a kind of adventure" (1948:215).

117. Information on Mono language survival is from Christopher Loether, Idaho State University, Pocatello.

118. Most of the information on the survival of Northern Paiute in this and the preceding paragraph was provided by Dr. Catherine Fowler, University of Nevada, Reno.

119. From Coso Hot Springs and the Coso Range, at the southwestern edge of Panamint territory. Kroeber wanted to avoid confusion with "Vanyume," the name of the Desert Serrano, which is a variant spelling of the same Southern Paiute word from which the term "Panamint" is taken. In the nineteenth century "Panamint" was used loosely to refer to various Uto-Aztecan speaking groups in the eastern Mojave Desert (Kroeber 1925:590).

120. Information on the survival of Panamint is from Dr. Jon Dayley, Boise State University, Boise, Idaho.

121. The spellings "Shoshone" and "Shoshoni" are both common. Contemporary Shoshoni people use "Shoshone" when referring to the people or the tribe (such as the Shoshone-Bannock Tribes of the Fort Hall Indian Reservation), but use "Shoshoni" when referring to language or culture. Although the editors of the *Handbook of North American Indians* have standardized to "Shoshone" for both people and language, the trend among linguists in recent years is to use only "Shoshoni," and that spelling is adopted here.

122. For a general survey of Comanche linguistics and history see Ives Goddard (2001:68–69) and Kavanaugh (2001).

123. Most of the information on Shoshoni language survival in this paragraph was provided by Dr. Christopher Loether, Idaho State University, and Dr. Jon Dayley, Boise State University.

124. John McLaughlin, who first proposed "Colorado River Numic," uses it consistently in his own work, but it has not yet been widely adopted (W. Miller, Elzinga, and McLaughlin 2005:414, fn. 1). "Ute-Chemehuevi," which seems an obvious alternative, was in fact Kroeber's term for all Southern Numic including Kawaiisu (Kroeber 1925:577), and its use in a more restricted sense would cause unnecessary confusion.

125. Information on the current status of Ute was provided by Tom Givón, University of Oregon. Pamela Bunte, CSU Long Beach, and John McLaughlin, Utah State University, provided information on Southern Paiute. Information on Chemehuevi was provided by Dirk Elzinga, Brigham Young University.

126. Jane Hill, in her (as of 2010) unpublished reclassification of the Uto-Aztecan languages (Hill 2009; see ¶3.30), places Takic and Tubatulabal under a single node "Californian," which she sees as coordinate with Numic and Hopi as the three primary divisions of Northern Uto-Aztecan. The deepest split in Californian is between Serrano-Kitanemuk and the others, which are then subdivided into Tubatulabal on the one hand and the remaining Takic groups (Gabrielino and Cupan) on the other.

127. Merriam recorded the Gabrielino self-designation as "Tong-vā," presumably [toŋve] or [toŋvey], and Harrington's principal Gabrielino consultant, Jesús Jauro, "used to hear his mother saying *to'oŋve* of a person talking . . . Gabrielino." The term appears to be a postcontact coinage based on the name of a village close to the site of San Gabriel Mission (W. McCawley 1996:9–10, 42). In the form "Tongva" (usually pronounced [táŋvə]), it has been adopted in recent decades as the indigenous alternative to "Gabrielino."

128. Sparkman's original manuscripts are preserved in the Bancroft Library (Sparkman 1898–1906) and contain material not included in the publications.

129. See ¶2.3.2, note 14, for the tangled history of the Boscana manuscripts.

130. Vanyume may also be attested in Merriam's vocabularies, where a variety of Serrano is documented called "Mo-he-ah´-ne-um" (Appendix A: X-23cc-dd). This may the same name as "Möhineyam," which Kroeber elicited in 1903–1904 as the native equivalent of Mohave "Vanyume" from an old woman he believed to be one of the last survivors of the tribe (1907b:70, 139–140).

131. This is apparently the village of Keishla (Quechla, Quechinga); see ¶3.32.2. Note also "Kij," the title Hale gave to his vocabulary of Gabrielino (1846:566–567).

132. Some Uto-Aztecanists prefer to call the classificatory unit the "Kern" or "Kern River" language, reserving "Tubatulabal" for the Pahkanapil dialect described by Voegelin (e.g., Manaster Ramer 1984).

133. "Bankalachi" appears to be the stem of Pahkanapil (*-pil* is the agentive suffix, cf. Voegelin 1935a:153), with the Yokuts tribal-name formative *-či*.

134. Some of the resemblances between the Yukian and Gulf languages are startlingly close. The pronoun system of Yukian (Table 53) corresponds in multiple ways to the pronoun systems of Chitimacha (Swadesh 1946) and Tunica (Haas 1946). For example, Yuki (Y) *ʔi* 1 sg object, Wappo (W) *ʔiʔ-* 1 sg object, *ʔiː-* 1 sg possessive = Chitimacha (C) *ʔiš* 1 sg, Tunica (T) *ʔi-* 1 sg; Y *ʔus* 1 pl excl subject, W *ʔísi* 1 pl excl subject = C *ʔuš* 1 pl; Y *moʔos* 2 pl subject, W *mísi* 2 pl subject = C *was* 2 pl. Note also the alternation between high and low vowels in Y *ʔi* 1 sg object and *ʔəp* 1 sg subject; W *ʔiʔ-* 1 sg object and *ʔáh* 1 sg subject; and T *ʔi-* 1 sg pronominal stem and *ʔa-* 1 sg subject in verbs.

135. For an insightful discussion of Kroeber's work with Ralph Moore, see Elmendorf (1981b). Between 1958 and 1994 the Kroeber-Uldall materials were in the personal possession of Harvey Pitkin, who organized and partially analyzed them, but with no published result. This valuable corpus is now primarily housed with the Harvey Pitkin Papers in the Library of the American Philosophical Society, although Kroeber's original field notebooks were returned to the Bancroft Library after being photocopied. In 1957, at Dell Hymes's request, Kroeber prepared a complete list of his Yuki material, indexed to drawer and item numbers as originally stored. A copy of this list is filed with the APS collection (Kroeber 1900–1958, Series II-A).

136. This is a useful first approximation to a Yuki dictionary, but since Kroeber's extensive materials could not be included, it is far from being a full record of what has been preserved of the Yuki lexicon. It is primarily valuable for the accurately transcribed forms collected from the last speakers by Sawyer and his colleagues. As this book was going to press, Marianne Mithun and her student Uldis Balodis, at UC Santa Barbara, announced plans to compile a full descriptive study of Yuki based on all extant documentation, including Kroeber's.

137. Or at least vowel length is consistently marked in Sawyer's transcriptions. Thompson, Park, and Li, however, write that they "were not able to hear this distinction, and Laura [Fish Somersal] could not confirm that it existed" (2006:1).

138. The evidence for the linguistic affiliation of the tribelets along the upper Salinas River between Paso Robles and Santa Margarita has recently been reviewed in detail by Milliken and Johnson (2003). They accept the concusion reached by Gibson (1983) that this region was primarily Chumash in speech at the time of first European contact, but find indications of a shift to Migueleño during the mission period.

139. Perhaps the most interesting of these is the nominal prefix or proclitic *t-* that occurs widely in Obispeño but has no counterpart elsewhere in Chumash (see Kroeber 1910:268).

140. Milliken and Johnson (2003:39) identify this speaker, whose name Henshaw heard as "Alikano," as a Choynok Yokuts who came to Mission San Luis Obispo at the age of six and was baptized "Galicano." Obispeño would have been his second or third language.

141. In recent years Applegate has made a considerable amount of Inezeño material available on the Internet at the Samala Chumash Language Tutorial, sponsored by the Santa Ynez Band (www.chumashlanguage.com).

142. The Ventureño lingua franca that developed at the mission, known to its speakers as Samala (*sʰamala*), incorporated a few features from other dialects but essentially was a continuation of the local variety, associated with the major village of Shisholop (Whistler 1981b). In his Inezeño dictionary (n.d.), Applegate equates *sʰamala* with the Chumash of Santa Ynez (*sʰamala hi no* 'I am Inezeño', *sʰamalan* 'to speak Inezeño'). It may have been a widely used term of self-reference among mission-era Chumash speakers. The Santa Ynez Band now refers to its heritage ethnicity and language as Samala, or Samala Chumash.

143. John Johnson believes that Ventureño dialect diversity may have been somewhat less complex: "Harrington's consultants (and previous vocabulary collectors) would refer to what amounted to the same dialect by different names, which leads to confusion. From my reading of Harrington's notes, there were the following dialects: Ventura, Matilija, Mupu or Santa Paula (Santa Paula–Ojai–Sespe), Santa Monica Mountains (Malibu–Thousand Oaks–Simi), Mugu (very possibly part of the Santa Monica Mts. Group), and Castac (Cashtéc–upper Piru), and probably all of the area labeled 'Emigdiano' in Kroeber's Handbook" (personal communication, 2003).

144. According to John Johnson, Merriam's informant for his "Alliklik" vocabulary was José Juan Olivas, who was also Harrington's source for Castac Ventureño. Olivas was married to a Kitanemuk speaker (personal communication, 2003).

145. A photograph of a page from one of Pico's manuscripts (Pico 1891) can be found in Ives Goddard (1996a:42, fig. 16).

146. "Chumashan Grammar in the Coast Dialect," undated. This manuscript was formerly catalogued as BAE MS 2966. It is now included in Harrington 1982–1990, vol. 3, reel 94 (see Appendix B). In addition to Librado, Harrington collected extensive data from five other Ventureño speakers: Simplicio Pico (son of Juan Estevan Pico) and Cecilio Tumamait, both raised in the Ventura mission community; José Juan Olivas, brought up at Piru; Candelaria Valenzuela, born at Seqpe; and

José Pelegrino Romero, a speaker of the Castac dialect (Whistler 1981b).

147. The most extensive Island Chumash data come from Harrington's work with Fernando Librado. Librado's family was from Santa Cruz Island, and in his notes Harrington was in the habit of referring not just to Librado's dialect but to the language as a whole as "Cruzeño." This usage has been adopted by some anthropologists and linguists, but it should be discouraged. It can easily lead to confusion when the discussion focuses on linguistic variation. Thus, in describing the documentation of Island Chumash, John Johnson (2001:58) characterizes as "Cruzeño" the two Roseño vocabularies obtained from natives of Santa Rosa Island.

148. Henshaw also obtained what he believed to be a long vocabulary of the Santa Rosa Island dialect (1884d). Through some misunderstanding, however, the speaker (Pa-li-ha-tcet)—who in fact provided Gould with authentic Roseño data—gave Henshaw a vocabulary that was mostly Barbareño. Henshaw's mistaken identification of the language of this vocabulary was left uncorrected in Heizer 1955 (Kathryn Klar, personal communication, 2010).

149. Although the established scholarly practice is to refer to Latin American indigenous languages in the local standard orthography (here Spanish), I make an exception with *Guaycura/Waikuri*, where an anglicized spelling is better known in the linguistic literature. As for the choice between *Waikura* and *Waikuri*, I follow Zamponi (2004) in preferring the latter.

150. Baegert's Waikuri corpus has recently been edited and reanalyzed by Zamponi (2004).

151. Massey (1949) included four "dialects" in Uchití: *Uchití* (Huchití) proper, on the southwest coast of the peninsula; *Cora*, on the east coast opposite; and *Periue* and *Aripe* along the coast north of La Paz.

152. Laylander sees no reason to suppose that Periue and Aripe were anything more than local varieties of Waicuri. However, the Cora area around Santiago and Bahía de las Palmas "fell within the prehistoric and early historic territory of the Pericú" (1997:28–29).

Part 4 Notes

1. See Dryer (2005) for a worldwide survey of prefixing versus suffixing in inflectional morphology. In North America, suffixing predominates in the West, while prefixing languages are in the majority in Mesoamerica. In eastern North America there is a balance between the two types.

2. Among Hokan languages, reduplication is prominent in Washo and Yuman, and present to some degree in many others; it is totally absent, however, in Yana and Seri. The process seems more deeply entrenched in Penutian, being particularly important in Klamath, but is absent in Maiduan. For a worldwide survey of the distribution of reduplication see Rubino (2005).

3. The typology followed here is that of Johanna Nichols and Balthasar Bickel (2005). The only languages with zero-marked clauses that they identify in North America are Haida and Nuuchahnulth (Nootka) on the Northwest Coast, Mixtec in southern Mexico, and Miskito and Bribri in Central America. The pattern is common in Southeast Asia, West and Central Africa, and New Guinea. The favored pattern in North America, head marking, is otherwise frequent only in Amazonia, New

Guinea, and northern Australia. The dependent marking pattern of Penutian and Northern Uto-Aztecan, although very sparsely represented elsewhere in North America (the only Mexican language Nichols and Bickel find to have it is Purépecha [Tarascan]), occurs with moderate frequency in South America (where Quechua has it) and is the dominant pattern in Eurasia and northern Africa.

4. Leonard Talmy has developed a system of schemata to model semantic interrelationships of this type, which he believes to be cognitively universal (Talmy 1985). Whatever the merits of his theoretical claims, the applicability of his schemata to the bipartite stem structures of Atsugewi—on which he worked as a field linguist during the 1960s—is beyond doubt.

5. While the term "instrumental" has become traditional in descriptions of the Pomo languages, it should be noted that all the prefixal elements include a reference to the undergoer of the action or to the type or manner of the action as well as to an actual instrument or means.

6. "One can hardly doubt that . . . lexical prefixes go back to former independent stems compounded with following verb stems, but the beginning of this process must be very old, dating back to the time of Proto-Hokan" (Jacobsen 1980:97). In part motivated by Washo data, Sapir speculated that, at least in the "Southern Hokan" languages, the first consonant of nearly all consonant-initial stems (nominal as well as verbal) was an analyzable element, and that the basic stem shape was C + VCV (Sapir 1921b, 1925a).

7. More generally, the role of discourse markers in organizing speech acts remains underappreciated, especially in small societies where nearly all information exchanges are deeply embedded in interpersonal relationships. Switch reference would have been merely one element in the complex network of verbal and nonverbal signals that regulated "information exchanges" in every traditional California society. While most of those signals are now unrecoverable, close analysis of narrative texts can sometimes be revealing. It has recently been shown, for example, that another Karuk discourse marker, *káruma*—which Bright and other earlier students of the language translated literally as 'the fact is' or 'though'—served to "highlight especially relevant information that advances the storyline of a narrative, contributing to dramatic tension" (Brugman and Macaulay 2009).

8. In fact, all the California and Oregon Athabaskan numerals, except the forms for eight and nine, are cognate with equivalent forms throughout Athabaskan. There seems little doubt that the Athabaskans who settled along the Oregon and California coasts brought with them a decimal count of great antiquity within the language family.

9. Although long-distance exchange networks of some sort must have existed in California for millennia (see, for example, the extremely ancient radiocarbon dates for the appearance of olivella shells in noncoastal sites reported by Fitzgerald, Jones, and Schroth 2005), there seems little doubt that the practice of setting the value of a traded object in precisely stated numbers of beads or shells (or strings of these) is associated with relatively recent cultural developments.

10. For a general model of the evolution of complex numeration systems from simple hand counting see Comrie (1999, 2005).

11. Thus in Luiseño fifteen is "all my hands and one of my feet," twenty is "my other foot finished," and forty is "twice my hands and feet are finished." Each form "recount[s] in full the

arithmetical process by which it is reached" (Kroeber and Grace 1960:118–120). This cumbersome system was abandoned very soon after the beginning of the mission period, and Jane Hill notes (2005:214) that Roscinda Nolasquez, the oldest and most traditional Cupeño speaker alive in the 1960s, always switched to Spanish when counting past five. Hill was able to reconstruct the indigenous Cupeño system only from notes collected by Paul-Louis Faye in the 1920s. Comrie (2007) argues that even the Cupeño numeral systems is mathematically decimal, not quinary: although ten (basically "two hands") can be analyzed as 5 + 5, the attested numerals above ten are expressed as multiples of ten, not of five. Only the Luiseño numeral system as attested by Sparkman (Kroeber and Grace 1960) can be analyzed as strictly quinary.

12. It is of note, however, that the Luiseño numeral for five, *mahár*, is of Gabrielino origin, as was the Chinigchinich religion (Kroeber and Grace 1960:118).

13. In northwestern California and southwestern Oregon a distinction must be made between the broad region in which clamshell beads were known as an item of trade and the much narrower area in which they served as the medium of exchange. The Briceland Sinkyone were the northernmost group to use clamshell beads as money; the next groups north—Garberville Sinkyone in the interior and the Mattole on the coast— used dentalia. The boundary was sharp and ritualized. Ike Duncan, Driver's Mattole informant, told him that if dentalia were taken south of Needle Rock (on the Lost Coast south of Shelter Cove) they would break of their own accord—"a novel type of factor limiting diffusion," Driver comments (1939:397).

14. The ethnographer E. M. Loeb provides further details:

Twenty among the Eastern Pomo is called *xai-di-lema-tek*, a full stick, and in counting small amounts [of clamshell beads] a stick is laid out for this primary unit. . . . The large counts run as follows among the Eastern Pomo: 80. *dol-a xai.* 4 sticks. 100. *lema-xai.* S5 sticks. 200. *hadagal-a-xai.* 15 sticks. 400. *kali-xai.* First (big) stick. 800. *xotc-guma-wal.* Two (big) sticks. 2400. *tsadi.* (Big) six. 3600. *hadagal-com.* Ten (missing) [i.e., nine big sticks, one less than ten] 4000. *hadagal.* Ten (big) sticks.In counting large quantities of beads two methods are employed.

According to the first, and older method, a small stick is laid out for every eighty beads. When five of these small sticks have been laid out, they are taken back, and a larger stick substituted for the Pomo large unit of four hundred. According to the second method a small stick is laid out for every hundred beads, four of these small sticks making the large unit. When four hundred has been reached the counting goes on in units of four hundreds until ten of the larger sticks have been used and four thousand beads have been counted. Now another group of ten sticks is prepared. They are all equal in size, a little larger than the former bundle of ten, and have some mark to distinguish them. Each stick represents four thousand. . . . When each of these latter ten sticks have been counted, you reach the number forty thousand, *xai-di-lema-xai.* This is known as the "big twenty."

My informant, [William] Benson, has himself seen counting in which five or six of the four thousand bead sticks were utilized. Large counts were commonly performed by the Pomo at the time of deaths and peace treaties. In a myth recounted by Barrett the first bear shaman gave forty thousand beads in pretended sympathy for the victim whose death he had caused. (Loeb 1926:229–230)

15. Mattole had two counts for higher numerals, a vigesimal one with 'stick' for 20, and a decimal one that used multiples of 10. Ike Duncan, Driver's Mattole informant, called the decimal count the "baby way" (Driver 1939:400).

16. In the California languages, the word used is an archaic form of the Athabaskan word for 'stick' (Hupa *tiḵʰin*, etc., with a classificatory prefix *ti-* and a relativizing suffix, rather than *ḵʰiŋ* 'stick'). In the Oregon languages, however, it is the normal word for 'stick' (Lower Rogue River *čʰən*, etc.).

17. According to Kroeber (1925:878–879), the Yuki basic count was octonary rather than quaternary because in their system either one or two sticks could be held between each pair of fingers. The full complement of sticks was thus eight (*pow mipat* 'one hand'). In Yuki culture, an elaborated version of stick counting continued to be employed by older individuals into the early twentieth century. Based on observations he had made around 1905, Kroeber reported that "the Yuki operate very skillfully by this method" and were so dependent on it that "when they are asked to count on the fingers like their neighbors, they work slowly and with frequent errors" (1925:878–879). When George Foster asked about the practice only a generation later, however, he could find no one who remembered it (1944:203).

18. In the post-mission varieties of Chumash attested from the late nineteenth and twentieth centuries, the higher count is universally decimal, reflecting the influence of Spanish. However, Father Señán's mission-period Ventureño *Confesionario* (Beeler 1967) contains a detailed description of the precontact system, apparently still in wide use. The count proceeded by units of 16, lexified as "chigípish," and the maximal counting unit was 32 ("dos chigípish"). Thus, according to Señán, our "55" would be given as "32 + 23," our "113" as "3 × 32 + 17," and our "200" as "6 × 32 + 8" (Beeler 1964:16–17).

19. In Sierra Miwok, 'twelve' is expressed by the formation *ʔoṭik-sake:n-ï* (Northern Sierra) or *ʔoṭik-ṣake:n-ï* (Central Sierra), based on *ʔoṭi-ko-* 'two', and 'eighteen' is expressed by *tak-ṣake[:] n-a* (Northern Sierra), based on a reduced form of *tolo:kos-u-* 'three'. Although Callaghan has analyzed these formations as consisting of the basic numeral + *sak-* 'continuative' + *e:n-ï* 'agentive', Blevins thinks it more likely that they reflect the multiplicative use of *ṣakken* 'six' or 'all (of a count)', the adverbial derivation in *-n* of the Eastern Miwok quantifier *ṣokke- ~ ṣïkke-* 'all, everything'. Although replaced in its primary meaning in all attested Eastern Miwok languages by forms based on a stem *temme-* 'big' or *temm(v)-* 'trade, go across (to the other hand)', *ṣakken* 'six' was borrowed with this meaning into San Francisco Bay Costanoan and into the northern dialect of Delta Yokuts, and into Rumsen Costanoan with the meaning 'five'.

20. The words for 'one' and 'two' in the Chunut and Toltichi counts are possibly borrowed from Spanish, by way of a mission-era trading jargon (see ¶4.15.1).

21. Stephen Marlett's recent paper "The Form and Use of Names in Seri" (Marlett 2008a) is the best general survey of naming, both as a linguistic category and as a set of social assumptions and practices, that exists in the California literature. It is accompanied (in the electronic version) by an appendix

that lists and analyzes all attested terms for places, individuals, legendary and historical figures, spirits, months, constellations, stars, and so on, in recent and modern Seri culture.

22. Both Northern Pomo *pʰóʔmaʔ* and Southeastern Pomo *-mfo* are derived from Proto-Pomo *pʰó- 'reside, live in a group', but there is no reconstructable Proto-Pomo formant for tribelet names. Confusion of Northern Pomo *pʰóʔmaʔ* 'people of . . .' with *pʰo:mo:* 'red earth hole', the name of a village in Potter Valley, led Powers (1877:146) to adopt "Pomo" as the overall name for Northern and Central Pomo, in turn prompting Barrett (1908a) to extend the term to the entire family.

23. Among the Yokuts, however, where children were always named after a living relative, a new name had to be assumed if one's namesake died. "Among the more southerly tribes," according to Kroeber, "the inconvenience caused by this practice was guarded against by the custom of each child receiving two names, one to be used as a reserve in emergency, as it were. If nevertheless both namesakes died, the person deprived of his designations was spoken of and addressed as *k'amun hoyowosh*, 'No-name'" (1925:499).

24. Compare also Powers, writing of the Nisenan: "One can very seldom learn an Indian's and never a squaw's name, though they will tell their American titles readily enough. It is a greater breach of decorum to ask a squaw her name than it is among us to ask a lady her age." (1877:315).

25. Although collections of personal names are rare in northern California ethnography, several dozen Hupa names were recorded by Curtin (1888–1889e) and by Sapir (1927b: notebook 2, 52–74), and a few others (or other attestations of the same names) are scattered through Goddard's publications.

26. Sapir was told that *kʰö:peh*, who was born at Ta'kimilding in the 1820s, was "not popular" and was "hatefully referred to" as *kʰe:peh*—that is, with reversal of the diminutive consonant shift of front-velar *kʸʰ* to *kʰ* and with normal Hupa *e:* rather than idiosyncratic [ö:] in the first syllable (Sapir 1927b: notebook 2, 71). This seems to indicate that undoing the symbolic phonetics in someone's name was interpreted as a deliberate insult. The bilabial stop (*p*), while a rare phoneme in Hupa, was apparently not thought of as the symbolic replacement of a more frequently occurring bilabial such as *m* or *w*.

27. Compare Powers on the Nisenan: "When a neophyte [boy] is initiated . . . a new name, his virile name, which is generally that of his father or some other near relative, is then added to his baby name" (1877:305–306). "Many people believe that half the squaws have no name at all. So far is this from the truth that everyone possesses at least one and sometimes two or three" (1877:315).

28. According to Powers, when a Yuki child did not "grow well, or otherwise seem to be prosperous and lucky" under one name, another could be given. He also reports that most Yuki men (or at least chiefs and other important men) had two permanent names, "one given in infancy, the other in later life . . . on account of circumstances in the person's history" (1877:126).

29. This practice of giving (or in some cases selling) one's own name appears to have been not uncommon in northern California. Powers reports that in the Shasta-Karuk area "a treaty is not accounted to be fully ratified and binding unless the high contracting powers exchange clothes. . . . Sometimes they also swap names, which renders the treaty very sacred" (1877:246–247).

30. The linkage of "pity" and "death" has been carried over into the Indian English of northwest California, where the conventional way of referring to a deceased tribal member is "poor [name]," as in "a large number of people attended poor Jimmie's funeral last Saturday." Many contemporary Yuroks use *ʔa:wokʷ* 'alas!', the Yurok exclamation for grief or loss, in place of "poor" (I recently received an e-mail from a Yurok acquaintance who told me that "a film has been made about awok Aileen Figueroa"), but this usage may not be traditional.

31. The lion's share of the information here is derived from Johanna Nichols's detailed survey of diminutive consonant symbolism in western North America (1971). References are to Nichols's primary sources.

32. See also the descriptions of "abnormal speech" in Quileute (Frachtenberg 1920) and Nez Perce (Aoki 1970:7–8).

33. Langdon reports that "Shoshoni uses a suffix *-pai* for Coyote and a suffix *-mai* for Bluejay, while in Chemehuevi Coyote uses *-aykʸ(A)*," but she comments that these rather perfunctory characterizations of the speech of mythical animals are of a distinctly different type from the exuberant consonantal shifts and interpolations found in the Northwest and in Yuman (1978c:15).

34. Gatschet includes transcriptions and translations of more than one hundred "incantation songs" that he obtained from various Klamath and Modoc shamans. While the songs name the specific animal spirits whose help is being invoked, "many Indians do not understand all these songs, which contain many archaic forms and words, and the conjurers themselves are generally loth to give their meaning, even if they should understand them. . . . The translations added by me are not literal; they render the meaning of the songs in a free and paraphrastic manner" (p. 160). He also includes texts of fifty-eight "cooing and wooing" songs (a well-defined genre of sexual taunts), twenty-two satiric songs, and fourteen otherwise unclassifiable songs, as well as phonetic renderings of a number of "war-whoops and dance-yells," humming tunes, and songs without identifiable words. No more thorough documentation exists of the song texts of any California group, especially from the nineteenth century.

35. In one of the rare exceptions, Gatschet includes a surprisingly modern discussion of the differences between formal and conversational styles in his Klamath grammar (1890, Part 1:677–681).

36. See also Kroeber (1925:667). Elliott (1999) lists all the attested Luiseño ceremonial couplets in modern transcriptions. The possibility of a historical connection to Mesoamerican *difrasismos* has not been fully explored, although Montes de Oca has raised the question (1997, 2001). Jane Hill reports vestiges of ceremonial couplets in the "chiefly language" of the Cupeño (2005:7, 416), including the first element in the formal title of the chief's ritual assistant, *tekw-ve've'esh* 'fire-tender'. She believes the synchronically unanalyzable *tekw-* can be traced back to a Proto-Uto-Aztecan couplet *te ku 'the wildfire, the domestic fire' (Hill 1985; 2005:7, n. 1).

37. The words in this set almost certainly represent direct borrowings of dialectal Spanish *chucho*, which replaced *perro* as the usual word for 'dog' in Spanish-Mexican California. This is especially true where they are found together with another word of undoubtedly Indian origin (as *hayu* in Central Pomo, Patwin, and Coast Miwok, *huč(u)mas* in Esselen, and *ʔawa:l* in Luiseño). The lop-eared breeds introduced by the Mexicans were often perceived by Indians to be a different animal from the erect-eared Indian dog (Bright 1960 [1976]:145).

38. The forms in this set are probably not direct borrowings of Spanish *chucho*. They are mostly attested in languages on the periphery of Spanish influence, and the occurrence of *suku-h*, with no alternative term, as far north as Wintu suggests that an aboriginal origin is possible. More likely, they represent the early nineteenth century diffusion by way of a trade jargon of a form based on *chucho* (see ¶4.15.1).

39. These words—if they indeed represent a coherent set—are more likely to be connected to the forms in set 2b than to be historically independent. Each, however, may have a separate history, with the Yana form most likely to be a distant echo of Spanish *chucho*, the Shasta form most likely to be of aboriginal origin (perhaps related to set 1), and the Maidu form indeterminate.

40. It is quite possible that Valley Yokuts *puʔus* 'dog', which is otherwise unique, originated as a borrowing of some reflex of Northern Uto-Aztecan *puHku*. Kawaiisu *pukuc* (also recorded as *puguzi*), with what is apparently a diminutive suffix, is especially close. Also possible, but less likely, is that Luiseño *ʔawá:-* (and almost identical forms in Cupeño and Cahuilla) is borrowed from Yuman *ʔaxat*.

41. Wiyot *wayic* 'dog' may be related to Klamath-Modoc *wač* 'pet, dog; horse'. If so, the historical connection must be an old one, going back to a period when California Algic—or at least the language ancestral to Wiyot—was spoken far to the north and east of its historical location.

42. Throughout the Kuksu area—which included all or part of Nisenan, Patwin, Pomo, Wappo, and Yuki territory—there was a common terminology for types of ceremonies (*hesi, kuksu, wayma*) and the spirit beings who were represented by the costumed dancers (*mo:ki, temeyu, way-saltu, yati, sili*, etc.). These terms, where their etymologies are known, have various origins. The names of the Racer and Cloud Runner spirits in the Hesi ceremony, *sili* and *yati*, are from the Nisenan words for 'tule' and 'cloud', respectively, and the ghosts represented in the *wayma*, or Ghost Society ceremony, are called *way-saltu*, Patwin for 'north spirit' (Kroeber 1932:395–396, Table 1).

43. See Callaghan's discussion of some of these terms in the context of her evaluation of evidence for a Yokuts-Utian subgroup within Penutian (2001:332, no. 50).

44. These words may be part of a very widely diffused set of terms that is of much older provenience than the bow and arrow. The core meaning of this wider set is not 'obsidian (point)', as the Maiduan and Klamath forms suggest, but rather 'knife' (especially one made of copper) and 'flint or copper' (the substances from which a knife could be made in northern North America in precontact times). It includes reconstructible protoforms in at least three families—Siouan *(a)wąze) 'iron, metal', Algonquian *ma:nθ- 'chert, flint, metal' and *ma:(n)θehsi 'flint knife', and Tsimshianic *mas(kʷ) 'copper-colored'– as well as resemblant lexemes as far afield as Muskogean (Choctaw *baš-li* 'cut with a knife', Alabama and Koasati *bas-li* 'strike stone, knap flint', *bas-ka* 'chip, flake') and Northern Iroquoian (Mohawk *(w)aʔšar-* 'knife'). Forms of similar shape and meaning, but with a front vowel, are equally widespread and include Proto-Athabaskan *we:šʳ (e.g., Lower Tanana *basr* 'knife, metal', Chipewan *bès* 'knife', Navajo *beésh* 'knife, flint, metal'), Proto-Tsimshianic *mes- (in Gitksan *mis-ʔín* 'copper, metal', Nishga *mis-ʔaws* 'red ochre'), Proto-Algonquian *meçkw- 'red-colored' and *wesa:w- 'yellow, copper-colored', and Proto–Northern Iroquoian *hwist- (in Mohawk

ohwísta?, Seneca *o:wísta?* 'money, metal'). Eyak *we:gsə-g* 'ulu, woman's scraper' is probably connected to one or both of these sets. So too, apparently, are numerous words for 'copper' and 'metal' in Siberian and Central Eurasian languages, most notably the forms that can be reconstructed as Proto-Uralic *waśka or *wáśkä 'copper, metal' and Proto-Indo-European *awes 'gold, reddish (metal)'. Compare also Ubykh *wësʷa 'copper' (Vogt 1963:204). If these resemblances are not accidental, there is a very interesting story yet to be told about the diffusion of primitive metallurgy across the Bering Strait. (For the possible origin and dispersion of these terms in Eurasia see Aalto 1959.)

45. Callaghan comments: "Confusion between 'seven' and 'eight' could arise from different methods of counting on the fingers. If one starts with the thumb or the little finger. 'eight' will refer to the middle finger on the second hand. If one starts with the index finger, counting the thumb last, the middle finger on the second hand will be number seven" (1994:170).

46. Other studies of Spanish loanwords in specific California languages include Bright 1979b and Hamp 1980 (Cahuilla and other Takic languages); Callaghan 1981 (Sierra Miwok); J. M. Crawford 1979 (Cocopa); Gamble 1989 (Wikchamni Yokuts); K. Hill 1984 (Serrano); Kroskrity and Reinhardt 1984 (Mono); McLendon 1969 (Eastern Pomo); Mixco 1977d (Kiliwa); Sawyer 1964a, 1964b (Wappo); Schlichter 1980 (Wintu); and Shipley 1959 (Northeastern Maidu). For a general survey see Shipley 1962.

47. The word *mahel(a)* could also be derived from *mokʰe:la*, the general word for 'woman' in most Valley Yokuts dialects (an undoubtedly indigenous form, based on a root *mokʰ-y-* 'wife, female relative' that has cognates throughout Penutian; cf. Silverstein 1972:165–167, 230). Evidently the process of pidgin formation that gave rise to *mahel(a)* took place at one (or more) of the missions that had a significant number of Valley Yokuts converts (such as San Juan Bautista and San Luis Obispo), and made use of the serendipitous resemblance of *mujer* and *mokʰe:la*. Whatever its origin, the term was in common use as the regional English variant of *squaw* during the nineteenth century, spelled *mahala* and pronounced [məhéɪlə] (OED). It survives in the place-name Mahala Creek, Humboldt County, and in *mahala mat*, the name of a native shrub in the Pacific Coast states, for both of which the spelling pronunciation [məhálə] is preferred (William Bright, quoted in Golla 2003:222, fn. 9).

48. *Bis* is a transparent borrowing of *bis!* 'encore!'; could *nas* be from *unas*? Klamath *Nas*, however, may have cognates in the Sahaptian languages (DeLancey 1992).

49. Sapir described the difficulties he experienced in attempting to communicate with Ishi in "a crude jargon of English, quasi-English, and Yahi" (Sapir 1916b:329, n. 4; 1923b:264).

50. For further observations on Ishi's Spanish words see Starn (2003) and Golla (2003:212–214).

Part 5 Notes

1. This correlation (or coincidence) was first noted by Boas, who called attention to the resemblances between the modern Yuki physical type and the one seen in burials on the southern Channel Islands (1905:356–357). Latin American researchers have recently argued that dolichocephaly is one of a cluster

of morphological traits that characterized the earliest human populations in the Americas (González-José et al. 2005). Even more recently, J. R. Johnson and Lorenz (2006) found that a well-differentiated mitochondrial DNA haplotype present in some modern Chumash descendants is also attested in ancient remains from southeastern Alaska (On Your Knees Cave, Prince of Wales Island) and among the Cayapá of coastal Ecuador, as well as in samples from western Mexico and Tierra del Fuego.

2. For example, Island Chumash (IC) *tanim*, Central Chumash (CC) *ʔališaw* 'sun'; IC *wa*, CC *xip* 'stone'; IC *mihi*, CC *ʔoʔ* 'water'; IC *nene*, CC *mitip'in* 'door, doorhole'; IC *tup'an*, CC *ʔax* 'bow, weapon'; IC *xis*, CC *yaʔ* 'arrow'; IC *wiyus*, CC *ʔalqap* 'mortar'; IC *tiki*, CC *šaq'* 'tortoise'; IC *šmačaw,* CC *ʔelye'wun* 'swordfish'. Klar (2010) lists fifty-five Island Chumash words for which she can "confidently say that there is no known cognate form in any other attested Chumashan language."

3. Another explanation for the mixed vocabulary of Island Chumash is that it reflects Island Chumash–Central Chumash bilingualism in the mainland mission communities, from which all the attestations come. But if this is true, the non-Chumash vocabulary is even more likely to be the residue of an ancient Channel Islands language.

4. Elmendorf (1968 [1993]:186) has pointed out that the skewing of Yukian cognate loss in Wappo toward semantic domains connected to men's activities may reflect a period of extensive intermarriage between Wappo women and non-Wappo men. (For more on the possible social and cultural factors at work in the evolution of Wappo see ¶3.35.4).

5. I follow Johanna Nichols (1997, 1999) in thinking that the language ancestral to all attested Indo-European languages (including the Anatolian branch) was most likely spoken east of the Caspian Sea, in the area of ancient Bactria-Sogdiana (between northern Afghanistan and southern Kazakstan), in the late fifth or early fourth millennium BC (ca. 5800–6200 BP).

6. A fuller list includes sets with the following glosses. *Trees and plants:* yellow pine, digger pine, sugar pine, cedar, fir, juniper, spruce, black oak, chokecherry, wild plum, buckeye, manzanita, green manzanita, madrone, willow, clover, white grass, nettle. *Animals:* chipmunk, rock squirrel, river otter, weasel. *Cultural features:* basket, burden basket, weave, disc beads, net, grind with pestle, shell acorns, (pierce with) arrow, porcupine quills. *Riverine directions:* upstream, downstream.

7. In a similar study, Jacobsen (1979a:563–570) separated out of Gursky's compilation of potential Hokan cognate sets (1974) those that involved only easily borrowable words shared by a pair of contiguous or nearly contiguous languages. Of forty such sets for all of Hokan, he found a "disproportionate" number (sixteen) to involve sharings between Karuk and Shasta. The glosses for these sets are cousin, eagle, to fish, fly, gopher, log, madrone, mushroom sp., nettle, sack, salmon, to shoot, to sting, sweat, weasel, and woodpecker. Only two other pairs of contiguous Hokan languages shared more than one potential borrowing, both of them also in the Northern California refuge area: Shasta-Achumawi (to fish, otter, squirrel, and two terms for baskets) and Palaihnihan-Yana (grandrelative, pine, wild plums, and spruce). Carrying out the same exercise for pairs of noncontiguous but nearby Hokan languages, Jacobsen again found that a Northern California pair—Karuk and Achumawi—had a whopping thirteen of the forty-nine sets of potential borrowings (cherry, clover, cocoon, crawfish, dead,

dentalium, shells, eel, hoop, juniper, pine, salmon, to tie, and trap), followed by Karuk-Yana with four sets (fir, hummingbird, lizard, and owl).

8. Jacobsen (1979a:565) also identifies the word for 'quail' as a unique sharing between Esselen and Salinan.

9. The full list includes sets with the following glosses. *Trees and plants:* acorn, acorn oak, white oak, buckeye, pepperwood, willow, clover, tule, (to dig, hoe) edible root. *Animals:* bear, coyote, wildcat. *Cultural features:* basket, beads, dream, to gather (acorns), path/road, shaman/poison, ghost.

10. The full list of environmentally or culturally significant cognate sets includes the following. *Trees and plants:* cottonwood, yellow pine, pine nut, oak sp., manzanita, wild onion, cattail/tule, wild potato, soaproot, thorn. *Animals:* bear, badger/porcupine, coyote, bobcat/mountain lion, jackrabbit, squirrel, gopher, fox (two terms). *Cultural features:* basket, twist, twine, weave, dig/hoe, acorn bread (cake, mush), trade/buy/sell, sew, salt, mash/bedrock mortar, pounding basket/pestle, bow (two terms).

11. A voiceless bilabial (or labiodental) fricative (*f*) also occurs in Southeastern Pomo and Northeastern Pomo, where it evidently has replaced Proto-Pomo *pʰ.

12. Compare both the consonants and vowels of Chimariko *ápxa* 'excrement', *ípxa* 'intestines' with Proto-Pomo (Oswalt) *ʔahpʰa* 'excrement', *ʔihpʰa* 'intestines' (Berman 2001c:1053).

13. The likelihood that Okwanuchu was a bilingual mix of Shasta and some other language supports this scenario, suggesting that the Shasta expansion south and east of Mount Shasta and into the upper McCloud drainage was quite recent, perhaps only a matter of a few generations before the historic period. The language that Shasta was replacing in Okwanuchu territory, however, was apparently not Palaihnihan. Olmsted has argued that it probably had independent (and notably conservative) status within Northern Hokan (Bright and Olmsted 1959:4).

14. Palaihnihan and Chimariko share another, probably older, feature of stem structure: the first elements of their bipartite stems are further analyzable into a lexical prefix with instrumental or vector-defining meaning attached to a phonologically prominent root of a quasi-nominal classificatory nature. The same structure, but without a locative-directional component, characterizes Pomo verb stems. Yuman follows roughly the same scheme, obscured somewhat by a tendency to lexically fossilize specific sequences of stem elements. The compound stems of Yana probably evolved from this ancient Hokan pattern.

15. There may be evidence of ancient contact bewteen Yana and Yukian in the numerals. Compare Yana *pay-* 'one' and *-pʰku-* 'each, only' to Yuki *powi* 'one', *pak'* 'each, one alone'; and Yana *pul-* 'three' to Yuki *mol-* 'three' (see Appendix D: 3.5 and 6.1).

16. Whistler's scheme for Pomo linguistic prehistory is also summarized in McCarthy (1985). For a critical assessment see Olmsted (1985). Despite the problems it raises with comparative Pomo linguistics, an early chronology for the expansion of Pomo correlates well with the 3000 BP date of separation of Northern Yukian and Wappo calculated by Elmendorf (1968 [1993]:178).

17. This four-way laryngeal feature contrast is otherwise found in North America only in the Kiowa-Tanoan languages (K. Hale 1967) and in Yuchi (Crawford 1973).

18. For another lexicostatistical study of Esselen and Hokan, see Webb 1980. To appreciate the similarities, as well as the

differences, between Salinan and Seri, compare the numerals in Appendix D.

19. The extent to which Rumsen and Esselen had influenced one another can be gauged by the bilingual word list obtained by the Spanish naval expedition in 1792 (Beeler 1978a:10–15; Cutter 1990:147–149). Of ninety-eight pairs of words, eight are identical in the two languages, and a further two are similar enough to be likely borrowings. Kroeber (1904:68) notes and comments on a few other Esselen-Rumsen resemblances. Callaghan (2006) has recently shown that the majority of these resemblant forms were probably borrowed into Esselen from Rumsen during mission times.

20. Callaghan (1988a), however, is not fully persuaded by Beeler's Esselen comparisons. In her view, the first element of the Karkin word for 'man' could just as well be compared to Chocheño *hunṭač* 'old man' and to similar words with this meaning in the San Francisco and Santa Clara varieties of San Francisco Bay Costanoan, although she admits the possibility that all these forms could be connected to Esselen.

21. Or northward-migrating, if Jane Hill (2002a) is correct (see ¶5.4.1).

22. An exception is Cecil Brown's data-rich and methodologically explicit comparison of Wintu to Proto-Mayan (1990). However, since this paper has not been published, but only circulated informally among the author's colleagues, it is not possible to evaluate its success in establishing the relationship.

23. It is somewhat puzzling that nearly half of the Alsea-like words in Wintuan are attested only in Northern Wintuan. Perhaps the absence of Patwin equivalents for so many of these words indicates that the Northern-Southern division of the family predated the Wintuan departure from Oregon. If so, perhaps the Pre-Patwin occupied the southern portion of an Oregon homeland, associated with the sites on the Rogue River that Clewett and Sundahl (1990:44) think may be ancestral to the Augustine tradition, while the Pre-Wintu were situated further to the northwest, closer to the Alsea. Such a scenario, however, would have to be reconciled with the borrowing of the Klamath-Modoc pronoun system into Proto-Wintuan, not just Pre-Wintu. (See also the discussion of Takelma prehistory in ¶5.3.3.)

24. Four of the pronouns of Klamath (K) and Wintu (W) are identical in form and meaning: 1 sg subject (K, W *ni*), 1 sg object (K, W *nis*), 2 sg object (K, W *mis*), 3 sg subject (K, W *pi*). With several others the similarities are close and systematic: 1 sg emphatic (K *no:*, W *niyo:*), 1 pl (K *na:l'-*, W *nele:-* and K *na:t-*, W *nite:-*), 2 pl (K *ma:l'-*, W *male:-* and K *ma:t-*, W *mite-*). Of particular interest is Wintu 2 sg subject *mi*. Although the modern Klamath 2 sg subject pronoun is *ʔi*, there are good reasons to suppose that this is an innovation replacing an earlier *mi*. Wintu *mi* could thus be a borrowing of the older Klamath form. For an extended discussion of the significance of these resemblances see DeLancey (1987). Interestingly, *mis* is also the 2 sg object pronoun in Northern Yukian (see Table 53). Shepherd (2005) has suggested that this form—which is irregular in the Yuki pronominal paradigm—was borrowed from Wintuan.

25. At least one other instance of the systematic borrowing of pronouns without any other significant evidence of linguistic contact has been noted in the Pacific Northwest. Kinkade (2005) has shown that the pronominal system of Alsea is essentially that of Coast Salish.

26. A connection between Proto-Yokuts culture and the late pre-Numic cultures of the Great Basin has also been proposed

by Dawson on the basis of basketry styles (Fowler and Dawson 1986:728–729).

27. A Mesoamerican homeland for Uto-Aztecan has been independently advocated by Wichmann (1999), who hypothesizes a genetic relationship between Mixe-Zoquean and Uto-Aztecan (partially following Whorf 1935, who included the two in his "Macro-Penutian" phylum along with Penutian, Totonacan, and Kiowa-Tanoan). The prehistoric connections of Mixe-Zoquean, a relatively small family centered on the Mexican Gulf Coast, are the subject of considerable debate among Mesoamericanists. A number of linguists have proposed a link to Mayan, and Campbell, who is normally quite cautious about proposals for distant genetic relationships feels that a "Macro-Mayan" group—Mixe-Zoquean, Totonacan, and Mayan—"ultimately . . . will be shown to be genetically related" (1997:323–324).

28. Probably no later than 500 BC. Among the loanwords in Kiowa-Tanoan (KT) identified by Hill as originating in Proto-Uto-Aztecan or Proto–Northern Uto–Aztecan are *p?aa* 'fresh corn' < PNUA *pa?yi* < PUA *pa?ci* 'corn, corn kernel, seed'; Taos *xwia-d-* 'hoe' < PUA *wika* 'planting stick, dibble'; Taos *xwia* 'to harvest' < PNUA *kwiyi* < PUA *kwisič* 'to carry, take'; KT *ʔia* 'corn' < PNUA *iya* (< *ica*) 'to plant'; KT *k?un*, *khǝ* 'corn, seed' < PNUA *kuma* 'corn'; KT *t?oi* 'person' < PNUA *toi-* 'male person'; KT *gwi(n)-* ~ *kwi(n)-* 'stand' < PNUA *wini* 'stand'; KT *kon* 'buffalo' < PNUA *kuhcuŋ* 'buffalo, cow'; and KT *t?ou* 'pine nut' < PNUA *tipat* 'piñon, pine nut' (Hill 2002a). Some of these resemblances were cited by Whorf and Trager (1937) in support of their "Azteco-Tanoan" hypothesis that Uto-Aztecan and Kiowa-Tanoan share a common ancestor.

29. For example Upper Piman *siwani* 'head of a Hohokam Great House' < Keresan *ši:wana* 'rain deity, kachina', probably by way of Zuni *šiwani* «rain priest»; Tepiman *kihe/a* 'some kind of brother' > Zuni as *kihe* 'ceremonial brother'; Tepiman and Northern Uto-Aztecan *ki* 'house' > Zuni *kiwihci* 'kiva'; and Tepiman *kok?oi* 'ghost, spirit of the dead' > Zuni *kokko*, the root for many words for kachinas (Hill 2002a).

30. If Joël's account of the Hopi origin of the Yuman word for 'bean' is correct (Joël 1978; see ¶5.2.12), the Yuman-speaking groups along the Colorado were in contact with Hopi speakers at the time they adopted agriculture, probably in the latter part of the first millennium AD. If the Western Anasazi area was the home ground for all the Northern Uto-Aztecan languages, it apparently had become dominated by Hopi in later centuries. A more parsimonious scenario, perhaps, would be to identify the Western Anasazi area with ancestral Hopi and Numic, and some area in the California region with ancestral Tubatulabal and Takic, and to see the two areas as "Northern Uto-Aztecan" only by propinquity—either as the end points of two separate migrations from a southern homeland (Jane Hill) or as the result of an early fragmentation of a northern homeland (Nichols, Fowler). An early bifurcation of this sort is implied in Ken Hale's and Wick Miller's classificatory work (Hale 1958–1959; Hale and Harris 1979; Miller 1983, 1984); and the close relationship between Hopi and Numic on the one hand, and Tubatulabal and Takic on the other, has been reaffirmed by recent comparative work by Manaster Ramer and by Hill herself (see especially Hill 2009). Hill has repeatedly pointed out the farming vocabulary uniquely shared between Hopi and Numic.

31. Recent analysis of skeletal collections from the Southern Channel Islands indicates a major population replacement

around 500 BC (Kerr 2004:139, cited in Glassow et al. 2007:210). If this correlates with the establishment of Uto-Aztecan speech communities on the islands, considerable dialectal diversity ought to have developed by the contact period, of which the four documented words of Nicoleño—apparently Uto-Aztecan but not attributable to any known Takic language—may be a trace (see ¶3.32.8). Santa Catalina, however, was reputed to be "pure Gabrielino in speech" (Kroeber 1925:620), and Harrington (1962) claimed that this observation was true of the other Southern Channel Islands as well.

32. Heizer was told that, in the fighting between the Saidukah and the Northern Paiutes, the former shouted, "Yahánahowíkunahónu." His source, "Skinny Dick," who had learned this phrase as a boy, said it was not in his language and speculated that it was some kind of "cussing." While Heizer thought it probable that the Saidukah were "merely another Paviotso band that was forced to give up its territory to a more aggressive group of the same language," he conceded that "it is possible that a linguist might discover that this phrase is in some other identifiable language." Other details about the Saidukah passed along in Northern Paiute tradition are that they dressed in leather coats and trousers, used mortars rather than metates, had spears but not arrows, and that the Achumawi of Pit River are their descendants (Heizer 1970:242; Sutton 1993:122–123). For earlier reports see Loud and Harrington (1929:162); R. Lowie (1924:205); and Steward (1937:626). For the meaning of "Saidukah" see D. Fowler and Fowler (1971:285, n. 73).

33. Hill's views on "agricultural regression" are derived in part from Bellwood (1997, 2005; see also J. Hill 2006:5–6). The possibility of a speedup of linguistic change in the sociolinguistic economy of California tribelets is explored in Basgall 1987 and Golla 2000.

34. To complicate matters still further, some Algonquianists continue to work with a model of Algonquian expansion that places the homeland in the lower Great Lakes area (M. Foster 1996:98–100).

35. The Columbia Plateau appears to be a typical "spread area" (J. Nichols 1992) within which single languages or groups of closely related languages tend to rapidly expand their territories and replace earlier linguistic diversity with considerable frequency. Modern Shuswap, Okanagan, and Kalispel are quite similar, and it seems highly likely that a relatively undifferentiated Proto–Interior Salish spread across the northern Columbia Plateau within the last five hundred to seven hundred years. Sahaptin and Nez Perce similarly appear to have recently expanded across the southern Columbia Plateau (Kinkade et al. 1998:68–69). In one or both of these areas the predecessor languages could well have been Algic (or perhaps Athabaskan, which in turn had earlier replaced Algic). Unfortunately, the reconstructible vocabulary of Proto-Algic sheds little light on the location and culture of its speakers. A word for 'salal' can be reconstructed, along with terms for 'atl-atl' (or 'spear') and 'water craft' (Andrew Garrett, personal communication).

36. It has been suggested that Wiyot might be the product of relatively recent language mixture, or at least was heavily influenced by a non-Algic substratum in the Humboldt Bay area, while Yurok, spoken in areas where the earlier population was probably much thinner, remained more "pure." There is certainly some evidence that the early Wiyots, as distinct from the Yuroks, borrowed significant aspects of their culture, particularly subsistence practices, from a much earlier tradition

(Moratto 1984:565–566). If Wiyot were a mixed or creolized version of Yurok, however, one would expect it to show a distinctly less "Algic" grammatical structure than Yurok, which is not the case. In fact, there are aspects of Wiyot grammar that are more archaic (i.e., similar to Algonquian) than Yurok. The differences between the two languages are much better explained as the product of independent innovations from a common source over a considerable period of time, that is, "normal" linguistic diversification.

37. This reconstruction is in essential agreement with the one proposed by Whistler (1979a), summarized in Moratto (1984:481–484). Whistler puts the Wiyot arrival around 900 AD, the Yurok about 1100 AD, and Athabaskan entry as late as 1300 AD. These dates strike me as too recent to explain the existing linguistic differences, particularly between California and Oregon Athabaskan. I would propose 100 AD or earlier for the original Ritwan spread down the coast and the settlement of early Wiyots on Humboldt Bay, 700–800 AD for the arrival of the Yuroks on the Klamath River, and no later than 800–900 AD for the intrusion of Athabaskans into the Trinity-Eel drainage.

38. There is evidence that an Athabaskan-speaking group formerly lived in the Nicola Valley, deep in Interior Salish territory about 150 miles south of the main body of Athabaskan languages in British Columbia and along the likely route of Pacific Coast Athabaskan migration. Nicola Athabaskan was already extinct in the late nineteenth century, and only a few dozen poorly transcribed words have been preserved (Boas 1924).

Notes to Appendices

1. Merriam's vocabularies and other linguistic notes were stored in space allocated to the Archaeology Research Facility in the basement of Hearst Gymnasium. To consult the data, researchers had to make prior arrangements, and they were not permitted to make photocopies. In addition, they had to agree to abide by the stipulation Merriam had made in his will that his materials could be published only if no alterations were made in his "practical" spelling of native terms. After the transfer of the collection to the Bancroft Library in the 1980s, the restrictions on copying and citation were eased.

2. For Harrington's life and career see ¶2.7.

3. There was some criticism at the time, particularly from Heizer, that these publications—most of which were based on typescripts prepared by Harrington—did not give Harrington sufficient credit as the author (Heizer 1975b, 1976).

4. Parts 1 through 9 of the microfilm, originally published by Kraus International Publications, are currently distributed through ProQuest Information and Learning (www.proquest.com). An additional ten microfilm reels containing Harrington's photograph collection was directly published by the National Anthropological Archives in 1994 and is no longer in print (Harrington 1994; Schaad 1994).

5. It was announced late in 2006 that the NAA will be collaborating with the Rosetta Project to make some of Harrington's sound recordings of California Indian languages available online. A grant from the Christensen Fund will enable the digitization of two hundred of the recordings (both wax cylinders and aluminum disks) and the creation of a set of online tools to facilitate their use. The digitized sound recordings will

appear both on the Rosetta Project language portal and in SIRIS, the Smithsonian's online public access catalog. Selected for digitization in this project are recordings of Cahuilla, Chimariko, Chumash, Costanoan, Juaneño, Luiseño, Miwok, Salinan, Tolowa, and Tubatulabal.

6. Merriam expressed his views on transcription in the introduction to his monograph *The Classification and Distribution of the Pit River Indian Tribes of California* (Merriam 1926a:2):

> My work in anthropology has been done *not* for the ultra specialist in linguistics, but for the average educated American who wants to learn about our aboriginal inhabitants. The alphabet employed therefore gives the usual sounds of the letters in the English alphabet.
>
> The only addition is the super ᶜʰ to denote the sound of *ch* in the German *buch*—a sound lacking in English but common in many Indian languages.
>
> Disquieting special and abnormal combinations and usages—such as *c* for *sh* [spelling shut, *cut*]; *c* for *th* [spelling that, *cat*]; *tch* for *ch* [spelling church, *tchurtch*]; *s* for *sh* [spelling sham, *sam*]; *ts* for *s* [spelling sad, *tsad*]; *dj* for *j* [spelling bluejay, *bludjay*]; *au* for *ow* [spelling how, *hau*]; *x* for aspirated *h* or *k*, and so on—have not been adopted.
>
> In writing Indian words many anthropologists are opposed to the use of the hyphen. Thus, no less an authority than Roland Dixon, in reviewing a scholarly contribution to the ethnology of California, states: "The advisability of such extensive hyphenation as is here used is open to question, and it is to be hoped that in further publications the forms will be given without this unnatural separation, convenient though it may be in some ways." (*Amn. Anthropologist,* vol. 6, p. 715, 1904.)
>
> I am of the opposite view, believing that the liberal employment of the hyphen in the separation of syllables is most helpful to both the transcriber and the student.

7. From Teeter (1964).

8. From Garrett, Blevins, and Conathan (2005).

9. In both Wiyot and Yurok all numerals are verbs. The forms for 1–4 are basic stems with a numeral root in first position and—except in the default set in Wiyot—a classificatory element in second position. The forms for 5–10 consist of a numerical adverb followed by a general verb of counting (a stem based on the root *həl-* in Wiyot, *tVm-* ~ *čVm-* in Yurok, and followed by the same classificatory element as in 1–4). The Wiyot default set is shown here; the numeral roots for 1–4 are *kuc-*, *ṛit-*, *ṛikʰ-*, and *ṛiyaʔw-*, and *-ər* is the third person pronominal subect inflection. Stems for 'one' and 'two' in some other commonly occurring sets are *kucatk-*, *ṛitatk-* 'it is (one, two) flat round object(s)' (classifier *-atk-*); *kucak-*, *ṛitak-* 'it is (one, two) long object(s)' (classifier *-ak-*); *kucewat-*, *ṛetəwat-* 'it is (one, two) string(s) of dentalia' (classifier *-əwat-*) (Reichard 1925, 84–85).

10. Although Yurok numeral verbs have the same underlying analysis as in Wiyot, the phonetic fusion between numeral root and classifier is much greater. For all practical purposes the forms belonging to each Yurok numeral set must be learned as individual lexemes. The default set, shown here, is used for counting body parts, clothes, chairs, utensils, and other miscellaneous objects. Modern speakers are familiar with six other sets of more specific application: people (*ko:raʔ* 'it is one person',

niʔił 'there are two people', etc.); animals (*kṛhtṛʼy, nṛʔṛʔṛył,* etc.); long straight things (*kohtaʼr, naʔaʼr,* etc.); round things (*kohtoh, noʔoh,* etc.); snake-like things (*kohtekʼ, naʔakʼ,* etc.); and flat things (*kohtokʼs, noʔokʼs,* etc.). An additional three sets are remembered, but rarely if ever used: houses (*kohteʼli, naʔaʼli,* etc.); boats (*kohtey, naʔey,* etc.); and bushy things (*kohtekʷʼoʼn, naʔakʷʼoʼn,* etc.). More than a dozen other sets are attested in materials collected from earlier generations of speakers. The correct employment of a large repertoire of these essentially unanalyzable variants was apparently one of the accomplishments of a speaker of "high" Yurok in traditional times (see ¶4.13.1).

11. *weʔsaγ* 'five' < *weʔs-saγ* 'one hand of a pair'

12. As with the numeral root in the forms for 1–4, the root of the counting verb (*tVm-* ~ *čVm-*) fuses with each classifier to produce a synchronically unanalyzable counting stem for the 5–10 forms of that set: *čoːʼm* 'there are (so many) things', *čoːʼmeł* 'there are (so many) people', *tṛmṛwṛʔṛył* 'there are (so many) animals', *tomakʷ* 'there are (so many) snake-like things', etc.

13. Most Athabaskan languages have a decimal count, and the numerals 1–8 and 10 can be reconstructed in Proto-Athabaskan. The Oregon Athabaskan numerals 1–7 and 10 are direct reflexes of the Proto-Athabaskan set, as are all Hupa numerals except 10.

14. From Golla (1976).

15. From Sapir and Golla (2001).

16. See ¶4.10.2.

17. See ¶4.10.2.

18. From Bright (1957) and Bright and Gehr (2004).

19. From Harrington (1982–1990, vol. 2, reel 21:0005) and Sapir (in Berman 2001c). The variation reflects the disintegration of the Chimariko speech community after 1850.

20. From Silver (1966) and Bright and Olmsted (1959).

21. From McLendon (1996).

22. See ¶4.10.2.

23. From K. Turner (1988b).

24. The variants in the right column are archaic forms used only in counting or as interjections (never adjectivally with a noun). They are rarely heard in modern Seri, and many younger speakers do not know them (Stephen Marlett, personal communication).

25. From Sapir (1922a).

26. From Barker (1963b, 1964).

27. "The numerals six, seven, eight, and nine are best considered as morphologically verbs provided with the compound prefix *haʔi:-* 'in the hand', and thus strictly signifying 'one (finger) is in the hand'; 'two, three, four (fingers) are in the hand'" (Sapir 1922a:265).

28. "No explanation can be given of *-kó* in *haʔi:-kó* 'nine', except that it may be an older stem for 'four', later replaced, for one reason or another, by the composite *kamkàm* 'two + two'" (Sapir 1922a:265).

29. "*ìxti:l* 'ten' is best explained as compounded of *i:-x-* 'hand' (but why not *i:u:x-* as in *i:u:x-tékʰ* 'my hand'?) and the dual *-tí:l*, and as being thus equivalent to 'two hands'" (Sapir 1922a:265).

30. See Sapir (1907a:266).

31. Northeastern Maidu from Shipley (1963) with some forms retranscribed from Dixon (1911) and Dixon and Kroeber (1907). Konkow (Mooretown Rancheria variety) retranscribed from Dixon and Kroeber (1907). Nisenan from Uldall and Shipley (1966) and Eatough (1999).

32. The Northeastern Maidu forms for seven, eight, and nine given here are retranscribed from Dixon (1911). Half a century later Shipley was able to collect only analytic terms for these numbers: *sáyc'ok'o-na-sítim* 'one after six' for 'seven', etc.

33. Dixon's Mooretown informant was evidently uncertain whether the basic value of an "arrow" was ten or twelve. In another set of Konkow numerals, *wikem noko* is given the value of eleven (Dixon and Kroeber 1907:679, 687, n. 11).

34. Compare Coast Miwok (Bodega Bay) *húya* 'four'. The reference to a necklace is possibly connected to the use of clamshell disk beads as a medium of exchange (see ¶4.10.2 and Farris 1990).

35. Wintu is from Pitkin (1985) and Schlichter (1981b), with analysis from Whistler (1979b). Nomlaki is from Whistler (1979b), based on Goldschmidt (1951).

36. That is, the index finger.

37. Patwin is "Common Patwin" abstracted from attested River and Hill Patwin subdialects by Whistler (1979b). Southern Patwin is from a vocabulary of the Suisun variety collected by J. A. Mason in 1916 from Platon Vallejo (Kroeber 1932: 354).

38. Contracted from **ser-po:ł-ʔete:-ta* (Whistler 1979b).

39. Contracted from **pan-ʔemu:h-ʔete:-ta* (Whistler 1979b).

40. Karkin is retranscribed from Arroyo (1837) in the light of Gerolt (1830), cf. Golla (1996d). Chocheño is from Miller and Callaghan (n.d.). Soledad is retranscribed from 19th century attestations following Callaghan (1990). Mutsun is from Okrand (1977). Rumsen is based on Broadbent (1957) and Callaghan (1990, 1992a).

41. Delta Yokuts from various manuscripts, analyzed and retranscribed by Kenneth Whistler and the author (see Kroeber 1959b). All other dialects from Kroeber (1963) and Newman (1944).

42. Yokuts numerals are generally cognate across the multitude of local dialects, with the exception of the dialects of the San Joaquin delta, at the far northern extremity of Yokuts territory, where most of the numerals above 3 were either borrowed from adjacent languages or were noncognate innovations. Delta Yokuts appears to comprise two dialect clusters, a northwestern cluster associated only with the tribelets of the marshes around Stockton and Tracy (Yachikamne, Tamukamne, and Cholovomne) and a somewhat more widely spread southeastern cluster associated with the tribelets located upstream from the marshes on the Eastern bank of the San Joaquin as far as the mouth of the Merced (Pasasamne, Lakisamne, and the Lower Merced varieties spoken by the converts at Mission Santa Cruz); see ¶3.26. The lexical discontinuity that is seen in the numerals suggests that the two tribelet clusters, although separated only by a few dozen miles, participated in different networks of trade and intermarriage.

43. The *poŋoy* variant is found in the Tule-Kaweah, Buena Vista, and Poso Creek dialect groups, *ponoy* is found elsewhere.

44. Apparently 'two times itself'. The *hot-poŋoy* variant is found in the Tule-Kaweah and Poso Creek dialect groups;

tapaŋiy (presumably reduced from **hot(a)-paŋiy*) is found only in the Buena Vista dialects; *hot-ponoy* is found elsewhere.

45. Apparently reduced from **yet'-sinil/siŋil* 'one hand'. The *yic'iŋil* variant is found in the Tule-Kaweah and Buena Vista dialect groups; *yec'elay* (also recorded *yec'iliy*) is found only in the Poso Creek dialect group; *yic'inil* is found elsewhere. The element *sinil ~ siŋil ~ selay/siliy* is not the usual noun for 'hand' in any Yokuts dialect but can be presumed to have had this or a related meaning in early Yokuts.

46. The variant *nomc'il* is found only in the Southern Valley dialects and in the Poso Creek dialects; *nomc'in* is found elsewhere.

47. The vowels differ among dialects. Some Nim Yokuts dialects have *mon'os*; the Buena Vista dialects have *mun'as*; the Poso Creek dialects have *men'us*. The final fricative also varies between *-s* and *-š*.

48. Valley dialects (both Northern and Southern) have *ṣo:pʰin-hot* ('three times itself'); *no:nipʰ* is found in all other Nim Yokuts dialects (i.e., Northern Foothills, Kings River, and Tule-Kaweah groups); *wuṭʰat'* is the variant in dialects of the Buena Vista group; *likiyi?* is the Poso Creek variant.

49. In general, the Yokuts numerals for 11–19 are formed on the verb bases 'make (1–9)' (Newman 1944:54–55) with a derivational suffix that is apparently related to, if not the same as, the "consequent gerundial" suffix *-m(i)* 'being in a state consequent to having acted upon' (Newman 1944:134–136). The base assumes a special shape, however, in *poč̣tom* 'twelve', where the expected stem is *pony-* 'two', and in *hač̣pam* 'fourteen' and *mun'č̣am* 'eighteen', where the expected stems, *hatp-* and *mun's-*, have a palatal (or retroflex?) affricate in place of an apical stop or fricative.

50. The variant *tiwa:p* is attested only in the Hometwoli dialect of the Buena Vista dialect group (Kroeber 1963:211).

51. The variant *ṣulokʰay* is attested in Hometwoli (Buena Vista dialect group) and *ṣuyukʰay* in Yaudanchi (Tule-Kaweah group) and is clearly related to *ṭʰulukʰay* 'seven' in the southern dialect of Delta Yokuts. The variant *poč̣tom* is attested in Chukaymina and Choynimni (Kings River dialect group), Dumna (Northern Foothill), Gashowu, and Wechihit and Tachi (Southern Valley) (Kroeber 1963:211).

52. A verbal noun derived from the stem *pʰič̣'-* 'count', that is, 'a (full) count' (Newman 1944:55, n. 44).

53. Bodega Miwok from Callaghan (1970) and Lake Miwok from Callaghan (1965), with analysis from Callaghan (1994).

54. Saclan from Arroyo (1837), by way of Beeler (1955b), as interpreted by Callaghan (1994). Plains Miwok from Callaghan (1984) and Sierra Miwok from Freeland (1951), with analysis from Callaghan (1994) and Blevins (2005a).

55. That is, big finger, thumb—the first digit counted on the second hand (Callaghan 1994:168).

56. See also the Cupeño numerals in Box 11.

57. *powi* (or *pəwi* in some dialects) is the general count term, *pak'* is used adverbially of a person ('by himself, alone'). For the distribution of this widespread loanword see ¶4.14.4.

58. From Klar (1980).

BIBLIOGRAPHY

Abbreviations

AA	*American Anthropologist*
AL	*Anthropological Linguistics*
BAE-AR	*Bureau of American Ethnology, Annual Report.* Washington, DC: Smithsonian Institution.
BAE-B	*Bureau of American Ethnology, Bulletin.* Washington, DC: Smithsonian Institution.
EDDMA	Ethnological Documents of the Department and Museum of Anthropology, University of California, Berkeley, 1875–1958. BANC FILM 2216, The Bancroft Library, University of California, Berkeley.
IJAL	*International Journal of American Linguistics*
JAF	*Journal of American Folk-Lore*
JCA	*Journal of California Anthropology*
JCA-PL	*Journal of California Anthropology, Papers in Linguistics*
JCGBA	*Journal of California and Great Basin Anthropology*
JCGBA-PL	*Journal of California and Great Basin Anthropology, Papers in Linguistics*
NAA	National Anthropological Archives. Department of Anthropology, Smithsonian Institution, Washington, DC.
SCOIL	Survey of California and Other Indian Languages. Department of Linguistics, University of California, Berkeley.
SSILA	Society for the Study of the Indigenous Languages of the Americas
UC-AR	*University of California, Anthropological Records.* Berkeley.
UC-PAAE	*University of California, Publications in American Archaeology and Ethnology.* Berkeley.
UC-PL	*University of California, Publications in Linguistics.* Berkeley.

Proceedings of the Hokan-Penutian Workshop, 1975–2000

A general meeting of specialists on California Indian languages, called variously the *Yuman Languages Workshop* *Hokan Languages Workshop, Hokan-Yuman Languages Workshop,* and *Hokan-Penutian Workshop,* was held annually from 1975 to 1996, with a final meeting in 2000. Written versions of many of the papers given at these meetings were published in volumes of proceedings, which are uniformly cited here as *Hokan-Penutian Workshop* (e.g., *1980 Hokan-Penutian Workshop*). The full titles, editors, and publishers of the individual proceedings volumes are given following this paragraph, and further details, including the contents of each volume, can be found in Hinton (2000). Full text files of all papers published in the Hokan-Penutian Workshop proceedings are available on the website of the Survey of California and Other Indian Languages (linguistics.berkeley. edu/~survey/).

1975 (UC San Diego). *Proceedings of the First Yuman Languages Workshop. Held at the University of California, San Diego, June 16–21, 1975,* edited by James E. Redden. University Museum Studies, Research Reports 7 (1976). Carbondale: University Museum, Southern Illinois University.

1976 (UC San Diego). *Proceedings of the 1976 Hokan-Yuman Languages Workshop. Held at the University of California, San Diego, June 21–23, 1976,* edited by James E. Redden. University Museum Studies, Research Reports 11 (1977). Carbondale: University Museum, Southern Illinois University.

1977 (U of Utah). *Proceedings of the 1977 Hokan-Yuman Languages Workshop, Held at the University of Utah, Salt Lake City, June 21–23, 1977,* edited by James E. Redden. Occasional Papers on Linguistics 2 (1978). Carbondale: Department of Linguistics, Southern Illinois University.

1978 (UC San Diego). *Papers from the 1978 Hokan Languages Workshop, Held at the University of California, San Diego, June 27–29, 1978,* edited by James E. Redden. Occasional Papers on Linguistics 5 (1979). Carbondale: Department of Linguistics, Southern Illinois University.

1979 (UCLA). *Proceedings of the 1979 Hokan Languages Workshop, Held at the University of California, Los Angeles, 1979,* edited by James E. Redden. Occasional Papers in Linguistics 7 (1980). Carbondale: Department of Linguistics, Southern Illinois University.

1980 (UC Berkeley). *Proceedings of the 1980 Hokan Languages Workshop, Held at the University of California, Berkeley, June 30–July 2, 1980*, edited by James E. Redden. Occasional Papers in Linguistics 9 (1981). Carbondale: Department of Linguistics, Southern Illinois University.

1981 (Sonoma State U). *Proceedings of the 1981 Hokan Languages Workshop and Penutian Languages Conference, Held at Sonoma State University, Rohnert Park, California, June 29–July 2, 1981.* Edited by James E. Redden. Occasional Papers in Linguistics 10 (1982). Carbondale: Department of Linguistics, Southern Illinois University.

1982 (UC Santa Cruz). *Proceedings of the 1982 Conference on Far Western American Indian Languages, Held at the University of California, Santa Cruz,* edited by James E. Redden. Occasional Papers in Linguistics 11 (1983). Carbondale: Department of Linguistics, Southern Illinois University.

1983–1985. *Papers from the 1983, 1984, and 1985 Hokan-Penutian Languages Conferences,* edited by James E. Redden. Occasional Papers in Linguistics 13 (1986). Carbondale: Department of Linguistics, Southern Illinois University.

1986 (UC Santa Cruz). [The 1986 Hokan-Penutian Workshop met as a session of the *Mary Haas Festival*, a special conference held at UC Santa Cruz celebrating Haas's role in establishing academic linguistics in California. Papers delivered in this session were published in the proceedings of the larger conference (Shipley 1988).]

1987 (U of Utah). *Papers from the 1987 Hokan-Penutian Languages Workshop and Friends of Uto-Aztecan Workshop, Held at University of Utah, Salt Lake City, June 18–21, 1987,* edited by James E. Redden. Occasional Papers on Linguistics 14 (1988). Carbondale: Department of Linguistics, Southern Illinois University.

1988 (U of Oregon). *Papers from the 1988 Hokan-Penutian Languages Workshop,* edited by Scott DeLancey. University of Oregon Papers in Linguistics: Publications of the Center for Amerindian Linguistics and Ethnography 1. Eugene: Department of Linguistics, University of Oregon.

1989 (U of Arizona). *Papers from the 1989 Hokan-Penutian Languages Workshop,* edited by Scott DeLancey. University of Oregon Papers in Linguistics: Publications of the Center for Amerindian Linguistics and Ethnography 2. Eugene: Department of Linguistics, University of Oregon.

1990 (UC San Diego). *Proceedings of the 1990 Hokan-Penutian Languages Workshop,* edited by James E. Redden. Occasional Papers on Linguistics 15 (1991). Carbondale: Department of Linguistics, Southern Illinois University.

1991 (UC Santa Cruz). *Papers from the American Indian Languages Conferences, Held at the University of California, Santa Cruz, July and August, 1991,* edited by James E. Redden. Occasional Papers on Linguistics 16 (1992). Carbondale: Department of Linguistics, Southern Illinois University.

1992 (UC Santa Barbara) *Papers from the 1992 Hokan-Penutian Languages Conference and the J. P. Harrington Conference, Held at the University of California, Santa Barbara, and the Museum of Natural History, Santa Barbara, June 24–27, 1992,* edited by James E. Redden. Occasional Papers on Linguistics 17 (1993). Carbondale: Department of Linguistics, Southern Illinois University.

1993 (Ohio State U). *Proceedings of the Society for the Study of the Indigenous Languages of the Americas, July 2–4, 1993, and the Hokan-Penutian Workshop, July 3, 1993, Both Held at the 1993 Linguistic Institute at Ohio State University in Columbus, Ohio,* edited by Margaret Langdon. Survey of California and Other Indian Languages, Report 8 (1994). Berkeley: Department of Linguistics, University of California.

1994 (U of Oregon) and 1995 (U of New Mexico). *Proceedings of the Hokan-Penutian Workshop, 1994–95,* edited by Victor Golla. Survey of California and Other Indian Languages, Report 9 (1996). Berkeley: Department of Linguistics, University of California.

1996 (UC Berkeley). *The Hokan, Penutian and J. P. Harrington Conferences and the Mary R. Haas Memorial, June 28–29, 1996, University of California, Berkeley,* edited by Leanne Hinton. Survey of California and Other Indian Languages, Report 10 (1997). Berkeley: Department of Linguistics, University of California.

2000 (UC Berkeley). *Proceedings of the Meeting of the Hokan-Penutian Workshop, June 17–18, 2000, University of California at Berkeley,* edited by Laura Buszard-Welcher. Survey of California and Other Indian Languages, Report 11 (2002). Berkeley: Department of Linguistics, University of California.

Cited Literature

Aalto, Pentti. 1959. Ein alter Name des Kupfers. *Ural-Altaische Jahrbücher* 31:33–40.

Adams, Douglas Q. 1985. Internal Reconstruction in Mutsun Morphology. IJAL 51:329–331.

Ahlborn, Richard E. 1992. The Mission San Antonio Prayer and Song Board. *Southern California Quarterly* 74:1–17.

Ahlers, Jocelyn C. 1999. *Proposal for the Use of Cognitive Linguistics in Hupa Language Revitalization.* PhD dissertation, University of California, Berkeley.

———. 2006. Word Formation in Elem Pomo. Paper presented at the Workshop on American Indigenous Languages, University of California, Santa Barbara, April 21–22, 2006.

———. 2007. Borrowing in Elem Pomo. Paper presented at the Annual Meeting of the Society for the Study of the Indigenous Languages of the Americas, Anaheim, California, January 4–7, 2007.

Alekseev, A. I. (Aleksandr Ivanovich). 1987. *The Odyssey of a Russian Scientist: I. G. Voznesenskii in Alaska, California, and Siberia, 1839–1849.* Translated by Wilma C. Follette; edited by Richard A. Pierce. Kingston, Ontario: Limestone Press.

Anderson, Alexander Caulfield. 1857. Klatskanai vocabulary received from A. C. Anderson, Cathlamet, Washington Territory, November, 1857. NAA MS 107a. 6 pp.

Anderson, Atholl. 2006. Polynesian Seafaring and American Horizons: A Response to Jones and Klar. *American Antiquity* 71:759–763. (Reply to Jones and Klar 2005, and also Klar and Jones 2005.)

Anderton, Alice J. 1988. *The Language of the Kitanemuks of California.* PhD dissertation, University of California, Los Angeles.

———. 1991. Kitanemuk: Reconstruction of a Dead Phonology Using John P. Harrington's Transcriptions. AL 33:437–447.

Angulo, Jaime de. See de Angulo, Jaime.

Anonymous. 1802. *Relación del Viage Hecho por las Goletas Sutil y Mexicana en el año 1792 para Reconocer el Estrecho de Fuca . . .* Madrid: Imprenta Real. (Sometimes attributed to Don Dionisio Alcalá Galiano, the commander of the *Sutil.* For discussion of the authorship see Cutter 1990:20–26.)

Aoki, Haruo. 1963. On Sahaptian-Klamath Linguistic Affiliations. IJAL 29:107–112.

———. 1970. *Nez Perce Grammar.* UC-PL 62.

Applegate, Richard B. 1972a. *Ineseño Chumash Grammar.* PhD dissertation, University of California, Berkeley.

———. 1972b. *Ineseño Chumash Dictionary.* MS.

———. 1974. Chumash Placenames. JCA 1:187–205.

———. 1975. *An Index of Chumash Placenames.* San Luis Obispo County Historical Society, Occasional Papers 9:19–46.

———. n.d. *Coast Miwok Language Tutorial.* Web site at www. jamatra.com/cm/.

Arnold, Jeanne E. 2001. The Chumash in World and Regional Perspectives. In *The Origins of a Pacific Coast Chiefdom: The Chumash of the Channel Islands,* edited by Jeanne E. Arnold, 1-19. Salt Lake City: University of Utah Press.

Arroyo de la Cuesta, Fr. Felipe. 1815. *Alphab.s Rivulus obeundus exprimationum causa horum Indorum Mutsum missionis Sanct. Johann. Baptistae exquisitarum a Fr. Phillip. ab Ar.yo de la Cuesta . . . 1815.* [The alphabetic rivulet to be gone to for translations of the expressions of these Mutsun Indians of the Mission of San Juan Bautista, by Fray Felipe Arroyo de la Cuesta]. BANC MSS C-C 19, The Bancroft Library, University of California, Berkeley. 94 pp. (Contains also catechism, Christian doctrine, etc., and music for Indian dance. With explanatory notes by Alexander S. Taylor and a letter, September 22, 1856, from Fr. Juan B. Comellas to Taylor, pasted on back cover. Partially published as Arroyo de la Cuesta 1862.)

———. 1810–1819. *El Oro Molido* [Refined Gold.] BANC MSS C-C 60, Bancroft Library, University of California, Berkeley. 172 pp. (Notebook compiled for his own use, 1810–1819. Contains guides for confession, hymns, and copies of prayers and religious instruction in Mutsun and Nopṭinṭe Yokuts. Partially recopied in Harrington, Appendix B, 2:057:0409–0657. Portions with material on Yokuts published in Beeler 1971.)

———. 1837. *Lengua de California. Santa Ynes, 1837.* BANC MSS C-C 63a-b, Bancroft Library, University of California, Berkeley. (A complex family of manuscripts and copies, some at the Bancroft and others elsewhere. The Bancroft's C-C 63a is the original, compiled by Arroyo during his retirement at Santa Ynez mission and dated March 6, 1837. It is in two parts. The first has a cover with the title in the handwriting of Alphonse Pinart and contains musical scores for portions of the Mass. The second part has a separate cover with the title "Lecciones de Indios" (in Arroyo's hand) and contains materials on Esselen; Antoniano and Migueleño Salinan; Obispeño, Purisimeño and Ineseño Chumash; Nopṭinṭe Yokuts; Luiseño; and five languages from the San Francisco Bay area: Huimen (Marin Miwok), Juichun (East Bay Costanoan), Saclan (Bay Miwok), Karkin (Costanoan), and Suisun (Southern Patwin). C-C 63b is a copy of "Lecciones de Indios" made for H. H. Bancroft by E. F. Murray at Santa Barbara, June 26, 1878, with the title, "Vocabularios de Idiomas de los Indios." A different copy of the second part, titled "Idiomas Californias," also by Murray, is in the Smithsonian [NAA MS 385]; another copy of this version, titled "Idiomas Californios," with a letter by Murray and a note and annotations by A. L. Kroeber, is in the Bancroft [BANC MSS 2003/235 c]. A. S. Gatschet's copy of the Salinan vocabularies, with English translations, is in the Smithsonian [NAA MS 850]. Portions of the original manuscript were published in Beeler 1955a, 1961b, 1971.)

———. 1861. *Grammar of the Mutsun Language.* Shea's Library of American Linguistics, no. 4. New York: Cramoisy Press.

———. 1862. *A Vocabulary or Phrase Book of the Mutsun Language.* Shea's Library of American Linguistics, no. 8. New York: Cramoisy Press. (Published version of a portion of Arroyo de la Cuesta 1815.)

Azpell, Thomas F. 1870. *Comparative vocabulary of Hoopa (Noh-tin-oah) and Klamath (Sa-ag-its)* [Yurok] *August 14, 1870.* NAA MS 83, National Anthropological Archives, Smithsonian Institution. 11 pp. (The Yurok vocabulary was published in Powers 1877.)

Baegert, Johann Jakob (Jacob), S.J. 1952. *Observations in Lower California.* Translated from the Original German with an Introduction, and Notes by M. M. Brandenburg and Carl L. Baumann. Berkeley: University of California Press. (Translated and annotated version of a German publication, 1771. Text of this edition available online through the eScholarship Program of the California Digital Library [ark. cdlib.org/ark:/13030/ft5r29n9xv/].)

Balodis, Uldis. 2009. *Third-Person Argument-Marking on Verbs in Kato.* Unpublished qualifying paper, Department of Linguistics, University of California, Santa Barbara.

Bancroft, Hubert Howe. 1874–1876. *The Native Races of the Pacific States of North America.* 5 volumes. [Vol. 3: *Myths and Languages.*] New York: Appleton.

Bancroft Library, University of California, Berkeley. 2007. *Finding Aid to the Ethnological Documents of the Department and Museum of Anthropology, University of California, Berkeley, 1875–1958,* microfilm edition, BANC FILM 2216. [Online at oac.cdlib.org/findaid/ark:/13030/kt1199q7hq]. ("Since [Valory 1971] is the arrangement in which the collection has been used and cited since 1971, the original order has been maintained in the microfilm edition.")

Barco, Miguel del, S.J. 1973. *Historia Natural y Crónica de la Antigua California.* Edited by Miguel León-Portilla. Mexico: UNAM.

Barker, M. A. R. (Muhammed Abd-al-Rahman). 1963a. *Klamath Texts.* UC-PL 30.

———. 1963b. *Klamath Dictionary.* UC-PL 31.

———. 1964. *Klamath Grammar.* UC-PL 32.

Barnhardt, W. H. 1859. *Comparative Vocabulary of the Languages Spoken by the 'Umpqua,' 'Lower Rogue River,' and 'Calapooia' Tribes of Indians, May 1859.* NAA MS 218, National Anthropological Archives, Smithsonian Institution. [Vocabulary of 170 items.]

Barrett, Samuel A. 1908a. *The Ethno-Geography of the Pomo and Neighboring Indians.* UC-PAAE 6(1):1–332.

———. 1908b. *The Geography and Dialects of the Miwok Indians.* UC-PAAE 6(2):333–368.

———. 1933. *Pomo Myths.* Bulletin of the Public Museum of the City of Milwaukee, 15. [Glossary, Pomo-English and English-Pomo, pp. 494–538.]

Barrows, David Prescott. 1900. *The Ethno-botany of the Coahuilla Indians of Southern California.* Chicago: University of Chicago Press. (Reprinted by Malki Museum Press, 1971.)

Bartlett, John Russell. 1848. *Dictionary of Americanisms: A Glossary of Words and Phrases Usually Regarded as Peculiar to the United States.* New York: Bartlett and Welford.

———. 1854. *Personal Narrative of Explorations and Incidents in Texas, New Mexico, California, Sonora, and Chihuahua: Connected with the United States and Mexican Boundary Commission, during the years 1850, '51, '52, and '53. By John*

Russell Bartlett, United States Commissioner during that period. New York: D. Appleton and Company.

———. n.d. *Miscellaneous Vocabularies of 32 Different Tribes.* NAA MS 1627, National Anthropological Archives, Smithsonian Institution. 225 numbered pp.

Basgall, Mark E. 1987. Resource Intensification among Hunter-Gatherers: Acorn Economies in Prehistoric California. *Research in Economic Anthropology* 9:21–52. (Reprinted in *Prehistoric California: Archaeology and the Myth of Paradise*, edited by L. Mark Raab and Terry L. Jones, 86–98. Salt Lake City: University of Utah Press, 2004.)

Bates, Craig D. 1983. The California Collection of I. G. Voznesensky. *American Indian Art Magazine,* Summer 1983:36–41, 79.

Bauman, James. 1980a. Chimariko Placenames and the Boundaries of Chimariko Territory. In *American Indian and Indoeuropean Studies: Papers in Honor of Madison S. Beeler*, edited by Kathryn A. Klar, Margaret Langdon, and Shirley Silver, 11–29. The Hague: Mouton.

———. 1980b. *Introduction to Pit River Language and Culture.* Anchorage: National Bilingual Materials Development Center, Rural Education, University of Alaska.

Bauman, James, Ruby Miles, and Ike Leaf. 1979. *Pit River Teaching Dictionary.* Anchorage: National Bilingual Materials Development Center, Rural Education, University of Alaska.

Bauman, James, and Shirley Silver. 1975. An Areal Survey of Phonological Processes in Northern California Languages. Paper presented at the Annual Meeting of the American Anthropological Association, San Francisco, December 1975.

Baumhoff, Martin A. 1958. California Athabascan Groups. UC-AR 16(5):157–238.

———. 1981. R. F. Heizer and the Merriam Collection. In *Contributions of Robert F. Heizer to California Ethnohistory*, edited by William S. Simmons and Polly McW. Bickel. Publications of the University of California Archaeological Research Facility 19:19–21.

Baumhoff, Martin A., and David L. Olmsted. 1963. Palaihnihan: Radiocarbon Support for Glottochronology. AA 65:278–284.

———. 1964. Notes on Palaihnihan Culture History: Glottochronology and Archaeology. In *Studies in Californian Linguistics,* edited by William Bright, 1–12. UC-PL 34.

Beals, Ralph L. 1933. *Ethnology of the Nisenan.* UC-PAAE 31(6):335–410.

Bean, Lowell John. 1974. Socal Organization in Native California. In *'Antap: California Indian Political and Economic Organization*, edited by Lowell John Bean and Thomas F. King, 13–34. Ramona, CA: Ballena Press. (Reprinted in Bean and Blackburn 1976:99–123.)

———, ed. 1992. *California Indian Shamanism.* Ballena Press Anthropological Papers no. 39. Menlo Park, CA: Ballena Press.

———, ed. 1994. *The Ohlone Past and Present: Native Americans of the San Francisco Bay Region.* Ballena Press Anthropological Papers no. 42. Menlo Park, CA: Ballena Press.

Bean, Lowell John, and Thomas C. Blackburn, eds. 1976. *Native Californians: A Theoretical Retrospective.* Ramona, CA: Ballena Press.

Bean, Lowell John, and Harry Lawton. 1976. Some Explanations for the Rise of Cultural Complexity in Native California with Comments on Proto-Agriculture and Agriculture. In *Native Californians: A Theoretical Retrospective*, edited by Lowell John Bean and Thomas C. Blackburn, 19–48. Ramona, CA: Ballena Press.

Bean, Lowell John, and Charles R. Smith. 1978. Gabrielino. In *Handbook of North American Indians.* Vol. 8: *California*, edited by Robert F. Heizer, 538–549. Washington, DC: Smithsonian Institution.

Bean, Lowell John, and Dorothea Theodoratus. 1978. Western Pomo and Northeastern Pomo. In *Handbook of North American Indians.* Vol. 8: *California*, edited by Robert F. Heizer, 289–305. Washington, DC: Smithsonian Institution.

Beckham, Stephen Dow. 1969. *George Gibbs, 1815–1873: Historian and Ethnologist.* PhD dissertation, University of California, Los Angeles.

———. 1971. *Requiem for a People: The Rogue Indians and the Frontiersmen.* Norman: University of Oklahoma Press.

Bee, Robert L. 1983. Quechan. In *Handbook of North American Indians.* Vol. 10: *Southwest*, edited by Alfonso Ortiz, 86–98. Washington, DC: Smithsonian Institution.

Beechey, Frederick W. 1831. *Narrative of a Voyage to the Pacific and Beering's Strait to Co-operate with the Polar Expeditions: Performed in His Majesty's Ship* Blossom *under the Command of Captain F. W. Beechey . . . in the years 1825, 26, 27, 28.* London: H. Colburn and R. Bentley.

Beeler, Madison S. 1954. Sonoma, Carquinez, Umunhum, Colma: Some Disputed California Names. *Western Folklore* 13:268–277.

———. 1955a. Saclan. IJAL 21:201–209.

———. 1955b. Yosemite and Tamalpais. *Names* 3:185–188.

———. 1957. On Etymologizing Indian Place-Names. *Names* 5:236–240.

———. 1959. Saclan Once More. IJAL 25:67–68.

———. 1961a. Senary Counting in California Penutian. AL 3(1):1–8.

———. 1961b. Northern Costanoan. IJAL 27:191–197.

———. 1964. Ventureño Numerals. In *Studies in Californian Linguistics*, edited by William Bright, 13–18. UC-PL 34.

———. 1967. The Ventureño Confesionario of José Señán, O.F.M. UC-PL 47.

———. 1970. Sibilant Harmony in Chumash. IJAL 36:14–17.

———. 1971. Nopṭinṭe Yokuts. In *Studies in American Indian Languages,* edited by Jesse O. Sawyer, 11–76. UC-PL 65.

———. 1972a. An Extension of San Francisco Bay Costanoan? IJAL 38:49–54.

———. 1972b. Inyo. *Names* 20:56–59.

———. 1974. [Review of Couro and Hutcheson 1974.] *Names* 22:137–141.

———. 1976. Barbareño Chumash Grammar: A Farrago. In *Hokan Studies: Papers from the First Conference on Hokan Languages,* edited by Margaret Langdon and Shirley Silver, 251–269. The Hague: Mouton.

———. 1977. The Sources for Esselen: A Critical Review. *Proceedings of the* [3rd] *Annual Meeting of the Berkeley Linguistics Society*, 37–45.

———. 1978a. Esselen. JCA-PL [1]:3–38.

———. 1978b. Inyo Once Again. *Names* 26:208.

———. 1979. Barbareño Chumash Text and Lexicon. In Mohammad Jazayery Ali, Edgar Polomé, and Werner Winter, eds., *Linguistic and Literary Studies in Honor of Archibald A. Hill,* vol 2, pp. 171–193. Lisse, Netherlands: Peter de Ridder.

Beeler, Madison S., and Kathryn A. Klar. 1977. Interior Chumash. JCA 4:287–305.

———. n.d. *Cruzeño Chumash Language: Lexicon and Grammar.* Contributions in Anthropology, Santa Barbara Museum of Natural History, Santa Barbara, California (forthcoming).

Beeler, Madison S., and Kenneth W. Whistler. 1980. Coyote, Hawk, Raven and Skunk (Barbareño Chumash). In *Coyote Stories II,* edited by Martha B. Kendall, 88–96. IJAL Native American Text Series, Monograph 6. Chicago: University of Chicago Press.

Bellwood, Peter. 1997. Prehistoric Cultural Explanations for Widespread Language Families. In *Archaeology and Linguistics,* edited by Peter McConvell and Nicholas Evans, 123–134. Melbourne: Oxford University Press.

———. 2005. *First Farmers.* Oxford: Blackwell.

Bendixen, Brigitte. 1980. *Phonological and Temporal Properties of Cocopa.* PhD dissertation, University of California, San Diego.

Bennyhoff, James A. 1968. A Delta Intrusion to the Bay in the Late Middle Period in Central California. Paper presented at the Annual Meetings of the Southwestern Anthropological Association and the Society for California Archaeology, San Diego, California. (Published in Hughes 1994.)

———. 1977. *The Ethnogeography of the Plains Miwok.* Center for Archaeological Research at Davis, Publication No. 5. (Publication of Bennyhoff's 1961 University of California, Berkeley, dissertation.)

Berman, Howard, ed. 1982a. *Freeland's Central Sierra Miwok Myths.* Survey of California and Other Indian Languages, Report 3. Berkeley: Department of Linguistics, University of California.

———. 1982b. A Supplement to Robins' Yurok-English Lexicon. IJAL 48:197–222.

———. 1982c. Two Phonological Innovations in Ritwan. IJAL 48:412–420.

———. 1983. Some California Penutian Morphological Elements. IJAL 49:400–412.

———. 1984. Proto-Algonquian-Ritwan Verbal Roots. IJAL 50:335–342.

———. 1986a. [Review of Callaghan 1984]. IJAL 52:305–309.

———. 1986b. A Note on the Yurok Diminutive. IJAL 52:419–421.

———. 1989. More California Penutian Morphological Elements. *Southwest Journal of Linguistics* 9:3–18.

———. 1990. New Algonquian-Ritwan Cognate Sets. IJAL 56:431–434.

———. 1996. The Position of Molala in Plateau Penutian. IJAL 62:1–30.

———. 2001a. Notes on Comparative Penutian. IJAL 67:346–349.

———, ed. 2001b. [Sapir's] Yurok Texts. In *The Collected Works of Edward Sapir.* Vol. 14: *Northwest California Linguistics,* edited by Victor Golla and Sean O'Neill, 1015–1038. Berlin: Mouton de Gruyter.

———, ed. 2001c. [Sapir's] Chimariko Linguistic Material. In *The Collected Works of Edward Sapir.* Vol. 14: *Northwest California Linguistics,* edited by Victor Golla and Sean O'Neill, 1039–1076. Berlin: Mouton de Gruyter.

———, ed. 2002. Merriam's Palewyami Vocabulary. IJAL 68:428–446.

Bethel, Rosalie, Paul V. Kroskrity, Christopher Loether, and Gregory Reinhardt. 1993. *A Practical Dictionary of Western Mono,* 2nd ed. Pocatello: Idaho State University, Department of Anthropology and American Indian Studies.

Bettinger, Robert L., and Martin A. Baumhoff. 1982. The Numic Spread: Great Basin Cultures in Competition. *American Antiquity* 47:485–503.

Bickel, Balthasar, and Johanna Nichols. 2005a. Fusion of Selected Inflectional Formatives. In *The World Atlas of Linguistic Structures,* edited by Martin Haspelmath, Matthew S. Dryer, David Gil, and Bernard Comrie, 86–89. Oxford, UK: Oxford University Press.

———. 2005b. Exponence of Selected Inflectional Formatives. In *The World Atlas of Linguistic Structures,* edited by Martin Haspelmath, Matthew S. Dryer, David Gil, and Bernard Comrie, 90–93. Oxford, UK: Oxford University Press.

———. 2005c. Inflectional Synthesis of the Verb. In *The World Atlas of Linguistic Structures,* edited by Martin Haspelmath, Matthew S. Dryer, David Gil, and Bernard Comrie, 94–97. Oxford, UK: Oxford University Press.

Biggs, Bruce. 1957. Testing Intelligibility among Yuman Languages. IJAL 23:57–62.

Blackburn, Thomas C. 1974. Ceremonial Integration and Social Interaction in Aboriginal California. In *'Antap: California Indian Political and Economic Organization,* edited by Lowell John Bean and Thomas F. King, 93–110. Ballena Press Anthropological Papers no. 2. Ramona, CA: Ballena Press.

———, ed. 1975. *December's Child: A Book of Chumash Oral Narratives.* Berkeley: University of California Press.

Blackburn, Thomas C., and Lowell John Bean. 1978. Kitanemuk. In *Handbook of North American Indians.* Vol. 8: *California,* edited by Robert F. Heizer, 550–574. Washington, DC: Smithsonian Institution.

Blevins, Juliette. 1993. Klamath Laryngeal Phonology. IJAL 59:237–279.

———. 2002. Notes on Sources of Yurok Glottalized Consonants. In *2000 Hokan-Penutian Workshop,* 1–18.

———. 2003. Yurok Syllable Weight. IJAL 69:4–24.

———. 2004. A Reconsideration of Yokuts Vowels. IJAL 70:33–51.

———. 2005a. Origins of Northern Costanoan ʃak:en 'six': A Reconsideration of Senary Counting in Utian. IJAL 71:87–101.

———. 2005b. Yurok Verb Classes. IJAL 71:327–349.

Blevins, Juliette, and Andrew Garrett. 2007. The Rise and Fall of *l* Sandhi in California Algic. IJAL 73:72–93.

———. n.d. Yurok Language Project, University of California, Berkeley. Internet web pages: linguistics.berkeley.edu/~yurok.

Blevins, Juliette, and Victor Golla. 2005. A New Mission Indian Manuscript from the San Francisco Bay Area. *Boletín: Journal of the California Mission Studies Association* 22(1):33–61.

Blitz, John H. 1988. Adoption of the Bow in Prehistoric North America. *North American Archaeologist* 9:123–145.

Boas, Franz. 1895. The Indians of British Columbia. Pp. 523–592 in *65th Annual Report of the British Association for the Advancement of Science for 1894.* London.

———. 1905. Anthropometry of Central California. *Bulletin of the American Museum of Natural History* 17(4):347–380.

———, ed. 1909. *Putnam Aniversary Volume.* New York: Stechert.

———, ed. 1911. *Handbook of American Indian Languages.* Part 1. BAE-B 40(1).

———, ed. 1922. *Handbook of American Indian Languages.* Part 2. BAE-B 40(2).

———. 1924. Vocabulary of an Athapascan Tribe of Nicola Valley, British Columbia. IJAL 3:36–38.

Boas, Franz, and Pliny Earle Goddard, eds. 1924. Vocabulary of an Athapascan Dialect of the State of Washington. IJAL 3:39–45.

Boas, Franz, Edward Sapir, Pliny Earle Goddard, and A. L. Kroeber. 1916. Phonetic Transcription of Indian Languages: Report of Committee of American Anthropological Association. *Smithsonian Miscellaneous Collections* 66(6), Publication 2415.

Bommelyn, Loren. 1989. *Xus we-yo: Tolowa (Tututni) Language Dictionary.* Crescent City, CA: Tolowa Language Committee.

———. 1995. *Now You're Talking Tolowa.* Arcata, CA: Center for Indian Community Development, Humboldt State University.

———. 1997. *The Prolegomena to the Tolowa Athabaskan Grammar.* MA thesis in Linguistics, University of Oregon.

Bommelyn, Loren, and T. Givón. 1998. Internal Reconstruction in Tolowa Athabaskan. Pp. 553–622 in *Cuatro Encuentro Internacional de Lingüística en el Noroeste, Tomo I: Lenguas Indígenas,* ed. Zarina Estrada Fernández et al. Hermosillo, Sonora: Editorial Unison.

Boscana, Fr. Gerónimo. 1846. *Chinigchinich: A Historical Account of the Origins, Customs and Traditions of the Indians at the Missionary Establishment of St. Juan Capistrano, Alta California; Called the Acagchemem Nation . . . By the reverend father friar Geronimo Boscana, of the order of Saint Francisco, apostolic missionary at said mission.* Translated from the original Spanish manuscript, by one who was many years a resident of Alta California [Alfred Robinson]. (In Robinson 1846, pp. 227–341.)

———. 1933. *Chinigchinich: A Revised and Annotated Version of Alfred Robinson's Translation of Father Gerónimo Boscana's Historical Account of the Belief, Usages, Customs and Extravagancies of the Indians of this Mission of San Juan Capistrano Called the Acagchemem Tribe.* Edited by P. T. Hanna. [Based on the text in Boscana 1846. Annotations, notes on Luiseño phonetics, and numerous Luiseño and Juaneño words and phrases by J. P. Harrington.] Santa Ana: Fine Arts Press. (Reprinted 1978, Malki Museum Press, with an introduction by William Bright; reprinted 2005, Malki Museum Press, with an introduction by John Johnson.)

———. 1934. *A New Original Version of Boscana's Historical Account of the San Juan Capistrano Indians of Southern California.* Edited by J. P. Harrington. [A Spanish manuscript apparently in Boscana's hand, but not the original of Robinson's translation in Boscana 1846. See Kessler 1979.] Smithsonian Miscellaneous Collections 92(4):1–42.

Bowen, Thomas. 1976. *Seri Prehistory: The Archaeology of the Central Coast of Sonora, Mexico.* Anthropological Papers of the University of Arizona 27.

———. 1983. Seri. In *Handbook of North American Indians.* Vol. 10: *Southwest,* edited by Alfonso Ortiz, 230–249. Washington, DC: Smithsonian Institution.

Bowen, Thomas, and Edward Moser. 1968. Seri Pottery. *The Kiva* 33(3):89–132.

Breschini, Gary S., and Trudy Haversat. 1994. *An Overview of the Esselen Indians of Central Monterey County, California.* Salinas, CA: Coyote Press.

———, eds. 1997a. *Contributions to the Linguistic Prehistory of Central and Baja California.* Salinas, CA: Coyote Press.

———. 1997b. Linguistics and Prehistory: A Case Study from the Monterey Bay Area. In *Contributions to the Linguistic Prehistory of Central and Baja California,* edited by Gary S. Breschini and Trudy Haversat, 127–141. Salinas, CA: Coyote Press.

———. 2004. *The Esselen Indians of the Big Sur Country: The Land and the People.* Salinas, CA: Coyote Press.

Bright, Elizabeth. 1952. Patwin field notes and recordings. In the collection of the Survey of California and Other Indian Languages, University of California, Berkeley. 10 notebooks, manuscripts, and tape recordings.

Bright, Jane O. 1964. The Phonology of Smith River Athapaskan (Tolowa). IJAL 30:101–107.

Bright, William. 1954. Some Northern Hokan Relationships: A Preliminary Report. In *Papers from the Symposium on American Indian Linguistics Held at Berkeley July 7, 1951,* pp. 63–67. UC-PL 10(1).

———. 1956. Glottochronologic Counts of Hokaltecan Material. *Language* 32:42–48.

———. 1957. *The Karok Language.* UC-PL 13.

———. 1958. Karok Names. *Names* 6:172–179.

———. 1960. *Animals of Acculturation in California Indian Languages.* UC-PL 4(4):215–246.

———, ed. 1964. *Studies in Californian Linguistics.* UC-PL 34.

———. 1965a. A Field Guide to Southern California Indian Languages. *UCLA Archaeological Survey, Annual Report* 7, pp. 393–407.

———. 1965b. The History of the Cahuilla Sound System. IJAL 31:241–244.

———. 1965c. Luiseño Phonemics. IJAL 31:342–345.

———. 1967. Karok mákkay < Scottish McKay. *Names* 15:79–80.

———. 1968. *A Luiseño Dictionary.* UC-PL 51.

———. 1974. Three Extinct American Indian Languages of Southern California. In *American Philosophical Society Year Book, 1974,* pp. 573–574. Philadelphia: American Philosophical Society.

———. 1975. The Alliklik Mystery. JCA 2:228–236.

———. 1976. *Variation and Change in Language: Essays by William Bright.* Edited by Anwar S. Dil. Palo Alto, CA: Stanford University Press.

———. 1977. Coyote Steals Fire. In *Northern California Texts,* edited by Victor Golla and Shirley Silver, 3–9. IJAL Native American Text Series 2(2). Chicago: University of Chicago Press.

———, ed. 1978a. *Coyote Stories.* IJAL-NATS Monograph 1. Chicago: University of Chicago Press.

———. 1978b. Sibilants and Naturalness in Aboriginal California. JCA-PL 1:39-63.

———. 1979a. A Karok Myth in "Measured Verse": The Translation of a Performance. JCGBA 1:117–123. (Reprinted in Bright 1984:91–100.)

———. 1979b. Hispanisms in Cahuilla. JCGBA-PL 1:101–116.

———. 1980a. Coyote Gives Acorns and Salmon to Humans. In *Coyote Stories II,* edited by Martha B. Kendall, 46–52. IJAL Native American Text Series, Monograph 6. Chicago: University of Chicago Press.

———. 1980b. Coyote's Journey. *American Indian Culture and Research Journal* 4:21–48. (Reprinted in Bright 1984:101–131.)

———. 1984. *American Indian Linguistics and Literature.* Berlin: Mouton de Gruyter.

———, ed. 1990a. *Collected Works of Edward Sapir.* Volume 5: *American Indian Languages 1.* Berlin: Mouton de Gruyter.

———. 1990b. "With One Lip, With Two Lips": Parallelism in Nahuatl. *Language* 66:437–452.

———, ed. 1992. *Collected Works of Edward Sapir.* Volume 10: *Southern Paiute and Ute Linguistics and Ethnography.* Berlin: Mouton de Gruyter.

———. 1994. *Preliminary Juaneño Vocabulary.* [Based on data of J. P. Harrington, collected ca. 1933, mostly from Anastasia de Majel.] (Posted at www.juaneno.com).

———. 2004. *Native American Placenames of the United States.* Norman: University of Oklahoma Press.

Bright, William, and Elizabeth Bright. 1959. Spanish Words in Patwin. *Romance Philology* 13:161–164. (Reprinted in Bright 1976:116–120.)

Bright, William, and Marcia Bright. 1969. *Archaeology and Linguistics in Prehistoric Southern California.* University of Hawaii Working Papers in Linguistics 1, no. 10. (Revised version in Bright 1976:189–205.)

Bright, William, and Susan Gehr. 2004. *Karuk Dictionary* [interim draft]. Happy Camp, CA: Karuk Tribe of California.

Bright, William, and Jane H. Hill. 1967. The Linguistic History of the Cupeño. In *Studies in Southwestern Ethnolinguistics: Meaning and History in the Languages of the American Southwest* [Festschrift in honor of Harry Hoijer], edited by Dell H. Hymes and William E. Bittle, 351–371. Studies in General Anthropology 3. The Hague: Mouton.

Bright, William, and John McLaughlin. 2000. Inyo Redux. *Names* 48:147–150.

Bright, William, and David L. Olmsted. 1959. A Shasta Vocabulary. *Kroeber Anthropological Society Papers* 20:1–55.

Brightman, Robert. 2004. Jaime de Angulo and Alfred Kroeber: Bohemians and Bourgeois in Berkeley Anthropology. In *Significant Others: Interpersonal and Professional Commitments in Anthropology*, edited by Richard Handler, 158–195. History of Anthropology 10. Madison: University of Wisconsin Press.

Brinton, Daniel G. 1891. *The American Race.* New York: D. C. Hodges.

Broadbent, Sylvia M. 1957. Rumsen I: Methods of Reconstitution. IJAL 23:275–280.

———. 1964. *The Southern Sierra Miwok Language.* UC-PL 38.

Broadbent, Sylvia M., and Catherine A. Callaghan. 1960. Comparative Miwok: A Preliminary Survey. IJAL 26:301–316.

Brown, Alan K. 1973. San Francisco Bay Costanoan. IJAL 39:184–189.

———. 1994. The European Contact of 1772 and Some Later Documentation. In *The Ohlone Past and Present: Native Americans of the San Francisco Bay Region*, edited by Lowell John Bean, 1–42. Ballena Press Anthropological Papers no. 42. Menlo Park, CA: Ballena Press.

———, ed. 2001. *A Description of Distant Roads: Original Journals of the First Expedition into California, 1769–1770, by Juan Crespí.* San Diego: San Diego State University Press.

Brown, Cecil H. 1990. Problems in Distant Genetic Comparison: The Case of Mayan/Wintu. Unpublished manuscript.

Brown, J. C. 2003. Floating Moras and Features in Southern Sierra Miwok. In *Proceedings of the 6th Workshop on American Indigenous Langauges*, edited by Jeanie Castillo, 3–12. Santa Barbara Working Papers in Linguistics 14.

Brugman, Claudia, and Monica Macaulay. 2009. Relevance, Cohesion, and the Storyline: The Discourse Function of the Karuk Particle *káruma. Journal of Pragmatics* 41:1189–1208.

Buckley, Eugene. 1991. Glottalized and Aspirated Sonorants in Kashaya. In *1990 Hokan-Penutian Workshop.*

———. 1994. Persistent and cumulative extrametricality in Kashaya. *Natural Language and Linguistic Theory* 12:423–464.

Buckley, Thomas. 1984. Yurok Speech Registers and Ontology. *Language in Society* 13:467–488.

Bunte, Pamela. 1979. *Problems in Southern Paiute Syntax and Semantics.* PhD dissertation, Indiana University, Bloomington.

Burrus, Ernest J., S.J. 1956. Pioneer Jesuit Apostles among the Indians of New Spain (1572–1604). *Archivum Historicum Societas Jesu* 25:574–597.

———. 1966. *Wenceslaus Linck's Diary of His 1766 Expedition to Northern Baja California.* Los Angeles: Dawson's Book Shop.

———. 1967. *Ducrue's Account of the Expulsion of the Jesuits from Lower California (1767–1769).* Sources and Studies for the History of the Americas, vol. 2. Rome: Jesuit Historical Institute.

Burrus, Ernest J., S.J., and Felix Zubillaga, S.J., eds. 1982. *Misiones mexicanas de la Compañía de Jesus 1618–1745: Cartas e informes conservados en la "Colección Mateu."* Madrid: Editorial José Porrua Turanzas.

Buschmann, Johann Carl Eduard. 1859. Die Spuren der Aztekischen Sprache in Nördlichen Mexico und Höheren Amerikanischen Norden. *Abhandlungen der Königlichen Akademie der Wissenschaften,* 1854, Supplement-Band II: 512–576. Berlin.

Buszard-Welcher, Laura, ed. 2002. *Proceedings of the Meeting of the Hokan-Penutian Workshop, June 17–18, 2000, University of California at Berkeley.* Survey of California and Other Indian Languages, Report 11. Berkeley: Department of Linguistics, University of California.

Buszard-Welcher, Laura, and Leanne Hinton. 2002. Survey of California and Other Indian Languages Receives Eero Vihman's Northern Pomo Materials. *SSILA Newsletter* 21(1):10–12.

Callaghan, Catherine A. 1962. Comparative Miwok-Mutsun with Notes on Rumsen. IJAL 28:97–107.

———. 1963. *A Grammar of the Lake Miwok Language.* PhD dissertation, University of California, Berkeley.

———. 1964a. Phonemic Borrowing in Lake Miwok. In *Studies in Californian Linguistics,* edited by William Bright, 46–53. UC-PL 34.

———. 1964b. [Field notes on the Tomales Bay dialect of Marin Miwok, from Mrs. Elgin.] MS.

———. 1965. *Lake Miwok Dictionary.* UC-PL 39.

———. 1967. Miwok-Costanoan as a Subfamily of Penutian. IJAL 33:224–227.

———. 1970. *Bodega Miwok Dictionary.* UC-PL 60.

———. 1971. Saclan: A Reexamination. AL 13:448–456.

———. 1972. Proto-Miwok Phonology. *General Linguistics* 12:1–31.

———. 1975. J. P. Harrington—California's Great Linguist. JCA 2:183–187.

———. 1976. Comment on "A Note on Harrington and Kroeber." JCA 3:147. (Reply to Heizer 1975b.)

———. 1977. Coyote the Imposter (Lake Miwok Text). In *Northern California Texts*, edited by Victor Golla and Shirley Silver, 10–16. IJAL Native American Text Series 2(2). Chicago: University of Chicago Press.

———. 1978a. Lake Miwok. In *Handbook of North American Indians*. Vol. 8: *California*, edited by Robert F. Heizer, 264–272. Washington, DC: Smithsonian Institution.

———. 1978b. Fire, Flood, and Creation (Lake Miwok Text). In *Coyote Stories*, edited by William Bright, 62–86. IJAL-NATS Monograph 1. Chicago: University of Chicago Press.

———. 1979. The Reconstruction of *Two* and Related Words in Proto-Miwok. IJAL 45:176–181. (Critique of Silverstein 1975. See Silverstein 1979b.)

———. 1980a. Coyote's Knee Rock (Lake Miwok Text). In *Coyote Stories II*, edited by Martha B. Kendall, 81–87. IJAL Native American Text Series, Monograph 6. Chicago: University of Chicago Press.

———. 1980b. An "Indo-European" Type Paradigm in Proto Eastern Miwok. In *American Indian and Indoeuropean Studies: Papers in Honor of Madison S. Beeler*, edited by Kathryn A. Klar, Margaret Langdon, and Shirley Silver, 31–41. The Hague: Mouton.

———. 1981. Spanish Loan Words in Northern Sierra Miwok. *Romance Philology* 35:335–343.

———. 1982. Proto Utian Derivational Noun Morphology. In *1981 Hokan-Penutian Workshop*.

———. 1983. Proto Utian Derivational Verb Morphology. In *1982 Hokan-Penutian Workshop*.

———. 1984. *Plains Miwok Dictionary*. UC-PL 105.

———. 1986a. Miwok Ablaut Grades. In *1983–85 Hokan-Penutian Workshop*, pp. 105–114.

———. 1986b. Miwok Cardinal Direction Terms. In *1983–85 Hokan-Penutian Workshops*.

———. 1986c. Patridominance and Proto Utian Words for 'Man', 'Woman', and 'Person'. In *1983–85 Hokan-Penutian Workshops*.

———. 1986d. Proto Utian Independent Pronouns. In *1983–85 Hokan-Penutian Workshops*.

———. 1987. *Northern Sierra Miwok Dictionary*. UC-PL 110.

———. 1988a. Karkin Revisited. IJAL 54:436–452.

———. 1988b. Proto Utian Stems. In *In Honor of Mary Haas: From the Haas Festival Conference on Native American Linguistics*, edited by William F. Shipley, 53–75. Berlin: Mouton de Gruyter.

———. 1990. Proto-Costanoan Numerals. IJAL 56:121–133.

———. 1991. Encounter with John P. Harrington. AL 33:350–356.

———. 1992a. The Riddle of Rumsen. IJAL 58:36–48.

———. 1992b. Utian and the Swadesh List. In *1991 Hokan-Penutian Workshop*, pp. 218–237.

———. 1994. Proto-Miwok Numerals. IJAL 60:161–176.

———. 1997a. Evidence for Yok-Utian. IJAL 63:18–64.

———. 1997b. Julpun: My Home Town Language. In *1996 Hokan-Penutian Workshop*, pp. 1–5.

———. 2001. More Evidence for Yok-Utian: A Reanalysis of the Dixon and Kroeber Sets. IJAL 67:313–345.

———. 2004. How Coyote Remade the World. In *Voices from Four Directions: Contemporary Translations of the Native Literatures of North America*, edited by Brian Swann, 226–239. Lincoln: University of Nebraska Press.

———. 2006. Evidence for an Esselen Substrate in Utian. Paper delivered at the 2006 Annual Meeting of the Society for the Study of the Indigenous Languages of the Americas, Albuquerque, New Mexico, January 5–8, 2006.

———. n.d.[a]. *Lake Miwok Grammar*. MS.

———. n.d.[b]. *Comparative Utian Grammar and Dictionary with Notes on Yokuts*. MS.

Callaghan, Catherine A., and Zinny Bond. n.d. *Marin Miwok Dictionary*. MS.

Callaghan, Catherine A., and Geoffrey Gamble. 1996. Borrowing. In *Handbook of North American Indians*. Vol. 17: *Languages*, edited by Ives Goddard, 111–116. Washington, DC: Smithsonian Institution.

Campbell, Lyle. 1997. *American Indian Languages: The Historical Linguistics of Native America*. New York: Oxford University Press.

Campbell, Lyle, and Marianne Mithun, eds. 1979. *The Languages of Native America: Historical and Comparative Assessment*. Austin: University of Texas Press.

Campbell, Lyle, and David Oltrogge. 1980. Proto-Tol (Jicaque). IJAL 46:205–223.

Charney, Jean O. 1993. *A Grammar of Comanche*. Lincoln: University of Nebraska Press.

Chase-Dunn, Christopher, and Kelly M. Mann. 1998. *The Wintu and Their Neighbors: A Very Small World-System in Northern California*. Tucson: University of Arizona Press.

Choris, Louis. 1822. *Voyage pittoresque autour du monde, avec des portraits de sauvages d'Amérique, d'Asie, d'Afrique, et des îles du Grand océan; des paysages, des vues maritimes, et plusieurs objets d'histoire naturelle; accompagné de descriptions par m. le baron Cuvier, et m. A. de Chamisso, et d'observations sur les crânes humains, par m. le docteur Gall*. Paris: Impr. de Firmin Didot.

Chung, Sandra. 1994. Remarks on Pablo Tac's *La lingua degli Indi Luiseños*. IJAL 40:292–307.

Chung, Sandra, and Jorge Hankamer, eds. 1991. *A Festschrift for William F. Shipley*. Santa Cruz: Syntax Research Center, University of California, Santa Cruz.

Clavigero, Francisco Saverio. 1789. *Storia della California*. 2 vols. Venice: Fenzo. [Data on Cochimi, 1:110–111, 264–266.] (Spanish translation, *Historia de la Antigua o Baja California*, edited by Miguel León-Portilla. Mexico City: Porrúa, 1970.)

Clewett, S. Edward, and Elaine Sundahl. 1990. A View from the South: Connections between Southwest Oregon and Northern California. In *Living with the Land: The Indians of Southwest Oregon*, edited by Nan Hannon and Richard K. Olmo, 37–45. [The Proceedings of the 1989 Symposium on the Prehistory of Southwest Oregon.] Medford: Southern Oregon Historical Society.

Collier, Mary E. T., and Sylvia B. Thalman, eds. 1996. [Isabel Kelly's] *Interviews with Tom Smith and Maria Copa*. Miwok Archaeological Preserve of Marin, Occasional Papers Number 6. San Rafael. (Publication of Kelly 1931–1932.)

Collins, James. 1985. Pronouns, Markedness, and Stem Change in Tolowa. IJAL 51:358–372.

———. 1989. Nasalization, Lengthening, and Phonological Rhyme in Tolowa. IJAL 55:326–340.

———. 1998. *Understanding Tolowa Histories: Western Hegemonies and Native American Responses*. New York: Routledge.

Collord, Thomas L. 1968. *Yokuts Grammar: Chukchansi*. PhD dissertation, University of California, Berkeley.

Comelias, Fr. Juan. 1860. Santa Cruz Vocabulary. In *The Indianology of California* [see A. Taylor 1860–1863], 13.8. (Reprinted in Powers 1877 and in Kroeber 1910:242–249.)

Comrie, Bernard. 1999. Haruai Numerals and their Implications for the History and Typology of Numeral Systems. In *Numeral Types and Changes Worldwide*, edited by Jadranka Gvozdanović, 81–94. Berlin: Mouton de Gruyter.

———. 2005. Numeral Bases. In *The World Atlas of Linguistic Structures*, edited by Martin Haspelmath, Matthew S. Dryer, David Gil, and Bernard Comrie, 530–533. Oxford, UK: Oxford University Press.

———. 2007. Endangered Numeral Systems of the Americas and Their Theoretical Relevance. Paper presented at the Annual Meeting of the Society for the Study of the Indigenous Languages of the Americas, Anaheim, California, January 2007.

Conathan, Lisa. 2002. Split Intransitivity and Possession in Chimariko. In *Proceedings of the 50th Anniversary Conference, June 8–9, 2002, University of California at Berkeley,* edited by Lisa Conathan and Teresa McFarland, 18–31. Survey of California and Other Indian Languages, Report 12. Berkeley: Department of Linguistics, University of California.

———. 2004. *The Linguistic Ecology of Northwestern California: Contact, Functional Convergence and Dialectology.* PhD dissertation, University of California, Berkeley.

———. 2006. Recovering Sociolinguistic Context from Early Sources: The Case of Northwestern California. AL 48:209–232.

Conathan, Lisa, and Tess Wood. 2003. Repetitive Reduplication in Yurok and Karuk: Semantic Effects of Contact. In *Papers of the Thirty-fourth Algonquian Conference,* edited by H. C. Wolfart, 19–33. Winnipeg: University of Manitoba.

———. n.d. Synopsis of A. L. Kroeber's Yurok Field Notes. In *Yurok Language Project.* Internet Web pages: linguistics. berkeley.edu/~yurok. University of California, Berkeley.

Cook, Sherburne F. 1957. The Aboriginal Population of Alameda and Contra Costa Counties, California. UC-AR 16(4):131–156.

———. 1974. The Esselen: Territory, Villages and Population. *Quarterly of the Monterey County Archaeological Society* 3(2). Carmel, CA.

———. 1976. *The Conflict between the California Indian and White Civilization.* Berkeley: University of California Press. (Contains "The Indians versus the Spanish Mission," 1–194.)

Cook, Sherburne F., and Cesare Marino. 1988. Roman Catholic Missions in California and the Southwest. In *Handbook of North American Indians.* Vol. 4: *History of Indian-White Relations,* edited by Wilcomb E. Washburn, 472–480. Washington, DC: Smithsonian Institution.

Corbusier, William. 1873–1875. Apache-Mojave or Yavape; and Apache-Yuma or Tulkepaia 1873–1875. NAA MS 2249-a, National Anthropological Archives, Smithsonian Institution.

———. 1885. Mojave or Hamokaba Vocabulary early 1885. NAA MS 2071, National Anthropological Archives, Smithsonian Institution.

———. 1923–1924. Wallapai Indian Words, Phrases and Sentences, and the Story How Wolf's Son Became a Star 1923 and 1924. 44 pp., typescript. NAA MS 2259, National Anthropological Archives, Smithsonian Institution.

Cortés, Fr. Juan (?). 1798–1805. Prayers and Catechism in the Language of the Mission of Santa Barbara, California. [Also an Act of Faith by Fr. Uria]. Transcript in the hand of John Gilmary Shea. 36 leaves. John G. Shea Papers, Box 7, Folder 13, Special Collections Division, Georgetown University Library,

Washington, DC. (Attributed to Fr. Estevan Tapis, but most likely a copy of the Cortés manuscript published in Kelsey 1979.)

Costansó, Miguel. 1770. *Diario histórico de los viages de mar y tierra hechos al norte de la California.* Mexico City: Imprenta del Superior Gobierno. [Includes (Barbareño) Chumash vocabulary.] (Published in English and Spanish as *The Narrative of the Portolá Expedition of 1769–1770,* edited by Adolph van Hemert Engert and Frederick J. Teggart, Berkeley: University of California, 1910. Also published as *The Costansó Narrative of the Portolá Expedition: First Chronicle of the Spanish Conquest of Alta California,* translated, with an introduction and bibliography, by Ray Brandes [includes facsimile edition of the original publication], Newhall, CA: Hogarth Press, 1970; reprinted 1985, San Bernardino: Borgo Press.)

Coulter, Thomas. 1841. [Vocabularies of Pima, San Diego (Diegueño), Santa Barbara (Barbareño Chumash), San Luis Obispo (Obispeño Chumash), and San Antonio (Antoniano Salinan).] In John Scouler, Observations on the Indigenous Tribes of the North West Coast of America. *Journal of the Royal Geographical Society* (London) 11:215–251. (Reprinted in Hale 1846:569–629, and in Gallatin 1848:126–129; Barbareño and Obispeño vocabularies reprinted in normalized phonetic orthography in Kroeber 1910:265–267.)

Couro, Ted, and Christina Hutcheson. 1973. *Dictionary of Mesa Grande Diegueño.* With introduction and notes by Margaret Langdon. Banning, CA: Malki Museum Press.

Couro, Ted, and Margaret Langdon. 1975. *Let's Talk 'Iipay Aa.* Banning, CA: Malki Museum Press.

Cowan, Robert Ernest. 1933. Alexander S. Taylor, 1817–1876— First Bibliographer of California. *California Historical Society Quarterly* 12:18–24.

Cowan, William, ed. 1991. *Papers of the Twenty-Second Algonquian Conference.* Ottawa: Carleton University.

Cowan, William, Michael K. Foster, and Konrad Koerner, eds. 1986. *New Perspectives in Language, Culture, and Personality.* Amsterdam: John Benjamins.

Crawford, James M. 1966. *The Cocopa Language.* PhD dissertation, University of California, Berkeley.

———. 1970. Cocopa Baby Talk. IJAL 36:9–13.

———. 1973. Yuchi Phonology. IJAL 39:173–179.

———. 1978. More on Cocopa Baby Talk. IJAL 44:17–23.

———. 1979. Spanish Loan Words in Cocopa. JCGBA-PL 1:117–132.

———. 1983. *Cocopa Texts.* UC-PL 100.

———. 1989. *Cocopa Dictionary.* UC-PL 114.

Crawford, Judith G. 1976. Seri and Yuman. In *Hokan Studies: Papers from the First Conference on Hokan Languages,* edited by Margaret Langdon and Shirley Silver, 305–324. The Hague: Mouton.

Cressman, Luther S. 1956. *Klamath Prehistory: The Prehistory of the Culture of the Klamath Lake Area, Oregon.* Transactions of the American Philosophical Society 46(4):375–513. Philadelphia. American Philosophical Society.

———. 1977. *Prehistory of the Far West: Homes of Vanished Peoples.* Salt Lake City: University of Utah Press.

Crook, Lt. (later Gen.) George. 1852–1861. Klamath River Vocabularies; Aliquah [Yurok], Arra-Arra [Karok], Hopah [Hupa] ca. 1852–1861. NAA MS 209, National Anthropological Archives, Smithsonian Institution. 31 pp.

Crum, Beverly, and Jon Dayley. 1993. *Western Shoshoni Grammar.* Occasional Papers and Monographs in Cultural

Anthropology and Linguistics 1. Pocatello, ID: Department of Anthropology, Boise State University.

Curtin, Jeremiah. 1884a. Yana vocabulary, October 11, 1884. NAA MS 2060, National Anthropological Archives, Smithsonian Institution. 149 pp.

———. 1884b. Wintun vocabulary, October 1884. NAA MS 1453, National Anthropological Archives, Smithsonian Institution. 93 pp.

———. 1884c. Wintu Myths, Tales and Words, 1884. NAA MS 2170, National Anthropological Archives, Smithsonian Institution. 250 sheets.

———. 1884d. Atsugei vocabulary, ca. 1884. NAA MS 2059, National Anthropological Archives, Smithsonian Institution. 72 pp.

———. 1884e. Saia [Nongatl] vocabulary, November 1884. NAA MS 1458, National Anthropological Archives, Smithsonian Institution. 119 pp.

———. 1884f. Vocabularies of Napa [Coast Miwok], Niles [Chocheño Costanoan], Stockton [Plains Miwok], and Suisun [Southern Patwin], November 1884. NAA MS 1456, National Anthropological Archives, Smithsonian Institution. 28 pp. (Mistakenly catalogued as "Wappo." Also contains items in Karuk, "Wailaki" [apparently Shastan, not Athabaskan], and "Tamukan" and "Tawitci" dialects of Delta Yokuts. Cf. Curtin 1889k.)

———. 1884–1885a. Modoc text. NAA MS 3799, National Anthropological Archives, Smithsonian Institution. 22 pp.

———. 1884–1885b. Modoc-English and English-Modoc vocabularies. NAA MS 1762, National Anthropological Archives, Smithsonian Institution. 30 pp.

———. 1884–1885c. Modoc myths, tales and words, collected in Oklahoma and California, 1885, 1888 [1884, 1885]. NAA MS 2569, National Anthropological Archives, Smithsonian Institution.

———. 1884–1889a. 32 Yanan myths. NAA MS 1296, National Anthropological Archives, Smithsonian Institution. 105 pp.

———. 1884–1889b. Yana vocabulary, 1884, 1889. NAA MS 953, National Anthropological Archives, Smithsonian Institution. 89 pp.

———. 1884–1889c. Personal names of the Wintun. NAA MS 2864, National Anthropological Archives, Smithsonian Institution. 600 cards.

———. 1884–1889d. Wintu words and names. NAA MS 1763, National Anthropological Archives, Smithsonian Institution. 23 pp.

———. 1885a. 55 Shasta myths. NAA MS 1295, National Anthropological Archives, Smithsonian Institution. ca. 102 pp.

———. 1885b. Autiréitcu-is (Shásti), July 13, 1885. NAA MS 709, National Anthropological Archives, Smithsonian Institution. 87 pp.

———. 1885c. Adzomawi Myths, 1887? [1885]. NAA MS 1298, National Anthropological Archives, Smithsonian Institution. 23 pp.

———. 1888–1889a. Wintun stories, ca. 1888–1889. NAA MS 3535, National Anthropological Archives, Smithsonian Institution. 218 pp.

———. 1888–1889b. Wintun vocabulary, 1888–1889. NAA MS 841, National Anthropological Archives, Smithsonian Institution. 78 pp.

———. 1888–1889c. Hupa vocabulary, December 1888–January 1889. NAA MS 1442, National Anthropological Archives, Smithsonian Institution. 107 pp.

———. 1888–1889d. Hupa vocabulary, December 1888–January 1889. NAA MS 2063, National Anthropological Archives, Smithsonian Institution. 117 pp.

———. 1888–1889e. Miscellaneous Hupa materials, ca. 1888. NAA MS 667, National Anthropological Archives, Smithsonian Institution.

———. 1889a. Tcimariko vocabulary, 1889. NAA MS 1451, National Anthropological Archives, Smithsonian Institution. 71 pp.

———. 1889b. Pulikla [Yurok] vocabulary, January and February 1889. NAA MS 1459, National Anthropological Archives, Smithsonian Institution. 79 pp.

———. 1889c. Fifteen untitled Karok stories, May 1889. NAA MS 269, National Anthropological Archives, Smithsonian Institution. ca. 195 pp.

———. 1889d. Ehnikan (Karok) vocabulary, June-July 1889. NAA MS 847, National Anthropological Archives, Smithsonian Institution. 81 pp.

———. 1889e. Karok vocabulary, June and July, 1889. NAA MS 1450, National Anthropological Archives, Smithsonian Institution. 111 pp.

———. 1889f. Kowihl (Wishoskan) [Wiyot] vocabulary, 1889. NAA MS 1457, National Anthropological Archives, Smithsonian Institution. 62 pp.

———. 1889g. Batawat [Wiyot] vocabulary. NAA MS 1455, National Anthropological Archives, Smithsonian Institution. 67 pp.

———. 1889h. Yuki vocabulary, September 1889. NAA MS 3281, National Anthropological Archives, Smithsonian Institution. 49 pp.

———. 1889i. [Yuki and Achumawi] vocabulary. NAA MS 1452, National Anthropological Archives, Smithsonian Institution. 118 pp. (Also contains a few Maidu and Wintu terms.)

———. 1889j. Ilmawi (Pit River) vocabulary, [September-] October 1889. NAA MS 1454, National Anthropological Archives, Smithsonian Institution. 54 pp.

———. 1889k. Numerals from 1–10 in languages spoken at Napa [Coast Miwok], San Jose [Chocheño Costanoan], Stockton [Plains Miwok], and Suisun [Patwin]; vocabulary of 17 words in Stockton. Redding, CA, November 4, 1889. NAA MS 3701, National Anthropological Archives, Smithsonian Institution. 2 pp. (Mistakenly catalogued as "Wappo." Cf. Curtin 1884f.)

———. 1898. *Creation Myths of Primitive America in Relation to the Religious History and Mental Development of Mankind.* Boston: Little, Brown. (Republished 2002 as *Creation Myths of Primitive America*, edited and with an introduction by Karl Kroeber. Santa Barbara, CA: ABC-CLIO.)

———. 1940. *The Memoirs of Jeremiah Curtin.* Edited with Notes and Introduction by Joseph Schafer. Madison: State Historical Society of Wisconsin.

Curtis, Edward S. 1907–1930. *The North American Indian: Being a Series of Volumes Picturing and Describing the Indians of the United States, The Dominion of Canada, and Alaska,* edited by Frederick W. Hodge. 20 volumes. [Volume 2 has vocabularies of Mojave and Yuma (123–128). Volume 9 has a vocabulary of Lower Columbia Athabaskan (199–200). Volume 13 has vocabularies of Hupa and Tolowa (243–253); Shasta, Achumawi, and Karuk (253–262); Yurok and Wiyot (263–272); and Klamath (272–276). Volume 14 has vocabularies of Kato and Wailaki (201–207); Yuki and Wappo (207–214); Eastern, Northern and Central Pomo (214–220);

Wintu, Nomlaki, and Patwin (220–229); Chico and Konkow Maidu (229–237); Central and Southern Sierra Miwok (237–243); and Chukchansi Yokuts (244–247). Volume 15 has vocabularies of Cupeño, Luiseño, and Cahuilla (173–179); Northern Diegueño (179–182); Mono and Paviotso (182–188); and Washo (188–192). All of these vocabularies were collected by William E. Myers.] Norwood, MA: Plimpton Press. (Reprinted 1970. New York: Johnson Reprint.)

Cutter, Donald C. 1960. *Malaspina in California*. San Francisco: J. Howell.

———. 1990. *California in 1792: A Spanish Naval Visit*. Norman: University of Oklahoma Press.

Dana, James Dwight. 1846. [Vocabularies of Saste (Shasta), Upper Sacramento (Nomlaki), Talatūi (Plains Miwok), and Pujūni, Sekumné, and Tsamak (Valley Nisenan).] In Hale 1846:569–629, 630–634. (Reprinted in Gallatin 1848:122–125, and in Powers 1877.)

Dangberg, Grace M. 1922. The Washo Language. *Nevada State Historical Society Papers* 3:145–152.

———. 1925. *Washo Grammar*. EDDMA, no. 4. 153 pp.

———. 1927. *Washo Texts*. UC-PAAE 22(3):391–443.

———. 1968. *Washo Tales: Three Original Washo Indian Legends*. Nevada State Museum, Occasional Papers No. 1. Carson City: Nevada State Museum.

Darden, Bill J. 1985. CV Phonology and Klamath. IJAL 51:384–387.

Darnell, Regna, and Judith Irvine, eds. 1994. *Collected Works of Edward Sapir*. Vol. 4: *Ethnology*. Berlin: Mouton de Gruyter.

David, Andrew, Felipe Fernández-Armesto, Carlos Novi, and Glyndwr Williams, eds. 2003. *The Malaspina Expedition 1789–1794. The Journal of the Voyage by Alejandro Malaspina*. Vol. 2: *Panama to the Philippines*. London: Hakluyt Society.

Davis, James T. 1961. *Trade Routes and Economic Exchange among the Indians of California*. University of California, Archaeological Survey, Report 54. (Reprinted in Heizer 1963:1–80. Republished 1974, edited by Robert F. Heizer. Ramona, CA: Ballena Press.)

Davis, John F. 1973. *A Partial Grammar of Simplex and Complex Sentences in Luiseño*. PhD dissertation, University of California, Los Angeles.

———. 1976. Some Notes on Luiseño Phonology. IJAL 42:192–216.

Davis, Nancy Yaw. 2000. *The Zuni Enigma: A Native American People's Possible Japanese Connection*. New York: Norton.

Davis, William E. 1970. A Swedish Gem in Idaho's Shining Mountains: Portrait of a Scholar. In *Languages and Cultures of Western North America: Essays in Honor of Sven S. Liljeblad*, edited by Earl H. Swanson, Jr., 1–14. Pocatello: Idaho State University Press.

Dayley, Jon P. 1989. *Tümpisa (Panamint) Shoshone Grammar*. UC-PL 115.

———. 1990. *Tümpisa (Panamint) Shoshone Dictionary*. UC-PL 116.

d'Azevedo, Warren L. 1986. Washoe. In *Handbook of North American Indians*. Vol. 11: *Great Basin*, edited by Warren L. d'Azevedo, 466–498. Washington, DC: Smithsonian Institution.

de Angulo [Mayo], Gui. 1995. *The Old Coyote of Big Sur: The Life of Jaime de Angulo*. Berkeley: Stonegarden Press.

de Angulo, Jaime. 1926. Two Parallel Modes of Conjugation in the Pit River Language. AA 28:273–274.

———. 1927. Texte en Langue Pomo. *Journal de la Société des Americanistes de Paris* 19:129–144.

———. 1928. Konomihu vocabulary, obtained at Selma, Oregon. MS. 30(H1c.5), Library of the American Philosophical Society, Philadelphia. 4 pp. (Copy in SCOIL archives, Angulo 006.)

———. 1929. The Patwin language. MS. 30(P4b.1–4), Library of the American Philosophical Society, Philadelphia. 125 pp.

———. 1930–1935. Pomo semasiology. MS. 30(H5.2), Library of the American Philosophical Society, Philadelphia. 32 pp. (Copy in SCOIL archives, Angulo 005)

———. ca. 1931. A comparison between the semasiologies of two languages of the so-called Hokan family (Pomo and Achumawi). MS. 30(H.1), Library of the American Philosophical Society, Philadelphia. 231 pp.

———. 1935. Pomo Creation Myth. JAF 48(189):203–262. (Same text as in de Angulo and Benson 1932.)

———. ca. 1935a. The reminiscences of a Pomo chief [autobiography of William Ralganal Benson; text in Central Pomo, translation and linguistic analysis]. MS. 30(H5.3), Library of the American Philosophical Society, Philadelphia. 306 pp.

———. ca. 1935b. The Pomo language. MS. 30(H5.1), Library of the American Philosophical Society, Philadelphia. 49 pp. (Typed copy, "The Pomo Language II: The Yukaya Dialect," SCOIL archives, Angulo 004.002.)

———. 1950. Indians in Overalls. *Hudson Review,* Autumn 1950. (Published in book form by the Turtle Island Founation, San Francisco, 1973.)

———. 1953. *Indian Tales, Written and Illustrated by Jaime de Angulo*. With a Foreword by Carl Carmer. New York: Hill and Wang.

———. n.d.[a]. Reminiscences of an Achumawi youth. MS. 30(H1a.5), Library of the American Philosophical Society, Philadelphia. 22 pp.

———. n.d.[b]. Conversational texts in Achumawi. MS. 30(H1a.1), Library of the American Philosophical Society, Philadelphia. 72 pp.

de Angulo, Jaime, and William Ralganal Benson. 1932. The Creation Myth of the Pomo Indians. *Anthropos* 27(1–2): 261–274; 27(5–6):779–795. (Same text as in de Angulo 1935.)

de Angulo, Jaime, and L. S. Freeland. 1920–1935. The Clear Lake dialect of the Pomo language in north-central California. MS. 30(H5.4), Library of the American Philosophical Society, Philadelphia. 219 pp. (2nd copy or draft in SCOIL archives, Angulo 003.001, 157 pp.)

———. 1928–1930. The Shasta language. MS. 30(H1c.1), Library of the American Philosophical Society, Philadelphia. 254 pp.

———. 1929a. Notes on the Northern Paiute of California. *Journal de la Société des Americanistes de Paris* 21:313–335.

———. 1929b. The Atsugewi language. MS. 30(H1b.1), Library of the American Philosophical Society, Philadelphia. 71 pp.

———. 1930. The Achumawi Language. IJAL 6:77–120. (See Olmsted 1966:5.)

———. 1931a. Karok Texts. IJAL 6:194–226.

———. 1931b. The Lutuami Language (Klamath-Modoc). *Journal de la Société des Americanistes de Paris* 23:1–45.

———. 1931c. Two Achumawi Tales. JAF 44:125–136.

———. 1931–1935. Appendix of addenda and corrigenda to the grammar of the Achumawi language. MS. 30(H1a.6), Library of the American Philosophical Society, Philadelphia. 67 pp. (Uldall 1933 was apparently once part of this document.)

————. ca. 1931. Achumawi texts. MS. 30(H1a.7), Library of the American Philosophical Society, Philadelphia. 156 pp.

————. n.d.[a]. Short vocabulary in Yurok. MS. 30(A7.1), Library of the American Philosophical Society, Philadelphia. 30 pp.

————. n.d.[b]. Parallel Achumawi and Atsugewi texts. MS. 30(H1a.2), Library of the American Philosophical Society, Philadelphia. 11 pp.

————. n.d.[c]. Conversational text in Atsugewi. MS. 30(H1b.2), Library of the American Philosophical Society, Philadelphia. 19 pp. (Seems originally to have been part of de Angulo and Freeland 1929b.)

de Angulo, Jaime, and Hans Jørgen Uldall. 1932. Pomo [phonetic sample of Eastern Pomo]. *Le Maître Phonétique* 37:506.

DeLancey, Scott. 1987. Klamath and Wintu Pronouns. IJAL 53:461–464.

————. 1988a. Morphological Parallels between Klamath and Wintu. In *1987 Hokan-Penutian Workshop,* pp. 50–60.

————. 1988b. Klamath Stem Structure in Genetic and Areal Perspective. In *1988 Hokan-Penutian Workshop,* pp. 31–39.

————. 1991. Chronological Strata of Suffix Classes in the Klamath Verb. IJAL 57:426–445.

————. 1992. Klamath and Sahaptian Numerals. IJAL 58:235–239.

————. 1996. Penutian in the Bipartite Stem Belt: Disentangling Areal and Genetic Correspondences. In *Proceedings of the 22nd Annual Meeting of the Berkeley Linguistics Society.* Berkeley: Department of Linguistics, University of California.

————. 1999. Lexical Prefixes and the Bipartite Stem Construction in Klamath. IJAL 65:56–83.

————. 2006. Inland Penutian: Problems and Possibilities in Mid-range Comparison. Keynote address, Workshop in American Indigenous Languages, University of California, Santa Barbara, April 2006.

DeLancey, Scott, Carol Genetti, and Noel Rude. 1988. Some Sahaptian-Klamath-Tsimshianic Lexical Sets. In *In Honor of Mary Haas: From the Haas Festival Conference on Native American Linguistics,* edited by William F. Shipley, 195–224. Berlin: Mouton de Gruyter.

DeLancey, Scott, and Victor Golla. 1997. The Penutian Hypothesis: Retrospect and Prospect. IJAL 63:171–202.

Demetracopoulou [Lee], Dorothy. 1933. The Loon Woman Myth: A Study in Synthesis. JAF 46(180):101–128.

Demetracopoulou [Lee], Dorothy, and Cora A. Du Bois. 1932. A Study of Wintu Mythology. JAF 45(178):375–500.

de Mofras, Eugène Duflot. See Duflot de Mofras, Eugène

Denny, J. Peter. 1991. The Algonquian Migration from Plateau to Midwest: Linguistics and Archaeology. In *Papers of the Twenty-Second Algonquian Conference,* edited by William Cowan, 103–124. Ottawa: Carleton University.

Devereux, George. 1949. Mohave Voice and Speech Mannerisms. *Word* 5:268–272. (Reprinted in Hymes 1964:267–271.)

————. 1951. Mohave Indian Verbal and Motor Profanity. In *Psychoanalysis and the Social Sciences,* edited by Geza Roheim, 99–127. New York: International University Press.

Diamond, Stanley, ed. 1960. *Culture in History: Essays in Honor of Paul Radin.* New York: Columbia University Press.

Dick, Russell, Ed Williams, and Arie Poldervaart. 1987. *Yerington Paiute Grammar.* Yerington, NV: Yerington Paiute Tribe. (Also published by Bilingual Education Services, Anchorage, Alaska.)

Diehl, Israel S. 1854. Partial copy by A. S. Gatschet of Diehl's vocabulary [of Nisenan, 1854], and original vocabulary by Diehl. NAA MS 646-d, National Anthropological Archives, Smithsonian Institution. 6 pp. [Marked "Utterly worthless— J.C.P." in the hand of James Constantine Pilling.]

Dixon, Roland B. 1900. *The language of the Maidu Indians of California.* PhD dissertation, Harvard University, Cambridge, MA.

————. 1904. [Review of P. Goddard 1903a, 1904.] AA 6:712–716.

————. 1905a. The Northern Maidu. *Bulletin of the American Museum of Natural History* 17 (Part 3):119–346.

————. 1905b. The Shasta-Achomawi: A New Linguistic Stock, with Four Dialects. AA 7:213–217.

————. 1906. Linguistic Relationships within the Shasta-Achomawi Stock. *Proceedings of the 15th International Congress of Americanists,* pp. 255-263. Quebec: Dussault-Proulx.

————. 1907. The Shasta. *American Museum of Natural History Bulletin* 7:381–498.

————. 1908–1910. Shasta texts. MS. 30(H1c.2), Library of the American Philosophical Society, Philadelphia. 6 notebooks. (Partially revised for publication in Dixon and Freeland 1928–1930.)

————. 1909. Outlines of Wintu Grammar. In *Putnam Aniversary Volume.,* edited by Franz Boas, pp. 461–479. New York: Stechert.

————. 1910. *The Chimariko Indians and Language.* UC-PAAE 5(5):293–380.

————. 1911. Maidu. In *Handbook of American Indian Languages,* Part 1, edited by Franz Boas, pp. 679–734. BAE-B 40(1).

————. 1912. *Maidu Texts.* Publications of the American Ethnological Society 4. Leiden: Brill.

————. 1931. Dr. Merriam's "Tló-hom-tah´-hoi". AA 33:264–267.

Dixon, Roland B., and L. S. Freeland. 1928-30. Shasta texts, originally collected by Roland B. Dixon; ed. and rev. by Lucy S. Freeland. MS. 30(H1c.3), Library of the American Philosophical Society, Philadelphia. 221 pp. (Based on Dixon 1908–1910.)

Dixon, Roland B., and Alfred L. Kroeber. 1903. The Native Languages of California. AA 5:1–26.

————. 1907. Numeral Systems of the Languages of California. AA 9:663–690.

————. 1913. New Linguistic Families in California. AA 15:647–655. (Peliminary abstract in *Science* 37:225.)

————. 1919. *Linguistic Families of California.* UC-PAAE 16(3):47–118.

Dorsey, J. Owen. 1884a. Notes on verbs in Tututni (Oregon Athapascan). Ca. 1884. NAA MS 4800:(4.1) (369), National Anthropological Archives, Smithsonian Institution. 7 pp.

————. 1884b. Dakube tede vocabulary from the Athapascans formerly living on Applegate Creek, "Rogue River John, a Dakube on his mother's side," October 1, 1884. NAA MS 4800:(4.1.1) (372), National Anthropological Archives, Smithsonian Institution. 19 pp. (9 pp. original notes; 10 pp. in Powell schedules).

————. 1884c. Galice Creek (Talt uct un tude) vocabulary and grammatical notes, Yacltun or Galice Creek Jim and Peter Muggins, September 18–October 9, 1884. NAA MS

4800:(4.1.2) (373), National Anthropological Archives, Smithsonian Institution. 53 pp. (25 pp. original notes; 28 pp. in schedules).

———. 1884d. Chasta Costa (Cistakawusta) vocabulary, Government George, Tatelatun or John, and Jake Orton, September–October 1884. NAA MS 4800:(4.1.3) (374), National Anthropological Archives, Smithsonian Institution. 26 pp. (8 pp. original notes; 18 pp. in Powell schedules).

———. 1884e. Upper Coquille (Miciqwutme tunne) [vocabulary] and grammatical notes, Coquille Thompson, Solomon, August and October 1884. NAA MS 4800:(4.1.4) (375), National Anthropological Archives, Smithsonian Institution. 112 pp. (60 pp. original notes; 52 pp. in Powell schedules).

———. 1884f. Chetco (Tceti tunne) vocabulary and grammatical notes, Baldwin Fairchild, September 20, 25; October 4–21, 1884. NAA MS 4800:(4.1.5) (376), National Anthropological Archives, Smithsonian Institution. 87 pp. (41 pp. original notes; 46 pp. in Powell schedules).

———. 1884g. Mikwunu tunne vocabulary and grammatical notes, William Simpson, October 15, 1884. NAA MS 4800:(4.1.6) (377), National Anthropological Archives, Smithsonian Institution. 44 pp. (23 pp. original notes; 21 pp. in Powell schedules).

———. 1884h. Tutu tunne or Tutu and Joshua vocabulary. NAA MS 4800:(4.1.7) (378), National Anthropological Archives, Smithsonian Institution. Ca. 375 pp. (100 pp. original notes, 275 pp. in Powell schedules).

———. 1884i. Tceme tunni or Joshua vocabulary and grammatical notes, Henry Clay and Alex. Catfish, August 1884. NAA MS 4800:(4.1.7) (379), National Anthropological Archives, Smithsonian Institution. Ca. 50 pp.

———. 1884j. Tutu vocabulary and grammatical notes. NAA MS 4800:(4.1.7) (380), National Anthropological Archives, Smithsonian Institution. Ca. 98 pp., 3 charts, in Powell schedules.

———. 1884k. Tutu vocabulary: original notes and vocabulary on slips. NAA MS 4800:(4.1.7) (381), National Anthropological Archives, Smithsonian Institution. Ca. 200 pp. and slips.

———. 1884l. Yukitce vocabulary and grammatical notes, formerly spoken by the Athapascans living on Euchre Creek, James Warner, Sr., September 2, 1884. NAA MS 4800:(4.1.8) (386), National Anthropological Archives, Smithsonian Institution. 31 pp. (20 pp. original notes; 11 pp. typed copy).

———. 1884m. Kwatami vocabulary and grammatical notes, spoken by the Athapascans formerly living on Sixes Creek, August 29, 1884. NAA MS 4800:(4.1.9) (387), National Anthropological Archives, Smithsonian Institution. 49 pp. (22 pp. original notes; 27 pp. in Powell schedules).

———. 1884n. Naltunnetunne vocabulary and grammatical notes, October 1884. NAA MS 4800:(4.1.10) (388), National Anthropological Archives, Smithsonian Institution. Ca. 177 pp. (100 pp. original notes; 77 pp. in Powell schedules).

———. 1884o. Qaunwate vocabulary from the Athapascans formerly living on Smith River, California, "Smith River John," September 20, 1884. NAA MS 4800:(4.1.11) (389), National Anthropological Archives, Smithsonian Institution. 15 pp. (4 pp. original notes; 11 pp. in Powell schedules).

———. 1884p. Takelma vocabulary and grammatical notes, spoken by the Takilman-speaking Indians formerly living in the Illinois valley and on Rogue River, Oregon September 3–October 24, 1884. NAA MS 4800:(4.4) (397), National Anthropological Archives, Smithsonian Institution. Ca. 65 pp. (24 pp. original notes, 41 pp in Powell schedules).

———. 1884q. Shasta (Sasti) vocabulary August-October 1884. NAA MS 4800:(4.5) (398), National Anthropological Archives, Smithsonian Institution. 24 pp. (13 pp. original notes, 11 pp. in Powell schedules).

———. 1886. Remarks on Applegate Creek Indians [Dakubetede] and Nabiltse, 1886. NAA MS 4800:(4.1.1) (371), National Anthropological Archives, Smithsonian Institution. 1 p. typescript.

———. 1890. The Gentile System of the Siletz Tribes. JAF 3:227–237.

Douthit, Nathan. 2002. *Uncertain Encounters: Indians and Whites at Peace and War in Southern Oregon, 1820s–1860s.* Corvallis: Oregon State University Press.

Driver, Harold E. 1936. *Wappo Ethnography.* UC-PAAE 36(3):179–220.

———. *Culture Element Distributions: X Northwest California.* UC-AR 1(6):297–433.

Drucker, Philip. 1937. *The Tolowa and Their Southwest Oregon Kin.* UC-PAAE 36(4):221–299.

———. n.d. Upper Takelma field notes [from Molly Orton and Elizabeth Harney]. EDDMA, no. 135. 32 pp.

Dryer, Matthew S. 2005. Prefixing versus Suffixing in Inflectional Morphology. In *The World Atlas of Linguistic Structures,* edited by Martin Haspelmath, Matthew S. Dryer, David Gil, and Bernard Comrie, 110–113. Oxford, UK: Oxford University Press.

Du Bois, Cora. 1935. *Wintu Ethnography.* UC-PAAE 36(1):1–148.

———. 1960. Paul Radin: An Appreciation. In *Culture in History: Essays in Honor of Paul Radin,* edited by Stanley Diamond. New York: Columbia University Press.

Du Bois, Cora, and Dorothy Demetracopoulou [Lee]. 1931. *Wintu Myths.* UC-PAAE 28(5):279–03. (Seventy-four northern Wintu myths collected from informants in the field during the summer of 1929. Twenty-four of the stories were recorded in Wintu and translated, another fifty tales were recorded in English. The compilers state that prior to their study, only nine Wintu tales, which were significantly different in style from theirs, had been recorded. See Curtin 1898.)

DuBois, Constance Goddard. 1908. *The Religion of the Luiseño and Diegueño Indians of Southern California.* UC-PAAE 8(3): 69–186.

Duflot de Mofras, Eugène. 1844. *Exploration du territoire de l'Oregon, des Californies et de la Mer Vermeille, exécutée pendant les années 1840, 1841 et 1842.* 2 vols. Paris: Bertrand. (English version: *Travels on the Pacific Coast,* edited by Marguerite E. Wilbur. Santa Ana, CA: Fine Arts Press, 1937. 2 vols.)

Duhaut-Cilly, Auguste Bernard. 1834-1835. *Voyage Autour du Monde, principalement à la California et aux Îles Sandwich, pendant les années 1826, 1827, 1828, et 1829.* Paris. [English version: *A Voyage to California, the Sandwich Islands, and Around the World,* translated and edited by Auguste Frugé and Neal Harlow. Berkeley: University of California Press, 1999.]

Eatough, Andrew. 1999. *Central Hill Nisenan Texts with Grammatical Sketch.* UC-PL 132.

Elliott, Eric B. 1994. 'How' and 'thus' in UA Cupan and Yuman: A Case of Areal Influence. In *1993 Hokan-Penutian Workshop,* pp. 145–169.

———. 1999. *Dictionary of Rincón Luiseño.* PhD dissertation, University of California, San Diego.

———. n.d. Faculty Member Special Profile: Eric Elliott. Pechanga/UCR Takic Language Revitalization Project, University of California, Riverside. (Accessed online, March 2010, at www.americanindian.ucr.edu/academic/special.html.)

Elmendorf, William W. 1963. Yukian-Siouan Lexical Similarities. IJAL 29:300–309.

———. 1964. Item and Set Comparison in Yuchi, Siouan, and Yukian. IJAL 30:328–340.

———. 1968. Lexical and Cultural Change in Yukian. AL 10(7):1–41. (Reprinted 1993, AL 35:171–242.)

———. 1981a. Features of Yukian Pronominal Structure. JCGBA-PL 3:3–16.

———. 1981b. Last Speakers and Language Change: Two Californian Cases. AL 23:36–49. (Reprinted 1993, AL 35:274–287.)

———. 1984. Yukian Sharings. Paper presented at the 1984 Hokan-Penutian Workshop, UC Berkeley, June 22–24, 1984.

———. 1997. A Preliminary Analysis of Yukian Root Structure. AL 39: 74–91.

Elmendorf, William W., and Alice Shepherd. 1999. Another Look at Wappo-Yuki Loans. AL 41.2 :209–229.

Elsasser, Albert B. 1978. Mattole, Nongatl, Sinkyone, Lassik, and Wailaki. In *Handbook of North American Indians,* vol. 8: *California,* edited by Robert F. Heizer, 190–204. Washington, DC: Smithsonian Institution.

Elston, Robert G. 1986. Prehistory of the Western Area. In *Handbook of North American Indians,* vol. 11: *Great Basin,* edited by Warren L. d'Azevedo, 135–148. Washington, DC: Smithsonian Institution.

Elzinga, Dirk. n.d. *An Online Chemehuevi Dictionary.* Department of Linguistics and English Language, Brigham Young University. (Contact author for access. See also H. Nelson et al. 2004.)

Enrico, John. 2004. Toward Proto-Na-Dene. AL 46:229–302.

Eshleman, Jason A., Ripan S. Malhi, John R. Johnson, Frederika A. Kaestle, Joseph G. Lorenz, and David Glenn Smith. 2004. Mitochondrial DNA and Prehistoric Settlements: Native Migrations on the Western Edge of North America. *Human Biology* 76:55–75.

Eshleman, Jason A., and David Glenn Smith. 2007. Prehistoric Mitochondrial DNA and Population Movements. In *California Prehistory: Colonization, Culture, and Complexity,* edited by Terry L. Jones and Kathryn A. Klar, 291–298. Lanham, MD: AltaMira Press.

Essene, Frank. 1942. *Culture Element Distributions: XXI. Round Valley.* UC-AR 8(1):1–97.

Euler, Robert C. 1975. The Pai: Cultural Conservatives in Environmental Diversity. In *Collected Papers in Honor of Florence Hawley Ellis,* edited by T. R. Frisbie, 80–87. Papers of the Archaeological Society of New Mexico, no. 2. Norman, OK: Hooper Publishing.

Everett, Willis E. 1882. Vocabulary of "Tu-u-tene" and nine confederated tribes, December 12, 1882. NAA MS 78, National Anthropological Archives, Smithsonian Institution. (170 pp. in Powell schedules. Additions and corrections in red ink by J. Owen Dorsey.)

Fages, Pedro. 1775. Continuación y suplemento á los dos impresos que de orden de este Superio Govierno han corrido . . . . Documentos relativos á las misiones de Californias, small folio series, vol. 4. Museo Nacional, Mexico City. (A signed contemporary copy dated November 30, 1775, is in the Archivo de Indias, Seville. Copies of both are in the Bancroft Library, University of California, Berkeley. For French translation of Seville copy, see Ternaux-Compans 1884. For English translation, see Priestley 1937.)

Farris, Glenn J. 1989. The Russian Imprint on the Colonization of California. In *Columbian Consequences,* vol. 1: *Archaeological and Historical Perspectives on the Spanish Borderlands West,* edited by David Hurst Thomas, 481–497. Washington, DC: Smithsonian Institution Press.

———. 1990. Vigesimal Systems Found in California Indian Languages. JCGBA 12:173–190.

Faye, Paul Louis. 1919–1920. Cupeño folk narrative and song texts; linguistic studies; notes on the Image Ceremony. EDDMA, no. 81. 412 pp. [Typed extract filed separately: "Two Cupeño Myth Texts," EDDMA, no. 8.]

———. 1919–1927. Cupeño ethnographic and linguistic field notes. EDDMA, no. 82. 2,484 pp.

Felger, Richard S., and Mary B. Moser. 1985. *People of the Desert and Sea: Ethnobotany of the Seri Indians.* Tucson: University of Arizona Press.

Fenton, William N. 1963. Horatio Hale M.A. (Harvard), F.R.S.C. (1817–1896). In *The Iroquois Book of Rites,* by Horatio Hale, reprinted with an introduction by William N. Fenton, vii–xxvii. Toronto: University of Toronto Press.

Fitzgerald, Richard T., Terry L. Jones, and Adella Schroth. 2005. Ancient Long-Distance Trade in Western North America: New AMS Radiocarbon Dates from Southern California. *Journal of Archaeological Science* 32:423–434.

Fletcher, Francis. 1628. *The World Encompassed by Sir Francis Drake.* London: Nicholas Bourne.

Forbes, Kari L. n.d. *An Ethnographic Study of the Contemporary Values of the Foothill Konkow, Butte County, California.* United States Forest Service, Bureau of Land Management, California Department of Forestry, and California Parks and Recreation.

Fortescue, Michael. 1999. *Language Relations across Bering Strait: Reappraising the Archaeological and Linguistic Evidence.* London: Continuum.

Foster, George M. 1944. *A Summary of Yuki Culture.* UC-AR 5(3):155–244.

Foster, Michael K. 1996. Language and the Culture History of North America. In *Handbook of North American Indians.* Vol. 17: *Languages,* edited by Ives Goddard, 64–110. Washington, DC: Smithsonian Institution.

Fowler, Catherine S. 1972a. *Comparative Numic Ethnobiology.* PhD dissertation, University of Pittsburgh.

———. 1972b. Some Ecological Clues to Proto-Numic Homelands. In *Great Basin Cultural Ecology: A Symposium,* edited by Don D. Fowler, 105–121. Desert Research Institute Publications in the Social Sciences 8. Reno: University of Nevada.

———. 1983. Some Lexical Clues to Uto-Aztecan Prehistory. IJAL 49:224–257.

Fowler, Catherine S., and Lawrence E. Dawson. 1986. Ethnographic Basketry. In *Handbook of North American Indians.* Vol. 11: *Great Basin,* edited by Warren L. d'Azevedo, 705–737. Washington, DC: Smithsonian Institution.

Fowler, Catherine S., and Sven Liljeblad. 1986. Northern Paiute. In *Handbook of North American Indians*. Vol. 11: *Great Basin*, edited by Warren L. d'Azevedo, 435–465. Washington, DC: Smithsonian Institution.

Fowler, Don D., and Catherine S. Fowler. 1970. Stephen Powers' "The Life and Culture of the Washo and Paiutes." *Ethnohistory* 17:117–149.

———. 1971. *Anthropology of the Numa: John Wesley Powell's Manuscripts on the Numic Peoples of Western North America, 1868–1880*. Smithsonian Contributions to Anthropology 14. Washington, DC: Smithsonian Institution.

Frachtenberg, Leo J. 1910. Kalapuya notebooks, Mary's River dialect. [The first ten pages of volume 4 consist of a Kwalhioqua (Lower Columbia Athabaskan) vocabulary and a short text.] NAA MS 1923-a, National Anthropological Archives, Smithsonian Institution. (Athabaskan vocabulary copied and reorganized as "Semantically grouped Willopah vocabulary." NAA MS 4797, National Anthropological Archives, Smithsonian Institution. 17 pp.)

———. 1918. Comparative Studies in Takelman, Kalapuyan, and Chinookan Lexicography: A Preliminary Paper. IJAL 1:175–182.

———. 1920. Abnormal Types of Speech in Quileute. IJAL 1:295–299.

Frawley, William, Kenneth C. Hill, and Pamela Munro, eds. 2002. *Making Dictionaries: Preserving Indigenous Languages of the Americas*. Berkeley: University of California Press.

Fredrickson, David A. 1984. The North Coastal Region. In *California Archaeology*, by Michael J. Moratto, pp. 471–527. New York: Academic Press.

Freeland, L. S. 1947. Western Miwok Texts with Linguistic Sketch. IJAL 13:31–46.

———. 1951. *Language of the Sierra Miwok*. Indiana University Publications in Anthropology and Linguistics, IJAL Memoir 6.

Freeland, L. S., and Sylvia M. Broadbent. 1960. *Central Sierra Miwok Dictionary with Texts*. UC-PL 23.

Freeland, Nancy. See: Freeland, L. S.

Freeze, Ray, and David Iannucci. 1979. Internal Classification of the Numic Languages of Uto-Aztecan. *Amérindia* 4:17–29.

Galiano, Don Dionisio Alcalá. See: Anonymous 1802.

Gallatin, Albert. 1848. Hale's Indians of North-West America, and Vocabularies of North America: With an Introduction. *Transactions of the American Ethnological Society* 2:xxiii–clxxxviii, 1–130.

Gamble, Geoffrey. 1978. *Wikchamni Grammar*. UC-PL 89.

———. 1980. "How People Got Their Hands" [Wikchamni text]. In *Coyote Stories II*, edited by Martha B. Kendall, 53–55. IJAL Native American Text Series, Monograph 6. Chicago: University of Chicago Press.

———. 1989. Spanish Loans in Wikchamni. In *General and Amerindian Ethnolinguistics: In Remembrance of Stanley Newman*, edited by Mary Ritchie Key and Henry M. Hoenigswald, 123–128. Berlin: Mouton de Gruyter.

———. 1991a. Palewyami: A Yokuts Key. In *A Festschrift for William F. Shipley*, edited by Sandra Chung and Jorge Hankamer, 61–81. Santa Cruz: Syntax Research Center, University of California, Santa Cruz.

———. 1991b. Yok-Utian: Old California Penutian? Paper presented at the Hokan-Penutian Conference, Santa Cruz, California.

———. 1992. Stanley S. Newman (1905–1984). IJAL 58:309–312.

———, ed. 1994. *Yokuts Texts*. Native American Texts Series 1. Berlin: Mouton de Gruyter.

Gamon, David. 1991. Kashaya Switch Reference. In *1990 Hokan-Penutian Workshop*, pp. 92–117.

Garibay K., Ángel María. 1970. *Llave del Nahuatl: colección de trozos clásicos, con gramática y vocabulario, para utilidad de los principiantes*. Third edition. México, D.F.

Garrett, Andrew. 2001. Reduplication and Infixation in Yurok: Morphology, Semantics and Diachrony. IJAL 67:264–312.

———. 2004. The Evolution of Algic Verbal Stem Structure: New Evidence from Yurok. Paper presented at the 30th Annual Meeting of the Berkeley Linguistics Society, February 13–16, 2004.

Garrett, Andrew, Juliette Blevins, and Lisa Conathan, compilers. 2005. *Preliminary Yurok Dictionary*. [Compiled from published sources and unpublished research.] March 2005. Berkeley: Yurok Language Project, Department of Linguistics, University of California, Berkeley. (Online at linguistics.berkeley.edu/~yurok).

Gatschet, Albert S. 1876a. Analytic Report upon Indian Dialects Spoken in Southern California, Nevada, and on the Lower Colorado River . . . based upon vocabularies collected by the expeditions for Geographical surveys west of the 100th meridian, Lieut. Geo. M. Wheeler . . . in charge. In *Annual Report of the U.S. Geological Survey West of the 100th Meridian*, 550–563. Washington, DC: Government Printing Office. [Includes vocabularies collected by Oscar Loew on Barbareño and Island Chumash; Cahuilla, Serrano, Juaneño, Gabrielino, Northern Paiute, Southern Paiute, and Chemehuevi; and Mojave, Diegueño, Quechan, and Hualapai. See the fuller publication of Loew's materials in Gatschet 1879a.]

———. 1876b. *Zwölf Sprachen aus dem Südwesten Nordamerikas (Pueblos- und Apache-Mundarten; Tonto, Tonkawa, Digger, Utah.) Wortverzeichnisse herausgegeben, erläutert und mit einer Einleitung über Bau, Begriffsbildung und locale Gruppirung der Amerikanischen Sprachen versehen*. Weimar: Böhlau. (Reprinted 1970 by Humanities Press. See Landar 1974.)

———. 1877a. Sasti-English and English-Sasti dictionary, September 1877. NAA MS 708, National Anthropological Archives, Smithsonian Institution. 135 pp. (Another dictionary, dated November 1877, 106 pp., is in NAA MS 706; a vocabulary, dated Sept. 18, 1877, 35 pp., is in NAA MS 1572; and a short vocabulary, dated 1876, 1 p., is in NAA MS 707.)

———. 1877b. Umpqua (Athapascan) vocabulary, recorded at Grande Ronde Indian Reservation, Polk Co., Oregon, Dec. 30, 1877. [Vocabulary of 410 items.] NAA MS 76, National Anthropological Archives, Smithsonian Institution. 35 pp.

———. 1877c. Der Yuma-Sprachstamm [part 1]. *Zeitschrift für Ethnologie* 9:341–350, 365–418. (See Gatschet 1883, 1886, and 1892a for parts 2–4.)

———. 1877d. Words, sentences and texts from the language of the Otakimme or Indians of Chico, California, August-September 1877. NAA MS 646-a, National Anthropological Archives, Smithsonian Institution. 131 pp.

———. 1877e. [Molala] Vocabulary November-December 1877. BAE MS 1000, National Anthropological Archives, Smithsonian Institution. 65 pp.

———. 1877f . Pit River of Northeastern California, September-October 1877 vocabulary. [Big Valley, Hot Springs, and Goose Lake dialects.] NAA MS 620, National Anthropological Archives, Smithsonian Institution. 11 pp.

———. 1877g. [Atfalati Kalapuya] Vocabulary November-December 1877. NAA MS 472-d, National Anthropological Archives, Smithsonan Institution. 64 pp. (Also Vocabulary of Ahantchuyuk Kalapuya, 22 pp., in NAA MS 473; Vocabulary of Yamel [Yamhill] Kalapuya, 25 pp., in NAA MS 474.)

———. 1877h. Indian Languages of the Pacific States and Territories. *Magazine of American History*, March 1877, pp. 145–171.

———. 1878. Sketch of the Klamath Language of Southern Oregon. *American Antiquarian* 1:81–84.

———. 1879a. Classification into Seven Linguistic Stocks of Western Indian Dialects Contained in Forty Vocabularies. *Report upon the United States Geographical Surveys West of the 100th Meridian, in charge of First Lieut. George M. Wheeler.* Vol. 7, *Archaeology*, pp. 403–485. Washington, DC: Government Printing Office. [Includes vocabularies collected by Oscar Loew on Shoshoni, Ute, Northern Paiute, Chemehuevi, Serrano, Cahuilla, Juaneño, Gabrielino, and Luiseño; Upland Yuman, Hualapai, Mojave, Diegueño, and Quechan; Wintu; and Barbareño Chumash. Some of these were included in Gatschet 1876a.]

———. 1879b. Adjectives of Color in Indian Languages. *American Naturalist* 13:475–485. [Chico Maidu and Klamath-Modoc data.]

———. 1882. Indian Languages of the Pacific States and Territories, and of the Pueblos of New Mexico. *Magazine of American History,* April, 1882. (Sequel to Gatschet 1877h.)

———. 1883. Der Yuma-Sprachstamm, zweiter Artikel. *Zeitschrift für Ethnologie* 15:123–147.

———. 1886. Der Yuma-Sprachstamm, dritter Artikel. *Zeitschrift für Ethnologie* 18:97–122.

———. 1889. [Wintu] Vocabulary 1889. NAA MS 1564, National Anthropological Archives, Smithsonian Institution. 25 pp.

———. 1890. *The Klamath Indians of Southwestern Oregon.* Contributions to North American Ethnology 2. Parts I and II (separately paginated). [Part I: Ethnographic Sketch of the Klamath People, pp. ix–cvi; Texts of the Klamath Language, pp. 1–197; Grammar, pp. 199–711. Part II: Klamath-English Dictionary, pp. 1–491; English-Klamath Dictionary, pp. 493–701.] Washington, DC: Government Printing Office. (A table of contents for the grammar, which otherwise lacks one, has been prepared by Scott DeLancey and is online at www.uoregon.edu/~delancey/bib/gatcon.html).

———. 1892a. Der Yuma-Sprachstamm, IV. *Zeitschrift für Ethnologie* 24:1–18.

———. 1892b. Vocabulary of the Pit River or Achomawi language of Northeastern California, December 1892. NAA MS 1533-a-c. 18 pp.

———. 1900. The Waikuru, Seri, and Yuma Languages. *Science* 12:556–558.

Gayton, Anna H. 1948. *Yokuts and Western Mono Ethnography. II: Northern Foothill Yokuts and Western Mono.* UC-AR 10(2):143–302.

Gehr, Susan. See Bright and Gehr 2004.

Geiger, Maynard, O.F.M. 1969. *Franciscan Missionaries in Hispanic California, 1769–1848: A Biographical Dictionary.* San Marino, CA: Huntington Library.

Geiger, Maynard, O.F.M., and Clement W. Meighan, eds. 1976. *As the Padres Saw Them: California Indian Life and Customs as Reported by the Franciscan Missionaries, 1813–1815.* Santa Barbara, CA: Santa Barbara Mission Archive Library. ("Anthropological Introduction" by Meighan, pp. 3–9; "Appendix A: Native Terms Used in Questionnaire," pp. 155–159.)

Gerolt, Karl von. 1830. Idioma Uimen, Idioma Suisun, Lengua Cacundo. Wilhelm von Humboldt, Wissenschaftliche Korrespondenz. MS 1061, Bl. 50–55, Archiv Schloss Tegel, Berlin. (See Mueller-Vollmer 1993.)

Gibbs, George. 1851. Sketch of the northwestern part of California accompanying a journal of the expedition of Col. Redick McKee, U.S. Indian Agent; during the summer and fall of 1851. Map 47, Tube 123, RG 77: Office of the Chief of Engineers, National Archives, Washington, DC.

———. 1851–1852. Vocabulary [of Nabiltse] 1851 or 1852. NAA MS 131, National Anthropological Archives, Smithsonian Institution. 2 pp.

———. 1852. Weitspek (Pohlik Klamath) [Yurok] and Hopah [Hupa] dictionaries and ethnographic notes 1852. NAA MS 954, National Anthropological Archives, Smithsonian Institution. 41 pp. (Yurok vocabulary published, with orthography standardized, in Powers 1877 as "Alikwa 1.")

———. 1852–1853. Pehtsik Klamath or Arra-Arra [Karuk] dictionary and ethnographic notes 1852–1853. NAA MS 846, National Anthropological Archives, Smithsonian Institution. 33 pp. (Vocabulary published, with orthography standardized, in Powers 1877.)

———. 1853a. Journal of the Expedition of Colonel Redick M'Kee, United States Indian Agent, Through North-Western California. Performed in the Summer and Fall of 1851. In *Historical and Statistical Information Respecting the History, Condition and Prospects of the Indian Tribes of the United States,* edited by Henry R. Schoolcraft. Vol. 3, pp. 99–177. Philadelphia: Lippencott. (Reprinted in Heizer 1972b.)

———. 1853b. Vocabularies of Indian Languages in Northwest California. [Includes vocabularies of Coast Miwok ("Tcho-ko-yem"), Hill Patwin ("Cop-éh"), four varieties of Pomo ("Kula-napo," "Yukai," "Chow-e-shak," and "Batem-da-kai-ee"), two varieties of Wiyot ("Wee-yot" and "Wish-osk"), Yurok ("Weits-pek"), Hupa, Tolowa, and Karuk ("Eh-nek").] In *Historical and Statistical Information Respecting the History, Condition and Prospects of the Indian Tribes of the United States,* edited by Henry R. Schoolcraft. Vol. 3, pp. 428–445. Philadelphia: Lippencott. (All but the Hupa and Tolowa reprinted, with orthography standardized, in Powers 1877.)

———. 1853c. Observations on Some of the Indian Dialects of Northern California. In *Historical and Statistical Information Respecting the History, Condition and Prospects of the Indian Tribes of the United States,* edited by Henry R. Schoolcraft. Vol. 3, pp. 420–423. Philadelphia: Lippencott.

———. 1854. *Report on the Indian Tribes of the Territory of Washington.* Secretary of War: Reports of Explorations 1:400–449. Washington, DC: Government Printing Office.

———. 1856. Vocabulary of the Willopah (dialect of Tahcully, Athapasca) [Lower Columbia Athabaskan]. . . . Feb. 1856. NAA MS 110. 7 pp. (Published in Boas 1895:588–592.)

———. 1861–1862. Comparative Vocabulary of Lutuami (Clamet)—from Hale, Palaik—from Hale, and Pitt River—recorded by Gibbs 1861–1862. NAA MS 549, National Anthropological Archives, Smithsonian Institution. 4 pp.

———. 1863a. *Instructions for Research Relative to the Ethnology and Philology of America.* Smithsonian Miscellaneous Collections 160. March 1863.

———. 1863b. Vocabularies of the Yuba [Maiduan] and Yukeh [Yuki] Languages of California. *Historical Magazine* 7:123–125. (Vocabularies collected by Lt. Edward Ross.)

———. 1863c. *Alphabetical Vocabularies of the Clallam and Lummi.* Shea's Library of American Linguistics, no. 11. New York: Cramoisy Press.

———. 1863d. *A Dictionary of the Chinook Jargon, or, Trade Language of Oregon.* Shea's Library of American Linguistics, no. 12. New York: Cramoisy Press. (Also issued as Smithsonian Miscellaneous Collections 161. March 1863.)

Gibson, Robert O. 1983. *Ethnogeography of the Salinan People: A Systems Approach.* Master's thesis, California State University, Hayward.

———. 1985. Ethnogeography of the Northern Salinan. In *Excavations at Mission San Antonio, 1976–1978,* edited by Robert L. Hoover and J. G. Costello, pp. 152–221. Los Angeles: UCLA, Institute of Archaeology, Monograph 26.

Gidley, Mick. 1998. *Edward S. Curtis and the North American Indian, Incorporated.* Cambridge, UK: Cambridge University Press.

———, ed. 2003. *Edward S. Curtis and the North American Indian Project in the Field.* Edited and with an introduction by Mick Gidley. Lincoln: University of Nebraska Press.

Gifford, Edward W. 1916. *Miwok Moieties.* UC-PAAE 12(4):170–193.

———. 1922. *California Kinship Terminologies.* UC-PAAE 18(1):1–285.

———. 1926. *California Anthropometry.* UC-PAAE 22(2):217–390.

———. 1931. *The Kamia of Imperial Valley.* BAE-B 97:1–94.

———. 1932a. *The Southeastern Yavapai.* UC-PAAE 29(3):177–252.

———. 1932b. *The Northfork Mono.* UC-PAAE 31(2):15–65.

———. 1933. *The Cocopa.* UC-PAAE 31(5):257–334.

———. 1936. *Northeastern and Western Yavapai.* UC-PAAE 34(4):247–354.

———. 1939. The Coast Yuki. *Anthropos* 34:292–375. (Reprinted by Sacramento Anthropological Society, Paper 2. Spring 1965.)

Gifford, Edward W., and Robert H. Lowie. 1928. *Notes on the Akwa'ala Indians of Lower California.* UC-PAAE 23(7):339–352.

Givón, Talmy. 1979. *Ute Dictionary.* Preliminary edition. Ignacio, CO: Ute Press, Southern Ute Tribe.

———. 1980. *Ute Reference Grammar.* Ignacio, CO: Ute Press, Southern Ute Tribe.

Givón, T[almy], and Loren Bommelyn. 2000. The Evolution of De-Transitive Voice in Tolowa Athabaskan. *Studies in Language* 24:41–76.

Glassow, Michael A., Lynn H. Gamble, Jennifer E. Perry, and Glenn S. Russell. 2007. Prehistory of the Northern California Bight and the Adjacent Transverse Ranges. In *California Prehistory: Colonization, Culture, and Complexity,* edited by Terry L. Jones and Kathryn A. Klar, 191–213. Lanham, MD: AltaMira Press.

Glenn, James R. 1991a. The Sound Recordings of John P. Harrington. AL 33:357–366.

———. 1991b. John Peabody Harrington. In *International Dictionary of Anthropologists,* edited by Christopher Winters, 270–272. Garland Reference Library of the Social Sciences, no. 638. New York: Garland Publishing.

Goddard, Ives. 1966. [Review of Teeter 1964.] IJAL 32:398–404.

———. 1975. Algonquian, Wiyot, and Yurok: Proving a Distant Genetic Relationship. In *Linguistics and Anthropology: In Honor of C. F. Voegelin,* edited by M. Dale Kinkade, Kenneth L. Hale and Oswald Werner, 249–262. Lisse, Netherlands: Peter de Ridder.

———. 1979. The Languages of South Texas and the Lower Rio Grande. In *The Languages of Native America: Historical and Comparative Assessment,* edited by Lyle Campbell and Marianne Mithun, 355–389. Austin: University of Texas Press.

———. 1986. Sapir's Comparative Method. In *New Perspectives in Language, Culture, and Personality,* edited by William Cowan, Michael K. Foster and Konrad Koerner, 191–210. Amsterdam: John Benjamins.

———. 1996a. The Description of the Native Languages of North America before Boas. In *Handbook of North American Indians.* Vol. 17: *Languages,* edited by Ives Goddard, 17–42. Washington, DC: Smithsonian Institution.

———. 1996b. The Classification of the Native Languages of North America. In *Handbook of North American Indians.* Vol. 17: *Languages,* edited by Ives Goddard, 290–323. Washington, DC: Smithsonian Institution.

———. 2001. The Languages of the Plains: Introduction. In *Handbook of North American Indians.* Vol. 13: *Plains,* edited by Raymond J. DeMallie, 61–70. Washington, DC: Smithsonian Institution.

Goddard, Pliny Earle. 1901–1908. Hupa texts (South Fork of the Trinity). 80 pp. (Forms part of Goddard 1902–1922a.)

———. 1902a. New River. [Short vocabulary and other notes. 3 pp., loose sheets, bundled together with a neat copy of Kroeber 1901 (6 pp.) and other information on New River Shasta in Kroeber's hand (2 pp). Cover note by Kroeber, dated 8/25/58, states that the latter and the copy of Kroeber 1901 "were evidently given by him to G. for his guidance . . . at Hupa or upriver from it on Trinity." A reference to Mrs. Jordan (Goddard 1902b) suggests that the date of collection was the summer of 1902.] Archives, Survey of California and Other Indian Languages, Department of Linguistics, University of California, Berkeley.

———. 1902b. [Shasta] vocabulary, collected . . . July 1902 from Mrs. Mary Jordan, a "New River Shasta" living (in 1902) near the head of the South Fork of the Salmon River. [Ca. 120 items.] (Forms part of Goddard 1902–1922a.)

———. 1902–1903. Tolowa field notes. MS. 30(Na20f.1), Library of the American Philosophical Society, Philadelphia. 18 notebooks.

———. 1902–1906. Kato materials. MS. 30(Na20b.1), Library of the American Philosophical Society, Philadelphia. 8 notebooks.

———. 1902–1907. Chilula field notes (Redwood Creek). MS. 30(Na20g.1), Library of the American Philosophical Society, Philadelphia. 5 notebooks.

———. 1902–1922a. Field notes in California Athabascan [and other] languages [Hupa, Kato, Wailaki, Sinkyone, Tolowa, Nongatl, and Pomo]. MS. 30(Na.3), Library of the American Philosophical Society, Philadelphia. 18 notebooks.

———. 1902–1922b. Athapaskan Field Note and Manuscript Collections. [Chilula texts; Wailaki Myths; Nongatl Texts; Wailaki Tales; Tolowa Tales and Texts; Mattole Word Lists (microfilm); Notes on California Athapaskan Geography and Ethnography; Hupa Tracings; Kato Linguistic Miscellany (with Edward Sapir); Description of Nongatl Fieldwork; Hupa Lexicon; Kato Text; also materials on San Carlos Apache and experimental phonetics, and typescript of Kroeber's "Goddard's California Athapaskan Texts" (published as Kroeber 1967).] EDDMA, no. 12. 1,313 pp., file cards, microfilm.

———. 1903a. *Life and Culture of the Hupa.* UC-PAAE 1(1):1–88.

———. 1903b. The Kato Pomo not Pomo. AA 5:375–376.

———. 1903–1906. Hupa materials. MS. 30(Na20a.2), Library of the American Philosophical Society, Philadelphia. 11 notebooks and loose sheets.

———. 1903–1908. Sinkyone field notes [1903–1908]. MS. 30(Na20i.1), Library of the American Philosophical Society, Philadelphia. 4 notebooks.

———. 1904. *Hupa Texts.* UC-PAAE 1(2):89–368.

———. 1905. *Morphology of the Hupa Language.* UC-PAAE 3.

———. 1906. Wailaki field notes [1906]. MS. 30(Na20c.1), Library of the American Philosophical Society, Philadelphia. 10 notebooks.

———. 1907. Mattole materials [1907]. MS. 30(Na20e.1), Library of the American Philosophical Society, Philadelphia. 2 notebooks.

———. 1907–1908. Nongatl field notes ("Pete" tribe) [1907–1908]. MS. 30(Na20h.1), Library of the American Philosophical Society, Philadelphia. 23 notebooks.

———. 1909. *Kato Texts.* UC-PAAE 5(3):65–238.

———. 1910. Saia. In BAE-B 30, p. 410.

———. 1911. Athapascan (Hupa). In *Handbook of American Indian Languages,* Part I, edited by Franz Boas, 85–158. BAE-B 40(1).

———. 1912. *Elements of the Kato Language.* UC-PAAE 11(1):1–176.

———. 1914a. *Notes on the Chilula Indians of Northwestern California.* UC-PAAE 10(6):265–288.

———. 1914b. *Chilula Texts.* UC-PAAE 10(7):289–379.

———. 1923a. *Habitat of the Wailaki.* UC-PAAE 20(6):95–109.

———. 1923b. *Wailaki Texts.* IJAL 2:77–135.

———. 1924. *Habitat of the Pitch Indians.* UC-PAAE 17(4):217–225.

———. 1929. *The Bear River Dialect of Athapascan.* UC-PAAE 24(5):291–334.

Goldschmidt, Walter. 1951. *Nomlaki Ethnography.* UC-PAAE 42(4):303–443.

———. 1978. Nomlaki. In *Handbook of North American Indians.* Vol. 8: *California,* edited by Robert F. Heizer, 341–349. Washington, DC: Smithsonian Institution.

Goldschmidt, Walter, and Harold E. Driver. 1940. *The Hupa White Deerskin Dance.* UC-PAAE 35(8):103–142.

Golla, Victor. 1970. *Hupa Grammar.* PhD dissertation, University of California, Berkeley.

———. 1976. Tututni (Oregon Athabaskan). IJAL 42:217–227.

———. 1977. Coyote and Frog (Hupa). In *Northern California Texts,* edited by Victor Golla and Shirley Silver, 10–16. IJAL Native American Text Series 2(2). Chicago: University of Chicago Press.

———, ed. 1984. *The Sapir-Kroeber Correspondence: Letters between Edward Sapir and A. L. Kroeber, 1905–25.* Survey of California and Other Indian Languages, Report 6. Department of Linguistics, University of California, Berkeley.

———. 1986. Sapir, Kroeber, and North American Linguistic Classification. In *New Perspectives in Language, Culture, and Personality,* edited by William Cowan, Michael K. Foster, and Konrad Koerner, 17–38. Amsterdam: John Benjamins.

———. 1988. Sapir's Yahi Work: An Historical Perspective. In *1987 Hokan-Penutian Workshop,* pp. 2–6.

———, ed. 1990. *Collected Works of Edward Sapir.* Vol. 8: *Takelma Texts and Grammar.* Berlin: Mouton de Gruyter.

———, ed. 1991a. *Collected Works of Edward Sapir.* Vol. 6: *American Indian Languages* 2. Berlin: Mouton de Gruyter.

———, ed. 1991b. *John P. Harrington and His Legacy: A Collection of Essays from the First Conference on the Papers of John Peabody Harrington, Santa Barbara Museum of Natural History, 24–26 June 1992.* AL 33(4). [Dated Winter 1991 but published in March 1994.]

———. 1991c. John P. Harrington and His Legacy. AL 33:337–349. (Introduction to Golla 1991b.)

———. 1996a. Sketch of Hupa, an Athapaskan Language. In *Handbook of North American Indians.* Vol. 17: *Languages,* edited by Ives Goddard, 364–389. Washington, DC: Smithsonian Institution.

———. 1996b. *Hupa Language Dictionary.* Arcata, CA: Hoopa Tribe and Center for Indian Community Development, Humboldt State University.

———. 1996c. Yukian, Gulf, and Greenberg. *SSILA Newsletter* 15(3):9–11.

———. 1996d. Some California Indian Vocabularies in Wilhelm von Humboldt's Collection. Paper presented at the Annual Meeting of the American Anthropological Association, San Francisco, California, November 20–23, 1996.

———. 1997. The Alsea-Wintu Connection. IJAL 63:157–170.

———. 2000. Language History and Communicative Strategies in Aboriginal California and Oregon. In *Languages of the North Pacific Rim,* vol. 5, edited by Osahito Miyaoka, 43–64. Suita, Japan: Faculty of Informatics, Osaka Gakuin University.

———. 2002. The History of the Term "Penutian." In *2000 Hokan-Penutian Workshop,* pp. 24–32.

———. 2003. Ishi's Language. In *Ishi in Three Centuries,* edited by Karl Kroeber and Clifton Kroeber, 208–225. Lincoln: University of Nebraska Press.

———. 2007a. North America. In *Encyclopedia of the World's Endangered Languages,* edited by Christopher Moseley, 1–95. London: Routledge.

———. 2007b. Linguistic Prehistory. In *California Prehistory: Colonization, Culture, and Complexity,* edited by Terry L. Jones and Kathryn A. Klar, 71–82. Lanham, MD: AltaMira Press.

———. 2011. A Navajo-like "4th Person" in California Athabaskan. MS in press.

———. n.d. Materials on Tututni (Lower Rogue River Athabaskan). MS.

Golla, Victor, Pamela Munro, and James A. Matisoff. 1997. Mary R. Haas 1910–1996. *Language* 73:826–837.

Golla, Victor, and Sean O'Neill, eds. 2001. *The Collected Works of Edward Sapir*. Vol. 14: *Northwest California Linguistics*. Berlin: Mouton de Gruyter. (Contains Sapir and Golla 2001.)

Golla, Victor, and Shirley Silver, eds. 1977. *Northern California Texts*. IJAL Native American Text Series 2(2). Chicago: University of Chicago Press.

González-José, Rolando, Walter Neves, Marta Mirazón Lahr, Silvia González, Héctor Pucciarelli, Miquel Hernández Martínez, and Gonzalo Correal. 2005. Late Pleistocene/ Holocene Craniofacial Morphology in Mesoamerican Paleoindians: Implications for the Peopling of the New World. *American Journal of Physical Anthropology* 128:772–780.

Good, Jeff, Teresa McFarland, and Mary Paster. 2003. Reconstructing Achumawi and Atsugewi: Proto-Palaihnihan Revisited. Paper presented at the Annual Meeting of the Society for the Study of the Indigenous Languages of the Americas, Boston, January 2–5, 2003.

Gorbet, Larry. 1976. *A Grammar of Diegueño Nominals*. Garland Studies in American Indian Linguistics. (Published version of *Relativization and Complementation in Diegueño: Noun Phrases as Nouns*. PhD dissertation, University of California, San Diego, 1974.)

Gordon, Lynn. 1986. *Maricopa Morphology and Syntax*. UC-PL 108.

Gordon, Matthew. 1996. The Phonetic Structures of Hupa. *UCLA Working Papers in Phonetics* 93:164–187.

———. 2001. Laryngeal Timing and Correspondence in Hupa. *UCLA Working Papers in Phonology* 5:1–70.

Gordon, Matthew, and Edmundo Luna. 2004. An Intergenerational Investigation of Hupa Stress. *Proceedings of the* [30th] *Annual Meeting of the Berkeley Linguistics Society*, pp. 105–117.

Goss, James A. 1968. Culture-Historical Inference from Utaztecan Linguistic Evidence. In *Utaztekan Prehistory*, edited by Earl H. Swanson, Jr., 1–42. Occasional Papers of the Idaho State Museum 22.

———. 1972. *Ute Lexical and Phonological Patterns*. PhD dissertation, University of Chicago.

Gould, Drusilla, and Christopher Loether. 2002. *An Introduction to the Shoshoni Language: dammen daigwape*. Salt Lake City: University of Utah Press.

Gould, Richard A. 1978. Tolowa. In *Handbook of North American Indians*. Vol. 8: *California*, edited by Robert F. Heizer, 128–136. Washington, DC: Smithsonian Institution.

Grant, Anthony P. 1993. The Vocabularies of Scouler, Tolmie and Coulter: A Reappraisal. In *1992 Hokan-Penutian Workshop*, pp. 20–44.

———. 2009. Morris Swadesh and the Uses of Adversity. Inaugural Lecture as Professor of Historical Linguistics and Language Contact, Edge Hill University [UK], April 22, 2009.

Grant, Campbell. 1978a. Chumash: Introduction. In *Handbook of North American Indians*. Vol. 8: *California*, edited by Robert F. Heizer, 505–508. Washington, DC: Smithsonian Institution.

———. 1978b. Eastern Coastal Chumash. In *Handbook of North American Indians*. Vol. 8: *California*, edited by Robert F. Heizer, 509–519. Washington, DC: Smithsonian Institution.

Gray, Dennis J. 1987. *The Takelma and Their Athapascan Neighbors: A New Ethnographic Synthesis for the Upper Rogue River Area of Southwestern Oregon*. University of Oregon Anthropological Papers 37.

Greenberg, Joseph H. 1987. *Language in the Americas*. Stanford, CA: Stanford University Press.

Greenberg, Joseph H., and Morris Swadesh. 1953. Jicaque as a Hokan Language. IJAL 19:216–222.

Greenwood, Roberta S. 1978. Obispeño and Purisimeño Chumash. In *Handbook of North American Indians*. Vol. 8: *California*, edited by Robert F. Heizer, 520–523. Washington, DC: Smithsonian Institution.

Grekoff, George V. 1997. Surface-Marked Privatives in the Evaluative Domain of the Chimariko Lexicon. In *1996 Hokan-Penutian Workshop*, pp. 35–55.

———. n.d. Notes on the Chimariko language. MS in the collection of the Survey of California and Other Languages, University of California, Berkeley. (For description see Wood and Hinton 2002.)

Gruber, Jacob W. 1967. Horatio Hale and the Development of American Anthropology. *Proceedings of the American Philosophical Society* 111:5–37.

Gudde, Erwin G. 1998. *California Place Names: The Origin and Etymology of Current Geographical Names*, 4th ed., revised and enlarged by William Bright. Berkeley: University of California Press.

Gunnerson, James H. 1962. Plateau Shoshonean Prehistory: A Suggested Reconstruction. *American Antiquity* 28:41–45.

Gursky, Karl-Heinz. 1965. Ein Lexicalischer Vergleich der Algonkin-Golf und Hoka-Subtiaba Sprachen. *Orbis* 14:160–215.

———. 1966a. On the Historical Position of Waikuri. IJAL 32:41–45.

———. 1966b. Ein Vergleich der Grammatischen Morpheme der Golf-Sprachen und der Hoka-Subtiaba-Sprachen. *Orbis* 15:511–537.

———. 1968. Gulf and Hokan-Subtiaban: New Lexical Parallels. IJAL 34:21–41.

———. 1974. Der Hoka-Sprachstamm: Eine Bestandsaufnahme des lexikalischen Beweismaterials. *Orbis* 23:170–215.

———. 1987. Achumawi und Pomo: Eine besondere Beziehung? *Abhandlungen der Völkerkundlichen Arbeitsgemeinschaft* 57:1–12. Nortorf, Germany: Völkerkundlichen Arbeitsgemeinschaft.

———. 1988. Der Hoka-Sprachstamm: Nachtrag I. *Abhandlungen der Völkerkundlichen Arbeitsgemeinschaft* 58:1–37. Nortorf, Germany: Völkerkundlichen Arbeitsgemeinschaft.

Gvozdanović, Jadranka, ed. 1999. *Numeral Types and Changes Worldwide*. Berlin: Mouton de Gruyter.

Haas, Mary R. 1946. A Grammatical Sketch of Tunica. In *Linguistic Structures of Native America*, edited by Cornelius Osgood, 337–366. Viking Fund Publications in Anthropology 6. New York: Viking Fund.

———. 1958. Algonkian-Ritwan: The End of a Controversy. IJAL 24:159–173.

———. 1963. Shasta and Proto-Hokan. *Language* 39:40–59.

———. 1964. California Hokan. In *Studies in Californian Linguistics*, edited by William Bright, 73–87. UC-PL 34.

———. 1966. Wiyot-Yurok-Algonkian and Problems of Comparative Algonkian. IJAL 32:101–107.

———. 1967. Language and Taxonomy in Northwestern California. AA 69:358–362. (Reprinted in Haas 1978:328–338.)

———. 1969. *The Prehistory of Languages*. Janua Linguarum Series Minor, 57. The Hague: Mouton.

———. 1970. Consonant Symbolism in Northwestern California: A Problem in Diffusion. In *Languages and Cultures of Western North America: Essays in Honor of Sven S. Liljeblad*, edited by Earl H. Swanson, Jr., 86–96. Pocatello: Idaho State University Press. (Reprinted in Haas 1978:339–352.)

———. 1976. The Northern California Linguistic Area. In *Hokan Studies: Papers from the First Conference on Hokan Languages*, edited by Margaret Langdon and Shirley Silver, 347–359. The Hague: Mouton. (Reprinted in Haas 1978:353–369.)

———. 1978. *Language, Culture, and History: Essays by Mary R. Haas.* Edited by Anwar S. Dil. Stanford, CA: Stanford University Press.

———. 1980. Notes on Karok Internal Reconstruction. In *American Indian and Indoeuropean Studies: Papers in Honor of Madison S. Beeler*, edited by Kathryn A. Klar, Margaret Langdon, and Shirley Silver, 67–76. The Hague: Mouton.

Hagan, William T. 1997. *Theodore Roosevelt and Six Friends of the Indian.* Norman: University of Oklahoma Press.

Haiman, John, and Pamela Munro, eds. 1983. *Switch Reference and Universal Grammar.* Amsterdam: Benjamins.

Hale, Horatio. 1834. *Remarks on the Language of the St. John's or Wlastukweek Indians, with a Penobscot Vocabulary.* Boston.

———. 1846. *Ethnography and Philology.* Vol. 6 of *United States Exploring Expedition During the Years 1838, 1839, 1840, 1841, 1842, Under the Command of Charles Wilkes, U.S.N.* Philadelphia: Lea and Blanchard. [Includes Hale's vocabularies of Kij(i) (Gabrielino) and Netela (Juaneño), pp. 566–567; Wihinasht (Northern Paiute), Kwalhioqua-Tlatskanai (Lower Columbia Athabaskan), Umpqua (Upper Umpqua Athabaskan), Lutuami (Klamath-Modoc), Palaihnih (Achumawi), La Soledad (Chalon Costanoan), San Miguel (Migueleño Salinan), and San Raphael (Marin Miwok), pp. 569–629. Also includes vocabularies collected by James Dwight Dana (q.v.), and vocabularies collected by Thomas Coulter (q.v.) reprinted from Scouler (1841).] (All these vocabularies are reprinted in Gallatin 1848, pp. 73–130. The Marin Miwok vocabulary is reprinted in Powers 1877, the Chumash vocabularies in Kroeber 1910, pp. 265–268, and the Gabrielino vocabulary in W. McCawley 1996, pp. 281–285.)

———. 1890. *An International Idiom: A Manual of the Oregon Trade Language, or "Chinook Jargon."* London: Whittaker.

Hale, Kenneth. 1958–1959. Internal Diversity in Uto-Aztecan, I and II. IJAL 24:101–107, 25:114–121.

———. 1967. Toward a Reconstruction of Kiowa-Tanoan Phonology. IJAL 33:112–120.

Hale, Kenneth, and David Harris. 1979. Historical Linguistics and Archeology. In *Handbook of North American Indians.* Vol. 9: *Southwest*, edited by Alfonso Ortiz, 170–177. Washington, DC: Smithsonian Institution.

Hall, Kira. 1991. Agentivity and the Animacy Hierarchy in Kashaya. In *1990 Hokan-Penutian Workshop*, pp. 118–135.

Hall, Roberta L. 1992. Language and Cultural Affiliations of Natives Residing Near the Mouth of the Coquille River Before 1851. *Journal of Anthropological Research* 48:165-84.

Halpern, Abraham M. 1935. Yuma linguistic and ethnographic notes [compiled by Halpern and assistants under a State Emergency Relief Administration project]. EDDMA, no. 122. 13 notebooks, 744 pp.

———. 1936a. Patwin and Wintu field notes [Colusa, Enterprise, Rumsey, and Stonyford]. Harvey Pitkin Papers, Series I-A, Library of the American Philosophical Society, Philadelphia.

9 notebooks. (A notebook belonging to this series is archived as Halpern.031 in SCOIL.)

———. 1936b. Achumawi field notes [Adin (Hill, Hamawi, Achumawi), Alturas I and II (Hamawi, Achumawi)]. Harvey Pitkin Papers, Series III-A, Library of the American Philosophical Society, Philadelphia. 3 notebooks.

———. 1936c. Nisenan and Konkow field notes [Auburn, Sugar Pine Hill (Central Hill Nisenan); Cherokee (Konkow)]. Harvey Pitkin Papers, Series III-A, Library of the American Philosophical Society, Philadelphia. 2 notebooks.

———. 1936–1937. Pomo-Patwin (Lower Lake) field notes. EDDMA, no. 148. 9 notebooks, 602 pp. (Basis of Halpern 1988. Notebook VII of this series is archived as Halpern 005.001 in SCOIL.)

———. 1939–1984. Survey of Pomo languages, 1939–1940, 1982–1984 [vocabulary, texts, other materials from Northern, Central, Southern, Southwestern (Kashaya), and Southeastern Pomo]. In the collection of the Survey of California and Other Indian Languages, Department of Linguistics, University of California, Berkeley. (See Halpern 1964 for a description of the 1939–1940 segment of this work.)

———. 1946a. Yuma. In *Linguistic Structures of Native America*, edited by Cornelius Osgood, 249–288. Viking Fund Publications in Anthropology 6. New York: Viking Fund.

———. 1946b. Yuma I–III. IJAL 12:25–33, 147–151, 204–212.

———. 1947. Yuma IV–VI. IJAL 13:18–30, 92–107, 147–166.

———. 1964. A Report on a Survey of Pomo Languages. In *Studies in Californian Linguistics,* edited by William Bright, 88–93. UC-PL 34.

———. 1976. Kukumat Became Sick—A Yuma Text. In *Yuman Texts,* edited by Margaret Langdon, 5–25. IJAL Native American Texts Series 1(3). Chicago: University of Chicago Press.

———. 1982. Southeastern Pomo Directionals. In *1981 Hokan-Penutian Workshop.*

———. 1988. *Southeastern Pomo Ceremonials: The Kuksu Cult and Its Successors.* UC-AR 29.

———. 1997. *Karʔúk: Native Accounts of the Quechan Mourning Ceremony.* Edited by Amy Miller and Margaret Langdon. UC-PL 128.

Hamp, Eric P. 1966a. On Two Californian Grammars. IJAL 32:176–188.

———. 1966b. Studies in Sierra Miwok. IJAL 32:236–241.

———. 1975. On Zuni-Penutian Consonants. IJAL 41:310–312.

———. 1980. Some Remarks on Bright's "Hispanisms in Cahuilla." JCGBA-PL 2:95–97.

Hannon, Nan, and Richard K. Olmo, eds. 1990. *Living with the Land: The Indians of Southwest Oregon.* The Proceedings of the 1989 Symposium on the Prehistory of Southwest Oregon. Medford: Southern Oregon Historical Society.

Hardy, Heather K. 1979. *Tolkapaya Syntax: Aspect, Modality and Adverbial Modification in a Yavapai Dialect.* PhD dissertation, University of California, Los Angeles.

Harrington, John P. 1916. Notes on Esselen Vocabularies. EDDMA, no. 13. 33 pp.

———. 1917. [Announcement of the relationship of Washo and Chumash.] AA 19:154.

———. 1928. *Exploration of the Burton Mound at Santa Barbara, California.* BAE-AR 44:23–168.

———. 1930. Karuk Texts. IJAL 6:121–161.

———. 1932a. *Tobacco among the Karuk Indians of California.* BAE-B 94.

———. 1932b. *Karuk Indian Myths.* BAE-B 107.

———. 1933. [Annotations; notes on Luiseño phonetics; numerous Luiseño and Juaneño words and phrases.] In *Chinigchinich: A Revised and Annotated Version of Alfred Robinson's Translation of Father Gerónimo Boscana's Historical Account of the Belief, Usages, Customs and Extravagancies of the Indians of this Mission of San Juan Capistrano Called the Acagchemem Tribe.* Edited by P. T. Hanna. Santa Ana, CA: Fine Arts Press.

———. 1942. *Culture Element Distributions: XIX, Central California Coast.* UC-AR 7:1–46.

———. 1944. Indian Words in Southwest Spanish. *Plateau* 17(2):27–40.

———. 1962. Introduction. In *California's Gabrielino Indians,* by Bernice Eastman Johnston, vii–viii. Los Angeles: Southwest Museum.

———. 1974. Sibilants in Ventureño. IJAL 40:1–9.

———. 1982–1990. *The Papers of John Peabody Harrington in the Smithsonian Institution, 1907–1957* [494 microfilm reels, issued in nine parts; see Appendix B]. Edited by Elaine Mills et al. Millwood, NY: Kraus International. (The microfilm is now distributed by ProQuest [www.proquest.com].)

———. 1994. *The Photograph Collection of John Peabody Harrington in the National Anthropological Archives, Smithsonian Institution* [10 microfilm reels], edited by Gerrianne Schaad. Washington, DC: National Anthropological Archives, in collaboration with Preservation Resources, Bethlehem, PA.

———. n.d. English-Yuki slip file. Harvey Pitkin Papers, Series II-B, Library of the American Philosophical Society, Philadelphia. 23 folders.

Harris, Zellig S. 1944. Yokuts Structure and Newman's Grammar. IJAL 10:196–211.

———. 1947. Structural Restatements I. IJAL 13:47–58. (Includes reanalysis of data from Newman 1944.)

Harwell, Henry O., and Marsha C. S. Kelly. 1983. Maricopa. In *Handbook of North American Indians.* Vol. 10: *Southwest,* edited by Alfonso Ortiz, 71–85. Washington, DC: Smithsonian Institution.

Haspelmath, Martin, Matthew S. Dryer, David Gil, and Bernard Comrie, eds. 2005. *The World Atlas of Linguistic Structures.* Oxford, UK: Oxford University Press.

Hattori, Eugene M. 1982. *The Archaeology of Falcon Hill, Winnemucca Lake, Washoe County, Nevada.* PhD dissertation, Western Washington University, Bellingham.

Hazen, William B. 1857. Linguistic material, 1857: Comparative vocabulary of Applegate, Ta-kil-ma, and Uppa [Shasta] [8 pp.]; individual Applegate Creek and Ta-kil-ma vocabularies [12 pp.]; correspondence with George Gibbs. NAA MS 154, National Anthropological Archives, Smithsonian Institution.

Heath, Jeffrey. 1977. Uto-Aztecan Morphophonemics. IJAL 43:27–36.

———. 1981. Tübatulabal Phonology. In George N. Clements, ed., *Harvard Studies in Phonology,* vol. 2:251–302. Bloomington: Indiana University Linguistics Club.

Heizer, Robert F. 1941a. Alexander S. Taylor's Map of California Indian Tribes, 1864. *California Historical Society Quarterly* 20:171–180. (Original map in The Bancroft Library, University of California, Berkeley.)

———. 1941b. The Distribution and Name of the Chumash Plank Canoe. *The Masterkey* 15:59–61.

———. 1941c. The Plank Canoe (Dalca) of Southern Chile. *The Masterkey* 15:105–107.

———. 1947. *Francis Drake and the California Indians, 1579.* UC-PAAE 42(3):251–302. (Reprinted in Heizer 1974.)

———, ed. 1951. *The French Scientific Expedition to California, 1877–1879.* University of California Archaeological Survey, Report 12, pp. 6–13.

———, ed. 1952. *California Indian Linguistic Records: The Mission Indian Vocabularies of Alphonse Pinart.* UC-AR 15:1–84.

———, ed. 1955. *California Indian Linguistic Records: The Mission Indian Vocabularies of H. W. Henshaw.* UC-AR 15:85–202.

———, ed. 1963. *Aboriginal California: Three Studies in Culture History.* Berkeley: Archaeological Research Facility, University of California. (Reprinting of J. T. Davis 1961, Kroeber 1961, and Heizer and Elsasser 1961.)

———. 1966. *Languages, Territories, and Names of California Indian Tribes.* Berkeley: University of California Press.

———. 1970. Ethnographic Notes on the Northern Paiute. In *Languages and Cultures of Western North America: Essays in Honor of Sven S. Liljeblad,* edited by Earl H. Swanson, Jr., 232–245. Pocatello: Idaho State University Press.

———, ed. 1972a. *The Eighteen Unratified Treaties of 1851–52.* Berkeley: University of California, Archaeological Research Facility.

———, ed. 1972b. *George Gibbs' Journal of Redick McKee's Expedition through Northwestern California in 1851.* Berkeley: University of California, Archaeological Research Facility.

———, ed. 1973. *Notes on the McCloud River Wintu* [by Livingston Stone, pp. 1–22]; and, *Selected Excerpts from Alexander S. Taylor's "Indianology of California"* [pp. 23–79]. Berkeley: University of California, Archaeological Research Facility.

———. 1974. *Elizabethan California.* Ramona, CA: Ballena Press. (Contains reprints of Heizer 1947, and Heizer and Elmendorf 1942.)

———, ed. 1975a. *Chumash Place Name Lists: Compilations by A. L. Kroeber, C. Hart Merriam, and H. W. Henshaw.* Berkeley: University of California, Archaeological Research Facility.

———. 1975b. A Note on Harrington and Kroeber. JCA 2:233–34. (Responded to by Klar 1976 and Callaghan 1976.)

———. 1976. Further on J. P. Harrington. JCA 3:82–83. (Reply to Klar 1976.)

———, ed. 1978. *Handbook of North American Indians.* Vol. 8: *California.* Washington, DC: Smithsonian Institution.

Heizer, Robert F., and William W. Elmendorf. 1942. Francis Drake's California Anchorage in the Light of the Indian Language Spoken There. *Pacific Historical Review* 11:213–217. (Reprinted in Heizer 1974.)

Heizer, Robert F., and Albert B. Elsasser, eds. 1961. *Original Accounts of the Lone Woman of San Nicholas Island.* University of California Archaeological Survey, Report 55. (Reprinted in Heizer 1963:121–181.)

Heizer, Robert F., and Thomas R. Hester. 1970. *Shasta Villages and Territory.* Papers on California Ethnography. Contributions of the University of California Archaeological Research Facility 9:119–158.

Heizer, Robert F., and John E. Mills. 1952. *The Four Ages of Tsurai: A Documentary History of the Indian Village on Trinidad Bay.* Translations of Spanish Documents by Donald C. Cutter. Berkeley: University of California Press. (Reprinted 1991 by the Trinidad Museum Society, with new introductory material by Axel Lindgren.)

Henkels, Stan. V. (booksellers). 1911. [Catalog No. 1033.] The Libraries of Henry Flanders . . . Prof. Horatio Hale, of Wilkes' expedition, Sarah Jane Hale, Editor of Godey's Lady's Book, Admiral Richard W. Meade and Rev. Andrew Hunter . . . embracing the best editions of English and American standard authors . . . also oil paintings and engravings to be sold . . . May 23d and 24th, 1911. [Item 570, "Original Manuscript Essay on the Language of the Oregon Indians, about 100 pp. 8vo, sheep." Item 593, "Original Manuscript Note Books, containing his Essays on the Philology of the Various Countries Visited by the Commodore Wilkes Expedition. 18 vols. 4to and 12mo. An interesting lot, containing much material on the Languages of the Natives of the Sandwich Islands, China, American Indians, &c."] Philadelphia: Stan. V. Henkels. (Henkels's sales records have been destroyed. The copy of the catalog owned by the American Antiquarian Society has these annotations: for item 570, "La.bya" and "[$]8.00 Kay"; and for item 593, "Dalton ua" and "[$]5.00 Jones.")

Henshaw, Henry W. 1883a. Washoe November, 1883. NAA MS 963-a, National Anthropological Archives, Smithsonian Institution. 152 pp.

———. 1883b. Panamint vocabulary December, 1883. NAA MS 786, National Anthropological Archives, Smithsonian Institution. 154 pp.

———. 1884a. [Yokuts] Vocabulary, 1884. NAA MS 863, National Anthropological Archives, Smithsonian Institution. 10 pp.

———. 1884b. Ineseño Chumash vocabulary, September 18, 1884. NAA MS 292, National Anthropological Archives, Smithsonian Institution. 80 pp. (Published in Heizer 1955:94–159, col. 4.)

———. 1884c. Santa Barbara [Barbareño Chumash] and La Purissima or Kagimuswas [Purisimeño Chumash] vocabularies, September 18, 1884. NAA MS 294, National Anthropological Archives, Smithsonian Institution. 78 pp. (Purisimeño [from incomplete neat copy, NAA MS 867] published in Heizer 1955:94–159, col. 2.)

———. 1884d. Comparative vocabularies [of Santa Clara Costanoan, Obispeño Chumash, and Santa Rosa Island Chumash]. NAA MS 296, National Anthropological Archives, Smithsonian Institution. 105 pp. (Contains: Santa Clara Costanoan vocabulary, September 27, 1884; published in Heizer 1955:160–185, col. 3. Obispeño Chumash vocabulary, October 19–28, 1884 [see Henshaw 1884–1888]. Santa Rosa Island Chumash [actually Barbareño Chumash], October 30–November 7, 1884 [neat copy, NAA MS 866]; published in Heizer 1955:94–159, col. 1.)

———. 1884e. [Mutsun Costanoan] Vocabulary, September 27, 1884. NAA MS 301, National Anthropological Archives, Smithsonian Institution. 16 pp.

———. 1884f. San Antonio and San Miguel [Salinan] vocabularies, September 28, 1884. NAA MS 3077-a, National Anthropological Archives, Smithsonian Institution. 113 pp. [Neat copies: San Antonio, NAA MS 3077-b; San Miguel, NAA MS 3077-c.]

———. 1884g. Rumsien [Rumsen Costanoan] and Obispeño Chumash vocabulary. NAA MS 647, National Anthropological Archives, Smithsonian Institution. 87 pp. (Rumsen Costanoan vocabulary published in Heizer 1955:160–185, col. 2. Obispeño Chumash included in material published in Heizer 1955:94–159, col. 6.)

———. 1884h. Barbareño Chumash vocabulary, November 10, 1884. NAA MS 291-a, National Anthropological Archives, Smithsonian Institution. 65 pp. [Neat copy, NAA MS 291-b.] (Published in Heizer 1955:94–159, col. 3.)

———. 1884i. San Buenaventura or Mis-ka-na-kan vocabulary, November 18, 1884. NAA MS 293-a, National Anthropological Archives, Smithsonian Institution. 73 pp. [Neat copy and typed copy, NAA MS 3075.] (Published in Heizer 1955:94–159, col. 5.)

———. 1884j. [Diegueño] Vocabulary, December 4, 1884. NAA MS 1105, National Anthropological Archives, Smithsonian Institution. 47 pp.

———. 1884k. [Diegueño] Vocabulary, December 7, 1884. NAA MS 1145, National Anthropological Archives, Smithsonian Institution. 52 pp.

———. 1884l. Vocabulary of the Language spoken at Santa Catarina [Paipai], December 10, 1884. NAA MS 1128, National Anthropological Archives, Smithsonian Institution. 76 pp.

———. 1884m. San Luis Rey [vocabulary], December 19, 1884. NAA MS 784, National Anthropological Archives, Smithsonian Institution. 70 pp.

———. 1884n. Gabrielino and Serrano vocabularies, December 29, 1884. NAA MS 787-a, National Anthropological Archives, Smithsonian Institution. 14 pp. [Neat copies: Gabrielino, NAA MS 787-b; Serrano, NAA MS 787-c.] (Gabrielino vocabulary published in W. McCawley 1996:287–288.)

———. 1884–1888. Obispeño Chumash vocabulary, October 19–28, 1884 [with additional material from the same speaker added in 1888]. NAA MS 868, National Anthropological Archives, Smithsonian Institution. 24 pp. (Published, together with other Obispeño material from Henshaw 1884g and 1888d, in Heizer 1955:93–159, col. 6. Heizer erroneously cites NAA MS 868 as 852-a.)

———. 1888a. Vocabulary [of Tomales Bay Coast Miwok]. NAA MS 565, National Anthropological Archives, Smithsonian Institution. 95 pp. (See Henshaw 1890:47–48.)

———. 1888b. Santa Cruz [Costanoan] and Tulareño [Yokuts] vocabularies, September 26–29, 1888 [entries from two Yokuts informants]. NAA MS 295, National Anthropological Archives, Smithsonian Institution. 73 pp. (Santa Cruz Costanoan vocabulary published in Heizer 1955:160–185, col. 4.)

———. 1888c. Esselen vocabulary, 1888 [with notes and marginalia by A. L. Kroeber and note by A. S. Gatschet]. NAA MS 382, National Anthropological Archives, Smithsonian Institution. 22 pp. (Published in Kroeber 1904:47–57. Additional Esselen material in Henshaw 1888d; see Henshaw 1890.)

———. 1888d. Soledad [Costanoan] vocabulary with some Obispeño Chumash entries. [Also contains some Esselen data (cf. note in NAA catalogue, and Henshaw 1890:49).] NAA MS 302, National Anthropological Archives, Smithsonian Institution. 47 pp. (Soledad Costanoan vocabulary published in Heizer 1955:160–185, col. 1. Obispeño Chumash included in material published in Heizer 1955:94–159, col. 6.)

———. 1890. A New Linguistic Family in California. AA (old style) 3:45–49.

———. 1892. Vocabulary of [Northern (?) Pomo; apparently collected at Ukiah], October 25, 1892. NAA MS 864, National Anthropological Archives, Smithsonian Institution. 73 pp.

———. 1892–1893. [Diegueño] Vocabulary, December 1892–January 1893. NAA MS 1143, National Anthropological Archives, Smithsonian Institution. 60 pp.

———. 1893. Kawia [Cahuilla] vocabulary, January, 1893. NAA MS 799, National Anthropological Archives, Smithsonian Institution. 19 pp.

Herzog, George, Stanley S. Newman, Edward Sapir, Mary Haas, Morris Swadesh, and Charles F. Voegelin. 1934. Some Orthographic Recommendations. AA 36:629–631.

Hester, Thomas R. 1978. Esselen In *Handbook of North American Indians.* Vol. 8: *California,* edited by Robert F. Heizer, 496–499. Washington, DC: Smithsonian Institution.

Hewes, Minna and Gordon. 1952. Indian Life and Customs at Mission San Luis Rey: A Record of California Mission Life Written by Pablo Tac, an Indian Neophyte (Rome, ca. 1835). *The Americas, a Quarterly Review of Inter-American Cultural History* 9:87–106. Washington, DC: Academy of American Franciscan History. (Translation of Tagliavini 1930a.)

Hill, Jane H. 1966. *A Grammar of the Cupeño Language.* PhD dissertation, University of California, Los Angeles.

———. 1985. On the Etymology of Classical Nahuatl *teekʷ-tli* 'lord, master'. IJAL 51:451–453.

———. 2001. Proto-Uto-Aztecan: A Community of Cultivators in Central Mexico? AA 103:913–934.

———. 2002a. Toward a Linguistic Prehistory of the Southwest: "Azteco-Tanoan" and the Arrival of Maize Cultivation. *Journal of Anthropological Research* 58:457–476.

———. 2002b. "Expert Rhetorics" in Advocacy for Endangered Languages: Who Is Listening, and What Do They Hear? *Journal of Linguistic Anthropology* 12:119–133.

———. 2003. Proto-Uto-Aztecan Cultivation and the Northern Devolution. In *Examining the Farming/Language Dispersal Hypothesis,* edited by Peter Bellwood and Colin Renfrew, 331–340. Cambridge, UK: McDonald Institute for Archaeological Research.

———. 2005. *A Grammar of Cupeño.* UC-PL 136. (Available online at repositories.cdlib.org/ucpress.)

———. 2006. Uto-Aztecan Hunter-Gatherers: Language Change in the Takic Spread and the Numic Spread Compared. Paper presented at the Conference on Historical Linguistics and Hunter-Gatherer Populations in Global Perspective, Max Planck Institute for Evolutionary Anthropology, Leipzig, 10–12 August, 2006.

———. 2008. Northern Uto-Aztecan and Kiowa-Tanoan: Evidence of Contact between the Proto-Languages? IJAL 74:155–188.

———. 2009. "External Evidence" in Historical Linguistic Argumentation: Subgrouping in Uto-Aztecan. MS.

Hill, Jane, P. J. Mistry, and Lyle Campbell, eds. 1998. *The Life of Language: Papers in Linguistics in Honor of William Bright.* Berlin: Mouton de Gruyter.

Hill, Jane H., and Rosinda Nolasquez. 1973. *Mulu'wetam: The First People. Cupeño Oral History and Language.* Banning, CA: Malki Museum Press.

Hill, Kenneth C. 1967. *A Grammar of the Serrano Language.* PhD dissertation, University of California, Los Angeles.

———. 1978. The Coyote and the Flood (Serrano). In *Coyote Stories,* edited by William Bright, 112–116. IJAL-NATS Monograph 1. Chicago: University of Chicago Press.

———. 1984. Hispanisms and Other Loanwords in Serrano. JCGBA-PL 4:91–106.

Hinkson, Mercedes Q. 1980. Patterns of Derivational Affixation in the Spanish Dialect of the Last Rumsen Speakers. In *American Indian and Indoeuropean Studies: Papers in Honor of Madison S. Beeler,* edited by Kathryn A. Klar, Margaret Langdon, and Shirley Silver, 77–84. The Hague: Mouton.

Hinsley, Curtis M. 1981. *Savages and Scientists: The Smithsonian Institution and the Development of American Anthropology, 1846–1910.* Washington, DC: Smithsonian Institution Press.

Hinton, Leanne. 1970. Unpublished field notes on La Huerta Diegueño. MS.

———. 1976. The Tar Baby Story. In *Yuman Texts,* edited by Margaret Langdon, 101–106. IJAL Native American Texts Series 1(3). Chicago: University of Chicago Press.

———. 1979. Irataba's Gift: A Closer Look at the ṣ > s > θ Soundshift in Mojave and Northern Pai. JCGBA-PL 1:3–37.

———. 1981. Upland Yuman Sibilant Shifts: The Beginning of the Story. JCGBA-PL 3:65–76.

———. 1984. *Havasupai Songs: A Linguistic Perspective.* Tübingen, Germany: Gunter Narr. (Based on the author's PhD dissertation, University of California, San Diego, 1977.)

———. 1988. Yana Morphology: A Thumbnail Sketch. In *1987 Hokan-Penutian Workshop,* pp. 7–16.

———. 1991. Takic and Yuman: A Study in Phonological Convergence. IJAL 57:133–157.

———. 1994. *Flutes of Fire: Essays on California Indian Languages.* Berkeley: Heyday Books.

———, ed. 1997. See *1996 Hokan-Penutian Workshop.*

———. 2000. The Proceedings of the Hokan-Penutian Workshops: A History and Indices. In *2000 Hokan-Penutian Workshop,* pp. 115–125.

Hinton, Leanne, and Margaret Langdon. 1976. Object-Subject Pronominal Prefixes in La Huerta Diegueño. In *Hokan Studies: Papers from the First Conference on Hokan Languages,* edited by Margaret Langdon and Shirley Silver, pp. 113–128. The Hague: Mouton.

Hinton, Leanne, and Pamela Munro, eds. 1998. *Studies in American Indian Languages: Description and Theory.* UC-PL 131.

Hinton, Leanne, and Alice Shepherd. 1998. Layers of Meaning in a Wintu Doctor Song. In *The Life of Language: Papers in Linguistics in Honor of William Bright,* edited by Jane Hill, P. J. Mistry, and Lyle Campbell, 271–280. Berlin: Mouton de Gruyter.

Hinton, Leanne, and William F. Weigel. 2002. A Dictionary for Whom? Tensions between Academic and Nonacademic Functions of Bilingual Dictionaries. In *Making Dictionaries: Preserving Indigenous Languages of the Americas,* edited by William Frawley, Kenneth C. Hill, and Pamela Munro, 155–170. Berkeley: University of California Press.

Hockett, Charles F. 1967. The Yawelmani Basic Verb. *Language* 43:208–222.

———. 1973. Yokuts as a Testing-Ground for Linguistic Methods. IJAL 39:63–79.

Hodge, F. W., ed. 1910. *Handbook of American Indians North of Mexico.* BAE-B 30.

Hoijer, Harry. 1956. The Chronology of the Athapaskan Languages. IJAL 22:219–232.

———. 1960. Athapaskan Languages of the Pacific Coast. In *Culture in History: Essays in Honor of Paul Radin,* edited by Stanley Diamond, 960–977. New York: Columbia University Press.

———. 1966. Galice Athapaskan: A Grammatical Sketch. IJAL 32:320–327.

———. 1973. Galice Noun and Verb Stems. *Linguistics* 104:49–73.

Holbrook, Kenny. 2001. Learning Maidu. *News from Native California.* Winter 2001–2002, pp. 18–19.

Holt, Catherine. 1946. *Shasta Ethnography.* UC-AR 3(4):299–350.

Hoover, Robert L., and J. G. Costello, eds. 1985. *Excavations at Mission San Antonio, 1976–1978.* Los Angeles: University of California, Institute of Archaeology, Monograph 26.

Hudson, Travis. 1977. Patterns of Chumash Names. JCA 4:259–272.

———. 1979. *Breath of the Sun: Life in Early California as Told by a Chumash Indian, Fernando Librado, to John P. Harrington.* Banning. CA: Malki Museum Press.

———. 1982. The Alliklik-Tataviam Problem. JCGBA 4:222–232.

Hudson, Travis, Thomas Blackburn, R. Curletti, and Jan Timbrook, eds. 1977. *The Eye of the Flute: Chumash Traditional History and Ritual as Told by Fernando Librado Kitsepawit to John P. Harrington.* Santa Barbara, CA: Santa Barbara Museum of Natural History. [Second edition, 1981. Banning. CA: Malki Museum Press.]

Hughes, Richard E. 1992. California Archaeology and Linguistic Prehistory. *Journal of Anthropological Research* 48:317–338.

———, ed. 1994. *Toward a New Taxonomic Framework for Central California Archaeology: Essays by James A. Bennyhoff and David A. Fredrickson.* Contributions of the Archaeological Research Facility, University of California, Berkeley, No. 52. (Ten previously unpublished papers, including Bennyhoff 1968.)

Hyde, Villiana. 1971. *An Introduction to the Luiseño Language.* Banning, CA: Malki Museum Press. (Second edition, edited by Ronald W. Langacker, San Bernardino, CA: Borgo Press, 1993.)

Hyde, Villiana, and Eric B. Elliott. 1994. *Yumáyk Yumáyk: Long Ago.* Berkeley: University of California Press.

Hymes, Dell H. 1957. A Note on Athapaskan Chronology. IJAL 23:291–297.

———. 1961a. Kroeber, Powell and Henshaw. AL 3(6):15–16.

———. 1961b. Alfred Louis Kroeber. *Language* 37:1–28.

———, ed. 1964. *Language in Culture and Society.* New York: Harper and Row.

———. 1979. How to Talk Like a Bear in Takelma. IJAL 45:101–106.

———. 1990. The Discourse Patterning of a Takelma Text: "Coyote and His Rock Grandmother." In *Collected Works of Edward Sapir.* Vol. 8: *Takelma Texts and Grammar*, edited by Victor Golla, 583–598. Berlin: Mouton de Gruyter.

Hymes, Dell. H., and William E. Bittle, eds. 1967. *Studies in Southwestern Ethnolinguistics: Meaning and History in the Languages of the American Southwest* [in honor of Harry Hoijer]. Studies in General Anthropology 3. The Hague: Mouton.

Hymes, Virginia D. 1955. Athapaskan Numeral Systems. IJAL 21:26–45.

Ibarra Rivera, Gilberto. 1991. *Vocablos Indigenas de Baja California Sur.* La Paz, Mexico: Gobierno de Baja California Sur.

Ives, Joseph C. 1860. *Report upon the Exploration of the River Colorado of the West.* Washington, DC.

Jacknis, Ira. 2003. Yahi Culture in the Wax Museum: Ishi's Sound Recordings. In *Ishi in Three Centuries,* edited by Karl Kroeber and Clifton Kroeber, 235–274. Lincoln: University of Nebraska Press.

Jacobs, Elizabeth D. 1968. A Chetco Athapaskan Myth Text from Southwestern Oregon. IJAL 34:192–193.

———. 1977. A Chetco Athapaskan Text and Translation. IJAL 43:269–273.

Jacobs, Elizabeth D., and Melville Jacobs. ca. 1935. Notes on U. Umpkwa Athapaskan in handwriting of Eliz. D. Jacobs (Bess Langdon) and Melville Jacobs, ca. 1935, Siletz, Oregon. [Vocabulary of 372 items.] MS. (My handwritten copy of the first page, and a photocopy of the remainder, of a manuscript that was in Harry Hoijer's possession in the mid-1960s, but that is now lost. The title was added to the original by Hoijer.)

Jacobs, Melville. 1931. *A Sketch of Northern Sahaptian Grammar.* University of Washington Publications in Anthropology 4(2):85–292. Seattle: University of Washington Press.

———. 1937. Historic Perspectives in Indian Languages of Oregon and Washington. *Pacific Northwest Quarterly* 28:55–74.

———. 1954. The Areal Spread of Sound Features in the Languages North of California. In *Papers from the Symposium on American Indian Linguistics held at Berkeley July 7, 1951,* pp. 46–56. UC-PL 10(1).

———. 1968. An Historical Event Text from a Galice Athabaskan in Southwestern Oregon. IJAL 34:183–191.

Jacobs, Roderick A. 1975. *Syntactic Change: A Cupan (Uto-Aztecan) Case Study.* UC-PL 79. (Based on the author's dissertation, University of California, San Diego, 1972.)

Jacobsen, William H., Jr. 1964. *A Grammar of the Washo Language.* PhD dissertation, University of California, Berkeley.

———. 1967. Switch-Reference in Hokan-Coahuiltecan. In *Studies in Southwestern Ethnolinguistics: Meaning and History in the Languages of the American Southwest* [Festschrift in honor of Harry Hoijer], edited by Dell H. Hymes and William E. Bittle, 238–263. Studies in General Anthropology 3. The Hague: Mouton.

———. 1976. Observations on the Yana Stop Series in Relationship to Problems of Comparative Hokan Phonology. In *Hokan Studies: Papers from the First Conference on Hokan Languages,* edited by Margaret Langdon and Shirley Silver, 203–236. The Hague: Mouton.

———. 1977. A Glimpse of the Pre-Washo Pronominal System. In *Proceedings of the 3rd Annual Meeting of the Berkeley Linguistics Society,* edited by Kenneth Whistler et al., 55–73. Berkeley: Berkeley Linguistics Society.

———. 1978. Washo Internal Diversity and External Relations. In *Selected Papers from the 14th Great Basin Anthropological Conference,* edited by Donald R. Tuohy, 115–147. Socorro, New Mexico: Ballena Press.

———. 1979a. Hokan Inter-Branch Comparisons. In *The Languages of Native America: Historical and Comparative Assessment,* edited by Lyle Campbell and Marianne Mithun, 545–591. Austin: University of Texas Press.

———. 1979b. Why Does Washo Lack a Passive? In *Ergativity: Towards a Theory of Grammatical Relations,* edited by Frans Plank, 145–160. London: Academic Press.

———. 1979c. Gender and Personification in Washo. JCGBA-PL 1:75–84.

———. 1980. Washo Bipartite Verb Stems. In *American Indian and Indoeuropean Studies: Papers in Honor of Madison S. Beeler*, edited by Kathryn A. Klar, Margaret Langdon, and Shirley Silver, 85–99. The Hague: Mouton.

———. 1983. Typological and Genetic Notes on Switch-Reference Systems in North American Indian Languages. In *Switch Reference and Universal Grammar,* edited by John Haiman and Pamela Munro, 151–183. Amsterdam: Benjamins.

———. 1986a. Washoe Language. In *Handbook of North American Indians.* Vol. 11: *Great Basin,* edited by Warren L. d'Azevedo, 107–112. Washington, DC: Smithsonian Institution.

———. 1986b. Washo Linguistic Prehistory. In *1983–85 Hokan-Penutian Workshops.*

———. 1996a. *Beginning Washo.* Nevada State Museum, Occasional Papers No. 5. Carson City: Nevada State Museum.

———. 1996b. Washo Pronouns. In *1994–96 Hokan Penutian Workshops,* pp. 175–176.

———. 1998. Headless Relative Clauses in Washo. In *Studies in American Indian Languages: Description and Theory,* edited by Leanne Hinton and Pamela Munro, 102–116. UC-PL 131.

Jany, Carmen. 2007. Complementation in Chimariko. IJAL 73:94–113.

———. 2009. *Chimariko Grammar: Areal and Typological Perspective.* UC-PL 142. (Published version of the author's PhD dissertation, University of California, Santa Barbara, 2007.)

Jensen, James D. 1973. *Stress and the Verbal Phonology of Tübatulabal.* PhD dissertation, Indiana University, Bloomington.

Jimeno, Fr. Antonio. 1856. [Vocabulary of] The Island of Santa Cruz Indians, Near Santa Barbara. The Bancroft Library, University of California, Berkeley. (Photostat copy in NAA. Published in A. Taylor 1860–1863 [May 4, 1860, erroneously attributed to "Timmeno"]. Published version reprinted in Powers 1877:560–567; Lucy-Fossarieu 1881; Kroeber 1910:265–268; and Heizer1973:40.)

Joël, Judith. 1964. Classification of the Yuman Languages. In *Studies in Californian Linguistics,* edited by William Bright, 99–105. UC-PL 34.

———. 1966. *Paipai Phonology and Morphology.* PhD dissertation, University of California, Los Angeles.

———. 1976. The Earthquake of '57—A Paipai Text. In *Yuman Texts,* edited by Margaret Langdon, 84–91. IJAL Native American Texts Series 1(3). Chicago: University of Chicago Press.

———. 1978. The Yuman Word for "Bean" as a Clue to Prehistory. JCA-PL [1]:77–92.

———. 1998. Another Look at the Paipai-Arizona Pai Divergence. In *Studies in American Indian Languages: Description and Theory,* edited by Leanne Hinton and Pamela Munro, 33–40. UC-PL 131.

Johnson, Adam. See Johnston, Adam.

Johnson, John R. 1978. The Trail to *Kashtiq.* JCA 5:188–198.

———. 1988. *Chumash Social Organization: An Ethnohistoric Perspective.* PhD dissertation, University of California, Santa Barbara.

———. 2000. Social Responses to Climate Change among the Chumash Indians of South-Central California. In *The Way the Wind Blows: Climate Change, History, and Human Action,* edited by Roderick J. McIntosh, Joseph A. Tainter, and Susan Keech McIntosh, 301–328. New York: Columbia University Press.

———. 2001. Ethnohistoric Reflections of Cruzeño Chumash Society. In *The Origins of a Pacific Coast Chiefdom: The Chumash of the Channel Islands,* edited by Jeanne E. Arnold, 53–70. Salt Lake City: University of Utah Press.

———. 2006. The Various *Chinigchinich* Manuscripts of Father Gerónimo Boscana. Paper presented at the 23rd Annual Conference of the California Mission Studies Association, San Diego, February 17–19, 2006.

Johnson, John R., and Dinah Crawford. 1999. Contributions to Luiseño Ethnohistory Based on Mission Register Research. *Pacific Coast Archaeological Society Quarterly* 35:79–102.

Johnson, John R., and David Earle. 1990. Tataviam Geography and Ethnohistory. JCGBA 12:191–214.

Johnson, John R., and Joseph G. Lorenz. 2006. Genetics, Linguistics, and Prehistoric Migrations: An Analysis of California Indian Mitochondrial DNA Lineages. JCGBA 26:33–64.

Johnson, John R., Amy Miller, and Linda Agren. 1991. The Papers of John P. Harrington at the Santa Barbara Museum of Natural History. AL 33:367–378.

Johnston, Adam. 1852a. Costanos [San Francisco Costanoan vocabulary] by Pedro Alcantara. In *Historical and Statistical Information Respecting the History, Condition and Prospects of the Indian Tribes of the United States,* edited by Henry R. Schoolcraft. Vol. 2, pp. 494–506. Philadelphia: Lippencott. (In "Notes to Vocabularies," p. 506, Johnston identifies Pedro Alcantara as "an aged . . . native of the Romonan tribe" living at Mission Dolores.)

———. 1852b. Cushna [N. Hill Nisenan vocabulary]. In *Historical and Statistical Information Respecting the History, Condition and Prospects of the Indian Tribes of the United States,* edited by Henry R. Schoolcraft, Vol. 2, pp. 494–508. Philadelphia: Lippencott. (In "Notes to Vocabularies," pp. 507–508, Johnston says that Cushna was spoken in the mountains of the South Yuba river.)

———. 1854. Languages of California. [Vocabularies of "Tuolumne" (Sierra Miwok), "Coconoons" (Delta Yokuts from the Merced River), "Kings river and around Tulare Lake" (Valley Yokuts), and "near to Mag. Reading's on the upper waters of the Sacramento river" (Nomlaki).] In *Historical and Statistical Information Respecting the History, Condition and Prospects of the Indian Tribes of the United States,* edited by Henry R. Schoolcraft, Vol. 4, pp. 405–415. Philadelphia: Lippencott.

Johnston, Bernice Eastman. 1962. *California's Gabrielino Indians.* Los Angeles: Southwest Museum.

Jones, Terry L., Richard T. Fitzgerald, Douglas J. Kennett, Charles H. Miksicek, John L. Fagan, John Sharp, and Jon M. Erlandson. 2002. The Cross Creek Site (CA-SLO-1797) and Its Implications for New World Colonization. *American Antiquity* 67:213–230.

Jones, Terry L., and Kathryn A. Klar. 2005. Diffusionism Reconsidered: Linguistic and Archaeological Evidence for Prehistoric Polynesian Contact with Southern California. *American Antiquity* 70:457–484. (See Klar and Jones 2005 for further discussion of the linguistic evidence, and Atholl Anderson 2006 for a reply.)

———, eds. 2007. *California Prehistory: Colonization, Culture, and Complexity.* Lanham, MD: AltaMira Press.

Jones, Terry L., Betty Rivers, Andrea M. Maliarik, Terry L. Joslin, and Douglas Alger. 2000. An Addendum to Harrington's Northern Salinan Place Names. JCGBA 22:3–11.

Jones, Terry L., Nathan E. Stevens, Deborah A. Jones, Richard T. Fitzgerald, and Mark G. Hylkema. 2007. The Central Coast: A Midlatitude Milieu. In *California Prehistory: Colonization, Culture, and Complexity,* edited by Terry L. Jones and Kathryn A. Klar, 125–146. Lanham, MD: AltaMira Press.

Kaestle, Frederika A., and David Glenn Smith. 2001. Ancient Mitochondrial DNA Evidence for Prehistoric Population Movement: The Numic Expansion. *American Journal of Physical Anthropology* 115:1–12.

Kaufman, Terrence. 1974. Middle American Languages. In *Encyclopaedia Britannica,* 15th ed., 11:959–963.

———. 1988. A Research Program for Reconstructing Proto-Hokan: First Gropings. In *1988 Hokan-Penutian Workshop,* pp. 50–168.

Kavanaugh, Thomas W. 2001. Comanche. In *Handbook of North American Indians.* Vol. 13: *Plains,* edited by Raymond J. DeMallie, 886–906. Washington, DC: Smithsonian Institution.

Keeling, Richard. 1991. *A Guide to Early Field Recordings (1900–1949) at the Lowie Museum of Anthropology.* Berkeley: University of California Press.

———. 1992. Music and Culture History among the Yurok and Neighboring Tribes of Northwestern California. *Journal of Anthropological Research* 48:25–48.

———. 1993. *Cry for Luck: Sacred Song and Speech Among the Yurok, Hupa, and Karok Indians of Northwestern California.* Berkeley: University of California Press. (Text available online through the eScholarship Program of the California Digital Library [ark.cdlib.org/ark:/13030/ft8g5008k8/].)

Kelly, Isabel T. 1931–1932. Coast Miwok field notes, San Rafael subgroup (from Maria Copa) and Bodega subgroup (from Tom Smith). EDDMA, nos. 139-140. 11 notebooks, 1,157 pp. (Also typescripts of these, filed as EDDMA, nos. 141–142, respectively. 537 pp. Published as Collier and Thalman 1996.)

———. 1932. Ethnography of the Surprise Valley Paiute. UC-PAAE 31(3):67–210.

———. 1978. Coast Miwok. In *Handbook of North American Indians.* Vol. 8: *California,* edited by Robert F. Heizer, 414–425. Washington, DC: Smithsonian Institution.

Kelsey, Harry. 1979. The *Doctrina* and *Confesionario* of Juan Cortés. [Edition of a manuscript in the Biblioteca Nacional de México, dated Santa Barbara, December 1798, and signed by Fr. Juan Cortés.] Altadena, CA: Howling Coyote Press.

———. 1986. Juan Rodríguez Cabrillo. San Marino, CA: Huntington Library.

Kendall, Daythal. 1977. *A Syntactic Analysis of Takelma Texts.* PhD dissertation, University of Pennsylvania, Philadelphia.

———. 1982. Some Notes toward Using Takelma Data in Historical and Comparative Work. In *1981 Hokan-Penutian Workshop.*

———. 1990. Takelma. In *Handbook of North American Indians.* Vol. 7: *Northwest Coast,* edited by Wayne Suttles, 589–592. Washington, DC: Smithsonian Institution.

———. 1997. The Takelma Verb: Toward Proto-Takelman-Kalapuyan. IJAL 63:1–17.

Kendall, Martha B. 1976. *Selected Problems in Yavapai Syntax: The Verde Valley Dialect.* New York: Garland. (Based on the author's PhD dissertation, Indiana University, 1972.)

———, ed. 1980. *Coyote Stories II.* IJAL Native American Text Series, Monograph 6. Chicago: University of Chicago Press.

———. 1983. Yuman Languages. In *Handbook of North American Indians.* Vol. 10: *Southwest,* edited by Alfonso Ortiz, 4-12. Washington, DC: Smithsonian Institution.

Kerr, Susan L. 2004. *The People of the Southern Channel Islands: A Bioarchaeological Study of Adaptation and Population Change in Southern California.* PhD dissertation, University of California, Santa Barbara.

Kessler, Cristina. 1979. A Note on the Mystery of the 'Long Lost Boscana Original'. JCGBA 1:193–195.

Kinkade, M. Dale. 1989. Charles Frederick Voegelin (1906–1986). AA 91:727–729.

———. 1990. History of Research in Linguistics. In *Handbook of North American Indians.* Vol. 7: *Northwest Coast,* edited by Wayne Suttles, 98–106. Washington, DC: Smithsonian Institution.

———. 2005. Alsea Pronouns. AL 47:61–67.

Kinkade, M. Dale, William W. Elmendorf, Bruce Rigsby, and Haruo Aoki. 1998. Languages. In *Handbook of North American Indians.* Vol. 12: *Plateau,* edited by Deward E. Walker, Jr., 49–72. Washington, DC: Smithsonian Institution.

Kinkade, M. Dale, Kenneth L. Hale and Oswald Werner, eds. 1975. *Linguistics and Anthropology: In Honor of C. F. Voegelin.* Lisse, Netherlands: Peter de Ridder.

Klar, Kathryn A. 1971. *Northern Chumash and the Subgrouping of the Chumash Dialects.* MA thesis, University of California, Berkeley.

———. 1975. Pismo and Nipomo. *Names* 23:26–30.

———. 1976. Harrington: A Reply to Heizer. JCA 3:145–147. (Reply to Heizer 1976.)

———. 1977. *Topics in Historical Chumash Grammar.* PhD dissertation, University of California, Berkeley.

———. 1980. Northern Chumash Numerals. In *American Indian and Indoeuropean Studies: Papers in Honor of Madison S. Beeler,* edited by Kathryn A. Klar, Margaret Langdon, and Shirley Silver, 113–119. The Hague: Mouton.

———. 1981. Proto-Chumash Person and Number Markers. In *1980 Hokan-Penutian Workshop.*

———. 1991. "Precious beyond the Power of Money to Buy": John P. Harrington's Fieldwork with Rosario Cooper. AL 33:379–391.

———. 1993. John P. Harrington's Phonetic Representations of Obispeño Chumash Palatal Consonants. In *1992 Hokan-Penutian Workshop,* pp. 17–19.

———. 2002. The Island Chumash Language: Implications for Interdisciplinary Work. In *Proceedings of the Fifth California Islands Symposium: 29 March to 1 April, 1999,* edited by David R. Browne, Kathryn L. Mitchell, and Henry W. Chaney, 654–658. Santa Barbara, CA: Santa Barbara Museum of Natural History.

———. 2010. Understanding Linguistic Prehistory on the Northern Channel Islands. Report prepared for Channel Islands National Park.

Klar, Kathryn A., and Terry L. Jones. 2005. Linguistic Evidence for a Prehistoric Polynesia—Southern California Contact Event. AL 47:369–400. (See Jones and Klar 2005 for discussion of the archaeological evidence, and Atholl Anderson 2006 for a reply.)

Klar, Kathryn A., Margaret Langdon, and Shirley Silver, eds. 1980. *American Indian and Indoeuropean Studies: Papers in Honor of Madison S. Beeler.* The Hague: Mouton.

Klar, Kathryn A., Kenneth W. Whistler, and Sally McLendon. 1999. The Chumash Languages: An Overview. In *Cultural*

Affiliation and Lineal Descent of Chumash Peoples in the Channel Islands and the Santa Monica Mountains, edited by Sally McLendon and John R. Johnson, Chap. 2. Report prepared for the Archeology and Ethnography Program, National Park Service, Washington, DC; Department of Anthropology, Hunter College, City University of New York; and Santa Barbara Museum of Natural History, Santa Barbara.

Klein, Sheldon. 1959. Comparative Mono-Kawaiisu. IJAL 25:233–238.

———. 1988. Narrative Style in Variants of a Kawaiisu Myth Text. In *In Honor of Mary Haas: From the Haas Festival Conference on Native American Linguistics,* edited by William F. Shipley. Berlin: Mouton de Gruyter.

———. 2002. Tying Loose Ends in Kawaiisu Phonology: Some Comments on Zigmond, Booth and Munro (1990). In *Proceedings of the 50th Anniversary Conference, June 8–9, 2002, University of California at Berkeley,* edited by Lisa Conathan and Teresa McFarland, 89–97. Survey of California and Other Indian Languages, Report 12. Berkeley: Department of Linguistics, University of California.

Kniffen, Fred B. 1928. *Achomawi Geography.* UC-PAAE 23(5):297–332.

———. 1939. *Pomo Geography.* UC-PAAE 36(6):353–400.

Kottman, Karl. 2005. Pablo Tac's Vocal Remembrance of "Californian." *Boletín: The Journal of the California Mission Studies Association* 22(2):22–52.

Kotzebue, Otto von. 1821. *A Voyage of Discovery, Into the South Sea and Beering's Straits.* London: Longman. 3 vols. [Translated from German by H. E. Lloyd.] (See Mahr 1932.)

Kozlowski, Edwin L. 1972. *Havasupai Simple Sentences.* PhD dissertation, Indiana University, Bloomingon.

Krauss, Michael E. 1976. [Introduction to forthcoming monograph on Kwalhioqua-Tlatskanai language.] University of Alaska. MS.

———. 1979. Na-Dene and Eskimo Aleut. In *The Languages of Native America: Historical and Comparative Assessment,* edited by Lyle Campbell and Marianne Mithun, 803–901. Austin: University of Texas Press.

———. 1990. Kwalhioqua and Clatskanie. In *Handbook of North American Indians.* Vol. 7: *Northwest Coast,* edited by Wayne Suttles, 530–532. Washington, DC: Smithsonian Institution.

Krauss, Michael E., and Victor Golla. 1981. Northern Athabaskan Languages. In *Handbook of North American Indians.* Vol. 6: *Subarctic,* edited by June Helm, 67–85. Washington, DC: Smithsonian Institution.

Kroeber, Alfred L. 1900–1910. Notes on Mojave ethnography and language. A. L. Kroeber Papers, BANC MSS C-B 925, The Bancroft Library, University of California, Berkeley. [Notebooks 7, 33–36, 50, 52, 54–55, 60–62, 86–88, 99, and 101, and other manuscripts.] (Microfilm: BANC FILM 2049, reel 103, frame 9, through reel 116, frame 115.)

———. 1900–1924. Notes on Patwin ethnography and language. Harvey Pitkin Papers, Series I-A and I-B, Library of the American Philosophical Society, Philadelphia. [Notebooks concerning various dialects or areas of Hill, River, Colusa, and Long Valley Patwin; also occasional information on Atsugewi, Yana, Salt Pomo, Lake Miwok, Kato, and Pomo. Patwin vocabulary file of 1,800 slips.] (See also Kroeber 1909b.)

———. 1900–1940. Notes on Yurok ethnography and language. A. L. Kroeber Papers, BANC MSS C-B 925, The Bancroft Library, University of California, Berkeley. [Notebooks 2–4, 9–48, and other manuscripts.] (Microfilm: BANC FILM 2049, reel 96, frames 501–603, and reel 125, frame 763. through reel 147.)

———. 1900–1958. Notes on Yuki ethnography and language. Harvey Pitkin Papers, Series II, Library of the American Philosophical Society, Philadelphia. [14 field notebooks (1900–1908, 1917); manuscripts, vocabularies and slip files, some incorporating data collected by Hans Jørgen Uldall in 1931–1932; transcriptions and translations of Yuki texts. The APS states: "The originals of Kroeber's Yuki notebooks were transferred to the Kroeber Papers, Bancroft Library, University of California, Berkeley in 1999. Photocopies of all were retained." As of 2010, however, these notebooks were not listed in the Bancroft Library's catalog of the A. L. Kroeber Papers, and not included in the microfilm of the collection.] (A few other Yuki materials are in A. L. Kroeber Papers, BANC MSS C-B 925, The Bancroft Library, University of California, Berkeley. Microfilm: BANC FILM 2049, reel 125, frame 661–686, and reel 163, frame 351 ff. See also Uldall 1931–1932.)

———. 1901. New River Shasta vocabulary. From Buck Kid's mother. A. L. Kroeber Papers, BANC MSS C-B 925, The Bancroft Library, University of California, Berkeley. [Notebook 12.] (Microfilm: BANC FILM 2049, reel 96, frames 405–500. Neat copy in Goddard 1902a.)

———. 1904. *Languages of the Coast of California South of San Francisco.* UC-PAAE 2(2):29–80.

———. 1906a. The Dialectic Divisions of the Moquelumnan Family in Relation to the Internal Differentiation of the Other Linguistic Families of California. AA 8:652–663.

———. 1906b. *The Yokuts and Yuki Languages.* In *Boas Anniversary Voume,* edited by Berthold Laufer, 64–79. New York: Stechert.

———. 1907a. *The Yokuts Language of South Central California.* UC-PAAE 2(5):165–378.

———. 1907b. *Shoshonean Dialects of California.* UC-PAAE 4(3):65–165.

———. 1907c. *The Washo Language of East Central California and Nevada.* UC-PAAE 4(5):251–317.

———. 1908a. *On the Evidence of the Occupation of Certain Regions by the Miwok Indians.* UC-PAAE 6(3):369–380.

———. 1908b. *A Mission Record of the California Indians.* UC-PAAE 8(1):1–27.

———. 1908c. *Ethnography of the Cahuilla Indians.* UC-PAAE 8(2):29–68.

———. 1909a. *Notes on the Shoshonean Dialects of California.* UC-PAAE 8(5):235–269.

———. 1909b. Patwin texts and notes, and preliminary linguistic analysis. Harvey Pitkin Papers, Series I-C, Library of the American Philosophical Society, Philadelphia.

———. 1910. *The Chumash and Costanoan Languages.* UC-PAAE 9(2):237–271.

———. 1911a. *The Languages of the Coast of California North of San Francisco.* UC-PAAE 9(3):273–435.

———. 1911b. *Phonetic Elements of the Mohave Language.* UC-PAAE 10(3):45–96.

———. 1915a. A New Shoshonean Tribe in California. AA 17:773–775.

———. 1915b. *Serian, Tequistlatecan, and Hokan.* UC-PAAE 11(4):279–290.

———. 1925. *Handbook of the Indians of California.* BAE-B 76.

———. 1929. *The Valley Nisenan.* UC-PAAE 24(4):253–290.

———. 1931. *The Seri.* Southwest Museum Paper 6.

———. 1932. *The Patwin and Their Neighbors.* UC-PAAE 29(4):253–423.

———. 1934. *Yurok and Neighboring Kin Term Systems.* UC-PAAE 35(2):15–22.

———. 1936. *Karok Towns.* UC-PAAE 35(4):29–38.

———. 1937. Thomas Talbot Waterman. AA 39:527–529.

———. 1940. Conclusions: The Present Status of Americanistic Problems. In *The Maya and Their Neighbors: Essays in Honor of Alfred Marston Tozzer,* edited by Clarence L. Hay, Ralph L. Linton, Samuel K. Lothrop, Harry L. Shapiro, and George C. Vaillant, 460–489. New York: D. Appleton-Century.

———. 1943. *Classification of the Yuman Languages.* UC-PL 1:20–40.

———. 1948. *Seven Mojave Myths.* UC-AR 11(1):1–70.

———. 1955. C. Hart Merriam as Anthropologist. In *Studies of California Indians,* by C. Hart Merriam, vii–xiv. Edited by the Staff of the Department of Anthropology of the University of California. Berkeley: University of California Press.

———. 1957. *Ethnographic Interpretations* 1-6. UC-PAAE 47(2):191–234.

———. 1958. An Atsugewi Word List. IJAL 213–214.

———. 1959a. *Ethnographic Interpretations* 7-11. UC-PAAE 47(3):235–310.

———. 1959b. Northern Yokuts. AL 1(8):1–19.

———. 1959c. Possible Athabascan Influence on Yuki. IJAL 25:59.

———. 1960a. Yurok Speech Uses. In *Culture in History: Essays in Honor of Paul Radin,* edited by Stanley Diamond, 993–999. New York: Columbia University Press.

———. 1960b. Powell and Henshaw: An Episode in the History of Ethnolinguistics. AL 2(4):1–5.

———. 1961. *The Nature of Land-Holding Groups in Aboriginal California.* University of California Archaeological Survey, Report 56:19–58. (Reprinted in Heizer 1963:81–120.)

———. 1963. *Yokuts Dialect Survey.* UC-AR 11(3).

———. 1967. Goddard's California Athabascan Texts. IJAL 33:269–275.

———. 1976. *Yurok Myths.* Berkeley: University of California Press.

———. n.d.[a]. Kato word list. Harvey Pitkin Papers, Series III-B, Library of the American Philosophical Society, Philadelphia.

———. n.d.[b]. Northern Paiute Verbs [slip file]. EDDMA, no. 132.

Kroeber, Alfred L., Anna H. Gayton, and L. S. Freeland. 1925. Southern Nisenan Ethnographic Notes and Vocabularies. [Collected from Tom Cleanso in Berkeley, January-February 1925.] EDDMA, no. 120. 5 notebooks, 1 map. 168 pp.

Kroeber, Alfred L., and Edward W. Gifford. 1949. *World Renewal: A Cult System of Native Northwest California.* UC-AR 13(1):1–156.

———. 1980. *Karok Myths.* Edited by Grace Buzaljko. Berkeley: University of California Press.

Kroeber, Alfred L., and George William Grace. 1960. *The Sparkman Grammar of Luiseño.* UC-PL 16. (See also EDDMA, nos. 26–29.)

Kroeber, Alfred L., and John P. Harrington. 1914. *Phonetic Elements of the Diegueño Language.* UC-PAAE 11(2):177–188.

Kroeber, Alfred L., and Thomas T. Waterman. 1917–1918. Notes on the Geography of Northwestern California: Yurok, Wiyot, Hupa, Chilula. EDDMA, no. 75. 91 pp. (Partially published in Waterman 1920 and Nomland and Kroeber 1936.)

Kroeber, Karl, ed. 2002. *Creation Myths of Primitive America,* edited and with an introduction by Karl Kroeber. Santa Barbara, CA: ABC-CLIO. (New edition of Curtin 1898.)

Kroeber, Karl, and Clifton Kroeber, eds. 2003. *Ishi in Three Centuries.* Lincoln: University of Nebraska Press.

Kroeber, Theodora. 1961. *Ishi in Two Worlds: A Biography of the Last Wild Indian in North America.* Berkeley: University of California Press.

———. 1970. *Alfred Kroeber: A Personal Configuration.* Berkeley: University of California Press.

Kroskrity, Paul V. 2002. Language Renewal and the Technologies of Literacy and Postliteracy: Reflections from Western Mono. In *Making Dictionaries: Preserving Indigenous Languages of the Americas,* edited by William Frawley, Kenneth C. Hill, and Pamela Munro, 171–192. Berkeley: University of California Press.

Kroskrity, Paul V., Rosalie Bethel, and Jennifer F. Reynolds. 2002. *Taitaduhaan: Western Mono Ways of Speaking.* Interactive CD ROM. Norman: University of Oklahoma Press.

Kroskrity, Paul V., and Gregory A. Reinhardt. 1984. Spanish and English Loanwords in Western Mono. JCGBA-PL 4:107–138.

Kuroda, S.-Y. 1967. *Yawelmani Phonology.* Research Monograph 43. Cambridge, MA: MIT Press.

Laird, Carobeth. 1975. *Encounter with an Angry God: Recollections of My Life with John Peabody Harrington.* Banning, CA: Malki Museum Press.

———. 1976. *The Chemehuevis.* Banning, CA: Malki Museum Press. ("A Brief Note on the Chemehuevi Language" and "Glossary," pp. 288–334.)

———. 1984. *Mirror and Pattern: George Laird's World of Chemehuevi Mythology.* Banning, CA: Malki Museum Press.

Lamb, Sydney M. 1953–1955. Mono [sound recordings] collected by Sydney Lamb; spoken by Lucy Kinsman et al. BLC no. LA 31, Berkeley Language Center, University of California, Berkeley. 10 hrs. 6 min.

———. 1955. [Field notebooks: Yuki, Huchnom, Wappo, Wiyot, Miwok.] Archived as Lamb.001.001, Survey of California and Other Indian Languages, Department of Linguistics, University of California, Berkeley. Two notebooks, original. (MS. Lamb.001.002 is a photocopy of the notebooks.)

———. 1957. *Northfork Mono Dictionary.* MS.

———. 1958a. Linguistic Prehistory in the Great Basin. IJAL 24:95–100.

———. 1958b. *Northfork Mono Grammar.* PhD dissertation, University of California, Berkeley.

———. 1964. The Classification of the Uto-Aztecan Languages: A Historical Survey. In *Studies in Californian Linguistics,* edited by William Bright, 106–125. UC-PL 34.

Landar, Herbert J. 1974. [Review of Gatschet 1970 (1876b).] IJAL 40:159–162.

Lang, Julian. 1994. *Ararapikva: Creation Stories of the People.* Berkeley, CA: Heyday.

Langacker, Ronald W. 1977. *An Overview of Uto-Aztecan Grammar.* Studies in Uto-Aztecan Grammar, vol. 1. Summer Institute of Linguistics Publications in Linguistics 56(1). Dallas: University of Texas at Arlington and SIL.

———, ed. 1982. *Studies in Uto-Aztecan Grammar,* vol. 3: *Uto-Aztecan Grammatical Sketches.* Summer Institute of Linguistics Publications in Linguistics 56(3). Dallas: University of Texas at Arlington and SIL.

———. 1998. Cognitive Grammar Meets the Yuman Auxiliary. In *Studies in American Indian Languages: Description and Theory,* edited by Leanne Hinton and Pamela Munro, 41–48. UC-PL 131.

Langdon, Margaret. 1970. *A Grammar of Diegueño: The Mesa Grande Dialect.* UC-PL 66. (Based on the author's dissertation, University of California, Berkeley, 1966.)

———. 1971. Sound Symbolism in Yuman Languages. In *Studies in American Indian Languages,* edited by Jesse O. Sawyer, 149–174. UC-PL 65.

———. 1974. *Comparative Hokan-Coahuiltecan Studies: A Survey and an Appraisal.* The Hague: Mouton.

———. 1975a. Kamia and Kumeyaay: A Linguistic Perspective. JCA 2:64–70.

———. 1975b. Boundaries and Lenition in Yuman Languages. IJAL 41:218–233.

———, ed. 1976. *Yuman Texts.* IJAL Native American Texts Series 1.3. Chicago: University of Chicago Press.

———. 1978a. Auxiliary Verb Constructions in Yuman. JCGBA-PL 1:93–130.

———. 1978b. The Origin of Possession Markers in Yuman. In *1977 Hokan-Penutian Workshop,* pp. 33–42.

———. 1978c. Animal Talk in Cocopa. IJAL 44:10–16.

———. 1979. Some Thoughts on Hokan with Particular Reference to Pomoan and Yuman. In *The Languages of Native America: Historical and Comparative Assessment*, edited by Lyle Campbell and Marianne Mithun, 592–649. Austin: University of Texas Press.

———. 1986. Hokan-Siouan Revisited. In *New Perspectives in Language, Culture, and Personality,* edited by William Cowan, Michael K. Foster and Konrad Koerner, 111–143. Amsterdam: John Benjamins.

———. 1991. Diegueño: How Many Languages? In *1990 Hokan-Penutian Workshop,* pp. 184–190.

———. 1993. An Early Diegueño Wordlist. In *1992 Hokan-Penutian Workshop,* pp. 61–68.

———. 1994. Kroeber and Harrington on Mesa Grande Diegueño (Iipay). In *1993 Hokan-Penutian Workshop,* pp. 170–182.

———. 1997a. Biography of A. M. Halpern (1914–1985). In *Karʔúk: Native Accounts of the Quechan Mourning Ceremony*, by A. M. Halpern, xv–xix. Edited by Amy Miller and Margaret Langdon. UC-PL 128.

———. 1997b. J. P. Harrington and Al Hayes. In *1996 Hokan-Penutian Workshop,* pp. 83–94.

Langdon, Margaret, and Dell H. Hymes. 1998. Mesa Grande 'Iipay Oratory and Narrative. In *The Life of Language: Papers in Linguistics in Honor of William Bright,* edited by Jane Hill, P. J. Mistry, and Lyle Campbell, 307–325. Berlin: Mouton de Gruyter.

Langdon, Margaret, and Pamela Munro. 1979. Subject and (Switch-)Reference in Yuman. *Folia Linguistica* 13:321–344.

Langdon, Margaret, and Shirley Silver, eds. 1976. *Hokan Studies: Papers from the First Conference on Hokan Languages.* The Hague: Mouton.

———. 1984. California t/ṭ. JCGBA-PL 4:139–165.

La Pérouse, Jean François de Galaup, Comte de. 1799. *Voyage de La Pérouse Autour de Monde.* 4 vols. Paris: Imprimerie de la République. (Reprinted 1937, Baltimore: Johns Hopkins Press. Translated 1969 [in part] by Charles N. Rudkin, *The First French Expedition to California,* Los Angeles: Dawson. Rudkin translation reprinted 1989, with introduction and commentary by Malcolm Margolin, as *Life in a California Mission: Monterey in 1786: The Journals of Jean François de la Pérouse,* Berkeley, CA: Heyday Books.) [Esselen and Rumsen word lists are on pp. 114–115 of the 1937 edition and on pp. 94–95 of the 1959 translation.]

Larsson, Lars J. 1987. Who Were the Konomihu? IJAL 53:232–235.

Latham, Robert Gordon. 1856. On the Languages of Northern, Western, and Central America. *Transactions of the Philological Society of London for 1856*, pp. 57–115.

———. 1860. *Opuscula: Essays Chiefly Philological and Ethnological.* London: Williams and Norgate.

Laylander, Don. 1997. The Linguistic Prehistory of Baja California. In *Contributions to the Linguistic Prehistory of Central and Baja California,* edited by Gary S. Breschini and Trudy Haversat, 1–94. Salinas, CA: Coyote Press.

Laylander, Don, and Jerry D. Moore, eds. 2006. *The Prehistory of Baja California: Advances in the Archaeology of the Forgotten Peninsula.* Gainesville: University Press of Florida.

Lee, Borim. 1991. *Prosodic Structures in Takelma Phonology and Morphology.* PhD dissertation, University of Texas at Austin.

Lee, Dorothy Demetracopoulou. 1938. Conceptual Implications of an Indian Language. *Philosophy of Science* 5:89–102.

———. 1940. The Place of Kinship Terms in Wintu ' Speech. AA 42:604–616.

———. 1942. Noun Categories in Wintu '. *Zeitschrift für Vergleichende Sprachforschung* 67:197–210.

———. 1943. The Linguistic Aspect of Wintu·' Acculturation. AA 45:435–440.

———. 1944a. Categories of the Generic and Particular in Wintu·'. AA 46:362–369.

———. 1944b. Linguistic Reflection of Wintu·' Thought. IJAL 10:181–187. (Reprinted in Lee 1959:121–130.)

———. 1946. Stylistic Use of the Negative in Wintu·'. IJAL 12:79–81.

———. 1959. *Freedom and Culture.* Englewood Cliffs, NJ: Prentice Hall.

Lee, Dorothy Demetracopoulou. See also Demetracopoulou, Dorothy.

Leeds-Hurwitz, Wendy. 1982. A Biographical Sketch of L. S. Freeland. In *Freeland's Central Sierra Miwok Myths,* edited by Howard Berman, 11–26. Survey of California and Other Indian Languages, Report 3. Berkeley: Department of Linguistics, University of California.

———. 1985. The Committee on Research on Native American Languages. *Proceedings of the American Philosophical Society* 129:129–160.

———. 2004. *Rolling in Ditches with Shamans: Jaime de Angulo and the Professionalization of American Anthropology.* Lincoln: University of Nebraska Press.

León-Portilla, Miguel. 1976. Sobre la lengua pericú de la Baja California. *Anales de Antropología* 13:87–101. Mexico City.

Lepsius, Carl Richard. 1863. *Standard Alphabet for Reducing Unwritten Languages and Foreign Graphic Systems to Uniform Orthography in European Letters,* 2nd rev. ed. London. (Facsimile edition 2005, Elibron Classics series, Adamant Media Corporation.)

Leventhal, Alan, Les Field, Hank Alvarez, and Rosemary Cambra. 1994. The Ohlone: Back from Extinction. In *The Ohlone Past and Present: Native Americans of the San Francisco Bay Region*, edited by Lowell John Bean, 297–336. Ballena Press Anthropological Papers no. 42. Menlo Park, CA: Ballena Press.

Levy, Richard S. 1972. Linguistic Evidence for the Prehistory of Central California. MS. (Revised as Levy 1979. Published as Levy 1997.)

———. 1976. *Costanoan Internal Relationships.* Publications of the University of California Archaeological Research Facility 17. Department of Anthropology, University of California, Berkeley.

———. 1978a. Eastern Miwok. In *Handbook of North American Indians.* Vol. 8: *California*, edited by Robert F. Heizer, 398–413. Washington, DC: Smithsonian Institution.

———. 1978b. Costanoan. In *Handbook of North American Indians.* Vol. 8: *California*, edited by Robert F. Heizer, 485–495. Washington, DC: Smithsonian Institution.

———. 1978c. Chochenyo Lexicon. MS.

———. 1979. A Linguistic Prehistory of Central California: Historical Linguistics and Culture Process. MS. (Revision of Levy 1972. Published as Levy 1997.)

———. 1997. *A Linguistic Prehistory of Central California: Historical Linguistics and Culture Process.* Coyote Press Archives of California Prehistory 44. Salinas, CA: Coyote Press.

Li, Charles, and Sandra Thompson. 1977. The Causative in Wappo: A Special Case of Doubling. *Proceedings of the* [3rd] *Annual Meeting of the Berkeley Linguistics Society*, pp. 175–182.

———. 1978. Relativization Strategies in Wappo. *Proceedings of the* [4th] *Annual Meeting of the Berkeley Linguistics Society*, pp. 106–113.

Li, Charles, Sandra Thompson, and Jesse O. Sawyer. 1977. Subject and Word Order in Wappo. IJAL 43:85–100.

Li, Fang-Kuei (Lǐ Fānggùi). 1927. Wailaki Athabaskan. [Texts with interlinear translations, vocabulary, collected in Round Valley during the summer of 1927; see Sapir 1927a.] Five field notebooks, ca. 100 pp. (Originals in the possession of William Seaburg. Microfilm copy, dated 1975, in the possession of Victor Golla. Partially published in Seaburg 1977a, 1977b.)

———. 1930. *Mattole, an Athabaskan Language.* University of Chicago Publications in Anthropology, Linguistic Series. Chicago: University of Chicago Press.

Liapunova, R. G. 1967. Ekspeditsiia I. G. Voznesenskogo i ee znachenie dlia etnografii Russkoi Ameriki [The expedition of I. G. Voznesenskii and its significance for the ethnography of Russian America]. In *Kultura i Byt Narodov Ameriki*, pp. 5–33. Sbornik Muzieia Antropologii i Etnografii 24. Leningrad: Akademiia Nauk SSSR [USSR Academy of Sciences].

Liedtke, Stefan. 2004. Florence Jones (1907–2003). *SSILA Newsletter* 21(4), January, p. 5.

Lightfoot, Kent D. 2005. *Indians, Missionaries, and Merchants: The Legacy of Colonial Encounters on the California Frontiers.* Berkeley: University of California Press.

Lightner, Thomas M. 1971. On Swadesh and Voegelin's "A Problem in Phonological Alternation." IJAL 37:201–220.

Liljeblad, Sven, and Catherine S. Fowler. 1986. Owens Valley Paiute. In *Handbook of North American Indians.* Vol. 11: *Great Basin*, edited by Warren L. d'Azevedo, 412–434. Washington, DC: Smithsonian Institution.

Littlejohn, Hugh W. 1928a. Nisenan Geography. [Completed manuscript (72 pp.) and field notes (117 pp.).] EDDMA, no. 18. 189 pp. (Maps are separately filed; see Littlejohn 1928c.)

———. 1928b. Nisenan Vocabularies. [Nisenan, Northwestern Maiduan, Northeastern Maiduan.] EDDMA, no. 19. 22 pp.

———. 1928c. Maps for Nisenan Geography. EDDMA, no. 32. 5 maps. (To accompany Littlejohn 1928a.)

Loeb, Edwin M. 1926. *Pomo Folkways.* UC-PAAE 19(2):149–405.

———. 1933. *The Eastern Kuksu Cult.* UC-PAAE 33(2):139–232.

Loether, Christopher P. 1991. *Verbal Art Among the Western Mono.* PhD dissertation, University of California, Los Angeles.

———. 2003. *A Grammar of Owens Valley Paiute for Community Members,* 2nd ed. Bishop, CA: Owens Valley Career Development Center.

Loew, Oscar. 1874–1875. Comparative Vocabulary of Mohave on the Colorado river at Ft. Mohave, Payute of southern Nevada, Indians of Inyo and Mono counties, California, and Kauvuya [Cahuilla]. NAA MS 819-b, National Anthropological Archives, Smithsonian Institution. (Edited and published in Gatschet 1876a and 1879a.)

———. 1875. [Vocabularies of Serrano, Gabrielino, Luiseño, Juaneño, Barbareño (and Island?) Chumash, and Wintu.] (Incorporated in Gatschet 1879a. Gabrielino reprinted in W. McCawley 1996:275–280; Barbareño Chumash reprinted in Kroeber 1910:265–268.)

Loud, Llewellyn L. 1918. *Ethnogeography and Archaeology of the Wiyot Territory.* UC-PAAE 14(3):221–436.

Loud, Llewellyn L., and M. R. Harrington. 1929. *Lovelock Cave.* UC-PAAE 25(1):1–183. [Appendix 2, "Notes on the Northern Paiute," by L. L. Loud, pp. 152–164.]

Lowie, Luella Cole, ed. 1965. *Letters from Edward Sapir to Robert H. Lowie, with an introduction and notes by Robert H. Lowie.* Berkeley, CA: L. C. Lowie.

Lowie, Robert H. 1924. Shoshonean Tales. *Journal of American Folklore* 37:1–242.

———, ed. 1936. *Essays in Anthropology Presented to A. L. Kroeber in Celebration of his Sixtieth Birthday, June 11, 1936.* Berkeley, CA.

———. 1939. *Ethnographic Notes on the Washo.* UC-PAAE 36(5):301–352.

———. 1963. *Washo Texts.* AL 5(7):1–30.

Lucy-Fossarieu, M. P. de. 1881. *Les langues indiennes de la Californie.* Compte Rendu du Congrès International des Sciences Ethnographiques, Paris, 1876. Imprimerie Nationale, Paris. (Vocabularies reprinted from A. Taylor 1860–1861.)

Luthin, Herbert W. 1988. A First Look at Secondary Stress in Yanan Discourse. In *1987 Hokan-Penutian Workshop*, pp. 17–27.

———. 1991. *Restoring the Voice in Yanan Traditional Narrative: Prosody, Performance and Presentational Form.* PhD dissertation, University of California, Berkeley.

———, ed. 2002. *Surviving through the Days: Translations of Native California Stories. A California Indian Reader.* Berkeley: University of California Press.

Luthin, Herbert W., and Leanne Hinton. 2003a. The Story of Lizard. In *Ishi in Three Centuries,* edited by Karl Kroeber and Clifton Kroeber, 293–317. Lincoln: University of Nebraska Press.

———. 2003b. The Days of a Life: What Ishi's Stories Can Tell Us about Ishi. In *Ishi in Three Centuries,* edited by Karl Kroeber and Clifton Kroeber, 318–354. Lincoln: University of Nebraska Press.

Lyneis, Margaret M. 1995. The Virgin Anasazi, Far Western Puebloans. *Journal of World Prehistory* 9:199–241.

Macaulay, Monica. 1988. A Preliminary Look at Karok Pitch Accent. In *1988 Hokan-Penutian Workshop,* pp. 41–61.

———. 1989. A Suffixal Analysis of the Karok "Endoclitic." *Lingua* 78:159–180.

———. 1992. Inverse Marking in Karuk: the Function of the Suffix *-ap.* IJAL 58:182–201.

———. 1993. Reduplication and the Structure of the Karuk Verb Stem. IJAL 59:64–81.

———. 2000. Obviative Marking in Ergative Contexts: The Case of Karuk *'ìin.* IJAL 66:464–498.

———. 2004. On the Karuk Directional Suffixes. In *Proceedings of the 30th Annual Meeting of the Berkeley Linguistics Society,* pp. 85–101.

Macri, Martha J., Victor K. Golla, and Lisa L. Woodward. 2004. J. P. Harrington Project: Academic and Community Participation. In *Language Is Life: Proceedings of the 11th Annual Stabilizing Indigenous Languages Conference, June 10–13, 2004, University of California at Berkeley,* edited by Wesley Y. Leonard and Stelómethet Ethel B. Gardner, pp. 1–12. Survey of California and Other Indian Languages, Report 15 (2004). Berkeley: Department of Linguistics, University of California.

Mahr, August C. 1932. *The Visit of the "Rurik" to San Francisco in 1816.* Stanford University Publications in History, Economics, and Political Science 2(2).

Major, Roy C. 2005. Chemehuevi Revisited. *Journal of the Southwest* 47:523–33.

Malécot, André. 1963–1964. Luiseño: A Structural Analysis. IJAL 29:89–95, 196–210; 30:14–31, 243–250.

Malhi, Ripan S., H. M. Mortensen, Jason A. Eshelman, Brian M. Kemp, Joseph G. Lorenz, Frederika A. Kaestle, John R. Johnson, C. Gorodezky, and David G. Smith. 2003. Native American mtDNA Prehistory in the American Southwest. *American Journal of Physical Anthropology* 120:108–24.

Manaster Ramer, Alexis. 1984. Kern Laws. IJAL 50:325–334.

———. 1992a. A Northern Uto-Aztecan Sound Law: **-c-* → *-y-.* IJAL 58:251–268.

———. 1992b. Tubatulabal 'man' and the Subclassification of Uto-Aztecan. *California Linguistic Notes* 23(2):30–31.

———. 1993. On Lenition in Some Northern Uto-Aztecan Languages. IJAL 59:334–341.

———. n.d. Giamina = Omomil. MS.

Mandelbaum, David G., ed. 1949. *Selected Writings of Edward Sapir.* Berkeley: University of California Press.

Margolin, Malcolm. 1978. *The Ohlone Way: Indian Life in the San Francisco–Monterey Bay Area.* Berkeley, CA: Heyday Books.

———. 1989. Introduction and Commentary. In *Life in a California Mission: Monterey in 1786: The Journals of Jean François de la Pérouse,* 1–50. Berkeley, CA: Heyday Books. (See La Pérouse 1799.)

Marlett, Stephen A. 1981. *The Structure of Seri.* PhD dissertation, University of California, San Diego.

———. 1990. Person and Number Inflection in Seri. IJAL 56:503–541.

———. 2000. Why the Seri Language is Important and Interesting. *Journal of the Southwest* 42:611–633.

———. 2001. Las relaciones entre las lenguas "hokanas" en México: ¿Cuál es la evidencia? Paper presented at the III Coloquio Internacional de Lingüística Mauricio Swadesh. Instituto de Investigaciones Antropológicas, Universidad Nacional Autónoma de México, August 29–September 4, 2001. [Available online at www.und.nodak.edu/instruct/smarlett/]

———. 2005. A Typological Overview of the Seri Language. *Linguistic Discovery* 3(1):54–73. [Online at journals.dartmouth. edu/cgi-bin/WebObjects/Journals.woa/2/xmlpage/1/ document/564]

———. 2008a. The Form and Use of Names in Seri. IJAL 74:47–82.

———. 2008b. The Seri-Salinan Connection Revisited. IJAL 74:393–399.

Marlett, Stephen A., and Mary B. Moser. 1996. Seri Contribution to the Intercontinental Dictionary Series. In *1994–95 Hokan-Penutian Workshop,* pp. 191–232.

Marsden, W. L. 1923. *The Northern Paiute Language of Oregon.* UC-PAAE 20(11):175–191.

Mason, J. Alden. 1912. *The Ethnology of the Salinan Indians.* UC-PAAE 10(4):97–240.

———. 1916a. *The Mutsun Dialect of Costanoan, Based on the Vocabulary of De la Cuesta.* UC-PAAE 11(7):399–472.

———. 1916b. Suisun [Southern Patwin] vocabulary. Harvey Pitkin Papers, Series I-B, Library of the American Philosophical Society, Philadelphia. (Published in Kroeber 1932:354–355.)

———. 1918. *The Language of the Salinan Indians.* UC-PAAE 14(1):1–154.

Massey, William C. 1949. Tribes and Languages of Baja California. *Southwestern Journal of Anthropology* 5:272–307.

———. 1966. Archaeology and Ethnohistory of Baja California. *Handbook of Middle American Indians* 4:38–58.

Mayo, Gui. See de Angulo, Gui.

McCarthy, Helen. 1985. Linguistics and Its Implications for California Ethnography and Culture History. In *Ethnography and Prehistory of the North Coast Range, California,* edited by Helen McCarthy, William R. Hildebrandt, and Laureen K. Swenson, 20–34. Center for Archaeological Research at Davis, Publication 8. Davis: Department of Anthropology, University of California, Davis.

McCawley, James D. 1969. Length and Voicing in Tübatulabal. *Proceedings of the Chicago Linguistic Society* 5:407–415.

McCawley, William. 1996. *The First Angelinos: The Gabrielino Indians of Los Angeles.* Banning and Novato, CA: Malki Museum Press and Ballena Press.

McGarry, Daniel D. 1950. Educational Methods of the Franciscans in Spanish California. *The Americas* 6:335–358.

McGee, W J. 1898. *The Seri Indians.* BAE-AR 17.

McLaughlin, John E. 1987. *A Phonology and Morphology of Panamint.* PhD dissertation, University of Kansas, Lawrence.

———. 2000. Language Boundaries and Phonological Borrowing in the Central Numic Languages. In *Uto-Aztecan: Structural, Temporal, and Geographic Perspectives. Papers in Memory of Wick R. Miller by the Friends of Uto-Aztecan,* edited by Eugene H. Casad and Thomas L. Willett, 293–303. Editorial Unison, Universidad de Sonora, Hermosillo.

McLendon, Sally. 1969. Spanish Loan Words in Eastern Pomo. *Romance Philology* 23:9–53.

———. 1973. *Proto Pomo.* UC-PL 71.

———. 1975. *A Grammar of Eastern Pomo.* UC-PL 74.

———. 1977. Bear Kills Her Own Daughter-in-Law, Deer (Eastern Pomo text). In *Northern California Texts,* edited by Victor Golla and Shirley Silver, 26–65. IJAL Native American Text Series 2(2). Chicago: University of Chicago Press.

———. 1978a. Ergativity, Case and Transitivity in Eastern Pomo. IJAL 44:1–9.

———. 1978b. Coyote and the Ground Squirrels. In *Coyote Stories*, edited by William Bright, 87–111. IJAL-NATS Monograph 1. Chicago: University of Chicago Press.

———. 1979. Clitics, Clauses, Closures and Discourse in Eastern Pomo. In *Proceedings of the 5th Annual Meeting of the Berkeley Linguistics Society*, pp. 637–646.

———. 1982. Meaning, Rhetorical Structure, and Discourse Organization in Myth. In *Analyzing Discourse: Text and Talk*, edited by Deborah Tannen, 284–305. Georgetown University Roundtable on Languages and Linguistics, 1981. Washington, DC: Georgetown University Press.

———. 1996. Sketch of Eastern Pomo. In *Handbook of North American Indians*. Vol. 17: *Languages*, edited by Ives Goddard, 507–550. Washington, DC: Smithsonian Institution.

McLendon, Sally, and Michael J. Lowy. 1978. Eastern Pomo and Southeastern Pomo. In *Handbook of North American Indians*. Vol. 8: *California*, edited by Robert F. Heizer, 306–323. Washington, DC: Smithsonian Institution.

McLendon, Sally, and Robert L. Oswalt. 1978. Pomo: Introduction. In *Handbook of North American Indians*. Vol. 8: *California*, edited by Robert F. Heizer, 274–288. Washington, DC: Smithsonian Institution.

Meigs, Peveril, III. 1939. The Kiliwa Indians of Lower California. *Ibero-Americana* 15:1–114.

Mengarini, Gregory, S.J. 1860. Santa Clara Vocabulary. In *The Indianology of California*, by Alexander S. Taylor, vol. 13, number 13. MICROFILM.E78.C15.T16, The Bancroft Library, University of California, Berkeley. (Reprinted in Powers 1877 and Heizer 1973:31–35).

Menzies, Archibald. 1924. Menzies' California Journal. *The California Historial Society Quarterly* 2:265–340.

Merriam, C. Hart. 1898–1938. *C. Hart Merriam Papers*. Vol. 1: *Papers Relating to Work with California Indians, 1850–1974* (the bulk from 1898–1938). BANC MSS 80/18-c, The Bancroft Library, University of California, Berkeley. (Microfilm: BANC FILM 1022.)

———. 1907. Distribution and Classification of the Mewan Stock of California. AA 9:338–357.

———. 1910. *The Dawn of the World: Myths and Weird Tales Told by the Mewan Indians of California*. Cleveland: Arthur H. Clark.

———. 1923. Application of the Athapaskan Term Nung-kahhl. AA 25:276–277.

———. 1926a. *The Classification and Distribution of the Pit River Indian Tribes of California*. Smithsonian Miscellaneous Collections 73(3).

———. 1926b. Source of the Name Shasta. *Journal of the Washington Academy of Science* 16:522–525.

———. 1929. The Cop-éh of Gibbs. AA 31:136–137.

———. 1930a. The New River Indians, Tló-hom-tah´-hoi. AA 32:280–293.

———. 1930b. A Remarkable Case of Word Borrowing among California Indians. *Science* 71:546.

———. 1930c. The Em´-tem´-bitch, a Shoshonean Tribe. AA 32:496–499.

———. 1955. *Studies of California Indians*. Edited by the Staff of the Department of Anthropology of the University of California. Berkeley: University of California Press.

———. 1966. *Ethnographic Notes on California Indian Tribes*. Compiled and edited by Robert F. Heizer. University of California Archaeological Survey, Report 68, Part 1, pp. 1–166.

———. 1967a. *Ethnographic Notes on California Indian Tribes: Ethnological Notes on Northern and Southern California Indian Tribes*. Compiled and edited by Robert F. Heizer. University of California Archaeological Survey, Report 68, Part 2, pp. 167–256.

———. 1967b. *Ethnographic Notes on California Indian Tribes: Ethnological Notes on Central California Indian Tribes*. Compiled and edited by Robert F. Heizer. University of California Archaeological Survey, Report 68, Part 3, pp. 257–450.

———. 1968. *Village Names in Twelve California Mission Records*. Edited by Robert F. Heizer. University of California Archaeological Survey, Report 74.

———. 1979. *Indian Names for Plants and Animals among Californian and other Western North American Tribes*. Assembled and edited by Robert F. Heizer. Soccoro, NM: Ballena Press.

Merriam, C. Hart, and Zenaida Merriam Talbot. 1974. *Boundary Descriptions of California Indian Stocks and Tribes*. Edited by Robert F. Heizer. Berkeley: Archaeological Research Facility, Department of Anthropology, University of California.

Michelson, Truman. 1914. Two Alleged Algonquian Languages of California. AA 16:361–367. (Criticism of Sapir 1913a; answered by Sapir 1915b. Reprinted in Bright 1990a:553–557.)

———. 1915. Rejoinder to Sapir. AA 17:194–198. (Answers Sapir 1915b; answered in turn by Sapir 1915c. Reprinted in Bright 1990a:558–561.)

Midtlyng, Patrick. 2005. Washo Morphophonology: Hiatus resolution at the edges -or- Let them be vowels. In *Proceedings from the 8th Workshop on American Indigenous Languages*, edited by C. Jany and L. Harper, 50–62. Santa Barbara Working Papers in Linguistics 16.

Midtlyng, Patrick, and Alan C. L. Yu. 2005. Phonetic Structures of Washo. *Journal of the Acoustical Society of America* 117:2490.

Milhau, John J. 1856. Vocabulary of Umpqua valley (proper) [192 items]. NAA MS 193-a, National Anthropological Archives, Smithsonian Institution.

Miller, Amy. 1990. Some Differences between Two Speakers of Jamul Diegueño. In *1990 Hokan-Penutian Workshop*.

———. 2001. *A Grammar of Jamul Tiipay*. Mouton Grammar Library 23. Berlin: Mouton de Gruyter. (Based on the author's PhD dissertation, University of California, San Diego, 1990.)

———. n.d. Rumsen Dictionary. MS.

Miller, Amy, and Catherine A. Callaghan. n.d. A Dictionary of Chocheño, based on the notes of J. P. Harrington. MS.

Miller, Henry. 1957. *Big Sur and the Oranges of Hieronymous Bosch*. New York: New Directions.

Miller, Jay, and William R. Seaburg. 1990. Athapaskans of Southwestern Oregon. In *Handbook of North American Indians*. Vol. 7: *Northwest Coast*, edited by Wayne Suttles, 580–588. Washington, DC: Smithsonian Institution.

Miller, Wick R. 1961. [Review of Kroeber and Grace 1960.] *Language* 37:186–189.

———. 1964. The Shoshonean Languages of Uto-Aztecan. In *Studies in California Linguistics*, edited by William Bright, 145–148. UC-PL 34.

———. 1966. *Anthropological Linguistics in the Great Basin*. Desert Research Institute Publications in the Social Sciences and Humanities 1:75–112.

———. 1970. Western Shoshoni Dialects. In *Languages and Cultures of Western North America: Essays in Honor of Sven S. Liljeblad*, edited by Earl H. Swanson, Jr., 17–36. Pocatello: Idaho State University Press.

———. 1983. Uto-Aztecan Languages. In *Handbook of North American Indians*. Vol. 10: *Southwest*, edited by Alfonso Ortiz, 113–124. Washington, DC: Smithsonian Institution.

———. 1984. The Classification of the Uto-Aztecan Languages Based on Lexical Evidence. IJAL 50:1–24.

———. 1986. Numic. In *Handbook of North American Indians*. Vol. 11: *Great Basin,* edited by Warren L. d'Azevedo, 98–106. Washington, DC: Smithsonian Institution.

———. 1996. A Sketch of Shoshone, A Uto-Aztecan Language. In *Handbook of North American Indians*. Vol. 17: *Languages,* edited by Ives Goddard, 693–720. Washington, DC: Smithsonian Institution.

Miller, Wick, Dirk Elzinga, and John E. McLaughlin. 2005. Preaspiration and Gemination in Central Numic. IJAL 71:413–444.

Milliken, Randall. 1987. *Ethnohistory of the Rumsen.* Papers in Northern California Anthropology 2. Berkeley: Northern California Anthropology Group. (Facsimile reprint. Salinas, CA: Coyote Press.)

———. 1990. *Ethnogeography and Ethnohistory of the Big Sur District, California State Park System, During the 1770–1810 Time Period.* Report submitted to the State of California, Department of Parks and Recreation. (Facsimile reprint. Salinas, CA: Coyote Press.)

———. 1994. The Costanoan-Yokuts Language Boundary in the Contact Period. In *The Ohlone Past and Present: Native Americans of the San Francisco Bay Region*, edited by Lowell John Bean, 165–182. Ballena Press Anthropological Papers no. 42. Menlo Park, CA: Ballena Press.

———. 1995. *A Time of Little Choice: The Disintegration of Tribal Culture in the San Francisco Bay Area, 1769–1810.* Menlo Park, CA: Ballena Press. (Based on *An Ethnohistory of the Indian People of the San Francisco Bay Area from 1770 to 1810.* PhD dissertation, University of California, Berkeley, 1991.)

———. 2002. The Spanish Contact and Mission Period Indians of the Santa Cruz–Monterey Bay Region. In *A Gathering of Voices: The Native Peoples of the Central California Coast,* edited by Linda Yamane, 25–36. Santa Cruz County History Journal, Issue 5. Santa Cruz, CA: Museum of Art and History.

———. 2008. *Native Americans at Mission San Jose.* Banning, CA: Malki-Ballena Press.

Milliken, Randall, and John R. Johnson. 2003. *Salinan and Northern Chumash Communities of the Early Mission Period.* Prepared for Contract No. 06A0148 and 06A0391, Environmental Branch, California Department of Transportation, District 5, San Luis Obispo, California. Davis: Far Western Anthropological Research Group, Inc.

Mills, Elaine L. 1981. *The Papers of John Peabody Harrington in the Smithsonian Institution, 1907–1957.* Vol. 1: *A Guide to the Field Notes: Native American History, Language, and Culture of Alaska/Northwest Coast.* Millwood, NY: Kraus International Publications.

———. 1985. *The Papers of John Peabody Harrington in the Smithsonian Institution, 1907–1957.* Vol. 2: *A Guide to the Field Notes: Native American History, Language, and Culture of Northern and Central California.* White Plains, NY: Kraus International Publications.

Mills, Elaine L., and Ann J. Brickfield. 1986. *The Papers of John Peabody Harrington in the Smithsonian Institution, 1907–1957.* Vol. 3: *A Guide to the Field Notes: Native American History, Language, and Culture of Southern California/Basin.* White Plains, NY: Kraus International Publications.

Mithun, Marianne. 1988. Lexical Categories and Number in Central Pomo. In *In Honor of Mary Haas: From the Haas Festival Conference on Native American Linguistics,* edited by William F. Shipley, 517–537. Berlin: Mouton de Gruyter.

———. 1990a. Third-Person Reference and the Function of Pronouns in Central Pomo Natural Speech. IJAL 56:361–376.

———. 1990b. The Role of Lexicalization in Shaping Aspectual Systems: Central Pomo. In *1990 Hokan-Penutian Workshop.*

———. 1991. Active/agentive Case Marking and Its Motivations. *Language* 67:510–546.

———. 1993. Switch Reference: Clause Combining in Central Pomo. IJAL 59:119–136.

———. 1998a. The Regression of Sibilant Harmony through the Life of Barbareño Chumash. In *The Life of Language: Papers in Linguistics in Honor of William Bright*, edited by Jane Hill, P. J. Mistry, and Lyle Campbell, 221–242. Berlin: Mouton de Gruyter.

———. 1998b. Fluid Aspects of Negation in Central Pomo. In *Studies in American Indian Languages: Description and Theory,* edited by Leanne Hinton and Pamela Munro, 77–86. UC-PL 131.

———. 1999. *The Languages of Native North America.* Cambridge, UK: Cambridge University Press.

———. In press. Core Argument Patterns and Deep Genetic Relations: Hierarchical Systems in Northern California. In *Typology of Argument Structure and Grammatical Relations,* edited by Bernard Comrie. Amsterdam: John Benjamins.

Mixco, Mauricio J. 1971. *Kiliwa Grammar.* PhD dissertation, University of California, Berkeley.

———. 1977a. J. P. Harrington's Cochimí Vocabularies. JCGBA 4:42–50.

———. 1977b. The Innovation of /h, hʷ/ in Kiliwa. IJAL 43:167–175.

———. 1977c. The Linguistic Affiliation of the Ñakipa and Yakakwal of Lower California. IJAL 43:189–200.

———. 1977d. The Kiliwa Response to Hispanic Culture. *Proceedings of the Third Annual Meeting of the Berkeley Linguistics Society,* pp. 12–23.

———. 1978. *Cochimí and Proto-Yuman: Lexical and Syntactic Evidence for a New Language Family in Lower California.* University of Utah Anthropological Papers 101.

———. 1979. Northern Cochimí Dialectology and Proto-Yuman. JCGBA-PL 1:39–64.

———. 1983. *Kiliwa Texts: "When I Have Donned My Crest of Stars."* University of Utah Anthropological Papers 107.

———. 1985. *Kiliwa Dictionary.* University of Utah Anthropological Papers 109.

———. 1996. *Kiliwa del Arroyo León, Baja California.* Archivo de Lenguas Indígenas de México 18. Mexico City: El Colegio de México.

———. 1997a. Mandan Switch Reference. AL 39:220–298.

———. 1997b. Haas's Hokan: Dead End, or Gateway to the Future? AL 39:680–694.

———. 2000. *Kiliwa.* Languages of the World/Materials 193. Munich: Lincom-Europa.

———. 2006. The Indigenous Languages. In *The Prehistory of Baja California: Advances in the Archaeology of the Forgotten Peninsula,* edited by Don Laylander and Jerry D. Moore, 24–41. Gainesville: University Press of Florida.

Montes de Oca, Mercedes. 1997. Los disfrasismos en el náhuatl, un problema de traducción o de conceptualización. *Amérindia: Revue d'Ethnolinguistique Amerindienne* 22:31–44.

———. 2001. Luiseño Couplets: A Naming Strategy. Paper presented at the Friends of Uto-Aztecan Working Conference, Santa Barbara, June 8–9, 2001.

Moore, Robert E. 2006. Disappearing, Inc.: Glimpsing the Sublime in the Politics of Access to Endangered Languages. *Language and Communication* 26:296–315.

Moratto, Michael J. 1984. *California Archaeology.* New York: Academic Press.

Moser, Edward. 1963. Seri Bands. *The Kiva* 28(3):14–27.

Moser, Edward, and Mary B. Moser. 1961. [Vocabulario Seri.] *Serie de vocabularios indígenas Mariano Silva Aceves* 5. México: Instituto Lingüístico de Verano.

———. 1976. Seri Noun Pluralization Classes. In *Hokan Studies: Papers from the First Conference on Hokan Languages,* edited by Margaret Langdon and Shirley Silver, 285–296. The Hague: Mouton.

Moser, Mary B., and Stephen A. Marlett. 1996. *Seri de Sonora.* Archivo de Lenguas Indígenas de México 19. Mexico City: El Colegio de México.

———. 2005. *Comcáac quih yaza quih hant ihíip hac: Diccionario seri–español–inglés.* Hermosillo: Universidad de Sonora; Mexico City: Plaza y Valdés Editores.

Moshinsky, Julius. 1974. *A Grammar of Southeastern Pomo.* UC-PL 72.

———. 1976. Historical Pomo Phonology. In *Hokan Studies: Papers from the First Conference on Hokan Languages*, edited by Margaret Langdon and Shirley Silver, 55–76. The Hague: Mouton.

Mueller-Vollmer, Kurt. 1993. *Wilhelm von Humboldts Sprachwissnschaft: Ein kommentiertes Verzeichnis des sprachwissenschaftliche Nachlasses.* Paderborn, Germany: Schöningh.

Munro, Pamela. 1976. *Mojave Syntax.* New York: Garland. (Based on the author's PhD dissertation, University of California, San Diego, 1974.)

———. 1990. Stress and Vowel Length in Cupan Absolute Nouns. IJAL 56:217–250.

———. 1994. Gulf and Yuki-Gulf. AL 36:125–222.

———. 1996. Sketch of Yavapai (especially Tolkapaya) [pronominal reference, case marking, and verbal inflection]. In *1994–95 Hokan-Penutian Workshop*, pp. 179–186.

———. 2000. The Gabrielino Enclitic System. In *Uto-Aztecan: Structural, Temporal, and Geographic Perspectives. Papers in Memory of Wick R. Miller by the Friends of Uto-Aztecan,* edited by Eugene H. Casad and Thomas L. Willett, 183–202. Editorial Unison, Universidad de Sonora, Hermosillo.

———. 2002. The Takic Foundations of Nicoleño Vocabulary. In *Proceedings of the Fifth California Islands Symposium: 29 March to 1 April, 1999,* edited by David R. Browne, Kathryn L. Mitchell, and Henry W. Chaney, 659–668. Santa Barbara, CA: Santa Barbara Museum of Natural History.

———. n.d. Gabrielino Dictionary. [Based on J. P. Harrington's field notes with analytical input from G. Anderson and W. Bright.] MS.

Munro, Pamela, Nellie Brown, and Judith G. Crawford. 1989. *A Mojave Dictionary.* Occasional Papers in Linguistics 10. Department of Linguistics, University of California, Los Angeles.

Munro, Pamela, with John Johnson. 2001. What Do We Know about Tataviam? Comparisons with Kitanemuk, Gabrielino, Kawaiisu, and Tubatulabal. Paper presented to the Friends of Uto-Aztecan Conference, Santa Barbara, California, July 9, 2001.

Murphy, Justin, and Alan C. L. Yu. 2007. Moraic anchoring of f0 in Washo. *Proceedings of the International Congress of the Phonetic Sciences* 16:1161–1164.

Natches, Gilbert. 1923. *Northern Paiute Verbs.* UC-PAAE 20(14):243–259.

Nelson, E. Charles, and Alan Probert. 1994. *A Man Who Can Speak of Plants: Dr Thomas Coulter (1793–1843) of Dundalk in Ireland, Mexico and Alta California.* Dublin: Privately published by E. Charles Nelson.

Nelson, Hans, Mike Manookin, and Dirk Elzinga. 2004. A Chemehuevi Lexicon. In *Proceedings of the E-MELD Workshop on Linguistic Databases and Best Practice, Wayne State University, June 15–18, 2004.* (Description of project. Available online at emeld.org/workshop/2004/proceedings.html.)

Nevin, Bruce E. 1998. Aspects of Pit River Phonology. PhD dissertation, University of Pennsylvania, Philadelphia. (Available online at the Rutgers Optimality Theory Archive: roa.rutgers.edu/files.)

Newman, Stanley S. 1932. The Yawelmani Dialect of Yokuts. IJAL 7:85–89.

———. 1944. *Yokuts Language of California.* Viking Fund Publications in Anthropology 2. New York: Viking Fund.

———. 1946. The Yawelmani Dialect of Yokuts. In *Linguistic Structures of Native America,* edited by Cornelius Osgood, 222–248. Viking Fund Publications in Anthropology 6. New York: Viking Fund.

———. 1964. Comparison of Zuni and California Penutian. IJAL 30:1–13.

Nichols, Johanna. 1971. Diminutive Consonant Symbolism in Western North America. *Language* 47:826–848.

———. 1992. *Linguistic Diversity in Space and Time.* Chicago: University of Chicago Press.

———. 1997. The Epicenter of the Indo-European Linguistic Spread. In *Archaeology and Language I: Theoretical and Methodological Orientations,* edited by Roger Blench and Matthew Spriggs. London: Routledge.

———. 1999. The Eurasian Spread Zone and the Indo-European Dispersal. In *Archaeology and Language II: Correlating Archaeological and Linguistic Hypotheses,* edited by Roger Blench and Matthew Spriggs. London: Routledge.

———. 2004. The Origin of the Chechen and Ingush: A Study in Alpine Linguistic and Ethnic Geography. AL 42:129–155.

Nichols, Johanna, and Balthasar Bickel. 2005. Locus of Marking in the Clause. In *The World Atlas of Linguistic Structures,* edited by Martin Haspelmath, Matthew S. Dryer, David Gil, and Bernard Comrie, 98–101. Oxford, UK: Oxford University Press.

Nichols, Michael J. P. 1974. *Northern Paiute Historical Grammar.* PhD dissertation, University of California, Berkeley.

———. 1981. Old California Uto-Aztecan. In *Survey Reports 1981,* edited by Alice Schlichter, Wallace L. Chafe, and Leanne Hinton, 5–41. Survey of California and Other Indian

Languages, Report 1. Department of Linguistics, University of California, Berkeley. (Reprinted in *Journal of the Steward Anthropological Society* 15(1–2):23–46, 1984.)

———. 1998. An Old California Word for 'Mountain Lion/ Wildcat'. In *Studies in American Indian Languages: Description and Theory,* edited by Leanne Hinton and Pamela Munro, 241–247. UC-PL 131.

Nomland, Gladys A. 1935. *Sinkyone Notes.* UC-PAAE 36(2):149–178.

———. 1938. *Bear River Ethnography.* UC-AR 2:91–124.

Nomland, Gladys A., and Alfred L. Kroeber. 1936. *Wiyot Towns.* UC-PAAE 35(5):39–48.

Norris, Evan. 1976. A Syntactic Sketch of Mono. MA thesis, California State University, Fresno.

———. 1980. Organization of Instrumental Prefixes in Eastern Mono. JCGBA-PL 2:25–40.

———. 1986. *A Grammar Sketch and Comparative Study of Eastern Mono.* PhD dissertation, University of California, San Diego.

Norwood, Susan. 1981. *Progressives in Yuman and Romance.* PhD dissertation, University of California, San Diego.

O'Connor, Mary Catherine. 1981. Some Uses of Case-Markings in Northern Pomo. In *1980 Hokan-Penutian Workshop.*

———. 1982. Asymmetry in the Switch-Reference System of Northern Pomo. In *1981 Hokan-Penutian Workshop.*

———. 1986. Two Kinds of Bound Anaphora in Northern Pomo: Are They Logophoric? In *1983–85 Hokan-Penutian Workshops.*

———. 1990a. Third Person Reference in Northern Pomo Conversation: The Indexing of Discourse Genre and Social Relations. IJAL 56:377–409.

———. 1990b. Suffixal Aspect and Tense-Aspect in Northern Pomo. In *1990 Hokan-Penutian Workshop.*

———. 1992. *Topics in Northern Pomo Grammar.* New York: Garland.

O'Connor, Mary Catherine, and Amy Rose Deal. 2005. A Linked Electronic Dictionary and Textbase for Northern Pomo. Paper presented at the Annual Meeting of the Society for the Study of the Indigenous Languages of the Americas, Oakland, California, January 2005.

Okrand, Marc. 1977. *Mutsun Grammar.* PhD dissertation, University of California, Berkeley.

———. 1979a. Metathesis in Costanoan Grammar. IJAL 45:123–130.

———. 1979b. Costanoan Philological Practices: Comment and Criticism. IJAL 45:181–187. (Critique of Silverstein 1975. See Silverstein 1979b.)

———. 1980. Rumsen II: An Evaluation of Reconstitution. In *American Indian and Indoeuropean Studies: Papers in Honor of Madison S. Beeler,* edited by Kathryn A. Klar, Margaret Langdon, and Shirley Silver, 169–182. The Hague: Mouton.

———. 1989. More on Karkin and Costanoan. IJAL 55:254–258.

———. 1991. A Note on San Francisco Costanoan. In *A Festschrift for William F. Shipley,* edited by Sandra Chung and Jorge Hankamer, 147–158. Santa Cruz: Syntax Research Center, University of California, Santa Cruz.

Olmsted, David L. 1954. Achumawi-Atsugewi Non-reciprocal Intelligibility. IJAL 20:181–184.

———. 1956. Palaihnihan and Shasta I: Labial Stops. *Language* 32:73–77.

———. 1957. Palaihnihan and Shasta II: Apical Stops. *Language* 33:136–138.

———. 1958. Atsugewi Phonology. IJAL 24:215–220.

———. 1959. Palaihnihan and Shasta III: Dorsal Stops. *Language* 35:637–644.

———. 1961. Atsugewi Morphology I: Verb Inflection. IJAL 27:91–113.

———. 1964. *A History of Palaihnihan Phonology.* UC-PL 35.

———. 1966. *Achumawi Dictionary.* UC-PL 45.

———. 1975. Jeremiah Curtin: His Life and Work as Linguist, Folklorist and Translator. *Historiographia Linguistica* 2:157–174.

———. 1984. *A Lexicon of Atsugewi.* Survey of California and Other Indian Languages, Report 5. Department of Linguistics, University of California, Berkeley.

———. 1985. Linguistic Evidence Concerning Pomo Migrations. In *Ethnography and Prehistory of the North Coast Range, California,* edited by Helen McCarthy, William R. Hildebrandt, and Laureen K. Swenson, 216–221. Center for Archaeological Research at Davis, Publication 8. Davis: Department of Anthropology, University of California, Davis.

Olmsted, David L., and Omer C. Stewart. 1978. Achumawi. In *Handbook of North American Indians.* Vol. 8: *California,* edited by Robert F. Heizer, 225–235. Washington, DC: Smithsonian Institution.

O'Neill, Sean P. 2001. *Spatial and Temporal Dimensions of Myth in Native Northwestern California: A Study in Linguistic and Cultural Relativism.* PhD dissertation, University of California, Davis.

———. 2006. Mythic and Poetic Dimensions of Speech in Northwestern California: From Cultural Vocabulary to Linguistic Relativity. AL 48:305–334.

———. 2008. *Cultural Contact and Linguistic Relativity among the Indians of Northwestern California.* Norman: University of Oklahoma Press.

Ortiz, Beverly. 1994. Chocheño and Rumsen Narratives: A Comparison. In *The Ohlone Past and Present: Native Americans of the San Francisco Bay Region,* edited by Lowell John Bean, 99–164. Ballena Press Anthropological Papers no. 42. Menlo Park, CA: Ballena Press.

Osgood, Cornelius, ed. 1946. *Linguistic Structures of Native America.* Viking Fund Publications in Anthropology 6. New York: Viking Fund.

Oswalt, Robert L. 1958. Russian Loanwords in Southwestern Pomo. IJAL 24:245–247.

———. 1960. Gualala. *Names* 8:57–58.

———. 1961. *A Kashaya Grammar (Southwestern Pomo).* PhD dissertation, University of California, Berkeley.

———. 1964a. The Internal Relationships of the Pomo Family of Languages. In *Actas y Memorias, XXXV Congreso Internacional de Americanistas, Mexico.* Tome II, pp. 413–427.

———. 1964b. *Kashaya Texts.* UC-PL 36.

———. 1976a. Comparative Verb Morphology of Pomo. In *Hokan Studies: Papers from the First Conference on Hokan Languages,* edited by Margaret Langdon and Shirley Silver, 13–28. The Hague: Mouton.

———. 1976b. Baby Talk and the Genesis of Some Basic Pomo Words. IJAL 42:1–13.

———. 1976c. Switch Reference in Maiduan: An Areal and Typological Contribution. IJAL 42:297–304.

———. 1977. Retribution for Mate-Stealing (Southern Pomo text). In *Northern California Texts,* edited by Victor Golla and Shirley Silver, 71–81. IJAL Native American Text Series 2(2). Chicago: University of Chicago Press.

———. 1979. An Exploration of the Affinity of Wappo and Some Hokan and Penutian Languages. In *1978 Hokan-Penutian Workshop,* pp. 56–71.

———. 1980. Ukiah. In *American Indian and Indoeuropean Studies: Papers in Honor of Madison S. Beeler,* edited by Kathryn A. Klar, Margaret Langdon, and Shirley Silver, 183–190. The Hague: Mouton.

———. 1981. On the Semantically Interlocking Nature of the Kashaya Verb Prefixes: The Case of *si-* 'water, drink, tongue'. In *1980 Hokan-Penutian Workshop.*

———. 1983. Interclausal Reference in Kashaya. In *Switch Reference and Universal Grammar,* edited by John Haiman and Pamela Munro, 267–290. Amsterdam: Benjamins.

———. 1985. The Infiltration of English into Indian. IJAL 51:527–529.

———. 1986. The Evidential System of Kashaya. In *Evidentiality: The Linguistic Coding of Epistemology,* edited by Wallace Chafe and Johanna Nichols, 29–45. Norwood, NJ: Ablex.

———. 1988a. The Floating Accent of Kashaya. In *In Honor of Mary Haas: From the Haas Festival Conference on Native American Linguistics,* edited by William F. Shipley, 611–622. Berlin: Mouton de Gruyter.

———. 1988b. History through the Words Brought to California by the Fort Ross Colony. *News from Native California* 2(3):20–22. (Reprinted in Hinton 1994:100–104.)

———. 1990. The Perfective-Imperfective Opposition in Kashaya. In *1990 Hokan-Penutian Workshop.*

———. 1998. Three Laryngeal Increments of Kashaya. In *Studies in American Indian Languages: Description and Theory,* edited by Leanne Hinton and Pamela Munro, 87–94. UC-PL 131.

Pandosy, Marie-Charles. 1862. *Grammar and Dictionary of the Yakima Language.* Translated by George Gibbs and John Gilmary Shea. Shea's Library of American Linguistics, no. 6. New York: Cramoisy Press.

Park, Susan. 1975. *Stephen Powers, California's First Ethnologist; and, Letters of Stephen Powers to John Wesley Powell Concerning Tribes of California,* edited by Robert F. Heizer. Contribution 28, University of California Archaeological Research Facility.

Parmenter, Ross. 1966. *Explorer, Linguist, and Ethnologist: A Descriptive Bibliography of the Published Works of Alphonse Louis Pinart, with Notes on his Life.* Introduction by Carl Schaefer Dentzel. Los Angeles: Southwest Museum.

Perry, Jean. 2003. When the World Was New: Ishi's Stories. In *Ishi in Three Centuries,* edited by Karl Kroeber and Clifton Kroeber, 275–292. Lincoln: University of Nebraska Press.

Phillips, Arthur M., III, Dorothy A. House, and Barbara G. Phillips. 1988. *Expedition to the San Francisco Peaks: C. Hart Merriam and the Life Zone Concept.* Flagstaff: Museum of Northern Arizona.

Piccolo, Francisco María, S.J. 1962. *Informe del estado de la nueva cristiandad de California.* Edited by Ernest J. Burrus, S.J. Madrid: Editorial José Porrua Turanzas.

Pico, Juan Estevan. 1891. Cuatro de julio de 1890 [Fourth of July, 1890]. NAA MS 3718, National Anthropological Archives, Smithsonian Institution. 20 pp. (Letter to Henry W. Henshaw, dated April 21, 1891, written in parallel columns in Ventureño Chumash and in English; typed English translation.)

Pierce, Joe E. 1962–1963. Native American Language Collection (OH 12). 57 tapes. Oregon State University, Corvallis, Oregon. ("Oral interviews with members of the Coquille and Siletz tribes made by Portland State University anthropologist Joe E. Pierce in 1962–63.")

Pierce, Joe E., and James M. Ryherd. 1964. The Status of Athapaskan Research in Oregon. IJAL 30:137–143.

Pilling, James Constantine. 1891. *Bibliography of the Algonquian Languages.* Washington, DC: Government Printing Office.

Pinart, Alphonse L. 1870–1885. Alphonse Louis Pinart Papers, 1870–1885. BANC MSS Z-Z 17, The Bancroft Library, University of California, Berkeley. 23 volumes. (Vol. 9: Diaries, June 24–October 26, 1878, travels in California.)

———. 1878a. Idioma Ex'xeien, dialecto del idioma Esselen . . . [The Ex'xien language, dialect of the Esselen language. These words were given by the Indian woman Omesia, formerly married to a man from the rancheria of Ex'seien or "the Rock." The Indian woman was born in the pueblo of Guacaron near the present site of Castroville. Recorded at Monterey, July 27, 1878.] BANC MSS C-C 62, no. 3 [former 35053], The Bancroft Library, University of California, Berkeley. (Published in Heizer 1952:73–82, "Esselen.")

———. 1878b. [Vocabulary of the Rumsen language of the Indians of Carmel. Obtained from the Indian Ventura, or Buenaventura, the blind Indian of Carmel who was born at Carmel in 1809. Monterey, July 27, 1878.] BANC MSS C-C 62, no. 4 [former 35057], The Bancroft Library, University of California, Berkeley. (Published in Heizer 1952:7–35, "Costanoan IV.")

———. 1878c. Vocabulario de la Lengua de la Misión de N. Sa. de la Soledad . . . [Vocabulary of the language of the Mission of Nuestra Señora de la Soledad. Obtained from Coleta, an Indian woman from the M de N S of Soledad who was born there, but now lives near the M of San Antonio. At M San Antonio, August 3, 1878.] BANC MSS C-C 62, no. 5 [former 35056], The Bancroft Library, University of California, Berkeley. (Published in Heizer1952:7–35, "Costanoan I.")

———. 1878d. Vocabulario de la Lengua de los Indios de la Misión de San Antonio de Padua . . . [Vocabulary of the language of the Indians of the Mission of San Antonio de Padua (Totaukui) or Tesxaya, obtained from Lorenzo, August 3, 1878.] BANC MSS C-C 62, no. 6 [former 35055], The Bancroft Library, University of California, Berkeley. (Published in Heizer 1952:73–82, "Salinan.")

———. 1878e. Vocabulario breve de la lengua Tulare de Sta. Cruz, ra. de Chalostaca (?), que interpreto la india Eulogia de nacion Tulare, la que vive actualmente en la rancheria del Potrero. Santa Cruz, el dia 23 de Agosto, 1878. [Short vocabulary of the Yokuts language of Santa Cruz, rancheria of Chalostaca (?), which was obtained from the Indian woman Eulogia of the Yokuts tribe, who now lives in the Indian village at the port. Santa Cruz, August 23, 1878.]. BANC MSS C-C 62, no. 7, The Bancroft Library, University of California, Berkeley.

———. 1878f. Vocabulario breve del Idioma de la misión Santa Cruz . . . [Short vocabulary of the language of Mission Santa Cruz obtained from the Indian woman Eulogia. M Santa Cruz, August 23, 1878. Gone over and added to with Rustico at Aptos, August 26, 1878.] BANC MSS C-C 62, no. 8 [former 34992], The Bancroft Library, University of California, Berkeley. (Published in Heizer 1952:7–35, "Costanoan II" from Eulogia, "Costanoan III" from Rustico.)

———. 1878g. Vocabulario del idioma Mitskanaxan de la misión de Santa Buenaventura . . . [Vocabulary of the Mitskanaxan language of Mission San Buenaventura. Obtained from the wife of Luis, Indian of the Mission. San Buenaventura, September 28, 1878.] BANC MSS C-C 62, no. 9 [former 34985], The Bancroft Library, University of California, Berkeley. (Published in Heizer 1952:36–72, "Chumash II.")

———. 1878h. [Vocabulary of the Alaxulapu language of Santa Ynes Mission. Obtained from Luis, aged Indian of Mission Santa Ynes who now lives in the village of San Buenaventura. San Buenaventura, September 28, 1878.] BANC MSS C-C 62, no. 10 [former 34981], The Bancroft Library, University of California, Berkeley. (Published in Heizer 1952:36–72, "Chumash I.")

———. 1878i. [Vocabulary of the Mupu language of Santa Paula and Camulos. Obtained from the wife of Roberto Salazar, an Indian woman of Santa Paula. Recorded at San Buenaventura, September 30, 1878. BANC MSS C-C 62, no. 11 [former 34983], The Bancroft Library, University of California, Berkeley. (Published in Heizer 1952:36–72, "Chumash III.")

———. 1878j. [Vocabulary of the language of Siuxton or Mission Santa Barbara. Obtained from Martina and Balthazar. Recorded at San Buenaventura, September 30, 1878.] BANC MSS C-C 62, no. 12 [former 34984], The Bancroft Library, University of California, Berkeley. (Published in Heizer 1952:36–72, "Chumash VII.")

———. 1878k. [Vocabulary of the čumaš language, dialect of Santa Rosa Island or Huyman. Obtained from Balthazar, Indian of the island of Santa Cruz now living in the rancheria of San Buenaventura. At San Buenaventura, September 30, 1878.] BANC MSS C-C 62, no. 13 [former 34986], The Bancroft Library, University of California, Berkeley. (Published in Heizer 1952:36–72, "Chumash VI.")

———. 1878l. [Vocabulary of the čumaš of Santa Cruz Island or Limue dialect. Obtained from Martina and Balthazar, Indian man and woman of the islands who now live in the rancheria of San Buenaventura. Recorded at San Buenaventura, September 30, 1878.] BANC MSS C-C 62, no. 14 [former 34988], The Bancroft Library, University of California, Berkeley. (Published in Heizer 1952:36–72 "Chumash V.")

———. 1878m. Vocabulario del idioma Alapamus o La Purisima . . . [Vocabulary of the Alapamus or La Purisima language. Obtained from Cecilio, an Indian of about 50 years of age now living in the rancheria of Santa Ynes. Recorded at Rancho Saka, October 6, 1878.] BANC MSS C-C 62, no. 15 [former 34989], The Bancroft Library, University of California, Berkeley. (Published in Heizer 1952:36–72, "Chumash IV.")

———. 1878n. Vocabulario breve del idioma Tulareño del Tejon rancheria de Tanesac & Vocabulario breve del idioma Tulareño del Tejon rancheria Iauxlemne. [Short vocabulary of the Yokuts language of the Tejon rancheria of Tanesac and Short vocabulary of the Yokuts language of the Tejon rancheria Iauxlemne.] BANC MSS C-C 62, no. 16 [former 34980], The Bancroft Library, University of California, Berkeley. ("Tanesac" is the Hometwoli variety of Buena Vista Yokuts; "Iauxlemne" is the Yawelmani, or Yawlumne, variety of Southern Valley Yokuts.)

———. 1894. Études sur les Indiens Californiens. *Revue de linguistique et de philologie comparée* 27:79–87. (Vocabulary of the Yachikamne dialect of Delta Yokuts. The original manuscript [1880?] has been lost, but a copy in Pinart's hand is in Pinart n.d.[b], box 1, folder 6, pp. 110ff. Published as

"On the Tcholovones of Choris," in an English translation by C. Hart Merriam and with an introductory note by R. F. Heizer, in Merriam 1955:133–138.)

———. n.d.[a]. Prayers and hymns translated into the languages of the Indians of California, mainly Tulareño [Yokuts] and Mutsun. [Undated]. BANC MSS C-C 75, The Bancroft Library, University of California, Berkeley. 48 pp. (Apparently copied from Arroyo de la Cuesta 1837.)

———. n.d.[b]. Alphonse Louis Pinart Native American Vocabularies. WA MSS S-285, Yale Collection of Western Americana, Beinecke Rare Book and Manuscript Library, Yale University. 5 boxes, 7.5 linear feet. (Vocabularies collected by Pinart together with vocabularies collected by others and transcribed by Pinart. Contents relating to California languages are arranged as follows: Box 1, folder 1, *Vocabularios de las lenguas indígenas de la Baja California.* Box 1, folders 6–10, *Vocabularios de las lenguas indígenas de la Alta California* (part I: Monterey, Mutsun, Yokuts; part II: Santa Barbara, San Antonio, Pomo, Shasta, Achumawi; part III: Patwin, Wintun, Maidu, Nisenan, Miwok; part IV: Karuk, Yurok, Klamath, Chimariko, Wiyot, Yuki; part V: Numic, Yuman). Box 2, folder 11, *Vocabulario de la lengua Seri.* A microfilm copy of folders 6–10, *Vocabularios de las lenguas indígenas de la Alta California,* is in the Anthropology Library, University of California, Berkeley.)

Pinart, Alphonse, and Henry R. Wagner. 1962. *Journey to Arizona in 1876.* Translated from the French by George H. Whitney. Biography and bibliography of Pinart by Henry R. Wagner. Introduction and Notes by Carl S. Dentzel. Los Angeles: Zamorano Club.

Pitkin, Harvey. 1962. A Bibliography of the Wintun Family of Languages. IJAL 28:43–54.

———. 1984. *Wintu Grammar.* UC-PL 94.

———. 1985. *Wintu Dictionary.* UC-PL 95.

———. n.d. Harvey Pitkin Papers, 1884–1968. Mss.Ms.Coll.78, American Philosophical Society, Philadelphia.

Poldervaart, Arie. 2004. *Paiute-English English-Paiute Dictionary.* Yerington, NV: Yerington Paiute Tribe.

Pope, Saxton T. 1920. *The Medical History of Ishi.* UC-PAAE 13:175–213.

Poser, William J. 1992. The Salinan and Yurumanguí Data in *Language in the Americas.* IJAL 58:202–229.

———. 1995. Binary Comparison and the History of Hokan Comparative Studies. IJAL 61:135–144.

Powell, John Wesley. 1871–1872. Kaivawit [Kaibab Southern Paiute] vocabulary. NAA MSS 1795, no. 4 and 11, 1494, 1491, and 2116-b, National Anthropological Archives, Smithsonian Institution. 196 pp. + 146 pp. + 109 pp. + 32 pp. (Original notes and recompilations of material collected during Powell's second and third trips down the Colorado and in the Grand Canyon, summers of 1871 and 1872. Published in D. Fowler and Fowler 1971:129–151.)

———. 1873a. Pa-vi-o'-tsi [Northern Paiute] vocabulary, May 1873. NAA MSS 1490 and 822, National Anthropological Archives, Smithsonian Institution. 61 pp. + 88 pp. (Published in D. Fowler and Fowler 1971:210–215.)

———. 1873b. Las Vegas [Southern Paiute] vocabulary, May-September 1873. NAA MSS 1493 and 821, National Anthropological Archives, Smithsonian Institution. 94 pp. + 66 pp. (Published in D. Fowler and Fowler 1971:152–160.)

———. 1873c. Ha-muk-aha-va vocabulary, "Mo-ja-ves" Las Vegas Valley, October 1873. NAA MS 1498, National Anthropological Archives, Smithsonian Institution. 4 pp.

———. 1877a. Linguistics. In *Tribes of California*, by Stephen Powers, 439–613. Contributions to North American Ethnology 3. Department of the Interior, U.S. Geographical and Geological Survey of the Rocky Mountain Region, J. W. Powell in charge. Washington, DC: Government Printing Office. (Extensive comparative vocabularies from various sources. The 1976 reprinting omits the Linguistics section.)

———. 1877b. *Introduction to the Study of Indian Languages with Words, Phrases and Sentences to Be Collected.* Washington, DC: Government Printing Office. (Instructions for collectors, with vocabulary to be obtained arranged in topical "schedules." Often referred to as the "Powell Schedule[s]." Supplanted by Powell 1880f.)

———. 1880a. Noje [Yana], vocabularies and stories, 1881 [1880]. NAA MS 3750, National Anthropological Archives, Smithsonian Institution. 9 pp. (For date of collection see Powell 1891:135.)

———. 1880b. Wintun myths and legends ca. November 1880. NAA MS 794-b, National Anthropological Archives, Smithsonian Institution. 205 pp. + 21 pp. (Twenty-three texts in English; separate Wintu vocabulary and other notes.)

———. 1880c. Numu Western Shoshonee [Northern Paiute] vocabulary, 1880. NAA MS 827, National Anthropological Archives, Smithsonian Institution. 71 pp. (Published in D. Fowler and Fowler 1971:234–240.)

———. 1880d. Nu-mu (Pa-vi-ot-so) Pai-yu-ti . . . of Humboldt Valley [Northern Paiute], November 28, 1880. NAA MS 832, no. 1–2, National Anthropological Archives, Smithsonian Institution. 50 pp. (Published in D. Fowler and Fowler 1971:240–245, 248–249.)

———. 1880e. Ute and Paiute stories [probably collected November 1880]. NAA MS 838, National Anthropological Archives, Smithsonian Institution. 19 pp. (Mostly Northern Paiute, with vocabulary. Published in D. Fowler and Fowler 1971:245–248.)

———. 1880f. *Introduction to the Study of Indian Languages with Words, Phrases and Sentences to Be Collected,* 2nd ed., with charts. Washington, DC: Government Printing Office. (Much expanded revision of Powell 1877b, with new phonetic alphabet.)

———. 1891. *Indian Linguistic Families of America North of Mexico.* BAE-AR 7:7–142.

———. n.d. Comparative Philology, Nu-a'-gun-tits and Chem-a-hue-vis. NAA MS 1496, National Anthropological Archives, Smithsonian Institution. 20 pp. (Comparative Southern Paiute and Chemehuevi vocabularies; copied from Powell 1873a and an original Chemehuevi MS that is now lost, probably also collected in 1873. Published in D. Fowler and Fowler 1971:276–278)

Powell, Laurence Clark. 1967. *Bibliographers of the Golden State.* School of Librarianship. University of California, Berkeley.

Powers, Stephen. 1872. *Afoot and Alone: A Walk from Sea to Sea by the Southern Route. Adventures and Observations in Southern California, New Mexico, Arizona, Texas, etc.* Hartford, CT: Columbian Book Co.

———. 1876. Life and Culture of the Washo and Paiutes. NAA MS 808, National Anthropological Archives, Smithsonian Institution, Washington, DC. (Published in Powers 1975:203–208. See also D. Fowler and Fowler 1970.)

———. 1877. *Tribes of California.* Contributions to North American Ethnology 3. Department of the Interior, U.S. Geographical and Geological Survey of the Rocky Mountain Region, J. W. Powell in charge. Washington, DC: Government Printing Office. (Includes "Linguistics" by J. W. Powell, pp. 439–613. Reprinted as Powers 1976, with linguistics section omitted.)

———. 1975. *The Northern California Indians.* A reprinting of nineteen articles on California Indians originally published 1872–1877. Edited and annotated by Robert F. Heizer. Contributions of the University of California Archaeological Research Facility 25, May 1975. Berkeley: Department of Anthropology, University of California. (Contains original versions of thirteen chapters of Powers 1877 and six other publications. Also Appendix 1: "Stephen Powers, Autobiographical Sketch.")

———. 1976. *Tribes of California,* with an introduction and notes by Robert F. Heizer. Berkeley: University of California Press. (Omits "Linguistics" by J. W. Powell.)

Press, Margaret L. 1979. *Chemehuevi: A Grammar and Lexicon.* UC-PL 92.

Priestley, Herbert Ingram, ed. and trans. 1937. *A Historical, Political, and Natural Description of California, by Pedro Fages, Soldier of Spain* [Obispeño Chumash vocabulary, pp. 80–83]. Berkeley: University of California Press. (Translation of Fages 1775.)

Proulx, Paul. 1981. The Linguistic Evidence on Algonquian Prehistory. AL 22(1):1–21.

———. 1984. Proto-Algic I: Phonological Sketch. IJAL 50:165–207.

———. 1985a. Proto-Algic II: Verbs. IJAL 51:59–94.

———. 1985b. Notes on Yurok Derivation. *Kansas Working Papers in Linguistics* 10(2):101–144.

———. 1994. Proto-Algic V: Doublets and their Implications. *Kansas Working Papers in Linguistics* 19(2):115–182.

Pullum, Geoffrey K. 1973. Yokuts Bibliography: An Addendum. IJAL 39:269–271. (Works that have reanalyzed data from Newman 1944.)

Quinby, Alysoun. 2003. Dialectology of River Yurok: A Preliminary Exploration. Senior honors thesis, Department of Linguistics, University of California, Berkeley.

Raab, L. Mark, and Terry L. Jones, eds. 2004. *Prehistoric California: Archaeology and the Myth of Paradise.* Salt Lake City: University of Utah Press, 2004.

Radin, Paul. 1919. *The Genetic Relationship of the North American Indian Languages.* UC-PAAE 14(5):489–502.

———. 1919–1920. Manuscript materials on Achumawi morphology and syntax; vocabulary. Radin 001-005. Survey of California and Other Indian Languaages, University of California, Berkeley.

———. 1924. *Wappo Texts.* UC-PAAE 19(1):1–147.

———. 1929. *A Grammar of the Wappo Language.* UC-PAAE 27.

———. 1932–1949. Notes on Patwin texts, grammar, and lexicon. MSS. 30(P4b.5-8) and 150(Pat.1:1–6, 2:1–6), Library of the American Philosophical Society, Philadelphia. 483 pp., ca. 3,600 slips.

Ramón, Dorothy, and Eric Elliott. 2000. *Wayta' Yawa'–Always Believe.* Banning, CA: Malki Museum Press. (Bilingual texts in Serrano and English.)

Raphael, Ray. 1993. *Little White Father: Redick McKee on the California Frontier.* Eureka, CA: Humboldt County Historical Society.

Ray, Verne F. 1963. *Primitive Pragmatists: The Modoc Indians of Northern California.* Seattle: University of Washington Press.

Redden, James E. 1966. Walapai I: Phonology; Walapai II: Morphology. IJAL 32:1–16, 141–163. (Based on author's PhD dissertation, Indiana University, 1965.)

———. 1976. Walapai Syntax: A Preliminary Statement. In *Hokan Studies: Papers from the First Conference on Hokan Languages,* edited by Margaret Langdon and Shirley Silver, 103–111. The Hague: Mouton.

———. 1981. Notes on Walapai Syntax III. In *1980 Hokan-Penutian Workshop.*

———. 1982. Relative Distance and Relative Specificity in Walapai Demonstratives. In *1981 Hokan-Penutian Workshop.*

———. 1983. Hualapai Predicate Nominatives. In *1982 Hokan-Penutian Workshop.*

———. 1986a. More on the Hualapai Auxiliaries *shyp-yu,* be, and *shyp-wi,* do. In *1983–1985 Hokan-Penutian Workshops.*

———. 1986b. The Hualapai Auxiliary *shyp-i,* say. In *1983–1985 Hokan-Penutian Workshops.*

———. 1986c. The Walapai Verbs *é.* In *1983–1985 Hokan-Penutian Workshops.*

———. 1990. Walapai Kinship Terminology. In *1990 Hokan-Penutian Workshop.*

———, ed. 1993. See Hokan-Pentutian Workshop (1977–1993).

Reichard, Gladys A. 1925. *Wiyot Grammar and Texts.* UC-PAAE 22(1):1–215.

Reichlen, Henry, and Robert F. Heizer. 1963. *The Scientific Expedition of León de Cessac to California, 1877–1879.* University of California Archaeological Survey Report 61:9–22.

Reid, Hugo. 1852 [1968]. *The Indians of Los Angeles County: Hugo Reid's Letters of 1852.* Edited and annotated by Robert F. Heizer. Los Angeles: Southwest Museum.

Rensch, Calvin. 1977. Classification of the Otomanguean Languages and the Position of Tlapanec. In *Two Studies in Middle American Comparative Linguistics.* Norman, OK: Summer Institute of Linguistics.

Richardson [Steele], Nancy, and Suzanne Burcell. 1993. *Now You're Talking—Karuk! A Beginner's Guide to Conversational Karuk.* Edited by Julian Lang. Arcata, CA: Center for Indian Community Development, Humboldt State University.

Riddell, Francis A. 1978. Maidu and Konkow. In *Handbook of North American Indians.* Vol. 8: *California,* edited by Robert F. Heizer, 370–386. Washington, DC: Smithsonian Institution.

Rigsby, Bruce J. 1965. *Linguistic Relations in the Southern Plateau.* PhD dissertation, University of Oregon.

Rivers, Betty, and Terry L. Jones. 1993. Walking along Deer Trails: A Contribution to Salinan Ethnogeography Based on the Field Notes of John Peabody Harrington. JCGBA 15:146–175.

Roberts, Edwards. 1888. *Santa Barbara and Around There.* Boston: Roberts Brother. (Contains "The Montecito Land Company," by George H. Gould, which includes a Santa Rosa Island Chumash vocabulary.)

Robins, Robert H. 1958. *The Yurok Language: Grammar, Texts, Lexicon.* UC-PL 15.

———. 1962. The Third Person Pronominal Prefix in Yurok. IJAL 28:14–18.

———. 1966. Word Classes in Yurok. *Lingua* 17: 210–229.

———. 1980. Grammatical Hierarchy and the Yurok Bipersonal Verb. In *Wege zu Universalienforschung: Sprachwissenschaftliche Beiträge zum 60. Geburtstag von Hansjakob Seiler,* edited by Gunter Brettschneider and Christian Lehmann, 360–364. Tübingen, Germany: Narr Verlag.

———. 1985a. A Rule Restatement of Yurok Allomorphy. IJAL 51: 559–561.

———. 1985b. Numerals as Underlying Verbs: The Case of Yurok. In *Studia linguistica, diachronica et synchronica Werner Winter sexagenario anno MCMLXXXIII,* edited by U. Pieper and G. Stickel, 722–733. Berlin: Mouton de Gruyter.

———. 1985c. The Young Man from Serper: A Yurok Folktale. In *Collectanea Philologica: Festschrift für Helmut Gipper,* edited by G. Heintz and P. Schmitter, 633–644. Baden-Baden, Germany: Koerner.

Robinson, Alfred, ed. and trans. 1846. *Life in California during a Residence of Several Years in That Territory.* New York: Wiley and Putnam. (Contains Boscana 1846.)

Rubino, Carl. 2005. Reduplication. In *The World Atlas of Linguistic Structures,* edited by Martin Haspelmath, Matthew S. Dryer, David Gil, and Bernard Comrie, 114–117. Oxford, UK: Oxford University Press.

Rude, Noel. 1987. Some Klamath-Sahaptian Grammatical Correspondences. *Kansas Working Papers in Linguistics* 12:67–83.

Russell, Charles W. 1858. *The Life of Cardinal Mezzofanti.* London: Longman and Green.

Russell, Craig H. 2004. Fray Juan Bautisto Sancho: Tracing the Origins of California's First Composer and the Early Mission Style. Parts 1 and 2. *Boletín: The Journal of the California Mission Studies Association* 21(1):68–101, 21(2):4–35.

Sadovszky, Otto J. von. 1976. Report on the State of the Uralo-Penutian Research. *Ural-Altaische Jahrbücher* 48:191–204.

———. 1996. *The Discovery of California: A Cal-Ugrian Comparative Study.* Budapest: Akademiai Kiado/Los Angeles: International Society for Trans-Oceanic Research.

Sandos, James A. 1985. Levantamiento!: The 1824 Chumash Uprising Reconsidered. *Southern California Quarterly* 67:109–133.

———. 2004. *Converting California: Indians and Franciscans in the Missions.* New Haven, CT: Yale University Press.

Sapir, Edward. 1907a. Notes on the Takelma Indians of Southwestern Oregon. AA 9:251–275. (Reprinted in Darnell and Irvine 1994:267–292.)

———. 1907b. Preliminary Report of the Language and Mythology of the Upper Chinook. AA 9:533–544.

———. 1907–1908. Kato linguistic miscellany (with P. E. Goddard). EDDMA, no. 12.11. 11 pp.

———. 1909. *Takelma Texts.* University of Pennsylvania, University Museum, Anthropological Publications 2:1–267. (Reprinted in Golla 1990:315–580.)

———. 1910a. *Yana Texts (Together with Yana Myths, Collected by Roland B. Dixon).* UC-PAAE 9(1):1–235.

———. 1910b. Upper Takelma. In *Handbook of American Indians North of Mexico,* edited by F. W. Hodge, 872. BAE-B 30.

———. 1911. [Review of Dixon 1910.] AA 13:141–143. (Reprinted in Bright 1990a:185–187.)

———. 1913a. Wiyot and Yurok, Algonkin Languages of California. AA 15:617–646. (Reprinted in Bright 1990a:453–483.)

———. 1913b. Southern Paiute and Nahuatl, a Study in Uto-Aztecan [part 1]. *Journal de la Société des Américanistes de Paris* 10:379–425. (Reprinted in Bright 1990a:351–397.)

———. 1914. *Notes on Chasta Costa Phonology and Morphology*. University of Pennsylvania, Anthropological Publications 2(2):271–340. (Reprinted in Golla 1991a:27–94.)

———. 1915a. Southern Paiute and Nahuatl, a Study in Uto-Aztecan [part 2]. AA 17:98–120, 306–28. (Reprinted in Bright 1990a:398–443.)

———. 1915b. Algonkin Languages of California: A Reply. AA 17:188–194. (Reply to Michelson 1914. Reprinted in Bright 1990a:485–489.)

———. 1915c. Epilogue [to Sapir-Michelson exchange]. AA 17:198. (Rejoinder to Michelson 1915. Reprinted in Bright 1990a:561.)

———. 1915d. The Nadene Languages: A Preliminary Report. AA 17:534–558. (Reprinted in Golla 1991a:105–131.)

———. 1915e. Yahi linguistic field notes. EDDMA, no. 68. 6 notebooks, 272 pp.

———. 1915f. *Abnormal Types of Speech in Nootka*. Canada, Department of Mines, Geological Survey, Memoir 62, Anthropological Series No. 5. Ottawa: Government Printing Bureau. (Reprinted in Mandelbaum 1949:179–196. Also reprinted in Golla 1991a:357–380.)

———. 1916a. *Time Perspective in Aboriginal American Culture: A Study in Method*. Canada, Department of Mines, Geological Survey, Memoir 90, Anthropological Series No. 13. Ottawa: Government Printing Bureau. (Reprinted in Mandelbaum 1949:389–462. Also reprinted in Darnell and Irvine 1994:31–120.)

———. 1916b. Terms of Relationship and the Levirate. AA 18:327–337.

———. 1917a. *The Position of Yana in the Hokan Stock*. UC-PAAE 13(1):1–34. (Reprinted in Bright 1990a:189–222.)

———. 1917b. The Status of Washo. AA 19:449–450. (Reprinted in Bright 1990a:223–224.)

———. 1918. *Yana Terms of Relationship*. UC-PAAE 13(4):153–173. (Reprinted in Darnell and Irvine 1994:567–588.)

———. 1920a. The Hokan and Coahuiltecan Languages. IJAL 1:280–290. (Reprinted in Bright 1990a:231–243.)

———. 1920b. A Note on the First Person Plural in Chimariko. IJAL 1:291–294. (Reprinted in Bright 1990a:245–249.)

———. 1920c. [Review of Mason 1918.] IJAL 1:305–309. (Reprinted in Bright 1990:251–255.)

———. 1920d. The Problems of Linguistic Relationship in America. (Abstract and notes for a paper presented to the American Association for the Advancement of Science, Chicago, December 1920. Published in Bright 1990a:94–104.)

———. 1921a. A Characteristic Penutian Form of Stem. IJAL 2:58–67. (Reprinted in Golla 1991a:261–273.)

———. 1921b. A Supplementary Note on Salinan and Washo. IJAL 2:68–72. (Reprinted in Bright 1990a:257–262.)

———. 1921c. A Bird's-Eye View of American Languages North of Mexico. *Science* 54:408. (Reprinted in Bright 1990a:93–94.)

———. 1921d. [The Sino-Dene Hypothesis. Excerpts from a letter to A. L. Kroeber, October 1, 1921.] In *The Sapir-Kroeber Correspondence: Letters between Edward Sapir and A. L. Kroeber, 1905–25*, edited by Victor Golla (1984), letter no. 332, pp. 374–383. Survey of California and Other Indian Languages, Report 6. Department of Linguistics, University of California, Berkeley. (Reprinted in Golla 1991a:133–140.)

———. 1922a. *The Takelma Language of Southwestern Oregon*. In *Handbook of American Indian Languages*, Part 2, edited by Franz Boas, 1–296. BAE-B 40(2). (Reprinted in Golla 1990:17–313.)

———. 1922b. *The Fundamental Elements of Northern Yana*. UC-PAAE 13(6):214–234.

———. 1923a. The Algonkin Affinity of Yurok and Wiyot Kinship Terms. *Journal de la Société des Américanistes de Paris* 15:3674. (Reprinted in Bright 1990a:491–530.)

———. 1923b. *Text Analyses of Three Yana Dialects*. UC-PAAE 20(15):263–294.

———. 1925a. The Hokan Affinity of Subtiaba in Nicaragua. AA 27:402–435, 491–527. (Reprinted in Bright 1990a:263–334.)

———. 1925b. The Similarity of Chinese and Indian Languages. *Science* 62, no. 1607, supplement of 16 October, xii. (Report of an interview. Reprinted in Golla 1991a:191–192.)

———. 1927a. An Expedition to Ancient America: A Professor and a Chinese Student Rescue the Vanishing Language and Culture of the Hupas in Northern California. *The University of Chicago Magazine* 20:10–12. (Reprinted in Darnell and Irvine 1994:735–738. Also reprinted in Golla and O'Neill 2001:1094–1096.)

———. 1927b. Hupa texts and slip file. Mss. 30(Na20a.4), Library of the American Philosophical Society, Philadelphia. 11 notebooks of ca. 125 pp. each; ca. 5,000 slips. (Texts published in Sapir and Golla 2001.)

———. 1928. A Summary Report of Field Work among the Hupa: Summer of 1927. AA 30:359–361. (Reprinted in Golla 1991a:195–198. Also reprinted in Golla and O'Neill 2001:1097–1098.)

———. 1929a. Male and Female Forms of Speech in Yana. In *Donum Natalicum Schrijnen*, edited by St. W. J. Teeuwen, 79–85. Nijmegen, Netherlands: Dekker & van der Vegt. (Reprinted in Mandelbaum 1949:169–178. Also reprinted in Bright 1990a:335–341.)

———. 1929b. Central and North American Languages. *Encyclopaedia Britannica*, 14th ed., vol. 5, pp. 138–141. (Reprinted in Bright 1990a:95–104.)

———. 1929c. A Linguistic Trip among the Navaho Indians. *Gallup Independent* (August 23, Gallup, NM) 1–2. (Reprinted in Darnell and Irvine 1994:739–741).

———. 1930–1931. *The Southern Paiute Language*. Part 1: *Southern Paiute, A Shoshonean Language*. Part 2: *Texts of the Kaibab Paiutes and Uintah Utes*. Part 3: *Southern Paiute Dictionary*. Proceedings of the American Academy of Arts and Sciences 65(1–3). (Reprinted in Bright 1992:17–752.)

———. 1931. The Concept of Phonetic Law as Tested in Primitive Languages by Leonard Bloomfield. In *Methods in the Social Sciences: A Case Book*, edited by Stuart A. Rice, 297–306. Chicago: University of Chicago Press. (Reprinted in Mandelbaum 1949:73–82. Also reprinted in Golla 1991a:199–202).

———. 1933. La Réalité Psychologique des Phonèmes. *Journal de Psychologie Normale et Pathologique* 30:247–265. (English translation, "The Psychological Reality of Phonemes," in Mandelbaum 1949:46–60.)

———. 1936a. Hupa Tattooing. In *Essays in Anthropology Presented to A. L. Kroeber in Celebration of his Sixtieth Birthday, June 11, 1936*, edited by Robert H. Lowie, 273–277. (Reprinted in Darnell and Irvine 1994:753–758.)

———. 1936b. Internal Linguistic Evidence Suggestive of the Northern Origin of the Navaho. AA 38:224–235. (Reprinted in Golla 1991a:209–220.)

Sapir, Edward, and Victor Golla. 2001. *Hupa Texts, with Notes and Lexicon.* In *The Collected Works of Edward Sapir.* Vol. 14: *Northwest California Linguistics,* edited by Victor Golla and Sean O'Neill, 19–1011. Berlin: Mouton de Gruyter.

Sapir, Edward, and Leslie Spier. 1943. *Notes on the Culture of the Yana.* UC-AR 3(3):239–298.

Sapir, Edward, and Morris Swadesh. 1953. Coos-Takelma-Penutian Comparisons. IJAL 19:132–137. (Reprinted in Golla 1991a:291–297.)

———. 1960. *Yana Dictionary.* Edited by Mary R. Haas. UC-PL 23.

Sarría, Padre Vicente Francisco de (?). 1819. Catecismo de la lengua Chalona de la Soledad. [In another hand: "By Padre Vicente Fco. de Sarria at Soledad about 1819." In Taylor's hand: "Vocabulary of the Chalon Indians of Soledad Mission in Monterey County, Cal., found at San Antonio Mission. Sent by Alex. S. Taylor. March 1860." The date 1819 cannot be correct if the author was Sarría, since he was at Soledad only between 1828 and 1835.] John G. Shea Papers, Box 10, Folder 4, Special Collections Division, Georgetown University Library, Washington, D.C. 2 pp. (The original of A. Taylor 1860.)

Sarris, Greg. 1994. *Mabel McKay: Weaving the Dream.* Berkeley: University of California Press.

Saubel, Katherine Siva, and Eric B. Elliott. 2004. *A Dried Coyote Tail: Iʹsill Heʹqwas Waʹxish. The Life of Katherine Siva Saubel.* Two volumes. Banning, CA: Malki Museum Press.

Sauvel [Saubel], Katherine Siva, and Pamela Munro. 1980. Professor Seiler and the Cahuilla Language. In *Wege zu Universalienforschung: Sprachwissenschaftliche Beiträge zum 60. Geburtstag von Hansjakob Seiler,* edited by Gunter Brettschneider and Christian Lehmann, 478–481. Tübingen, Germany: Narr Verlag. (A Cahuilla text, with analysis.)

———. 1981. *Chem'ivillu': Let's Speak Cahuilla.* Los Angeles: American Indian Studies Center, University of California, Los Angeles.

Sawyer, Jesse O. 1960. Field notes on the Tomales Bay dialect of Marin Miwok, from Mrs. Elgin. Ms. [Part of] Sawyer.007. Survey of California and Other Indian Languages, Department of Linguistics, University of California, Berkeley.

———. 1964a. Wappo Words from Spanish. In *Studies in Californian Linguistics,* edited by William Bright, 163–169. UC-PL 34.

———. 1964b. The Implications of Spanish /r/ and /rr/ in Wappo History. *Romance Philology* 18:165–177.

———. 1965. *English-Wappo Vocabulary.* UC-PL 43.

———. 1975. Nomlaki word list collected from Sylvester Simmons, 1/7/75. Ms. Sawyer.001. Survey of California and Other Indian Languages, Department of Linguistics, University of California, Berkeley.

———. 1978. Wappo. In *Handbook of North American Indians.* Vol. 8: *California,* edited by Robert F. Heizer, 256–263. Washington, DC: Smithsonian Institution.

———. 1980. The Non-Genetic Relationship of Wappo and Yuki. In *American Indian and Indoeuropean Studies: Papers in Honor of Madison S. Beeler,* edited by Kathryn A. Klar, Margaret Langdon, and Shirley Silver, 209–219. The Hague: Mouton.

———. 1991. *Wappo Studies.* Edited by Alice Shepherd, with annotations by William W. Elmendorf. Survey of California and Other Indian Languages, Report 7. Berkeley: Department of Linguistics, University of California. [Contains "Wappo Notes" (11–84) and "The Colors of Wappo and Yuki" (85–111).]

Sawyer, Jesse O., and Alice Schlichter. 1984. *Yuki Vocabulary.* UC-PL 101.

Saxon, Leslie. 1993. A Personal Use for Athapaskan 'Impersonal' *ts'e-*. IJAL 59: 342–354.

Schaad, Gerrianne, ed. 1994. *The Photograph Collection of John Peabody Harrington in the National Anthropological Archives, Smithsonian Institution: A Catalog to the Microfilm.* Washington, DC: National Anthropological Archives.

Schlichter, Alice. 1979. Wintu Internal Variation. IJAL 45:236–244.

———. 1980. English and Spanish Loanwords in Wintu. In *American Indian and Indoeuropean Studies: Papers in Honor of Madison S. Beeler,* edited by Kathryn A. Klar, Margaret Langdon, and Shirley Silver, 221–227. The Hague: Mouton.

———. 1981a. Notes on the Wintu Shamanistic Jargon. In *Survey Reports 1981,* edited by Alice Schlichter, Wallace L. Chafe, and Leanne Hinton, 95–130. Survey of California and Other Indian Languages, Report 1. Department of Linguistics, University of California, Berkeley. (Reprinted in Bean 1992.)

———. 1981b. *Wintu Dictionary.* Survey of California and Other Indian Languages, Report 2. Department of Linguistics, University of California, Berkeley.

———. 1981c. The Proto-Wintun Pronominal System. Typescript in author's possession, July 1981. 44 pp.

———. 1985. *The Yukian Language Family.* PhD dissertation, University of California, Berkeley.

Schlichter, Alice. See also Shepherd, Alice.

Schoolcraft, Henry R., ed. 1851–1857. *Historical and Statistical Information Respecting the History, Condition and Prospects of the Indian Tribes of the United States,* vol. 1–6. Philadelphia: Lippencott.

Scouler, John. 1841. Observations on the Indigenous Tribes of the North West Coast of America. *Journal of the Royal Geographical Society (London)* 11:215–251. (Contains a vocabulary of [Upper] Umpqua collected by William Fraser Tolmie and vocabularies of Diegueño, Juaneño, Gabrielino, Barbareño and Obispeño Chumash, and Antoniano Salinan collected by Thomas Coulter. See A. Grant 1993.)

Seaburg, William R. 1976–1982. Tolowa fieldnotes and sound recordings [9 notebooks, 692 pp.; 46 5″ reel-to-reel tape recordings]. Jacobs Research Collection, University of Washington Libraries. (See Seaburg 1982.)

———. 1977a. A Wailaki Text with Comparative Notes. IJAL 43:327–332.

———. 1977b. The Man Who Married a Grizzly Girl (Wailaki). In *Northern California Texts,* edited by Victor Golla and Shirley Silver, 114–120. IJAL Native American Text Series 2(2). Chicago: University of Chicago Press.

———. 1982. *Guide to Pacific Northwest Native American Materials in the Melville Jacobs Collection and in Other Archival Collections in the University of Washington Libraries.* University of Washington Libraries, Communications in Librarianship, Number 2.

———. 1994. *Collecting Culture: The Practice and Ideology of Salvage Ethnography in Western Oregon, 1877–1942.* PhD dissertation, University of Washington, Seattle.

Seaburg, William R., and Pamela T. Amoss, eds. 2000. *Badger and Coyote Were Neighbors: Melville Jacobs on Northwest Indian Myths and Tales.* Corvallis: Oregon State University Press.

(Contains "Melville Jacobs: An Introduction to the Man and His Work," pp. 1–36.)

Seiden, William. 1963. *Havasupai Phonology and Morphology.* PhD dissertation, Indiana University, Bloomington.

Seiler, Hansjakob. 1970. *Cahuilla Texts with an Introduction.* Indiana University Publications, Language Science Monographs 6. Bloomington: Indiana University Press; The Hague: Mouton.

———. 1977. *Cahuilla Grammar.* Banning, CA: Malki Museum Press.

———. 1985. Absolutive Suffix and Reanalysis in Cahuilla. IJAL 51:578–581.

Seiler, Hansjakob, and Kojiro Hioki. 1979. *Cahuilla Dictionary.* Banning, CA: Malki Museum Press.

Shaterian, Alan. 1983. *Yavapai Phonology and Dictionary.* PhD dissertation, University of California, Berkeley.

Shaul, David L. 1982. A Phonemic Analysis of Esselen. In *1981 Hokan-Penutian Workshop.*

———. 1983. Esselen Noun Thematic Suffixes. In *1982 Hokan-Penutian Workshop.*

———. 1984. Esselen Linguistic Prehistory. *Journal of the Steward Anthropological Society* 15(1–2):47–58.

———. 1988. Esselen/Utian Onomastics. In *In Honor of Mary Haas: From the Haas Festival Conference on Native American Linguistics,* edited by William F. Shipley, 693–704. Berlin: Mouton de Gruyter.

———. 1989. [Review of Hinton 1984.] AA 91:266–267.

———. 1995a. The Huelel (Esselen) Language. IJAL 61:191–239.

———. 1995b. The Last Words of Esselen. IJAL 61:245–249.

Shaul, David L., and Jane H. Hill. 1998. Tepimans, Yumans, and other Hohokam. *American Antiquity* 63:375–396.

Shepherd, Alice. 1989. *Wintu Texts.* UC-PL 117.

———. 2005. *Proto-Wintun.* UC-PL 137. (Available online at repositories.cdlib.org/ucpress/.)

Shepherd, Alice. See also Schlichter, Alice.

Sherzer, Joel. 1976. *An Areal-Typological Study of American Indian Languages North of Mexico.* North Holland Linguistic Series. New York: American Elsevier.

Shipek, Floence C. 1982. Kumeyaay Socio-Political Structure. JCGBA 4:296–303.

———. 1986. Myth and Reality: The Antiquity of the Kumeyaay. In *1983–1985 Hokan-Penutian Workshops.*

Shipley, William F. 1957. Some Yukian-Penutian Lexical Resemblances. IJAL 23:269–274.

———. 1959. [Review of Einar Haugen, *Bilingualism in the Americas.*] Romance Philology 13:84–86.

———. 1961. Maidu and Nisenan: A Binary Survey. IJAL 27:46–51.

———. 1962. Spanish Elements in the Indigenous Languages of California. *Romance Philology* 16:1–21.

———. 1963. *Maidu Texts and Dictionary.* UC-PL 33.

———. 1964. *Maidu Grammar.* UC-PL 41.

———. 1966. The Relation of Klamath to California Penutian. *Language* 42:489–498.

———. 1969. Proto-Takelman. IJAL 35:226–230.

———. 1978. Native Languages of California. In *Handbook of North American Indians.* Vol. 8: *California,* edited by Robert F. Heizer, 80–90. Washington, DC: Smithsonian Institution.

———. 1980a. Rumsen Derivation. In *American Indian and Indoeuropean Studies: Papers in Honor of Madison S. Beeler,* edited by Kathryn A. Klar, Margaret Langdon, and Shirley Silver, 237–244. The Hague: Mouton.

———. 1980b. Penutian among the Ruins: A Personal Assessment. *Proceedings of the* [6th] *Annual Meeting of the Berkeley Linguistics Society,* pp. 437–441.

———, ed. 1988. *In Honor of Mary Haas: From the Haas Festival Conference on Native American Linguistics.* Berlin: Mouton de Gruyter.

———. 1995. Wick R. Miller. IJAL 61:240–245.

———. 2002. The Awáswas Language. In *A Gathering of Voices: The Native Peoples of the Central California Coast,* edited by Linda Yamane, 173–181. Santa Cruz County History Journal, Issue 5. Santa Cruz: The Museum of Art and History.

Shipley, William F., and Richard A. Smith. 1979a. The Roles of Cognation and Diffusion in a Theory of Maidun Prehistory. JCGBA-PL 1:65–73.

———. 1979b. Proto-Maidun Stress and Vowel Length: The Reconstruction of *One, Two, Three,* and *Four.* IJAL 45:171–176. (Critique of Silverstein 1975. See Silverstein 1979b.)

———. 1982. Nouns and Pronouns, Maidun and Otherwise. In *1981 Hokan-Penutian Workshop.*

Siegl, Bernard C. 1994. *The Cal-Ugrian Theory: An Assessment of a New Linguistic Classification.* MA thesis, California State University, Fullerton.

Silver, Shirley. 1966. *The Shasta Language.* PhD dissertation, University of California, Berkeley.

———. 1974. Some Northern Hokan Plant-Tree-Bush Forms. JCA 1:102–109.

———. 1976. Comparative Hokan and the Northern Hokan Languages. In *Hokan Studies: Papers from the First Conference on Hokan Languages,* edited by Margaret Langdon and Shirley Silver, 193–202. The Hague: Mouton.

———. 1978. Shastan Peoples. In *Handbook of North American Indians.* Vol. 8: *California,* edited by Robert F. Heizer, 211–224. Washington, DC: Smithsonian Institution.

———. 1980. Shasta and Konomihu. In *American Indian and Indoeuropean Studies: Papers in Honor of Madison S. Beeler,* edited by Kathryn A. Klar, Margaret Langdon, and Shirley Silver, 245–263. The Hague: Mouton.

Silver, Shirley, and Wick R. Miller. 1997. *American Indian Languages: Cultural and Social Contexts.* Tucson: University of Arizona Press. (Includes original data from Achumawi, Pomo, Shasta, and Shoshoni.)

Silver, Shirley, and Clara Wicks. 1977. Coyote Steals the Fire (Shasta Text). In *Northern California Texts,* edited by Victor Golla and Shirley Silver, 121–131. IJAL Native American Text Series 2(2). Chicago: University of Chicago Press.

Silverstein, Michael. 1972. *Studies in Penutian I. California, 1. The Structure of an Etymology.* PhD dissertation, Harvard University, Cambridge, MA.

———. 1975. On Two California Penutian Roots for *Two.* IJAL:369–380.

———. 1979a. Penutian: An Assessment. In *The Languages of Native America: Historical and Comparative Assessment,* edited by Lyle Campbell and Marianne Mithun, 650–691. Austin: University of Texas Press.

———. 1979b. Two bis. IJAL 45:187–205. (Reply to Callaghan 1979; Okrand 1979b; and Shipley and Smith 1979b.)

Sitjar, Padre Buenaventura. 1861. *Vocabulario de la Lengua de los Naturales de la Mision de San Antonio, Alta California.* Edited by J. G. Shea. Shea's Library of American Linguistics, no. 7. New York: Cramoisy Press. (Published version of Sitjar and Pieras 1771–1797a.)

Sitjar, Padre Buenaventura, Padre Pedro Cabot, and (?) Padre Francisco Dumetz. 1770–1835. Vocabulary of [Antoniano Salinan] Indian Words, 1770–1835 [with signed and dated annotations by Alexander S. Taylor identifying the authors]. S265, Manuscripts Collection, Boston Athenaeum. 89 pp. (Taylor's attribution of coauthorship to Padre Dumetz, who never served at Mission San Antonio, is apparently a mistake. Padre Juan Sancho is probably meant.)

Sitjar, Padre Buenaventura, and Padre Miguel Pieras. 1771–1797a. Vocabulario de la lengua de los naturales de la misión San Antonio, Alta California. [Vocabulary of the Indians of San Antonio Mission. Title and explanatory notes by Alexander S. Taylor.] BANC MSS C-C 34, The Bancroft Library, University of California, Berkeley. 472 pp. (Copy in John G. Shea Papers, Box 7, Folder 6, Special Collections Division, Georgetown University Library, Washington, DC. Published as Sitjar 1861.)

———. 1771–1797b. [Confesionario in Antoniano Salinan and Spanish. 16 leaves. Also vocabulary, prayers, at the end.] John G. Shea Papers, Box 7, Folder 5, Special Collections Division, Georgetown University Library, Washington, DC.

Sloan, Kelly. 1991. Syllables and Templates: Evidence from Southern Sierra Miwok. PhD dissertation, Massachusetts Institute of Technology, Cambridge, MA.

Smith, Norval. 1985. Spreading, Reduplication and the Default Option in Miwok Nonconcatenative Morphology. In *Advances in Nonlinear Phonology*, edited by Harry van der Hulst and Norval Smith, 363–380. Dordrecht, Netherlands: Foris.

———. 2007. A Contribution to Delta Yokuts Vocabulary: Some Items from Tamukan. JCGBA 27:45–51.

Smith, Richard A. 1977. Bear and Deer Woman (Nisenan). In *Northern California Texts*, edited by Victor Golla and Shirley Silver, 132–146. IJAL Native American Text Series 2(2). Chicago: University of Chicago Press.

Snapp, Allen, John Anderson, and Joy Anderson. 1982. Northern Paiute. In *Studies in Uto-Aztecan Grammar,* vol. 3: *Uto-Aztecan Grammatical Sketches,* edited by Ronald W. Langacker, 1–92. Summer Institute of Linguistics Publications in Linguistics 56(3). Dallas: University of Texas at Arlington and SIL.

Sparkman, Phillip Stedman. 1898–1906. Notes on the Luiseño language and culture; Luiseño grammar and dictionaries [several drafts]; Luiseño religious terminology; [ethnographic] sketch of Luiseño tribe(s). EDDMA, nos. 25–30, 51. ca. 3,200 pp.

———. 1905. A Sketch of the Grammar of the Luiseño Indians. AA 7:656–662.

———. 1908. *The Culture of the Luiseño Indians.* UC-PAAE 8(4):187–234.

Spier, Leslie. 1930. *Klamath Ethnography.* UC-PAAE 30.

———. 1933. *Yuman Tribes of the Gila River.* Chicago: University of Chicago Press.

———. 1946. *Comparative Vocabularies and Parallel Texts in Two Yuman Languages of Arizona.* University of New Mexico Publications in Anthropology 2.

Spier, Robert F. G. 1978a. Foothill Yokuts. In *Handbook of North American Indians.* Vol. 8: *California,* edited by Robert F. Heizer, 471–484. Washington, DC: Smithsonian Institution.

———. 1978b. Monache. In *Handbook of North American Indians.* Vol. 8: *California,* edited by Robert F. Heizer, 426–436. Washington, DC: Smithsonian Institution.

Sproat, Richard. 1981. Southern California Reflexives: An Example of Translation Borrowing? JCGBA-PL 3:77–94.

Stanton, William. 1975. *The Great United States Exploring Expedition of 1838–1842.* Berkeley: University of California Press.

Starn, Orin. 2003. Ishi's Spanish Words. In *Ishi in Three Centuries,* edited by Karl Kroeber and Clifton Kroeber, 201–207. Lincoln: Unversity of Nebraska Press.

———. 2004. *Ishi's Brain: In Search of America's Last "Wild" Indian.* New York: W. W. Norton.

Starostin, Sergej A. 1989. Nostratic and Sino-Caucasian. In *Explorations in Language Macrofamilies,* edited by V. Shevoroshkin, 42–66. Bochum, Germany: Brockmeyer.

Steele, Susan. 1979. Uto-Aztecan: An Assessment for Historical and Comparative Linguistics. In *The Languages of Native America: Historical and Comparative Assessment,* edited by Lyle Campbell and Marianne Mithun, 444–544. Austin: University of Texas Press.

———. 1990. *Agreement and Anti-Agreement: A Syntax of Luiseño.* Dordrecht, Netherlands: Kluwer.

Sterling, Keir B. 1974. *Last of the Naturalists: The Career of C. Hart Merriam.* New York: Arno Press.

Stern, Theodore. 1998. Klamath and Modoc. In *Handbook of North American Indians.* Vol. 12: *Plateau,* edited by Deward E. Walker, Jr., 446–466. Washington, DC: Smithsonian Institution.

Steward, Julian H. 1933. *Ethnography of the Owens Valley Paiute.* UC-PAAE 33(3):233–350.

———. 1937. Linguistic Distributions and Political Groups of the Great Basin Shoshoneans. AA 39:625–634.

Stewart, Kenneth M. 1983. Mohave. In *Handbook of North American Indians.* Vol. 10: *Southwest,* edited by Alfonso Ortiz, 55–70. Washington, DC: Smithsonian Institution.

Stewart, Omer C. 1939. *The Northern Paiute Bands.* UC-AR 2(3):127–149.

———. 1943. *Notes on Pomo Ethnogeography.* UC-PAAE 40(2):29–62.

Stirling, Mathew W., and K. Glemser. 1963. John Peabody Harrington, 1884–1961. AA 65:370–381.

Story, Gillian. 1989. The Athapaskan First Duoplural Subject Prefix. In *Athapaskan Linguistics: Current Perspectives on a Language Family,* edited by Eung-Do Cook and Keren Rice, 487–531. Berlin: Mouton de Gruyter.

Sturtevant, William C. 1959. Authorship of the Powell Linguistic Classification. IJAL 25:196–199.

———. 1981. R. F. Heizer and the Handbook of North American Indians. In *Contributions of Robert F. Heizer to California Ethnohistory,* edited by William S. Simmons and Polly McW. Bickel, 1–5. Publications of the University of California Archaeological Research Facility 19.

Suárez, Jorge. 1983. *La lengua tlapaneca de Malinaltepec.* Mexico: UNAM.

Sutton, Mark Q. 1993. The Numic Expansion in Great Basin Oral Tradition. JCGBA 15:111–128.

———. 2009. People and Language: Defining the Takic Expansion into Southern California. *Pacific Coast Archaeological Society Quarterly* 41:31–93.

Swadesh, Morris. 1946. Chitimacha. In *Linguistic Structures of Native America,* edited by Cornelius Osgood, 312–336. Viking Fund Publications in Anthropology 6. New York: Viking Fund.

———. 1954a. Perspectives and Problems of Amerindian Comparative Linguistics. *Word* 10:306–332.

———. 1954b. On the Penutian Vocabulary Survey. IJAL 20:123–133.

———. 1956. Problems of Long-Range Comparison in Penutian. *Language* 32:17–41.

———. 1959. Linguistics as an Instrument of Prehistory. *Southwestern Journal of Anthropology* 15:20–35.

———. 1965. Kalapuya and Takelma. IJAL 31:237–240.

———. n.d. Chimariko in the Light of Sapir's Data. MS.

Swadesh, Morris, and Robert Melton. 1953. Penutian and Athabaskan linguistic material. 28 sound tape reels, recorded in 1953 in California, Oregon and Washington. 85-555-F ATL 18238-18265, Archives of Traditional Music, Indiana University, Bloomington. ("Elicitations in Nez Perce, Sahaptin, Yakima, Chinook, Tsimshian, Santiam, Galice, Dootoodn [Tututni], Coos, Suislaw, Molale, Paiute, Chinook (upper), Klamath, Wintun, Concow, Nomlaki, Patwin, Miwok, Chukchansi, and Nisenan.")

Swadesh, Morris, and C. F. Voegelin. 1939. A Problem in Phonological Alternation. *Language* 15:1–10. (Tubatulabal phonology.)

Swann, Brian, ed. 2004. *Voices from Four Directions: Contemporary Translations of the Native Literatures of North America.* Lincoln: University of Nebraska Press.

Swanson, Earl H., Jr., ed. 1968. *Utaztekan Prehistory.* Occasional Papers of the Idaho State Museum, no. 22.

———. 1970. *Languages and Cultures of Western North America: Essays in Honor of Sven S. Liljeblad.* Pocatello: Idaho State University Press.

Swanton, John R. 1915. Linguistic Position of the Tribes of Southern Texas and Northeastern Mexico. AA 17:17–40.

———. 1940. *Linguistic Material from the Tribes of Southern Texas and Northeastern Mexico.* BAE-B 127.

Tagliavini, Carlo. 1926. *La lingua degli indi Luiseños segondo gli appunti grammaticali inediti di un chierico indigeno, conservati tra i manuscritti Mezzofanti nell' Archiginnasio di Bologna.* Bologna, Italy: Nicola Zanichelli. (English translation in Kroeber and Grace 1960:221–237.)

———. 1930a. L'Evangelizzazione e i costumi degli Indi Luiseños secondo la narrazione di un chierico indigeno. *Proceedings of the 23rd International Congress of Americanists* (New York, 1928), pp. 633–648. (English translation in Hewes and Hewes 1952.)

———. 1930b. Frammento d'un dizzionaretto Luiseño-Spagnuolo scritto da un indigeno. *Proceedings of the 23rd International Congress of Americanists* (New York, 1928), pp. 905–917.

Talmy, Leonard. 1972. *Semantic Structures in English and Atsugewi.* PhD dissertation, University of California, Berkeley.

———. 1985. Lexicalization Patterns: Semantic Structure in Lexical Forms. In *Language Typology and Syntactic Description III,* edited by Timothy Shopen, 57–149. Cambridge, UK: Cambridge University Press.

Tanner, Helen Hornbeck. 1991. Erminie Wheeler-Voegelin (1903–1988), Founder of the American Society for Ethnohistory. *Ethnohistory* 38:58–72.

Tarpent, Marie-Lucie. 1997. Tsimshianic and Penutian: Problems, Methods, Results, and Implications. IJAL 63:65–112.

Tarpent, Marie-Lucie, and Daythal Kendall. 1998. On the Relationship between Takelma and Kalapuyan: Another Look at "Takelman." Paper presented at the annual meeting of the Society for the Study of the Indigenous Languages of the Americas, New York, January 9–11, 1998.

Tatsch, Sheri J. 2006. *Nisenan: Dialects and Districts of a Speech Community.* PhD dissertation, University of California, Davis.

Taylor, Alexander S. 1856. Vocabulary of the Indians living near Dent's Ferry and vicinity on the Stanislaus river in the Sierra Nevada of Calaveras county, . . . taken by Alex. S. Taylor, 1st of November 1856 from José Patricio, aged 25, Rancheria Ta-kin near Dent's Ferry of the Stanislau. [Vocabulary of a dialect of Delta Yokuts, ca. 220 words.] BANC MSS C-B 418 (James L. Warren papers), box 8, no. 4, The Bancroft Library, University of California, Berkeley. (Published in *The California Farmer,* March 23, 1860. Reprinted in Powers 1877, pp. 572 ff. Reprinted in Kroeber 1959b, vocab. E.)

———. 1860. Vocabulary of the Chalon Indians of Soledad Mission in Monterey County, Cal. found at San Antonio Mission. Sent by Alexr S. Taylor, March 1860. [A short catechism, not a vocabulary.] John G. Shea Papers, Box 10, Folder 4, Special Collections Division, Georgetown University Library, Washington, DC. 7 pp. (Copy in Sarría 1819, in Taylor's hand.)

———. 1860–1863. *The Indianology of California,* or, Fragmentary notes, selected and original, on the Indian tribes of the countries formerly called Alta and Baja California, in four series of 150 separate numbers, published in *The California Farmer* from 1860 to 1863 by Alexander S. Taylor. [Partly mounted clippings.] The Bancroft Library, University of California, Berkeley. (Available on microfilm BANC E78.C15.T16. Most of the vocabularies in the articles are reprinted in Lucy-Fossarieu 1881; selected articles, including some vocabularies, are reprinted in Heizer 1973. Most of the original vocabularies are in BANC MSS C-B 418 [James L. Warren papers], box 8-9, Bancroft Library, University of California, Berkeley.)

———. 1862a. The Indian Languages of Santa Barbara, California. [Manuscript with mixture of English, Latin, and some Indian language, probably Chumash, dated 10/10/1862 by Alexander S. Taylor.] John G. Shea Papers, Box 10, Folder 6, Special Collections Division, Georgetown University Library, Washington, DC. 8 pp.

———. 1862b. Mission of Santa Ynez in Santa Barbara County by Alex. S. Taylor. From the old "Ritual Romano" of the Mission used by the old missionaries. [A copy in Taylor's hand, dated 10/10/1862.] John G. Shea Papers, Box 10, Folder 10, Special Collections Division, Georgetown University Library, Washington, DC. 4 pp.

Taylor, E. G. R. 1932. Francis Drake and the Pacific: Two Fragments. [Includes Richard Maddox's "Account of California."] *Pacific Historical Review* 1:360–369.

Taylor, Walter W. 1961. Archaeology and Language in Western North America. *American Antiquity* 27:71–91.

Teeter, Karl V. 1958. Notes on Humboldt County, California, Place Names of Indian Origin. *Names* 6:55–56.

———. 1959. Consonant Harmony in Wiyot (with a Note on Cree). IJAL 25:111–113.

———. 1964. *The Wiyot Language.* UC-PL 37.

———. 1974. Some Algic Etymologies. IJAL 40:197–201.

Teeter, Karl V., and John D. Nichols. 1993. *Wiyot Handbook.* Memoir 10, Algonquian and Iroquoian Linguistics. Winnipeg: Department of Linguistics, University of Manitoba.

Teit, James A. 1910. Willapa word lists; and notes. Mss. 30(Na9.1-2), Library of the American Philosophical Society, Philadelphia. 13 pp. and 4 pp. (Published, with some omissions, in Boas and Goddard 1924.)

Ternaux-Compans, M. 1884. [French translation of Fages 1775.] *Nouvelles Annales des Voyages et des Sciences Géographiques* 101:145–182, 311–347.

Thomas, David Hurst, ed. 1989. *Columbian Consequences.* Vol. 1: *Archaeological and Historical Perspectives on the Spanish Borderlands West.* Washington, DC: Smithsonian Institution Press.

Thompson, Chad. 1990. The Diachrony of the Deictics in Athabaskan. Paper presented at the 1990 Athapaskan Conference, University of British Columbia.

Thompson, Sandra A., Joseph Sung-Yul Park, and Charles N. Li. 2006. *A Reference Grammar of Wappo.* UC-PL 138. (Online at repositories.cdlib.org/ucpress/ucpl.)

Thoresen, Timothy H. H. 1975. Paying the Piper and Calling the Tune: The Beginnings of Academic Anthropology in California. *Journal of the History of the Behavioral Sciences* 11:255–275.

———. 1976. Kroeber and the Yurok, 1900–1908. In *Yurok Myths,* by A. L. Kroeber, xix–xxix. Berkeley: University of California Press.

Thornes, Timothy J. 2003. *A Northern Paiute Grammar with Texts.* PhD dissertation, University of Oregon.

Tolmie, William Fraser. See Scouler 1841.

Tozzer, Alfred M. 1933. Zelia Nuttall. AA 35:75–82.

Troike, Rudolph C. 1976. The Linguistic Classification of Cochimí. In *Hokan Studies: Papers from the First Conference on Hokan Languages,* edited by Margaret Langdon and Shirley Silver, 159–164. The Hague: Mouton.

———. 1996. Sketch of Coahuilteco, a Language Isolate of Texas. In *Handbook of North American Indians.* Vol. 17: *Languages,* edited by Ives Goddard, 644–665. Washington, DC: Smithsonian Institution.

Turner, Katherine. 1980. The Reconstituted Phonemes of Salinan. JCGBA-PL 2:53–92.

———. 1983. Meeting on Central and Southern California Areal Linguistics and Prehistory. *1982 Hokan-Penutian Workshop.*

———. 1987. *Aspects of Salinan Grammar.* PhD disseration, University of California, Berkeley.

———. 1988a. Salinan Linguistic Materials. JCGBA 10:265–270.

———. 1988b. Salinan Numerals. In *In Honor of Mary Haas: From the Haas Festival Conference on Native American Linguistics,* edited by William F. Shipley, 805–818. Berlin: Mouton de Gruyter.

Turner, Katherine, and David L. Shaul. 1981. J. P. Harrington's Esselen Data and "The Excelen Language." JCGBA-PL 3:95–124.

Turner, Paul R. 1967. Seri and Chontal (Tequistlateco). IJAL 33:235–239.

———. 1976. Pluralization of Nouns in Seri and Chontal. In *Hokan Studies: Papers from the First Conference on Hokan Languages,* edited by Margaret Langdon and Shirley Silver, 297–304. The Hague: Mouton.

Turner, William W. See Whipple 1855.

Uldall, Hans Jørgen. 1931–1932. Linguistic notes on Yuki [slip files, manuscripts, including transcriptions of texts]. Harvey Pitkin Papers, Series II, Library of the American Philosophical Society, Philadelphia. (See Kroeber 1900–1958.)

———. 1932. Preliminary Report on Yuki Tones; Atlantic City, December 31, 1932. [With annotations by A. L. Kroeber]. Ms. 30(Yk.1), Library of the American Philosophical Society, Philadelphia. 19 pp.

———. 1933. A Sketch of Achumawi Phonetics. IJAL 8:73–77. (See de Angulo and Freeland 1931–1935.)

———. 1954. Maidu Phonetics. IJAL 20:8–16.

Uldall, Hans Jørgen, and William Shipley. 1966. *Nisenan Texts and Dictionary.* UC-PL 46.

Ultan, Donald. 1961–1962. Patwin field notes and recordings [computer printout, arranged by notebook number, 1–7]. Harvey Pitkin Papers, Series I-B, Library of the American Philosophical Society, Philadelphia.

———. n.d. Patwin-English vocabulary [computer printout]. Harvey Pitkin Papers, Series I-B, Library of the American Philosophical Society, Philadelphia. 6 folders.

Ultan, Russell. 1964. Proto-Maidun Phonology. IJAL 30:355–370.

———. 1967. *Konkow Grammar.* PhD dissertation, University of California, Berkeley.

———. 1973. A Case of Sound Symbolism in Konkow. In *Studies in American Indian Languages,* edited by Jesse O. Sawyer, 295–301. UC-PL 65.

Underriner, Janne L. 2002. *Intonation and Syntax in Klamath.* PhD dissertation, University of Oregon.

Vajda, Edward J. 2009. A Siberian Link to the Na-Dene Languages. *Anthropological Papers of the University of Alaska* 6.

Valory, Dale. 1971. *Guide to Ethnological Documents (1–203) of the Museum and Department of Anthropology, University of California, Berkeley, Now in the University Archives.* Archaeological Research Facility, Department of Anthropology, University of California, Berkeley. (Now incorporated into the online finding aid for the microfilm of this collection. See Bancroft Library 2007.)

Vihman, Eero. 1976. On Pitch Accent in Northern Pomo. In *Hokan Studies: Papers from the First Conference on Hokan Languages,* edited by Margaret Langdon and Shirley Silver, 77–83. The Hague: Mouton.

Voegelin, C. F. 1935a. *Tübatulabal Grammar.* UC-PAAE 34(2):55–190.

———. 1935b. *Tübatulabal Texts.* UC-PAAE 34(3):191–246.

———. 1946. Notes on Klamath-Modoc and Achumawi Dialects. IJAL 12:96–101.

———. 1958. Working Dictionary of Tübatulabal. IJAL 24:221–228.

Voegelin, C.F, F. M. Voegelin, and Noel W. Schutz, Jr. 1967. The Language Situation in Arizona as Part of the Southwest Culture Area. In *Studies in Southwestern Ethnolinguistics: Meaning and History in the Languages of the American Southwest* [Festschrift in honor of Harry Hoijer], edited by Dell H. Hymes and William E. Bittle, 403–451. Studies in General Anthropology 3. The Hague: Mouton.

Voegelin, Erminie Wheeler. 1938. *Tübatulabal Ethnography.* UC-AR 2(1):1–84.

———. 1942. *Culture Element Distributions: XX Northeast California.* UC-AR 7(2):47–251.

Vogt, Hans. 1963. *Dictionnaire de la langue Oubykh.* Instituttet for Sammenlignende kulturforskning [Oslo], Skrifter, Serie B, 52.

Wagner, Henry R. 1929. *Spanish Voyages to the Northwest Coast of America in the Sixteenth Century.* San Francisco: California Historical Society.

Wallace, William J. 1978. Hupa, Chilula and Whilkut. In *Handbook of North American Indians*. Vol. 8: *California*, edited by Robert F. Heizer, 164–179. Washington, DC: Smithsonian Institution.

Walsh, Jane MacLaren. 1976. *John Peabody Harrington: The Man and His California Indian Fieldnotes*. Ballena Press Anthropological Papers 6. Ramona, CA: Ballena Press.

Walters, Diane. 1977. Coyote and Moon Woman (Apwarukeyi text). In *Northern California Texts*, edited by Victor Golla and Shirley Silver, 147–157. IJAL Native American Text Series 2(2). Chicago: University of Chicago Press.

Warner, Natasha, Quirina Luna, and Lynnika Butler. 2007. Ethics and Revitalization of Dormant Languages: The Mutsun language. *Language Documentation and Conservation* 1(1):58–76. (Electronic journal published by the University of Hawaii Press. Accessible at hdl.handle.net/10125/1727.)

Warren, Claude N., and Robert H. Crabtree. 1986. Prehistory of the Southwestern Area. In *Handbook of North American Indians*. Vol. 11: *Great Basin,* edited by Warren L. d'Azevedo, 183–193. Washington, DC: Smithsonian Institution.

Wash, Suzanne. 1991. Patterns of the Generic and Particular in Wintu Narrative Texts. In *1990 Hokan-Penutian Workshop,* pp. 136–143.

———. 1995. *Productive Reduplication in Barbareño Chumash*. MA thesis, University of California, Santa Barbara.

———. 2001. *Adverbial Clauses in Barbareño Chumash Narrative Discourse*. PhD dissertation, University of California, Santa Barbara.

Watahomigie, Lucille J., Jorigine Bender, Philbert Watahomigie, Sr., and Akira Y. Yamamoto. 2001. *Hualapai Reference Grammar,* revised and expanded edition. Endangered Languages of the Pacific Rim (ELPR), Publication series A2-003. Osaka (Japan): Faculty of Informatics, Osaka Gakuin University.

Waterhouse, Viola G. 1976. Another Look at Chontal and Hokan. In *Hokan Studies: Papers from the First Conference on Hokan Languages*, edited by Margaret Langdon and Shirley Silver, 325–343. The Hague: Mouton.

Waterman, Thomas T. 1911. *The Phonetic Elements of the Northern Paiute Language*. UC-PAAE 10(2):13–44.

———. 1920. *Yurok Geography*. UC-PAAE 16(5):177–314.

———. 1923. *Yurok Affixes*. UC-PAAE 20(18):369–386.

———. 1925. Village Sites in Tolowa and Neighboring Areas of Northwestern California. AA 27:528–543.

———. n.d. Tubatulabal texts, vocabulary, and ethnographic notes. [Field notebooks. No date, but probably before 1913.] EDDMA, no. 34. 113 pp. 1 map.

Webb, Nancy M. 1971. *A Statement of Some Phonological Correspondences among the Pomo Languages*. IJAL Memoir 36.

———. 1980. Esselen-Hokan Relationships. *1979 Hokan-Penutian Workshop*.

Weigel, William F. 2006. *Yowlumne in the Twentieth Century*. PhD dissertation, University of California, Berkeley.

Whipple, Amiel W. 1850. Extract from a Journal of an Expedition from San Diego, California, to the Rio Colorado. [Vocabularies of Die{g}ueño and Quechan.] Report of the Secretary of War, pp. 2–28. Washington: Government Printing Office. (Reprinted in *Historical and Statistical Information Respecting the History, Condition and Prospects of the Indian Tribes of the United States*, edited by Henry R. Schoolcraft, vol. 2, pp. 103–104, 118–121. Philadelphia: Lippencott.)

———. 1855. Vocabularies of North American Languages collected by A. W. Whipple; classified, with accompanying remarks, by Wm. W. Turner. In *Report upon the Indian Tribes*, by Amiel W. Whipple, Thomas Ewbank, and William W. Turner, 54–103. U.S. Department of War, Reports of Explorations and Surveys (Pacific Railroad Reports), vol. 3, part 3, pp. 1–127. Washington, DC: Government Printing Office. (Vocabularies of Shoshone, Comanche, Chemehuevi, Cahuilla, Luiseño, Juaneño, Quechan ["Cuchan"], Mojave, Maricopa, and Diegueño.)

Whistler, Kenneth W. 1976. Nomlaki field notes. Material collected from Joe Freeman (Paskenta Hill Nomlaki) [photocopies of the originals]. Ms. Whistler.002, Survey of California and Other Indian Languages, Department of Linguistics, University of California, Berkeley.

———. 1977a. Wintun Prehistory: An Interpretation Based on Linguistic Reconstruction of Plant and Animal Nomenclature. *Proceedings of the* [3rd] *Annual Meeting of the Berkeley Linguistics Society*, pp. 157–174.

———. 1977b. Deer and Bear Children (Patwin Text). In *Northern California Texts*, edited by Victor Golla and Shirley Silver, 158–178. IJAL Native American Text Series 2(2). Chicago: University of Chicago Press.

———. 1978. Mink, Bullethawk and Coyote (Patwin Text). In *Coyote Stories*, edited by William Bright, 51–61. IJAL-NATS Monograph 1. Chicago: University of Chicago Press.

———. 1979a. Linguistic Prehistory of the Northwest California Coastal Area. In *A Study of Cultural Resources in Redwood National Park*, edited by Polly McW. Bickel, 11–26. Denver: Report to the National Park Service.

———. 1979b. Patwin Numerals: A Reconstruction and Its Cultural Implications. Paper delivered at UC Santa Barbara, March 29, 1979.

———. 1980a. *Proto-Wintun Kin Classification: A Case Study in Reconstruction of a Complex Semantic System*. PhD dissertation, University of California, Berkeley.

———. 1980b. An Interim Barbareño Chumash Dictionary. MS. 96 pp.

———. 1981a. Ablaut in Hill Patwin. In *Survey Reports 1981,* edited by Alice Schlichter, Wallace L. Chafe, and Leanne Hinton, 42–94. Survey of California and Other Indian Languages, Report 1. Department of Linguistics, University of California, Berkeley.

———. 1981b. Ventureño Dialects. Paper presented to the Group in American Indian Languages, University of California, Berkeley, October 30, 1981.

———. 1986. Evidentials in Patwin. In *Evidentiality: The Linguistic Coding of Epistemology*, edited by Wallace Chafe and Johanna Nichols, 60–74. Norwood, New Jersey: Ablex.

———. 1988. Pomo Prehistory: A Case for Archaeological Linguistics. *Journal of the Steward Anthropological Society* 15(1–2):64–98.

Whistler, Kenneth W., and Victor Golla. 1986. Proto-Yokuts Reconsidered. IJAL 52:317–358.

White, Raymond C. 1963. *Luiseño Social Organization*. UC-PAAE 48(2):91–194.

White, Robin B. 1973. *Klamath Phonology*. (Studies in Linguistics and Language Learning, 12.) Seattle: University of Washington.

Whitney, William Dwight. 1867. *Language and the Study of Language: Twelve Lectures on the Principles of Linguistic Science*. New York.

Whorf, Benjamin L. 1935. The Comparative Linguistics of Uto-Aztecan. AA 37:600–608.

Whorf, Benjamin L., and George L. Trager. 1937. The Relationship of Uto-Aztecan and Tanoan. AA 39:609–624.

Wichmann, Søren. 1999. On the Relationship between Uto-Aztecan and Mixe-Zoquean. *Kansas Working Papers in Linguistics* 24(2):101–113.

Wickersham, James. 1888. Athapascan language. Talked by a small band of Tinneh (Tena) at Boisfort, S.W. from Olympia, Wash. Terr'y [Lower Columbia Athabaskan]. MS. Alaska State Historical Library. 6 pp.

Willie, MaryAnn. 1991. *Pronouns and Obviation in Navajo.* PhD dissertation, Linguistics, University of Arizona, Tucson.

Willys, Rufus Kay. 1929. French Imperialists in California. *California Historical Society Quarterly* 8:116–129.

Winter, Werner. 1957. Yuman Languages I: First Impressions. IJAL 23:18–23.

———. 1967. The Identity of the Paipai (Akwa'ala). In *Studies in Southwestern Ethnolinguistics: Meaning and History in the Languages of the American Southwest* [Festschrift in honor of Harry Hoijer], edited by Dell H. Hymes and William E. Bittle, 372–378. Studies in General Anthropology 3. The Hague: Mouton.

———. 1998. ʔ in Yuman Nouns. In *Studies in American Indian Languages: Description and Theory,* edited by Leanne Hinton and Pamela Munro, 72–76. UC-PL 131.

Wood, Esther J. [Tess]. 2007. *The Semantic Typology of Pluractionality.* PhD dissertation, University of California, Berkeley. (Includes a case study of Yurok.)

Wood, Esther J. [Tess], and Leanne Hinton. 2002. A Report on George Grekoff's Collection of Chimariko (and Other) Materials. In *2000 Hokan-Penutian Workshop,* pp. 109–114.

Woodward, Mary. 1964. Hupa Phonemics. In *Studies in Californian Linguistics*, edited by William Bright, 199–216. UC-PL 34.

Wrangell, F. P. von, and Peter S. Kostromitinov. 1839. Statistische und ethnographische Nachrichten über die russischen Besitzungen an der Nordwestküste von Amerika. In *Beiträge zur Kenntniss des Russischen Reiches und der angränzenden Länder Asiens*, edited by Karl Ernst von Baer and Gregor von Helmersen, 80–96 [with accompanying Coast Miwok and Kashaya Pomo vocabularies pp. 234–235.] St. Petersburg: Kaiserliche Akademie der Wissenschaft. (Translated in Wrangell and Kostromitinov 1974, 1980. Vocabularies reprinted, with notes by F.L.O. Roehrig, in Powers 1877.)

———. 1974. Ethnographic Observations on the Coast Miwok and Pomo by Contre-Admiral F. P. von Wrangell and P. Kostromitinov of the Russian Colony Ross, 1839. Translated by Fred Stross; ethnographic notes by R. F. Heizer. Berkeley: Archaeological Research Facility, University of California. (English translation of two excerpts from Wrangell and Kostromitinov 1839.)

———. 1980. Russian America: Statistical and Ethnographical Information. With additional material by Karl Ernst von Baer. Edited by R. A. Pierce. Materials for the Study of Alaska History 15. Kingston (Ontario): Limestone Press. (Full English translation of Wrangell and Kostromitinov 1839.)

Yamane, Linda. 1995. *When the World Ended/How Hummingbird Got Fire/How People Were Made: Rumsien Ohlone Stories.* Berkeley, CA: Oyate.

———, ed. 2002. *A Gathering of Voices: The Native Peoples of the Central California Coast.* Santa Cruz County History Journal, Issue 5. Santa Cruz, CA: Museum of Art and History.

Youst, Lionel, and William R. Seaburg. 2002. *Coquelle Thompson, Athabaskan Witness: A Cultural Biography.* Norman: University of Oklahoma Press.

Yu, Alan C. L. 2005. Quantity, Stress, and Reduplication in Washo. *Phonology* 22:437–475.

Yu Qiuju. 2004. *A Comparative Study of Proto-Mongolian and Proto-Sahaptian.* MA thesis, University of Regina (Canada).

Zamponi, Raoul. 2004. Fragments of Waikuri (Baja California). AL 46:156–193.

Zigmond, Maurice L. 1981. *Kawaiisu Ethnobotany.* Salt Lake City: University of Utah Press.

———. 1986. Kawaiisu. In *Handbook of North American Indians.* Vol. 11: *Great Basin,* edited by Warren L. d'Azevedo, 398–411. Washington, DC: Smithsonian Institution.

Zigmond, Maurice L., Curtis G. Booth, and Pamela Munro. 1990. *Kawaiisu: A Grammar and Dictionary, with Texts.* Edited by Pamela Munro. UC-PL 119.

INDEX

Note: Page numbers in *italics* indicate illustrations. Page numbers in *italics* followed by *m* indicate maps; page numbers in *italics* followed by *t* indicate tables; page numbers in *italics* followed by *b* indicate boxes.

ablaut, 210

Achumawi, *96m*, 96–98, 305n. 40; dialects of, 97; documentation of, *30b*, 41, 44–45, *46b*, 97–98, 265, 277, 306n. 42; geography of, *96m*, 96–97, 305–306n. 41; linguistic structure of, 99, *99t*, 306n. 44; nomenclature for, 100; personal names in, 222; phonemes of, 99, *99t*, 306n. 43, 306n. 44

affricates, 205–206; laryngeal contrasts in, 204–205

Ahlers, Jocelyn: Kawaiisu Grammar Project, *55b*; on Hupa metaphors, 78; Southeastern Pomo documentation by, 107

Aiticha Kings River Yokuts, 151

Alaskan languages: borrowing from, 230, *233b*

Algic, *2m*, 8, *50b*, *55b*, 61–68, *62m*; prehistory of, 256–257, 319nn. 34–37. *See also* Wiyot; Yurok

Alsea, 130, 250, 318n. 25

Amamix, Agapito, 20–21

American Anthropologist, 40

American Phonemic orthography, 284, *284t–286t*

Anasazi, 255

Anderson, Sally, 81

Anderton, Alice, 54, 56

Andreas, Jim (Tubatulabal), 187

animals: names of, 227–228, 315–316nn. 37–41; represented speech of, 225, 315n. 33

Antoniano Salinan, 19, 114, *115m*, 267, 277

Apachean, 69, 303n. 8

apical affricates, 205

apical stops, 205

Applegate, Richard: Coast Miwok documentation by, 157, 309n. 90; on Inezeño (Samala), 196, 198

approximants, 207

Apwaruge (Dixie Valley) Atsugewi, *96m*, 98

Arapaho, 36

Army Specialized Training Program, 53–54

Arroyo de la Cuesta, Father Felipe, 19–20, 22; Chumash documentation by, 195, 196; Costanoan documentation by, 163, 164, 165, 297n. 16, 297n. 18; Esselen documentation

by, 113; Luiseño documentation by, 181; Miwok documentation by, 156, 159; Yokuts documentation by, 297n. 19

Aspasniahan Esselen triblet, 112, *113m*

aspiration, 204–205

Astariwawi (Hot Springs) Achumawi, *96m*, 97

Athabaskan (Na-Dene), *55b*, 68–82; California Athabaskan, *2m*, 8, *50b*, *76m*, 76–82, *77t*, *82t*, 257–258, 276; language family, *50b*, 68–69; Lower Columbia Athabaskan, *2m*, 69–70, 257–258; migration and, 5; numerals in, 287, 320n. 13; Oregon Athabaskan, *2m*, 8, *50b*, 70–75, *70t*, *71m*, *75t*, 257–258, 276; Pacific Coast Athabaskan, 68–75, *69m*, *70t*, *71m*, *75t*; prehistory of, 257–258, 319n. 38

Atondo, Isidro, 12

Atsnil Delta Yokuts, 153

Atsuge (Hat Creek) Atsugewi, *96m*, 98

Atsugewi, 98–100; attitudes toward, 305n. 40; documentation of, *37b*, 98–99, 265, 277, 306n. 42, 313n. 4; geography of, *96m*, 98; linguistic structure of, 99, *99t*, 217, 306n. 43; nomenclature for, 100

Atwamwi (Atwamsini) Achumawi, *96m*, 97

augmentative affix, 223

Awaswas Costanoan, *163m*, 165–166, 310n. 108, 310n. 109

Babel, Molly, *55b*

baby talk, 224–225

backed velar stops, 205–206

Baegert, Jacob, 13–14

Baja California: Jesuit missionaries in, 12–14, *14m*; languages of, *125m*, 125–127, 200–201, *201t*, 240

Bald Hill Wintu, *141m*, 142

Balokay Northern Pomo, 109

Bannock, 173

Barbareño Central Chumash, *16b*, *194m*, 196–197, *199t*, 276

Barbour, George W., 26

Barco, Miguel del, 14

Barker, M.A.R. (Philip R.), 133, 308n. 75, 308n. 77

Barrett, Samuel A., 41, 107, 108, 111, 154

Barrows, David Prescott, 182

Bartlett, John Russell, 26

Basehart, Harry, *52*

Basque, 69

Bauman, James, 98

Bay Miwok, 159, *159m*, 229

Bean, Lowell John: on triblet model, 3–4

Bear Creek valley: as dual-language area, 7

Bear River Athabaskan. *See* Mattole–Bear River

Beeler, Madison, 54, 114, 163–164, 197, 220

Belisano, Pacifico (Esselen), 113

Bendixen, Brigitte, 56

Bennyhoff, James A., 222

Bensell, Ida (Euchre Creek), 73, 303n. 12

Benson, William Ralganal (Eastern Pomo), 107, 109

Berman, Howard: on Chimariko, 89; on Hokan relationships, 242, 244; on Miwok, 159–160; on Palewyami Yokuts, 149; on Penutian relationships, 128; on Ritwan, 61; on Yurok, 58, 66–67

Bibliothèque de Linguistique et d'Ethnographie Américaines, 299n. 37

bilabial fricative, 206

bilingualism, 4; Eastern Pomo–Northern Pomo, 81; Kammatwa-Watiru, 92, 305n. 35; Kato–Northern Pomo, 81. *See also* multilingualism

bipartite verb stems, 216–217, 245, 313nn. 4–6

bird names, 228

Blevins, Juliette: on Mission-era documents 154, 165; on numerals, 220, 229; on Yokuts, 154; Yurok documentation by, 67–68

Bloomfield, Leonard, 49

bluejay names, 228

Boas, Franz, 36, 39, 40, 45, 49, 302n. 83

Bokeya Central Pomo, 109

Bommelyn, Loren, 57, 74

Borjeño (Borjino) Cochimí, 125

borrowing, 204; from California Indian languages, 230, 233, *234b–237b*; from English, 230, *232b*; from Eskimo, 230, *232b*; infrequency of, 5; postcontact, 230–237; precontact, 227–229; from Russian, 230,

decimal numeral system, 218–219, 313n. 8
DeLancey, Scott, 57, 128, 130, 216–217
Delta-California Yuman, *118t*, *119m*, 120–121
Delta (Far Northern Valley) Yokuts, 31, 149, *149m*, *150t*, 153–154, 309nn. 84–86, 321n. 41
Demetracopoulou (Lee), Dorothy, 42, 142, 227
dependent-marking languages, 203, 210–211, 212, 313n. 3
Desert Cahuilla, *178m*, 182
Desert Serrano (Vanyume), *178m*, *179t*, 183, 312n. 130
Devereux, George, 122
Didiu Cochimí, 125
Diegueño (Kumeyaay), 3, *37b*, *118t*, *119m*, 120–121, 267, 280, 307n. 57, 307n. 58
diminutives, 222, 223–225, *224b*, 315n. 30, 315n. 31
Dixon, Carrie B. (Wintu), *143*
Dixon, Roland B., 38–39, *39*, 92, 94, 101, 138; Chimariko documentation by, 89, 300n. 55, 300n. 56
doctrinas, 18–19, 20, 22
dog terms, 227–228
dolichocephaly, 240, 316–317n. 1
Dominicans, 13, 14
Dorsey, Rev. James Owen, 34–35, *35*, 72, 73, 131
Dos Pueblos Central Chumash, 196
double-marking languages, 210
Drake, Francis, 12, *13*
Du Bois, Cora, 42, 94–95, 141–142
dual-language areas, 7–8
dubitative marker, 218
Ducrue, Benno, 14
Duflot de Mofras, Count Eugène, 25
Dumna Northern Hill Yokuts, 153
Duncan, Ike (Mattole–Bear River), *79*

Eastern Miwok, 158–160, *159m*, 309–310n. 93; moiety organization of, 222; numerals in, 321n. 54, 321n. 55
Eastern Mono, 171, *171m*, *172m*, 311n. 116
Eastern Panamint, 174
Eastern Pomo, *105m*, *106m*, *106t*, 107–108, *112t*, 216–217, 266
Eastern Shoshoni, 175
Eel River Athabaskan, *76m*, 76, *77t*, 79–81, 303–304nn. 16; documentation of, 3, 80–81, 264, 304n. 17; Mattole–Bear River contact with, 78–79; Wiyot contact with, 62
Eel River Wailaki, 80
Ekheahan Esselen tribelet, 112, *113m*
El Conejo Central Chumash, 197
El Oro Molido (Arroyo), 20
Elem Southeastern Pomo, *106m*, 107
Elliott, Eric, 57, 181–183
Elmendorf, William W.: on early borrowing involving Yukian, 241, 247; on the Yuki-Wappo relationship, 192–193, *193t*; on a Yukian-Siouan relationship, 188
Elzinga, Dirk, 176
Emeneau, Murray B., 53
Emigdiano Central Chumash, 267
Encinales, Pedro (Salinan), *116*
English: borrowing from, 230, *232b*; Karuk borrowing in, 233
Entimbich Kings River Yokuts, 151, 171, 311n. 115
Erikson, Erik H., *67*
Escamilla, Ramon, *55b*
Eskimo: borrowing from, 230, *233b*
Eslenahan Esselen tribelet, 112, *113m*
Esmerileua region, *115m*, 116

Esselen, *2m*, 112–114; documentation of, 18–19, 23, 34, *37b*, 112–114, 267, 277, 306–307nn. 50–52; geography of, 112, *113m*; linguistic structrure of, 114, *114t*; nomenclature for, 114; numerals in, 289; phonemes of, 114, *114t*; prehistory of, 247–248, 318n. 19, 318n. 20
Esselen Tribe of Monterey County, 307n. 53
Essene, Frank, 302n. 89
ethnonyms, 213, 220–221
Euchre Creek Oregon Athabaskan, 73
Excelen Esselen tribelet, 112, *113m*
exponence, 211
expressive symbolism, 223–226
Eyak, 68–69

Fages, Pedro, 16, *17b*, 195, 297n. 11
Fall River Achumawi, *96m*, 97
farming terms, 248, 254
Faye, Paul Louis, 182
Fernandeño. *See* Gabrielino-Fernandeño (Tongva)
finger counting, 229, 316n. 45
flaps, 207
Fletcher, Francis, 12
Fletcher, Stuart, *55b*
Folsom, Jack (Achumawi), *45*
Fort Ross, 23, 230
Foster, George, 226
Fowler, Catherine, 57, 254, 256, 311n. 118
Frachtenberg, Leo J., *41*
Franciscans, 14–22; missions of, 14–16, *18m*; questionnaire of 1812 of, 21–22
Freeland, Lucy S. (Nancy), 45, 86, 107, 158, 160, 173, 301n. 71
French Gulch Wintu, 141, *141m*
fusion, 211

Gabrielino-Fernandeño (Tongva), *37b*, *178m*, 179–180, 209, 223, 226, 271, 279, 293, 312n. 127
Galiano, Dionisio Alcalá, 23
Galice-Applegate Oregon Athabaskan, *71m*, 72–73, 276
Gálvez, José de, 15
Gamble, Geoffrey, 130, 151, 154–155, 220, 227
Garrett, Andrew: Yurok documentation by, 67–68; 300n. 50
Gashowu Yokuts, 149, *149m*, 152
Gatschet, Albert Samuel, 33, *135*, 299n. 42; Klamath-Modoc documentation by, 33, 133–134, 225, 308n. 69, 315n. 35
Gayton, Anna, 171, 311n. 115
gemination, 207
gender-linked registers, 102, 227
Gerolt, Karl von, 20, 297–298n. 21
Giamina (Omomil), 187–188, 254
Gibbs, George, 26–27, *27*, 97, 298–299nn. 31–33; Hupa-Chilula documentation by, 77–78; Karuk documentation by, 85; Kashaya documentation by, 110; Nabiltse documentation by, 72; Patwin documentation by, 144; Pomo documentation by, 107, 109; at Smithsonian Institution, 27; Wiyot documentation by, 62–63, 65; Yurok documentation by, 65, 68
Gifford, Edward W., 41–42, 86
Givón, Tom, 57, 311n. 125
glottal fricative *(h)*, 207
glottal stop, 207
glottalization, 204–205; approximant, 207; nasal, 207
Goddard, Pliny Earle, 3, *39*, 39–40, 300nn. 58–60; Hupa-Chilula documentation by, 40, 78

Golla, Victor, 302n. 93; on Athabaskan diversity, 5; Hupa-Chilula documentation by, 78, 302n. 93; Lower Rogue River Athabaskan documentation by, 73; on Penutian relationships, 128; Yokuts classification of, 148–149, *150t*
Good, Dwight A., *55b*
Gorbet, Larry, 56
Gordon, Lynn, 56
Gordon, Matthew, 78
Gosiute Shoshoni, 175
Goss, James, 176
grammar, 203–204, 209–218; ablaut in, 210; adverbial derivation in, 215–216; bipartite stems in, 216–217, 313nn. 4–6; case marking in, 211–212; exponence in, 211; fusion in, 211; instrumental affixes in, 216; morphological complexity in, 211; morphological processes in, 209–210; morphological subject/object marking in, 210–211, 313n. 3; plurality marking in, 213–215; reduplication in, 209–210; stem compounding in, 216–218; stem derivation in, 215–218; structural patterns in, 210–211, 313n. 3; suppletion in, 210; switch reference in, 218, 313n. 7; synthesis in, 211
grammatical markers, 211
Grekoff, George, 89, 305n. 31
Guilicos (Guilucos) Wappo, 191
Gursky, Karl-Heinz: on Hokan classification, 83–84

Haas, Mary R., 53–54, *54*, 302nn. 90–92
Habenapo Eastern Pomo tribelet, *106m*, 107
Haida, 69, 303n. 6
Halchidhoma, 122
Hale, Horatio, 24–25, *25*, 97, 116, 134, 173, 298n. 28, 298n. 29; Lower Columbia Athabaskan documentation by, 69, 70; Upper Umpqua Athabaskan documentation by, 71
Hale, Kenneth, 52
Halpern, Abraham M., 53, *53*, 302n. 89, 303n. 94; Achumawi documentation by, 98; Pomo classification of, 106–107, 246; Pomo documentation by, 107, 108, 109, 110, 306n. 49
Halyikwamai Cocopa, 120
Hammawi (Likely) Achumawi, *96m*, 97
Hamp, Eric P., 54
Handbook of the Indians of California (Kroeber), 3, 38
Hanesakh Takelma, 131
Hardy, Heather, 56
Harriman Alaska Expedition, 43
Harrington, Carobeth Tucker, 46–47, 176
Harrington, John Peabody, *41*, 46–47, *47*, *195*, 273–281, 301n. 74; Central Chumash documentation by, 195, 196–197, 276–277; Chemehuevi documentation by, 176, 278–279; Chimariko documentation by, 89, 276; Cochimí documentation by, 126, 280; Costanoan documentation by, 19–20, 164, 165, 166, 278; Esselen documentation by, 113, 277; Giamina documentation by, 188; Island Chumash documentation by, 198, 277; Karuk documentation by, 85–86, 277; manuscripts of, 273–281, *274b*, 301n. 76, 301n. 77; microfilmed manuscripts of, 274–281, 319n. 4; place-name documentation by, 221; publications of, 301n. 75; Salinan documentation by, 116, 277; Shastan documentation by, 93, 278; sound recording collection of, 275, 319–320n. 5; Takic documentation by, 180, 181, 182, 183, 279; transcription system of,

284, *284t–286t*; Tubatulabal documentation by, 186, 279; Yana documentation by, 101; Yokuts documentation by, 149, 150, 151, 152, 280; Yuki documentation by, 190, 280; Yuman documentation by, 118, 119, 121, 122, 280–281

Havasupai, *119m*, 122–123, 226, 248

Hayes, Alfred, *56b*

Hayfork Wintu, *141m*, 142, 268, 276, 279

head-marking languages, 203, 210–211, 313n. 3

Hearst, Phoebe Apperson, 36, 40

Heizer, Robert, x, 12, 28, 31, 44, 91, 240, 259, 318n. 32

Henshaw, Henry Wetherbee, 33, 34, *35*, 104, 113, 195, 197, 299n. 46, 299n. 47

Hewett, Edgar Lee, 46

Hewisedawi (Goose Lake) Achumawi, *96m*, 97

"high" languages, 226–227

Hill, Jane H., 54; Cupeño documentation by, 182; on Numic, 256; on Uto-Aztecan, 5, 169–170, 254, 255, 318n. 28

Hill, Kenneth, 54, 183

Hill Konkow, 137, *137m*, 268

Hill Patwin, 143–145, *144m*, *147t*, 268

Hinton, Leanne, 56, 59, 102, 107, 121, 255

Hockett, Charles F.: on Yokuts, 154

Hoffman, Meredith, *55b*

Hoijer, Harry, 54, *56*, 302n. 93, 303n. 94

Hokan, *2m*, 8–9, 82–127, 304n. 19, 304n. 20; Central California Coast diffusion area of, 242–243, 317n. 8; Chimariko, *2m*, 87–90, *88m*, 89, *89t*, *90t*; Cochimí, *2m*, *125m*, 125–127; Esselen, *2m*, 23, 112–114, *113m*, *114t*; Karuk, *2m*, *29b*, *37b*, *46b*, *55b*, 84–87, *85m*, 86, *86t*; Kaufman's classification of, 84, *84t*, 242, 305n. 26; Northern California diffusion area of, 242, 317n. 6; numerals in, 288–289; Palaihnihan, *2m*, *46b*, *55b*, 95–100, *96m*, *99t*; phylum, 82–84; plural stems in, 214–215; Pomo, *2m*, *29b*, *37b*, *55b*, *105m*, 105–111, *106m*, *106t*, *112t*; prehistory of, 242–248, 315nn. 9–11, 317n. 17; Salinan, *2m*, 19, *30b*, *37b*, 42, *55b*, 114–117, *115m*, *117t*; Sapir's classification of, *50b*, 82–83, *83t*, 304nn. 21–24; Seri, *2m*, *125m*, 126, 127, *127t*, 289, 307n. 65, 307n. 66, 320. 24; Shastan, *2m*, 90–95, *91m*, *95t*; switch reference in, 218; Washo, *2m*, *37b*, *55b*, 102–105, *103m*, *104t*; Yana, *2m*, *100m*, 100–102, *102t*; Yuman, *2m*, *37b*, *56b*, 117–125, *118t*, *119m*, *123t*, 307n. 62

Hokan Conference, 83, 304–305n. 25

Hokan-Siouan, 82–83

Holder, Ralph (Eastern Pomo), *108*

Hometwoli, 150

Hopi, 254, 255, 318n. 30

Houser, Michael J., *55b*

Howalek Eastern Pomo tribelet, 107

Hualapai, *119m*, 122–123, 225, 248, 289

Huave, 249

Huchnom Yukian, *189m*, 190

Hughes, Richard E., 239

Hulse, Frederick, 302n. 89

Huocon (Coconoon) Delta River Yokuts, 153

Hupa-Chilula, 76–78, *76m*, *77t*; animal talk in, 225; diminutives in, 223, *224b*, 315n. 26; documentation of, *37b*, 40, *50b*, *55b*, 76–78, 264, 276, 303n. 13; Hupa names for, 4; New River Hupa/Chimariko shift to, 87; non-Hupa varieties of, 77; numerals in, 287; personal names in, 222, 315n. 25; phonemes of, 81–82, *82t*, 208; pronominal categories of, 304n. 18; second-language education in, 78; Wiyot contact with, 62

Hupa Documentation Project (UC Berkeley), *55b*

"Hupa": origin of name, 244

Hymes, Dell H., 52, 57, 223

Hymes, Virginia, 220

Illinois River Valley: as dual-language area, 7

Ilmawi (Cayton Valley) Achumawi, *96m*, 97

Imperial Valley Kamia, 120, 307n. 57

Imunahan Esselen tribelet, 112, *113m*

Indiana University, 57

Indo-European, 317n. 5

Inezeño Central Chumash, *194m*, 196, 266, 276, 312n. 141

instrumental affixes, 216

intergroup conflict: language boundaries and, 5

Interior Chumash, *194m*, 198

Interior Ventureño, 197

International Journal of American Linguistics, 40, 52

International Phonetic Alphabet, 283, *284t–286t*

interpreters, 6–7

Introduction to the Study of Indian Languages (Powell), 299n. 41

Ipai Diegueño, *119m*, 120–121, *224b*, 267

Ishi, 40, *40*, *101*, 225, 230, 306n. 46, 316n. 49, 316n. 50

Island Chumash, 12, *30b*, 194, *194m*, 198, 240–241, 277, 313n. 147, 313n. 148, 317n. 2, 317n. 3

Island Takic, *178m*, 184

isolating marker, 211

Itsatawi (Goose Valley) Achumawi, *96m*, 97

Ives, Lieutenant Joseph C., 26

Jacobs, Elizabeth (Bess), 57, 73, *73*

Jacobs, Melville, 57, *73*, 128

Jacobs, Roderick, 57

Jacobsen, William H., Jr., 57; on grammatical typology, 216–218; Salinan documentation by, 116; Washo documentation by, 103–105; on Washo prehistory, 246

James, Jerry (Wiyot), 63, *64*

Jamul Diegueño, 121, 214, 218

jargons: shamanistic jargon, 7, 229; trade jargon, 230

Jenny Creek Shasta, 92

Jesuits, 12–14, *14m*

Jicaque (Tol), 83

Joël, Judith, 54, 119, 248

Johnson, Frances (Takelma), 131, *132*

Johnson, John, 221–222

Joshua Oregon Athabaskan, 73

Juaneño, *15b*, 19, *178m*, 180–181, 226, 255

Kacha Northern Pomo, 109

Kahwan Cocopa, 120

Kai Pomo (Shelter Cove Sinkyone), 7–8

Kalapuyan: Takelma relationship to, 129

Kale Southern Pomo, 110

Kalisamne, 153

Kamdot Southeastern Pomo, *106m*, 107

Kamia, *119m*, 120, 307n. 57

Kammatwa, 92, 305n. 35

Karkin Costanoan, 6, *163m*, 163–164, 295n. 8, 310n. 97; Esselen relationship to, 247; numerals in, 291

Karuk, *2m*, 84–87; diminutives in, 223, *224b*; discourse markers in, 313n. 7; documentation of, *29b*, *37b*, *46b*, *55b*, 85–86, 265, 277, 305n. 27; English loanwords in, *232b*; geography of, 84–85, *85m*; Hupa-Chilula contact with, 77; linguistic structure of, 86–87, *86t*, 217; nomenclature for, 87;

numerals in, 288; phonemes of, 86–87, *86t*, 243; prehistory of, 243; second-language education in, 86; Tolowa contact with, 74

"Kashaya": for Pomo, 4

Kashaya (Southwestern Pomo), 23, *105m*, 110–111, 266; loanwords in, 230, *233b*; second-language education in, 111

Katimin, 277

Kato, 6, 7–8, 76, *76m*, *77t*, 81; documentation of, *37b*, 81, 264, 276; pronominal categories of, 304n. 18

Kaufman, Terrence: on Hokan classification, 84, *84t*, 242, 305n. 26

Kaveltcadom, 122

Kawaiisu Grammar Project (UC Berkeley), *55b*

Kawaiisu Southern Numic, *171m*, 175–176

Kayaw Eastern Pomo tribelet, 107

Kechayi Northern Hill Yokuts, 153

Kelly, Isabel, 156–157

Kendall, Martha B. (Bonnie), 52, 57

Kern Valley Indian Council, 187

Keswick Wintu, 141, *141m*

Keweevkapaya Yavapai, 123

Kidd, Malinda (New River Shasta), 94, 305n. 38

Kidd, Saxy (New River·Hupa), 78

Kigil (Quiguil) Salinan district, 115, *115m*

Kiliwa, 118, *118t*, *119m*, 126, 280

Kings River Yokuts, 149, *149m*, 151

Kino, Father Eusebio, 13

Kitanemuk, *178m*, 183, 255, 279

Klamath-Modoc, *2m*, 133–136; documentation of, 33, *46b*, *55b*, 133–134, 265, 277, 308n. 69, 308n. 76, 308n. 77, 315n. 35; geography of, 133, *134m*; linguistic structure of, 134–135, *135t*, 136t, *210*, *213t*, 217, 251, 308n. 77, 318n. 24; nicknames in, 223; nomenclature for, 135–136; numerals in, 290; phonemes of, 135, *135t*, 308n. 77; prehistory of, 251, 318n. 24; second-language education in, 135

Klamath River: as dual-language area, 7

Klamath River Shasta, 91, *91m*

Klar, Kathryn, 183–184, 195, 198–199, 240

Klein, Sheldon, 175–176

knife: terms for, 316n. 44

Koi Southeastern Pomo, *106m*, 107

Komli Northern Pomo, 109

Konkow, 136–138, *137m*, 268; diminutives in, *224b*; numerals in, 290, 321n. 33; personal names in, 222

Konomihu, 6, 90, *91m*, 92–93, 244, 278

Kosalektawi (Alturas) Achumawi, *96m*, 97

Kostromitinov, Peter S., 23, 110, 157

Koyeti Southern Valley Yokuts, 152

Kozlowski, Edwin, 57

Kroeber, A. L. (Alfred L.), 35–38, *36*, *41*, 299–300n. 49, 299n. 48; Chumash documentation by, 196; Costanoan documentation by, 164; Esselen documentation by, 113, 306–307n. 52; field notes of, *37b*; Giamina documentation by, 187–188; Inezeño documentation by, 196; Karuk documentation by, 85; Kitanemuk documentation by, 183; Luiseño documentation by, 181; Miwok documentation by, 159, 160; Mojave documentation by, 122; Nisenan documentation by, 139; Northeastern Pomo documentation by, 108; Northern Wintuan documentation by, 143; on Northern Yukian and Athabaskan, 188; on Numic prehistory, 255; psychoanalytic practice of, 300n. 51; Salinan documentation by, 116; Sapir's relationship with, 49–50, 302n. 82; Seri classification

Mono Language Program (UCLA), 172
monoexponential markers, 211
Monqui, 14, *125m*, 200
Moore, Ralph (Yuki), *190*
Moore, Robert E., 57, 301n. 77
Moquelumnan (Miwok), 35, *36t*, 162
Moratto, Michael J., 239, 253, 257
morphology, 209–218; California Athabaskan,
82, 304n. 18; Chimariko, 89–90, *90t*, 212,
305n. 34; Chumash, 199, *199t*; complexity
of, 211; Costanoan, 167, 210, 310–311n.
110; Esselen, 114; Karuk, 87, 217; Klamath-
Modoc, 135, *136t*; Numic, 177–178; Oregon
Athabaskan, 75; Palaihnihan, 99, 217; Pomo,
111, *112t*, 212, 216–217, 218; Shastan, 95;
Takelma, 132–133, *133t*, 210; Takic, 184,
215–216; Tubatulabal, 187, *187t*; Washo,
104–105, 217; Wintuan, 146–147, *147t*,
148t, *213t*, 250, 318n. 24; Wiyot, 64–65;
Yokuts, 155–156, 210, *213t*; Yukian, 192,
193t, 312n. 134; Yuman, 124, 217; Yurok,
67–68, 217–218
Moser, Edward, 127, *127*
Moser, Mary Becker, 127
Moshinsky, Julius, 107
Mountain Cahuilla, *178m*, 182
Mountain (Northeastern) Maidu, *137m*, 138,
139, *139t*, *140t*, 268, 320n. 31, 321n. 32
mountain quail names, 228
Mugu Central Chumash, 197
multilingualism, 4, 6–8, 296n. 9; among
Yuroks, 65; areal, 7–8; at Carquinez Strait, 8;
at Eastern Clear Lake, 8; personal, 6–7; social
function of, 6–7; at South Fork of Eel River,
7–8; at Stonyford, 8
Munro, Pamela, 56, 122, 180, 182
Museum of Anthropology (University of
California), 36, 38
Mutsun, 19–20, *30b*, 162, *163m*, 165–166,
168t, 267, 278, 291, 310–311n. 110, 310nn.
104–107
Mutsun Language Foundation, 167
Myers, William E., 47–49, *48*, 301–302n. 78
mythic animals, 225, 315n. 33

Na-Dene. *See* Athabaskan (Na-Dene)
Nabiltse, *71m*, 72–73
names: animal, 227–228, 315–316nn. 37–41;
ceremonial, 228, 316n. 42; ethnonymic, 213,
220–221; language, 4 (*See also at specific
languages*); personal, 204, 222–223, 315nn.
23–29; Seri, 314–315nn. 21; toponymic, 12,
204, 220–221, *234b*–*237b*, 296n. 2; triblet,
221
nasals, 207
Natches, Gilbert (Northern Paiute), 173
Navajo, 304n. 18
neutral territory, 6, 7–8
Nevada Northern Paiute, 173
Nevin, Bruce, 98
New River Hupa/Chimariko, 87, *88m*
New River Shasta, *37b*, 90, *91m*, 93–94, 265,
305n. 37
New River valley: as dual-language area, 7
Newbold, Lindsey, *55b*
Newman, Stanley S., *52*, 52–53; Yokuts
documentation by, 52–53, 152, 153, 154
Nichols, J. P. Michael, 174, 254
Nichols, Johanna, 313n. 3, 315n. 31, 317n. 5
Nim-Yokuts, 148–149, *150t*, 309n. 82
Nisenan, *37b*, 42, *137m*, 138–139, 252, 268,
277, 308n. 78, 308n. 79; numerals in, 290;
personal names in, 315n. 24, 315n. 27;
regional dialects of, 4, 295n. 5

Noble, Sally (Chimariko), *89*
Nomlaki (Wintun), *141m*, 143, 268, 290
Nongatl Eel River Athabaskan, *76m*, 80, 264,
303–304n. 16, 304n. 17; Mattole–Bear River
contact with, 78–79; Wiyot contact with,
62
nonlinear marker, 211
Noptinte (Nopthrinthre) Northern Valley
Yokuts, 153
Norris, Evan, 172
North American Indian, The (Curtis), 47–49
North Fork Wailaki, 80
Northeastern ("Mountain") Maidu, *137m*, 138,
139, *139t*, *140t*, 268, 320n. 31, 321n. 32
Northeastern Mono, 171
Northeastern Pomo, 6, *105m*, 108, 295–296n. 8
Northern Hill Nisenan, *137m*, 139
Northern Hill Yokuts, *149m*, 153
Northern Paiute, *171m*, 173–174, 292
Northern Paiute Language Project (UC
Berkeley), *55b*
Northern Pomo, 81, *105m*, *106m*, *106t*, 108–
109, 266, 277, 315n. 22
Northern Shoshoni, 175
Northern Sierra Miwok, *159m*, 160
Northern Sinkyone, 79
Northern Takelma, 131
Northern Ute, 176
Northern Valley Yokuts, 20, 149, *149m*, 152–
153, 309n. 83
Northern Wintuan, 140–143, *141m*, 229
Northern Yana, *100m*, 100–101
Northern Yukian, 188–191, *189m*, 209; vs.
Wappo, 192–193
Norwood, Susan, 56
noun: Central Chumash, 199, *199t*; Chimariko,
89; Costanoan, 167, *168t*; Esselen, 114;
Karuk, 87; Klamath-Modoc, 135; Maiduan,
139, *140t*; Miwok, 161, *162t*; Numic, 177;
Oregon Athabaskan, 75; Palaihnihan,
99; Salinan, 117; Seri, 127; Shastan, 95;
Takelma, 132; Takic, 184; Tubatulabal, 187;
Washo, 104; Wintuan, 146, *147t*; Wiyot, 64,
303n. 3; Yana, 102; Yokuts, 155; Yukian,
192; Yuman, 124; Yurok, 67–68
numeral system, 204, 218–220; Algic, 287;
Athabaskan, 287, 320n. 13; borrowed, 229;
Cahuilla, 293; Chalon, 291; Chemehuevi,
292; Chimariko, 288; Chocheño, 291;
Chumash, 294; Cocopa, 289; Costanoan,
229, 291, 321n. 40; decimal, 218–219, 313n.
8; Esselen, 289; Gabrielino, 293; Hokan,
288–289; Hualapai, 289; Hupa-Chilula, 287;
Karkin, 291; Karuk, 288; Klamath-Modoc,
290; Konkow, 290, 321n. 33; Lower Rogue
River, 287; Maiduan, 290, 320–321nn.
31–33; Miwok, 220, 229, 292, 314n. 19,
321nn. 53–55; Mohave, 289; Mutsun, 291;
Nisenan, 290; Nomlaki, 290; Northern
Paiute, 292; Numic, 292; octonary, 220,
314n. 17; Palaihnihan, 288; Panamint, 292;
Patwin, 291, 321n. 37; Penutian, 290–292;
Pomo, 289; Proto-Athabaskan, 320n. 13;
quaternary, 220; quinary, 218–219, *219b*,
313–314n. 11, 314n. 12; Rumsen, 291;
Salinan, 289; senary, 220; Seri, 289, 320n.
24; Shastan, 288; Takelma, 290, 320nn.
27–30; Takic, 293; Toltichi, 220, 314n. 20;
Tubatulabal, 293; Uto-Aztecan, 292–293;
vigesimal, 219–220, 314nn. 13–16; Washo,
288; Wintuan, 229, 290, 291, 321n. 35,
321n. 37; Wiyot, 287, 320n. 9; Yana, 288,
317n. 15; Yokuts, 291, 321nn. 41–52;
Yukian, 220, 293, 314n. 17, 314n. 18, 317n.

15, 321n. 57; Yuman, 289; Yurok, 287,
320n. 9, 320n. 10
Numic, *2m*, 33, *37b*, *46b*, *55b*, 170–178, 278–
279; Central, 170, *170t*; classification of,
170t, 311n. 113; documentation of, 172–176,
270; internal diversity of, 5; Kawaiisu, *171m*,
175–176; linguistic structure of, 177–178,
178t; Mono, *37b*, *171m*, 171–173, *172m*,
311n. 116; nomenclature for, 178; Northern
Paiute, *171m*, 173–174, 292; numerals in,
292; Panamint, *171m*, 174–175, 292, 311n.
119; phonemes of, 177, *177t*; prehistory
of, 255–256, 318–319nn. 30–33; Shoshoni,
171m, 175, 311n. 121; Southern, *50b*, 170–
171, *170t*, *171m*, 175–177; Western, 170,
170t, *171m*, 171–174; Yok-Utian contact
with, 130
Nutunutu Southern Valley Yokuts, 152

Obispeño (Northern Chumash), 16, *17b*, 194,
194m, 195, 276, 294, 297n. 11, 312n. 139
object marking, 210–211
O'Connor, M. Catherine, 109
octonary numeral system, 220, 314n. 17
Ohlone, 168, 311n. 112
Okrand, Marc, 165–168
Okwanuchu, 94–95, 305n. 38
Oleyomi Lake Miwok tribelet, 157
olivella shells, 219, 313n. 9
Olmsted, David, 52, 98, 306n. 42
Omomil (Giamina), 187–188, 254
O'Neal, Lottie (Okwanuchu), *94*
O'Neill, Sean, 78
Oregon Athabaskan, *2m*, 8, *50b*, 69, 70–75, *70t*,
71m, 257–258, 276; linguistic structure of,
74–75, *75t*; second-language education in,
74; survival of, 74
Oregon Northern Paiute, 173
Oregon Shasta, 91, *91m*
orthography, xiii–xiv, 283–284, *284t*–*286t*,
299n. 36, 303n. 2
Osborn, Blind Sam (Mono), *172*
Oswalt, Robert L., *110*; on Pomo, 106, *106t*,
109, 110, 246; on Russian loanwords, 230,
233b
Otomanguean, 84
Owens Valley Paiute (Eastern Mono), 171,
171m, *172m*

Pacific Coast Athabaskan, 68–75, *69m*, *70t*,
71m, *75t*
Pahkanapil Tubatulabal district, *185m*, 185–
186, 279
Pai languages (Upland Yuman), *118t*, *119m*,
122–123
Paipai (Akwa'ala), 117, 118–120, *118t*, *119m*,
281
Paiute Tribe of Utah, 177
Palagewan Tubatulabal district, 185, *185m*
Palaihnihan, *2m*, *46b*, *55b*, 95–100, *96m*, *99t*,
308n. 74; documentation of, 97–99, 265,
277; linguistic structure of, 99, *99t*, 217;
nomenclature for, 99–100; numerals in, 288;
prehistory of, 96, 244–245, 317n. 14
palatal affricates, 205
palatal nasal, 207
Palewyami, 149
Panamint, *171m*, 174–175, 292, 311n. 119
Parrish, Essie (Kashaya Pomo), *110*
Pasasamne Delta Yokuts, 153, 154
Pass (Wanikik) Cahuilla, *178m*, 182
Paster, Mary, *55b*
Patwin, *37b*, 140–141, 143–145, *144m*,
147t, 268, 291; Miwok contact with, 253;

classification, *50b*, 82–83, *83t*, 304nn.
21–24; Hupa-Chilula documentation by, *50b*,
78; Kroeber's relationship with, 49–50, 302n.
82; Penutian classification of, *50b*, 128;
Seri classification of, 126, 248; Southern
Numic documentation by, *50b*, 176; Takelma
documentation by, 49, *50b*, 131, 302n. 80,
308n. 72; Uto-Aztecan classification of, *50b*,
169; Yana documentation by, *50b*, 101,
306n. 47; Yurok documentation by, *50b*, 66
Sarhentaruc Esselen tribelet, 112, *113m*
Sastean (Shastan), 35, *36t*, 95
Saubel, Katherine Siva, 182
Sawyer, Jesse O., 190–191
Schlichter, Alice. *See* Shepherd, Alice
schwa, 209
scientific expeditions, 22–23, 24–25
Scott Valley Shasta, 91, *91m*, 278, 305n. 37
Scouler, John, 24
Seaburg, William, 57
Seiden, William, 57
Seiler, Hansjakob, 58, 182
semantic couplets, 226, 315n. 36
Señán, Fray José, 21, 22
senary numeral system, 220
Seri, *2m*, *125m*, 307n. 65; documentation of,
127, 307n. 66; geography of, 126; linguistic
structure of, 127, *127t*; names in, 314n. 21;
nomenclature for, 127; numerals in, 289,
320n. 24; phonemes of, 127, *127t*; plural
marking in, 215; prehistory of, 248
Serra, Father Junípero, 15
Serrano, *37b*, *178m*, *179t*, 183, 209, 255, 279
shaman, 6, 7, 227
Shasta, *37b*, 90, *91m*, 223; linguistic structure
of, 95, *95t*; shamanistic register in, 227
Shasta Valley Shasta, 91, *91m*
Shastan, *2m*, 90–95; dialects of, 92;
documentation of, *30b*, *37b*, *46b*, *55b*,
92–95, 265, 278; geography of, 90–92, *91m*;
Konomihu, 6, 90, *91m*, 92–93, 244, 278;
linguistic structure of, 95, *95t*; New River
Shasta, *37b*, 90, *91m*, 93–94, 265, 305n.
37; nomenclature for, 95; numerals in, 288;
Okwanuchu, 94–95, 305n. 39; prehistory
of, 244, 317n. 13; regional dialects of, 91,
91m; Shasta, *37b*, 90, *91m*, 95, *95t*, 223, 227;
survival of, 92; villages of, 91–92
Shaterian, Alan, *56b*
Shaul, David L., 114, *114t*, 225
Shea, John Gilmary, 19, 27, 28
Shelter Cove Sinkyone, 79
Shepherd, Alice: Northern Wintuan
documentation by, 142–143, 146, *147t*–*148t*;
on Northern Yukian, 189; on shamanistic
jargon, 7, 227
Shigom Eastern Pomo tribelet, 107
Shinal Eastern Pomo tribelet, 107, 109
Shipley, William, 138, 139
Shodakay Northern Pomo, 109
Shokowa Central Pomo, 109
Shoshonean (Northern Uto-Aztecan), 35, *36t*,
169
Shoshoni, *171m*, 175, 311n. 121
sibilant fricative, 206
Sierra Miwok, *37b*, *159m*, 160, 215, 223, 278,
309–310n. 95
Silva, Cecile (Wikchamni), *151*
Silver, Shirley K., 92, 98, *98*, 242–244, 257–258
Silverstein, Michael, 57, 307n. 67; on
"Californian grammars," 54
Simmons, Hoxie (Rogue River Athabaskan),
72, *72*
Siniard, Roy, *55b*–*56b*

Sinkyone Eel River Athabaskan, 79, 264;
Mattole–Bear River contact with, 78–79
Sitjar, Father Buenaventura, 19, 116
Sixes Oregon Athabaskan, 73
Smith, Richard A., *55b*
Solórsano, Ascención (Mutsun), 19, 20
Somersal, Laura Fish, *191*
song texts, 225–226, 315n. 34
Soto, Steve (Palewyami), *151*
South Fork Chimariko, *88m*, 88–89
Southeastern Mono, 171
Southeastern Pomo, 6, *105m*, *106m*, *106t*, 107,
266, 277, 314–315n. 22
Southern Hill Nisenan, *137m*, 139, 268
Southern Numic, 170–171, *170t*, *171m*,
175–177
Southern Paiute, 176, 177
Southern Patwin, *144m*, 145–146, 268
Southern Pomo, *105m*, 109–110, 266, 277,
306n. 49
Southern Sierra Miwok, *159m*, 160
Southern Sinkyone, 79
Southern Ute, 176–177
Southern Valley Yokuts, 149, *149m*, 152
Southern Wintuan. *See* Patwin
Southern Yana, 40, *100m*, 101
Southwestern Pomo (Kashaya), 23, *105m*, 110–
111, 266; loanwords in, 230, *233b*
Spanish: borrowing from, 230, *231b*, 316n. 46,
316n. 47; Costanoan borrowings in, 230;
missionary policy on, 16, 18, 296n. 4, 296n.
5; Salinan borrowings in, 230, 233
Sparkman, Philip Stedman, 38, 181, 312n. 128
Spence, Justin, *55b*
Spott, Robert (Yurok), *67*
Steele, Susan, 57, 181
Stevenson, Matilda Coxe, 46
Stillwater Valley Wintu, 141, *141m*
Stonyford: multilingualism at, 8
stops, 205–206; laryngeal contrasts in, 204–205
structural linguists, 49–53
subject marking, 210–211
subsistence practices: tribelet unit and, 3;
Washo, 5
suffixation, 203, 313n. 1
Suisun Southern Patwin, 145
Super, Violet (Karuk), *58*
suppletion, 210
survey expeditions, 25–26
Survey of California (and Other) Indian
Languages (UC Berkeley), 53–54, *55b*–*56b*,
58
Swadesh, Morris, 53, 302n. 91
switch reference, 111, 203, 218, 313n. 7
synthesis, 211

Ta-kin Northern Valley Yokuts, 152–153
Tac, Pablo, 20–21, 181
Tachi Southern Valley Yokuts, 152
Tagliavini, Carlo, 21
Takelma, *2m*, 129, *129t*, 130–133; diminutive
prefixes in, 223, 225; documentation of, *50b*,
131–132, 278, 308n. 72; geography of, 130–
131, *131m*, 303n. 10; linguistic structure of,
132–133, *132t*, *133t*, 210, 308n. 72, 308n.
73; Lowland, 130–131, *131m*; nomenclature
for, 133; Northern, 131, *131m*; numerals in,
290, 320nn. 27–30; phonemes of, 132, *132t*,
308n. 72, 308n. 73; possessive affixes of,
132, *133t*; prehistory of, 249–250; Upland,
131, *131m*
Takic, *2m*, *37b*, *55b*, 178–185, 279; Cahuilla,
37b, *178m*, 182–184, *184t*, 255, 279,
293; classification of, 179, *179t*, 311n.
126; Cupeño, *178m*, 181–182, 279;

documentation of, 180, 181, 182–184;
Gabrielino-Fernandeño (Tongva), *37b*,
178m, 179–180, 209, 223, 226, 279, 293,
312n. 127; geography of, *178m*, 178–179;
Hope contact with, 255; internal diversity
of, 5; Island, *178m*, 184; Juaneño, *15b*, 19,
178m, 180–181, 226, 255; Kitanemuk, *178m*,
183, 255, 279; linguistic structure of, 184,
184t, 215–216; Luiseño, 19–20, 21, *37b*,
178m, 180–181, 209, *224b*, 226, 255, 279;
nomenclature for, 185; numerals in, 293;
personal names in, 223; phonemes of, 184,
184t, 209; prehistory of, 255, 318n. 30,
318–319n. 31; Serrano, *37b*, *178m*, 183, 209,
255, 279; Tataviam, *178m*, 183–184, 312n.
130; Vanyume, *178m*, 183, 312n. 130
Takic Language Program (UC Riverside), 181
Taldash Oregon Athabaskan, 72
Talmy, Leonard, 98–99, 217, 313n. 4
Tamukamne (Tamcan) Delta Yokuts, 153, 154
Tamyen San Francisco Bay Costanoan, *163m*,
164–165, 310n. 101, 310n. 102
Tataviam, *178m*, 183–184
Tatsch, Sheri, 308n. 78, 308n. 79
Taylor, Alexander S., 27–28, 299n. 35, 307n.
56
Taylor, Walter W., 246
Teeter, Karl, 63, 303n. 2
Telamni Valley Yokuts, 152
Tequislatecan, 84
Thompson, Coquelle (Upper Coquille), 72
Thompson, Sandra, 57, 191
Thornes, Timothy J., 57, 174
Tipai Diegueño, *119m*, 120–121, 217, 267
Tlatskanai Lower Columbia Athabaskan, 69–70
Tlingit, 68–69
Tolkapaya Yavapai, 123
Tolmie, William Fraser, 24
Toloim (Toloip, Bankalachi) Tubatulabal
district, *185m*, 186
Tolowa. *See* Chetco-Tolowa
Toltichi Northern Hill Yokuts, 153, 220, 314n. 20
tone, 209
Tongva (Gabrielino-Fernandeño), *37b*, *178m*,
179–180, 209, 223, 226, 279, 312n. 127
Toosarvandani, Maziar, *55b*
toponyms, 204, 220–221
Totonacan, 249
trade jargon, 230
transcription systems, 283–284, *284t*–*286t*,
303n. 2, 320n. 6
tribelets, 2–4, 295n. 1; names for, 221; single-
tribelet, 6
Tribes of California (Powers), *29b*–*30b*, 33
Trinidad Yurok, 65, *66*
Trinity River Chimariko, 87–88, *88m*, 276
Trinity Wintu, 267
Tsetacol district, *115m*, 116
Tsnungwe Tribe, 78, 89, 305n. 32
Tubatulabal, *2m*, 185–187, 312n. 132; contact
with, 186; documentation of, *37b*, *55b*,
186–187, 271, 279; geography of, *185m*,
185–186; linguistic structure of, 187, *187t*,
210; nomenclature for, 187; numerals
in, 293; Pahkanapil, *185m*, 185–186,
279; Palagewan, 185, *185m*; phonemes
of, 187, *187t*; prehistory of, 255; Toloim
(Bankalachi), *185m*, 186
Tuholi, 150
Tulamni Yokuts, *149m*, 149–150
Tule-Kaweah Yokuts, 149, *149m*, 150–151
Tuleyoma Lake Miwok tribelet, 157
Tümpisa (Timbisha) Panamint, 174
Turner, Katherine, 117
Tututni Oregon Athabaskan, 72

Indexer: Nancy Newman
Composition: P. M. Gordon Associates
Text: 8.6/12 Charis SIL
Display: Akzidenz Grotesk
Printer and Binder: Thomson-Shore